THE AMERICAN URBAN READER

The American Urban Reader brings together the most exciting work on the evolution of the American city, from colonial settlement and western expansion to post-industrial cities and the growth of the suburbs. Each of the chronologically and thematically organized chapters includes thoughtfully selected scholarly essays from historians, social scientists, and journalists, which are supplemented by relevant primary documents that offer more nuanced perspectives and convey the diversity and interdisciplinary nature of the study of the urban condition. A comprehensive companion website offers valuable further reading, compelling supplementary links, slideshows of additional images, and a dialogue-opening blog written by one of the editors.

Lisa Krissoff Boehm and Steven H. Corey together bring 35 years of classroom experience in urban studies and history, and have selected a range of work that is dynamically written and carefully edited to be accessible to students and appropriate for anyone seeking a deeper understanding of how American cities have developed.

For additional information and classroom resources please visit *The American Urban Reader* companion website at **www.routledge.com/textbooks/9780415803984**.

Steven Hunt Corey is Professor and Chair of the Department of Urban Studies at Worcester State College, Worcester, MA.

Lisa Krissoff Boehm is Professor of Urban Studies and Director of the Honors Program at Worcester State College in Worcester, MA. She is the author of *Popular Culture and the Enduring Myth of Chicago, 1871–1968* (Routledge) and *Making a Way out of No Way: African American Women and the Second Great Migration*.

THE AMERICAN URBAN READER

HISTORY AND THEORY

Steven H. Corey and Lisa Krissoff Boehm

EDITORS

Routledge
Taylor & Francis Group

NEW YORK AND LONDON

First published 2011
by Routledge
270 Madison Avenue, New York, NY 10016

Simultaneously published in the UK
by Routledge
2 Park Square, Milton Park, Abingdon, Oxon OX14 4RN

Routledge is an imprint of the Taylor & Francis Group, an informa business

Typeset in Sabon by Wearset Ltd, Boldon, Tyne and Wear
Printed and bound in the United States of America on acid-free paper by Edwards Brothers, Inc.

Library of Congress Cataloging in Publication Data

The American urban reader : history and theory / edited by Steven H. Corey and Lisa Krissoff Boehm.
p. cm.
Includes bibliographical references and index.
1. Urbanization–United States. 2. Cities and towns–United States. 3. Sociology, Urban–United States.
I. Corey, Steven H. II. Boehm, Lisa Krissoff, 1969-
HT123.A66644 2010
307.760973–dc22
2009054300

ISBN 13: 978-0-415-80394-6 (hbk)
ISBN 13: 978-0-415-80398-4 (pbk)

For
Lisa Signorelli (SHC)

For
David and Peter Krissoff Boehm (LKB)

CONTENTS

PART V. MANAGING THE METROPOLIS

PART VI. THE URBAN ENVIRONMENT

PART VII. TRANSPORTATION AND PHYSICAL MOBILITY

PART VIII. URBAN MIGRATIONS AND SOCIAL MOBILITY

PART IX. RACE AND THE POST-WAR METROPOLIS

PART X. EXURBIA AND POSTINDUSTRIAL CITIES

FIGURES

ACKNOWLEDGMENTS

We have discussed the possibility of writing this textbook for about eight years now. It is wonderful to see it come to fruition. We want to thank all of those who supported this work. Routledge's history editor, Kimberly Guinta, shared our vision and contacted Steve Corey to see if he was available at this time. Matthew Kopel, senior editorial assistant at Routledge, patiently answered endless inquiries pertaining to permissions and style.

Research grants made this work possible. The Worcester State College Faculty Mini-Grant program allowed for travel to archives and professional conferences, and provided funds towards the purchase of research materials and rights for the book and companion website. We are most grateful for the generous financial support of the American Antiquarian Society's Center for Historic American Visual Culture.

Our department provided the intellectual home for this work to take place. Our wonderful students have given us the opportunity to develop as teachers over the years, and continue to make every day worthwhile. We have learned so much from the students, and we are proud of their collective achievements. Department administrator Linda Sweeney tirelessly copied countless essays and primary documents, many of which did not make their way into this volume. Department colleagues Frances "Tuck" Amory, Anne "Shiko" Gathuo, Joyce Mandell, and Maureen Power provided daily encouragement. Friends across the campus proved supportive of our work. Thank you to Don Vescio for technological assistance and Jerry Sorge for helping to organize the grant disbursement. Departmental co-founder, the late Vincent "Jake" Powers, provided the inspiration for how to teach vital urban history to students.

Many librarians and archivists and administrators gave their time and expertise to the work. Paul J. Erickson, of the American Antiquarian Society helped secure helpful funding for the project. Georgia "Gigi" Barnhill, Jon Benoit, Andrew Bourque, Lauren Hewes, Jackie Donovan Penny, and Elizabeth Pope were always kind and courteous with our numerous requests for materials. Vincent Golden helped to locate key documents related to the Tredegar Iron Works strike of 1847. We would also like to thank Patrizia Sione (Kheel Center at Cornell University), Barbara Semedo (Brookings Institution), Bill Welge and Jennifer Day (Oklahoma Historical Society), John Powell (Newberry Library), and Nelson L. Dawson (Kentucky Historical Society). Thank you also to the staffs of the Brown University Libraries, the Goddard Library at Clark University, the Library of Congress, the Newberry Library in Chicago, the New-York Historical Society, the New York Public Library, the North Kingstown Free Library, the Oklahoma Historical Society, the University of Rhode Island Library, and the Worcester State College Library. Thank you to all of the authors here for allowing their works to be included, and for the hard-working permissions staffs of the publishers. Thank you also to families of Wayne Andrews, Harriette Arnow, Arthur M. Schlesinger, Sr., and Richard C. Wade.

The framework of this book was born at key conferences where we discussed teaching urban history. At the 122nd Annual Meeting of the American Historical Association in Washington D.C., January 3–6, 2008, we served on a panel with historians Amy Howard

(University of Richmond), Michael Lewis (Salisbury University), and Gregory Wilson (University of Akron). At the request of editor David Goldfield, our remarks evolved into papers that we published as the January 2010 version of the *Journal of Urban History* (*JUH*), the first ever edition of that journal devoted to teaching. Since graduate school, we have both fought against the all-too-frequent hesitancy to discuss teaching. It was refreshing to start a conversation with Howard, Lewis, and Wilson on-line and watch it blossom into a thorough dialogue at the conference and through the writing of articles for the *JUH*. The thought process continued on through the 2009 Urban History Association conference in Houston, where we spoke at a panel with Janice Bedarneck (University of Dayton). We also benefitted greatly from conversations with scholars including Russell Chabot, Bruce Cohen, Tom Conroy, Jared Day, Corey Dolgon, Maura Doherty, Amy Finstein, Julie Frechette, Charlotte Haller, Tona Hangen, Sean Holmes, D. Bradford Hunt, Fortunata Makene, Joyce Mandell, Mark Motte, Emily Straus, Kristin Waters, and Carl Zimring. Thank you to John Bodnar for contributing the foreword to this reader. So many of the scholars included in this volume as contributors also offered advice and encouragement regarding the need for this volume. Students Emily Parker and Johanie Rodriguez contributed ideas to this volume.

Families and friends of course provided the backbone of the practical support and encouragement necessary to complete the daily labors involved with writing and editing. Steven Corey would like to dedicate his share of the book to Lisa Signorelli for decades of loving support, encouragement, and companionship, as well as the entire Signorelli family. He also thanks Lori Corey, Keith Corey and Katie Minahan, David Kieffner, Mark Pesce, Stephen Beganyi, Melissa Devine, Shannon Chandley and Thomas Silvia, Petra Daniel Laurie, Daniel Lynch and Stanzie Kensinger, and Deborah Milbauer. Lisa Krissoff Boehm would like to thank her husband, Chris Boehm, for technological expertise, parenting back-up, on-the-fly grammatical assistance, and the patience to allow her or me to edit this reader while simultaneously completing another book. David and Peter Krissoff Boehm, to whom this book is dedicated, provided wonderful comic relief with their rare sense of sarcasm, creative dance moves, and general "son-shine." Madelon and Joel Krissoff, Sylvia and Abe Krissoff, Jonathan and Nikolette Krissoff, Sarah Krissoff, Shari Hack, Richard Hack, Bill and Chris Krissoff, Austin Krissoff, and Lynne and Harvey Golomb were a reservoir of support yet again. Friends, too numerous to name here, listened to updates on the book progression with utmost patience.

FOREWORD
John Bodnar*

The majority of Americans have lived in cities now for nearly a century. The fact that the United States began as a nation with a largely agrarian population and evolved into a country of city dwellers is well known. Less understood is what this momentous transformation meant to the nation's history and how it was understood by the people who lived it. The distinctive contribution of this innovative reader by Steven H. Corey and Lisa Krissoff Boehm is its recovery of the vast scale of this story—both its analytical and personal sides—and the powerful impact the growth of cities made on the lives and minds of so many citizens. This book makes it clear that Americans not only settled in cities but thought about them a great deal.

The American Urban Reader offers a particularly powerful view of the residents of metropolitan areas and the trials and tribulations they faced. As city spaces became more crowded with migrants of various ethnic and racial backgrounds, Americans expended an enormous amount of time to identify who they wanted to live near them in their neighborhoods and who they did not. Cities became cauldrons of ethnic and racial accommodation and tension. Neighbors rendered assistance to some and erected barriers to keep out those who appeared alien or threatening. And they did so over the entire course of our urban experience—a point that the editors make well by extending the story of immigration and race from the nineteenth century into contemporary times.

American cities—as documented here—were not only sites of conflict and social disorder, however, but also laboratories where citizens attempted to work out solutions to enormous social problems, a point that has not been readily appreciated. It was on city streets and in urban universities that reformers, scholars, and political leaders fashioned solutions to the vexing problems of modern American life such as public health, charity and welfare, transportation, and education.

Even more striking was the degree to which citizens funneled so many aspects of city life into their imaginations. Corey and Boehm explain well how a preoccupation with urban growth actually helped to initiate a number of academic specialties in history, economics, and sociology. Historians have published a considerable number of studies—many sampled here—that identify colorful urban types that moved through the city such as pickpockets, boarders, and prostitutes. Pioneering works in sociology were authored by social workers like Jane Addams and sociologists like W. E. B. Du Bois. Novelists never tired of creating characters who moved from rural regions to city streets and thinking out loud regarding the impact of this change on the ordinary person. *The American Urban Reader* is exceptional in the way it captures not only the conditions of city life but the massive impact of the urban landscape on the American cultural imagination.

Finally, the book takes due note of the fact that the urban transformation of America is not simply a historic or completed process. It reveals the rise of suburban and exurban regions and the emergence of new cities with reasons for being that could not even be imagined in the nineteenth century. Thus, the growth of an industrial city like Chicago is contrasted with the dynamic entertainment driven metropolis of Las Vegas. One can only wonder near the end of this story what will come next.

NOTE

* John Bodnar is Chancellor's Professor, Indiana University, and his latest book is *The "Good War" in American Memory* (Johns Hopkins University Press, 2010).

PREFACE

The essays in this anthology, *The American Urban Reader: History and Theory* (*AUR*), are examples of the finest scholarship in U.S. urban history and urban studies. We have assembled works that convey the richness and strikingly broad breadth and depth of the various subfields of social history and related humanities and social science disciplines which deal with urban life. We have also attempted to balance time and geographic space in sampling the spectrum of the American (which for this volume means the United States) urban experience from colonial settlements to contemporary exurban enclaves, as well as many other configurations in between, from coast to coast. We have supplemented the essays with documents from actual observers of and participants in the events, movements, and social conditions covered in the larger themes of each section of the anthology. In a departure from traditional historical anthologies, we have also included writings that discuss social science theory and advocate for better contemporary public policy. We have added such works in order to convey the diversity and interdisciplinary nature of the study of the urban condition.

Given the abundance of writing on urban, metropolitan, and suburban affairs, selecting articles and primary documents for this volume was no easy task. Given the space constraints, we have omitted many wonderful and insightful contributions that we had hoped to include. Our original list of articles and documents could have filled multiple volumes. This attests to the richness of recent scholarship on the city. We have included additional material, including supplementary documents, photographs, and weblinks, in the accompanying website for this volume.

The themes we have chosen to anchor each chapter are at once chronological and thematic. We start with selections that probe into various definitions of and competing viewpoints on the urban condition. We follow with historical overviews on city growth, beginning with the colonial period and proceeding on to the modern day. Urbanists writing for roundtables published in the *Journal of Urban History* and those taking part in discussions on the H-Urban list on H-Net, have commented on the modern focus (late nineteenth to twentieth century) of the bulk of new urban history. But without the added perspective of scholarship on the colonial era through the early nineteenth century, we cannot truly understand contemporary urban places. We follow with primary documents related to the readings that provide chronological, geographical, and social diversity and the kinds of nuances only this type of source offers. We expect the document sections will give readers a more interactive experience, and that they will open the themes up nicely for classroom discussions. Research papers could use these documents as a starting point, and students also may want to draw on the book-length works in which the essays were originally published. Note, whenever possible, we have retained the original spelling and grammar of the documents. We have also included a bibliography of recommended works, divided by theme, in the back matter of the volume. We expect that the *AUR* will be paired with one or more of these works depending on the focus of the class.

The book highlights persistent themes in urban history, including immigration, migration, industrialization, urban politics, transportation, environmental concerns, the growth of the modern "ghetto," and suburbanization. We devote substantial space to issues of class, race, gender, sexual orientation, and ethnicity. For an expanded exploration of suburbanization, we recommend Becky Nicolaides' and Andrew Weise's *The Suburb Reader* (New York: Routledge, 2006). For reasons of space and consistency, we consider the impact of suburbanization from the point of view of the central city, but do not delve into the creation of a suburban way of life to a considerable extent. We ultimately did not have the space to deal extensively with the connected themes of architecture or urban art, although architecture makes more than a passing appearance here in some articles.

Students love urban studies, urban sociology, and urban history, although at times they do not know it. Students regretfully often arrive at college associating history (in particular) with the rote memorization of dates and facts. History professors have to dispel these preconceptions in the first few days of class. As practiced today, urban history is a very interdisciplinary field. This book is not simply urban history, however. This book comes from our collective thirty-five years of higher education experience teaching urban studies, history, geography, American studies, education, and women's studies courses at our home institution of Worcester State College in Worcester, Massachusetts, and our previous teaching positions at Indiana University, University of Michigan-Dearborn, University of Rhode Island, and Yeshiva University in Manhattan. We owe a debt to the historians and social scientists that have taught us over the years. Without forward-thinking professors, we would not have been able to find the comfort level necessary to take on the modern city in an interdisciplinary way. Both of the editors pursued interdisciplinary master's degrees before we entered our history Ph.D. programs. Urban history provided a good fit for the type of social history we were doing by the time we completed our graduate studies.

The historiography of American cities has grown considerably since Arthur M. Schlesinger's publication of *The Rise of the City, 1878–1898* in 1933. By that point, urban sociology was well underway and held sway over how academics and many college-educated people dealt with issues connected to the urban setting. The growth of social history during the twentieth century, as is discussed at length in our essay, "Examining America's Urban Landscape: From Social Reform to Social History," in Part I of the volume, gave weight to the scholarly value of viewing the world from "the bottom up." Urban history often views the city right from street level, which offers an intriguing view, indeed. Urban history is social history with an urban focus. In the modern day, when most Americans reside or work in metropolitan settings, the importance of understanding urban life cannot be overestimated.

PART I

DEFINITIONS AND PERSPECTIVES

EDITORS' INTRODUCTION TO PART I

This part of *The American Urban Reader* provides an overview of how scholars and social commentators have conceived of cities and assessed the nature of urban life in the United States. It begins with our own original essay, which examines the ways in which reformers who sought to improve problems associated with urban life and academics who have attempted to define the meaning of urbanization have framed their investigations of cities. We argue that in their effort to understand issues associated with industrialization, immigration, and explosive metropolitan growth, social reformers influenced academics.

Sociologists and other social scientists who drew heavily on the work of urban activists were decades ahead of historians in assessing life in the American city. The myopic view of cities within the historical profession began to change in the 1930s and 1940s when a small group of social historians published cutting-edge works on colonial and nineteenth-century cities. Leading the pack was noted American historian Arthur M. Schlesinger, Sr., who argued that the city, no less than the frontier, shaped the course of U.S. history. We are pleased to include one of Schlesinger's clearest syntheses of urban history with the selection of "The City in American Civilization" from his 1949 book, *Paths to the Present*.

While historians were just beginning to explore the history of cities systematically, sociologists were well under way, formulating comprehensive theories on urban life. At the forefront of this movement were members of the Chicago School, who sought to examine the city as an object of detached analysis. The Chicago School, known for such luminaries as Robert Park, Ernest W. Burgess, and Louis Wirth, set the stage for the way in which future generations of social scientists and public policy makers understood the city.

Two of the most important works of the Chicago School were Ernest W. Burgess' "The Growth of the City: An Introduction to a Research Project," published in 1925, and Louis Wirth's 1938 "Urbanism as a Way of Life." To illustrate the sustained influence of these authors, we have selected essays from two contemporary scholars who build from and reassess the Chicago School's contributions to social theory. In the selection "Urbanism and Suburbanism as Ways of Life: A Reevaluation of Definitions," originally published in 1962 and updated with a postscript three decades later, noted sociologist Herbert Gans questions whether a sociological definition of a city can be formulated. In "Beyond *Blade Runner*," Mike Davis reconstitutes Ernest W. Burgess' concentric zone model around the late-twentieth-century climate of fear in Los Angeles.

The fifth essay in this part, "Crossing the City Line" by Robert Orsi, helps contextualize the contemporary fear of cities. Orsi expands the traditional approach of historians and social scientists by assessing the relationship between religion and urban life. He deftly ties together the influences of Louis Wirth and other scholars who attempt to come to grips with social and psychological consequences of urbanism. Orsi notes that city folk have to live with the consequences of the negative opinions and projections that outsiders have about urban life. Even the concept of "city religion" seems like an oxymoron to many people, even though much of what is characteristic of modern religion in the United States originated in cities.

The documents in this part explore the interplay of social investigation, fear, and safety in cities. The first is an excerpt from John H. Griscom's 1845 report, *The Sanitary Condition of the Laboring Population of New York*, which provides an overview of the work of sanitary reformers and Protestant ministers regarding the living conditions of the working poor. Next is a brief sampling of the advice that guidebooks gave to tourists who visited large cities in the nineteenth century. In addition to pointing out the best places to view the city's panorama, tips on protecting one's valuables, and staying safe were common features of this literature. A selection from the urbanist Jane Jacobs reminds us of the positive role sidewalks play in providing safety and cultural assimilation for urban children. The large gulf that existed between modern industrial cities and the agrarian countryside during the late nineteenth and early twentieth centuries is depicted in the once infamous "Tillman's Allegorical Cow" cartoon [**Figure 1.3**]. Although it was drawn to show how capitalists who supported the gold standard lived off the hard work of farmers, it also summarized the distrust many rural people held toward Wall Street and all wealthy people in Eastern cities.

Examining America's Urban Landscape: From Social Reform to Social History

Steven H. Corey and Lisa Krissoff Boehm

The United States is an urban nation. As such, it is impossible to understand American civilization without studying and appreciating its cities. Arguably, the social diversity, cultural vitality, and economic innovation of the United States are largely the products of urban life. The importance of cities is not surprising in light of the prodigious immigration and migration during the nineteenth century. Since 1920, the majority of Americans have lived in urban settings. The year 2008 marked the first time that the majority of the world population resided in cities, and this demographic change prompted renewed interest in urban history and urban studies.

Even during the American colonial era, cities, or more accurately towns, exerted a disproportionate influence over the overwhelmingly rural landscape. Given the prominence of cities in colonial America and the United States, it is not surprising that many social observers and academics have attempted to chronicle the evolution of urban spaces and analyze a host of issues associated with urban life. This essay, and *The American Urban Reader: History and Theory* in its entirety, highlights selected trends in this rather voluminous literature on American cities.

It is of course impossible to make mention of every genre of writing on the urban condition within a single essay, or even within a single anthology. Our training as social historians and experience as professors in an interdisciplinary social science department led us to concentrate on how ordinary men and women have lived in, perceived, and responded to urban surroundings, as well as the ways in which social and political elites have interpreted and attempted to shape urban growth and development. Therefore, we have framed *The American Urban Reader* as a collection of scholarly essays from social historians and social scientists, supplemented with primary documents that provide a broader view of leading issues, trends, and opinions on urban life throughout American history.

This essay has a much narrower focus than the volume as a whole. Here, we investigate the relationship between the evolution of urban life since the nineteenth century and the establishment of, and transformations within, some of the academic disciplines that study the American city. More specifically, the essay considers how issues associated with urban life spawned an array of social commentary and reform efforts that influenced sociologists and, subsequently, historians, and a broad assortment of other academicians. In an attempt to consider the evolution of the field of urban history, we examine how a wide range of scholars, journalists, and social activists have framed their understanding of American cities. Beginning with a discussion of urban social reform, the essay moves on to cover the early work of new urban-oriented subfields within sociology, history, and other social sciences.

Cities and the quest to understand and transform them played a direct role in the establishment of sociology as an academic discipline in the late nineteenth and early twentieth centuries. Urban themes also fundamentally shaped the writing of American history in the latter half of the twentieth century, although urban history was not fully developed as a subfield. In fact, during the 1960s and 1970s, the study of urban history ignited the American historical profession, both as a discrete area of scholarly inquiry and as a means to understand and address contemporary social policy concerns. In higher education today, social historians largely outnumber other types of historians (much to the consternation of some of their colleagues in other subfields). Urban history, which may be considered the social history of particular places, urban groups, urban movements, or urban phenomenon, has become so ubiquitous it is often difficult to recognize as a distinct historical subfield.

Some urban historians, as well as scholars from other disciplines who utilize urban history, bemoan the field's under-theorization and absence of a canon. As this essay argues and *The American Urban Reader* demonstrates, however, the state of urban history is both vibrant and in keeping with the long-standing interests and diversity of urban research. By tracing the roots of urban sociology and its offspring, urban history, through both popular and scholarly inquiry, this essay contextualizes these approaches by historicizing select theories on, and historiographic trends concerning, the growth and development of American cities.

The Rise of the City

Beginning in the early nineteenth century, American cities and their inhabitants became the subject of intense investigation by social and political reformers, later joined by a fervent new brand of change-oriented journalists (often referred to as muckrakers). After the 1860s, scholars in the social sciences and humanities entered the discussion. The backdrop for this intellectual activity was the dramatic increase in the number and size of cities. The large metropolitan regions had significant weight in popular culture, those that became associated with anti-urban sentiments were known as "shock cities." In particular, the huge growth of Chicago, redolent with crime, flooded with immigrants, and intriguingly located in America's rural-identified heartland, fueled growing scholarly contemplation of urban

life, and birthed the Chicago School of urban sociology in the gothic-styled halls of the University of Chicago. Statistics on nineteenth-century urban growth can only hint at the difficulties facing the United States as the nation transformed from an overwhelmingly agrarian society to one on the verge of becoming evenly divided between the country and the city.

The very first census of the U.S. population, conducted in 1790, revealed that the fledgling country contained just twenty-four urban places, each defined as a legally incorporated area with a population of 2,500 or more persons. By the standards of their day, these urban areas, which contained just over 5 percent of the nation's population, were equivalent to cities. These sites obviously had far fewer people in them than today's urban centers; only two of them had more than 25,000 people, while exactly half held between 2,500 and 5,000 inhabitants. They served, nonetheless, as conduits of growth for the new nation. By 1900, there were 1,737 urban areas containing almost 40 percent of the nation's population—with eighty-two cities containing 25,000–50,000 people, another seventy-two containing 50,000–500,000 inhabitants, three containing 500,000–1,000,000, and another three (New York City, Chicago, and Philadelphia) with populations over one million.

Cities were epicenters of unprecedented social and economic change. Each year thousands of migrants from the countryside and immigrants from foreign countries poured into cities and competed with each other and native-born residents for jobs, housing, and other vital resources. At the same time, a variety of new and expanding commercial activities, such as industrial manufacturing and real estate speculation, challenged traditional urban enterprises and folkways. Small-scale craft production and the unabashed use of public spaces to raise plants and livestock went on without planning or regulation, thus leading to social and political conflicts over acceptable civic behavior and basic political rights such as taxation, suffrage, and representation. These disagreements and challenges caught the attention of social commentators who, more often than not, viewed them as negative consequences of the newly emerging urban way of life.

Famously, Thomas Jefferson, writing to Benjamin Rush in 1800, exclaimed, "I view great cities as pestilential to the morals, health and liberties of man."[1] Jefferson is often cited as the champion of the yeoman farmer and the morally invigorating life found by spending the bulk of one's time out-of-doors. Anti-urban attitudes such as Jefferson's transcended the early years of the Republic. In their influential, yet often disputed, book, *The Intellectual Versus the City: From Thomas Jefferson to Frank Lloyd Wright*, historians Morton and Lucia White argue, "enthusiasm for the American city has not been typical or predominant in our intellectual history. Fear has been the more common reaction."[2] **[For more on fear and American cities, see the essays "Beyond *Blade Runner*" by Mike Davis and "Crossing the City Line" by Robert Orsi in Part I.]** Thomas Bender, in *Toward an Urban Vision: Ideas and Institutions in Nineteenth Century America*, however, offers a nuanced view, exploring the ways in which the producers of high culture may have expressed more favorable attitudes towards the urban than once understood.[3]

We can see by examining popular attitudes in the nineteenth and twentieth centuries, however, that our national conception of cities, especially in terms of their effect on morality or psychological health, remains at best a contested one. Historian Andrew Lees notes that, beginning in the 1820s, a wide range of authors in Europe and the United States began to deal specifically with urban issues in the course of their work; most notably the clergy who served city parishes, doctors and public health officials, writers of descriptive books, and essayists. Not all observations of American cities were critical. Many individuals expressed excitement about the new opportunities for economic, social, and personal advancement found in urban settings. In fact, Lees argues that "Americans were just as favorably disposed toward their cities as Europeans were toward theirs, and that a good case can be made that the balance of opinion was more favorable in the United States than it was anywhere else."[4] However, the tenor and tone of the works that most influenced the academic tradition routinely placed cities in an unfavorable light, especially when compared to more traditional rural life.

Not surprisingly, middle and upper class individuals who engaged in religiously based social activism experienced first-hand the substandard living arrangements and working conditions of the urban poor. While many ministers and their followers sympathized with the underprivileged, many still attributed the plight of the destitute to individual depravity. Yet a new brand of social research and activism, emerging in Europe and the United States in the early-to-mid-nineteenth century, slowly chipped away at notions that the impoverished or sick held all responsibility for their own suffering. While commentators on both sides of the Atlantic, particularly England's Herbert Spencer (1820–1903), began to popularize Social Darwinism and its "survival of the fittest" mentality to justify social inequality, a small but influential number of reformers went beyond simply identifying problems, condemning individual behavior by documenting in detail the very conditions they sought to fix, and providing specific solutions. These efforts represented the earliest systematic studies of urban life, setting the stage for subsequent academic efforts.

In the United States, this newer way of thinking predated the progressive and social survey movements of the late nineteenth and early twentieth centuries, although it constituted less of a national phenomenon. Nor were the links between social and political reform activities throughout this period necessarily direct. Indeed, when assessing the connections between the social survey movement, made famous by the *Pittsburgh Survey* undertaken between 1907 and 1908 (see below), and the rise of empirical social research methods, sociologist Martin Bulmer argues, "Various traditions in the history of social investigation may have coexisted, or followed one another in time, but there were no necessary connections between them."[5] However, the prodigious growth of cities in the nineteenth century did lead social reformers and government officials to take note of a series of problems common to many cities. In the areas of public health, housing, immigration, and politics, those working to improve urban conditions began to follow similar trajectories and occasionally borrowed directly from one another. These activities were an attempt to understand and control a wide variety of conditions associated with rapid urbanization. They also shaped the course of social science. In time, many academics became less interested in advocacy and reform as a means of understanding and influencing society, and more interested in the development of rigorous scholarship.

The first round of urban investigations came in the field of public health, most notably with the work of sanitary reformers in the 1830s–1860s. Cities in this period faced unprecedented overcrowding and unpleasant living conditions, primarily from the interaction of manufacturing and the extraordinary influx of new people, which served to intensify preexisting class inequality, poverty, malnutrition, and physical squalor. These circumstances promoted the spread of disease and shortened the average life span. Reformers began their work by compiling statistics on births, marriages, and deaths in order to track larger public health trends. Throughout the 1830s and 1840s, a veritable "statistical movement" emerged in Great Britain and the United States around health and other social concerns, which led in part to the establishment of the Royal Statistical Society in 1834, the American Statistical Association in 1839, and government agencies on both sides of the Atlantic charged with collecting data and protecting the welfare of the general public.[6]

A small cadre of health officials and medical professionals also altered the way people viewed the relationship between poverty, disease, and the physical environment, particularly in cities. Before the advancement and acceptance of the germ theory in the latter half of the nineteenth century, a wide variety of theories competed as to the cause of sickness and epidemics. Not surprisingly, many explanations focused on the lifestyles and activities of victims, especially those perceived as living immoral lives. Beginning in the 1840s, however, health reformers advanced the so-called "sanitary idea" that ill health caused poverty and that disease had definite environmental origins. People came to consider disease as a product of an individual's interaction with his or her surroundings rather than sinful habits.

Leading this sanitary movement were England's Edwin Chadwick (1800–1890) and New York City's John H. Griscom (1809–1874). In 1842, Chadwick had published the groundbreaking *Report on the Sanitary Condition of the Labouring Population of Great Britain*. Three years later, Griscom published *The Sanitary Condition of the Laboring Population of New York: With Some Suggestions for Improvement* [see Document 1.1]. Both volumes documented the wretched living conditions faced by the urban poor and emphasized the physical sources of sickness. By stressing the need for proper sanitation to prevent illness, these two landmark studies galvanized reformers and contributed to the widespread association between a clean environment, good health, and the escape from poverty.[7]

Frederick Engels' *The Conditions of the Working Class in England in 1844*, published in 1845, became the work that perhaps most solidly connected the concerns of the sanitary movement with the academic scholarship explored in the second half of this essay. Writing up his observations of Manchester, England, a city ravaged by the industrial revolution and the resulting overcrowding of workers and their families, Engels (1820–1895) startled readers and prompted scholars to examine cities at street level, gleaning knowledge from the seemingly mundane details of everyday life. Engels' work directly or indirectly inspired the members of the legendary Chicago School, detailed below, generations of realist American urban novelists such as Upton Sinclair, Theodore Dreiser, Ann Petry, and Nelson Algren, and influential social commentators ranging from Jacob Riis to Alex Kotlowitz.

The most dramatic and comprehensive survey of an American municipality during the nineteenth century was the 1865 *Report of the Council of Hygiene and Public Health of the Citizens' Association of New York Upon the Sanitary Condition of the City*. By the middle of the century, New York was not only the nation's largest urban area, it also bore the reputation for being the filthiest city in the Western world. Physicians and other members of the Citizens' Association of New York worked as a team to map and compare every dwelling and parcel of property in New York City against a checklist of twenty-two criteria, ranging from street cleanliness to the presence of overcrowding, sickness, and high mortality. The results were nothing short of staggering, revealing a city in decay where thousands of people died each year from preventable disease. Like Manchester, New York was a city divided by class, with its filthiest and deadliest sections housing the poor. Wealthy and middle-class residents were not immune to the deadly effects of "offensive nuisances" such as slaughterhouses, manure yards, and fat-rendering plants located near their homes or commuter routes [see **Figure 6.2 "Encroachment of Nuisances Upon Populous Up-Town Districts"**]. The report generated such intense public outcry that the following year the New York state government created the Metropolitan Board of Health, the first modern health department in the United States, in order to clean up New York City.[8]

The year 1865 also witnessed the formation of the American Social Science Association (ASSA) in Boston, Massachusetts. This powerful group and its publication, the *Journal of Social Science* (which commenced in 1869) provided a conduit between the study of cities and advocacy for fixing urban problems. Additionally, the ASSA fostered fledgling formal academic disciplines, especially economics, history, political science, and sociology. At the request of the Massachusetts Board of State Charities, prominent Boston-area reformers organized the ASSA in the model of the British National Association for the Promotion of Social Science to better understand and address statistical and philanthropic matters, including sanitary conditions, employment, education, crime, and mental illness. Throughout the 1870s–

1890s, the nation's most influential social reformers and academics gathered at ASSA annual meetings, held in cities throughout the United States, to exchange information and formulate plans of action. The *Journal of Social Science* published pieces by such public intellectuals as Frederick Douglass, Florence Kelley, Charles Loring Brace, and W. E. B. Du Bois. Members of the ASSA also spun off a number of more specialized social reform organizations, including the National Prison Association (established in 1870), the National Conference of Charities and Corrections (established in 1874), and the American Health Association (also established in 1874). ASSA members routinely engaged social concerns directly, speaking out about the dire conditions faced by the urban poor and becoming well-known outside academia for their efforts. Social science professors even brought their students into the streets to study conditions first-hand.[9]

The marriage between social activism and the traditionally conservative university curriculum did not last. While social reformers sought to influence the behavior of others through moral suasion and government regulation, academics were more concerned about establishing legitimacy and authority within their own newly emerging disciplines, as well as avoiding conflict with administrative officials and wealthy donors who might object to politically charged activism. As such, the various divisions of the ASSA fractured, and ASSA members contributed to the founding of the American Historical Association (established in 1884), the American Economic Association (established in 1885), the American Political Science Association (established in 1903), and the American Sociology Society (established in 1905). By 1912, the ASSA ceased to exist and what little remained of the body eventually folded into the National Institute of Social Sciences. Nonetheless, cities and their residents remained the subject of inquiry and reform.

Two areas in particular that generated investigations and activism were the effects of widespread immigration on the cultural life of the nation and the rise of political machines led by party bosses, many of whom rose to power by securing the loyalty of newly naturalized immigrants residing in cities. Following the influx of people during colonial settlement, the first great wave of immigration to the young United States occurred in the 1840s–1850s, with some 4.3 million people arriving, largely from Ireland, Germany, Great Britain, and Canada. Many of these immigrants settled in cities and joined the large numbers of native-born Americans who had moved from the countryside in search of economic opportunity. By 1860, almost 20 percent of the total U.S. population was urban. Immigration leveled off in the 1860s–1870s at about 2.5 million per decade, and then shot up again to 5.2 million in the 1880s. By 1890, almost 15 percent of the total U.S. population was foreign-born, the highest percentage of the nineteenth century. Nearly 3.7 million more immigrants came in the 1890s and total immigration numbers peaked at 8.7 million in the decade between 1900 and 1910, with two-thirds of these people coming from Southern and Eastern Europe. The foreign-born and their children comprised a sizable portion of the urban population, and in some cities by the late 1890s made up a majority of the local residents. For example, immigrants and their children comprised 79 percent of the population of Chicago in 1890. In 1920, just over 13 percent of all Americans were foreign-born and more than half (51.2 percent) lived in cities.

The settling of so many people in urban spaces resulted in chronic overcrowding. In the tradition of the Citizens' Association and the ASSA, journalists, housing reformers, and officials representing government commissions documented and assessed the reasons for such wretched conditions, often recommending specific steps to bring about change. Perhaps the most famous of these investigations was the 1890 work of journalist and Progressive Era reformer Jacob Riis, *How the Other Half Lives: Studies Among the Tenements of New York* [see Document 3.5, "The Mixed Crowd"]. Riis (1849–1914), himself a Danish immigrant, spent years as a police reporter and worked closely with charity aid workers, public health officials, and others interested in assisting New York's poor. Although steeped in denigrating stereotypes of ethnic groups, the book did provide the city's privileged classes with unforgettable stories and heart-wrenching insights into the daily life of immigrant New Yorkers. Riis' work encouraged the passage of the Tenement House Law of 1901, which required improved light and ventilation in multi-family properties and called for the establishment of New York City's Tenement House Department.

Riis was part of a much larger national reform movement during the so-called Progressive Era of approximately 1889–1920. Progressives attempted to reign in abuses of power; they brought business-like practices to notoriously corrupt city government. Many progressives turned away from the idea of Social Darwinism, coming to believe that immigrants, the impoverished, and others in need within the city were deserving recipients of their efforts. Progressives believed that with the development of social services, these once marginal urban dwellers could themselves become society's leaders. Social settlement house workers spearheaded this movement within the city by moving directly into immigrant neighborhoods to provide assistance. Settlement house workers contributed to the creation of the academic study of sociology, informing generations of academics with their findings and their methodologies.

Jane Addams (1860–1935) and Ellen Gates Starr (1859–1940) arrived in Chicago in 1889 and established the nation's most influential settlement house, Hull-House, on the city's Near West Side [see Document 5.5 "Hull-House, A Social Settlement" (1894) and Document 5.6 "Growing up with a City" (1926)]. Jane Addams and Ellen Gates Starr were both graduates of Rockford Female Seminary in Rockford, Illinois. Starr spent much of her life working on labor issues and leading programs at Hull-House, where she expressed a special interest in bookbinding and taught the skill to students of all ages. Hull-House offered a broad range of programs to the newly arrived immigrants and their families living in the surrounding area. The services included health care, kindergarten, literature courses, and clubs for young working women. Addams' and Starr's 1888 visit to London's Toynbee Hall led to the creation of Hull-House. Jane Addams achieved acclaim for her work on behalf of the poor and her international peace advocacy. Addams, perhaps the best-known woman of her day, inspired like-minded people in other cities; by 1900 there were approximately 500 settlement houses in the United States. Addams' many books include *Hull-House Maps and Papers* (1895), a thoroughly researched edited collection complete with multi-colored maps indicating wage, ethnicity, and other neighborhood differentials. *Hull-House Maps and Papers* and Addams' *Twenty Years at Hull-House* (1910) are still taught at colleges and universities, which demonstrates how advocates for social reform can influence academic pursuits. Addams was linked with a number of influential academics, including John Dewey (1859–1952) who taught at the University of Chicago between 1894 and 1904 and founded the Chicago School of Pragmatism there. Dewey challenged generations of educators to rethink the structure of higher education and the public school.[10]

Fighting government corruption was another area of interest for urban reformers. By the middle of the nineteenth century, explosive population growth, economic expansion, and the physical transformation of urban space brought about increasing demands by citizens for new government regulations and municipal services. As the nature of local and state government shifted in emphasis from touting individual responsibility to support for providing employment for individuals and lucrative contracts for private sector companies, opportunities for graft and malfeasance blossomed. At the center of this transformation of government were political parties and their bosses, who oversaw the election of politicians and the distribution of patronage (i.e., jobs) and other spoils of office for loyal party members. One of the most notorious of these bosses was New York City's William M. Tweed (1823–1878).

Tweed used his connections as a member of Tammany Hall—the political machine associated with the Democratic Party which manifested influence from the 1790s to the 1960s—to swindle millions of dollars from city coffers. Political bosses operated in other locations and in other eras, although the heyday of the political boss was between the Civil War and the Great Depression. Well-known bosses include Democrat Daniel P. O'Connell in Albany (who wielded party power between the 1920s and the 1970s), Democrat Richard J. Daley in Chicago (1953–1976), Republican George Cox in Cincinnati (approximately 1880s–1911), and Democrat Thomas Pendergast in Kansas City (approximately 1925–1936) [see **Document 5.2 "William Tweed's Confession"**].

Tweed's nefarious activities, and similar antics by Democrat and Republican politicians in communities all across the country, led to citizen reform organizations and investigations by journalists and state legislative bodies. Such corruption placed cities in a precarious position since, as legal creations of their state government, they could and often did find their right to self-government revoked or severely restricted. Reactions to political machines within Boston, Chicago, Cleveland, Kansas City, New York City, Philadelphia, St. Louis, and other cities inspired an array of municipal reforms during the Progressive Era that called for adherence to "good government" and sound business practices. Progressives promoted the implementation of civil service programs, whereby public employees were hired and promoted on the basis of merit rather than party affiliation.

A new style of journalism called muckraking provided commentary on the changing city and offered practical direction for emerging public policy. English newspaper editor William T. Stead's *If Christ Came to Chicago!*, imagined what Christ would have thought about Chicago if he had visited at the time of the city's momentous World's Fair of 1893. Stead (1849–1912) concluded that Christ would have found Chicago a reprehensible city, its values steeped in base concerns. Stead wrote:

This vast and heterogeneous community, which has been collected together from all quarters of the known world, knows only one common bond. Its members came here to make money. They are staying here to make money. The quest of the almighty dollar is their Holy Grail.[11]

Another muckraker journalist, Lincoln Steffens (1866–1936), writing in the pages of *McClure's Magazine* alongside his notable colleagues Ida Tarbell and Ray Stannard Baker, focused on ineffectual and unethical city governments. Steffens' opinions inspired a generation of urban political reformers and a collection of his essays, published as *The Shame of the Cities* (1904), remains a staple in urban studies, history, urban planning, and political science courses to this day [see **Document 5.3 "Philadelphia: Corrupt and Contented"**]. Arguably, the most famous and influential of these writers was Upton Sinclair (1878–1968), whose novel *The Jungle* (1906) sought to expose the destitute life of the working class in Chicago and the brutality of the American wage labor system. Rather than responding to his indictment of capitalism, the public reacted with outrage to his depictions of unsanitary practices within the meatpacking industry. Sinclair lamented in his autobiography, "I aimed at the public's heart, but by accident I hit it in the stomach."[12] As a result of intense public pressure, and sagging sales of processed meats, the federal government enacted the Meat Inspection Act and the related legislation, the Pure Food and Drug Act, in mid-1906.

At the same time that these campaigns against urban problems fueled actual political reform, they also inspired academics. While critics of higher education commonly deride the professoriate as being ensconced in an ivory tower, a place wholly separate from the real world, leading scholars have long been aware of and influenced by the challenges of their local, national, and global surroundings. Urban historians, sociologists, and theorists must, of necessity, grow ties with the "real world" rather than hiding from it. Although academics busied themselves with establishing their disciplines

during the 1880s and 1890s, they still did not ignore the plight of cities around them. Many promising young scholars joined their friends and colleagues in social settlements and various reform movements, conducting surveys of communities all across the United States.

British businessman and social investigator Charles Booth (1840–1916) led the way by inspiring a new generation of researchers to investigate cities first-hand. Despite a lack of formal academic training, Booth directed a group of scholars gathering data on private households throughout London, England. Booth's team gathered information on social conditions, religion, wages, and occupations for what would become the multi-volume *Life and Labour of the People of London*, conducted between 1886 and 1903.[13] Heavily laden with statistics, charts, and richly detailed colored maps, *Life and Labour* harkened back to the work of the sanitarians in the early half of the nineteenth century and heavily influenced the social survey movement of the 1890s–1920s. *Life and Labour* was also quite similar to Jane Addams' *Hull-House Maps and Papers* (1895) and other investigative works published by settlement house workers. Booth's study was so well-received that in 1892 the Royal Statistical Society awarded him their first Guy Medal (named for the British statistician William Guy) and elected him to serve as their president between 1892–1894.

Although not necessarily confined to cities, the survey movement resulted in thousands of separate studies on the social structure, economic characteristics, and leading problems of municipalities throughout the United States. The most famous of these was the Pittsburgh Survey, conceived in 1906 as the first major attempt within the United States to investigate the social life of one place by a research team. Seventy-four people conducted the field research, including social reformers from Pittsburgh, Hull-House's Florence Kelly, South End (Boston) House's Robert Woods, and other settlement house leaders from across the country. These social reformers were joined by academics, such as the University of Wisconsin's John R. Commons and his student John

Fitch. The Pittsburgh Survey examined housing conditions, the way in which gender affects work, the ethnic and racial composition of the workforce, union issues, and the multifaceted influence of manufacturing—particularly the power and influence of the steel industry—in six volumes published from 1909–1914. Excerpts from these volumes also appeared as articles in the widely read periodical, *Survey* (formerly *Charities and the Commons*).

Although the Pittsburgh Survey was widely publicized, some contemporary scholars argue it had little initial impact on the development of empirical research methods in academic social science. Such methods, particularly in the field of sociology, were evolving independently in the early twentieth century. Sociologist Martin Bulmer posits that the Pittsburgh Survey, like much the social survey movement in the United States, was ultimately more akin to the journalism of Riis and Steffens. According to Bulmer, the content of the Pittsburgh Survey lacked integration, although it was factual and systematic in scope. The survey remained, however, undeniably important for bringing a wide range of middle-class professionals from settlement houses "into the orbit of social investigation."[14]

Another innovative contribution to social science research was *The Philadelphia Negro: A Social Study* (1899) by the African American sociologist W. E. B. Du Bois (1868–1963). Du Bois studied at Fisk University, Harvard University (where he earned his Ph.D.), and the University of Berlin. Du Bois' work was related to that of Charles Booth and Jane Addams. Du Bois moved to Philadelphia in 1896 with his wife and lived above a cafeteria in the city's Seventh Ward, well known for its large black population. Du Bois conducted in-depth interviews, compiled statistical data, and used maps to describe the living and working conditions of black Philadelphians. Primarily trained as a historian, Du Bois' outlook included a broad sweep of the social sciences, and his published work contributed in a direct way to the field of sociology. As sociologist Elijah Anderson argues, Du Bois represents an essential link in the empirical chain between academic social science and the settlement house movement. Anderson notes that Du Bois' studies are seminal, not just for their investigations of the urban poor, but also for being among the first to formally consider race in urban America. However, as Bulmer notes, because Du Bois was black and taught for a lengthy time at a black institution of higher education (Atlanta University—now Clark Atlanta University), his work initially had less impact than it should have within the white social science community.[15]

Sociologists and the City

The evolution of mainstream academic research on cities began in Europe. The establishment of the modern university and the emergent academic disciplines and professions paralleled the rise of the industrial city. German theorists in particular paved the way for work done in the United States. The 1887 publication of sociologist Ferdinand Tönnies' treatise on societal change, *Gemeinschaft und Gesellschaft* (*Community and Society*), remains a watershed moment in urban scholarship. In this volume, Tönnies (1855–1936) theorized that the modern world was transitioning away from communities built upon kinship relations (*gemeinschaft*), to the multivalent, urban society (*gesellschaft*), in which everyday life was defined by contracts and non-familial connection. Modern commentaries typically portray Tönnies as saddened by this movement towards *gesellschaft* community, but this interpretation of his stance may be overdrawn.[16]

French sociologist Emile Durkheim (1858–1917) was clearer in his classic work, *The Division of Labor in Society* (1893). Durkheim differentiated the mechanical solidarity of the rural village from what he termed the organic solidarity of urban life, where everyone in a functioning society had a particular role to fill. Taken at face value, this theory appeared to give a more positive coloration to the urbanization of modern life than did Tönnies' argument, but Durkheim also famously introduced the concept of *anomie*, or disorientation based on the challenges and multiple stimuli of urban life. Durkheim theorized that the pressures of *anomie* can lead ultimately to increased suicide levels. This idea was brought to fruition in the writing of Georg Simmel (1858–1918), especially in his essay "The Metropolis and Mental Life" (1905).[17]

The influence of German scholars on urban theory in the United States came through the establishment of graduate programs in the social sciences, most notably at the Johns Hopkins University and the University of Chicago, in the late nineteenth century. Sociologists at Chicago, in particular, took the lead in urban research by adding empirical evidence from direct field research to the ideas of their German counterparts. Adherents of the so-called Chicago School sought to examine the city as an object of detached analysis and, as such, abandoned the nineteenth-century tradition of merging urban investigations with social activism. In the process they laid the intellectual framework for how most American social scientists, and even many urban historians, viewed cities.

Robert E. Park (1864–1944), a student of Georg Simmel and John Dewey, is widely regarded as the founder of the Chicago School. Park's collection of essays, *The City: Suggestions for the Study of Human Nature in the Urban Environment*, written with his colleagues at Chicago, Ernest W. Burgess (1886–1966) and Roderick D. McKenzie (1885–1940), forever changed scholarly research on urban environments. In addition to finding inspiration from German sociologists, the Chicago School also borrowed liberally from the sciences, especially biology, and perceived the city in ecological terms, akin to a living organism. The concept of social ecology sought to explain patterns of urbanization with models that could be applied universally to all cities. The most famous was Ernest W. Burgess' concentric zone model, which laid out a physical outline of a typical industrial American city in the 1920s [see **Mike Davis' "Beyond Blade Runner" in Part I for a modified view of Burgess' model**].

Members of the Chicago School took to the streets and neighborhoods of America's second city, producing an impressive number of case studies that made it the most studied city in the country, if not the world. Influential students of Robert E. Park used his views in their case studies. Harvey Zorbaugh's 1929 work, *The Gold Coast and the Slum*, followed the idea of the city as an organism and highlighted the interdependency of wealthy and poor Chicagoans. William I. Thomas' and Polish sociologist Florian Znaniecki's *The Polish Peasant in Europe and America* (published in separate volumes between 1918 and 1920) was heralded as one of the most important works of sociology in the period.

Beyond Chicago, sociologists also explored the nature of urban life in smaller cities. This was an important development and one worth reviving today; too often modern urban studies focus only on megacities (cities of ten million or more residents), ignoring the smaller, and perhaps more representative, locales. The most famous work on smaller-sized cities was Robert S. Lynd's (1892–1970) and Helen Merrell Lynd's (1896–1982) study of Muncie, Indiana published in 1929 as *Middletown: A Study in American Civilization*. As is common in the social survey movement, the Lynds sought to study everything they could about one community. They examined paid work, home, schools, leisure, religious, and civic activities within the anonymous community they referred to only as Middletown. Only in later years was Middletown revealed to be Muncie. *Middletown* established a scholarly model for community sociology. *Middletown* was also very popular with a general audience. During the 1930s, the Lynds returned to Muncie to study the impact of the Great Depression. The result was *Middletown in Transition: A Study in Cultural Conflicts* (1937), which further theorized social and economic change in urban America. Since then, numerous other studies of Muncie have been undertaken, making it the most thoroughly documented small city in the United States. The complete collection of documents gathered on Muncie now comprises the Middletown Studies Collection & Digital Archives administered by Ball State University.[18]

Urban theory advanced further in 1938 when another member of the Chicago School, Louis Wirth (1897–1952), published "Urbanism as a Way of Life" in the *American Journal of Sociology*. Wirth refined the distinctions put forward by the German theorists regarding the differences between urban and rural life when he argued that the size, density, and heterogeneity of an urban area influenced the outlook and behavior of its inhabitants. As one of the definitive statements of the Chicago School, "Urbanism as a Way of Life" remains one of the most important and widely read essays in all of urban sociology. Wirth's work influenced generations of social scientists and social workers eager to understand life in cities and reform urban problems. Building from Wirth, many of these professionals focused on negative aspects of urban life, especially perceptions of family decline, the breakdown of primary groups and ties, the concept of *anomie*, and social deviance.[19]

However, in 1962, sociologist Herbert J. Gans challenged Wirth's argument in his book chapter "Urbanism and Suburbanism as Ways of Life" in which he argued that there was no single urban, or even suburban, way of life [see **"Urbanism and Suburbanism as Ways of Life: A Reevaluation of Definitions" in Part I**]. Gans examined five major types of inner-city residents, the "cosmopolites," the "unmarried and childless," the "ethnic villagers," the "deprived," and the "trapped and downwardly mobile" and found that residential instability, rather than population size, density, and heterogeneity of cities caused the social features of the urbanism identified by Wirth. Drawing on his own study of a suburban Levittown development, Gans expanded the focus of urban inquiry beyond the inner city to the outer city, i.e., residential neighborhoods and adjacent suburbs, where he found relationships between people to be "quasi-primary," or more intimate than secondary ties, yet more guarded than primary. For Gans, socioeconomic class status and lifecycle stage were more important than settlement type, and this conclusion led him to assert that a sociological definition of the city, as was formulated by Wirth, could not be made.

Enter the Historians: The City as Frontier

While sociologists were busy conducting field research, theorizing the nature of urban life, and formalizing the vibrant subfield of urban sociology, historians were just beginning to contemplate the impact of cities on America's development. This tardiness led noted urban scholar Richard C. Wade (1921–2008) to muse in retrospect that "Historians have arrived at the study of the city by slow freight."[20] Beginning in the 1930s and early 1940s, Arthur M. Schlesinger, Sr. (1888–1965) and a small number of historians commenced the first wave of scholarly interest in American urban history. In 1933, Schlesinger's *The Rise of the City* appeared as part of the multi-volume "A History of American Life" series published by Macmillan and edited by Schlesinger and his colleague Dixon Ryan Fox (1887–1945). The June 1940 edition of *The Mississippi Valley Historical Review* carried Schlesinger's seminal article "The City in American History," which signaled the emergence of urban history as a vibrant and viable field of study within the larger historical profession [see the updated version of this essay in Part I].[21]

Historians had not completely ignored cities before Schlesinger. A few acknowledged and even briefly commented upon urban growth when writing about related themes such as industrialization, immigration, labor, capital accumulation, and regional difference. In the main, though, historians concerned themselves with political and economic narratives that stressed American distinctiveness. Cities, commonly associated with Europe and its ills, did not fit neatly into this script and were left to social scientists for rigorous inquiry. It is no surprise, then, to find that early in Schlesinger's career, while a professor of history at Iowa State University in 1921, he turned to the *American Journal of Sociology* to publish his article "The Significance of Immigration in American History."[22] Other historians also recognized the importance of the city, and in 1932 a committee of the American Historical Association (AHA) formally concluded that cities and urbanism needed further study. That same decade, Carl

Bridenbaugh, Constance McLaughlin Green, Robert Albion, Sidney Pomerantz, and, of course, Schlesinger, published on colonial and select nineteenth-century cities.[23]

The backdrop for this first round of heightened interest in cities was the conclusion of the U.S. Census Bureau in 1920 that, for the first time in history, the majority of Americans lived in urban areas. The shift from a majority rural to a majority urban nation was not only a significant turning point in America's evolution, it also influenced the writing of American history. This paradigm shift paralleled the finding three decades earlier by the Census Bureau that the line of frontier settlement had ceased to exist. The demise of the frontier led a young history professor at the University of Wisconsin named Frederick Jackson Turner (1861–1932) to deliver what would become his most famous work, "The Significance of the Frontier in American History," at the meeting of the AHA concurrent with the World's Columbian Exhibition in Chicago during July 1893. Turner's argument that the abundance of "free land" on the frontier had shaped America's uniquely democratic institutions did not immediately take hold. However, Turner's clarity and ability to synthesize large periods of time and space while extolling the perceived virtues of American exceptionalism propelled his interpretation of national development to the forefront of the historical profession during the early twentieth century.

Ever perceptive to social transformations, Turner—by the early 1920s a Harvard professor in the twilight of his scholarly career—knew that an urban reinterpretation was near. He even made notes for a paper outlining the significance of the city in American history. Although he never finished this work, Turner did express concern to his eventual replacement in the Harvard history department, Arthur M. Schlesinger, Sr., that any such revaluation must lie squarely in the American rather than European political and historical tradition.[24] Schlesinger's 1940 work, "The City in American History," did just that, by weaving the narrative synthesis of U.S. history trumpeted by Turner and Charles Beard (1874–1948) into

the history of cities. Schlesinger stated that the themes of the frontier and economic conflict were central organizing concepts behind the growth of cities. In bold strokes, Schlesinger argued that the city, no less than the country, was responsible for shaping American culture. He also bridged the long-standing divide between urban and rural ways of life by arguing that, in the end, the distinction between city and country blurred as each became more and more like the other.

Almost immediately, though, there were those who cautioned against such revisionist history without the development of a corresponding theory of urbanism to provide a framework. In 1941, William Diamond argued that while Schlesinger's essay did much to advance Turner's call for an urban reinterpretation, it still lacked clear definitions of central terms, especially "urban" and "city," which have multiple meanings. Diamond pointed out that historians could learn much from urban sociologists, such as those at the University of Chicago, particularly in terms of creating categories of classification and analysis. Even urban sociologists had not advanced far enough for the demanding Diamond, who asserted that little effort had been made to formulate a comprehensive theory of urbanism. He did deign to label Louis Wirth's 1938 essay, "Urbanism as a Way of Life," an "exceedingly interesting attempt" at theorization.[25]

In what would become a familiar pattern in American urban historiography, Diamond's critique had little impact on the production of scholarly monographs, the majority of which continued to be case studies of individual communities that were, as historian Michael Frisch noted in 1979, "idiographic" in approach, devoid of generalizations about the nature of urban life. In 1960, Eric Lampard suggested a new direction for urban historians and urban sociologists, calling for rigorous examination of urbanization as a societal process and an end to the traditional focus on the perceived "problems" or deviance of cities in contrast to romantic notions of rural life. Although he was critical of the sociological conception of "ideal types," he did advocate the "ecological complex" model advanced by sociologists in the field of human ecology such as Amos H. Hawley and Leo F. Schnore, which defined community structure as the interplay between population and environment mediated by technology and organization.[26]

Lampard found his attempt at theorization largely ignored. Part of the reason lies in the long-standing reluctance of American historians in general to engage in rigid structural analysis, Marxist or otherwise, or highly theoretical approaches that are the hallmark of sociology and other social science disciplines. In fact, many contemporary historians do not even consider themselves social scientists and instead stress a narrative approach more common to the humanities. As Michael Frisch argues, analytical power implied descriptive weakness for those American urban historians who were "committed to the more traditional goal of the fullest possible historical explanation … rather than a framework of conditions necessary to such explanation."[27] In practice, then, most urban historians followed Blake McKelvey's reasoning that there should be "no qualms about writing local history," since the goal of the historian, in contrast to the sociologist, is to "trace the forces and directions of human social movement through time and place [rather] than to define inflexible patterns."[28]

A mild undercurrent of debate persists as to whether history is really a social science or a humanistic discipline. Urban historians, who draw overtly and covertly from sociology, geography, psychology, and other social sciences, most often take advantage of the growing acceptance of interdisciplinarity within history, and may label themselves social scientists. This tendency is supported by the high number of urban historians with membership in the Social Science History Association (formally organized in 1974), which features a network devoted to urban concerns. On the other hand, urban historians with a deep connection to the humanities are also easy to find within the field. Oral history, a growing methodology within urban history and urban studies, shares obvious methodological connections with English and American Studies, for oral history transcripts and recordings are carefully parsed just like poems, short stories, or novels would be within literary and cultural studies.

The 1960s and 1970s witnessed a second round of interest in American urban history, set against the backdrop of the tremendous political and social change that swept the nation and transformed the historical profession. Leading this wave of new scholarship was Richard C. Wade, who influenced an entire generation of urban scholars with his noteworthy 1958 article "Urban Life in Western America, 1790–1830," and the books *The Urban Frontier: The Rise of Western Cities, 1790–1850* (1959) and *Slavery in the Cities: The South, 1820–1860* (1964)[29] [see **"Urban Life in Western America, 1790–1830" in Part II**]. Wade, a former graduate student of Schlesinger's at Harvard, set Turner on his head by proclaiming that the establishment of towns spearheaded the American frontier. Wade traced this line of reasoning all the way back to Josiah Strong. In 1885, Strong had surmised that Western growth was launched by the presence of the railroads, solidified by the growth of towns, and, finally, bolstered by the farms that followed town development.[30]

Another pathbreaking work in this period was Sam Bass Warner's *Streetcar Suburbs: The Process of Urban Growth in Boston, 1870–1900* (1962), which demonstrated how urban sprawl preceded the automobile [see **"From Walking City to the Implementation of the Street Railways," in Part VII**]. *Streetcar Suburbs* provided a conceptual framework for the evolution of urban physical space and differentiation by class within a single Boston case study. *Streetcar Suburbs* shaped how scholars across numerous disciplines understand suburban growth and the impact of transportation on American cities. Warner, whose collective body of work comes as close as any urban historian to fulfilling the promise of understanding urbanization as a process, was widely influential in shaping the so-called "new urban history" along with his colleague Stephan Thernstrom, author of *Poverty and Progress: Social Mobility in a Nineteenth Century*

City (1964). Thernstom, in particular, is credited with a move toward quantification within social history, which led to a long-lived debate regarding the relative reliability of quantitative versus qualitative data. The resonance of this particular infighting has considerably lessened over the decades. Together, Warner and Thernstrom provided models of scholarship that broke with traditional ways of presenting America's past, frequently referred to as "consensus history." So-called consensus history stressed the common unity of the American political, social, and cultural experience and held little room for tension and conflict, especially for those often found on the margins of power, such as working people, minorities, and women.

The promises of quantitative research and the new urban history began to be realized with the work of Theodore Hershberg, who founded and directed the Philadelphia Social History Project between 1969 and 1981. Through generous federal funding, a team of scholars and their assistants gathered and processed census returns and other quantifiable material on the city of Philadelphia, forming a database suited to interdisciplinary and multidisciplinary research. Hershberg conceived of the city in active terms, fulfilling Eric Lampard's call for scholars to think of the city as a process, rather than simply as a place. While the results of the Philadelphia Social History Project were impressive, resulting in a treasure trove of databases, several scholarly books, sixteen doctoral dissertations, and at least 100 articles and papers, it was not enough to sustain the promise of the new urban history. Like Thernstrom and Warner before him, Hershberg grew tired of working within the confines of the new urban history label.[31]

Other fields of historical inquiry have also profoundly shaped the course of urban scholarship. Immigration history is one such subfield, although it commonly lacks proper recognition for its direct relation to urban history. Books that set forth an urban take on immigration, including Oscar Handlin's *Boston's Immigrants, 1790–1965* (1941) and *The Uprooted* (1951), John Bodnar's *The Transplanted: A History of Immigrants*

in Urban America (1985), and Bernard Bailyn's, *The Peopling of North America: An Introduction* (1986), all had enormous influence on the future of urban history. Case studies of the immigrants in particular cities, for which works like Kathleen Neils Conzen's astute commentary, *Immigrant Milwaukee, 1836–1860: Accommodation and Community in a Frontier City* (1976), set the standard, also strengthened the connections between urban and immigration history.

The historical narrative of regional migrants also rounded out the understanding of urban populations. Joe Trotter, Jr.'s *Black Milwaukee: The Making of an Industrial Proletariat, 1915–1945* (1985), Nell I. Painter's *Exodusters: Black Migration to Kansas after Reconstruction* (1977), and James R. Grossman's *Land of Hope: Chicago, Black Southerners, and the Great Migration* (1989) told the story of black migration to cities. White migration, especially the story of the millions of white southern migrants who flooded into the Midwest, aptly captured by Chad Berry's *Northern Migrants, Southern Exiles* (2000), is less often placed in the context of urban history, yet it is a vital component of the story [see **Part VIII for excerpts from Chad Berry's book and Lisa Krissoff Boehm's** *Making a Way out of No Way: African American Women and the Second Great Migration* (2008)]. The study of migrants can be enhanced by examining gender and sexual orientation. Cities proved to be especially alluring to single females, as Joanne Meyerowitz documents in her first book, *Women Adrift: Independent Wage Earners in Chicago, 1880–1930* (1988). The impact of George Chauncey's *Gay New York: Gender, Urban Culture and the Making of the Gay Male World, 1890–1940* (1994) is difficult to overstate[32] [see **Chauncey's essay in Part IV**].

While many of these works share themes and settings common to the new urban history, they compose part of a much larger movement within the American historical tradition, called the "new social history." The new social history grew out of interest in and concern over social and political issues facing the United States in the 1960s and 1970s, especially those affecting groups of people traditionally outside of mainstream historical research. This "history from the bottom up" has encouraged an explosion of scholarship that, in essence, has resulted in the dominance of social history within the American historical profession over the last few decades. As Thomas Bender notes, though, this new American history is much more than the triumph of social history, it is a broader transformation in which "the domain of the historical has been vastly extended, inherited narratives displaced, new subjects and narratives introduced."[33]

Urban history cannot help but have an overlapping agenda with urban geography. Geographer John W. Reps' *The Making of Urban America: A History of City Planning in the United States* (1965) remains essential reading for serious urban historians. James T. Lemon's *The Best Poor Man's Country: A Geographical Study of Early Southeastern Pennsylvania* (1972) and *Liberal Dreams and Nature's Limits: Great Cities of North America Since 1600* (1996) relates key facts about the growth of American cities since colonial settlement. William Cronon introduced a generation of historians to the basic tenets of geography, including the way in which cities relate to their hinterlands, with his widely read *Nature's Metropolis: Chicago and the Great West* (1991). Cronon segues neatly into environmental history and environmental studies, fields which continue to influence, and be influenced by, urban history. Additionally noteworthy in the cross-pollination of urban and environmental history are the works of Samuel P. Hays, Martin V. Melosi, Christine M. Rosen, and Joel A. Tarr.[34] [see **Part V for essays by Melosi and Tarr**].

Another trend that began in the 1960s and gained pace in the 1970s was the establishment of urban studies programs at colleges and universities across the nation. Polarizing and geographically widespread riots took place in American cities during the 1960s. They combined with a host of other social, political, and economic trends to produce a so-called "urban crisis" that seemed to threaten the viability of cities. Institutions of higher education sought to offer new curricula, majors, and programs to promote the understanding and management of this extensive social change [see **Parts V, VIII, and IX for essays and documents on various aspects of the "urban crisis"**]. These programs differed greatly in their structure and approach. Some offered graduate or undergraduate courses through standalone departments, while others were fed by faculty located in a variety of departments. Emphasis varied widely, including professional or academic tracks and interdisciplinary or multidisciplinary focuses. Some programs highlighted public policy analysis, while others had strengths in social work, public administration, non-profit management, education, or planning. Very few of the urban studies programs boasted of strengths in urban history. In 1969, a group of leaders from these urban studies programs formed the Council of University Institutes for Urban Affairs in Boston, Massachusetts. In 1981, this body became the Urban Affairs Association (UAA). The UAA remains as one of the leading professional organizations for urban scholars.

The present-day practice of urban studies often centers upon the question of whether or not a Los Angeles School of Urbanism—popularly identified, like the city itself, as simply the L.A. School—has come to replicate the influence had by the Chicago School during the early twentieth century. Allen J. Scott's and Edward W. Soja's *The City: Los Angeles and Urban Theory at the End of the Twentieth Century* (1996) perhaps best approaches the debate over whether L.A. typifies the contemporary city or is a place without precedents or antecedents. What does L.A.'s history tell us about other American cities, if anything? The Huntington Library, the University of California-Los Angeles, and the L.A. School of Urbanism at the University of Southern California all promote the L.A. School at an institutional level. They question whether or not Los Angeles, the city that first comes to mind when one discusses urban sprawl and automobile-based congestion, has something to tell us about American cities generally. The University of Southern California's website states, "In a nutshell, the difference between Chicago and L.A. is this: whereas traditional Chicago-based concepts of urbanism imagine a city organized around its central core, in L.A. urbanism, the urban peripheries are organizing what is left of the center. For many, this difference is emblematic of a shift toward postmodern urbanism."[35]

The L.A. School owes quite a bit to writer, activist, and academic Mike Davis, whose innovative works, including *City of Quartz: Excavating the Future in Los Angeles* (1990) and *The Ecology of Fear: Los Angeles and the Imagination of Disaster* (2000), brought new focus to the impact of the city [see **Davis' essay in Part I**]. Perhaps the most important lesson of L.A. is not its sprawling landscape but the extent of its global connections, especially the influence of Asian capital, Asian immigrants, and Mexican and South American immigrants within the city. The L.A. School asks if Los Angeles is *the* city of the *world*, and not just the United States. The possibility that the rest of the world might become more like L.A. frightens many urbanists. Imagining more of the world's cities being consumed by an L.A.-style sprawl worries more than only the pessimistic pundits. Greater world reliance on the automobile and fossil fuels would bring staggering ramifications. Here, again, Mike Davis offers a possible picture of our global future through the nexus of rapid urbanization and capitalist globalization in *Planet of Slums* (2007). Another vision of the future where the rest of the world catches up to trends set in motion in the urban United States is Fareed Zakaria's *The Post-American World* (2008). While not an urbanist in his academic training or other writings, Zakaria's book has raised calls for a rigorous examination of the implications of the new global and highly urbanized economy.[36]

The depth and breadth of urban scholarship has come a long way from the streets of London and Manchester, in the United Kingdom, and New York, Chicago, and Pittsburgh within the United States. In 1988, the Urban History Association (UHA) was formed by 264 charter members in order to stimulate scholarship on world cities in all periods of history. Richard C. Wade served as the UHA's first president; the organization now holds biennial meetings and awards prizes for books, articles, and dissertations. Despite this progress, many urban historians believe there are unresolved theoretical issues. For example, in 1990, approximately 250 urban historians gathered in Chicago to commemorate the fiftieth anniversary of Schlesinger's article, "The City in History." The event proved bittersweet, for it revealed that urban historians remained divided about the success of their chosen field. Some lamented the lack of coherence within the field, which seemed not to have a real sense of a canon. Yet the more upbeat found the widespread impact of urban history an exhilarating challenge. Margaret Marsh attempted to explain this duality by pointing out how the goals of "new urban history" were not always complementary:

> The first was a passionate commitment to find in history a set of keys that would enable policy makers to gain a more enlightened perspective on contemporary urban problems. In this quest, for so it must be defined, scholars drew much of their inspiration from an earlier group of activist scholars, the social ecologists of the Chicago school of the 1920s. Another influence on the "new" urban historians came from a more recent empirical trend in the social sciences, particularly political science and sociology.[37]

Marsh concluded by stressing the importance of agency as a way of successfully rejuvenating urban history. Continued focus on agency would add the voices of the marginalized to the historical story. She urged scholars to "develop a research agenda that, in illuminating issues central to the human experience, makes our own contributions both larger and more compelling."[38]

Sixteen years later, however, many of the same themes continued to reverberate in a lively exchange on the state of urban history between noted academics Clay McShane, Carl Abbott, and Timothy Gilfoyle. McShane conducted a thorough review of trends in urban history by examining five separate databases, which included analysis of the field's leading scholarly publication, the *Journal of Urban History*, and book prizes awarded by the UHA. McShane concludes that there is no urban history canon, contested or otherwise. This results in a serious disconnect between urban history and the rest of the history profession. More intriguingly, McShane argues that, given the large number of works with an urban theme that have been recognized by historical societies outside of the UHA, it is quite possible that urban history has simultaneously triumphed among the profession at large, while much of the scholarly output has been disregarded by urban history's own practitioners. Abbott and Gilfoyle, however, see the state of the field in more positive terms. In fact, they argue that the presence of urban themes in other historical subfields is an indication of strength, not weakness, for the field. In a summation of the dialogue, McShane acknowledged that where he sees fragmentation, Carl Abbott sees vitality. For McShane, "the two are not incompatible."[39] Given the long and winding evolution of the field of urban history within the United States, perhaps this is the most astute and judicious assessment that can be made.

Scholars whose work focuses on American cities have greatly contributed to the mission of understanding the nation's past, and helped clarify the contemporary state of affairs within major metropolitan areas and the nation as a whole. If, as it has been argued, social history makes up one of the most influential elements of today's historical studies, and urban history proves to be one of the central themes within social history, urban history ought to be a component of history courses taught at all levels of the educational system. All too often, however, when urban historians explain their subfield to a lay audience, they are first met with puzzled looks and many questions. History, as presented in middle schools and high schools across the nation, has too often devolved into rote memorization of dates and facts for standardized tests. A fixation on dates and facts may make for easier accountability through politically mandated assessments, but the reliance on this tired practice allows little room for innovative theories and thinking. And a preference for teaching factoids and historical "firsts" dwindles opportunities for relaying the moving stories of immigration, migration, and the varied reasons for the establishment and growth of cities. Urban history, urban sociology, and urban geography comprise an inherently compelling building block of knowledge, essential for all learned persons. The field has evolved from the work of social reformers to become one of the most vital aspects of the academy. Relevant to all those who live in or are affected in any way by cities, urban history and urban studies proves to be an engaging field with resonance far beyond the classroom.

NOTES

1. Barbara B. Oberg, ed., *The Papers of Thomas Jefferson*, Volume 32 (Princeton, NJ: Princeton University Press, 2005), 167.
2. Morton and Lucia White, *The Intellectual Versus the City: From Thomas Jefferson to Frank Lloyd Wright* (Cambridge, MA: Harvard University Press and MIT Press, 1962), 1.
3. Thomas Bender, *Toward an Urban Vision: Ideas and Institutions in Nineteenth Century America* (Baltimore, MD: Johns Hopkins University Press, 1991).
4. Andrew Lees, *Cities Perceived: Urban Society in European and American Thought, 1820–1940* (New York: Columbia University Press, 1985), 103. See also pp. 9–10.
5. Martin Bulmer, "The Social Survey Movement and Early Twentieth-Century Sociological Methodology," in Maurine W. Greenwald and Margo Anderson, eds., *Pittsburgh Surveyed: Social Science and Social Reform in the Early Twentieth Century* (Pittsburgh, PA: University of Pittsburgh Press, 1996), 15.
6. Andrew Lees uses the term "statistical movement" in reference to Great Britain, although it certainly applies to activities within the United States as well. See Lees, *Cities Perceived*, 20.
7. Edwin Chadwick, *Report ... From the Poor Law Commissioners, on an Inquiry into the Sanitary Condition of the Labouring Population of Great Britain; With Appendices* (London: W. Clowes and Sons, 1842); John H. Griscom, *The Sanitary Condition of the Laboring Population of New York: With Some Suggestions for its Improvement* (New York: Harper & Brothers, 1845; reprint, Arno & New York Times, 1970). For the influence of Chadwick and Griscom's reports see Martin V. Melosi, *The Sanitary City: Urban Infrastructure in America from Colonial Times to the Present* (Baltimore, MD: Johns Hopkins University Press, 2000), 43–48, 60–62. An assessment of

public health activities on emerging urban environmental values is discussed in Christopher J. Preston and Steven H. Corey, "Public Health and Environmentalism: Adding Garbage to the History of Environmental Ethics," *Environmental Ethics* 27 (Spring 2005): 3–21.

8. Citizens' Association of New York, *Report of the Council of Hygiene and Public Health of the Citizens' Association of New York Upon the Sanitary Condition of the City*, 2nd ed. (New York: D. Appleton and Co., 1866; reprint, New York: Arno Press, 1970), xxii–xxx, xxxix–xlvii, lxi–lxvii, xcii–xcvi. A brief summary of the *Report of the Council of Hygiene* and its impact is discussed in John Duffy, *A History of Public Health in New York City, 1625–1866* (New York: Russell Sage Foundation, 1968), 558–566; Gret Brieger, "Sanitary Reform in New York City: Stephen Smith and the Passage of the Metropolitan Health Bill," in Judith Walzer Leavitt, *Sickness & Health in America: Readings in the History of Medicine and Public Health* (Madison, WI: University of Wisconsin Press, 1985), 339–413; James C. Mohr, *Radical Republicans and Reform in New York During Reconstruction* (Ithaca: Cornell University Press, 1973), 61–69.

9. F. B. Sanborn, "Mother of Associations: A History of the American Social Science Association," *Journal of Social Science*, 46 (1909): 2–6; Dorothy Ross, "The Development of the Social Sciences," in James Farr and Raymond Seidelman, *Discipline and History: Political Science in the United States* (Ann Arbor, MI: University of Michigan Press, 1998), 85; Betsy Jane Clary, "The Evolution of the Allied Social Science Associations," *American Journal of Economics and Sociology*, 67 (5) (2008): 987.

10. Charlene Haddock Seigfried, "Socializing Democracy: Jane Addams and John Dewey," *Philosophy of the Social Sciences*, 29 (2) (1999): 207–230.

11. William T. Stead, *If Christ Came to Chicago!: A Plea for the Union of All Who Love in the Service of All Who Suffer, 1894* (Chicago: Chicago Historical Bookworks, 1990), 123.

12. Carl S. Smith, *Chicago and the American Literary Imagination, 1880–1920* (Chicago: University of Chicago Press, 1984), 170.

13. There are several editions of this work published with various titles by Macmillan and Company in London between 1889 and 1903. For Booth's impact see Harold W. Pfautz, *Charles Booth on the City: Physical Patterns and Social Structure* (Chicago: University of Chicago Press, 1967) and Bulmer, "The Social Survey Movement and Early Twentieth-Century Sociological Methodology," 15–18.

14. Bulmer, "The Social Survey Movement and Early Twentieth-Century Sociological Methodology," 18.

15. Elijah Anderson, "Introduction to the 1996 Edition of The Philadelphia Negro," in W. E. B. Du Bois, *The Philadelphia Negro: A Social Study* (Philadelphia: University of Pennsylvania Press, 1899, 1996): xviii–xix; Bulmer, "The Social Survey Movement and Early Twentieth-Century Sociological Methodology," 22.

16. Mathieu Deflem, "Ferdinand Tönnies (1855–1936)," in Edward Craig, ed., *Routledge Encyclopedia of Philosophy* (London: Routledge, 2001).

17. See Hans Polis, "Anomie in the Metropolis: The City in American Sociology and Psychiatry," *Osiris*, 2nd Series, 18 (2003): 196, 198.

18. Robert S. Lynd and Helen Merrell Lynd, *Middletown: A Study in American Culture* (New York: Harcourt, Brace, and Company, 1929) and Robert V. Kemper, "Middletown," *Encyclopedia of American Urban History*, Volume 2, edited by David Goldfield (New York: Sage, 2007), 475–476.

19. Louis Wirth, "Urbanism as a Way of Life," *American Journal of Sociology*, 44 (10) (1938): 1–24; Hans Polis, "Anomie in the Metropolis: The City in American Sociology and Psychiatry," 200–201; J. John Palen, *The Urban World*, 8th ed. (Boulder, CO: Paradigm Publishers, 2008), 16, 151–152.

20. Richard C. Wade, "An Agenda for Urban History," in Herbert J. Bass, ed., *The State of American History* (Chicago: Quadrangle Books, 1970), 43.

21. Arthur M. Schlesinger, *The Rise of the City, 1878–1898* (New York: Macmillan, 1933) and Arthur M. Schlesinger, "The City in American History," *Mississippi Valley Historical Review*, 27 (1940): 43–66.

22. Arthur M. Schlesinger, "The Significance of Immigration in American History," *American Journal of Sociology*, 27 (1) (1921): 71–85.

23. The AHA committee is mentioned in Bayrd Still, *Urban America: A History With Documents* (Boston: Little, Brown, and Company, 1974), 543. Writing in 1941, William Diamond cited a "vast number of books" written on cities and urbanization in the 1930s. See, William Diamond, "On the Dangers of an Urban Reinterpretation of History," in Eric F. Goldman, ed., *Historiography and Urbanization: Essays in American History in Honor of W. Stull Holt* (Baltimore, MD: Johns Hopkins University Press, 1941; Port Washington, NY: Kennikat Press, 1968), 67. For a sampling of urban monographs in the 1930s see, Robert Albion, *The Rise of the Port of New York, 1815–1860* (New York: Charles Scribner's Sons, 1939); Carl Bridenbaugh, *Cities in the Wilderness: The First Century of Urban Life in America, 1625–1742* (New York: Ronald Press, 1938); Constance McLaughlin Green, *Holyoke, Massachusetts, A Case Study of the Industrial Revolution in America* (New Haven, CT: Yale University Press, 1936); and Sidney Pomerantz, *New York, An All American City 1783–1803* (New York: Columbia University Press, 1938).

24. For Turner's notes on the significance of the city in

American history, see Bayard Still and Diana Kleb-anow, "The Teaching of American Urban History," *The Journal of American History*, 55 (4) (1969): 843. The letter from Turner to Schlesinger is reprinted in Wilbur R. Jacobs, *The Historical World of Frederick Jackson Turner: With Selections From His Correspondence, Narrative by Wilbur R. Jacobs* (New Haven, CT: Yale University Press, 1968), 163–165; on Schlesinger replacing Turner, see Ray Allen Billington, *Frederick Jackson Turner: Historian, Scholar, Teacher* (New York: Oxford University Press, 1973), 386–387.

25. Diamond, "On the Dangers of an Urban Reinterpretation of History," 81, 90 (footnote #64), 100.

26. Eric E. Lampard, "American Historians and the Study of Urbanism," *The American Historical Review*, 67 (1) (1961): 58–60.

27. Michael Frisch, "American Urban History as an Example of Recent Historiography," *History and Theory*, 18 (1979): 355.

28. Blake McKelvey, "Urban History Today," *The American Historical Review*, 57 (4) (1952): 920; Frisch, "American Urban History as an Example of Recent Historiography," 920.

29. Richard C. Wade, "Urban Life in Western America, 1790–1830," *The American Historical Review*, 64 (1) (1958): 14–30; Richard C. Wade, *The Urban Frontier: The Rise of Western Cities, 1790–1850* (Cambridge, MA: Harvard University Press, 1959); Richard C. Wade, *Slavery in the Cities: The South, 1820–1860* (New York: Oxford University Press, 1964).

30. Wade, "An Agenda for Urban History," 60.

31. Theodore Hershberg, ed., *Philadelphia: Work, Space, Family, and Group Experience in the Nineteenth Century* (New York: Oxford University Press, 1981), v–xvi, 3–35; Bas van Heur, "New Urban History," *Encyclopedia of American Urban History*, Volume 2, edited by David Goldfield (New York: Sage, 2007), 538–539; "Theodore Hershberg, Biography," Center for Greater Philadelphia, www.cgp.upenn.edu/th_bio.html, accessed September 28, 2009.

32. See Joe Trotter, Jr., *Black Milwaukee: The Making of an Industrial Proletariat, 1915–1945* (Urbana, IL: University of Illinois Press, 1985); Nell I. Painter, *Exodusters: Black Migration to Kansas after Reconstruction* (New York, NY: Knopf, 1977); James R. Grossman, *Land of Hope: Chicago, Black Southerners, and the Great Migration* (Chicago: University of Chicago Press, 1989); Chad Berry, *Northern Migrants, Southern Exiles* (Urbana, IL: University of Illinois Press, 2000); Lisa Krissoff Boehm, *Making a Way out of No Way: African American Women and the Second Great Migration* (Jackson, MI: University Press of Mississippi, 2009); Joanne Meyerowitz, *Women Adrift: Independent Wage Earners in Chicago,* 1880–1930 (Chicago: University of Chicago Press, 1988); George Chauncey, *Gay New York: Gender, Urban Culture and the Making of the Gay Male World, 1890–1940* (New York: Basic Books, 1994).

33. Thomas Bender, "Strategies of Narrative Synthesis in American History," *The American Historical Review*, 107 (1) (2002): 129.

34. John W. Reps, *The Making of Urban America: A History of City Planning in the United States* (Princeton, NJ: Princeton University Press, 1965); James T. Lemon, *The Best Poor Man's Country: A Geographical Study of Early Southeastern Pennsylvania* (Baltimore, MD: Johns Hopkins University Press, 1972); James T. Lemon, *Liberal Dreams and Nature's Limits: Great Cities of North American Since 1600* (New York: Oxford University Press, 1996); William Cronon, *Nature's Metropolis: Chicago and the Great West* (New York: W. W. Norton, 1991). Joel A. Tarr provides an overview of the works of Cronon, Hays, Melosi, and other urban environmental scholars in Joel A. Tarr, "Urban History and Environmental History in the United States: Complimentary and Overlapping Fields," www.h-net.org/~environ/historiography/usurban.htm, accessed April 7, 2009. For further insights on urbanization as a process see Samuel P. Hays, "From the History of the City to the History of Urbanized Society," *Journal of Urban History*, 19 (4) (1993).

35. See University of Southern California's L.A. School at http://college.usc.edu/la_school.

36. Mike Davis, *Planet of Slums* (London: Verso, 2006) and Fareed Zakaria, *The Post-American World* (New York: W. W. Norton, 2008). In October 2009, the New England Studies Association organized their annual meeting around Zakaria's work with the theme, "The Post-American City."

37. Margaret Marsh, "Old Forms, New Visions: New Directions in United States Urban History," *Pennsylvania History*, 59 (1) (1992): 21.

38. Marsh, "Old Forms, New Visions," 26.

39. Clay McShane, "Response to Abbot and Gilfoyle," *Journal of Urban History*, 32 (4) (2006): 606. See also Clay McShane, "The State of the Art in North American Urban History," *Journal of Urban History*, 32 (4) (2006): 582–606; Carl Abbott, "Borderland Studies: Comments on Clay McShane's 'The State of the Art in North American Urban History,'" *Journal of Urban History*, 32 (4) (2006): 598–601; Timothy Gilfoyle, "Urban History: A Glass Half Full or Half Empty? Comments on Clay McShane's 'The State of the Art in North American Urban History,'" *Journal of Urban History*, 32 (4) (2006): 602–605.

The City in American Civilization

Arthur M. Schlesinger, Sr.

Source: *Paths to the Present* (New York: Macmillan, 1949).

EDITORS' INTRODUCTION

In stark contrast to sociologists and academics in other related disciplines, American historians arrived at the study of urban life, in the words of the late Richard C. Wade (1921–2008), "by slow freight."[i] Not until the publication of Arthur M. Schlesinger's 1933 book, *The Rise of the City*, and his seminal 1940 article, "The City in American History," did an actual subfield of urban history begin to emerge.[ii] Although a few academically trained historians dealt with issues and themes related to urbanization, notably immigration and industrialization, amateur and booster historians were responsible for the bulk of city histories written at the local level.

The following essay from *Paths to the Present* (1949) is one of Schlesinger's clearest and most comprehensive calls for an urban reinterpretation of American history. He begins by citing Professor Frederick Jackson Turner's "frontier thesis," arguably the most influential in American historical writing, which placed the "Great West" at the center of the nation's unique social evolution and democratic achievement. Turner presented his thesis, which explained the significance of the closing of the American frontier, at a special meeting of the American Historical Association held at the 1893 Columbian Exposition in Chicago. The Columbian Exposition, otherwise known as the Chicago World's Fair, was designed in large measure to celebrate the progress of Western civilization. Although not widely accepted at first, Turner's thesis became ubiquitous and largely self-evident to many American historians by the early twentieth century. However, criticism of Turner's emphasis on the frontier was inevitable, and not altogether unexpected. Writing to his friend and colleague Arthur Schlesinger in 1925, Turner himself stated that an alternative "urban reinterpretation" of American history seemed likely.[iii] In the following selection, Schlesinger boldly outlines such an approach by carefully balancing the influence of the city with the frontier. Schlesinger concentrates on the origins and manifestations of the rural versus urban discord prominent throughout much of the nineteenth and early twentieth centuries and argues that, in the end, the distinction between city and country eventually blurs, as each becomes more and more like the other.

Arthur Meier Schlesinger was born in 1888 in Xenia, Ohio. He received his bachelor's degree from the Ohio State University and doctorate from Columbia University, where he

---

i Richard C. Wade, "An Agenda for Urban History," in Herbert J. Bass, ed., *The State of American History* (Chicago: Quadrangle Books, 1970), 43.

ii Arthur M. Schlesinger, *The Rise of the City, 1878–1898* (New York: Macmillan, 1933); "The City in American History," *Mississippi Valley Historical Review,* 27 (June 1940): 43–66.

iii Wade, "An Agenda for Urban History," 46; Wilbur R. Jacobs, *The Historical World of Frederick Jackson Turner: With Selections From His Correspondence* (New Haven: Yale University Press, 1968), 163–165. While Turner's frontier thesis has long lost its luster, it is still serves as a convenient point of departure for understanding much of American history including urbanization. For example, see William Cronon, *Nature's Metropolis: Chicago and the Great West* (New York: W. W. Norton, 1991), 46–54.

studied under noted historians Charles Beard and James Harvey Robinson. Schlesinger taught at the University of Iowa before moving to the history department at Harvard University in 1924, where he replaced the newly retired Frederick Jackson Turner (at Turner's request) and remained there for the rest of his career. In addition to *The Rise of the City* and *Paths to the Present*, Schlesinger was the author of *New Viewpoints in American History* (New York: Macmillan, 1922), several monographs on colonial history, and co-editor with fellow social historian Ryan Dixon Fox of the widely influential "A History of American Life" series published by Macmillan from the 1920s through the 1940s. He died in 1965, and that year Harvard University formally named the Woman's Archive at Radcliffe College after him and his wife, Elizabeth Bancroft Schlesinger, who were strong supporters of women's rights. Their son, the late Arthur M. Schlesinger, Jr. (1918–2007), was also a noted historian and member of the history department at Harvard University and the Graduate Center of the City University of New York (along with Richard C. Wade), as well as special assistant to President John F. Kennedy.

THE CITY IN AMERICAN CIVILIZATION

"The true point of view in the history of this nation is not the Atlantic Coast," declared Frederick Jackson Turner in his famous essay of 1893, "it is the Great West." Professor Turner, writing in Wisconsin, had formed his ideas in an atmosphere of profound agrarian unrest, and the announcement of the Superintendent of the Census in 1890 that the frontier line could no longer be traced impelled him to the conclusion that "the first period of American history" had closed. His brilliant paper occasioned a fundamental reappraisal of the mainsprings of national development.

Today, however, it seems clear that in the zeal to correct older notions he overlooked another order of society which, rivaling the frontier even in the earliest days, eventually became the major force. The city marched westward with the outposts of settlement, always injecting exotic elements into pioneer existence, while in the older sections it steadily extended its dominion over politics, economics and all the other interests of life. The time came, in 1925, when Turner himself confessed the need of "an urban reinterpretation of our history." A true understanding of America's past demands this balanced view—an appreciation of the significance of both frontier and city. The broad outline of the particular role of the city are here suggested.

I

The Atlantic shore constituted the original frontier. Though the great bulk of colonists took up farming, the immediate object of the first settlers was to found a village or town, partly for mutual protection and partly as a base for peopling the near-by country. Other advantages presently gave these places more lasting reasons for existence. There persons could enjoy friendly intercourse with their neighbors as in Europe and there, too, ply a variety of occupations. These communities, besides taking in farm produce for consumption and export, developed local manufactures, arts and crafts and carried on fisheries and an active overseas trade. Without the articles so provided—hardware, firearms, medicine, books and the like—the colonial standard of living would have greatly suffered.

In time the coastline became beaded with towns, many of them so well situated with respect to geographic and trading advantages as to grow into the great cities of today. The establishment of settlements like Albany, New York, and Lancaster, Pennsylvania, moreover, foreshadowed the rise of urban communities inland. If colonial towns seem small by modern standards, it is well to remember that this was also true of contemporary English provincial towns, for industrialization had not yet concentrated populations in the homeland. Philadelphia with thirty thousand people on the eve of Independence was one of the metropolises of the British Empire.

From the outset townsfolk were plagued with what would today be called urban problems. There were disadvantages as well as advantages in living closely together, and as these disadvantages became flagrant, the citizens were moved to action. Though they seldom assumed community responsibilities willingly, their record compares favorably with that of provincial cities in the mother country. To combat the increase of crime the public-spirited in some places maintained night watches out of their own purses, while in others the city fathers required persons to take turns guarding the streets by night on pain of fines. Sooner or later, however, the taxpayers accepted such policing as a normal municipal charge. The fire hazard early prodded the authorities to regulate the construction of chimneys, license chimney sweeps and oblige householders to keep water buckets; and when these measures fell short of the requirements in the eighteenth century, the people formed volunteer companies which, long after the colonial period, continued to be the chief agency of fire fighting. The removal of garbage generally devolved upon roving swine and goats, while drainage remained pretty much an unsolved problem, though occasional individuals laid private sewers. The pressure of urban needs also fertilized American inventiveness, producing Franklin's lightning rod and the fireplace stove.

Thanks to the special conditions of town life, the inhabitants developed a sense of collective responsibility in their daily concerns that increasingly distinguished them from the individualistic denizens of the farm and frontier. Other circumstances served to widen the distance. As cities grew in size and substance, they engaged in economic rivalry with one another which tended to ignore the interests of the intervening countryside. Boston, New England's metropolis, possessed special mercantile advantages which enabled her for nearly a century to maintain a position of primacy in British America, with New York, Philadelphia and lesser centers hardly more than commercial satellites. These other ports, however, contended as best they could for their share of ocean-borne traffic and briskly cultivated their local trading areas. [...]

Happily for America's future independence, Britain's new revenue policy after 1763 struck deeply at the roots of urban prosperity. The business classes rallied promptly to the defense of their interests and, heedless of the dangers of playing with fire, secured the backing of the artisan and mechanic groups. Throughout the decade of controversy the seaports set the pace of resistance, supplying most of the militant leaders, conducting turbulent demonstrations at every crisis, and mobilizing farmer support when possible. Even in rural commonwealths like Virginia and Maryland the most effective steps of opposition were taken when the colonists consulted together at the provincial capitals while attending legislative sessions. Boston's foremost position in the proceedings may well have arisen from the fact that, having recently fallen behind Philadelphia and New York in the commercial race, she was resolved at any cost to stay the throttling hand of Parliament. [...]

The colonial town, however, was more than an embodiment of political and economic energies or a means of gratifying the gregarious instinct. Cities, then as now, were places where one found a whole gamut of satisfactions. Ports of entry for European settlers and goods, they were also ports of entry for European thought and standards of taste. At the same time their monopoly of printing presses, newspapers, bookstores and circulating libraries exposed the residents to a constant barrage of mental stimuli. Hence the spirit of innovation expressed itself quite as much in intellectual as in commercial undertakings. It was townsfolk who led in founding schools and colleges. The protracted battle to establish inoculation as a preventive against smallpox was fought out in the cities. The first great victory for freedom of the press was won by a Philadelphia lawyer defending a New York editor. Besides, mere numbers of people made it possible for the professions to become more clearly differentiated, so that a merchant need no longer plead cases before the courts nor a clergyman practice medicine. Before the colonial period ended, bar associations and medical societies were flourishing in New York,

Boston and elsewhere, and medical schools were drawing students to Philadelphia and New York. [...]

The city, both in its internal life and external relations, deeply affected colonial society politically, economically and culturally. Though in 1776 only about one in twenty-five Americans dwelt in places of eight thousand or more, the urban influence, thanks to its concentrated character, carried far greater weight than its fractional representation in the population indicated. Moreover, city residents evolved a pattern of life which not only diverged from, but increasingly challenged, that of countryside and frontier. These restless, aspiring urban communities foreshadowed the larger role that cities would play in the years ahead.

II

That role townsfolk began to assume in the struggle for a strong central government following the Revolution. [...] The framing and ratification of the Constitution represented in considerable degree their triumph over the debtor groups and small farmers of the interior. In the circumstances the first Congress under the new instrument was greeted with petitions from Philadelphia, New York, Boston and Baltimore for a tariff to protect American manufactures.

The underlying strife between city and country led also to the formation of the first national parties under the Constitution. Hamilton's famous financial plan, intended to benefit urban capitalists and thus indirectly the nation, formed the rallying point of the Federalists, while Jefferson, imbued with physiocratic notions, organized the Republican opposition. The Virginia planter, unlike the New York lawyer, dreaded the growth of a powerful moneyed class, and in the spread of cities he foresaw a repetition of the social miseries of the Old World. "For the general operations of manufacture," he declared, "let our work-shops remain in Europe." He could even regard calmly the destructive yellow-fever epidemics in Philadelphia and other ports in the 1790's, since the pestilence might teach people to avoid populous centers. [...]

III

The westward surge of population beginning shortly after the Revolution has obscured the fact that the leading Atlantic cities, though hard hit by the war, soon resumed their growth, and that with the coming of the nineteenth century the rate of urban development in the nation at large far surpassed that of rural development. Between 1800 and 1860 the number of townsfolk increased twenty-four times while the rural population merely quadrupled. By 1810 one out of every twenty Americans lived in communities of eight thousand or more, by 1840 one out of every twelve, and by 1860 nearly one in every six.

Paradoxically enough, westward migration itself helped to bring this about, for the transappalachian region bred its own urban localities. Serving at first chiefly as distributing centers for commodities from the seaboard, these raw settlements quickly developed into marts where local manufacturer and farm dweller exchanged products. Pittsburgh early began to make glass, shoes, iron castings, nails and textiles, and already in 1814 the *Pittsburgh Gazette* was complaining of the sooty atmosphere. By that time Cincinnati, farther down the river, boasted of two woolen mills and a cotton factory, and its meat-packing business was winning it the sobriquet of Porkopolis. Emboldened by such achievements, apparently every cluster of log huts dreamed of equal or greater eminence. The Indiana pioneers, for example, hopefully named their forest hamlets Columbia City, Fountain City, Saline City, Oakland City and Union City or, setting their sights still higher, called them New Philadelphia, New Paris, Rome City and even New Pekin.

Meanwhile, in the East, scores of cities sprang into being, generally at the fall line of the rivers, where water power was available for manufacturing. As the budding industrialists looked about for new worlds to conquer, they, together with the Eastern merchants and bankers, perceived their El Dorado in the settling West. Soon New York, Philadelphia and Baltimore were racing for the trade of the transappalachian country. This clash of urban imperialisms appeared most strikingly perhaps in the rivalry for transportation routes to the interior. The Baltimoreans led off by building a turnpike to tap the eastern terminus of the Cumberland Road, which the federal government by 1818 had completed as far as Wheeling on the Ohio. In order to counter this move, Pennsylvania promoted Philadelphia's wagon trade with the West by subsidizing a chain of roads to Pittsburgh. New York City, utilizing her natural advantages, now secured state backing for an all-water artery through upstate New York from the Hudson to Lake Erie. [...]

Middle Western towns, following the Eastern example, meanwhile entered upon a somewhat similar struggle, each seeking to carve out its own economic dependencies and spheres of influence and to profit from the new ties with the seaboard. By 1840 a network of artificial waterways joined Cleveland and Toledo on Lake Erie with Portsmouth, Cincinnati and Evansville on the Ohio. As in the East, however, the arrival of the steam locomotive changed the situation. Now every up-and-coming municipality strove by hook or crook to become a railroad center, sometimes plunging heavily in debt for the purpose. And looking to the commercial possibilities of the remoter West, Chicago, St. Louis, Memphis and New Orleans concocted rival plans for a Pacific railroad—a maneuvering for position that had political repercussions in Congress and contributed to the passage of the Kansas-Nebraska Act in 1854, which it was thought would facilitate the building of a transcontinental line from St. Louis. This law, by authorizing slavery by "popular sovereignty" in a region hitherto close to it, helped to set the stage for the Civil War.

The progress in transportation facilities, confined largely to the North, spurred urban development throughout that part of the country. The Erie Canal, reinforced by the rail arteries to the West and the magnificent harbor at the mouth of the Hudson, established conclusively New York's pre-eminence on the seaboard and in the nation. From only sixty thousand inhabitants in 1800 its population (not counting Brooklyn) climbed to eight hundred thousand by 1860, outdistancing Philadelphia and placing it next to London and Paris in size, while Philadelphia with more than half a million was in 1860 larger than Berlin. Brooklyn, Baltimore and Boston came next in size. Indicative of the westward movement of the urban frontier was the fact that at the latter date all the other places of over hundred thousand—New Orleans, Cincinnati, St. Louis and Chicago—were in the heart of the country. Chicago, though the smallest of these cities in 1860, had already gathered the economic sinews which would make it New York's chief rival before the century closed. Anthony Trollope, observing the Midwest in 1861, remarked that except for a few river and lake sites "settlers can hardly be said to have chosen their own localities. These have been chosen for them by the originators of the different lines of railway." Urban communities greatly augmented the demand for farm products, accelerated the invention of labor-saving implements like the steel plow and the reaper and thus furthered commercial agriculture, which in turn speeded city growth.

To master the new complexities of urban living demanded something more than the easygoing ways of colonial towns. Enlarged populations called for enlarged measures for the community safety and welfare, whether by government or otherwise. As might be expected, the bigger cities set the pace. After the lethal yellow-fever visitations of the 1790's frightened Philadelphia into installing a public water works, other places fell into line, so that more than a hundred systems came into existence before the Civil War. Unfortunately, ignorance of the yet to be discovered germ theory of disease fastened attention on clear water instead of pure water, thus leaving the public health still inadequately protected. To cope with the growing lawlessness the leading cities now supplemented night watches with day police. In 1822 Boston instituted gas lighting and in 1823 set the example of a municipally owned sewerage system. About the same time regular omnibus service was started on the streets of New York, to be followed in the next decade by horsecars running on tracks.

Fire fighting, however, continued generally in the hands of volunteer companies. Though Boston organized a paid municipal department in 1837 and Cincinnati and other Western towns greatly improved the apparatus by introducing steam fire engines in the 1850's, New York and Philadelphia, thanks to the political pull of volunteer brigades, resisted changes in equipment and waited respectively till 1865 and 1871 to municipalize their systems. The cities did nothing at all to combat the evil of slums, an unexpected development due to the great inrush of foreign immigrants into the Atlantic ports in the forties and fifties. Even more serious for the ordinary citizen was the growth of political machines, rooted in the tenement-house population, the fire companies and the criminal classes, and trafficking in franchises for the new public utilities. Appointments to government office for partisan services, first practiced in Eastern cities, preceded and led directly to the introduction of the spoils system into state and national politics.

The "diversities of extreme poverty and extreme wealth," which Edwin H. Chapin etched so sharply in *Humanity in the City* (1854), distressed the tenderhearted and gave rise to most of the reform crusades of the pre-Civil War generation. Compact living facilitated the banding together of such folk and also the collection of funds. Never before had America known so great an outpouring of effort to befriend the poor and the handicapped. Under urban stimulus arose the movement for free schools, for public libraries, for married women's property rights, for universal peace, for prison reform, for a better deal for the insane. The new conditions of city life begot a social conscience on the part of townsfolk which would be lasting of effect and which increasingly differentiated them from their brethren on the farm and frontier. [...]

Whatever the attractions of town life, the elevenfold leap in urban population between 1820 and 1860 aroused increasing dismay and foreboding among rural folk who saw their own sons and daughters succumbing to the lure. "Adam and Eve were created and placed in a garden. Cities are the results of the fall," cried Joseph H. Ingraham, a popular religious novelist. Country preachers joined in denouncing these human agglomerations "cursed with immense accumulations of ignorance and error, vice and crime," while farm journals implored the young not to sacrifice their manly independence in order "to fetch and carry" and "cringe and flatter" for a miserable pittance. Political attitudes further mirrored the deepening distrust.

IV

In the generation following the Civil War the city took supreme command. Between 1860 and 1900 the urban population again quadrupled while the rural merely doubled. With one out of every six people inhabiting communities of eight thousand or over in the earlier year, the proportion rose to nearly one out of four in 1880 and to one out of three in 1900. Considerably more than half of the urban-moving throng gravitated to places of twenty-five thousand and upwards. Since every town dweller added to this effectiveness by association with his fellows, even these figures understate the city's new role in the nation. Nevertheless the sheer growth of particular localities is amazing. By 1890 New York (including Brooklyn) had about caught up with Paris, while Chicago and Philadelphia, with over a million each as compared with New York's two and a half million, then outranked all but five cities in Europe. In the Far West, Los Angeles jumped from fewer than 5000 in 1860 to more than 100,000 in 1900, and Denver from nothing at all to 134,000, while in the postwar South, Memphis with a bare 23,000 in the former year surpassed 100,000 in the latter. "The youngest of the nations," wrote Samuel L. Loomis in 1887, "has already more large cities than any except Great Britain and Germany." Thanks to the progress of settlement in the West and the burgeoning of industry in a South emancipated from slavery, the city had at last become a national instead of a sectional institution.

As urban centers grew in size and wealth, they cast an ever stronger spell over the American mind. Walt Whitman, returning to Greater New York in September, 1870, after a short absence, gloried in the "splendor, picturesqueness, and oceanic amplitude of these great cities." [...] Conceding that Nature excelled in her mountains, forests and seas, he rated man's achievement equally great "in these ingenuities, streets, goods, houses, ships—these hurrying, feverish, electric crowds of men." Little wonder that the young and the ambitious yielded to the temptation. "We cannot all live in cities, yet nearly all seem determined to do so," commented Horace Greeley, adding that with "millions of acres" awaiting cultivation "hundreds of thousands reject this and rush into the cities."

The exodus from the older countryside was especially striking. While the cities of Maine, Vermont, Massachusetts, Rhode Island, New York, Maryland and Illinois gained two and a half million people between 1880 and 1890, the rural districts of these states lost two hundred thousand. The drain of humanity from backwoods New England left mute witnesses in deserted hill villages and abandoned farms. In the nation as a whole, 10,063 townships out of 25,746 in thirty-nine states and territories shrank in population during the decade. Some of the rural decline was due to the shifting of agriculturists from older regions to the free unworked lands of the trans-Mississippi West, but the phenomenon was so widespread—and, indeed, as characteristic of Europe during these years as of America—as to evidence the more potent and pervasive influence of the city. True, the 1880's merely climaxed a historic trend. In the century from 1790 to 1890 the total population had grown 16-fold while the urban segment grew 139-fold. Hence the celebrated announcement of the Superintendent of the Census in 1890 that a frontier line no longer existed can hardly be said to have marked the close of "the first period of American history." Rather it was a tardy admission that the second period was already under way. [...]

These civic advances, however, came at a price already beginning to be evident before the Civil War. Americans had developed their political institutions under simple rural conditions; they had yet to learn how to govern cramped populations. Preyed upon by unscrupulous men eager to exploit the expanding public utilities, municipal politics became a byword for venality. As Francis Parkman wrote, "Where the carcass is, the vultures gather together." New York's notorious Tweed Ring denoted a sickness that racked Philadelphia, Chicago, St. Louis, Minneapolis and San Francisco as well. "With very few exceptions," declared Andrew D. White, "the city governments of the United States are the worst in Christendom—the most expensive, the most inefficient, and the most corrupt."

Through an irate citizenry succeeded now and then in "turning the rascals out," the boss and the machine soon recovered control. Nevertheless, the good-government campaigns ventilated the abuses of municipal misrule and aroused the humane to the worsening plight of the urban poor. Under reform prodding, the New York legislature from 1865 onward adopted a series of laws to combat the slum evil in America's metropolis, though with disappointing results. More fruitful were the steps taken by private groups in Manhattan and elsewhere to establish social settlements and playgrounds and to replace the indiscriminate almsgiving of earlier times with a more rational administration of charity. Religion, awakening to the social gospel, helped out with slum missions and institutional churches. In the city, too, trade-unions made a new start, organizing the swelling army of urban workers on a nationwide basis, joining with the reformers in securing factory legislation and gradually winning concessions from the employing class. Occasional voices with a foreign accent advocated socialism or anarchism as the remedy for the city's gross disparities of wealth and want, while Edward Bellamy in *Looking Backward* offered a home-grown version of communism in his fanciful account of Boston as it would be in the year 2000.

The increasing tension of living was evidenced in a variety of ways. Masses of people reared in a rustic environment had suddenly to adapt themselves to the frantic urban pace. One outcome was a startling growth of neurasthenia, a word coined by Dr. George M. Beard of New York in his work *American Nervousness* (1881), which traced the malady to the hurry and scurry, the din of the streets, the frenzied struggle for existence, the mental excitements and endless distractions. From the ranks of the high-strung, Mary Baker Eddy gathered most of her converts to the new religion of Christian Science, and for much the same reason townsfolk now gave enthusiastic support to organized sports. Flabby muscles unfitted most persons for direct participation, but they compromised by paying professional contestants to take their exercise for them. If, as a magazine writer said, nervousness had become the "national disease of America," baseball, partly as an antidote, became America's national game.

The stress of existence seemed only to enhance creative powers, however. The cities, re-enacting their role of the "fireplaces of civilization"—Theodore Parker's phrase—provided compelling incentives to cultural achievement, multiplying colleges, public libraries and publishing houses and founding art museums, art schools and conservatories of music. [...] Civic pride prompted the holding of two great expositions, one at Philadelphia in 1876 and the other at Chicago in 1893. That the second and grander took place in an inland metropolis revealed how decisively urbanization had altered the face of traditional America.

The new age of the city rested upon an application of business enterprise to the exploitation of natural resources such as mankind had never known. The city, as insatiable as an octopus, tended to draw all nutriment to itself. Railroads, industrial combinations, investment capital, legislative favors, comprised the means. There arose a complex of urban imperialisms, each striving for dominion, each battling with rivals and each perforce yielding tribute to the lord of them all. "Every produce market, every share market," observed James Bryce, "vibrates to the Produce Exchange and Stock Exchange of New York."

As the city forged ahead, imposing its fiat on less developed regions, the rift between country and town widened portentously. [...]

This feeling of rural inferiority, this growing sense of frustration, underlay the political eruptions in the farming regions: the Granger movement in the 1870's, the Farmers' Alliances of the eighties and the Populist conflagration in the nineties. Each time specific economic grievances like steep freight rates, high interest charges and low crop prices stirred the smoldering embers into blaze. These were tangible hardships which the farmers demanded the government remove by such measures as railroad regulation and silver inflation. It fell to the greatest of the agrarian champions, addressing the Democratic national convention in 1896, to hurl the ultimate challenge at urban imperialism. "Burn down your cities and leave our farms, and your cities will spring up again as if by magic," cried William Jennings Bryan of Nebraska in a speech that won him the nomination, "but destroy our farms and the grass will grow in the streets of every city in the country." In the election that followed, the big cities in the East and Midwest, including New York which for the first time went Republican, responded by casting decisive majorities against the Democrats and free silver. [...]

V

Urban dominance was further enhanced by the emergence of great metropolitan districts or regions. These "city states" had begun to form in the nineteenth century as swifter means of transportation and communication flung the inhabitants outward into the suburbs, but it was the coming of the automobile and motor truck and the extension of electricity and other conveniences into the surrounding territory that gave these supercommunities their unprecedented size and importance.

Each consisted of one or more core cities with satellite towns and development rural areas, the whole knit together by economic, social and cultural ties. The hundred and thirty-three metropolitan regions in 1930 grew to a hundred and forty by 1940, when they contained almost half the total population. [...]

Of all the new trends in urban development, however, none had such profound effects as the altered relationship of country and city. Historians generally attribute the decline of the free-silver movement in the late nineties to the discovery of fresh sources of gold supply and an uptrend of crop prices, but probably the more fundamental cause was the amelioration of many of the social and psychological drawbacks of farm existence. The introduction of rural free delivery of mail after 1896, the extension of good roads due to the bicycle craze, the expanding network of interurban trolleys, the spread of party-line neighborhood telephones after the basic Bell patents expired in 1893, the increase of country schools—all these, coming shortly before 1900, helped dispel the aching isolation and loneliness, thereby making rustic life pleasanter.

Yet these mitigations seem trifling compared with the marvels which the twentieth century wrought. The automobile brought farm families within easy reach of each other and of the city; the motorbus facilitated the establishment of consolidated schools with vastly improved instruction and equipment; while the radio introduced new interests and pleasures into the homes themselves, shedding its benefits impartially on country and town. At the same time the mechanical energy used in agriculture grew eightfold between 1900 and 1935, thus lightening the husbandman's toll and adding to his opportunities for leisure. [...]

Just as rural life became more urbanized, so urban life became more ruralized. Wooded parks, tree-shaded boulevards, beautified waterfronts, municipal golf courses, athletic fields and children's playgrounds multiplied, while an increasing army of white-collar workers and wage earners piled into motorcars and buses each night to go farther and farther into the suburbs. Within the metropolitan regions population actually grew faster in the rustic outskirts between 1930 and 1940 than in the central cities. Retail trade too felt the centrifugal tug, and even factories showed a tendency to move into outlying villages where taxes, rent and food cost less. The extension of giant power will doubtless speed the trend, affording more and more townsfolk a chance to live and work and bring up their children in country surroundings. The dread specter of atomic-bomb attacks may operate to the same end in the interests of national military security.

Thus the twentieth century has been spinning a web in which city and country, no longer separate entities, have been brought ever closer together. When the city encroaches sufficiently on the country and the country on the city, America may hope to arrive at a way of life which will blend the best features of both the traditional ways. [...]

From humble beginnings in the early seventeenth century the city thus traced a varied course. In Europe the modern urban community emerged by gradual stages out of the simple town economy of the Middle Ages; by comparison, the American city leaped into being with breath-taking speed. At first servant to an agricultural order, then a jealous contestant, then an oppressor, it now gives evidence of becoming a comrade and co-operator in a new national synthesis. Its economic function has been hardly more important than its cultural mission or its transforming influence upon rural conceptions of democracy. The city, no less than the frontier, has been a major factor in American civilization. Without an appreciation of the role of both the story is only half told.

Urbanism and Suburbanism as Ways of Life: A Reevaluation of Definitions

Herbert J. Gans

Source: *People, Plans, and Policies* (New York: Columbia University Press and Russell Sage Foundation, 1991). Originally published in Arnold M. Rose (ed.), *Human Behavior and Social Processes: An Interactionist Approach* (Houghton Mifflin, 1962).

EDITORS' INTRODUCTION

Is there a distinct urban way of life? If so, what accounts for the differences between the actions and attitudes of people in cities versus rural areas? Noted sociologist Louis Wirth, part of the University of Chicago's influential Chicago School, contended that such distinctions existed and in 1938 published "Urbanism as a Way of Life," one of the most important and widely read essays on cities, in which he argued that the size, density, and heterogeneity of an urban area influences the outlook and behavior of its inhabitants. As one of the definitive statements of the Chicago School style of urban inquiry, "Urbanism as a Way of Life" influenced generations of urban sociologists, social scientists, and social workers eager to understand urban life and/or reform problems that they tended to associate with cities. Building on Wirth, many of these professionals focused on negative aspects of urban life, especially perceptions of family decline and the breakdown of primary group ties. Many urbanists performed studies related in some way to the concept of *anomie* (a term popularized by sociologist Emile Durkheim), which can be defined as the absence of social norms and disassociation from others in the community, and social deviance, especially in the form of mental illness, vice, and crime.[i]

In 1962, sociologist Herbert J. Gans reassesed Wirth's argument in "Urbanism and Suburbanism as Ways of Life: A Reevaluation of Definitions." Gans asserted that there was no single urban or even suburban way of life. Gans examined five major types of inner city residents, the "cosmopolites," the "unmarried and childless," the "ethnic villagers," the "deprived," and the "trapped and downwardly mobile" and found that residential instability, rather than number (or size), density, and heterogeneity of cities caused the social features of the urbanism identified by Wirth. Drawing on his own study of a suburban Levittown development, Gans expanded the focus of urban inquiry beyond the inner city to the outer city, i.e., residential neighborhoods and adjacent suburbs, where he found relationships between people to be "quasi-primary," or more intimate than secondary ties yet more guarded than primary. For Gans, socioeconomic status, class, and lifecycle stage were more important than settlement type, which led him to assert that a sociological definition of the city, as formulated by Wirth, could not be made.

Looking back at his essay in 1991, Gans added a postscript (included in the essay below) where he notes the ways in which his original article was time bound. Although he underestimated the potential of suburban growth and failed to consider the increasing

---

i Louis Wirth, "Urbanism as a Way of Life," *American Journal of Sociology*, 44 (10) (1938): 1–24; Hans Polis, "Anomie in the Metropolis: The City in American Sociology and Psychiatry," *Osiris*, 2nd Series, 18 (2003): 200–201; J. John Palen, *The Urban World*, 8th ed. (Boulder, CO: Paradigm Publishers, 2008), 16, 151–152.

polarity between the rich and the poor in American cities, Gans contends that the main tenants of his essay concerning the relationship between social structure and the physical environment were still sound after almost three decades. Widely regarded as one of the nation's preeminent sociologists and the leading proponent of "public sociology," Herbert J. Gans retired in 2007 as the Robert S. Lynd Professor of Sociology at Columbia University. He is the author of hundreds of scholarly articles and a dozen books including *The Urban Villagers* (Glencoe: Free Press, 1963), *The Levittowners* (New York: Pantheon, 1967), *People and Plans: Essays on Urban Problems and Solutions* (New York: Basic Books, 1968), *People, Plans, and Policies: Essays on Poverty, Racism, and Other National Urban Problems* (New York: Columbia University and Russell Sage Foundation, 1991), from which this essay is taken, *The War Against the Poor: The Underclass and Antipoverty Policy* (New York: Basic Books, 1995), and *Democracy and the News* (New York: Oxford University Press, 2003).

URBANISM AND SUBURBANISM AS WAYS OF LIFE

A Reevaluation of Definitions

THE CONTEMPORARY SOCIOLOGICAL conception of cities and of urban life is based largely on the work of the Chicago School and its summary statement in Louis Wirth's essay "Urbanism as a Way of Life."[1] In that paper, Wirth developed a "minimum sociological definition of the city" as "a relatively large, dense and permanent settlement of socially heterogeneous individuals." From these prerequisites, he then deduced the major outlines of the urban way of life. As he saw it, number, density, and heterogeneity created a social structure in which primary-group relationships were inevitably replaced by secondary contacts that were impersonal, segmental, superficial, transitory, and often predatory in nature. As a result, the city dweller became anonymous, isolated, secular, relativistic, rational, and sophisticated. In order to function in an urban society, he or she was forced to combine with others to organize corporations, voluntary associations, representative forms of government, and the impersonal mass media of communications. These replaced the primary groups and the integrated way of life found in rural and other preindustrial settlements.

Wirth's paper has become a classic in urban sociology, and most texts have followed his definition and description faithfully.[2] In recent years, however, a considerable number of studies and essays have questioned his formulations.[3] In addition, a number of changes have taken place in cities since the article was published in 1938, notably the exodus of white residents to low- and medium-priced houses in the suburbs and the decentralization of industry. The evidence from these studies and the changes in American cities suggest that Wirth's statement must be revised.

There is yet another and more important reason for such a revision. Despite its title and intent, Wirth's paper deals with urban-industrial society, rather than with the city. This is evident from his approach. Like other urban sociologists, Wirth based his analysis on a comparison of settlement types, but unlike his colleagues, who pursued urban-rural comparisons, Wirth contrasted the city to the folk society. Thus, he compared settlement types of pre-industrial and industrial society. This allowed him to include in his theory of urbanism the entire range of modern institutions which are not found in the folk society, even though many such groups (for example, voluntary associations) are by no means exclusively urban. Moreover, Wirth's conception of the city dweller as depersonalized, atomized, and susceptible to mass movements suggests that his paper is based on, and contributes to, the theory of the mass society.

Many of Wirth's conclusions may be relevant to the understanding of ways of life in modern society. However, since the theory argues that all of society is now urban, his analysis does not distinguish ways of life in the city from those in other settlements within modern society. In Wirth's time, the comparison of urban and preurban settlement types was still fruitful, but today, the primary task for urban (or community) sociology seems to me to be the analysis of the similarities and differences between contemporary settlement types.

This paper is an attempt at such an analysis; it limits itself to distinguishing ways of life in the modern city and the modern suburb. A reanalysis of Wirth's conclusions from this perspective suggests that his characterization of the urban way of life applies only—and not too accurately—to the residents of the inner city. The remaining city dwellers, as well as most suburbanites, pursue a different way of life which I shall call "quasi-primary." This proposition raises some doubt about the mutual exclusiveness of the concepts of city and suburb and leads to a yet broader question: whether settlement concepts and other ecological concepts are useful for explaining ways of life.

The Inner City

WIRTH ARGUED that number, density, and heterogeneity had two social consequences which explain the major features of urban life. On the one hand, the crowding of diverse types of people into a small area led to the segregation of homogeneous types of people into separate neighborhoods. On the other hand, the lack of physical distance between city dwellers resulted in social contact between them, which broke down existing social and cultural patterns and encouraged assimilation as well as acculturation—the melting-pot effect. Wirth implied that the melting-pot effect was far more powerful than the tendency toward segregation and concluded that, sooner or later, the pressures engendered by the dominant social, economic, and political institutions of the city would destroy the remaining pockets of primary-group relationships. Eventually, the social system of the city would resemble Tönnies' *Gesellschaft*—a way of life which Wirth considered undesirable.

Because Wirth had come to see the city as the prototype of mass society, and because he examined the city from the distant vantage point of the folk society—from the wrong end of the telescope, so to speak—his view of urban life is not surprising. In addition, Wirth found support for his theory in the empirical work of his Chicago colleagues. As Greer and Kube[4] and Wilensky[5] have pointed out, the Chicago sociologists conducted their most intensive studies in the inner city.[6] At that time, it consisted mainly of slums recently invaded by new waves of European immigrants and rooming-house and skid-row districts, as well as the habitat of Bohemians and well-to-do "Gold Coast" apartment dwellers. Wirth himself studied the Maxwell Street Ghetto, a poor inner-city Jewish neighborhood then being dispersed by the acculturation and mobility of its inhabitants.[7] Some of the characteristics of urbanism which Wirth stressed in his essay abounded in these areas.

Wirth's diagnosis of the city as *Gesellschaft* must be questioned on three counts. First, the conclusions derived from a study of the inner city cannot be generalized to the entire urban area. Second, there is as yet not enough evidence to prove—or, admittedly, to deny—that number, density, and heterogeneity result in the social consequences which Wirth proposed. Finally, even if the causal relationship could be verified, it can be shown that a significant proportion of the city's inhabitants were, and are, isolated from these consequences by social structures and cultural patterns which they either brought to the city or developed by living in it. Wirth conceived the urban population as consisting of heterogeneous individuals, torn from past social systems, unable to develop new ones, and therefore prey to social anarchy in the city. While it is true that a not insignificant proportion of the inner-city population was, and still is, made up of unattached individuals,[8] Wirth's formulation ignores the fact that this population consists mainly of relatively homogeneous groups, with social and cultural moorings that shield it fairly effectively from the suggested consequences of number, density, and heterogeneity. This applies even more to the residents of the outer city, who constitute a majority of the total city population.

The social and cultural moorings of the inner-city population are best described by a brief analysis of the five major types of inner-city residents. These are: 1. the "cosmopolites"; 2. the unmarried or childless; 3. the "ethnic villagers"; 4. the "deprived"; and 5. the "trapped" and downward-mobile.

The "cosmopolites" include students, artists, writers, musicians, and entertainers, as well as other intellectuals and professionals. They live in the city in order to be near the special "cultural" facilities that can be located only near the center of the city. Many cosmopolites are unmarried or childless. Others rear children in the city, especially if they have the income to afford the aid of servants and governesses. The less affluent ones may move to the suburbs to raise their children, continuing to live as cosmopolites under considerable handicaps, especially in the lower-middle-class suburbs. Many of the very rich and powerful are also cosmopolites, although they are likely to have at least two residences, one of which is suburban or exurban.

The unmarried or childless must be divided into two subtypes, depending on the permanence or transience of their status. The temporarily unmarried or childless live in the inner city for only a limited time. Young adults may team up to rent an apartment away from their parents and close to job or entertainment opportunities. When they marry, they may move first to an apartment in a transient neighborhood, but if they can afford to do so, they leave for the outer city or the suburbs with the arrival of the first or second child. The permanently unmarried may stay in the inner city for the remainder of their lives, their housing depending on their income.

The "ethnic villagers" are ethnic groups which are found in such inner-city neighborhoods as New York's Lower East Side, living in some ways as they did when they were peasants in European or Puerto Rican villages.[9] Although they reside in the city, they isolate themselves from significant contact with most city facilities, aside from workplaces. Their way of life differs sharply from Wirth's urbanism in its emphasis on kinship and the primary group, the lack of anonymity and secondary-group contacts, the weakness of formal organizations, and the suspicion of anything and anyone outside their neighborhood.

The first two types live in the inner city by choice; the third is there partly because of necessity, partly because of tradition. The final two types are in the inner city because they have no other choice. One is the "deprived" population: the emotionally disturbed or otherwise handicapped; broken families; and, most important, the poor-white and especially the nonwhite population. These urban dwellers must take the dilapidated housing and blighted neighborhoods to which the housing market relegates them, although among them are some for whom the slum is a hiding place or a temporary stopover to save money for a house in the outer city or the suburbs.[10]

The "trapped" are the people who stay behind when a neighborhood is invaded by nonresidential land uses or lower-status immigrants, because they cannot afford to move or are otherwise bound to their present location.[11] The "downward-mobiles" are a related type; they may have started life in a higher class position, but have been forced down in the socioeconomic hierarchy and in the quality of their accommodations. Many of them are old people, living out their existence on small pensions.

These five types may all live in dense and heterogeneous surroundings; yet they have such diverse ways of life that it is hard to see how density and heterogeneity could exert a common influence. Moreover, all but the last two types are isolated or detached from their neighborhood and thus from the social consequences that Wirth described. [...]

Wirth's description of the urban way of life fits best the transient areas of the inner city. Such areas are typically heterogeneous in population, partly because they are inhabited by transient types who do not require homogeneous neighbors or by deprived people who have no choice or may themselves be quite mobile. Under conditions of transience and heterogeneity, people interact only in terms of the segmental roles necessary for obtaining local services. Their social relationships may thus display anonymity, impersonality, and superficiality.[12]

The social features of Wirth's concept of urbanism seem, therefore, to be a result of residential instability, rather than of number, density, or heterogeneity. In fact, heterogeneity is itself an effect of residential instability, resulting when the influx of transients causes landlords and realtors to stop acting as gatekeepers—that is, wardens of neighborhood homogeneity.[13] Residential instability is found in all types of settlements, and presumably its social consequences are everywhere similar. These consequences cannot, therefore, be identified with the ways of life of the city.

The Outer City and the Suburbs

THE SECOND effect which Wirth ascribed to number, density, and heterogeneity was the segregation of homogeneous people into distinct neighborhoods[14] on the basis of "place and nature of work, income, racial and ethnic characteristics, social status, custom, habit, taste, preference and prejudice."[15] This description fits the residential districts of the *outer city*.[16] Although these districts contain the majority of the city's inhabitants, Wirth went into little detail about them. He made it clear, however, that the sociopsychological aspects of urbanism were prevalent there as well.[17]

Because existing neighborhood studies deal primarily with the exotic sections of the inner city, very little is known about the more typical residential neighborhoods of the outer city. However, it is evident that the way of life in these areas bears little resemblance to Wirth's urbanism. Both the studies which question Wirth's formulation and my own observations suggest that the common element in the ways of life of these neighborhoods is best described as *quasi-primary*. I use this term to characterize relationships between neighbors. Whatever the intensity or frequency of these relationships, the interaction is more intimate than a secondary contact, but more guarded than a primary one.[18] [...]

Postwar suburbia represents the most contemporary version of the quasi-primary way of life. Owing to increases in real income and the encouragement of home-ownership provided by the F.H.A., families in the lower middle class and upper working class can now live in modern single-family homes in low-density subdivisions, an opportunity previously available only to the upper and upper-middle classes.[19]

The popular literature of the 1950s described the new suburbs as communities in which conformity, homogeneity, and other-direction are unusually rampant.[20] The implication is that the move from city to suburb initiates a new way of life which causes considerable behavior and personality change in previous urbanites. My research in Levittown, New Jersey, suggests, however, that the move from the city to this predominantly lower-middle-class suburb does not result in any major behavioral changes for most people. Moreover, the changes which do occur reflect the move from the social isolation of a transient city or suburban apartment building to the quasi-primary life of a neighborhood of single-family homes. Also, many of the people whose life has changed report that the changes were intended. They existed as aspirations before the move or as reasons for it. In other words, the suburb itself creates few changes in ways of life.[21]

A Comparison of City and Suburb

IF OUTER-URBAN and suburban areas are similar in that the way of life in both is quasi-primary, and if urban residents who move out to the suburbs do not undergo any significant changes in behavior, it is fair to argue that the differences in ways of life between the two types of settlements have been overestimated. Yet the fact remains that a variety of physical and demographic differences exist between the city and the suburb. However, upon closer examination, many of these differences turn out to be either spurious or of little significance for the way of life of the inhabitants.[22]

The differences between the residential areas of cities and suburbs which have been cited most frequently are:

1. Suburbs are more likely to be dormitories.

2. They are further away from the work and play facilities of the central business districts.

3. They are newer and more modern than city residential areas and are designed for the automobile rather than for pedestrian and masstransit forms of movement.

4. They are built up with single-family rather than multifamily structures and are therefore less dense.

5. Their populations are more homogeneous.

6. Their populations differ demographically: they are younger; more of them are married; they have higher incomes; and they hold proportionately more white-collar jobs.[23]

Most urban neighborhoods are as much dormitories as the suburbs. Only in a few older inner-city areas are factories and offices still located in the middle of residential blocks, and even here many of the employees do not live in the neighborhood.

The fact that the suburbs are farther from the central business district is often true only in terms of distance, not travel time. Moreover, most people make relatively little use of downtown facilities, other than workplaces.[24] Many downtown stores seem to hold their greatest attraction for the upper-middle class;[25] the same is probably true of typically urban entertainment facilities. Teenagers and young adults may take their dates to first-run movie theatres, but the museums, concert halls, and lecture rooms attract mainly upper-middle-class ticket buyers, many of them suburban.[26]

The suburban reliance on the train and the automobile has given rise to an imaginative folklore about the consequences of commuting on alcohol consumption, sex life, and parental duties. Many of these conclusions are, however, drawn from selected high-income suburbs and exurbs and reflect job tensions in such hectic occupations as advertising and show business more than the effects of residence.[27] It is true that the upper-middle-class housewife must become a chauffeur in order to expose her children to the proper educational facilities, but such differences as walking to the corner drugstore and driving to its suburban equivalent seem to me of little emotional, social, or cultural import.[28] In addition, the continuing shrinkage in the number of mass-transit users suggests that even in the city many younger people are now living a wholly auto-based way of life.

The fact that suburbs are smaller is primarily a function of political boundaries drawn long before the communities were suburban. This affects the kinds of political issues which develop and provides somewhat greater opportunity for citizen participation. Even so, in the suburbs as in the city, the minority who participate routinely are the professional politicians, the economically concerned businesspeople, lawyers, and salespeople, and the ideologically motivated middle- and upper-middle-class people with better than average education.

The social consequences of differences in density and house type also seem overrated. Single-family houses in quiet streets facilitate the supervision of children; this is one reason why middle-class parents who want to keep an eye on their children move to the suburbs. House type also has some effects on relationships between neighbors, insofar as there are more opportunities for visual contact between adjacent homeowners than between people on different floors of an apartment house. However, if occupants' characteristics are also held constant, the differences in actual social contact are less marked. Homogeneity of residents turns out to be more important than proximity as a determinant of sociability. If the population is heterogeneous, there is little social contact between neighbors, either on apartment-house floors or in single-family-house blocks; if people are homogeneous, there is likely to be considerable social contact in both house types. One need only contrast the apartment house located in a transient, heterogeneous neighborhood and exactly the same structure in a neighborhood occupied by a single ethnic group. The former is a lonely, anonymous building; the latter, a bustling microsociety. I have observed similar patterns in suburban areas: on blocks where people are homogeneous, they socialize; where they are heterogeneous, they do little more than exchange polite greetings.[29]

Suburbs are usually described as being more homogeneous in house type than the city, but if they are compared to the outer city, the differences are small. Most inhabitants of the outer city, other than well-to-do homeowners, live on blocks of uniform structures as well; for example, the endless streets of row houses in Philadelphia and Baltimore or of two-story duplexes and six-flat apartment houses in Chicago. They differ from the new suburbs only in that they were erected through more primitive methods of mass production. Suburbs are, of course, more predominantly areas of owner-occupied single homes, though in the outer districts of most American cities home-ownership is also extremely high.

Demographically, suburbs as a whole are clearly more homogeneous than cities as a whole, though probably not more so than outer cities. However, people do not live in cities or suburbs as a whole, but in specific neighborhoods. An analysis of ways of life would require a determination of the degree of population homogeneity within the boundaries of areas defined as neighbourhoods by residents' social contacts. Such an analysis would no doubt indicate that many neighbourhoods in the city as well as the suburbs are homogeneous. Neighborhood homogeneity is actually a result of factors having little or nothing to do with the house type, density, or location of the area relative to the city limits. Brand new neighborhoods are more homogeneous than older ones, because they have not yet experienced resident turnover, which frequently results in population heterogeneity. Neighborhoods of low- and medium-priced housing are usually less homogeneous than those with expensive dwellings because they attract families who have reached the peak of occupational and residential mobility, as well as young families who are just starting their climb and will eventually move to neighborhoods of higher status. The latter, being accessible only to high-income people, are therefore more homogeneous with respect to other resident characteristics as well. Moreover, such areas have the economic and political power to slow down or prevent invasion.

The demographic differences between cities and suburbs cannot be questioned, especially since the suburbs have attracted a large number of middle-class child-rearing families. The differences are, however, much reduced if suburbs are compared only to the outer city. In addition, a detailed comparison of suburban and outer-city residential areas would show that neighborhoods with the same kinds of people can be found in the city as well as the suburbs. Once again, the age of the area and the cost of housing are more important determinants of demographic characteristics than the location of the area with respect to the city limits. [...]

A Reevaluation of Definitions

THE ARGUMENT presented here has implications for the sociological definition of the city. Such a definition relates ways of life to environmental features of the city qua settlement type. But if ways of life do not coincide with settlement types, and if these ways are functions of class and life-cycle stage rather than of the ecological attributes of the settlement, a sociological definition of the city cannot be formulated.[30] Concepts such as "city" and "suburb" allow us to distinguish settlement types from each other physically and demographically, but the ecological processes and conditions which they synthesize have no direct or invariate consequences for ways of life. The sociologist cannot, therefore, speak of an urban or suburban way of life.

Conclusion

MANY OF the descriptive statements made here are as time bound as Wirth's.[31] In the 1940s Wirth concluded that some form of urbanism would eventually predominate in all settlement types. He was, however, writing during a time of immigrant acculturation and at the end of a serious depression, an era of minimal choice. Today, it is apparent that high-density, heterogeneous surroundings are for most people a temporary place of residence; other than for the Park Avenue or Greenwich Village cosmopolites, they are a result of necessity, rather than choice. As soon as they can afford to do so, most Americans head for the single-family house and the quasi-primary way of life of the low-density neighborhood, in the outer city or the suburbs.[32]

Changes in the national economy and in government housing policy can affect many of the variables that make up housing supply and demand. For example, urban sprawl may eventually outdistance the ability of present and proposed transportation systems to move workers into the city; further industrial decentralization can forestall it and alter the entire relationship between work and residence. The expansion of urban-renewal activities can perhaps lure a significant number of cosmopolites back from the suburbs, while a drastic change in renewal policy might begin to ameliorate the housing conditions of the deprived population. A serious depression could once again make America a nation of doubled-up tenants.

These events will affect housing supply and residential choice; they will frustrate, but not suppress, demands for the quasi-primary way of life. However, changes in the national economy, society, and culture can affect people's characteristics—family size, educational level, and various other concomitants of life-cycle stage and class. These in turn will stimulate changes in demands and choices. The rising number of college graduates, for example, is likely to increase the cosmopolite ranks. This might in turn create a new set of city dwellers, although it will probably do no more than encourage the development of cosmopolite facilities in some suburban areas.

The current revival of interest in urban sociology and in community studies, as well as the sociologist's increasing curiosity about city planning, suggests that data may soon be available to formulate a more adequate theory of the relationship between settlements and the ways of life within them. The speculations presented in this essay are intended to raise questions; they can be answered only by more systematic data collection and theorizing.

Postscript

WHEN I reread this essay again after many years, I was struck by how much the first sentence remains largely true. While no single school, including the ecological school, is now dominant in urban sociology, Louis Wirth's "Urbanism as a Way of Life" remains the most often cited article and probably the most often read one as well. It still supplies the simplest and seemingly most accurate definition of the city, and a rationale, not to mention an outline, for studying urban sociology—all the research and writing questioning Wirth's ideas notwithstanding. In fact, although over half of all Americans now live in the suburbs, urban sociology courses remain resolutely urban, although often because they deal with the urban sociology of the poor and the minorities who remain stuck in the city. Whatever the merit of that approach (which I use myself), we still do not have a sociology of the suburbs or even a respectable sociological literature on suburbia.

I pointed out in my article, originally published in 1962, that it was as time bound as Wirth's, and I was by and large right. Even though I seem to have predicted the yuppies in my penultimate paragraph, I did not consider the possibility that someday suburbia would be the majority form of residence, and that it would then be inhabited by people of all ages and households of all types, rather than mainly young families with young children. I did mention the decentralization of industry, but did not think that it might one day become a flood. Now, about two-thirds or more of those living in the suburbs also work there, and even fewer than a third need to come to the city's central business district, except perhaps for high culture, since museums and concert halls have by and large not decentralized (yet). Professional sports teams have, however, even if they are still called by the name of the city nearest to where they play.

I should also have thought about the possibility that when the suburbs became more popular, the mainly urban essayists and intellectuals who criticized them—and by implication their middle-American residents—for undue conformity, homogeneity, and other sociocultural diseases would have to end the suburban critique. This they did, shortly after I published this article, but they found new targets with which to continue the cultural class war. Such targets are always available, however, beginning and still ending with television viewing and television programming.

Having underestimated the extent of the suburban move, I also failed to consider the likelihood of a city inhabited increasingly by the very rich and the poor. Nor did I consider that black ghettos would also be found in what I called the outer city, even if they are ghettos of the black working class and lower middle class more than of the black poor, and are thus not altogether different than when they were inhabited by the white working and lower middle classes. It did not even occur to me that housing might one day become expensive, so that most American home buyers could no longer afford either a new or a secondhand single-family house, that suburbia would be filling up with row houses and condominiums—and that the major housing problem of the poor was the inability to pay high rents, which was one cause of the tragic increase in homelessness exacted by the Reagan administration on the poor, the cities, and even many suburbs.

Actually, my prediction of the yuppies was partly luck, for while I expected more young people to come into the inner city after college, some having done so already in the 1950s, I did not expect the large number who came and for whom old neighborhoods near the central business district and elsewhere were gentrified. They have come largely because of the dramatic increase in *professional* service employment in the central business districts of many cities, although because they spend so much time on the streets and in expensive "boutiques," their visibility is greater than their actual number. Moreover, that number could decline sharply in the 1990s, not only because when they marry and have children many move to the suburbs, but also because if the boom times in professional service employment end, their number—and visibility—will shrink quickly and considerably.

I could list other ways in which the 1962 article was time bound; for example, it paid no more attention than Wirth's article to the various political battles—about race, or class, or just property values—that take place in cities and suburbs, and thus could not consider that as all resources became scarcer, these battles would increase in

number and intensity. Still, in its basic conception, the article remains accurate as I write this postscript in the spring of 1990. The basic differences are not between city and suburb, but between the inner city and the rest of the metropolitan area, and the major reasons are more or less as I stated them.

NOTES

1. Louis Wirth, "Urbanism as a Way of Life," *American Journal of Sociology* (July 1938), 44:1–24; reprinted in Paul Hatt and Albert J. Reiss, Jr., eds., *Cities and Society* (Glencoe, Ill.: Free Press, 1957), pp. 46–64.

2. Richard Dewey, "The Rural–Urban Continuum: Real but Relatively Unimportant," *American Journal of Sociology* (July 1960), 66:60–66.

3. I shall not attempt to summarize these studies, for this task has already been performed by Dewey, Reiss, Wilensky, and others. The studies include: Morris Axelrod, "Urban Structure and Social Participation," *American Sociological Review* (February 1956), 21:13–18; Dewey, "The Rural–Urban Continuum;" William H. Form et al., "The Compatibility of Alternative Approaches to the Delimitation of Urban Sub-areas," *American Sociological Review* (August 1954), 19:434–440; Herbert J. Gans, *The Urban Villagers* (New York: Free Press of Glencoe, 1962); Scott Greer, "Urbanism Reconsidered: A Comparative Study of Local Areas in a Metropolis," *American Sociological Review* (February 1956), 21:19–25; Scott Greer and Ella Kube, "Urbanism and Social Structure: A Los Angeles Study," in Marvin B. Sussman, ed., *Community Structure and Analysis* (New York: Crowell, 1959), pp. 93–112; Morris Janowitz, *The Community Press in an Urban Setting* (Glencoe, Ill.: Free Press, 1952); Albert J. Reiss, Jr., "An Analysis of Urban Phenomena," in Robert M. Fisher, ed., *The Metropolis in Modern Life* (Garden City, N.Y.: Double-day, 1955), pp. 41–49; Albert J. Reiss, Jr., "Rural-Urban and Status Differences in Interpersonal Contacts," *American Journal of Sociology* (September 1959), 65:182–195; John R. Seeley, "The Slum: Its Nature, Use, and Users," *Journal of the American Institute of Planners* (February 1959), 25:7–14; Joel Smith, William Form, and Gregory Stone, "Local Intimacy in a Middle-Sized City," *American Journal of Sociology* (November 1954), 60:276–284; Gregory P. Stone, "City Shoppers and Urban Identification: Observations on the Social Psychology of City Life," *American Journal of Sociology* (July 1954), 60:36–45; William F. Whyte, *Street Corner Society* (Chicago: University of Chicago Press, 1955); Harold L. Wilensky and Charles Lebeaux, *Industrial Society and Social*

Welfare (New York: Russell Sage Foundation, 1958); Michael Young and Peter Willmott, *Family and Kinship in East London* (London: Routledge and Kegan Paul, 1957).

4. Greer and Kube, "Urbanism and Social Structure," p. 112.

5. Wilensky and Lebeaux, "Industrial Society," p. 121.

6. By the *inner city* I mean the transient residential areas, the Gold Coasts and the slums that generally surround the central business district, although in some communities they may continue for miles beyond that district. The *outer city* includes the stable residential areas that house the working- and middle-class tenant and owner. The *suburbs* I conceive as the latest and most modern ring of the outer city, distinguished from it only by yet lower densities and by the often irrelevant fact of the ring's location outside the city limits.

7. Louis Wirth, *The Ghetto* (Chicago: University of Chicago Press, 1928).

8. Arnold M. Rose, "Living Arrangements of Unattached Persons," *American Sociological Review* (August 1947), 12:429–435.

9. Gans, *Urban Villagers.*

10. Seeley, "The Slum."

11. *Ibid.* The trapped are not very visible, but I suspect that they are a significant element in what Raymond Vernon has described as the "gray areas" of the city in his *Changing Economic Function of the Central City* (New York: Committee on Economic Development, Supplementary Paper No. 1, January 1959).

12. Whether or not these social phenomena have the psychological consequences Wirth suggested depends on the people who live in the area. Those who are detached from the neighborhood by choice are probably immune, but those who depend on the neighborhood for their social relationships—the unattached individuals, for example—may suffer greatly from loneliness.

13. Needless to say, residential instability must ultimately be traced to the fact that, as Wirth pointed out, the city and its economy attract transient—and, depending on the sources of outmigration, heterogeneous—people. However, this is a characteristic of urban-industrial society, not of the city specifically.

14. By neighborhoods or residential districts I mean areas demarcated from others by distinctive physical boundaries or by social characteristics, some of which may be perceived only by the residents. However, these areas are not necessarily socially self-sufficient or culturally distinctive.

15. Wirth, "Urbanism as a Way of Life," p. 56.

16. For the definition of *outer city*, see note 6.

17. Wirth, "Urbanism as a Way of Life," p. 56.

18. Because neighborly relations are not quite primary and not quite secondary, they can also become *pseudo-primary*, that is, secondary ones disguised with false affect to make them appear primary.

Critics have often described suburban life in this fashion, although the actual prevalence of pseudo-primary relationships has not been studied systematically in cities or suburbs.

19. Harold Wattel, "Levittown: A Suburban Community," in William M. Dobriner, ed., *The Suburban Community* (New York: Putnam, 1958), pp. 287–313.

20. Bennett Berger, *Working Class Suburb: A Study of Auto Workers in Suburbia* (Berkeley: University of California Press, 1960). Also Vernon, *Changing Economic Function of the Central City.*

21. Berger, *Working Class Suburb.*

22. Wattel, "Levittown." They may, of course, be significant for the welfare of the total metropolitan area.

23. Otis Dudley Duncan and Albert J. Reiss, Jr., *Social Characteristics of Rural and Urban Communities, 1950* (New York: Wiley, 1956), p. 131.

24. Donald L. Foley, "The Use of Local Facilities in a Metropolis," in Hatt and Reiss, *Cities and Societies*, pp. 237–247. Also see Christen T. Jonassen, *The Shopping Center versus Downtown* (Columbus: Bureau of Business Research, Ohio State University, 1955).

25. Jonassen, "The Shopping Center," pp. 91–92.

26. A 1958 study of New York theatergoers showed a median income of close to $10,000, and 35 percent were reported as living in the suburbs. That year, the median U.S. family income was $5087. John Enders, *Profile of the Theater Market* (New York: Playbill, undated and unpaged).

27. A. C. Spectorsky, *The Exurbanites* (Philadelphia: Lippincott, 1955).

28. I am thinking here of adults; teenagers do suffer from the lack of informal meeting places within walking or bicycling distance.

29. Herbert J. Gans, "Planning and Social Life: Friendship and Neighbor Relations in Suburban Communities," *Journal of the American Institute of Planners* (May 1961), 27:134–140.

30. Because of the distinctiveness of the ways of life found in the inner city, some writers propose definitions that refer only to these ways, ignoring those found in the outer city. For example, popular writers sometimes identify "urban" with "urbanity," that is, "cosmopolitanism." However, such a definition ignores the other ways of life found in the inner city. Moreover, I have tried to show that these ways have few common elements and that the ecological features of the inner city have little or no influence in shaping them.

31. Even more than Wirth's they are based no data and impressions gathered in the large eastern and midwestern cities of the United States.

32. Personal discussions with European planners and sociologists suggest that many European apartment dwellers have similar preferences, although economic conditions, high building costs, and the scarcity of land make it impossible for them to achieve their desires.

Beyond *Blade Runner*

Mike Davis

Source: *Ecology of Fear: Los Angeles and the Imagination of Disaster*
(Metropolitan Books, Henry Holt & Co., 1998).

EDITORS' INTRODUCTION

Why do so many Americans fear cities? How does this apprehension influence the cultural, economic, political, and social contours of urban space? In the following essay, historian, social commentator, and activist Mike Davis surveys the geopolitical landscape of Los Angeles at the end of the twentieth century by updating Ernest Burgess' 1924 concentric zone hypothesis [see Steven H. Corey and Lisa Krissoff Boehm, "Examining America's Urban Landscape: From Social Reform to Social History" in Part I]. Burgess, a member of the Chicago School, developed his concentric zone model, one of the most famous in all of social science, to illustrate that city growth is a consequence of ecological factors and is not haphazard. In addition to traditional ecological determinants of class, land value, and race, Davis adds the new and provocative factor of fear.

Trained as a historian, Mike Davis is commonly associated—directly or indirectly—with the so-called L.A. School of urban theory. Although there are multiple, and often contradictory, definitions of the L.A. School, at the macro level they all hold, as Raul Homero Villa and George J. Sanchez note, the "greater Los Angeles metropolitan area region as preeminently, perhaps singularly, exemplary of the tendential urban process at work in … major cities across the globe."[i] In contrast to the Chicago School, which focused on the dominant central city, adherents of the L.A. School discuss the fragmented spatial and social patterns of the multicultural Los Angeles metropolitan region as a whole. The urban periphery—that is the area other than downtown, and in some cases, outside the city limits—is actually central to understanding the new postmodern city. As Michael Dear states, "It is no longer the center that organizes the hinterland but the hinterland that determines the center."[ii] In the following essay, Davis illustrates the reconfiguration of Los Angeles based on the prejudices and fears of the hinterland.

Davis, in fact, was one of the first people to identify the existence of an L.A. School. He gained international notoriety through the success of his award winning *City of Quartz: Excavating the Future in Los Angeles* (New York: Verso, 1990), which detailed class and racial tensions that led to the 1992 riots in Los Angeles that accompanied the Rodney King trial. *City of Quartz* has been translated into eight languages and received the Issac Deutscher Award from the London School of Economics, and was named as a best book in urban politics by the American Political Science Association. Mike Davis teaches history at the University of California, Irvine, and is a Distinguished Professor in the Department of Creative Writing at the University of California, Riverside. He is also author of many books, including *Magical Urbanism: Latinos Reinvent the U.S. City* (New York: Verso, 2000), *Dead Cities, And Other Tales* (New York: W. W. Norton, 2002) and *Planet of Slums* (New York: Verso, 2006).

---

i Raul Homero Villa and George Sanchez, eds., *Los Angeles and the Future of Urban Cultures: A Special Issue of the American Quarterly* (Baltimore, MD: Johns Hopkins University Press, 2005), 1.

ii Michael J. Dear, ed., with J. Dallas Dishman, *From Chicago to L.A.: Making Sense of Urban Theory* (New York: Sage, 2002), 3.

ECOLOGY OF FEAR

Every American city boasts an official insignia and slogan. Some have municipal mascots, colors, songs, birds, trees, even rocks. But Los Angeles alone has adopted an official nightmare.

In 1988, after three years of debate, a galaxy of corporate and civic celebrities submitted to Mayor Bradley a detailed strategic plan for Southern California's future. Although most of *L.A. 2000: A City for the Future* is devoted to hyperbolic rhetoric about Los Angeles's irresistible rise as a "world crossroads" comparable to imperial Rome or LaGuardian New York, a section in the epilogue, written by historian Kevin Starr, considered what might happen if the city failed to create a new "dominant establishment" to manage its extraordinary ethnic diversity. "There is, of course, the *Blade Runner* scenario: the fusion of individual cultures into a demotic polyglotism ominous with unresolved hostilities."[1]

Blade Runner—Los Angeles's dystopic alter ego. Take the Grayline tour in 2019: the mile-high neo-Mayan pyramid of the Tyrell Corporation drips acid rain on the mongrel masses in the teeming ginza far below. Enormous neon images float like clouds above fetid, hyperviolent streets, while a voice intones advertisements for extraterrestrial suburban living in "Off World." Deckard, a postapocalypse Philip Marlowe, struggles to save his conscience and his woman in an urban labyrinth ruled by malevolent biotech corporations.

With Warner Brothers' release of the more hardboiled "director's cut" a few months after the Rodney King riots, Ridley Scott's 1982 film version of Philip K. Dick's novel (*Do Androids Dream of Electric Sheep?*) reasserted its sway over our increasingly troubled sleep. Ruminations about the future of Los Angeles now take for granted the dark imagery of *Blade Runner* as a possible, if not inevitable, terminal point for the former Land of Sunshine.

Yet for all of *Blade Runner*'s glamor as the reigning star of sci-fi dystopias, its vision of the future is strangely anachronistic and surprisingly unprescient. Scott, in collaboration with "visual futurist" Syd Mead, offered a pastiche of imaginary landscapes that Scott himself has conceded to be "overkill."[2] Peel away the overlays of Yellow Peril (Scott is notoriously addicted, as in his subsequent film *Black Rain*, to urban Japan as the face of Hell) and noir (all those polished black marble interiors), peel away the high-tech plumbing retrofitted to street-level urban decay—what remains is the same vista of urban gigantism and human mutation that Fritz Lang depicted in *Metropolis*.

The sinister man-made Everest of the Tyrell Corporation as well as all the souped-up rocket-squad cars darting around the air space are obviously the progeny—albeit now swaddled in darkness—of the famous city of the bourgeoisie in that 1931 Weimar film. But Lang himself was only plagiarizing from contemporary American futurists: above all, architectural artist Hugh Ferriss, who, together with Chrysler Building designer Raymond Hood and Mexican architect-archaeologist Francisco Mujica (visionary of urban pyramids like the Tyrell tower), popularized the coming "Titan City" of hundred-story skyscrapers with suspended bridge highways and rooftop airports. Ferriss and company, in their turn, largely reworked already existing fantasies—common in Sunday supplements since 1900—of what Manhattan might look like at the end of the century.[3]

Blade Runner, in other words, remains yet another edition of the core modernist fantasy of the future metropolis—alternately utopia or dystopia, *ville radieuse* or Gotham City—as monster Manhattan. Such imagery might best be called "Wellsian" since as early as 1906, in his *Future in America*, H. G. Wells was trying to envision the late twentieth century by "enlarging the present"—represented by New York—to create "a sort of gigantesque caricature of the existing world, everything swollen up to vast proportions and massive beyond measure."[4]

Ridley Scott's caricature may have captured ethnocentric anxieties about multiculturalism run amok, but it failed to engage the real Los Angeles—especially the great unbroken plains of aging bungalows, stucco apartments, and ranch-style homes—as it erodes socially and physically into the twenty-first century. In fact, his hypertrophied Art Deco Downtown seems little more than a romantic conceit when compared to the savage slums actually being born in the city's inner belt of decaying postwar suburbs. *Blade Runner* is not so much the future of the city as the ghost of past imaginations. [...]

In what follows, I offer an extrapolative map of a future Los Angeles that is already half-born. Since the 1992 riots, premonitions of Butler's low-rise dystopia, with urban decay metastasizing in the heart of suburbia, have become commonplace. But the map itself—although inspired by the writings of Butler and Gibson—most closely resembles a diagram that Ernest W. Burgess, a sociologist at the University of Chicago, popularized during the 1920s.[5] As one historian has described it: "There is no more famous diagram in social science than that combination of half-moon and dartboard depicting the five concentric urban zones which appear during the rapid expansion of a modern American city such as Chicago."[6]

For those unfamiliar with the Chicago school of sociology's canonical study of the "North American city" (actually, 1920s Chicago generalized as archetype), Burgess's dartboard represents the spatial hierarchy into which the struggle for the survival of the urban fittest supposedly sorts social classes and their respective housing types. As imagined by academic social Darwinism, it portrays a "human ecology" organized by the "biological" forces of concentration, centralization, segregation, invasion, and succession. My remapping takes Burgess back to the future. It preserves such "ecological" determinants as income, land value, class, and race but adds a decisive new factor: fear.

Scanscape

Is there any need to explain *why* fear eats the soul of Los Angeles? Only the middle-class

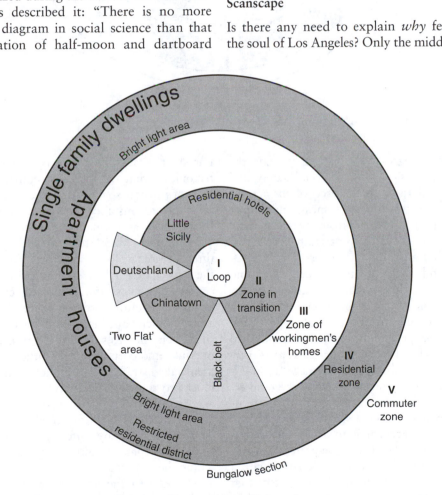

Figure 1.1 "The Most Famous Diagram in Social Science."

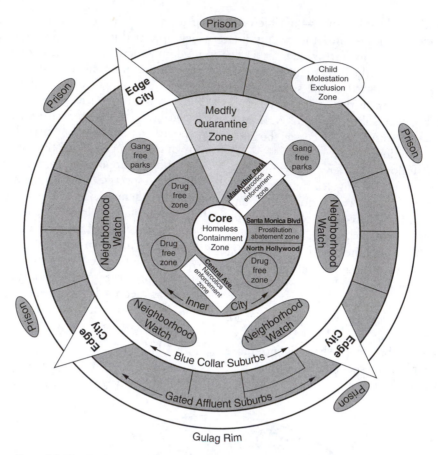

Figure 1.2 The Ecology of Fear.

dread of progressive taxation exceeds the current obsession with personal safety and social insulation. In the face of intractable urban poverty and homelessness, and despite one of the greatest expansions in American business history, a bipartisan consensus insists that any and all budgets must be balanced and entitlements reduced. With no hope for further public investment in the remediation of underlying social conditions, we are forced instead to make increasing public and private investments in physical security. The rhetoric of urban reform persists, but the substance is extinct. "Rebuilding L.A." simply means padding the bunker.

As city life grows more feral, the various social milieux adopt security strategies and technologies according to their means. As with Burgess's dartboard, the pattern resolves itself into a series of concentric zones with a bull's eye in Downtown. To the extent that these security measures are reactions to urban unrest, it is possible to speak about a "riot tectonics" that episodically convulses and reshapes urban space. After the 1965 Watts rebellion, for instance, downtown Los Angeles's leading landowners organized a secretive "Committee of 25" to deal with perceived threats to redevelopment efforts.[7] Warned by the LAPD that a black "inundation" of the central city was imminent, the committee abandoned efforts to revitalize the city's aging financial and retail core. Instead, it persuaded city hall to subsidize the transplanting of banks and corporate front offices to a new financial district atop Bunker Hill, a few blocks to the west. The city's redevelopment agency, acting as a private planner, bailed out the committee's lost investments in the old business district by offering discounts far below real market value on parcels of land within the new core.

The key to the success of this strategy, celebrated as Downtown's "renaissance," was the physical segregation of the new core and its land values behind a rampart of regraded palisades, concrete pillars, and freeway walls. Traditional pedestrian connections between Bunker Hill and the old core were removed, and foot traffic was elevated above the street on "pedways"—as in Hugh Ferriss's imaginary Titan City—access to which was controlled by the security systems of individual skyscrapers. This radical privatization of Downtown public space, with its ominous racial overtones, occurred without significant public debate.

The 1992 riots vindicated the foresight of Fortress Downtown's designers. While windows were being smashed throughout the old business district, Bunker Hill lived up to its name. By flicking a few switches on their command consoles, the security staffs of the great bank towers were able to cut off all access to their expensive real estate. Bullet-proof steel doors rolled down over street-level entrances, escalators instantly froze, and electronic locks sealed off pedestrian passageways. As the *Los Angeles Business Journal* pointed out, the riot-tested success of corporate Downtown's defenses has only stimulated demand for new and higher levels of physical security.[8]

One consequence of this demand has been the continuing erosion of the boundary between architecture and law enforcement. The LAPD have become central players in the Downtown design process. No major project now breaks ground without their participation. Police representatives have exerted effective pressure against the provision of public toilets ("crime scenes" in their opinion) and the toleration of street vending ("lookouts for drug dealers"). The riots also provided suburban police departments with a pretext for enhancing their involvement in planning and design issues. In affluent Thousand Oaks, for example, the sheriff's liaison to the planning commission persuaded the city to outlaw alleys as a "crime prevention priority."[9]

Video monitoring of Downtown's redeveloped zones, meanwhile, has been extended to parking structures, private sidewalks, and plazas. This comprehensive surveillance constitutes a virtual *scan-scape*—a space of protective visibility that increasingly defines where white-collar office workers and middle-class tourists feel safe downtown. Here Los Angeles, however, has no monopoly on Orwellian technology. Nearly one hundred British town centers, thanks to an initiative of the former Tory government, are now enclosed within the panoptic gaze of closed-circuit television monitors mostly operated by private contractors.[10]

These "City Watch" programs, zealously promoted by surveillance technology industry leader ADT, may soon become the international norm. Hollywood, for example, has just established California's first official "Videotape Surveillance Zone" in the drug-ridden Yucca Street neighborhood just west of the famed Capital Records building.[11] The legendary Hollywood sign, meanwhile, is guarded against vandals and hikers by state-of-the-art motion detectors and infrared cameras with radar-activated zoom lenses. "Intruders' pictures are recorded on a computer disk as evidence and city park rangers are alerted. Then loudspeakers warn trespassers that they are being watched and that authorities are on their way."[12]

Inevitably, video monitoring will sooner or later be linked with home security systems in a seamless continuity of surveillance over daily routine. Indeed, up-market lifestyles may soon be defined by the ability to afford "electronic guardian angels" to watch over the owner and all significant others in her or his life. A Beverly Hills security expert, who retails clandestine video systems that allow affluent working parents to monitor their low-paid nannies and maids, compared the boom in sales following the 1997 trial of Louise Woodward (the British nanny accused of murdering a Boston-area infant) to the middle-class run on local gunstores after the 1992 riots.[13] Science and technology journals, for their part, have recently heralded the advent of "digital super-surveillance" based on gadgets like pocket radars, millimeter-wave video cameras, infrared automatic tracking, code grabbers and rotaters, retinal scanners, voice keys, finger mappers, and thermal facial imagers. "Brave New World," according to the *New Scientist*, is now off the shelf:

It is a world where there will be nowhere to hide, nor anywhere to hide anything. There are already devices under development that will see through walls and strip-search suspects from a distance, looking under their clothes and inside their bodies. Individuals may be identified by their unique smells and tracked down, or "recognised" electronically, even before they have had time to complete a crime. And thanks to cheap digital video cameras and powerful new search algorithms, individuals will be tracked by computers. There will be no anonymity even in the once welcoming crowds.[14] [...]

Half-Moons of Repression

In the original Burgess diagram, "pie slices" or "half-moons" representing ethnic enclaves ("Deutschland," "Little Sicily," or "the Black Belt") and specialized architectural ecologies ("residential hotels" or "the two-flat area") are wedged into the city's concentric socioeconomic structure. In contemporary metropolitan Los Angeles, new species of enclaves are emerging in sympathy with the militarization of the landscape. For want of any generally accepted name, we might call them "social control districts." They merge the sanctions of the criminal or civil code with landuse planning to create what Michel Foucault would undoubtedly have recognized as a yet higher stage in the evolution of the "disciplinary order" of the modern city. Growing like weeds in a constitutional no man's land, Southern California's social control districts can be distinguished according to their specific juridical modes of imposing spatial "discipline."

"Social Control Districts"

[...] *Abatement* districts, currently enforced against graffiti and prostitution in sign-posted neighborhoods of Los Angeles and West Hollywood, extend the traditional police power over nuisance (the legal fount of all zoning) from noxious industry to noxious behavior. Financed by fines collected (on prostitution offenses) or special sales taxes levied (on spray paints, for example), they devote additional law enforcement resources to specific social problems. Going a step further, business leaders in Little Tokyo and Hollywood have proposed the establishment of self-taxing "improvement districts" which would be able to hire private security guards to supplement the police. Needless to say, this would further erode the already fuzzy boundary between public and private policing in Los Angeles.

Since the 1992 riots, moreover, the LAPD has buttressed abatement programs by interventions in the zoning process. Using computer software to identify hot spots of prostitution, petty crime, and drug use, the police now routinely veto building and operating permits for "crime magnet" businesses. "Most commanding officers don't want new bars in their area, or new liquor locations or new dance halls," a police spokesperson explained to the *Los Angeles Times*. "What you have is an increased police interest in using zoning laws as vehicles to stop these businesses when they have problems." The LAPD considers this a logical extension of "community-based policing," but some Latino community leaders have complained that it really constitutes discrimination against Spanish-speaking mom-and-pop businesses like meat markets and *tiendas* (corner grocery stores) that need liquor sales to break even. Drinkers simply shop at supermarkets instead.[15]

Enhancement districts, represented all over Southern California by the "drug-free zones" and "gun-free zones" surrounding public schools, add extra federal or state penalties ("enhancements") to crimes committed within a specified radius of public institutions. In other cases, new laws, targeted at specific groups and locations, criminalize otherwise legal behavior. As a condition of probation, for example, prostitutes are now given maps demarcating areas, including parts of Hollywood, South Central, and the San Fernando Valley, where they can be arrested simply for walking down the street. In Costa Mesa (Orange County) prostitutes are further humiliated by having their clothes confiscated after arrest. They are released from jail wearing flimsy white paper jumpsuits.[16]

From the circumscription of a group's otherwise legal behavior, it is a short step to *containment* districts designed to quarantine potentially epidemic social problems or, more usually, social types. In Southern California these undesirables run the gamut from that insect illegal immigrant, the Mediterranean fruit fly, to homeless people. Since the early 1980s, the city of Los Angeles has tried to prevent the spillover of cardboard "condos" into surrounding council districts or into the more upscale precincts of Downtown by keeping homeless people "contained" (the official term) within the 50-square-block area of skid row. In 1996, the city council formalized the status quo by declaring a portion of skid row's sidewalks an official "sleeping zone." As soup kitchens and skid row missions brace themselves for a new wave of homelessness in the wake of recent state and federal welfare reforms, the LAPD maintains its traditional policy of keeping street people herded within the boundaries of the nation's largest outdoor poorhouse.

Obverse to containment is the formal *exclusion* of pariah groups from public space or even the city limits. The tactics are sometimes ingenious. In Anaheim, for instance, a city-supported citizens' group ("Operation Steer Clear") dumped tons of steer manure in local parks in the hope that the stench would drive away drug dealers and gang members. "Anticamping" ordinances, likewise, have been passed by a spate of Southland cities, including the "Peoples' Republic" of Santa Monica, with the goal of banishing the homeless from sight. Since such exclusion ordinances merely sweep a stigmatized social group onto the next community's doorstep, each city, in a chain reaction, adopts comparable legislation in order to avoid becoming the regional equivalent of a human landfill.

Similarly, Los Angeles and a score of smaller cities have used sweeping civil injunctions—whose constitutionality was upheld by the California Supreme Court in January 1997—to prevent gangs from congregating in parks or on street corners. Although one high-ranking LAPD official has complained that these "gang-free zones" merely push gang activity into adjoining neighborhoods, they are highly popular with vote-conscious district attorneys and city council members who love the image that the injunctions broadcast of decisive action and comprehensive deterrence.[17] In a typical example, a Los Angeles judge banned Eighteenth Street homeboys in one neighborhood from "associating in public view" in groups larger than two, even in their own front yards. He also imposed an 8 P.M. curfew on juvenile gang members and banned the use of cellular phones and pagers. In addition, his injunction prohibited Eighteenth Street members from whistling in public—a form of signaling, the city attorney alleged, used by lookouts for drug dealers.[18]

As civil libertarians have pointed out, the social control district strategy penalizes individuals, even in the absence of a criminal act, merely for group membership. "Status criminalization," moreover, feeds off middle-class fantasies about the nature of the dangerous classes. And fearful fantasies have been growing in hothouse fashion. In the mid-1980s, for example, the ghost of Cotton Mather suddenly appeared in suburban Southern California. Allegations that local daycare centers were actually covens of satanic perversion wrenched courtrooms back to the seventeenth century. In the course of the McMartin Preschool molestation trial—the longest and most expensive such ordeal in American history—children testified about molester-teachers who flew around on broomsticks and other manifestations of the Evil One.

The creation by the little city of San Dimas of the nation's first "child-molestation exclusion zone" was one legacy of the accompanying collective hysteria, which undoubtedly mined huge veins of displaced parental guilt. This Twin Peaks-like suburb in the eastern San Gabriel Valley was signposted from stem to stern with the warning: "Hands Off Our Kids! We I.D. and Fingerprint Our Kids for Safety." It is unclear whether the armies of lurking pedophiles in the mountains above San Dimas were deterred by these warnings, but any post-Burgess mapping of urban space must acknowledge the power that bad dreams now wield over the public landscape.

NOTES

1. *L.A. 2000: A City for the Future*, final report of the Los Angeles 2000 Committee (Los Angeles, 1988), p. 86.
2. Quoted in Paul Sammon, *Future Noir: The Making of* Blade Runner (New York, 1996), p. 75.
3. Cf. Hugh Ferriss, *The Metropolis of Tomorrow* (New York, 1929); and Francisco Mujica, *History of the Skyscraper* (New York, 1930).
4. H. G. Wells, *The Future in America* (New York, 1906), pp. 11–12.
5. Ernest Burgess, "The Growth of the City: An Introduction to a Research Project," *Publications of the American Sociological Society* 18 (1924): 85–97; and Robert Park and Ernest Burgess, *The City* (Chicago, 1925). Urban ecology was resuscitated after World War II with Amos Hawley's *Human Ecology: A Theory of Community Structure* (New York, 1950).
6. Dennis Smith, *The Chicago School: A Liberal Critique of Capitalism* (London, 1988), p. 28.
7. Mike Davis, "The Infinite Game: Redeveloping Downtown L.A.," in Diane Ghirardo (ed.), *Out of Site: A Social Criticism of Architecture* (Seattle, 1991).
8. Jim Hathcock, "Security Firms Overwhelmed by Sudden Demand for Riot Protection," *Los Angeles Business Journal* 27 July 1992.
9. *LAT* 6 August 1993 (Ventura County edition).
10. See Nicholas Fyfe, "City Watching: Closed Circuit Television Surveillance in Public Spaces," *Area* 28, no. 1 (1996).
11. Ibid.
12. *New Scientist*, 24 August 1994, p. 18.
13. Interviewed by Warren Olney on "Which Way L.A." KCRW (FM), Santa Monica, 14 November 1997.
14. "Technospy: Nowhere to Hide," *New Scientist*, 4 November 1995, p. 4.
15. *LAT* 26 September 1993.
16. *LAT* 4 May 1994 and 11 October 1995.
17. For the critical views of LAPD deputy chief Michael Bostic, see *LAT* 23 November 1997.
18. *LAT* 22 May 1997.

Crossing the City Line

Robert A. Orsi

Source: *Gods of the City: Religion and the American Urban Landscape*
(Bloomington: Indiana University Press, 1999).

EDITORS' INTRODUCTION

Are cities virtuous places? America's urban centers have long been a focal point of fascination and sensationalism, routinely tempered with moral outrage, indignation, and condemnation by outside observers and domestic commentators alike. The social and literary construction of cities and their inhabitants as deviant, sinful, and aberrant from mainstream America accompanied the rise of the increasingly urban, industrial, and diverse nation in the nineteenth and twentieth centuries. A dichotomy was often made between the virtuous and morally uplifting countryside and the secular and godless city. Urban areas, however, were not and are not without redemption. Indeed, as religious scholar Robert A. Orsi argues in the following essay, much of what constitutes modern American religion developed in the city.

As Orsi notes, those who feared cities projected their own apprehensions onto urban spaces and confused the vitality and diversity of the streets with religious declination and disorder. Rather, streets are complex spaces where urban residents interact and forge their own culture. What people do religiously in cities is a product of the type of city they live in and their life circumstances. As a result, there is no single urban religious style, just as there is no single form of urbanism in the United States. Orsi's investigation into the role of religion in American cities serves to further historicize the fear of urban life that Mike Davis documents within contemporary Los Angeles, as well as the underlying urban–rural dichotomy that characterized classic urban theory and informed the assumptions and models of the Chicago School. Orsi's work also serves as an example of how scholars can better integrate theory and religion in the study of urban life.[i] Religion is often ignored in works claiming to provide a complete history of cities.

Robert A. Orsi is a professor of religion at Northwestern University and the editor of *Gods of the City: Religion and the American Urban Landscape* (1999). He is also the author of several award-winning works, including *The Madonna of 115th Street: Faith and Community in Italian Harlem, 1880–1950* (New Haven: Yale University Press, 1985), *Thank You Saint Jude: Women's Devotion to the Patron Saint of Hopeless Causes* (New Haven: Yale University Press, 1996), and *Between Heaven and Earth: The Religious Works People Make and the Scholars Who Study Them* (Princeton: Princeton University Press, 2004).

---

i Jon Butler, "Theory and God in Gotham," *History and Theory*, 45 (2006): 60.

CROSSING THE CITY LINE

Ever since the publication in 1938 of Louis Wirth's influential article "Urbanism as a Way of Life," American sociologists and urban scholars have debated whether the conditions of urban life — population density and heterogeneity, for example, or the frantic pace and welter of distractions in cities — give rise to distinct subjectivities. Is there a characteristic city self? Does the city (isolated from other determinants) make people more or less tolerant, more or less nervous? Does the sorry environment of a slum leach into the hearts and souls of the people who must live there and affect their sense of themselves and of what is possible in the world, a complex of influences that sociologist Gerald D. Suttles called the "social order of the slum"? This debate over the social-psychological consequences of urbanism has generated an extensive but ultimately inconclusive literature. That everyone seems to have an opinion about the issue, however, indicates how high the stakes are in setting or erasing the boundaries between city people and everyone else.[1]

This intense boundary work has deep roots in American civilization. For social, historical, topographical, religious, and cultural reasons as the industrial city took shape on the ground, it also emerged as a discursive construction in several overlapping idioms, a charged imaginative creation of fantasy, terror, and desire. For two hundred years, despite (or perhaps because of) the ceaseless urbanizing of the population, the city was cast as the necessary mirror of American civilization, and fundamental categories of American reality — whiteness, heterosexuality, domestic virtue, feminine purity, middle-class respectability — were constituted in opposition to what was said to exist in cities. A revolution in American reading habits and tastes in the first half of the nineteenth century generated a new competitive marketplace for popular reading material, and as secular and religious publishers competed to shape and appeal to the tastes of an emergent mass audience of readers, religious writers were explicitly concerned to arouse and direct emotionally charged moral responses at a time when disestablishment appeared to threaten public religious authority. Accounts of the "mysteries and miseries" of the great cities, described in graphic detail and sometimes illustrated, became a staple of popular reading and moral pedagogy; they amplified the cry of evangelicals for renewed moral authority.

In the feverish imaginations of antebellum anti-Catholic literary provocateurs, city neighborhoods appeared as caves of rum and Romanism, mysterious and forbidding, a threat to democracy, Protestantism, and virtue alike. Journalism, anti-Catholic and anti-immigrant polemics, temperance pamphlets, and evangelical tracts together created a luridly compelling anti-urban genre that depicted the city as the vicious destroyer of the common good, of family life and individual character, and counterposed the city to an idealized image of small-town life. The *National Police Gazette*, with its salacious "true tales" of urban depravity, was first published in 1845. Historian R. Laurence Moore has dubbed this genre of urban writing "moral sensationalism."[2]

The literature of urban moral sensationalism titillated readers at the same time that it appeared to endorse familiar moral and religious judgments. Indeed, prohibition on one level generated desires on another: the constant reiteration of the dangers and otherness of the city re-created the urban landscape as an object of fascination and a fantasied space of freedom from social constraint. Campaigns for the suppression of vice became vehicles of pornographic excitement. The "city" — rendered as the site of moral depravity, lascivious allure, and the terrain of necessary Christian intervention — became from this moment an enduring commodity of American popular culture and the compulsive domain of prohibited desires and unattainable satisfactions. One consequence of the wide circulation of this literature and its direction of desire toward the cities was the complex, multiply fissured, and unstable representation of the "city" that is still characteristic of American public language. The resonance and strange allure of the term "inner city" today in the minds of those with little or no experience of urban life, as well as in Hollywood fantasies, are contemporary products of this history.

So city people in the United States have always had to live in other people's ideas of where they live as well as in real places on the ground. [...] Spaces on the urban landscape are both geographical sites where real people live and constructions of terror and desire among those who live elsewhere, including elsewhere in the city. Whatever "the South Bronx," "Harlem," "East L.A.," "South Phoenix," and other such culturally marked urban places mean to residents (and they have meant many things over the years to many different groups of people), these locations have been cast by outsiders simultaneously as squalid, dangerous slums and exotic locales of forbidden sensual delights ("therapy for deeper white needs," as critic Nathan Irvin Huggins describes 1920s Harlem, where "the most forbidden was most available"); as secure "urban villages" populated by contentedly domestic industrial peasants; and as fragmented, anomic no-man's lands. City people know this. [...] Part of the work of city religion is contending with the consequences of such fantasies.[3] [...]

Religion in the Spaces of the City

Until recently, the phenomenology of city religions was not a specific field of scholarly inquiry. This reflects the wider cultural occlusion of strangers in the cities. The very idea of "city religion" struck many as an oxymoron, and the term has been absent from major encyclopedias and dictionaries of American religion. Mircea Eliade, the great historian of religions and a lifelong resident of cities himself, argued that what passed for religion in contemporary Western urban settings were degraded and impotent "survivals" of real religiosity, which necessarily existed in intimate and ongoing connection to the rhythms and revelations of the sacred in nature. Modern men and women, whose lives are governed by function, speed, efficiency, and novelty, have been alienated from the ontological grounds of human experience, said Eliade — from being itself, as being is disclosed and experienced in the hierophanies (or self-disclosures) of the sacred in nature: in the rhythms of the moon, for example, or the pulse of the oceans. The modern city, by this account, is the end product of a long history of spiritual alienation and decline, the outcome of processes of secularization. As moral philosopher Alasdair MacIntyre explained, "When the working class were gathered from the countryside into the industrial cities, they were finally torn from a form of community in which it could be intelligibly and credibly claimed that the norms which govern social life had universal and cosmic significance, and were God-given. They were planted instead in a form of community in which the officially endorsed norms so clearly are of utility only to certain partial and partisan human interests that it is impossible to clothe them with universal and cosmic significance." The task of the study of urban religion, then, if one follows these theorists, becomes either to chart the progress of this decline or to identify isolated pockets of resistance to it.[4]

The strongest theoretical work on urban religions has concentrated on the traditional cities of Asia, Meso-America, and South Asia, carefully explicating the relationships among the plans and architecture of these ancient cities and their respective cosmologies, social hierarchies, and ritual calendars. Although this scholarly tradition reminds us that city culture is not a product of the last two centuries in the West, it has largely ignored the religious lives of people in the turbulent, chaotic industrial city, where cosmology, ritual, architecture, and demarcations of space are not so carefully and intentionally synchronized, if at all. Indeed, it is often precisely the disjunctures between environment and religious idiom that occasion crises, cultural creativity, and religious innovation.[5]

The belief that religion is not natural to cities is pervasive in contemporary American culture. The religious ethos of white middle-class Americans at the end of the twentieth century is dominated by a spirit of "expressive individualism," according to the authors of *Habits of the Heart*, a romantic sensibility akin to Eliade's that is more likely to identify mountaintops and ocean beaches as places evocative of religious feelings than street corners and the basements of housing projects; and religion, in this common understanding, is a matter of feeling rather than of practice, authority, discipline within a tradition, or of feeding the spirits. If there is religion in the cities — "real" religion, that is — then it is either the courageous faith of those who go and live and serve among the poor, or the alluring vitality, spiritual exoticism, and primeval powers of the other. The history and phenomenology of urban religions remain so little explored in large part because of the authority of the narrative of urban religious decline and alienation and of these variant strains of romantic religion in American culture.[6]

Yet the truth is that much of what is characteristic of modern American religion has developed in cities. Pentecostalism, settlement houses, Christian Science, the various modern forms of American Judaism, gospel and soul music, immigrant street shrines and festivals, and the American encounter with the many religious traditions of Asia and Africa, to cite just a few examples, are all phenomena of the cities. Important international religious movements either found indigenous expression in U.S. cities, as with Hasidic Judaism in Brooklyn (where Chagall-like rebbes float above red-brick Brooklyn tenements in paintings sold in galleries on Eastern Parkway), or were recast into more vital forms here before being transplanted back to their cultures of origin, as happened with Swami Prabhupada's Hare Krishna movement. African spiritualities and religious practices took complex urban forms in Vodou and Santería in the spaces and traffic between New York and Port-au-Prince and between Miami and Havana, respectively. Familiar idioms of popular Protestantism assumed new shapes as the rural white population moved into cities, as we have seen; much of what constitutes the distinctive character of modern American Protestantism arose in response to the cities.

Are there distinctly urban religious experiences and practices? [...] "Urban religion" does not refer simply to religious beliefs and practices that happen to take place in cities (and that might as well take place elsewhere). Urban religion is what comes from the dynamic engagement of religious traditions (by which I mean constellations of practices, values, and beliefs, inherited and improvised, in ongoing exchanges among generations and in engagement with changing social, cultural, and intellectual contexts) with specific features of the industrial and post-industrial cityscapes and with the social conditions of city life. The results are distinctly and specifically urban forms of religious practice, experience, and understanding.

The spaces of the cities, their different topographies and demographics, are fundamental to the kinds of religious phenomena that emerge in them. Relevant geographical factors include the arrangement of ethnic neighborhoods in relation to each other; the location of markets, schools, different sorts of recreational sites, and workplaces; the possibilities for and forms of intersection of neighborhoods; and the architectural details of different urban landscapes — including stoops, fire escapes, rooftops, and hallways. In the new post-industrial world cities, other factors are the displacement, diffusion, and even erasure of determinate, particular space by recent developments in telecommunications and transportation technologies, the intensification of global traffic in ideas and artifacts, and the extension of city boundaries over such vast terrain as to obliterate the meaning or necessity of an urban "there." This has all made for complex and contradictory experiences of place for those who travel these new pathways and live in these new "placeless places," and new challenges to their religious creativity.

These specific features of the urban (and perhaps post-urban) landscape, which differ from city to city, are not simply the setting for religious experience and expression but become the very materials for such expression and experience. City folk do not live *in* their environments; they live *through* them. Who am I? What is possible in life? What is good? These are questions that are always asked, and their answers discerned and enacted, in particular places. Specific places structure the questions, and as men and women cobble together responses, they act upon the spaces around them in transformative ways. This is the architectonic of urban religion. Religion is always, among other things, a matter of necessary places, sites where the humans and their deities, ancestors, or spirits may most intimately communicate; religious practice in city and countryside alike engages the vicissitudes of the environments that humans find themselves thrown into and makes meaningful places out of contingent spaces. [...]

The young James Baldwin, for example, constantly scanned the horizon of avenues, temples, bars, beauty parlors, churches, and candy stores of Harlem for clues to who he was; in the process, he created a distinctly religious sense of the city for himself. His fears and desires shaped what he saw, and what he was seeing in turn oriented his fears and desires. Conflicting views of the South Bronxes existed as the products of the interaction of understanding, experience, and imagination. Urban religion is the site of converging and conflicting visions and voices, practices and orientations, which arise out of the complex desires, needs, and fears of many different people who have come to cities by choice or compulsion (or both), and who find themselves intersecting with unexpected others (and with unexpected experiences of their own subjectivities) on a complex social field and in a protean physical landscape that insists on itself with particular intensity.[7]

Consider what becomes of Harlem's Lenox Avenue when it is seen through the eyes of the recently converted boy John Grimes in Baldwin's autobiographical novel, *Go Tell It on the Mountain*: "And the avenue, like any landscape that has endured a storm, lay changed under Heaven, exhausted and clean, and new. Not again, forever, could it return to the avenue it had once been. Fire, or lightning, or the latter rain, coming down from these skies which moved with such pale secrecy above him now, had laid yesterday's avenue waste, had changed it in a moment, in the twinkling of an eye, as all would be changed on the last day, when the skies would open up once more to gather up the saints." Likewise, Moishe Sacks, the leader of a South Bronx synagogue that forms the center of Jack Kugelmass's essay, describes his Sabbath walks through the neighborhood thus: "Every Saturday when I walk to shul, particularly as I get to the area around the shul where all the buildings are gone, even with all the garbage and rubble, it reminds me of the area around the *kotel maravi*, the Western Wall, in Jerusalem. To me this place is my holy place. It's my kotel maravi."[8]

Life in the industrial and post-industrial city demanded (and demands) constant resourcefulness, flexibility, creativity, and existential inventiveness. Modernist intellectuals and artists of the nineteenth century believed that the vitality, pace, and complexity of the industrial city would give rise to distinct art forms capable of bringing the "explosive forces" of urban society to life in art — an aspiration that resulted in a series of formal experiments that included "cubist painting, collage and montage, the cinema, the stream of consciousness in the novel, the free verse of Eliot and Pound and Apollinaire, futurism, vorticism, constructivism, dada, poems that accelerate like cars, paintings that explode like bombs," in Marshall Berman's words. So it has been with urban religious creativity: the world of the modern city has necessitated, encouraged, or simply made possible a tremendous explosion of religious innovation and experimentation.[9]

If this association of urban religions with an exuberant (even if sometimes ambiguous) modernism strikes readers as strange, this may be because in American discourse the dominant metaphors for the cultural experience of city-dwelling immigrants and migrants have tended to be horticultural. Newcomers to the city are "uprooted" or "transplanted" chthonic peasants who pine for their lost earth and re-create their "villages" and shtetls in the cities. But migrants and immigrants to American cities, many of whose journeys to the United States took them not only through farmland or rural areas, but through other cities around the globe, showed themselves to be skilled in the arts of cultural and especially religious improvisation — as resourceful as their ancient counterparts in Rome, Athens, Benares, and Jerusalem. They were makers of their religious worlds of meaning and practice.

African American migrants from the South, for example, built a complex religious culture in northern cities that included Pentecostal practice and experience, New Thought and other metaphysical schools, vernacular healing idioms, the revitalization and reorganization of long-established Protestant denominations touched now by the rhythms and ways of southern migrants, cosmologically derived dietary regimes, African nationalisms, and new faiths such as the Black Jews of Harlem or the Nation of Islam, which drew eclectically on other religious traditions (to name only some of the idioms available in African American city neighborhoods). Such rich environments encouraged a continual, explosive religious creativity, for when "migrants reestablished religious practices and asserted new identities, their experience and exposure to other belief systems altered their religious traditions," as historian Jill Watts writes of the circumstances surrounding Father Divine's movement. The great migration of African Americans northward was, among other things, the occasion for an outpouring of religious creativity.[10]

There is no single urban religious style or idiom; just as there are many different urbanisms reflecting particular economies, demographics, politics, histories, and topographies, so there are many different kinds of urban religions. What people do religiously in cities is shaped by what kinds of cities they find themselves in, at what moment in the histories of those cities, and by their own life experiences, cultural traditions, and contemporary circumstances. Miami's religious history is not like New York's or San Antonio's or Chicago's (although they share common features). The labor histories of migrants and immigrants to Miami, the worlds they left, and the social and physical environments they encountered in Florida

are all specific to that city and to those people, as are the forms of religious improvisation and response that have emerged on this ground.

Some city faiths draw individuals into a shared common world through discipline and ritual, while others sanction the radically individualistic quests possible in cities. Some connect migrants and immigrants to the places they came from; others heighten the distance between here and there, now and then. Particular urban religious idioms, such as the Nation of Islam, forcefully proclaim themselves to be new expressions of ancient faiths, while others insist on their identities as ancient and "traditional" faiths. Many urban religious are ambivalently situated among the divergent and competing possibilities available to city dwellers, alternately mitigating and exacerbating the dilemmas of immigrant and migrant experience. They offer not resolution, but creative engagement and response. [. . .]

It was through their religious displays that urban people announced in their own voices the heterogeneity of cities. Studies of religious practices in specific city neighborhoods that ignore the broader ideological and architectural contexts within which urban religions take shape may fail to recognize that it was through public religious practice — by bringing the Madonna out into the streets, for instance, or transforming apartments in neglected housing projects into ebullient domains of the spirits — that immigrants and migrants staked a claim to living in a particular kind of nation. It has been by their religious practice as much as their politics that migrants and immigrants joined the national debate about pluralism, multiculturalism, and heterogeneity.

Urban street life is a spectacle of recognizable signs, a semiotics of place, that divides the initiated from the uninitiated. Even apparently chaotic street patterns mask "a highly organized street culture, whose boundaries and conventions were well-known to the initiated." This is one of the reasons that style is so important to urban people and to urban religion — why people dress themselves, their gods, and their children so carefully for public display during religious events. It is through style — through the intricate intentionalities of public self-representation, and especially through style in religion — that city people have made meanings and impressed those meanings on themselves and others, have met and contested the gaze of reformers and bureaucrats, and have presented themselves at the borders and junctures of adjacent urban social worlds.[11]

The spaces of the city are not simply venues of display, however. Rather, urban people negotiate a delicate balance between revelation and self-effacement, display and concealment, in their use of the cityscape. [...]

Outsiders have consistently mistaken the vitality and heterogeneity of city streets for disorderliness, neglecting the ways that these streets are spaces of an indigenous moral watchfulness and order. Jane Jacobs understood that neighborhoods police themselves through finely woven and carefully sustained webs of interpersonal connections, bonds that are often constituted, disclosed, celebrated, and negotiated in public religious events. Jacobs represented this dimension of urban culture with a domestic image: the streets raised children. This phrase has been used by others, of course, to register the familiar unease with the mores of the inner city and to issue a dire pronouncement: left to the streets, children will be corrupted by the city. But Jacobs means just the opposite, because she understood that it was in the streets of neighborhoods not destroyed by the many forces converging against the modern American city that people acknowledged and accepted responsibility for their world. This is why the diminution of the streets by height and by urban renewal programs was so destructive to the communities on which they were inflicted. It is in the streets that urban people have encountered themselves as moral agents and as makers of their cultural worlds. Streets are "conduits of sociability." The streets were prooftext for Malcolm X's religious message: Just look around you, he urged his listeners on Harlem afternoons, to see what the white man has done to you. People have studied the streets to learn what was possible and what not; children have discovered here the

temptations of transgression but also the reach of authority.[12]

The streets are not simple spaces, then. If they were, there would be no need to take the gods out into them. Migrants from the Spanish-speaking Caribbean revealed a deep apprehension of *la calle* as well as a deep fondness for it in conversations with a *New York Times* reporter in 1980. *La calle* taught their children to be cold, they said, to be disrespectful to their elders, to value material goods over family connectedness. As they spoke, *la calle* took shape as an agent in their stories of life in New York. These men and women understand the spaces of the city as their inevitable partner in making a moral world for themselves and their children; their response to this inevitability was ambivalence. The streets were to be contended with, encountered, rendered part of the moral universe of families and neighborhoods.[13]

Religious figures of all sorts — clergy with established congregations, upstart leaders of new religious movements trying to build followings by raiding the flocks of others, Pentecostal street preachers, Vodou practitioners, and so on — have long understood the importance of making their presence known in the spaces of the city, to keep an eye on those in their care, to establish and maintain their own authority, and most of all to listen to the voices of these spaces, to attend to what is going on, and to catch the signs and portents offered up by the urban landscape. In the 1940s and 1950s, for example, Harlem's streets, parks, stoops, and churches buzzed with unhappiness and disappointment, a palpable political and moral atmospherics that the editors of a memoir by Malcolm X's assistant minister, Benjamin Karim, describe as a pervasive "street-corner discontent." Harlem was being created in this way as a community of concern and protest; issues of human rights and economic justice were being debated and the nature of religious truth was contested, all in the flow of conversation, gesture, and presence in its spaces. By moving attentively through these spaces, walkers on the sidewalks joined the neighborhood discourse.[14]

African American ministers and Roman Catholic priests have been especially connected to the urban environment, interacting with their respective flocks (and with those who were not but who could be part of their flocks) and establishing links between their congregations and the necessary powers within and beyond the neighborhoods. Malcolm X was a master of the art of street presence. He loved moving through the spaces of Harlem. Catholic urban experience in the cities of the industrial North and Midwest was so thoroughly articulated to place that Catholics identified their neighborhoods by the names of their churches: they came from "St. Stan's" or "St. Bridget's." Catholics "used the parish to map out — both physically and culturally — space within all of the northern cities," creating disciplined moral worlds in which "neighborhood, parish, and religion were constantly intertwined." They celebrated this Catholic ecology in an annual round of processions, carnivals, and block parties. Catholic priests and nuns roamed these city worlds in their distinctive garb, extending the moral authority of the church into saloons, parks, and candy stores. It was one of the intentions of the Franciscans in the South Bronx, for example, to cause a stir on the streets by appearing in their unfamiliar medieval garb, which the friars hoped would so startle and intrigue local people that it might be a step toward shattering the dreadful isolation and givenness of their local world. The environmental authority of African American and Roman Catholic religious figures is particularly evident during community crises, when ministers and priests circle through the neighborhoods to calm the crowds in the streets.[15]

The city comes alive for immigrants and migrants as they move through its emptied spaces in a dynamic fundamentally different from the city's allure in the experience of missionaries, pilgrims, and sexual voyagers. These latter encounters have depended on the absence or occlusion of the other. In contrast, to take one example, Frank Bartleman, a pioneer of Pentecostalism, understood the area around Azusa Street in Los Angeles to be a charged and active terrain: people on their way to the revival found themselves already overcome by God's spirit present in the streets surrounding the chapel and fell into trances on the sidewalks. The city itself comes alive in this imagining and in other experiences of urban religion — suffused with the energies of the sacred. But this is the result of presence, not absence — the presence of divinities and of the people who engage them in the city's spaces.[16]

NOTES

1. Louis Wirth, "Urbanism as a Way of Life," *American Journal of Sociology* 44, no. 1 (July 1938): 1–24; see also Georg Simmel, "The Metropolis and Mental Life," in *The Sociology of Georg Simmel*, trans. and ed. Kent H. Wolff (New York: Free Press, 1950), 409–24. An important entry in the long debate prompted by Wirth and other urbanists of his generation is Herbert Gans, "Urbanism and Suburbanism as Ways of Life: A Reevaluation of Definitions," in Arnold M. Rose, ed., *Human Behavior and Social Processes: An Interactionist Approach* (Boston: Houghton Mifflin, 1962), 625–48; see also Claude S. Fisher, "Toward a Subcultural Theory of Urbanism," *American Journal of Sociology* 80, no. 6 (1974): 1319–41. For a classic statement of the moral power of slum environments, see Gerald D. Suttles, *The Social Order of the Slum: Ethnicity and Territory in the Inner City* (Chicago: University of Chicago Press, 1968).

2. R. Laurence Moore defines and discusses "moral sensationalism" in relation to antebellum accounts of the city in *Selling God: American Religion in the Marketplace of Culture* (New York: Oxford University Press, 1994), 12–39; my understanding of the ideological conflicts of this period are informed by, among other works, Jenny Franchot, *Roads to Rome: The Antebellum Protestant Encounter with Catholicism* (Berkeley and Los Angeles: University of California Press, 1994); David S. Reynolds, *Walt Whitman's America: A Cultural Biography* (New York: Knopf, 1995); and Robert H. Wiebe, *The Opening of American Society: From the Adoption of the Constitution to the Eve of Disunion* (New York: Knopf, 1984).

3. Nathan Irvin Huggins, *Harlem Renaissance* (New York: Oxford University Press, 1971), 91; Huggins notes that after World War I, "Afro-Americans and Harlem could serve a new kind of white psychological need" (89).

4. Alasdair MacIntyre, *Secularization and Moral Change* (New York: Oxford University Press, 1967), 14–15, quoted in Christiano, *Religious Diversity and Social Change*, 122; Christiano offers a helpful discussion and incisive critique of the secularization thesis on pp. 118–33. For a

review of the current state of religious historical scholarship on urban religion, with useful bibliographies, see Butler, "Protestant Success in the New American City, 1870–1920."

5. Mircea Eliade, *The Sacred and the Profane: The Nature of Religion*, trans. Willard R. Trask (New York: Harper and Row, 1961; orig. pub. 1957), 13, 24, 51, 116–59, 178–79, and 201–13. Eliade writes, "The religious sense of urban populations [in industrial societies] is gravely impoverished. The cosmic liturgy, the mystery of nature's participation in the Christological drama, have become inaccessible to Christians living in a modern city. Their religious experience is no longer open to the cosmos" (178–79). For a discussion of the continuing centrality of some version of the secularization thesis to the study of urban religions, see Callum G. Brown, "Review Essay: Religion in the City," *Urban History* 23, no. 3 (December 1996): 372–79. Influential studies of religion and ancient cities include Wheatley, *City as Symbol*; idem, *The Pivot of the Four Quarters: A Preliminary Enquiry into the Origins and Character of the Ancient Chinese City* (Chicago: University of Chicago Press, 1971); idem and Thomas See, *Form Court to Capital: A Tentative Interpretation of the Origins of the Japanese Urban Tradition* (Chicago: University of Chicago Press, 1978); Eliade's discussion of "city-cosmos" in *Sacred and Profane*, 47f.; Jonathan Z. Smith, *To Take Place: Toward Theory in Ritual* (Chicago: University of Chicago Press, 1987); Johanna Broda, David Carrasco, and Eduardo Matos Moctezuma, *The Great Temple of Tenochtitlan: Center and Periphery in the Aztec World* (Berkeley and Los Angeles: University of California Press, 1987); David Carrasco, ed., *To Change Place: Aztec Ceremonial Landscapes* (Niwot: University Press of Colorado, 1991). For an attempt to apply this theoretical orientation to the modern city, see Ira G. Zepp, Jr., *The New Religious Image of Urban America: The Shopping Mall as Ceremonial Center* (Westminster, Md.: Christian Classics, 1986).

6. Robert N. Bellah, Richard Madsen, William M. Sullivan, Ann Swidler, and Steven M. Tipton, *Habits of the Heart: Individualism and Commitment in American Life* (New York: Harper and Row, 1986), 32–35, 48–50, 333–34; on the enduring power of nature in American religious imaginings, see Catherine L. Albanese, *Nature Religion in America: From the Algonkian Indians to the New Age* (Chicago: University of Chicago Press, 1990).

7. Baldwin engages the meanings of the spaces of Harlem in many of his writings; for an especially powerful example, see the opening pages of "Down at the Cross: Letter from a Region in My Mind," in *The Fire Next Time* (New York: Dell, 1985; orig. pub. 1962), 27f. [Reference to the South Bronx draws on material earlier in Orsi's full work.]

8. James Baldwin, *Go Tell It on the Mountain* (New York: Dell, 1977; orig. pub. 1953), 215–16; Jack Kugelmass, *The Miracle of Intervale Avenue: The Story of a Jewish Congregation in the South Bronx* (New York: Schocken, 1986), 173.

9. Berman, *All That Is Solid*, 145.

10. Jill Watts, *God, Harlem USA: The Father Divine Story* (Berkeley and Los Angeles: University of California Press, 1992), 110; see also Milton C. Sernett, *Bound for the Promised Land: African American Religion and the Great Migration* (Durham: Duke University Press, 1997).

11. The phrase in the text is from Chauncey, *Gay New York*, 191. Jacobs refers to an "underlying order of cities," *Death and Life*, 15.

12. Jacobs, *Death and Life*, 74–88. "Conduits of sociability" is from Peiss, *Cheap Amusements*, 57.

13. David Vidal, "Hispanic Residents Find Some Gains amid Woes," *New York Times*, May 12, 1980.

14. Benjamin Karim, with Peter Skutches and David Gallen, *Remembering Malcolm* (New York: Carroll and Graf, 1992), 44.

15. The phrases in the text on Catholic parishes are from John T. McGreevy, *Parish Boundaries: The Catholic Encounter with Race in the Twentieth-Century Urban North* (Chicago: University of Chicago Press, 1996), 15, 22; see also Eileen M. McMahon, *What Parish Are You From? A Chicago Irish Community and Race Relations* (Lexington: University Press of Kentucky, 1995). Benjamin Karim writes that "walking, mostly, kept Malcolm fit, and the many people he knew or would meet on Harlem's streets — the storekeepers, businessmen, mothers and children, the clergy, panhandlers — kept his spirits high"; *Remembering Malcolm*, 71.

16. Frank Bartleman, *How Pentecost Came to Los Angeles, As It Was in the Beginning: Old Azusa Mission — From My Diary* (n.p., 1928), 53. Bartleman writes, "When men came within two or three blocks of [Azusa Mission] they were seized with conviction."

DOCUMENTS FOR PART I

1-1. *THE SANITARY CONDITION OF THE LABORING POPULATION OF NEW YORK* (1845)

John H. Griscom

Source: John H. Griscom, *The Sanitary Condition of the Laboring Population of New York. With Some Suggestions for Improvement* (New York: Harper & Brothers, 1845).

EDITORS' INTRODUCTION

Along with religious missionaries, medical and civic leaders who sought to prevent epidemics by improving public health were the first to address the living conditions of the urban poor. Dr. John D. Griscom conducted the research for *The Sanitary Condition of the Laboring Population of New York* in 1844 with the assistance of other physicians and ministers throughout the city. This work was the first sanitary survey of the city, modeled after Edwin Chadwick's *Report on the Sanitary Condition of the Labouring Population of Great Britain* (1842).

The sanitary reform movement of the early nineteenth century advanced the idea that ill health caused poverty and that disease had decidedly environmental origins. Sanitarians held that filth and decaying waste products generated miasmas or poisonous effluvium that spread illness. The solution for a healthier city was to clean sources of dirt and foul odors, particularly from damp cellars and other forms of substandard housing. Although sanitarians failed to accurately explain the origins of disease—that would happen later in the century with germ theory—they did advance the modern association between cleanliness and good health.[i]

Sanitarians also pioneered the use of social statistics as evidence to justify reform, and linked environmental factors to social behavior. In the report below, Griscom provides an explanation as to why the city's poorest residents, especially immigrants, women, and children, were its sickest. He describes in detail the specific danger of tenement houses, or multiple unit residential dwellings, which spread disease and compromised personal virtue. Griscom's recommendation for stricter sanitary and housing laws, to be enforced by a sanitary police, were decades ahead of its time. In fact, only after the formation of the Metropolitan Board of Health in 1866 was sanitation a priority for the city, and not until the Tenement House Law of 1901 did the average New Yorker experience significant improvements in their day-to-day living conditions.

Objects Briefly Stated

Of the three objects contemplated in the Declaration of Independence as necessary to be secured by government, the first named is "Life." Higher purposes cannot be conceived for which government should be instituted.

[...]

As upon the individual, when sick, falls as increased pecuniary burden, with (in general) a suspension of income, so upon the state or city, must rest, not only the expense of removing an unsound condition of public health, but also, from the attendant loss of character, a diminution of its resources.

When individuals of the pauper class are ill, their entire support, and perchance that

---

i For an overview of the sanitary movement see, Martin V. Melosi, *The Sanitary City: Urban Infrastructure in America from Colonial Times to the Present* (Baltimore, MD: Johns Hopkins University Press, 2000), 43–48, 60–62.

of the whole family, falls upon the community. From a low state of general health, whether in an individual or in numbers, proceed diminished energy of body and of mind, and a vitiated moral perception, the frequent precursor of habits and deeds, which give employment to the officers of police, and the ministers of justice.

[...]

The objects of this communication, briefly stated, are these;—1st, to show that there is an immense amount of sickness, physical disability, and premature mortality, among the poorer classes;—2d, that these are, to a large extent, unnecessary, being in a great degree the results of causes which are removable;—3d, that these physical evils are productive of moral evils of great magnitude and number, and which, if considered only in a pecuniary point of view, should arouse the government and individuals to a consideration of the best means for their relief and prevention; and 4th, to suggest the means of alleviating these evils and preventing their recurrence to so great an extent.

[...]

Distinction Between Public Health and Individual Health

At all seasons of the year, there is an amount of sickness and death in this, as in all large cities, far beyond those of less densely peopled, more airy and open places, such as country residences. Even in villages of small size, there is an observable difference over the isolated country dwelling, in the proportionate amount of disease prevailing; proving conclusively that the congregation of animal and vegetable matters, with their constant effluvia, which has less chance of escape from the premises, in proportion to the absence of free circulation of air, is detrimental to the health of the inhabitants.

These circumstances have yet to be investigated in this city, as they should be. Our people, especially the more destitute, have been allowed to live out their brief lives in tainted and unwholesome atmospheres, and be subject to the silent and invisible encroachments of destructive agencies in every direction, without one warning voice being raised to point them to the danger, and without an effort to rescue them from their impending fate.

[...]

It is of course among the poor labouring classes that such knowing is most wanted. The rich, though they may be equally ignorant of the laws of life, and of the best means of its prevention, live in larger houses, with freer ventilation, and upon food better adapted to support health and life. Their means of obtaining greater comforts and more luxuries, are to them, though perhaps unconsciously, the very reason for their prolonged lives.

[...]

The investigations...so necessary and desirable for this city, have been carried on in other countries, with a degree of enthusiasm, sustained by talent and learning, which does honor to Philanthropy. No one can rise from the perusal of the works of Edwin Chadwick of London, or of Parent Du Chatelet of Paris, or of many others who have laboured in this field of humanity, with out feeling a portion of the ardor which inspires them, and wishing he had been thrown into the same pursuit, that some of the leaves of the same laurel might encircle his own brow.[1] It is in the cause of Humanity, of the poor, the destitute, the degraded, of the virtuous made vicious by the force of circumstances, which they are now investigating, and exposing to the knowledge of others.

It is often said that "one half of the world does not know how the other half lives." The labor of raising the veil which now separates the two halves, by which the misery and degradation of the one, have been concealed from the view of the other, has been theirs and their associates. Howard,[2] called by distinction the *Philanthropist*, revealed to the gaze of the astonished multitude the interior of the prisons of England, and straightaway the process of reform commenced in them, and continued until the prison system of the present day, has become one the most striking examples of the spirit of the times. But Chadwick and Du Chatelet, especially the former, are diving still deeper into the subject of moral and physical reform. They are probing to the bottom the foul ulcers upon the body of society, and endeavoring to discover the causes of so much wretchedness and vice, which fill the prisons and the workhouses. Howard's labours tended to *cure* the disease, Chadwick's to *prevent* it.

[...]

System of Tenantage of the Poor

The tenements, in order to admit a greater number of families, are divided into small apartments, as numerous as decency will admit. Regard to comfort, convenience, and health, is the last motive... These closets, for they deserve no better name, are then rented to the poor, from week to week, or month to month, the rent being almost invariably required in advance, at least for the first few terms. The families moving in first, after the house is built, find it clean, but the lessee has no supervision over their habits, and however filthy the tenement may become, he cares not, so that he receives his rent.

[...]

In these places, filth is allowed to accumulate to an extent almost incredible. Hiring their rooms for short periods only, it is very common to find the poor tenants moving from place to place, every few weeks. By this practice they avoid the trouble of cleaning their rooms, as they can leave behind them the dirt which they have made. The same room, being occupied in rapid succession, by tenant after tenant, it will easily be seen how the walls and windows will become broken, the doors and floors become injured, the chimneys filled with soot, the whole premises populated thickly with vermin, the stairway, the common passage of several families, the receptacle for all things noxious, and whatever of self-respect the family might have had, be crushed under the pressure of the degrading circumstances by which they are surrounded.

[...]

Ventilation—Amount of Air Necessary for Each Person

We now naturally come, in the course of this inquiry, to two important questions, preparatory to the suggestion I intend to make, of remedy for these evils.

1st. What is the effect of this degraded and filthy manner of life upon the health of the individuals, and the duration of their lives?

2nd. What is the influence upon their morals, their self-respect, and appreciation of virtue?

The answers to these queries must have an important bearing upon the moral obligations, the pecuniary expenses, and the order and character of the City Government. If it can be shown that much sickness and many premature deaths are the results of these residences, it will be evident that the care of the sick, and the support of the widows and orphans, must add greatly to the expenses of the city; and it can be proved that degraded habits, bad associations, and immoral practices (through the results only of circumstances, and not of education) are their consequences, it will be equally apparent, there will thus be continued, a class in the community more difficult to govern, more disposed to robbery, mobs, and other lawless acts, and less accessible to the influences of religious and moral instruction.

With regard to the first question, an argument can hardly be necessary. Almost everyone can recall to mind, some proof of the effects of nauseous odors, of the inhalation of foul air, or of sleeping in a small confined apartment, upon his own health and feelings. These effects may have only been temporary, but they serve to show that a prolonged continuance of them, must, in reason, produce permanently bad results upon the continuance of mental and corporeal powers.... Every city resident who takes a stroll into the country, can testify to the difference between the atmosphere of the two situations:—the contrast of our out-door (to say nothing of the in-door) atmosphere, loaded with the animal and vegetable exhalations of our streets, yards, sinks, and cellars—and the air of the mountains, rivers, and grassy plains, needs no epicurean lungs to detect it.

[...]

Number of Sick Paupers—Greater Proportion Females

If the habitations of damp, dark cellars, and of narrow alleys and courts, and the breathing of a vitiated atmosphere, are *rightly* asserted to be promotive of disease, then the most subject to these causes should be sick in the greatest numbers. Now the *male* part of this class breathe a totally different air throughout the day, and their labors in the streets, along the rivers, or upon buildings, and *only at night* are they subject to the worse atmosphere.... One the other hand, *the females, both day and night*, inhale the polluted atmosphere of the dwellings, and are more continually under all the other bad influences of their unfortunate situations.

Due the official results correspond with these premises?

It will be seen upon examining the Dispensary[3] returns, that in some years the proportion of female to males, prescribed for at the Dispensaries, has been 12 to 10 1/2—in others, 12 to 8 1/2, and in one instance 19 to 11. This comparison is more rendered more striking when we take into account the greater amount of intemperance among the males.

The Annual Reports of the City Inspector[4] show that nearly one-half the deaths caused by consumption[5] are of the *foreign part of the population*, and that more than *one-third* the whole number of deaths are of foreigners. Such an immense disproportion can only be accounted for on the supposition that some extraordinary cause of death prevail among the strangers who come to reside among us. Now it is pretty well ascertained fact, that a large majority of the cellar and court population of this city consists of persons of foreign birth and their children. Of the Dispensary patients, about 60 *per cent* are natives of other countries, and if it were possible to ascertain the parentage of the children receiving aid from these institution, we should find a larger portion than this directly dependent upon foreigners.
[...]

Answer from Reverend Isaac Orchard

In one of these houses, in a garret, with sloping roof and low ceiling, one small, broken window, no bedstead, nor other bedding than a few bundle of rags upon the floor, I have found three families of men, women, and children: there they lived, and there they all slept. Now, if a woman accustomed to humble life, or decent poverty, be constrained to remove to such a place, what must be the effect on her mind, morals, and her habits? At first, she will recoil from undressing in the presence of a strange man, but soon she will do it without a blush. Is she a wife? There are other wives and their husbands in the room, without even a curtain to hide the most private transactions. That which transpires cannot be unobserved, though seeking the darkest recess, and soon it will be imitated without secrecy and without scruple. Children too will see them, and think, and imitate—and thus become depraved in their thoughts, desires, and practices. Can any one doubt that there must be a rapid declension in morals, in both parents and children?
[...]

Suggestion of a New Arrangement for, and Proper Duties of a Sanitary Police

From what has been related respecting the effects of the habitations of the poor, upon their health, viz., 1st, the living in damp, dark, underground, and other ill-ventilated apartments. 2d. The dirty and injured condition of the floors, walls, yards, and other parts of the premises. 3d. The crowding too many persons in single rooms of inadequate size and accommodations. To correct the first of these evils, there appears but one way, and that is to place all the dwellings of the city under the inspection of competent officers, who shall have the power *to enforce the law of domiciliary cleanliness*. For this purpose, those places known or suspected to be kept usually in improper condition, should be visited periodically, say once in one, two, or three months. The law should be so arranged as to make cleaning bear upon the owner or lessee, and not upon the tenant directly, who is generally so poor, as to be unable to perform the necessary purgation and rectification of the premises.
[...]

The effect of such a law upon the habits of the tenant would not be *direct*,—his personal condition can only be reached by moral law,—but the landlord, under this compulsory process, urged by the fear of having his premises out-lawed would, in letting them, stipulate with his tenants to keep them clean, to whitewash the walls and ceilings, wash the floors, remove the collections of dirt and garbage, and keep the yards and cellars in good order. And knowing that the health officer will pay them frequent visits, armed with the power of the law, it is altogether reasonable to suppose that the tenants themselves would be stimulated to maintain a better appearance of person and domicils—that many would feel a pride in a good and cleanly aspect—that the smothered feelings of self-respect, love of praise, and desire for the comforts of cleanliness, would, in hundreds of bosoms, be re-awakened into life and energy.

NOTES

1. Edwin Chadwick was an English sanitary reformer who also advocated for changes in Britain's poor laws. Alexandre Parent Duchâtlet, was a French public health theorist who worked on the sewers of Paris and prostitution.

2. John Howard (1726–1790), noted British reformer who toured Europe examining prisons and advocating for the single-cell method of incarceration. His most famous work, *The State of the Prisons*, was originally published in 1777.

3. Dispensaries were clinics that provided health care for people at little or no cost. Griscom uses numbers from the Northern, Eastern, and New York Dispensaries.

4. The City Inspector was New York's chief public health officer until the creation of the Metropolitan Board of Health in 1866.

5. Common nineteenth-century term for tuberculosis.

1-2. ADVICE TO STRANGERS

Robert Macoy

Source: Robert Macoy, *History of and How to See New York and Its Environs* (New York: R. Macoy, 1876).

EDITORS' INTRODUCTION

As New York City grew, so too did its tourist industry. Although visitors, sailors, merchants, émigrés, and immigrants arrived from all over the globe during the nineteenth century, the city's officials did little to facilitate their travel. Hotels, railroad companies, and other commercial establishments advertised their services and promoted popular destinations in newspapers and pamphlets. Guidebooks also provided tourists with information on where to go, what to see, and how to spend money. The following excerpt is from one guidebook, published in conjunction with the nation's centennial celebrations, which describes how best to take in the majesty of New York while traveling safely through its streets. This advice is particularly important in light of the numerous pickpockets and other criminals discussed in Timothy Gilfoyle's essay "The 'Guns' of Gotham" **[in Part IV]** and stereotypes about the dangers of the streets in Jane Jacob's "The Use of Sidewalks: Assimilating Children" **[see Document 1.3]**.

Standing on the dome [of the Masonic Temple, at Twenty-third Street and Sixth Avenue] the,

VISITOR IS SURROUNDED BY A PANORAMA,

the extent of which can in no other way be realized. Looking beyond the interminable rows of streets, and endless array of buildings, he sees Brooklyn, Greenpoint, Astoria, the Islands, and Public Institutions located thereon, then the Heights of the Jersey shore, and the towns and villages, nestling at their feet; the Harbor of New York, where the navies of the world might find a resting place; the Narrows and Lower Bay, and thus back to the point of starting; and he may know, that within the range of his vision are

MORE THAN TWO MILLIONS OF PEOPLE,

and wealth beyond calculation; that among them are represented every phase of social life, from the millionaire to the tramp; that while among them, virtue and social and civil order largely predominate, there, none the less, are also the homes of abject poverty and revolting crime.

To the holiday visitor, seeking recreation, or the gratification of a curiosity to see the great city, as well as to the student of human nature in its varying aspects, the Great Metropolis affords an ample field, and to assist those who wish to know what to see, and how to see it with the greatest degree of comfort and convenience, is the object of this work. [...]

Advice to Strangers

To our friends from the country who are visiting the city for the first time, we offer a few suggestions that may assist them in their efforts to see the city to the best advantage, and with the greatest of economy of time and convenience:

If possible, reach the city in the day-time.

Avoid being too free with strangers.

On reaching the depot or landing, take the car or stage which passes nearest your stopping place.

If a carriage is engaged, make a bargain with the driver before entering the vehicle. Your trunk or valise may accompany you; or have your baggage checked by an authorized agent of an Express Company, whom you will find on the car or boat, and for which take his receipt. This will relieve you of further trouble, as your baggage can be delivered at any place in the city or vicinity, within a few hours and at a stipulated price.

If you are obliged to make inquiries on the street, apply to a policeman or go into a respectable place of business.

Avoid all crowds, particularly at night.

Careful attention to your own business will insure freedom from annoyance or interruption.

1-3. THE USE OF SIDEWALKS: ASSIMILATING CHILDREN (1961)

Jane Jacobs

Source: Jane Jacobs, *The Death and Life of Great American Cities* (New York: Random House, 1961).

EDITORS' INTRODUCTION

As Robert Orsi argues earlier in this part with his essay, "Crossing the City Line," people who do not live in the city often confuse the energy of the streets with disorder. In this selection, the late Jane Jacobs (1916–2006) tackles one of the most enduring, yet woefully inaccurate of all urban legends; namely, that the streets corrupt and endanger the lives of children who play in them. She uses as her foil the long-standing association between open spaces, especially urban parks, and moral order. Few urban theorists have achieved the stature of Jane Jacobs. Although she received no formal training as a planner, *The Death and Life of Great American Cities* is arguably the most influential book ever written on the subject. Many of Jacobs' points and her overall common-sense approach to planning and appreciation for city life is echoed today in the principles of New Urbanism **[see Document 10.3 "Charter of the New Urbanism"]**. Jacobs was also a noted community activist in her adopted cities of New York and Toronto. In addition to *The Death and Life of Great American Cities*, Jacobs was the author of several other books on urban and economic affairs.

The Uses of Sidewalks: Assimilating Children

Among the superstitions of planning and housing is a fantasy about the transformation of children. It goes like this: A population of children is condemned to play on the city streets. These pale and rickety children, in their sinister moral environment, are telling each other canards about sex, sniggering evilly and learning new forms of corruption as efficiently as if they were in reform school. This situation is called "the moral and physical toll taken of our youth by the streets," sometimes it is called simply "the gutter."

If only these deprived children can be gotten off the streets into parks and playgrounds with equipment on which to exercise, space in which to run, grass to lift their souls! Clean and happy places, filled with the laughter of children responding to a whole-some environment. So much for the fantasy.

Let us consider a story from real life, as discovered by Charles Guggenheim, a documentary-film maker in St. Louis. Guggenheim was working on a film depicting the activities of a St. Louis children's day-care center. He noticed that at the end of the afternoon roughly half the children left with the greatest reluctance.

Guggenheim became sufficiently curious to investigate. Without exception, the children who left unwillingly came from a nearby housing project. And without exception again, those who left willingly came from the old "slum" streets nearby. The mystery, Guggenheim found, was simplicity itself. The children returning to the project, with its generous playgrounds and lawns, ran a gauntlet of bullies who made them turn out their pockets or submit to a beating, sometimes both. These small children could not get home each day without enduring an ordeal that they dreaded. The children going back to the old streets were safe from extortion, Guggenheim found. They had many streets to select from, and they astutely chose the safest. "If anybody picked on them, there was always a store-keeper they could run to or somebody to come to their aid," says Guggenheim. "They also had any number of ways of escaping along different routes if anybody was laying for them. These little kids felt safe and cocky and they enjoyed their trip home too." Guggenheim made the related observation of how boring the project's landscaped grounds and playgrounds were, how deserted they seemed, and in contrast how rich in interest, variety and material for both the camera and the imagination were the older streets nearby. [...]

"Street gangs" do their "street fighting" predominately in parks and playgrounds. When the *New York Times* in September 1959 summed up the worst adolescent gang outbreaks of the past decade in the city, each and every one was designated as having occurred in a park. Moreover, more and more frequently, not only in New York but in other cities too, children engaged in such horrors turn out to be from super-block projects, where their everyday play has successfully been removed from the streets (the streets themselves have largely been removed). The highest delinquency belt in New York's Lower East Side, is precisely the parklike belt of public housing projects. The two most formidable gangs in Brooklyn are rooted in two of the oldest projects. Ralph Whelan, director of the New York City Youth Board, reports, according to the *New York Times*, an "invariable rise in delinquency rates" wherever a new housing project is built. The worst girls' gang in Philadelphia has grown up on the grounds of that city's second-oldest housing project, and the highest delinquency belt of that city corresponds with its major belt of projects. In St. Louis the project where Guggenheim found the extortion going on is considered relatively safe compared with the city's largest project, fifty-seven acres of mostly grass, dotted with playgrounds and devoid of city streets, a prime breeding ground of delinquency in that city. Such projects are examples, among other things, of an intent to take children off the streets. They are designed as they are partly for just this purpose.

The disappointing results are hardly strange. The same rules of city safety and city public life that apply to adults apply to children too, except that children are even more vulnerable to danger and barbarism than adults.

In real life, what significant change *does* occur if children are transferred from a lively city street to the usual park or to the usual public or project playground?

In most cases (not all, fortunately), the most significant change is this: The children have moved from under the eyes of a high numerical ratio of adults, into a place where the ratio of adults is low or even nil. To think this represents an improvement in city child rearing is pure daydreaming.

City children themselves know this; they have known it for generations. "When we wanted to do anything antisocial, we always made for Lindy Park because none of the grownups would see us there," says Jesse Reichek, an artist who grew up in Brooklyn. "Mostly we played on the streets where we couldn't get away with anything much."

Life is the same today. My son, reporting how he escaped four boys who set upon him, says, "I was scared they would catch me when I had to pass the playground. If they caught me *there* I'd be sunk!"

A few days after the murder of two sixteen-year-old boys in a playground on the midtown West Side of Manhattan, I paid a morbid visit to the area. The nearby streets were evidently back to normal. Hundreds of children, directly under the eyes of innumerable adults using the sidewalks themselves and looking from windows, were engaged in a vast variety of sidewalk games and whooping pursuits. The sidewalks were dirty, they were too narrow for the demands put upon them, and they needed shade from the sun. But here was no scene of arson, mayhem or the flourishing of dangerous weapons. In the playground where the nighttime murder had occurred, things were apparently back to normal too. Three small boys were setting a fire under a wooden bench. Another was having his head beaten against the concrete. The custodian was absorbed in solemnly and slowly hauling down the American flag.

On my return home, as I passed the relatively genteel playground near where I live, I noted that its only inhabitants in the late afternoon, with the mothers and the custodian gone, were two small boys threatening to bash a little girl with their skates, and an alcoholic who had roused himself to shake his head and mumble that they shouldn't do that. Farther down the street, on a block with many Puerto Rican immigrants, was another scene of contrast. Twenty-eight children of all ages were playing on the sidewalk without mayhem, arson, or any event more serious than a squabble over a bag of candy. They were under the casual surveillance of adults primarily visiting in public with each other. The surveillance was only seemingly casual, as was proved when the candy squabble broke out and peace and justice were re-established. The identities of the adults kept changing because different ones kept putting their heads out the windows, and different ones kept coming in and going out on errands, or passing by and lingering a little. But the numbers of adults stayed fairly constant—between eight and eleven—during the hour I watched. Arriving home, I noticed that at our end of our block, in front of the tenement, the tailor's, our house, the laundry, the pizza place and the fruit man's, twelve children were playing on the sidewalk in sight of fourteen adults.

To be sure, all city sidewalks are not under surveillance in this fashion, and this is one of the troubles of the city that planning ought properly to help correct. Underused sidewalks are not under suitable surveillance for child rearing. Nor are sidewalks apt to be safe, even with eyes upon them, if they are bordered by a population which is constantly and rapidly turning over in residence—another urgent planning problem. But the playgrounds and parks near such streets are even less wholesome.

Nor are all playgrounds and parks unsafe or under poor surveillance. But those that are wholesome are typically in neighborhoods where streets are lively and safe and where a strong tone of civilized public sidewalk life prevails. Whatever differentials exist in safety and wholesomeness between playgrounds and sidewalks in any given area are invariably, so far as I can find, in the favor of the much maligned streets.

SENATOR TILLMAN'S ALLEGORICAL COW.

Figure 1.3 Senator Tillman's Allegorical Cow, 1896. Source: Congressional Record: The Proceedings and Debates of the Sixty-*Third Congress, First Session* (Washington, DC: Government Printing Office) 50—Part 6 (October 1913).

The deep distrust between rural and urban America during the late nineteenth and early twentieth centuries is reflected in this cartoon conceived by the outspoken United States Senator Benjamin R. Tillman (Democrat, South Carolina). In 1896, Tillman commissioned artist Tom Fleming to depict Wall Street bankers symbolically milking a cow fed on the produce of southern and western farmers. Supporters of William Jennings Bryan, who was both the Democratic Party and Populist Party nominee for president in 1896, handed out millions of copies of the allegorical cow during the election. Republican William McKinley won the election in large measure due to the support of urban industrial voters. The cow cartoon reappeared when Bryan ran for president again in 1900 and 1908; making it one of the most widely circulated cartoons in American history. Tillman had the cartoon reprinted in *The Congressional Record* in 1913 to illustrate his point that the gamblers and speculators of Wall Street, along with other moneyed interests in New England and the Middle Atlantic states, were still milking the nation of its wealth.

PART II

URBAN ROOTS
Colonial Settlement and Westward Expansion

EDITORS' INTRODUCTION TO PART II

The United States was shaped by urbanization long before the majority of its people lived in cities. From the beginning of colonial settlement, people lived in and depended upon urban configurations of all sizes, for protection as well as economic, political, and social interaction. Even before the arrival of Europeans, some Native Americans lived in urban settlements. Although the highest percentage of colonial settlers living in an urban area peaked at just 10 percent in 1690, cities played a critical role and exerted a disproportionate influence over European and later American settlement of the North American continent. The essays and documents in this section describe principle features of city building and characteristics of urban life during the seventeenth through nineteenth centuries, with first-hand accounts and innovative scholarship by historians writing in the twentieth century.

Today, well over 75 percent of all Americans live in "urban" areas, traditionally defined by the United States Bureau of the Census as incorporated municipalities or designated counting districts containing 2,500 or more people, which includes cities of all sizes and their outlying areas, plus many towns, villages, and boroughs (suburban or otherwise). The U.S. government set 2,500 as the threshold for being urban in 1790, at the time of the very first federal census.[i] At that time, most people lived in much smaller agrarian communities that earned the classification of "rural." In fact, the first census counted only five cities (New York, Philadelphia, Boston, Charleston, and Baltimore) with more than 10,000 inhabitants, with just 5 percent of the total national population (200,000 out of 3.9 million people) living in urban areas. Not until 1830 did the overall urban population of the United States again reach the 10-percent level it had in the colonial era. Three decades later, the census for 1860 revealed that the nation's total urban percentage had reached 20 percent, or 6.2 million people, with 392 urban areas, 93 of them containing more than 10,000 people, and nine of which had 100,000 or more inhabitants. Finally, by 1920 the census revealed that for the first time in the nation's history, the majority of the population (51 percent) lived in any one of 2,722 urban areas, 68 of which were cities with 100,000 or more people, and three of them (New York, Chicago, and Philadelphia) serving as home to over one million residents.

The first essay in this part, by Pauline Maier, speculates on the role of distinction and variance in shaping characteristics of American versus European urbanization through an examination of eighteenth-century Boston and New York City. Second is Richard C. Wade's classic 1958 essay, "Urban Life in Western America, 1790–1830," which provides an overview of city building along the Ohio and Mississippi River Valleys in the late eighteenth and early nineteenth centuries. More than any other historian, Wade directly confronts the anti-urban bias of traditional historiography by asserting that cities, in the form of frontier towns, first settled the American West and paved the way for later agricultural successes. Finally, David R. Goldfield provides an overview of cities in the colonial South by surveying settlement patterns along the Atlantic and Gulf coasts and adjacent inland regions. Goldfield provides a partial reassessment of Wade with his own theory on the stages of colonial urban growth and the subsequent impact on future southern cities.

The documents in this part reflect the urban attitudes and assumptions of European and American-born white men. The first document is an excerpt from John Winthrop's "A Model of Christian Charity"—better known as the "City Upon a Hill" sermon—given in 1630 to fellow Puritan migrants on their way to settling Boston in the Massachusetts Bay Colony. Next is a description of Philadelphia's early years by Dr. Benjamin Bullivant, who traveled from Boston to Delaware and back in 1697. Another traveler's impressions, this time of the remains of ancient Indian mounds of Cahokia, east of modern-day St. Louis, is provided in the form of a letter by Henry M. Brackenridge to Thomas Jefferson in 1813. Though abandoned long before the first European explorers and settlers arrived in the region, Cahokia was at one time the heart of an expansive Native American trading network that archeologists estimated contained 35,000 or more people. A map of Savannah in 1800, and two illustrations, one of Boston in 1768, and the other New Orleans in the 1850s, complete the documents and provide an artistic glimpse into the way people organized and viewed their urban surroundings.

NOTE

i.   The Census Bureau has modified the definition of urban several times since 1790, most notably after the 1940 census in order to include large and densely settled areas outside of an incorporated municipality. Starting with the 2000 census, the Bureau defines "urban" as all territory, population, and housing units specifically within an urban area (UA) or urban cluster (UC). For more detail see United States Bureau of the Census, *Historical Statistics of the United States: Colonial Times to 1970*, Bicentennial Edition, Part 1 (Washington D.C., 1975), 2–3; U.S. Census Bureau, Geography Division, "Census 2000 Urban and Rural Classification," created April 30, 2002, revised December 30, 2008 (www.census.gov/geo/www/ua/ua_2k.html).

Boston and New York in the Eighteenth Century

Pauline Maier

Source: *The Proceedings of the American Antiquarian Society*, 91, Part 2 (1981): 177–195.

EDITORS' INTRODUCTION

American society was overwhelmingly rural and agrarian during the colonial era. No more than 10 percent of the entire population lived in urban areas, more accurately towns, by the end the seventeenth century, and by the time the colonies achieved independence from Great Britain, the percentage had fallen in half. In fact, just five cities contained more than 10,000 people by the time of the American Revolution, with Philadelphia leading with roughly 25,000, New York 22,000, Boston 16,000, Charleston (Charles Town), South Carolina at 12,000, and Newport, Rhode Island with 11,000. Although urban areas were few in number and relatively small, both in terms of population and geographic size by today's standards, as colonial historians Carl Bridenbaugh, Gary Nash, and others have shown, they exerted a considerable amount of influence over the countryside, especially in political, economic, and cultural affairs.[i] What accounts for this urban hegemony? What functions did American cities perform, and were they unique from each other and their European counterparts?

In the following essay, historian Pauline Maier addresses the issue of what constituted a city in the colonial era by comparing and contrasting eighteenth-century life in Boston and New York. She explores the major characteristics and functions of these two seaports with an eye as to how they developed separate economic, political, and intellectual spheres of influence and personalities which went on to define each city in the nineteenth and twentieth centuries. Maier even speculates on the larger meaning of urbanism in the United States versus Europe by stressing that differences between cities are as important as commonalities. Such variance helps to account for America's diversity and resilience to major economic and political crises throughout history.

Pauline Maier is the William R. Kenan, Jr., Professor of American History at the Massachusetts Institute of Technology. She is the author of *From Resistance to Revolution: Colonial Radicals and the Development of American Opposition to Britain, 1765–1776* (New York: Knopf, 1972), *The Old Revolutionaries: Political Lives in the Age of Samuel Adams* (New York: Knopf, 1980), *American Scripture: Making the Declaration of Independence* (New York: Knopf, 1997), and notable articles in the *William and Mary Quarterly* and the one reproduced here from the *Proceedings of the American Antiquarian Society*.

---

i Population figures are averaged from a variety of sources: James A. Henretta and Gregory H. Nobles, *Evolution and Revolution: American Society, 1600–1820* (Lexington, MA: D. C. Heath, 1987), 75–76; Carl Bridenbaugh, *Cities in the Wilderness: The First Century of Urban Life in America, 1625–1742* (New York: Ronald Press, 1938; New York: Oxford, 1964), 143–144; Carl Bridenbaugh, *Cities in Revolt: Urban Life in America, 1743–1776* (New York: Alfred Knopf, 1955), 216–217. For urban influence see also Henretta and Nobles, *Evolution and Revolution*; Bridenbaugh, *Cities in the Wilderness* and *Cities in Revolt*; Gary B. Nash, *The Urban Crucible: Social Change, Political Consciousness, and the Origins of the American Revolution* (Cambridge, MA: Harvard University Press, 1979); and Gary and Benjamin L. Carp, *Rebels Rising: Cities and the American Revolution* (New York: Oxford University Press, 2007).

BOSTON AND NEW YORK IN THE EIGHTEENTH CENTURY

MY TITLE was inspired by George Rudé's *Paris and London in the Eighteenth Century*, though my concerns were not his. In the course of working on urban politics in the Revolutionary period I became aware of how remarkably different were Boston and New York—different not just in their people and politics but in feeling, in character, in that wonderfully all-encompassing thing called culture. Their differences were neither incidental nor ephemeral: to a remarkable extent the distinctive traits each city had developed by the end of the eighteenth century survived into the nineteenth and even the twentieth century. And so I propose to consider those differences, how they began and persisted over time, and their more general importance in American history.

Any such exercise assumes that the subjects of inquiry were comparable, that is, that they had some essential identity in common upon which distinctions were grafted. The existence of such a common identity for two early American ports on the Atlantic seaboard is in part obvious. But there remains a problem relevant to their comparability that is worth beginning with, one that has troubled me and, I suppose, other students of the period since first encountering Carl Bridenbaugh's path-breaking books *Cities in the Wilderness* and *Cities in Revolt*. That is, by what right do we classify together Boston, New York, and similar communities as 'cities' before 1800?

Consider the gulf between Rudé's subjects and mine. He wrote about two of the greatest cities in the Western world, population centers that no one hesitates to call urban. Paris already had over a half million people in 1700. It grew only modestly over the next century, while London expanded at a quick pace—from 575,000 people in 1750 to almost 900,000 fifty years later. By contrast Boston's population stood at 6,700, New York's nearer 5,000 when the eighteenth century began. One hundred years later New York had over 60,000 and Boston almost 25,000 people.[1] It takes no very sophistic-ated statistical analysis to suggest that a 'city' of 6,700 was something very different from one of a half million, that New York at its eighteenth-century peak was still in many ways distinct from London, whose population was some fifteen times greater. If 'city' denotes a community's size, Boston and New York would not qualify.

The word 'city' has not, however, distinguished places by size so much as by function. Historically it designated independent communities that served as centers for a surrounding countryside and as points of contact with the outside world. The word derives from the Latin word *civitas*, which the Romans used, as it happens, for a colonial situation—for the separate states or tribes of Gaul, and then for their most important towns. There were also *civitates* in Roman Britain, but the Angles and Saxons used instead the word *burh* or *borough*, adopting *city* in the thirteenth century for foreign or ancient cities, for large indigenous communities such as London, and later for the chief boroughs of a diocese, those that became cathedral towns.[2]

Cities perform their centralizing function in many ways, most of which were exercised by Boston and New York. Like other major colonial cities, they were provincial capitals as well as important cultural centers where newspapers and pamphlets were published, discussed, and distributed. But above all they were commercial centers, Atlantic coastal ports where the produce of the countryside was collected and shipped to the West Indies, Africa, or Europe and exchanged for products or credits that could in turn be exchanged for goods of foreign origin needed by colonists in both city and country. Later cities became the merchandising centers for manufactures of either rural or urban origin, whose 'reach' and therefore whose volume of business grew with the development of more advanced transportation systems; they became the homes of banks, of insurance companies, of stock exchanges.[3] As they did so, they drew upon the efforts of increasing numbers of people. But it was not the size of their populations that made them cities so much as the functions Boston and New York shared with

Paris and London even when their people were counted in thousands, not tens or hundreds of thousands.

From the beginning, moreover, colonial cities had a cosmopolitan character that distinguished them from more rural towns, of whose people it could be said, as George Homans wrote of thirteenth-century English villagers, that they 'had upon the whole more contact with one another than they had with outsiders.'[4] While their ships traded at ports-of-call in the Caribbean and the larger Atlantic world, the cities played host to numbers of transients or 'strangers,' whether in the laboring force or among the more substantial persons of affairs who found business to transact at Boston or New York. Already in the seventeenth century Boston merchants found themselves in conflict with their colony's Puritan leaders, whose effort to isolate Massachusetts from Old World contamination proved incompatible with the demands of commerce. 'The well-being of trade,' Bernard Bailyn has observed, 'demanded the free movement of people and goods.'[5] In the end the merchants won, but their victory was never such as made Boston altogether hospitable to new immigrants, particularly those of non-English origin. Only the French Huguenots—the Faneuils, Bowdoins, Rivoires, and their like—found a welcome there and were easily assimilated.

New York's population was more diverse in origin, including persons of Dutch as well as of French and English origin along with lesser numbers of Germans, Irishmen, Jews, and other Europeans as well as substantial numbers of Africans. Manhattan and the nearby counties of Long Island had the largest concentration of blacks anywhere in North America above the plantation colonies. The city also absorbed substantial numbers of migrants from New England.[6]

The diversity of New York's peoples has, however, often been exaggerated, for they were, like Boston's people, predominantly Northern European Calvinists who shared, out of diverse historical experiences, a militant hostility to 'papism' and to Catholic Absolutism in France and Spain. Even Manhattan's Sephardic Jews shared in some measure this 'Protestant' culture, for they had suffered from the same forces that the Dutch had fought in their long struggle for national independence—the Spanish monarchy and the Catholic Church.[7] With people already so alike, the 'melting pot' could melt: by the mid-eighteenth century, Peter Kalm noted, younger persons of Dutch descent, particularly on Manhattan, spoke mostly English, attended the English church, 'and would even take it amiss if they were called Dutchmen and not Englishmen.' French Huguenots who first arrived at New York in the seventeenth century also gradually became Anglicans,[8] helping to make the city by the late eighteenth century far more culturally unified than it had been one hundred years earlier or would be a century later, when Italian Catholics, the Ashkenazic Jews of Eastern Europe, and other decidedly alien people were added in great numbers to the older 'native stock.'

In the course of the eighteenth century, Boston and New York also gave evidence of a new anonymity among their people that reflected the growth of their populations. That development was slow in coming. Certainly there remained much of the small town about Philadelphia, the largest of American cities in 1771 when Esther DeBerdt Reed reported to her father in London that 'the people must either talk of their neighbors, of whom they know every particular of what they both do and say, or else of marketing.... We hardly dare tell one another our thoughts,' she added, 'lest it should spread all over town; so, if anybody asks you how we like Philadelphia, you must say very well.'[9] The newspapers published in colonial cities in their very dearth of local news also testify to the way eighteenth-century urban people knew their news without reading about it. There were, however, signs of change. Thomas Bender cites the appearance of craftsmen's ads in New York newspapers of the 1750s as evidence that artisans were finding it necessary to announce their existence to townsmen who might in an earlier day have known of it without such formal notice. The publication of city directories at New York in 1786 and Boston in 1789 attests again to an increasing unfamiliarity of city people with each other.[10] Soon thereafter authorities addressed themselves to the problem of locating people within the increasingly anonymous urban masses. In 1793 New York's Common Council ordered that buildings along the streets be numbered according to a prescribed method. From that regulation it was but a short step to the 1811 report of a New York commission that surveyed the island and planned the expanse of practical if monotonously regular numbered streets that would in time stretch from the old and irregular colonial city on the lower tip of Manhattan up toward the Harlem River, and which has been logically taken as the beginning of New York's emergence as a 'modern' city.[11]

In all these ways—in the functions that marked them as cities, in their relative cosmopolitanism and common Protestant culture, in the gradual development by the late eighteenth century of a social anonymity that has since become so much a part of urban life—Boston and New York were almost interchangeable. And yet they had acquired, like children, distinctive traits that they would carry with them into later life. The appearance of differences early in the cities' histories is striking, their persistence over time the more so. Both need to be explained. Their reasons lie, I suggest, in the ideals or purposes of the cities' founders, and in the peculiar, unpredictable way those early traditions were reinforced by eighteenth-century circumstances.

Boston's Puritan fathers came to America with a mission defined against the avarice and corruption of contemporary England. They sought to establish close-knit communities where love of God and concern for neighbor took precedence over selfish gain. Their ideology proved well suited to the business of colonizing. Because the Puritans sought to found permanent homes in America, whole families migrated, not the men alone. The population of New England therefore grew naturally at a far faster rate than elsewhere in seventeenth-century North America.[12] The Puritans' commitment to their 'callings' and their emphasis on industry also contributed to the cause of success

in this world as much as in the next, and Boston became the premier city of British North America.

Its early achievement proved impossible to sustain, however, and as the eighteenth century proceeded Boston gradually yielded its leadership to Philadelphia and New York. It is commonplace to say that geography determined Boston's destiny: the proximity of the Appalachian mountains to the Atlantic coast in New England, the rocky quality of soil along the coastal belt, the course of its rivers, which too often ran on a north-south axis and so provided no ready path to the interior, all these limited the extent and the richness of that hinterland upon which Boston's importance depended. But its fate, we now know, is not so simply explained. An 'almost biblical series of misfortunes' afflicted Boston in the mid-eighteenth century, most of which were related to the series of colonial wars that brought disaster to Boston even as they blessed with prosperity the artisans and merchants of New York and Philadelphia. [...]

It is too much to say that Boston never recovered, but its record in the late colonial period was overall one of decline. And hard times served the cause of tradition, for the Spartan ideals of the founders could ennoble necessity by calling it virtue. New England's ministers continued to cite the first generation of settlers as a model of achievement, as they had done from the late seventeenth century, and to chastise the children for failing to take up their fathers' 'Errand into the Wilderness,' explaining the calamities that fell upon them as punishments for the sinful shortcomings of those who had inherited that New World Israel. The ideals of the fathers provided, in short, a way of understanding and of organizing experience, of ordering history, and so continued to influence the life of the region and of its major city.

New York was founded instead as an outpost of the Dutch West India Company in its search for profit. No greater mission brought the Dutch from Holland: indeed, the Dutch were on the whole unwilling to migrate, finding their homeland hospitable as the English Puritans did not. The Dutch

West India Company therefore turned elsewhere for settlers—to the oppressed Protestants of France, to Africa—in the hope that they might help make New Netherland economically viable. The commitment to material gain that marked Company rule continued after the British conquest. The financial needs of the later Stuart kings, the hopes of greater fortunes that motivated the governors appointed by them and their successors, the ambitions of colonists who flattered royal officials in a quest for land grants, contracts, or lucrative appointments, all these only enhanced New York's materialistic bent. The city became a nest of those after profit however won—of pirates and privateers, of slave traders and smugglers—a community whose spokesmen on into the Revolutionary era emphasized interest while those of Boston cultivated virtue.[13]

New Yorkers did well—and then did better. The city sat at the mouth of the great Hudson River, which, with the Mohawk, provided ready access to a rich and extensive market even before the canal era added the trans-Appalachian West to Manhattan's 'back yard.' It benefitted also from wartime contracts and privateering returns, and except for occasional years of recession continued the ascent that would in time make it the foremost American city. [...]

Politics moderated the distance between rich and poor in Boston. There the governing town meeting brought together persons of different station and blessed men with power for their eloquence, reason, and character as well as their wealth. Boston had a board of selectmen and a series of other municipal officers who were chosen by the town meeting, and those who sought such preferment learned, if they did not instinctively know, that respect was a prerequisite of political support. New York was governed differently. By the terms of the Montgomery Charter of 1731, the governor and provincial council named the city's mayor, recorder, clerk, and treasurer. Municipal ordinances were passed by a Common Council that consisted of the mayor and recorder along with the city's aldermen, who were elected by voice vote within the several wards into which New York had been

divided. Qualified voters also chose a set of assistants, several minor officials, and the vestry-men who cared for the poor. But they had no continuing, direct voice in governing the city as in Boston. [...]

The existence of a wealthy upper class with a taste for European ways had, however, some cultural advantages, for its patronage set eighteenth-century New York on its way toward becoming an American center for the performing arts. Manhattan claimed two playhouses in 1732; by the time of the Revolution it had as many as seven. Not that all New Yorkers were free from scruples born of their Protestant heritage. William Hallam's London Company of Comedians, which came to the city in 1753, was denied official permission to perform until after it issued assurances that its members were 'not cast in the same Mould' as their 'Theatrical Predecessors,' that 'in private Life' and 'publick Occupation' they were of a different moral order. In retrospect, however, it seems more important that the company went to New York because people in Virginia predicted a 'genteel and favourable Reception' in Manhattan, where 'the Inhabitants were generous and polite, naturally fond of Diversions rational, particularly those of the Theatre,' and that Hallam's company finally enjoyed a successful and profitable run in the city. New York also saw occasional musical performances, as in January 1737 when the *New-York Gazette* advertised a 'consort ... for the benefit of Mr. Pachebell, the harpsicord parts performed by himself.' And two years later an advertisement announced 'A New Pantomine Entertainment.... To which will be added an Optick,' which was a primitive predecessor of motion pictures. Cockfighting was also popular, as was horse-racing, with wagers part of the event—all of which remained far from Boston, a city less open to such forms of commercial entertainment. Indeed, theatre was introduced at Boston only during the 1790s, having been earlier outlawed by an act of 1750.[14]

Boston was distinguished instead by its traditional respect for learning and for the printed word. Before the Puritan fathers were more than a decade in America they founded Harvard College and established a printing press in Cambridge.[15] New York City was settled in 1626—four years before Boston—but had no press for almost seventy years, until William Bradford was lured to Manhattan in 1693. Even a casual survey of the Evans bibliography of early American imprints testifies to the immense and continuing superiority of eighteenth-century Boston as a place of publication. Few books and pamphlets came out of New York, and those were heavily weighted toward the official publications of the provincial government. As for newspapers, the first to be published on a continuous schedule in British North America was the *Boston News-Letter*, begun in 1704. And Boston had two other papers, the *Boston Gazette* (1719) and the *New-England Courant* (1721) before the *New-York Gazette* began publication in 1725.[16]

New Yorkers' sense of a good education apparently differed from that of Bostonians: the City of New York was 'so conveniently Situated for Trade and the Genius of the people so inclined to merchandise,' wrote the Rev. John Sharpe in 1713 after some twelve years on Manhattan, 'that they generally seek no other Education for their children than writing and Arithmetick. So that letters must be in a manner forced upon them not only without their seeking, but against their consent'—a proposal unlikely to meet with success. [...]

New York was, quite simply, a different kind of place than Boston, shaped by different values that were sustained by economic success. [...] These distinctions were reflected in John Adams's perceptions of New York, which he visited on the way to the Continental Congress in Philadelphia, with eyes fully open and with Boston as a constant standard of comparison. Like all travellers, Adams was impressed by New York's beauty, for it was in ways long since lost a garden city whose clean and spacious streets were lined with trees, and where the noise of frogs, especially on hot nights when rain was expected, provided a major annoyance.[17] He remarked on the striking views or 'prospects' the city offered of the Hudson

and East Rivers, of Long Island and what he called the 'Sound River,' and of New Jersey. He found New York's streets 'vastly more regular and elegant than those in Boston, and the houses are more grand, as well as neat.' [...] Adams was struck, too, by the evidence of wealth, as in the costly accoutrements of John Morin Scott's breakfast table, which he inventoried lovingly ('rich plate, a very large silver coffee-pot, a very large silver tea-pot, napkins of the very finest materials'), or the 'rich furniture' at the home of Isaac Low. Still, the continuous socializing he found 'very disagreeable on some accounts.' It seems never to have crossed the New Yorkers' minds that a Bostonian might be more anxious to see the twenty-year-old King's College, or the city's churches, printers' offices, and bookshops. And 'with all the opulence and splendor of this city,' Adams reported that there was 'very little good breeding to be found.... I have not seen one real gentleman, one well-bred man, since I came to town.' There was, moreover, 'no conversation that is agreeable' at their 'entertainments': there was 'no modesty, no attention to one another,' for the New Yorkers of that still-pastoral island had already acquired the conversational style of the modern metropolis. 'They talk very loud, very fast, and altogether,' Adams observed. 'If they ask you a question, before you can utter three words of your answer, they will break out upon you again, and talk away.'[18]

There are in these observations testimony not merely to style, but to the pace, the bewildering restlessness that already possessed New Yorkers long before the nineteenth century. Even the sleighs they rode in the winter to friends' homes out of town or to 'Houses of entertainment at a place called the Bowery ... fly with great swiftness,' Madam Knight noted on her visit there in 1704, 'and some are so furious that they'll turn out of the path for none except a Loaden Cart.' What was the hurry? And why were New Yorkers always building, tearing down, rearranging, reconstructing their city, leaving not even the bones of their ancestors in peace? They seem forever to have done things with what struck outsiders as excess: convinced that 'merchandizing' was a good employment, they went into trade in such numbers, reported the visitor John Miller in 1695, 'that whosoever looks on their shops would wonder'—like a modern stroller down Madison Avenue—'where there are so many to sell, there should be any to buy.'[19] The monumental energy of colonial New Yorkers prefigured that of later Americans, who within a century of winning independence built from thirteen modest colonies a nation whose western boundary had pushed from the Appalachians to the Pacific. The enterprise of New Yorkers contributed generously to that development. Indeed, the very physical circumstances of New Yorkers identified them with the nation in 1776: they were concentrated within the lowest mile of a thirteen-and-a-half-mile-long island much as their countrymen were settled along the eastern edge of a vast continent whose expanses of empty land invited and even demanded expansion. People such as these had no time to celebrate the past. They were too engrossed with inventing the future.

How different the situation of the Bostonians, housed on a modest peninsula already fully settled by the time of the Revolution, suffering from a generation of decline, a people convinced that the model of their future lay in the past. In fact, nineteenth-century Boston, true to its colonial origins, became the literary capital of the new nation and also a financial center whose importance yielded to New York only in the 1840s. Meanwhile New Englanders, fleeing the rural poverty of their native region, settled and populated much of the West. There remains considerable irony nonetheless in the fact that Boston served for the generation of 1776 as a model for the new republic. Its democratic politics, tradition of disinterested public service, and modest style, inculcated by Puritanism and continued through hardship, coincided neatly with the demands of classical republicanism—so much so that Samuel Adams could see in the United States a final realization of New England's historic mission.[20] New York played a far more ambiguous role in the politics of the Revolution than did Boston, and the city never took on a similar symbolic importance—perhaps because infinite possibilities are more difficult to comprehend than the limited values of an established and well-defined historical tradition. New York has in fact remained difficult to grasp, to summarize. 'By preference, but also in some degree by necessity,' Nathan Glazer and Daniel Patrick Moynihan observed in *Beyond the Melting Pot*, 'America has turned elsewhere for its images and traditions. Colonial America is preserved for us in terms of the Doric simplicity of New England, or the pastoral symmetry of the Virginia countryside. Even Philadelphia is manageable. But who can summon an image of eighteenth-century New York that will *hold still in the mind?*'[21] And yet the importance of openness, optimism, opportunity, and energy, even of materialism and of visual over literary entertainments to the nation that emerged from the American eighteenth century is undeniable.

Neither Boston nor New York had an enduring importance for the United States like that of London for Britain or of Paris for France. The United States was too diverse, too dynamic to allow any one economic, political, and cultural center to emerge on the European model. Even the economic dominance New York achieved in the early nineteenth century gave way or was shared with Chicago and Los Angeles, which themselves took on qualities that distinguished them from each other and from their 'parent cities' on the Atlantic coast. Students of the city have been more interested in the attributes that distinguish urban from rural life and in those traits that cities share than in the differences that distinguish one city from another. But in a nation predominantly urban, whose people are geographically mobile, differences are at least as important as commonalities. They mean that American cities provide homes for persons of widely different styles and interests, who serve to reinforce the traits that originally attracted them. The differences between cities have also shaped the way they responded to major economic and political crises in American history, not least of all the Revolution itself. The characteristics that separated Boston from New York in the eighteenth century were therefore part of an important urban pattern, and contributed to the texture and complexity that came to characterize the nation they helped to found and to build.

NOTES

1. George Rudé, *Paris and London in the Eighteenth Century* (London, 1970), pp. 7, 35–36; Carl Bridenbaugh, *Cities in the Wilderness: The First Century of Urban Life in America, 1625–1742* (New York, 1964), p. 143n; Douglass C. North, *The Economic Growth of the United States, 1790–1860* (New York, 1961), p. 49 (table 5).

2. *The Oxford English Dictionary*, 2 (Oxford and London, 1961): 443–45. I am here bypassing the narrow and more legalistic meaning the word assumed in North America, where it was applied to separately incorporated communities governed by the traditional English mayor and court of aldermen. [...] The definition was not, however, respected in common usage. Boston was, for example, commonly referred to as a city in the eighteenth century, and by a man no less learned than Cotton Mather. See Samuel G. Drake, *The History and Antiquities of the City of Boston* (Boston, 1851), p. 569n.

3. For a still-useful treatment of urban economic development, see N. S. B. Gras, *An Introduction to Economic History* (New York and London, 1922), esp. ch. 5, pp. 181–269.

4. Homans, *English Villagers of the Thirteenth Century* (Cambridge, Mass., 1941), p. 403, cited in Thomas Bender, *Community and Social Change in America* (New Brunswick, 1978), p. 61.

5. Bailyn, *New England Merchants in the Seventeenth Century* (Cambridge, Mass., 1955), pp. 105–6.

6. Robert V. Wells, *The Population of the British Colonies in America before 1776: A Survey of Census Data* (Princeton, 1975), pp. 114–15; Edgar J. McManus, *A History of Negro Slavery in New York* (Syracuse, N.Y., 1966), p. 25; and Gov. Robert Hunter, Aug. 11, 1720, in Stokes, *Iconography of Manhattan Island*, 4:493.

7. See Israel Goldstein, *A Century of Judaism in New York: B'Nai Jesburun 1825–1925, New York's Oldest Ashkenazic Congregation* (New York, 1930), p. 8.

8. Peter Kalm, *Peter Kalm's Travels in North America: The English Version of 1770* (1937; repr. New York, 1966), 1:142; and Robert M. Kingdon, 'Why Did the Huguenot Refugees in the American Colonies Become Episcopalian?' *The Historical Magazine of the Protestant Episcopal Church* 49 (1980): 317–35, esp. p. 317, where he comments on the 'unusually rapid' assimilation of Huguenots, who 'seem to have lost the use of their language and other cultural traits,... to have dropped the custom of inter-marrying among themselves,' and 'even ... stopped using distinctively French names, more rapidly than members of other non-English groups of immigrants,' and also pp. 325–26 on the gradual defection of Manhattan's Huguenots to the Church of England's Trinity Church.

9. Reed to Dennys Deberdt, Philadelphia, January 17, 1771, in [William B. Reed,] *The Life of Esther DeBerdt, Afterwards Esther Reed, of Pennsylvania* (Philadelphia, 1853), p. 166.

10. Bender, *Community and Social Change*, p. 74.

11. Stokes, *Iconography of Manhattan Island*, 1:387, 407–8.

12. The importance of sex ratios to relative population growth was discussed first by Wesley Frank Craven in *White, Red, and Black: The Seventeenth-Century Virginian* (New York, 1971), esp. pp. 26–27.

13. *The Urban Crucible: Social Change, Political Consciousness, and the Origins of the American Revolution* (Cambridge, Mass., 1979), pp. 304–5, and Pauline Mair, *The Old Revolutionaries: Political Lives in the Age of Samuel Adams* (New York, 1980), esp. pp. 97–100.

14. Mary C. Henderson, *The City and the Theatre, New York Playhouses from Bowling Green to Times Square* (Clifton, N.J., 1973), esp. pp. 8–9, 14; Stokes, *Iconography of Manhattan Island*, 4: 639–40, 641, 544 (and also 546), 558–59, 545, and passim. Samuel Eliot Morison, *Harrison Gray Otis, 1765–1848: The Urbane Federalist* (Boston, 1969), pp. 59–61.

15. Drake, *History and Antiquities of ... Boston*, pp. 241–42.

16. Stokes, *Iconography of Manhattan Island*, 1:184; Frank Luther Mott, *American Journalism: A History, 1690–1960* (New York, 1962), pp. 11, 15, 30.

17. See esp. *Peter Kalm's Travels in North America*, 1:131–32.

18. Madam Knight's comments on the city and its sociability are in *The Journal of Madam Knight*, introduced by George Parker Winship (New York, 1935), pp. 54–56. Adams's diary for August 20–26, 1774, in Charles Francis Adams, ed., *The Works of John Adams*, 2 (Boston, 1850): 345–55, esp. pp. 345–47, 349, 352, 353.

19. *The Journal of Madam Knight*, pp. 55–56; John Miller, *A Description of the Province and City of New York; with Plans of the City and Several Forts as they Existed in the Year 1695*, ed. John Gilmary Shea (New York, 1862), p. 35.

20. Maier, *The Old Revolutionaries*, pp. 4–45, 49.

21. Glazer and Moynihan, *Beyond the Melting Pot* (Cambridge, Mass., 1963), p. 2. Emphasis mine.

Urban Life in Western America, 1790–1830

Richard C. Wade

Source: *The American Historical Review*, 64 (1) (1958): 14–30.

EDITORS' INTRODUCTION

The settlement of the American "West" began with towns, several of which grew into great cities. Many of the towns, in turn, existed on paper and in the minds of speculators long before the arrival of their first inhabitants. From the small towns, and the cities which evolved from some of them, the agrarian countryside emerged. Or so historian Richard C. Wade argued in his landmark 1958 essay from *The American Historical Review*, reprinted below. With these fundamental insights, Wade, a graduate student of Arthur M. Schlesinger, Sr., turned Frederick Jackson Turner's famous "frontier thesis" on its head and ignited a new wave of interest in urban history in particular and urban studies in general during the 1960s and 1970s.

In this selection, Wade contemplates the founding of towns and cities along the Ohio and Mississippi River Valleys and their contribution to defining the qualities and nature of life in the transmontane West region. By West, Wade is referring to the trans-Allegheny West, the region beyond the Appalachian Mountain Range that served as the official western border of the American colonies under the British Proclamation Line of 1763. Today, of course, these same cities typically are considered part of the Midwest, the Middle Atlantic region, and the upper South.

The location of each town derived from a combination of perceived natural advantages and anticipated trade routes. These settlements, however, did not arise in a vacuum. Commercial agents, military officials, and land speculators surveyed and planned each town after pre-existing models, principally the city of Philadelphia with its checkerboard pattern of streets crossing at right angles, regardless of the actual physical characteristics and limitations of the natural terrain. Eastern capital, travelers' accounts, and exaggerated newspaper promotion fueled a process that predicted a future sprawling metropolis at almost every river bend. While few of these envisioned great cities actually emerged, the pattern of urban promotion and "city making mania" took root and moved further west with each generation.[i] Civic leaders in the West also looked eastward, again primarily to the "mother city" of Philadelphia, to recruit physicians, teachers, and ministers, as well as to adopt best practices in municipal government. Over time, two distinct types of society, one urban and one rural, emerged in tandem to define Western life in the United States.

Richard Clement Wade, widely regarded as the father of American urban history, was the founder and first president of the Urban History Association. He was born in Des Moines, Iowa in 1921 and raised in Winnetka, Illinois, a northern suburb of Chicago. He received his Ph.D. from Harvard University in 1956 and taught at Washington University in St. Louis in the early 1960s. Wade moved to the University of Chicago until 1971, when

---

i For more on city making in the Great Lakes region and other parts of the expanding "Great West," as well as the reinterpretation of Turner's frontier thesis, see William Cronon, "Dreaming the Metropolis," in *Nature's Metropolis: Chicago and the Great West* (New York: W. W. Norton, 1991), 23–54.

he became Distinguished Professor of History at the Graduate Center of the City University of New York. More than any other historian, Wade influenced generations of urban studies scholars with his emphasis on the interdisciplinary examination of urban life. His classic works include *The Urban Frontier: The Rise of the Western Cities, 1790–1830* (Cambridge, MA: Harvard University Press, 1959), *Slavery in the Cities: The South, 1820–1860* (New York: Oxford University Press, 1964), and *Chicago: Growth of a Metropolis* (Chicago: University of Chicago Press, 1969) with Harold M. Mayer. Wade also enjoyed public service and taking part in Democratic Party politics. He served as a member of the Chicago Housing Commission from 1967 to 1971, the manager of Robert F. Kennedy's upstate New York campaign for the United States Senate in 1964, and an advisor to Senator George McGovern's 1972 presidential campaign. He died at his home in New York City in 2008.[ii]

URBAN LIFE IN WESTERN AMERICA, 1790–1830

THE towns were the spearheads of the American frontier. Planted as forts or trading posts far in advance of the line of settlement, they held the West for the approaching population. Indeed, in 1763, when the British drew the Proclamation Line across the Appalachians to stop the flow of migrants, a French merchant company prepared to survey the streets of St. Louis, a thousand miles through the wilderness. Whether as part of French and Spanish activity from New Orleans or part of Anglo-American operations from the Atlantic seaboard, the establishment of towns preceded the breaking of soil in the transmontane West.

In 1764, the year of the founding of St. Louis, settlers made the first plat of Pittsburgh. Twelve years later and four hundred miles down the Ohio, Louisville sprang up at the Falls, and the following decade witnessed the beginnings of Cincinnati and Lexington. Before the century closed, Detroit, Buffalo, and Cleveland were laid out on the Great Lakes. In fact, by 1800 the sites of every major metropolis in the old Northwest except Chicago, Milwaukee, and Indianapolis had been cleared and surveyed.

Furthermore, these urban outposts grew rapidly even in their infant decades. By 1815 Pittsburgh, already a thriving industrial center, had 8,000 inhabitants, giving it a slight margin over Lexington. Cincinnati estimated its population at 4,000 at the end of the war with Great Britain, while farther west Louisville and St. Louis neared half that figure. [...]

Not all the towns founded in the trans-Allegheny region in this period fared as well, however. Many never developed much beyond a survey and a newspaper advertisement. Others, after promising beginnings, slackened and settled down to slow and unspectacular development. Still others flourished briefly then faded, leaving behind a grim story of deserted mills, broken buildings, and aging people—the West's first harvest of ghost towns. Most of these were mere eddies in the westward flow of urbanism, but at flood tide it was often hard to distinguish the eddies from the main stream. Indeed, at one time Wheeling, Virginia, St. Genevieve, Missouri, New Albany, Indiana, and Zanesville, Ohio, were considered serious challengers to the supremacy of their now more famous neighbors.

Other places, such as Rising Sun, Town of America, or New Athens, were almost wholly speculative ventures. Eastern investors scanned maps looking for likely spots to establish a city, usually at the junction of two rivers, or sometimes at the center of fertile farm districts. They bought up land, laid it out in lots, gave the place a name, and waited for the development of the region to appreciate its value. Looking back over this period one editor called it a "city-making

---

ii For more on Wade's influence and career see his obituaries by William Grimes in the *New York Times*, July 25, 2008 and Kenneth T. Jackson in the Organization of American Historians' *OAH Newsletter*, 36 (4) (2008): 27.

mania," when everyone went about "anticipating flourishing cities in vision, at the mouth of every creek and bayou."[1] This speculation, though extensive, was not always profitable. "Of the vast number of towns which have been founded," James Hall declared, "but a small minority have prospered, nor do we think that, as a general rule, the founders of these have been greatly enriched by their prosperity."[2]

Despite many failures, these abortive attempts to plant towns were significant, for they reveal much about the motives of the people who came West in the early period. Many settlers moved across the mountains in search of promising towns rather than good land, their inducements being urban opportunities rather than fertile soil. Daniel Drake, who was among the earliest urbanites of the frontier, later commented on this process:

> It is worthy of remark, that those who made these beginnings of settlement, projected towns, which they anticipated would grow into cities.... And we may see in their origins, one of the elements of the prevalent tendency to rear up towns in advance of the country which has ever since characterized Ohio. The followers of the first pioneers, like themselves had a taste for commerce and the mechanic arts which cannot be gratified without the construction of cities.[3]

[...] The West's young cities owed their initial success to commerce. All sprang from it, and their growth in the early years of the century stemmed from its expansion. Since the Ohio River was the chief artery of trade and travel, the towns along its banks prospered most. Pittsburgh, where the Allegheny meets the Monogahela, commanded the entire valley; Cincinnati served the rich farm lands of Kentucky and Ohio; Louisville fattened on the transshipment of goods around the Falls; and St. Louis, astride the Mississippi, was the focus of far-flung enterprises, some of which reached to the Pacific Ocean. Even Lexington, landlocked in a country of water highways, grew up as the central mart of Kentucky and Tennessee.

Though these cities were firmly established by the first decade of the century, the coming of the steamboat greatly enhanced their size and influence.[4] By quickening transportation and cutting distances, steam navigation telescoped fifty years' urban development into a single generation. The flow of commerce down river was now supplemented by a northward and eastward movement, giving cities added opportunities for expansion and growth. "The steam engine in five years has enabled us to anticipate a state of things," a Pittsburgher declared enthusiastically, "which in the ordinary course of events, it would have required a century to have produced. The art of printing scarcely surpassed it in beneficial consequences."[5] The "enchanter's wand" not only touched the established towns but created new ones as well. A French observer noted that "in the brief interval of fifteen years, many cities were formed ... where before there were hardly the dwellings of a small town.... A simple mechanical device has made life both possible and comfortable in regions which heretofore have been a wilderness."[6]

As these commercial centers grew, some inhabitants turned to manufacturing. Indeed, this new interest spread so rapidly in Pittsburgh that in 1810 a resident likened the place to "a large workshop," and already travelers complained of the smoke and soot.[7] Between 1803 and 1815 the value of manufactured goods jumped from $350,000 to over $2,600,000, and the city's iron and glass products became known throughout the new country.[8] Watching this remarkable development, the editor of Niles' Register exclaimed: "Pittsburgh, sometimes emphatically called the 'Birmingham of America,' will probably become the *greatest manufacturing town in the world*"[9] Lexington also turned increasingly to industry, her ropewalks and textile mills supplying the whole West. Beginnings were more modest in other places, but every city had at least a few ambitious enterprises.

Some of this urban expansion rested on a speculative base, and the depression of 1819 brought a reckoning. Lexington, already suffering from its land-locked position, received fatal wounds, while Pittsburgh, the West's foremost city, was crippled for a decade.

Elsewhere, however, the setback proved only momentary and the mid-twenties saw the old pace renewed. Population growth again provides a convenient index of development. Cincinnati quickly overtook its faltering rivals, the number of its residents leaping from 6,000 in 1815 to over 25,000 in 1830. By the latter date the census recorded Pittsburgh's recovery. Though the figure had dropped to 7,000 during the depression, it rose to 13,000 in 1830. Farther west Louisville and St. Louis enjoyed spectacular expansion, the former boasting over 10,000 inhabitants at the end of the period, while the Mississippi entrepôt passed the 6,000 mark. Lexington alone lagged, its population remaining stable for the next two decades.

Even these figures, however, do not convey the real growth. In most places municipal boundaries could no longer contain the new settlers, and many spilled over into the suburbs. For instance, Allegheny, Bayardstown, Birmingham, Lawrenceville, Hayti, and East Liberty added nearly 10,000 to Pittsburgh's population, bringing the total to 22,000.[10] The same was true of Cincinnati where 2,000 people lived in the Eastern and Northern Liberties.[11] In Louisville, Preston's and Campbell's "enlargements" and Shipping-port and Portland swelled the city's total to 13,000.[12] Ultimately, the urban centers annexed these surrounding clusters, but in the meantime local authorities grappled with early manifestations of the suburban problem.

As the cities grew they staked out extensive commercial claims over the entire West.[13] Timothy Flint calculated that Cincinnati was the central market for over a million people, while a resident asserted that its trade was "co-extensive with steamboat navigation on the western waters."[14] Louisville's economic penetration was scarcely less impressive. As early as 1821, a local editor declared that "the people of the greater part of Indiana, all Kentucky, and portions of Tennessee, Alabama, Illinois, Missouri, now report to this place for dry goods, groceries, hardware and queensware."[15] St. Louis' empire touched Santa Fe on the south, Canada on the north, and the Pacific on the west. "It is doubtful if history affords the example of another city," wrote Hiram M. Chittenden, "which has been the exclusive mart for so vast an area as that which was tributary to St. Louis."[16]

In carving out these extensive dependencies, the young metropolises overwhelmed their smaller neighbors. The rise of St. Louis destroyed the ambitions of Edwardsville across the Mississippi, which once harbored modest hopes of importance. Pittsburgh's recovery in the late twenties condemned Wheeling and Steubenville to minor roles in the upper Ohio region. And Louisville's development swallowed two Kentucky neighbors while reducing Jeffersonville and New Albany on the Indiana side of the river to mere appendages.

Not satisfied with such considerable conquests, the cities reached out for more. Seeking wider opportunities, they built canals and turnpikes and, even before 1830, planned railroads to strengthen their position. Cincinnati, Pittsburgh, and St. Louis tried to tap the increasing trade on the Great Lakes by water links to the North. Pennsylvania's Iron City also hoped to become a major station on the National Road, and for a decade its Washington representatives lobbied to win that commercial bond with the East. Lexington, suffocating in its inland position, frantically strove for better connections with the Ohio River. A turnpike to Maysville was dashed by Jackson's veto, technical difficulties made a canal to the Kentucky River impractical, but some belated hope rose with the possibility of a railroad to Louisville or Cincinnati.

The intensive search for new advantages brought rivalry and conflict. Though the commerce of the whole West lay untouched before them, the cities quarreled over its division. Thus Louisville and Cincinnati fought over a canal around the Falls of the Ohio. The Kentucky town, feeling that its strength depended upon maintaining the break in transportation, obstructed every attempt to circumvent the rapids. Only when Ohio interests threatened to dig on the Indiana side did Louisville move ahead with its own project. Likewise, harsh words flew between Wheeling and Pittsburgh as they contended for the Ohio River terminus of the National Road. Smaller towns, too, joined the struggle. Cleveland and Sandusky, for instance, clashed over the location of the Ohio Canal, the stake being nothing less than control of the mounting trade between the Valley and the lakes. And their instinct to fight was sound, for the outcome shaped the future of both places.

Urban rivalries were often bitter, and the contestants showed no quarter. In the late twenties when only the success of Transylvania University kept Lexington's economy from complete collapse, Louisville joined the attack which ultimately destroyed the school. In a similar vein Cincinnatians taunted their upriver competitor as it reeled under the impact of the depression of 1819. "Poor Pittsburgh," they exclaimed, "your day is over, the sceptre of influence and wealth is to travel to us; the Cumberland road has done the business."[17] But even the Queen City found her supremacy insecure. "I discovered two ruling passions in Cincinnati," a traveler remarked, "enmity against Pittsburgh, and jealousy of Louisville."[18] This drive for power and primacy, sustained especially by merchants and articulated by editors, was one of the most consistent and striking characteristics of the early history of Western cities.

As they pursued expansive policies, municipalities also ministered to their own growing pains. From the beginning, urban residents had to contend with the problems of living together, and one of their first acts was to petition the territory or state for governing authority to handle them. The legislatures, representing rural interests and generally suspicious of towns, responded with charters bestowing narrow grants of power which barely met current needs and failed to allow for expansion. As localities grew, however, they developed problems which could be met only with wider jurisdiction. Louisville's charter had to be amended twenty-two times before 1815 and Cincinnati's underwent five major changes between 1815 and 1827. Others, though altered less often, were adjusted and remade until finally scrapped for new ones. Reluctantly, and bit by bit, the states turned over to the cities the responsibility of managing their own affairs, though keeping them starved for revenue by strict tax and debt limitations.

Despite inadequate charters and modest incomes, urban governments played a decisive role in the growth of Western cities. Since these were commercial towns, local authorities paid special attention to mercantile requirements. They not only constructed market houses but also extended municipal regulation over a wide variety of trading activity. Ordinances protected the public against adulterated foods, false measurements, and rigged prices. Some municipalities went even farther and assumed responsibility for seeing that "justice is done between buyer and seller."[19] In search of this objective, officials fixed prices on some goods, excluded monopolies from the market, and tried to equalize opportunities for smaller purchasers. To facilitate access to the exchange center, they lavished time and money on the development of wharves and docks and the improvement of streets.

Municipalities also tackled a wide variety of other problems growing out of urban life. Fire protection, at first casually organized, was placed on a more formal basis. Volunteer companies still provided the manpower, but government participation increased markedly. Local councils legislated against many kinds of fire hazards, and public money furnished most of the equipment. Moreover, some places, haunted by the image of Detroit's disaster in 1805, forbade the construction of wooden buildings in the heart of the city, a measure which not only reduced fire risks but also changed the face of downtown areas. The development of adequate police was much slower. By 1830 only Lexington and Louisville had regular patrols, and these were established with the intent more of control of slaves than the general protection of life and property. In other towns law enforcement was lax by day and absent at night, though the introduction of gas lighting in Pittsburgh and Cincinnati in the late twenties made the after-dark hours there less dangerous than before.

Congested living created new health hazards and especially increased the likelihood of epidemics. Every place suffered, but none like Louisville, which earned a grim reputation as the "Graveyard of the West" because of the constant visitations of yellow fever and malaria.[20] Cities took preventive measures, such as draining stagnant ponds and clearing streets and lots, and also appointed boards of health to preside over the problem. Municipal water systems, introduced in Pittsburgh and Cincinnati before 1830, made life healthier and certainly more comfortable, while the discussion of installing underground sewers pointed to still more extensive reform in sanitation.

In meeting urban problems, Western officials drew heavily on Eastern experience. Lacking precedents of their own, and familiar with the techniques of older cities, they frankly patterned their practice on Eastern models. There was little innovation. When confronted by a new question, local authorities responded by adopting tested solutions. This emulation characterized nearly every aspect of development—from the width of streets to housing regulations. No major improvement was launched without a close study of established seaboard practices. St. Louis' council, for example, instructed its water committee to "procure from the cities of Philadelphia and New Orleans such information as can be obtained on the subject of conveying water and the best manner of clearing it."[21] When Cincinnati discussed introducing underground sewers, an official group was designated to "ascertain from the city authorities of New York, Philadelphia, Baltimore and Boston, how far the sinking of common sewers is approved in those cities."[22] Pittsburgh undertook gas lighting only after exhaustive research and "very full enquiries at New York and Baltimore."[23]

Though the young towns drew upon the experience of all the major Atlantic cities, the special source of municipal wisdom was Philadelphia. Many Western urbanites had lived or visited there; it provided the new country with most of its professional and cultural leadership; it was the model metropolis. "She is the great seat of American affluence, of individual riches, and distinguished philanthropy," a Pittsburgh editorial declared in 1818. "From her ... we have everything to look for."[24] Newspapers often referred to it as "our mother city."[25]

From street plans to cultural activity, from the shape of market houses to the habits of people, the Philadelphia influence prevailed. Robert Peterson and John Filson, who had a hand in the founding of Louisville, Lexington, and Cincinnati, borrowed the basic grid pattern of the original plats from the Pennsylvania metropolis.[26] Market location and design came from the same source, as did techniques for fire fighting and police protection. Western towns also leaned on Philadelphia's leadership in street lighting, water-works, and wharving. Even the naming of suburbs—Pittsburgh's Kensington and Cincinnati's Liberties—came from the mother city. The result was a physical likeness which struck many travelers and which Philadelphians themselves recognized. Gideon Burton, for instance, remembered his first impression of Cincinnati in the 1820's: "How beautiful this city is," he remarked, "how much like Philadelphia."[27]

The Quaker City spirit, moreover, went beyond streets, buildings, and improvements, reaching into a wide range or human activity. Businessmen, yearly visitors in the East, brought marketing and promotion techniques from there;[28] young labor movements lifted their platforms from trade union programs in the mother city; employment agencies were conducted "principally on the Philadelphia plan."[29] The same metropolis trained most of the physicians of the West and a large share of the teachers and ministers. Caspar Wistar's famed Sunday evening gatherings of the intelligentsia provided the idea for Daniel Drake's select meetings of Cincinnati's social and cultural elite. Moreover, Philadelphia furnished the model of the perfect urbanite, for the highest praise that Western town dwellers could bestow upon a fellow citizen was to refer to him as their own "Benjamin Franklin."[30] In short, Philadelphia represented the highest stage of urban development, and progress was measured against this ideal. [...]

As transmontane cities developed they created societies whose ways and habits contrasted sharply with those of the countryside. Not only was their physical environment distinct, but their interests, activities, and pace of life also differed greatly. In 1811 a farmer near Lexington expressed the conflict as contemporaries saw it in a dialogue between "Rusticus" and "Urbanus." The latter referred to the "rude, gross appearance" of his neighbor, adding: "How strong you smell of your ploughed ground and corn fields. How dismal, how gloomy your green woods. What a miserable clash your whistling woodland birds are continually making." "Rusticus" replied with the rural image of the town dweller. "What a fine smooth complexion you have Urbanus: you look like a weed that has grown up in the shade. Can you walk your streets without inhaling the noxious fumes with which your town is pregnant? ... Can you engage in calm contemplation, when hammers are ringing in every direction—when there is as great a *rattling* as in a storm when the hail descends on our house tops?"[31] [...]

Urban ways were further distinguished from rural habits by the collective approach to many problems. City living created issues which could not always be solved by the highly individualistic methods of agrarian society. Local governments assumed an ever wider responsibility for the conduct of community affairs, and voluntary associations handled a large variety of other questions. Merchants formed chambers of commerce to facilitate cooperation on common problems; professional people organized societies to raise the standards of their colleagues and keep out the untrained. Working people, too, banded together in unions, seeking not only greater economic strength but also fraternity and self-improvement. Religious and philanthropic clubs managed most charity and relief work, while immigrants combined to help new arrivals. In addition, other associations grew up to promote literature and music, encourage debating, advocate social innovations, support public causes, and conduct the welter of amusements which larger cities required. Just as conditions in the countryside placed greatest emphasis on individual effort, so the urban situation made cooperative action seem more appropriate.

Rural and metropolitan West were also separated by distinctive social and cultural developments. The towns very quickly produced a surprisingly rich and diversified life, offering opportunities in many fields similar to those of Eastern cities but lacking on the farm or frontier.[32] They enjoyed a virtual monopoly of printing presses, newspapers, bookstores, and circulating libraries. Theaters sprang up to encourage local players and traveling troupes, while in larger places museums brought the curious and the scientific to the townfolks.[33] In addition, every week brought numerous lectures and debates on all kinds of topics, keeping urban residents abreast of the latest discoveries and developments in every field. By 1815 these amenities had already lost their novelty. Indeed, some thought the civilizing process was getting out of hand. "Twenty sermons a week—," a Cincinnatian wearily counted, "Sunday evening Discourses on Theology—Private assemblies—state Cotillion parties—Saturday Night Clubs, and chemical lectures—... like the fever and the ague, return every day with distressing regularity."[34]

Of course, the whole transmontane region matured culturally in this period, but the towns played a strategic role. "Cities have arisen in the very wilderness...," a St. Louis editor noticed in 1821, "and form in their respective states the *foci* of art and science, of wealth and information."[35] A Cincinnatian made a similar observation. "This *city*, in its growth and cultural improvements has anticipated the western country in general."[36] The hinterland, already bound to urban communities by trade, readily admitted its dependence. The *Pittsburgh Gazette* merely stated the obvious when it remarked in 1819 that the surrounding region "looks up to Pittsburgh not only as a medium through which to receive the comforts and luxuries of foreign commodities, but also a channel from which it can most naturally expect a supply of intellectual wealth."[37] Thus while the cities' merchants staked out markets in the countryside, their civic leaders spread a cultural influence into the same area.

This leadership extended into almost every field. For example, the educational opportunities of town children greatly exceeded those of their rural neighbors. Every municipality developed a complex of private tuition schools topped by an academy and, in every place except Louisville, a college. Moreover, the cities organized the movement for public schooling. Ohio's experience is illustrative. The movement for state legislation started in Cincinnati, received its major impetus from the local press, and was carried in the Assembly through the efforts of representatives from Hamilton county. It is also significant that the first superintendent of common schools in Ohio was Samuel Lewis of Cincinnati. Nor was this urban leadership surprising. The cities, as the great population centers, felt the educational pressure first and most acutely. In addition, they alone had the wealth needed to launch ambitious projects for large numbers of children. Hence the towns were ready for comprehensive public programs long before the countryside.

The most striking illustration of the cultural supremacy of the cities, however, was Lexington's unique reign as the "Athens of the West."[38] The area's largest town until 1810, it was early celebrated for its polish and sophistication and was generally conceded to be the region's capital of arts and science. But the coming of the steamboat and the depression of 1819 combined to undermine its economic position. To offset this commercial and industrial decline, Lexington's civic leaders inaugurated a policy of vigorous cultural expansion.[39] They built schools, subsidized Transylvania University, and advertised the many opportunities for advancement in learning and letters in the metropolis. Throughout the twenties this campaign was a spectacular success. The town became the resort of the most talented men of the new country. Educators, scientists, painters, lawyers, architects, musicians, and their patrons all flocked there. Transylvania University attained national eminence, attracting most of its faculty from the East and drawing students from better than a dozen states. Like a renaissance city of old Italy, Lexington provided the creative atmosphere for a unique flowering that for a decade astonished travelers and stimulated the best minds of the West.

The graduating class of the medical school in 1826 demonstrated the extent of the university's reputation and influence. With sixty-seven degrees granted in that year, twenty-eight of the recipients came from Kentucky, ten from Tennessee, five each from Virginia, South Carolina, and Alabama, three from Ohio, two each from Mississippi, Illinois, and Louisiana, and one each from North Carolina and Georgia. During the twenties the college trained many of the West's most distinguished people. In politics alone it turned out at least seventeen congressmen, three governors, six United States senators, and the president of the Confederacy. In the same decade the school produced scores of lawyers, clergymen, and physicians, who did much to raise professional standards in the new country. Few universities have left such a clear mark on a generation; in its heyday Transylvania fully deserved its title of the "Harvard of the West."[40] [...]

The glitter of this city drew young people from all over the transmontane region, including many from the countryside. In doing so, it provoked a familiar lament from the rural areas whose children succumbed to the bewitchment of Lexington. "We want our sons to be practical men," wrote a Kentucky farmer, "whose minds will not be filled with those light notions of refinement and taste, which will induce them to believe that they are of a different order of beings, or that will elevate them above their equals."[41] Later, agrarian representatives in the legislature joined the attack on Transylvania by voting to cut off state financial assistance.

No less striking than cultural cleavages were the differences in rural and urban religious development. Progress in the cities was steadier and more substantial—though less spectacular—than in the back country. Traveling ministers might refer to Pittsburgh as "a young hell, a second Sodom,"[42] and Francis Asbury might complain in 1803 that he felt "the power of Satan in those little, wicked western trading towns,"[43] but both churches and membership multiplied rapidly in urban centers. Furthermore, the growth owed nothing to the sporadic revivals which burned across the countryside at the beginning of the century. These movements were essentially rural, having their roots in the isolation of agricultural living and the spiritual starvation of people unattended by regular services. The city situation, with its constant contacts and settled church organizations, involved neither of these elements. Instead, religious societies proliferated, sects took on such additional functions as charity and missionary work, and congregations sent money back East to aid their seminaries. Far from being sinks of corruption, Western cities quickly became religious centers, supplying Bibles to the frontier, assisting foreign missions, and, in the twenties, building theological schools to provide priests and ministers for the whole region.

Political life also reflected the growing rural-urban division. Though the rhetoric of the period often obscured them, differences existed from the very beginning. Suspicion of the towns led states to avoid economic and cultural centers when locating their capitals. Nearly all these cities sought the prize, but none was successful. The *Missouri Gazette* candidly stated the issue in 1820. "It has been said that St. Louis is obnoxious to our Legislature—that its growth and influence ... are looked on with a jealous eye, and its pretensions ... ought to be discouraged."[44] The same clash had earlier occurred in Kentucky, where state leaders virtually invented Frankfort to keep the capital away from Louisville or Lexington. [...]

The cities' political influence rested on their ability to produce leadership. As the economic and intellectual centers of transmontane life they attracted the talented and ambitious in all fields. Politics was no exception. Nearly all the great spokesmen of the West had important urban connections and their activity often reflected the demands of their town constituents. Henry Clay was one of Lexington's most prominent lawyers when he went to the United States Senate in 1806. Thomas Hart Benton held local offices in St. Louis before moving on to the national scene, and William Henry Harrison, though he lived in nearby North Bend, had deep roots in Cincinnati affairs through most of his long public life. Moreover, all were alive to the interests of their city. Benton's successful attack on government factories in the Indian territory culminated a long and intense campaign by St. Louis merchants to break federal trade control on the Missouri. Clay's enthusiasm for an ample tariff on hemp derived at least as much from the pressure of Lexington's manufactures as from that of the growers of the Blue Grass. And Harrison, as state senator, led the campaign for public schools in Ohio largely at the behest of his Cincinnati supporters. These were not isolated cases; an examination of the careers of these men demonstrates the importance of their urban connections.

By 1830, then, the West had produced two types of society—one rural and one urban. Each developed its own institutions, habits, and living patterns. The countryside claimed much the larger population and often gave to transmontane affairs an agrarian flavor. But broadcloth was catching up with buckskin. The census of 1830 revealed the disproportionate rate of city growth. While the state of Ohio had four times as many inhabitants as it counted in 1810, Cincinnati's increase was twelvefold. The story was the same elsewhere. Louisville's figure showed a growth of 650 per cent compared with Kentucky's 50 per cent, and Pittsburgh tripled in size while Pennsylvania did not quite double its population. By 1830 the rise of these cities had driven a broad wedge of urbanism into Western life.

Though town and country developed along different paths, clashes were still infrequent. The West was large enough to contain both movements comfortably. Indeed, each supported the other. The rural regions supplied the cities with raw materials for their mills and packinghouses and offered an expanding market to their shops and factories. In turn, urban centers served the surrounding areas by providing both the necessities and comforts of life as well as new opportunity for ambitious farm youths. Yet the cities represented the more aggressive and dynamic force. By spreading their economic power over the entire section, by bringing the fruits of civilization across the mountains, and by insinuating their ways into the countryside, they speeded up the transformation of the West from a gloomy wilderness to a richly diversified region. Any historical view which omits this aspect of Western life tells but part of the story.

NOTES

1. *Missouri Republican* (St. Louis), Aug. 29, 1825.
2. Hall, *The West: Its Commerce and Navigation* (Cincinnati, 1848), p. 227.
3. Drake, "Dr. Drake's Memoir of the Miami County, 1779–1794," Beverley Bond, Jr., ed., Historical and Philosophical Society of Ohio, *Quarterly Publications*, XVIII (1923), 58.
4. Louis C. Hunter, *Steamboats on the Western Rivers, An Economic and Technological History* (Cambridge, Mass., 1949), pp. 27–32.
5. Morgan Neville, "The Last of the Boatmen," *The Western Souvenir for 1829* (Cincinnati, Ohio, n.d.), p. 108.
6. [Jean Baptiste] Marestier, *Mémoire sur les Bateaux à vapeur des États-Unis d'Amérique* (Paris, 1824), pp. 9–10.
7. Zadock Cramer, *Pittsburgh Almanack for the Year of Our Lord 1810* (Pittsburgh, Pa., 1810), p. 52.
8. Pittsburgh's industrial foundations are discussed in Catherine Elizabeth Reiser, *Pittsburgh's Commercial Development, 1800–1850* (Harrisburg, Pa., 1951), pp. 12–21.
9. *Niles' Register*, May 28, 1814.
10. *Pittsburgh Gazette*, Nov. 16, 1830.
11. *Cincinnati Advertiser*, Aug. 18, 1830.
12. United States *Census*, 1830, pp. 114–15.
13. For an appreciation of the economic importance of the cities in the growth of the West, see Frederick Jackson Turner, *Rise of the New West, 1819–1829* in *The American Nation: A History*, A. B. Hart, ed., XIV (New York, 1906), 96–98.
14. Flint, "Thoughts Respecting the Establishment of a Porcelain Manufactory at Cincinnati," *Western Monthly Review*, III (1830), 512; Benjamin Drake and Edward W. Mansfield, *Cincinnati in 1826* (Cincinnati, Ohio, 1827), p. 71.
15. *Louisville Public Advertiser*, Oct. 17, 1829.
16. Chittenden, *The American Fur Trade of the Far West* (2 vols., New York, 1902), I, 99.
17. *Pittsburgh Gazette*, Dec. 18, 1818.
18. *Pittsburgh Gazette*, Feb. 5, 1819.
19. *Pittsburgh Gazette*, Mar. 9, 1810.
20. Benjamin Casseday, *The History of Louisville from Its Earliest Settlement till the Year 1852* (Louisville, Ky., 1852), p. 49.
21. St. Louis City Council, Minutes, Court House, St. Louis, June 12, 1829.
22. Cincinnati City Council, Minutes, City Hall, Cincinnati, Oct. 6, 1827.
23. Pittsburgh City Council, City Council Papers, City Hall, Pittsburgh, May 10, 1827.
24. *Pittsburgh Gazette*, Oct. 27, 1818.
25. For example, see *Pittsburgh Gazette*, June 23, 1818.
26. For example, see Rufus King, *Ohio First Fruits of the Ordinance of 1787* (Boston, 1888), p. 209.
27. Burton, *Reminiscences of Gideon Burton* (Cincinnati, Ohio, 1895). The strategic location of Western cities in the life of the new country reminded some visitors of the regional supremacy of Philadelphia. Lewis Condict, for example, referred to Lexington as "the Philadelphia of Kentucky." "Journal of a Trip to Kentucky in 1795," *Proceedings of the New Jersey Historical Society*, n.s., IV (1919), 120.
28. *Cincinnati Enquirer*, Apr. 22, 1923.
29. *Pittsburgh Mercury*, Aug. 7, 1827.
30. The phrase was constantly used in characterizing John Bradford of Lexington and Daniel Drake of Cincinnati, but it was applied to others as well.
31. *Kentucky Reporter* (Lexington), July 2, 1811.
32. For a day-to-day account of the cultural offerings of a Western city between 1820 and 1830 see the highly informative but unpublished diary of William Stanley Merrill in the library of the Historical and Philosophical Society of Ohio (Cincinnati).
33. The development of the theater in Western cities is outlined in Ralph Leslie Rush, *The Literature of the Middle Western Frontier* (New York, 1925), I, 352–400. For a detailed study of a single town see William G. B. Carson, *The Theatre on the Frontier, The Early Years of the St. Louis Stage* (Chicago, 1932), pp. 1–134.
34. *Liberty Hall* (Cincinnati), Dec. 9, 1816.
35. *Missouri Gazette* (St. Louis), Dec. 20, 1820.
36. *Liberty Hall* (Cincinnati), June 29, 1819.
37. *Pittsburgh Gazette*, Apr. 30, 1813.
38. For Lexington's growth and brief supremacy see Bernard Mayo, "Lexington, Frontier Metropolis," in *Historiography and Urbanization*, Eric F. Goldman, ed. (Baltimore, Md., 1941), pp. 21–42.
39. See, for example, *Kentucky Reporter*, Oct. 4, 1820.
40. The reputation of Lexington in Cincinnati is charmingly portrayed in the letters of young Ohioans attending Transylvania University to their friends back home. See especially the William Lytle Collection in the library of the Historical and Philosophical Society of Ohio (Cincinnati).
41. *Kentucky Reporter* (Lexington), Feb. 16, 1824.
42. *Pittsburgh Gazette*, Sept. 23, 1803.
43. Francis Asbury, *Journal of Rev. Francis Asbury, Bishop of Methodist Episcopal Church* (n.p., 1821), III, 127.
44. *Missouri Gazette* (St. Louis), Dec. 6, 1820.

Pearls on the Coast and Lights in the Forest: The Colonial South

David R. Goldfield

Source: *Cotton Fields and Skyscrapers: Southern City and Region, 1607–1980* (Baton Rouge, LA: Louisiana State University Press, 1982).

EDITORS' INTRODUCTION

Despite a tendency to associate urbanization prior to the Civil War with the Northeast and Midwest, the South also developed through the process of city building. Scholars, most notably historian David Goldfield, consider whether towns and cities in the colonial South grew in the same manner as their counterparts in New England and Europe. The following essay from Goldfield's work, *Cotton Fields and Skyscrapers: Southern City and Region, 1607–1980*, addresses the legacy of colonial settlement and the subsequent development of southern cities through an overview of the founding and evolution of urban areas along the southern Atlantic and Gulf coasts and adjacent inland regions.

In contrast to Richard Wade's discussion of trans-Appalachian towns, Goldfield emphasizes the role of farmers and agricultural surplus in the success of southern cities. Goldfield also pays special attention to the impact of geography and natural features that often undermined legislative attempts and speculative desires to establish urban enclaves in the remote countryside. He then formulates a three-stage model of southern development that culminates in the rise of Charleston as the region's preeminent city, the growth of backcountry towns, and the establishment of links between the coast and the frontier that set the stage for the economic and social development of southern cities to the present.

David R. Goldfield is the Robert Lee Bailey Professor of History at the University of North Carolina, Charlotte. In addition to *Cotton Fields and Skyscrapers*, he is also the author of *Southern Histories: Public, Personal, and Sacred* (Athens, GA: University of Georgia Press, 2003) and *Still Fighting the Civil War: The American South and Southern History* (Baton Rouge, LA: Louisiana State University Press, 2002). He is currently the editor of the *Journal of Urban History*, the most important journal in the field, and is a past president of the Urban History Association.

PEARLS ON THE COAST AND LIGHTS IN THE FOREST

The Colonial Era

Like pearls on a string, the cities of colonial America lined the Atlantic coast from Boston to Savannah. We recall the maps in those otherwise forgettable textbooks of our childhood years: the cities in geographic single file, clinging to their watery niches. The distance between Boston and Savannah, though, was more than in miles. The New England settlers wrote to their British comrades across the sea of a wilderness that was abundant but very difficult, a challenge appropriate for testing the mettle of God's chosen. The letters from the southern latitudes likened the country to paradise—a lush, easy place where modest effort brought forth great rewards. It was not only a different way of looking at the world that separated northern and southern colonies; they were in fact different worlds.

Climate, geography, and geology facilitated life in the colonial South; they inhibited it in the colonial North. The rivers in the southern colonies ran deep into the interior, creating luxuriant bottomlands as they ran their courses. The mountain spine that divided eastern America from the Ohio country was conveniently deep into the southern interior. Even here, there lay a fertile valley—a highway for travel and a soil for cultivation. The climate, though a bit uncomfortable during the summer months, allowed a long growing season. The kaleidoscopic beauty of late October in the lower Shenandoah or the colorful floral array of Charleston in late March lifted southern hearts when New England was painted gray. Climate and geography made the South distinctive. The civilization, more particularly the urban civilization that grew from these natural conditions, would indelibly bear the character of land and weather.

Several decades ago, historians debated whether cities or farms were the first settlements on the American frontier. Richard C. Wade's book on the trans-Appalachian frontier of the late eighteenth and early nineteenth century was among the most influential statements on the subject. He contended that cities, not farms, were the spearheads of civilization on the frontier. Wade's "cities," however, were for the most part military outposts, artifically sustained by eastern supplies and capital. Were it not for the farmers who followed closely on the heels of the departing Indians, these settlements would have returned to forests. An agricultural surplus was necessary for the emergence of cities.

As British policymakers discovered ruefully, however, the existence of an agricultural surplus was a prerequisite but not a guarantee for urban development. Yet the British had several good reasons for wanting their colonists to "plant in towns." First, they could not conceive of civilization as they knew it to exist without towns. The colonies, in the midst of the wild frontier, could easily lose the trappings of Western culture and assume the manners and tastes of their surrounding environment. Second, the colonists as individual settlers were vulnerable against enemy attack—Indian, French, or Spanish. The English mind, only

recently removed from the reality of walled cities and fortified towns, equated urban life with security. [...]

Finally, there were commercial-administrative reasons why the English government and its New World representatives urged the growth of towns. From their European experience, they saw towns, at the very least, serving as marketplaces—convenient gathering points—for agricultural and industrial production. The towns facilitated and financed production in a reciprocal arrangement: as the farms grew, so did the cities, encouraging expansion of cultivation, which in turn stimulated urban growth. In addition, the commercial legislation, weighted toward the mother country in a colonial economy, was most readily administered at urban focal points. The difficulties involved with overseeing the economic activities of a diffuse population were obvious.

Besides simple encouragement, there were periodic schemes designed to promote urban settlement in the face of an apparent southern colonial resistance to do so. In the 1660s, when the nonurban appearance of the Chesapeake colonies (Maryland and Virginia) was a source of both incredulity and concern in official circles, the Carolina proprietors published lengthy directives for the creation of agricultural villages that would also function as commercial centers. The combination of farming and urban activities was common throughout Europe and, as New England demonstrated, appeared in the New World as well, where such settlements solved the problems of food supply and commercial-administrative function. Later, in 1730, Governor Robert Johnson of South Carolina, looking more to security than to commercial-administrative problems, recommended the establishment of ten frontier towns to protect and thereby encourage interior settlement.

These plans, and the more general official encouragement, were unsuccessful. And here the influence of the distinctive geographic and climatic conditions of the colonial South is evident. The rivers that spread like fingers from the coastal plain to the interior discouraged concentrated settlement. The fertile lands along the winding rivers proved ideal for agriculture, and their abundance from coast to fall line enticed thousands of settlers. For the traditionally land-starved Englishman, the plentiful supply of good land made huddling together in small villages unnecessary, unattractive, and unremunerative.

In addition, these rivers were navigable deep into the interior. This allowed the planters to market their own crops, removing one of the primary functions of towns. Ships, even oceangoing vessels in the Chesapeake colonies, sailed up to the docks of individual farmers, unloaded their goods from England, and took on tobacco or rice. The planter doubled as merchant, eliminating the middleman and therefore maximizing his profits (and risk as well).

This scenario was especially apt for the Chesapeake colonies, where the Chesapeake Bay and the rivers of the Virginia colony were like so many miniature seas. The respective colonial governments of Maryland and Virginia, in futile attempts to override nature, passed fourteen acts promoting town growth during the last half of the seventeenth century. By 1710, the failure of urban settlement was so complete that officials permanently abandoned legislative town-building efforts. As the Reverend Hugh Jones wrote in 1724, "neither the interest nor inclinations of the Virginians induce them to cohabit in towns."

The situation was much the same further south. The Carolina proprietors' agricultural village scheme failed. The abundance of good land, especially on the irregular coastal plain in North Carolina, resulted in scattered farms rather than the hoped-for villages. Governor Johnson's military villages fared little better in South Carolina sixty years later. Only one of Johnson's ten towns—Orangeburg—was permanently established. The nine others simply could not counteract the centrifugal tendencies of the population, even on the hazardous frontier.

If towns were to emerge in the colonial South—and they did—legislation and wishes were obviously poor incentives. The same geographic pattern that encouraged dispersed settlement would also dictate the nature and extent of the urban settlements that eventually emerged amidst the farms. As the Chesapeake and Carolina regions settled into staple production patterns, which abundant land and accommodating soil made possible by 1700, towns developed to service staple agriculture at various levels. The type of staple agriculture in turn determined the type of urban settlement.

The connection between staple production and urbanization was apparent with tobacco, the leafy monarch of the Chesapeake. The weed's popularity in Europe was such that as early as the 1620s tobacco grew in the streets of Jamestown, the forlorn first town of the Virginia colony. The marketing demands of the crop complemented the Chesapeake's geographic condition. Tobacco marketing in the colonial era did not require intermediaries. When the tobacco fleet arrived from England in October and November, the planter simply packed his crop into hogsheads (roughly four hundred pounds each) and rolled them to the nearest dock (frequently his own) where he bargained with the captain for the price.

By the early eighteenth century, however, Europeans had developed a discriminating taste for tobacco that required more quality control at the colonial end of the trade. Also, tobacco cultivation had become so extensive that the individual deals struck between captain and planter were becoming less feasible if the ships were not to remain in the colonies most of the fall and winter. Perhaps most important, the tobacco trade had become big business by the 1700s. London and Liverpool merchants were not content to entrust their profit margins to itinerant captains or refractory planters, so they sent agents to the Chesapeake to establish bases of operations to end the uncertainties of the traveling tobacco show.

The result in town building from these initiatives was quite small. Geography again limited what might have been an urban boom under the new arrangements, because the continued availability of good cropland, especially in Virginia, restricted population in the towns. Moreover, the numerous estuaries and rivers that dotted the Chesapeake made communication difficult if a traveler's or a cargo's destination was not along the same river. [...]

But urban Chesapeake was to get new life in the 1740s with the introduction of a new agriculture. The decline of tobacco prices and the increased food demands in Europe encouraged the cultivation of wheat in certain areas of the Chesapeake colonies. The marketing of wheat, unlike tobacco, required several procedures that could be conducted best in central locations, *i.e.*, towns, and the processing and subsequent storage requirements of the crop facilitated the growth of larger urban settlements. Baltimore was a direct beneficiary of wheat cultivation, being able to tap the wheatfields of Pennsylvania and western Maryland. In the Piedmont and Valley regions of Virginia, where farmers began to shift to grains, Richmond, Fredericksburg, and Staunton grew as wheat markets to supplement an unstable tobacco trade. Whereas the tobacco trade had rarely sustained towns of more than three hundred residents, the wheat trade succeeded in building cities like Baltimore that exceeded six thousand people by the time of the Revolution. In the 1780s, tobacco regained profits and favor in southern and eastern Maryland and in Virginia, so these areas remained over-whelmingly rural.

The interaction between geography, staple cultivation, and urban development was equally apparent further south, where the string of pearls on the Atlantic thinned out considerably. There was Norfolk, a struggling little seaport of six hundred persons in 1775, existing as a rendezvous for the British navy and by the grace of royal commercial regulations. Williamsburg also appeared on the map, but despite its importance as a colonial capital, it could never generate more than two hundred permanent residents, and the only trading of importance conducted in Williamsburg was of a political nature. That Williamsburg achieved a reputation beyond its meager numbers is a tribute to the people who occasionally visited there to pass laws and swat mosquitoes and to its unique town plan, which introduced Baroque civic design to the New World.

The city, planned by Theodorick Bland, provided an excellent interplay between government buildings and street layout. The linear pattern featured one major thoroughfare—Duke of Gloucester Street—along which were located the major structures and activities of the community. At one end of the street, at the College of William and Mary, the linear pattern broke off into branches, a common Baroque device. However, Bland's interesting plan was insufficient to sustain a population, and only latter-day tourism has rescued the community from weeds.

Williamsburg was an interesting but insignificant (in terms of urban development) knot on the strand, and there was virtually nothing to fill the strand in the neighboring colony of North Carolina. The hazardous shoals of the Outer Banks precluded the emergence of an important seaport, and the small ports, more administrative than trading centers, like Edenton, New Bern (the colonial capital), and Wilmington served only their immediate hinterlands in the fertile coastal plain, much as the small Chesapeake tobacco ports did. Geography more than crop cultivation accounted for the colony's urban anemia. The navigable rivers flowing into backcountry North Carolina emptied into South Carolina, so the lumber and wheat cultivation that characterized interior North Carolina ultimately benefited the urban growth of Charleston.

Charleston was the major southern colonial urban center, with a population of ten thousand by the time of the Revolution. Its development reflected the history of crop cultivation and geography in the Carolina region. The city's early growth resulted from the deerskin trade, which demanded extensive storage facilities and produced sufficient capital to enable the city to become an important credit center as well, moving beyond the level of simple marketing functions. With this foundation, as well as an extensive commercial network in the backcountry, Charleston merchants helped to develop the rice, slave, and lumber trades that generated relatively rapid urban growth after 1730. When England allowed South Carolinians to export rice directly to southern Europe in that year, Charleston merchants reaped the benefits. Rice, like wheat, required extensive marketing, storage, and processing facilities. Finally, as the hub of rice cultivation, Charleston was also the leading slave market in the colonial South. The human cargo provided additional capital for its merchants, which in turn enhanced the city's influence as a credit center.

Rice cultivation spun a culture of its own in Charleston. City and country merged in the Carolina capital. The rice planters, some of whom had begun their careers in Charleston and all of whom had economic ties to the city, built comfortable townhouses of brick or cypress and yellow pine to complement their spacious country homes. Indeed, some interesting architectural forms appeared late in the colonial period as the planters attempted to duplicate the comfort and privacy of their plantation homes on a city lot. The result was a home with narrow street frontage and the ubiquitous porch or veranda extending back on the side of the long lot. These lots were sufficiently deep for servants' quarters, stables, a kitchen, and the usual garden. The symmetrical, well-proportioned exterior design of the houses and the hand-carved woodwork and paneled rooms in their interiors reflected the influence of the Georgian architecture then popular in England. As a combination urban plantation home and Georgian townhouse, the Charleston residence of the rice planter was a home away from home in more ways than one.

Charleston was a seasonal residence. Its life beat to an agricultural rhythm—vibrant in the winter months, languid during the rest of the year except for a few months in late summer when the "sickly season" in the low country brought planters and their families to the city. The activities during the winter season swirled about the planters in a perpetual round of balls, theater performances, dinner parties, and concerts. It was as if these sometime city residents were absorbing all of the social life they could to last them through the isolation of the growing season, when there would not be another white family for miles. [...]

Recalling the strand of pearls along the coast, it is perhaps easy to forget that urban civilization penetrated the interior forests of colonial America and in some instances would rival coastal counterparts in the nineteenth century.

Backcountry Carolina settlement began unpretentiously as military garrisons in the early eighteenth century. The forts soon expanded their security functions to supply soldiers and frontier traders. They were also convenient collection points for the important deerskin trade to Charleston. Here too, the nature of the deerskin trade—the need for storage and processing facilities—stimulated urban growth. After the 1730s when the deerskin trade declined in importance, these backcountry towns easily shifted to marketing wheat, hemp, and indigo to Charleston merchants.

Charleston entrepreneurs did not wait for backcountry resources to pour into their laps, however. After years of organizing the deerskin and later the rice commerce, they learned that organization meant efficiency. They nurtured the frontier outposts and lined their own pockets with the profits.

Camden, South Carolina, located 125 miles northwest of Charleston along a major trade road to the backcountry deerskin commerce, was one such Charleston protégé. Charleston merchants sent agents to the interior town, much as London merchants sent representatives to the Chesapeake tobacco towns, to serve as formal links between coast and backcountry and to ensure an orderly, steady flow of commerce in both directions. By the 1740s, Camden had transcended its initial function as a collecting point to engage in some minor industry. When the transformation of the backcountry from trapping to farming resulted in wheat cultivation in the Camden area, merchants in Camden erected mills to process wheat, which they then shipped to Charleston.

The growth of Camden reflected the growth of functions. No longer an appendage of Charleston, it was becoming an urban settlement in its own right with the development of backcountry agriculture. The town boasted a sawmill, a circuit court, a warehouse, two meetinghouses, a jail, and some fine residences. Commercial, industrial, and administrative functions had transformed the backwoods outpost into a full-fledged trading partner with Charleston.

The Camden experience was repeated throughout the colonial South wherever a primary coastal center, linked to the interior by roads or rivers, helped to build commercial bases in the backcountry. In Virginia, communities like Alexandria, Norfolk, Richmond, and Petersburg, located at the heads of river navigation, were no rivals to imperial Charleston, but they too stimulated interior development in such towns as Dumfries and Colchester, downriver from Alexandria, and Leedstown and Hobbes Hole, down the Rappahannock from Fredericksburg.

Here, in outposts of fifty to one hundred citizens, the line between rural and urban was surely blurred—a characteristic of a frontier society. Frequently, these types of communities began as mere extensions of a plantation where an enterprising planter had established a gristmill, some warehouses, and a country store for the benefit of neighbors and the profit of himself. In fact, descriptions of larger plantations, especially those in the Carolina low country, read much like accounts of small towns. One such plantation, not atypical, included a dairy, a large gristmill, a sawmill, and a store stocked with the latest inventory from Charleston. The clearing in the forest, the farm with a gristmill and a store shared characteristics of both urban and rural environments, but were neither.

By the 1750s, however, a remarkable wave of immigration to the Carolina backcountry established and expanded previously marginal settlements into full-fledged urban places with their economic livelihood firmly grounded with the farmers in the surrounding countryside. During the 1750s, settlers from western Pennsylvania and Virginia streamed into back-country Carolina attracted by land and the security against Indian attack. Immigration increased during the 1760s to include an ethnic mix that still characterizes these backcountry areas today. The German and Swiss settled in already-existing outposts such as New Windsor and Saxa Gotha; the Scotch-Irish in Ninety-Six and the Waxhaws; and the Welsh Baptists,

Irish Quakers, and French Huguenots in similar interior settlements, giving the backcountry a unique international flavor.

The development of Saxa Gotha indicated the vagaries of backcountry urbanization. The town was one of Governor Johnson's frontier settlements of the 1730s, but it languished until some seventy Swiss families moved there in the 1740s, and soon a church and school appeared as landmarks of civilization. The town's location on a river that penetrated further into the backcountry led to the establishment of a gristmill once farmers began cultivating the surrounding region. Charleston merchants also established their interests in the town by the 1760s, and inns, warehouses, and homes soon filled out the growing community. By that time, the story of Saxa Gotha was similar to the evolution of Camden, though on a much smaller scale. [...]

The diligence of Charleston merchants in establishing commercial links to the interior received additional inspiration when a rival city appeared on the strand to the south of the Carolina port. Savannah was indeed a gem of the ocean. At least, that is what its imaginative mentor, James Oglethorpe, had in mind when he planned the city in 1733. The outlines of his good sense can still be seen in the tree-lined streets and periodic interruptions of parks and rest places. Well into the nineteenth century, Savannah was one of the few cities in the country that provided sufficient open spaces for its citizens.

The same ideas that influenced the Carolina proprietors and South Carolina's Robert Johnson affected Oglethorpe: the belief in the importance of urban settlement, yet the recognition that rural features were necessary to temper the urban landscape. In Oglethorpe's view, the city and the country could be mutually reinforcing environments. The result—a middle landscape—would integrate the best from both worlds. Oglethorpe grew up with a generation that was beginning to see the problems of concentrated urban settlement. Indeed, a half century before Savannah appeared on the Georgia coast, William Penn had designed Philadelphia as a "green garden town" with spacious lots, an orderly gridiron street pattern, and five squares that served as America's first public parks.

Oglethorpe was aware of Penn's plan—Savannah copied the Philadelphia gridiron street pattern—and sought to improve upon it. The city was constructed of building-block units, or wards, each of which contained ten or a dozen house lots with an open square at the center. Since the city controlled surrounding lands, the expansion of Savannah could be easily regulated with the simple addition of wards as the need arose. This allowed for considerable expansion without the formless sprawl that was already evident in Philadelphia. In order to provide food for the community and to inject pastoral activities and values in the urban milieu, Oglethorpe surrounded the city with garden plots and larger farms. [...]

As both city and countryside developed, the idea of the urban farmer became less plausible. The collection of plots and farms into larger units and the permanent residence of citizens either on the farm or in the city were becoming more common by the time of the Revolution. The city itself, however, with its relatively slow growth, was able to preserve the basic features of the "green garden town" plan, the disappearance of which had so frustrated William Penn.

English settlers were not the only southern colonists who appreciated the middle landscape ideal. The French in their European communities had compromised urban and rural life-styles. The wide avenues and formal gardens that were characteristic of urban planning during the reign of Louis XIV, as well as the smaller, less formal squares, were simultaneous attempts at the elegant and the pastoral. The French influence in the colonial South was confined to the Gulf Coast, an area that remained of only peripheral concern to the empire. After the establishment of Mobile in 1710, the French embarked on their most ambitious scheme in the area with the founding of New Orleans in 1722 by Jean Baptiste Le Moyne, sieur de Bienville. He held lofty aspirations for the city at the Mississippi delta. He intended a great capital, and his plan reflected these intentions. The focal point of Bienville's city was the *place d'armes*, a formal open ground now called Jackson Square. The formal *place*, a common French planning device at the time, was centered perfectly on the river and dominated by St. Louis Cathedral. Later, government buildings and apartments of wealthy and prominent citizens joined the church on the *place*. Architecture historian Christopher Tunnard has called this grouping "the most important architectural plaza in the United States."

New Orleans did not achieve the hoped-for grandeur. The siting of the town may have been militarily efficacious, but for almost every other purpose it was unfortunate. Settlers constantly battled floods, tropical diseases, and virtual isolation from other settlements. The potentially rich farmlands in the area were hardly worked, so the city's economic potential went largely unfulfilled during the colonial period. Still, as early as 1727, there were nearly one thousand people in this mainly administrative and military outpost. By the late eighteenth century, Americans were arriving in significant numbers, bringing with them more aggressive business methods and staple-crop cultivation.

The isolation of New Orleans, though extreme, was not unique to that city. By the time of the American Revolution, urban civilization existed in the colonial South, but certainly not in an integrated urban network or a well-defined urban system with a distinctive hierarchy of urban places. Transportation, whether by roads or rivers, was problematic and seasonal. The type of steady reciprocal commercial flow characteristic of an urban network was missing in certain areas. Indeed, in some regions, towns of any size were missing. All settlements were small, with the exceptions of Charleston and New Orleans, and limitations on size implied limitations of functions that would preclude the evolution of an urban hierarchy. The frontier environment, in addition, was too unstable to support an urban network. Settlements were founded and frequently disappeared. Finally, the metropolis or primary city so necessary for the development of any system was absent. [...]

The pattern of urbanization in the colonial South was similar to urban development in feudal Europe, which is not surprising considering the primitive surroundings and the lower-order economic activities. That pattern was decentralized, revolving around relatively parochial economies. The pattern reached an extreme in the Chesapeake, where geographic configurations produced a new economic region every ten miles or so. The towns of Virginia and Maryland, though in the same geographic area, probably had more communication with London than they had with each other. [...]

The evolution of the urban South during the colonial period went through three general periods. During the seventeenth century, urban development was slight. The abundance of fertile land, the limited nature of staple-crop cultivation, and geographic patterns counteracted the directives and intentions of royal officials. The first half of the eighteenth century was the seedbed for sustained urban development in the colonial South. Staple cultivation burgeoned—wheat and rice production in particular—and increased manipulations by England's merchants and legislators stimulated urban growth. Finally, beginning in the 1740s, the establishment of Charleston as the colonial South's most important city, the growth of backcountry towns and cultivation, and the links between coast and frontier marked the third stage of urban development.

Urbanization throughout much of the period, though, was insignificant—indeed all of colonial America remained overwhelmingly rural up to and considerably beyond the Revolution. Yet the colonial period is a crucial era for southern urbanization because the themes that characterized the distinctive development of the South's cities up to the present first appeared at that time.

To begin with, whatever direction southern urbanization would take in the post-Revolutionary era, it seemed evident that the peculiar characteristics of the region—its geography, climate, and crop cultivation, for some major examples—would mold the character of its cities. If the region were distinctive, so would its cities be distinctive. The colonial era had demonstrated that within the same colonial empire, very different patterns could emerge.

Second, a biracial society was emerging. Certainly, blacks, both free and slave, resided in areas outside the colonial South. The black population was greater in the South, however, and here staple-crop agriculture, particularly such labor-intensive crops as tobacco and rice, encouraged the use of black labor. The abundance of land—and large tracts of it—made the use of gang labor feasible and efficient. In a colonial society where labor was scarce, the African provided an excellent adaptation to soil, climate, and geography. Such a fixed capital investment ensured adherence to staple agriculture.

Slavery, however, was an urban institution as well. In the colonial era, when the line between slavery and freedom was unclear, the urban slave probably enjoyed more freedom than he would at any future time. Southern urban residents were just beginning to cope with the implications—legal and philosophical—of a biracial society by the time of the Revolution. [...]

The importance of the metropolis in determining the urban and economic future of a region was a third theme that first emerged in the colonial era. By the eighteenth century, the colonial administration in London had sufficient influence to enhance or inhibit urban growth in the American colonies. The power of legislation, especially commercial legislation, was understood in the colonies. Where possible, detrimental laws were avoided, but where this was not possible, oblivion and economic ruin were realistic concerns. This point was evident with all colonists, regardless of region, and more so in the cities where the economic stakes were highest. When avoidance was impossible, or when threatening measures seemed imminent, revolution was the alternative. Of course, the origin of the American Revolution was not as simple as that. But the colonists' long experience with the real and potential power of the metropolis was a crucial factor in fomenting revolutionary sentiment once that power was used in an adverse way.

The metropolis could affect urbanization

in more subtle ways as well. Capital accumulation and consequently credit were constant problems in colonial economic life, and some colonies resorted to inflationary paper money to "solve" the difficulties of inadequate capital. The absence of banks in the colonial economy threw the responsibility of capital accumulation and credit upon urban merchants and planter-merchants. The system worked adequately in Charleston, for example, but ultimately the reins of capital were held in London. The coastal financiers were typically middlemen in the credit network. In fact, some planters dealt directly with London capitalists, bypassing local lenders. London had the banks, controlled the specie circulation (chronically short in the colonies), and therefore had as much influence on economic growth as the colonial financiers. This situation merely describes a typical colonial condition. It was, nevertheless, a well-remembered legacy of the colonial era. Banking, in fact, was a dominant issue during the first half century of national existence.

These then were to become the persistent themes of southern urbanization: the influence of the rural landscape and especially of staple agriculture, the presence of a biracial society, and the impact of the metropolis. The same forces, of course, affected the entire region. And that is the point. In the next period of southern history, the antebellum era, southerners would capitalize on the first, accommodate themselves to the second, and fight the third. In the process, they would become increasingly set apart from the rest of the nation, and so would their cities.

DOCUMENTS FOR PART II

2-1. A MODEL OF CHRISTIAN CHARITY (1630)

John Winthrop

Source: Samuel Eliot Morison, ed., *Winthrop Papers*, Volume II, 1623–1630 (Boston: The Massachusetts Historical Society, 1931). Courtesy of the Massachusetts Historical Society, Boston, Massachusetts.

EDITORS' INTRODUCTION

In April 1630, the Reverend John Winthrop led a group of Puritans from England on eleven ships bound for the Massachusetts Bay Colony. Their goal was to create a model for how to reform and purify the Church of England. Prior to landing in Massachusetts, Winthrop delivered his famous "A Model of Christian Charity" sermon aboard the ship *Arbella* in which he reminded his fellow Puritans of the importance of their undertaking. Although the sermon revolved around the themes of justice and mercy, it is most remembered for Winthrop's concluding remarks where he draws from biblical verse (Matthew 5:14) in arguing that in their efforts in New England they will be as "a City upon a Hill" with the eyes of all people upon them. This theme has become one of the most influential and enduring self-reflections in all of American history and forms the underpinning for much of U.S. foreign policy.

Winthrop and his followers eventually settled on the Shawmut Peninsula in Massachusetts and renamed it Boston, after a town in Lincolnshire, England where many Puritans once lived. Boston was a covenanted community, composed of individuals in a special compact with one another and God. The Puritans adopted the town or township form of government, also transplanted from England, with a congregation of believers at the center. The Puritan form of settlement became the archetype American municipality, replicated with each generation throughout New England and portions of the Middle Atlantic and Midwest.

The following version of Winthrop's sermon is from a manuscript printed in the seventeenth century for mass circulation. The twentieth-century editors of the *Winthrop Papers*, who worked with the Massachusetts Historical Society (which included Samuel Eliot Morison and Arthur M. Schlesinger, Sr.), retained the original seventeenth-century spelling, grammar, and inconsistent capitalization, and supplemented it with select biblical references in the citations. The contemporary reader will note the common inversion of the letters "u" and "v" in certain words, the use of "c" instead of "t" and the addition of the letter "e" in several places.

A MODELL OF CHRISTIAN CHARITY

Written

On Boarde the Arrabella

On the Attlantick Ocean.

By the Honorable JOHN WINTHROP, Esquire.

In His passage, (with the great Company of Religious people, of which Christian Tribes he was the Brave Leader and famous Governor;) from the Island of Great Brittaine, to New-England in the North America.

Anno 1630.

CHRISTIAN CHARITIE.
A MODELL HEREOF.

God Almightie in his most holy and wise providence hath soe disposed of the Condicion of mankinde, as in all times some must be rich and some poore, some highe and eminent in power and dignitie; others meane and in subieccion.

THE REASON HEREOF.

I. REAS: *First*, to hold conformity with the rest of his workes, being delighted to shewe forthe the glory of his wisdome in the variety and differance of the Creatures and the glory of his power, in ordering all these differences for the preservacion and good of the whole, and the glory of his greatnes that as it is in the glory of princes to haue many officers, soe this great King will haue many Stewards counting himselfe more honoured in dispenceing his guifts to man by man, then if hee did it by his owne immediate hand.

2. REAS: *Secondly*, That he might haue the more occasion to manifest the worke of his Spirit: first, vpon the wicked in moderateing and restraineing them: soe that the riche and mighty should not eate vpp the poore, nor the poore, and dispised rise vpp against theire superiours, and shake off theire yoake; 2ly in the regenerate in exerciseing his graces in them, as in the greate ones, theire loue mercy, gentlenes, temperance etc., in the poore and inferiour sorte, theire faithe patience, obedience etc:

3. REAS: *Thirdly*, That every man might haue need of other, and from hence they might be all knitt more nearly together in the Bond of brotherly affeccion: from hence it appeares plainely that noe man is made more honourable then another or more wealthy etc., out of any perticuler and singular respect to himselfe but for the glory of his Creator and the Common good of the Creature, Man... There are two rules whereby wee are to walke one toward another: JUSTICE and MERCY.
[...]

When God giues a speciall Commission he lookes to haue it stricktly obserued in every Article... Thus stands the cause betweene God and vs, wee are entered into Covenant with him for this worke, wee haue taken out a Commission, the Lord hath giuen vs leaue to drawe our owne Articles wee haue professed to enterprise these Accions vpon these and these ends, wee haue herevpon besought him of favour and blessing: Now if the Lord shall please to heare vs, and bring vs in peace to the place wee desire, then hath hee ratified this Covenant and sealed our Commission, [and] will expect a strickt performance of the Articles contained in it, but if wee shall neglect the observacion of these Articles which are the ends wee haue propounded, and dissembling with our God, shall fall to embrace this present world and prosecute our carnall intencions, seekeing great things for our selues and our posterity, the Lord will surely breake out in wrathe against vs be revenged of such a periured people and make vs knowe the price of the breache of such a Covenant.

Now the onely way to avoyde this shipwracke and to provide for our posterity is to followe the Counsell of Micah, to doe Justly, to loue mercy, to walke humbly with our God,[1] for this end, wee must be knitt together in this worke as one man, wee must entertaine each other in brotherly Affeccion... wee shall finde that the God of Israell is among us, when tenn of vs shall be able to resist a thousand of our enemies, when hee shall make vs a prayse and glory, that men shall say of succeeding plantacions: the lord make it like that of New England: for wee must Consider that wee shall be as a Citty vpon a Hill,[2] the eies of all people are vppon vs; soe that if wee shall deale falsely with our god in this worke wee haue vndertaken and soe cause him to withdrawe his present help from vs, wee shall be made a story and a by-word through the world, wee shall open the mouthes of enemies to speake euill of the ways of god and all professours for Gods sake; wee shall shame the faces of many of gods worthy seruants, and cause theire prayers to be turned into Cursses vpon vs till wee be consumed out of the good land whether wee are goeing...

> Therefore lett vs choose life,
> that wee, and our Seede,
> may liue; by obeying his
> voyce, and cleaueing to him,
> for hee is our life, and
> our prosperity.

NOTES

1. Micah, vi. 8.
2. Matthew, v. 14.

2-2. PHILADELPHIA IN 1697

Benjamin Bullivant

Source: Benjamin Bullivant, *A Journall with Observations on my Travail from Boston in N.E. to N.Y. New Jersies & Philadelphia in Pennsylvania* A.D. 1697, as excerpted by Wayne Andrews, "The Travel Diary of Dr. Benjamin Bullivant," *New-York Historical Society Quarterly*, 60 (1) (1956): 69–71. Courtesy of the New-York Historical Society, New York, New York.

EDITORS' INTRODUCTION

William Penn founded Philadelphia in 1682 as a commercial port between the Delaware and Schuylkill Rivers for the new colony of Pennsylvania. Philadelphia and the colony as a whole grew quickly as large numbers of Quakers, Scotch-Irish, and German immigrants settled the region. In 1760, less than a century later, Philadelphia was the largest town in British North America and one of the largest urban areas in the entire British Empire except for London. William Penn laid out the streets of Philadelphia in a grid pattern that became a model for other cities as the colonies and later the United States expanded. **[See David Goldfield's essay "Pearls on the Coast and Lights in the Forest," and Richard Wade's essay "Urban Life in Western America, 1790–1830," in this part.]**

The following description of Philadelphia, made by Dr. Benjamin Bullivant just fifteen years after its founding, reflects the quick growth and vibrancy of the port. Bullivant, born in England, worked as a physician and apothecary. He also served as Attorney General under Royal Governor Edmund Andros during the short-lived Dominion of New England (1686–1689), which also included the provinces of New York, East Jersey, and West Jersey. Between June and August 1687, Bullivant traveled from Boston south to Newcastle (Delaware) and back, visiting and describing the principle port towns along the way. The excerpt below, edited by Dr. Wayne Andrews, retains its seventeenth-century spelling and grammar. Andrews served as the curator of manuscripts for the New-York Historical Society in 1956 and later Archives of American Art Professor at Wayne State University in Detroit from 1964 to 1983.

Philadelphia in Pensylvania is seated on Delaware River 150 myles from the Sea, it is now but 15 yeares since they begann to Build, and yet do all ready shew a very magnificent City. The Streetes are regularly layd out along the Delaware, & thwarting Into the Land, Broad, & even, Leadeing forth into smooth roades, that carry you into the Country, & at about 2 myles distance from ye River delaware, direct from the City, is another Large River, called Schuilkill beyond which some are building & this is the extent of ye City bounds to the Land from Delaware, and it is probable enough the Vacancy betwixt the 2 Rivers may in time be made into fayr streetes, & Joyned into one City as is designed & layed out by the Proprieto^r, & Surveyed [by] m^r Penn in his printed draught of ye City of Philadelphia which when fin-

ished, will be almost a square in forme. The Delaware is fresh & good water so are they^r pumps & wells, here is also sundry sort of fish, Sturgeon & flesh of all sorts plenty enough. There are some few large and stately dwellings of some eminent Merchants, But ordinarily theyr houses exceeded not our second rate buildings in London, and many Lower. But generally very pretty with posts In the streets as in London and shops after the English mode they have a market twice a week with butchers stalls, & Blocks, and a market Bell, Rung also att certain howres of the day by a woman to give the time of the day. Here is a very large, tall, Brick meeteing house for the quakers neare ye market place, & not fair distant a Neate little church for ye Ch of England, English fashion, handsomely pailed in, and a sufficient decent buryall place annexed to itt. Philadelphia hath somewhat upwards of 500 families dwelling now in itt, & very many Buildings goeing forw^d it seems allready to exceede most shire towns in England, it hath no fortifications, though very capable of it, (on ye River side) being so farr distant from ye sea, & mostly quakers they say it is not they^r practice to trust in carnall weapons & find by good usadge of the Indians they are a safeguard to them, & rather seeke shelter amongst the english than annoy them wth a warr being at a greate distance from all European enemies. I was presented at Philadelphia wth sundry Nosegayes of as large & beautifull flowers as are ordinarily in the London gardens. The gouuerno^r of this province is the Honb^le Coll Markham,[1] who lives in a small, but very Neate dwelling, and is a person of much Courtesie, and Learned, he hath his Lady with him, and some children. here is gathered the Black stone in which is found the Salamanders wool, so called because it will not burn, thought it may be spunn into thread for service.[2] Philadelphia hath the purest bread and strongest beere in America the Beefe, Veale & pork tollerable but short of England mutton & Lamb indifferent, but scarce at some times of ye yeare. Butter and cheese very good. They have two markets a weeke, wednesdays and Saturdays, and the most like an old England market of any in this part of the world, it is at this Instant very hott weather, which obliges people to go very thinly habited of the Negros & Indians I saw many quite naked, except what covered the Secrets of nature. Vessells of 500 tunns lay theyr sides to the wharfes, & unlode by theyr own takle. The Quakers are very generous in they^r Entertainments and furnish they^r houses very Neatly and stick not to give theyr daughters to men of the world, and indeed they are many of them prettey women, here are apples, peares, peaches, apricots, mulberries, & cherries in abundance. They pay little or no taxes of any Sort whatsoever nor any Customes or Excise have no militia, only a Night watch in Philadelphia, Justices & Constables County Courts, Provinciall Courts and assemblies.

NOTES

1. William Markham (c. 1635–1704/5), Lieutenant-Governor or Governor of the Province and the Lower Counties 1693–99.
2. Asbestos.

2-3. ENVISIONING GREAT AMERICAN INDIAN CITIES (1813)

Henry Marie Brackenridge

Source: *Transactions of the American Philosophical Society*, Vol. 1, New Series (1818): 151–159.

EDITORS' INTRODUCTION

Just east of St. Louis, Missouri, across the Mississippi River, are numerous earthen mounds that comprise the remains of the ancient American Indian city of Cahokia. At one time, more than 200 of these mounds or pyramids radiated twenty miles or so from the center of Cahokia, the largest such concentration in North America, with more than half arranged within a five-square-mile area around vast open plazas. During its height in the twelfth century (AD or CE), Cahokia was the center of an extensive Indian nation whose influence extended throughout the Mississippi and Missouri River Valleys as far north as the Dakotas, east to present-day New York and Florida and south and west to Mexico. Cahokia was the largest Native American city north of Mexico, with 10,000–20,000 or more people at its center, and another 30,000 or so in surrounding communities stretching out in a fifty mile radius. At its height, Cahokia was as large as the city of London and, until the rise of Philadelphia in the late eighteenth century, the largest city in the territory that would become the United States.

Cahokia had collapsed by the time of European exploration, leaving subsequent generations to speculate on the purpose of the mounds, their composition, and the people who built them. The following document is one such assessment from the writer Henry Marie Brackenridge (1786–1871), who presented his ideas to Thomas Jefferson (1743–1826) in the form of a letter written in 1813 and subsequently reprinted in several journals and magazines of that era. Brackenridge envisioned Cahokia (his original spelling of "Cohokia" and other words are retained in the document below) as part of a series of large ancient cities with populations exceeding those of his own day located throughout the Mississippi and Ohio River Valleys. Seeing this area through an urban lens was not uncommon in the early nineteenth century as Richard C. Wade illustrates in his essay, "Urban Life in Western America, 1790–1830" in this part. However, while many nineteenth-century settlers and investors envisioned an urban future, Brackenridge sought to stake out a past where ancient American cities and their inhabitants compared favorably to other civilizations of the ancient world and the celebrated Teocalli—or Mesoamerican pyramids—of Mexico.[i]

On The Population and Tumuli of the Aborigines of North America. In a letter from H.M. Brackenridge, Esq. to Thomas Jefferson.

Baton Rouge, July 25, 1813.

Sir,

From a knowledge that research into the history of the primitive inhabitants of America, is one of your favourite amusements, I take the liberty of making this communication. My attention to the subject, was first awakened on reading, when a boy, the observations contained in the "Notes on Virginia," and it has become, with me, a favourite theme of speculation. I often visited the mound, and other remains of Indian antiquity in the neighbourhood of Pittsburgh, my native town, attracted by a pleasing interest, of which I scarcely knew the cause, and afterwards read, and heard with delight, whatever related to these monuments of the first, or rather earlier, inhabitants of my native country. Since the year 1810 (without previously intending it) I have visited almost every thing of this kind, worthy of note on the Ohio and Mississippi; and from examination and reflection, something like hypothesis, has taken the place of the vague wanderings of fancy. The following is a sketch of the result of those observations.

I. Throughout...the valley of the Mississippi, there exist the traces of a population far beyond what this extensive and fertile portion of the continent, is supposed to have possessed: greater, perhaps, than could be supported of the present white inhabitants, even with careful agricultural practiced in the most populous parts of Europe.
[...]

II. In the valley of the Mississippi, there are discovered the traces of two distinct traces of people, periods of population, one much more ancient than the other. The traces of the last are the most numerous, but mark a population less advanced in civilization; in fact, they belong to the same race that existed in the country when the French and the English effected their settlement on this part of the continent.
[...]

III. The first and most ancient period, is marked by...extraordinary tumuli or mounds. I have reason to believe that their antiquity is great. The oldest Indians have no tradition as their authors, or the purpose, or which they were originally intended; yet they were formerly, I might also say instinctively, in the habit of using them for one of the purposes for which they were at first designed, to wit, as places of defence... These tumuli as well as the fortifications, are

---

i   For more on Cahokia, see Timothy R. Pauketat, *Cahokia: Ancient America's Great City on the Mississippi* (New York: Viking, the Penguin Library of American Indian History, 2009) and Bilonie Young and Melvin Fowler, *Cahokia: The Great Native American Metropolis* (Urbana, IL: University of Illinois Press, 2000).

to be found at the junction of all the considerable rivers, in the most eligible positions for towns, and in the most extensive bodies of fertile land. Their number exceeds, perhaps, *three thousand*; the smallest not less than twenty feet in height, and one hundred in diameter at the base. Their great number, and the astonishing size of some of them, may be regarded as furnishing, with other circumstances, evidence of their antiquity. I have been sometimes induced to think, that at the period when those mounds were constructed, there existed on the Mississippi, a population as numerous as that which once animated the borders of the Nile, or of the Euphrates, or of Mexico and Peru.

IV. The most numerous, as well as the most considerable of these remains, are found precisely in the part of the country where the traces of a numerous population might be looked for, to wit, from the mouth of the Ohio (on the east side of the Mississippi) to the Illinois river, and on the west side from the St. Francis to the Missouri. I am perfectly satisfied that cities similar to those of *ancient Mexico*, of several hundred thousand souls, have existed in this part of the country. Nearly opposite St. Louis there are the traces of two such cities, in the distance of five miles, on the bank of the Cohokia, which crosses the American bottom at this place. There are not less than one hundred mounds, in two different groups; one of the mounds falls little short of the Egyptian pyramid Mycerius… The following is an enumeration of the most considerable mounds on the Mississippi and on the Ohio; the greater part I examined myself with such attention as the short time I had to spare would permit.

1. At Great Creek, below Wheeling.
2. At Pittsburgh.
3. At Marietta.
4. At Cincinnati.
5. At New Madrid—one of them 350 feet diameter at the base.
6. Bois Brulie bottom, fifteen miles below St. Genevieve.
7. At St. Genevieve.
8. Mouth of the Marameck.
9. St. Louis—one with two stages, another with three.
10. Mouth of the Missouri.
11. On the Cohokia river—in two groups.
12. Twenty miles below—two groups also, but the mounds of a smaller size—on the back of a lake, formerly of the bed of the river.
13. Near Washington (M.T.) 146 feet in height.
14. At Baton Rouge, and on the bayou Manchac—one of the mounds near the lake is chiefly composed of shells—the inhabitants have taken away great quantities of these for the purpose of making lime.
15. The mound on Black River, of two stages, with a group around it.

At each of these places there are groups of mounds; and at each there probably existed a city. On the other considerable rivers which are tributaries to the Ohio and Mississippi, in Kentucky, Tennessee, state of Ohio, Indiana territory, &c. they are equally numerous. But the principle city and center of the population was between the Ohio, Mississippi, Missouri, and Illinois.
[…]
Such are the appearances of antiquity in the western country, which I consider as furnishing proof of an ancient and numerous population. The resemblance to those of New Spain would render probable the existence of the same arts and customs; perhaps of an intercourse. The distance from the large mound on Red River, to the nearest in New Spain, is not so great but that they might be considered as existing in the same country.
[…]
The antiquity of these mounds is certainly very great; this is not inferred from the growth of trees, which prove an antiquity of a few centuries, but from this simple reflection; a people capable of works requiring so much labour, must be numerous, and if numerous, somewhat advanced in the arts; we might therefore look for works of stone or brick, the traces of which would remain for at least eight or ten centuries. The great mound of Cohokia, is evidently constructed with as much regularity as any of the Teocalli of New

Spain, and was doubtless cased with brick or stone, and crowned with buildings; but of these no traces remain… Some might be startled if I should say that the mound of Cohokia is as ancient as those of Egypt! The Mexicans possessed but imperfect traditions of the construction of their Teocalli; their traditions attributed to the Toultees, or to the Olmess, who probably migrated from the Mississippi.

Who will pretend to speak with certainty as to the antiquity of America—the races of men who have flourished and disappeared—of the thousand revolutions, which, like other parts of the globe, it has undergone? The philosophers of Europe, with a narrowness and selfishness of the mind, have endeavoured to deprecate everything which relates to it. They have called it the *New World*, as though its formation was posterior to the rest of the habitable globe. As few facts suffice it to repel this idea:—the antiquity of her mountains, the remains of volcanoes, the alluvial tracts, the wearing away of cataracts, &c. and the number of primitive languages, greater perhaps than in all the rest of the world besides.

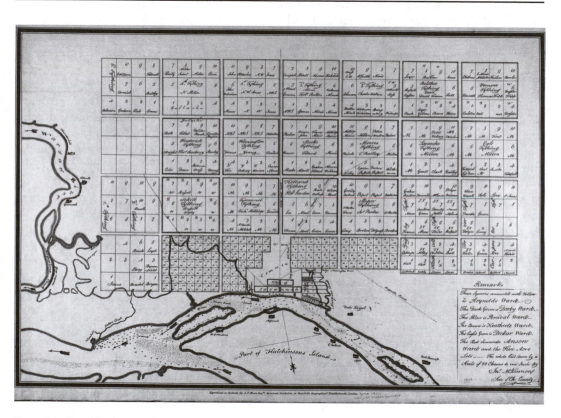

Figure 2.1 City of Savannah, Georgia (circa 1800). Source: Courtesy of the Hargrett Rare Book and Manuscript Library/University of Georgia Libraries.

General James Oglethorpe and 112 other colonists founded the city of Savannah, Georgia on February 12, 1733. Oglethorpe envisioned the colony of Georgia as a haven for British debtors and persecuted Protestants in continental Europe. He established Savannah as the colonial capital and laid it out in a gridiron pattern modeled after Philadelphia, with residential lots in groups of ten to twelve, often with a trust lot for public buildings. Each ward featured an open square in the center. The pattern was easily expandable and by the middle of the nineteenth century, there were twenty-four squares in the city. This rare map by John McKinnon details the development of the city's squares circa 1800.

Figure 2.2 "A View of Part of the Town of Boston, in New-England and Brittish Ships of War: Landing Their Troops! 1768." Source: Clarence S. Brigham, *Paul Revere's Engravings* (Worcester: American Antiquarian Society, 1954). Courtesy of the Center for Historic American Visual Culture at the Antiquarian Society.

Paul Revere (1734–1818) was a noted silversmith and patriot during the American Revolution. He was also an engraver who established a successful printmaking business that won acclaim for the depiction of political events, such as the Boston Massacre of March 1770. The engraving above portrays the landing of British troops on the Long Wharf in Boston on October 1, 1768. In addition to the military presence, the engraving shows a city crowded around its economic lifeline, the harbor, dominated by churches and mixed use residential and commercial buildings.

VIEW OF NEW ORLEANS.

Figure 2.3 "View of New Orleans Taken from the Lower Cotton Press" (circa 1850–1855). Source: Bernhard Dandorf, "View of New Orleans Taken from Lower Cotton Press," (Louis Schwarz, Publisher, circa 1851–1855). Courtesy of the Center for Historic American Visual Culture at the American Antiquarian Society.

The French founded New Orleans in May 1718 and named it after Phillippe II, duc d'Orleans and regent of France. Spain took over in 1762 and it remained in their hands until 1801 when the French resumed control before selling it to the United States in 1803. The export of southern cotton helped make New Orleans the fourth largest port in the world by 1840. During the 1850s, German lithographer Bernhard Dandorf (1809–1902) made this print of commercial activity along on the Mississippi River (the modern-day Press Street area). Cotton presses used steam power to pack cotton into bales for shipment to northern and European factories.

THE NEW CITY

Industry and Immigrants, 1820s–1920s

EDITORS' INTRODUCTION TO PART III

The history of the United States is intertwined with industry and immigration. Both are central to the nation's story. From the start, the "New World" offered a home to Europeans fleeing the ravages of war and economic upheaval. The First Industrial Revolution, born in Great Britain, soon took root in New England, where the fledgling nation's first factories were established. Entrepreneurs understood the implications of turning from human and animal power to water energy and fossil fuels to produce goods on a larger scale. Samuel Slater's Pawtucket, Rhode Island, mill, established in 1793, was a small operation, but its existence heralded a marked change in the American (and eventually the world) economy. Elsewhere in New England, such as on the banks of the Merrimack and the Connecticut Rivers, far-sighted businessmen established extensive manufacturing facilities. This industrial model spread to the Middle Atlantic states, the Midwest, and eventually the South. Right away, however, increased production had noticeable effects on the landscape as illustrated by John T. Cumbler's essay, "From Milling to Manufacturing: From Villages to Mill Towns" in this part. The public's desire for machine-made goods increased the demand for supplemental labor, fueling migration from the countryside and immigration from overseas. Demographic change and industrial growth brought environmental challenges and enhanced local markets for American merchandise.

Conditions in American cities were far from ideal. As immigration grew, housing failed to keep up with demand and conditions deteriorated. Many Americans lived in poverty generation after generation. As Christine Stansell demonstrates in her essay, "Women in the Neighborhoods," women carved out their own worlds within the city as part of a cash-and-barter economy of necessity that swirled about the teeming tenements. Castle Garden and Ellis Island were immigration processing centers in New York City that channeled millions of newcomers into the country. Frederick M. Binder and David M. Reimers explore this story in their essay, "Old and New Immigrants in Greater New York City, 1880 to World War I." The backgrounds of the masses disembarking from the ships in New York's harbor changed markedly over time. Beginning in the late nineteenth century, more and more immigrants heralded from Eastern and Southern Europe. Fewer were of Protestant stock. Could the United States absorb an unlimited number of immigrants?

Increased diversity challenged Americans. Thousands flocked to join the American Protective Association, founded in 1887 and focused on limiting the number of Catholics entering the United States, and the Immigration Restriction League, founded in 1894. Many Republican political leaders, fueled by the strong anti-immigrant leanings of their constituents, promoted literacy tests for all newcomers, as well as physical examinations for immigrants traveling to America in the least-expensive steerage cabins of ships.

The Chinese found themselves in the center of the anti-immigrant debate, particularly on the country's west coast, where they were more numerous. The Chinese Exclusion Act of 1882 cut off most of the immigration from China; all Asian immigration was reduced by law until late in the twentieth century. These debates are covered in **Document 3.4,** in which Senator Aaron Sargent of California and an anonymous defender of Chinese immigration present arguments for and against restrictions. The case of the Chinese demonstrates how American immigration fears were heightened with racial difference. Although a very small minority, the Chinese sojourners soon experienced a thunderous wave of discrimination. Economic and cultural exclusion limited immigrants from China to niche labor opportunities and isolated Chinatowns into ethnic islands, as discussed by Ronald T. Takaki in his essay for this part. Japanese immigrants went through similar trials, faced with the exclusionary Gentlemen's Agreement of 1908, and the subsequent Ladies' Agreement of 1922, which ended the immigration of Japanese wives (many of them the well-known picture brides) to join husbands in the United States.

It is important to note that slavery existed in cities as well as plantations, and in the North as well as the South. In **Document 3.1,** the Vesey Slave Revolt, Charleston, South Carolina (1822), we learn about the lengths that white Charlestonians would go to maintain order in their city. Having a large enslaved population created myriad tensions as we can see in **Document 3.2** on the Tredegar and Armory Iron Works in Richmond, Virginia (1847), where ironwork owners attempted to have free whites work alongside black slaves.

Anti-immigration sentiment and discomfort over changing economic realities also played out in nineteenth-century cities. In Louisville, Kentucky (1855), German and Irish immigrants struggled for the right to vote, and conflict with the native-born population erupted in street violence as demonstrated in **Document 3.3.** The popularity of Jacob Riis' *How The Other Half Lives* (1890) demonstrates the centrality of the immigrant question for the nation. The social and ethnic diversity of immigration is reflected in **Document 3.5,** which is a chapter from Riis' landmark book. As Carl Smith's essay, "The Pullman Strike and Making Sense of the Age," reveals, in 1894 Chicago exploded into chaos when the Pullman Palace Car Company owner George Pullman failed to reduce rents in his model town when he slashed employee wages. Finally, **Document 3.6** illustrates the harsh and unsafe working conditions of sweatshops, in this case New York City's Triangle Shirtwaist Company. The Triangle Shirtwaist Fire of 1911, in which approximately 146 workers lost their lives, was the symbol of an age, and encouraged greater oversight and improvement of working conditions.

From Milling to Manufacturing: From Villages to Mill Towns

John T. Cumbler

Source: *Reasonable Use: The People, the Environment, and the State, New England, 1790–1930* (New York: Oxford University Press, 2001).

EDITORS' INTRODUCTION

Historian John T. Cumbler blends environmental, labor, and urban history in this essay. Enormous changes occurred in the United States when investors began to establish industrial firms in the late 1790s. America's first industrial revolution followed the trend towards mechanization, which had started in England. The physical landscape was irrevocably changed by the early factories, which rerouted waterways to power their machines, created dams, spilled industrial waste into the water, the soil, and the skies, and drew thousands of workers to live near the factories, so they could show up for work on time every day. As Cumbler explains here, small rural localities were transformed into industrial villages, and ultimately, cities.

These changes were not entirely unwelcomed; weary farmers were looking for a more reliable way to make a living. The highly rocky and undulating landscape of New England proved no match for the richer soils of New York State and points further west. Women and children, seeking to supplement the incomes of their families, peopled the very first factories. Increasingly, men joined them, and ultimately immigrants came to America specifically to secure jobs in U.S. industry. The move away from the family farm—a move that ultimately left just 2 percent of Americans making their living from farming in the twentieth century—began the movement of manpower into industrial plants.

Cumbler bases his narrative in the Connecticut River Valley. The Connecticut River, the largest river in New England, flows predominantly southward through New Hampshire, Vermont, Massachusetts, and Connecticut. Other industrial firms had flowered in Rhode Island and eastern Massachusetts, along the Blackstone River Valley and its tributaries, and very well-known corporations located slightly later along the Merrimack River, flowing through Waltham and Lowell. Given the fledgling America's strained relations with its former colonial power, Great Britain, and the embargo with England initiated by President Thomas Jefferson in 1807–1809, and the ravages of the War of 1812, forward-thinking Americans turned their unreliable agricultural economy into one focused on industrial products. The business progress was not always resolute; after the War of 1812 and resumption of trading relations with Great Britain, many small mills collapsed. Other firms bought out struggling businesses and buttressed their trade, growing even more profitable.

While industry brought needed jobs to displaced farmers, it wrought terrible damage on the surrounding landscape. The changes were quickly noticeable. Trees were cleared for the establishment of larger towns, used to frame new factories, utilized to erect new dwellings for the burgeoning workforce, and burned for heat. Industrial waste poured into the environment, joined by the exponential growth of human refuse and waste from the increased population. Not everyone was forward-thinking enough to imagine what further damage continued industrialization and urban growth would do to the landscape. Those who were, Cumbler argues, evolved into the very first environmental activists.

John T. Cumbler is a professor of history at the University of Louisville. He is the author of numerous works, including, *Working-Class Community in Industrial America: Work, Leisure, and Struggle in Two Industrial Cities, 1880–1930* (Westport, CT: Greenwood Press, 1979), *A Social History of Economic Decline: Business, Politics, and Work in Trenton* (New Brunswick: Rutgers University Press, 1989), *Northeast and Midwest United States: An Environmental History* (Santa Barbara: ABC-CLIO, 2005), and *From Abolition to Rights for All: The Making of a Reform Community in the Nineteenth Century* (Philadelphia: University of Pennsylvania Press, 2008). In addition, Cumbler served as the John Adams' Distinguished Fulbright Professor in the Netherlands.

FROM MILLING TO MANUFACTURING

From Villages to Mill Towns

The new world of New England was one of factories and factory towns, as well as farms and forests. It was a world where farmers, looking to those factory towns for markets, plowed their fields deep and intensively managed their land. It was a world where lumbermen stripped mountainsides of their forest cover to meet the cities' growing appetite for lumber. It was a world of managed and controlled nature.[1] It was also a world of rapid change, and increasingly after 1800, the force behind that change was the coming of the manufacturing mills.

Levi Shepard's 1788 duck-cloth factory was of a different type than the traditional mills of New England. Although mills that spun or fulled cloth had long been part of rural New England, Levi Shepard had a different market in mind when he encouraged local farmers to bring him their flax. Shepard wanted to take material from the countryside and, with the help of "workers employed," "manufacture" it into a commodity for sale.[2] Shepard's decision to focus on manufacturing for distant markets represented a new world.[3]

Mills and Manufacturing

Manufacturing in rural New England began small. It grew out of, while at the same time it transformed, traditional rural society. The processing of goods of the countryside was an integral part of traditional New England life, whether in 1650 or 1800. In 1790, the *Hampshire Gazette* commented that although "a large quantity of woollen cloth are made in private families and brought to market in our trading towns, a great part of [the woollen cloth] is not calculated for market."[4]

The shift from milling produce for local use to manufacturing occurred initially for most of rural New England with the shift of small traders, merchants, and millers from processing for local farmers to processing for external markets.[5] Edmund Taylor of Williamsburg on the Mill River, for example, at the turn of the century added carding and picking machines to his gristmill. As he did for grain, Taylor processed the material from the countryside, keeping a portion of it as his pay. Once established, Taylor added a cotton textile factory to his enterprises, using the surplus water from his gristmill.[6]

The Bellows Falls Company of Vermont, besides running a country store, was using waterpower to run "wool carding machines" for local farmers. Like many other traditional millers and country store owners who dammed up a stream and put in a waterwheel to run a sawmill, gristmill, fulling mill, or even carding machines, the Bellows Falls Company processed produce for the local community. Customers brought to the mill products of their farm, which they had processed at the mill and then took home with them. Although the Bellows Falls Company may have kept some of the wool it carded and shipped it into the stream of commerce flowing out of the valley, the local community saw the mill's primary function as processing products for the valley's residents.[7]

In the early years of the nineteenth century, manufacturing in New England underwent a radical transformation and in doing so began the first stage of the long and complicated process of industrializing the New England countryside. When Thomas Jefferson imposed an embargo on goods coming into and going out of the United States through the War of 1812, imported manufactured goods became scarce in America. Shopkeepers and traders who found that they could no longer get finished cloth or paper began to look at the old gristmill and sawmill sites with new eyes. In 1808, Job Cotton took over Joseph Burnell's sawmill on the Mill River and brought in cotton textile spinning machines. On the Chicopee River, the Chapin brothers—William, Levi, and Joseph—built a small mill that by 1810 had two carding machines, a drawing frame, and two short spinning frames "of very rude construction." The Chapins employed eight to ten workers, who produced yarn that was put out to local women to weave. The workers had no regular payday. The company exchanged yarn and cloth at the local stores, and those it employed had credit at the stores.[8] By the time war broke out in 1812, old mill sites throughout New England were being converted into textile mills.[9] Anticipating increased demand for manufactured woolens, Stephen Cook in 1815 replaced his gristmill with a woolen manufactory, and Isaac Biglow made plans to build a cotton factory of five thousand spindles beside his gristmill.[10]

Peace with England in 1815 brought not only an end of war and of war orders for cotton and wool but also a flood of English manufactured goods to the American market. Most of the small cotton mills went under in the ensuing years. Job Cotton's mill closed its doors and stood idle, and Isaac Biglow never used his cotton factory as intended but outfitted it instead to make paper.[11] The years following the peace brought the first real depression to inland New England since Shays's rebellion. The depression may have closed Job Cotton's mill, but it did not return the valley to its more traditional past.

Although the general depression in the postwar years wiped out most of the small manufacturing operations, the better-capitalized mills with big dams, overshot waterwheels, and newer machinery weathered the depression and continued to grow. The new large dams and multistory factory buildings that utilized heavy, powered machinery to turn out woven cotton and woolen cloth needed wooden beams and flooring, machines, belts, and pulleys, candles and paper.

As New England began to manufacture goods for far-off markets, the very manufacturing process itself began consuming massive amounts of the region's resources and generated more manufacturing. Manufacturing needed machinery, and increasingly that machinery was locally produced. These mills not only gathered up massive amounts of waterpower and resources, they also gathered up hundreds and even thousands of people into new industrial cities, taking in food and water and disposing of waste.

Manufacturing along the Connecticut River Valley

At the turn of the nineteenth century, traveler Timothy Dwight noted that mill streams everywhere were giving rise to an "unusual number of works erected for various manufacturing purposes, powder, paper, glass, etc."[12] Another Dwight, Theodore, noted in 1830 that indeed New England's gristmills had given over "within a few years [to] manufactures." "On the road up the Connecticut River ... everyone must be struck with the size and number of the manufacturers which have been multiplied and magnified to such an extent all over the country."[13]

Most of these early manufacturing mills were located on small rivers and tributaries. Over the century, as engineering skill improved, technology developed, and more capital became available, manufacturers had the ability to capture more power from the larger rivers. As they did so, they moved to the falls of water on the region's great rivers. Around these falls grew industrial towns, then cities. These cities in turn reached out into the countryside, pulling more and more of it into their grasp. Included in the resources needed was water. And the Connecticut River had vast amounts of water.

Manufacturing along the southern Connecticut River Valley began early. Already by 1830, Middletown's "various manufacturers carried on with success," while Hartford had thriving paper, iron, and brass works as well as an established armaments industry. In the nineteenth century, tinware producers in Berlin, Connecticut, expanded to include brassware and hardware, and this metal-working industry spread to towns up and down the valleys between Middletown and Hartford.[14] On the west side of the river at Windsor Locks, paper mills and silk mills were built, while at Enfield, carpet making became a major industry.[15]

By the nineteenth century, Springfield's industry, led by the U.S. Armory, grew to be a crucial part of the town's activity. G. and C. Merriam bought the copyright to Noah Webster's dictionary and began to manufacture the nation's best-known reference book. Across the Connecticut River in West Springfield, along the tributary Westfield River, large-scale tannery factories transformed tanning into a huge enterprise consuming massive amounts of tree bark. The Clark Carriage and Wagon shops and several new cotton and woolen factories in Agawam village all employed large numbers of hands. The region's expanded manufacturing demanded factories and homes. New circular sawmills were built to cut lumber coming downriver. Unlike the older sawmills, these new mills were large-scale operations with dozens of workers constantly at work cutting and sawing. North of Springfield on the east side of the Connecticut, a number of manufacturing enterprises rose up along its tributary the Chicopee River. Ironworks triggered Chicopee's rise as a manufacturing center. During the early years of the century, a number of small cotton mills opened for carding and spinning cotton, although most did not survive the depression of 1816. In 1825, through the intervention of Edmund Dwight, Boston's textile investors (known to historians as the Boston Associates) began to take an interest in the waterpower of the Chicopee River.[16] The Chicopee was dammed, and the first of

the huge multistory textile mills and attendant boardinghouses were built. More mills soon followed, so that by the end of the 1830s, Chicopee had four major textile manufacturing companies that employed hundreds of workers.[17] Edmund Dwight also persuaded Nathan Ames to move his edge-tool manufacturing company to Chicopee. Ames's company prospered, and in 1845, with his connections to Dwight, Ames bought up the local machine shops and began to produce textile machines as well.[18] Upriver in Palmer, the Thorndike Manufacturing Company, again the product of Boston investment, in 1837 built a gigantic stone mill that soon employed 450 workers producing cotton ticks, denims, and stripes.[19]

At Bellows Falls, Vermont, Bill Blake obtained waterpower rights in 1802 from the Company Rendering the Connecticut River Navigable by Bellows Falls and built a paper mill there, rebuilding it in 1812. He built still another paper mill in 1814 in Wells River, Vermont. Blake's mills proved successful, and soon he had teams throughout Vermont and New Hampshire buying up rags for his paper mills, which were turning out paper for sale around the country.[20]

On the outskirts of Springfield, John Ames built an extensive paper-making factory in the early 1820s that employed dozens of local workers to cut and sort rags and work the new multistage, water-powered paper-making machines. In 1827, another Ames, David, took over a small one-vat, three-hand, screw-press paper company in Chicopee and expanded it into a major manufacturing enterprise, introducing power-driven paper-making machinery and exporting paper out of the region. By the 1840s, towns up and down the valley were turning out paper for books, newspapers, stationery, envelopes, wrapping, and collars.

Factories grew up along tributaries to the Connecticut. In the 1830s, wing dams on either side of the river north of Springfield at Hadley Falls provided power for a series of traditional mills, along with the newer cotton and woolen mills. With an initial investment of $50,000, a group of Springfield and Enfield investors formed the Hadley Falls Company in 1827 in order to build a large cotton textile mill powered by water brought in by a wing dam. By 1832, the company was running 2,700 spindles and employing forty-six women, "daughters of local farmers," and twenty-three men.[21]

North of the falls at Hadley, the tributary Mill River had a number of silk manufacturing companies, which briefly encouraged local farmers to grow mulberry trees to feed the silk worms.[22] Farther north, cotton textile and woolen factories sprang up at Bellows Falls, along with Blake's paper mills, while at Lebanon, New Hampshire, woodworking shops and factories produced tools, furniture, and agricultural implements from lumber harvested from local forests. Between 1810 and 1850, manufacturing mills, machine shops, and woodworks multiplied along the rivers and streams running into the Connecticut.[23] At Franconia, New Hampshire, a significant ironworks developed.[24] By the middle of the nineteenth century, blacksmith shops and iron foundries had shifted to waterpower for operating bellows and, in the foundries, for milling iron casting. With this shift, more ironworks were located on waterpower sites.

The expansion of sheep raising in Vermont and New Hampshire provided wool for the expanding woolen factories sprouting up around the falls of almost every northern New England river.[25] At Hartford, Vermont, Albert Dewey dammed the falls of the Quechee River and began woolen manufacturing, producing 450 yards daily.[26] Dewey's factory on the Quechee was only one of many that sprang up in northern New England in the thirty years after the War of 1812 to take wool from the region's farmers.[27] In 1811, Colonel James Shepherd opened a small woolen factory on the Mills River, where spinning and weaving was done by hand. By 1818, Shepherd had expanded and installed power spinning mules and weaving machines. By the end of the 1820s, the company was converting fleece from Shepherd's and his neighbors' large flocks of sheep into broadcloth, which was then sold throughout the country.[28]

Factories and Farms

Factories transformed the land around them from farms and fields to other factories, tenements, roads, and canals. As they produced goods for export, they also became import centers themselves, not only of food and lumber but also of people. The mills and their machines needed operatives, who came from many of those same hills that furnished the lumber for the mills.

These manufacturing and commercial centers were surrounded by commercial farmers, while poor country cousins abandoned or scraped by on overworked hill-country farms. Where once there were villages with teachers, doctors, ministers, traders, merchants, artisans, clerks, and lawyers, all with their own gardens, cows, pigs, and chickens, now there were cities with hundreds of operatives and tradespeople, very few of whom could afford the time or had the space to raise their own food. The food that fed the growing cities of New England came from the region's farms, but these were very different farms from those of the eighteenth century. New England's cities took the farm produce from farmers who specialized in feeding urban people.[29] The milk, cheese, butter, and vegetables that poured into the cities to feed the operatives came from farmers who specialized in dairy products or commercial garden vegetables.[30] In 1846, for example, Jesse Chickering noted one of the changes that had occurred in Massachusetts agriculture: The "dense state of the population in the villages" had given rise to an "increase ... of vegetables raised, such as potatoes, apples for eating, garden vegetables, and fruit."[31] New England farmers had always raised fruits and vegetables, but increasingly, nineteenth-century farmers focused their activity on perishable market produce, and the markets for that produce were local.[32] In a midcentury promotional bulletin, the Hadley Falls Company noted that "the position of a city in the midst of the splendid farms and fruitful meadows of the Connecticut Valley would be highly favorable for obtaining supplies; and the existence of such a market for their produce would be greatly beneficial to the interests, and stimulating to the industry, of the people of that part of the state engaged in agriculture."[33] As the *Hampshire Gazette* recognized in 1831, farms around the new industrial centers prospered when they shifted to sending food to feed the workers gathered to work in the mills. "Go view the manufacturing villages," it urged, "go and view the farms which surround them ... see the universal prosperity which reigns there."[34] [...]

Forests and Factories

In addition to the produce from the surrounding countryside, the factory towns also consumed acres and acres of the region's forests. Hills and mountains far up the valley yielded up their forests so that dams, mills, and tenements could be built and heated, and tools and furniture could be fabricated.[35] To encourage manufacturers to build mills at their dam site, the Hadley Falls Company used a report detailing the wealth of available lumber from the valley's northern forests. The company noted in its promotional report that "there is not likely to be any lack of building materials at Holyoke. Lumber is brought greater or lesser distances down the Connecticut River from the forests on its banks."[36]

As the mills and mill towns grew in number and size, lumber floated in ever increasing volume down from the hills and mountains of Vermont and New Hampshire. The combination of burning and cutting forest land to clear farms and cutting timber for construction and fuel meant the baring of northern New England's valleys, hills, and mountains. Between 1820 and 1860, Massachusetts and Vermont went from over 60 percent forest covered to just over 40 percent, while New Hampshire went from over 60 percent to less than 50 percent.[37] [...]

Increasingly after the 1870s, New England's railroads turned to coal for fuel, and after midcentury, homes and industry in the region's cities did so too. The burning of coal eased the demand for cordwood while it increased air pollution. But the burning of coal did not end the pressure on the region's forests. It was not until the 1870s that New

Hampshire's forest area stopped declining, while Vermont continued to lose forests until 1880, when only 35 percent of the state was forested.[38] [...]

On July 24, 1882, Theodore Lyman—a wealthy Boston Brahmin, Civil War veteran, Harvard Overseer, amateur scientist, Massachusetts commissioner of fisheries, and independent Mugwump candidate for Congress—in answer to a question about protective tariffs, quoted his father, who had been mayor of Boston in the 1830s. "My father use to say very truly as long as New England was overlaid by ten feet of gravel, she would have to manufacture or starve." Lyman went on to say that New England had "an extraordinary amount of manufactures and of the greatest variety.... I can hardly believe my eyes such is the enormous growth." "What would Massachusetts be like" without its industry? Lyman wondered. "You would see no mills and no dams, nothing but a few grist mills here and there and houses whose occupants raised such crops as they could from the scanty soil."[39] Of course, before the massive manufacturing establishments arrived, Massachusetts had both dams and mills, but by the 1880s, New Englanders could scarcely imagine a world without industrial enterprises; when they did, some of them viewed it as empty and miserly.

NOTES

1. Although developmental economists have argued that traditionalist farmers were more destructive to the environment than were market-oriented farmers who used more modern agricultural techniques, it is a mistake to overcredit market-oriented farmers as being more environmentally sensitive because of their long-term economic interests. Individually, traditionalists as well as market-oriented farmers may have acted in ways that were destructive to the environment. See Carolyn Merchant, *Ecological Revolutions: Nature, Gender, and Science in New England* (Chapel Hill, 1989), 154–156. See also Donald Worster, *The Dust Bowl: The Southern Plains in the 1930s* (Oxford, 1979).
2. See Christopher Clark, *The Roots of Rural Capitalism: Western Massachusetts, 1780–1860* (Ithaca, 1990). See also Timothy Dwight, *Travels Through New England and New York* (Cambridge, 1969), 4:348.

3. Although Levi Shepard represented a new focus in the valley, employing labor to manufacture goods for distant markets, his technology was very familiar. Shepard built his factory at the back of his home lot. All the machinery was worked by hand, with a boy or girl hired to turn the wheel, yet Shepard's market was not local.

4. *Hampshire Gazette*, Sept. 29, 1790.

5. See Jonathan Prude, *The Coming of Industrial Order: A Study of Town and Factory Life In Rural Massachusetts, 1813–1860* (Cambridge, 1983), for an example of the impact of mills on the surrounding countryside.

6. Charles J. Dean, "The Mills of Mill River," manuscript, 1935, Forbes Library, Northampton, MA, 21.

7. Besides carding, fulling, sawing, and grinding, some local millers were also manufacturing tools for local farmers. Rufus Hyde and his sons built a mill dam to power a trip-hammer. The Hydes used the trip-hammer to hammer out axes and scythes. They also used the waterwheel to turn their grindstones that sharpened axes sold to local farmers. Ibid., 23.

8. Vera Shlakman, *Economic History of a Factory Town: A Study of Chicopee, Massachusetts, Smith College Studies in History*, vol. 20, nos. 1–4 (Northampton, 1934–1935), 22.

9. Dean, "Mills of Mill River," 30–33.

10. *Stephan Cook v. William Hull* (Oct. 1825), MA Reports, Pickering, 3:269; *Isaac Biglow and Others v. Mellen Battle and Others* (Oct. 1818), MA Reports, Tyng, 15:313.

11. *Biglow v. Battle*, Dean, "Mills of Mill River," 30, 31.

12. Dwight, *Travels*, 2:197, 4:342, and 4:343–346.

13. Theodore Dwight, *Notes of a Northern Traveler* (Hartford, 1831), 97, 831.

14. Ibid., 94; Dwight, *Travels*, 2:195; Alexander Johnson, *Connecticut: A Study of a Commonwealth-Democracy* (Boston, 1895), 357, 358, 363.

15. Edwin M. Bacon, *The Connecticut River and the Valley of the Connecticut: Three Hundred and Fifty Miles from Mountain to Sea, Historical and Descriptive* (New York, 1906), 430.

16. Edmund Dwight's family had been merchants and investors in the early canal projects along the Connecticut. Edmund, married to an Eliot, moved to Boston in 1816 and joined the inner circle of wealthy Bostonians just expanding into investments in textile production. See Shlakman, *Economic History*, 27–47.

17. By 1841, Chicopee had the Chicopee, Cabot, Perkins, and Dwight manufacturing corporations, employing 2,500 hands. The town also had a number of skilled workers in the Belcher Iron Works and the Ames Manufacturing Company, which produced metal tools, cutlery, knives, and swords. Shlakman, *Economic History*, 25–36; see also Bacon, *Connecticut River*, 423.

18. Shlakman, *Economic History*, 27.

19. Will L. Clark, ed., *Western Massachusetts: A History, 1636–1925* (New York, 1926), 2:946, 947, 971.

20. Lyman S. Hayes, *The Connecticut River Valley in Southern Vermont and New Hampshire: Historical Sketches* (Rutland, 1929), 290, 292, 293. See R. H. Clapperton, *The Paper Making Machine: Its Invention, Evolution, and Development* (Oxford, 1967).

21. Robert Bennett, "The Roots of the Holyoke Water Power Company" (Holyoke, 1985) manuscript, Holyoke Public Library, 2:7.

22. Silk manufacturing continued in several towns along the central and lower valleys. Bacon, *Connecticut River*, 418. Dean, "Mills of Mill River," 54–58.

23. Harold Wilson, *The Hill Country of Northern New England: Its Social and Economic History* (New York, 1967), 145.

24. On the Franconia ironworks, see Jerold Wikoff, *The Upper Valley: An Illustrated Tour along the Connecticut River before the Twentieth Century* (Chelsea, VT, 1985), 118, 119, 120; Dwight, *Travels*, 4:117. On the locating of ironworks on water-power sites, see *Paul Sibley and another v. Thomas Hoar and another* (Oct. 1855) MA Reports, Gray 4:222.

25. There were almost a million and a half sheep in Vermont and over a half million in New Hampshire by the 1830s.

26. Wikoff, *Upper Valley*, 123.

27. Margaret Richards Pabst, "Agricultural Trends in the Connecticut Valley Region of Massachusetts, 1800–1900," *Smith College Studies in History*, vol. 26, nos. 1–4 (Northampton, Oct. 1940–July 1941), 53, 54. A history of Ryegate, Vermont, at the turn of the century noted that "before 1850 woolen mills could be found in [many of northern Vermont's towns]." Quoted in Wilson, *Hill Country*, 45.

28. Dean, "Mills of Mill River," 33.

29. Valley farmers continued to raise wheat and grains, but their relative importance to the region's agriculture declined after 1840, with production itself declining after 1850. Dairy products jumped in value over the first half of the nineteenth century. Pabst, *Agricultural Trends*, 54. This shift to perishable vegetables, fruits, and dairy products was encouraged after the opening up of the Erie Canal and the penetration into New England and New England's traditional markets of staple agricultural goods—particularly grain—from central New York and the upper Midwest.

30. The impact on gender roles of the shift of vegetables and dairy products from home use to market produce is an area of research that needs more work. Carolyn Merchant's *Ecological Revolutions* explores some of these issues.

31. Quoted in Pabst, *Agricultural Trends*, 53.

32. In 1885, when Massachusetts took a census of its agricultural products, it found that for farm communities around the industrial centers, dairy

products followed by garden vegetables accounted for the majority of farm income. Hampton County had a total of $175,571 in meats and game, $234,264 in cereals, $302,426 in vegetables, $950,208 in dairy, and $126,021 in poultry. Hampshire County had a total of $210,689 in meats and game, $228,341 in cereals, $266,978 in vegetables, $1,050,825 in dairy (mostly milk), and $111,843 in poultry. The produce of individual towns reflected a dramatic shift toward dairy, mostly milk, and toward vegetables, particularly cabbage, potatoes, and squashes, and to a lesser extent toward poultry. State of Massachusetts Bureau of Labor Statistics, *Census of Massachusetts, 1885, vol. 3, Agricultural Products and Property* (Boston, 1887), 568, 569, 570, 571, 216–294 (hereafter, *MBLS, Census*).

33. Hadley Falls Company, "Report of the History and Present Condition of the Hadley Falls Company at Holyoke, MA," 1853, manuscript, Holyoke Public Library, 19 (hereafter, "Hadley Falls Company Report").

34. Quoted in Pabst, *Agricultural Trends*, 26.

35. By midcentury, New Hampshire was sending almost 20 million feet of timber down the river. Wikoff, *Upper Valley*, 64; Dwight, *Travels*, 2:72; Roland Harper, "Changes in the Forest Area of New England In Three Centuries," *Journal of Forestry* 16 (Apr. 1918): 443,449. At Hartland, Vermont, David Summer erected extensive lumber mills and sent cut lumber downriver to Massachu-

setts and Connecticut towns, where he had lumber yards to store and sell his product. Hayes, *Connecticut River Valley*, 41.

36. "Hadley Falls Company Report" 20.

37. Harper, "Changes in the Forest Area," 447. Increasingly after 1840, railroads began consuming massive amounts of the region's lumber both for construction and for fuel. In 1846, G. B. Emerson in his classic report to the State of Massachusetts on its trees and shrubs noted that the 560 miles of railroad in the state were consuming 53,710 cords of wood annually. "Hadley Falls Company Report," 449.

38. Vermont's forests dropped from 60 to 45 percent of the state's land area between 1820 and 1850 and to 35 percent by 1880. Harper, "Changes in the Forest Area," 449; See *Henry Irvine v. Daniel Stone* (Nov. 1850) MA Reports, Cushing, 6:508, for a case involving bringing coal to Boston to be used as a heating fuel. The cost of shipping coal from Philadelphia, where it was brought in from the mines northwest of the city, to Boston was $3.75 a ton for stove coal plus $735 freight for 202 tons of coal. At these prices, coal soon became competitive with northern cord wood. By midcentury, most New England cities had coal yards that sold to local businesses. *Commonwealth v George E. Mann* (Oct. 1855) MA Reports, Grey, 4:212.

39. *Boston Herald*, July 22, 1882; Lyman Scrapbooks.

Women in the Neighborhoods

Christine Stansell

Source: *City of Women: Sex and Class in New York,
1789–1860* (New York: Knopf, 1986).

EDITORS' INTRODUCTION

This selection, drawn from the two opening chapters of Christine Stansell's ground-breaking work, *City of Women*, introduced readers to the history of urban women. Stansell examines the world of working-class New York City between the late 1700s and the Civil War, concluding that women, while subject to the pressures of their low economic status and a patriarchal culture, were far from victims. In contrast to New Englanders, who turned to large-scale factories when farming faltered, New Yorkers relied on commercial ports, expanding national and international trade, and entrepreneurship for its economy. The highly organized craft system established in colonial New York City eroded in the face of the pressures of the world market and left many families without assurance of an adequate living. Small production houses were hurt by increased competition and low-priced, factory-produced goods. The erstwhile artisans lost the opportunity for advancement with this reduced need for highly trained workers. Middle class families foundered, and more women needed to contribute to their household incomes in order to make ends meet.

Stansell's book makes innovative arguments that established a common starting point for the scholars who study urban women. She makes a keen observation regarding the lack of privacy in these women's lives; so many of their daily tasks—and the tasks of their children—took them outside of their own dwellings. Women and children did the work that modern urban residents pay their utility companies to perform today. Women and children brought in water to their households, gathered wood for cooking, and purchased or scavenged coal to warm their lodgings. Women contributed in a monetary way to their households by working outside the home for wages, caring for boarders, or producing goods out of raw supplies brought to their homes by middlemen. This latter practice, known as "outwork," constituted a popular choice, although caring for children and performing household chores while trying to keep up with the time demands of outwork proved daunting. The urban women might also pawn household goods for ready cash, or sell homemade food or even alcohol. The women moved easily in and out of their neighbors' apartments, and claimed the stoops of their tenements as their own by their constant presence there. While men were slightly more obvious to city visitors, with their regular business taking them frequently into the streets, Stansell has demonstrated a public female realm, which formed, quite literally, a city of women. Urban women were not invisible, they were simply overlooked by many academics prior to the publication of this important study.

Stansell, a former professor at Princeton University, is the Stein-Freiler Distinguished Service Professor at the University of Chicago. She is the author of *Powers of Desire: The Politics of Sexuality* (co-authored with Ann Snitow and Sharon Thompson, New York: Monthly Review Press, 1983) and *American Moderns: Bohemian New York and the Creation of a New Century* (New York: Henry Holt, 2000), Stansell served as a Radcliffe Institute Fellow 2006–2007. She contributes regularly to the *New Republic*.

WOMEN IN THE NEIGHBORHOODS

By the 1820s, men and women of the urban bourgeoisie were coming to see households as more than just lodgings. The "home," their own term for the domestic setting, had become for them a pillar of civilization, an incubator of morals and family affections, a critical alternative to the harsh and competitive world of trade and politics. The home was based on a particular configuration of family members: woman at home, man at work, children under maternal supervision or at school. In its psychological form, it embodied the emotional self-sufficiency of the conjugal family and the suitability of women to private life; as a material setting, it elaborated the physical elements of the household into an embellished inner space cut off from the public world.[1]

In this sense, the home was absent from the lives of urban laboring women, who observed no sharp distinctions between public and private. Rather, their domestic lives spread out to the hallways of their tenements, to adjoining apartments and to the streets below. Household work involved them constantly with the milieu outside their own four walls; lodgers, neighbors, peddlers and shopkeepers figured as prominently in their domestic routines and dramas as did husbands and children. It was in the urban neighborhoods, not the home, that the identity of working-class wives and mothers was rooted. [...]

The particular kind of urban neighborhood which so disturbed civic-minded bourgeois New Yorkers was different from earlier forms. One new element was the extensive community of women that developed within the transient and disruptive circumstances of urban migration. Of course, the most visible inhabitants of the neighborhoods were men. They were the preponderance of drunken brawlers and street loungers and the most noticeable workers, as they trudged to and from the docks or labored at the open doors of the craft shops that dotted the streets. Another, less noticeable round of female activity, however, went on around this masculine sphere, a cycle of pinching and saving, of cleaning and borrowing and lending, of taking—and of being taken. With unremitting labor, wives, mothers and female neighbors kept the "tenement classes" going from day to day—whether stitching shirts for the clothing shops or bargaining down street peddlers. Out of the precarious situations into which immigration, poverty and (for many) the erosion of male support thrust them, women formed particular attachments to each other and to their children that made the neighborhoods important resources in the negotiations and battles of daily urban life.

Industrialization and Working-Class Formation

The residents of these gregarious neighborhoods helped to transform New York into what was, by 1860, the largest manufacturing city in America and the capital of the country's finance and commerce.[2] Its small workshops, stacked floor by floor in the new cast-iron warehouses that lined the narrow, crowded streets, were as important to America's Industrial Revolution as the better-known mills of New England. Between 1820 and 1860, the population quadrupled to over 800,000; the city's border moved a mile and a half north from City Hall to Forty-second Street. "How this city marches northward!" marveled diarist George Templeton Strong after a walk in 1850. "Wealth is rushing in upon us like a freshet."[3]

New York's spectacular rise began in the 1820s. The disruption of shipping in the war had seriously damaged the port, but recovery was steady, and by 1820 the maritime economy was sturdy and thriving. In the next few years, in a series of remarkable leaps, its merchants gained control of the American import/export economy. In 1825, the completion of the Erie Canal, the final step to preeminence, linked the city to the Great Lakes and secured its position as an entrepôt for the enormous hinterland the canal penetrated.[4] "Not a tree will be felled which does not necessarily operate to increase the trade and riches of New York," a contemporary observed in 1819.[5]

These commercial developments stimulated a phenomenal growth of the small manufacturing sector that had appeared in the 1790s. The opening of the Erie Canal, with its profitable possibilities for new inland markets, alerted many more craftsmen to the advantages of mass production and the entrepreneurial-minded began to expand their operations. The steady flow of people into the city allowed ambitious master craftsmen to restructure and enlarge their work forces and to cut labor costs by hiring unskilled and semiskilled immigrants and women as wage laborers rather than journey-men who had served regular apprenticeships. When skilled workers faced this competition they, too, accepted lowered wages and intermittent work.

The genius of the city's entrepreneurs, its favored situation in trade and, above all, its cheap labor brought about New York's Industrial Revolution. In contrast to the pattern usually associated with industrial development—the mechanization of work in factories—New York employers generally did not adopt new machines but rather incorporated handicraft workers into wage-labor arrangements. With the exception of a few trades where journeymen continued to craft custom goods for a luxury market, wage labor and its attendant insecurities came to affect most New York laboring people in the years after 1820. Metropolitan industrialization greatly reduced the chances that journeymen might own their own shops, and greatly enlarged the scale of proletarian dependency: the state in which workers own no means of a livelihood other than their own ability to labor. The distinction between skilled and unskilled, artisan and laborer had been meaningful in the eighteenth century when chances were good that a journeyman might in due time become a proprietor of his own shop. It became far less so in the nineteenth century, as craftsmen and laborers alike were pulled into the working class, and as proprietorship itself became a shaky business. [...]

Between 1820 and 1860, the working class became largely immigrant: English, German and (most of all) Irish. The foreign-born population soared from 18,000 in 1830 to more than 125,000 in 1845, a proportional increase from 9 percent of the city's residents to 35 percent; by 1855, the Irish accounted for 28 percent of New York's populace, the Germans for 16 percent.[6] Before 1846, the newcomers tended to be poor but not necessarily penniless: The Irish, for instance, were often Protestant farmers and skilled craftsmen from the North, although canal and railroad construction projects also drew thousands of Catholic peasants and cottiers who ended up as day laborers in the States. After the first crop failures of the potato famine in Ireland in 1845, however, distress became desperation, and Irish refugees began to arrive bereft of all but the clothes on their backs. Depression in the grain-exporting regions of northern Germany also sent a small, steady flow of poor German peasants into the tide of pauperized Irish. In 1855, an estimated three-quarters of the work force were immigrants.[7] [...]

A small black population also figured in the ranks of the working poor. Strictly speaking, slavery did not altogether end in New York until 1827. It had long been declining in the city, however, and beginning with the Revolution (when the British occupying the city had announced a general emancipation), the black community consisted primarily of freed men and women. As in other Northern cities, racial segregation was marked. Although blacks lived in pockets scattered throughout the whole city (a pattern of dispersal among whites that accounts for the frequency of interracial domestic feuds in the court records), they were often denied the use of public conveyances and almost always barred from working in the crafts. Black men worked as seamen, day laborers, waiters, barbers and whitewashers, generally in menial, ill-paid and casualized situations.[8]

The political economy of the city of women was distinct, although not unrelated to that of race, ethnicity and occupation. Family situations propelled women into the working class, and the relations of gender gave a distinct shape to the female experience of proletarianization. A woman's age, marital status, the number and age of her children and, above all, the presence or absence of male support determined her position in working-class life. Any woman, whether the wife of a prosperous artisan or a day laborer's daughter, was vulnerable to extreme poverty if, for some reason, she lost the support of a man. With the expansion of manufacturing employment after 1830, young single women might earn some kind of a living for themselves, but married women with children experienced the loss of men's wages, either through death or desertion, as devastating. The seasonal moves that men made to find work enhanced their women's vulnerability. Tramping artisans and migrant laborers could die on the road or take advantage of the moment to abandon their families, and even loyal husbands could find it hard to get news and money back to children and wives in New York. The frequency of occupationally related accidents and disease in men's employments contributed to a high rate of male mortality, which also left many women as the breadwinners for their families.[9] Men, too, suffered when their wives died or left them. The loss of women's housekeeping services, along with whatever income they contributed, created hardships for widowers and deserted husbands. Nonetheless, a woman's absence alone was not sufficient to imperil a husband's livelihood, while a wife cast on her own faced the specter of the Almshouse.

Domestic Labor in the Tenements

For all laboring women, native-born and immigrant, black and white, wives of skilled men and daughters of the unskilled, working-class life meant, first and foremost, the experience of living in the tenements. The tenements were remote from the middle-class home, and they were also different from the households of the urban laboring classes in the late eighteenth century. The difference was not in standards of living, although there has been great historical debate over whether the material conditions of the laboring classes improved or declined with industrial capitalism. Certainly, eighteenth-century New York, as compared to the nineteenth

century, was no golden age of prosperity for working people. What did distinguish the industrial metropolis from the eighteenth-century port was not the existence of poverty but rather its context and scale, as the uncertainties of wage work spread out from the lowest ranks of laborers to artisans accustomed to some measure of domestic security, and encompassed multitudes of immigrants who arrived each decade.

Women experienced this partly as a change in the nature of housekeeping. We have seen that after the Revolution urban domestic production had become the privilege of a minority of prosperous artisans' wives; after 1820 it virtually disappeared along with its symbols, the peripatetic pigs and cows who trotted about the streets. Even those women still prosperous enough to carry on household production, the wives of successful artisan entrepreneurs, largely abandoned it for commercial goods. Poorer women lacked the steady income, the space or the facilities to engage in household crafts. Another pattern took hold in the tenements, the catch-as-catch-can struggle to make ends meet. A ceaseless round of scraping, scrimping, borrowing and scavenging came in some measure to dominate the housekeeping of all working-class women.

Tenement life overrode distinctions between ethnic and occupational groups and played an important role in the creation of a metropolitan working-class culture. Tenements were one response to the acute housing shortage that began in New York with the surge in immigration in the 1820s and lasted unabated through the mid-1850s. Tenements differed from earlier housing for the poor in that they were constructed or refurbished specifically for multiple occupancy. Before 1850, landlords had generally subdivided existing buildings, usually single-family houses, into "reconstructed" tenements to accommodate more people and generate more rents[10]—"dilapidated, crazy old houses," one urban reformer called them.[11] Landlords rented out hives out hives of subdivided space, packing people into attics, outlying stables and sheds, and damp basements. In 1842, a public health survey found that more than 7,000 people lived in cellars, and by midcentury, the number had grown to 29,000.[12] The old wooden tenements stood for decades. The infamous Old Brewery, a five-story tenement in the heart of the Five Points, supposedly housed more than 1,000 people in its labyrinth of rooms, cellars, subcellars and hidden passageways.[13] Several families might occupy a large room; it was common for one family to crowd into a single room. In 1839, for instance, an evangelical tract distributor in lower Manhattan visited six families living in a garret. A sick woman lay on a few rags on the floor. "The place where she lay was so low that the shingles of the roof could be reached by the hand," he related.[14] In another tenement in 1845, a reporter for a *Tribune* series on labor found a shoemaker living with his family in a room in which a man could not fully stand. The furnishings were his workbench, a cradle made from a dry-goods box, one pan and a few broken chairs.[15]

In the early 1830s, a few speculators erected buildings specifically for occupancy by the poor. In the next decade, builders began to construct working-class tenements divided into standard units of space. Recalling the English model of workers' block housing, regimented lines of the bare brick buildings appeared in the upper reaches of the east side in the newly settled wards above Fourteenth Street. The typical apartment in a new tenement had a front room, which served as kitchen and parlor, and one or two sleeping cubicles, often windowless.[16] Even so, the new construction did not meet the demand: Lodgers and whole families doubled up in the back rooms, "space filtered from within working class neighborhoods," as Elizabeth Blackmar has put it.[17] Lodgings in the standardized tenements could be even worse than the odd-size crannies of the reconstructed tenements, since builders often erected tenements in the centers of blocks, nearly flush with the back walls of those that fronted the streets, thus blocking off light and air. The rear buildings themselves lacked direct light and cross-ventilation. Often adjoining the privies, the rear tenements were the recourse of the very poor and became the scenes of some of the worst horrors of metropolitan housing.[18]

In the worst tenements, there was little that went on that visitors from charitable organizations could recognize as housekeeping. The households of the poorest people—the day laborers, free blacks, underpaid craftworkers and single mothers who crowded into the back rooms of their neighbors and into basements and attics—were packed with people but bare of domestic effects. There was no furniture to speak of, few clothes to wash, little food to prepare. The reports of social investigators at midcentury described an overwhelming domestic inertness in the tenements. The poor "crowded beneath mouldering, water-rotted roofs, or burrowed among rats in clammy cellars," observed one; another exclaimed that tenement dwellers "exist almost comfortably in conditions which others of refinement would find intolerable."[19] The Irish seemed especially bad housekeepers: "accustomed in their own country to live like pigs, they can stow themselves away into all sorts of holes and corners, and live on refuse,"[20] noted a sardonic journalist. What such observers could not see was that despite the odds against them, most women, no matter how poor, took pride in neat and clean lodgings. Even the Irish, commented an English workingman with all the prejudices of his countrymen, were proud of their domestic amenities, their "'bits of carpits on their flures.'"[21] A well-swept hearth and scoured floor were symbols of self-esteem still within the reach of even the very poor: The *mise en scène* of many a charity visitor's account is a bare room where a woman or child is scrubbing the floor.

Slightly more prosperous working people were likely to win bourgeois encomiums as the "respectable" poor; especially if they approximated the family patterns of the prosperous: father at work, mother at home, children in some apprenticed position or at school. "Their habitations, though generally small and crowded, and in very unpleasant situations, nevertheless present the appearance of neatness and order, which widely distinguishes their occupants from the more wretched portion of society," a tract-distributing minister reported in 1834. "Their children are many of them decently clad and sent to school, and when they arrive at a suitable age, are generally apprenticed to some mechanical art."[22] Respectable families could maintain furnished interiors which also garnered the charity visitors' approval: chairs, bedsteads and icons of decency like clocks and prints on the wall.[23] [...]

What the charity visitors were unable to see was that keeping house in the tenements in any circumstances was hard work. Dirt and trouble abounded.[24] [...] For all the lack of substantial household effects, domestic labor in these tiny rooms absorbed the energies of women morning to night. The poorer the family, the heavier was woman's work. Cleaning was only a small part of complicated and arduous family economies. The major effort went into acquiring necessities—food, fuel and water—a task that took up hours of the day and entailed scores of errands out of the house. This work was by nature public, knitting together the household with the world of the streets. It generated its own intricate network of exchange among neighbours and between parents and children and created the material basis for a dense neighborhood life.

Women and children spent a great deal of time on work that, in the twentieth century, utilities would perform. Although by the 1840s the privileged classes were beginning to enjoy the first fruits of domestic technology—running water, piped gas and water closets—the tenements had no utilities.[25] Privies were in the back courts; light came from candles and kerosene lamps; water, from rain barrels, street-corner pumps and, for a fortunate few, sinks in downstairs hallways. New York completed its much-touted Croton water system in 1842, and gas was introduced in the early 1830s, but tenement landlords seldom went to the expense of piping either into their buildings; the few who purchased water only ran it to the first floor. The burden of "the almost entire absence of household conveniences" usually fell on young children not otherwise employed; like their peers in rural America and Ireland, they toted water up the stairs and hauled slops back down (less fastidious mothers tossed their slops right out the window). Children also ran the many errands required when there was never enough money in hand for the needs of the moment. Mothers sent them out to fetch a stick of wood for the fire, thread for their sewing, potatoes for dinner. Purchases were necessarily piecemeal, "by the small," and often on credit: one candle, an ounce of tea, three cents' worth of Godfrey's Cordial for a colicky baby.[26]

Children's street scavenging also produced objects for domestic use. Scavenging seems to have been a widespread practice among the laboring classes in the eighteenth century, but after 1820, those who could afford to probably began to desist from sending children out to the streets, since child scavengers were liable to be arrested for vagrancy, and the habit of mixing scavenging with petty theft and prostitution had become common. The poor, however, had no choice. For them, scavenging was an essential way to make ends meet, even if the chore might lead their children into thieving or illicit sex. Scavenging was the chore of those too young to earn income through wage work or street selling.

Six- or seven-year-olds were not too small to set out with friends and siblings to gather fuel for their mothers. Small platoons of children scoured the docks for food—tea, coffee, sugar and flour spilled from sacks, barrels and wagons. Streets, shipyards and lumberyards, building lots, demolished houses and the precincts of artisan shops and factories held chips, ashes, wood and coal to take home or peddle to neighbors.[27] As children grew more skilled, they learned how to pillage other odd corners of the city. "These gatherers of things lost on earth," a journalist called them in 1831. "These makers of something out of nothing."[28]

Street scavenging has probably been a practice of the urban poor for centuries, but this was a specifically nineteenth-century form, which depended on a demand for raw materials from an urban manufacturing system where commercial lines of supply were not fully in place. Besides taking trash home or peddling it to neighbors, children sold it to junk dealers, who in turn vended it to manufacturers and artisans to use in industrial processes. On the waterfront, children foraged for loose cotton, which had shredded off bales on the wharves where the Southern packet ships docked, as well as for shreds of canvas and rags; junk dealers bought the leavings and sold them to manufacturers of paper and shoddy (shoddy, the cheapest kind of cloth, made its way back to the poor in the form of "shoddy" ready-made clothing). Broken bits of hardware—nails, cogs and screws—went to iron and brass founders and coppersmiths to be melted down; bottles and bits of broken glass to glassmakers. Old rope was shredded and sold as oakum, a fiber used to caulk ships. The medium for these exchanges was a network of secondhand shops along the waterfront. In 1850, public authorities made some efforts to close down the junk trade, but police harassment seems to have had little effect. [...]

Pawning was also a feature of domestic work. Through pawning, women made use of less-needed goods in the service of procuring necessities. The traffic was especially heavy toward the end of the week, since rent was usually due on Saturday morning. "Sunday clothes are put in pawn during the week, and redeemed again on Saturday night" when wages were paid.[29] Clothes were the most common pledge—winter clothes in summer, extra clothes in winter, Sunday clothes any time. A substantial wardrobe was one edge against adversity. The pawning cycle functioned fairly smoothly as long as income was steady enough for a woman to redeem the possessions when she needed them—shoes, for instance, when the cold weather came. In hard times, however, women gave up absolute necessities, a sign a family was in trouble: pots, pans, bedding and treasures of respectability like watches, clocks and books. [...]

In the tenements, even laundry was a feature of public life, strung up high above the streets and alleys. The solitary housewife would not emerge within the urban working class until the late 1920s, when cheap utilities first became available in the tenements. In the first half of the nineteenth century, the boundaries between private and public life were fluid and permeable. Laboring women made their lives as wives and mothers on the streets as much as by their hearthsides.

NOTES

1. Cott, *Bonds of Womanhood*, pp. 63–100; Ryan, *Cradle of the Middle Class*, pp. 14–15.
2. Carl N. Degler, "Labor in the Economy and Politics of New York City, 1850–1860; A Study of the Impact of Early Industrialism" (Ph.D. diss., Columbia University, 1952), pp. 3–4.
3. *The Diary of George Templeton Strong*, ed. Allan Nevins and Milton Halsey Thomas, 4 vols. (New York, 1952), 2:24 (entry for October 27, 1850).
4. For discussions of economic change in the city, see Albion, *The Rise of New York Port*; David T. Gilchrist, ed., *The Growth of the Seaport Cities 1790–1815; Proceedings of a Conference Sponsored by the Eleutherian Mills-Hagley Foundation* (Charlottesville, Va., 1966); Ernst, *Immigrant Life*; Flick, *History of the State of New York*, 5:327–28.
5. John M. Duncan, *Travels Through Part of the United States*, 2 vols. (New York, 1823), 1:25.
6. Ernst, *Immigrant Life*, pp. 23, 192–93; Stott, "Worker in the Metropolis," pp. 54–60.
7. Another estimate places the number of foreign-born in the *nonclerical* work force at 85 percent in 1855. Stott, "Worker in the Metropolis," pp. 58–60.
8. On Germans, see Ernst, *Immigrant Life*, pp. 84–92. On blacks, see Leo H. Hirsch, Jr., "The Negro and New York, 1783 to 1865," *Journal of Negro History* 16 (October 1931): 382–473; Ottley and Weatherby, *The Negro in New York*, 1–91.
9. Richard Stott stresses that the city's male labor market was *regionally* based, thus necessitating that men travel frequently outside the city for work. "Worker in the Metropolis," p. 101. Contemporary testimony about the mobility of male laborers can be found in the Society for the Reformation of Juvenile Delinquents, *Fifteenth Annual Report* (New York, 1850), p. 9; Matthew Carey, "Essay on the Public Charities of Philadelphia," *Miscellaneous Essays* (Philadelphia, 1830), pp. 172–73.

   Both Sally Alexander in "Women's Work in Nineteenth Century London: A Study of the Years 1820–50," in *The Rights and Wrongs of Women*, ed. Juliet Mitchell and Ann Oakley (Harmondsworth, Eng., 1976), p. 80, and Barbara Taylor in *Eve and the New Jerusalem*, pp. 203, 244, 336, note the growing instability of male support among British laboring people. See also the general comments on the numbers of women in New York bereft of male support in the Association for the Asylum for Lying-In Women (AALW), *Sixth Annual Report* (New York, 1829) and Commissioner of the Almshouse, *Annual Report* (New York, 1847), p. 39. On male mortality see Carol Groneman Pernicone, "'The Bloody Ould Sixth': A Social Analysis of a New York City Working-Class Community in the Mid-Nineteenth Century" (Ph.D. diss., University of Rochester, 1973), p. 29.

10. The best account of tenement development is Blackmar, "Housing and Property Relations," pp. 169–492. Richard Stott points out that by 1864, 70 percent of New York's population lived in multiple family dwellings; in 1859, two-thirds of the city's families lived in buildings occupied by three or more other families. "Workers in the Metropolis," p. 305.

11. Association for the Improvement of the Condition of the Poor (AICP), *Fourteenth Annual Report* (New York, 1857), p. 18. Blackmar gives an interesting account of the evolution of multiple occupancy. "Housing and Property Relations," pp. 184–88.

12. City Inspector, *Annual Report of the interments ... in New York ... and a Brief View of the Sanitary Conditions of the City* (New York, 1843), p. 163; AICP, *Sixteenth Annual Report* (1859), p. 46; Ernst, *Immigrant Life*, p. 49.

13. A sensational account of the Old Brewery and similar tenements is in Herbert Asbury, *The Gangs of New York* (New York, 1927), pp. 12–17; the *Daily Tribune* (New York), June 19, 1850 contains a contemporary account. See also Groneman Pernicone, "The 'Bloody Ould Sixth,'" pp. 39–40.

14. New York City Tract Society (NYCTS), *Thirteenth Annual Report* (1839), p. 25.

15. *Daily Tribune*, September 9, 1845.

16. Blackmar, "Housing and Property Relations," pp. 436–37; Smith Rosenberg, *Religion and the Rise of the American City*, pp. 176–77.

17. Blackmar, "Re-Walking the 'Walking City': Housing and Property Relations in New York City, 1780–1840," *Radical History Review* 21 (Fall 1979): 131–48.

18. Ernst, *Immigrant Life*, pp. 49–51; Stokes Collection Typescript, passim, NYPL; New York Assembly, *Report*.

19. Ibid., p. 13; AICP (1862), quoted in Groneman Pernicone, "'The Bloody Ould Sixth,'" p. 15.

20. George C. Foster, *New York Naked* (New York, 1850), p. 118.

21. James Dawson Burn, *Three Years Among the Working Classes* (London, 1865), p. 15; see also Stott, "Worker in the Metropolis," pp. 313–14.

22. George B. Arnold, minister-at-large, in 1834, quoted in Stokes Collection Typescript, p. 593.

23. Catharine Maria Sedgwick describes the interior of a respectable artisan household where pawning had not taken its toll in *The Poor Rich Man, and the Rich Poor Man* (New York, 1839), p. 105, and in *Clarence; Or, a Tale of Our Own Times* (New York, 1849), p. 320. See also Stott, "Worker and the Metropolis," pp. 311–13 for the cheap furniture market.

24. This account of tenement conditions is drawn chiefly from John H. Griscom, *The Sanitary Condition of the Laboring Population of New York* (New York, 1845); New York Assembly, *Report*; Citizens' Association of New York, *Report of the Council of Hygiene and Public Health ... Upon the Sanitary Condition of the City* (New York, 1865).

25. Susan Strasser, *Never Done: A History of American Housework* (New York, 1982), pp. 6, 67–72, 85. On the absence of utilities, see Duffy, *History of Public Health*, pp. 209, 275, 524; New York City Inspector, *Annual Report ... and a Brief View of the Sanitary Condition of the City*, p. 201; New York Assembly, *Report*, p. 35; Citizens' Association, *Report*, passim.

26. Griscom, *Sanitary Condition*, p. 8; [Sedgwick], *Poor Rich Man*, pp. 99, 157; Foster, *New York in Slices; By an Experienced Carver* (New York, 1849), p. 82; Matthew Carey, *A Plea for the Poor* (Philadelphia, 1837), p. 12. The reference to Godfrey's Cordial comes from Records of the County Coroner, case #414 (1855), NYMA; tea, from New York Assembly, *Report*, pp. 25–26. On throwing slops see Duffy, *History of Public Health*, pp. 361, 364–65.

27. As early as 1823, the SPP had denounced chip picking along the waterfront. SPP, *Report of a Committee ... on the Expediency of Erecting an Institution for the Reformation of Juvenile Delinquents* (New York, 1823), p. 17. For other references see Joseph Tuckerman's comments on similar patterns in Boston in *An Essay on the Wages Paid to Females* (Philadelphia, 1830), p. 22; Samuel I. Prime, *Life in New York* (New York, 1847), p. 87; [Sedgwick], *Poor Rich Man*, p. 87; Virginia Penny, *The Employments of Women* (Boston, 1863), pp. 122, 435, 444, 467, 484–85; Solon Robinson, *Hot Corn: Life Scenes in New York Illustrated* (New York, 1854), p. 207; *Daily Tribune*, March 16, 1850; William H. Bell Diary, NYHS; Phillip Wallys, *About New York: An Account of What a Boy Saw on a Visit to the City* (New York, 1857), pp. 43–44.

28. *New York Mirror*, quoted in Stokes Collection Typescript, p. 461.

29. *Jonathan's Whittlings of War* (New York), May 24, 1854.

Old and New Immigrants in Greater New York City, 1880 to World War I

Frederick M. Binder and David M. Reimers

Source: *All Nations Under Heaven: An Ethnic and Racial History of New York City* (New York: Columbia University Press, 1995).

EDITORS' INTRODUCTION

All Nations Under Heaven covers the multi-ethnic history of New York City from the colonial period to the late twentieth century. As one of the leading U.S. ports, New York City has historically been one of America's most diverse cities. Founded by the Dutch as New Amsterdam in 1625 as a trading center, the settlement was diverse from the outset. By 1643, at least eighteen different languages were spoken on the tiny island settlement of Manhattan. New York City later became home to the Castle Garden (1830–1892) and Ellis Island (1892–1954) immigrant processing centers. Although many sojourners came to New York bound for inland locales, millions of others settled permanently in the metropolitan region.

Social historians like Binder and Reimers often divide immigration into two categories—"old" and "new" immigrants. "Old" typically refers to those who entered the country during the 1830s–1880s. These old immigrants came primarily from northern and western Europe, particularly Ireland, Great Britain, Germany, and Scandinavia. Old immigrants were juxtaposed with native-born Americans, despite the fact that the two groups shared similar geographic origins. The "new" were those who arrived between the 1890s and the early 1920s, before the passage of sweeping immigration restrictions. While people from northern and western Europe continued to arrive in large numbers, the "new" immigration was notable for the high number of people from southern and eastern Europe, with a high number of Catholics, Greek Orthodox, Jews, and Muslims. Long-settled white Americans considered the "new immigrants" far different than the earlier wave. Their nativism led to a series of new laws that severely curtailed the number of legal immigrants allowed into the nation. In the latter half of the twentieth century, movements of people from Asia, Africa, and Latin America entered the country. However, historians do not agree on a standard terminology to describe this more contemporary period of immigration.

This essay primarily tells the story of the so-called new immigrants from the 1880s to World War I (1914–1918), although the authors add the story of African American New Yorkers as well. Binder and Reimer's chapter provides historical perspective to our current debates surrounding immigration. The "new" immigrants of the early twentieth century have been replaced by an even more recent group. Some of these immigrants have had long relationships with the United States. As historian Ronald Takaki and others have shown, some Mexican Americans suddenly found themselves to be "foreigners in their native land" after the acquisition of Spanish colonized lands in California and the Mexican-American War's Treaty of Guadalupe Hidalgo in 1848.[i] Since the legislative changes of the late twentieth century, we also see a growing influx of newcomers from

---

i Ronald Takaki, *A Different Mirror: A History of Multicultural America* (Boston: Little, Brown and Company, 1993), 166.

Asia, including an increasing number of Chinese, Koreans, Filipinos, and East Indians. These new Americans are joined by Cubans, Africans, Brazilians, Cape Verdeans, Caribbean immigrants, and a wide variety of others. The United States policy placed particular emphasis on highly educated immigrants, and thus drew off the educated classes of a variety of nations. The United States still proved alluring to residents of Mexico, Central America, and South America, many of whom filled low-paying positions in America's service and construction industries.

Frederick M. Binder is Professor Emeritus in the department of history at The College of Staten Island of the City University of New York. He is the author of *The Color Problem in Early National as Viewed by John Adams, Jefferson, and Jackson* (The Hague: Mouton, 1963), *The Age of the Common School, 1830–1865* (New York: Wiley, 1974) and, in addition to *All the Nations Under Heaven*, is co-editor with David M. Reimers of *The Way We Lived: Essays and Documents in American Social History* (Boston: Houghton Mifflin, 1988–2008). David M. Reimers is Professor Emeritus in the department of history at New York University. In addition to his work with Frederick M. Binder, he is the author of numerous books including *Still the Golden Door: The Third World Comes to America* (New York: Columbia University Press, 1985), *Unwelcome Strangers: American Identity and the Turn Against Immigration* (New York: Columbia University Press, 1998) and, with Leonard Dinnerstein, *Ethnic Americans: A History of Immigration* (New York: Columbia University Press, 1999).

OLD AND NEW IMMIGRANTS IN GREATER NEW YORK CITY, 1880 TO WORLD WAR I

As the twentieth century approached, New York maintained its position as the nation's largest city. For a brief period Chicago, rapidly recovering from its famous fire, appeared to be a viable challenger. But with the merger of Manhattan with its four outlying boroughs to form Greater New York City in 1898, the city easily outdistanced its midwest rival. Consolidated New York contained more than three million inhabitants, and on the eve of World War I housed a population twice as large as Chicago's.[1]

New York also remained America's leading port. While the city slipped from its commercial high point of 1850, when 70 percent of America's exports and imports went through its harbor, nearly half of the nation's shipping came through New York at the turn of the century. And about two of every three new immigrants entered the United States through Ellis Island, just off shore of Manhattan's southern tip, after it opened as a reception center in 1892.[2]

World commerce gave the city financial supremacy as well. Led by J. P. Morgan & Co., New York was home to the nation's leading banks. The New York Stock Exchange anchored Wall Street, and giant law firms emerged after the Civil War to serve the needs of the metropolis and the nation.[3] These enterprises required the employment of large numbers of professional and other white collar workers, who, in turn, further contributed to the city's growth.

While shipping, commerce, and finance gave New York a preeminence among American cities, they did not necessarily attract new immigrants as settlers. Laboring jobs and manufacturing, which usually did not require a knowledge of English and a high level of skill, provided that lure. Rapid industrial growth characterized New York from 1815 to 1880, after which crowded streets and high rents hindered development of most space-demanding industries. Meat packing and steel located in cities like Pittsburgh and Chicago, while light manufacturing flourished in New York. Publishing, metal working, food processing and the manufacture of clothing and luxury items required a large-scale labor force that the incoming immigrants helped provide. Overall the number of wage earners in industry doubled between 1880 and 1910.[4]

Of all the industries attracting immigrants, clothing was by far the leader. Prior to the

1890s the ready-to-wear clothing industry was, with the exception of women's cloaks, primarily producing menswear. Technological progress, however, led to a spectacular rise in the manufacture of women's suits and shirtwaists by the 1890s. During the final decades of the century much of the finishing work on garments—final trimming and basting and making buttonholes—was farmed out to Yiddish-speaking subcontractors. They, in turn, recruited mostly unskilled immigrants to labor in their homes or in tenement-flat workshops, which became universally known as "sweatshops." There as many as twenty men, women, and children were crammed together, peddling on machines, cutting, and hand sewing with needles and thread they had to supply themselves for eighty-four hours or more per week. Long hours, seasonal unemployment, child labor, barely subsistence wages, and airless flats; these were the conditions under which thousands of newly arrived immigrants labored.[5] [...]

At the state level, legislators enacted laws providing pensions for widowed mothers with children and instituting workmen's compensation benefits. Largely through the efforts of Frances Kellor, the first state-controlled employment bureau opened in 1911. In addition, Albany legislators responded to New York City's disastrous Triangle fire of 1911 that claimed the lives of 146 workers, most of them young, immigrant, Jewish women. The Triangle Shirtwaist Company had ignored existing fire regulations and had maintained unsafe, though not illegal, working conditions. Pressure by union workers, led by the dynamic Rose Schneiderman and an aroused public opinion, resulted in the passage of new factory safety regulations.[6]

As the job mix of New York altered, so too did the ethnic composition of the city's workforce. After 1880, Germans and Irish still settled in the city. For example, 55,000 Germans arrived in the 1880s and twice that number in the next decade, making them the largest ethnic group in New York.[7] But by the turn of the century immigration from Great Britain, Germany, and Ireland ebbed as the economic and social climates in those countries generally improved. The trickle of "New Immigrants" from southern and eastern Europe, who had begun to increase their numbers around 1880, became a flood after 1900.[8]

Meanwhile, those who arrived as part of the "Old Immigration" continued their struggles to achieve upward mobility, some with considerable success. German immigrants and their descendants found prosperity in the city's expanding economy, and a substantial white collar middle class—and even a social and economic elite—emerged by the 1880s. [...]

Harlem, in upper Manhattan, attracted middle class German Jews and Protestants. Still other German New Yorkers left Manhattan entirely and found homes in the outer boroughs, especially in Brooklyn. In 1900 about 60 percent of the city's Germans resided in Manhattan but only 42 percent could be found there ten years later. Two thirds of the second generation resided outside of Manhattan in 1910.[9] These new areas of settlement were made accessible by the city's continuing transportation revolution. Faster electric street cars and elevated lines replaced the old horsedrawn cars. After 1904 came the subways, which began to shape new neighborhoods even before World War I.[10] Bridges were no less important to the expanding city. The Brooklyn Bridge, called at the time the "eighth wonder of the world," was completed in 1883, followed by the Manhattan (1903) and Williamsburg (1909) bridges. All these spans connected Manhattan to Brooklyn.

Between 1900 and 1910 the number of foreign-born Germans in the city declined from 332,000 to 278,000, and then the number of second generation German New Yorkers also began to fall. The *Staats-Zeitung* remained the nation's largest German-language daily, but the number of German publications was declining.[11] The movement out of Manhattan's *Kleindeutsch-land* did not mean the immediate disintegration of varied German institutional life. German gymnastic, musical, and shooting societies were still numerous and quite active at the turn of the century. Yet by 1910 the decline of German presence in the city was noticeable.

The Irish, poorer to begin with, were slower to move up from their poverty than the Germans. Most Irish remained working class on the eve of World War I, with many men holding laborers' jobs and some young women still engaged in domestic employment. Rough and poor Irish neighborhoods continued to dot the city landscape, most notably Hell's Kitchen on Manhattan's West Side. It was here that the Tenderloin, home of gambling, drinking, prostitution, and rampant police corruption, had been a vice center for decades. Newspaper stories from 1881 described Hell's Kitchen, the area approximately from 57th to 34th Streets between Ninth and Twelfth Avenues, as a center of poverty and crime, with many residents living in squalid conditions. One room had "no carpet save one of filth [that] covered the floor.... Furniture, if fit to be called by that name, was none. A bundle of rags and straw in a corner sufficed for a bed." The occupants, generally of Irish descent, were described as "honest and industrious," whose principal fault "seems to be a love for the intoxicating cut."[12] Thirty years later little had changed. Efforts of reformers during the Progressive era brought a measure of relief to Hell's Kitchen, particularly through housing legislation, but it still remained a poor and unsafe neighborhood, "so notorious that vaudeville comedians used it as source of humor."[13]

Yet, as the years passed American-born Irish children were staying in school (both public and parochial) longer and finding better jobs upon leaving. A middle class—the "lace curtain Irish"—had emerged by the late 19th century, and its members were the backbone of the social and fraternal organizations associated with parish life. They held memberships in such national bodies as the Irish Catholic Benevolent Union and the Ancient Order of Hibernians, subscribed to at least one of the city's five Irish-American newspapers, and sent their children to one of the Catholic secondary schools.[14] [...]

The Irish were also a bit slower than Germans to move up and out of Manhattan, but their mobility became quite marked after 1900. They relocated to better neighborhoods on both sides of Manhattan and crossed over into the Bronx, leaving behind the slums of the Sixth Ward.[15] Many of these uptown Irish had succeeded as entrepreneurs, especially as owners of saloons, while others became skilled workers. At the turn of the century the Central Federated Union, the local association of the American Federation of Labor (AFL), was dominated by Irish craftsmen.[16] Irish women also became active in the labor movement. Leonora O'Reilly helped establish the New York chapter of the Women's Trade Union League in 1904, and Annie Moriarty tried to organize the city's growing number of Irish women teachers.[17]

But it was always politics and the Roman Catholic Church that held the greatest attraction for Irish New Yorkers. They had moved into politics as foot soldiers of Tammany Hall before the Civil War. Subsequently, they dominated the Hall and much of New York City's municipal political life off and on for many years. The appeal of politics to the Irish was obvious, since a growing city provided both jobs and lucrative construction contracts. In 1888 it was estimated that control of city hall meant 12,000 jobs; the creation of Greater New York ten years later raised that figure to 60,000.[18] In the fire and police departments, the civil service, and the schools (where young Irish women became prominent), Irish New Yorkers claimed more than one third of the city's public jobs in 1900.[19] Connections to the political machine by the Irish were vital to obtaining jobs in a non-civil service era, but the English they spoke gave them an additional advantage over most immigrants. Mastery of English was a requisite for most municipal employment as well as for such private sector jobs as fare collectors on the city's subways, which were then privately owned. Many of these positions were blue collar and hardly provided middle class incomes, but they offered steady employment in an economy that experienced periodic recessions and depressions. Moreover, some jobs, especially in the police department, presented the possibility for graft, which was widespread at the turn of the century. For example, policemen regularly took bribes for permitting prostitution to flourish and saloons to operate illegally. Historian Timothy J. Gilfoyle concluded, "While the police did not control every prostitute and madame in New York, the most lucrative operations were subject to police approval."[20] [...]

Of course, local politicians got their share of the boodle because they worked closely with the police to "regulate" prostitution.[21] Even more rewarding was inside knowledge of future city contracts. A few politicians acquired substantial fortunes through their connections to city hall. While reformers decried such practices as scandalous, Tammany boss George Washington Plunkitt put it more benignly with a suggestion for his epitaph: "George Washington Plunkitt— He seen his opportunities and he took 'em."[22] [...]

Because there were more voters than jobs, Irish politicians offered other services beyond employment. Machine benefits begun in the mid-nineteenth century, including baskets of food at Christmas, fuel for cold winter days, help in finding housing, and picnics, singing and sport clubs for amusement, continued well into the twentieth. Big Tim Sullivan, leader of the Bowery district, was born in poverty to Irish immigrant parents and lived for years in some of the city's worst neighborhoods. The one-time saloon owner rose rapidly within the Tammany organization to become a master of urban politics. During the depression winter of 1894 he fed thousands of poor people Christmas dinners. He also gave away food and clothing, worked hard to see that deserving voters got jobs, and still found time to run his burlesque and vaudeville house.[23] [...]

Christmas baskets, fraud, jobs, and appeals to non-Irish voters could not always secure control of City Hall. Periodic reform movements, representing voter disgust at widespread graft, succeeded at times in capturing that main prize. However, despite setbacks, Tammany Hall and the Irish politicians who ran it remained the preeminent powers in New York City politics well into the fourth decade of the twentieth century.

After 1880 Irish New Yorkers continued their domination of the Roman Catholic Church. As Italian and Polish Catholics poured into the city, the Irish clergy criticized their particular practices of Catholicism and their folk traditions, but the church did expand its parishes, schools, and charities to serve them. Under Archbishop Michael Corrigan and later John Cardinal Farley, the Archdiocese initiated a major church-building campaign.[24]

While Irish men dominated the church, Irish women became nuns and served as teachers in the parochial schools and as nurses in the church's hospitals. Their labors made Catholic institutional life possible in New York City. The Catholic Sisters of Charity began their New York activities before the Civil War, and they expanded as the city grew. They tended the sick, administered hospitals, taught parochial school children, and staffed orphanages and other institutions serving the city's poor. Among the most notable of the city's Catholic hospitals was St Vincent's, which opened in response to the cholera epidemic of 1849. [...]

As immigration from Germany and Ireland slowed, the countries of southern and eastern Europe sent increasing millions across the Atlantic Ocean in search of a better life. Of these so-called "new immigrants"—Italians, Greeks, Czechs, Slavs, and Jews—some went to Canada and Latin America, but the vast majority came to the United States. Just as social and economic changes spurred emigrants to leave northern and western Europe between 1820 and 1880, those forces now spread eastward and southward. Commercial agriculture consolidated estates in the Austro-Hungarian Empire and forced thousands of peasants to leave. In Southern Italy and Sicily conditions had been bleak for generations, even before landlords began squeezing peasants off the land. To make matters worse, taxes were unbearable, population growth high, and prospects for alternative employment poor. World-wide competition for wheat and grapes after 1870 drove prices for these products down and tariff wars a few years later only added to the peasants' woes.[25] In both areas peasants drifted into the cities, but some eventually chose emigration to

America. In addition, those European workers who labored in small handcraft industries, sometimes operating out of their homes, experienced growing competition from factory production. Everywhere rising population created additional pressures for emigration.[26]

Ethnic tensions in central and eastern Europe added to economic discontents, but no group experienced more discrimination than Russia's Jews. Already required, with few exceptions, to a live in a limited Pale of Settlement, the czar's May Laws of 1882 forced a half-million of his Jewish subjects to relocate from rural villages to cities and towns. Other decrees subjected Jews to long-term military service, banned them from certain professions, and severely restricted their access to universities. Slavic anti-Semitism reached a new high with the pogroms, government-sanctioned riots and bloodbaths against Jews that began in the early 1880s. As they watched their homes and business burned and fellow Jews murdered, many became convinced that emigration to America was their only salvation.[27]

For potential emigrants desire to come to America was often heightened by news of the bounties that awaited them. Railroads and steamship lines printed thousands of pamphlets in dozens of foreign languages explaining the wonders of the New World. And letters from those who had gone before urged their relatives and countrymen to join them. Mary Antin, a Russian Jewish immigrant, recalled in later years "America was in everybody's mouth ... people who had relatives in the famous land went around reading their letters for the enlightenment of less fortunate folk.... All talked of it."[28] At times letters contained prepaid tickets, which made the voyage possible for many of Europe's poor.[29]

Eastern Europeans lived far from Bremen, Liverpool, Rotterdam, and other ports where ships sailed for America, but improved railroad systems eased the journeys of many. Some emigrants, eager to leave but too poor to afford train fare, made their way to the ports on foot or by horse or donkey-drawn carts. Improvements in oceangoing steamships cut the cost and the time required for the American journey to a matter of days. Steerage, in which most immigrants travelled on the big ocean liners, was hardly luxurious. Edward Steiner described his voyage in 1906:

> Crowds everywhere, ill smelling bunks, uninviting washrooms—this is steerage. The food, which is miserable, is dealt out of huge kettles into the dinner pails provided by the steamship company.... On many ships, even drinking water is grudgingly given, and on the steamship *Staatendam* ... we had literally to steal water for the steerage from the second cabin.[30]

Yet passage on the steamships was a far cry from the unsafe conditions of sailing-ship days, and few perished enroute.[31]

The federal government had assumed total control of immigration during the 1880s, and in 1892 opened Ellis Island as a reception center for the newcomers. As passengers saw the Statue of Liberty and Ellis Island looming in front of them, they were exhilarated but at the same time feared being rejected. The average immigrant usually remained at Ellis Island for only a few hours, however, before embarking on a journey to a new life. Unscrupulous agents still waited to exploit innocent newcomers, but efficient immigrant aid societies were now available to offer assistance. After passing inspection at Ellis Island, the immigrants boarded ferry boats for a short trip to New Jersey or Manhattan. Most went on, seeking friends and families ready to receive them in other cities, but hundreds of thousands remained in New York City.

As has been pointed out, the "New Immigration" largely consisted of people from southern and eastern Europe. Of these the Jews and Italians arrived in such great numbers and played so major a role in the city that a separate chapter will be devoted to them. However, it is important to recognize that, in this great tidal wave of immigration, all the nations and places of Europe were represented. The 1911 Commission on Immigration found in one New York school district, which contained 20,000 of the city's over one half million pupils, that three quarters of the students were foreign born.[32] [...]

Like the mid-century Irish and Germans, the latest immigrants lived in crowded quarters side by side with peoples who spoke different languages and possessed different cultures. The Dillingham Commission, established by Congress to investigate immigration, found one Manhattan block where second generation Americans of English, German, and Irish descent lived among foreign-born Canadians (other than French), English, Finnish, French, Germans, Hebrew, Irish, Southern Italians, Magyars, Scots, and Swedes.[33] This block's mixture was not terribly exceptional in heterogeneous New York, where neighborhoods were in constant fluctuation as newcomers replaced the older residents.[34]

But all was not diversity; some areas earned reputations for being the centers of a particular group. One observer described how the "Servo-Croatian colony in New York is situated along Eleventh Avenue from Thirty Fourth to Forty-eight Streets and on the adjacent cross streets between Tenth and Eleventh Avenues."[35] Another observer pointed out that although the city's Hungarian population was comparatively small, Magyars lived in "three distinct quarters," the largest being on the Lower East Side of Manhattan.[36] Czechs were associated with Manhattan's East River blocks from 65th to 78th streets. While noting that a variety of groups lived in these blocks, one commentator said, "it is the Cech [sic] who gives this quarter of the city an atmosphere all its own."[37]

Immigrants who had arrived in small numbers before 1880 swelled their migration after that date. The first Greeks, who arrived as refugees from the turmoil of their War for Independence in the 1820s, were followed after 1880 by considerable numbers from the rural provinces.[38] Because these immigrants came from territories of the Ottoman Empire and other regions outside of Greece as well as from Greece itself, the actual size of the ethnic Greek community in New York City cannot be determined. Their number probably reached 20,000 or so by the time of World War I, scattered across several New York neighborhoods; no one district emerged as a strictly Greek enclave.[39]

Poles joined their countrymen in the Williamsburg-Greenpoint section of Brooklyn. The first Polish Catholic church was St. Stanislaus, but as the community grew and spread out, more churches as well as fraternal orders, parish schools, and a Polish National Home were created.[40] Though the Catholic church and religious observance were of utmost importance in the lives of these immigrants, they also eventually celebrated their ethnic holidays, Constitution Day (May 3rd) and Pulaski Day (October 11th), as major social events.

New immigrants worked in a variety of trades, but frequently clustered into selected occupations. New York Czechs (Bohemians), for example, labored as metal workers and in the garment trades, but were especially known for manufacturing pearl buttons and making cigars. One Czech journalist estimated that 95 percent of first Czech immigrants, including many women, found jobs in the tobacco industry.[41] In their homeland women had traditionally worked in cigar factories, while the men engaged in agriculture and in crafts. In America, necessity drove many husbands to take up their wives' trade. One worker noted, "Women could make better cigars than men, and it was therefore necessary that the wives help their husbands."[42] [...]

The Greek community largely consisted of unskilled males usually from rural areas, but once in New York Greeks worked in several occupations. Labor bosses for a time funneled young boys into jobs as bootblacks, while their elders became peddlers, fur workers, cigarette manufacturers, and operators of confectioneries and restaurants. The worst conditions were those encountered by the bootblacks who labored long hours for little pay.[43] [...]

Following the German and Irish models, southern and eastern Europeans organized churches, fraternal associations, and clubs. Holy Trinity, formed in 1891, was the city's first church for Greeks, and New York ultimately became the center of America's Greek Orthodox Church.[44] The focal point of Greek male social life was the coffeehouse, which one historian described as having air "choked with clouds of smoke rising from cigarettes, pipes, and cigars." [...]

New York's Arab community, largely Syrian-Lebanese, also dates from the era of the "new immigrants." By 1900 half the Syrians in America resided in New York City. The first Arabs did not arrive in the city until the 1870s, but that population grew to several thousand by 1920, mostly located on the Lower West Side of Manhattan.[45] [...] New York's Syrian population was overwhelmingly Christian and large enough to support several churches, newspapers, and ethnic organizations, such as the Syrian Ladies Aid Society, which helped new immigrants. Male immigrants made their living by peddling, factory work, and running small businesses, while the women who worked were concentrated in factories manufacturing negligees, kimonos, lace, and embroidery. Syrian craftsmen were noted for rugs and tapestries.[46]

Unlike some other immigrants who arrived before 1880, the Chinese did not increase their numbers substantially. American racism dictated the future of the city's Chinese residents as the Chinese exclusion movement, especially active in California and the West during the 1870s, gained strength. In 1870, Congress restricted naturalization to blacks and whites, and the courts later held that Asians were not white. Finally, in 1882 Congressional legislation banned most Chinese immigration.[47]

Immigration restriction made it virtually impossible for Chinese, including the wives of immigrants already here, to come to New York, and Chinatown, as it developed after 1880, was a bachelor society where men outnumbered women by a ratio of better than six to one. It was run by the six companies of the Chinese Consolidated Benevolent Association, dominated by the merchant elite. Life in the early twentieth century for males, many with wives back in China, revolved around laundries, restaurants, and small shops. The men resided in small, crowded apartments in which they, nonetheless, led a lonely existence. Some Chinatown residents turned to gambling and patronizing prostitutes, practices which angered white New Yorkers and convinced them that the Chinese were a degraded race. At the same time, Chinatown developed as a tourist center after 1900, an exotic place for visitors to gawk.[48]

While the period after 1880 is noted primarily for the massive influx of immigrants from southern and eastern Europe, those years were also ones of rapid growth of the city's Scandinavian population, which soared by 50 percent between 1900 and 1920.[49] The center of New York's Scandinavians and Finns was along Brooklyn's waterfront. By 1910 "Finn Town," in Brooklyn already had 1,000 residents, and around 1916 another wave of Finnish migrants arrived. This working class group was "infused with a socialist-labor ideology" and rapidly organized cooperatives for housing and saving.[50]

Sailors formed the basis of New York's Norwegian community. In the 1880s many jumped ship while in Brooklyn or Manhattan for jobs on better paying American vessels. Joined by migration from Norway, their numbers increased rapidly after 1880, although, since they were mostly male, they tended toward a somewhat transient existence. They waited for jobs aboard incoming ships or worked at crafts, such as carpentry, related to their maritime background.[51] Yet as leaders emerged and the numbers of women grew, Norwegian institutional life took root. The community had, as historian David Mauk notes, "gone on land." [...]

Among other newcomers to New York in the late nineteenth and early twentieth centuries were southern blacks. Some had begun to arrive following the Civil War, but more than 80,000 left the South between 1870 and 1890, and 107,796 followed in the 1890s. Nearly 100,000 came north during the first decade of the twentieth century. These migrants were escaping an intensified southern racism as well as a deteriorating economic situation and hoped to improve their lot in the North. New York City became one of the main termini for this migration, facilitated by frequent train service from Maryland, Virginia, and the Carolinas. New York and Brooklyn combined had fewer than 20,000 blacks in 1860, but the figure reached 33,888 in 1890 and 60,666 ten years later. By 1910 the five-borough city claimed over 90,000 black residents.[52]

Of the 3,552 foreign-born blacks residing in New York in 1900, most had immigrated from the West Indies. This small group then constituted the largest such settlement in the United States. Most had arrived during the previous decade, prompted by improved transportation, exaggerated stories of New York City's bounties, and poor economic conditions in the Caribbean. Harlem's emergence as the "capital" of black America, beginning around 1910, increased the lure of New York as West Indian laborers and domestics joined with skilled workers and professionals in seeking a better life.[53]

West Indians retained considerable ethnic identity as their churches and organizations differentiated them from native-born African Americans. They avoided intermarriage with American blacks, who in turn considered them haughty and aloof. But like the American blacks, West Indians faced racial discrimination, which limited their housing and employment opportunities.[54] [...]

New York State's civil rights laws were not rigorously enforced in the late nineteenth century. Court decisions as well as political hedging further confused the issue. Judicial interpretations of the New York 1873 Civil Rights Act apparently sanctioned all-black schools, and the state legislature did not explicitly ban them when it reenacted the Common School Act in 1894. Finally, in 1900 the state outlawed segregated schools. Black children subsequently attended schools in their local neighborhoods, and black teachers even taught white pupils on occasion. However, as residential segregation increased over time, neighborhood schools also became increasingly segregated and overcrowded.[55]

Civil rights laws did not cover religion, and white churches continued to practice segregation. A few black Christians did attend predominately white congregations, but most realized they were not welcome there, and ultimately they migrated to the black churches. When a new YMCA opened on West 53rd Street in the Tenderloin District, it was assumed to be for blacks only.[56]

Job discrimination in the early twentieth century was rampant. Blacks found themselves blocked from training as skilled workers, not wanted in trade unions, and rebuffed when they applied for construction or other skilled laboring jobs. Similar problems faced them when they applied to work in sales or for such white collar employment as clerks, bookkeepers, and typists. Not many had moved into these occupations by 1910.[57] One exception, however, was the federal and city governments through which in 1900 more than 400 blacks found employment as clerks. Social worker Mary Ovington reported 176 African Americans employed in the city's post offices, but noted, "The clerkship, that to a white man is only a stepping-stone, to a Negro is a highly coveted position."[58] Manhattan had no black police or firemen as late as 1910, and overall blacks were underrepresented in municipal employment. In 1911, when the city appointed Samuel J. Battle as the first black policeman, people were taken on guided tours to see the "strange phenomenon." Battle remembered children taunting him, "There goes the nigger cop."[59]

Studies completed in 1911 and 1912 by a black sociologist and white social worker revealed only modest changes in the occupational status of the city's blacks since the 1850s. Most blacks worked as domestic servants and unskilled laborers.[60] Black women, more apt to work outside the home than white women, were confined to domestic labor. About one third of married black women worked for wages, some 90 percent as domestic or personal servants. Many others worked at home by taking in lodgers, a practice more common among blacks than whites and necessitated by high rents blacks paid for apartments and the low wages they earned from menial jobs.[61] Opportunities varied little for the unmarried black woman. A small black elite of professionals and businessmen had expanded somewhat since the Civil War, which led sociologist George Haynes to conclude in 1912 that the group's future was promising. But most black businesses lacked capital and confined themselves to serving a black community with little purchasing power.[62] Numerically, the most successful of black businesses, such as barber-shops, were outgrowths of personal and domestic service and required only small amounts of capital. They existed to serve a strictly black clientele. Blacks were totally excluded from the city's banking, large manufacturing, retail, and financial institutions, unless they worked as janitors or maids.

The growth of the black population and the segregated nature of New York society did create a demand for growing numbers of black teachers, lawyers, doctors, ministers, and other professionals. Because African Americans achieved a modest success on the stage, vaudeville performers and musicians found some opportunities open.[63] [...] However, attention to this emerging business, professional, and entertainment elite should not obscure the fact that blacks were underrepresented in the professions, that black business enterprises had limited futures, and that these black performers at times had to play stage roles degrading to their race. Indeed, as far as earnings and recognition by the larger white society was concerned, to belong to the black elite one could be a skilled worker or a waiter in an expensive and exclusive hotel or restaurant as well as be a professional or entrepreneur.

NOTES

1. David Hammack, *Power and Society: Greater New York at the Turn of the Century* (New York, 1982), chapter 7.
2. Ellis Island was temporarily closed after a fire but reopened in 1897.
3. Hammack, *Power and Society*, pp. 31–9.
4. Ibid., pp. 39–40. Piano, clock, and printing manufacturing did require large space, and the city was fortunate to keep these industries in Manhattan and Brooklyn.
5. Irving Howe, *The World of Our Fathers* (New York, 1976), pp. 80–84.
6. Bonnie Mitelman, "Rose Schneiderman and the Triangle Fire," *American History Illustrated* 167 (July 1981): 38–47.
7. Dorothee Schneider, *Trade Unions and Community: The German Working Class in New York City, 1870–1900* (Urbana, 1994), pp. 7–8.
8. Ira Rosenwaike, *Population History of New York City* (Syracuse, 1972), p. 68.
9. Thomas Henderson, *Tammany Hall and the New Immigrants* (New York, 1976), pp. 73–74.
10. For the subway's impact, see, Clifton Hood, *722 Miles: The Building of the Subways and How They Transformed New York* (New York, 1993).
11. Henderson, *Tammany and the New Immigrants*, p. 74.
12. Quoted in Richard O'Connor, *Hell's Kitchen* (New York, 1958), p. 65.
13. Ibid., p. 182.
14. Kerby Miller, *Emigrants and Exiles* (New York, 1985), pp. 495, 506, and 533; Jay Dolan, *Immigrant Church: New York's Irish and German Catholics, 1815–1865* (South Bend, 1983), pp. 111–13.
15. Henderson, *Tammany and the New Immigrants*, pp. 74–79; Kate Claghorn, "The Foreign Immigrant in New York City," *Industrial Commission*, Vol. 15 (Washington, 1908), p. 471.
16. Henderson, *Tammany and the New Immigrants*, p. 83.
17. Janet Nolan, *Ourselves Alone: Women's Emigration from Ireland, 1885–1920* (Lexington, Ky.: 1989), pp. 84–85.
18. Chris McNickle, *To Be Mayor of New York* (New York, 1993), p. 9.
19. Steven Erie, *Rainbow's End: Irish-Americans and the Dilemmas of Urban Machine Politics, 1840–1985* (Berkeley, 1988), pp. 88–90.
20. Timothy J. Gilfoyle, *City of Eros: New York City, Prostitution, and the Commercialization of Sex, 1790–1920* (New York, 1992), p. 253.
21. Gilfoyle, *City of Eros*, chapter 12.
22. Quoted in Erie, *Rainbow's End*, p. 10. For Tammany see also Gustavus Myers, *The History of Tammany Hall* (New York, 1971, originally 1917); Oliver Allen, *The Tiger: The Rise and Fall of Tammany Hall* (New York, 1993).
23. Daniel Czitrom, "Underworlds and Undergods: Big Tim Sullivan and Metropolitan Politics in New York, 1889–1913," *Journal of American History* 78 (Sept. 1991): 536–58.
24. Mary Brown, "Italian Immigrants and the Catholic Church in the Archdiocese of New York, 1880–1950," PhD. diss., Columbia University, 1987, pp. 115–18 and 155.
25. Gary R. Mormino and George E. Pozzetta, *The Immigrant World of Ybor City* (Urbana, 1987), chapter 1.
26. For conditions in Europe see John Bodnar, *The Transplanted: A History of Immigrants in Urban America* (Bloomington, 1985), chapter 1; Philip Taylor, *The Distant Magnet: European Emigration to USA* (New York, 1971), chapters 2–3.
27. Gerald Sorin, *A Time for Building: The Third Migration, 1880–1920* (Baltimore, 1992), pp. 23 and 33; Ronald Sanders, *Shores of Refugee: A Hundred Years of Jewish Emigration* (New York, 1988), chapters 1–2.
28. Quoted in Howard Sachar, *A History of the Jews in America* (New York, 1992), p. 119.
29. Taylor, *The Distant Magnet*, chapter 4.
30. Quoted Sachar, *A History of the Jews in America*, p. 127.
31. Ibid., chapter 8.
32. U.S. Commission on Immigration, Vol. 31, *The Children of Immigrants in Schools* (Washington, 1911), p. 612.

33. U.S. Immigration Commission, *Immigrants in Cities*, Vol. 26–27, part 1 (Washington, 1911), p. 168.

34. See Richard Lieberman, "Social Change and Political Behavior: The East Village of New York City, 1880–1905," PhD diss., New York University, 1976, chapter 2.

35. Marie Sabsovich Orenstein, "The Servo-Croats of Manhattan," *The Survey* 29 (Dec. 7, 1912): 277.

36. Louis Pink, "The Magyar in New York," *Charities* 13 (Dec. 3, 1904): 262–63.

37. Thomas Capek, Jr., *The Cech (Bohemian) Community of New York* (San Francisco, 1969, originally 1921), p. 20.

38. Michael Contopoulos, "The Greek Community of New York City: Early Years to 1910," PhD diss., New York University, 1972, chapters 3–4.

39. Charles Moskos, *Greek Americans: Struggle and Success* (Englewood Cliffs, 1980), pp. 23–24.

40. Sister Adele Dabrowski, "A History and Survey of the Polish in Brooklyn Community," MA thesis, Fordham University, 1946, pp. 78–79 and 152.

41. Capek, *The Cech Community*, pp. 23–24.

42. Quoted in Eileen Boris, *Home Work: Motherhood and the Politics of Industrial Homework*, p. 27.

43. Moskos, *Greek Americans*, pp. 24–25; and Contopoulos, "The Greek Community," chapter 6. The number of Greek women increased after 1910, but men still outnumbered women 2.8 to 1 in 1930.

44. Moskos, *Greek Americans*, pp. 23–24.

45. Gregory Orfalea, *Before the Flames: A Quest for the History of Arab Americans* (Austin, 1989), pp. 75–78.

46. Orfalea, *Before the Flames*, p. 767; Harriet D. Bodemer, "The Syrian Colony in Brooklyn," MA thesis, Fordham University, 1943, pp. 47–48; WPA Files, "Arabs in New York"; and Miller, *Our Syrian Population*.

47. The 1882 ban was temporary, but it was extended in subsequent years and finally repealed in 1943. Then China was granted a small immigration quota. Certain classes of Chinese could still come to America, and ways were found to get around the ban to permit "paper sons" (supposed sons of Chinese-American citizens) to emigrate to America. But in general the limits imposed severe restrictions on Chinese immigration. See Ronald Takaki, *Strangers from a Different Shore: A History of Asian Americans* (Boston, 1989), pp. 416–18.

48. Ibid., pp. 251–52.

49. Louis Winnick, *New People in Old Neighborhoods: The Role of New Immigrants in Rejuvenating New York's Communities* (New York, 1990), p. 95.

50. Ibid., pp. 77–78, 84, and 85.

51. David Mauk, "The Colony That Rose from the Sea: The Norwegians in the Red Hook Section of Brooklyn, 1850–1910," PhD diss., New York University, 1991, chapters 2–3.

52. Seth Scheiner, *Negro Mecca: A History of the Negro in New York City, 1865–1915* (New York, 1965), p. 221.

53. Calvin Holder, "The Causes and Composition of West Indian Immigration to New York City, 1900–1952," *Afro-Americans in New York Life and History* 11 (Jan. 1987): 8–17.

54. Philip Kasinitz, *Caribbean New York: Black Immigrants and the Politics of Race* (Ithaca, 1992), pp. 24–25, 33–35, and 41–52.

55. Gilbert Osofsky, *Harlem: The Making of a Ghetto* (New York, 1966), pp. 147–48; Connolly, *A Ghetto Grows in Brooklyn*, pp. 26–29; Marsha Hunt Hiller, "Race Politics in New York City, 1890–1930," PhD diss., Columbia University, 1972, pp. 36–50.

56. Osofsky, *Harlem*, pp. 41–42.

57. Ibid., pp. 95–100, 86–87; George Haynes, *The Negro at Work in New York City: A Study of Economic Progress* (New York, 1968, originally 1912), pp. 25–26.

58. Mary Ovington, *Half a Man: The Status of the Negro in New York* (New York, 1960, originally 1911), p. 88.

59. Quoted in Osofsky, *Harlem*, p. 166.

60. Haynes, *The Negro in New York*, chapter 4; Ovington, *Half a Man*, chapter 4.

61. Haynes, *The Negro in New York*, pp. 61–65.

62. See ibid., part II, chapters 1–3. Haynes optimistically subtitled his book "A Study in Economic Progress," but his data revealed a more sobering picture. In some activities, like catering and barbering, blacks had lost their former white clientele. See Ovington, *Half a Man*, p. 108.

63. Ovington, *Half a Man*, pp. 112–37.

Ethnic Islands: The Emergence of Urban Chinese America

Ronald T. Takaki

Source: *Strangers from a Different Shore: A History of Asian Americans*
(Boston: Little, Brown, 1989).

EDITORS' INTRODUCTION

The late Ronald Takaki (1939–2009), Emeritus Professor of Ethnic Studies at the University of California, Berkeley, was responsible for introducing a great many Americans to a revised history of the United States that honors the nation's diverse past. For far too long, American history has been recounted through stories of Jamestown, Plymouth, and rural frontier settlements, featuring only Americans of white, European descent as historical actors. Takaki's landmark work, *A Different Mirror: A History of Multicultural America* has been in demand as a college textbook since it was first published by Little, Brown in 1993. Takaki's *Strangers from a Different Shore* introduced readers to an extended history of Asian Americans, many of whom, like the Chinese featured in this essay, made homes in urban settings.

Arriving on America's Pacific coast, Asian immigrants often passed through Angel Island, the immigration processing center for the western United States which operated between 1910 and 1940. A large group of Asian immigrants also settled in Hawaii. Asians who settled in cities on the mainland of the United States often found themselves living in "ethnic islands," settlements composed of people from their own background who were isolated culturally and economically from the dominant American culture. The Chinese Exclusion Act of 1882 coalesced nativist and racist sentiments with worries about labor competition into a landmark law. The Chinese Exclusion Act became the first federal law to prohibit the immigration of one specific group of people based on nationality. Chinese settlers composed only 2 percent of the American population at this time, yet they were subject to a disproportionate share of American anti-immigrant preoccupation. The law specifically restricted Chinese immigrants who were seeking wage labor positions, although there were exceptions for Chinese businessmen. Some resourceful immigrants found ways to immigrate despite restrictions. When earthquakes ripped through San Francisco in 1906, and the resulting fires destroyed the city's legal records, some Chinese then claimed to have been born in San Francisco. As citizens, they could bring their wives and children into the United States. Chinese communities had suffered greatly due to the lack of women immigrants. Legal loopholes, such as those created by the loss of San Francisco records and the creation of "paper sons" Takaki describes here, helped the Chinese American community stabilize. By 1920, the Chinese had settled in cities from Los Angeles to Boston. Yet 40 percent of all Chinese lived in just two major cities, San Francisco and New York. Chinese urban dwellers crowded into limited housing and carved out economic opportunity in service industries. Chinatown itself became a commodity, sold to curious whites as a tourist attraction, and creating a long-term market for an Americanized version of Chinese food.

ETHNIC ISLANDS

The Emergence of Urban Chinese America

The Chinese had been forced to retreat into ethnic islands — their own separate economic and cultural colonies. During the early decades of the twentieth century, the Chinese became increasingly urban and employed in restaurants, laundries, and garment factories. Isolated from American society, their communities in the cities became places of curiosity for white tourists, and a new industry began to develop in Chinatowns. Tourism became a new "necessity," reinforcing both the image and condition of the Chinese as "strangers" in America.

Angel Island

"Rather than banish the Chinaman," Jacob Riis recommended in 1890 in *How the Other Half Lives*, "I would have the door opened wider — for his wife; make it a condition of his coming or staying that he bring his wife with him. Then, at least, he might not be what he now is and remains, a homeless stranger among us." But the door to Chinese immigration had been closed by the government here, creating an isolated, predominantly male community. The exclusion law and the *Ah Moy* court decision had prohibited the entry of Chinese women, including the wives of Chinese laborers already in the United States.[1] [...]

The women had become "widows" of men living in America. They sent the stranded sojourners, their husbands, "letters of love, soaked with tears." One Chinese migrant in Oregon responded, writing a letter that began, "My Beloved Wife":

It has been several autumns now since your dull husband left you for a far remote alien land. Thanks to my heart body I am all right. Therefore stop your embroidering worries about me.

Yesterday I received another of your letters. I could not keep tears from running down my cheeks when thinking about the miserable and needy circumstances of our home, and thinking back to the time of our separation.

Because of our destitution I went out, trying to make a living. Who could know that the Fate is always opposite to man's design? Because I can get no gold, I am detained in this secluded corner of a strange land. Furthermore, my beauty, you are implicated in an endless misfortune. I wish this paper would console you a little. This is all what I can do for now....

This letter was never finished and never mailed, left in a desk drawer of the Kam Wah Chung Store in Oregon.[2]

What happened to the nameless writer of this unmailed letter might have paralleled the life stories of the owners of the Kam Wah Chung Store — Lung On and Ing Hay. They had come to America as sojourners in the 1880s. They worked first as wage earners and then opened their own merchandise store. Gradually, over the years, as they built their business and developed personal and social ties to their new community, they felt a detachment from their homeland and their families. In 1899, Lung's father instructed his son in a letter: "Come home as soon as you can. Don't say 'no' to me any more.... You are my only son. You have no brothers and your age is near forty.... You have been away from home for seventeen years, you know nothing about our domestic situation.... Come back, let our family be reunited and enjoy the rest of our lives." In a letter to "My Husband-lord," Lung's wife scolded her absent mate: "According to Mr. Wang, you are indulging in sensuality, and have no desire to return home. On hearing this I am shocked and pained. I have been expecting your return day after day.... But, alas, I don't know what kind of substance your heart is made of.... Your daughter is now at the age of betrothal and it is your responsibility to arrange her marriage." Her appeal must have moved her husband, for Lung wrote to his cousin Liang Kwang-jin on March 2, 1905: "We are fine here, thank you. Tell my family that I will go back as soon as I accumulate enough money to pay the fare." But a few weeks later, Lung learned from a letter written by his cousin, dated March 4, that certain events in the life history of his family in China had already passed him by: "Two years ago your mother died. Last year your daughter married. Your aged father is immobile. He will pass away any time now. Your wife feels left out and hurt.... Come back as soon as you receive this message." Meanwhile, Ing's father had also written to his son in 1903: "Men go abroad so that they might make money for support of their families, but you have sent neither money nor a letter since you left."[3]

Separated from their families in China, the men missed the company of their own small children — their sounds and laughter. Perhaps this was why Lung On and Ing Hay regularly saved pictures of children cut from calendars, advertisements, and newspapers and placed them safely in a box. Discovered decades later in one of the desk drawers of the abandoned store, this box of pictures told sad tales of Chinese-immigrant fathers living far away from their children. The two shopkeepers also pampered the white children in the neighborhood. Years later, one of them, Mrs. John W. Murray recalled: "Doc Hay always gave us children Chinese candy, oranges and other goodies."[4]

Back home, Chinese women fingered and studied old yellowing photographs of their men, so young and so handsome. Look at these dreamers and the twinkle in their eyes, filled with possibilities and promises, they said proudly. But, aiya, what did they look like now, after twenty years in Gam Saan? [...]

Desperate to be reunited with their loved ones, some men looked for loopholes in the law. Aware Chinese merchants were permitted to bring their families here, Chinese laundrymen, restaurant owners, and even common laborers sometimes tried to pose as "paper merchants." A Chinese who had sworn in his oath to the immigration authorities that he was a "merchant" turned out to be a hotel cook; another was actually a gardener. Other Chinese would bribe merchants to list them as partners or would buy business shares in order to claim they were merchants. "A number of the stores in the cities are organized just for that purpose," explained an immigration commissioner. "They are organized just to give the Chinese a chance to be a merchant."[5]

Most Chinese men, however, believed they would never be able to bring their wives to America. Then suddenly a natural disaster occurred that changed the course of Chinese-American history. Early in the morning of April 18, 1906, an earthquake shook San Francisco. "Aih yah, dai loong jen, aih yah dai loong jen," residents of Chinatown screamed, "the earth dragon is wriggling." In terror, they jumped out of their beds, fled from collapsing buildings, and ran down buckling streets. [...]

The fires destroyed almost all of the municipal records and opened the way for a new Chinese immigration. Chinese men could now claim they had been born in San Francisco, and as citizens they could bring their wives to the United States. Before the earthquake, the number of women had consistently remained at 5 percent or less of the Chinese population. In 1900 there were only 4,522 Chinese females in America. Only handfuls of them entered the country each year: between 1900 and 1906, their numbers ranged from twelve to 145 annually. But after the catastrophe in San Francisco, they began arriving in increasing numbers — from 219 in 1910 to 356 in 1915 to 573 in 1920 to 1,050 in 1922 and 1,893 two years later. One out of every four Chinese immigrants was female during this period, compared to only one out of twenty during the nineteenth century. Some 10,000 Chinese females came between 1907 and 1924. But this immigration was halted suddenly by that year's immigration act. One of the law's provisions prohibited the entry of aliens ineligible to citizenship. "The necessity [for this provision]," a congressman stated, "arises from the fact that we do not want to establish additional Oriental families here." This restriction closed tightly the gates for the immigration of Chinese women. [...] The provision applying the restriction to wives of citizens was repealed in 1930. By then, women represented 20 percent of the Chinese population, providing the beginning of a viable base for the formation of Chinese-American families.[6]

Meanwhile, Chinese sons had also begun coming to America. According to U.S. law, the children of Americans were automatically citizens of the United States, even if they were born in a foreign country. Thus children fathered by Chinese Americans visiting China were American citizens by birth and eligible for entry to their country. Many young men came to the United States as sons of American citizens of Chinese ancestry. Others came as imposters: known as "paper sons," they had purchased the birth certificates of American citizens born in China and then claimed they were citizens in order to enter the United States. [...] Exactly how many Chinese men falsely claimed citizenship as "paper sons" will never be known, but it was later calculated that if every claim to natural-born citizenship were valid, every Chinese woman living in San Francisco before 1906 would have had to have borne eight hundred children.[7]

But the purchase of a birth certificate did not mean entry, for the "paper sons" were detained at the immigration station on Angel Island in San Francisco, where they had to pass an examination and prove their American identity. To prepare for the examination, they studied "crib sheets," or *Hau-Kung*, and memorized information about the families of their "fathers": they had to remember "everyone's name, the birthday, and if they passed away, when." When they approached the Golden Gate, they tore up their crib sheets and threw them overboard. [...]

By the thousands, Chinese had begun entering the United States again. After sailing through the Golden Gate and disembarking on Angel Island, the newcomers were placed in the barracks of the immigration station. Their quarters were crowded and unsanitary, resembling a slum. "When we arrived," said one of them, "they locked us up like criminals in compartments like the cages in the zoo. They counted us and then took us upstairs to our rooms. There were two to three rooms in the women's section.... Each of the rooms could fit twenty or thirty persons." The men were placed in one large room. There were 190 "small boys up to old men, all together in the same room," a visitor reported in 1922. "Some were sleeping in the hammock like beds with their belongings hanging in every

possible way ... while others were smoking or gambling." The days were long and tedious, and "lights went out at a certain hour, about 9 P.M." But their "intestines agitated," many could not fall asleep. The inmates could see San Francisco to the west and Oakland to the east; they had journeyed so far to come to America and yet they had not been allowed to enter. [...]

But the newcomers were not released until they had convinced the authorities their papers were legitimate. And not everyone passed the examination. Approximately 10 percent of all the Chinese who landed on Angel Island were forced to board oceangoing ships and sent back to China. [...]

The lucky ones were allowed to hurry onto ferries and to sail happily to San Francisco. By 1943, some 50,000 Chinese had entered America through Angel Island. But they did not then go to the California foothills to become miners, the Sierra Nevada Mountains to work on the railroad, or the valleys of San Joaquin and Sacramento to join the migrant farm laborers. Unlike the earlier pioneers from China, they went to the cities, seeking shelter and employment in Chinatowns.

Gilded Ghettos: Chinatowns in the Early Twentieth Century

The geographical distribution of the Chinese in America changed significantly during the early decades of the twentieth century. By 1940, of the 77,504 Chinese on the mainland, 43,987, or 57 percent, resided in the Pacific states and 16,404, or 21 percent, in the Middle Atlantic states. Between 1900 and 1940, Chinatowns in the mountain and western regional cities like Butte, Boise, Rock Springs, Denver, and Salt Lake City were in decline. While the percentage of the Chinese population residing in cities with 100,000 or more inhabitants was only 22 percent in 1880 and 33 percent in 1900, it rose rapidly to 56 percent within twenty years and to 71 percent by 1940. Predominantly a rural people in the nineteenth century, the Chinese became mainly an urban group. By 1940, 91 percent of the Chinese population, compared to only 55 percent of the Japanese (and 57 percent of the total U.S. population), was classified by the Census Bureau as "urban."[8]

The urbanization of the Chinese population reflected several different developments. A Chinatown could survive, as Rose Hum Lee noted, only in a city with a population of at least 50,000, in an area with a diversified rather than a single industry, and in a state with a Chinese population of at least 250. Most of the Chinatowns in small western towns did not have these requirements. Secondly, the decline of the small Chinatowns was a consequence of the immigration exclusion laws and the absence of Chinese women. [...]

Pushed from the small towns, the Chinese were pulled to the metropolitan cities where employment was available in an ethnic-labor market. In the nineteenth century, Chinese laborers could be found in every sector of the American economy — agriculture, mining, manufacturing, and transportation. By 1920, they had virtually vanished from these areas of employment. The mainstay of California agriculture in the late nineteenth century, Chinese farm laborers did less than one percent of the harvesting in 1920. By then, there were only 151 Chinese miners, compared to 17,609 in 1870; only one hundred Chinese workers in cigar making and boot and shoe manufacturing, compared to more than 2,000 in 1870; only 488 Chinese railroad workers, compared to over 10,000 Chinese employed by the Central Pacific Railroad in the 1860s.

The Chinese were located in a different sector of the labor market from whites. By 1920, 58 percent of the Chinese were in services, most of them in restaurant and laundry work, compared to only 5 percent for native whites and 10 percent for foreign whites. Only 9 percent of Chinese were employed in manufacturing, compared to 26 percent for native whites and 47 percent for foreign whites. [...]

Explaining why so many Chinese had entered the laundry business, one of them said: "It is a very hard job, sure enough. But there is nothing else to do. This is the kind of life we have to take in America. I, as one of the many, do not like to work in the laundry, but what else can I do? You've got to take it; that's all." The Chinese laundryman personified the forced withdrawal of the Chinese into a segregated ethnic-labor market. They had not always been laundrymen; in fact, in 1870 of the 46,274 Chinese in all occupations, only 3,653, or 8 percent were laundry workers. By 1920, of 45,614 gainfully employed Chinese, 12,559, or 28 percent (nearly one out of three) were laundry workers. The number of Chinese laundries soared in the first half of the twentieth century. In Chicago, for example, there were 209 of them in 1903 and 704 twenty-five years later. In New York City by 1940, 38 percent of all gainfully employed Chinese were engaged in laundry work; Chinese laundries were "located on almost every street corner." Chinese laundrymen had to spread themselves out, to Chicago, New York, Baltimore, Los Angeles, and other cities and to different districts within a city, where there were not too many laundries.[9] [...]

Once he had secured his loan and opened his business, the Chinese laundryman found himself working long hours. During his visit to a Chinese laundry, sociologist Paul Siu recorded the activities of the day. Like most laundrymen, Tong and his partners lived in the back of the shop, and they woke early in the morning. At 8:00 A.M., Tong went out to collect the laundry. Hong and Wah worked inside, attending the steam boiler and washtub. Ming sorted and marked laundry in the office. The noise of the washing machine drowned out their conversation. Tong returned with a load of dirty laundry in a wooden trunk and left again. The first wash was done, and Hong and Wah rinsed and wrung it then hung it to dry. About ten Tong was back, bringing a second load with him. It took an hour and a half to wash, rinse, wring, and then hang the clothes in the drying rooms. Around ten-thirty, Hong began to cook lunch. For lunch on busy days, they had cold meats and cakes with coffee. In the afternoon, they turned to the next set of tasks: Hong and Ming did most of the starching work, while Wah and Tong did the damping and ironing. Afterward Hong set the collars and cuffs on a machine, a chore that took him the whole afternoon and deep into the night. At eleven thirty, all the men ate their dinner. After supper, they all sat in the yard to cool off before they went to bed, and they finally were able to fall asleep at one in the morning.[10] [...]

Isolated in white neighborhoods, Chinese laundries were connected to larger segregated ethnic islands in American cities — the Chinatowns. In 1920, concentrations of Chinese were present in Los Angeles, Oakland, Chicago, Seattle, Portland, Sacramento, and Boston. Forty percent of all Chinese lived in two cities — San Francisco and New York. The metropolitan Chinatowns developed a different character and purpose from the initial nineteenth-century Chinatowns. They were no longer way stations to service single-male workers in transit to the gold fields, farms, and railroads. While they remained a place of refuge for a bachelor society, Chinatowns became residential communities for families, Chinese economic enclaves, and tourist centers.[11]

In Chinatown in 1934, 276 families lived in 652 rooms, or cubicles, or 2.4 rooms per family. They had seventy bathrooms, or four families per bathroom, and 114 kitchens, or 2.4 families per kitchen. The average number of persons per bathroom was 20.4 and per kitchen 12.3. Six years later, 15,000 Chinese lived in a confined area only five blocks by four blocks in size, their residential spaces wedged between, above, and below shops, restaurants, and stores. Of the 3,830 dwelling units in Chinatown, a city housing authority report revealed, approximately 3,000 had no heating. "Buildings constructed after the fire to house single men on a bare existence basis — that is, containing tiny windowless rooms with hall toilets and kitchens and often no bath facilities anywhere — now housed families." Chinatown was a slum. Eighty-two percent of Chinese dwellings were substandard, compared to only 20 percent for the rest of the city's population. The tuberculosis rate in Chinatown was three times higher than the rate for the other residential areas of San Francisco. The children were forced to play in the streets, for Chinatown had no parks.[12]

A ghetto, Chinatown confirmed views of the Chinese as unhealthy, unassimilable, and undesirable immigrants, yet this same negative imagery opened the way to the development of Chinatown as a tourist center — a "quaint" and "mysterious" section of the city, a "foreign colony" in America. There, advertisements promised, white tourists could experience the "sounds, the sights, and the smells of Canton" and imagine themselves in "some hoary Mongolian city in the distant land of Cathay." They could "wander in the midst of the Orient while still in the Occident" and see throngs of people with "strange faces" in the streets and also "a few Ah Sins, bland and childlike as Bret Harte's immortal hero," sitting in restaurants and eating "chop suey."[13]

NOTES

1. Jacob Riis, *How the Other Half Lives: Studies Among the Tenements of New York* (rpt. Cambridge, Mass., 1970), p. 69.
2. Chinese rhyme, Hom (ed. and trans.), *Songs of Gold Mountain*, p. 124; letter by unknown Chinese migrant, in the Kam Wah Chung Company Papers, John Day, Oregon.
3. Chu-chia to Lung On, July 1899; wife to Lung On, n.d.; Lung On to Liang Kwanjin, March 2, 1905; Liang Kwan-jin to Lung On, March 4, 1905; Ing Du-hsio to Ing Hay, April 9, no year, translations by Chia-Lin Chen, Kam Wah Chung Company Papers.
4. Mrs. John W. Murray to Chia-Lin Chen, October 30, 1971, reprinted in Chen, "A Gold Dream in the Blue Mountains: A Study of the Chinese Immigrants in the John Day Area, Oregon, 1870–1910," unpublished M.A. thesis, Portland State University, 1972, pp. 123–124.
5. Esther Wong, "The History and Problem of Angel Island," March 1924, pp. 7–8, Survey of Race Relations, Stanford University, Hoover Institution Archives; "Interview with Mr. Faris, Deputy Commissioner of Immigration in Seattle," ibid., pp. 2–11.
6. Eliot G. Mears, *Resident Orientals on the American Pacific Coast* (Chicago, 1928), p. 408; Helen Chen, "Chinese Immigration into the United States: An Analysis of Changes in Immigration Policies," unpublished Ph.D. thesis, Brandeis University, 1980, p. 105; Nee, *Longtime Californ'*, p. 25; R. D. McKenzie, *Oriental Exclusion: The Effect of American Immigration Laws, Regulations, and Judicial Decisions upon the Chinese and Japanese on the American Pacific Coast* (Chicago, 1928) pp. 46, 94, 192, 194; S. W. Kung, *Chinese in American Life:*

Some Aspects of Their History, Status, Problems, and Contributions (Seattle, 1962), pp. 92, 100, 192–195; Wen-Hsien Chen, "Chinese Under Both Exclusion and Immigration Laws," unpublished Ph.D. thesis, University of Chicago, 1940, pp. 28–29. In a note to the author, July 1988, H. M. Lai points out that Chinese from remote areas like Grass Valley were also able to secure forged birth certificates.

7. Richard Kock Dare, "The Economic and Social Adjustment of the San Francisco Chinese for the Past Fifty Years," unpublished M.A. thesis, University of California Berkeley, 1959, p. 54.

8. Fuju Liu, "A Comparative Demographic Study of Native-Born and Foreign-Born Chinese Populations in the United States," unpublished Ph.D. thesis, Michigan State College, 1953, pp. 96, 97. "Urban area," as defined by the 1940 census report, "is made up for the most part of cities and other incorporated places having 2,500 inhabitants or more." *Sixteenth Census of the United States, 1940, Population*, vol. 2, part 1, p. 8.

9. Siu, "Chinese Laundryman," pp. 25, 146; Kung, *Chinese in American Life*, p. 57; Peter Kwong, *Chinatown, N.Y.: Labor & Politics, 1930–1950* (New York, 1979), p. 61; Wong Wee Ying, interview, May 7, 1982, Chinese Women of America Research Project, Chinese Culture Foundation of San Francisco, p. 4.

10. Siu, "Chinese Laundryman," pp. 88–89.

11. Lee, "Decline of Chinatowns," p. 428; Nee, *Longtime Californ'*, p. 62.

12. Lim P. Lee, "The Need for Better Housing in Chinatown," *Chinese Digest*, December 1938, p. 7; Carey McWilliams, *Brothers Under the Skin* (rpt. Boston, 1964, originally published in 1942), pp. 108–110; "The Life Story of Edward L. C. as written by himself," circa 1924, p. 5, Survey of Race Relations, Stanford University, Hoover Institution Archives.

13. Herman Scheffaner, "The Old Chinese Quarter," *Liuing Age* (August 10, 1907) pp. 360, 362; "Historic Chinatown," *San Francisco Chronicle*, October 1, 1917 and December 24, 1917.

The Pullman Strike and Making Sense of the Age

Carl Smith

Source: *Urban Disorder and the Shape of Belief: The Great Chicago Fire, the Haymarket Bomb, and the Model Town of Pullman* (Chicago: University of Chicago Press, 1995).

EDITORS' INTRODUCTION

Professors teaching urban history note the rich array of sources on Chicago, especially the city's late nineteenth-century past. Chicago was America's infamous city, whose reputation for crime-ridden streets, congested tenements filled with newly arrived immigrants, and the open vice of the Levee district riveted Americans who were afraid and fascinated at the same time about what their nation was becoming.[i] The resonance of this symbolic image for America was akin to that of Manchester, England in the 1840s, which was, according to historian Asa Briggs, the "shock city" of its day. The Great Chicago Fire of 1871 began in the barn of Catherine and Patrick O'Leary at the juncture of DeKoven and Jefferson Streets. This conflagration destroyed over 2,000 acres of the city and secured Chicago an important place in the nation's popular culture. In order to revive the image of the city, Chicago entrepreneurs organized the Columbian Exposition of 1893, a world's fair. The Pullman Strike of 1894, however, destroyed much of the positive effect of the 1893 exposition.

In this selection, Carl Smith provides commentary on the Pullman Strike, which began on May 11, 1894. This pivotal event intrigued Americans, drawn to the epic battle between Pullman Palace Car Company owner, George Pullman, heretofore known for his paternalism towards his workers, and the insolvent and increasingly violent strikers. The strike was one of the watershed events of the era, symbolizing the economic instability and social unrest of the time. Workers protested long hours and pay cuts, insisting on simultaneous rent reductions within Pullman, Illinois. This model company town, built by George Pullman between 1880 and 1884, lay just outside of Chicago and was annexed by the city in 1889. Thousands of eager visitors to the Columbian Exposition toured Pullman's orderly streets. George Pullman, however, refused to alter rents in the face of a growing national depression, and the laborers, under the direction of Eugene V. Debs and the American Railway Union, launched a formal strike against their employer. Railroad workers throughout the country refused to connect Pullman cars to trains, and train traffic snarled. The federal government intervened in July 1894, and President Grover Cleveland sent troops into Chicago to maintain order and restore train service. Although the union broke under pressure, the federal panel which later investigated the strike found fault with George Pullman and his paternalistic company town. Pullman was ordered to divest his holdings in the town that bore his name, and when he died in 1897, he was buried at the Graceland Cemetery under steel and concrete to protect him from possible desecration.

Carl Smith serves as the Franklyn Bliss Snyder Professor of English & American Studies at Northwestern University. He has authored three major books on Chicago history, all of which transcend the local story to tell us something very important about

---

i See Lisa Krissoff Boehm, *Popular Culture and the Enduring Myth of Chicago, 1871–1968* (New York: Routledge, 2004).

the national urban past. *Urban Disorder and the Shape of Belief*, from which this selection is taken, won the Urban History Association's prize for Best Book in North American Urban History and the Society of Midland Authors' first prize for non-fiction. Smith authored the books *Chicago and the American Literary Imagination, 1880–1920* (Chicago: University of Chicago Press, 1984) and *The Plan of Chicago: Daniel Burnham and the Remaking of the American City* (Chicago: University of Chicago Press, 2006). Smith has also designed two award-winning websites featuring rich primary document sources and commentary for the Chicago History Museum's exhibitions, *The Great Chicago Fire and the Web of Memory*, and *The Dramas of Haymarket*.[ii]

MAKING SENSE OF THE AGE

"The Pullman strike," Jane Addams recollected in *Twenty Years at Hull-House*, "afforded much illumination to many Chicago people. Before it, there had been nothing in my experience to reveal that distinct cleavage of society, which a general strike at least momentarily affords." She described it elsewhere in literary terms as "a drama which epitomized and, at the same time, challenged the code of social ethics under which we live, for a quick series of unusual events had dispelled the good nature which in happier times envelopes the ugliness of the industrial situation." She most regretted "the sharp division into class lines, with the resultant distrust and bitterness." Addams recalled also how much the strike entered public consciousness on a personal level. "Every public-spirited citizen in Chicago during that summer," Addams explained, "felt the stress and perplexity of the situation and asked himself, 'How far am I responsible for this social disorder?'"[1]

If Addams perhaps overestimated the readiness of her fellow citizens to consider their own responsibility for the bitter feelings and class conflict that surrounded the Pullman strike, she was correct in her perception that many serious-minded people in Chicago and across the nation shared "the stress and perplexity of the situation" and tried to explain what it meant. Like the Great Chicago Fire and the Haymarket bombing before it, the Pullman strike became a major topic for analysis in itself and in relation to historical change in America, especially that change most fully represented in city life. The discussion of the strike soon opened into a consideration of the nature of the present, particularly the American urban present, at the close of the nineteenth century, that revealed a tension between old and new bases of conceptualizing modern reality.

On the one hand, many of the terms that were used to characterize the individuals, groups, and ideas that seemed to be determining events, and the interpretive narratives that were offered to explain these events, had been in the cultural imagination for some time. The understanding of Haymarket heavily influenced the analyses of the Pullman strike, just as concerns expressed in the fire literature and in commentaries on the railroad strike of 1877 shaped the view of what had happened at Haymarket. Once again different spokespersons tried to win public support for their opinions by claiming that they represented the real America. And, as before, they maintained that what the opposition said was the reverse of the truth, and that ideas, methods, goals, and leaders of the other side promoted disorder and disaster. All of this gives much of the debate over the meaning of Pullman a certain familiar quality that reveals the staying power of certain ideas and forms of expression in the discussion of urban disorder in post—Civil War America. On the other hand, some questioned the old terms and categories in light of the fact that they no longer seemed to apply to what appeared to be a new kind of social order.

---

ii See *The Great Chicago Fire and the Web of Memory* website at www.chicagohistory.org/fire/ and *The Dramas of Haymarket* at www.chicagohistory.org/dramas/.

A Walkout in Utopia

The Pullman strike was really not one strike but two, a small walkout limited to company employees and a nation-wide sympathetic boycott by members of the American Railway Union of trains pulling Pullman cars. The first was rooted in long-standing discontents with the company, but its immediate cause was the Panic of 1893. The international economic downturn that began in the spring was delayed locally by the Columbian Exposition, but it soon descended on Chicago in full force. The closing of the exposition and the continuing flow of new-comers into the city in a time of general depression created massive unemployment. Without food, shelter, or hope of income, by mid-November people were taking meals at soup kitchens and sleeping on the hard stone stairways and floors of City Hall and, as in 1873, police stations. [...]

The employees of the Pullman Company faced tough times as the demand for the products they manufactured dropped off. The flow of praise for the model town as immune to all the conflict and upsets suffered elsewhere continued into the spring of 1894, but negative reports appeared more frequently in the Chicago newspapers.[2] The company's visibility, not to mention its reputation for being the answer to the problems that beset capital and labor, made its difficulties a compelling subject, especially for those journalists who were already skeptical about the Pullman idea. "Great destitution and suffering prevails in Pullman," the Chicago Times declared in early December of 1893, contending that the "sullen gloom" that "envelope[d] the whole town" was born not so much of poverty but "of bitterness and a feeling of resentment at what is openly called the slavery imposed by the conditions of employment by the Pullman company." Like Richard Ely, the Times maintained that the company's housing policies and prices made for a shifting and resentful population. What stability there was in the community derived not from the imposed system of social control, but from the workers' loyalty to each other. [...]

The Times's anti-Pullman articles contained a few exaggerations, but they were not far from the mark in describing conditions in the town. In response to a drop in orders, the company had begun to cut wages in August of 1893, and the number of employees fell from 4,500 to 1,100 between July and November. Pullman's decision to take new contracts even at a loss raised employment to 3,100 by April of 1894, but this was done by spreading work and with a continuing decline in pay. Insisting that the administration of the factories had no connection to the housing, the company refused to reduce rents. Unable to make ends meet, employees protested and organized. There had been strike actions or threats of strikes by workers in different trades since the early 1880s, but none of the actions were of significant breadth and duration.[3] By the spring of 1894, company operatives across the trades had combined under the auspices of the American Railway Union, which had been founded in Chicago only a year before but which now boasted 150,000 members nationwide and was fresh from a major victory in a strike against the Great Northern Railroad.

A committee of workers met with Pullman executive Thomas Wickes in company headquarters on Michigan Avenue in early May to ask for adjustments in wages and rents and to complain about the practices of shop foremen. Accompanied George Howard, vice president of American Railway Union, they spoke again with Wickes and with other representatives of the company two days later. George Pullman joined this second meeting after it began, but neither he nor his subordinates promised any substantial relief. The chances of reaching an accord diminished when the company, after promising no reprisals, fired three workers who were on the committee. This quickly led to a strike on May 11. As the lines were drawn in this "industrial war," the rhetoric on all sides became more confrontational. American Railway Union president Eugene Victor Debs proclaimed, "The whole country is in an inflammable condition."[4] [...]

On June 20 the American Railway Union informed the Pullman Company that beginning June 26 its members would no longer handle trains that included Pullman cars. In response to this threat, the General Managers Association of the twenty-four railroads serving Chicago met on June 25 to plan tactics. They empowered John M. Egan to direct their strategy, which was based on the argument that the boycott was an illegal and unjustified violation of contract.[5] At first, the American Railway Union was very successful and appeared to have the upper hand.... But the federal government was more than ready to take management's side. Attorney General Richard Olney, a Boston corporate lawyer who had represented and served on the boards of several leading railroads, maintained that the boycott obstructed interstate commerce and the United States mail, and on July 2 the United States Circuit Court issued an exceptionally broad injunction, restraining, commanding, and enjoining Debs, his union, and "all other persons combining and conspiring with them" from interfering or encouraging anyone else to interfere with railroad traffic.

President Grover Cleveland ordered troops into Chicago from Fort Sheridan, over the objections of Governor Altgeld and Chicago mayor John P. Hopkins, who was, coincidentally, a former Pullman employee who had risen quickly in the company and in George Pullman's esteem until the two of them had a falling out.[6] In a talk on the strike he gave at Princeton ten years later that was also published in *McClure's*, Cleveland sounded like those who had spoken against the Haymarket accused when he called the Pullman strike a "conspiracy" that "immensely increased executive anxiety and foreboded the most calamitous and far-reaching consequences."[7] The soldiers arrived just after midnight on Independence Day, 1894. Their commander, General Nelson Miles, summoned more troops from posts in Michigan, Kansas, and Nebraska, and within a week there were almost 2,000 army regulars in the city, many of them living in an encampment of tents pitched on the lakefront near the Pullman Building.[8] For the third time in a little more than twenty years, Chicago was under military occupation.

While Altgeld continued to protest against this federal intervention and Debs counseled

against physical confrontation, violence broke out in several areas throughout the city, leading to the shooting of two rioters and the destruction of over 700 cars at the Panhandle yards in South Chicago. [...]

As in 1877, the violence was in all likelihood not the work of union leaders, who posted their own guards to protect the Pullman factories, but of thrill-seeking troublemakers, unemployed and otherwise discontented workers with no direct connection to the strike or the boycott, and individuals resentful of the power of the railroads. The anti-union journalists were still not ready to make distinctions between vandals and strikers, however. Most newspapers called the boycott an unprovoked war not on the Pullman Company or even the railroads, which had no disputes with the Pullman operatives, but against the basis of the social order. Debs answered that "the struggle with the Pullman company has developed into a contest between the producing classes and the money power of the country."[9] [...]

On July 7 a mob tried to obstruct a train at 49th and Loomis that was being protected by the state militia. They pelted the soldiers with stones, provoking a bayonet charge and a series of encounters that left several people on both sides wounded and four more rioters dead. The same day General Miles and the federal marshal decided to despatch mail trains from six major depots. The military presence, the arrest of Debs and other leaders for contempt, the breakdown of communications between strike committees throughout the country, the lack of support from other national unions (notably the American Federation of Labor and the Knights of Labor), the adamant stance of the Pullman Company, the unified will and power of the General Managers Association, and the general ebbing of the riot fever together caused the American Railway Union boycott to collapse.[10] By July 10 the militia had broken a blockade of trains in the stockyards, and within a few days the union was totally beaten. On July 18, with the battle won, Attorney General Olney ordered the army to evacuate.

Convicted of contempt, Debs served six months in the McHenry County jail in rural

Woodstock, where his reading supposedly included *Looking Backward* and *The Cooperative Commonwealth*. Debs later stated that the whole experience was crucial in his conversion to socialism.[11]... Despite the efforts of several prominent attorneys, including Clarence Darrow and the distinguished former Illinois senator Lyman Trumbull (now in his eighties), both of whom had advised Governor Altgeld the year before in his decision to issue the Haymarket pardon, the Supreme Court unanimously upheld the federal government, handing down its decision in May of 1895. As prescribed by law, President Cleveland appointed a three-member Strike Commission to investigate what had happened. The commission was headed by United States Commissioner of Labor Statistics Carroll D. Wright, who had led the 1884 Pullman tour by state labor commissioners. In mid-August the commission began taking testimony. It heard from over a hundred witnesses on both sides, including Debs and Pullman.[12]

The panel went beyond the events of June and July to investigate the underlying causes of the original strike against the Pullman Company. If George Pullman and the railway managers expected vindication for themselves and the same kind of condemnation of labor organizers that had come out of the Haymarket trial, they were badly disappointed. The tone of the official findings by these sober experts was appropriately restrained, but the message was sharp and clear. George Pullman's policies had left his workers "without local attachments or any interested responsibility in the town, its business, tenements, or surroundings." His grand design, far from offering a model for a sound social order, had torn the whole country apart. The commissioners criticized the Pullman Company's refusal to arbitrate, saying that they were "impressed with the belief, by the evidence and by the attendant circumstances as disclosed, that a different policy would have prevented the loss of life and great loss of property and wages occasioned by the strike." They recommended the establishment of a permanent United States Strike Commission and other actions to prevent economic disputes from turning into social disorders.[13]

NOTES

1. Jane Addams, *Twenty Years at Hull-House*, p. 158; "A Modern Lear," p. 107.

2. In an article headlined "Where Peace Reigns," one local paper confidently observed, "Just now, when the whole country is trembling with the fever of a diseased labor condition, one finds a sort of satisfaction in studying the status of a town that is based and founded on labor, and yet one in which there is no serious clash between the interests of those who work for wages and the men who live from the profits of labor employed." *Chicago Sunday Herald* (29 April 1894), PSNL. Miscellaneous Scrapbooks, Series A, vol. 17.

3. Buder, *Pullman*, p. 149. For a summary of strike action among Pullman workers, see Leyendecker, *Palace Car Prince*, pp. 180–81. In fairness to the company, it should be noted that it did not raise rents in good times, nor did it aggressively try to evict tenants who fell behind. There seems to have been little public discussion of whether the landlords of operatives outside of Pullman should reduce rents.

4. *Chicago Tribune* (15 May 1894), PSNL Strike Scrapbooks, vol. 1.

5. The General Managers Association had been inactive since the mid-1880s but was reorganized under new leadership early in 1893, almost simultaneously with the formation of the American Railway Union. Both developments were based in the recognition by the respective memberships that their individual interests would be best served by a common national strategy. Stromquist, *A Generation of Boomers*, p. 251.

6. Hopkins was perhaps the most notable case of an operative whose talent and initiative George Pullman tried to develop and reward. He started as a laborer in the lumberyards, but Pullman quickly promoted the highly capable employee and helped him get started in his own stores in the Arcade. Hopkins's highest post in the company was paymaster. A Democrat, Hopkins favored annexation to Chicago and helped carry Pullman for Cleveland in 1888. See Almont Lindsey, *The Pullman Strike: The Story of a Unique Experiment and a Great Labor Upheaval* (Chicago: University of Chicago Press, 1942), pp. 80–81. This book is the most detailed history of the strike. For a brief summary, with excellent visual material on the town and the walkout, see Susan E. Hirsch, "The Metropolis of the West," in Hirsch and Goler, *A City Comes of Age*, pp. 76–82. On Altgeld's role in the strike, including his sympathy toward the Pullman residents suffering from the strike (whom he visited personally and for whom he helped raise contributions in the summer of 1894), his antagonism toward George Pullman and the Pullman Company, and the sharp criticisms he endured for his stance, see Barnard, *"Eagle Forgotten,"* pp. 271–317.

7. Grover Cleveland, *The Government in the Chicago Strike of 1894* (Princeton: Princeton University Press, 1913), p. 2. The article appeared in *McClure's* in July 1904.

8. See Lindsey, *The Pullman Strike*, pp. 206–7, for disputes between Miles and Major General John M. Schofield, commander of the army, on the placement of troops. In all, Cleveland sent out two-thirds of the army, or about 16,000 troops, along with some sailors and marines to deal with the strike across the nation. See Edward M. Coffman, *The Old Army: A Portrait of the American Army in Peacetime, 1784–1898* (New York: Oxford University Press, 1986), p. 251.

9. John M. Egan called the charge that men were recruited by the railroads to burn cars "the vilest rot." *Report on the Chicago Strike*, pp. 158, 282; *Chicago Times* (30 June 1894), PSNL. Strike Scrapbooks, vol. 2; Eugene V. Debs, "The Federal Government and the Chicago Strike," in *Writings and Speeches of Eugene V. Debs* (New York: Hermitage Press, 1948), p. 150. Debs originally prepared this last article as a response to Cleveland's essay in *McClure's*, but it was rejected, and he published it instead in the socialist journal *Appeal to Reason* in August of 1904. Almont Lindsey writes, "They [the mobs] were prepared to take advantage of any situation that would yield excitement and plunder. Unemployment and insecurity—products of the panic of 1893—had fostered a spirit of recklessness and despair, which in turn must have contributed to the recklessness of the crowds that assembled as much from curiosity as from any desire to do violence." *The Pullman Strike*, p. 205. The composition of the various mobs and their motives is hard to figure precisely, especially given the eagerness of the railroads and the government to pin the blame on Debs and the unions, and Debs's inability to restrain each and every worker no matter how eloquently he argued that disorder could only harm the union in the public eye. Lindsey sees no firm proof of agents provocateurs, but notes that there is some evidence that a few of the cars were fired by deputy marshals and that, though the railroads were careless in protecting their property, nothing very valuable was damaged. It is also possible that even if they did not deliberately plan the violence, the 5,000 belligerent and unprofessional deputies who were hired and armed by the railroads were as much a provocation as a deterrent to disorder.

10. Lindsey, *The Pullman Strike*, pp. 208–10. The main reason for the lack of wider union solidarity was that the strike seemed at this point to be a lost cause, but the personal, philosophical, and tactical disagreements among different unions and their leaders complicated the issue. On the intricate union politics of the time—and the tensions between Debs and Gompers in particular—see Nick Salvatore, *Eugene V. Debs: Citizen and Socialist* (Urbana: University of Illinois Press, 1982), pp. 135–37.

11. Debs, "How I Became a Socialist," in *Debs: His Life, Writings and Speeches* (Girard, Kans.: The Appeal to Reason, 1908), p. 82.

12. Wright served as chairman ex officio, while the other two members were John D. Kernan of New York and Nicholas E. Worthington of Illinois (the law prescribed one member from the local state).

13. *Report on the Chicago Strike*, pp. xxii, xlii; *Chicago Tribune* (13 November 1894), PSNL Strike Scrapbooks, vol. 9. The Commission set the cost of destroyed property and of the marshals at just under $700,000, the loss of earnings by the railroads at $4,672,916. It calculated that about 3,100 Pullman employees lost at least $350,000 in wages, and that some 100,000 workers on the twenty-four railroads centered in Chicago lost an estimated $1,389,143. *Report on the Chicago Strike*, p. xiii. The report is a remarkable document, not only for the blummess of its findings, which had the effect of countering the anti-union feeling in official circles, but as a coherently focused collection of testimony by principals and other parties deeply involved in the strike and the events surrounding it.

DOCUMENTS FOR PART III

3-1. VESEY SLAVE REVOLT, CHARLESTON, SOUTH CAROLINA (1822)

Source: *An Account of the Late Intended Insurrection among a Portion of the Blacks of this City.* Second Edition (Charleston: Corporation of Charleston, Printed by A. E. Miller, 1822). Courtesy of the American Antiquarian Society, Worcester, Massachusetts.

EDITORS' INTRODUCTION

This pamphlet, most likely written by Charleston Mayor James Hamilton, Jr., and published by the city of Charleston, was meant to inform white Charlestonians about the details of a slave uprising. According to the pamphlet, one slave reported a planned uprising of other slaves and free blacks for June 16, 1822, which led to a series of arrests (eventually numbering 131 in total). Among the free blacks arrested was Denmark Vesey who had come to the United States in 1781 as a slave and had purchased his freedom with the winnings of a lottery. Government officials executed Vesey and thirty-five others to discourage any further disturbances. At that time, the majority of people in Charleston were African American, and thus white officials remained vigilant about possible threats. Documents related to the Vesey uprising are thin, and some historians even question the existence of a conspiracy.[i]

On Thursday the 27th, Denmark Vesey, a free black man, was brought before the Court for trial,

Assisted by his Counsel, G.W. Cross Esq.

It is perhaps somewhat remarkable, that at this stage of the investigation, although several witnesses had been examined, the *atrocious* guilt of *Denmark Vesey* had not been as yet fully unfolded. From the testimony of most of the witnesses, however, the Court found enough, and amply enough, to warrant the sentence of death, which, on the 28th, they passed on him. But every subsequent step in the progress of the trials of others, lent new confirmation to his overwhelming guilt, and placed him beyond a doubt, on the criminal eminence of having been the individual, in whose bosom the nefarious scheme was first engendered. There is ample reason for believing, that this project was not, with him, of recent origin, for it was said, he had spoken of it for upwards of four years.

These facts of his guilt the journals of the court will disclose—that no man can be proved to have spoken of or urged the insurrection prior to himself. All the channels of communication and intelligence are traced back to him. His house was the place appointed for the secret meetings of the conspirators, at which he was invariably a leading and influential member; animating and encouraging the timid, by the hopes of prospects of success; removing the scruples of the religious, by the grossest prostitution and perversion of the sacred oracles, and inflaming and confirming the resolute, by all the savage fascinations of blood and booty. [...]

He was sentenced for execution of the 2d of July.

---

i Sources differ as to the date of the planned uprising, and some point to an initial date of mid-July, which was moved forward due to secrecy concerns. A few place Vesey's immigration to the U.S. in 1771 rather than 1781. Others question the existence of a conspiracy at all, wondering if the investigations, trial, and executions were staged in order to impart order in Charleston. See Richard C. Wade, *Slavery in the Cities: The South 1820–1860* (Oxford: Oxford University Press, 1967), Thomas Wentworth Higginson, *Denmark Vesey, The Atlantic* (originally published in *The Atlantic Monthly*, 7(44) (1861): 728–744, www.theatlantic.com/issues/1861jun/higgin.htm (January 12, 2009), John Lofton, *Denmark Vesey's Revolt* (Kent, OH: Kent State University Press, 1983), Edward A. Pearson, ed., *Designs Against Charleston: The Trial Record of the Denmark Vesey Slave Conspiracy of 1822* (Chapel Hill: University of North Carolina Press, 1999), David Robertson, *Denmark Vesey* (New York: Knopf, 1999), Robert S. Starobin, ed., *Denmark Vesey: The Slave Conspiracy of 1822* (New York: Prentice-Hall, 1970).

3-2. TREDEGAR AND ARMORY IRON WORKS, RICHMOND, VIRGINIA (1847)

Source: *The Richmond Inquirer*, May 29, 1847 (including reprints from the *Richmond Republican* and *The Daily Richmond Whig*). Courtesy of the American Antiquarian Society, Worcester, Massachusetts.

EDITORS' INTRODUCTION

John Cumbler's essay, "From Milling to Manufacturing: From Villages to Mill Towns," explores the rise of industrialization in New England. While that region was the birthplace of American manufacturing, other sections of the country also developed factories. Even the pre-Civil War South turned to factory production in a limited scope, often with the use of slave labor. In fact, although many contemporary scholars have argued that slavery and factory work were antithetical, in some cases slavery made southern industry possible. Historian Kathleen Bruce, in her study of Virginia iron ore manufacturing, argues that it was precisely because of slave labor that the Richmond industry survived. Richmond iron manufacturers hired skilled white laborers from the North, who trained slaves to work within plants. Bruce concludes that the Virginia iron industry transformed after the 1850s into an industry strictly serving the South. She writes that:

> The climax of Virginian iron manufacture came in 1861, when, though small in volume, it entered for four years upon the national stage of American history, since without it and without the allied industry of Richmond coal, which had been active from the eighteenth century, it is difficult to see how the Confederacy could have persisted.[i]

The document below contains a series of articles culled from several different newspapers all reprinted on a single day in *The Richmond Inquirer*, we learn that many white factory workers had qualms about working side-by-side with slaves. Some of these workers had come from northern industries for these jobs. Free workmen balked at teaching their skill-set to men in bondage, fearing they would not be hired by other mills who might blacklist them for sharing industry secrets across racial lines. They also worried that by training less-expensive workers, they would ultimately be fired in favor of their enslaved trainees.

Tredegar and Armory Iron Works

In common with our associates of the press, we deeply regret the unfortunate controversy which has recently occurred between the workmen of the Tredegar and new Armory Iron Works and their employers. We quote the publications which we find in the *Republican* of Thursday, to show the origin of a movement which our whole community must condemn:

Richmond, May 23d, 1847
Resolved, That we, the Workmen of Tredegar Iron Works, do pledge ourselves that we will not go to work, unless the negroes be removed from the Puddling Furnace, at the new mill—like-wise from the Squeezer and Rolls in the old mill.

2d. *Resolved*, further, That we, the Pudlers, will not work for less than $4.50 per ton.

(Signed by the Puddlers of Tredegar Works.)

Resolved, That we, the Puddlers of the New Mill, will act on the above resolution.

(Signed by the Puddlers of Armory Works.)

We, the Helpers of Puddling Furnaces, do act with the above resolution.

(Signed by the Helpers at Puddling Furnaces.)

---

i Kathleen Bruce, *Virginia Iron Manufacture in the Slave Era* (New York: Augustus M. Kelley, 1968), vii–viii. There were also other factories that employed slaves. See Charles B. Dew, *Bond of Iron: Master and Slave at Buffalo Forge* (New York: W. W. Norton & Company, 1994) which chronicles the iron-making operations of Buffalo Forge, in Rockbridge County, Virginia.

Richmond, May 22d, 1847

We, the Heaters, do stand out for one dollar per ton for all sizes.

(Signed by the Heaters.)

We, the Rollers, do not intend to work until the above resolution is complied with.

(Signed by the Rollers.)

And the following note was communicated with the resolutions, to Mr. J.R. Anderson, the lessee of the Tredegar Works:

Mr. Anderson and Managers:

Gentlemen—You need not light up the Furnaces Monday, nor any time, until you comply with our resolution.

Two questions are raised in the above resolutions, viz: a demand for higher wages and the employment of negroes, but from the following additional resolution adopted on Wednesday, it is evident that the latter is the only point in issue. Indeed, it is emphatically avowed in so many words:

"At a called meeting of the Workmen of the Tredegar Iron Works,–

"*Resolved*, That whereas it has been rumored that we, the said workmen, intended to raise a mob to injury of our employers, in consequence of the difficulty that has arisen between us and the said employers, from their wishing to employ and instruct colored people in our stead in the said Tredegar Iron Works, the undersigned, workmen of the said Tredegar Works, take this method of showing to the public that we have not attempted to raise a mob, (as was rumored,) or otherwise to injure any of our employers—*having no other object in view at the time that we resolved to strike, but that of trying to prohibit the employment of colored people on the said Works.*"

On Wednesday Mr. Anderson addressed the following letter to his workmen:

To my late Workmen at the Tredegar Iron Works.

On Saturday last, I received by the hands of Gatewood Talley, information that you had determined, by a mutual combination, that you would not work for me again until I had discharged my negroes from the Squeezer and Puddle Rolls, where they had been working several years, and until the "Armory Iron Company" had discharged theirs from the puddling furnaces—and that the Puddlers and Heaters required their pay to be increased. I requested Mr. Talley to say to you, that I regretted that you had given up constant employment at good wages, always promptly paid in cash, but that I fully recognized the right of any individual to leave my employment at any time—at the same time, I had no idea of relinquishing my right to discharge or employ any one [sic] at my pleasure—that I had not designed to put negroes to puddling at the Tredegar works, but that now I should be compelled by your quitting my employment to do so, and that I had never intended to discharge any of my hands who did their duty—that in reference to the price of puddling, I had advanced the price two or three years ago when iron advanced; and when iron fell last summer, I might with propriety have reduced the wages, but have not done so to this day—that the heaters and puddlers, who complained of low wages, could earn with ordinary diligence, from $2 to $2.75, whilst the rollers may earn from $3 to $5 per day—and that I could not accede to any demand they had made. If I were to yield to your demands, I would be giving up the rights guaranteed to me by the constitution and laws of the State in which we live. This, I hope, you will never expect me to do; and having heard nothing further from you since my reply was conveyed to you on the 22d inst., I must infer that you do not intend to work for me any longer. I therefore give you notice, that I wish all who occupy my houses to give me possession of them as soon as practicable, and I have given directions for your accounts to be made out. I will waive all claim on account of the usual notice not being given, and will, in advance of the usual pay day, pay each man all that is due to him as soon as he delivers to me the possession of his house. Those who do not occupy my houses will be paid off to-morrow, and all I have to add, is, that you will bear in mind that you have *discharged yourselves*—that I gave assurance beforehand to two of your members, Henry Thomas and Lott Joy, that I would never discharge one of you who continued to do his duty to me; and now, having endeavored to do my duty as your employer, I wish that you may, one and all of you, never regret that you have given up the employment you had from me.

Your obedient servant,
J.R. Anderson

Tredegar Iron Works, May 26, 1847

These are all the facts which have been made public—and we cannot entertain the least doubt that the community, with a knowledge of what has transpired, will fully sustain Mr. Anderson in his just, liberal and proper course. As public journalists, we feel called upon to give an expression of what we deem public sentiment upon a question involving the value of slave labor and the rights and privileges of masters and employers. The principle set up in this case is not confined to Mr. Anderson or the Tredegar Works alone, but is of a general application to all kinds of business, and is, therefore, a matter of vital interest to the whole community. If it be sanctioned, it will render slave property utterly valueless, and place employers in the power of those employed, the latter dictating to the former what species of labor they shall employ in their service. We agree with the *Whig*, which says:

"It is probably that this view of the subject had not presented itself to the minds of the heretofore orderly, industrious and worthy workmen at the Tredegar works, and that they have permitted their over-wrought feelings to carry them beyond the bounds of prudence and propriety. Whether this be so or not, however, it is not less certain that the claim they set up, (as we told one of them personally a few days ago, who desired us to insert an article in vindication of their position, which we respectfully declined,) is wholly inadmissible in this latitude. The right of employers to select such kinds of labor as they may prefer, is one of which the law itself cannot deprive them—much less combinations of individuals, formed either for the purpose of intimidation, or with the less criminal, though unworthy design of inducing, for other reasons, acquiescence in their demands. The sympathies of all communities are naturally and properly most generally in favor of the hard working-man, whose toils ought to be fairly requited; but in *this* community, no combination, formed for the *purpose* avowed by the authors of the recent strike, can receive the slightest toleration. We hope that better counsels and wiser determinations may prevail among the workmen—and that we may soon hear that the harmony and good feeling heretofore existing between them and their employers has been entirely restored."

3-3. RIOTS, LOUISVILLE, KENTUCKY

Source: *New York Daily Times* and *Louisville Journal*.

EDITORS' INTRODUCTION

On August 6, 1855, a date known as "Bloody Monday," riots broke out in Louisville, Kentucky in conjunction to debates about whether the foreign-born, including naturalized citizens, ought to be allowed to vote in the election held that day. Scores of people were severely injured in the melee, at least twenty-two people were killed, and some estimates place the number much higher. Rioters looted businesses and set homes on fire. Anti-immigrant articles appeared in the *Louisville Journal*, whose sentiments leaned clearly toward the increasingly popular American Party. This party was referred to as the Know-Nothings, a xenophobic, anti-Catholic body that derived its nickname from members' secret password, "I know nothing." Note below how differently the *Louisville Journal* and the *New York Daily Times* (later the *New York Times*), which looked more favorably upon immigration, reported the story. In 2006, after the 150th anniversary of the riots, the Ancient Order of Hibernians, the German American Club, the German Heritage Auxiliary, and other civic organizations placed a marker in the riot area to memorialize the event.

"The First Blood Shed," *Louisville Journal,* **as reprinted by the** *New York Daily News,* **August 11, 1855**

The Anti-Americans may assert and protest and swear as strongly as they will, that the fearful riots of Monday were begun by the Americans, but in disproof of this, the broad, palpable, undeniable and undenied fact stands out, that the first bloodshed, the first killing, the first murdering, both in the upper and in the lower parts of the city were the work of the foreign born population. The foreigners may have imagined that they did not have fair play at the polls, but they were the first to resort to assassination. They may have falsely imagined that an attack upon themselves was contemplated, but they were the first to resort to assassination. They may have erroneously supposed that they were rendering an important service to God and mankind, but they were the first to resort to assassination. And when foreign-born citizens with not the shadow of justification, assassinate American citizens in our streets, what can be expected but that the aroused spirit of our countrymen will rage and thirst for revenge?

Even by the admission of one of the Anti-American organs of yesterday, the Irish in the lower part of the city on Monday evening, with no other provocation than the knocking down of an Irishman in the street, opened a general fire from the windows of their houses, discharging volley after volley among the American citizens. And who will say that so common a thing as a blow given by and individual in the street afforded a pretext for a general discharge of Irish musketry from concealed places upon American throngs? Can it be thought strange if some of our countrymen, enraged by the spilling of the blood of their kindred under such circumstances of atrocity, took quick vengeance into their own hands and carried it to a lamentable extent?

This disparity between the number of foreign-born and native-born citizens killed is but small, and the Coroner can bear witness, and many hundreds of others can bear witness, that the first persons killed in both extremities of the city were Americans—shot down by dogs by unseen foes. Unquestionably a large number of the Americans, infuriated by the massacre of their friends, have evinced a disposition to go much too far in the work of retaliation—and therein they are guilty; but this shall not deter us from the assertion and reiteration of the great fact that American bosoms were stained with blood before American hands were.

New York Daily News, **August 13, 1855**

We quote copiously again to-day from the Louisville newspapers,—not only such facts as are asserted concerning the origin and progress of the late Riots, but also the controversial opinions and assertions of the journals representing the several parties. Nothing could be more directly and explicitly contradictory than their statements. The Louisville *Journal,* the organ and champion of the Know-Nothings, asserts that the whole difficulty began with the foreign populations,—that they committed the first aggressions,—made the first assaults,—shed the first blood, and are, therefore, justly responsible for the whole affair. The *Courier* and the *Democrat,* both warmly hostile to the Know-Nothings, deny that the foreigners commenced the riot, and declare that it was started by drunken rowdies who assailed the Irish and Germans with abuse and blows wherever they could meet them. And they further quote paragraphs from the *Journal* of the day previous to the election, saying that the native American voters were to have the first chance at the polls, and that if *any* were excluded, it must be those of foreign birth—as proof that injustice and wrong were designed from the outset and led to these natural results.

Nothing, certainly, could be more inappropriate than the language of the *Journal* referred to;—and if not designed to provoke violence, it was well calculated to exasperate those against whom it was directed. Nothing can justify any preference of one citizen over another at the polls. If all are *citizens*; all have an equal right to vote; and any attempt to discriminate,—to admit one and exclude another, or to assert the *right* of one to precedence over the other, on any ground whatever, is a gross violation of right and a direct provocation to resentment and outrage.

It is not shown by any positive proof that these articles had any actual connection with the riots. But it was very injudicious, to say the least, and may fairly be regarded as among the causes which stimulated the ill-feeling that vented itself in violence and bloodshed.

3-4. DEBATES ON CHINESE IMMIGRATION (1876)

Source: *Immigration of Chinese, Speech of Hon. Aaron A. Sargent of California, In the Senate of the United States*, May 2, 1876. Courtesy of the American Antiquarian Society, Worcester, Massachusetts.

Source: Augustus Layres (writing under the pseudonym Friends of Right, Justice, and Humanity), *Facts Upon the Other Side of the Chinese Question, With a Memorial to the President of the U.S., From Representative Chinamen in America*, 1876. Courtesy of the American Antiquarian Society, Worcester, Massachusetts.

EDITORS' INTRODUCTION

During the nineteenth century, debates about immigration comprised one of the most contentious political issues, especially in cities, where immigrants congregated in high numbers. Organized labor, nativists (those with prejudice against anyone not born in the United States), and others joined the movement to curb immigration. The newcomers themselves, and those who befriended them, made repeated arguments for allowing immigration. In 1882, however, the United States passed the Chinese Exclusion Act, the first federal law targeting one particular immigrant group. Although the Chinese comprised just 0.002 percent of the United States population, racial difference and the lack of cultural understanding strengthened white prejudice. California, where just over 40 percent of the 148,000 Chinese in the United States lived, stood at the forefront of this battle. One of the charges against the Chinese was that they were working as "coolie" laborers, a type of slavery or indentured servitude. The extent of this worry far exceeded the reality, and free Chinese laborers were routinely maligned as coolies by their detractors. Chinese women were repeatedly categorized as prostitutes, and indeed Chinese prostitution constituted a rampant problem, as the majority of Chinese men arrived in the United States as bachelors or left wives behind in China.

The first item, labeled (A), below is an excerpt from a speech given on May 2, 1876 by United States Senator Aaron A. Sargent of California. The month prior, Sargent urged that President Ulysses S. Grant "cause negotiations to be entered upon with the Chinese government to effect such change in the existing treaty between the United States and China as will lawfully permit the application of restrictions upon the great influx of Chinese subjects to this country."[i] The ban against Chinese immigration, passed in 1882, was not lifted until 1943, when Chinese aligned with the Allies in World War II and allowed into the country again in very small numbers. The second document, labeled (B), written under the pseudonym Friends of Right, Justice, and Humanity, was attributed to Augustus Layres, and signed simply "—X."

---

* *Immigration of Chinese, Speech of Hon. Aaron A. Sargent of California, In the Senate of the United States*, May 2, 1876.

(A) But when the question is as to the introduction of large numbers of people into the country whose admission is not a matter of right, but of policy, then we ought to consider whether they are a disturbing element, and whether exclusion is not the best and surest prevention against disorders which are difficult to cure when once fastened upon us.

Is the desire of the Chinese to select our country as a place of residence so clear a natural right that, rather than gainsay it, we are willing to submit to the disorders which must grow out of the prejudice known to exist against them? As to this prejudice, is it not based upon some reason? I intend to state some of the objections to their coming which account for the bitter opposition shown in California and elsewhere where they have already appeared in numbers. Are the people of the East quite certain that, if the Chinese were to land in their midst in the proportion of one in every eight of the population of several States, they would be as easy to the future as now? They should try to put themselves in our place, and deal with this question as if they too had among them this strange and dangerously unassimilative people, increasing in numbers from year to year.

General Exclusion Only Remedy for Evils

The importation of coolies is now forbidden by statute. But it is found impossible to reach the cases of violation of its provisions, because neither side will disclose the existence of cooly [sic] contracts.

The importation of females for immoral purposes is also forbidden by statute. But the law is a dead-letter, because of the impossibility of obtaining proof of its violation.

And yet it is the almost universal conviction of Californians that nine-tenths of the Chinese male immigration is in violation of the former, and ninety-nine hundredths of the female immigration is in violation of the latter statue. There can be no remedy but general exclusion; and the policy, justice, and necessity of that supreme measure I propose to discuss.

The resolution before the Senate looks to a modification of certain provisions of the existing treaty between the United States and China. Those provisions are as follows:

Article V

The United States of America and the Emperor of China cordially recognize the inherent and inalienable right of man to change his home and allegiance, and also the mutual advantage of free migration and emigration of their citizens and subjects respectively from the one country to the other, for purposes of curiosity, of trade, or to any other foreign country, without their free and voluntary consent, respectively.

Article VI

Citizens of the United States visiting or residing in China shall enjoy the same privileges, immunities, and exemptions, in respect to travel or residence, as may there be enjoyed by the citizens or subjects of the most favored nation; and, reciprocally, Chinese subjects visiting or residing in the United States shall enjoy the same privileges, immunities, and exemptions, in their respect to travel or residence, as may there be enjoyed by the citizens or subjects of the most favored nation. But nothing herein contained shall be held to confer naturalization upon citizens of the United States in China, nor upon the subjects of China in the United States.

The question of the restriction of Chinese immigration to the United States concerns at present the people of the Pacific coast more than it does Eastern communities. Our people are not always wise or deliberate in their treatment of the subject, and their irritability often leads them to extravagance of speech and exhibitions of heated prejudices which produce an effect at the East the very opposite of what they intend. The unreasonable-ness, or even violence, of discontented people does not, however, make the cause of their discontent any the less important. The remedy for the evils, if evils they are, of Chinese immigration lies entirely in the hands of the Federal

Government. The treaty-making power must first be appealed to seek such modifications of our treaty with China as will pave the way for legislation under the power of Congress to regulate commerce. It is very desirable, therefore, that all appeals to the Federal Government should be clearly based on reason, humanity, and national interest. The Chinese are to a very limited extent the objects of hatred and prejudice east of the Rocky mountains, and all arguments against their influx must be free from the familiar cries with which place-hunting demagogues assail the ears of mobs in California. That the presence of Chinese in this country in any considerable numbers is most undesirable is my firm conviction, as I think it is of the great body of those in California who aid in the protection of them in their treaty rights. The question of national duty in the premises comes to as at the threshold of any discussion, and we are obliged to consider it.

(B) Sundry Charges and Conclusion

We dismiss as unworthy of consideration the charges that "*The Chinese are pagans; are not a homogeneous race, do not adopt our manners, our food, our style of dress, etc.*"

It will be a sad day, indeed, for this great Republic, when it shall prescribe personal qualities of this kind as conditions to immigration. America will again become wild then, and her qualifications for simple residents as recommended by the Anti-Chinese Committee are unknown even in the most despotic countries.

The Chinese are accused of being *filthy, diseased, immoral*, and *vicious* people, who fill our prisons and crowd our hospitals.

The Report of the Board of Directors of the California State Prison, for 1875, gives the total number of prisoners as 1,083, of whom only 187 are Chinese, notwithstanding they find but little mercy in our courts. The County Hospital Report shows also but a small proportion of Chinese patients. The City Record of mortality among them is very small, and Dr. Toland has testified that they are personally clean.

But if these evils exist, why do not the Municipal Authorities remedy them? Legislation is not exhausted as it is alleged, only faithful police officers who do not accept bribes are required, as shown by the investigation.

Again, if these charges be true, how does it happen that the Chinese have "*monopolized*" as you say, a great portion of the domestic and commercial service, and in the very best houses, for nearly twenty years? Can it be that our wealthy and honored citizens will confide their households to filthy, diseased, immoral, and criminal servants? Either our citizens are not what they seem or it is not true what you say in regard to the Chinese.

But it is enough. This Anti-Chinese Crusade, started by sectarian fanaticism, encouraged by personal prejudice and ambition for political capital, has already culminated in personal attack, abuse, and incendiarism against the inoffensive Chinese. Anti-Coolie Clubs are now arming and preparing to follow the late example of the people of Antioch, who have banished the Chinese and burned their quarters.

It is high time that the Municipal, State, and National authorities, in common with law abiding citizens, should awake to the imminent danger that threatens to break the peace and to disgrace both State and nation. They must assert their authority in defense of our treaty obligations with China, for the protection of Chinese emigrants and in behalf of law and order.

—X

3-5. THE MIXED CROWD (1890)

Jacob Riis

Source: Jacob Riis, *How the Other Half Lives: Studies Among the Tenements of New York* (New York: Scribner & Sons, 1890).

EDITORS' INTRODUCTION

Jacob Riis (1849–1914), a Danish immigrant who came to the United States in 1870, documented the American immigrant experience in his short stories, muckraking journalism, and his important books *How the Other Half Lives* (1890), *The Children of the Poor* (1892), *The Making of an American* (1901), *The Battle With the Slums* (1902), and *Children of the Tenements* (1903). Riis brought critical attention to the condition of overcrowded, impoverished neighborhoods. His photographs were taken with a magnesium flash that literally and figuratively brought life to the dark side of urban life. Riis' photographs and writings allowed the middle class and upper class, not otherwise acquainted with the slums, a way to see how other Americans lived. Despite his good intentions, Riis' writing betrayed clear biases against many of the ethnic groups portrayed in his works because of the use of derogatory language and excessive stereotypes.

The Mixed Crowd

When once I asked the agent of a notorious Fourth Ward alley how many people might be living in it I was told: One hundred and forty families, one hundred Irish, thirty-eight Italian, and two that spoke the German tongue. Barring the agent herself, there was not a native-born individual in the court. The answer was characteristic of the cosmopolitan character of lower New York, very nearly so of the whole of it, wherever it runs to alleys and courts. One may find for the asking an Italian, a German, a French, African, Spanish, Bohemian, Russian, Scandinavian, Jewish, and Chinese colony. Even the Arab, who peddles "holy earth" from the Battery as a direct importation from Jerusalem, has his exclusive preserves at the lower end of Washington Street. The one thing you shall vainly ask for in the chief city of America is a distinctively American community. There is none; certainly not among the tenements. Where have they gone to, the old inhabitants? I put the question to one who might fairly be presumed to be of the number, since I had found him sighing for the "good old days" when the legend "no Irish need apply" was familiar in the advertising columns of the newspapers. He looked at me with a puzzled air. "I don't know," he said. "I wish I did. Some went to California in '49, some to the war and never came back. The rest, I expect, have gone to heaven, or somewhere. I don't see them 'round here."

Whatever the merit of the good man's conjectures, his eyes did not deceive him. They are not here. In their place has come this queer conglomerate mass of heterogeneous elements, ever striving and working like whiskey and water in one glass, and with the like result: final union and a prevailing taint of whiskey. The once unwelcome Irishman has been followed in his turn by the Italian, the Russian Jew, and the Chinaman, and has himself taken a hand at opposition, quite as bitter and quite as ineffectual, against these later hordes. Wherever these have gone they have crowded him out, possessing the block, the street, the ward with their denser swarms. But the Irishman's revenge is complete. Victorious in defeat over his recent as over his more ancient foe, the one who opposed his coming no less than the one who drove him out, he dictates to both their politics, and, secure in possession of the offices, returns the native his greeting with interest, while collecting the rents of the Italian whose house he has bought with the profits of his saloon. As a landlord he is picturesquely autocratic. An amusing instance of his methods came under my notice while writing these lines. An inspector of the Health Department found an Italian family paying a man with a Celtic name twenty-five dollars a month for three small rooms in a ramshackle rear tenement—more than twice what they were worth—and expressed his astonishment to the tenant, an ignorant Sicilian laborer. He replied that he had once asked the landlord to reduce the rent, but he would not do it.

"Well! What did he say?" asked the inspector.

"'Damma, man!' he said; 'if you speaka thata way to me, I fira you and your things in the streeta.'" And the frightened Italian paid the rent.

Injustice to the Irish landlord it must be said that like an apt pupil he was merely showing forth the result of the schooling he had received, re-enacting, in his own way, the scheme of the tenements. It is only his frankness that shocks. The Irishman does not naturally take kindly to tenement life, though with characteristic versatility he adapts himself to its conditions at once. It does violence, nevertheless, to the best that is in him, and for that very reason of all who come within its sphere soonest corrupts him. The result is a sediment, the product of more than a generation in the city's slums, that, as distinguished from the larger body of his class, justly ranks at the foot of tenement dwellers, the so-called "low Irish."

It is not to be assumed, of course, that the whole body of the population living in the tenements, of which New Yorkers are in the habit of speaking vaguely as "the poor," or even the larger part of it, is to be classed as vicious or as poor in the sense of verging on beggary. York's wage-earners have no other place to live, more is the pity. They are truly poor for having no better homes; waxing poorer in purse as the exorbitant rents to which they are tied, as ever was serf to soil, keep rising. The wonder is that they are not all corrupted, and speedily, by their surroundings. If, on the contrary, there be a steady working up, if not out of the slough, the fact is a powerful argument for the optimist's belief that the world is, after all, growing better, not worse, and would go far toward disarming apprehension, were it not for the steadier growth of the sediment of the slums and its constant menace. Such an impulse toward better things there certainly is. The German rag-picker of thirty years ago, quite as low in the scale as his Italian successor, is the thrifty tradesman or prosperous farmer of to-day.[1]

The Italian scavenger of our time is fast graduating into exclusive control of the corner fruit-stands, while his black-eyed boy monopolizes the boot-blacking industry in which a few years ago he was an intruder. The Irish hod-carrier in the second generation has become a bricklayer, if not the Alderman of his ward, while the Chinese coolie is in almost exclusive possession of the laundry business. The reason is obvious. The poorest immigrant comes here with the purpose and ambition to better himself and, given half a chance, might be reasonably expected to make the most of it. To the false plea that he prefers the squalid houses in which his kind are housed there could be no better answer. The truth is, his half chance has too long been wanting, and for the bad result he has been unjustly blamed.

As emigration from east to west follows the latitude, so does the foreign influx in New York distribute itself along certain well-defined lines that waver and break only under the stronger pressure of a more gregarious race or the encroachments of inexorable business. A feeling of dependence upon mutual effort, natural to strangers in a strange land, unacquainted with its language and customs, sufficiently accounts for this.

The Irishman is the true cosmopolitan immigrant. All-pervading, he shares his lodging with perfect impartiality with the Italian, the Greek, and the "Dutchman," yielding only to sheer force of numbers, and objects equally to them all. A map of the city, colored to designate nationalities, would show more stripes than on the skin of a zebra, and more colors than any rainbow. The city on such a map would fall into two great halves, green for the Irish prevailing in the West Side tenement districts, and blue for the Germans on the East

Side. But intermingled with these ground colors would be an odd variety of tints that would give the whole the appearance of an extraordinary crazy-quilt. From down in the Sixth Ward, upon the site of the old Collect Pond that in the days of the fathers drained the hills which are no more, the red of the Italian would be seen forcing, its way northward along the line of Mulberry Street to the quarter of the French purple on Bleecker Street and South Fifth Avenue, to lose itself and reappear, after a lapse of miles, in the "Little Italy" of Harlem, east of Second Avenue. Dashes of red, sharply defined, would be seen strung through the Annexed District, northward to the city line. On the West Side the red would be seen overrunning the old Africa of Thompson Street, pushing the black of the negro rapidly uptown, against querulous but unavailing protests, occupying his home, his church, his trade and all, with merciless impartiality. There is a church in Mulberry Street that has stood for two generations as a sort of milestone of these migrations. Built originally for the worship of staid New Yorkers of the "old stock," it was engulfed by the colored tide, when the draft-riots drove the negroes out of reach of Cherry Street and the Five Points. Within the past decade the advance wave of the Italian onset reached it, and to-day the arms of United Italy adorn its front. The negroes have made a stand at several points along Seventh and Eighth Avenues; but their main body, still pursued by the Italian foe, is on the march yet, and the black mark will be found overshadowing to-day many blocks on the East Side, with One Hundredth Street as the centre, where colonies of them have settled recently.

Hardly less aggressive than the Italian, the Russian and Polish Jew, having over run the district between Rivington and Division Streets, east of the Bowery, to the point of suffocation, is filling, the tenements of the old Seventh Ward to the river front, and disputing with the Italian every foot of available space in the back alleys of Mulberry Street. The two races, differing hopelessly in much, have this in common: they carry their slums with them wherever they go, if allowed to do it. Little Italy already rivals its parent, the "Bend," in foulness. Other nationalities that begin at the bottom make a fresh start when crowded up the ladder. Happily both are manageable, the one by rabbinical, the other by the civil law. Between the dull gray of the Jew, his favorite color, and the Italian red, would be seen squeezed in on the map a sharp streak of yellow, marking the narrow boundaries of Chinatown. Dovetailed in with the German population, the poor but thrifty Bohemian might be picked out by the sombre hue of his life as of his philosophy, struggling against heavy odds in the big human bee-hives of the East Side. Colonies of his people extend northward, with long lapses of space, from below the Cooper Institute more than three miles. The Bohemian is the only foreigner with any considerable representation in the city who counts no wealthy man of his race, none who has not to work hard for a living, or has got beyond the reach of the tenement.

Down near the Battery the West Side emerald would be soiled by a dirty stain, spreading rapidly like a splash of ink on a sheet of blotting paper, headquarters of the Arab tribe, that in a single year has swelled from the original dozen to twelve hundred, intent, every mother's son, on trade and barter. Dots and dashes of color here and there would show where the Finnish sailors worship their djumala (God), the Greek pedlars the ancient name of their race, and the Swiss the goddess of thrift. And so on to the end of the long register, all toiling together in the galling fetters of the tenement. Were the question raised who makes the most of life thus mortgaged, who resists most stubbornly its levelling tendency—knows how to drag even the barracks upward a part of the way at least toward the ideal plane of the home—the palm must be unhesitatingly awarded the Teuton. The Italian and the poor Jew rise only by compulsion. The Chinaman does not rise at all; here, as at home, he simply remains stationary. The Irishman's genius runs to public affairs rather than domestic life; wherever he is mustered in force the saloon is the gorgeous centre of political activity. The

German struggles vainly to learn his trick; his Teutonic wit is too heavy, and the political ladder he raises from his saloon usually too short or too clumsy to reach the desired goal. The best part of his life is lived at home, and he makes himself a home independent of the surroundings, giving the lie to the saying, unhappily become a maxim of social truth, that pauperism and drunkenness naturally grow in the tenements. He makes the most of his tenement, and it should be added that whenever and as soon as he can save up money enough, he gets out and never crosses the threshold of one again.

NOTE

1. The Sheriff Street Colony of rag-pickers, long since gone, is an instance in point. The thrifty Germans saved up money during years of hard work in squalor and apparently wretched poverty to buy a township in a Western State, and the whole colony moved out there in a body. There need be no doubt about their thriving there.

3-6. TRIANGLE SHIRTWAIST FIRE, NEW YORK CITY (1911)

Source: *The Ladies' Garment Worker*, April 1911. Permission of the Kheel Center at Cornell University.[i]

EDITORS' INTRODUCTION

On March 25, 1911, the Triangle Shirtwaist Company, located in the Washington Square area of New York City, was engulfed in flames and 146 of the 500 workers at the facility lost their lives. The majority of the victims were Italian or Jewish immigrants, mostly women and teenagers. The awful incident became a rallying point for those fighting for safer workplaces in the years to come. New immigrants often worked in highly dangerous industrial settings in the nineteenth and early twentieth centuries, and, unfortunately, sweatshop work conditions still persist in the United States and factories abroad. Frances Perkins, who would later become Secretary of Labor in the cabinet of President Franklin Roosevelt, watched the fire and the young people jumping to their deaths out of factory windows. The tragedy influenced her lifetime of work on behalf of laborers. The incident made an indelible mark in the collective memory of New Yorkers. Modern media commentators have even linked the events of 1911 to the terrorist attacks of 9/11, noting similarities in both the human tragedies and the high level of local and international attention.

Notice of the Fire

When ready to go to press we learn of the awful calamity at the Triangle Waist Company. While most of the garment manufacturing establishments in New York City are not any better as far as fire protection is concerned, it is significant that the worst calamity happened at the Triangle, known among the workpeople in the trade as the "prison." The name is probably due the extraordinary discipline with poor earning for which the firm is famous.

It is not strange that in this most democratic of all countries in the world the employers can so easily use the arm of the law to protect themselves against any inconveniences which their workpeople may cause them, but the law is nowhere when the life and limb of the worker is to be protected.

The writer of these lines, when approaching the factory some two years ago in an attempt to organize the workpeople of that firm, was pounced upon by two plainclothed

---

i See on-line exhibit on the Triangle Shirtwaist Company Fire at www.ilr.cornell.edu/trianglefire/.

policemen and taken to the police cell. No one, however, knows whom to blame for this calamity.

It is evident that the worker can expect next to nothing in the way of protection from the legal authorities. Whether it is the Supreme Court or the good people who are interested in the architectural beauties of the city, nothing will be done until the workers will begin in earnest to attend to their own business. They must declare a strike at all such fire traps until adequate protection is provided.

Pickets should be posted at the entrance of such places with sign boards bearing the following inscription: *Please do not go to work in this place until proper fire protection is provided for the workpeople.*

Let the authorities find our action contrary to the Sherman Anti-Trust Laws or any other of the innumerable laws provide to safeguard the interest of the capitalists, and which the authorities are ever ready to guard jealousy. We will cheerfully go to prison but there will be no more fire traps. Such a strike will put an end to such a state of things within 48 hours.

There are in the same building a number of cloak shops, who before the general strike, worked until 6 o'clock on Saturdays. Thanks to the change in hours all these left at 1 o'clock, otherwise the victims would have been more numerous.

PART IV

City Life from the Bottom Up, 1860s–1940s

EDITORS' INTRODUCTION TO PART IV

The study of the city's past—the field of urban history—evolved in the twentieth century alongside the general discipline of history, and reflected changes in the parent field. As explored in the Part I essay by Steven H. Corey and Lisa Krissoff Boehm, "Examining America's Urban Landscape: From Social Reform to Social History," the formal study of history grew increasingly open to interdisciplinary ideas and also included far more quantitative work than in the past. The cultural environment of the period, including the civil rights, women's rights, anti-war, student, and other social movements, irrevocably altered academic life. Heretofore, the so-called ivory tower, and particularly the professorate, was predominated by a group of people who were both wealthier and whiter (and more often males and Protestants) than the American population in general. With the growth of economic opportunity in the twentieth century, college education became an option open to more Americans, including the working class, immigrants and the children of immigrants, and women. Some decided to stay permanently within the hallowed halls of academia, and located jobs as professors. The viewpoints of these newcomers transformed formal study by bringing in a host of diverse concerns, particularly in regards to the study of a wider range of American experiences. Peter Stearns, writing in the *Journal of Social History*, summarizes, "The fundamental twin premises—that ordinary people not only have a history but contribute to shaping history more generally, and that a range of behaviors can be profitably explored historically beyond (though also including) the most familiar political staples—are still valid."[1]

What became known as the "new social history," and is now regarded simply as social history, considered the American past from a new vantage point. As Stearns points out, the methodology also relied on new sources. Where once historians solely had tackled such documents as the papers of presidents, the archival holdings of corporations, and the letters of statesmen when crafting their studies, they now redefined "primary source" and read a wider range of materials. Popular works, advertisements, oral histories, the letters and diaries of everyday people, union minutes, and city directories, once of suspect historical value, all became suitable fodder for respectable historical study. Instead of viewing history "from the top down," the new social historians looked at history "from the bottom up." This shift in directional focus changed almost everything.

Historians Wendy Gamber, Timothy Gilfoyle, and George Chauncey offer unforgettable examples of history from the bottom up. Gamber takes us into the world of the nineteenth-century boarding house—a world very common to the urbanites of this time but never before given its historical due. To highlight her findings, a selection from Thomas Butler Gunn's *The Physiology of New York Boarding-Houses* (1857) is included. Timothy Gilfoyle, using a memoir penned by a petty thief as his starting point, creates a wide-ranging narrative of the life of the poor and criminal classes of New York City. He takes his readers from the hardscrabble streets of Five Points, to the opium dens, and through the nightmarish prison system. Pickpocketing ranked among the most prevalent of crimes in nineteenth-century cities, as evidenced in *The National Police Gazette*'s illustration from 1857 of such criminals at work. The danger of the streets extended beyond petty crime, as shown in the open passages of Theodore Dreiser's iconic *Sister Carrie* (1900). Carrie Meeber, a naïve country migrant, was led astray by two men soon after she arrived in Chicago. George Chauncey relates the little-known story of gay New York, broadening our understanding of life in America's largest metropolis. Chauncey demonstrates that the big city proved alluring for homosexuals from small-town America, as it did for young women like Sister Carrie. In *Strange Brother* (1931) by Blair Niles, we see how a gay settlement house worker named Mark Thornton attempted to find solace by fleeing the fictional Narova City for New York.

NOTE

1. Peter Stearns, "Social History Present and Future," *Journal of Social History*, 37, (1) (Fall 2003): 9.

The "Guns" of Gotham

Timothy Gilfoyle

Source: *A Pickpocket's Tale: The Underworld of Nineteenth Century New York* (New York: W. W. Norton, 2006).

EDITORS' INTRODUCTION

Timothy Gilfoyle, a professor of history at Loyola University in Chicago, is the author of the well-regarded work, *City of Eros: New York City, Prostitution, and the Commercialization of Sex, 1790–1920* (New York: W. W. Norton, 1992). With that work, Gilfoyle introduced many readers to the seedier side of New York City streets and the elaborate social systems that grew up around the sex industry. In *A Pickpocket's Tale*, Gilfoyle takes readers deeper into the urban underworld by revealing the life of George Appo, a petty-thief born in 1856 to an Irish mother and a Chinese father. Appo penned a slim memoir, a selection from which begins this essay. Using George Appo's life as a jumping off point, Gilfoyle launches into a thorough and compelling history of the world of crime in the late 1800s.

Crime history tends to quickly veer off into stories of prurient interest rather than items of true historical importance. Gilfoyle deftly avoids this issue in his writing, bringing forth readable books and articles of true social history. In the wider work from which this selection is taken, all of the institutions George Appo becomes acquainted with during the course of his life are discussed in depth, including the famed Five Points neighborhood, the Five Points House of Refuge, the *Mercury* packet ship (a veritable prison with sails for wayward youth), Sing-Sing, Clinton State Prison, the city's network of opium dens, the Eastern Penitentiary, the Tombs, Blackwell's Island, and the New York County court system. The work also details the inner-workings of the crimes themselves. Here we see the methodology of the pickpocket. The crowded streets, full-to-bursting street-cars, and the loose clothing of the period gave pickpockets ample opportunities. The reliance on cash heightened temptation, for a single score could bring in quite a few dollars. Prior to the Civil War, lawmakers and cultural observers treated pickpocketing as a minor crime, and even occasionally deemed this crime "romantic," part of the compelling atmosphere of the city. In the 1860s, attitudes changed, and prosecutors punished pickpockets more harshly than they did violent crimes.

A Pickpocket's Tale is an excellent example of what became known as "the new social history," for here we literally see the street from its basest level. Where once the word history meant only the tales of warfare, the biographies of kings, the building of nations, or the lives of presidents, historians began to consider the history of the masses. The change in viewpoint accompanied sweeping cultural changes outside academia; with the civil rights movement, the women's movement, and the empowering of the working and middle class, more Americans received an education and different types of people entered into the professorate. These professors' personal views of the world influenced the kinds of questions they asked of the past. Even those who were not themselves working class or members of a minority group were often made more aware of the struggles of those who were. Sensitivity towards issues related to gender and sexual orientation also grew with time. Everyday urban life held fascination for scholars, and they gleaned from the available documents a much more nuanced understanding of the American life. Gilfoyle here demonstrates all we can learn from a short memoir; from the viewpoint of a small-time thief, we take front row seats at a theatrical show on nineteenth-century life.

A Pickpocket's Tale received the Dixon Ryan Fox Prize from the New York State Historical Association and was a selection for the Book-of-the-Month Club and mentioned by the *Chicago Tribune* and the *London Times* as one of their best books of 2006. *City of Eros* also won the Dixon Ryan Fox Prize and the Allan Nevis Prize from the American Historical Association. Gilfoyle is the book review editor for the *Journal of Urban History*, the author of *Millennium Park: Creating a Chicago Landmark* (Chicago: University of Chicago Press, 2006), co-author (with Patricia Cline Cohen and Helen Lefkowitz Horowitz) of *The Flash Press: Sporting Male Weeklies in 1840s New York* (Chicago: University of Chicago Press, 2008), and is editing George Appo's memoir for Rutgers University Press.

THE "GUNS" OF GOTHAM

When I was released from Sing Sing Prison [on 2 April 1876], I had to go to St. Luke's Hospital to be operated on by Professors Otis and Peters. After nearly three months under good medical treatment, I left the hospital. As I had no means or way to obtain the necessities of life, I naturally went back to stealing for a living. But the two years in state prison made me wiser than before so I left New York and went to Philadelphia, where I remained about four months and then returned to New York looking very prosperous.

The year was the Centennial Year, 1876, and near to a close, the time being November. New York City was full of strangers from all parts of the world, and the crooks were all doing well, in general, at their business. In fact, New York was overrun with crooks from the West.... I soon became intimately acquainted with the crooks and learned many ways and means to earn money dishonestly with not so much risk as picking pockets, but I could not read nor write and my mode of talking was too slangy. Therefore, I could not operate with safety and success as my general appearance was against me, so I had to continue picking pockets.[1]

THE SECOND HALF of the nineteenth century was the era of the "gun"—the pickpocket—in American cities. "Of all the departments of crime as now practiced," admitted America's most famous private detective, Allan Pinkerton, in 1884, "there is not one which contains a larger number of adept operators than that of pickpockets." As regards New York, Pinkerton was right. From 1861 to 1863 the municipality successfully convicted only 74 individuals for larceny. But a decade later, from 1873 to 1875, 519 felons landed in the state penitentiary for the same offense. The period from 1866 to 1887 might better be described as the age of larceny. During those two decades larceny comprised between one-third and one-half of all crimes in New York State. In the words of one pickpocket, the decades following the Civil War were "the halcyon days for us."[2]

Yet pickpocketing was a poorly defined crime. Although the act was among the most common and frequently mentioned transgressions in the nineteenth-century city, it never appeared in any criminal code. Picking a pocket or snatching a purse was larceny, "one of the primordial crimes of Western culture," according to the legal historian George Fletcher. Larceny, however, was never authoritatively defined until the twentieth century. Judges punished such acts on the simple assumption that they knew what it was—taking the goods of another. Hence no clear boundaries separated larceny from burglary and robbery.[3]

Similarly the precise dimensions of the pickpocket's world remain impossible to measure. Purloined goods were rarely recovered, and even smaller proportions of pickpockets were ever prosecuted. In the seventeen known years in which George Appo worked as a pickpocket, for example, he was arrested for and convicted of larceny four times. To the average law-abiding citizen, four convictions were considerable. But Appo picked hundreds—quite possibly thousands—of pockets *without* being apprehended. Once, while working a county fair outside Toronto, Appo pickpocketed approximately twenty-five different individuals.[4] His four arrests for pickpocketing quite likely account for less—maybe much less—than 1 percent of all his thefts.

Pickpockets like Appo were part of a distinctive criminal order. Numerous observers described pickpockets as "professional thieves" and "artists," part of a social underground fraternity with hidden rules and practices. Allan Pinkerton believed that criminal subcultures replicated the American middle class by dividing into specialized professions, each concerned with their own particular status and reputation. Petty crooks operated in social isolation, noted writer James D. McCabe, Jr., but pickpockets were different: They "have certain habits, attitudes, haunts; they act in certain ways when placed in certain positions." For George Appo such people were "good fellows," individuals who refused to cooperate with law enforcement authorities, who eschewed testifying against enemies. "What constitutes a Good Fellow in the eyes and estimation of the underworld is a nervy crook, a money getter and spender," wrote Appo. A good fellow valiantly accepted the consequences and punishment of an arrest, even if the crime was committed by another.[5] A good fellow was a member of a fraternity of thieves.

This fraternity shared a distinctive, arcane language. One reporter confessed that he found pickpockets impossible to comprehend, sounding as if they spoke a foreign tongue. Pickpockets referred to their accomplices (numbering two to six) as "mobs." The streets, parks, or trolleys where they worked were "beats." Pocketbooks were "leathers," and money was a "roll." The actual larceny was a "touch," which was performed by a "wire," a "pick," a "bugger," or a "tool," while "stalls" distracted or jostled the victim. The "cover" made sure the theft took place unobserved. The novelist Herman Melville described the underworld vocabulary as "the foulest of all human lingoes, that dialect of sin and death, known as the Cant language, or the Flash."[6] [...]

When necessary pickpockets went on a "jump-out," traveling to fairs, circuses, racetracks, sporting events—in essence, any large assembly or festivity in a nearby town.

Swarms of pickpockets followed traveling circus shows as they moved about the country. Some concentrated on certain types of public gatherings, such as funerals, weddings, and parades. Such "rovers" literally roamed the United States in search of such gatherings, forcing police officials to take special precautions. For example, before the ceremonies surrounding Ulysses S. Grant's funeral, the opening of the Statue of Liberty, and the Centennial of the Constitution, New York's chief detective, Thomas Byrnes, ordered the summary arrest of all known pickpockets, including Appo. The practice—known as "caging"—was "truly a bold one," admitted Byrnes, "but the ends certainly justified the means." Detectives literally waited at the city's railway stations and arrested suspects on their arrival. The policy continued into the twentieth century.[7]

Pickpocket mobs working in specialized locations were probably the most successful in the fraternity. Arrest records indicate that individuals working alone—like Appo—were more likely to get caught. More than three-quarters of those prosecuted labored by themselves, and most were simply "working the street." Quite likely arrested pickpockets like Appo enjoyed no relationship with a "percentage copper"—a police officer who tolerated their pilferings for a bribe or "percentage" of their haul. Still, many ignored the danger. "If I needed a dollar quick I'd take any risk," admitted one pickpocket. "I'd jump on a car, and tackle the first sucker I saw."[8]

Streetcars—with more than 90 million annual riders nationwide by the 1880s—were among the most favored workplaces for pickpockets. Riders complained that the cars were so bumpy and crowded that it was impossible to feel the arms or hands of adjacent passengers. By the 1860s, New York streetcars conspicuously posted signs warning BEWARE OF PICKPOCKETS! Many passengers felt their pockets immediately on reading the warning, allowing conscientious thieves to determine which ones to pick. Nearly a decade later, a state assembly report admitted that well-known pickpockets routinely boarded streetcars, "hustled" passengers with ease, and made "scarcely any concealment of the matter." If a conductor resisted or warned passengers, pickpockets simply took "the first opportunity to knock him on the head." Conversely, sympathetic drivers frequently worked in league with pickpockets.[9]

Pickpockets did not often knock people on the head, however. The craft attracted individuals who avoided violence. "Knockdown pickpockets"—individuals who physically assaulted pedestrians, snatched the object, and immediately ran away—were rare.... Pickpocket dress and fashion placed a premium on blending into the general populace. Law enforcement officials like George Washington Walling argued that leading pickpockets were "stylishly dressed, easy in their manners and correct in speech." Pickpockets like Jim Caulfield confirmed as much, emphasizing that they always tried to be neat, clean, and as fashionable as possible. An attractive personal appearance, he admitted, was part of "the capital of a grafter."[10]

Pickpockets may have differed over precisely where and how they worked, but they shared certain demographic characteristics. First, picking pockets was a young man's game. More than three-quarters (80 percent) of those arrested were male, more than half (56 percent) being fifteen to twenty-four years of age. Like Appo, however, many pickpockets continued working well into adulthood. (Appo's final conviction occurred when he was twenty-six.) Fully a quarter of all arrested pickpockets during these years were twenty-five to twenty-nine years old, and another 17 percent continued their stealthful ways throughout their thirties. Less than 4 percent were forty or over.[11] [...]

Females were part of this criminal fraternity. Detective Allan Pinkerton, for example, believed that female thieves were as successful as their male competitors. His counterpart and rival detective, Thomas Byrnes, even considered female pickpockets to be more dangerous. Like their male counterparts, many women worked in "mobs" and directed their pirating toward men. Most significantly female pickpockets tended to be poorer than men, the majority occupying the lowliest wage-labor positions, such as servants and prostitutes; more than half were associated with a brothel, concert saloon, barroom, or boardinghouse. Sex was the lure.[12] Michael Springer, for example, agreed to treat several females in an East Tenth Street restaurant. After ordering wine and sitting down beside one young woman, Springer suddenly felt her hand in his pants. "What are you doing with your hand in my pocket?" he asked. Sexual stimulation was not her purpose—Springer was missing $273.[13]

Pickpockets prospered in nineteenth-century New York and other urban centers for many reasons. First, the forced, physical intimacy of the new, densely packed industrial city made picking pockets easy. "It's only a big city that can furnish one of this craft with his daily supply of purses and pocketbooks, jewelry and small wares," declared one observer. Moreover, fashion encouraged pickpocketing. For most of the nineteenth century, men tended to carry valuables in their coats, not their pants. Before the Civil War frock coats tended to be long, extending to the midthigh, if not the knee, and providing a protective cover for the front pants pocket. But after 1860 the shortened length of frock coats facilitated pickpocketing. Although overcoats were longer, they included external pockets with no flaps. By midcentury many New Yorkers argued that a majority of the city's pickpockets were newsboys and bootblacks who learned the technique during cold weather when pedestrians wore overcoats with external change pockets.[14]

During the final decades of the century, frock coats were replaced by the popular sack coat. "Every man in America, multimillionaire as well as laborer, wears a sack coat," wrote one designer. "It is the great American business coat, and in other countries is recognized as the badge of the American." Sack coats were short, extended to the waist, included a small collar, and offered comfort and easy movement. Most important, with a plentiful number of pockets, the sack was a coat waiting for a pickpocket.[15] [...]

Female clothing was even easier to pilfer. Nineteenth-century women generally wore layers of clothing, some with long skirts and hoops underneath, making it difficult to detect the touch of a pickpocket. On street-cars and other forms of public transit, the dresses of seated women frequently fell over the legs of passengers sitting beside them. Pickpockets then simply slid a hand underneath the dress and cut out the pocket.[16]

A third contributing factor to the rise of pickpocketing was tolerance by law enforcement officials. "The old system," wrote journalist Lincoln Steffens, "was built upon the understood relations of the crooks and the detective bureau." "Professional" criminals were allowed to operate "within reason." For pickpockets specific blocks or streetcars were divided among themselves, each of whom had a "monopoly." In return for such privileges, pickpockets reported on others who violated such agreements, and were expected to return stolen goods on police request.[17] [...]

But the greatest incentive for pickpockets was the exorbitant amount of cash in people's pockets. Nineteenth-century businessmen, bank messengers, and ordinary pedestrians routinely carried large quantities of money and other valuables on their persons. This was especially true in the Wall Street area before 1880. "It is remarkable," concluded another detective, "how careless business men are about their watches, however valuable they may be." Some cases involved extraordinary sums. In 1866 a Williamsburg Bank messenger was picked clean on his way to the Park National Bank of New York with a satchel containing fourteen thousand dollars in cash and checks.... Appo himself admitted that it was easy to get rich quick. After a few days of pickpocketing, he usually accumulated six to eight hundred dollars. [...]

Necessity demanded that pedestrians carry significant sums of money. (Credit cards did not become a financial instrument until the twentieth century.) Only a minority of Americans entrusted their money to banks, so few people rendered payments with personal checks. Even then, many merchants refused such forms of payment, especially from strangers. Hence to purchase most goods—expensive or cheap—shoppers had to carry cash. This reality made the streets of New York and other American cities pickpocket heaven.

The perception that pickpocketing was an increasingly common urban experience produced a hostile public reaction. Prior to the Civil War, pickpockets evoked little public fear. Novelists like George Thompson treated such thievery as a unique urban adventure, while George Foster portrayed the best pickpockets as "genteel." Even the detective Thomas Byrnes described pickpockets as "an interesting class of thieves." One newspaper openly acknowledged that "a tinge of romance [was] connected with the profession of picking pockets."[18]

The romance disappeared after 1870. In that decade, New Yorkers were besieged with numerous publications warning residents of the dangers presented by pickpockets and other criminals. Charles Loring Brace's *The Dangerous Classes of New York and Twenty Years Among Them* (1872) and Edward Crapsey's *The Nether Side of New York; or, the Vice, Crime and Poverty of the Great Metropolis* (1872) were but two examples reflecting a new consciousness of the city's criminal dangers. The New York State Assembly even created a special select committee in 1875 to investigate and address Gotham's growing crime rate. [...]

Criminal prosecutions of pickpockets reflected this growing fear. Between 1859 and 1876 the number of pickpockets brought to trial by the district attorney nearly quintupled, increasing from 52 to 242. Since no systematic sentencing policy existed in New York's criminal courts, judges enjoyed wide discretion to crack down whenever and on whomever they wanted. Examples abound reflecting the judicial intolerance of street crime. One thirty-four-year-old pickpocket received a five-year sentence for picking $210. A twenty-two-year-old stole ten cents; the judge sentenced him to two and a half years in the penitentiary. Upon learning that a thirty-five-year-old female was an experienced pickpocket, the judge sentenced her to five years in prison, specifically "to protect the community from pickpockets." Even pleas of poverty and contrition fell upon deaf ears. Young, unemployed men begged judges for mercy, only to be sent to Sing Sing for terms ranging from two to five years.[19]

Youthful mischief likewise engendered little judicial sympathy. One fourteen-year-old Irish immigrant was convicted of stealing one dollar; for that he was sent to the House of Refuge for a year. When two teenagers, in separate cases, were convicted of pilfering fifty cents, they each received three-year sentences. Similarly one nineteen-year-old was sent to Sing Sing for five years for stealing eighty cents; another was given four years for absconding with five cents.[20]

These harsh punishments reflected a new conception of larceny. During the second half of the nineteenth century, Anglo-American courts expanded the law of larceny to encompass a broader range of cases and common law. Whereas earlier larceny law was based on "stealthful or forcible conduct," new interpretations of such criminal behavior encompassed taking that was outwardly innocent. As criminal law increasingly protected social interests, police and courts intervened prior to the occurrence of harm. Hence larceny came to be defined as a crime against property, and police began arresting suspects as soon as they simply touched another with the intent to steal.[21]

In fact larceny (and hence pickpocketing) was treated more severely in New York City than in the rest of New York State. In 1860 the legislature passed a law applicable only to the city whereby any "stealing, taking and carrying away" of property from a person was to be treated as grand larceny, even if the property was less than twenty-five dollars in value. Simply touching a potential victim, or even his or her clothing, now constituted an assault with intent to steal, irrespective of whether any violence was inflicted. One judge later remarked that these statutes deliberately addressed a defect in criminal law that previously rendered pickpocket convictions difficult if not impossible.[22] [...]

In general the New York nineteenth-century judiciary was extraordinarily lenient in meting out punishments from 1830 to 1880. Violent crimes like assault and battery were punished with fines, probation, and indeterminate sentences 25 percent of the time. Serious offenses like rape and manslaughter were rarely penalized with prison terms approaching the available statutory maximum. In the most comprehensive examination of New York City's 1,560 murders from 1800 to 1875, the historian Eric Monkkonen found that only 10.7 percent of all murderers were caught, tried, and convicted. Of those convicted 75 percent were sentenced to seven or fewer years in prison; only 2 percent (thirty-one total) were executed.[23]

Not so with pickpockets. After 1870 New York's judges punished such convicts not only with increasing severity but with more rigor than murderers. Of the twenty-one convicted pickpockets sentenced in the Court of General Sessions in 1859 and 1864 for stealing one hundred dollars or more, only two, or 10 percent, received sentences of three years or more. By contrast after 1871 54 percent of pickpockets convicted of stealing one hundred dollars or more received such stern sentences. Meanwhile, two-thirds of those convicted of stealing one dollar or less were sentenced to one or more years, and nearly half drew sentences in excess of two years. Perhaps most significant was that sentences longer than four years were rare before 1870, but thereafter 12 percent were given such punishments.[24]

Appo confronted this changing judicial reality on multiple occasions. Recorder John K. Hackett, for example, was well known for his unremitting hatred of pickpockets. Once, while sitting on the bench, he proclaimed "that the law ought to condemn them to be shot." On another occasion Hackett instructed a jury that simply because a purloined watch was not found in the possession of a pickpocket was no reason to acquit, because "pickpockets generally went in couples." The jury rendered a verdict of guilty; Hackett happily sentenced him to five years in Sing Sing.[25] This was not unusual. Between 1871 and 1874 Hackett issued harsh sentences to a variety of pickpockets.... And on 3 April 1874, Hackett sentenced seventeen-year-old George Dixon, better known as George Appo, to two and a half years in Sing Sing.[26]

NOTES

1. Appo, 8–9.

2. Allan Pinkerton, *Thirty Years a Detective* (Chicago, 1884), 36; Hutchins Hapgood, ed., *The Autobiography of a Thief* (New York, 1903), 13–49 (pervasive pickpocketing), 35 (halcyon days); Josiah Flynt, *Notes of an Itinerant Policeman* (Boston, 1900), 67–68; Flynt, *The World of Graft* (New York, 1901), 2–15; Lawrence M. Friedman, *Crime and Punishment in American History* (New York, 1993), 108–10. Nearly half (48 percent) of all crime in 1866–67 was some type of larceny, and never dropped below 36 percent until after 1887. In 1927 robbery (25 percent) surpassed larceny (24 percent) for the first time. See NYSS, *Proceedings Before the Special Committee of the New York State Senate* (Albany, 1876), 1192a (statistics before 1876); and table no. 1 in NYSCC, *Report to the Commission of the Sub-Commission on Penal Institutions—1928* (Albany, 1928), 33. "Gun" was reportedly an abbreviated form of the Yiddish word for "thief," or *gonnif*. See Edwin H. Sutherland, *The Professional Thief: By a Professional Thief* (Chicago, 1932), 44.

3. George F. Fletcher, *Rethinking Criminal Law* (Boston, 1978), 3–5 (primordial), 30–42, 90, 100–12.

4. Appo, 29.

5. Appo, 81, 84, 94–96; James D. McCabe, Jr., *The Secrets of the Great City* (Philadelphia, 1868), 359–60; Allan Pinkerton, *Professional Thieves and the Detective* (New York, 1880), 69; *NPG*, 29 Apr. 1882 (artist).

6. Hapgood, *Autobiography*, 51–53 (special part); Pinkerton, *Thirty Years*, 33–39, 48–50; Herman Melville, *Pierre, or The Ambiguities* (New York, 1852; reprint, 1984), 281; McCabe, *Secrets*, 358 ("foreign tongue"), 359 ("bugger"), 369 ("beats"); A. E. Costello, *Our Police Protectors: History of the New York Police* (New York, 1885), 417; *Tribune*, 2 July 1883, 25 Dec. 1887. For lists of underworld slang, see Timothy J. Gilfoyle, "Street-Rats and Gutter-Snipes: Child Pickpockets and Street Culture in New York City, 1850–1900," *Journal of Social History* 37 (2004), note 28. For examples of street gang or group organization of pickpockets, see People v. Charles Cassel, 9 July 1869; People v. Witt and Malloy, 8 Aug. 1876, both in DAP; unmarked clipping, 8 July 1889, vol. 62, DAS; Thomas Byrnes, *Professional Criminals of America* (New York, 1886), 36–37; Phil Farley, *Criminals of America* (New York, 1876), 202–3. For examples of married and heterosexual couples working as pickpockets, see People v. John Williams and Bella Williams, 16 Sept. 1864; People v. Bridget McGuire, 19 Dec.

7. 1859; People v. Ellen Wilson, 5 Sept. 1872, all in DAP; *World* clipping, 2 Aug. 1885, vol. 13, DAS.

7. Hapgood, *Autobiography*, 53 (jumps out), 78–82; Munro, *New York Tombs*, 172; Flynt, *Graft*, 39 (jump out); Pinkerton, *Thirty Years*, 31–37; Benjamin P. Eldridge and William B. Watts, *Our Rival, the Rascal* (Boston, 1897), 16; McCabe, *Secrets*, 366–70; *NPG*, 27 May 1882; *Tribune*, 25 Dec. 1887. On preventive arrests, see *Tribune*, 7 Aug. 1885; *World*, 8 Aug. 1885; unmarked clipping, 22 Apr. 1889, vol. 60, DAS; Byrnes, *Professional Criminals*, 34–35; Helen Campbell, Thomas W. Knox, and Thomas Byrnes, *Darkness and Daylight: or, Lights and Shadows of New York Life* (Hartford, Conn., 1891), 704 (rovers). On preventive arrests of Appo, see *World*, 6, 7 Aug. 1885; *Brooklyn Eagle*, 2 May 1889.

8. Hapgood, *Autobiography*, 51; People v. Charles Cassell, 8 July 1869; People v. John Riley, 21 Nov. 1864; People v. John Brown, 13 Dec. 1864. For pickpockets in churches, see People v. Maria Anderson, 2 June 1874; People v. Henry Maler, 8 June 1876; People v. John Danaker, 17 Feb. 1869; People v. James Watson, 8 Apr. 1869; People v. Maria Brown, 19 Apr. 1869, all in DAP. Arrest and prosecution statistics in this chapter are based on the sampling of 1,176 individuals arrested for pickpocketing from 1859 to 1876 and described in chapter 2, note 20; and Gilfoyle, "Street-Rats and Gutter-Snipes," notes 19 and 20. Of 1,176 individuals prosecuted, trial and other testimony revealed that at least 279 (24 percent) worked with one or more accomplices, 51 percent worked on the street, 14 percent in a concert saloon or restaurant, and 13 percent on a street-car or other form of public transit.

9. People v. Henry Gibson, 6 Dec. 1871; People v. John McClane, 9 July 1872; People v. James Carson, 5 Dec. 1876, all in DAP; *Harper's Weekly*, 20 May 1871 (in league); *Increase of Crime*, 24 (hustle passengers); McCabe, *Secrets*, 367 (Beware); Sutherland, *Professional Thief*, 44 (warning signs). On crowded streetcars, see *Herald*, editorial, 2 Oct. 1864; *Tribune*, editorial, 2 Feb. 1866.

10. *Star* clipping, 8 Oct. 1883 (delicately); unmarked clipping, 8 Aug. 1895, vol. 144; *Times* clipping, 7 July 1890 (knockdown pickpockets), vol. 75, all in DAS; Hapgood, *Autobiography*, 39–40; George W. Walling, *Recollections of a New York Chief of Police* (New York, 1887), 330; *NPG*, 27 May 1882; Byrnes, *Professional Criminals*, 34; *Tribune*, 25 Dec. 1887; Farley, *Criminals of America*, 202. Only 11 percent (114 in number) of those arrested in the sample were "knockdown pickpockets."

11. Of 1,176 individuals prosecuted for pickpocketing, 940 were male (80 percent) and 236 female (20 percent). The breakdown by age was:

Ages	Total	Percentage of Total	Percentage of Adults
10–14	57	5	–
15–17	109	9	–
18–19	179	15	18
20–24	372	32	37
25–29	203	17	20
30–34	110	9	11
35–39	57	5	6
40–44	22	2	2
45–49	11	1	1
50 and above	5	0.4	0.5
Unknown	51	4	5

For examples of pickpockets identifying themselves as "gentlemen" and "entrepreneurs," see People v. Charles Gibbons, 7 Apr. 1876; People v. James O'Brien, 17 Jan. 1876, both in DAP. To categorize the occupations given by prosecuted pickpockets, I relied on the classification scheme devised by Michael B. Katz in *The People of Hamilton, Canada West: Family and Class in a Mid-Nineteenth-Century City* (Cambridge, Mass., 1975), 343–48; and "Occupational Classification in History," *Journal of Interdisciplinary History* 3 (1972), 63–88. With roman numeral I identifying occupations with high socioeconomic ranking to roman numeral V for those with low socioeconomic ranking, pickpockets fell into the following categories: [See table below].

Roman numeral VI includes "unclassified occupations." Newsboys and bootblacks were not included in Katz's classification, and I recategorized servants and laundresses from "unclassifiable occupations" to category V.

12. Campbell, *Darkness*, 705–6 (Byrnes); Pinkerton, *Thirty Years*, 37 (female thieves); Byrnes, *Professional Criminals*, 35–36; Farley, *Criminals of America*, 206–7. On female mobs, see People v. Ellen Daley and Mary Ann Williams, 5 Aug. 1859, DAP; unmarked clipping, 30 June 1885, vol. 13; unmarked clipping, 11 Aug. 1895, vol. 144, both in DAS. Among the 241 females prosecuted for larceny or grand larceny, 43 percent were arrested in a panel house (a house of prostitution where male clients were systematically robbed), brothel, saloon, or concert saloon. Another 22 percent were arrested in the street.

13. People v. Catharine Smith, 25 Nov. 1864; People v. Catherine Columbus, 16 Nov. 1864; People v. Josephine Thompson, 9 Mar. 1869, all in DAP.

14. *Star* clipping, 8 Oct. 1883 (big city), DAS; *Tribune*, 12 Aug. 1876; Slick, *Snares of New York*, 39; *Tribune*, 12 Aug. 1876.

15. R. I. Davis, *Men's Garments, 1830–1900: A Guide to Pattern Cutting* (London, 1989), 54, 60 (decline of frocks); H. Matheson, *H. Matheson's Scientific and Practical Guide for the Tailor's Cutting Department* (New York, 1871), 14 (popular garment); Frederick T. Croonberg, *The Blue Book of Men's Tailoring* (1907; reprint, New York, 1977), 14–15 (Every man; plenty of pockets); R. L. Shep, "Introduction" in Louis Devere, *The Handbook of Practical Cutting on the Centre Point System* (London, 1866, 1868; reprint, Lopez Island, Wash., 1986).

16. Hapgood, *Autobiography*, 34; *Sun*, 4 Mar. 1861; Munro, *New York Tombs*, 41.

17. Steffens, *Autobiography*, 222–26, 288.

18. *Star* clipping, 8 Oct. 1883, DAS; *NPG*, 27 Dec. 1845, 3 Jan. 1846, 10 Jan. 1846, 4 Apr. 1846; George Thompson, *Adventures of a Pickpocket; or Life at a Fashionable Watering Place* (New York, 1849); George G. Foster, *New York by Gas-Light* (New York, 1850), 85; Campbell, *Darkness*, 704.

19. On the sample from the DAP and related methodology, see note 9 above; People v. Joseph Brunner, 17 Nov. 1876; People v. John McGrath, 17 Nov. 1876; People v. Hoy, 17 June 1879; People v. Ellen Wilson, 5 Sept. 1872, all in DAP. For cases involving unemployed men pleading for mercy, see People v. James Delany, 6 July 1876 (2.5 years); People v. Joseph Carroll, 29 June 1876 (4.5 years), both in DAP. On judges issuing severe penalties against "knockdown pickpockets" to deter others, see *Times* clipping, 7 July 1890, vol. 75, DAS.

20. People v. Henry Ducketts (14 years old), 24 June 1879; People v. John Kelly (19 years old), 16 Mar. 1871; People v. John Golden (17 years old), 14 Jan. 1874; People v. Alfred Johnson (19 years old), 3 June 1874; People v. Lawrence Dixon (19 years old), 6 Feb. 1874, all in DAP. For an earlier charge against Ducketts when he was nine, see People v. Henry Ducketts, 21 Apr. 1874, DAP.

21. For statutes defining pickpocketing and various forms of larceny, see Laws of 1860, chapter 508, sections 33, 34; revised in Laws of 1862, chapter 374, sections 2, 3 (assault with intent to steal); revised in Laws of 1882, chapter 410, sections 3 (attempted larceny), 63 (grand larceny), 531 (larceny in the second degree), 686 (punishment

Total in Category	I	II	III	IV	V	VI	Unknown
1,176	14 (13M/1F)	90 (85M/5F)	406 (390M/16F)	249 (228M/21F)	265 (142M/123F)	69 (13M/56F)	69
Total % (of 1,107)	1.3	7.6	37	23	24	6	1
Male % (of 871)	1.5	9.7	49	26	16	1.5	
Female % (of 222)	–	2.3	7	9	55	25	

for unsuccessful attempt), 1447. Grand larceny was the felonious taking and carrying away of another's personal property valued in excess of twenty-five dollars. Larceny in the second degree included unlawful appropriation of property of any value from a person. Courts upheld convictions of attempted larceny even if nothing was in the victim's pocket or the perpetrator gained control of no property. See *Commonwealth of Massachusetts v. McDonald*, 5 Cush. 365; *People v. Jones*, 46 Mich. 441; *State of Connecticut v. Wilson*, 30 Conn. 500; 1862 LEXIS 24; *Rogers v. Commonwealth of Pennsylvania*, 5 Serge. & Rawle 463; *People v. Bush*, 4 Hill 133. For examples and a good summary of the above statues and cases, see *People of the State of New York v. Thomas Moran*, 123 N.Y. 254; 25 N.E. 412; 20 Am.St.Rep. 732; 1890 N.Y. LEXIS 1730; Fletcher, *Rethinking Criminal Law*, 4–5.

22. Unmarked clipping, 10 June 1883, DAS; Board of Police Justices of the City of New York, *Second Annual Report for the Year 1875* (New York, 1876), 9; *NPG*, 31 Dec. 1881.

23. William Francis Kuntz II, *Criminal Sentencing in Three Nineteenth-Century Cities* (New York, 1988), 358–59, 370; Monkkonen, *Murder in New York City*, esp. 167; Monkkonen, "Racial Factors in New York City Homicides," 113 (2 percent); Monkkonen, "The American State from the Bottom Up," 521–31.

24. The data and information below are based on the sample in DAP, 1859–74, described in chapter 2, note 20. In 1871, 1872, and 1874, 101 individuals were convicted of larceny, 54 of whom were sentenced to three or more years in prison. Court of General Sessions indictments in 1859 and 1864 frequently did not include the final punishment on convicted defendants. Only twenty-one indictments and convictions involving individuals who stole $100 or more in valuables provided a final sentence.

25. *Truth*, 4 June 1883, DAS (shot); Matthew Hale Smith, *Sunshine and Shadow in New York* (Hartford, Conn., 1868), 569; People v. John Smith, 25 Nov. 1872, DAP. For other examples of long sentences, see People v. John Jackson, 17 Nov. 1876; People v. Henry Lee, 15 June 1876, all in DAP.

26. Entry for 20 Mar. 1874, 475–76, First District, PCDB (Appo); entry for "George Dixon," 15 Apr. 1874, 396, vol. 11, SSAR; entry for 13 Apr. 1874, vol. 3, Sing Sing admissions, 1842–1874 (n.p.), Executive Register of Commitments to Prisons, NYSArc; People v. John Williams, 15 Sept. 1871 (5 years for a $60 watch); People v. Emma Wilson and Catherine Love, 16 Oct. 1874 (3 years for a $6 watch); People v. Jane Crane, 20 Oct. 1874 (3 years for $2.30); People v. Jane Loughlin, May 1876, all in DAP; *Morning Journal* clipping, 20 Dec. 1886 (25 years), vol. 29, DAS. For other examples of lengthy Hackett sentences to teenagers, see entry for George Smith, age nineteen (2.5 years), 11 Sept. 1875, 56; entry for John McCauly, age eighteen (2 years), 17 Sept. 1875, 80, both in vol. 13, SSAR. Near the end of his career, Hackett allegedly became insane and issued even heavier sentences.

Percentage Breakdown of Prison Sentences

Year	Total Cases	Total Sentenced	<1 year	1–1.9	2–2.9	3+	Suspend.	H. of Ref.
1859	54	26	35	8	31	27	0	0
1864	118	40	35	8	28	3	0	0
1869	91	47	9	15	30	38	0	9
1871	144	84	12	7	14	52	11	4
1872	144	74	9	16	38	31	9	5
1874	316	245	14	12	42	20	1	11
1876	301	219	10	20	33	27	0	11
TOTAL	1,168							

THE POCKET BOOK DROPPER.

Figure 4.1 "The Pocket Book Dropper," *The National Police Gazette* May 27, 1848. Courtesy of the Center for Historic American Visual Culture at the American Antiquarian Society.

The Boardinghouse in Nineteenth-Century America

Wendy Gamber

Source: *The Boardinghouse in Nineteenth-Century America* (Baltimore: Johns Hopkins University Press, 2007).

EDITORS' INTRODUCTION

Wendy Gamber, professor of history at Indiana University, Bloomington, offers a compelling critique of the idealization of home within nineteenth-century cities. This essay examines the effects of the market economy on private living through the often overlooked history of the boardinghouse, a ubiquitous part of the urban landscape. In the crowded city, women (and it was predominantly a women's business) turned to taking in boarders to earn essential income. Boarding possibilities ranged from "hotbunking" in a rented tenement bed shared by a laborer on another shift (workers might even lay down in a bed still warm from the previous occupant), to renting a bedroom and a separate parlor from a "genteel" woman offering rooms in a "private" home on a well-regarded street. Whatever the case, the fees earned from boarding others provided critical household income to many families, and allowed a high percentage of urban dwellers to obtain shelter. In the nineteenth century, one third to one half of urbanites were engaged in the economy of boarding, either as the ones providing the space or the ones paying the rent. Many participating in the system were both renters and boardinghouse keepers, for it was standard practice to sub-let rooms to others within a rented apartment or home. **[See Document 4.1, Thomas Butler Gunn, *The Physiology of New York Boarding-Houses* (1857).]**

Gamber's compelling form of scholarship, including her first book, *The Female Economy: The Millinery and Dressmaking Trades, 1930–1970* (University of Illinois Press, 1997) could only be possible in the academic climate of the late twentieth and early twenty-first centuries in which flourishing historical subfields have allowed for works informed by multiple perspectives, deeply influenced by women's studies. Here, Gamber explores the distinction between public and private space, and probes the question of what constitutes "home." The concept of home evolved over the course of the nineteenth century; the idea that home was a haven from the workaday outside world was not a constant. First, men's labor had to separate itself from the household physically. Then the concept of women's separate sphere had to develop and come into general usage. Once these ideas were firmly established, the boarding house, with its laxity between private and public, family and guests, love and money, seemed to challenge common social mores. To some, it might appear immoral for a wife and mother to charge unrelated adults for a room in her home and a place at her table. With the gaining momentum of the concept of home as haven, Americans associated homes with rest and leisure. The labor of housewives was to be done without any outward association with work; housework was, in a sense, pastoralized. Gamber asks whether the boarding house arrangement—cash for the trappings of home—exposed the fraudulence of thinking of a home as a haven. The presence of paid servants, often brought in by higher-class boardinghouse keepers, muddied the transaction even further. Boardinghouses also challenged typical gender norms and the usual separation between men and women socially. What should others make of the mixed-gender arrangements—here we have unrelated adults under one roof, sleeping nearby one another, socializing in the evenings, and forming friendships with limited supervision. Gamber demonstrates how the boardinghouse proved to be a popular choice for young married couples; in a boardinghouse, the young wife did not have to bother with cleaning and cooking, and might find some leisure time for herself.

HOUSES AND HOMES

Writing in the late 1990s about the increasing prevalence of grown children living with their parents, the etiquette expert Judith Martin ("Miss Manners") deplored the tendency of both parties to view their circumstances as "some sort of landlord-boarder arrangement." While she acknowledged that grown-ups residing in multigenerational households deserved greater autonomy and privacy than did minors, she insisted nevertheless that "a family household is not a boarding house, where people are supposed to pretend they have no interest in one another's private lives."[1]

Miss Manners is known for her fondness for quaint anachronisms, and her boardinghouse analogy, which probably only dimly resonated with her readers, is no exception. Indeed, the idea that the home, or, as Miss Manners put it, the "family household," is not a boardinghouse has a long history. It was a staple of nineteenth-century popular discourse, a moral certainty to which commentators as diverse as Sarah Josepha Hale, a prolific author of domestic fiction and "editress" of the genteel *Godey's Lady's Book*, and the iconoclastic poet Walt Whitman subscribed. Hundreds of self-appointed cultural authorities—journalists, humorists, writers of "fact" and fiction—joined Hale and Whitman in chronicling the disappointments, annoyances, and even dangers of boardinghouse life. They wrote for different purposes, with varying degrees of sophistication and satire, and they spoke to different, albeit often overlapping, audiences. But all agreed that boardinghouses were not homes.

Home, in their eyes, represented far more than a place of residence. Ideally the private abode of the nuclear family, it furnished a refuge from a market-driven world, governed proper relations between the sexes, provided moral guidance and emotional support to its inhabitants, and upheld republican government and social order. Its antithesis—in theory if not in fact—was the boardinghouse, a public establishment where strangers of both sexes mingled freely, fueling crime, vice, and social anarchy. Worst of all, in boarding-houses the moral contagions of the market invaded social relationships that ideally remained untainted by base economic concerns. For in boardinghouses women washed, cleaned, and cooked for money, services that elsewhere they presumably provided out of love. In an era dominated by powerful—if often illusory—dichotomies between home and market, public and private, love and money, boardinghouses emerged as unsavory counterparts to idealized homes. Or, to put it another way, they offered nineteenth-century Americans a means of defining home by representing everything that home was not.

"Be It Ever So Humble…"

Without a doubt the nineteenth century was the golden age of the home.[2] Ministers, journalists, authors of prose and poetry, lyricists, and editors of ladies' and general interest magazines, along with ordinary Americans, celebrated the virtues of home. They sang songs like "Home, Sweet Home" (perhaps the century's most popular ballad), recited poems like "My Own Fireside," and read novels that depicted heaven as a home.[3] Historians have most often identified these sentiments with the white, native-born bourgeoisie. Certainly, middle-class writers dominated popular discourse; certainly, members of the middle class were best positioned to turn domestic longings into material realities. Nevertheless, celebration of home transcended class, ethnic, and racial lines. "Wouldst thou listen to its gentle teaching, All thy restless yearning [home] … would still!" exclaimed the African American *Christian Recorder*. "Home! Sweet home! … Home is the flowery pathway of life, where the nobler passions of humanity blossom, in unspotted purity; the sacred shrine where all our longing, vagrant, pilgrim fancies love to worship," the *Boston Pilot* rhapsodized for the benefit of its largely Irish Catholic readers.[4]

It had not always been this way. As late as the 1830s and 1840s, home in the sentimental sense represented a novel and, in many senses, alien concept. Before that time, *home*, generally interchangeable with *household*, had no special meaning. And boarding, which would become the bête noire of midcentury moralists, was a familiar practice. Taverns and boardinghouses accommodated travelers and served as more or less permanent residences for some people. Members of eighteenth- and early nineteenth-century households, rural and urban, commonly included nonrelatives, often apprentices, who received room and board in exchange for their labor, or "helpers," who participated in less formal agreements.[5] Such arrangements neither precluded exploitation nor ensured domestic harmony. But only with the rise of home as a cultural icon did numerous Americans begin to perceive boarding as a social problem.

Yet, if the nineteenth century was the golden age of the bourgeois home, it was also the age of the boardinghouse. In cities and many towns, people of all classes were at least likely to live in boardinghouses as in homes. What historians call the market revolution, a series of related developments that included the expansion of commercial agriculture, the beginnings of industrialization, the emergence of a working class dependent on wages, the rise of a salaried white-collar middle class, and massive urban growth, could never have been accomplished without boardinghouses and the labor of those who kept them. As rural populations outstripped local land supplies, as overfarming exhausted the soil, as farm machinery and manufactured goods reduced demand for agricultural and household labor, as bad harvests and unpredictable commodity prices spawned foreclosures, and as urban adventure beckoned, increasing numbers of men and women abandoned the American countryside to become merchants, clerks, salesmen, mechanics, and seamstresses in New York, Boston, Philadelphia, and countless smaller cities. At the same time, thousands of immigrants, propelled by famine, political upheaval, and economic dislocation, left Ireland, Germany, Britain, and France (and later Eastern Europe) for the United States. Some journeyed west to take up farming, but most had little choice but to pursue urban employments—as day laborers, domestic servants, and factory hands. As city populations expanded dramatically (by some estimates as much as 800% during the first half of the nineteenth century), so too did the number of establishments that offered room and board to rural migrants, European newcomers, and assorted people who could not or would not live in "homes."[6]

Social historians have estimated that somewhere between a third and a half of nineteenth-century urban residents either took in boarders or were boarders themselves.[7] A more precise reckoning is not possible, in part because few who kept boarders openly advertised that fact, in part because landladies—stung by accusations that allied them with a heartless marketplace—often adopted vague and confusing terminology. Contemporaries nevertheless recognized boarding's ubiquity. "Like death, no class is exempt from it," humorist Thomas Butler Gunn quipped in 1857; a year earlier Whitman had claimed, "it is probable that nearer three quarters than two thirds of all the adult inhabitants of New York city … live in boarding-houses." Gunn and Whitman's hyperbole aside, the boardinghouse was so common that even its detractors described it, albeit not entirely accurately, as an "American institution," a symbol of the uniquely transient nature of American life.[8]

The same developments that increased the demand for "American institutions"—the expansion of urban manufactures and commerce, the dramatic increase in the numbers of city residents in need of shelter, and the emergence of economies based less on custom than on cash—helped give rise to the domestic ideal that nineteenth-century Americans came to call the home. As employers—no longer bound by craft traditions—increasingly declined to house their employees, homes became the private abodes of loving families. As artisan workshops gave way to factories and retail stores, "home" became distinct from "work." Merchants, clerks, laborers, and mechanics left their residences each morning for counting-houses, dry goods stores, workrooms, and docks, returning home in the evening and perhaps for their midday meals. As the exigencies of the marketplace seemingly enveloped all interactions, the private home became a sanctuary. It was a place where love, not money, reigned supreme.

Powerful as they were, these beliefs rested on convenient fictions. Regardless of commentaries that distinguished "home" from "work," housewives of all classes, save the very wealthy, worked hard indeed. They washed, cooked, swept, scrubbed, and stitched, arduous tasks in an era that featured few labor-saving devices. The authors of advice manuals and prescriptive fiction resolved the apparent contradiction between domestic ideology and everyday reality by defining unpaid household labor as something other than work. "What do you think I am doing?" exclaims a character in Hale's *Keeping House and House Keeping* (1845). "I am learning to make puddings, pastry, and bread! What I once thought such a drudgery now makes every day pass pleasantly." What one historian aptly terms "the pastoralization of housework"—a perception that bedevils stay-at-home parents to this day—found widespread support, even among housewives themselves. A woman hastily scribbling a letter or diary entry by candlelight might describe a twelve-hour marathon of washing, sewing, cooking, and cleaning and conclude that she had not "done anything."[9]

The prevalence of paid labor within homes provided potentially more troublesome challenges to the notion that "home" and "work" were distinct categories of experience. Even solidly middle-class housewives frequently contributed to family coffers by taking in sewing, laundry—and boarders. They rarely, however, recognized this remunerated labor as real work, typically reporting their occupations to census takers as "keeping house." What is more, considerable numbers invited wage laborers—domestic servants—into their homes. To be sure, bourgeois matrons did all they could to preserve the privacy of the family, an entity from which servants, as opposed to the "helps" of an earlier era, were decidedly excluded. They routinely banished servants—during those rare hours when they were not at "work"—to dreary basements or stifling attics and barred them from the family table—except as waitresses. Nevertheless, the presence of servants, like housewives' gainful employment, suggests that homes were neither truly private nor truly removed from the market.[10]

Those who penned syrupy tributes to domestic bliss confronted a related dilemma. Did the true value of home reside in its material manifestation, its emotional essence, or both? A veritable mountain of prescriptive literature warned against luxury and ostentation. But few writers expected their readers to live lives of material deprivation. Even as they emphasized sentiment over rampant materialism, most had particular physical structures in mind when they conjured up visions of home. Most often, they meant a single-family, detached, owner-occupied, increasingly suburban, dwelling situated somewhere between the opulent mansions of the idle rich and the squalid tenements of the urban poor. [...]

Nineteenth-century newspapers listed quantities and prices of pork, beef, cotton, and flour under the heading of "domestic markets," distinguishing commodities bought and sold within the boundaries of the United States from "importations." Few would have applied the phrase to the middle-class home. Yet, in more ways than one, homes were indeed domestic marketplaces. Nevertheless, the idea that home and market were distinct, even oppositional, entities stubbornly persisted.[11]

If the home furnished a refuge from the market; indeed, if its very existence justified the ruthless pursuit of self-interest in the marketplace, what then of the boardinghouse? It would be going too far to claim that boarding-houses alone resolved the tensions and contradictions so glaringly evident in the rhetoric that surrounded the home. But they certainly helped to do so. As nineteenth-century commentators struggled to understand the meaning of home, boardinghouses seemed to provide them with a ready contrast, encompassing all that homes were not. If homes were private, boardinghouses were public. If homes nurtured virtue, boardinghouses bred vice. Above all, boardinghouses were creatures of the marketplace. Paying cash for housekeeping services (and accepting cash for providing them) defied the social logic of the domestic ideal. In the period that enshrined the home as the foundation of moral life and simultaneously embraced the market as the overarching model for economic relations, distinguishing between home and boardinghouse provided Americans with one means of determining what could and what could not be sold.

Women's labor stood at the heart of this social equation, for boardinghouse keeping was women's work. Even when husbands and fathers styled themselves proprietors, wives and daughters, sometimes assisted by female servants, performed the labor that keeping boarders entailed. That boardinghouse keeping should have provoked hostility is at first surprising. It offered no dramatic challenge to existing sexual divisions of labor; little distinguished keeping a boardinghouse from keeping house. Relocated to the marketplace, house-wifery underwent a kind of magical, albeit malevolent, transformation. If women's unpaid labors of love made houses into homes, women's market labor converted boardinghouses into hovels, even brothels. Yet as landladies and boarders would discover, maintaining the always permeable boundaries between love and money, home and market, boardinghouse and home proved difficult indeed.

American Institutions

Ubiquitous in the nineteenth century, the "American institution" largely has disappeared from the national landscape. Thus a word of explanation may be in order. Perhaps bed-and-breakfasts provide the closest present-day analogy, for boardinghouses, unlike lodging houses, provided meals, usually served at a common table, and housekeeping services in addition to shelter. Hotels, on the other hand, served food and drink to passersby as well as guests. Hotels were usually purpose built; thus they tended to be more luxurious, expensive, and architecturally elaborate than were boardinghouses. (Hence they were almost always run by men.) Boardinghouses, apart from the imposing structures erected by corporate employers, most often were converted dwellings—or simply "homes" with extra rooms to let. "Public" boardinghouses mimicked their more illustrious counterparts by offering meals ("board") to non-residents; "private" establishments accommodated only the needs of the people who lived in them. To be sure, there was considerable overlap between these various sorts of institutions. The same building might be described as a small hotel by one observer, as a large boardinghouse by another. Some land-ladies accommodated both boarders and lodgers. Conversely, the proprietors of otherwise private boardinghouses welcomed "day boarders" who slept elsewhere. And, as we shall see, boarders and boardinghouse keepers drew infinitely flexible distinctions between public and private establishments, between taking in boarders and running a boardinghouse, between living in a boardinghouse and boarding with a private family.[12]

These distinctions represented only the tip of the proverbial iceberg, for there were many different kinds of boardinghouses. Contemporaries usually contented themselves with distinguishing between "genteel" and "mechanic" establishments or with assigning labels such as first, second, and third class (categories that had no fixed or official meaning). Beneath these surfaces lurked a bewildering heterogeneity. Thomas Butler Gunn, the author of *The Physiology of New York Boarding-Houses* (1857), was one of the few observers who grasped the enormous complexity of this varied social universe. Possibly a relation of the renowned physician John C. Gunn, possibly a man who had medical training himself, he rejected dichotomous and tripartite taxonomies in favor of "physiology," classifying his subject into no fewer than thirty categories. These included the usual class and ethnic suspects ("the cheap boarding-house," "the Irish immigrant boarding-house," "the Chinese boarding-house," and "the German 'gasthaus'") but also occupational, philosophical, regional, and moral affinities ("the actor's boardinghouse," "the medical students' boarding-house," "the boarding-house wherein spiritualism becomes predominant," "the vegetarian boarding-house," "the boarding-house frequented by Bostonians"). Clearly writing tongue-in-cheek, Gunn nevertheless captured something of the variety of available boarding experiences. An enthusiastic reviewer for *Frank Leslie's Illustrated Newspaper* certainly thought so: "He has taken the roof off every class of boarding-house in the city, and revealed to the world their inmates in all their wide variety of character and occupation, their style of living, and exposed the whole system in every degree of social status." Newspaper advertisements confirm that there was indeed a boarding-house for everyone: Swedenborgians, tailors, amateur musicians, "respectable colored people," Southerners, teetotalers, and disciples of the food reformer Sylvester Graham.[13] Even smaller cities and towns offered potential boarders a semblance of the variety they would find in places like New York, Philadelphia, Boston, Chicago, and San Francisco.

Like the houses they inhabited, boarders' experiences varied, often in direct proportion to the accommodations they could afford. They generally had little good to say—in part because many boardinghouses deserved their disagreeable reputations. ... Writers, both famous and unremarkable, usually based their observations not on imagination but on experience, rendering easy distinctions between "prescription" and "reality," "fact" and "fiction" problematic. Most probably knew a good deal more about boardinghouses than about homes. ... Not coincidentally, they typically invoked homes as abstract ideals—ideals they literally helped to construct—but reserved their thickest description for boardinghouses, depicting eccentric housemates, filthy bed linens, "grave-like bedrooms," and intolerable "cuisine" in vivid, if not loving, detail. However realistic their portrayals, he notion that boardinghouses could never be more than "substitutes for home," ... influenced their perceptions. Homes, however vague and romanticized, provided them with yardsticks by which to measure boarding life—and boarding almost always came up short.[14] [...]

"Our Family at 34": Susan Parsons Brown (1856–1861)

Susan Parsons Brown left her hometown of Epsom, New Hampshire, for Boston at the tail end of March 1856. Snow still lay on the ground, so her father took her by horse sled to the house of a family friend. From there another friend of the family drove her by wagon to Concord. At Concord, Brown boarded a train that took her to Boston.[15]

This was not the first time that Brown had been away from home or even the first time she had visited Boston. At thirty-two, the former Lowell mill girl and peripatetic teacher was a veteran of such journeys. Still, her move to Boston represented the most dramatic contrast with her previous rural and small-town life. There she quickly found work. After a brief and disappointing stint in a wholesale millinery workroom, where "all days pass very much alike," she accepted the position of English teacher for the city's Jewish school.[16]

Unlike characters in Victorian melodramas, Brown was hardly alone in the city, even if she was away from home. Boston and nearby Cambridge teemed with relatives and friends with Epsom connections. Nor did moving to the city mean permanent exile. Brown returned to Epsom during school vacations, and her parents, sometimes separately, sometimes together, frequently visited her in Boston. Brown's story is not one of urban anomie but of urban community—a community linked by intricate ties between city and country. Through church, school, and respectable entertainments, she strengthened old acquaintances and forged new ones. But Brown's primary attachments were to what she called "our family at 34," the inhabitants of her boardinghouse at 34 Oxford Street. Her story offers a compelling example of how one lodger fashioned her boardinghouse into a home.

Very likely, Brown chose "34" because its keeper, Mrs. R. H. Haskell, was no stranger but rather the daughter of a family friend and a recent migrant to the city herself. (Possibly, the forty-four-year-old Haskell was even a relation.) Brown joined a household fairly bursting at the seams. In addition to Brown and her landlady, the "family" included two married couples, at least seven young clerks and salesmen who worked downtown in dry goods stores, a Miss Richardson, who seems to have been an invalid, and a servant. City directories suggest that Haskell's husband was still alive during Brown's first two years in Boston, but Brown never mentioned him; nor did she note his death. This was not unusual; it was common for keepers' husbands to disappear from boarders' view. Boardinghouse keeping was women's work; landladies, not their spouses, typically met potential boarders, collected rents, and presided over dining tables.

Although the composition of Brown's boardinghouse family would change frequently, the general pattern would remain the same: a married couple or two, a few single women, and a majority of young salesmen and male clerks who worked downtown on Summer, Winter, and Washington Streets in the city's commercial district.[17]

Although she always referred to her as Mrs. Haskell or Mrs. H, Brown acted more or less as a sister or daughter to her landlady. For a time, she and Haskell slept in the same room (a situation that perhaps spoke less of intimacy than of a shortage of available space). She accompanied Haskell on "bonnet hunting" expeditions, on social calls, and to Fourth of July fireworks. She ran errands for her. When Haskell left for a two-week visit to her mother in Pittsfield, Brown took over the management of the household, baking pies and cakes on Satur-

days and interviewing prospective lodgers.[18] When Haskell faced financial difficulties, Brown lent her money. (She did not, however, hesitate to charge interest.)[19]

Brown forged relationships not just with her landlady but with the whole of the "family" at 34. She carefully recorded the arrival of new boarders and the departure of old ones. Each New Year's Day she took an inventory of the household's inhabitants, noting that "the family at 34 consists of…" or "our family at 34 consists of…" Brown's nomenclature was more than merely semantic; the inhabitants of 34 did indeed act something like a family. When Brown was sick, "Dr. Downs" (Mr. Downs, a fellow boarder and singing master) gave her medicine.[20] Sometimes the entire household joined together for May Day excursions, New Year's games of blind man's bluff, or an occasional "popped corn party."[21] On one New Year's Day, the boarders gathered in the parlor for a "presentation" in Mrs. Haskell's honor.[22]

More often, the family split into smaller, usually mixed-sex groups. All told, Brown spent surprisingly little time in the company of the other women, married and single, who lived at 34. She sallied forth into the world—on walks around the Common, to church, to lectures, to meetings—usually accompanied by one or more male boarders, even venturing to attend Catholic services with one Mr. Staple. She saw no moral danger in these excursions; after all, she was with members of her "family." Indeed, Brown played a central role in maintaining 34's respectability by organizing an "English grammar class" for the household's young male clerks. (In this she was not unique; Elizabeth Dorr, a teacher who boarded in nearby Dorchester, volunteered to give a German housemate lessons in English pronunciation.) Their dutiful attendance suggests the depth of their own commitment to self-improvement.[23]

Some of Brown's relationships with male boarders were mere friendships. Brown took a sisterly, even motherly, interest in Charles Dodge, a clerk some ten years her junior. She mended his coats and took pride in his accomplishments. "Dodge cast his *first* vote," she noted on Election Day in 1856.[24] Her interest in other boarders was more than sisterly. Although she was in her early thirties, Brown did not lack for suitors. She seems to have been choosy rather than desperate. A previous acquaintance from Epsom, John Cate French, courted her in Boston; in June 1856, however, they had "much conversation" in Mrs. Haskell's parlor "and parted 'friends.'"[25] For a brief period later that summer, a courtship with Alexander Lyle, one of the dry goods salesmen, blossomed. He and Brown sat in the parlor "chatting until the wee hours" on several occasions. The romance soon fizzled, and "*Mr. Lyle left boarding here*" [Brown's emphasis] the following February.[26] By June, Brown had identified another prospect, a new boarder named Alexander Forbes. Brown welcomed Forbes and his roommate, both recently arrived from Scotland, with a bouquet of flowers, because they were "newcomers & strangers."[27] The twenty-one-year-old Forbes, a clerk at Turnbull and Churchill's downtown dry goods store, quickly joined Brown's social circle. Soon he was accompanying her to church, Young Men's Christian Association (YMCA) meetings, and public lectures.

If Brown's initial interest limited itself to friendly sympathy, the tide quickly shifted toward romance. Soon Brown and Forbes were "chatting" in the parlor until the "wee hours."[28] Forbes, for his part, scrawled a hasty note to Brown on a scrap of newspaper torn from the *Boston Herald*. Perhaps he furtively passed it to her at breakfast or dinner, or slipped it into her hand as they passed on the stairs: "Miss Brown I love you." Finally, in December 1857, Brown obliquely noted that she and Forbes had "decided on a question that has been in agitation."[29] In other words, they were engaged. They did not marry until August 1859, a year and a half later. After a ceremony and brief honeymoon in Epsom, they returned to Mrs. Haskell's boardinghouse to begin married life. ("The first night of our married life in 34," the new Mrs. Forbes noted in her diary on August 13, 1859.) In this they were typical of newlyweds, who often chose boardinghouses over homes.

Their marriage changed the allocation of boardinghouse space and sociability. They moved together into a new room, and as a married couple they could invite fellow boarders of either sex into their "private" domicile within the larger household.[30]

With its mixed assemblage of men and women, married and single, 34 was typical of middle-class boarding establishments. At first glance, its composition and ever-changing cast of characters suggests the fulfillment of moralists' dire warnings. In nineteenth-century parlance, 34 was a "promiscuous" or mixed-sex establishment. Haskell and her boarders lived in close proximity, even on terms of physical intimacy—evident when Brown noted in a diary entry that Dodge's "colic" (probably manifested by vomiting) had awakened the household.[31] Yet, all evidence suggests that 34 Oxford Street was an eminently respectable residence; very likely it was on the YMCA's list of respectable boarding places for young men new to the city.[32]

Brown was not an especially expressive diarist. Nevertheless, it is clear that she considered 34 Oxford Street home and its inhabitants her family. How did she negotiate the dichotomy between house and home, between "den" and respectable domicile? Brown must have encountered conventional definitions of *home* when she attended Edwin Hubbell Chapin's lecture, "Woman and her Work" which she pronounced "very excellent."[33] Still, home—as glorified in novels, household manuals, and ladies' magazines—may have been a less than familiar concept to her. Her reading tended toward the classics rather than the domestic, toward Shakespeare rather than *Godey's Lady's Book*. And Brown was no stranger to boarding. She had lived in a boardinghouse during her eight-month stint in 1843 as a weaver in Lowell; as a teacher in various New Hampshire towns she had always boarded with local families.[34] Her own family in Epsom sometimes took in boarders.[35] For Brown, as for many other Americans of her time, the isolated nuclear family and the idealized home were far more alien than living in the midst of the assorted and mostly transient individuals who made up the family at 34.

Nor can Brown's expansive (and in the view of bourgeois moralists, misguided) definition of family be attributed solely to rural innocence. She was no naïf; she was thoroughly familiar with the moral dangers of the city. Numerous YMCA speakers, whose lectures she attended, must have made the theoretical case. Yet Brown had more immediate knowledge. Vice even crossed the threshold of 34 in the person of James Haining, a fellow boarder whom Brown feared was "going the way to destruction." A young man might take one of many "ways to destruction" in antebellum America—drinking, gambling, sex, Sabbath-breaking, laziness, extravagance—Haining's particular vices are anyone's guess. In any case, he left 34, perhaps not voluntarily, before he could do much damage. Mrs. Haskell quite likely evicted him, for maintaining the respectability of one's establishment was an essential part of the work of boardinghouse keeping. Still hoping for Haining's reformation, Brown sent him a book titled *The Young Men of the Bible* before he left Boston for New York.[36] Whether this gesture had the desired effect is unclear. Possibly it did, for less than a year later "Jas. Haining returned from N. Y. to board here again," resuming his employment at Turnbull and Churchill's (the same dry goods store where Alexander Forbes worked).[37]

Perhaps Brown perceived no tension between boardinghouse and home because she didn't have to. Mrs. Haskell's domicile most likely was *not* a "boardinghouse"; rather—although twenty-five to thirty boarders crossed her threshold each year and although she housed seven to ten of them at any one time—in Brown's view she very likely offered accommodations in a "private family."[38] Middle-class establishments that housed boarders were *private families;* working-class ones were *boardinghouses*. This flexible definition of family assuaged anxieties about living arrangements and clearly distinguished respectable establishments from disreputable ones. "Privacy" was an elastic concept that conferred an aura of respectability on otherwise "promiscuous" households.

Within two years of the Forbes's marriage, Mrs. Haskell gave up boardinghouse keeping, and the couple, in keeping with social expectations, moved to "our own house." "Our own house" was not exactly what one might expect. Strictly speaking, it was not their own; they rented it for $550 a year. Nor was it the private dwelling that "our own house" might imply. Instead, it was a boardinghouse of their own.

NOTES

1. Judith Martin, "Miss Manners: Adult Children Living at Home Can be Desirable Experience," *Bloomington Herald-Times*, March 22, 1998; Martin, "Miss Manners: Multigenerational Households Find Compromise Difficult," *Bloomington Herald-Times*, August 16, 1998.

2. See, e.g., Nancy F. Cott, *The Bonds of Womanhood: "Woman's Sphere" in New England, 1780–1835* (New Haven, CT: Yale University Press, 1977), 63–100; Mary P. Ryan, *Cradle of the Middle Class: The Family in Oneida County, New York, 1790–1865* (Cambridge: Cambridge University Press, 1981), 186–229; Gwendolyn Wright, *Moralism and the Modern Home: Domestic Architecture and Cultural Conflict in Chicago, 1873–1913* (Chicago: University of Chicago Press, 1980), and *Building the Dream: A Social History of Housing in America* (New York: Pantheon, 1981); Clifford Edward Clark Jr., *The American Family Home, 1800–1960* (Chapel Hill: University of North Carolina Press, 1986); and Elizabeth Blackmar, *Manhattan for Rent, 1785–1850* (Ithaca, NY: Cornell University Press, 1989).

3. Richard Crawford, *America's Musical Life: A History* (New York: W. W. Norton, 2001), 178–80; Alaric A. Watts, "My Own Fireside," in *Home Life Made Beautiful*, ed. Margaret Sangster (New York: Christian Herald, 1897), 33–34; Alice Fahs, [on Elizabeth Stuart Phelps's *The Gates Ajar* (1868)] *The Imagined Civil War: Popular Literature of the North and South, 1861–1865* (Chapel Hill: University of North Carolina Press, 2001), 147–48.

4. "Home Influences," *Christian Recorder*, May 1, 1869; "The Pleasures of Home," *Boston Pilot*, June 9, 1838, 158.

5. Clark, *The American Family Home*, 11–12; Blackmar, *Manhattan for Rent*, 55, 57–60; Laurel Thatcher Ulrich, *A Midwife's Tale: The Life of Martha Ballard, Based on Her Diary* (New York: Vintage, 1991), 21, 80–82, 161, 223–26.

6. Sean Wilentz, "Society, Politics, and the Market Revolution, 1815–1848," in *The New American History*, ed. Eric Foner (Philadelphia: Temple University Press, 1990), 51–71; Charles Sellers, *The Market Revolution: Jacksonian America, 1815–1846* (New York: Oxford University Press, 1991); Melwyn Stokes and Stephen Conway, eds., *The Market Revolution in America: Social,*

Political, and Religious Expressions, 1800–1880 (Charlottesville: University Press of Virginia, 1996); Karen Haltunnen, *Confidence Men and Painted Women: A Study of Middle-Class Culture in America, 1830–1870* (New Haven, CT: Yale University Press, 1982), 35. For the best and most sustained scholarly treatments of boardinghouses, see Paul Groth, *Living Downtown: The History of Residential Hotels in the United States* (Berkeley and Los Angeles: University of California Press, 1994); Rachel Amelia Bernstein, "Boarding-House Keepers and Brothel Keepers in New York City, 1880–1910" (Ph.D. diss., Rutgers University, 1984); Mark Peel, "On the Margins: Lodgers and Boarders in Boston, 1860–1900," *Journal of American History* 72 (March 1986): 813–34; Blackmar, *Manhattan for Rent*, 60, 63–7, 88, 134–38; and Kenneth A. Scherzer, *The Unbounded Community: Neighborhood Life and Social Structure in New York City, 1830–1875* (Durham: Duke University Press, 1992). Boardinghouses receive brief attention in Christine Stansell, *City of Women: Sex and Class in New York, 1789–1860* (New York: Knopf, 1986), 9, 13, 53, 85, 185–86; Richard B. Stott, *Workers in the Metropolis: Class, Ethnicity, and Youth in Antebellum New York City* (Ithaca, NY: Cornell University Press, 1990), 169–71, 179–80, 204–9, 241–43; Gwendolyn Wright, *Building the Dream: A Social History of Housing in America* (New York: Pantheon, 1981), 37–38, 125; Susan Strasser, *Never Done: A History of American Housework* (New York: Pantheon, 1982), 145–61; Ruth Schwartz Cowan, *More Work for Mother: The Ironies of Household Technology from the Open Hearth to the Microwave* (New York: Basic Books, 1983), 108–9; Elizabeth Collins Cromley, *Alone Together: A History of New York's Early Apartments* (Ithaca, NY: Cornell University Press, 1990), 16, 21–27; Timothy J. Gilfoyle, *City of Eros: New York City, Prostitution, and the Commercialization of Sex, 1790–1920* (New York: W. W. Norton, 1992), 73, 78, 165–72; and Joanne J. Meyerowitz, *Women Adrift: Independent Wage Earners in Chicago, 1880–1930* (Chicago: University of Chicago Press, 1988), 24, 70–76.

7. John Modell and Tamara K. Hareven, "Urbanization and the Malleable Household: An Examination of Boarding and Lodging in American Families," *Journal of Marriage and the Family* 35 (1973): 467–79; Michael B. Katz, *The People of Hamilton, Canada West: Family and Class in a Mid-Nineteenth-Century City* (Cambridge, MA: Harvard University Press, 1975), 36, 222–36, 264–70; Peel, "On the Margins," 816–17; and Groth, *Living Downtown*, 92.

8. Thomas Butler Gunn, *The Physiology of New York Boarding-Houses* (New York: Mason Brothers, 1857), 12; Emory Holloway and Ralph Adimari, eds., *New York Dissected by Walt Whitman: A Sheaf of Recently Discovered News-paper Articles by the Author of Leaves of Grass* (New York: Rufus Rockwell Wilson, 1936), 96–7; "Boarding Out," *Harper's Weekly* (March 7, 1857), 146; Helen A. Hawley, "Concerning an American Institution," *Chautauquan* 13 (1891): 230. Neither boardinghouses nor complaints about them were unique to the United States. See Sharon Marcus, *Apartment Stories: City and Home in Nineteenth-Century Paris and London* (Berkeley and Los Angeles: University of California Press, 1999), 104–8.

9. On the history of housework, see Strasser, *Never Done*; Cowan, *More Work for Mother*; and Jeanne Boydston, *Home and Work: Housework, Wages, and the Ideology of Labor in the Early Republic* (New York: Oxford University Press, 1990). Sarah Josepha Hale, *Keeping House and House Keeping: A Story of Domestic Life* (New York: Harper and Brothers, 1845), 132. *Pastoralization* is Boydston's term; see esp. 142–63.

10. On this point, see esp. Blackmar, *Manhattan for Rent*, 112.

11. See, e.g., *Boston Courier*; December 28, 1849. Jeanne Boydston, *Home and Work: Housework, Wages, and the Ideology of Labor in the Early Republic* (New York: Oxford University Press, 1990), esp. 142–63. Sentimental ideology was vulnerable to other contradictions. It coexisted with thriving markets in human flesh (though sentimental ideology provided abolitionists with powerful arguments). Men might turn to the language of sentiment to describe their adventures—and especially their failures—in the marketplace; women and men profited by selling the artifacts of sentimental culture. On these issues, see Walter Johnson, *Soul by Soul: Life Inside the Antebellum Slave Market* (Cambridge, MA: Harvard University Press, 1999); Amy Dru Stanley, "Home Life and the Morality of the Market," in *The Market Revolution in America: Social, Political, and Religious Expressions, 1800–1880*, ed. Melwyn Stokes and Stephen Conway (Charlottesville: University of Virginia Press, 1996), 74–96; Amy Dru Stanley, *From Bondage to Contract: Wage Labor; Marriage, and the Market in the Age of Slave Emancipation* (Cambridge: Cambridge University Press, 1998), 17–35; Scott A. Sandage, "The Gaze of Success: Failed Men and the Sentimental Marketplace, 1873–1893," in *Sentimental Men: Masculinity and the Politics of Affect in American Culture*, ed. Mary Chapman and Glenn Hendler (Berkeley and Los Angeles: University of California Press, 1999), 181–201; and Elizabeth White Nelson, *Market Sentiments: Middle-Class Market Culture in Nineteenth-Century America* (Washington, DC: Smithsonian Books, 2004).

12. See Peel, "On the Margins," 813–15; Groth, *Living Downtown*, 5–7; and Elisabeth Anthony Dexter, *Career Women of America, 1776–1840* (1950; reprint, Clifton, NJ: Augustus M. Kelley, 1972), 123, for discussions of these distinctions.

13. Gunn, *Physiology of New York Boarding-Houses*; John C. Gunn, *Gunn's Domestic Medicine; or, Poor Man's Friend, in the Hours of Affliction, Pain, and Sickness*, 5th rev. ed. (New York: Saxton and Miles, 1845). Both Thomas Butler Gunn's use of physiology as his organizing device and his description of the medical students' boardinghouse suggest some familiarity with medical practice. *Frank Leslie's Illustrated Newspaper*, July 11, 1858, 95. On occupational and ethnic identities, see Scherzer, *Unbounded Community*; 104–5; and Peel, "On the Margins," 824–27. A Mrs. McCollick advertised her boardinghouse as being run "on Temperance principles"; *New York Tribune*, May 13, 1841. See also the advertisement placed in an unidentified newspaper by Miss A. A. Burr, who, "being herself of the New Church," hoped to attract fellow worshippers to her New York boardinghouse by offering them "very reasonable terms" (enclosed in letter from Margaretta Lammot du Pont to Alfred V. du Pont, March 6, 1853, folder 2, box 2, Du Pont Family Papers, HML); Stephen Nissenbaum, *Sex, Diet, and Debility in Jacksonian America: Sylvester Graham and Health Reform* (Westport, CT: Greenwood Press, 1980). On boardinghouses that reflected political and regional, albeit not necessarily partisan, identities, see James Sterling Young, *The Washington Community, 1800–1828* (New York: Columbia University Press, 1966), 98–109, 123–42.

14. Lawrence J. Friedman, *Inventors of the Promised Land* (New York: Alfred A. Knopf, 1975), 168; George G. Foster, *New York by Gas-Light: With Here and There a Streak of Sunshine* (New York: Dewitt and Davenport, 1850), 10; Gunn, *Physiology*, 34, 36. Britons who condemned boardinghouses in their own country were similarly vague about the characteristics of homes. See Marcus, *Apartment Stories*, 107–8.

15. Forbes Diary, March 31, 1856.

16. Ibid., April 29 and June 2, 1856.

17. *Boston Directory* (Boston: George Adams, 1855–57); *Boston Directory* (Boston: Adams, Sampson, and Co., 1858–60).

18. Forbes Diary, August 8, 15, 16, 19, 1856.

19. Ibid., August 1, 1859; November 14, 1856; May 3, 1858.

20. Ibid., February 2, 1859.

21. Ibid., May 12, 1857; January 11, 1859.

22. Ibid., January 1, 1859.

23. Ibid., 1857–60; for social activities and grammar class, see December 23, 1857; March 22, April 28, May 7, June 10, August 20, October 19, November 2, and December 31, 1858; January 1, 10, and 17, 1859; September 21, 1856; Elizabeth Dorr Diary, June 21, 1854, MHS.

24. Forbes Diary, November 4, 1856; March 2, 1857.

25. Ibid., June 18, 1856.

26. Ibid., July 16, 1856.

27. Ibid., June 23, 1857.

28. Ibid., December 26, 1857.

29. Ibid., December 30, 1857.

30. Ibid., August 7, 13, and 16, September 6, and November 11, 1859.

31. Ibid., November 8, 1856.

32. When Brown began keeping boarders herself a few years later, she posted vacancies in the YMCA's reading rooms; see Forbes Diary, July 1, 1865. Given the frequency with which the residents of 34 attended YMCA activities, it is likely that Haskell had done so as well.

33. Forbes Diary, April 22, 1858. No text of Chapin's "Woman and Her Work" seems to have survived. Very likely the sentiments it expressed resembled those of his *Duties of Young Women*, which was reprinted several times. Chapin's views on the home were utterly unoriginal. See *Duties of Young Women* (Boston: George W. Briggs, 1848), 161–76.

34. Thomas Dublin, *Transforming Women's Work: New England Lives in the Industrial Revolution* (Ithaca, NY: Cornell University Press, 1994), 99–100.

35. See, e.g., Forbes Diary, October 10, 1857.

36. Ibid., February 5, May 11 and 22, 1859.

37. Ibid., January 15 and 16, 1860.

38. This is how Brown would advertise her own boardinghouse after her marriage; see chapter 2.

Urban Culture and the Policing of the "City of Bachelors"

George Chauncey

Source: *Gay New York: Gender, Urban Culture, and the Making of the Gay Male World, 1890–1940* (New York: Basic Books, 1994).

EDITORS' INTRODUCTION

George Chauncey joined the faculty of Yale's department of history in 2006, after fifteen years at the University of Chicago. *Gay New York* was an instant success when published in 1994, winning the Merle Curti Prize for the best book in social history from the Organization of American Historians and the organization's Frederick Jackson Turner Prize for the best first book in history, as well as the *Los Angeles Times* Book Prize and the Lambda Literary Award. This book profoundly influenced thinking about gay males in urban settings. Chauncey has also served as a legal witness in an important Supreme Court case, testifying on the history of anti-gay discrimination for *Romer* v. *Evans* in 1994, a case with broad implications which involved the question of the legality of gay rights statues within Colorado communities. Chauncey also served as lead author in a legal brief for *Lawrence* v. *Texas* (2003) which led to the overturning of the majority of the nation's remaining sodomy laws. His latest book takes the examination of gay America from World War II to the early gay liberation era.

Gay New York is important not only for the detailed story it reveals about gay spaces and places within New York, but also for its reception by academic and mainstream audiences. Chauncey was not the first to broach the subject of homosexuality in a historical study. Martin Duberman, John D'Emilio, Carol Smith-Rosenberg, Vern L. Bullough, Michael Sherry, and a host of independent scholars have provided much insight on this aspect of the American past. But Chauncey's work caught the attention of those inside and outside academe in a way that no other work had yet accomplished.

Gay New York is also a fine work of American urban history. Chauncey deftly connects his narrative of gay Americans coming to the city with concurrent migrations of other rural or small-town Americans coming to the city and the immigrants flowing in from other countries. All of these newcomers headed for the city in order to take advantage of economic and cultural opportunities. Chauncey marks the outbreak of World War I as a watershed moment in this history; with mobilization for war and the increasing diversity of urban populations came a heightened interest in urban morality. In his descriptions of the organizational response to these perceived moral threats, Chauncey concludes that scrutiny of gay behavior, which was termed "male perversion," grew out of worries over prostitution and the sexual behavior of servicemen, who were perceived as "innocents abroad," under *in loco parentis* care of President Wilson and the armed services. The paradigm of the day defined homosexual encounters between servicemen and urban dwellers as incidents in which vulnerable people were led astray by unscrupulous urbanites. Chauncey places the history of homosexual America in the context of broader American urban history. With the influx of people from the American countryside, the prosaic small towns, and locations as varied as Kurland, Russia and Galway, Ireland, the great city of New York was irrevocably changed. Chauncey writes, "This reconstitution of the population had vast ramifications for the city's politics and for the social organization and culture of class, nationality, and sexuality."[i]

---

i George Chauncey, *Gay New York: Gender, Urban Culture, and the Making of the Gay Male World, 1890–1940* (New York: Basic Books, 1994), 137.

URBAN CULTURE AND THE POLICING OF THE "CITY OF BACHELORS"

The men who built New York's gay world at the turn of the century and those who sought to suppress it shared the conviction that it was a distinctly urban phenomenon. "Only in a great city," declared one man who had moved to New York in 1882, could an invert "give his overwhelming yearnings free rein *incognito* and thus keep the respect of his every-day circle.... In New York one can live as Nature demands without setting every one's tongue wagging."[1] In his hometown he had needed to conform at all times to the social conventions of the community, for he had been subject to the constant (albeit normally benign and unselfconscious) surveillance of his family and neighbors. But in the city it was possible for him to move between social worlds and lead a double life: by day to hold a respectable job that any queer would have been denied, and by night to lead the life of a fairy on the Bowery.

This freedom was precisely what troubled the Committee of Fifteen, an anti-vice society established in 1900 to suppress female prostitution in New York's saloons. It noted ominously that in the city

> the main external check upon a man's conduct, the opinion of his neighbours, which has such a powerful influence in the country or small town, tends to disappear. In a great city one has no neighbours. No man knows the doings of even his close friends; few men care what the secret life of their friends may be.... [T]he young man is left free to follow his own inclinations.[2]

The Committee was particularly concerned about the ease with which men developed liaisons with female prostitutes in New York, but it was distressed as well by other, more unconventional manifestations of such "freedom." Its agents visited saloons primarily in search of female prostitutes, but they repeatedly stumbled upon resorts where fairies gathered, such as Paresis Hall on the Bowery and Billy's Place on Third Avenue, which they believed would never have been tolerated in smaller communities.

To some observers, sympathetic and hostile alike, the fairy became an emblem of modernity and of the collapse of traditional forms of social control. Doctors who studied the problem of inversion inevitably associated it with the growth of cities and sometimes attributed it either to the cities' increasingly alien character or to the nervous exhaustion (or "neurasthenia") produced by the demands of urban industrial culture. In 1895, for instance, the American translator of a French article on inversion claimed that the "forms of vice" the article described were "as yet little familiar [to Americans], at least so far as concerns [our] native-born population." But he warned that "the massing of our population, especially the foreign element, in great cities" would inevitably lead to an increase in inversion and similar vices.[3] Some theorists in the first generation of American urban sociologists, who echoed many of the concerns of the reformers with whom they often worked, expressed similar anxieties about the enhanced possibilities for the development of a secret homosexual life that urban conditions created. Urbanization, they warned, resulted in the breakdown of family and other social ties that kept an individual's behavior under control in smaller, more tightly organized and regulated towns. The resulting "personal disorganization," the sociologist Walter Reckless wrote in 1926, led to the release of "impulses and desires ... from the socially approved channels," and could result "not merely in prostitution, but also in perversion."[4]

As the early sociologists suspected, the emergence of an extensive and multifaceted gay male world was made possible in part by the development of distinctive forms of urban culture. But the gay world was shaped as well by the efforts of those sociologists, the Committee of Fifteen, its successor, the Committee of Fourteen (established 1905), and a host of other authorities to understand and discipline that broader culture. The making of the gay world can only be understood in the context of the evolution of city life and the broader contest over the urban moral order.

Like the first generation of sociologists, many subsequent analysts have focused on the supposed anonymity of the city as the primary reason it became a center of unconventional behavior. To be sure, the relative anonymity enjoyed in Manhattan by gay tourists from the heartland—and even from the outer boroughs—was one reason they felt freer there than they would have at home to seek out gay locales and behave openly as homosexuals. But to focus on the supposed anonymity of the city (a quality that is, in any case, always relative and situational) is to imply that gay men remained isolated from (or "anonymous" to) one another. The city, however, was the site not so much of anonymous, furtive encounters between strangers (although there were plenty of those) as of an organized, multilayered, and self-conscious gay subculture, with its own meeting places, language, folklore, and moral codes. What sociologists and reformers called the social *disorganization* of the city might more properly be regarded as a social *reorganization*. By the more pejorative term, investigators actually denoted the multiplication of social possibilities that the massing of diverse peoples made possible. "Disorganization" also evoked the declining strength of the family, the neighborhood, the parish, and other institutions of social control, which seemed, in retrospect at least, to have enforced older patterns of social order in smaller communities.[5] But it ignored, or was incapable of acknowledging, the fact that new forms of social order were emerging in their place. Although the anonymity of the city was important because it helped make it possible for gay men to live double lives, it was only a starting point. It will prove more useful to focus on the ways gay men utilized the complexity of urban society to build an alternative gay social order.[*]

The complexity of the city's social and spatial organization made it possible for gay men to construct the multiple public identities necessary for them to participate in the gay world without losing the privileges of the straight: assuming one identity at work, another in leisure; one identity before biological kin, another with gay friends. The city, as the sociologist Robert Park observed in 1916, sustained a "mosaic of little [social] worlds," and their segregation from one another allowed men to assume a different identity in each of them, without having to reveal the full range of their identities in any one of them. "This [complexity] makes it possible for individuals to pass quickly and easily from one moral milieu to another," Park mused, which "encourages the fascinating but dangerous experiment of living at the same time in several different contiguous, but otherwise widely separated, worlds ... [and] tends ... to produce new and divergent individual types."[7] Though Park's model overestimated the cohesiveness and isolation of each "little world"—and underestimated the degree to which they were mutually constitutive and to which dominant social groups intervened in the social worlds of the subordinate—it captured some of the significance for gay men of the complexity of the city's social organization. [...]

It is impossible to determine how many men moved to New York at the turn of the century in order to participate in the gay life emerging there, but gay men and other contemporary observers believed the numbers were large. Case histories of "inverts"

Whether the processes described here should be regarded as an effect of urban culture or of industrial capitalism has been subject to debate. Both positions have merit. It clearly was not the massing of people or the spatial expansion of cities alone that facilitated the emergence of gay subcultures. Changes in urban social organization and in the role of particular cities in the broader economy were also critical. The decline of the system of household-based artisanal production in New York City in the nineteenth century, which resulted in a breakdown in preindustrial modes of social control, was equally significant, for instance. Thus there is considerable merit to the argument made by some urban theorists that "urban culture" is a misnomer for the forms of social organization characteristic of industrial capitalist culture. The latter conceptualization of the phenomenon, however, fails to account fully for the social and spatial complexity peculiar to cities even in an industrial capitalist society. Although limited gay social networks developed in rural areas, and even small towns usually had a handful of surreptitious gay meeting places by the early twentieth century— hotel men's bars, bus stations, and certain street corners or blocks, most commonly, as well as the homes of a few of the town's "confirmed bachelors"—only large cities had the social and spatial complexity necessary for the development of an extensive and partially commercialized gay subculture.[6]

published in medical journals early in the century were peppered with accounts of men who came to New York because they were aware of homosexual interests they had to hide in their hometowns or because they were forced to flee when their secret was discovered. Numerous doctors not only identified inversion as a distinctly urban phenomenon but commented especially on the number of inverts in New York. As early as the 1880s, George Beard thought that many male inverts lived there, and in 1913 the psychiatrist A. A. Brill confidently estimated there were "many thousands of homosexuals in New York City among all classes of society."[9] Two researchers investigating homosexual life in the late 1930s found that most of the men they interviewed who had moved to New York from smaller towns had done so because "their local communities frowned upon homosexuality, and New York [seemed to them] to be the capital of the American homosexual world."[10] The researchers noted that many such migrants had indeed been able to find "work, a homosexual circle of acquaintance, [and] a definite social life."[11]

Whatever the numbers, gay men's migration was clearly part of the much larger migration of single men and women to the city from Europe and rural America alike. A disproportionate number of the people who moved to the cities were young and unmarried, and while for many of them migration was part of a carefully considered strategy designed to address the broader economic needs of their families, for many it also provided a welcome relief from family control.[12] The city was a logical destination for men intent on freeing themselves from the constraints of the family, because of its relatively cheap accommodations and the availability of commercial domestic services for which men traditionally would have depended on the unpaid household labor of women.

"For the nation's bachelors," the *New York Times Magazine* declared in 1928, "this city is the Mecca. Not only is it the City of Youth, but it is the City of the Single," with some 900,000 unmarried men and 700,000 single women counted among its residents. "It is certain," the article continued, "they are not all in a [Madison Square] Garden line-up waiting for admission to the next fight, neither are they all concentrated in speakeasies and along the docks.... The city has something for every kind of bachelor."[13] Some of those bachelors were working-class immigrants crowded in the tenement districts and waterfront; others were American-born rural youths barely making enough to rent a furnished room; still others were successful entrepreneurs living in the city's luxurious new apartment hotels. Together the bachelors constituted 40 percent or more of the men fifteen years of age or older living in Manhattan in the first third of the century.[†]

The existence of an urban bachelor subculture facilitated the development of a gay world. Tellingly, gay men tended to gather in the same neighborhoods where many of the city's other unmarried men and women clustered, since they offered the housing and commercial services suitable to the needs of a nonfamily population. Gay male residential and commercial enclaves developed in the Bowery, Greenwich Village, Times Square, and Harlem in large part because they were the city's major centers of furnished-room housing for single men. Lesbian enclaves developed for similar reasons in the 1920s in Harlem and the Village, then the city's two primary centers of housing for single women. Rooming houses and cafeterias served as meeting grounds for gay men, facilitating the constant interaction that made possible the development of a distinctive subculture. To the horror of reformers, many small entrepreneurs ignored the "disreputable" character of

† The number of unmarried men and women in the city increasingly distinguished it from the nation as a whole. Immigrants were disproportionately young and single, but even the native-born Americans of the city were much less likely to marry than their rural counterparts. Only a third of the native-born white men aged twenty-five to thirty-four with American parents were unmarried in the nation as a whole in 1900, compared to half of those in Manhattan; only 15 percent of those aged thirty-five to forty-four were unmarried in the nation, versus 30 percent of those living in Manhattan.[14]

their gay patrons precisely because they were patrons. A smaller number actively encouraged the patronage of openly gay men because it attracted other customers.

The expanding bachelor subculture in the city's furnished-room and tenement districts precipitated a powerful reaction by social-purity forces, which would have enormous consequences for the development of the gay world. The emerging bachelor subculture was only one of the ominous features of a changing urban landscape that many native-born middle-class Americans found increasingly threatening. The rapid growth in the number and size of cities in the late nineteenth century was itself a source of concern, but even more anxiety-provoking was their increasingly "alien" character. As America's greatest port, New York City had always been an immigrant metropolis. Even as early as 1860, Irish Catholic immigrants constituted a quarter of the city's white population, and the nineteenth century was punctuated by nativist reactions to them. Beginning in the 1880s, the national background of the immigrants began to shift from northern and western Europe—the historic source of the so-called old-stock Americans—to southern and eastern Europe. Germans and the Irish continued to migrate in large numbers, but by the 1890s the majority of people immigrating to New York, in particular, were from Italy or Russia (the latter primarily Russian Jews). Almost a third of Manhattan's residents in 1910 were foreign-born Jews or Italians and their children.[15]

This reconstitution of the population had vast ramifications for the city's politics and for the social organization and culture of class, nationality, and sexuality. The growing number of immigrants and their cultural difference from the northwestern Europeans who had already settled in the States led many Americans of "older stock" to fear that they would lose control of their cities and even the whole of their society. This provoked a generation of struggle over urban political and social power. These conflicts became inextricably linked to the class conflict of the late nineteenth century, for, to an astonishing extent, the industrial working class forged in the late-nineteenth-century United States was an immigrant class. The peasants and laborers who left their European homelands became the workhorses of the second industrial revolution in the United States. The sharp class conflict of the late nineteenth century, then, was construed in ethnic as well as class terms, and conflicts over political and cultural power became inextricably intertwined with conflicts of class, ethnicity, and race. The Anglo-American middle class increasingly defined its difference from immigrants in the interrelated—and mutually constitutive—terms of race and class. As immigrants seemed to overwhelm the nation's cities, growing numbers of Anglo-American middle-class families fled to suburbs such as Brooklyn. They increasingly feared, as the historian Paul Boyer has shown, that the city posed a threat not just to the morality of individuals but to the survival of American society as a whole.[16]

In the closing decades of the nineteenth century and the opening decades of the twentieth, an extraordinary panoply of groups and individuals organized to reform the urban moral order. Although their efforts rarely focused on the emerging gay world, most of them nonetheless had a significant effect on its development. Some sought to reconstruct the urban landscape itself in ways that would minimize the dissipating effects of urban disorder: reforming the tenements, putting up new residential hotels in which single men and women could lead moral lives, creating parks to reintroduce an element of rural simplicity and natural order to the city, building playgrounds and organizing youth clubs to rescue young people from city streets and gangs, and constructing grand boulevards and public buildings that would inspire a new order in the city itself and command respect for an orderly society.[17]

Other reform efforts had a more coercive edge. Native-born Americans usually controlled the state legislatures in which smaller towns and rural districts were disproportionately represented, but they could not count on locally controlled urban police forces to enforce the vision of moral order they had codified in state law. Indeed, the integration of New York City's police force into the local political structure, the subordination of individual officers to local ward bosses, and their role in enforcing the elaborate system of extortion and profiteering that allowed the Bowery resorts to exist were continuing sources of outrage and frustration to the reformers.[18]

Beginning in the 1870s, they responded to this problem by organizing a host of private anti-vice and social-purity societies to enforce the laws themselves and to institutionalize a new regime of surveillance and control. Sometimes working together, sometimes highly competitive, each society claimed the authority to combat a different threat to the city's moral order. At the height of its powers under the leadership of the Reverend Charles Parkhurst in the 1890s, the Society for the Prevention of Crime, founded in 1877, worked to compel the police to enforce anti-vice laws by exposing the links between police corruption and the vice resorts of the Bowery and Tenderloin. In later decades it focused its more limited resources on studying criminal behavior. The Society for the Suppression of Vice, which Anthony Comstock founded in 1872 under the auspices of the Young Men's Christian Association of New York and led until his death in 1915, fought to suppress stage shows and literature it deemed obscene. The Committee of Fourteen, founded in 1905, took the lead in the fight against prostitution; it was the largest and most effective of the groups until its demise at the onset of the Depression. The Society for the Prevention of Cruelty to Children, founded in 1872 by Eldridge Gerry as an offshoot of the Society for the Prevention of Cruelty to Animals, sought to protect children in general. It concentrated its efforts on "saving" children from immigrant parents who they thought neglected or abused them. In immigrant neighborhoods, as the historian Linda Gordon notes, it was known simply as "The Cruelty" because of its agents' reputation for taking children from homes it deemed undesirable.[19]

The policing of gay culture in the early twentieth century was closely tied to the efforts of these societies to police working-class culture more generally. The societies' efforts to control the streets and tenements and to eliminate the saloon and brothel were predicated on a vision of an ideal social order centered in the family. The reformers' targets reflected their growing anxiety about the threat to the social order posed by men and women who seemed to stand outside the family: the men of the bachelor subculture who gathered without supervision in the "dissipating" atmosphere of the saloons; the women whose rejection of conventional gender and sexual arrangements was emblematized by the prostitute; the youths of the city whose lives seemed to be shaped by the discordant influences of the streets rather than the civilizing influences of the home; and, on occasion, the gay men and lesbians who gathered in the niches of the urban landscape constructed by those groups. The reform campaigns constituted a sweeping assault on the moral order of working-class communities, and especially of single women and rough working-class men, although middle-class entrepreneurs and intellectuals also became their targets at times. The Anti-Saloon League, for instance, mounted a frontal attack on one of the central institutions of male sociability in many working-class neighborhoods. Similarly, the Committee of Fourteen defined "prostitution" more broadly than many working-class youths did. As the historian Kathy Peiss has shown, the Committee frequently regarded working-class conventions of treating as a form of prostitution, for it labeled women who were willing to offer sexual favors (of any sort) to men in exchange for a night on the town, or even as part of an ongoing relationship, as "amateur prostitutes."[20] Thus their campaign against "prostitution" led the reformers to attack not just brothels but saloons, cabarets, and other social venues where men and women transgressed Victorian gender conventions by interacting too casually.

The social-purity activists were also keen to prevent the violation of racial boundaries, which they imagined inevitably had a sexual element. W. E. B. Du Bois learned as much in 1912, when the Committee tried to close

Marshall's Hotel on West Fifty-third Street, because, according to the Committee, it tolerated "that unfortunate mixing of the races which when the individuals are of the ordinary class, always means danger [that is, interracial sex]."[21] Similarly, the Society for the Suppression of Vice's definition of indecent literature was not limited to erotic photographic or written depictions of sexual acts, which even most opponents of suppression agreed were "indecent." Their targets also included birth control literature, medical studies of homosexuality, and plays and short stories with lesbian or other unorthodox sexual themes, which other people might classify as "scientific," "artistic," or "serious."[22] The reform societies' campaigns against "prostitution" and other "social evils," in other words, actually constituted much broader campaigns to reconstruct the moral world by narrowing the boundaries of acceptable sociability and public discourse.

Some of the organizations secured quasi-police powers from the state legislature in order to pursue their objectives; others used their connections with the city's business leaders to put economic pressure on tenement landlords, hotel operators, and the brewing companies to close clubs and saloons where men and women interacted too freely or women worked as prostitutes. Reformers hired agents who put the immigrant neighborhoods under surveillance: visiting the saloons, streets, and tenements where men and women gathered; reviewing the moral tenor of the films, stage shows, burlesque routines, and club acts seen by New Yorkers; attending the masquerade balls and other social events organized by the city's immigrant, bohemian, and gay social clubs to regulate the kinds of costumes worn and dancing allowed. They also monitored the police and devised elaborate administrative mechanisms to force them to uphold moral regulations they otherwise would ignore. Ironically, the records of the anti-vice societies serve as one of the richest sources for this study. Although requiring careful interpretation, they constitute some of the most comprehensive surveys available of the social and sexual life of the city's working-class districts from the 1870s (and especially the 1890s) until the 1920s, after which state agencies began to take greater responsibility for regulating the urban moral order.

The role of the anti-vice societies in enforcing the state's sodomy law is emblematic. A legacy of English statutes, laws against sodomy and the "crime against nature," had existed since colonial days, but the state had done little to enforce the sodomy law in the first century of independence. As the scholars Timothy Gilfoyle and Michael Lynch discovered, only twenty-two sodomy prosecutions occurred in New York City in the nearly eight decades from 1796 to 1873. The number of prosecutions increased dramatically in the 1880s, however. By the 1890s, fourteen to thirty-eight men were arrested *every year* for sodomy or the "crime against nature." Police arrested more than 50 men annually in the 1910s—more than 100 in 1917—and from 75 to 125 every year in the 1920s. Although the dramatic increase in arrests resulted in part from intensified concern among the city's elite about homosexuality and a new determination on the part of the police, much of it stemmed from the efforts of the Society for the Prevention of Cruelty to Children, which involved itself in the cases of men suspected of sodomy with boys in order to ensure their indictment and successful prosecution by the district attorney. The fragmentary court records available suggest that at least 40 percent—and up to 90 percent—of the cases prosecuted each year were initiated at the complaint of the SPCC. Given the SPCC's focus on the status of children in immigrant neighborhoods, the great majority of sodomy prosecutions were initiated against immigrants in the poorest sections of the city; in the 1940s and 1950s, African-Americans and Puerto Ricans would become the primary targets of sodomy prosecutions for similar reasons.[23]

The role of the SPCC in the prosecution of men for sodomy exemplified the role of the other moral-reform groups in the policing of homosexuality before World War I. Although the SPCC had a tremendous impact on the number and character of sodomy prosecutions, it did not make homosexuals a special target. It was only in the course of its more general campaign to protect the city's children from assault that men were arrested for having sex with boys. The other societies also contributed substantially to the policing of homosexuality, but they, too, usually did so only in the course of pursuing some other, more central mission, and rarely focused on homosexuality per se. The Society for the Prevention of Crime and its allied organization, the City Vigilance League, investigated and denounced the male prostitutes of Paresis Hall in 1899, for instance, but only as part of their general campaign against the police corruption that allowed prostitution to flourish in New York. The superintendent of the Society reported to his board of directors in 1917 that one of its agents had been solicited by "a man of unnatural sexual desires" near its offices on Union Square and that "evidence of many such cases could probably be got." In response, the board instructed him to proceed against such cases only on an individual basis when they came to his attention and not to "enter upon [a] campaign against such vice."[24] Similarly, the sporadic efforts of the Committee of Fourteen to prevent men's use of the streets and saloons for homosexual trysts and social gatherings, while not insignificant, usually were only an incidental aspect of its more general effort to regulate the streets and commercial amusements that served as sites for sexual encounters or unchaperoned meetings between young men and women.[25] Until World War I, the societies did not identify homosexuality as a social problem so threatening that it merited more than incidental attention.

World War I and the Discourse of Urban Degeneracy

World War I was a watershed in the history of the urban moral reform movement and in the role of homosexuality in reform discourse. The war embodied reformers' darkest fears and their greatest hopes, for it threatened the very foundations of the nation's moral order—the family, small-town stability, the racial and gender hierarchy—even as it offered the reformers an unprecedented opportunity to implement their vision. It also led them to focus for the first time on homosexuality as a major social problem. For the Committee of Fourteen and other social-purity groups, which had monitored New York's sexual underworld closely since the turn of the century, were convinced that the war had resulted in a substantial growth in the scale and visibility of gay life in the city.

Military mobilization had an enormous impact on New York, the major port of embarkation for the European theater. Hundreds of thousands of servicemen passed through the city during the war; one official estimated that five thousand to ten thousand soldiers from two camps on Long Island alone visited New York every day, and twice that many came on weekends.[26] The streets were filled with soldiers and sailors. "They were to be seen singly," one of the Committee of Fourteen's investigators reported in 1917, "or (and mostly) in couples, trios and quartettes walking about the streets either soliciting girls or being solicited by the girls and women.... There were many thousand ... in the proportion of three soldiers to ten ... civilians."[27] They congregated especially in the Union Square area, on Fourteenth Street near Third and Fourth Avenues, at Times Square, and on MacDougal Street in the Village, as well as in Riverside and Battery Parks and other waterfront areas—places known as cruising areas for gay men as well as prostitutes.[28]

The presence of so many soldiers from rural backgrounds in New York and other cities augured to purity crusaders a moral crisis of alarming proportions. The war to make the world safe for democracy threatened to expose hundreds of thousands of American boys from farms and small towns to the evil influences of the big city. The manner in which the reformers construed this crisis was profoundly shaped by the discourse of urban degeneracy that had been central to their moral vision throughout the Progressive Era. Indeed, the social disorganization, anomie, and unraveling of family ties associated with urbanism colored the responses to the war on every side, from the solemn pledge President Wilson made to the mothers of America that Uncle Sam would act in loco parentis, protecting their sons from urban evils, to the gleeful taunt of urban musicians (who viewed the change altogether more positively), "How You Gonna Keep 'Em Down on the Farm After They've Seen Paree?" The dominant wartime discourse portrayed American troops as naive rural boys, "innocents abroad," and depicted New York itself as a seductive big-city woman who threatened to infect those small-town boys with venereal diseases and unwholesome city ways. As a longtime social-purity activist warned at the moment of American entry into the war, soldiers who were not protected from temptation "not only will ... bring back into the social structure a vast volume of venereal disease to wreck the lives of innocent women and children, but they will bring back into it other attitudes and practices which will destroy homes, cause misery, and degenerate society."[29] Urban immorality was considered by activists to be a virulent plague threatening to invade the bodies and minds of the nation's youth, and, through them, the nation itself.

NOTES

1. Paraphrased in Ralph Werther, *The Female-Impersonators* (New York: Medico-Legal Journal, 1922), 200–201. It is entirely possible that Werther was the source of these sentiments, rather than the person to whom he attributed them, but that would not undermine my point that gay men viewed the city in these terms.

2. Erwin R. A. Seligman, ed., *The Social Evil: With Special Reference to Conditions Existing in the City of New York* (1902; New York: Putnam's, 1912), 8. On the Committee of Fifteen, see Jeremy P. Felt, "Vice Reform as a Political Technique: The Committee of Fifteen in New York, 1900–1911," *New York History* 54 (1973): 24–51.

3. C. Judson Herrick, note concerning his translation of Marc André Raffalovich, "Uranism, Congenital Sexual Inversion," *Journal of Comparative Neurology* 5 (March 1895): 65. G. Frank Lydston also commented in 1889 that there was "in every community of any size a colony of male sexual perverts; they are usually known to each other and are likely to congregate together" ("Sexual Perversion, Satyriasis and Nymphomania," *Medical and Surgical Reporter* 61 [1889]: 254); see also James Kiernan, "Classification of Homosexuality," *Urologic and Cutaneous Review* 20 (1916): 350.

4. Walter C. Reckless, "The Distribution of Commercialized Vice in the City: A Sociological Analysis," in *The Urban Community*, ed. Ernest W. Burgess (Chicago: University of Chicago Press, 1926), 192, 202.

5. The major proponent of this alternative view of urbanism is Claude Fischer, *To Dwell Among Friends: Personal Networks in Town and City* (Chicago: University of Chicago Press, 1982), especially 64–66; idem, *The Urban Experience* (New York: Harcourt Brace Jovanovich, 1976), especially 35–39.

6. Contributors to this debate include Fischer, *The Urban Experience*, 25–36, and Manuel Castells, "Is There an Urban Sociology?," *Urban Sociology: Critical Essays* (New York: St. Martin's, 1976). On the breakdown of social control in nineteenth-century cities upon the decline of artisanal modes of production and the increasing class segregation of cities, and the related decision of employers and reformers to establish professional police forces in New York and other cities in the 1840s–60s, see John C. Schneider, *Detroit and the Problem of Order, 1830–1880: A Geography of Crime, Riot, and Policing* (Lincoln: University of Nebraska Press, 1980), 83–86 and passim; for a detailed study of this process in New York City, see Sean Wilentz, *Chants Democratic: New York City and the Rise of the American Working Class, 1788–1850* (New York: Oxford University Press, 1984).

7. Robert Park, "The City: Suggestions for the Investigation of Human Behavior in the Urban Environment" (1916), as reprinted in *Classic Essays on the Culture of Cities*, ed. Richard Sennett (New York: Meredith, 1969), 126.

8. George M. Beard, *Sexual Neurasthenia*, ed. A. D. Rockwell (New York: E. B. Treat, 1884), 102; A. A. Brill, "The Conception of Homosexuality," *Journal of the American Medical Association* 61 (1913): 335. For an account of a man forced to flee his home, see Douglas C. McMurtrie, "Some Observations on the Psychology of Sexual Inversion in Women," *Lancet-Clinic* 108 (1912): 488.

9. Martin Goodkin to author, Aug. 3, 1988; Maurice Leznoff, "The Homosexual in Urban Society" (master's thesis, McGill University, 1954), 40–49.

10. George W. Henry and Alfred A. Gross, "Social Factors in the Case Histories of One Hundred Underprivileged Homosexuals," *Mental Hygiene* 22 (1938): 602.

11. See, for example, Joanne J. Meyerowitz, *Women Adrift: Independent Wage Earners in Chicago, 1880–1930* (Chicago: University of Chicago Press, 1988).

12. "The Bachelors of New York," *New York Times Magazine*, Sept. 9, 1928. Although the *Times* was probably not thinking of gay bachelors in particular, some of its gay readers seem to have understood the article in such terms. Alexander Gumby,

a black gay man who ran a famous salon frequented by Harlem's intellectuals, many of them gay, in the 1920s, clipped the article and put it in a scrapbook he titled "Odd, Strange and Curious," now a part of the Alexander Gumby papers at the Columbia University Library.

13. James Ford, *Slums and Housing: With Special Reference to New York City: History, Conditions, Policy* (Cambridge, Mass.: Harvard University Press, 1936), 336; *Twelfth Census of the United States Taken in the Year 1900, Vol. II, Population, Part II* (Washington, D.C.: United States Census Office, 1902), 254, 333; see also *1890 Census, Part I*, 883; *1910 Census, Vol. I*, 630; *1920 Census, Vol. II*, 504; *1930 Census, Vol. II*, 962; *1940 Census, Vol. IV, Part III*, 683.

14. *Thirteenth Census of the United States Taken in the Year 1910, Vol. I, Population 1910, General Report and Analysis* (Washington, D.C.: Government Printing Office, 1913), 948.

15. An immense number of historical studies document and analyze these trends. The major points are usefully summarized and argued in Paul Boyer, *Urban Masses and Moral Order in America, 1820–1920* (Cambridge, Mass.: Harvard University Press, 1978), 123–31; see also, to cite just three other studies, John Higham, *Strangers in the Land: Patterns of American Nativism, 1860–1925* (New Brunswick, N.J.: Rutgers University Press, 1955); Kenneth T. Jackson, *Crabgrass Frontier: The Suburbanization of the United States* (New York: Oxford University Press, 1985); Thomas Kessner, *The Golden Door: Italian and Jewish Immigrant Mobility in New York City* (New York: Oxford University Press, 1977).

16. A number of historians have analyzed this process. See, for example, Boyer, *Urban Masses;* Daniel M. Bluestone, *Constructing Chicago* (New Haven, Conn.: Yale University Press, 1991); David Scobey, "Empire City: Politics, Culture, and Urbanism in Gilded Age New York" (Ph.D. diss., Yale University, 1989).

17. For an overview of the role of the police, see Samuel Walker, *A Critical History of Police Reform* (Lexington, Mass.: Lexington Books, D. C. Heath, 1977).

18. My comments on the general character of the societies are based on my research in their organizational records (as described in the Note on Sources) and on Timothy J. Gilfoyle, "The Moral Origins of Political Surveillance: The Preventive Society in New York City, 1867–1918," *American Quarterly* 38 (1986): 637–52; idem, *City of Eros: New York City, Prostitution, and the Commercialization of Sex, 1790–1920* (New York: Norton, 1992), 185–96; Boyer, *Urban Masses;* Mary Ryan, *Women in Public: Between Banners and Ballots, 1825–1880* (Baltimore: Johns Hopkins University Press, 1990), ch. 3; John D'Emilio and Estelle Freedman, *Intimate Matters: A History of Sexuality in America* (New York: Harper & Row, 1988), ch. 7 and 9; and Linda

Gordon, *Heroes of Their Own Lives: The Politics and History of Family Violence* (New York: Viking, 1988).

19. Kathy Peiss, "'Charity Girls' and City Pleasures: Historical Notes on Working-Class Sexuality, 1880–1920," in *Passion and Power: Sexuality in History*, ed. Kathy Peiss and Christina Simmons (Philadelphia: Temple University Press, 1989), 57–69.

20. W. E. B. Du Bois to the Committee, letter dated Sept. 23, 1911 (the actual year must have been 1912); Frederick H. Whitin to Du Bois, Oct. 11, 1912, Du Bois folder, box 11, COF. Du Bois wrote to protest the Committee's campaign against Marshall's, which had once been a popular nightspot when many of Manhattan's African-American residents had lived in the midtown area, because it was "about the only place where a colored man downtown can be decently accommodated." The Committee continued to worry that illicit sexual intentions offered the only explanation for the social mingling of blacks and whites; see, for example, their investigator's observation in 1928 that Small's Paradise, a famous Harlem nightspot on Seventh Avenue, "was rather crowded with white and colored people, dancing and drinking.... Mixed couples are allowed to enter this place," he noted ominously (report on Small's Paradise, 2294 1/2 Seventh Ave., basement, July 24, 1928, 2 A.M., box 36, COF).

21. Linda Gordon, *Woman's Body, Woman's Right: A Social History of Birth Control in America* (New York: Penguin, 1976); David J. Pivar, *Purity Crusade: Sexual Morality and Social Control, 1868–1900* (Westport, Conn.: Greenwood, 1973). I discuss the attacks on scientific books on homosexuality, lesbian plays and short stories, and the like in chapters 9, 11, 12.

22. I have not offered more precise figures here because the sources are dismayingly vague and contradictory. The number of sodomy cases between 1796 and 1873 is based on the comprehensive survey of the Manhattan district attorney case files conducted by Timothy Gilfoyle in the course of his research on prostitution in nineteenth-century New York, and is reported in Michael Lynch, "New York City Sodomy, 1796–1873," as cited in D'Emilio and Freedman, *Intimate Matters*, 123. The immense number of cases prosecuted in the twentieth century made a comprehensive survey of the case files impossible, so I have relied instead on published reports and a sampling of the manuscript case files. The annual reports of the Board of City Magistrates and Board of Police Justices give figures for the number of arrests and convictions for sodomy in New York for the late nineteenth and early twentieth centuries, but those numbers often conflict; one reports that thirteen men were arrested for the crime against nature in 1896, for instance, while the other reports thirty-eight arrests. (I have based my estimates on the lower figure given, so they

should be taken as conservative estimates.) It is even more difficult to determine the percentage of cases in which the SPCC played a role, since that is not noted in the annual reports. My estimates are based on my review of actual district attorney case files concerning sodomy prosecutions from 1890 to 1940 (see the Note on Sources for more information about those files). Because the district attorney did not index cases by charge, I reviewed his alphabetical list of all cases prosecuted for every year surveyed and then ordered the cases identified as sodomy cases. Only a fraction of the sodomy cases were identified as such in the docket books, however, so my estimate could not be based on a full survey of the sodomy prosecutions. There is no reason to believe that the two hundred sodomy cases I did review were unrepresentative, but given the limitations of the evidence I have not attempted to offer more precise or "definitive" figures for the percentage of cases initiated by the SPCC. It is clear that the SPCC played an active role and that men who had sex with boys were the primary targets of sodomy prosecutions, but precise figures are unavailable.

23. Superintendent's Report to the Board of Directors, n.d. [Apr. 9, 1917], and Minutes of a regular meeting of the Board of Directors, Apr. 9, 1917, box 13, Society for the Prevention of Crime papers, Rare Book and Manuscript Library, Columbia University.

24. My comments on the role of the moral-reform societies in policing homosexual matters are based on my review of the manuscript records of the Society for the Prevention of Crime (most of which are held at the Rare Book and Manuscript Library, Columbia University) and the Society for the Suppression of Vice (Library of Congress). The particular actions taken by the societies are documented later in this chapter and in subsequent chapters.

25. T. S. Settle to Raymond Fosdick, chair, War Department Commission on Training Camp Activities, Sept. 4, 1917, box 24, COF.

26. J. A. S., report on street conditions, Nov. 17, 1917, box 25, COF.

27. See the hundreds of reports submitted by Committee of Fourteen investigators during the war.

28. M. J. Exner, "Prostitution in its Relation to the Army on the Mexican Border," *Social Hygiene* 3 (April 1917): 205, as quoted in Allan M. Brandt, *No Magic Bullet: A Social History of Venereal Disease in the United States Since 1880* (New York: Oxford University Press, 1985), 57. My characterization of World War I discourse is based primarily on the accounts provided by Brandt's superb study, as well as David Kennedy's *Over Here: The First World War and American Society* (New York: Oxford University Press, 1980). I have, however, stressed the continuity between the Progressive Era depiction of urban immorality and wartime moral discourse more than these authors have.

4-1. *THE PHYSIOLOGY OF NEW YORK BOARDING-HOUSES* (1857)

Thomas Butler Gunn

Source: Thomas Butler Gunn, *The Physiology of New York Boarding-Houses* (New York: Mason Brothers, 1857).

EDITORS' INTRODUCTION

Here Thomas Butler Gunn, an Englishman turned New Yorker, pens a humorous portrait of boardinghouse life in New York City in the mid-nineteenth century. As Wendy Gamber has shown in this part, boardinghouses comprised a common dwelling-type in nineteenth-century cities, and up to 30 percent of urban households took in boarders. Gunn's book chronicles daily life in a wide variety of establishments, from dirty boarding-houses, to those where one does not get enough to eat, and even those establishments where one is required to fawn over the female boardinghouse keeper. In this selection, he mocks life at a vegetarian-oriented boardinghouse. He openly pokes fun at the proprietors, who he accuses of following all the latest fads and religions. By the end of the summer stay, Gunn almost imagines embracing the vegetarian lifestyle and marrying a vegetarian woman. He leaves the house promptly, drinks champagne, and devours a ham sandwich.

More than half a million of human beings are said to be resident in this capital of the Western World. Now each individual of them has, or may become subject to Boarding-House domiciliation. Like death, no class is exempt from it. A topic of more universal interest, commending itself equally to author-craft and the public, could scarcely be hoped for. Is it not then, remarkable, that ours should be the first to grapple with it in a fitting and comprehensive manner?

A volume such as we can conceive rather than produce—penned with profound and philosophic knowledge of the subject, scrupulous veracity and delectable wit and wisdom—would needs be priceless. We wish we could cast such a one on the restless waters of the sea of life around us. To the lips of the student of human nature a chalice, fraught with instruction and delight, should be freely offered; to the alien and stranger a book of good counsel and comfort; and to mankind in general, we, like the serpent in Eden—yet possessing, withal, no latent guile—would proffer knowledge. In default of this much-to-be-desired volume, we respectfully tender ours.

[…]

Chapter XXI: The Vegetarian Boarding-House (As It Was)

In commencing the present Chapter we would especially disclaim any intention of describing a certain Establishment yet extant among us. Of that we know no more than that it is said to be conducted on an approach to—though not strictly—Vegetarian principles; and that its proprietor has a reputation of a gentleman and a man of science. Our Vegetarian Boarding-House is an entirely different affair; and, to the best of our knowledge, ceased to exist upwards of four years ago. Yet its peculiarities are worthy of preservation.

The tenement was one of those old-fashioned, comfortable-looking, red-brick ones margining the Battery. We became a boarder in consequence of this location, though we acknowledge curiosity as our principle inducement. It was sultry July weather, and we hadn't dollars enough to compass rustication. We always loved the Battery before the city authorities made a big dirt-pile of it. The sparkling waters of the bay rippling in golden sunlight, the pleasant rustle of leaves overhead, and the shadow-checquered [sic] grass under foot were suggestive of other than city life—and as for abstinence from flesh diet, one doesn't feel very carnivorous in summer, and could give one's self a dispensation at a restaurant, if desirable. So, obtaining an introduction to the proprietor, we became an innate of the Vegetarian Boarding-House.

He was a tall, spare man, with a large nose, light watery eyes and but little hair, though he wore a straggling hay-colored beard. Like the wise men of old he hailed from the East. His life seemed to have been spent similarly to those of the Athenians in Scripture in inquiring for *new things*. Not an *ism* whether philosophic, philanthropic or theologic, but had, in its turn, subjugated him. He had shower-bathed his soul with Unitarianism, frozen it up tight in Transcendentalism, thawed it out with Universalism, besmoked it in Swedenborgianism, knocked it higher than a kite with Millerism, let it putrify in Mormonism, flayed it with Shaking-Quakerism, buried it under General Negation, and dug it up with Spiritualism. He had kept a Water-Cure Establishment, visited Icaria, lived in a Phalanstery, and officiated as 'Elder' at Salt Lake. He had been ridden on a rail and tarred and feathered, as an Abolition-lecturer, down South. He had anticipated Neal Dow in the advocation of the Maine Law. At the time of our sojourn in his Boarding-House he devoted himself, almost exclusively, to Vegetarianism and the Woman's Rights movement.

His wife—taken *after* the Mormon episode—was a little rigid woman, without eyebrows. If the reader can imagine an elderly frog laboring under the combined miseries of a severe stomach-ache and the conviction that he was going insane and better commit suicide, that will convey some idea of the expression of her countenance. She always dressed in black, wore very scanty frocks, black cotton stockings, and thick shoes. She

had accompanied her husband in what may be designated his theologic and social *benders*, in some cases preceding him. She was a keen politician (Whole-Ticket-Died-in-the-Wool-Anti-Union-Pro-Amalgamation-Anti-States-Rights-and-No-Backing-Out Stripe), and studied anatomy with the view of practicing as a Doctress. Happily for society in general, she had no children.

Our landlady had as much faith in cold water as Preiss-nitz[1] or a mermaid. Her house, her person, her very cat was overwashed. If it had rained in-doors all day long the house couldn't have been wetter. From garret to basement, both chambers and stair-case were always in a more of less hydropathic condition. You turned out for an unsuspecting walk of half an hour's duration, to find, on regaining your apartment, the chairs blocking the passage, the *disjecta membra* of your bedstead reclining against the wall, and a stout negress on her hands and knees, scrubbing away with perseverance and energy worthy of a better cause. Perhaps Mrs. ____ would be superintending—and quite ready to crush you with sanatory [sic] authorities in case of objection. Our floor was rendered so damp by these proceedings that we shouldn't have been surprised at seeing a plentiful crop of mushrooms or toad-stools spring up under the washing stand, or to have found an eel in the pockets of the old coat which served us for a dressing gown.

[...]

Our meals—at which we formed a snug family party—were served with uniform cleanliness, and excellently prepared. Every thing was of the herbaceous of farinaceous description, of course. We had no meats, no fish, no gravy soups. Tea and coffee were also rejected, as stimulants. But every variety of vegetable appeared at our table, as also fruit and pastry. (No butter entered into the composition of the latter, that being a tabooed article.) Bananas, melons, peaches, grapes, oranges, cherries, pine-apples; all the daintier forms of Vegetarian fare were provided with a liberal hand. The display, indeed, exceeded our expectations. We saw Vegetarian diet under its most attractive (summer) aspect. Whether the fraternity were confined to turnips, etc., during the winter season, we can not determine. In spring they generally went out to graze at a country Establishment, located somewhere in Connecticut, and owned by a relative of the landlord's.

4-2. *SISTER CARRIE* (1900)

Theodore Dreiser

Source: Theodore Dreiser, *Sister Carrie* (New York: Doubleday, 1900).

NOTE

1. Vincenz Priessnitz, a famous nineteenth-century proponent of hydrotherapy.

EDITORS' INTRODUCTION

The following selection comes from Chapter 1 "The Magnet Attracting—A Waif Amid Forces," of Theodore Dreiser's *Sister Carrie*, originally published in 1900 by Doubleday. In George Chauncey's essay, "Urban Culture and the Policing of the 'City of Bachelors,'" one sees another example of how the city offered the possibility of economic and personal freedom to migrants from small-town and rural America. Dreiser's American classic ignited controversy upon its initial publication. Young Carrie Meeber came to the city, threw off the yoke of her sister and brother-in-law's restrictive household, and launched an out-of-wedlock relationship with Charles Drouet, whom she met on the train to Chicago. Later on in the novel, she engages in a relationship with George Hurstwood, who seems even more sophisticated to the naïve Carrie. The scandalous nature of this publication arises both from Carrie's nontraditional love affairs and her ultimate feat of survival. In other novels in which young women went astray in the city, the authors punished their wayward characters with an untimely death by the end of the work. Dreiser allows Carrie to survive her lover Hurstwood, and even to achieve fame and monetary success in the city. In this famous scene, an anxious Carrie leaves her family behind and immediately falls under the sway of Charles Drouet.

The Magnet Attracting—A Waif Amid Forces

When Caroline Meeber boarded the afternoon train for Chicago, her total outfit consisted of a small trunk, a cheap imitation alligator-skin satchel, a small lunch in a paper box, and a yellow leather snap purse, containing her ticket, a scrap of paper with her sister's address in Van Buren Street, and four dollars in money. It was in August, 1889. She was eighteen years of age, bright, timid, and full of the illusions of ignorance and youth. Whatever touch of regret at parting characterized her thoughts, it was certainly not for advantages now being given up. A gush of tears at her mother's farewell kiss, a touch in her throat when the cars clacked by the flour mill where her father worked by the day, a pathetic sigh as the familiar green environs of the village passed in review, and the threads which bound her so lightly to girlhood and home were irretrievably broken.

To be sure there was always the next station, where one might descend and return. There was the great city, bound more closely by these very trains which came up daily. Columbia City was not so very far away, even once she was in Chicago. What, pray, is a few hours—a few hundred miles? She looked at the little slip bearing her sister's address and wondered. She gazed at the green landscape, now passing in swift review, until her swifter thoughts replaced its impression with vague conjectures of what Chicago might be.

When a girl leaves her home at eighteen, she does one of two things. Either she falls into saving hands and becomes better, or she rapidly assumes the cosmopolitan standard of virtue and becomes worse. Of an intermediate balance, under the circumstances, there is no possibility. The city has its cunning wiles, no less than the infinitely smaller and more human tempter. There are large forces which allure with all the soulfulness of expression possible in the most cultured human. The gleam of a thousand lights is often as effective as the persuasive light in a wooing and fascinating eye. Half the undoing of the unsophisticated and natural mind is accomplished by forces wholly superhuman. A blare of sound, a roar of life, a vast array of human hives, appeal to the astonished senses in equivocal terms. Without a counselor at hand to whisper cautious interpretations, what falsehoods may not these things breathe into the unguarded ear! Unrecognized for what they are, their beauty, like music, too often relaxes, then weakens, then perverts the simpler human perceptions.

Caroline, or Sister Carrie, as she had been half affectionately termed by the family, was possessed of a mind rudimentary in its power of observation and analysis. Self-interest with her was high, but not strong. It was, nevertheless, her guiding characteristic. Warm with the fancies of youth, pretty with the insipid prettiness of the formative period, possessed of a figure promising eventual shapeliness and an eye alight with certain native intelligence, she was a fair example of the middle American class—two generations removed from the emigrant. Books were beyond her interest—knowledge a sealed book. In the intuitive graces she was still crude. She could scarcely toss her head gracefully. Her hands were almost ineffectual. The feet, though small, were set flatly. And yet she was interested in her charms, quick to understand the keener pleasures of life, ambitious to gain in material things. A half-equipped little knight she was, venturing to reconnoiter the mysterious city and dreaming wild dreams of some vague, far-off supremacy, which should make it prey and subject—the proper penitent, groveling at a woman's slipper.

"That," said a voice in her ear, "is one of the prettiest little resorts in Wisconsin."

"Is it?" she answered nervously.

The train was just pulling out of Waukesha. For some time she had been conscious of a man behind. She felt him observing her mass of hair. He had been fidgeting, and with natural intuition she felt a certain interest growing in that quarter. Her maidenly reserve, and a certain sense of what was conventional under the circumstances, called her to forestall and deny this familiarity, but the daring and magnetism of the individual, born of past experiences and triumphs, prevailed. She answered.

He leaned forward to put his elbows upon the back of her seat and proceeded to make himself volubly agreeable.

"Yes, that is a great resort for Chicago people. The hotels are swell. You are not familiar with this part of the country, are you?"

"Oh, yes, I am," answered Carrie. "That is, I live at Columbia City. I have never been through here, though."

"And so this is your first visit to Chicago," he observed.

All the time she was conscious of certain features out of the side of her eye. Flush, colorful cheeks, a light moustache, a grey fedora hat. She now turned and looked upon him in full, the instincts of self-protection and coquetry mingling confusedly in her brain.

"I didn't say that," she said.

"Oh," he answered, in a very pleasing way and with an assumed air of mistake, "I thought you did."

Here was a type of the traveling canvasser for a manufacturing house—a class which at that time was first being dubbed by the slang of the day "drummers." He came within the meaning of a still newer term, which had sprung into general use among Americans in 1880, and which concisely expressed the thought of one whose dress or manners are calculated to elicit the admiration of susceptible young women—a "masher." His suit was of a striped and crossed pattern of brown wool, new at that time, but since become familiar as a business suit. The low crotch of the vest revealed a stiff shirt bosom of white and pink stripes. From his coat sleeves protruded a pair of linen cuffs of the same pattern, fastened with large, gold plate buttons, set with the common yellow agates known as "cat's-eyes." His fingers bore several rings—one, the ever-enduring heavy seal—and from his vest dangled a neat gold watch chain, from which was suspended the secret insignia of the Order of Elks. The whole suit was rather tight-fitting, and was finished off with heavy-soled tan shoes, highly polished, and the grey fedora hat. He was, for the order of intellect represented, attractive, and whatever he had to recommend him, you may be sure was not lost upon Carrie, in this, her first glance.

Lest this order of individual should permanently pass, let me put down some of the most striking characteristics of his most successful manner and method. Good clothes, of course, were the first essential, the things without which he was nothing. A strong physical nature, actuated by a keen desire for the feminine, was the next. A mind free of any consideration of the problems or forces of the world and actuated not by greed, but an insatiable love of variable pleasure. His method was always simple. Its principal element was daring, backed, of course, by an intense desire and admiration for the sex. Let him meet with a young woman once and he would approach her with an air of kindly familiarity, not unmixed with pleading, which would result in most cases in a tolerant acceptance. If she showed any tendency to coquetry he would be apt to straighten her tie, or if she "took up" with him at all, to call her by her first name. If he visited a department store it was to lounge familiarly over the counter and ask some leading questions. In more exclusive circles, on the train or in waiting stations, he went slower. If some seemingly vulnerable object appeared he was all attention—to pass the compliments of the day, to lead the way to the parlor car, carrying her grip, or, failing that, to take a seat next her with the hope of being able to court her to her destination. Pillows, books, a footstool, the shade lowered; all these figured in the things which he could do. If, when she reached her destination he did not alight and attend her baggage for her, it was because, in his own estimation, he had signally failed.

A woman should some day write the complete philosophy of clothes. No matter how young, it is one of the things she wholly comprehends. There is an indescribably faint line in the matter of man's apparel which somehow divides for her those who are worth glancing at and those who are not. Once an individual has passed this faint line on the way downward he will get no glance from her. There is another line at which the dress of a man will cause her to study her own. This line the individual at her elbow now marked for Carrie. She became conscious of an inequality. Her own plain blue dress, with its black cotton tape trimmings, now seemed to her shabby. She felt the worn state of her shoes.

"Let's see," he went on, "I know quite a number of people in your town. Morgenroth the clothier and Gibson the dry goods man."

"Oh, do you?" she interrupted, aroused by memories of longings their show windows had cost her.

At last he had a clew to her interest, and followed it deftly. In a few minutes he had come about into her seat. He talked of sales of clothing, his travels, Chicago, and the amusements of that city.

"If you are going there, you will enjoy it immensely. Have you relatives?"

"I am going to visit my sister," she explained.

"You want to see Lincoln Park," he said, "and Michigan Boulevard. They are putting up great buildings there. It's a second New York—great. So much to see—theatres, crowds, fine houses—oh, you'll like that."

There was a little ache in her fancy of all he described. Her insignificance in the presence of so much magnificence faintly affected her. She realized that hers was not to be a round of pleasure, and yet there was something promising in all the material prospect he set forth. There was something satisfactory in the attention of this individual with his good clothes. She could not help smiling as he told her of some popular actress of whom she reminded him. She was not silly, and yet attention of this sort had its weight.

"You will be in Chicago some little time, won't you?" he observed at one turn of the now easy conversation.

"I don't know," said Carrie vaguely—a flash vision of the possibility of her not securing employment rising in her mind.

"Several weeks, anyhow," he said, looking steadily into her eyes.

There was much more passing now than the mere words indicated. He recognized the indescribable thing that made up for fascination and beauty in her. She realized that she was of interest to him from the one standpoint which a woman both delights in and fears. Her manner was simple, though for the very reason that she had not yet learned the many little affectations with which women conceal their true feelings. Some things she did appeared bold. A clever companion—had she ever had one—would have warned her never to look a man in the eyes so steadily.

"Why do you ask?" she said.

"Well, I'm going to be there several weeks. I'm going to study stock at our place and get new samples. I might show you 'round."

"I don't know whether you can or not. I mean I don't know whether I can. I shall be living with my sister, and—"

"Well, if she minds, we'll fix that." He took out his pencil and a little pocket notebook as if it were all settled. "What is your address there?"

She fumbled her purse which contained the address slip.

He reached down in his hip pocket and took out a fat purse. It was filled with slips of paper, some mileage books, a roll of greenbacks. It impressed her deeply. Such a purse had never been carried by any one attentive to her. Indeed, an experienced traveler, a brisk man of the world, had never come within such close range before. The purse, the shiny tan shoes, the smart new suit, and the air with which he did things, built up for her a dim world of fortune, of which he was the centre. It disposed her pleasantly toward all he might do.

He took out a neat business card, on which was engraved Bartlett, Caryoe & Company, and down in the left-hand corner, Chas. H. Drouet.

"That's me," he said, putting the card in her hand and touching his name. "It's pronounced Drew-eh. Our family was French, on my father's side."

She looked at it while he put up his purse. Then he got out a letter from a bunch in his coat pocket. "This is the house I travel for," he went on, pointing to a picture on it, "corner of State and Lake." There was pride in his voice. He felt that it was something to be connected with such a place, and he made her feel that way.

"What is your address?" he began again, fixing his pencil to write.

She looked at his hand.

"Carrie Meeber," she said slowly. "Three hundred and fifty-four West Van Buren Street, care S. C. Hanson."

He wrote it carefully down and got out the purse again. "You'll be at home if I come around Monday night?" he said.

"I think so," she answered.

How true it is that words are but the vague shadows of the volumes we mean. Little audible links, they are, chaining together great inaudible feelings and purposes. Here were these two, bandying little phrases, drawing purses, looking at cards, and both unconscious of how inarticulate all their real feelings were. Neither was wise enough to be sure of the working of the mind of the other. He could not tell how his luring succeeded. She could not realize that she was drifting, until he secured her address. Now she felt that she had yielded something—he, that he had gained a victory. Already they felt that they were somehow associated. Already he took control in directing the conversation. His words were easy. Her manner was relaxed.

They were nearing Chicago. Signs were everywhere numerous. Trains flashed by them. Across wide stretches of flat, open prairie they could see lines of telegraph poles stalking across the fields toward the great city. Far away were indications of suburban towns, some big smokestacks towering high in the air.

Frequently there were two-story frame houses standing out in the open fields, without fence or trees, lone outposts of the approaching army of homes.

To the child, the genius with imagination, or the wholly untraveled, the approach to a great city for the first time is a wonderful thing. Particularly if it be evening–that mystic period between the glare and gloom of the world when life is changing from one sphere or condition to another. Ah, the promise of the night. What does it not hold for the weary! What old illusion of hope is not here forever repeated! Says the soul of the toiler to itself, "I shall soon be free. I shall be in the ways and the hosts of the merry. The streets, the lamps, the lighted chamber set for dining, are for me. The theatre, the halls, the parties, the ways of rest and the paths of song–these are mine in the night." Though all humanity be still enclosed in the shops, the thrill runs abroad. It is in the air. The dullest feel something which they may not always express or describe. It is the lifting of the burden of toil.

Sister Carrie gazed out of the window. Her companion, affected by her wonder, so contagious are all things, felt anew some interest in the city and pointed out its marvels.

"This is Northwest Chicago," said Drouet. "This is the Chicago River," and he pointed to a little muddy creek, crowded with the huge masted wanderers from far-off waters nosing the black-posted banks. With a puff, a clang, and a clatter of rails it was gone. "Chicago is getting to be a great town," he went on. "It's a wonder. You'll find lots to see here."

She did not hear this very well. Her heart was troubled by a kind of terror. The fact that she was alone, away from home, rushing into a great sea of life and endeavor, began to tell. She could not help but feel a little choked for breath—a little sick as her heart beat so fast. She half closed her eyes and tried to think it was nothing, that Columbia City was only a little way off.

"Chicago! Chicago!" called the brakeman, slamming open the door. They were rushing into a more crowded yard, alive with the clatter and clang of life. She began to gather up her poor little grip and closed her hand firmly upon her purse. Drouet arose, kicked his legs to straighten his trousers, and seized his clean yellow grip.

"I suppose your people will be here to meet you?" he said. "Let me carry your grip."

"Oh, no," she said. "I'd rather you wouldn't. I'd rather you wouldn't be with me when I meet my sister."

"All right," he said in all kindness. "I'll be near, though, in case she isn't here, and take you out there safely."

"You're so kind," said Carrie, feeling the goodness of such attention in her strange situation.

"Chicago!" called the brakeman, drawing the word out long. They were under a great shadowy train shed, where the lamps were already beginning to shine out, with passenger cars all about and the train moving at a snail's pace. The people in the car were all up and crowding about the door.

"Well, here we are," said Drouet, leading the way to the door. "Good-bye, till I see you Monday."

"Good-bye," she answered, taking his proffered hand.

"Remember, I'll be looking till you find your sister."

She smiled into his eyes.

They filed out, and he affected to take no notice of her. A lean-faced, rather commonplace woman recognized Carrie on the platform and hurried forward.

"Why, Sister Carrie!" she began, and there was embrace of welcome.

Carrie realized the change of affectional atmosphere at once. Amid all the maze, uproar, and novelty she felt cold reality taking her by the hand. No world of light and merriment. No round of amusement. Her sister carried with her most of the grimness of shift and toil.

"Why, how are all the folks at home?" she began; "how is father, and mother?"

Carrie answered, but was looking away. Down the aisle, toward the gate leading into the waiting-room and the street, stood Drouet. He was looking back. When he saw that she saw him and was safe with her sister he turned to go, sending back the shadow of a smile. Only Carrie saw it. She felt something lost to her when he moved away. When he disappeared she felt his absence thoroughly. With her sister she was much alone, a lone figure in a tossing, thoughtless sea.

4-3. *STRANGE BROTHER* (1931)

Blair Niles

Source: Blair Niles, *Strange Brother* (New York: Liveright Press, 1931).

EDITORS' INTRODUCTION

This novel was written under a pseudonym by Mary Blair Rice, a founding member of the Society of Women Geographers and a prolific author. The book traces the relationship between a heterosexual divorcée named June and a homosexual man named Mark, who teaches in a settlement house. After their meeting in a Harlem nightclub, the two become fast friends. Mark teaches June about the difficulties he has faced as a gay man, both in his small home town and even in the more tolerant, anonymous, and diverse New York City. In this section, Mark first admits to June that he is a homosexual. This document relates to the article by George Chauncey, in this part, which reveals the gay world created in New York City between the world wars.

June was hoping that somehow she would be sincere and fearless in this dark place to which Mark's emotion had carried her.

"And you have a soul like that, I think," Mark said. "That's why I could talk to you right away as I have. There may be a lot of things you don't know about, but you give me the impression that you're ready to look straight at anything that's life, and accept it. You don't look at me as if I were something in the Zoo. You see I'm always one of three things to most people who know about me: I'm a curiosity—a sort of sideshow—or I'm a joke, or a horror. Often people who don't know I am different will say to me that the whole tribe of us ought to be run in, locked up, or maybe put out of the way altogether. We are the modern witches—that's what we are!...

"Oh, don't please think I go on like this with everybody. Why, my bread and butter depends on people's not knowing! I teach, you see, in a Settlement. The man in charge there—"

Mark remembered Herbert Rokeby's thin penetrating voice pervading the dining-room, saying that everything must be regular, that he insisted on everything being regular.

"Mr. Rokeby, the man in charge, would put me out if he knew; put me out as if I were a leper!"

"How you have suffered!" June exclaimed, "to feel like this... to feel that it's such a monstrous thing...when it's only..." she hesitated, "only a misfortune."

And after a silence she added, "If you don't mind, tell me, has it always been so? Were you always what you call—different?"

"I'm sure of it. When I look back, I can see that it was true of me from the beginning, though I didn't know it; didn't positively know it until I was sixteen. And then... it came to me all in a moment, suddenly, like a blow. A man told me—a man who loved me. I heard it as gently and wisely as any one [sic] could hear such a thing. But I was stunned—literally stunned."

And back of Mark's words there was the memory of how, at the end of that day when he'd been helping Tom pack to go away to Calcutta, he and Tom had taken the glasses of root beer and gone out to rest under the maple trees.

Tom had spoken then, quietly, breaking the truth to him tenderly. Tom, it seemed, had known about him all along. He understood what Mark had not realized. And now that Tom was going away, he wanted before he left, to convince Mark that if a thing were real, you need never be ashamed of it—no matter what people said. "If you live courageously," Tom had said, "out of what seems disaster you may achieve victory. That is the creed to live by."

He had said too that Mark must learn to stand alone and to make for himself a full life, accepting whatever was reality. And thus clear-eyed he would conquer. But Tom had said that Mark must go to some place like New York, where he could fight the battle with himself, unhandicapped by small-town talk.

Small-town talk…Tom's words had made Mark recall gossip that he had heard in Narova City. Experiences of the past had returned to be re-lived, flashing through his mind with the incredible speed of memory; and taking on new meaning in the light of what Tom had said.

PART V

MANAGING THE METROPOLIS

EDITORS' INTRODUCTION TO PART V

One of the most remarkable facets of American urban life during the nineteenth century was the expansion and transformation of municipal government. During the colonial era, local communities had limited authority to manage their own affairs. After the American Revolution, individual states granted their cities and towns the right to incorporate as municipal entities. Municipal status allowed cities and towns the authority to pass local ordinances, levee taxes, enforce fines, and otherwise manage their own legal affairs. During the nineteenth century, cities officials across the country used these powers to hire private contractors and public employees to meet the basic health, education, and public safety needs of a rapidly expanding urban population. As such, the actual physical and economic landscape of cities changed with the construction of schools, roads, sewers, and other forms of infrastructure, as well as creation of new job opportunities in education, police and fire protection, sanitation, and other fields.

Concurrent with the rise of municipal governance was the extension of voting access—albeit slow and uneven—and the broadening of civil and legal rights for immigrants, racial minorities, women, and others traditionally excluded from the decision making process. In the late eighteenth century, only a minority of adults, usually propertied men and occasionally widows, were able to vote and hold office. Although only a few states allowed women to vote by the end of the nineteenth century, working-class voters, many of them naturalized immigrants and the children of immigrants, influenced the outcome of elections and even held political office in many large cities. The rise of the working-class electorate solidified political machines and party bosses. While not strictly urban, machines became synonymous with large cities, especially those that were able to spend vast amounts of money on public works projects, where opportunities for graft and corruption allowed a handful of individuals to enrich themselves through extralegal activities.

Not surprisingly, these municipal and political trends played themselves out to the extreme in New York City. As the largest metropolitan area in the nation, New York was both a trendsetter and the object of superlatives for all that was positive and negative about big city government. The construction of Central Park is a case in point. Although widely regarded as the first great public park in the United States, its design and construction reflected political and social unease within the city. As **Document 5.1** describes and **Figure 5.1** illustrates, advocates for the park envisioned a pastoral setting where New Yorkers of all classes could benefit from tranquil vistas and peaceful social intercourse. However, as Roy Rosenzweig and Elizabeth Blackmar point out in their essay, the park's management became embroiled in political controversy as different constituencies vied to shape the use of public space.

Debate over Central Park highlighted the larger struggle between municipal and state officials as to whether or not New York City could even manage its own affairs. Adding fuel to arguments for limiting self-governance in New York City were the actions of the notorious party boss William M. Tweed who extorted millions of dollars through the political machinery of Tammany Hall, which controlled the city's Democratic Party. **Document**

5.2 samples the extent of Tweed's corruption as he explained to city investigators in detail how he and others stole millions of dollars from public coffers between the 1850s and 1870s. As **Document 5.3** demonstrates, political corruption was not limited to New York or even the Democratic Party as noted muckraker Lincoln Steffens proved in his investigation of Republican-dominated Philadelphia at the turn of the twentieth century.

Social reformers sought their own solutions to urban ills. Following the Columbian Exposition of 1893, Daniel Burnham and Chicago businessmen set out to improve the physical infrastructure of their city. The 1909 Plan of Chicago led to great improvements within that city and simultaneously sparked a national movement for urban redevelopment. Jane Addams and Ellen Gates Starr launched Hull-House in 1889 on Chicago's Near West Side to serve the city's immigrant communities. Addams also recruited wealthy society figure Louise de Koven Bowen to assist at Hull-House. Bowen wrote of the practical knowledge and self-esteem she garnered by volunteering at Hull-House in a self-reflective memoir. [**See Documents 5.4, 5.5, and 5.6.**]

State-dependant cities experienced a fundamental transformation during the Great Depression. In his essay, Thomas Kessner explores how New York Mayor Fiorello H. La Guardia forged a partnership between America's cities and the federal government with the use of New Deal relief programs that put people back to work building an urban infrastructure. The relationship between cities and the federal government expanded following World War II with legislation that enabled slum clearance and public housing development. [**See Document 9.1, "Housing Act of 1949."**] The federal–city partnership expanded with the social programs of President Lyndon B. Johnson's War on Poverty. Despite this aid, cities still faced many obstacles in rejuvenating their economic base. For many commentators, cities reached their nadir in the 1970s when deindustrialization combined with decentralization and a declining tax base. One of the most dramatic examples of this reversal of fortune came when New York City teetered on the verge of bankruptcy in the mid-1970s. [**See Figure 5.2 for the iconic *New York Daily News* headline from October 1975, "Ford to City: Drop Dead."**]

Despite the bad publicity, American cities proved resilient. **Document 5.7** demonstrates how Charlotte, North Carolina and Kansas City, Missouri attempted to stave off municipal decline by building from their pre-existing advantages. As Jon Teaford explores in his essay, during the 1970s and 1980s big city mayors and other civic leaders anticipated a long awaited urban renaissance. Even the unprecedented devastation of Hurricanes Katrina and Rita in August and September 2005 failed to entirely erode the resolve of the citizens and leaders of New Orleans, Louisiana. The multi-layered problem of rebuilding the city is explored by Arnold Hirsch and A. Lee Levert in their timely article "The Katrina Conspiracies: The Problem of Trust in Rebuilding an American City." [**See also Document 5.8 "President Arrives in Alabama, Briefed on Hurricane Katrina."**]

The "Spoils of the Park"

Roy Rosenzweig and Elizabeth Blackmar

Source: *The Park and the People: A History of Central Park*
(Ithaca: Cornell University Press, 1992).

EDITORS' INTRODUCTION

Central Park is one of the great icons of urban America and an invaluable source of rec-reation, entertainment, and respite for New York City residents and visitors alike. Built between 1857 and 1870, it was the first great public park in the United States and a model for other large parks all over the world. From the very start, competing visions of urban life determined the location, look, and use of Central Park. Noted landscape archi-tects Frederick Law Olmsted and Calvert Vaux designed the park with the intention of bringing the soothing elements of the countryside into the city. Its tree-lined meadows, water features, and serpentine pathways serve as a striking contrast to the modern build-ings, busy sidewalks, and perpendicular grid of street life. **[See Figure 5.1, "A Correct Map of the New York Central Park, 1865" and Document 5.1, "On the Social Uses of Central Park."]** The park, however, is equally artificial, meticulously superimposed over the original swampy and rocky topography that was once home to roughly 1,600 people. The construction of the park displaced a small yet well-established African-American community, Seneca Village, a variety of small wooden dwellings occupied by Irish and German immigrants—pejoratively referred to at the time as "shantytowns"—and an array of noxious manufacturing and agricultural endeavors such as bone boiling works, pig-geries, and gardens that helped feed residents throughout the city. **[See Figure 6.2 "Encroachment of Nuisances Upon Populous Up-Town Districts."]**

Management of the park also reflected the contours of nineteenth-century political power. In an effort to curb the growing influence of New York City's Democratic Party, whose strength lay in a burgeoning working class and immigrant voter base, Republi-cans who controlled the state government in Albany passed a series of measures to undercut the city's ability to govern itself under the principle of "home rule" or local autonomy. In 1857, upstate Republicans created the Central Park Commission under the direction of Andrew H. Green, who served as president and comptroller from 1857 to 1871. By the early 1870s, the city regained home rule rights to Central Park under the so-called "Tweed Charter," named after William M. Tweed, the notoriously corrupt party boss who led the dominant faction of the Democratic Party called Tammany Hall. **[See Document 5.2 "William Tweed's Confession."]** During this same period, a national economic depression strained city coffers while residents simultaneously demanded greater public services and reduced taxes. As a result, the management of the park became deeply intertwined with city politics, as illustrated in the following excerpt from Roy Rosenzweig and Elizabeth Blackmar's book *The Park and the People: A History of Central Park*. Rather than this transition resulting in the park's decline, though, it brought a greater democratization of public space. In the process, the genteel nature of the park's use and supervision eventually gave way to one more representative of the people and the city it was intended to serve.

The Park and the People received several awards, including the Urban History Asso-ciation Prize for Best Book on North American Urban History (1993) and the Historic Preservation Book Award (1993). The late Roy Rosenzweig (1950–2007) was the Mark and Barbara Fried Professor of History and New Media at George Mason University, where he also served as founder and director of the Center for History and New Media. He was the author of *Eight Hours for What We Will: Workers and Leisure in an Industrial City, 1870–1920* (Cambridge: Cambridge University Press, 1983) and other articles, books, CD-ROMs, and websites on American history, public history, and museums. He is well known for his work as consulting editor on Pantheon Books' Who Built America: Working People & the Nation's Economy, Politics, Culture & Society' series. Elizabeth Blackmar is professor of history at Columbia University and author of *Manhattan for Rent, 1785–1850* (Ithaca: Cornell University Press, 1989) and other works on social and urban history.

THE "SPOILS OF THE PARK"

At 5:15 P.M. on April 20, 1870, the Board of Commissioners of the Central Park adjourned its final meeting, expressing "apprehension" and "deep concern" about the future. The commissioners entrusted the board's property to Andrew Green, one of two members who would join the new Board of Commissioners of the Department of Public Parks. Two weeks earlier, the Democratic-controlled legislature had approved a new city charter that would dramatically alter the city's subservient relationship to the state. This so-called Tweed charter—a backhanded tribute to Tammany boss William Tweed, whose political skills and timely bribes had secured the restoration of home rule—transferred control of Central Park. Henceforth, the mayor would appoint the park commissioners, and debates over its management would remain in the thick of city politics.[1]

Anti-Tammany editors marked this moment in 1870 as initiating the destruction of the park that had so triumphantly represented the values of elite New Yorkers. For the *New York Times* in the 1860s, the park had been the "antipode" of the city and its "official corruption"; now the paper worried that Tweed and his "unclean horde" would take over the park, bringing "the total and irretrievable ruin of a magnificent work of art." By the next year the *Times* was charging that "park administration" under the leadership of Tweed's closest adviser, Peter Sweeny, "has become thoroughly demoralized ... overthrowing the best and only well-executed work in the City." Subsequent historians have shared this gloomy verdict.

With the passage of the Tweed charter, a typical recent account notes, "the shadow that fell on Central Park became dark night."[2]

Popular culture, too, has upheld the link between Tweed's depredations and the park. The 1945 musical *Up in Central Park* (and the 1948 film, with Vincent Price as Boss Tweed) retold the story of political greed and corruption, albeit with a kind of raucous jollity. The romance between the daughter of an Irish ward heeler and a crusading *Times* reporter ends happily with a rousing chorus singing the praises of the "Big Back Yard of the City."[3] But most contemporary (as well as retrospective) accounts agree that the park continued to deteriorate long after Tweed's brief regime ended in 1871.

Such charges found their fullest and most famous expression in 1882 when Frederick Law Olmsted published a pamphlet titled *The Spoils of the Park*. Central Park had taken on a "slovenly and neglected aspect," Olmsted charged, because city politicians and their "ignorant" appointed commissioners had surrendered park service to "that form of tyranny known as influence and advice and that form of bribery known as patronage." City officials had failed to keep the park under the supervision of trained professionals who could protect and fulfill its true purpose as a public work of landscape art and the site of healthful and moral recreation.[4] [...]

Olmsted provided as evidence twenty-three vignettes in which commissioners bowed to political pressure or park workers violated their public duty. "I don't get any salary for being here," he quoted one commissioner; "it would be a pretty business if I couldn't oblige a friend now and then." As an example of the "tyranny of influence," Olmsted decried proposals for new entrances and roads that would "tell to the advantage of somebody's real estate." And as evidence of park workers' insubordination, Olmsted recalled that the mechanical detectors he had installed to make sure that night watchmen did not sneak off their beats to sleep in park sheds had been smashed "by sledges" within a week.[5]

In attributing the decline primarily to patronage, Olmsted put forth an analysis that influenced the reformers of his generation and also later historians. Yet the tendency to frame park politics—or city politics for that matter—only as a duel between "corrupt" politicians and "public-spirited" citizens obscures the larger issues that shaped the management of Central Park as a public institution, the struggle over who would control the public purse and whose interests would be served by government. In the mid-nineteenth century, wealthy and professional men and women—many of them Republicans—had advocated a wider arena of state action and had experimented with centralized governmental authority. As they expanded public services, new executive commissions, like the one that controlled Central Park from 1857 to 1870, restrained popular sovereignty. But for genteel reformers, this expansion of government also carried a risk. As happened when the Tweed Ring captured Central Park, new city bureaucracies could fall into the "wrong hands" and veer from their advocates' cardinal values of efficiency and taste. In politicians' hands, the resources of an expanded public sector could be used to court the votes of working-class and immigrant New Yorkers.[6]

In looking for managerial solutions to the problems posed by party rule, Olmsted and others tried to imagine a public order insulated from political brokering and from the competitive free-market economy. To Olmsted the original state-appointed Central Park commission had come to represent a model for shielding public administration from politicians; in the same way Olmsted imagined the public space of Central Park as

shielding citizens from the tensions of city streets. The park could not embody a pristine civic order, however. The money and labor that maintained it were embedded, after all, in the same conflicting interests that underlay the larger political economy and culture of the city itself.

Moreover, the three groups Olmsted now blamed for the park's decline—politicians, park workers, and landowners—did not agree that "spoils" represented only self-interest. Politicians saw patronage as essential to preserving party loyalty and, hence, the electoral system itself. Park workers who resisted degrading work rules believed that the municipal government that employed them had an obligation to meet the standard of fair wages and hours. And landowners argued that public improvements like Central Park, which benefited their property, sustained the city's economic growth.

In the boom years after the Civil War, politicians as unlike as Andrew Green and William Tweed thought the public sector could accommodate these different interests. Prosperity inspired confidence in local government's ability to coordinate economic growth, to provide new public institutions, and to support an improved standard of living for more city residents. But in the 1870s, with fiscal crisis and economic depression, the city's manufacturers, bankers, and wealthiest taxpayers rejected this growth-oriented vision of government and attacked the "excesses of democratic politics" as a drain on their own private resources. Reformers who took up the cry of "spoils" regarded Central Park's decline as symptomatic of a larger decay.

In focusing on freeing the park from politicians, Olmsted and others ignored the more fundamental cause of the deterioration of the landscape. Public institutions required public money, and as Commissioner Salem Wales observed, Central Park was an "expensive luxury" to maintain.[7] When propertied taxpayers demanded budget cuts, city officials slashed park maintenance funds as well as park workers' wages. The fight over the "spoils" of the park in the 1870s thus rested on the larger issue of who would control public resources.

Cashing in on the Park

Through the Civil War, bankers had collected interest on war bonds in gold, railroad investors had accumulated fortunes from government-subsidized land grants and troop transport, and city manufacturers had gotten rich by supplying the army with uniforms and boots. For working people wartime inflation was a severe burden, from which their living standards did not immediately recover; but in the aggregate, post-Civil War New York City prospered as never before in its history. The gaudy carriage parade in Central Park displayed wealthy New Yorkers' exuberant confidence in the value of public works. Not only had the city matched European capitals by building the park, such public improvements had promoted new levels of economic growth and cultural attainment.

In the expansive context of the Gilded Age, New Yorkers with varying and often deeply antagonistic interests looked to state and local government to support their personal and civic ambitions. Republicans and Democrats quarreled over which party would control the public sector, but elected representatives of both parties endorsed new governmental ventures to protect public health, improve public schools, regulate the labor and housing markets, and build parks, boulevards, and museums. If politicians could work compromises, and if the economic pie continued to expand, it seemed that prosperity could satisfy all appetites—those of landowners, bankers, merchant philanthropists, contractors, and workers.

In December 1865 Andrew Green, as the Central Park commission's comptroller, outlined an ambitious agenda for city planning. The commission had proved itself with the park and was now prepared to manage uptown streets and other public places. In a report to the board, Green described a street plan that would reach along the West Side from 59th Street to Washington Heights, including a principal north-south thoroughfare ("the Boulevard," now Broadway), a "riverside drive" along the top of the Hudson River bluffs, and a new "public pleasure ground" adjacent to the Hudson River. This "riverside park," like Central Park, would spare the city the cost of cutting regular cross streets into the steep and rocky bluffs.[8]

Green, viewing the park board's mission as analogous to that of the 1811 Street Commission that laid out Manhattan's grid, had little doubt that a well-planned city required the overarching intelligence of "a single mind or a single interest"—his own. City businessmen endorsed the expansion of the board's planning authority as a way of countering the chaotic competition of city building. Radical Republican legislators applied the Central Park model of commission government to other city departments, including the fire department and the board of health in 1866. By 1869 state lawmakers had expanded the park commission's authority into the southwestern Westchester district that later became part of the borough of the Bronx.[9]

Green was torn between the satisfaction of controlling vast stretches of the city's public landscape and his habitual commitment to economy, and he distinguished between *planning* for future development and *building* new public works. Property owners would petition and pay assessments for the actual construction of parks and boulevards, he suggested, only when "a compensating use can be made of the[ir] property." Although he was a real estate lawyer himself, Green misjudged the ambitions of uptown landowners, who enthusiastically endorsed (and indeed took credit for securing) the expanded responsibilities of the Central Park commission. Rather than wait for the "compensating use" of their own building projects, landowners urged that new public works begin at once. John McClave, a house carpenter who had become one of the city's most successful real estate operators, spoke for many uptowners when he announced that "he had no faith in buying farms and mapping them out into streets and avenues unless they are contiguous to the grand improvements." "The only way to create an intrinsic value in real estate is to put capital upon it"—especially public capital.[10]

In advocating new public grounds and spacious boulevards, landowners drew on the precedent of Central Park: parks would spare the city (and proprietors) the cost of building streets and would pay for themselves by establishing new elite residential quarters that would expand the city's tax base. In the optimistic climate of a boom economy, few downtown taxpayers protested when state lawmakers, heeding the uptown lobbyists, approved the creation of Riverside and Morningside parks and authorized the boulevard bonds.[11]

With this signal that uptown real estate was ripe for new buyers (and with greenback dollars fanning the flame), many uptown landowners decided to cash in on the promise of Central Park and its radiating "grand drives" as a real estate amenity. After the economic dry spell that reached from the panic of 1857 through 1863, land speculation ignited. Estate administrators and old-time New York families with large tracts jumped into the market and sold off uptown parcels to brokers and smaller investors. On the East Side, James Lenox reaped as much as $3 million by selling lots on the thirty-acre Lenox Hill estate his father had acquired in 1818. In 1868 executors of the Talman estate on the West Side sold two blocks between 66th and 68th streets for $200,000; a month later the southern block alone was resold for $172,000. That same year a block along the southern border of Central Park went for $840,000.[12]

New investors in 1866 were spending $5,000 to $7,000 for lots on uptown cross streets that had brought $400 in 1857. A Fifth Avenue plot facing Central Park that cost $13,000 in 1867 sold for $24,000 the following year. Brokers made fortunes by trading other people's land; between 1857 and 1868, John McClave claimed, he handled $15 million worth of uptown property and earned nearly $1 million in commissions. Other large landowners—the Zabriskie and Jones families, for example—tenaciously clung to their uptown land, expecting yet higher prices once the territory had been fully improved with paved streets, sewers, and gas lines.[13]

Newspapers and Clinton W. Sweet's *Real Estate Record and Building Guide*, closely following the real estate boom, welcomed landowners' efforts to coordinate their interests. In 1866 landowners west of Central Park formed the West Side Association to promote uptown improvements. Among the early members were some of the city's most solid citizens, including the former park commissioner John A. C. Gray and the former mayor Fernando Wood, who, after reaching the nadir of political repute in his support of southern secession, had abandoned politics and returned to the respectable ranks of investors. East Side landowners quickly followed the trend toward coordinating "sectional interests" and formed their own real estate association. These landowners' groups formally disassociated themselves from party politics, but many uptowners and building contractors did identify their interests with Tammany's recapture of city government under Tweed's 1870 charter. If the city controlled its own affairs, including uptown improvements and the further embellishment of Central Park, landowners might overcome Andrew Green's (and hence the park commission's) reluctance to push forward the construction (and not just the planning) of public works.[14]

While uptown landowners cashed in on Central Park and endorsed local Democrats' plans for uptown improvements, city workers made their own claims to a share of the new prosperity. By 1867 park laborers, who had earned as little as ninety cents a day in 1861, recouped the losses of the past decade's inflation and secured a two-dollar daily wage. Skilled construction workers in the private sector made even more substantial gains when they threatened disruptive strikes if contractors did not meet their demands for union work rules and the eight-hour day. At the end of the Civil War, the city's trade unionists also moved toward independent politics, joining the National Labor Union and establishing a statewide Workingmen's Assembly to lobby the legislature for an eight-hour law. Most employers and business groups believed that permitting more leisure time would only subvert discipline among workers. But in 1867 lawmakers from both parties acknowledged the labor movement's militance by passing an eight-hour bill, albeit one that failed to provide for enforcement. In 1870 the law was narrowed to apply to *public* workers alone.[15]

New York City Democrats appealed to their labor constituents with the promise of jobs on an expanded public improvements program as well as with their backing of the eight-hour law. By 1870, one historian has estimated, city government employed one-eighth of the voters.[16] Thus, Tammany Democrats rebuilt their political control of New York City and its administrative departments by means of public works that tacked together a tentative coalition between real estate interests and labor.

Creating an Orderly Park

The Tweed charter gave the new Department of Public Parks jurisdiction over Central Park, all the small parks, and the improvements on the West Side. With Peter Sweeny (the reputed "brains" of the Tweed Ring) at its helm, the new board employed men in numbers that matched those of the early days of Central Park's construction, an average of 1,587 workers in 1870 and 2,970 in 1871. In its first year, the Sweeny board spent more than $600,000 improving the park, and another $340,000 maintaining it.[17]

Some of this money went to complete architectural features inherited from the old commission, including the Carousel, Dairy, Belvedere Castle, Bethesda Terrace, and stables. Funds were allocated to repair walks and drives worn down by heavy use. (Carriage traffic eroded an inch and a half of paving from the drives each year.) Many of the picturesque plantings, which had been placed quickly and temporarily to meet budget constraints and the expectations of the first visitors, were, as Olmsted and Vaux noted, in need of "extensive revision." The new board, however, interpreting in its own way "the principle that distance, expanse, and extent should be constantly aimed at," now directed a rigorous program of planting, pruning, and thinning trees and clearing out "shrubbery that obstructs the view." Even the suspicious *Times* conceded in the summer of 1870 that the new commissioners "seem determined to make some show for the money they spend." But when the Department of Public Parks issued its first annual report, Andrew Green, who had been effectively isolated on the board by the Tammany commissioners, issued a disclaimer. The report, he charged, showed "a singular want of comprehension of the methods, purposes, and designs of the original commission."[18]

The Sweeny board had, in fact, rejected the earlier design in favor of new aesthetic goals for managing Central Park. The new Democratic commissioners, including Robert Dillon (who had urged an "artificial" style at the time of the design competition), envisioned the park as the urbane symbol of the city's cultural accomplishments; they ignored the advice of Olmsted and Vaux, who were dismissed as the park's landscape architects in November 1870. The board's first annual report proudly displayed illustrations of new architectural attractions: menagerie buildings, the interior of the Arsenal fitted up for a museum, plans for a crystal-palace-like conservatory at Fifth Avenue and 74th Street, and the Sheepfold designed by Jacob Wrey Mould (and today incorporated into the Tavern on the Green restaurant).[19]

With respect to the natural landscape, the Sweeny board simply wanted a bright, clean, and orderly park that showed the effect of good housekeeping. Responding to criticisms of the park's rusticity, workers straightened paths for convenience, exposed bridges to the parkgoers' view, pruned the low branches of trees to open new vistas, planted shade trees (that blocked old vistas), and brushed moss and leaf mold off the rocks. Gardeners cleared out the "catbriers and tangled weeds" (as they considered the native plants) and created ara-besque flower beds with more than thirty-eight thousand bulbs and other flowers in "conspicuous portions of the Park." Whatever distress these interventions caused New Yorkers sympathetic to the aesthetic motives of the original plan, many editors, parkgoers, and adjacent landowners welcomed them as improvements.[20] [...]

Despite the parks department's expansive program, the Tammany administration invested its greatest efforts in the Department of Public Works, headed by Tweed himself. While West Siders complained of delays on *their* public improvements, Tweed ordered street paving, sewers, and gas lines through the Upper East Side and Harlem. In these territories, where a close circle of his supporters had bought land, the sooner streets were built, the sooner and more profitably these speculators could sell. At the end of the century, Tammany politician George Washington Plunkitt dubbed such favors "honest graft." Reformers later spent years trying (unsuccessfully) to add up the extent of the Tweed administration's "dishonest graft"—the "boodle" politicians pocketed or used to bribe the press and other lawmakers. Roughly $20 million, one investigating committee suggested, had come out of the difference between the actual and billed costs of the courthouse and other enterprises; Tweed ring members had spent a portion of this sum on generous printing orders and advertising that persuaded publishers to look the other way. (The lavishly illustrated 427-page parks department report printed by William C. Bryant and Company in January 1871 was typical of such enticements). Members of the Tweed Ring who stole public money or used it for bribes were far from the only beneficiaries of the program of public improvements: the spoils of the progrowth political coalition had been widely distributed.[21]

City laborers won jobs and the eight-hour day on public works without a cut in their two-dollar wage. Skilled construction workers found steady work as developers followed street improvements and raised more than two thousand buildings a year. Still, workers' incomes, which ranged from five to eight hundred dollars a year, paled in contrast to the spoils of land speculation. By the conservative calculation of the city's assessors, land values increased by $341 million between 1865 and 1871. Uptown landowners and speculators garnered the biggest gains as assessed land values north of 40th Street—even though dramatically undervalued—tripled in that same period. Few doubted that Central Park had spurred the uptown boom.[22] [...]

By the mid-1870s, economic depression had sundered the political alliance of real estate and labor. Uptown landowners themselves held contradictory interests in the city's fiscal policies: as taxpayers, they welcomed budget cuts that would reduce taxes; as real estate investors, they wanted public improvements. To resolve this contradiction, members of the West Side Association abandoned their earlier tacit support for a large city work force and instead launched a litany of familiar complaints about inefficiency. The city was "paying four times the proper and legitimate cost" of improvements, landowner Simeon Church informed a state senate committee in 1875. To prove his point, Church told the story of a gentleman acquaintance who jumped out of his carriage to strike rock with a hammer alongside a street gang and did more work in fifteen minutes than the workmen would do in an hour. (No one asked if this gentleman could have kept up his furious pace for eight or ten hours.) Complaining that park workers sat around as at "picnic parties," other landowners decried city employment practices as an "outrage upon the rights of property and an outrage on the rights of the men who [did private] contract work" and earned as little as ninety cents for a for ten-hour day.[23] [...]

Redefining the Political Public

At the heart of debates over municipal governance in the 1870s stood the question of the identity and interests of New York's "political public." To men like Olmsted, preoccupied with the issue of "spoils," the relationship between voters and public officials seemed not an expression of popular will but rather a fundamentally corrupt exchange. The party patronage bargain placed public services in the hands of unqualified and incompetent administrators and workers. Olmsted regarded the legitimate "public" (and especially parkgoers) primarily as consumers who had lost the full value of services to which they were entitled and which only men like himself could give them. Other reformers, sharing Olmsted's contempt for party politics, argued instead that propertied taxpayers constituted the legitimate political public because they paid for city government. A taxpayers' revolt, which first appeared during the economic boom of the 1860s, gained steam in virtually every northeastern city during the depression of the 1870s. Although propertied families had themselves been among the strongest advocates of new municipal services—from better schools to parks—many now considered the tax burden of an expanded public sector an imposition arising from the "excesses" of democratic politics.[24]

In 1876 Governor Samuel Tilden tapped this reform sentiment and appointed a twelve-man commission to make recommendations on the governance of cities in New York. The following spring the Tilden Commission issued a report that took off the gloves in the class battle over control of municipal resources. City government, it asserted, should be regarded as a closed municipal corporation. Control of revenues should be restricted to a board of finance elected by property owners and tenants who paid at least $250 in rent—more than half the annual income of the majority of city workers.[25] It was an attempt, in effect, to institutionalize the 1871 coup of the Committee of Seventy—the bankers and merchants who had seized control of city government from the Tweed Ring and appointed Tilden's close friend Andrew Green as their financial officer. The Tilden Commission further recommended that all public works not financed by assessments on adjacent landowners be built only with current tax revenues; in other words, it ruled out new projects that would be financed—as had the construction of Central Park—through bonds.

With this report propertied taxpayers and reformers announced that they were no longer willing to let the representatives of a democratic electorate determine which public goods and services city residents needed. Nor would they contribute to a public sector that provided decent working conditions for city employees. Business would flee the city, one municipal society warned, unless a new system of government checked the power of "those who have everything to gain by voting away the prosperity of others." The reformers did not believe that working people contributed to the city's wealth through their labor and the rents that covered landlords' tax bills. Gone was Calvert Vaux's vision of "true and intelligent republicanism" in which

disparities of wealth would be a "comparatively unimportant matter" because all citizens could enjoy the comforts of public institutions—from parks and libraries to public baths and theaters—through which a "man of small means *may* be almost on the same footing as the millionaire." Gone too was the confidence that such public improvements as Central Park both marked and propelled the city's progress. The progrowth coalition of land speculators, contractors, and workers had been repudiated.[26]

The Tilden Commission cast its proposals to dismantle democratic local government in the form of a constitutional amendment to reorganize the administration of municipal corporations. In the fall of 1878 New York City voters rejected the movement by electing Tammany representatives to the state legislature and common council. Nonetheless, bankers and wealthy taxpayers could not be ignored. When Tammany's own "reform" chief, John Kelly, succeeded Green as city comptroller in December 1876, he acknowledged the weight of businessmen's judgments and rigorously pursued retrenchment. As both "reform comptroller" *and* Tammany boss, Kelly made the Department of Public Parks the special target of fiscal and party discipline.... Kelly slashed the department's appropriations by 25 percent. Then in the fall of 1877 Kelly informed the board president that he was withholding Frederick Law Olmsted's salary.[27]

There is a certain irony in Kelly's step. In effect, he reduced the codesigner to the status of an ordinary park worker, rigidly applying the same disciplinary rules that Olmsted himself had advocated for public employees. Olmsted, the comptroller charged, had missed work for more than two days—indeed, for nearly a month—to pursue "multifarious employment outside the City of New York" (including the Buffalo and Montreal park systems, on which Olmsted worked during this period). Kelly deliberately ignored Olmsted's growing national reputation. Perhaps he was venting his spleen at Olmsted as the "representative man" of Tammany's harshest gentleman critics at the Union League. But Kelly claimed that Central Park no longer needed the expensive advice of a landscape archi-tect. The office had become a "sinecure," echoed a new Tammany park commissioner, and in the face of budget cuts, the board could better use the money to pay "poor laborers and policemen."[28]

Kelly probably did not anticipate the outcry Olmsted's firing would trigger in the press. Olmsted's well-connected friends mobilized a protest that moved from the parlors of private homes and the lounges of the Century Club and the Union League to the editorial and letters columns of the *Tribune*, *Post*, *World*, and *Herald*. However much they might welcome budget cuts and efficient executive authority in principle, reformers did not intend that the burden of retrenchment should fall on one of their own—or on their own park.[29]

Calvert Vaux viewed the protests with mixed feelings. Although he and Olmsted had dissolved their partnership in 1872, Vaux had few doubts that his former partner's dismissal was unfortunate for Central Park. He was nonetheless distressed to see his own contri-bution once again erased by such men as E. L. Godkin, who wrote in a two-column protest letter to the *Tribune* that it would be no exag-geration to say that Olmsted, "who designed the Park and has for twenty years nearly watched over its execution, holds a leading position among the professors of this art. The credit due to him is heightened by the fact that no other American has worked in the same field with equal success." Vaux felt he had no choice but to correct the record in his own letter to the *Tribune*. Satirically invoking the metaphor of the division of "their joint artistic property" in Central Park first articu-lated by Olmsted in 1863, Vaux complained that Godkin had assumed the status of "administrator" of a joint estate—the divider, one might say, of the spoils of reputation—and had directed "to F. L. Olmsted, every-thing; to C. Vaux the cut direct."[30]

The "Secret and Decline and Decay"

The retrenchment of the 1870s took its toll both on the park and on the individuals most closely identified with it. Yet if Olmsted and Vaux found decreasing

demand for the talents of public landscape architects, they were spared the worst effects of the depression. Tens of thousands of New York wage earners were unemployed, and some were driven to despair. In August 1875 Andreas Fuchs, a forty-year-old shoemaker, shot himself to death in a secluded part of Central Park, explaining in a note left for his wife and children, "I have no work and do not know what to do." (By 1879 suicides in the park had become so frequent that the police had standing orders to search the shrubbery and out-of-the-way spots each morning for victims.) By 1881 William Martin had left the park board and had lost his real estate fortune and even his private residence to foreclosure. After taking desper-ate measures of his own, Martin was threat-ened with disbarment for abusing his fiduciary responsibilities as an estate admin-istrator by "borrowing" the heirs' money.[31] [...]

The physical deterioration of their preem-inent public institution dismayed genteel New Yorkers. Editorials in national journals and letters to local newspapers complained of worn-down carriage drives, muddy paths, overgrown vegetation, unrepaired bridges, and of the taste of the park's new adminis-trators. The carriage parade proceeded apace on weekday afternoons, but the back-drop of landscape art was peeling away. In the late 1860s the city had been spending about $250,000 per year for the mainte-nance of Central Park. Ten years later it spent $100,000 less on taking care of *all* city parks. Although deflation compensated for some of the 60 percent drop in spending, the responsibility for twenty-three additional parks and squares meant a drastic cut in the money available for maintaining Central Park.[32] [...]

Still, the Sweeny board had not ruined Central Park. It had, in fact, lavished money on upkeep, and that was the crux of the problem. Even after Tweed went to jail for his theft and Sweeny retired from politics, the structure of the political system that had supported their regime remained. Working-class New Yorkers would vote for politicians who promised jobs and decent hours and decent pay on public works. And during boom times, propertied New Yorkers would support the generous investment of "public capital" to propel the city's economy. But the policies and taxes that supported higher public wages cut into private profits. "Governments," the Tilden Commission had concluded, are not created for "sentimental purposes." "They are contrivances to furnish protection to the industrious citizen" who wishes "to pursue his private avocations."[33] During the depression, bankers, merchants, industrialists, and landowners mobilized politically to defend their private interests by minimizing their economic contribution to the public sector.

If Central Park was only one of many public institutions that suffered from budget cuts, it was the one nearest to the hearts of the city's most comfortable citizens. Nonetheless, propertied New Yorkers chose to sacrifice its maintenance to the discipline of the marketplace. Because they feared losing control of city government to Tammany politicians and their immigrant working-class supporters, they tried, as the historian C. K. Yearley puts it, "to starve the party by starving the state."[34] Wealthy New Yorkers continued to use the park and to defend the designers' original vision, but they would never again confidently regard it as the symbol of their own standing as the "representative class" of a unified public. The era of Tweed and retrenchment marked a retreat from the optimism with which elite New Yorkers had advocated creating a public park that would accommodate their own desires and needs *and* elevate those citizens below them. They realized that providing working people with, in Olmsted's terms, the "mental & moral capital" of leisure time and space might encroach on their own financial capital. Precisely because Central Park was "public," new groups— park workers seeking a living wage, park officials advocating a different aesthetic, or politicians running the party system—made new claims on its administration. Whatever the problems of patronage, the restoration of home rule had given a voice to new constituencies that would work to open city politics and the park itself to a broader public. [...]

The park that had in the 1860s represented elite accomplishment would become in the 1880s and 1890s a more genuinely democratic public space.

NOTES

1. BCCP *Min.*, Apr. 20, 1870. On the politics behind the 1870 charter, see Seymour J. Mandelbaum, *Boss Tweed's New York* (1965), 66–75; Alexander B. Callow, *The Tweed Ring* (1966), 222–35.
2. *NYT*, Mar. 13, 1870, Mar. 22, 1871; Eugene Kinkead, *Central Park, 1857–1995: The Birth, Decline, and Renewal of a National Treasure* (1990), 77; See also *NYT*, Apr. 5, 1870; *World*, Mar. 15, 18, Apr. 4, 1870.
3. *NYT*, Mar. 22, 1871; Kinkead, *Central Park*, 77; Herbert and Dorothy Fields, *Up in Central Park* (1945).
4. Frederick Law Olmsted, *Spoils of the Park*, reprinted in Frederick Law Olmsted and Theodora Kimball, eds. *Forty Years of Landscape Architecture: Central Park* (1928; reprint) Cambridge, MA, 1973), 140, 144–45, 154.
5. Ibid., 127, 148, 131.
6. On genteel or liberal reformers, see John G. Sproat, *"The Best Men": Liberal Reformers in the Gilded Age* (1968); Eric Foner, *Reconstruction: America's Unfinished Revolution* (1989), 488–509; Geoffrey Blodgett, "Frederick Law Olmsted: Landscape Architecture as Conservative Reform," *Journal of American History* 62 (Mar. 1976): 869–89.
7. *Trib.*, Dec. 30, 1880.
8. Andrew H. Green, *Communication to the Commissioners of Central Park Relative to the Improvement of the Sixth and Seventh Avenues, from the Central Park to the Harlem River, the Laying Out of the Island from 155th Street, and Other Subjects* (1866), 68, and for uptown plan, 38–75. For Green's planning vision, see David Hammack, "Comprehensive Planning before the Comprehensive Plan: A New Look at the Nineteenth-Century American City," in *Two Centuries of American Planning*, ed. Daniel Schaffer (Baltimore, 1988); David Scobey, "The Streets and Social Order: Changing Relations of Class, Power, and Space in Gilded Age New York" (Ph.D. diss., Yale University, 1989), chap. 6.
9. Green, *Communication*, 42; BCCP *11AR* [1867], 129–31; James C. Mohr, *The Radical Republicans and Reform in New York during Reconstruction* (Ithaca, 1973), 117–18 and passim; George Alexander Mazaraki, "The Public Career of Andrew Haswell Green" (Ph.D. diss., New York University, 1966), 101–12.
10. Green, *Communication*, 53; *RERBG*, Oct. 31, 1868; and for landowners taking credit, see, e.g., *RERBG*, Apr. 2, 1870. For typical landowners' petitions for improvements, see BCCP *Min.*, Jan. 9, Feb. 26, Mar. 26, Aug. 3, Nov. 12, 1868, Apr.

8, 1869. See also *Her.*, Nov. 23, 1864, Jan. 16, Apr. 22, 1865; Martha J. Lamb, "Riverside Park: The Fashionable Drive of the Future," *Manhattan* 4 (1884): 55–56, which credits uptown developer William R. Martin with first proposing Riverside Park.

11. Although the legislature authorized the park board to create the parks, delays developed when landowners objected to assessments. See, e.g., *RERBG*, June 4, 1870; *NYT*, Mar. 28, 1871; "Report of William R. Martin, President of the Department, on the Treatment of the Uptown Parks," BDPP *Min.*, doc. 70 (June 9, 1876).

12. Eugene Moehring, *Public Works and the Patterns of Urban Real Estate Growth in Manhattan, 1835–1894* (1981), 308, 283–87, 302–12; *NYT*, Mar. 11, 1868; Henry Stevens, *Recollections of Mr. James Lenox of New York and the Formation of His Library* (London, 1886), 4. See also *Trib.*, Apr. 11, 1863, June 3, 1867; *Her.*, Feb. 25, Nov. 23, 1864, Sept. 24, 1865; *Sun*, Sept. 4, 1867; *NYT*, Mar. 11, 1868, July 27, 1869; *RERBG*, Jan. 16, Feb. 13, 20, 1869; Real Estate Record and Guide, *A History of Real Estate, Building, and Architecture in New York City during the Last Quarter of a Century* (1898; rpt. 1967), 58–65; M. Christine Boyer, *Manhattan Manners: Architecture and Style, 1850–1900* (1985), 30–35.

13. Moehring, *Public Works*, 286; *RERBG*, Oct. 31, 1868; *Her.*, June 16, 1879.

14. *RERBG*, May 9, June 13, 27, 1868; Iver Bernstein, *The New York City Draft Riots: Their Significance for American Society and Politics in the Age of the Civil War* (1990), 206–9. See also West Side Association, *Proceedings of Six Public Meetings, 1870–1871* (1871).

15. On park wages and petitions, see BCCP *12AR* [1868], 13; BCCP *Min.*, Jan. 14, June 5, 1868; *Her.*, June 27, 1868. On labor movement and eight-hour day, see Bernstein, *New York City Draft Riots*, 209–15, 244–55; David Montgomery, *Beyond Equality: Labor and the Radical Republicans, 1862–1872* (1967; Urbana, Ill., 1981), 170–96, 237–49, 323–33; Mohr, *Radical Republicans and Reform*, 119–39; George Gorham Groat, "The Eight Hour and Prevailing Rate Movement in New York State," *Political Science Quarterly* 21 (Sept. 1906): 416–17. The parks department also formally adopted the eight-hour day: BDPP *Min.*, May 24, 1870.

16. Morton Keller as cited in Martin Shefter, *Political Crisis/Fiscal Crisis: The Collapse and Revival of New York City* (1987), 16.

17. *FYLA*, 536; BDPP *Min.*, Oct. 10, 1871. The Sweeny board served from April 20, 1870 to November 22, 1871. For its budgets, see "Communication of Commissioner William R. Martin," BDPP *Min.*, doc. 64 (Mar. 5, 1875): 13–14; Edward Dana Durand, *The Finances of New York City* (1898), 147, 148. Andrew Green estimated that the Sweeny board spent a total of $3.1 million on all parks in 17 months: *NYT*, Oct. 19, 1871.

18. For continuation of the earlier board's projects, see *NYT*, Apr. 30, July 31, Sept. 18, 1870; BDPP *Min.*, doc. 5 (Dec. 27, 1870); *FYLA*, 88 (Green), 265 (revisions), 266 (Sweeny board's program); *NYT*, June 29, 1870. For Green's isolation, see Mazaraki, "Public Career of Green," 119–29.

19. See BDPP, *1AR* [1870], 11–17, and report of Jacob Wrey Mould, 397–412; BDPP *Min.*, Dec. 6, 1870 (Dillon); on dismissal, BDPP *Min.*, Nov. 11, 1870; *NYT*, Dec. 21, 1870, *FYLA*, 88–89. See also *World*, June 19, 1870.

20. BDPP, *1AR* [1870], 295, 300 (quots.), and 26–27, 39–40, 296–99. For praise, see *Star*, Aug. 3, 1871; *Globe*, June 14, 1871; *CA*, June 14, July 22, 1871; *Mail*, June 14, 1871; *Turf, Field and Farm*, July 21, 1871; *Pomeroy's Democrat*, June 25, 1871; and Strong, *Diary*, 4:361, 373, 375, 377. Even the *NYT*, July 4, 1871, commended the park's "strikingly beautiful appearance" before returning to its drumbeat of criticism, e.g., on Sept. 1, 1871. For critique of the Sweeny board's management of the natural features, see FLO and CV to BDPP, BDPP *2AR* [1871], app. B, rpt. in *FYLA*, 240–70; *SP*, 134–35.

21. For "honest graft," see Moehring, *Public Works*, 312–22; Callow, *Tweed Ring*, 179–81; *Her.*, Apr. 9, 1875 (Tweed's own holdings); and on West Siders' complaints, e.g., *World*, Mar. 30, Aug. 7, 1870. For "dishonest graft," see Callow, 164–65; Durand, *Finances of New York*, 139–40; BDPP, *1AR* [1870]; and for an alternative interpretation, Leo Hershkowitz, *Tweed's New York: Another Look* (1977).

22. Durand, *Finances of New York*, 373; BDPP, doc. 64 (1875): 31 (land values); Boyer, *Manhattan Manners*, 36 (new buildings). Even Andrew Green personally benefited from the postwar economic boom with a substantial salary raise, a free trip to Europe, and apparently an advance on a book on Central Park that he never wrote; see Report of the Committee of Law Department, BA *Docs.*, no. 5 (June 3, 1875), 28–29, 38–39; Report of the Commissioner of Accounts, ibid., no. 6 (June 17, 1875), 16–25. Charges of greater corruption implied in John Foley, *Andrew H. Green and Thomas C. Fields: Secret Management of the Central Park Commission* (1874) are unsubstantiated. Foley was a lobbyist unhappy with Green's actions as city comptroller, particularly his refusal to pay the Tweed regime's printing bills: Mazaraki, "Public Career of Green," 194–99. When Commissioner Fields left the country to avoid prosecution, it was for his shenanigans as a fire commissioner: *NYT*, Feb. 4, Oct. 26, 1872, Sept. 20, 1875, Jan. 26, 1885.

23. "Report of the Committee of the Senate of the State of New York, Appointed to Investigate the Several Departments of the Government in the City and County of New York," Sen. *Docs.*, 99, vol. 7, no. 79 (Mar. 16, 1876): 419, 425, 385. See also *NYT*, Mar. 8, 1874.

24. Mandelbaum, *Boss Tweed's New York*, 171; Clifton K. Yearley, *The Money Machines: The Breakdown and Reform of Government and Party Finance in the North, 1860–1920* (Albany, 1970), 3–35; Jon C. Teaford, *The Unheralded Triumph: City Government in America, 1870–1900* (Baltimore, 1984), 284–89.

25. "Report of the Commission to Devise a Plan for the Government of Cities in the State of New York," Ass. *Docs.*, 100, vol. 6, no. 68 (Mar. 6, 1877). See also Mandelbaum, *Boss Tweed's New York*, 169–71; Michael McGerr, *The Decline of Popular Politics: The American North, 1865–1928* (1986), 49–50, 65, 71–72.

26. Mandelbaum, *Boss Tweed's New York*, 170–71, 172 (municipal society); Calvert Vaux, *Villas and Cottages: A Series of Designs Prepared for Execution in the United States*, (1857; 2d ed., 1864; rpt. 1970), 50. Yearley, *Money Machines*, 27–28, argues that the middle class was particularly squeezed by taxes on real property.

27. Mandelbaum, *Boss Tweed's New York*, 172–81; John Kelly to William Martin, Dec. 4, 1877, FLO Mss.; *FYLA*, 110.

28. *Her.*, Jan. 10, 1878. For Olmsted's work on the Montreal and Buffalo parks, see Roper, *FLO*, 317–33, 348, 356–59, 384–85; *FLOP* 6 (forthcoming).

29. See, e.g., Howard Martin to FLO, Jan. 11, 15, 1878, Louisa Schuyler to FLO, Jan. 13, 1878, FLO Mss.; petition, *FYLA*, 112–13; *World*, Jan. 10, 13; 1878; *Her.*, Jan. 12, 14, 1878; *Post*, Jan. 11, 26, 1878; *Mail*, Jan. 14, 1878. The *Express*, Jan. 14, 1878, supported the firing.

30. *Trib.*, Jan. 11 (Godkin), CV to *Trib.*, Feb. 19, 1878.

31. *Her.*, Aug. 22, 1875; *World*, Aug. 23, 1875 (Fuchs); *NYT*, Sept. 9, 1879 (suicides), June 29, 1880, Mar. 25, 1882 (Martin).

32. On deterioration, see, e.g., *NYT*, Nov. 15, 1875, Aug. 12, 1877, Feb. 1, Sept. 7, 8, 1879; *Trib.*, Mar. 3, 1879; *Her.*, May 28, 1877, May 26, Oct. 18, 1879. For budgets, see BDPP *Min.*, Sept. 24, 1879; *Trib.*, Dec. 31, 1877; an untitled report apparently prepared for a board of estimate hearing, Dec. 26, 1882, 84:12, MP; Commissioners of Account of Mayor Smith Ely, May 21, 1878, 81:24, MP.

33. Ass. *Docs.*, 100, no. 68: 19. "People look back to the despised Ring Regime," the *Herald* noted on June 16, 1879, "and say no matter how the Ring plundered and robbed New York, it gave New York at least a splendid park."

34. Yearley, *Money Machines*, 275. The *Times* complained that the city was "starving this beautiful playground of the people," but advocated starving the party in the park: Nov. 7, 1874, Apr. 28, 1875, Nov. 22, 1876.

New Deal City

Thomas Kessner

Source: *Fiorello H. La Guardia and the Making of Modern New York*
(New York: McGraw Hill Publishers, 1989).

EDITORS' INTRODUCTION

Prior to the 1930s, American cities received little monetary assistance (or other forms of direct attention) from the United States government. Federal policies, like those of individual states themselves, favored the economic interests of rural regions. This lack of funding changed dramatically during the Great Depression of the 1930s, when municipal leaders lobbied for and secured aid from both federal and state sources in order to pay for a variety of relief measures that helped unemployed, homeless, and under-nourished citizens. At the forefront of this movement were dynamic and foresighted mayors such as Detroit's Frank Murphy, who championed the needs of the poor and working class. Murphy testified before Congress on the dire fiscal condition of cities, and spearheaded the formation of the United States Conference of Mayors in 1932 and early 1933. Without question, the most influential figure in the transformation of federal–city policy was New York City's indomitable Mayor Fiorello H. La Guardia, whose close ties to President Franklin Delano Roosevelt (FDR) and his administration fundamentally altered the relationship between Washington, D.C. and urban America.

On January 1, 1934, less than one year after FDR became president and amidst the depths of the Great Depression, Fiorello H. La Guardia took over New York City on the heels of several notorious political scandals involving the former mayor James "Jimmy" Walker and the Tammany Hall faction of the city's Democratic Party. La Guardia, who served as a Republican in the United States House of Representatives during the 1910s and 1920s, enjoyed a reputation as a compassionate humanitarian and honest reformer and thus earned the support of non-Tammany Democrats and independent voters when he ran for mayor in 1933 under the banner of the Fusion Party. The following essay from Thomas Kessner's *Fiorello H. La Guardia and the Making of Modern New York*, describes how the mayor forged a new partnership between cities and the federal government by using his reform experience and connections to key members of FDR's "New Deal" coalition. The term "New Deal" describes a series of broad measures initiated by the president to stimulate the economy. Many New Dealers themselves, especially Henry Hopkins, Francis Perkins, and First Lady Eleanor Roosevelt, were familiar with the problems facing cities through their own experiences as social reformers in New York. La Guardia, with his trademark political savvy, counted upon trusted New Dealers' continued influence and access to the purse strings in Washington. He provided the federal government with models for public works projects. As such, New York City served as the urban laboratory for the New Deal, proving that federal programs could successfully give the unemployed a new sense of pride and self-worth while rebuilding cities and the nation's economy.

Thomas Kessner is Distinguished Professor of History at the Graduate Center of the City University of New York (CUNY) and the first Director of the Fiorello H. La Guardia Archives. His other works include *Capital City: New York City and the Men Behind America's Rise to Economic Dominance, 1860–1900* (New York: Simon & Schuster, 2003); *Today's Immigrants, Their Stories: A New Look at the Newest Americans* (with Betty Caroli), (New York: Oxford University Press, 1982); and *The Golden Door: Italian and Jewish Immigrant Mobility in New York City, 1980–1915* (New York: Oxford University Press, 1977).

EXTENDING THE LOCUS: NEW YORK GOES TO WASHINGTON

The U.S. Constitution makes no mention of a federal responsibility for the cities. Traditionally, municipalities were treated as wards of their states, as an Iowa court decision stated in 1868: "Municipal corporations owe their origins to, and derive their powers and rights wholly from, the [state] legislature. It breathes into them ... life.... As it creates, so may it destroy. Municipal corporations are the mere tenants at the will of the legislature." In another decision, this one after the turn of the century, the Supreme Court concurred, announcing that "the State ... at its pleasure may modify or withdraw all ... [city] powers ... expand or contract the territorial area, unite the whole or a part with another municipality, repeal the charter and destroy the corporation. All this may be done ... without the consent of the [city's] citizens, or even against their protest."

In his 1925 state of the union address, President Calvin Coolidge cautioned against federal intervention in local matters. "It does not at all follow that because abuses exist it is the concern of the Federal Government to attempt their reform." And ignore them he did, with an assiduousness that made a virtue of neglect. At the International Conference of Cities in 1931, the U.S. delegation was the only one to report that its government took no direct responsibility for its cities. Three years later C. A. Dykstra, a student of the American city, looked out at urban America with its unemployed masses and chaotic finances and wrote, "At this moment the city trembles," while the federal government continued to do nothing.[1]

Franklin Roosevelt brought into office the mixed feelings about cities of a Dutchess County squire raised on the expansive acres of rural property. As governor he had devoted his energies to countryside issues, and the Jimmy Walker scandals did little to endear the downtown districts to him. Nor was he particularly comfortable on the sidewalks of New York. "Al Smith," he admitted to Raymond Moley, "knows these city people better. He can move them. I can't."[2]

But big-city mayors did their best to try to move Roosevelt. In May of 1933, pleading that their resources were exhausted, they implored Washington to reverse its policy of fastidious neglect to rescue strapped American municipalities. Although the scion of Hyde Park hesitated to add urban debts to the staggering federal budget, headlines detailing the imminent financial collapse of Detroit, Chicago, and New York changed his mind. He directed the Reconstruction Finance Corporation (RFC) to make millions available in the form of loans to imperiled cities, and he initiated a vast public works program under Interior Secretary Harold Ickes. Unfortunately, the supercautious Ickes tied up the billions entrusted to him in bureaucratic red tape.

Meanwhile unemployment was rising, cities were broke, and people were starving. "What this relief business needs," one newspaper remarked "is less RFC and more PDQ." Reformers pleaded for openhanded assistance with a sense of urgency. One night Harry Hopkins, New York State's temporary emergency relief administrator, together with his friend William Hodson, cornered Secretary of Labor Frances Perkins at the Women's University Club in a cramped space under the stairs. They asked for her support for an ambitious program of direct federal relief. Miss Perkins brought the two reformers to the White House, where they persuaded the president to create a $500 million Federal Emergency Relief Administration (FERA) to distribute assistance grants through the states. "It is socialism," bellowed Representative Robert Luce, but amidst the crying need of the times the epithet had lost its sting. Too many real radicals were running around for the New Deal Congress to worry about another Roosevelt reform. The bill passed by a comfortable margin.[3]

Hopkins went to Washington to head the new agency. "For a social worker," William E. Leuchtenburg has written about the new relief czar, "he was an odd sort. He belonged to no church, had been divorced and analyzed, liked race horses and women, was given to profanity and wisecracking, and had little patience with moralists."

Shrewd, cynical, and brusque, Hopkins was tactless with senators but tender with the distressed. He spent money with zest and brought with him a sweeping commitment to the rights of the poor. Harold Ickes was still searching for the perfect program while Hopkins, a half hour after accepting his appointment, set up a temporary desk in a federal building hallway to distribute federal largesse immediately. In his first two hours, working amidst discarded crates and packing boxes, chain-smoking and gulping coffee, assisted by a staff that he threw together on the way, he handed out $5 million and continued to spend with a sense of mission. He had little patience with the penny-pinchers and the dispensers of long-term solutions. "People have to eat in the short run," he would say. He insulted the bureaucratic pashas, bent conventions that hindered quick action, and was fully prepared to be sent packing within a few months, "so I'll do as I please."[4]

And as the 1933 Depression winter approached, Hopkins argued for even more relief for the unemployed. Handing out relief checks was not enough. In an industrial society work was the key to a person's identity, and relief without work corroded a man's spirit. Instead of doles he wanted the government to create projects that would yield jobs for the unemployed. Such work relief might be more expensive but, Hopkins declared, it "preserves a man's morale ... saves his skill ... [and] gives him a chance to do something useful." He won Roosevelt's approval for a Civil Works Administration that would make work for 4 million unemployed by funding federal improvements. But while previous assistance programs had been administered through the states, the new CWA offered outright grants directly to municipalities.

In November 1933 Hopkins invited mayor-elect Fiorello La Guardia to help plan the new CWA. La Guardia had been a familiar and passionate friend of the unemployed, and he would soon be managing the nation's largest city. Hopkins wanted his support for any program designed for the cities. Thus, weeks before he actually took office, La Guardia was called upon to assist in designing the most significant program of urban assistance in the nation's history.[5]

La Guardia also cast an interested eye in the direction of Interior Secretary Harold Ickes's Public Works Administration (PWA), which was finally beginning to make large-ticket public works allocations. In the past, New York City had failed to claim its portion of federal grants. Its applications were invariably weak, thrown together by hacks who inspired little confidence in Washington. La Guardia changed that. Teaming the best public planner in the nation with one of the brightest experts on public finance, he dispatched Robert Moses and Adolf Berle to Washington to deliver the message that New York was prepared to compete for federal projects and prove that it could manage them with integrity and efficiency.

Then La Guardia himself came to the capital. The Washington press corps turned out to greet their old friend and as usual he had a story for them. He was here, he declared, to claim New York's fair share of public allotments. He happened to have in his pocket—veteran journalists knew about *that* pocket—a few proposals for the secretary of the interior, for subways, bridges, slum clearance, street repair, airfields.... The list was long, but each of the requests was carefully laid out, with a firm price tag and a prudent projection of labor needs; and each of the projects promised to leave a large permanent public monument to the New Deal upon its completion.

Ickes was impressed with the tough, knowledgeable New Yorker. This was someone with whom he could do business. He felt assured that any money that would go to a La Guardia administration would be spent carefully and honestly. "I liked his appearance," the secretary confided to his diary on November 23. "He is short and quite stocky and apparently full of vigor. His career in Congress shows that he has real ability and high courage.... [H]e ought to give New York a great administration."[6]

What Ickes might not have realized was how critical a part La Guardia actually intended for Washington to play in his administration. For La Guardia was determined to bring New York under the economic umbrella of the New Deal. Shortly after assuming office he told Congress that the crash had "put every municipality to the wall," and the states were not able or willing to help much. The federal government would have to step in, and La Guardia intended to make New York City a model for federal-urban cooperation. "What I want to do," La Guardia's adviser, Adolf Berle, wrote President Roosevelt, "is to navigate New York City into a friendly cooperative basis with both the state and the National Administrations, and if there is any line to be taken here I should be glad of a steer."[7]

Back in New York City, La Guardia assembled planning groups of engineers, architects, and other experts and put them to work on proposals for CWA grants. "I come to you," he told the pleased professionals, "because I want ... help from people who know something ... rather than from the politicians." No longer would New York projects be developed with rewarding a small clique of favored Democratic friends in mind. He instructed the planners to design projects that could be completed swiftly because the entire CWA program would last only a few months. And because CWA would pay for workers but required a municipal contribution for the cost of materials, he asked for labor-intensive projects.

Three weeks after his election and more than a month before taking office, La Guardia signed deals with contractors to furnish equipment and completed detailed plans for the useful employment of some 200,000 CWA workers to construct covered municipal markets, clean and refurbish the city's parks, reclaim its rotting docks, set up temporary shelters for the homeless, and repair public buildings. One shrewd two-stage plan applied for CWA labor to clear slums and then asked PWA for money to build low-cost public housing on the cleared sites. By the time La Guardia took office, New York had captured 20 percent of all job slots allocated by the CWA.[8] [...]

The coming of the CWA to the city, wrote one social worker, "sounded like the opening of the gates of Heaven to the unemployed." For months the needy had been forced through ego-smashing means tests to qualify for assistance. Now there were real jobs for them with salary checks. During its brief few months—roughly coinciding with the first 100 days of the La Guardia administration—CWA contributed more than $50 million to the city's needy, tiding hundreds of thousands of families over one of the bitterest winters in New York history. And its 4000 separate projects put a fresh new face on the streets, parks, and public buildings of the metropolis.[9]

In this first major test handling a federal program, La Guardia demonstrated how much New York had changed. Hundreds of relief suggestions and requests from the mayor's friends, supporters, and relatives were passed to the Department of Welfare, to be evaluated on their merits with all of the rest of the applications. On one of his first unannounced site visits La Guardia found a crowd of park workers "resting" during hours. He walked over and fired sixty of them for "loitering."[10]

In other cities federal programs were being filtered through the political machine, or frittered away on useless projects. In Chicago, Harry F. Gosnell, the respected Negro leader, charged that blacks were threatened with a cutoff of relief funds if they voted Republican during the 1933 elections. San Francisco Mayor Edmond O. Hansen stated flatly that it was "necessary to register as a Democrat" to qualify for relief in some parts of his home state. In Boston, the relief administrator refused to accept any direction from Washington; he wanted the federal authorities to drop off the money and disappear. So completely did Massachusetts State Treasurer Charles Hurley control CWA appointments through the State Relief Board that the press referred to CWA as "Charlie's Workers Administration." The administration would suffer no such embarrassments in La Guardia's New York. A few weeks into the new municipal administration, national studies singled out New York for the most honest and effective CWA in the country, and state investigators reported that "New York City ... is remarkably free from political control or influence."[11] [...]

Building with Relief

To manage New York's public works La Guardia wanted the Man Who Could Get Things Done, president of the State Parks Commission, Robert Moses. La Guardia was awed by the job that Robert Moses had accomplished with the New York State parks. He once told Paul Windels that he liked to drive along the Long Island parkways that Moses had built, for inspiration. And they were inspiring! For Moses thought in terms that few other public officials had even dared to dream: huge public undertakings that changed not only the physical landscape but the terms of social reference by which entire communities related to their surroundings.

In the early 1920s Moses had fixed his thoughts on Long Island and dreamed of a state park on Jones Beach, another on Fire Island, and three more state parks on the south shore of Long Island, and four parks on the Sound, and two more at the island's center. In fact, he dreamed of tens of thousands of acres of new parks. And parkways connecting them, so that a family driving from New York City could drive up to the island parks and beaches along beautiful roads. He had dreamed, in fact, of 124 miles of parkways, carefully landscaped to form "ribbon parks." In the summer of 1924 Moses took Governor Al Smith for a tour of his dream. "Why don't I make you President of the Long Island State Park Commission," asked Governor Smith. Why, yes, he would take the job, said Moses. And then he went out and converted his dream into real grass.

In the process he had learned how to use the law to get things done, to drive men to get things done, to find the best engineers and architects and back them to the hilt to get things done, to reward executives who worked under him with power and perquisites in order to cement their loyalty and spur their devotion to get things done; to use every bit of information and shrewdness to cow legislators into getting things done, to curry favor with the powerful and the press to get things done. And over all of this to spin the gossamer of higher purpose. Moses was ready for new dreams. The challenge of equipping New York with modern physical surroundings and parks offered a proper scale for his interests. La Guardia wanted this uniquely gifted Man Who Could Get Things Done to manage his public works program. [...]

La Guardia and Moses were alike in many respects, in their audacious sense of urban possibility, their dedication to the large job, and the fear and grudging admiration that they inspired among those who worked for them. In Moses, La Guardia found a man at least as driven, ambitious, and work-addicted as he. La Guardia once wrote his parks commissioner that he had sponsored Moses for membership in the Circus of Saints and Sinners. "It is quite an affair and I am sure it will be in keeping with your high and exalted position." Moses wrote back, thanking the mayor, but "if you don't mind there is so much to do that I am going to forego all parties, luncheons, speaking engagements, etc., except those of a strictly official nature. I cut them all out some time ago as a matter of fact." Between the two power-driven men it was like a famous marriage: They could hardly stand to be with each other and they could not at all stand to be without each other.

Theirs would be a great, painful, tempestuous, and ultimately effective collaboration.[12] [...]

Moses, using PWA funds and CWA workers and whatever he could squeeze out of the mayor, meanwhile carried out his own ambitious park agenda, oblivious to the behind-the-scenes controversy about him. Despite a fierce winter, laborers who just a short while back had spent their workdays looking for a place to warm up, were put on double and triple shifts. On February 23 New York had eighteen inches of snow on the ground. Offices closed, cars could not pass through many streets, but the Parks Department did not stop working *outdoors*. Through ice and snow and below-zero cold, the refurbishing of the parks never halted. An atmosphere of excitement took hold of the architects and engineers who saw their plans almost immediately turned into finished improvements. In one feverish sixteen-day stretch, working with one eye pitched out the windows of their Arsenal headquarters, a team of fifteen architects completed plans for a new Central Park zoo.[13] [...]

After the CWA was phased out in March, half the parks laborers were dismissed, but Moses' ramrods kept the rest working, and when on the first balmy Saturday of the new spring New Yorkers visited their parks, they were amazed. Seventeen hundred renovation projects had been completed; everything in the parks had been repainted, every lawn reseeded, and every tennis court resurfaced. Miles of walks, bridle paths, and playing surfaces had been refinished. Hundreds of comfort stations, drinking fountains, wading pools and park benches were repaired, thousands of dead trees uprooted, sandboxes refilled and nineteen miles of fences put up. Moses put uniforms on park employees, including the relief workers assigned to the parks. When the welfare commissioner protested that they were not Parks Department personnel, Moses told him, "I won't have them slopping around in any old clothes." Parks were meant to be fun, not grave reminders of down-and-out reliefers in their sackcloth.[14]

From empty plots that had for the longest time been strewn with the refuse of careless New Yorkers bloomed colorful flowers. Seven new municipal golf courses were opened. Central Park was brought back to life. The roaming rat packs were exterminated. Squatters who had taken up residence from Hoover's days in the dry reservoir bed were evicted, making way for a Great Lawn. Play areas, pools, sports courts and a Tavern-on-the-Green were all added. Moses had spent $26 million on parks, all of it, he assured New Yorkers, "judiciously." The biblical Moses had smitten the rock and brought forth water; La Guardia's Moses, joked wags, smote the rock and brought forth water, flowers, trees, and playing fields. And he did it while cutting administrative costs to half what they had been under Tammany.

He made new parks as well. La Guardia had no money for parks, so Moses did it without money. Every strip of public land that was not being put to use was fair game, as the Parks Department surveyed the city record for idle property and La Guardia instructed the Sinking Fund Commission, which held control over much of this property, to turn it over. By May sixty-nine new small parks and play areas had been developed. In 1918 the city had raised through public subscription more than $200,000 for a war memorial. It was never enough for the elaborate arch that had been contemplated, and the money remained in a city account for all these years. Now it was put to use in a war memorial playground for each borough.

On the Lower East Side, where from Jimmy Walker's time the city had dawdled with the huge Chrystie-Forsyth tract, the new administration created a fine playground for the slum children. Even Arnold Rothstein's estate was converted to public use. The murdered gambler had died with tax arrears of $334,000. The bill was cleared by forgiving the back taxes in return for a seventy-four-acre chunk of Rothstein's estate in middle Queens.

There had been 119 playgrounds in New York in the summer of 1933. In the summer of 1934 there were 179.[15]

Urban Spokesman

THE Depression persisted into its sixth winter. Legions of the poor and desperate continued to stalk the city streets, warmed only by their resentments. Federal investigators who regularly dipped into the mood of the people found a harder edge to these New Yorkers. There was a disquieting desperation, a willingness to follow a leader, any leader. City Welfare Commissioner William Hodson feared that unless jobs were made available soon the masses might pursue "a new social order," and Communists were making gains through their unemployment councils. "The next idol," warned another social worker, "is likely to be someone who has a promise...." Months earlier, La Guardia had led a delegation of mayors to Roosevelt's beloved Hyde Park and, there among the autumnally bare fruit trees and generous lawns, delivered his message: "stripped of all pretty phrases and stock quotations," the cities could no longer care for their own.[16]

In early April Congress, in its single largest appropriation ever, allocated $4.8 billion, for a Works Projects Administration, and

Roosevelt placed open-fisted Hopkins at its helm. "Boys…" proclaimed Harry Hopkins, "[w]e've got to get everything we want—a works program, social security, wages and hours, everything—now or never." This was no guarded Ickes program, and La Guardia expressed its generous spirit: "Will some of these billions be wasted? Sure. In such a gigantic undertaking there's bound to be a small percentage of waste. But I am sure that when the history of these trying times is written it will not begrudge one penny to aid the hungry and the jobless."[17]

The mayor would come to the capital on the Potomac, alone without any advisers, and drop in to discuss projects with Roosevelt. "Our Mayor is probably the most appealing person I know," Roosevelt once said. "He comes to Washington and tells me a sad story. The tears run down my cheeks and tears run down his cheeks and the first thing I know, he was wangled another fifty million dollars." While cabinet members were having trouble getting on the calendar, La Guardia would slip into Washington on short notice and in a half hour complete plans for yet another batch of projects. Together the protean mayor and his indulgent patron forged programs for a modern New York, worth hundreds of millions of dollars. "He has a confidential relationship with President Roosevelt enjoyed by no Democrat," wrote *Albany Times Union* political columnist John Heffernan. "The doors of the White House open at his radiant approach, and the President is never too busy to sit down and have a chat with him." Heffernan thought that it had something to do with Roosevelt's determination to destroy Tammany. But there was much more to this relationship, as Heffernan himself sensed: "New York's Mayor has boxed the political compass as capriciously as Franklin Roosevelt, who can be Right today, and Left tomorrow and when he's in the middle, boys, he's neither up nor down." Liberal pragmatists both, the president and the mayor respected each other.[18]

Trustworthy, articulate, loyal, and savvy, La Guardia also had the uncanny ability to take the heat off the president when a fresh program with a mind-boggling price tag came down the pike. After Roosevelt introduced his four billions-plus relief agenda in 1935, even before conservatives had a chance to express their anguish for the Republic and its free institutions, there came the chunky New Yorker bounding into Washington demanding more. Straightaway, the president's proposal appeared moderate by comparison. "The Mayor took his program to Washington to lay it before the President personally," reported the papers, regarding La Guardia's request for a cool $1 billion for his city. "It was understood here," stage-whispered one correspondent, that the administration welcomed the mayor's excessive proposals, which made their requests seem modest, considering the level of need.[19]

When the inevitable chorus of complaints rose to criticize this or that New Deal program, Washington's favorite rasp attacked the "fault-finders and whiners" who called on the government to keep out of the people's business as an excuse for ignoring the people's starvation. Fiorello went down South to respond to Pulitzer Prize-winning Robert E. Lee biographer Douglass Southall Freeman's charge that the New Deal was a threat to American liberties: "I admire the vision and courage of a Federal government that reaches out and gives succor to localities in time of dire need." "MAYOR DEFENDS NEW DEAL" ran the headlines.[20]

By May 1935 New York had rented a three-room D.C. flat for its peripatetic mayor, who flew into Washington for meetings with the president, Ickes, Hopkins, or Secretary of the Treasury Henry Morgenthau as often as twice a week (generally planning to return to his city hall office by afternoon), wisecracking to reporters that the District of Columbia was "no further than the Bronx," anyway.[21]

In the same month Roosevelt finally acknowledged that the cities deserved a significant voice in planning national economic recovery. He created a mayor's chair on the Allotment Advisory Committee that controlled public works allocations. To no one's surprise, the administration selected its favorite mayor for the committee. […]

Through his influence on the Allotment Advisory Committee, La Guardia also managed to steer one-fourth of all federal highway allocations toward the cities, even if the technical definition of "highway" had to be stretched to include avenues and parkways. Of the more than twenty members on the committee, La Guardia was the only one aside from the president to attend each of the twenty-two meetings. He had learned in his congressional days the value of doing the detailed drudge work. While others worked for the spotlight, he worked for results and often as not got them.

PWA grants had become expensive gift horses, paying outright for 30 percent of labor and material costs on approved projects while making the rest of the money available as loans at 4 percent interest. La Guardia, complaining that cities could not absorb such debt, persuaded President Roosevelt to change the formula to 45 percent outright gift and 55 percent loan, at 3 percent. Crowed La Guardia: For the "first time the conditions of cities have been considered by the Federal Government in any general plan for the whole country." Secretary of Treasury Morgenthau prodded the president to rescind the interest rate reduction, but La Guardia and the cities were becoming a formidable power in national councils. A few weeks later La Guardia was named to a special committee that awarded reductions in the rate of interest that Washington charged on loans.[22]

Recognizing La Guardia's special role, the cities also singled him out to lead them. For years, power had lagged behind demographics, as rural interests continued to dominate state legislatures and national congresses, while population flowed into the cities. The United States had changed from a nation of farms to one of cities, and spurred by the Depression, mayors from across the nation joined together in a national organization to articulate their needs and demand their fair share. In November of 1935 they selected New York's tart-tongued chief magistrate and the New Deal's favorite municipal officer as president of the U.S. Conference of Mayors, an office that he continued to hold for the next ten years. New York did not suffer for Fiorello's larger enthusiasms. Even before his municipal colleagues digested his confidential memos detailing new WPA programs, La Guardia was developing plans for more than $300 million in new projects for New York. By October 1935 New York had won 200,000 WPA job slots while other cities were still reading the fine print on the applications.

In leading the cities' fight for direct access to federal assistance without going through their states, La Guardia had the Conference of Mayors petition Harry Hopkins to create independent WPA units for the twenty-five largest cities on an equal level with the forty-eight state-directed operations. On June 26, 1936, Hopkins announced his decision. WPA would award the privilege of administering its own federal relief operation to only one of the twenty-five municipalities, La Guardia's New York. The Empire City would be treated as the "forty-ninth state." New York had won Hopkins's confidence by developing a wide range of WPA projects and administering them with integrity. The decision represented a personal victory for a tireless mayor who had developed the trust and power to place his city at the forefront of the emerging partnership between Washington and the cities.[23] [...]

In all of this, in taking the federal money and translating it into projects, in maintaining a good trusting relationship with Washington while insisting on his city's prerogatives, in setting a model and speaking for urban America, La Guardia proved nimble and adept. [...]

Cities were no longer as free and easy as before. Fastening upon his city a broad conception of municipal responsibility, La Guardia understood that the new lineaments of a large, salient, serious city government depended on federal assistance. And no other mayor harvested federal opportunities for fruitful cooperation with more persistence or imagination. Mastering what historian Henry Graff has called "the art of spending public money, before that skill became commonplace," the first La Guardia administration brought to New York City a list of grants, loans, and WPA projects that fills pages: the East River Drive, the Triborough, First Houses, Williamsburg Projects, Marine

Parkway, the Lincoln Tunnel, the Queens Midtown Tunnel, piers, public schools, libraries, hospitals, sewage disposal plants, prisons, Hunter and Brooklyn colleges, public baths, subway extensions, health centers, garbage treatment plants, water mains, boardwalks, swimming pools, beaches, zoos, health centers, parks, parkways, the Public Health Research Institute, huge indoor market areas, and miles and miles of repaved city streets. The city was rebuilt with a promise of even more to come. And behind all of these projects a plump man kept his feet on the pedals and pumped furiously, flooding the Great Dispenser in Washington with insistent demands for more and more. "I wish you would keep your shirt on," Harry Hopkins once shouted at the mayor in exasperation. "You and I can talk to each other without having snappy wires going back and forth."[24]

Just a couple of years back New Yorkers applied for relief by promising ward heelers that they would vote Democratic on election day. This relief offered narrow, private benefits, for Tammany and the lucky recipient, but the city was atrophying. Fiorello La Guardia seized the opportunity of the Depression unemployment crisis to transform construction from a private to a public enterprise and cities from neglected wards of the state to wards of a more bountiful federal government. At the start of his administration La Guardia had to beg for home rule from Albany to straighten out a $30 million budget crisis. Two years later he was negotiating directly with Washington for ten times that amount. The massive new works that he brought to New York supplied jobs, stimulated dormant industries, and enriched the public and private life of the region; they also symbolized the possibilities for a creative federal partnership in creating the modern city.

NOTES

1. Mark Gelfand, *A Nation of Cities: The Federal Government and Urban America, 1933–1965* (New York: Oxford University Press, 1975), 5–6, 22–23; Newbold Morris, *Let the Chips Fall: My Battles Against Corruption* (New York: Appleton-Century-Crofts, 1955), 97.

2. Gelfand, *A Nation of Cities*, 24, 54–55.

3. Howard Chudacoff, *Evolution of American Urban Society*, (Second edition, Englewood Cliffs, New Jersey: Prentice-Hall, 1981), 238; Arthur M. Schlesinger, Jr., *The Coming of the New Deal*, Vol. 2 of *The Age of Roosevelt* (Boston: Houghton Mifflin, 1957–1960), 264–265.

4. William E. Leuchtenburg, *Franklin D. Roosevelt and the New Deal* (New York: Harper & Row, 1963), 120; Chudacoff, *Evolution of American Urban Society*, 239; Edward R. Ellis, *Nation in Torment: The Great American Depression, 1929–1939* (New York: Coward McCann, 1970), 490.

5. Schlesinger, *Coming of the New Deal*, 268 (quote); *Times, American*, November 11, 1933; Joseph Verdicchio, "New Deal Work Relief and New York City: 1933–1938," (Ph.D. dissertation, New York University, 1980), 6–80; William A. Wallace to FHL, November 12, 1933, Box 2716, NYMA.

6. *Times*, November 29, 1933 (also editorial in *Times* of September 15, 1933, on New York City's past difficulties obtaining funds in Washington); FHL to Robert Moses, November 16, 1933, Moses Papers, NYPL; *The Secret Diary of Harold Ickes*, Vol. I (New York: Simon & Schuster, 1953), 126.

7. Gelfand, *A Nation of Cities*, 28; Adolf A. Berle, Jr., to FDR, January 9, 1934, FDR Library, Hyde Park.

8. *World-Telegram*, November 29, 1933; *Times*, November 30, 1933; Verdicchio, "New Deal and New York City," 107.

9. Barbara Blumberg, *The New Deal and the Unemployed: The View From New York City* (Lewisburg: Bucknell University Press, 1979), 32; Verdicchio, "New Deal and New York City," 104.

10. *Times*, February 1, 1934, quoted in Verdicchio, "New Deal and New York City," 115.

11. Roger Biles, *Big City Boss in Depression and War* (DeKalb: Northern Illinois University Press, 1984), 77; Charles Trout, *Boston: The Great Depression and the New Deal* (New York: Oxford University Press, 1977), 148–151; *Times*, April 21, 1936; Verdicchio, "New Deal and New York City," 115–117. See also Walter DeLamater to FHL, January 7, 1934, FHL to DeLamater, January 20, 27, 1934, Box 2626, NYMA.

12. Verdicchio, "New Deal and New York City," 159–161; FHL to Ickes, August 2, 1934, Box 2547, NYMA (on West Side Highway); *Times*, May 17, 20, November 18, 1934 (on other grants); Caro, *Power Broker*, 372.

13. *World-Telegram*, December 14, 1934.

14. *World-Telegram*, December 14, 1934; Caro, *Power Broker*, 372–374, 376–378.

15. Blumberg, *New Deal*, 38–39; FHL in United States Conference of Mayors, *Proceedings* (1935): 247.

16. Hopkins quoted in Blumberg, *New Deal*, 41; FHL quoted in Albany *Times-Union*, April 30, 1935.

17. *Times*, October 29, 1940; Albany *Times-Union*, June 28, 1935.

18. *Times*, February 12, 1935.

19. *Herald-Tribune*, July 20, 1935 (quotes); *Times*, July 21, 1935.

20. Heckscher, *La Guardia*, 83; *Times*, May 30, 1935; *American*, May 30, 1935.

21. United States Conference of Mayors, *Proceedings* (1935): 248; FDR to FHL, June 12, 1935, charges against FHL quoted in Salvatore A. Cotillo to FDR, July 1, 1935, both in Personal File 1376, FDRP-HP; FDR to FHL, June 10, 1935, FHL to FDR, June 12, 1935 (quote), both in Box 2573, NYMA; *Times*, June 1–3, July 2, 1935; Brooklyn *Eagle*, June 2, 1935; *News*, June 1, 1935.

22. Gelfand, *Nation of Cities*, 47–48 (quotes); United States Conference of Mayors, *Proceedings* (1935): 248; *Times*, May 8, 24, July 23, 1935.

23. *Sun*, November 20, 1935 (on Conference of Mayors); Blumberg, *New Deal*, 48–49.

24. S. J. Woolf, "Mayor Two Years and Still Optimistic," *New York Times Magazine* (January 5, 1936): 22; Henry Graff, "The Kind of Mayor La Guardia Was," *New York Times Magazine* (October 22, 1961): 46; Hopkins quoted in Auerbach, "La Guardia," 43.

Messiah Mayors and the Gospel of Urban Hype

John C. Teaford

Source: *The Rough Road to Renaissance: Urban Revitalization in America, 1940–1985* (Baltimore: Johns Hopkins University Press, 1990).

EDITORS' INTRODUCTION

The United States decennial census for 1940 revealed that, for the first time, the era of robust urban growth initiated during the nineteenth century had slowed to a trickle and, for many of America's largest cities, even come to an end. Rather than the double digit increases typically found with each census, the rate of urban population growth between 1930 and 1940 had slowed by roughly a third to just 8 percent across the entire nation. While the national rate of urbanization would improve in subsequent decades, it never approached the boom levels of the nineteenth century. In fact, after World War II, most major cities experienced a decentralization of population outward from the urban core to outlying peripheral areas, notably new suburban communities. As a result, cities entered a period of perceived decline and, in many cases, perceived physical decay or "blight" highlighted by sagging retail sales in the traditional central business district and a decreased tax base.[i]

The tactics used in the immediate post-war years for rebuilding cities differed from the massive public works programs of the 1930s New Deal. Civic and business leaders had to form partnerships, coming up with new and creative ways to revitalize cities and forge a new urban renaissance. Legislation like the Blighted Areas Redevelopment Act of 1947 and the Housing Act of 1949, which launched a nation-wide urban renewal program, paved the way for these possibilities. The United States government funded (in whole or in part) measures to tear down dilapidated multi-family housing in "overcrowded" neighborhoods, construct new high-rent apartments chock-full of the latest amenities, build new interstate highways, and finance the construction of new single-family homes outside of city limits. Two intriguing examples of these took place in St. Louis and Pittsburgh where upgrades to infrastructure and other physical features improved the overall environmental quality of life in and around these metropolitan areas. Despite these efforts, cities continued to experience decentralization, as witnessed by the growth and development of the suburbs, and the flight of white residents. Inner cities also experienced a variety of social and economic maladies, highlighted by race riots and deindustrialization during the 1960s and 1970s—all of which combined to form a so-called national "urban crisis." By the late 1970s, though, there were signs that downtowns might indeed be on the rebound.

The following essay by noted historian Jon Teaford provides the view of the urban renaissance of the mid-1970s through mid-1980s from city hall. Central to this revival were the bold actions and upbeat attitudes of dynamic, big-city mayors who, presented a public façade of confidence and a "can-do spirit" reminiscent of the attitude of New York City's Fiorello La Guardia during the Great Depression. While the reality and extent of the

---

i The term blight has a changing definition. Originally it was applied to any area seen as dilapidated, although in its contemporary usage the term often refers to a physical location in which real estate prices continue to devalue over time. The term "slum" is also often used in a myriad of ways. The legal definition has been employed to describe a broad array of neighborhood types. Middle-class neighborhoods of single-family homes have been legally declared "slums."

urban renaissance can be debated, these mayors certainly instilled a new sense of optimism in their citizens, inspired confidence, and once again made many people proud to live and/or work in large cities.

Jon C. Teaford is Professor Emeritus, Department of History at Purdue University. In addition to *The Rough Road to Renaissance*, he is the author of numerous books including *The American Suburb: The Basics* (New York: Routledge, 2007), *The Twentieth-Century American City: Problems, Promise, and Reality* (Baltimore: Johns Hopkins University Press, 1986), and *The Unheralded Triumph: City Government in America, 1870–1900* (Baltimore: Johns Hopkins University Press, 1983).

MESSIAH MAYORS AND THE GOSPEL OF URBAN HYPE

On August 26, 1976, Boston's Mayor Kevin White joined with entrepreneur James Rouse in opening the Rouse-developed Quincy Market, a festive collection of boutiques, gourmet groceries, trendy restaurants, and colorful pushcarts occupying the city's 150-year-old recycled public market. Located in the supposedly crime-ridden city core with insufficient parking facilities and no department-store anchor, the marketplace seemed to defy all conventional retailing wisdom. Neither White nor Rouse was confident of success, but when they arrived on opening day, more than fifty thousand customers were already on the scene to launch what one observer described as "a gigantic four-day party, with mimes and steel bands and dancing into the night."

The enthusiasm did not wane during the following months and years. In 1978 one national magazine claimed that at night the marketplace became "a huge, floating cocktail party for singles, suburbanites, and partying businessmen." By 1979 Quincy Market's promoters were boasting that it attracted more foot traffic than Disney World, and according to one Bostonian the marketplace was "Disney World with class," "a glittering rebuke to the notion that inner cities could not attract tourists and shoppers with their cameras, their appetites, and their money." On the tenth anniversary of the auspicious opening, the market's designer reminisced about the joyous event, proclaiming that "it was the day the urban renaissance began."[1]

Across the nation many commentators agreed with this assessment. A longtime veteran of the urban revitalization war with service in the Fight-Blight campaign and the Greater Baltimore Committee offensive, James Rouse himself was to become the guru of the festival marketplace, claiming that its appearance represented a turning point in the seemingly endless battle to revive the city. After decades of effort, Rouse perceived victory at hand. Though some were less enthusiastic than was the ebullient developer, the birth of the festival marketplace certainly marked the beginning of a fresh optimism about central cities. The emerging downtown real estate boom of the late 1970s and early 1980s lent further support to hopes for revival, and the gentrification of inner-city neighborhoods also seemed to offer proof that the cities were coming back. For Rouse and many like-minded urbanites the portents of recovery were increasingly clear. [...]

The age of doomsayers had passed, and everywhere urban boosters trumpeted the new positive message that central cities could be fun and profitable. Even signs of blight and social disorder could be repackaged in positive language favorable to the city. The vandalism of New York City's subways by spraycan-wielding youths was proclaimed "graffiti art," a blossoming of indigenous urban culture rather than a symptom of decay and lawlessness. [...]

No publicists or pollyannas, however, were more positive than were the new wave of big-city mayors. They preached a message of revival, and every new office tower, behemoth convention center, and lively Quincy Market represented a glittering incarnation of their words of redemption. Moreover, they were not reluctant to attribute the city's improved fortunes to their own leadership and political acumen. In fact, they were the messiahs of their own gospel of urban hype. Endlessly, they presented the same message: the cities were coming back, and they were the saviors responsible for this rebirth.

Even sober and often pessimistic scholars believed that the worst had passed. By the mid-1980s scholarly articles were appearing that asked "Where Has Urban Crisis Gone?" "Whatever Happened to the Urban Crisis?" and "What Urban Crisis?"[2] Though these commentators recognized that problems persisted, "crisis" no longer seemed an appropriate description for the state of urban America. The crisis was over, and many older central cities appeared to have stemmed their decline.

Thus after more than four decades of intensive debate over how to revive the faltering central city, the prevailing rhetoric was positive, and morale in the once-beleaguered hubs seemed to be high. Whether reality matched the rhetoric was another question that many mayors, journalists, and even some scholars chose to ignore. The evangelists of urban hype had declared victory, and at urban festivals and marketplaces throughout the nation's northeastern quadrant there was literally dancing in the streets.

The Mayors and Their Message

In 1985 political scientist Barbara Ferman published a study titled *Governing the Ungovernable City*.[3] It told of mayors who had overcome the barriers to effective urban leadership that had seemed so insuperable just a decade earlier. And it testified to the new spirit in city hall. In the late 1960s and early 1970s big-city mayors like John Lindsay had appeared to be at the mercy of the chaotic events of the time. They did not govern the city; they reacted to the myriad crises that wracked the metropolis. By the late 1970s and early 1980s, however, the messiah mayors did seem to be in control, confidently charting the urban course rather than being pushed helplessly to and fro. They easily won reelection, remained in the mayor's seat year after year, and effectively hobbled opposition. Their electoral successes

rested largely on their reputations as urban saviors. They had redeemed their cities from the fiscal doom of the mid-1970s and bolstered municipal credit ratings. They had created a more favorable business climate and thus had nurtured a new downtown building boom. Moreover, they had supposedly kept a lid on social disorder, and their cities had not suffered a recurrence of rioting. In other words, they could claim to have saved the central city from the endemic crises of the past, and they could count on the voters' gratitude.

Perhaps the most lauded of the messiah mayors was Baltimore's William Donald Schaefer. Thomas D'Alesandro III, Schaefer's immediate predecessor, had retired in exasperation in 1971 after only one frustrating term in the mayor's office. By contrast, Schaefer was to win four terms as mayor, survive fifteen years in that position, and would step down only to assume the higher office of Maryland governor. Though he was a white man in a predominantly black city, in the 1983 Democratic primary Schaefer was able to defeat his black mayoral opponent, outpolling him among voters of both races. Schaefer's foe had recruited Martin Luther King III and Atlanta's Mayor Andrew Young as well as other black leaders from throughout the country to campaign for him, but a majority of Baltimore's blacks seemed unimpressed. Speaking to over two thousand paying guests at a "Blacks for Schaefer" dinner, a former black mayoral candidate lauded the incumbent as a modern Joshua "bringing down the walls that separate people in Baltimore," and one seasoned observer reported that in the early 1980s "Schaefer had an approval rating of ninety percent throughout the city" with the figure "higher among blacks than among whites."[4] [...]

Schaefer's counterpart in New York City was Edward Koch. Elected the city's chief executive in 1977, by 1980 *New York* magazine was describing him as "the most popular mayor in memory."[5] The following year Koch won both the Democratic and Republican mayoral primaries, carrying more than 60 percent of the vote in each contest, and he went on to triumph in the general election with a 75 percent majority, the largest in modern New York history. Like Schaefer, Koch was a "character," about whom innumerable stories circulated. He was outspoken, often tactless, and unlike the Baltimore mayor he especially alienated black political leaders. Moreover, he suffered from a serious case of egomania. But just as Schaefer's life was Baltimore, Koch seemed to work unceasingly with an undeniable love for his city. And his quirks were appealing to an electorate satiated by the smooth charm of Lindsay and the colorless ineffectuality of Beame. According to *Time*, Koch was "New York's nut uncle, the bachelor workhorse with opinions on everything [and] who will not stop talking."[6]

Elsewhere the messiah mayors had less media appeal but were equally attractive to the voters. In 1977 Richard Caliguiri became mayor of Pittsburgh and launched Renaissance II. Another conciliatory, low-profile mayor was winning a reputation as the savior of beleaguered Cleveland. Campaigning with the slogan "Together we can do it," in 1979 George Voinovich defeated the controversial incumbent Dennis Kucinich, garnering a majority among both blacks and whites in the racially divided city.[7] Two years later he won reelection with a 77 percent majority, carrying all the city's wards. [...]

Detroit's perennial savior was the black mayor Coleman Young. First elected in 1973, Young won reelection in 1977, 1981, and 1985, capturing over 60 percent of the vote in the latter two contests.... Reflecting the success of Young's coalition building with the white business establishment, auto tycoon Henry Ford II proclaimed that without Young, "this city would be dead."[8]

Only one of the glamorous crusaders of the late 1960s was able to adapt to the new age and assume the trappings of a messiah mayor. A political chameleon par excellence, Boston's Mayor Kevin White fashioned a new image for himself in the second half of the 1970s. No longer Boston's Lindsay, he was now that city's Koch, an unbeatable mayor who could cope with financial emergencies and father such monuments of revival as Quincy Market. His arrogance offended some Bostonians, and one city council member complained, "Kevin thinks he's the one true God."[9] But after his fourth victory in 1979 the *Boston Globe* correctly identified the longtime mayor as "one of the most powerful in Boston's history."[10]

Less sympathetic observers labeled the perennial Boston mayor a "boss" and attacked his efforts to build a personal machine. After his reelection in 1975, White established a permanent campaign organization with precinct captains and ward coordinators who between elections were expected to identify and answer neighborhood complaints. On election day, however, they were to make sure that the voters turned out for the mayor. As a reward, the White administration granted these lieutenants city jobs and promotions. Though it was a personal organization dedicated to one man rather than to a party, White's arrangement was a throwback to the machine politics of an earlier era.[11] In 1979 White's mayoral opponent tried to capitalize on this, using the slogan "We can Beat the White Machine" and calling for a "change from the politics of fear and spoils to the politics of access and openness."[12] But White defended his attempt to restore the power of urban political leaders. "Since 1970," the mayor argued, "there's been an unstructured assault on the political profession's right to govern, to lead. Until we recapture a very diffuse political process, nobody can do anything!" According to the embattled chief executive, "When I'm faced with this kind of situation, you bet your life I'm going to pull together all the scraps of power I can assemble."[13] [...]

In Boston, Mayor Kevin White confronted persistent budget problems, yet he kept the city from bankruptcy. Exacerbating White's budget woes was passage of a statewide tax limitation, Proposition 2½, in November 1980. Massachusetts voters mandated that local property taxes could not exceed 2.5 percent of the fair market value, a restriction that could mean the loss of 75 percent of Boston's property tax revenues. Within a month after the proposition's passage, Standard and Poor's, the bond-rating firm, lowered Boston's credit rating because the tax ceiling might have "a severe impact on the city and the quality of life" there. The glum city treasurer admitted, "If I was in their shoes, I might have done the same thing."[14] At the same time, Mayor White's ten-member committee charged with examining possible budget cuts submitted its report proposing a 25 percent reduction in police and fire budgets, a 50 percent drop in the allocation for hospitals and health, and the slashing of 60 percent from park and recreation funds.[15] White proceeded to lay off unprecedented numbers of municipal employees, but fortunately direct financial aid from the state increased markedly. Moreover, the city sold its convention center to the state, adding $40 million to the municipal account and saving Boston taxpayers from the necessity of alone having to shoulder the center's deficits.[16] Throughout the remaining White years, the budget crunch continued to be front-page news, but as in Detroit the mayor was able to salvage his city by taking tough measures. [...]

By the early 1980s the older central cities were not suddenly basking in good fortune, but through a policy of fiscal restraint the messiah mayors were coaxing some kind words from credit-rating agencies and wary bankers. The mayors' gospel was one of sacrifice and austerity, not of expanded services or a bountiful, benevolent public sector. They fashioned fiscal survival through layoffs, tax hikes, privatization, and divestment of functions to the state or to joint city-suburban authorities. Repeatedly they told the city electorate that the citizenry had to pay more and to get less in return. And the chastened voters generally seemed to buy this message. Achieving this popular tolerance for a policy of higher taxes and fewer police was probably the messiah mayors' most miraculous accomplishment.

Yet the mayors' message was not only one of deprivation and self-denial. Sweetening their rhetoric was a heavy strain of ballyhoo about the long-awaited arrival of the central-city renaissance, a rebirth that supposedly would soon fatten starved budgets and relieve residents of some of their tax burden. Aiding the mayors in realizing this dream was the federal government's Urban Development Action Grant Program (UDAG). Initiated in 1978, UDAG offered distressed central cities money to stimulate economic development. Moreover, the program was highly flexible, allowing municipalities to use the grants in virtually any manner so long as they nurtured private investment that created new jobs and taxes. Though overall federal funding was declining, this relatively unencumbered grant of cash was just what the mayors wanted. Now the public sector could enter into partnerships with private developers and leverage billions of dollars of needed investment. The city could, for example, use the money to provide public infrastructure improvements to facilitate private construction projects, and it could subsidize interest payments on loans or offer direct subsidies to developers. With such financial lures older central cities might well attract new development dollars.[17] [...]

Any signs of retail life downtown fueled the hype of messiah mayors and their ilk. Especially encouraging were the new shopping malls and festival marketplaces that arose in some central business districts during the late 1970s and early 1980s. In 1976 Boston's Quincy Market led the way, but other well-publicized signals of retail revitalization soon appeared elsewhere. For example, in August 1977 Quincy Market's developer, James Rouse, opened his Gallery at Market East in Philadelphia. A four-level enclosed shopping mall with 125 stores and restaurants as well as an 850-car garage, it was a clone of the latest in suburban retailing. As its public relations director observed, "It's like a suburban mall in an urban area, but it also has some good food."[18] Yet according to the city's press office, the Gallery was a symbol of "the New Philadelphia, a Philadelphia that is vibrant and progressive." And at its opening the mayor claimed that the Gallery "reestablishe[d] Market Street East as the most vital downtown shopping area in the United States."[19]

What firmly secured James Rouse's title as the savior of downtown retailing, however, was the inauguration of Baltimore's Harborplace in 1980. Part of Mayor Schaefer's Inner Harbor project to revitalize an area of rotting wharves and warehouses, Harborplace applied the Quincy Market formula with enormous success. According to police estimates, four hundred thousand people jammed the Inner Harbor area on the marketplace's opening day, and during the next year, its forty-five specialty shops, twenty food markets, and thirty-seven restaurants served eighteen million visitors, more than the total number attracted to Walt Disney World, and its sales were more than twice those of a typical regional mall. Moreover, it seemed to realize Rouse's goal for the inner city, making it "a warm and human place, with diversity of choice, full of festival and delight."[20]

Especially blessed was Saint Louis, for it was soon to enjoy a double boost to its downtown retailing, acquiring both a Rouse-developed festival marketplace in the mold of Harborplace and a downtown shopping mall reminiscent of suburbia and Philadelphia's Gallery. Early in August 1985, St. Louis Centre opened with four levels of two hundred shops anchored on either end by the city's major department stores. After only three weeks of business, a sales clerk in the mall expressed the prevailing euphoria in Schoemehl's Saint Louis when he observed: "For years we've been hearing about what a dead city this is, and now, suddenly, it's had new life breathed back into it."[21] Meanwhile, that same month Rouse's Union Station welcomed its first customers, appealing to the shoppers' nostalgia for the railroad just as Harborplace cashed in on the romance of Baltimore's bygone seafaring tradition. Within the mammoth headhouse and train shed of Saint Louis's ninety-year-old rail depot, Rouse carved out space for eighty shops, twenty-two restaurants, and a 550-room hotel. "This is a remarkable structure and place that people really have a deep affection for," rhapsodized a member of the Schoemehl administration. But he continued on a more practical note: "Having it come back to life means an immense amount of economic activity that simply would not have happened otherwise."[22]

Harborplace and Quincy Market were especially welcome to the messiah mayors, for these popular attractions fit into the city leaders' long-term goal of boasting tourism and convention business. Repeatedly, economic development experts spoke of the postindustrial economy and the growth of the service sector. In other words, the future of urban America was not in factories but in service, and one of the service industries most pregnant with possibilities was tourism. Unlike the steel mills and hog-butchering establishments, it was a clean industry without environmental drawbacks. In fact, tourism and convention goers meant glittering hotels, posh restaurants, and an aura of fun and excitement to counter the long-standing grim images of the older hubs. If the messiah mayors wished to repackage their domains in glitzy new wrappings, tourism and the convention trade would provide the necessary materials. Moreover, the hospitality industry employed large numbers of unskilled workers, something the older central cities had in abundance. In one city after another, then, festival marketplaces, convention centers, and hotels were all ingredients of a new formula for revitalization success. Older cities could come back if they became exciting magnets for the tourist dollar. [...]

No mayor proved more successful at drawing new tourists to his town than did Baltimore's William Schaefer. His Inner Harbor project included the oldest American warship, a science museum, and the National Aquarium as well as Harborplace. Opened in 1981, the National Aquarium attracted four million visitors during its first three years, offering such tourist delights as a shark tank, a tropical rain forest with thirty species of fish and almost one hundred colorful tropical birds, as well as an outdoor seal pool. And to publicize the aquarium, the irrepressible Mayor Schaefer donned a bathing suit and with appropriate ceremony dove into the seal tank.[23]

The Schaefer administration adopted a conscious policy of creating "animation" in the city, organizing a constant round of ethnic festivals, farmers' markets, concerts, street performers, and children's programs. To stir excitement during one promotion campaign, it even painted the curbs pink.

The head of the city's Office of Promotion and Tourism said that the festivities were intended to make Baltimoreans "begin to feel good about themselves, so that then they would feel good about their city." Moreover, she boasted, "Everything we do is called 'common denominator entertainment'—things that will bring people together and not pull them apart."[24] Through this policy of perpetual circuses, Baltimore's messiah mayor thus hoped to patch over the divisions within the city and boost spirits depressed by the decades of decline. Further, if Baltimoreans felt good about their city, so would outsiders, thereby bringing additional profits to the city's cash registers.

Throughout the Northeast and Midwest, mayors and urban boosters were pursuing the Baltimore philosophy. In the postindustrial city, anything and everything must be done to draw outside dollars. Unlike in the early twentieth century, excellent port facilities or ready access to supplies of iron ore and coal were no longer sufficient for urban success. Now Coleman Young, mayor of America's once-supreme industrial giant, was advocating casino gambling as a substitute for the fortunes that Chrysler, General Motors, and Ford had formerly generated. Answering critics of the idea, Young observed, "I don't believe that any enterprise that offers the prospect of 50,000 jobs can be cavalierly dismissed."[25] If roulette wheels could boost beleaguered Detroit, then the city should permit them. And if diving into seal pools and painting curbs pink worked, then why not dive and paint?

Though downtown was the showpiece of any renaissance city of the late 1970s and the 1980s, urban boosters could also identify encouraging signs in some of the core residential neighborhoods. In fact, gentrifying districts in a number of cities seemed to provide strong evidence that the tide had turned and the urban comeback was genuine. Especially in New York City, a tight housing market sent upper-middle-income urbanites scurrying for homes in neighborhoods that they would not have dared visit a decade earlier. A wave of so-called yuppies engulfed Manhattan's Upper West Side in the late 1970s and the 1980s,

turning former slums into prime real estate. In 1976 a middle-class couple bought an Upper West Side brownstone for $65,000. "This block was a hellhole," according to the wife, "it was terrible to walk down the street." Eight years later the brownstone was worth $400,000 and was within a stone's throw of an ample supply of gourmet delicatessens and trendy boutiques.[26]

With housing costs soaring in Manhattan, Brooklyn also acquired a new allure. The Park Slope neighborhood welcomed chic migrants from the overcrowded island across the East River. In 1986 one Brooklyn resident observed, "When you see Bloomingdale's head-to-toe going to the park, then you know Park Slope is changing."[27] Meanwhile, the Greenpoint section of Brooklyn seemed to be taking off as well, becoming the possible site for a real estate binge. "In Greenpoint certain blocks have gone nuts," a resident exclaimed in 1986. "One house in this neighborhood just sold for $250,000."[28] [...]

Yet messiah mayors and city functionaries also had to deal with residential districts less attractive to yuppies and gentrifying restorationists. In the early 1970s a proliferation of feisty neighborhood organizations had forced municipal officials to take notice of their demands, and in order for the Caliguiris, Schaefers, and Voinovichs to achieve some semblance of harmony and perpetuate their long reigns in city hall, they had to recognize these neighborhoods and tout them almost as loudly as the central business district. Critics of the messiah mayors complained of their downtown orientation, writing of the "corporate center strategy" that dominated renaissance efforts.[29] But the popular executives of the 1980s were generally too smart politically to fall prey to downtown tunnel vision. A Cincinnati city councilman expressed the political reality facing many urban leaders when he observed: "Politicians in this town don't want to be accused of being anti-neighborhood, so you keep groups quiet by feeding them dollars."[30] Revitalized neighborhoods had to be part of the new message of salvation; voters demanded it. Thus messiah mayors included some neighborhood programs in their packages of revitalization initiatives, though their professions of faith in the neighborhood gospel were perhaps less sincere than their gung ho preaching on the rebirth of downtown.

The central-city economy of the mid-1980s was generally better than it had been in the mid-1970s, but compared with suburbia or the nation as a whole, even the most prosperous of the older central cities seemed sluggish at best. Moreover, the central-city office construction boom of the 1980s was no greater than that of the late 1960s and early 1970s. At the close of the 1980s no soaring giants had topped such creations of the early 1970s as Chicago's Sears Tower or New York City's World Trade Center. Instead, the 1980s office construction bonanza could be seen as a continuation of an office boom that had been in progress since the late 1950s and had suffered only a momentary interruption in the mid-1970s. If new office towers and an expanding business and professional service sector were symptoms of urban rebirth, then the gestation period for this new life had begun at least a quarter of a century earlier.

But the office sector was not the only sign of economic hope for the central city. The much-publicized growth in tourism and convention business and the accompanying boom in hotel construction also signaled revitalization. In Boston more than 4,000 new hotel rooms opened for visitors between 1980 and 1985, more than the total constructed during the entire half century from 1930 to 1980. Moreover, Boston's hotel employment soared 109 percent between 1976 and 1985.[31] In downtown Baltimore the number of available hotel rooms tripled between 1980 and 1986 as did the figures for tourist visits and expenditures.[32] Unknown to convention goers prior to 1980, Baltimore was capturing an increasing share of the meeting business, and the Saint Louis "Meeting Place" campaign also seemed to be placing the Missouri metropolis on the convention map. With newly fashioned "fun" images, former models of dullness and despair like Baltimore and Saint Louis were reaping financial rewards.

But for every older central city winning in the convention game, there was a loser. For example, tourism and convention business was not fueling a rebirth in Philadelphia; instead, the hotel business in the City of Brotherly Love was as dismal as ever. In 1985 downtown Philadelphia had 6,200 hotel rooms compared with 6,300 a decade earlier. Despite charging the lowest room prices in the Northeast, the occupancy rate in 1985 dropped below 55 percent, the worst in the Boston-Washington megalopolis. Between July 1, 1984, and June 30, 1985, the fifteen major downtown hotels lost a total of $36.5 million, leading the *Philadelphia Inquirer* to pronounce the local lodging industry "desperately ill."[33] [...]

By the late 1980s it was apparent to any objective observer that America's older central cities had not yet triumphed wholly over the forces of blight and decentralization that they had been battling for five decades. Flashy new skylines proved that central-city downtowns had not died as the founders of the Urban Land Institute had feared they would. There were millions of feet of additional office space in the central business districts, and millions of workers congregated there each weekday. But in most of the older hubs suburban shoppers were a relatively rare sight, and the first-run movie houses had long before switched off their marquee lights. Some film palaces survived as performing arts centers, but most were gone as was much of the downtown nightlife. The function of the central business district had narrowed. In the 1980s it was the center of business and professional services and finance, but no longer the hub of shopping or amusement.

Moreover, beyond the central business districts, vacant lots and abandoned buildings were constant reminders of the scars inflicted by persistent blight and decentralization. Some neighborhoods were gentrified, but these were, in the words of one urban expert, "islands of renewal in seas of decay."[34] A number of residential areas had survived the preceding half century relatively unscathed, and others seemed to be sprouting new life after the long battle against decline. Yet no city lacked its wastelands that lent credence to the worst fears of those who had warned of urban decay decades before. A visitor to these no-man's-lands could only conclude that America's cities had taken a wrong turn along the road to renaissance and become irretrievably lost.

Yet, if nothing else, the messiah mayors had boosted the spirits of many urban dwellers and made them proud of their cities. They had also rehabilitated the bleak images of the older cities and convinced many Americans that places like Baltimore were fun and cities like Pittsburgh were highly livable. Further, the messiah mayors had seemingly overcome some of the political problems that had undermined the efforts of earlier executives. They had fashioned enough of an urban consensus to keep themselves in power year after year and had made the formerly ungovernable cities governable. Whereas the disruption of traditional political patterns had made the road to renaissance rougher for earlier mayors, the Kochs, Schaefers, and Youngs filled some of the dangerous potholes and eliminated some of the obstacles in the way of revitalization. These messiahs may not have worked as many miracles as they claimed, but they were generally adept enough at political sleight-of-hand to keep up the illusion of success.

NOTES

1. Benjamin Thompson, "Making a Marketplace," *Boston Magazine* 78 (August 1986): 111; Gurney Breckenfeld, "Jim Rouse Shows How to Give Downtown Retailing New Life," *Fortune* 97 (10 April 1978): 90; and Michael Ryan, "Boston Learns to Love the Great American Marketplace," *Boston Magazine* 71 (April 1979): 120, 124. See also Morton S. Stark, "Mixed-Use and 'Theme' Centers," *Stores* 62 (April 1980): 50–52; and Michael Demarest, "He Digs Downtown," *Time* 118 (24 August 1981): 42, 44–48, 53.

2. Alexander Ganz, "Where Has the Urban Crisis Gone? How Boston and Other Large Cities Have Stemmed Economic Decline," *Urban Affairs Quarterly* 20 (June 1985): 449–68; M. Gottdiener, "Whatever Happened to the Urban Crisis?" ibid. 20 (June 1985): 421–27; and Eric Monkkonen, "What Urban Crisis? A Historian's Point of View," ibid. 20 (June 1985): 429–47.

3. Barbara Ferman, *Governing the Ungovernable City: Political Skill, Leadership, and the Modern Mayor* (Philadelphia: Temple University Press, 1985).

4. *Baltimore Sun*, 7 July 1983, p. D12; and Kevin O'Keeffe, *Baltimore Politics, 1971–1986: The Schaefer Years and the Struggle for Succession* (Washington, D.C.: Georgetown University Press, 1986), p. 94.

5. Rinker Buck, "How Am I Doing? An In-Depth Look at Mayor Koch's Record," *New York* 13 (8 September 1980): 18.

6. Roger Rosenblatt, "A Mayor for All Seasons," *Time* 117 (15 June 1981): 24.

7. *Cleveland Plain Dealer*, 7 November 1979, p. 15A. See also ibid., 1 November 1979, pp. 1A, 6A; 2 November 1979, pp. 1A, 18A, 34A; 4 November 1979, pp. 1A, 22A; 5 November 1979, pp. 1A, 14A, 29A–30A; 7 November 1979, pp. 1A, 14A; and 8 November 1979, p. 4C; and Todd Swanstrom, *The Crisis of Growth Politics: Cleveland, Kucinich, and the Challenge of Urban Populism* (Philadelphia: Temple University Press, 1985), pp. 210–24.

8. "Copious Coping," *Time*, p. 30.

9. Howie Carr, "Kevin versus the Council: Case History of a Feud," *Boston Magazine* 72 (December 1980): 98.

10. *Boston Globe*, 7 November 1979, p. 1.

11. Ferman, *Governing the Ungovernable City*, pp. 92–95.

12. *Boston Globe*, 3 November 1979, p. 1; and 7 November 1979, p. 22.

13. Ferman, *Governing the Ungovernable City*, p. 92.

14. *Boston Globe*, 3 December 1980, p. 21.

15. Ibid., 4 December 1980, pp. 1, 40.

16. Richard P. Nathan, Fred C. Doolittle, and Associates, *The Consequences of Cuts: The Effects of the Reagan Domestic Program on State and Local Governments* (Princeton, N.J.: Princeton Urban and Regional Research Center, 1983), pp. 133–35; Mary John Miller, J. Chester Johnson, and George E. Peterson, *The Future of Boston's Capital Plant* (Washington, D.C.: Urban Institute Press, 1981), p. 5; and John Strahinich and J. William Semich, "The Money Pit," *Boston Magazine* 78 (September 1986): 154, 157.

17. J. Thomas Black, Allan Borut, Robert M. Byrne, and Michael J. Morina, *UDAG Partnerships: Nine Case Studies* (Washington, D.C.: Urban Land Institute, 1980), pp. 100–108.

18. *Philadelphia Evening Bulletin*, 11 August 1977, p. 52.

19. Ibid., 12 August 1977, p. 50. See also ibid., 7 August 1977, p. 26; ibid., 11 August 1977, p. 20; Jurgen F. Haver, "Philadelphia Story—Ongoing Renewal," *Stores* 62 (April 1980): 53–57; Morton S. Stark, "Shopping Center Futures—Tide Turning?" ibid. 62 (March 1980): 20; and *New York Times* 25 March 1978, pp. 25–26.

20. Demarest, "He Digs Downtown," p. 42. For further accounts of Harborplace, see Douglas M.

Wrenn, *Urban Waterfront Development* (Washington, D.C.: Urban Land Institute, 1983), pp. 152–55; McNulty et al., *Return of the Livable City*, pp. 23–33; Harold R. Snedcof, *Cultural Facilities in Mixed-Use Development* (Washington, D.C.: Urban Land Institute, 1985), pp. 243–45; Joseph D. Steller, Jr., "An MXD Takes Off: Baltimore's Inner Harbor," *Urban Land* 41 (March 1982): 14–15; "A New Market Complex with the Vitality of an Old Landmark: Harborplace in Baltimore," *Architectural Record* 168 (October 1980): 100–105; David A. Wallace, "An Insider's Story of the Inner Harbor," *Planning* 45 (September 1979): 20–24; and Jacques Kelly, "The Master Builders," *Baltimore Magazine* 78 (June 1985): 90–103, 167.

21. *St. Louis Post-Dispatch*, 26 August 1985, p. 3A. See also Jacquelyn Bivens, "Full Steam Ahead in Saint Louis," *Chain Store Age Executive* 59 (May 1983): 80, 85, 87–90.

22. *St. Louis Post-Dispatch*, 29 August 1985, p. 7F. See also ibid., pp. 1F-6F; ibid., 30 August 1985, pp. 1A, 18A-19A; ibid., 10 January 1988, pp. 11–21; Edmund Faltermayer, "How Saint Louis Turned Less into More," *Fortune* 112 (23 December 1985): 44–46, 50, 54, 58; "Spirit of Saint Louis," *Progressive Architecture* 66 (November 1985): 84–93; and Charlene Prost, "Comeback City," *Planning* 51 (October 1985): 4–10.

23. Todd Englander, "Big-League Mayors Who Pitch for Their Cities," *Meetings and Conventions* 21 (May 1986): 52; and *Baltimore Wow!* (Baltimore: City of Baltimore, 1984), pp. 35–36.

24. Sandra Hillman, "Leveraging Prosperity in Baltimore," in Green, *City as Stage*, p. 98; and McNulty et al., *Return of the Livable City*, pp. 31–32.

25. *Detroit Free Press*, 13 February 1988, p. 7A. For a similar proposal for Cincinnati, see *Cincinnati Enquirer*, 8 November 1979, p. C1.

26. Amy Singer, "When Worlds Collide," *Historic Preservation* 36 (August 1984): 32.

27. Jane Peterson, "Anguish and Joy in a Changing Neighborhood," ibid. 35 (July–August 1983), p. 26.

28. Linda Greider, "Secrets of Great Old Neighborhoods," ibid. 38 (February 1986): 29. See also *New York Times*, 13 September 1987, sec. 12, pp. 4–7.

29. See, for example, Marc V. Levine, "Downtown Redevelopment as an Urban Growth Strategy: A Critical Appraisal of the Baltimore Renaissance," *Journal of Urban Affairs* 9, no. 2 (1987): 103–23; Joe R. Feagin, "The Corporate Center Strategy," *Urban Affairs Quarterly* 21 (June 1986): 617–28; and Richard Child Hill, "Crisis in the Motor City: The Politics of Economic Development in Detroit," in Susan S. Fainstein, Norman I. Fainstein, Richard Child Hill, Dennis R. Judd, and Michael Peter Smith, eds., *Restructuring the City: The Political Economy of Urban Redevelopment* (New York: Longman, 1983), pp. 80–125.

30. Susan Morse, "Neighborhood Spirit Shapes a City," *Historic Preservation* 40 (July–August 1988): 27.

31. Rachelle L. Levitt, ed., *Cities Reborn* (Washington D.C.: Urban Land Institute, 1987), pp. 18, 21.

32. Levine, "Downtown Redevelopment," p. 109.

33. Gregory R. Barnes, "Philly Hotels Face Survival Struggle," *Hotel and Motel Management* 201 (13 January 1986): 3, 48.

34. Brian J. L. Berry, "Islands of Renewal in Seas of Decay," in Paul E. Peterson, ed., *The New Urban Reality* (Washington, D.C.: Brookings Institution, 1985), p. 69.

The Katrina Conspiracies: The Problem of Trust in Rebuilding an American City

Arnold R. Hirsch and A. Lee Levert

Source: *Journal of Urban History*, 35(2) (January 2009): 207–219.

EDITORS' INTRODUCTION

In August and September 2005, Hurricanes Katrina and Rita wreaked havoc in communities situated along the Gulf of Mexico from Florida all the way to Texas. In terms of property damage, Hurricane Katrina, which made landfall twice, once in Florida and the second time in southeastern Louisiana and Mississippi, was the most expensive hurricane to hit the United States. Katrina was arguably the largest and most widespread disaster in American history. Approximately 2,000 people in seven states died from the storm, and over a million more relocated to temporary evacuation shelters, or longer-term residential quarters, located in all fifty states, the District of Columbia, and Puerto Rico. Many of these people have never returned. Four weeks after Katrina, Hurricane Rita made landfall in Louisiana and Texas, hampering recovery efforts already underway, creating more property damage, and contributing to the deaths of over 100 people in four states.

The focal point of hurricane destruction for most people in the United States was the city of New Orleans, also known as the "Crescent City," given its location on a bend of the Mississippi River. At first, it seemed as though Katrina's devastating winds and tidal surge, which leveled structures along the Mississippi coast, had spared New Orleans and its almost 500,000 residents. However, shortly after Katrina hit, the levee system failed, and water from Lake Pontchartrain submerged 80 percent of the city. Despite the first mandatory evacuation in the Crescent City's history, thousands of residents did not have the resources to leave, or remained by choice. As the floodwaters rose, their situation quickly deteriorated. Media outlets began to report on the dire condition of those in the Louisiana Superdome, set up as a last-resort emergency center, and the Ernest N. Morial Convention Center, which began as an unofficial shelter. Dramatic coverage also focused on the thousand of residents trapped in their homes seeking sanctuary from floodwaters on rooftops or elevated spans of highway. Stories, exaggerated or otherwise, of violence, looting, and property damage also dominated media coverage of New Orleans, feeding off and reinforcing old stereotypes about race, poverty, and urban behaviors. As such, New Orleans became the focus of an intense national debate over disaster relief and recovery, and to no small degree, over whom to blame for the suffering of so many people. Finger pointing ran the gamut from faulting the victims themselves for not leaving the city in time to blaming the political leadership of Mayor C. Ray Nagin, Louisiana Governor Kathleen Blanco, and President George W. Bush, especially after the latter praised Federal Emergency Management Agency (FEMA) Director Michael Brown for doing "a heck of job" with recovery efforts. **[See Document 5.8 "President Arrives in Alabama, Briefed on Hurricane Katrina (2005)."]**

Rebuilding efforts have been no less controversial. While some argued that it is foolish to reconstruct a city situated largely below sea level, the overwhelming majority of people across the country agreed with government officials and civic leaders who vowed to bring New Orleans back and make it better than ever. However, the scale of recovery and the city's long and complex history of race relations fueled skepticism over planning and public–private cooperation to rebuild the city. The following essay by Arnold Hirsch and A. Lee Levert explores how the historic lack of trust between blacks and whites in New Orleans generated rumors of intentional levee destruction and shaped explanations for the slow pace of relief. As Hirsch and Levert argue, old patterns of thought and behavior inadequately prepared people to address the unprecedented destruction of the city. Pre-Katrina fears of exclusion and race domination also shaped post-Katrina political elections and attitudes toward the rebuilding process.

Arnold R. Hirsch is the Ethel and Herman L. Midlo Professor for New Orleans Studies and University Research Professor in the department of history at the University of New Orleans. Hirsch has written articles on a variety of urban topics and served as the co-editor and contributor to *Creole New Orleans: Race and Americanization* (Baton Rouge: Louisiana State University Press, 1992) and *Urban Policy in Twentieth-Century America* (New Brunswick: Rutgers University Press, 1993). A. Lee Levert is an independent scholar who has published a variety of articles on Louisiana history and culture. She holds a J.D. and an M.A. in history and has worked at the Louisiana State Museum, the Historic New Orleans Collection, and, currently, at the Loyola University New Orleans Archives.

The devastation wrought by Hurricane Katrina across the North American Gulf Coast left a stunned nation groping for explanations. Few—very few—went so far as the Idaho weatherman who pointed an accusatory finger at the Japanese mafia (Yakuza) for its use of an electromagnetic generator devised by the old Soviet Union "to create and control storms." A theory that unilaterally repealed the "second law of thermodynamics," while arguing that the inundation of New Orleans was payback for the incineration of Hiroshima sixty years before, did not find a wealth of believers.[1]

There were other theories and theorists, of course, of greater but still variable credibility. Crossing the political spectrum from the wacky Left to the radical Right, people offered, exchanged, and accepted tales of perfidy and betrayal on a scale that could scarcely be imagined.

African Americans heard from Nation of Islam leader Louis Farrakhan, for example, who emerged from a meeting with New Orleans mayor C. Ray Nagin demanding an investigation into alleged links between the Bush administration and a suspected plot to sabotage the levees. If established, such links would permit Farrakhan to press charges of mass murder.

Emanating from multiple sources, allegations that the levees had been deliberately breached to flood poor black areas and spare well-to-do white ones gained wide cur-

rency. Interviews with Katrina's refugees, both on the nightly news and in authoritative documentary films, reinforced such charges with conviction and belief. Eye- and earwitnesses seemingly confirmed the presence of strange figures scurrying about the levees in the hours between Katrina's passing and the flooding of the Lower Ninth Ward. Even more heard at least one explosion. That the "big bang," it appears, came from a runaway barge that crashed into—and destroyed what remained—of the Industrial Canal levee still failed to sway locals from their belief in sabotage. One unidentified resident stated the case plainly: "They had a bomb. They bombed that sucker."[2]

Given the certainty of conviction, motives seemed self-evident. Whites, having only recently "lost" control of the city demographically and politically, seemed poised to "take over" once more. Dutch Morial had been elected the city's first black mayor in 1978; no white candidate had won that office since.[3] Black voting majorities had also recently (1985) produced a black majority on the City Council and, at least, the hope of a more responsive government. Complicating matters, elections for all of these offices loomed on the horizon just a few months away. With the forced, near total evacuation of the city, questions arose quickly as to the size, character, and mood of the electorate that would (or could) take part in the contest. Talk of a "whitening" of the city subsequently became election fodder for both groups.[4]

The perceived motives for the opportunistic breakup of black New Orleans extended beyond the political realm as well. Suspicions in the community ran to real estate interests and developers who coveted black-occupied land. Moreover, those seeking to gentrify the city at black expense were accompanied by the persistence, many African Americans believed, of the sort mindless racism that simply wished to do them harm.

The significance of such conjecture lay not in the truth of the allegations but in their plausibility and acceptance, no matter how outlandish. It was also much more than a matter of laying blame or seeking "causes" for the magnitude of Katrina's horror. Whether fantasy or common sense, the conclusions drawn regarding the course of destruction that accompanied the storm were both rooted in history and determinative of the direction that recovery and reform would take. More than that, they compromised the chances for success as well. The utter lack of trust, and the inability to deal in good faith across racial lines, would short-circuit those attempts at reconstruction that challenged racial verities. Old patterns of thought and behavior—on the part of both blacks and whites—were simply inadequate to address the unprecedented situation in the Crescent City, and yet they preempted any new departures.

The opportunity to start over provides a chance to do better. What would the new New Orleans be like? Any attempt to answer that question requires, first of all, an appreciation for the enormity and complexity of the problems involved. Eighty percent of the city of New Orleans was under water after Lake Pontchartrain emptied into it, nearly 2,000 people had died (as best we can tell today), and its political, civic, and economic structures had virtually disappeared.[5] It had reverted almost to a state of nature—or at least as close to one as we are ever likely to see. Given the city's dysfunctional economic and political structures, its poverty and dearth of resources, it is hard to imagine any people asked to do more with less.

One need only make the comparison to another era of urban revitalization to see that the unprecedented scale and nature of the Katrina catastrophe is not well understood. The nation's flirtation with urban renewal in the 1950s and 1960s witnessed the development of projects and plans that were years in the making. Renewal cut a large swath through densely settled urban land, cost millions of dollars, called for the displacement and resettlement of thousands, and finally, had to confront the race issue in virtually every neighborhood it touched.[6]

In contrast, Katrina almost literally wiped the entire city of New Orleans off the map. There was no targeted selection of needy neighborhoods in New Orleans; there was, instead, the submersion of 80 percent of the city for a period of several weeks. The job facing post-Katrina New Orleanians did not involve rehabilitation or renovation as much as it demanded a total reconstruction. The city's weak-kneed economy simply disappeared. Its politics (ineffectual, corrupt, and racially polarized) served the city as a cement life jacket, permitting not even a gulp of fresh air before submerging it in a toxic brew of problems for which it offered few solutions and less hope.[7]

Where urban renewal tried to build upon strengths and expand healthy areas, the recovery of post-Katrina New Orleans involved repopulating and rebuilding virtually the entire city. Even those neighborhoods that escaped relatively unscathed had the lives and daily routines of their residents deeply impacted. The physical resurrection of the Crescent City thus also had to be far more than a bricks-and-mortar program. Not only did the social revivification of the city involve reuniting families over a period of weeks, months, and yes, now years, but those who returned relatively quickly had to relearn the urban landscape. Where could you get a meal? Groceries? Gas for your car? How to run errands or begin to clean up with businesses open only a couple of hours a day, if at all (the lack of help and accessibility crippled even those eagerly trying to reopen their doors)? Urban renewal was never like this. And there were no ready-made plans that encompassed the rebuilding of an entire city, with earmarked resources, on an accelerated timetable.

Even after considering all of that, there was still the problem of race. One need only contemplate the post–World War II difficulties that ate at inner-city neighborhoods from block-busting in Baltimore, to the selection of public-housing sites in Chicago, to the dearth of decent housing that pinched middle-class blacks everywhere, in order to see that such considerations overwhelmed the laser-like, focused programs that involved only the most carefully selected projects during the era of renewal.[8]

And the results? Even given the time, resources (political and economic), and seeming manageability of the problems facing it, urban renewal is neither regarded highly nor remembered fondly. Slums and so-called blight not only persisted but grew faster than they could be eradicated by any clearance or prevention program. Periodic, almost cyclical discussions of the various "pathologies" of the ghetto, represented by such concepts as the "culture of poverty" in the 1960s and the "underclass" of the 1980s and 1990s, reinforced conventional wisdom and left an idiosyncratic white perspective to direct ameliorative efforts.[9] Such developments did little but leave the intellectual cupboard bare of any potentially fresh approach to the problem. And that would explain, at least in part, the persistence and "invisibility" of the minority poor and their "rediscovery" in the reports emanating from the Louisiana Superdome and Convention Center.

Moreover, in the age of renewal, the announcement of a development sent shock waves rippling through the affected neighborhood. The displacement and relocation of the poorest African Americans into adjacent communities repeatedly triggered white resistance in myriad forms and contested virtually every effort to develop black living space, whether public or private.[10] The refusal to tolerate unfettered black mobility led each project to seek its own accommodation to local conditions. To address the problem today, it is understood that the effects of displacement on a New Orleans–Katrina scale could not be handled piece-meal, on a neighborhood-by-neighborhood basis. It would be necessary to tackle the whole thing at once. Who would care to define and proclaim the racial homelands in our major cities? It is a problem that cannot even be faced, let alone resolved.

But it must still be said that Katrina represented opportunity as well as tragedy. That opportunity, however, had to be recognized before it could be seized—a prospect made all the more difficult by the city's unspeakable trauma. Familiar, comfortable patterns of thought and behavior would need to be jettisoned in favor of the untried and unknown. If such was not too much to ask, it certainly proved too much to expect.

The easy, uncritical bruiting about of rumors regarding the deliberate, malevolent destruction of the Industrial Canal levee testified to the prepositioning of those obstacles. Whites, of course, had their own cherished tales. They included accounts of rape, murder, child molestation, sniping, and looting. Lamentably, many such reports proved all too true, but inflammatory exaggerations and outright fabrications aggravated the situation.

Filmmaker Spike Lee devoted considerable attention to the "bombing" allegations emanating from the Ninth Ward by allowing local residents to voice their suspicions with little contradiction in his documentary *When the Levee Broke*. Uptown whites, particularly those who were fortunate enough to have laid claim to the high ground that edged the Mississippi River's banks above the French Quarter (the "sliver on the river" according to some, the "isle of denial" to others) thought it scandalous that anyone could think them capable of such crimes and, worse, prevent them from offering a defense. They could not see, however, that it was Lee's intention neither to make patently false accusations nor to defend whites against them. He was exposing a pattern of belief that was as real as the hurricane itself and one that could be ignored only at its own peril.

There were good reasons, moreover, for African Americans in New Orleans to expect the worst even as they hoped for better. First, they had history as a teacher. Not only had the political and economic elites of New Orleans coldly planned the intentional demolition of levees to flood neighboring parishes to save themselves, but they had actually already done so once before. Journalist John Barry recalled in *Rising Tide* (his detailed account of the great 1927 flood) that the U.S. Army Corps of Engineers had earlier advised the city's financial community to "blow a hole in the levee" should the river ever "threaten" the city. Ultimately, New Orleans's civic leadership took ten days and thirty-nine tons of explosives to punch a hole in the levee system in what later officials called an unnecessary attempt to relieve pressure on the city. When, in 1965, Hurricane Betsy ravaged the same area, including the black-occupied Lower Ninth Ward, the previously demonstrated willingness to flood out white residents in St. Bernard and Plaquemines parishes gave rise to rumors identical to those that swept the neighborhood in Katrina's wake forty years later. New Orleans's use of "bombs" to divert flooding may have been questionable, but it was hardly unknown. Such allegations were thus rooted in fact, renewed over the years, and reinforced by contemporary divisions. It did not take much to make such tales appear real.[11]

Such experiences raised new difficulties both during and after the crisis brought on by Katrina. The horrific conditions and televised human drama evident in the Louisiana Superdome and the city's convention center highlighted the callousness of government at every level and shocked most of the United States into recognizing the seemingly perpetually joined problems of poverty and race once more. Still, it apparently took nearly a week for the depth and scope of the tragedy to penetrate the Republican President's consciousness, and the Governor of Louisiana, Democrat Kathleen Blanco, barely made her presence felt beyond a Mayor Richard J. Daley-style warning to that the late-arriving National Guard would "shoot-to-kill."[12] New Orleans' black Democratic mayor, C. Ray Nagin, stepped into the yawning leadership vacuum and promptly disappeared after expressing hope for the "cavalry's" timely arrival.[13] Thus, there was an utter failure of

leadership regardless of partisan affiliation, color, gender, or class

It would be wrong to assume, however, that adversarial posturing represented the full extent of black/white interactions. Indeed, at the height of the crisis, to cite just a single example, the so-called Cajun Navy emerged from the swamps of south Louisiana with their own boats and equipment and, at great personal risk, engaged in systematic rescue efforts, plucking New Orleanians off the roofs of their flooded homes and out of the toxic waters that filled the city. A volunteer citizens' armada, they jumped in where the Federal Emergency Management Agency and other authorities feared to tread. The Cajun Navy was ultimately credited with rescuing some 4,000 endangered residents in eastern New Orleans.[14]

Conversely, the unquestionably heroic actions of uncounted African Americans also kept Katrina's death toll far below what it might have otherwise been. Proportionately, the greatest number of casualties and suffering could be found among the elderly, sick, and disabled who were unable to flee. Here, despite a highly publicized cases of a doctor and two nurses who were charged (the charges were later dropped) with murder and of another in which a pair of nursing-home operators were tried (and acquitted) for deserting their wards at the height of the crisis (several dozen of the home's residents drowned), there is also evidence of unusual selflessness in the service of (other-race) others. The anecdotal evidence is overwhelming that the large number of nurses, personal and professional, and other such service personnel employed in the city refused to leave their wards, often staying with and saving patients at the cost of being cut off from their own families.[15]

But those wisps of empathy and threads of a common humanity, though essential to the reknitting of New Orleans's society, remained subordinate to a dominant, reflexive fear and hostility. It is important to realize that in the first hours and days after the levees crumbled, the reactions of both whites and blacks were reflexive and, hence, especially revelatory. Just as surely as a knee will jerk upward when properly struck, New Orleans twitched violently along preconditioned lines in Katrina's wake. The earliest responses exposed fundamental assumptions and perceptions normally hidden from view—and those that would be buried again beneath the verbiage of later, more deliberate responses. Furthermore, despite the encouraging interracial initiatives noted above, the unmistakable intensity of an in-group, "we-versus-they" perspective seemed to deepen the closer one that stood in the path of the hurricane's eye.

Humanitarian needs, however, had to be immediately addressed by state and local authorities. If Governor Blanco and Mayor Nagin offered little help, a Republican congressman from Baton Rouge, Richard Baker, literally could not contain himself. Exuding the rank opportunism afforded by the moment, Baker plumbed new depths of cynicism with a statement wholly inappropriate in tone and substance. "We finally cleaned up public housing in New Orleans," he told the *Wall Street Journal*. "We couldn't do it, but God did."[16]

Even more blunt were the locally generated sentiments borne of the chaos, fear, and disorder that seemed to be everywhere. One white professional who could observe both looters and those he believed to be such from his uptown porch (observers often distinguished looters from those foraging for food, clothing, and medical necessities simply by the color of their skin) sat holding a small arsenal as he was interviewed. When asked about the source of New Orleans's problems, he volunteered, "Two blocks away from here people are living hand to mouth.... I don't know of another city where, if you're in a two-million-dollar house, you're not sure that everything around you for two miles is a two-million-dollar house."[17] Familiarity, under these conditions, bred not just contempt but a good deal of suspicion and fear as well.

It is impossible, in the limited allotments of time and space permitted here, to catalog the full range of difficulties revived and aggravated by the intersection of the hurricane's destructive force with New Orleans's racial history. But it is possible to expose and, at least, begin to explore one fundamental aspect of the city's race relations: who would repopulate the city, and how would that be done? As clearly implied by Congressman Baker and the white homeowner above, housing and the allocation of urban space would be two key issues receiving the closest scrutiny. Having endured a forced evacuation, the repopulation of New Orleans would necessarily be a conscious rather than a haphazard process. There was also something else. It would also be, of necessity, a political process. The quantity, cost, quality, and location of public housing; the desire to shrink the vulnerable city's "footprint"; the amount of and ease with which Louisiana residents could obtain state aid for their return home (Louisiana residents filing applications for such assistance remained scattered among some forty-five states more than two years after Katrina's landfall); and the selection of neighborhoods to be favored by the city's planning resources represented only a handful of the uncounted considerations that linked housing and race in post-Katrina New Orleans.

Finally, of course, there was the question of politics itself. The battles over housing, development, and access to aid and the land were viewed, by both blacks and whites, as a power struggle of signal importance. The seemingly "Pavlovian" statements made and actions taken during the immediate crisis and the cooler, more calculated ones later (sometimes masquerading as policy) with regard to housing and mobility issues revealed the now carefully hidden assumptions that not only cast a long shadow over any reconstruction proposal but also reified the racial divisions and interests that remained the greatest threat to the emergence of a new city.

A full understanding of these issues in New Orleans must come to grips with their multifaceted character. First, for African Americans, freedom of movement, the right to go where one pleases, is both evidence and symbolic of freedom itself. Although circumstances were quite different in the post-Katrina period compared with that following emancipation, the former slaves' ability to locate and relocate their families, flee to safety, travel in groups, and otherwise improve their lot, virtually defined freedom for them even as whites viewed such matters as security issues for themselves. Whether uprooted by war or natural disaster, the sheer movement of black people, their gathering in concentrated settlements, their encroachment on "white" territory, or their freedom simply to roam about the countryside had, therefore, never gone uncontested or unregulated.[18] A subsequent pattern of instinctive, seemingly almost intuitive reactions on the part of local whites tended to isolate and confine blacks within the city rather than to whisk them to safety and extend humanitarian assistance. They also generated violent, or near violent, confrontations that fueled differing "racial" perceptions of Katrina's impact and significance.

The best known of these incidents involves the attempt of perhaps several hundred people (overwhelmingly black, though not exclusively so) to leave the rapidly deteriorating conditions around the Louisiana Superdome and to cross the Crescent City Connection (the bridge linking the city's east and west banks) on foot on September 1, 2005. A small contingent emerged from the town of Gretna, in Jefferson Parish, at the opposite end of the bridge, to cut them off. Gretna's defenders, led by a pair of uniformed Sheriff's deputies, greeted Katrina's neediest refugees with a shotgun blast over their heads and the vow that "there would be no Superdomes" in their city.[19]

Forced to back off the bridge at gunpoint, these storm victims still fared better than some of those Katrina refugees who tried to flee across the Industrial Canal's Danziger bridge to the east. There, on September 5, 2005, police rushed to the scene where snipers, it was erroneously reported, had wounded an officer. They opened fire on an unarmed group crossing the span, killing two and injuring four others. Governor Blanco went further, placing National Guard troops on other bridges and possible points where pedestrians might exit the city. Suburban Jefferson Parish similarly denied access to residents from neighboring Orleans Parish by setting up roadblocks. (This was a recurring practice. New Orleans Mayor Sidney Barthelemy had to endure Jefferson Parish Sheriff Harry Lee's blockage of streets crossing parish lines early in his 1986–1994 administration.)[20]

The quick resort to deadly violence in the face of rumored racial disorders made the Danziger incident reminiscent, perhaps, of the slave insurrection panics that erupted throughout the South in 1835 and in 1856 to 1857. At the least, it is not much of a stretch to hear in the contemporary complaints of local officials echoes of their postemancipation predecessors. Indeed, historian Leon Litwack noted that in the nineteenth century, municipal authorities tended to regard any influx of black migrants as an "inundation" of "vagrants, thieves, and indigents," who threatened to "place an intolerable burden on taxpayers and charitable services."[21] Those promising "no Superdomes" certainly understood those arguments.

Once the immediate crisis had passed, authorities and citizens alike pondered an uncertain future. Congressman Baker's opportunistic suggestion to let God handle public housing at least had the virtue of raising the key question in the context of public policy. Where are poor people to live? Not only did this issue have to be explicitly addressed, but it was clear that the outcome, whatever it might be, would result from conscious political discussion and choice.

On the local level, one particularly revealing effort tried desperately to dress up nineteenth-century thought in twenty-first-century science. St. Bernard Parish, perhaps more rural than suburban, and nearly all white, bumped up against the city's Ninth Ward on its southeastern border. It enjoyed a serious growth spurt in the late 1960s, spurred on by the twin incentives of court-ordered school desegregation in the city and the insurance settlements that were converted into down payments on new homes following Hurricane Betsy in 1965. Virtually leveled by Katrina forty years later, St. Bernard sought to control its future development by passing an ordinance that prohibited the owners of single-family homes that had not been rented out before the hurricane from renting to anyone who was not a blood relative. Ostensibly intended to "promote home ownership" and preserve the parish's "quality of life," the ordinance aimed, its proponents argued, at preventing monied interests from buying up large tracts of land and dumping cheap rental units on the market.[22]

Most observers failed to buy the cover story. The Greater New Orleans Fair Housing Center charged that it was an effort to "perpetuate segregation" and filed suit in U.S. District Court. Others simply pointed to the region's tangled racial history and noted, with almost palpable discomfort and certainly with cause, that enforcement would involve more than simple observation. One critic noted the need for DNA tests "on everyone who wants to rent a house."[23] Given such thin disguises and blunt actions, it is not surprising that New Orleans's African Americans would question either the motives or the judgment of those offering such a "welcome home." And reasonable people who could not bring themselves to find a cosmic relationship between the middle passage and the path taken by many hurricanes across the Atlantic to punish the United States, or to see the similarities between the hulls of slave ships and the configuration of the Louisiana Superdome, may be forgiven for harboring some suspicions.[24]

Public housing was perhaps the policy area that best illustrated the damage done by the high degree of mutual distrust that sprang from racial polarization and adversarial politics. Certainly, Congressman Baker's public comments provided black New Orleanians cause for concern. Before Katrina, New Orleans was a city of just under 500,000 that had roughly 7,100 public-housing units, of which some 5,600 were occupied. Federal and local authorities were, in fact, already deep into discussions concerning the demolition of the city's largest remaining projects and their replacement by new mixed-income developments.

The evacuation, however, had emptied the projects, and initially, the federal government and the Housing Authority of New Orleans (HANO)—the former had taken control of the latter in 2002—did not permit the tenants to return. That a significant number of the apartments could have been repaired thus raised suspicions in the minds of the minority poor as to whether they would be welcomed back at all. Indeed, to the extent that Katrina lent any urgency at all to the long-standing housing crisis for the poor in the Crescent City, it was to speed ongoing negotiations on demolition not to press already existing, serviceable, affordable, and subsidized units into use. The result was that more than a year after Katrina cut her path of destruction across the Gulf Coast, only 1,600 HANO families had returned to the city, and another 400 units stood ready to be occupied. But HANO had also, by that time, contracted for the demolition of some 4,500 apartments in four remaining large projects.[25]

Government officials had determined, quite rightly, that it needed to surrender the policy of concentrating the poor in massive, segregated, and decaying projects in favor of more mixed developments. But there was a certain comfort level despite the poverty, crime, and other dangers found there. The close ties nurtured by familial and social networks often supplied those who called it "home" for generations what little help they could count on. The fear and insecurity of living on the margins outside of the projects provided the governing context.

Dubious tenants, therefore, responded with lawsuits, appeals, and Attorney William Quigley's argument that the government's permanent displacement of thousands represented an assault on the city's culture and history. While survival itself under such hostile conditions may well be celebrated, it was an essentially negative stance that contemplated only the prevention of the loss of existing housing. It was an argument that held no vision of a better future and represented an opportunity lost. Forced to play defense against virtually every aggressive initiative emanating from government or the private sector, well-meaning advocates for the poor had precious little to advocate.[26]

It is now nearly two and a half years into the post-Katrina era. Those who had been least affected are staggering toward a modest recovery. Here and there (especially if "there" is uptown or involves the centers of the tourist trade), there are some signs of revival and even new life. But vast, desolate stretches of an abandoned city remain; there are no "ruins" as such, only an emptiness where busy neighborhoods once stirred—and the darkness at night. Quality of life and, especially, safety issues are troublesome.

The federal government initially promised to provide "whatever it takes" to restore New Orleans. It has come up short. There are more expressions of disappointment and anger than surprise with regard to the president's lack of involvement; but the state and city were also the victims of bad timing and the ugly politics of the age. The two Louisiana congressional districts hit hardest by Katrina were the first and second districts—precisely those that covered most of metropolitan New Orleans. Republican Bob Livingston represented the first district and stood poised to become Speaker of the House in 1998 when the revelation of past personal improprieties forced his resignation. Democrat William Jefferson held the second district seat, and while he remains in Congress, Katrina's aftermath found him under investigation and politically hobbled by the discovery of $90,000 in cash in his freezer. He has since been indicted on a variety of charges, including the solicitation of bribes. One can only imagine the difference in assistance that would have been forthcoming if these rising stars had tended to the district's business rather than their own. Whether taking the high road of bipartisanship or pursuing the narrow path of rigid party rule, New Orleans's delegation would have been well positioned to press its claims.

There was little relief to be had, moreover, from electoral politics on the local level. The pace of reconstruction remains glacially slow, and the trends revealed by two post-Katrina elections are not promising. In the spring of 2006, following an unstructured, twenty-three-candidate, nonpartisan, open primary, the city held its first post-Katrina mayoral election. In pitting African American incumbent C. Ray Nagin

against the state's white Lieutenant Governor, Mitch Landrieu, New Orleans demonstrated how identity politics could be reduced to pure tactics, an empty vessel to be filled by the candidate du jour and the needs of the moment.

In 2002, Nagin won office running as a surrogate "white" candidate, a business executive who stood on a typical "good-government" platform.[27] He enjoyed solid backing from white civic and social elites and used their endorsements and funds to defeat the "black" candidate, police chief Richard Pennington. Nagin's white support (especially his largest donors) disappeared with Katrina's floodwaters, however, and following the April 2006 primary, he alone survived as the African American community's last, best hope against yet another feared "white takeover."

Nagin proved only too willing and able to shed the image of the reform-minded, elite-supported corporate executive. With the multicrisis brought on by Katrina providing the context, his campaign's use of the "race card" reflected the shrewd calculation of a tactician, not the commitment of an ideologue. His apparent determination (once he was dumped by big-money white contributors) was simply that racial polarization was the only way to keep his job. It was not a difficult calculation. He won in 2002 by collecting 90 percent of the white vote; he would attract but 6 percent in his post-Katrina reelection. This was the context for his Martin Luther King Jr. Day speech in which he tweaked white sensibilities and energized black troops with his claim that New Orleans was, and would remain, a "Chocolate City."

His capitulation to the politics of division, fear, and scarcity did not, however, make him a popular figure in the black community, nor did it provide him with an agenda. African Americans bore the brunt of his failures during the Katrina crisis itself, and his black opposition in the 2006 primary excoriated him. But his main black challenger, Pentacostal preacher Tom Watson, endorsed him in the general election after branding him a murderer responsible for the deaths of 1,200 storm victims in the primary. It was testimony not only to the depth and power of race as an issue but also to its ability to trump accountability. It also gave him enough votes to beat Mitch Landrieu.

For their part, Landrieu and most whites seemed content with the politics of displacement. Whether acting out of sheer opportunism, fear, or mistaken calculation, Landrieu's mayoral campaign relied more on the perceived iconic status of the candidate's father, Moon Landrieu, as a civil rights mayor to attract black votes than its own ability to make self-interested appeals. Clearly, there were elements in the black community that had been alienated from the current administration and could be wooed; even among many of those who eventually came around to vote for Nagin, there was no close personal connection. And after Nagin's victory, it quickly became apparent how lightly those racial ties bound him. He continued to take counsel from many of the same white developers, businessmen, and civic elites as before. Otherwise, he has kept a low profile, fighting few battles for "the race" even as events heat up in the street. As this is being written, protestors are placing themselves between bulldozers and those public-housing units facing imminent court-ordered demolition.[28] The mayor is nowhere to be found. And for those watching the buildings coming down, there are few convincing, credible voices contradicting the notion that it is all part of a grand design to prevent their families and friends from coming home.

Just as clearly, the liberal Landrieu feared losing white voters by appearing too eager in his pursuit of black ones. Ultimately, he looked at the city's post-Katrina demographics and tried to have it both ways. Landrieu carried nearly one in four black primary voters on the strength of his own liberal-moderate record, his father's role in advancing the early civil rights revolution, and the hurricane-induced reduction in black population, registration, and turnout. In the end, Landrieu and Nagin found themselves with few programmatic differences and applying the same campaign logic, if not tactics. Solidifying their own racial bases, they would rely on unity and turnout to produce a victory. Surely, such a course doomed any white candidate to defeat before Katrina, but now, white New Orleans believed a door had been opened. Uncertainty governed estimates of population size, composition, location, and commitment; it also governed the unusual voting procedures adopted under post-Katrina circumstances producing still more guesswork and hope for an unexpected victory. The difference came in means. Nagin had to heighten race consciousness and issues, while Landrieu preferred to mute them. Indeed, in the end, the elder Landrieu's civil rights record may have cost as many embittered white votes as it won grateful black ones.

Nagin eked out a narrow victory, and black New Orleans had its mayor. They enjoyed something less than a political honeymoon; it was more like a one-night stand. And in November 2007, the city held its first post-Katrina election for the City Council and a host of other local offices. Without a single black member until one was appointed to fill a vacancy in 1973, the seven-member council became majority black in 1985. It remained so until the first post-Katrina body was sworn in. Sporting a dominant 5–2 majority of women to men, it is also tilted in favor of whites by a 4–3 margin. Similarly, black district representatives who held seats in the state house and senate found themselves beaten by white challengers.[29]

One might wish the city's political forces were coherent and efficient enough to produce an intended result with some purpose behind it. But these results seem to fall in the realm of visceral reactions, the application of long-nursed grudges, and the utter inability of leadership to overcome the burden of the past even as unprecedented circumstances demanded it.[30] But, then, maybe that Idaho weatherman was onto something.

NOTES

1. "Cold-War Device Used to Cause Katrina?," *USA Today*, September 20, 2005.
2. *When the Levees Broke: A Requiem in Four Acts*, directed by Spike Lee (Home Box Office, 2006).

3. Arnold R. Hirsch, "Simply a Matter of Black and White: The Transformation of Race and Politics in Twentieth-century New Orleans," in Arnold R. Hirsch and Joseph Logsdon, eds., *Creole New Orleans: Race and Americanization* (Baton Rouge, LA, 1992), chap. 6; Arnold R. Hirsch, "Race and Politics in Modern New Orleans: The Mayoralty of Dutch Morial," *Amerikastudien/American Studies* 35 (1990): 461–85.

4. "Whites Take a Majority on New Orleans' Council," *New York Times*, November 19, 2007.

5. "Blanco Tours New Orleans," *Times-Picayune*, September 7, 2005; "FEMA Denied State's Request for Rescue Rafts as Katrina Approached," *Times-Picayune*, January 30, 2006.

6. For background on urban renewal, see Mark Gelfand, *A Nation of Cities* (New York, 1975); John Mollenkopf, *The Contested City* (Princeton, NJ, 1983); Jon Teaford, *The Rough Road to Renaissance: Urban Revitalization in America, 1940–1985* (Baltimore, 1990); Robert Caro, *Robert Moses and the Fall of New York* (New York, 1974); Scott Greer, *Urban Renewal and American Cities* (Indianapolis, IN, 1964); and James Q. Wilson, ed., *Urban Renewal: The Record and the Controversy* (Cambridge, MA, 1966). Individual case studies abound, and a provocative review essay that covers recent housing policy historiography is D. Bradford Hunt, "Rethinking the Retrenchment Narrative in U.S. Housing Policy History," *Journal of Urban History* 32 (September 2006): 937–50.

7. For general histories of Hurricane Katrina and its aftermath, see Douglas Brinkley, *The Great Deluge: Hurricane Katrina, New Orleans, and the Mississippi Gulf Coast* (New York, 2006); Michael Eric Dyson, *Come Hell or High Water: Hurricane Katrina and the Color of Disaster* (Cambridge, MA, 2006); Ivor van Heerden and Mike Bryan, *The Storm: What Went Wrong and Why During Hurricane Katrina—The Inside Story from One Louisiana Scientist* (New York, 2007); Center for Public Integrity Investigation, *City Adrift: New Orleans Before and After Katrina* (Baton Rouge, LA, 2007); See also Jed Horne, *Breach of Faith: Hurricane Katrina and the Near Death of a Great American City* (New York: 2006); Chester Hartman and Gregory D. Squires, eds., *There Is No Such Thing as a Natural Disaster: Race, Class and Hurricane Katrina* (New York, 2006); Sally Forman, *Eye of the Storm: Inside City Hall During Katrina* (Bloomington, IN, 2007); and Chris Rose, *One Dead in Attic* (New Orleans, 2005).

8. W. Edward Orser, *Blockbusting in Baltimore: The Edmondson Village Story* (Lexington, KY, 1994); Arnold R. Hirsch, *Making the Second Ghetto: Race and Housing in Chicago, 1940–1960* (Chicago, 1998); Mary Pattillo, *Black on the Block: The Politics of Race and Class in the City* (Chicago, 2007).

9. Michael B. Katz, ed., *The "Underclass" Debate* (Princeton, NJ, 1993); Oscar Lewis, "The Culture of Poverty," in G. Gmelch and W. Zenner, eds., *Urban Life: Readings in the Anthropology of the City* (Long Grove, IL, 1996); Nicholas Lemann, *The Promised Land: The Great Black Migration and How It Changed America* (New York, 1991).

10. Stephen Grant Meyer, *As Long as They Don't Move Next Door: Segregation and Racial Conflict in American Neighborhoods* (Lanham, MD, 2000); Hirsch, *Making the Second Ghetto*; Orser, *Blockbusting in Baltimore*; Kenneth D. Durr, *Behind the Backlash: White Working Class Politics in Baltimore, 1940–1980* (Chapel Hill, NC, 2003).

11. John M. Barry, *Rising Tide: The Great Mississippi Flood of 1927 and How It Changed America* (New York, 1997), 222, 257, 339.

12. "Blanco Demands Apology," *Times-Picayune*, September 1, 2005; "Troops Told 'Shoot to Kill' in New Orleans," *ABC News Online*, September 2, 2005.

13. "Mayor Nagin Speaks Out," *Times-Picayune*, September 10, 2005.

14. Brinkley, *Great Deluge*, 381.

15. A grand jury refused to indict Dr. Anna Pou on charges that she murdered nine of her patients in the days after Hurricane Katrina. Pou still faces four civil suits in connection with the deaths. "Grand Jury Refuses to Indict Anna Pou," *Times-Picayune*, July 25, 2007. Sal and Mabel Mangano also were "found innocent of negligent homicide in the drowning deaths of 25 elderly residents in their St. Bernard Parish nursing home during Hurricane Katrina." "Manganos Not Guilty in St. Rita's Nursing Home Case," *Times-Picayune*, September 7, 2007. For anecdotal evidence of the assistance extended across racial lines, see Eileen Guillory, "Facing the Storm: An Oral History of Elderly Survivors of Katrina" (paper presented at the Fifteenth International Oral History Association Conference, Guadalajara, Mexico, September 23–26, 2008).

16. "Some GOP Legislators Hit Jarring Notes in Addressing Katrina," *Washington Post*, September 10, 2005.

17. Dan Baum, "Porch Duty: Report from Carrollton," *The New Yorker*, September 12, 2005.

18. Leon F. Litwack, *Been in the Storm So Long: The Aftermath of Slavery* (New York, 1979), 296–326.

19. Brinkley, *Great Deluge*, 469.

20. Lyle Kenneth Perkins, "Failing the Race: The Historical Assessment of New Orleans Mayor Sidney Barthelemy, 1986–1984" (MA thesis, Louisiana State University, 2002), 22–23.

21. Litwack, *Been in the Storm So Long*, 314.

22. "St. Bernard Sued over Rent Limit; Group Says New Law Upholds Segregation," *Times-Picayune*, October 4, 2006.

23. Ibid.

24. Black activist Daniel Buford lectures that "hurricanes follow the path of the slave ships." "Hurricanes Follow Path of Slave Ships," *Louisiana Weekly*, September 26, 2005. Jesse Jackson, upon

seeing the Convention Center where thousands had been stranded for days after the storm, said, "This looks like the hull of a slave ship." "Katrina's Racial Storm," *Chicago Tribune*, September 8, 2005. On February 28, 2008, a federal judge ordered St. Bernard Parish to pay $32,500 in damages to the New Orleans Fair Housing Action Center and a local landowner who brought suit and challenged the September 2006 ordinance in court. Parish officials were not compelled to admit any "wrongdoing" and claimed "victory" on that basis. See "Judge OKs Accord in Housing Bias Suit," *Times-Picayune*, February 29, 2008.

25. "Far from Full: Lost in the Debate about the Demolition of N.O. Housing Developments Is One Fact: There Are Hundreds of Units Available Right Now," *Times-Picayune*, December 16, 2007.

26. "HANO Gets OK to Raise 4500 Units," *Times-Picayune*, September 22, 2007; "HANO Balks at Tearing Down Lafitte," *Times-Picayune*, December 11, 2007.

27. For a more detailed account of the 2006 mayoral election, see Arnold R. Hirsch, "Fade to Black: Hurricane Katrina and the Disappearance of Creole New Orleans," *Journal of American History* 34, no. 3 (December 2007): 752–61.

28. "Judge Puts Demolitions in Hands of Council," *Times-Picayune*, December 15, 2007.

29. "Election Results Reflect Racial Shift," *Times-Picayune*, November 19, 2007.

30. One straw in a cross-cutting political wind was the recent 7–0 vote of the City Council to demolish those contested public-housing units. Defying expectations that they would be racially divided, the Council's unity held forth the promise of a different future—if they could deliver not only on the demolition but also the subsequent provision of more and better affordable housing.

DOCUMENTS FOR PART V

5-1. ON THE SOCIAL USES OF CENTRAL PARK (1864)

Frederic B. Perkins

Source: Frederic B. Perkins, *The Central Park: Photographed by W. H. Guild, Jr., With Descriptions and a Historical Sketch by Fred. B. Perkins* (New York: Carleton, 1864). Courtesy of the American Antiquarian Society, Worcester, Massachusetts.

EDITORS' INTRODUCTION

The earliest supporters of Central Park came in large number from the upper class who sought an attractive setting for their own leisure activities and alternatives to the moral degradation of the lower classes' cheap amusements and drinking establishments. The following excerpt is from one such booster of the park, Frederic Beecher Perkins. Perkins published the volume before Central Park was formally completed. He provides social, moral, and intellectual justifications for the park, especially in terms of how rich and poor New Yorkers alike could benefit from the design of Frederick Law Olmsted and Calvert Vaux. Frederic B. (Beecher) Perkins was a member of the widely influential Beecher family, which included his grandfather, the temperance reformer Lyman Beecher, the abolitionist and author Harriet Beecher Stowe, and Henry Ward Beecher, minister of the Plymouth Congregational Church in Brooklyn, New York, whom he cites at the start of the selection. Frederic Perkins' daughter Charlotte Perkins Gilman was a noted feminist author.

Socially,—as Henry Ward Beecher, the friend of all good amusements and enjoyments, might like to view it,—the Park is what I have already called it—a great democratic pleasure ground; a proof of the ease and the natural method by which a democracy can create, for its own enjoyment, gardens as elaborate, costly, and magnificent, as those of monarchs. No visitor needs to send in a card to the proprietor, or in request permission to inspect his "valuable collection." To be a visitor is to exercise ownership in it. It is his who will but enter and enjoy. Only by staying outside, indeed, can we avoid exercising ownership in it. Nor is they any distinction of persons, other than ethical. Disorder and disgustfulness are excluded; otherwise, the poorest owns as much of the Park as the richest. The dirty-faced body of the shanty runs, squalls, and grubs in the gravel as freely as the rich man's bescrubbed and bedizened infant—and far more so; and far more does he enjoy it too. What is a lace ruffle about his drawers, or a feather in his hat, or a fiery-red mantle, to a little child compared with nice dirt, and freedom to disport himself therein? Truly, less than nothing, and vanity. Indeed, not only does the poor man have whatever the rich man can, in the Park, but much that he cannot. Hundreds of sweet, quiet, nooks, pleasant corners of water scenery, little shadow bowers, higher "coinages of vantage," accurately chosen view-points— all these *must* be walked to. Nature will be wooed in humility. She is like Elisha of old; they that come with chariots and horses, and gold and raiment, may perhaps, receive some word as by a messenger, as Naaman did. If he had gone humbly on foot, doubtless Elisha would have spoken with him. Nature will not be visible for more than six feet high. So the Park is a pleasure-ground, because it was made to be; and a democratic one, because, being of natural rather than artificial features, it must be. By silent, constant ministrations, it is in sundry ways teaching the greater social ethics—equality of privilege, liberty under law, the greatest good for, as well as of, the greatest number.

Morally,—as Dr. Tying might be, with graver analysis, disposed to consider it,—every one of the usefulness of the Park is a direct promotive of good morals; for good morals are bettered by good health, by innocent enjoyment, by sight and intercourse of what is beautiful. Yet still the most striking ethical significance of the Park is in this: that it proves and expresses great, and essential, and foreseeing, and deliberate kindheartedness in our citizens of to-day, who provide for posterity a scene of recreation and a source of health which cannot, in the nature of things, grow to a just completeness until many of its originators are dead.

Last of all—Intellectually, in sum and total, altogether; as, after venturing to specify all those eminent men, I must necessarily attempt to set forth that which the Park it:

It becomes, perhaps, most admirably, when considered as a wonderful symmetrical combination of means, successfully contrived to serve many purposes; that is, a great monument of Creative Intellect; both for conceptive imagination, and for realizing executive talent. For foresight imagination, wisdom, system, complexity, order, and energy, the history of the works of the Park are a very noble study. Even in the original design, prepared in 1858, the necessity of including the land up to One Hundred and Tenth Street, was understood and silently allowed for, so that now, when this space is actually to be added, it exactly completes the design of the Park; and in adjusting all its features allowance was consistently made for a state of things at least twenty years in the future. In preparing that design, its makers were obliged to body forth with

their own thoughts the green meadows, structures, the lakes and fountains, sweeping drives and winding pathways, shadowing out all this beauty over an actuality of the extremest bareness and filth. So wisely and systematic was the plan contrived that it meets all requirements of passengers and commerce, of the baby in arms, the capitalist's coach and the horseman's steed. So wisely and strongly was the administrative machine constructed, that its economy has been marked and great, the work done with singular faithfulness and regularity, and the whole kept almost unstained by the rotting influence of political interference.

Unfinished as it is, Central Park already links fast to the names of its two designers, the high praise of having created by far the greatest public work on the American continent, for grandeur, beauty, purity, and success.

That Mr. Olmsted and Mr. Vaux have not remained at the head of their great work is much to be regretted, however, efficient subsequent administration may be. The originating mind should complete its own work. Yet it is gratifying to be known, that their plan could in fact scarcely be radically without the utter overturn and destruction of the face of the Park; that their designs are still carried forward in good faith, their methods of work and government still followed, and their plan for additional ground between One Hundred and Sixth and One Hundred and Tenth Streets on record, and approved by the Commissioners.

While, therefore, they are gone, their intellect still presides over the work; and the experience and ability of the hands into which the succession has fallen, are such as to warrant the harmonious completion of this grand enterprise.

5-2. WILLIAM TWEED'S CONFESSION (1878)

Special Committee of the Board of Alderman and William M. Tweed

Source: Board of Aldermen, *Report of the Special Committee of the Board of Aldermen Appointed to Investigate the "Ring" Frauds Together with the Testimony Elicited During the Investigation*, Document No. 8, January 4, 1878 (New York: Martin B. Brown, 1878).

EDITORS' INTRODUCTION

William M. Tweed (1823–1878), often referred to as "Boss Tweed," was a New York City politician whose controversial career as an elected official and party boss has made him synonymous with urban political corruption. Tweed, the son of a furniture maker, won his first election as a city alderman in 1852 shortly after he became a leader in a local volunteer firefighting company. Tweed held a variety of city, county, state, and even federal offices; most notably as a member of the U.S. Congress from 1853–1855, the Board of Supervisors from 1857–1870, a state Senator from 1868–1871, as well as concurrent city government titles of Deputy Street Commissioner, 1863–1870 and Commissioner of Public Works, 1870–1871.

Tweed's real political influence lay in his role as a party boss where he was able to exchange government services and favors for money, jobs for loyal followers, and other forms of power. He was a member of Tammany Hall, the leading faction of the city's Democratic Party, which secured its control over the city by appealing to the needs of working New Yorkers such as newly arrived immigrants. However, Tweed used his position to steal from taxpayers and extort money from those wishing to do business in the city as the head of the so-called "Ring" (also known as the "Tweed Ring" and the "Forty Thieves"), which extorted at least $30 million, and perhaps a good deal more. In 1871, a series of newspaper investigations exposed Tweed and his career came to a crashing halt. After being sentenced to twelve years in prison, Tweed escaped to Spain where authorities apprehended him. He eventually returned to New York, dying in debtor's prison in 1878.

The following document provides a remarkable account of how Tweed and his ring operated. The document comes from a report prepared for the Board of Aldermen by a special committee to account for the stolen money and the status of legal proceedings against members of the ring. In the first part, we find a review of the committee's findings, in the second actual excerpts from testimony by Tweed. Tweed, while cooperating with the committee, admitted to bribing state senators in order to secure a new charter for the city under the auspices of the Charter of 1870, paying off city officials to obtain authorization and funding for the Brooklyn Bridge, and manipulating local elections at the ward level.

Report of the Special Committee

THE RING IN THE BOARD OF SUPERVISORS.

According to William M. Tweed, whose evidence is in the main corroborated by that of Mr. Henry F. Taintor, the accountant who was employed in behalf of the people to work up and analyze the evidence concerning the Ring frauds; the first point of the attack of the Ring was upon the County Treasury, and as far as your Committee is able to ascertain, the first frauds were committed by a corrupt combination in the Board of Supervisors in the year 1860. This "Supervisors' Ring" existed from that time until, on account of internal dissentions, some of the members of it procured a law to be passed in 1870, by which the Board of Supervisors was abolished. The personel [sic] of this Ring changed slightly from year to year, and was composed at one time or other of the following persons: William M. Tweed, Walter Roche, John R. Briggs, Henry Smith, John Fox, James Hayes, Andrew J. Bleakley, and Isaac J. Oliver. The three first-named individuals originated the combination by agreeing to sustain each other in the Board and to vote together on bills presented for approval. Their united votes were sufficient to determine almost any question which came before the Board. In the subsequent years the other persons mentioned were from time to time added to their number and shared with them in the fraudulent gains.

HOW THE FRAUDS WERE PERPETRATED.

Almost every person who did work or furnished supplies for the county at this time were informed by some member of the Ring that, in order to insure a continuance of the public patronage, increased orders and prompt payment, it would be necessary for them to add to their bills a certain percentage in excess of their true face, which increases or percentage it was understood and agreed should be paid to the corrupt combination of members of the Board aforesaid.

The amount so added at this time was generally fifteen per cent. of the face of the bills.
[…]

BOARD OF AUDIT IN 1870.

After the Board of Audit of 1870 had been appointed in compliance with the statute [the Charter of 1870 which eliminated the Board of Supervisors], they agreed among themselves that they would require of all persons who dealt with the city in any way (except a few whom they feared to approach) to add fifty per cent. to the true face of their bills. The other fifty per cent. being intended for distribution among the members of the Board.
[…]

POWER OF THE RING.

With the City Government in their hands, the [state] Legislature under their control, and the City Treasury at their command, the Ring was now at the height of their power. They did not even hesitate to change the will of the people as expressed at elections, whenever such change seemed to them desirable. The bench of the Supreme Court ceased, under their influence, to preserve its purity, and no one who refused to submit to their dictation had the slightest chance for political preferment. To such an extent had rascality become prevalent that even in the Assembly of this State, certain members organized a band for the express purpose of selling their votes, and were known as "The Black Horse Cavalry." Persons who performed no service for the city, but who were serviceable to the Ring for purely political purposes, were placed upon the pay rolls as city and country officials and supported from the public treasury.

Several pretended attempts of self-styled reformers to expose this disgraceful combination were easily dealt with by the simple expedient of giving them fat offices.

AMOUNT STOLEN.

Mr. Taintor testifies that between January 1, 1868, and July 1, 1871, so far as he has developed the matter, $30,000,000 were fraudulently diverted from the treasury by the corrupt practices of the Ring, and that this does not include the amount stolen by the Ring in the Board of Supervisors, between 1860 and 1866. It is safe to assume that from 1860 until July, 1871, the people of the city have been robbed of fifty millions of dollars at least.

THE EXPOSURE AND DOWNFALL OF THE RING.

In the Spring of 1871, and when the operations of the Ring had reached this enormous magnitude, they were suddenly brought to light through the columns of one of the city journals, which published not only an outline of the facts heretofore recited, but also an accurate list of the principle persons who had been engaged in the frauds. Public attention was at once fixed upon this all-absorbing subject, and every possible device was suggested whereby might be assured the arrest of the thieves and the recovery of the millions stolen by them. There was a very widespread feeling of distrust manifest towards the law officers then in office, and several associations of citizens were formed, who assumed to take the prosecution of these offenders into their own hands. Committees were appointed, the most eminent counsel—selected from both political parties—were retained, accountants and detectives were employed, and a formidable campaigned was commenced, having for its object the condign and speedy punishment of the thieves, and the wrestling from them their ill-gotten gains.

[...]

At present all the thieves, with one single exception, are at large, several of them are living in and near New York, in elegant ease, if not in ostentatious luxury, and all of them claim entire immunity from all sorts of suits or demands from the City or the People, on the ground that they have all been used as witnesses. Some dozen of the thieves have thus been let loose upon the community, in order that they might be used as witnesses against one or two of the others.

Nor has the pecuniary result of these suits been any more satisfactory.

The eminent counsel which had been especially retained to conduct these prosecutions originally began them in the name of the People of the State instead of the name of the Mayor, etc., of the City of New York. In those actions warrants of arrest were obtained against several of the principle members of the Ring, and bail bonds in large amounts were given by them. All of these actions failed because the Court of Appeals held that the right of action was not in the State but in the municipality.

Thereupon the Legislature passed an act—chapter 49 of the Laws of 1875—practically transferring to the State the cause of action to recover moneys fraudulently obtained from the city, and new actions were begun. Meanwhile much invaluable time had been lost, the bail-bonds taken in the original actions were, of course, not available, and the defendants had taken care

to go where no new bail-bonds could be exacted of them.

[...]

An examination…shows that the energy with which these [new] suits seems to have been prosecuted at first has in very many cases entirely expended itself, and that for the last two or three years very little seems to have been accomplished in the progress of these cases, with a view either to the recovery of the stolen money or the prosecution of the thieves.

[...]

Your Committee respectfully suggests that your Honorable Board furnish the Attorney General of the State with a copy of the testimony taken in the course of this investigation, and of this report, and that you earnestly request him to take immediate and active steps to punish those of the Ring thieves who have heretofore escaped, and either to compel them to make such restitution as is now possible, or else to rid the community whom they have robbed of their presence.

[...]

Testimony of William M. Tweed

SIXTH DAY.
September 15, 1877

Q. Now, Mr. Tweed, you say that you paid money to certain members of the Senate, for the purpose of influencing their action with regard to the Charter of 1870?

A. I do say so; yes sir.

Q. Personally?

A. Yes, sir…

Q. Before it was passed?

A. Before it was passed.

Q. Well, now, will you state what members of the Senate you paid money to in this very connection, with regard to the Charter of 1870?

[...]

A. It must be told in the form of a little narrative, as there are little many points bearing on the subject… The origination of this charter was from the fact that a great many Democrats in New York had become dissatisfied… the matter became very violent among ourselves, so a meeting was called of the Tammany Hall General Committee of

that year, by myself, who was then chairman of that committee... I went to Albany, I found that Mr. Hastings[1] and others, republicans, were very anxiously at work to keep up this rivalry in the democratic organization... I stated my business with him, which was to ask his advice about the passage of the charter, and to get him to aid us in helping it along. After some little discussion, he finally consented to aid me, dropping his opposition to our side of the house, and suggested that the best way to do it would be that I should see certain Senators, and, if possible, have a caucus of the Republican Senators called, and get them committed to our charter. We had arranged it so as to have no difficulty to pass it in the lower house. We passed it in the lower house, and at Mr. Hastings' suggestion, I saw a number of Senators, more particularly Senators Norris Winslow, William Woodin, Bowen, Minier, and Senator James Wood.
[...]

I talked the matter over with Mr. Winslow, and he thought they ought to have $50,000 apiece. I said we would pay for it, but I said we couldn't afford to pay that; finally we talked the matter over, and, in one or two days, Hastings suggested that if I got Woodin it would be well for me, as he was an influential man, a powerful speaker, and stood very high in his party.
[...]

I spoke to Woodin, and said, "I will win anyhow; I have got the thing all fixed, but I would rather win by a very large majority, and have all the Republicans go with me, and be on my side." Then I suggested the caucus, and suggested that the Republicans should resolve in the caucus to support me in this measure... finally he consented to go with the others. I said, "Shall I hand you $40,000?" He said, "Do the same with this as you are doing with the rest." I said, "I am going to hand the rest to Mr. Winslow." The Republicans held their caucus, and resolved to stand by the charter... when the bill came up every Republican voted for it except Mr. Thayer, and every Democrat voted for it except Mr. Genet. The Senate was full—thirty-two Senators; thirty of them voted for it, and only two against it.

Q. This was the charter which had been prepared by the leaders of Tammany Hall?
A. Yes, sir.
Q. Were these the only Senators whom you had dealings with in connection with this matter?
A. No, sir; I bought some of the others also.
Q. How did you buy them?
A. I bought some of the Democrats by giving them places?
Q. What Democrats, and what places? All about it.
A. I couldn't tell what places. Places—employment of men in the department, where they put their name on the pay-roll, and drew their money once a month.

SEVENTH DAY.
September 18, 1877
Q. What was your connection with the Brooklyn Bridge?
A. Well, it is a long story.
Q. Condense it; just tell me your connection with it.
[...]
A. I don't know the year... 1868, I think—Mr. Henry C. Murphy, who was a brother Senator, called on me and stated he was president of that bridge, and desired to have the Common Council authorize the Comptroller to issue the bonds, or give them money to the amount of one and a-half million dollars for the benefit of the bridge. I told him I had nothing to do with the Common Council at that time, and wasn't a member of it. "But," he said, "can't you influence them?" I told him I hadn't done any lobbying business there, but I might, if necessary. Shortly after he called again. In the meantime I had conversed with a gentleman occupying a position in the Board of Aldermen which entitled him to credence, and he told me the appropriation could be passed by paying for it. I asked him how much was necessary... I informed Mr. Murphy of that fact. He told me to go ahead and make the negotiation. I did so, and the money was authorized to be appropriated or bonds issued...

Q. Did you tell Mr. Henry C. Murphy that you were going to get the necessary ordinance passed by paying for it?

A. That was the understanding.

Q. Did you tell him subsequently that you had done it?

A. Yes, sir.

Q. And that you had paid either fifty or sixty thousand dollars to the Board of Alderman?

A. I think it was sixty or sixty-five.

[…]

Q. Now, Mr. Tweed, with regard to elections—to the management of elections for the city and country officers—and generally, the elections for the city and county: When you were in office, did the Ring control the election in this city at that time?

A. They did, sir; absolutely.

Q. Please tell me what the *modus operandi* of that was. How did you control the election?

A. Well, each ward had a representative man, who would control matters in his own ward, and whom the various members of the general committee were to look up to for advice how to control elections.

Q. The General Committee of Tammany Hall?

A. Of the regular organization.

Q. What advice? What do you mean by that?

A. Why, what to do.

Q. What were they to do, in case you wanted a particular man elected over another?

A. Count the ballots in bulk, or without counting them announce the result in bulk, or change from one to the other, as the case may have been.

Q. Then these elections really were no elections at all? The ballots were made to bring about any result that you determined upon beforehand?

A. The ballot made no result; the counters made the result.

NOTE

1. Mr. Tweed was referring to Hugh Hastings, editor of *The Commercial Advertiser* an influential Republican newspaper.

5-3. PHILADELPHIA: CORRUPT AND CONTENTED (1903)

Lincoln Steffens

Source: Lincoln Steffens, "Philadelphia: Corrupt and Contented," *McClure's Magazine*, XXI (July 1903): 249–263.

EDITORS' INTRODUCTION

Lincoln Steffens (1866–1936), is widely considered one of the foremost muckraking journalists of the early twentieth century. Steffens, the son of a banker, grew up in Sacramento, California in comfortable surroundings. He attended college at the University of California, Berkeley and studied abroad in Europe for several years before taking a position with *McClure's Magazine* in 1901. Deeply influenced by social science, Steffens contemplated the nature of political corruption in American cities. His editor, S. S. McClure, sent Steffens on a fact-finding tour, resulting in a series of six articles on St. Louis, Minneapolis, Pittsburgh, Philadelphia, Chicago, and New York. These articles formed the core of a single volume, *The Shame of the Cities*, originally published in 1904 and still in print over a century later.

Steffens began his investigation of Philadelphia with a working hypothesis that American cities resembled each other in political structure. Through his research, he determined that no matter which form of checks and balances were in place, the same old style of political corruption would persist. Steffens argued that political bosses were a natural phenomenon. Steffens also found limited benefits to reforms which utilized a business model. Businesses, of course, could also be corrupt.[1] This selection on Philadelphia helps debunk a popular notion that machines were the product of cities politically dominated by immigrants and the Democratic Party. As Steffens reminded his readers, Philadelphia was the most American of the large cities, and like the rest of the state and nation, Republican, yet political machines still reigned.

OTHER American cities, no matter how bad their own condition may be, all point with scorn to Philadelphia as worse—"the worst governed city in the country." St. Louis, Minneapolis, Pittsburg submit with some patience to the jibes of any other community; the most friendly suggestion from Philadelphia is rejected with contempt. The Philadelphians are "supine," "asleep"; hopelessly ring-ruled, they are "complacent." "Politically benighted," Philadelphia is supposed to have no light to throw upon a state of things that is almost universal.

This is not fair. Philadelphia is, indeed, corrupt; but it is not without significance. Every city and town in the country can learn something from the typical political experience of this great representative city. New York is excused for many of its ills because it is the metropolis, Chicago because of its forced development; Philadelphia is our "third largest" city and its growth has been gradual and natural. Immigration has been blamed for our municipal conditions; Philadelphia, with 47 per cent of the population native born of native born parents, is the most American of our greater cities. It is "good," too, and intelligent. I don't know how to measure the intelligence of a community, but a Pennsylvania college professor who declared to me his belief in education for the masses as a way out of political corruption, himself justified the "rake-off" of preferred contractors on public works on the ground of a "fair business profit." [...]

Philadelphia is representative. This very "joke," told, as it was, with a laugh, is typical. All our municipal governments are more or less bad and all our people are optimists. Philadelphia is simply the most corrupt and the most contented. Minneapolis has cleaned up. Pittsburg has tried to, New York fights every other election, Chicago fights all the time. Even St. Louis has begun to stir (since the elections are over) and at the worst was only shameless. Philadelphia is proud; good people there defend corruption and boast of their machine. My college professor, with his philosophic view of "rake-offs," is one Philadelphia type. Another is the man, who, driven to bay with his local pride, says: "At least you must admit that our machine is the best you have ever seen."

All Through With Reform

Disgraceful? Other cities say so. But I say that if Philadelphia is a disgrace, it is a disgrace not to itself alone, nor to Pennsylvania, but to the United States and to American character. For this great city, so highly representative in other respects, is not behind in political experience, but ahead, with New York. Philadelphia is a city that has had its reforms. Having passed through all the typical stages of corruption, Philadelphia reached the period of miscellaneous loot with a boss for chief thief, under James McManes and the Gas Ring 'way back in the late sixties and seventies. This is the Tweed stage of corruption from which St. Louis, for example, is just emerging. Philadelphia, in two inspiring popular revolts, attacked the Gas Ring, broke it, and in 1885 achieved that dream of American cities—a good charter. The present condition of Philadelphia, therefore, is not that which precedes, but that which follows reform, and in this distinction lies its startling general significance. What has happened since the Bullitt Law or charter went into effect in

i Lincoln Steffens, *The Autobiography of Lincoln Steffens*, Volume 1 (New York: Harcourt, Brace, and Company, 1931), 409.

Philadelphia may happen in any American city "after reform is over." [...]

The Bullitt Law, which concentrates in the Mayor ample power, executive and political, and complete responsibility. Moreover, it calls for very little thought and action on the part of the people. All they expected to have to do when the Bullitt Law went into effect was to elect as Mayor a good business man, who with his probity and common sense would give them that good business administration which is the ideal of many reformers.

Business Men as Mayors

The Bullitt Law went into effect in 1887. A committee of twelve—four from the Union League, four from business organizations, and four from the bosses—picked out the first man to run under it on the Republican ticket, Edwin H. Fitler, an able, upright business man, and he was elected. Strange to say, his administration was satisfactory to the citizens, who speak well of it to this day, and to the politicians also; Boss Mc-Manes (the ring was broken, not the boss) took to the next national convention from Philadelphia a delegation solid for Fitler for President of the United States. It was a farce, but it pleased Mr. Fitler, so Matthew S. Quay, the State boss, let him have a complimentary vote on the first ballot. The politicians "fooled" Mr. Fitler, and they "fooled" also the next business Mayor, Edwin S. Stuart, likewise a most estimable gentleman. Under these two administrations the foundation was laid for the present government of Philadelphia, the corruption to which Philadelphians seem so reconciled, and the machine which is "at least the best you have ever seen." [...]

The machine controls the whole process of voting, and practices fraud at every stage. The assessor's list is the voting list, and the assessor is the machine's man. The assessor pads the list with the names of dead dogs, children, and non-existent persons. One newspaper printed the picture of a dog, another that of a little four-year-old negro boy, down on such a list. A ring orator in a speech resenting sneers at his ward as "low down" reminded his hearers that that was the ward of Independence Hall, and, naming over signers of the Declaration of Independence, he closed his highest flight of eloquence with the statement that "these men, the fathers of American liberty, voted down here once. And," he added, with a catching grin, "they vote here yet." Rudolph Blankenburg, a persistent fighter for the right and the use of the right to vote, sent out just before one election a registered letter to each voter on the rolls of a certain selected division. Sixty-three per cent. were returned marked "not at," "removed," "deceased," etc. From one four-story house where forty-four voters were addressed, eighteen letters came back undelivered; from another of forty-eight voters, came back forty-one letters; from another sixty-one out of sixty-two; from another forty-four out of forty-seven. Six houses in one division were assessed at one hundred and seventy-two voters, more than the votes cast in the previous election in any one of two hundred entire divisions.

The repeating is done boldly, for the machine controls the election officers, often choosing them from among the fraudulent names; and when no one appears to serve, assigning the heeler ready for the expected vacancy. The police are forbidden by law to stand within thirty feet of the polls, but they are at the box and they are there to see that the machine's orders are obeyed and that repeaters whom they help to furnish are permitted to vote without "intimidation" on the names they, the police, have supplied. [...]

Bosses Appointed from the U. S. Senate

Deprived of self-government, the Philadelphians haven't even self-governing machine government. They have their own boss, but he and his machine are subject to the State ring and take their orders from the State boss, Matthew S. Quay, who is the proprietor of Pennsylvania and the real ruler of Philadelphia, just as William Penn, the great proprietor, was. Philadelphians, especially the local bosses, dislike this description of their government, and they point for refutation to their charter. But this very Bullitt

Law was passed by Quay, and he put it through the Legislature, not for reform reasons, but at the instance of David H. Lane, his Philadelphia lieutenant, as a check upon the power of Boss McManes. [...]

Philadelphia Machine Upside Down

The Philadelphia organization is upside down. It has its root in the air, or, rather, like the banyan tree, it sends its roots from the center out both up and down and all around, and there lies its peculiar strength. For when I said it was dependent and not sound, I did not mean that it was weak. It is dependent as a municipal machine, but the organization that rules Philadelphia is, as we have seen, not a mere municipal machine, but a city, State, and national organization. The people of Philadelphia are Republicans in a Republican city in a Republican State in a Republican nation, and they are bound ring on ring on ring. The President of the United States and his patronage; the National Cabinet and their patronage; the Congress and the patronage of the Senators and the Congressmen from Pennsylvania; the Governor of the State and the State Legislature with their powers and patronage; and all that the Mayor and City Councils have of power and patronage;—all these bear down upon Philadelphia to keep it in the control of Quay's boss and his little ring. This is the ideal of party organization, and, possibly, is the end toward which our democratic republic is tending. If it is, the end is absolutism. Nothing but a revolution could overthrow this oligarchy, and there is its danger. With no outlet at the polls for public feeling, the machine cannot be taught anything it does not know excepting at the cost of annihilation. [...]

Making Graft Safe

But the greatest lesson learned, and applied was that of conciliation and "good government." The people must not want to vote or rebel against the ring. This ring, like any other, was formed for the exploitation of the city for private profit, and the cementing force is the "cohesive power of public plunder." But McManes and Tweed had proved that miscellaneous larceny was dangerous, and why should a lot of cheap politicians get so much and the people nothing at all? The people had been taught to expect but little from their rulers: good water, good light, clean streets well paved, fair transportation, the decent repression of vice, public order and public safety, and no scandalous or open corruption. It would be good business and good politics to give them these things. [...]

But each of these 15,000 persons was selected for office because he could deliver votes, either by organizations, by parties, or by families. These must represent pretty near a majority of the city's voters. But this is by no means the end of the ring's reach. In the State ring are the great corporations, the Standard Oil Company, Cramp's Ship Yard, and the steel companies, with the Pennsylvania Railroad at their head, and all the local transportation and other public utility companies following after. They get franchises, privileges, exemptions, etc.; they have helped finance Quay through deals: the Pennsylvania paid Boss, David Martin, Quay said once, a large yearly salary; the Cramps get contracts to build United States ships, and for years have been begging for a subsidy on homemade ships. The officers, directors, and stockholders of these companies, with their friends, their bankers, and their employees are of the organization. Better still, one of the local bosses of Philadelphia told me he could always give a worker a job with these companies, just as he could in a city department, or in the mint, or post-office. Then there are the bankers who enjoy, or may some day enjoy, public deposits; those that profit on loans to finance political financial deals; the promoting capitalists who share with the bosses on franchises; and the brokers who deal in ring securities and speculation on ring tips. Through the exchange the ring financiers reach the investing public, which is a large and influential body. The traction companies, which bought their way from beginning to end by corruption, which have always been in the ring, and whose financiers have usually shared in other big ring deals, adopted early the policy of bribing the people with "small blocks of stock." [...]

But we are not yet through. Quay has made a specialty all his life of reformers, and he and his local bosses have won over so many that the list of former reformers is very, very long. Martin drove down his roots through race and religion, too. Philadelphia was one of the hot-beds of "know-nothingism." Martin recognized the Catholic, and the Irish-Irish, and so drew off into the Republican party the great natural supply of the Democrats; and his successors have given high places to representative Jews. [...]

If there is no other hold for the ring on a man there always is the protective tariff. "I don't care," said a manufacturer. "What if they do plunder and rob us, it can't hurt me unless they raise the tax rates, and even that won't ruin me. Our party keeps up the tariff. If they should reduce that, my business would be ruined."

5-4. *WACKER'S MANUAL OF THE PLAN OF CHICAGO* (1913)

Walter D. Moody

Source: Walter D. Moody, *Wacker's Manual of the Plan of Chicago* (Chicago: Chicago Plan Commission, 1913). Courtesy of the Newberry Library, Chicago, Illinois.

EDITORS' INTRODUCTION

Walter D. Moody (1874–1920) served as Managing Director of the Chicago Plan Commission. The commission was confident that Chicago was "destined to become the center of the modern world, if the opportunities in her reach are intelligently realized, and if the city can receive a sufficient supply of trained and enlightened citizens."[i] Daniel Hudson Burnham, the mastermind behind the breathtaking and influential architecture of the Columbian World's Fair held in Chicago in 1893, brought his ideas for civic improvement to the Commercial Club of Chicago, securing their solid support. Burnham, an architect, city planner, and the formal plan's chief author, wanted to build a series of parks, wide open avenues, and new cultural and government buildings in Chicago. The resulting *Plan of Chicago*, published with accompanying drawings by the Commercial Club in 1909, inspired cities all over the United States to invest in physical changes; this movement became known as the "City Beautiful" movement. Here, we learn about the plan in a book designed for Chicago schools. Moody wanted school children to play an active role in bringing the ideas of the plan to fruition. One can easily connect the idea of the Chicago Plan to that of Olmsted's Central Park. **[See Rosenzweig and Blackmar "The 'Spoils of the Park'" in Part V.]** Fresh air and easy access to outdoor recreation promised to offer relief for the perceived anxieties of urban life. A physically improved city also aids business by speeding-up the movement of people, ideas, and capital and encourages a higher number of tourists to visit the city.

Chapter XI, The Plan of Chicago; Its Purpose and Meaning

The Plan of Chicago, as it has been worked out, is a plan to direct the future growth of Chicago in a systematic and orderly way. Its purpose is to make Chicago a real, centralized city instead of a group of overcrowded, overgrown villages. It will hold her position among the great cities of the world, that Chicago is to be given opportunities for indefinite growth in wealth and commerce,

---

i Walter D. Moody, *Wacker's Manual of the Plan of Chicago* (Chicago: Chicago Plan Commission, 1913), no page. See Carl Smith, *The Plan of Chicago: Daniel Burnham and the Remaking of the American City* (Chicago: University of Chicago Press, 2006).

and that Chicago is to become the most convenient, healthful and attractive city on earth. History shows that this work will give to us, the owners and builders of Chicago, world-wide fame that will be everlasting.

We have seen that in the history of the cities of the past their building according to a definite plan has to do chiefly with two elements, namely, congestion, which means the crowding of large numbers of people into small areas; and traffic, which means the movement of merchandise and people from one part of the city to another. We modern people, owing to the advance of science during our times, recognizes [sic] another element as of great importance, namely, the creation and preservation of conditions promoting public health. We know that if a city is to continue strong and progressive, or even if it is to continue to exist at all, its people must be healthy and its children robust.

Above everything else, then, the Plan of Chicago is concerned with our vital problems of congestion, traffic and public health. The plan will do away with congestion in the city and its streets, and so promote the health and happiness of all. It will make traffic easy and convenient, and so make it easier and cheaper to carry on business, thus increasing the wealth of the city and its people faster than will be possible otherwise. The plan will give Chicago more and larger parks and playgrounds, and better and wider streets, and thus make the whole people more healthy and better able to carry on the work of commerce and civilization of our great city.

All over the world today cities are growing as they never did before. Steam and electric transportation have made it easy to transport food for multitudes. Modern manufacturing methods draw large numbers of men together in cities to cheaply produce clothing, machinery and the varied supplies men need in their daily lives throughout the world. No country in the world, however, has given rise so rapidly to large cities as the United States, where it was shown by the census of 1910 that forty out or every one hundred people now reside in cities, and, of these, twelve reside in the three cities of New York, Philadelphia and Chicago.

Wise men who have made a study for years of city growth tell us that this moving of mankind toward the cities is only starting, and that it is sure to continue, probably with a stronger and stronger tide, for many years to come. At the same time other men of science, devoting their lives to a study of the effect of city life upon humanity, declare to us that the physical condition of people in the cities, as compared with the people of the open country, is deteriorating. City life, they say, saps the energy of men, and makes them less efficient in the work of life. The remedy for this, they tell us, lies in providing increased means of open-air recreation, better sanitation in city houses, and more light and air in city streets. The Plan of Chicago provides for complying with this imperative demand. To preserve ourselves and our city by meeting this call for better health conditions is an aim of the Plan of Chicago.

Another appeal for the adoption of the Plan of Chicago is that made to the business instinct of our people. To carry it out means to attract to our city millions of dollars now being spent every year in other cities. When we have created a great attractive city here people will be drawn to it from all over our country, as today people are attracted to Paris. They will visit Chicago with their families and friends and remain indefinitely to enjoy the delights of the city, with vast resultant benefit to all our citizens.

In drawing the Plan of Chicago, the architects constantly kept in mind the needs of the future city in the three great elements of congestion, traffic and public health. They took the city as it has grown up and applied to it the needs of the future in transportation in recreation and in hygiene.

Because we are a commercial people, and live in a great commercial city, first thought was given to transportation. The architects' first care, therefore was to create a proper system of handling the business of Chicago in its streets, and upon its street railways, its steam railroads and its water courses. The greatest part of the plan, then, refers to improving the existing streets, to cutting new ones where necessary, to arranging the city's railway and water terminals most effectively, and to the quick and cheap handling of all the business of Chicago.

This plan of transportation completed, the architects set about a plan of making Chicago more attractive, of providing parks for the people in places where they should be provided, of giving the people recreation grounds both within the city and in the outer district nearby, of improving and beautifying the lake front of the city, and so arranging all things that the future people of Chicago may be strong and healthy, and so ambitious to extend the fame and the commerce of their city.

Finally, in their planning, the architects recognized the need of giving the people of Chicago a way to express in solid form their progressive spirit. The people of Chicago have always been proud of their city, of its importance and its power. The architects strove, therefore to provide a means whereby the civic pride and glory of Chicago could be shown to the world in imposing buildings of architectural grandeur. Thus they provided a civic center upon a vast scale, to be improved with towering buildings serving as the seat of the city government, uniting and giving life to the whole plan of the metropolis, and standing as a notice to the world of the tremendous might and power of a city loved and revered by its millions of devoted and patriotic citizens.

5-5. *HULL-HOUSE, A SOCIAL SETTLEMENT* (1894)

Jane Addams and Ellen Gates Starr

Source: Jane Addams and Ellen Gates Starr, *Hull-House, A Social Settlement at 225 Halsted Street, Chicago: An Outline-Sketch*, 1894. Courtesy of the Newberry Library, Chicago, Illinois.

EDITORS' INTRODUCTION

In 1894, Jane Addams (1860–1935) and Ellen Gates Starr (1859–1940), published a slim volume to explain the settlement house they had founded in Chicago in the fall of 1889. The authors related the settlement concept itself and the activities of the house in great detail. The booklet discusses the extension classes offered at the house, the working people's chorus, working girls' club, on-going lectures, women's club, children's dinner club, medical services, labor bureau, and host of other activities. Jane Addams, a graduate of Rockford Female Seminary (Illinois) was a noted Progressive-Era reformer and perhaps the best known woman of her day. Addams and Starr's 1888 visit to London's Toynbee Hall inspired them to found Hull-House, wherein people interested in social change lived within the neighborhood they hoped to change. Hull-House provided a model for other U.S. communities. Addams' numerous articles and well received books, including *Hull-House Maps and Papers* (1895), *Democracy and Social Ethics* (1902), *Newer Ideals of Peace* (1907), *Spirit of Youth and the City Streets* (1909), *Twenty Years at Hull-House* (1910), *A New Conscience and an Ancient Evil* (1912), *The Long Road of Women's Memory* (1916), *Peace and Bread in Time of War* (1922), *The Second Twenty Years at Hull-House* (1930), brought her ideas and reflections on her experiences to an eager audience. Jane Addams was awarded the Nobel Peace Prize in 1931.[i]

---

i Victoria Bissell Brown, "Jane Addams," 14–22, and Jennifer L. Bosch, "Ellen Gates Starr," 838–842, in Rima Lunin Schultz and Adele Hast, eds., *Women Building Chicago, 1790–1990* (Bloomington: Indiana University Press, 2001).

The two original residents of Hull-House are entering upon their fifth year of settlement in the 19th Ward. They publish this outline that the questions daily asked by neighbors and visitors may be succinctly answered. It necessarily takes somewhat the character of a report, but is much less formal. It aims not so much to give an account of what has been accomplished, as to suggest what may be done by and through a neighborhood of working people, when they are touched by a common stimulus and possess an intellectual and social centre about which they may group their various organizations and enterprises. This centre or 'settlement' to be effective must contain an element of permanency, so that the neighborhood may feel that the interest and fortunes of the residents are identical with their own. The settlement must have an enthusiasm for the possibilities of its locality, and an ability to bring into it and develop from it those lines of thought and action which make for the 'higher life.'

The original residents came to Hull-House with a conviction that social intercourse could best express the growing sense of the economic unity of society. They wished the social spirit to be the undercurrent of the life of Hull-House, whatever direction the stream might take. All the details were left for the demands of the neighborhood to determine, and each department has grown from a discovery made through natural and reciprocal social relations.

[…]

Ward Book and Maps

A ward book has been kept by the residents for two years in which have been noted matters of sociological interest found in the ward. Many instances of the sweating evil and child labor have been recorded as well as unsanitary tenements. A resident has charted the information collected during the slum investigation in the form of two sets of maps, one set on the plan of Charles Booth's wage maps of London and one set showing the nationalities of the district. The latter indicates nineteen different nationalities within the third of a square mile lying east and south of Hull-House. Arrangements have been made for the publication of these maps with a series of papers written by the residents.

After the passage of the factory and workshop bill, which includes a clause limiting women's labor to eight hours a day, the young women employés [sic] in a large factory in the near neighborhood of Hull-House formed an EIGHT HOUR CLUB for the purpose of encouraging women in factories and workshops to obey the eight-hour law.

5-6. *GROWING UP WITH A CITY* (1926)

Louise de Koven Bowen

Source: Louise de Koven Bowen, *Growing up with a City* (New York: The Macmillan Company, 1926).

EDITORS' INTRODUCTION

Louise de Koven Bowen (1859–1953), heir to a sizable real estate fortune, had deep ties with the city of Chicago; her grandfather had lived in Fort Dearborn and her mother was born within its palisades. Bowen found herself called to a formal civic role through her engagement with Hull-House. She said of her work there, "I often felt at this Hull-House club that not even in church did I ever get the inspiration or the desire for service, so much as when I was presiding at a meeting of the club and sat on the platform and looked down on the faces of 800 or 900 women gathered together, all intensely in earnest and all most anxious perhaps to put over some project in which they were interested." Bowen donated the money used to build a hall for the Hull-House women's club, which came to be named Bowen Hall. She also donated seventy-two acres of land in Waukegan, Illinois to Hull-House for a camp. Bowen, founder of the first Chicago boy's club, a trustee and treasurer of the Hull-House Association, president of the Woman's City Club, president of the Juvenile Protective Association, supporter of the first juvenile court in the United States, advocate for women's suffrage, and a member of a variety of other boards, was also the author of *The Colored People of Chicago* (1913) and *Safeguards for City Youth at Work and Play* (1914). In 1923, Chicago papers discussed her possible candidacy for mayor of the city. In 1925, Bowen chaired the Women's World's Fair held in Chicago.[i] **[See Carl Smith, "The Pullman Strike and Making Sense of the Age" in Part III for the Pullman Strike mentioned by Bowen below.]**

Hull-House

All through this earlier part of my life my attention had been turned toward the lack of adequate housing for people of a great city, and I felt most strongly that better homes were the most necessary things in the world. About this time I had heard vaguely of Hull-House and of its founder, Jane Addams. My curiosity was greatly aroused by what I had heard of her, a young girl, rather delicate, very well educated, who had traveled a great deal, but who had such a sympathy for her fellow men that she had established herself, with a friend, Miss Ellen Gates Starr, in an old house belonging to the Hull family, and which had been given her, rent free, by Miss Helen Culver, its owner. This house was situated at the corner of Halsted and Polk Streets.

About this time I had a young friend who was tired of social life, and who was anxious to do something worth while [*sic*]. She asked my advice about going to live at Hull-House, and finally established herself there for the winter; meantime, I had heard Jane Addams speak at a meeting concerning the great strike at the Pullman Company; I remember she likened Mr. Pullman to King Lear, and she seemed so fair and so dispassionate in her setting forth the reason of this strike and her feeling that Mr. Pullman had wanted to do everything for his employees but that he wanted to do it in his own way, that I was much impressed by her sympathy for the working man, and the sense of justice which made her see Mr. Pullman's side. Soon after I went over to Hull-House to visit my friend, and I was much interested in some stories she told me of her work in the neighborhood, and I remember giving some money to be used for the poor, the first donation I had ever made to Hull-House. I then met Miss Addams, and she asked me if I would come over there and do some work; when I asked what kind, she said she wished I would join the Hull-House Woman's Club, composed of the women of the neighborhood, which had recently been formed. When I asked what I should do, Miss Addams suggested that I lead the women in making motions and in helping them to think on the subjects which came before them, and in helping them express their thoughts. This all seemed to me rather vague, and I was rather frightened at the prospect; I knew almost nothing of parliamentary law, but immediately joined a class on the North Side with a good teacher and about ten women as members. I studied very hard, had a great many meetings and finally felt that at least I knew the parliamentary ropes. I then joined the Hull-House Woman's Club, and when a question came up for discussion I usually made the motion and talked to it, and the women were quick to learn and to follow. Some time later I was made secretary of this club and still later was elected President. For about seventeen years I filled some official position in the

i Louise de Koven Bowen, *Growing up with a City* (New York: The Macmillan Company, 1926), 85. See also, Sharon Z. Alter, "Bowen, Louise deKoven," in Rima Lunin Schultz and Adele Hast, eds., *Women Building Chicago, 1790–1990* (Bloomington: Indiana University Press, 2001), 101–106.

club, many years being president, and I have always felt that any experience I acquired in speaking was entirely due to practice in this club. I can see the crowded room now, filled with tired women, a few of them with shawls over their heads, some of them with babies in their arms or clinging to their skirts; there was always a good deal of noise, the women were restless, the air was heavy and stuffy, but no one wanted a window open. On the front row sat the eldest members of the club, most of them wore little black bonnets with ribbons tied under their chins. They had an invariable habit of going to sleep, and when I was speaking and saw them begin to nod it always acted as a tonic because I brightened up and tried to be so entertaining or startling in my remarks that they would come to with a little jerk, and the test of my speaking was—could I keep that front bench looking intelligent and awake?

5-7. ON THE WAY UP: CHARLOTTE AND KANSAS CITY (1976)

Source: "On the Way Up: Four Cities Show How it Can Be Done," *U.S. News and World Report* (5 April 1976): 62–64.

EDITORS' INTRODUCTION

The 1970s were a particularly difficult decade for America's largest cities. As the national economy experienced inflation and the loss of jobs, many municipalities found themselves in dire fiscal condition as operating expenses grew and tax bases dwindled. The movement of people and jobs to suburban communities also threatened any chance for a quick recovery. Cities responded with cuts to services and, in severe cases, massive layoffs of public employees.

Fortunately, there were communities that rode out the storm and even prospered. The document below is from a special investigation on the status of big cities from *U.S. News and World Report*. In addition to chronicling the ills of New York, Detroit, Chicago, and St. Louis, the magazine also reported on success stories like Charlotte and Kansas City. In contrast to other metropolitan regions, for instance the case of Oakland, California discussed by Robert Self in Part IX, Charlotte was able to avoid the "white noose" of suburban growth that choked traditional central cities. Kansas City also bucked larger national trends by retaining its ties to agriculture and leveraging millions of dollars to build new stadiums and hotels. This helped the city move toward an urban renaissance. **[See Jon C. Teaford's essay "Messiah Mayors and the Gospel of Urban Hype" in this part.]**

Charlotte: Building, Growing, and Booming

Charlotte prospers, many believe, because of a liberal annexation law that keeps it from getting hemmed in, and because of its strength as a financial and distribution center for a booming North Carolina manufacturing region.

But, further: It managed to resolve the busing-for-integration issue before the city was torn apart.

Unlike other cities being strangled by rigid geopolitical limits, State law allows Charlotte to annex contiguous urbanized areas without a vote by those inside or outside. Since 1960, the city has added 42 square miles this way.

"We don't have that white noose around the neck of the central city that's happened in a lot of Northern cities and large urban areas," notes black City Councilman Harvey B. Gantt. "People who move in to take advantage of the city also have to pay their fair share of costs."

City Finance Director John B. Fennell agrees that the law has contributed to Charlotte's sound financial position.

He says Charlotte has seen its property-tax base rise from 3.6 billion dollars in 1975 to 4.4 billion in 1976. Instead of increasing tax rates, Charlotte has lowered them, from a rate of $1.02 per $100 to 88 cents today.

Keeping downtown "viable." Charlotte has a diversified economy and serves as a financial and distribution center for the heavily textile Carolinas and to some extent the Southeast. Trucking here is second only to Chicago's.

Growth has been rapid and forecasts are it will continue.

The population rose to 284,738, up 3.7 per cent, from 1970 to 1973. By 1995, a planning study predicts, the county's population of 397,850 will almost double.

Unlike many large cities, the downtown area remains viable. Not only does a quarter of the county's population work here, but ties to downtown have tightened.

Since 1970, about 185 million dollars has been invested in the central city, including two office-banking towers in 1974. Construction still goes on as work is done on a 5.7-million-dollar county Hall of Justice and a 15-story, 15.5-million-dollar hotel.

Increasingly seen as a boon to the city is Charlotte's desegregation program, one of the toughest in the nation and employing massive court-ordered busing.

Working with school officials last year, the Citizens Advisory Group—interested parents, school and civic representatives—helped devise a plan widely viewed as being more fair and stable than previous attempts.

J. Dennis Lord, a professor at the University of North Carolina at Charlotte, says: "White flight has not been a disaster."

Growing... renovating. Charlotte's growth and prosperity have not been without growing pains, a grappling to preserve quality of life.

"When I moved here 10 years ago, it seemed to me Charlotte desired more than anything else to be a 'junior Atlanta.' What seemed to be the panacea for life and vibrance in the inner city was a strong convention trade," says Dennis Rash, dean of students at UNC in Charlotte, and chairman of Friends of the Fourth Ward, a preservation group. He senses a change.

For example, local banks have worked to develop a unique financing plan to begin renovation of the fourth war—a 28-square-block area a few minutes from downtown which in the 1920s and '30s was the "in" place to live. The area is now 50 per cent vacant and deteriorating with only 600 residents, but Mr. Rash predicts 8,500 in 10 years, many of them in new townhouses.

Many people view Charlotte as a big small town that's turning into a truly urban, big city.

James L. Cox, director for urban studies and community services at UNC in Charlotte, says of the city:

"I think Charlotte has potential, a chance to avoid many of the problems faced by other cities. It's really a question of whether it can deliver on that potential."

Kansas City: Shedding Its "Cow Town" Image

Kansas City, Mo., is often touted as one of the brightest stars among American cities—and for many reasons.

The once-famous "cow town" is still closely tied to agriculture, a fact which has been an economic blessing over the years. While the city has a good diversification in its economy, a large share of its commercial activity services the huge surrounding farming industry.

The bulk of wheat sold to Russia under grain deals, for example, has been marketed through Kansas City. The city's stockyards still do a brisk business, but Kansas City has outgrown the cow-town image. Its growth as an industrial and financial center has dwarfed the cattle industry.

But there's much more to Kansas City's advancement than that. In many ways, it is light-years ahead of larger, older cities in warding off urban malaise.

During the early 1950s, the Kansas City government began a period of progressive reform that has continued with few interruptions to the present.

While pulling itself back up by its bootstraps, Kansas City took steps that have proved farsighted. Among these was a judicious diversification of the city's revenue sources and an ambitious program of annexing available land to the city.

Under a tax-reform program in the 1950s, Kansas City began reducing its reliance on the property tax by creating new taxes. Today, the city relies on property taxes for only 11 per cent of its total revenue. Compare this with that of other cities: New York 21 per cent; Minneapolis, 28 per cent; San Francisco, 23 per cent; Dallas, 34 per cent.

Consider also the following per capita property-tax costs: Kansas City, $43.99; Boston, $503.16, and San Francisco, $234.26. It is not difficult to imagine what this means when individuals and corporations are making decisions as to where to locate.

Better way of life. Besides economic assets, Kansas City also boasts a better quality of life. It is a clean town, crossed with freeways, and remarkably easy to travel around in without becoming snarled in traffic.

There are 150 parks in easy reach of the 500,000 residents of the city and 800,000 others who live in the metropolitan area. The entertainment and cultural agenda will equal any city twice its size.

Kansas City was built was an eye for esthetics. The city claims it is second only to Rome in the number of fountains that garnish its parks and boulevards.

Another area hard to measure but equally important to municipal well-being: Kansas City has long benefited from a sense of civic responsibility and confidence in municipal government on the part of local businessmen.

A salesmen recently visited Kansas City and was staying at the city's new 350-million-dollar Crown Center. He commented: "Kansas City is just nothing like you would expect. The downtown is a thriving place. It has new convention centers, new basketball and ice arenas, a new twin football and baseball stadium. What really surprises you is all this is going on in Kansas City."

"All this" is part of a 5.3-billion-dollar city renaissance that also includes a new international airport, a foreign-trade zone, 148-acre amusement park, a new medical school and hospital, community colleges, grade schools, and the restoration of an "old town" along the Missouri River water-front. Local businesses will pay for 75 per cent.

Reluctance to borrow. Among Kansas City's conservative fiscal policies has been a tenacious resistance to over-indebtedness. General obligation bonds now total 97 million dollars which is 189 million short of its legal limit. The result of such solvency has been an AA rating for most of Kansas City bonds. Investors are being attracted away from other cities. The rate of interest Kansas City has had to pay on bonds is declining. On a recent issue it was only 4.97 per cent.

Aggressive annexation carried out in the 1950s and the '60s has also paid off. Says A.G. Hays, assistant director of finance: "Even back then the city council saw that many other cities were getting sealed off by suburbs and they took steps to prevent Kansas City from becoming a victim of the same problem."

Though Kansas City has a population of just under 500,000, it is the country's eight largest in land size. From 62 square miles in 1950, it went to 130 square miles in 1960 and 316 today. For decades, the city will be able to absorb residential and commercial expansion within its boundaries and, thus, avoid loss of assessed valuation.

Summing up the success of Kansas City, Charles N. Kimball, president of the Midwest Research Institute, says: "We are blessed in Kansas City with a do-it-yourself-minded establishment that can produce a multibillion-dollar building boom and still not lose sensitivity to the need to solve human problems. We have learned from mistakes of older cities. Growth here is being managed; it won't be allowed to destroy the way of life."

Mr. Kimball admits that Kansas City is considered an unlikely place for such success because its area encompasses two cities, two States, seven metropolitan counties and 30 other government bodies.

"We should be engulfed in red tape, bet we aren't," Mr. Kimball asserts. "Kansas City is like a bumblebee: It shouldn't fly, but it does."

5-8. PRESIDENT ARRIVES IN ALABAMA, BRIEFED ON HURRICANE KATRINA (2005)

President George W. Bush

Source: Press Release, September 2, 2005, President Arrives in Alabama, Briefed on Hurricane Katrina.

EDITORS' INTRODUCTION

On September 2, 2005, President George W. Bush landed at the Mobile Regional Airport in Mobile, Alabama to view the destruction of Gulf Coast communities by Hurricane Katrina. At a press conference, President Bush praised the Coast Guard, the National Guard, and others involved in relief efforts. Despite the fact that much of the city of New Orleans lay under water, Bush joked with those in attendance. He commented that he looked forward to the day he could sit on the porch of U.S. Senator Trent Lott's rebuilt home. President Bush then praised the work of Federal Emergency Management Agency (FEMA) Director Michael Brown for doing "a heck of job." Although the people gathered at the news conference applauded the statement, the remark soon met with a torrent of criticism. The incident brought scrutiny into Brown's qualifications. For many, President Bush's confidence in "Brownie" underscored just how out of touch the White House and the Bush administration were with the American public.

THE PRESIDENT: Well, first I want to say a few things. I am incredibly proud of our Coast Guard. We have got courageous people risking their lives to save life. And I want to thank the commanders and I want to thank the troops over there for representing the best of America.

I want to congratulate the governors for being leaders. You didn't ask for this, when you swore in, but you're doing a heck of a job. And the federal government's job is big, and it's massive, and we're going to do it. Where it's not working right, we're going to make it right. Where it is working right, we're going to duplicate it elsewhere. We have a responsibility, at the federal level, to help save life, and that's the primary focus right now. Every life is precious, and so we're going to spend a lot of time saving lives, whether it be in New Orleans or on the coast of Mississippi.

We have a responsibility to help clean up this mess, and I want to thank the Congress for acting as quickly as you did. Step one is to appropriate $10.5 billion. But I've got to warn everybody, that's just the beginning. That's a small down payment for the cost of this effort. But to help the good folks here, we need to do it.

We are going to restore order in the city of New Orleans, and we're going to help supplement the efforts of the Mississippi Guard and others to restore order in parts of Mississippi. And I want to thank you for your strong statement of zero tolerance. The people of this country expect there to be law and order, and we're going to work hard to get it. In order to make sure there's less violence, we've got to get food to people. And that's a primary mission, is to get food to people. And there's a lot of food moving. And now the—it's one thing to get it moving to a station, it's the next thing to get it in the hands of the people, and that's where we're going to spend a lot of time focusing.

We've got a lot of rebuilding to do. First, we're going to save lives and stabilize the situation. And then we're going to help these communities rebuild. The good news is—and it's hard for some to see it now—that out of this chaos is going to come a fantastic Gulf Coast, like it was before. Out of the rubbles of Trent Lott's house—he's lost his entire house—there's going to be a fantastic house. And I'm looking forward to sitting on the porch. (Laughter.)

GOVERNOR RILEY: He'll be glad to have you.

THE PRESIDENT: Out of New Orleans is going to come that great city again. That's what's going to happen. But now we're in the darkest days, and so we got a lot of work to do. And I'm down here to thank people. I'm down here to comfort people. I'm down here to let people know that we're going to work with the states and the local folks with a strategy to get this thing solved.

Now, I also want to say something about the compassion of the people of Alabama and Mississippi and Louisiana and surrounding states. I want to thank you for your compassion. Now is the time to love a neighbor like you'd like to be loved yourselves.

Governor Riley announced the fact that they're going to open up homes in military bases for stranded folks. And that's going to be very important and helpful.

My dad and Bill Clinton are going to raise money for governors' funds. The governors of Louisiana, Mississippi and Alabama will have monies available to them to help deal with the long-term consequences of this storm.

The faith-based groups and the community-based groups throughout this part of the world, and the country for that matter, are responding. If you want to help, give cash money to the Red Cross and the Salvation Army. That's where the first help will come. There's going to be plenty of opportunities to help later on, but right now the immediate concern is to save lives and get food and medicine to people so we can stabilize the situation.

Again, I want to thank you all for—and, Brownie, you're doing a heck of a job. The FEMA Director is working 24—(applause)—they're working 24 hours a day.

Again, my attitude is, if it's not going exactly right, we're going to make it go exactly right. If there's problems, we're going to address the problems. And that's what I've come down to assure people of. And again, I want to thank everybody.

And I'm not looking forward to this trip. I got a feel for it when I flew over before. It—for those who have not—trying to conceive what we're talking about, it's as if the entire Gulf Coast were obliterated by a—the worst kind of weapon you can imagine. And now we're going to go try to comfort people in that part of the world.

Thank you. (Applause.)

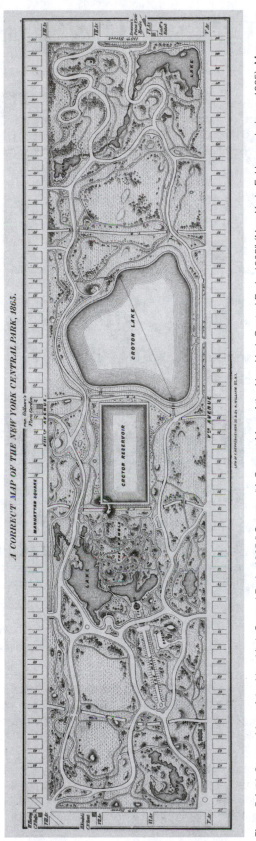

Figure 5.1 "A Correct Map of the New York Central Park, 1865." Source: "A Correct Map of the New York Central Park, 1865" (New York: F. Heppenheimer, 1865). Map Collection, American Antiquarian Society. Courtesy of the Center for Historic American Visual Culture at the American Antiquarian Society.

Central Park is located on 843 acres in the middle of the island of Manhattan between 59th and 110th Streets (south to north) and Fifth and Eight Avenues (east to west). In 1858, Frederick Law Olmsted and Calvert Vaux won a public contest for the park's design commission with their "Greensward" plan that called for a pastoral landscape in the English romantic tradition. This map, made while the park was under construction (it was finished in 1870), shows the open meadows, pedestrian walkways, equestrian paths, watercourses, and other distinctive features of the Greensward plan.

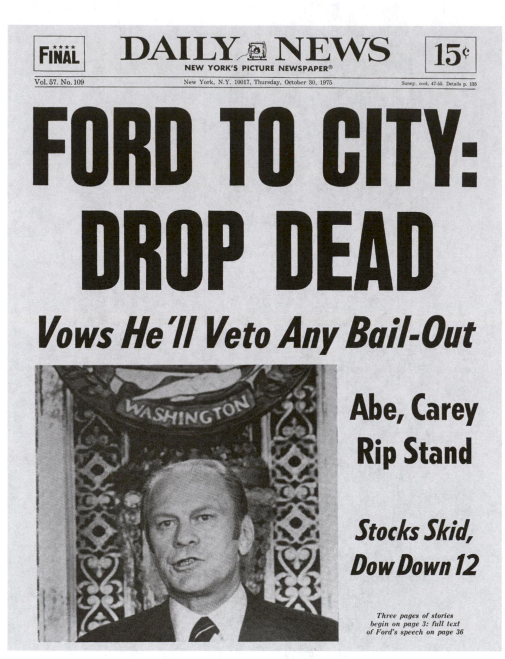

Figure 5.2 "Ford to City: Drop Dead." Source: *New York Daily News* (October 30, 1975), 1. Reprinted with permission of the New York Daily News.

During the mid-1970s, American municipalities faced the greatest fiscal crisis since the Great Depression. In 1975, New York City ran out of money despite massive budget cuts and layoffs of city employees. In May 1975, banks and other lenders announced they would not extend the city any more loans. In June, the state created the Municipal Assistance Corporation (MAC) to pay off existing creditors. However, the city needed more money to stave off bankruptcy. The crisis came to a head in October when President Gerald R. Ford announced that he had no intention of bailing out the city. Eventually the state created the Emergency Financial Control Board to manage New York City's spending. Ford's position sent a clear signal that the federal-city partnership of the New Deal had ended.

PART VI

THE URBAN ENVIRONMENT

EDITORS' INTRODUCTION TO PART VI

Inherent to the process of urbanization is the alteration of the physical landscape. American cities grew dramatically in the nineteenth and twentieth centuries as people extracted vast quantities of natural resources from the environment, and then transformed and consumed them to shape their living, working, and leisure spaces. This manipulation of the environment fueled the industrial revolution and subsequent advancements in science and technology that form the material basis of modern urban life. Although the benefits that accompany industrialization and urbanization were widely celebrated by civic and business leaders, these processes also resulted in environmental degradation and numerous social conflicts—such as the inequitable distribution of wealth and power—that remain unresolved.

The intense interest in urban affairs that developed in the 1960s and the rise of the "new urban history" and "new social history" in the 1970s coalesced into a body of scholarship around environmental history and policy. This new work reflected popular concerns over threats to natural resources and human health. Cities were a perfect place to examine the intersection of social and environmental history since, as noted historian Samuel B. Hayes argued, they gave rise to the contemporary environmental movement in the United States as part of a much wider environmental culture that developed after World War II.[1] The essays in this part highlight human and environmental consequences of urbanization and reflect contemporary scholarship in urban and environmental history, sociology, and ethnic studies. Historian Joel A. Tarr examines the contamination of resources necessary to sustain life, notably fresh water and clean air, and the creation of sanitary infrastructure to remediate pollution in Pittsburgh, Pennsylvania. Martin V. Melosi and Joseph A. Pratt trace the impact of cheap fossil fuels on the growth of cities and their surrounding metropolitan areas through a study of Houston, Texas. And finally, sociologists David N. Pellow and Lisa Sun-Hee Park examine environmental inequity and racism by documenting the disproportionate association between toxic waste and hazardous manufacturing with working-class ethnic minorities in California's Silicon Valley.

The illustrations and documents in this part highlight the often precarious relationship between human beings and their built environments. This proves especially true in terms of pollution and poor public health. As we argue in our essay in Part I, "Examining America's Urban Landscape: From Social Reform to Social History," beginning in the 1840s, sanitary reformers in Europe and the United States documented the relationship between the spread of disease in cities and filthy air and water, raw sewage, and the overall foul living conditions of the working poor. A graphic illustration of such conditions in 1857 is provided in **Figure 6.1**, "Bridge Over the Monongahela River," that shows the smoky skyline of Pittsburgh, a subject which Joel Tarr addresses in his essay. The most extensive public health study of an American city in the nineteenth century was the *Report of the Council of Hygiene and Public Health of the Citizens' Association of New York Upon the Sanitary Condition of the City* published in 1865. A map from this report, "Encroachment of Nuisances Upon Populous Up-Town Districts" is also included as **Figure 6.2** to illustrate how the use of mixed space in Manhattan allowed for manure yards, rendering works, and other noxious establishments to operate next to residential areas.

While the nineteenth century witnessed great strides in sanitation and public health, disasters such as hurricanes, floods, and earthquakes highlighted the limits of human attempts to control and suppress nature. And the devastation caused the natural disasters was augmented by human miscalculations. The San Francisco Earthquake of 1906 is one such calamity that, along with its accompanying fires, killed hundreds (if not thousands) of people and destroyed the downtown and two-thirds of all business districts and residential neighborhoods. A sample of the devastation is provided with **Figure 6.3**, "Demolished and Titled by the Earthquake, Homes on Howard Street at 17th, 1906." The recent loss of life and infrastructure devastation along the Gulf Coast region of the United States by Hurricanes Katrina and Rita are also covered in documents and essays in Part V.

The change in attitude toward environmental protection that followed World War II forms the central theme of **Document 6.1**, "Special Message to the Congress on Conservation and Restoration of Natural Beauty (1965)," by President Lyndon B. Johnson. In this sweeping statement on the relationship between nature and the American way of life, President Johnson explains that the federal government should make cities more livable by decreasing water, land, and air pollution. While the subsequent environmental movement of the late 1960s and 1970s even surpassed Johnson's call to action, there were still millions of Americans who were underserved by environmental regulations. As **Document 6.2** from the United Church of Christ's landmark 1987 study *Toxic Wastes and Race in the United States* demonstrates, there is a close correlation between race and the location of environmental hazards in American cities. The release of this report was instrumental in bringing the larger issue of environmental justice into the nation's political dialogue regarding public health and social equity.

NOTE

1.   Samuel P. Hays, *Explorations in Environmental History* (Pittsburgh: University of Pittsburgh Press, 1998): 85–86.

The Metabolism of the Industrial City: The Case of Pittsburgh

Joel A. Tarr

Source: *Journal of Urban History* 28 (5) (July 2002): 511–545.

EDITORS' INTRODUCTION

Cities are the product of human interaction with natural resources and, as such, are part of the earth's overall environment and web of life. As the noted sanitary engineer Abel Wolman argued in his 1965 *Scientific America* essay "The Metabolism of Cities," modern urban areas have populations that sustain themselves by drawing materials from, and introducing potentially harmful waste products into, the planet's closed ecological system.[i] Borrowing and adopting his title from Wolman, historian Joel A. Tarr expands upon the biological concept of metabolism by examining the interactive relationship between the city and the natural environment through the use, misuse, and remediation of water and air resources in Pittsburgh, Pennsylvania during the nineteenth and twentieth centuries.

From humble origins as a small village surrounding Fort Pitt in the eighteenth century, Pittsburgh became one of America's preeminent industrial cities in the late nineteenth century, leading the nation in the production of pig iron and steel products. This manufacturing progress, however, came at great expense to the natural beauty and purity of physical features and the health of those living in the area. By the second half of the nineteenth century, Pittsburgh's rivers were filthy from untreated sewage and industrial discharge and its skies full of smoke and soot. **[See Figure 6.1 "Bridge Over the Monongahela River, Pittsburgh, Penn."]** As Tarr notes, many people in the city also lacked basic sanitary services such as potable water and sewers. Not surprisingly, such conditions bred disease, disproportionately affecting working-class immigrant and African American residences. Tarr traces the gradual improvements to Pittsburgh's water supply and wastewater disposal system, as well as smoke and air pollution, in the context of advances in and debates over technology, science and engineering, sanitary reform, and public health policies which all combined to make the city more environmentally sustainable.

Joel A. Tarr is the Richard S. Caliguiri University Professor of History & Policy at Carnegie Mellon University in Pittsburgh, Pennsylvania. He holds joint appointments in the department of history, the department of engineering and public policy, and the H. John Heinz III School of Public Policy Management. He is the author of numerous works on technology and the urban environment including *The Horse in the City: Living Machines in the 19th Century* (Baltimore: Johns Hopkins University Press, 2007) with Clay McShane, *Devastation and Renewal: An Environmental History of Pittsburgh and Its Region* (Pittsburgh: University of Pittsburgh Press, 2003) editor, and *The Search for the Ultimate Sink: Urban Pollution in Historical Perspective* (Akron: University of Akron Press, 1996). In 2008, the Society for the History of Technology (SHOT) recognized Tarr for his pioneering scholarship by awarding him the Leonardo da Vinci Medal, their highest recognition.

---

i Abel Wolman, "The Metabolism of Cities," *Scientific America* (September 1965): 179–190.

THE METABOLISM OF THE INDUSTRIAL CITY

The Case of Pittsburgh

The concept of metabolism has been adopted from biology and refers to physiological processes within living things that provide the energy and nutrients required by an organism as the conditions of life itself. These processes can be described in terms of the transformation of inputs (sunlight, chemical energy, nutrients, water, and air) into biomass and waste products. While essentially a concept originating in science, I have found it useful as a means to comprehend the environmental history of cities. Just as living things require the inputs mentioned above, so do cities. That is, cities cannot exist without those inputs—urbanites require clean air, water, food, fuel, and construction goods to subsist while urban industries need materials for production purposes. These materials may initially come from the area of the urban site itself, but increasingly over time they are derived from the urban hinterland or even farther. That is, as the city grows, it extends its ecological footprint deeper and deeper into its hinterland.

The ecologist Eugene Odum has written that "the city is a parasite on the natural and domesticated environments," since it does not grow food, and dirties its air and water. One can also note that it reshapes and consumes the land. Odum observes that a parasite "does not live for very long if it kills or damages its host." Therefore, for a parasite to survive, it must develop systems of exchange that benefit both its host and itself.[1] While some may object to characterizing the city as a parasite on the environment, thus raising the ancient specter of the evil city and the natural countryside, from a purely descriptive perspective, the concept is a valid one. Cities do consume their environments and cannot survive unless they reach a point of equilibrium with their sites and their hinterlands in regard to the consumption of air, water, and land resources.[2] Today we call such a goal seeking a sustainable city.

Cities and their metropolitan areas have had major effects on the natural environment since their appearance, but these impacts have accelerated over the past two centuries with the development of industrialism and rapid urbanization. In the United States, urban development has advanced, and today a large majority of the population lives in sizable metropolitan areas. These metropolitan areas are growing not only population-wise but also in terms of aerial extent. In these habitats, city builders have reshaped and often destroyed natural landscapes and eliminated animal, bird, marine, and insect species, while urban demands for resources have profoundly affected hinterlands.

The relationship between the city and the natural environment has actually been interactive, with cities having massive effects on the natural environment, while the natural environment, in turn, has profoundly shaped urban configurations. Not only did nature cause many of the annoyances of daily urban life, such as bad weather and pests, but it also produced natural disasters and catastrophes such as floods, fires, volcanic activity, and earthquakes. Often, however, the actions of urbanites—such as building on flood plains and steep slopes, under the shadow of volcanoes, or in earthquake-prone zones—have exacerbated the dangers they are exposed to from natural hazards.[3]

This essay will focus on the metabolism of one major industrial city—Pittsburgh—in the years from about 1800 to 2000. In doing so, it will explore issues relating to resources of water and air, and the ways in which they were used, misused, and remediated. That is, the essay will consider the ways in which the city has moved from a lack of concern with environmental goods toward a more sustainable level.

Pittsburgh is sited in southwestern Pennsylvania, west of the Allegheny Mountains. The physical geography of the region consists of an uplifted plateau of about twelve hundred feet in height that has been dissected by an extensive river and stream network flowing from the Allegheny Mountains. The cutting action of rivers and streams carved a complex topography of hills and steep valleys with a general relief of five hundred feet but also sharp variations.

Human action as well as natural forces have shaped and reshaped the landscape. Development has taken place especially along the floodplains and terraces in the major valleys as well as in interior valleys and hollows. The region's greatest mineral resource is bituminous coal, but it also has natural gas and petroleum deposits that were historically important. The city's population reached a high of approximately 676,000 in 1950, but today (2000) it is down to about half that total. The six-county metropolitan area is at a plateau of about 2.25 million, where it has remained for several decades. Territorially, through annexation, the city grew to fifty-five square miles during the nineteenth and twentieth centuries but has remained stagnant since about 1930. Conversely, the urbanized area of the mature metropolitan region has continued to expand along its periphery. During this period, the city and the region's environment—its water, air, and land resources—have undergone dramatic changes.

Water Supply and Wastewater Disposal

Cities require fresh water to exist.[4] These supplies fill a number of functions, such as human and domestic needs, commercial and industrial purposes, street flushing, and fire fighting. One of the most serious environmental problems Pittsburgh has faced throughout its history is pollution of its neighboring rivers. As a riverine city, Pittsburgh has been both blessed by abundant supplies and cursed by the extensive pollution of these supplies. This pollution, from both domestic and industrial sources, has severely affected the quality of the water drawn from the rivers for both drinking water and industrial uses, as well as from wells. In addition, pollution has sharply curtailed the availability of the rivers for recreational purposes.

Like other urbanites at the beginning of the nineteenth century, Pittsburghers drew their water from local sources such as wells, rivers, and ponds, as well as from rainwater gathered in cisterns. Both private and public water suppliers provided water to the city almost from its very beginnings. The debate over improved water supply focused initially on the issue of public versus private provision. ... In 1822, citizens again petitioned the councils, requesting that the municipality build a waterworks to supply Allegheny River water to the city. The petitions maintained that municipal ownership was required to guarantee improved fire protection and to secure lower fire insurance rates, to service domestic and manufacturing needs, and to meet public health requirements.[5] The insistence on public rather than private provision highlights the widespread belief that water was too important to city life to be left to the private profit-making sector.

In 1826, the Pittsburgh Select and Common Councils responded to citizens' demands and approved the construction of a waterworks that would, according to the council presidents, provide protection against fire and "beneficial effects to every manufactory and ... family in the city." The city completed the waterworks in 1828. The system utilized a steam pump to draw water from the Allegheny River and raise it to a million-gallon reservoir for gravity distribution throughout the city. Responding to new demands caused by a major fire and the annexation of contiguous towns, the councils expanded the system in 1844 and in 1848. By the end of 1850, the city had laid twenty-one miles of water pipe, with the system serving 6,630 dwellings, stores, and shops. System expansion continued, especially after the major annexations of territory in 1868 and 1872. In 1879, the city opened a new waterworks that pumped water from the Allegheny River and stored it in two reservoirs for gravity distribution throughout the city. From 1895 to 1915, the city expanded the water supply network from 268 to 743 miles.[6]

The funding of the waterworks was the single largest expenditure made by the city during its first fifty years. Pittsburgh was not unusual in the extent to which waterworks costs constituted a substantial part of the total municipal budget. The building of New York's Croton Aqueduct in 1842, for instance, increased the city's debt from $500,000 to more than $9 million and caused many citizens to predict financial disaster.[7] Pittsburgh's willingness to make such a large expenditure for a public good can be explained by the joining of a variety of interest groups—merchants and industrialists, homeowners, fire insurance companies, and those concerned with the public health—to demand the construction of an adequate waterworks. Waterworks were ordinarily the most expensive capital project undertaken by nineteenth-century American cities, indicating their importance to urban metabolism.

Access to water services, however, was unevenly distributed throughout the city, an important issue of what today we call environmental justice. Working-class districts had poorer water supplies than did affluent neighborhoods, often relying on local springs or wells subject to pollution. Piped water was frequently accessed through a spigot in the back yard (frequently located near the privy vaults) rather than through indoor plumbing. The infamous Painter's Row, tenements owned by U.S. Steel on the South Side, had one spigot in the yard serving ninety-one families.[8]

An administrative ruling acerbated the situation in regard to water access. In 1872, the City Water Commission ruled that the size of the pipe laid on a particular street would be determined by the amount of potential revenue. This ruling resulted in either insufficient supply or no supply to poor neighborhoods. Such a policy, however, was not unusual for American cities. Robin L. Einhorn has called it the "segmented system"—a system that provided benefits to those who paid for them but that also "made the American urban landscape a physical expression of political inequality."[9] Typhoid death rates were high throughout the city but were highest in working-class immigrant and African American areas.[10]

A supply of potable water was only one part of the city's metabolic system—wastewater from households and industries as well as storm water had to be disposed of. Household wastes and wastewater were usually placed in cesspools and privy vaults, and these were a frequent source of problems.[11] Many portions of Pittsburgh's heavily industrialized South Side, for instance, utilized springs for water that were located close to neighborhood privy vaults. Private scavengers under contract to the city were responsible for maintaining sanitary conditions by cleaning privy vaults and removing garbage. In the process of performing this task, however, they frequently fouled the streets and polluted the rivers. As the city grew, domestic waste disposal problems increased; in the late nineteenth century, the Pittsburgh Board of Health identified privy vault nuisances as the major health issue facing the city.[12] [...]

Increasingly, it became obvious that only the construction of a sewerage system would alleviate wastewater disposal problems. A variety of public and private sewers existed. Until the 1840s, all municipal sewers were above ground and made of wood or brick. [...] By mid-century, however, demands for improved services, particularly from the city's commercial interests, persuaded the municipality to construct underground sewers in the business district. By 1866, this district possessed a "fairly adequate" system of main sewers. Other sections of the city were provided with services in a more uneven and haphazard fashion. By 1875, the city had constructed about twenty-five miles of sewers, mostly for storm water drainage. These sewers, however, suffered from design faults and were often either undersized or oversized and subject to constant clogging. The city had no topographical maps until the 1870s, and sewers did not conform to topography; neither did they follow an overall engineering plan. Rather, the municipality built sewers as a result of council members' attempts to meet their constituent demands. In addition, householders often constructed their own sewers, many of which went unrecorded. In 1881, a noted New York civil engineer, J.J.R. Croes, hired to consult on improving the system, commented to a meeting of the Western Pennsylvania Engineers' Society that "you have no sewers; you don't know where they are going, or where they are to be found." Without sewers, the great majority of households in the city continued to depend on cesspools and privy vaults for disposal of domestic waste.

Debate raged about possible designs of the sewer system. Should it be a separate, small-pipe system that carried only domestic and industrial wastes, the technology advocated by the famous sanitarian Col. George E. Waring Jr.? Or should it be a larger, combined system that could accommodate both waste water and storm water, a design favored by many noted sanitary engineers?[13] The city's public health and engineering professionals divided over this question. Physicians argued that the separate system was preferable because it would protect health by removing wastes from the household before they had begun to generate disease-causing sewer gas. Storm water was a secondary matter and could be handled by surface conduits.

Sanitary engineers took a different position, maintaining that domestic wastes and storm water were equally important and that a large-pipe system that would accommodate both was more economical. The virtues of the combined system in terms of both health considerations and storm water removal convinced city officials and by the late 1880s Pittsburgh had begun to build such a system.[14] Between 1889 and 1912, civil engineers from the new Bureau of Engineering of the Public Works Department constructed more than 412 miles of sewers, almost all of the combined type. The construction of the planned centralized sewerage system signified a movement away from the "piecemeal, decentralized approach to city-building characteristic of the 19th century."[15] In constructing a large centralized combined sewer network, Pittsburgh was following the lead of other large American cities such as Boston, Chicago, and New York.[16]

Many citizens resisted connecting to the new sewer lines and attempted to keep their old privy vaults and cesspools. The Board of Health used the sanitary code to compel connection. In a series of acts in the late nineteenth and early twentieth centuries, the council barred the construction of cesspools where sewer service was available, outlawed the draining of water closets into privy vaults, and prohibited the connection of privy wells to public sewers. Resistance to connecting to the system continued, particularly in working-class areas, because of householder opposition to paying sewer assessments.[17]

Building of a sewer system reduced nuisances but increased contamination of the city's water supply. By 1900, most of the Pittsburgh population received its water from either the Allegheny or the Monongahela River, and over the years the watersheds of these streams had become increasingly populated. By 1900, for instance, more than 350,000 inhabitants in seventy-five upriver municipalities discharged their untreated sewage into the Allegheny River, the river that provided water supplies for most of Pittsburgh's population. Some of Pittsburgh's own sewers discharged into the river at sites located above water supply pumping stations. The resulting pollution gave Pittsburgh the highest typhoid fever death rate of the nation's large cities from 1882 to 1907—well over 100 deaths per 100,000 population. In contrast, in 1905, the average for northern cities was 35 per 100,000 persons.[18] [...]

The Health Department advised that drinking water be boiled, but new immigrants often ignored such advice since they viewed the water as uncontaminated. "You cannot make the foreigner believe that Pittsburgh water is unwholesome," observed one physician, noting that roughly half of all foreign-born men sickened with typhoid within two years of arriving in the city.[19] Pittsburgh had one of the highest rates of bottled water consumption in the nation, but these supplies were out of reach for most working-class people. Thus, as a 1909 *Pittsburgh Survey* article observed, "those who could not afford to buy bottled water continued to drink filth." According to the municipal Health Department, Pittsburgh appeared "as two cities, one old and congested with a high mortality, and the other new and spacious with a very low death rate."[20]

Beginning in the 1890s, agitation increased among women's groups, engineers, and physicians about the need to protect the water supply from infectious disease. The new science of bacterial water analysis had convinced many of these citizens that mortality and morbidity from infectious waterborne disease could be prevented. In the 1890s, engineers and civic groups cooperated to investigate the quality of the water supply using the new methods of bacterial science. These studies conclusively demonstrated the relationship between typhoid and water quality, and in 1896, the councils approved an ordinance authorizing the mayor to create a Pittsburgh Filtration Commission to further study the matter and make public policy recommendations.[21] The commission's investigations reconfirmed the link between water and disease, and its 1899 report recommended construction of a slow-sand filtration plant as the most economical means of dealing with the threat to the public health. ... Once in operation, the filtration system had dramatic effects, and by 1912, Pittsburgh's death rate from typhoid fever equaled the average for the largest American cities.[22] [...]

Although Pittsburgh was filtering its own water after 1907, the city continued to dump its untreated sewage into its neighboring rivers, endangering the water supply of downstream communities. In the beginning of 1910, the city requested the State Department of Health to grant it a permit allowing it to extend its sewerage system. The department, headed by a physician, Samuel G. Dixon, first responded by requesting a "comprehensive sewerage plan for the collection and disposal of all of the sewage of the municipality." In addition, the department argued that to attain efficiency of treatment, the city should consider changing its sewerage from the combined to the separate system.[23] [...]

The city of Pittsburgh responded to Dixon's order by hiring the engineering firm of Allen Hazen and George C. Whipple to act as consultants for the required study. Hazen and Whipple were among the nation's most distinguished sanitary engineers and were already known for their espousal of water filtration as an alternative to sewage treatment to protect drinking water quality. Hazen had actually served as chief consultant on the construction of Pittsburgh's sand filtration plants. The engineers based their study primarily on an evaluation of the costs of building a treatment system and of converting Pittsburgh sewers to the separate system.

In their report, issued on January 30, 1912, Hazen and Whipple argued that Pittsburgh's construction of a sewage treatment plant would not free the downstream towns from threats to their water supplies nor from the need to filter them, since other communities would continue to discharge raw sewage into the rivers. The method of disposal by dilution, they maintained, sufficed to prevent nuisances, particularly if storage reservoirs were constructed upstream from Pittsburgh to augment flow during periods of low stream volume. Hazen and Whipple argued that there was no case "where a great city has purified its sewage to protect public water supplies from the stream below."[24]

Hazen and Whipple's most powerful argument concerned the lack of economic feasibility of converting Pittsburgh's sewerage system to separate sewers and building a sewage treatment plant. There was no precedent, they claimed, for a city's replacing the combined system with the separate system "for the purpose of protecting water supplies of other cities taken from the water course below." They calculated that financing such a project would have caused the city to exceed its municipal indebtedness level and thus violate state law. Moreover, because the sewage treatment plant was intended for the protection of the downstream communities, it would not give Pittsburgh any direct benefits. Furthermore, downstream cities would still have to filter their water to protect against waterborne pathogens. No "radical change in the method of sewerage or of sewage disposal as now practiced by the city of Pittsburgh is necessary or desirable," they concluded.[25] [...]

Given the political context and the financial limitations on the city, Dixon had no realistic means by which to enforce his order. In 1913, he capitulated and issued Pittsburgh a temporary discharge permit.

The city continued to receive such permits until 1939, and it was not until 1959 that Pittsburgh and seventy-one other Allegheny County municipalities ceased discharging raw sewage into the abutting rivers and began treating their wastes.[26] Thus, nearly half a century was to pass before Dixon's vision of sewage-free rivers would even begin to be realized.

This particular case has implications larger than those that relate only to Pittsburgh. The dispute pitted public health physicians against sanitary engineers and illustrated their different conceptions of the choice dictated by the urban environment. Sanitary engineers believed that they had a superior conception of the relative needs and values of cities in regard to public health because of their understanding of municipal financial limitations—thus sewage treatment was a luxury, less critical than other urban public health needs. Many public health officials believed, on the other hand, that sewage disposal was not a proper use of streams, especially if drinking water quality was involved.[27] From the perspective of urban metabolism and urban sustainability, the short-term nature of the engineering option is clear, however driven by fiscal necessities.

Smoke and Air Pollution

A vital part of the urban metabolism is clean air, but effective metabolism also requires a constant source of energy, which often conflicts with the goal of maintaining clean air. The primary air quality concern of cities before World War II was smoke pollution, which consisted primarily of particles generated by the burning of fossil fuels, especially bituminous coal. These particles blocked the sunlight, irritated the lungs, discolored clothing and other materials including building facades, and threatened the public health.

Heavy smoke pollution was a problem for many cities, especially for those such as Pittsburgh and St. Louis that were located close to large deposits of bituminous coal. Smoke pollution in Pittsburgh resulted from a conjunction of the factors of topography, urbanization, industrialization, and the availability at low cost of large sources of high-volatile bituminous coal. The coal was used for domestic and commercial heating purposes, for processing raw materials and manufacturing goods, and for providing fuel for transportation systems.[28] Early in the nineteenth century, Pittsburgh gained a reputation as the "smoky city."

The increase of smoke pollution as Pittsburgh grew and industrialized compelled public authorities to make some gestures at control. In 1868, the City Councils passed a statute banning the use of bituminous coal or wood by railroads within the city limits, and in 1869, they forbade the construction of beehive coke ovens. Neither statute, however, was strictly enforced. During the 1880s, the discovery and exploitation of local supplies of natural gas provided the city with approximately six years of clean air. Exhaustion of the local gas supply, however, caused a return to soft coal as a fuel and to heavy smoke palls, stimulating various elite and professional groups to press for smoke control.[29] The Woman's Health Protective Association joined with the Western Pennsylvania Engineer's Society to push for smoke control statutes. The City Councils responded by passing a series of ordinances in the 1890s and at the beginning of the twentieth century that regulated dense smoke from industrial, commercial, and transportation sources, but not from domestic sources. In 1911, the City Council created a Bureau of Smoke Regulation for enforcement purposes.[30] [...]

Although it had some limited success, the smoke control movement failed to control the smoke nuisance to any appreciable degree during the first third of the century. During the 1920s and 1930s, therefore, smoke and fuel researchers and regulators redefined the problem. They agreed that industries and railroads had made advances in eliminating dense smoke through technological and fuel improvements, by care in firing methods, and through cooperation with smoke bureaus. The smoke problem persisted, smoke investigators held, because of a failure to control domestic furnaces. Experts argued that smoke from household furnaces was especially objectionable because "the amount of black smoke produced by a pound of coal is greatest when fired in a domestic furnace and that domestic smoke is dirtier and far more harmful than industrial smoke."[31]

Domestic furnaces had not been regulated for several reasons, the most important of which were the political and administrative problems involved in controlling the heating habits of a multitude of householders. In 1940, there were 175,163 dwellings in Pittsburgh, of which 141,788 burned coal and 30,507 consumed natural gas; 53,388 of those burning coal had no central heating plant and used stoves to heat their homes. Smoke regulators lacked an effective administrative mechanism to control domestic smoke without hundreds of smoke inspectors. Politically, the issue was difficult because control threatened to impose higher costs for capital equipment and fuel on householders. And because of a historical equation between smoke and prosperity in Pittsburgh and other industrial cities, it was difficult to develop a public consensus for stringent controls.[32] In short, the problem was one of devising a strategy to change individual behavior in regard to fuel use in the name of the collective social goal of clean air.

The climate of opinion in Pittsburgh in the late 1930s, however, discouraged discussion of smoke control. A city dependent on heavy industry, Pittsburgh was badly scarred by the Depression; clear skies suggested closed factories and unemployed workers. In addition, many local businesses were related to the coal mining industry, which also suffered severely from the Depression. As a sign of its belief that smoke equaled prosperity and its relief at the return of full employment, in 1939 the Pittsburgh City Council actually eliminated the Bureau of Smoke Regulation. [...]

At the end of the decade, however, the Pittsburgh smoke control forces received a dramatic assist from the city of St. Louis, also an industrial center dependent on bituminous coal. [...] In February 1941, the *Pittsburgh Press* began a concerted series of articles and editorials pointing to St. Louis' success and asserting that Pittsburgh could also achieve clean air.[33] Most effective in mobilizing opinion were two pictures published on the *Press'* front page showing a smoke-darkened St. Louis street before smoke regulation and the same street sunlit after the control ordinances had become operative. Egged on by the paper, readers, especially irate housewives, began bombarding Pittsburgh Mayor Cornelius D. Scully with hundreds of letters a day demanding action. Delegations of civic officials and politicians visited St. Louis on a "civic pilgrimage" to examine the administrative machinery of smoke control and to assess its potential political costs. Most returned convinced of its technical feasibility. [...]

The antismoke campaigners stressed the achievement of St. Louis in attaining clean air and emphasized that the benefits of smoke control would outweigh the costs both for the community and for its citizens. In February 1941, the mayor appointed a Commission for the Elimination of Smoke that represented a broad spectrum of the community. In his charge to the commission, Mayor Cornelius D. Scully declared that "Pittsburgh must, in the interest of its economy, its reputation and the health of its citizens, curb the smoke and smog which has made this season, and many others before it, the winter of our discontent." The commission included representatives of business, labor, government, the media, the health professions, and voluntary associations with a civic and a welfare orientation; the inclusion of three women reflected the campaign leadership's perception of the importance of women in achieving smoke control. A technical advisory group stood ready to present recommendations concerning control of specific sources such as railroads and metallurgical companies and to gather information on questions such as the availability of smokeless fuel and smokeless equipment.[34]

While the commission was holding its hearings, the Civic Club and the League of Women Voters conducted a countywide campaign of public arousal and education through a network of voluntary associations. While voluntary organizations of all types were represented in the network, women's groups were most numerous, reflecting the deep involvement of women in the smoke elimination campaign. As homemakers, women of all classes knew how much extra cleaning smoke necessitated, with the burden falling most severely on working-class women who lived close to the mills. Middle- and upper-class women in the Civic Club and the League of Women Voters coordinated luncheons and lectures and provided speakers to interested groups.[35] [...]

Controlling smoke, however, would not be costless. Among the groups who would be most affected were coal miners and low-income workers. The representative of the Mine Workers on the commission, however, appeared to accept the argument that smoke control would not substantially affect mine employment because the need for smokeless coal would actually result in the mining of larger amounts of bituminous.[36] As for working-class consumers, the commission took the position that smoke control would bring more benefits than costs to the working class because it suffered the most from the effects of smoke pollution.[37]

In spite of disagreements within the commission, all members, including coal industry and labor representatives, signed the final report. The report listed the names of two hundred voluntary organizations including fifty-six women's clubs, twenty-four business organizations, and many labor and civic groups as supporters of smoke control. The report held that smoke elimination would "bring about a new era of growth, prosperity and well-being" for the city and would impose "little or no additional burden on the low-income groups of the city."[38]

The commission report recommended a strategy based on control of smoke at the source. Over a staged two-year period, all fuel users would have to either burn smokeless fuels or utilize smokeless mechanical equipment. By controlling the quality of the fuel inputs into the city's metabolic engine, air quality would improve.[39] The commission also recommended the creation of a Bureau of Smoke Prevention to be housed in the Department of Health and headed by a "qualified engineer" with the power to impose fines and to seal equipment in case

of law violations. Only public opinion, concluded the report, would determine if the city would become smoke free.[40] [...]

Successful implementation, however, would not have taken place without the support of the newly elected mayor, David Lawrence, and the efforts of two newly created and allied organizations—the United Smoke Council, consisting of eighty allied organizations from Pittsburgh and Allegheny County, and the Allegheny Conference on Community Development (ACCD), formed in 1943. The council's function was to continue public educational efforts about the need for smoke control.[41] The mission of the ACCD was the development of "an over all community improvement program" for Pittsburgh, in which smoke control played a vital part. The ACCD was especially critical because of its concentration of corporate power and its help in providing the planning essential for policy implementation.[42] [...]

The improvements in Pittsburgh air quality that occurred after the implementation of the smoke control ordinance, however, were not necessarily the result of the type of fuel and equipment substitutions projected by the 1941 policy makers. [...] While the use of low-volatile and processed coal (Disco) and smokeless coal-burning equipment did play a role in reducing smoke in 1947–1948, they steadily declined in significance. Increasingly, low-priced natural gas, furnished by pipelines from the Southwest and stored in underground storage pools, became the dominant fuel used for Pittsburgh domestic heating.[43] The rates of change for the city are striking. In 1940, 81 percent of Pittsburgh households burned coal and 17.4 percent natural gas (from Appalachian fields); by 1950, the figures were 31.6 percent for coal and 66 percent for natural gas. This represented a change in fuel type and combustion equipment by almost half the city households, most of which took place after 1945[44] (see Figure 7). In addition, railroad conversion from steam to diesel-electric locomotives between 1950 and 1960 also greatly reduced railroad contributions to the city's smoke burden.

Because of the shift to natural gas in Pittsburgh, the reduction in smoke pollution would undoubtedly have eventually occurred without the smoke control law. The price of natural gas made it very competitive with coal from an economic perspective, and heating with gas was much more convenient. But while not as critical as some Pittsburgh boosters would have one believe, the Pittsburgh smoke control ordinance undoubtedly accelerated the rate of change to clean fuel. Comparisons in rates of fuel change made between Pittsburgh and other cities make this clear. The clean air initiative was also important as a motivating factor in the famous Pittsburgh Renaissance, convincing Pittsburghers that positive change was possible.[45] [...]

Conclusions

This essay has attempted to develop the concept of metabolism in relationship to the environmental history of the city of Pittsburgh. In so doing, it has examined the domains of water and air in regard to their use, misuse, and attempted restoration. To a great extent, the use and misuse of environmental resources was predicated on a value system that emphasized production and material progress rather than environmental protection. Reaction against abuses of the natural system began in the late nineteenth century, led particularly by women's groups and socially minded engineers. Progress, however, was slow and even nonexistent, as the forces of industrial development overwhelmed those whose priorities emphasized environmental protection and restoration.

The years since the end of the Second World War, however, have witnessed increasing momentum on the part of groups and individuals concerned with environmental quality. While some environmental improvements were primarily stimulated by concern over urban redevelopment rather than by environmental values, substantial improvements were accomplished. Improved air and river water quality as well as increased species and fish diversity are encouraging improvements. Environmental values are receiving more attention and have been embraced by a larger sector of the public. Progress, however, has been halting,

and many aspects of the environment wait to be redeemed. In addition, even in areas where there has been partial land use change, new developments often have little design or aesthetic distinction and pay little homage to environmental qualities. Thus, although the metabolism of the city has begun to move toward a point of balance, many areas of the city and the region await action to help them reach sustainability.

NOTES

1. Eugene P. Odum, *Ecology and Our Endangered Life-Support Systems* (Sunderland, MA: Sinauer Associates, 1989), 17.
2. Another way of expressing the concept of society-nature interaction is to think of a society as making "colonizing interventions," where such interventions are "the sum of all purposive changes made in natural systems that aim to render nature more useful for society." Thus, metabolism and colonization are "intricately interwoven," reflecting aspects of nature-society interactions. See Verena Winiwarter, "Where Did All the Waters Go? The Introduction of Sewage Systems in Urban Settlements," in Christoph Bernhardt, ed., *Environmental Problems in European Cities in the 19th and 20th Century* (New York: Waxman, 2001), 107.
3. Mike Davis, *Ecology of Fear: Los Angeles and the Imagination of Disaster* (New York, 1998); B. R. Stephenson, *Visions of Eden: Environmentalism, Urban Planning, and City Building in St. Petersburg, Florida, 1900–1995* (Columbus, 1997); Theodore T. Steinberg, *Acts of God: The Unnatural History of Natural Disasters* (New York, 2000).
4. For a comprehensive study of water supply and wastewater disposal issues in American history, see Martin Melosi, *The Sanitary City: Urban Infrastructure in America from Colonial Times to the Present* (Baltimore: Johns Hopkins University Press, 2002).
5. Richard A. Sabol, "Public Works in Pittsburgh Prior to the Establishment of the Department of Public Works" (research paper, Department of History, Carnegie Mellon University, 1980), 5; Frank Kern, "History of Pittsburgh Water Works, 1821–1842" (research paper, Department of History, Carnegie Mellon University, 1982), 1–4.
6. Erwin E. Lanpher and C. F. Drake, *City of Pittsburgh: Its Water Works and Typhoid Fever Statistics* (Pittsburgh: City of Pittsburgh, 1930), 23–25. Extensive waste and leaky pipes plagued the system, resulting in frequent water shortages.
7. James H. Thompson, "A Financial History of the City of Pittsburgh, 1816–1910," (Ph.D. dissertation, University of Pittsburgh, 1948), 44–45; Paul

Studenski and Herman E. Kross, *Financial History of the United States* (New York: McGraw-Hill, 1952), 13.

8. Susan J. Kleinberg, *The Shadow of the Mills: Working-Class Families in Pittsburgh, 1870–1907* (Pittsburgh: University of Pittsburgh Press, 1989), 87–93.

9. Robin L. Einhorn, *Property Rules: Political Economy in Chicago, 1833–1872* (Chicago: University of Chicago Press, 1991), 104.

10. Clayton R. Koppes and William P. Norris, "Ethnicity, Class, and Mortality in the Industrial City: A Case Study of Typhoid Fever in Pittsburgh, 1890–1910," *Journal of Urban History* 2 (May 1985): 269–75.

11. Charles Davis, in discussion following George H. Browne, "A Few of Pittsburgh's Sewers," *Transactions Engineers' Society of Western Pennsylvania* 1 (January 1880-June 1882): 229; Terry F. Yosie, "Retrospective Analysis of Water Supply and Wastewater Policies in Pittsburgh, 1800–1959," (Doctor of arts dissertation, Carnegie Mellon University, 1981), 14–16, 48–49. The nuisances created led to municipal regulation of privies as early as 1816.

12. Davis, in discussion following Browne, "A Few of Pittsburgh's Sewers," 229.

13. Browne, "A Few of Pittsburgh's Sewers," and "Discussion," 214–49.

14. For a discussion of the conflict in Pittsburgh between engineers and the Board of Health, see ibid., 219–21.

15. Jon A. Peterson, "The Impact of Sanitary Reform Upon American Urban Planning," *Journal of Social History* 13 (Fall 1979): 84–89.

16. Combined sewer overflow events are a frequent cause of bacterial pollution in the Pittsburgh area rivers today.

17. The so-called Street Acts, passed by the city councils in 1887–1889, provided that street and lateral sewer improvements would be made on the petition of one-third of the abutting property owners in a neighborhood. All abutters, however, would be assessed for improvements. In 1891, the state supreme court declared these acts unconstitutional. See Thompson, "Financial History," 178–79; Yosie, "Retrospective Analysis of Water Supply," 112–13.

18. *Fourth Annual Report of the State Department of Health* (Harrisburg, PA, 1911), 1476.

19. Quoted in Nancy Tomes, *The Gospel of Germs: Men, Women, and the Microbe in American Life* (Cambridge: Harvard University Press, 1998), 189–90.

20. Quoted in Koppes and Norris, "Ethnicity, Class, and Mortality in the Industrial City," 271. For a study of a similar situation in Pittsburgh's neighboring city of Allegheny, see Bruce W. Jordan, "The Allegheny City Water Works, 1840–1907," *Western Pennsylvania Historical Magazine* 70 (January 1987): 29–52. Pittsburgh annexed Allegheny in 1907.

21. *Report of the Joint Commission of the Chamber of Commerce of Pittsburgh, Engineer's Society of Western Pennsylvania, Allegheny County Medical Society, and Iron City Microscopical Society* (Pittsburgh, 1894).

22. C. E. Drake, "Statistics of Typhoid Fever in Pittsburgh," in *City of Pittsburgh, Its Water Works* (Pittsburgh, 1931), 29–38.

23. "The Greater Pittsburgh Sewerage and Sewage Purification Orders," *Engineering News* 63 (1910): 179–80; "Pittsburgh Sewage Purification Orders," ibid., 70–71; "The Sewerage Problem of Greater Pittsburgh," *Engineering Record* 61 (1910): 183–84; see also G. Gregory, "A Study in Local Decision Making: Pittsburgh and Sewage Treatment," *Western Pennsylvania Historical Magazine* 57 (1974): 25–42.

24. "The Most Important Sewerage and Sewage Disposal Report Made in the United States," *Engineering Record* 65 (1912): 209–12; "Pittsburgh Sewage Disposal Reports," *Engineering News* 67 (1912): 398–402.

25. Ibid., 400–401.

26. Pennsylvania Commissioner of Health, *Eighth Annual Report* (Harrisburg, 1913), 901–902; Gregory, "A Study in Local Decision Making," 41–42.

27. "The Pollution of Streams," *Engineering Record* 60 (1909): 157–59.

28. Comments were made about smoke in Pittsburgh as early as 1800. For a review of nineteenth-century developments, see John O'Connor Jr., "The History of the Smoke Nuisance and of Smoke Abatement in Pittsburgh," *Industrial World* (March 24, 1913).

29. Robert Dale Grinder, "From Insurgency to Efficiency: The Smoke Abatement Campaign in Pittsburgh before World War I," *Western Pennsylvania Historical Magazine* 61 (1978): 187–202. See Angela Gugliotta, "How, When, and for Whom Was Smoke a Problem in Pittsburgh," in Joel A. Tarr, ed., *Perspectives on Pittsburgh Environmental History* (Pittsburgh: University of Pittsburgh Press, forthcoming).

30. See, for example, J.W. Henderson, Bureau Chief, Pittsburgh Bureau of Smoke Regulation, "Smoke Abatement Means Economy," *Power* (July 24, 1917); R. Dale Grinder, "The Battle for Clean Air: The Smoke Problem in Post–Civil War America," in Martin V. Melosi, ed., *Pollution and Reform in American Cities, 1870–1930* (Austin: University of Texas, 1980), 89.

31. Victor J. Azbe, "Rationalizing Smoke Abatement," in *Proceedings of the Third International Conference on Bituminous Coal* (Pittsburgh, 1931), II, 603.

32. Osborn Monnett, *Smoke Abatement, Technical Paper 273, Bureau of Mines* (Washington, 1923); H.B. Meller, "Smoke Abatement, Its Effects and Its Limitations," *Mechanical Engineering* 48 (November 1926): 1275–83.

33. *Pittsburgh Press* and *Pittsburgh Post-Gazette*, February 3, 4, 12, 1941.

34. *Pittsburgh Press*, March 13, 1941.

35. See, for example, *Pittsburgh Press* and *Pittsburgh Post-Gazette*, March 13, April 30, June 24, 1941; M. Jay Ream to _____, April 3, 1941, Civic Club Records; "Notes Taken on Smoke at Annual Meeting," May 8, 1941, Civic Club Records. See also "List of Organizations Co-Operating with Civic Club on Smoke Elimination," ibid.

36. "Hearings before the Pittsburgh Smoke Commission," April 15, 1941, 38–39, ibid.

37. See, for instance, "Proceedings of the Fifth Meeting of the Pittsburgh Smoke Commission," March 31, 1941, 23, 69–78; "Proceedings of the Sixth Meeting," April 7, 1941, 38–39.

38. Ibid., 19.

39. In addition to smoke, the suggested ordinance provided for enforcement against other air pollutants such as fly ash, noxious acids, gases, and fumes. This provision was also included in the St. Louis ordinance and represented an advance in air pollution control as compared to earlier ordinances that had focused on dense smoke only.

40. *Pittsburgh Press*, July 7, 1941.

41. See "The United Smoke Council of the Allegheny Conference," in United Smoke Council Records, and "Minutes," Meeting of the United Smoke Council of Pittsburgh and Allegheny County, October 18, 1945, United Smoke Council Records.

42. "Minutes, Meeting of the United Smoke Council of Pittsburgh and Allegheny County," November 3, 1945.

43. See "Jobs for Inches," *Business Week*, December 29, 1945, 19; "Natural Gas Is on the Up," ibid., March 13, 1948, 26; *Annual Reports* of the Philadelphia Company (Equitable Gas Company) (1946), 15; (1948), 16–17; (1949), 21–22. See also Christopher James Castaneda, *Regulated Enterprise: Natural Gas Pipe-lines and Northeastern Markets, 1938–1954* (Columbus: Ohio State University Press, 1993), 75–89, 118.

44. Data on household fuel use are available from the 1940 and 1950 Censuses of Housing. See U.S. Department of Commerce, Bureau of the Census, *Housing: Characteristics by Type of Structure, 16th Census of the U.S.* (Washington, 1945), and *Census of Housing: 1950*, vol. 1, *General Characteristics 17th Census* (Washington, 1953).

45. The evidence suggests that the coal producers and miners were correct in warning that the smoke control law would hasten the loss of their domestic markets and their jobs. Pittsburgh Representatives of the United Mine Workers charged in the postwar period that there was a conspiracy in Pittsburgh to drive out coal in favor of natural gas. See *Pittsburgh Press*, December 21, 1945; March 8, 9, 1947; April 23, 1947; December 2, 5, 1947; and July 3, 1948. In its 1949 *Annual Report*, the Equitable Gas Company, which served more households in Pittsburgh than any other gas utility, observed that smoke abatement legislation and the high cost of coal were increasing their domestic sales.

Houston: The Energy Metropolis

Martin V. Melosi and Joseph A. Pratt

Source: *Energy Metropolis: An Environmental History of Houston and the Gulf Coast* (Pittsburgh: University of Pittsburgh Press, 2007).

EDITORS' INTRODUCTION

America's dependence on fossil fuels became abundantly clear with the spike in gasoline prices following Hurricanes Katrina and Rita in 2005, and subsequent worldwide speculation in oil futures that once again made energy a major public policy concern as it had been during the first "Energy Crisis" of 1973 and the second in 1979. For better or for worse, cheap and abundant energy from coal, oil, and natural gas has shaped the American urban landscape and provided the basis for dramatic metropolitan growth during the twentieth century in the form of automobile sprawl. No other city in the United States has been as influenced by the production, distribution, and consumption of energy as Houston, Texas. Famous for its lack of conventional zoning, Houston has grown dramatically from a small frontier town in the early nineteenth century to the largest city in Texas and the fourth largest city in the United States—with a population of over two million people—in the early twenty-first century. The city itself now sits at the heart of the nation's sixth largest metropolitan area containing roughly 5.7 million inhabitants.

Houston's story, however, is much more than that of urban sprawl. It is one of the most ethnically and racially diverse cities in America and home to world-class cultural, education, and medical institutions, impressive modern architecture, and multinational corporations. As Martin V. Melosi and Joseph A. Pratt argue, Houston is also the Bayou City, whose physical setting within the Gulf Coast region of southeastern Texas is critical to understanding the interplay between energy, urbanization, and the natural environment, an area of inquiry long neglected by historians. In this selection, the introduction from their book *Energy Metropolis: An Environmental History of Houston and the Gulf Coast* (2007), Melosi and Pratt sketch the impact of energy on the evolution of American cities and explore the urbanization of the Texas Coastal Zone. Among the principle features of the interaction between human and natural forces in this region has been pollution from energy related activities and extensive urbanization that has left the zone susceptible to tornadoes and hurricanes. Two examples of this urban fragility are Hurricane Ike, which severely disrupted Galveston, Texas in September 2008, and the great and unnamed hurricane of 1900 that all but destroyed that city.

Martin V. Melosi is the Distinguished University Professor of History and Director of the Center for Public History at the University of Houston. In addition to *Energy Metropolis*, his works include *Garbage in the Cities: Refuse, Reform and the Environment* (College Station, TX: Texas A&M Press, 1981; Pittsburgh, University of Pittsburgh Press, 2005), *Effluent America: Cities, Industry, Energy, and the Environment* (Pittsburgh: University of Pittsburgh Press, 2001), and *The Sanitary City: Urban Infrastructure in America from Colonial Times to the Present* (Baltimore: Johns Hopkins University Press, 2000; Pittsburgh: University of Pittsburgh Press, 2008), winner of multiple awards from the American Society of Environmental History, the Urban History Association, and other professional organizations. Joseph A. Pratt is the Cullen Professor of History and Business at the University of Houston and a leading historian of the petroleum industry. Pratt has authored or co-authored nine books in addition to *Energy Metropolis* and served as a consultant for the Public Broadcasting Service (PBS) mini-series on the oil industry, *The Prize*, and for the *American Experience* documentary on the Trans-Alaskan Pipeline. He is also the founder of the Houston History Project and editor of *Houston History*, a magazine of popular history.

ENERGY METROPOLIS

An Environmental History of Houston and the Gulf Coast

Cities are by their very nature energy intensive. The concentration of human and material resources for purposes of survival, construction of infrastructure for transportation and communication, and the production and consumption of goods and services are essential characteristics of communal living. As William Cronon and others have demonstrated, the connection of city and hinterland often extends the impact of urban development beyond the city's political borders while creating interdependence between the built and natural world.[1] The production and use of energy have been potent forces in driving this process of change.

The historical impact of energy reaches beyond the conversion of resources to stationary and motive power to make machines run; to illuminate streets and interiors; to move trains, cars, buses, and trucks; and to generate heat and refrigerated air. Broadly understood, energy encompasses all processes of production and consumption that allow people to function in the physical world. A key challenge in urban and environmental history is to identify and analyze the central impacts of energy production and use on the evolution of cities.

One general impact is clear: changes in energy supply and demand have greatly affected the economic context within which cities have grown. New technologies using new sources of energy have shaped the transportation and communication revolutions that have transformed the world economy in the last two centuries. The impact of new sources of energy on the American economy has been particularly pronounced in the years since the mid-nineteenth century, when the widespread use of fossil fuels encouraged the most significant transportation innovation of that century, the completion of a national system of railroads. Coal fueled the trains that transformed the American landscape, introduced a new scale of business activity, and created a much broader national market. Then oil fueled the cars and planes that extended that transformation. The burning of coal, oil, and natural gas generated the bulk of electricity and provided most of the fuel for modern industrialization. Taken together, these fossil fuels have provided far and away the most significant supplies of energy in the modern economy; their adaptation to industrial uses and transportation systems fundamentally altered the economy by broadening the scale of markets and the scope of business activities. [...]

Fossil fuels helped transform the modern city, altering the physical environment in new and significant ways. The most obvious impact was a fundamental change in land-use patterns in and around cities, which reached out and absorbed once-rural land surrounding the sprawling urban centers. The concentrated usage of energy in the production of goods brought a new scale of industrial pollution to cities. Growing energy use for transporting people and goods added another layer of pollution to the mix, particularly in cities that grew rapidly only after the advent of the automobile. In these and many other ways, as the lure of jobs and better opportunities from urban industrial growth attracted larger populations, the environmental impacts of increasing energy use also grew dramatically.

Although the strong and complex connections between energy use, urban growth, and environmental issues are intuitively obvious, they have been slighted by historians. Perhaps the connections are simply too deeply embedded to be easily analyzed. Also, the study of energy history has not yet developed as fully as the vibrant fields of urban and environmental histories. One way to begin to examine more thoroughly these related issues is to focus on extreme cases, which show most dramatically the relationship between energy, environment, and urbanization.

To more fully examine the intersection of energy, environment, and urbanization, this essay offers the example of Houston. The Bayou City is currently the nation's fourth-largest city, and it sits at the center of the seventh-largest metropolitan area in the United States. It is the home to over 100 racial and ethnic groups, making it one of the most diverse cities in the nation.[2]

As both a consumer and producer of energy, especially oil and natural gas, the city has few rivals around the world. Other parts of the nation can boast of significant oil-producing and -refining areas, most notably the original oil fields in Pennsylvania; the substantial refining complexes in Cleveland and New Jersey; southern California's concentrations of refineries, oil fields, and transportation hubs; and the refining region of southern Louisiana. None of these areas, however, matches the Houston region in its concentration of oil refining, petrochemical production, oil and natural gas transportation, and oceangoing tankers. For better and for worse, the Houston area has developed around oil and oil refining, and it provides a unique case of an energy-intensive metropolis more than other Sun Belt cities such as Atlanta, Dallas-Fort Worth, Oklahoma City, Phoenix, or Los Angeles.

Oil shaped Houston's modern economic and environmental history. In every industrial region, leading industries produce particular patterns of pollution. In the case of Houston, the production, processing, and shipment of oil and natural gas gave the city a distinctive identity within the national economy while also creating distinctive levels and forms of air, water, and ground pollution.

In every large city, the predominant fuel used in regional transportation and industry emits significant pollution. In twentieth-century Houston, oil and natural gas supplied the bulk of the fuel used to transport people and to produce and transport goods. Because petroleum was both the major industry and the major fuel for modern Houston, this self-proclaimed "energy capital of America" has also been the de facto "oil pollution capital of America."[3]

Houston's emergence as a major metropolis was shaped by fundamental changes in the national and international energy industries. Since the late nineteenth century, fossil fuels have steadily replaced wind, water, and animal power; in the process, local sources of energy have been replaced by sources supplied by an increasingly specialized and concentrated energy economy.[4] Oil and natural gas surged forward during the twentieth century to become the dominant energy source in the industrial world, and Houston, more than any other city, benefited economically from this development. Houston became synonymous with oil much as Pittsburgh was with steel or Detroit was with automobiles or the Silicon Valley became with microprocessing. It was a center for specialized activities needed by the national and international petroleum industry, one of the most dynamic industries of the twentieth century.

Nature endowed the Houston region with the abundant natural resources, innumerable sunny days, the lack of harsh winters, and the geographical location that allowed it to prosper as a center of oil production and refining. But good luck and good timing also help explain its dominant role in the development of oil and natural gas. With the discovery in 1901 of the epoch-defining Spindletop oil field in nearby Beaumont, Texas, the region's oil-related economy sprang to life. Houston and surrounding areas on the Gulf Coast quickly became the focal point for the expansion of the oil and gas industries in the southwestern United States, an area that produced the bulk of the world's oil from the turn of the twentieth century through the 1960s. Just as the nation entered the automobile age, with its surging demand for refined oil products, Houston found itself perfectly positioned to become the center for the regional and then the national petroleum industry. Even the subsequent movement of the locus of world oil production to the Middle East could not easily displace the economic advantages embedded in the region's infrastructure during the long dominance of southwestern oil. Adding strength to the regional economy after the 1930s was the spectacular growth of the natural gas industry in the United States, which was centered in Houston.

Over the course of the twentieth century, the regional economy diversified steadily to include more and more oil-related activities. The region's sturdy oil-related industrial core evolved to include the production, refining, and shipment of oil; the production and shipment of natural gas; the production and shipment of petrochemicals; management and research in oil, natural gas, and petrochemicals; specialized construction for these industries; the manufacture of tools and supplies needed by the petroleum complex; specialized technical and management services; and highway and residential construction undertaken in part to meet the needs of the workforce of the oil-related complex. From these activities came both the economic growth and the severe industrial pollution that characterized the modern history of the Gulf Coast region surrounding Houston.

The industrial heart of this oil-related complex was refining. The giant petroleum refineries and petrochemical plants that processed crude oil and natural gas into a variety of products also created tens of thousands of industrial jobs that attracted generations of workers to the region. The center of the massive refining complex that stretched from Corpus Christi, Texas, to New Orleans was the Houston Ship Channel, which reached southeastward from Houston forty miles to the Gulf of Mexico. In the mid-twentieth century, this region along the Gulf Coast produced as much as a third of the nation's refined goods and half of its petrochemicals. Into and out of this highly specialized industrial complex flowed millions of barrels of crude oil and refined oil and tons of petrochemical products per day, and the processing and shipping of these products gave the region its identity in the national economy. Even in the late twentieth century, after automation sharply

reduced the number of employees in the refineries and the Houston economy successfully diversified into other economic activities, refining remained a major contributor to regional prosperity.

The manufacturing jobs in these and other oil-related factories gave the region a distinctive industrial working-class tone to a greater extent than Dallas, Fort Worth, Austin, or San Antonio. This was a place where people from the rural hinterland of Texas and Louisiana came in search of greater opportunities for themselves and their children. Bringing with them the racial attitudes inherited from the strict and violent segregation practiced in the small-town and rural South, they helped make Houston the largest Jim Crow city in the nation by 1950. But despite segregated housing and public services and segregated workforces in the area's refineries and factories, these workers—black and white—also brought the migrants' faith that those who worked hard could create a better future for their families in Houston. This fundamental optimism that the city held opportunities for those willing to work hard floated in the air of Houston along with the fumes from the refineries. Jobs, not air pollution, remained the primary concern of millions of people who migrated to the region in the twentieth century.

Sustained growth, of course, brought a new set of challenges. Where would those who flocked to the city live? How would the urban services needed by a growing population be provided? Transportation was one key issue facing the booming region. A prototypical Sun Belt city, Houston grew up with the automobile. With no widespread investment in public transit before the coming of oil in 1901 and the opening of the Houston Ship Channel in 1914, the city expanded rapidly just as cars came into general use. It is symbolically fitting that the decade of the city's fastest growth in the twentieth century was the 1920s, when auto use took off in the region and around the nation and the ship channel refining complex boomed. In that decade, the first substantial suburbs connected to the central city by jobs and roads were the refinery towns east of the city throughout the industrial corridor along the ship channel—Pasadena, Galena Park, Baytown, Deer Park, and Texas City.

In subsequent decades, the city expanded in every other direction. Favorable state laws, such as the Municipal Annexation Act (1963), also allowed the city to aggressively annex adjoining areas and thus further enlarge its territory. By 1999, this generous annexation policy had allowed Houston to reserve approximately 1,289 square miles (excluding the areas of the city within it) for future annexation.[5] Land surrounding the city provided living space for the millions of migrants to the region; inexpensive gasoline provided the fuel needed to commute longer and longer distances; and inexpensive electricity produced primarily by abundant and low-cost natural gas allowed for the air-conditioning that made the city livable during its long, harsh summers. Local, state, and federal governments responded to citizens' demands to build more and more roads reaching farther and farther out from the city. Individuals responded by hustling up the resources to acquire cars and, if possible, homes in the suburbs. The region as a whole moved easily and with little public debate toward a "mass transit" strategy of more highways filled by more cars, often with one driver per car.

Over decades of sustained outward urban growth, both energy costs and environmental costs became embedded in regional transportation systems. Once infrastructure for the transportation of goods and people had been built, change was most difficult, in spite of shifting political calculations of economic and environmental costs. By the end of the twentieth century, most people living in a thirty-mile radius of the central city had become "Houstonians" who were tied into the economic and cultural life of the city primarily through a sprawling system of roads and freeways. The specialized transportation system of pipelines, tanker trucks, railroads, barges, and oceangoing tankers used by the region's petroleum-related core of industries bound together the region's economy and tied it into national and global markets.

The Houston region grew from a frontier town in the early nineteenth century, to a small city of about 45,000 in 1900, and finally to an expansive metropolis of more than five million in 2006. Urban growth has been a core objective of the city from its modest start, spearheaded by John Kirby Allen and Augustus Chapman Allen in 1836, until this very day. Shipping, rail, and especially automotive and truck transportation helped push Houston's borders and Houston's influence beyond its initial location along Buffalo Bayou.

Although the region expanded geographically before oil, the booming new industry and the growing use of the automobile greatly accelerated the city's expansion out into the surrounding countryside in the twentieth century. By the turn of the twenty-first century, "Houston"—as defined by economic and commuting ties, not by political boundaries—had become one of the world's largest cities in area, spanning perhaps 2,000 square miles that stretched thirty or forty miles from downtown Houston in every direction over a broad area of the Texas Gulf Coast. Much of this land had been farmland in the early twentieth century, but by the year 2000, from Katy to Conroe to Baytown to Galveston to Sugar Land, each exit looked much the same, the homes in each subdivision merged into several generic floor plans, and all roads led into and out of Houston. The city exhibited the worst kind of urban sprawl—patternless, unplanned (Houston is the largest city in the United States without zoning), and highly decentralized. In the post-World War II years, Houston had half the population density of Los Angeles and reached into ten counties.

Of course, cars commuting around the sprawling city combined with the refineries and petrochemical plants to produce serious air and water pollution. Adding to the city's environmental woes is its susceptibility to severe weather conditions such as tornadoes and hurricanes, and a propensity to flood often and intensely. Volumes of water exacerbate nonpoint pollution problems, as all kinds of toxic materials—from lawn fertilizers to heavy metals—run into the city's extensive network of bayous and ultimately spill into the Gulf of Mexico. Severe pollution problems arose from the transportation of the millions of barrels of crude oil and refined products per day that flowed through these plants on their way through the global oil economy. In this sense, the Houston region served not only as the nation's refining center but also as one of the national economy's primary dumping grounds for oil-related and other forms of pollution.

Just as Houston earned great economic benefit from its specialized role as a center of oil-related activities, it also paid a high environmental price. Petrochemicals presented their own special set of problems from air and water emissions, along with the disposal of a variety of solid and liquid wastes. Altogether, the region suffered the triple dilemma of dealing simultaneously with mounting oil-related pollution from the exhausts of gasoline-powered automobiles, the production of oil and chemical products from local plants, and myriad urban pollutants.

Efforts to find an acceptable balance between the costs and benefits of petroleum processing and petroleum pollution proved difficult. For most of the region's history, a broadly shared societal consensus that included a majority of the population, rich and poor, favored oil development largely unrestrained by pollution controls. "Opportunity" and "economic growth" were the twin tenets of the local religion of boosterism, and the church did not have much tolerance for doubters who voiced concerns about the quality of life.

Those who called for stricter controls of pollution had to overcome more than regional attitudes favoring growth. Local politics, as well as civic leadership, were dominated by business leaders whose idea of a "healthy business climate" included low taxes, weak unions, and very limited regulation. Several scholars have provided the useful label "free enterprise city" to describe the dominance of Houston's political and civic cultures by conservative businessmen.[6] Granted such business power is hardly unique among cities in capitalist America, and further granted that much of the power and the behavior of the local elite can be explained with reference to their commitment to segregation as easily as to their

commitment to free enterprise, the fact remains that business and civic leaders in Houston historically represented a strong and consistent barrier to the passage and enforcement of effective pollution controls.

Political realities also included the entrenched power in the political process at the state and federal levels of the well-organized interests of the major industries that produced the bulk of the region's industrial pollution. The basic decisions about Houston's oil-related development were made by private corporations in the global energy economy. In Houston, as around the world, price dictated the key decisions on energy use and, to an extent, the approach to pollution control. But the political process played a pivotal role in channeling government promotion and blocking government regulation. The economic importance of oil in the state of Texas, in general, and in the city of Houston, in particular, skewed political decisions toward policies that promoted the oil industry and away from policies that constrained the industry, at least until the federal government preempted much of the traditional authority of states over pollution control after the 1960s. The state's one-party political system through the 1960s also proved to be a barrier to change, as those who advocated states' rights in defense of Jim Crow had ample reason to support the states' rights arguments of those who fought against federal government involvement in pollution control.[7]

An important part of the economic/environmental history of the region has been the ongoing efforts to create more effective pollution controls while also encouraging continued economic growth. Only in the recent past have segments of the American public recognized that more efficient energy use in response to higher prices has broken the traditional coupling of growth in energy use and economic growth. Only recently have segments of the American public—including some civic leaders and grassroots organizations in Houston—recognized that high levels of pollution are not only a threat to public health and the quality of life but also can become a barrier to economic growth and the creation of jobs in the region and the nation. For most of Houston's history—in politics and in practice—there was little effort to "balance" energy and environmental needs, since pollution control was treated as distinctly secondary to economic growth. Yet there are at least tentative signs that a new balance, with greater concern for environmental quality, is politically possible.

Unlike many other oil-producing regions around the world that have been seemingly "cursed" by the problems of oil-led development, the Houston area has grown spectacularly since the discovery of oil in the region in 1901.[8] Since that time, the region has successfully absorbed the dynamic oil industry, using it as the engine of growth that transformed the city. Historically, the timing of the discovery and development of oil was fortuitous for Houston, which got in on the ground floor at the birth of the modern petroleum industry. The giant refineries built in the region in the early twentieth century could not be easily moved as oil production itself subsequently moved away from the region.

The area around Houston was a thriving regional center before the discovery of oil. The rise of shipping and commercial development along Buffalo Bayou in the nineteenth century was an essential precedent for the construction of the Houston Ship Channel and the emergence of Houston as an international focal point for oil production, refining, and petrochemicals. The business community proved well equipped to take on the new economic activities spawned by the industry. It had an established legal system capable of managing the demands of the new industry, and well-developed local corporate law firms. Most important, oil development went forward under the direction of transplanted Texans and native Texans who reinvested much of the profits from the giant new oil fields in regional developments such as giant refineries and pipelines connecting these refineries to other major oil fields outside the region.

The long-term prosperity generated by the regional economy also reflected its historical capacity to diversify away from oil production—from a regional perspective, the most difficult to retain branch of the oil industry.

In the mid-twentieth century, such diversification occurred within the expanding oil-related core, where first refining and oil-tool manufacturing, then petrochemicals, and finally the production and transportation of natural gas provided dynamic areas of economic expansion. Then in the 1960s and accelerating in the mid-1980s, after the dramatic drop in oil prices led to a devastating regional depression, diversification outside of oil bolstered the region's growth.

Yet even much of this "new, nonoil economy" in Houston had indirect ties to the oil industry. The coming of the Lyndon B. Johnson Space Center to Clear Lake, south of Houston, was orchestrated by an alliance of George Brown of Brown & Root (a construction company with many strong ties to oil industry markets), the president of Humble Oil, and Vice President Lyndon Johnson. The growth of the Texas Medical Center, which became a major employer in Houston by the 1980s, was fostered by the philanthropic support of many Houstonians who had made their original fortunes in oil, as was the growth of Rice University and the University of Houston. Even the real estate development industry that built the Houston suburbs had strong ties to the oil industry; for example, Friendswood Development, a major regional developer that built much of Clear Lake and Kingwood, originally was affiliated with Exxon and named after one of its important regional oil fields, and the Woodlands north of the city was inspired by the efforts of oilman George Mitchell. [...]

The Physical Setting

As an energy-intensive metropolis, Houston has been shaped by natural and human forces. However, to fully understand the environmental history of this urban area—including Galveston—requires attention to its physical realities, especially its location within the Gulf Coast region of southeastern Texas. The circumstance of where the metropolis is situated speaks volumes about its dynamic history.[9]

Houston is foremost a product of the Texas Coastal Zone, an area of approximately 20,000 square miles consisting of about 2,100 square miles of bays and estuaries, 375 miles of coastline, and 1,425 miles of bay, estuary, and lagoon shoreline. The shoreline itself is composed of interconnected natural waterways, restricted bays, lagoons, and estuaries with modest freshwater inflow, elongated barrier islands, and a very low astronomical tidal range.[10]

Texas actually has two shorelines—one running along the Gulf of Mexico and another along the bays. Bolivar Peninsula, Galveston Island, and Follets Island are grass-covered barrier flats and sandy beaches of one to three miles in width that separate the bay areas from the Gulf of Mexico. Galveston Island is the best known of the barrier islands, approximately thirty miles long and two-and-a-half miles wide, with no underlying bedrock and consisting of mud flats on the side facing the bay. As David McComb has noted, "Lying parallel to the coast two miles away, Galveston stands as a guardian protecting the land and the bay from the Gulf."[11]

Behind the barrier islands, Galveston Bay (composed of four major subbays: Galveston Bay, Trinity Bay, East Bay, and West Bay) and some smaller bays comprise almost 600 square miles of surface area. West Bay is a lagoon separating Galveston from the mainland. Galveston Bay and its continuation as Trinity Bay constitute an estuary. The entire Galveston Bay watershed, or drainage basin, covers 33,000 square miles of land and water from the Dallas-Fort Worth Metroplex to the Texas coast—a substantially larger area than the water that the bay encompasses. Extensive marshy areas less than five feet above sea level extend along the landward side of West and East bays. Bolivar Roads and San Luis Pass are natural passes that connect the bays to the Gulf. Rollover Pass, extending through the Bolivar Peninsula, connects the Gulf of Mexico and East Bay.[12]

Above the bays, two major river valleys—the Trinity and the San Jacinto—and several minor valleys of headward-eroding streams—Cedar Bayou, Buffalo Bayou, Clear Creek, Dickinson Bayou, Halls Bayou, Chocolate Bayou, and Bastrop Bayou—cut into the coastal plain. The Brazos River and Oyster Creek flow through the western portion of the Texas Coastal Zone, but not within deep valleys.[13]

The Houston-Galveston area consists of approximately 2,268 square miles of land, which is a broad region of flat coastal plain situated between the coastal marshes and the areas of pine and hardwood forests along either side of the Trinity River and north of downtown Houston. The coastal plain itself inclines from the Gulf at two to five feet per mile. The maximum elevation of the coastal plain is about ninety feet above sea level in the northwestern part of the coastal zone.[14]

Situated approximately forty-nine feet above sea level on prairie some fifty miles from the Gulf of Mexico, the city of Houston is linked geographically, geologically, and climatically to the Texas coast. The coastal plain of which Houston is a part comprises gently dipping layers of sand and clay. The slope of the impermeable layers of clay, shale, and gumbo interbedded with permeable, water-bearing sands and gravel is greater than the slope of the land surface. These conditions are favorable for artesian water, and the city historically has drawn water from the Chicot and Evangeline aquifers running southeast to northwest from the Gulf Coast through the city and to its north. Extraction of the groundwater, however, can lead, and has led, to land subsidence and saltwater intrusion if water is drawn out too aggressively.[15]

On the surface, water from Houston drains into the Gulf of Mexico via an elaborate network of bayous. With an average yearly rainfall of forty-two to forty-six inches from often torrential downpours, the area is subjected to frequent flooding. Since urbanization removes much of the filtering capacity of the soil, runoff has exaggerated Houston's tendency to flood as the city continued to expand. Since the city also is susceptible to hurricanes and tornadoes, water and the pollutants it often carries have been the greatest natural threat to Houstonians and its neighbors.[16]

Along with its extensive waterways, Houston also is a heavily vegetated city. Large portions of the region are forested, with substantial tree growth along the bayous. Loblolly pine is the tree species that dominates the region. Much of the west side of the area, which contains acres of native prairie, has been converted to developed private property where trees have been planted. On the north and northeast sides, the natural land cover has densely vegetated canopies over approximately 50 percent of the area. To the south, the area is covered with a combination of prairie, marsh, forest, and abandoned agricultural lands. At the highly developed city center, however, the ground and canopy cover has diminished markedly. A "heat island" effect is most pronounced in this area. A study by the National Aeronautics and Space Administration (NASA) in August 2000 found "hot spots" of approximately 149 degrees Fahrenheit in the warmest locations and 77 degrees Fahrenheit in cooler areas.[17]

In many respects, Houston's climate is one of its most identifiable features. An ill-fated publicity campaign once used the phrase "Houston is Hot!" to promote the city. Indeed, Houston's climate is subtropical and humid, with prevailing winds bringing heat from the deserts of Mexico and moisture from the Gulf. The sun shines for much of the year, with an annual growing season of almost 300 days. The average low temperature is 72 degrees Fahrenheit in the summer and 40 degrees Fahrenheit in the winter; the average high is 93 degrees Fahrenheit in the summer and 61 degrees Fahrenheit in the winter. Humidity in June is typically about 63 percent.[18]

As one geologic study noted, "The attributes that make the Texas Coastal Zone attractive for industrialization and development also make it particularly susceptible to a variety of environmental problems."[19] The deepwater ports, intercoastal waterways, good water supplies, large tracts of arable land, and relatively mild climate have been valuable assets. In addition, the region has a variety of other exploitable resources, including timber, sulfur and salt, sand and gravel, shells for lime, abundant wildlife, shellfish and finish, and petroleum reserves.[20] The agricultural, commercial, industrial, and recreational possibilities for the region, however, have come with a price due to natural and human impacts.

Probably the most dramatic natural events have been tropical hurricanes and tornadoes. As far back as 1776, a hurricane of unknown intensity destroyed a mission in the Galveston area. In the nineteenth century, major hurricanes struck the upper coast in 1854, 1867, and 1886.[21] The "Great Storm" that hit Galveston on September 8, 1900, is the best known of the South Texas hurricanes, especially since it killed more people than any other natural disaster in the history of the United States— 6,000 people in Galveston alone and probably 10,000 to 12,000 total—and devastated the city itself.[22] Although no storm since that time recorded loss of life even close to the one in 1900 (the death toll from Hurricane Katrina in 2005 exceeded 1,800 people), hurricanes and tropical storms have been regular visitors to the upper Texas coast. In recent years, powerful storms such as Hurricane Carla (1961), Tropical Storm Claudette (1979), Hurricane Alicia (1983), Tropical Storm Allison (2001), and Hurricane Rita (2005) have wracked southeast Texas.[23] Along with loss of life, property damage, and severe flooding, the storms also have contributed to substantial shoreline retreat.[24] However, human action also encourages shoreline recession. For example, until a 1970 bill was passed by the Texas legislature, beach sediments were removed for road building. Building of jetties also disrupts the normal transportation of sediment and produces recession, as in the case of the Sabine Pass jetties and jetties along Bolivar Peninsula.[25]

Human impacts on the Texas Coastal Zone are wide ranging. Extensive dredging of channels and passes has resulted in the discharge of sediment into bays, ultimately modifying natural bay circulation patterns, and affected water quality and estuarine plants and animals. Because of increased cultivation, the construction of irrigation and drainage canals and urban paving result in many streams accelerating the transport of sediment into bays as well as increasing nonpoint pollutants, including pesticides and herbicides from runoff. Straightening and lining streams with concrete—as in the case of several bayous in Houston—encourage flash flooding. Thermal effluents from various manufacturing processes and power generation can be lethal to fish. Aggressive withdrawal of groundwater causes land subsidence and saltwater intrusion, and activates faults. Discharge of organic materials, trace metals, and other materials too numerous to mention from a variety of sources—including oil production, pipelines, spills, and chemical production—adds significantly to the pollution load of all water courses.[26]

Human actions also have had significant impacts on the major habitats of the bays and environs, including oyster reefs, submerged aquatic vegetation, intertidal marsh vegetation and animal life, and freshwater wetlands. For example, between 1950 and 1989, approximately 54 percent of the freshwater marshes in the Galveston Bay watershed were lost because of draining wetlands and conversion to upland areas.[27]

Houston and other upper Texas coast cities are subject, first and foremost, to the geologic, geographic, and climatic features that help to define them in physical terms. As one observer said, "Harris County doesn't have earthquakes ... doesn't have blizzards ... doesn't have avalanches. We have flooding." The unique physical characteristics of southeast Texas go hand in hand with the human modifications to the region that define its environmental history—its potential, its shortcomings, and its evolution. Part of what makes Houston an energy-intensive metropolis existed before people put their stamp on this part of the world—forces that resist as well as accommodate urban development.

NOTES

1. William Cronon, *Nature's Metropolis: Chicago and the Great West* (New York: W. W. Norton, 1991); Kathleen Brosnan, *Uniting Mountain and Plain: Cities, Law, and Environmental Change along the Front Range* (Albuquerque: University of New Mexico Press, 2002).

2. There is as yet no comprehensive economic history of Houston. For a general political history, see David G. McComb, *Houston: The Bayou City* (Austin: University of Texas Press, 1969). See also

Marilyn McAdams Sibley, *The Port of Houston: A History* (Austin: University of Texas Press, 1968); and Lynn M. Alperin, *Custodians of the Coast: History of the United States Army Engineers at Galveston* (Galveston, Tex.: U.S. Army Corps of Engineers, 1977).

3. A pioneering work of energy, growth, and environment in a region is James C. Williams, *Energy and the Making of Modern California* (Akron, Ohio: University of Akron Press, 1997). An excellent account of the early politics of oil-led development in California is Paul Sabin, *Crude Politics: The California Oil Market, 1900–1940* (Berkeley: University of California Press, 2004).

4. For a collection of essays about energy transitions, see Lewis J. Perelman, August W. Giebelhaus, and Michael D. Yokell, eds., *Energy Transitions: Long-Term Perspectives* (Boulder, Colo.: Westview Press, 1981). For an essay on Houston, see Joseph A. Pratt, "The Ascent of Oil: The Transition from Coal to Oil in Early Twentieth-Century America," in Perelman et al., *Energy Transitions*, 9–34.

5. Martin V. Melosi, "Community and the Growth of Houston," in *Effluent America: Cities, Industry, Energy, and the Environment*, ed. Martin V. Melosi (Pittsburgh: University of Pittsburgh Press, 2001), 194–95.

6. See Joe R. Feagin, *Free Enterprise City: Houston in Political and Economic Perspective* (New Brunswick, Conn.: Rutgers University Press, 1988).

7. On the national level, see Robert Engler, *The Politics of Oil, Private Power and Democratic Directions* (New York: Macmillan, 1961). For Houston, see Feagin, *Free Enterprise City*. For Texas, see George Green, *The Establishment in Texas Politics: The Primitive Years, 1938–1957* (Westport, Conn.: Greenwood Press, 1979). For Houston, see also Joseph A. Pratt, "8F and Many More: Business and Civic Leadership in Modern Houston," *Houston Review of History and Culture* 2, no. 1 (2004): 2–7, 31–44.

8. Short discussions of many oil-producing regions are found in Augustine A. Ikein, *The Impact of Oil on a Developing Country: The Case of Nigeria* (New York: Praeger, 1990). See also Tony Hodges, *Angola: Anatomy of an Oil State* (Bloomington: Indiana University Press, 2001).

9. I would like to acknowledge the efforts of Steven MacDonald in identifying and collecting research material for this section of the book.

10. W. L. Fisher, J. H. McGowen, L. F. Brown Jr., and C. G. Groat, *Environmental Geologic Atlas of the Texas Coastal Zone—Galveston-Houston Area* (Austin: Bureau of Economic Geology, University of Texas at Austin, 1972), 1.

11. David G. McComb, *Galveston: A History* (Austin: University of Texas Press, 1986), 6, 7–8. See also Houston Geological Society, *Geology of Houston and Vicinity, Texas* (Houston: Houston Geological Society, 1961), 3, 7; Robert R. Lankford and

John J. W. Roger, comps., *Holocene Geology of the Galveston Bay Area* (Houston: Geological Society, 1969), vii, 1; and Fisher et al., *Environmental Geologic Atlas*, 7.

12. Fisher et al., *Environmental Geologic Atlas,* 7; Jim Lester and Lisa Gonzalez, eds., *Ebb and Flow: Galveston Bay Characterization Highlights* (Galveston, Tex.: Galveston Bay Estuary Program; 2001), 12; Joseph L. Clark and Elton M. Scott, *The Texas Gulf Coast: Its History and Development*, Vol. 2 (New York: Lewis Historical, 1955), 14–16; Houston Geological Society, *Geology of Houston*, 3.

13. Fisher et al., *Environmental Geologic Atlas*, 7.

14. Ibid.; G. L. Fugate, "Development of Houston's Water Supply," *Journal of the American Water Works Association* 33 (October 1941): 1769–70.

15. Planning and Development Department, *Public Utilities Profile for Houston, Texas* (Summer 1994), III-15; Fugate, "Houston's Water Supply," 1769–70. The geologic formations from which Houston obtains groundwater supplies are upper Miocene, Pliocene, and Pleistocene in origin. See Nicholas A. Rose, "Ground Water and Relations of Geology to Its Occurrence in Houston District, Texas," *Bulletin of the American Association of Petroleum Geologists* 27 (August 1943): 1081.

16. See "Houston," in *Twentieth Century Cities*, part 4 of Association of American Geographers, *Contemporary Metropolitan America*, ed. John S. Adams (Cambridge, Mass.: Ballinger, 1976), 109, 121–24; Houston Chamber of Commerce, *Houston Facts '82* (Houston: Houston Chamber of Commerce, 1983).

17. U.S. Environmental Protection Agency (EPA), *Heat Island Effect: Houston's Urban Fabric*, www.epa.gov/heatisland/pilot/houst_urbanfabric. html; U.S. EPA, *Heat Island Effect: Houston*, www.epa.gov/heatisland/pilot/houston.html.

18. U.S. EPA, *Heat Island Effect: Houston*; World Travels, Houston Climate and Weather, www. wortltravels.com/Cities/Texas/Houston/Climate.

19. Fisher et al., *Environmental Geologic Atlas*, 1.

20. Ibid., 1, 7.

21. Espey, Huston & Associates, prep., Archival Research: Houston-Galveston Navigation Channels, Texas Project—Galveston, Harris, Liberty and Chambers Counties, Texas, April 1993, 8.

22. McComb, *Galveston*, 121–49.

23. David Roth, "Texas Hurricane History," National Weather Service, Lake Charles, La., 2004, www. srh.noaa.gov/lch/research/txhur.php.

24. Espey, Huston & Associates, *Archival Research*, 10.

25. Eugene Jaworski, "Geographic Analysis of Shoreline Recession, Coastal East Texas," College Station, Texas A&M University, Environmental Quality Note 3, June 1971, 1–13.

26. Fisher et al., *Environmental Geologic Atlas*, 15, 20; Robert R. Stickney, *Estuarine Ecology of the Southeastern United States and Gulf of Mexico* (College Station: Texas A&M University Press, 1984), 247–80.

27. Lester and Gonzalez, *Ebb and Flow*, 9–11.

The Emergence of Silicon Valley: High-Tech Development and Ecocide, 1950–2001

David Naguib Pellow and Lisa Sun-Hee Park

Source: *The Silicon Valley of Dreams: Environmental Justice, Immigrant Workers, and the High-Tech Global Economy*
(New York: New York University Press, 2002).

EDITORS' INTRODUCTION

Silicon Valley is located in the southern portion of the San Francisco Bay Area and includes over a dozen cities and municipalities primarily within Santa Clara County including Palo Alto, and San Jose, California's third largest city behind Los Angeles and San Diego, and tenth largest in the United States. The term "Silicon Valley" emerged in the 1970s to describe the large number of silicon chip and semiconductor industries in the Santa Clara Valley. Although the region is now the center of America's digital and information age industry, the term itself is also synonymous with the country's entire high-tech sector. Silicon Valley enjoys immense wealth and attracts people from all over the world who seek a chance to fulfill their dreams by turning their ideas and innovations into fortunes.

The high-tech industry enjoys a global reputation as an advanced form of economic development free of the industrial pollution and human exploitation of the past. However, Silicon Valley also has an underside that, as sociologists David Naguib Pellow and Lisa Sun-Hee Park argue in *The Silicon Valley of Dreams*, contains increasing social inequality and the exploitation of workers, human suffering from preventable illnesses and premature death, and widespread ecological devastation. The transformation of the Santa Clara Valley from an agricultural area to an electronics and military-related manufacturing hub began with the building of armaments factories and the opening of the first West Coast plant for International Business Machines Corporation (IBM) in San Jose during World War II. Between 1950 and 1974, approximately 800 electronics businesses relocated to or opened in Santa Clara County, attracting thousands of job seekers from diverse ethnic and racial backgrounds. The region's commercial boosters hailed these and other high-technology manufacturing establishments as pleasant and pollution free enterprises in comparison to noxious smoke billowing factories of the Midwest and East Coast cities. In this selection from *The Silicon Valley of Dreams*, Pellow and Park shatter the illusion of "clean" high-tech industries while at the same time linking the toxic contamination of Silicon Valley with social inequality; a combination of which, they argue, produces environmental inequalities and environmental racism.[i]

David Naguib Pellow is the Don Martindale Endowed Chair of Sociology at the University of Minnesota. His research interests include environmental justice, racial and ethnic inequality, immigration, and labor studies. In addition to *The Silicon Valley of Dreams*, his other works include *Garbage Wars: The Struggle for Environmental Justice in Chicago* (Cambridge, MA: MIT Press, 2004), *Power, Justice, and the Environment: A Critical Appraisal of the Environmental Justice Movement* (Cambridge, MA: MIT Press, 2005)

---

i David Naguib Pellow and Lisa Sun-Hee Park, *The Silicon Valley of Dream; Environmental Justice, Immigrant Workers, and the High-Tech Global Economy* (New York: New York University Press, 2002), xi, 2, 62.

co-edited with Robert J. Brulle, and *Resisting Global Toxics: Transnational Movements for Environmental Justice* (Cambridge, MA: MIT Press, 2007). Lisa Sun-Hee Park is an associate professor of sociology at the University of Minnesota. Her interests also include environmental justice, immigration and welfare policy, and Asian-American studies. She is the author of *Consuming Citizenship: Children of Asian Immigrant Entrepreneurs* (Palo Alto: Stanford University Press, 2005) which won the 2006 Outstanding Book Award from the American Sociological Association, Asia and Asian America Section.

THE EMERGENCE OF SILICON VALLEY

Immigrants and People of Color Seek Opportunities in the Valley of Dreams

Long an elite and exclusive private institution, Stanford University had no less stringent expectations of the firms it was allowing to locate in its industrial park. The university sought to ensure that the companies and their personnel would "blend in" with the suburban environment. They sought

> "light industry of a non-nuisance type ... which will create a demand for technical employees of a high salary class that will be in a financial position to live in this area." The well-paid, well-educated worker in the industrial park made a "very desirable kind of resident" for the community, according to the president of the Stanford Board of Trustees; employers should expect the suburban environs of the park to "attract a better class of workers."[1]

The terms "desirable" and "better class" are classic *code words* that denote Stanford's wish to attract white, middle-class workers and to repel undesirables, the multiracial blue-collar "riffraff" generally associated with manufacturing industries.[2] This was a textbook pitch reminiscent of the turn-of-the-century "city beautiful" efforts by Frederick Law Olmsted and others, who were openly classist and racist in their consultations with cities regarding what a desirable citizen population might be.[3] The *San Jose News* did its part to promote Santa Clara County's clean and lily-white image when it boasted that political and business leaders were able to attract entrepreneurs to the area who used "[i]mproved production tech-

niques and new types of industries which eliminated or reduced industrial nuisances."[4] In 1968, while the Black Panther Party, the Brown Berets, La Raza Unida, and the San Francisco State University strike were in full force, the *San Jose News* proudly proclaimed that Santa Clara "is a white collar county ... and 93.6 per cent of the county population [is] white."[5] Little did the Stanford University administrators, newspaper editors, and urban planners in the county realize that the region would soon be transformed into one of the most environmentally polluted and racially and ethnically diverse in the nation.

Chicanos

The 1960s and 1970s saw the emergence of public protests in San Jose's Chicano community when activists and residents put the spotlight on police brutality, economic discrimination, and the lack of services in their neighborhoods. Punctuating some of these concerns, one Chicano activist, Sal Alvarez, told an audience at a West Valley College symposium in 1969 that "Mexicans in San Jose got cheated out of land under urban renewal ... [and] the killing of Mexican Americans by police in California is a very serious problem and a worry in San Jose."[6] Community-based and national organizations like United People Arriba, the Council on Latin American Affairs, and La Raza Unida were active in San Jose and Santa Clara County. Apartment complexes, construction companies, schools, and police departments charged with discrimination against Chicanos were the primary targets of the protest movement.[7]

A 1973 Rand Corporation study reported that while much of San Jose was experiencing prosperity, "poor [largely Latino] neighborhoods [had] deteriorated relative to better-off neighborhoods and segregation had increased."[8] Housing quickly became a social and environmental justice issue as activists linked poor housing quality and poor health with racism. The fate that befell so many African American neighborhoods around the nation during the 1950s due to urban renewal efforts also came to pass in the barrio of Sal si Puedes in east San Jose.[9] Urban renewal was the federal effort to improve municipalities by razing degraded and blighted housing and by connecting cities and states through the interstate highway system. These changes devastated and destroyed many communities, earning urban renewal the nicknames "Negro removal" and "Mexican removal." For example, most of the houses of Sal si Puedes were razed as part of an urban renewal program that included the construction of a new freeway.[10] In the 1980s, other neighborhoods populated by people of color in San Jose would fall prey to urban renewal—ironically, for the construction of the Tech Museum, the city's monument to the electronics and computer industries, and its own physical proclamation of its status as the "Capitol of Silicon Valley."[11]

The Chicano community of Alviso, in North San Jose, was also the site of many conflicts over environmental and social justice concerns. In March 1973, activists set up a tollbooth on the Gold Street Bridge, charging twenty-five cents for cars to pass—a symbolic protest to call attention to the lack of paved streets in Alviso. The streets were not paved until 1980, twelve years after Alviso was annexed by San Jose.[12]

Asian/Pacific Islander Americans and Immigrants

According to the 1980 census, an estimated 11,700 Vietnamese immigrants were living in San Jose. By 1987 that number had jumped to around 75,000.[13] During the 1980s, there was a marked rise in white resentment and hate crimes directed at the Vietnamese population in particular, and at Asian/Pacific Islander Americans and immigrants in Silicon Valley in general.[14] During this period, many manufacturing workers were being laid off in the United States and there was increased tension over the heightened competition with Japan in the auto and electronics industries. Much of this tension was channeled into scapegoating any and all Asians, regardless of their specific ancestry.[15]

At the same time, some Asian immigrants were doing well in the high-technology sector, as white-collar workers. Chinese software engineers set up many businesses by networking with firms and entrepreneurs overseas and, by 1992, Asians made up a third of the engineering work-force in Silicon Valley.[16] Very few of these upwardly mobile Asian workers broke through the glass ceiling into the ranks of management. David Lam, founder of Lam Research, a company that makes equipment used in chip making, explained, "Many Asian engineers are not being looked at as having management talent. They are looked upon as good work horses, and not race horses."[17]

As financially stable as some Asians appeared to be, most were working-class and many of them experienced plenty of setbacks. In 1983, Atari Corporation, the video game maker, announced that it was closing its Silicon Valley plant and shifting production overseas to Hong Kong and Taiwan. Most of those production employees thrown out of work were Latino, Chinese, and Vietnamese. One of these workers was Hoa Ly. In 1978, Ly escaped Saigon in a fishing boat jammed with fifty-five other refugees. He spent half a year in a Malaysian refugee camp and later moved to Silicon Valley, where he got a job in printed circuit board assembly at Atari for which he was paid $7 per hour. Since his mother and father both worked by his side at Atari, when the company closed down his whole family was suddenly out of work. The Atari case was also quite significant because it was a high-profile example of the empty "no layoff pledge" many Silicon Valley companies made during the 1970s, when business and political leaders were claiming that this industry was immune to recession.[18]

Since the 1980s, the popular sentiment regarding immigrants took at least two, perhaps contradictory, directions. The first was a continuation of the traditional nativist approach to immigration, and this anti-immigrant movement gained sanction at the highest levels, as the efforts to pass Proposition 187 (denying undocumented residents access to public services) and the implementation of the Welfare and Immigration Reform Acts of 1996 moved forward. Television commercials depicted gangs of "illegals" crossing the Rio Grande under cover of night, and presidential hopeful Pat Buchanan warned of a "foreign invasion" from Mexico. In Silicon Valley, as elsewhere, this backlash took the form of Immigration and Naturalization Service (INS) raids of workplaces. In April 1984, when the INS opened a new office in Silicon Valley, they conducted raids on two electronics firms in San Jose and the city of Santa Clara on the same day. Using classic nativist rhetoric, Harold Ezell, the INS's Western regional commissioner, stated, "Probably 25 percent of the working population in this area is here illegally, particularly in the Silicon Valley area. We intend to make our presence known. Our officers will be *freeing up jobs for U.S. citizens* and people who are here legally."[19] Neither the newspaper article nor the INS acknowledged that, without the abundance of undocumented immigrant labor, many Silicon Valley industries would relocate overseas or south of the U.S./Mexico border. The second direction in popular sentiment was the general consensus among labor, business, and politicians that the Immigration bill of 1990 and the H1-B visa expansion in 2000 (allowing white-collar high tech workers to immigrate to work at a particular firm for a limited period) were good for the U.S. economy, because of the alleged "shortage" of skilled workers.[20] The AFL-CIO called for an amnesty for the nation's estimated 5 million undocumented immigrants and Federal Reserve Board Chairman Alan Greenspan warned that, without a new wave of skilled immigrant workers, the integrity of the U.S. economy would be threatened.[21] Soon the national and California state legislation and policy making around these questions lumped documented and undocumented immigrants together for punitive measures. This indiscriminate grouping of these populations rendered the distinctions moot in many cases and revealed the deep similarities between the racist nature of immigration policy at the turn of the twentieth century and the twenty-first.[22] One of the major differences for Silicon Valley and the state of California, however, was that, for the first time since indigenous peoples occupied the land, people of color were now the majority. Of the 1.6 million people in Santa Clara County in the year 2000, 49 percent were white, 24 percent were Latino, 23 percent were Asian, and 4 percent were African American.[23] [...]

From "Clean Industry" to the Valley of Toxic Fright

The postindustrial, post-smokestack, campus-like suburban planning made it easy for developers and industry owners to claim that the electronics sector was "clean" and "pollution free." The clean image of the electronics industry was touted by executives, politicians, and newspapers everywhere. Harold Singer, an official of the San Francisco Bay Regional Water Quality Control Board, once stated, "the horizon above San Jose is unmarred by smokestacks, and people here are proud of that. They have worked hard at making the valley a base of the computer-electronics industry and an unpolluted place to live."[24]

As recently as the year 2000, the *Smithsonian Magazine* described the "clean rooms" where microchips are made as "the most fanatically clean, most thoroughly sanitized places on the planet," where "one could eat one's oatmeal off the floor."[25] The highly toxic wafers from which microchips are cut are viewed by industry promoters as "pristine,"[26] and the chemical-laden water that washes semiconductor components in the electronics "fab" plants is described as "pure."[27] Even former U.S. President Bill Clinton rubbed shoulders with CEOs in Silicon Valley in the 1990s, publicly proclaiming that the high-tech industry "will move America forward to a stronger economy, a cleaner environment and technological leadership."[28] These accounts leave the uninformed reader with the impression that high-tech firms are the paragon of hygiene and safety, sanitation and environmental responsibility.

The history behind this image—and more importantly, the need and desire to create this image—seems to be lost on most observers of Silicon Valley's environmental problems. In the 1940s, as large defense industries such as General Electric, IBM, and Westinghouse Electric were locating and/or expanding in the Valley, the agricultural interests were quite concerned about the environmental impacts of this new form of development. In 1950, the San Jose Chamber of Commerce wrote:

> there were some sincere and intelligent people who looked askance at this industrial development. They had genuine fears that smokestacks would "encircle the city"; that "blighted areas" would spring up in industrial sections; that orchards would be torn up "by the hundreds"; and that by past standards, this accelerated trend in the establishment of a new industry might result in an unbalanced, top-heavy economy destined to collapse at some undetermined time in the future.[29]

The author of a study of the Bay Area conducted during the 1950s described the level of accuracy of these dire predictions:

> The fears that orchards would be torn up by the hundreds were indeed well founded; and smokestacks, though they by no means encircled the city, did undeniably contribute to the development of a new problem. The Chamber [of Commerce] sought to assure the skeptical that industrial growth was not incompatible with desirable living conditions. Yet it was not long before the Santa Clara County Board of Supervisors found it necessary to designate the entire county an air pollution control district; the skies over the Santa Clara Valley were becoming a dirty gray. In March, 1950, the county health officer, declared that "smog," the murky atmospheric condition familiar to Los Angeles, was not only a Santa Clara County problem but also a "Bay Area problem." The new factories in San Jose and Santa Clara were producing air pollutants.[30]

Thus the very beginnings of the electronics and defense industries were marred by environmental problems, the greatest irony of all being that they involved "smokestacks." So it seems that in the 1950s and 1960s, when Palo Alto and other cities in the Valley demanded that new industries be smokestack-less, these concerns were rooted in the real experience of having observed this sector befoul the local environment. Whether or not the municipalities were aware of it, these expectations and claims of nonpollution were either naïve promises or lies, while the production processes internal to these corporations actually became even more toxic than before. This heavily polluted past also challenges earlier claims by Silicon Valley boosters that the region was "pollution free" prior to the electronics boom of the 1960s.[31]

The End of Innocence

In the 1960s and 1970s, a sort of amnesia fell over the Valley's residents and policy makers; they all seemed to arrive at a consensus that the new industry was somehow pristine. This image was shattered in December 1981, when it was discovered that the drinking water well that supplied 16,500 homes in the Los Paseos neighborhood of South San Jose was contaminated with the deadly chemical trichloroethane (TCA), a solvent used to remove grease from microchips and printed circuit boards after they are manufactured. Officials estimated that 14,000 gallons of TCA and another 44,000 gallons of various toxic waste materials had been leaking from an underground storage tank for at least a year and a half.[32] The responsible party was the Fairchild Semiconductor corporation.

Lorraine Ross, a resident of the neighborhood (and a mother), was catapulted into the role of environmental activist. She and her neighbors mapped out a disturbing and pervasive cluster of cancers, miscarriages, birth defects, infant heart problems, and fatalities in the neighborhood that public health authorities and the industry were forced to take seriously. Two health studies were carried out immediately, both of which confirmed the presence of higher than expected frequencies of congenital birth defects (three times the normal rate), spontaneous abortions, and heart defects. However, neither study would take the bold step of pin-pointing industrial chemicals as the cause.[33] One reason for the delayed discovery of the presence of chemicals was that at the time, state and federal regulations did not require testing for industrial chemicals. Tests were only required for viruses, bacteria, pesticides, and herbicides.[34] A painful irony here is that TCA was commonly used as a substitute cleaner for TCE (trichloroethylene). TCE is a suspected carcinogen that was nearly phased out of the industry in the late 1970s—the result of the Campaign to Ban TCE, led by occupational health advocates in San Jose.[35] This community organizing success was reversed when the industry phased out the targeted chemical and substituted a comparably hazardous one.

Back in the Los Paseos community of San Jose, Lorraine Ross was organizing against Fairchild, berating the city council that year with the question, "Fairchild or my child?": "It takes a lot of nerve for them to invade a pre-existing residential neighborhood, pour dangerous chemicals into a leaking tank, poison the surrounding environment and hide the fact from the people affected by their negligence."[36]

Ross was not alone. She was a leader of a burgeoning antitoxics/environmental justice and occupational health movement taking shape in Silicon Valley. Organizations like the Santa Clara Center for Occupational Safety and Health (SCCOSH) had prior to the contamination of Los Paseos been involved in leading community workshops on chemical solvents such as those spilled at Fairchild.[37] The Silicon Valley Toxics Coalition (SVTC), an environmental justice group that had formed in response to the Fairchild spill, was also at the forefront of the campaign to bring that company to justice. In 1983, Fairchild closed down its plant in South San Jose, a victory for Ross and the environmental justice movement. Since then, the company has spent more than $40 million on the cleanup. Similar chemical accidents and resulting toxic illness and death tolls have occurred in the communities near the IBM and Teledyne Semiconduc-

tor plants; the IBM spill is one of the largest in the county, having leaked toxics since 1956.[38] IBM had to install a more extensive chemical detection system for ground water monitoring as a result of efforts by the Silicon Valley Toxics Coalition, Communities for a Better Environment (a San Francisco–based group), the Santa Clara Valley Water District, and the County Board of Supervisors.[39] This result actually set two new precedents. The first was that the so-called "clean industry" could no longer be viewed as pristine. The second was that this industry was not trustworthy and that only the presence of a strong local environmental justice movement could ensure that necessary reforms would materialize.

Challenges to the "clean industry" image in the Valley abound. The USEPA has estimated that a large area of land, contaminated by eleven electronics plants in the Mountain View area alone (a community with a large population of immigrants, people of color, and working-class persons) will take $60 million and 300 years to clean up. As we mentioned in chapter 2, that site is located at Moffett Field, the old Naval base that sat on the land owned by one of the few remaining Ohlones in the area, Lope Inigo. As for the once pure water and fertile land of the Valley, 57 private and 47 public drinking wells were contaminated as of 1992, and 66 plots of land have been declared too toxic for human beings to walk on.[40]

Soon after the Fairchild spill made news headlines, various arms of the federal government also took on the charge of addressing this problem. In 1985, the Congressional Committee on Public Works and Transportation held a hearing on toxic concerns in the electronics industry in San Jose.[41] The USEPA also undertook its own study of the human health risks associated with industrial pollution in Santa Clara County. The agency released a preliminary draft of this "Integrated Environmental Management Project" in 1985, which concluded that pollution-related health risks in the area were "comparatively low."[42] Clearly elated, a spokesman for the Semiconductor Industry Association (SIA) informed the media that, based on the EPA's findings, industrial chemicals in Silicon Valley "do not pose a significant threat to human life."[43] Environmentalists and journalists immediately became suspicious and discovered that a scandal was afoot. According to one report, long before the study was released, the SIA had hired a high-ranking official of the Republican Party who lobbied the EPA into lowering risk estimates and excluding tests from the study that would indicate whether solvents caused chronic diseases, birth defects, and miscarriages.[44] This effort seems to have paid off, as it appears to have shaped the "findings" in the EPA's study. But it was a major source of embarrassment for the EPA when high-profile environmental groups and political leaders denounced the report as flawed and biased in favor of industry. The true significance of this event was that environmentalists learned that they had to remain vigilant and be wary of "scientific studies," because the USEPA and any other agency could be bought and paid for by industry to silence or "disprove" dissenting perspectives concerning the true costs of the Silicon Valley "miracle."

After testing other companies for toxins, county authorities found that sixty-five of seventy-nine (or 82 percent) had hazardous chemicals in the ground beneath their plants. Some of these included IBM, Intel, Hewlett-Packard, DEC, Tandem, Raytheon, NEC, AMD, Signetics, TRW, and many others. Today Santa Clara County is home to twenty-nine Superfund sites, more than any other county in the nation, and twenty-four of those sites are the result of pollution by electronics firms.

The earlier claims that computer/electronics was a "clean industry" rang painfully hollow, because, as the Silicon Valley Toxics Coalition's Ted Smith put it, this industry had "buried its smokestacks underground."[45] Other leaders stated similar concerns:

> Voicing the shock shared by cities that had assumed the electronics industry was nonpolluting, San Jose's mayor, Janet Gray Hayes, said, "I remember thinking about smokestacks in other industries. I didn't expect this problem in my own backyard."[46] She continued, "When I first became Mayor and we embarked on an economic development program, there was no doubt in my mind that this was a clean industry. We now know that we are definitely in the midst of a chemical revolution."[47] [...]

Environmental Inequalities

When the nature and extent of high tech's toxicity became public knowledge, a decline in the location of such industries in white communities was complemented by a shift to lower-income communities and communities of color.[48] For example, after the discovery of toxic waste in the water tables in Palo Alto, residents organized and supported new regulations so strict that some companies moved out or decided against locating there, and shifted their toxic production to less restrictive communities (with higher percentages of working-class people and persons of color) such as Mountain View.[49] Similarly, during the early 1980s in Sonoma County (north of San Francisco), citizens opposed *all* high-tech development because of the newly discovered associated pollution threats. And in 1984, a Fremont-based group, Sensible Citizens Reacting Against Hazardous Materials (SCRAM), organized to block CTS Printex's attempts to locate a plant in that town.[50] This dynamic was a stark departure from the fights and bidding wars among municipalities in their efforts to attract the "clean industry" in previous decades. But this is also a pattern we see in myriad other "environmental protection" practices that impact communities of color across the United States and around the world. In other words, immigrants and people of color bear the cost of both environmental destruction (when industry extracts or pollutes natural resources) *and* environmental protection (when white, affluent communities discover that an industry is toxic and protect themselves by shifting the burden onto lower-income neighborhoods and communities of color).[51]

However, some polluting businesses that originally located in marginal neighborhoods were forced to reform because communities of color were also organizing. For example, Lorenz Barrel and Drum was located in a working-class and Latino neighbohood in south San Jose. For forty years this company treated the electronics industry's hazardous waste. The site was located a half block away from Mi Tierra, one of San Jose's first community gardens. A local neighborhood group, Students and Community Against Lorenz Pollution (SCALP), formed and pressured authorities to take action.[52] In 1986, federal authorities shut the company down, citing criminal violations. The soil and ground water on site were found to be contaminated with at least fourteen toxic chemical compounds.[53] The site was "remediated" for a $5.2 million price tag, but was covered with an asphalt cap—the "cleanup" method of choice in low-income communities and communities of color—rather than subjected to a true abatement and restoration operation as preferred under law.[54] Even so, more than 25,000 drums containing hazardous waste and 3,000 cubic yards of contaminated soil were removed. A year later, the company's owner was sentenced to two years in jail, assessed fines of $2.04 million, and ordered to spend up to $100,000 on health monitoring for current and former neighbors and employees. So while environmental racism placed these residents and workers at risk, they were able to achieve some modicum of justice through collective action.

While residents and the general public may not have been knowledgeable concerning the hazards associated with electronics production before the 1980s, ample evidence suggests that the industry was aware of the facts early on. Years later, in 1976 (five years before the Fairchild spill was made public), a study submitted to the Santa Clara County Board of Supervisors disclosed that tons of "poisonous and explosive chemicals" were being illegally dumped in communities and into the sewer system throughout the region. These hazardous materials were from electronics firms and many of these dumps were located in communities of color and low-income neighborhoods inside the county and beyond.[55] So communities of color were being polluted

well before the public outrage against the electronics industry made headlines in the early 1980s, and the industry was well aware of it.

After communities began demanding that toxic sites be placed on the EPA's Superfund list, evidence of another pattern of environmental inequality emerged. Many of these federally designated toxic Superfund sites are in communities of color and working-class neighborhoods. [...]

Whether from depletion or pollution, Santa Clara County industries seem always to have been intent on maintaining a dependence upon—and a lack of respect for—water, land, immigrants, and people of color. Environmental racism in the Valley meant not only that people of color were being exposed to toxics and pollutants at home and work, but also that this process was part and parcel of a broader context of general ecological degradation in the region. European contact, the missions, mining, farming and canning, and computer/electronics production each brought the promise of economic prosperity and new social liberties springing forth from the bountiful wealth of natural resources that only California could offer. But in each case, economic gains were concentrated among a few while poverty and immiseration were shared among the many; racial and ethnic cleavages reemerged and deepened; and the integrity of the natural environment suffered as yet untold assaults. Nothing is new about the latest proclamation of salvation in Silicon Valley; it is old wine in new bottles and represents only the most recent manifestation of a long history of environmental injustice, California style.

NOTES

1. Findlay 1992, 132; David Packard, President of Stanford University Board of Trustees, quoted in *Daily Palo Alto Times*, February 17, 1960.
2. See Omi and Winant (1994) for an insightful discussion of the range of racial "code words" used as proxies for more direct words like "race" or "African Americans," "Asian Americans," etc.
3. Delgado and Stefancic 1999.
4. Choate 1968a.
5. Choate 1968c.

6. Fraser 1969.
7. Hanson 1969; Larimore 1969; Flood 1968.
8. Heritage Media Corporation 1996, 215.
9. The barrio of Sal si Puedes was home to many Chicanos. The name translates to "get out if you can" and the neighborhood earned this label because of the many mud holes in its streets before they were paved and because of the preponderance of substandard housing and poverty (see Clark 1970, 35).
10. Findlay 1992, 39; Clark 1970, vii.
11. Heritage Media Corporation 1996, 229. Recent research has also begun to make links among race, environmental quality, and transportation systems. Robert Bullard and his collaborators have traced the history of America's two-tiered, racially biased transportation system, from early conflicts over "separate but equal" accommodations, through "urban renewal," to today's urban sprawl that amplifies the problems of pollution and ecological damage (see Bullard and Johnson 1997; Bullard, Johnson, and Torres 2000).
12. Alviso 2001.
13. Rios 1987.
14. Dickey 1984.
15. This tension led to the Pentagon blocking Fujitsu Ltd., a Japanese corporation, from purchasing Fairchild Semiconductor Corporation in 1987, because of the alleged "national security risk" involved (see Sanger 1987). A senior White House staff member told a reporter, "This is a test case. If Japan can come in and buy this company, it can come in and buy them all over the place. We don't want to see the semiconductor industry under Japanese control" (Kilborn 1987). Popular bumper stickers in Santa Clara County, Detroit, and other areas where competition was fiercest included those reading: "Toyota, Datsun, Honda and Pearl Harbor" or "Hungry and Out of Work? Eat a Foreign Car." Never mind the fact that Fairchild Semiconductor Corporation was already controlled by the Schlum-berger company, which was itself run by a French family; or that Intel Corporation was run by Andrew Gove, a Hungarian immigrant. One writer spoke of the "Japanese domination" of the 64K random access memory (RAM) chip in the 1980s as "the technological equivalent of Pearl Harbor" (Johnston 1982).
16. Pollack 1992.
17. Ibid.
18. IBM had a fifty-year-old tradition of no layoffs before it began letting employees go (via early retirements and buyouts) in the 1980s. When, in 1993, IBM announced that it would lay off employees for the first time in its history, they planned to cut up to seven thousand jobs, ending the fifty-year legacy of "full employment" adopted by IBM founder Tom Watson Sr. One computer peripheral manufacturer boasted in a classified ad for new workers about its "Recession Proof Strategy" (see San Jose Mercury News, February 1, 1982, 8CL). For more on layoffs, see "Electronics Job Losses Total 55,000 so far in '92," San Jose Mercury News, August 26, 1992; also see "IBM Ends No-Layoff Policy," San Jose Mercury News Wire Services, February 16, 1993.
19. Goldston 1984.
20. Marshall 1990.
21. Freedberg 2000.
22. See Park and Yoo 2001.
23. Goodell 2000.
24. Cummings 1982.
25. Page 2000, 40.
26. Ibid., 40.
27. Ibid., 43.
28. Kadetsky 1993, 519.
29. Industrial Survey Associates 1950, 4.
30. Scott 1959, 273.
31. Mandich (1975, 41) references these early boosters' claims of a pristine Valley during the 1950s and 1960s.
32. Siegel 1984, 58–59.
33. At that time, no toxicological study had proven a link between pollution and miscarriages or birth defects. One reason for this alleged lack of proof was the corruption and corporate bias endemic in the private laboratories and federal agencies conducting these tests (see Environmental Health Coalition 1992; Klinger 1982). For example, in one suspicious incident, of the 150 potentially toxic water samples the California Department of Health Services collected during the summer of 1980, the only one lost or destroyed was the sample from the water well Fairchild contaminated (Harris 1982). Perhaps CDHS officials were afraid of what they might find, particularly given the release of a report that very same summer revealing that the county cancer death rate had jumped 20 percent during the 1970s (see Klinger 1980). A more recent example of related corruption in environmental health testing was the indictment of employees of the Intertek Corporation for altering or falsifying some 250,000 environmental tests in 1996 and 1997. In many cases, false clean bills of health were issued for sites known to have significant environmental contamination, like the Rocky Mountain Arsenal in Denver, Colorado, and the Oakland Army Base in California (Ayres 2001).
34. Timberlake 1987, 142. Lorraine Ross and other activists in the Los Paseos neighborhood also discovered that toxicological knowledge about solvents was in its infancy during the mid-1970s, when the underground chemical storage tanks were built for Fairchild just two thousand feet from a public well (Yoachum 1982).
35. The group PHASE (Project on Health and Safety in Electronics) was at the forefront of this campaign. PHASE later changed its name to the Santa Clara Center for Occupational Safety and Health (SCCOSH), a group that continues to work closely with the Silicon Valley Toxics Coalition.
36. Timberlake 1987, 141.
37. SCCOSH 1982.

38. Champion 1988.

39. Benson 1986a.

40. Thurm 1992. Even more threatening than the contamination of the many smaller drinking wells was the pollution of the Anderson Reservoir—the county's prime drinking water source—by rocket fuel manufacturer United Technologies Corporation. In 1989, UTC spilled an estimated 10,000 gallons of groundwater contaminated with TCE into a creek that feeds into the reservoir (Calvert 1989).

41. *Hazardous Waste Contamination of Water Resources* 1985.

42. Kutzmann 1985.

43. Ibid.

44. Steinhart 1985.

45. Smith and Woodward 1992.

46. Johnston 1982, p. 470.

47. Cummings 1982.

48. Szasz and Meuser 2000.

49. *San Jose Mercury News*, April 28, 1988. Mountain View has one of the lowest median family incomes and highest percentages of people of color of any city in Santa Clara County (U.S. Bureau of the Census 1990).

50. Siegel 1984, 64.

51. With regard to solid waste, the white, affluent city of Palo Alto rejected all landfill proposals in 1976, thus shifting the burden of disposing of its own municipal solid waste to other communities.

52. Douglas 1987.

53. U.S. Department of Health and Human Services 1989a.

54. Lavelle and Coyle 1992.

55. Keller 1976. Two legally sanctioned dumps were located in the heavily African American, Latino, and Asian immigrant communities of Richmond and Martinez, north of Santa Clara County.

DOCUMENTS FOR PART VI

6-1. SPECIAL MESSAGE TO THE CONGRESS ON CONSERVATION AND RESTORATION OF NATURAL BEAUTY (1965)

President Lyndon B. Johnson

Source: *Public Papers of the Presidents of the United States, Lyndon B. Johnson: Containing the Public Messages, Speeches, and Statements of the President, 1965*, Book I—January to May 31, 1965 (Washington, D.C.: United States Government Printing Office, 1966).

EDITORS' INTRODUCTION

The Great Society is the name given to President Lyndon B. Johnson's domestic agenda which emphasized civil rights, fair housing, the rejuvenation of cities, and the War on Poverty. While the environmental goals and policies of the Johnson administration have received much less attention, they were no less visionary than his other plans. The February 8, 1965 message to Congress enumerates the many environmental problems that faced the country, such as dwindling open space, unsightly highways, and air pollution. **[See Figure 6.4.]** President Johnson used language reminiscent of nineteenth and early twentieth century reformers who sought cleaner and healthier cities. He also articulated the vision of wilderness conservation advocates, who feared that industrialization and urbanization would destroy the natural landscape. Johnson called for a more integrated approach to the reconfiguration of urban space, designing suburbs, and preserving architecture. These ideas are akin to the tenets of New Urbanism. **[See Document 10.3.]**

Special Message to the Congress on Conservation and Restoration of Natural Beauty. *February 8, 1965*

To the Congress of the United States:

For centuries Americans have drawn strength and inspiration from the beauty of our country. It would be a neglectful generation indeed, indifferent alike to the judgment of history and the command of principle, which failed to preserve and extend such a heritage for its descendants.

Yet the storm of modern change is threatening to blight and diminish in a few decades what has been cherished and protected for generations.

A growing population is swallowing up areas of natural beauty with its demands for living space, and is placing increased demand on our overburdened areas of recreation and pleasure.

The increasing tempo of urbanization and growth is already depriving many Americans of the right to live in decent surroundings. More of our people are crowding into cities and being cut off from nature. Cities themselves reach out into the countryside, destroying streams and trees and meadows as they go. A modern highway may wipe out the equivalent of a fifty acre park with every mile. And people move out from the city to get closer to nature only to find that nature has moved farther from them.

The modern technology, which has added much to our lives can also have a darker side. Its uncontrolled waste products are menacing the world we live in, our enjoyment and our health. The air we breathe, our water, our soil and wildlife, are being blighted by the poisons and chemicals which are the by-products of technology and industry. The skeletons of discarded cars litter the countryside. The same society which receives the rewards of technology, must, as a cooperating whole, take responsibility for control.

To deal with these new problems will require a new conservation. We must not only protect the countryside and save it from destruction, we must restore what has been destroyed and salvage the beauty and charm of our cities. Our conservation must be not just the classic conservation of protection and development, but a creative conservation of restoration and innovation. Its concern is not with nature alone, but with the total relation between man and the world around him. Its object is not just man's welfare but the dignity of man's spirit.

In this conservation the protection and enhancement of man's opportunity to be in contact with beauty must play a major role.

This means that beauty must not be just a holiday treat, but a part of our daily life. It means not just easy physical access, but equal social access for rich and poor, Negro and white, city dweller and farmer.

Beauty is not an easy thing to measure. It does not show up in the gross national product, in a weekly pay check, or in profit and loss statements. But these things are not ends in themselves. They are a road to satisfaction and pleasure and the good life. Beauty makes its own direct contribution to these final ends. Therefore it is one of the most important components of our true national income, not to be left out simply because statisticians cannot calculate its worth.

And some things we do know. Association with beauty can enlarge man's imagination and revive his spirit. Ugliness can de-mean the people who live among it. What a citizen sees every day is his America. If it is attractive it adds to the quality of his life. If it is ugly it can degrade his existence.

Beauty has other immediate values. It adds to safety whether removing direct dangers to health or making highways less monotonous and dangerous. We also know that those who live in blighted and squalid conditions are more susceptible to anxieties and mental disease.

Ugliness is costly. It can be expensive to clean a soot smeared building, or to build new areas of recreation when the old landscape could have been preserved far more cheaply.

Certainly no one would hazard a national definition of beauty. But we do know that nature is nearly always beautiful. We do, for the most part, know what is ugly. And we can introduce, into all our planning, our programs, our building and our growth, a conscious and active concern for the values of beauty. If we do this then we can be successful in preserving a beautiful America. [...]

The Cities

Thomas Jefferson wrote that communities "should be planned with an eye to the effect made upon the human spirit by being continually surrounded with a maximum of beauty."

We have often sadly neglected this advice in the modern American city. Yet this is where most of our people live. It is where the character of our young is formed. It is where American civilization will be increasingly concentrated in years to come.

Such a challenge will not be met with a few more parks or playgrounds. It requires attention to the architecture of building, the structure of our roads, preservation of historical buildings and monuments, careful planning of new suburbs. A concern for the enhancement of beauty must infuse every aspect of the growth and development of metropolitan areas. It must be a principal responsibility of local government, supported by active and concerned citizens.

Federal assistance can be a valuable stimulus and help to such local efforts.

I have recommended a community extension program which will bring the resources of the university to focus on problems of the community just as they have long been concerned with our rural areas. Among other things, this program will help provide training and technical assistance to aid in making our communities more attractive and vital. In addition, under the Housing Act of 1964, grants will be made to States for training of local governmental employees needed for community development. I am recommending a 1965 supplemental appropriation to implement this program.

We now have two programs which can be of special help in creating areas of recreation and beauty for our metropolitan area population: the Open Space Land Program, and the Land and Water Conservation Fund.

I have already proposed full funding of the Land and Water Conservation Fund, and directed the Secretary of the Interior to give priority attention to serving the needs of our growing urban population.

The primary purpose of the Open Space Program has been to help acquire and assure open spaces in urban areas. I propose a series of new matching grants for improving the natural beauty of urban open space.

The Open Space Program should be adequately financed, and broadened by permitting grants to be made to help city governments acquire and clear areas to create small parks, squares, pedestrian malls and playgrounds.

In addition I will request authority in this program for a matching program to cities for landscaping, installation of outdoor lights and benches, creating attractive cityscapes along roads and in business areas, and for other beautification purposes.

Our city parks have not, in many cases, realized their full potential as sources of pleasure and play. I recommend on a matching basis a series of federal demonstration projects in city parks to use the best thought and action to show how the appearance of these parks can better serve the people of our towns and metropolitan areas.

All of these programs should be operated on the same matching formula to avoid unnecessary competition among programs and increase the possibility of cooperative effort. I will propose such a standard formula.

In a future message on the cities I will recommend other changes in our housing programs designed to strengthen the sense of community of which natural beauty is an important component.

In almost every part of the country citizens are rallying to save landmarks of beauty and history. The government must also do its share to assist these local efforts which have an important national purpose.

We will encourage and support the National Trust for Historic Preservation in the United States, chartered by Congress in 1949. I shall propose legislation to authorize supplementary grants to help local authorities acquire, develop and manage private properties for such purposes.

The Registry of National Historic Landmarks is a fine federal program with virtually no federal cost. I commend its work and the new wave of interest it has evoked in historical preservation. [...]

Highways

More than any country ours is an automobile society. For most Americans the automobile is a principal instrument of transportation, work, daily activity, recreation and pleasure. By making our roads highways to the enjoyment of nature and beauty we can greatly enrich the life of nearly all our people in city and countryside alike.

Our task is two-fold. First, to ensure that roads themselves are not destructive of nature and natural beauty. Second, to make our roads ways to recreation and pleasure.

I have asked the Secretary of Commerce to take a series of steps designed to meet this objective. This includes requiring landscaping on all federal interstate primary and urban highways, encouraging the construction of rest and recreation areas along highways, and the preservation of natural beauty adjacent to highway rights-of-way. [...]

The Recreation Advisory Council is now completing a study of the role which scenic roads and parkways should play in meeting our highway and recreation needs. After receiving the report, I will make appropriate recommendations.

The authority for the existing program of outdoor advertising control expires on June 30, 1965, and its provisions have not been effective in achieving the desired goal. Accordingly, I will recommend legislation to ensure effective control of billboards along our highways.

In addition, we need urgently to work towards the elimination or screening of unsightly, beauty-destroying junkyards and auto graveyards along our highways. To this end, I will also recommend necessary legislation to achieve effective control, including Federal assistance in appropriate cases where necessary.

I hope that, at all levels of government, our planners and builders will remember that highway beautification is more than a matter of planting trees or setting aside scenic areas. The roads themselves must reflect, in location and design, increased respect for the natural and social integrity and unity of the landscape and communities through which they pass. [...]

Pollution

One aspect of the advance of civilization is the evolution of responsibility for disposal of waste. Over many generations society gradually developed techniques for this purpose. State and local governments, landlords and private citizens have been held responsible for ensuring that sewage and garbage did not menace health or contaminate the environment.

In the last few decades entire new categories of waste have come to plague and menace the American scene. These are the technological wastes—the by-products of growth, industry, agriculture, and science. We cannot wait for slow evolution over generations to deal with them.

Pollution is growing at a rapid rate. Some pollutants are known to be harmful to health, while the effect of others is uncertain and unknown. In some cases we can control pollution with a larger effort. For other forms of pollution we still do not have effective means of control.

Pollution destroys beauty and menaces health. It cuts down on efficiency, reduces property values and raises taxes.

The longer we wait to act, the greater the dangers and the larger the problem.

Large-scale pollution of air and waterways is no respecter of political boundaries, and its effects extend far beyond those who cause it.

Air pollution is no longer confined to isolated places. This generation has altered the composition of the atmosphere on a global scale through radioactive materials and a steady increase in carbon dioxide from the burning of fossil fuels. Entire regional airsheds, crop plant environments, and river basins are heavy with noxious materials. Motor vehicles and home heating plants, municipal dumps and factories continually hurl pollutants into the air we breathe. Each day almost 50,000 tons of unpleasant, and sometimes poisonous, sulfur dioxide are added to the atmosphere, and our automobiles produce almost 300,000 tons of other pollutants.

In Donora, Pennsylvania in 1948, and New York City in 1953 serious illness and some deaths were produced by sharp increases in air pollution. In New Orleans, epidemic outbreaks of asthmatic attacks are associated with air pollutants. Three-fourths of the eight million people in the Los Angeles area are annoyed by severe eye irritation much of the year. And our health authorities are increasingly concerned with the damaging effects of the continual breathing of polluted air by all our people in every city in the country.

In addition to its health effects, air pollution creates filth and gloom and depreciates property values of entire neighborhoods. The White House itself is being dirtied with soot from polluted air.

Every major river system is now polluted. Waterways that were once sources of pleasure and beauty and recreation are forbidden to human contact and objectionable to sight and smell. Furthermore, this pollution is costly, requiring expensive treatment for drinking water and inhibiting the operation and growth of industry.

In spite of the efforts and many accomplishments of the past, water pollution is spreading. And new kinds of problems are being added to the old:

—Waterborne viruses, particularly hepatitis, are replacing typhoid fever as a significant health hazard.
—Mass deaths of fish have occurred in rivers over-burdened with wastes.
—Some of our rivers contain chemicals which, in concentrated form, produce abnormalities in animals.

—Last summer 2,600 square miles of Lake Erie—over a quarter of the entire Lake—were almost without oxygen and unable to support life because of algae and plant growths, fed by pollution from cities and farms.

In many older cities storm drains and sanitary sewers are interconnected. As a result, mixtures of storm water and sanitary waste overflow during rains and discharge directly into streams, bypassing treatment works and causing heavy pollution.

In addition to our air and water we must, each and every day, dispose of a half billion pounds of solid waste. These wastes—from discarded cans to discarded automobiles—litter our country, harbor vermin, and menace our health. Inefficient and improper methods of disposal increase pollution of our air and streams.

Almost all these wastes and pollutions are the result of activities carried on for the benefit of man. A prime national goal must be an environment that is pleasing to the senses and healthy to live in.

Our Government is already doing much in this field. We have made significant progress. But more must be done. [...]

White House Conference

I intend to call a White House Conference on Natural Beauty to meet in mid-May of this year. Its chairman will be Mr. Laurance Rockefeller.

It is my hope that this Conference will produce new ideas and approaches for enhancing the beauty of America. Its scope will not be restricted to federal action. It will look for ways to help and encourage state and local governments, institutions and private citizens, in their own efforts. It can serve as a focal point for the large campaign of public education which is needed to alert Americans to the danger to their natural heritage and to the need for action. [...]

Conclusion

In my thirty-three years of public life I have seen the American system move to conserve the natural and human resources of our land.

TVA transformed an entire region that was "depressed." The rural electrification cooperatives brought electricity to lighten the burdens of rural America. We have seen the forests replanted by the CCC's, and watched Gifford Pinchot's sustained yield concept take hold on forestlands.

It is true that we have often been careless with our natural bounty. At times we have paid a heavy price for this neglect. But once our people were aroused to the danger, we have acted to preserve our resources for the enrichment of our country and the enjoyment of future generations.

The beauty of our land is a natural resource. Its preservation is linked to the inner prosperity of the human spirit.

The tradition of our past is equal to today's threat to that beauty. Our land will be attractive tomorrow only if we organize for action and rebuild and reclaim the beauty we inherited. Our stewardship will be judged by the foresight with which we carry out these programs. We must rescue our cities and countryside from blight with the same purpose and vigor with which, in other areas, we moved to save the forests and the soil.

6-2. *TOXIC WASTES AND RACE IN THE UNITED STATES* (1987)

Commission for Racial Justice, United Church of Christ

Source: *Toxic Wastes and Race in the United States: A National Report on the Racial and Socio-Economic Characteristics of Communities with Hazardous Waste Sites* (New York: Public Data Access, Inc., 1987). Reprinted with permission of the United Church of Christ.

EDITORS' INTRODUCTION

"Environmental racism" is a term that refers to the disproportionate placement of environmental risks in communities of color, and the exclusion of representatives from those communities in the environmental decision making process. The earliest articulation of the term came in the 1987 report from the United Church of Christ's Commission for Racial Justice, *Toxic Wastes and Race in the United States.* The "Major Findings" and the table "Fifty Metropolitan Areas" from the report highlight the over-represented fact that blacks, Hispanics, Asian/Pacific Islanders, and Native Americans were over-represented in populations living near uncontrolled waste sites. Environmental hazards, however, are not exclusive to minority communities. In fact, as the summary asserts, more than half of all Americans live in communities with uncontrolled toxic waste sites.

Major Findings

This report presents findings from two cross-sectional studies on demographic patterns associated with (1) commercial hazardous waste facilities and (2) uncontrolled toxic waste sites. The first was an analytical study which revealed a striking relationship between the location of commercial hazardous waste facilities and race. The second was a descriptive study which documented the widespread presence of uncontrolled toxic waste sites in racial and ethnic communities throughout the United States. Among the many findings that emerged from these studies, the following are most important:

Demographic Characteristics of Communities with Commercial Hazardous Waste Facilities

–Race proved to be the most significant among variables tested in association with the location of commercial hazardous waste facilities. This represented a consistent national pattern.

–Communities with the greatest number of commercial hazardous waste facilities had the highest composition of racial and ethnic residents. In communities with two or more facilities or one of the nation's five largest landfills, the average minority percentage of the population[1] was more than three times that of communities without facilities (38 percent vs. 12 percent).

–In communities with one commercial hazardous waste facility, the average minority percentage of the population was twice the average minority percentage of the population in communities without such facilities (24 percent vs. 12 percent).

–Although socio-economic status appeared to play an important role in the location of commercial hazardous waste facilities, race still proved to be more significant. This remained true after the study controlled for urbanization and regional differences. Incomes and home values were substantially lower when communities with commercial facilities were compared to communities in the surrounding counties without facilities.

–Three out of the five largest commercial hazardous waste landfills in the United States were located in predominantly Black[2] or Hispanic communities. These three landfills accounted for 40 percent of the total estimated commercial landfill capacity in the nation.

Demographic Characteristics of Communities with Uncontrolled Toxic Waste Sites

–Three out of every five Black and Hispanic Americans lived in communities with uncontrolled toxic waste sites.

–More than 15 million Blacks lived in communities with one or more uncontrolled toxic waste sites.

–More than 8 million Hispanics lived in communities with one or more uncontrolled toxic waste sites.

–Blacks were heavily over-represented in the populations of metropolitan areas with the largest number of uncontrolled toxic waste sites. These areas include:

Memphis, TN	(173 sites)
St. Louis, MO	(160 sites)
Houston, TX	(152 sites)
Cleveland, OH	(106 sites)
Chicago	(103 sites)
Atlanta, GA	(94 sites)

–Los Angeles, California had more Hispanics living in communities with uncontrolled toxic waste sites than any other metropolitan area in the United States.

–Approximately half of all Asian/Pacific Islanders and American Indians lived in communities with uncontrolled toxic waste sites.

–Overall, the presence of uncontrolled toxic waste sites was highly pervasive. More than half of the total population in the United States resided in communities with uncontrolled toxic waste sites.

NOTES

1. In this report, "minority percentage of the population" was used as a measure of "race".
2. In this report, the terminology used to describe various racial and ethnic populations was based on categories defined by the U.S. Bureau of the Census: Blacks, Hispanics, Asian/Pacific Islanders and American Indians.

FIFTY METROPOLITAN AREAS WITH GREATEST NUMBER OF BLACKS LIVING IN COMMUNITIES WITH UNCONTROLLED TOXIC WASTE SITES (ranked by number of persons)

METROPOLITAN AREA	BLACKS LIVING IN WASTE SITE AREAS	# SITES IN AREA	TOTAL POPULATION IN METROPOLITAN AREA (TH)			PERCENTAGE OF GROUP WHICH LIVES IN WASTE SITE AREAS			BLACK PERCENTAGE OF POPULATION IN AREAS WITH SITES	W/O SITES	ALL AREAS
			BLK	WH	ALL	BLK	WH	ALL			
1. CHICAGO, IL	913,430	103	1,200	1,519	3,228	76.1	59.1	68.3	41.4	28.1	37.2
2. PHILADELPHIA, PA	370,425	46	642	1,005	1,731	57.7	57.5	57.4	37.3	36.8	37.1
3. NEW YORK, NY	361,458	77	1,762	3,836	7,177	20.5	23.6	22.6	22.3	25.2	24.6
4. DETROIT, MI	326,175	34	802	627	1,470	40.7	47.5	44.2	50.2	58.0	54.5
5. HOUSTON, TX	317,398	152	455	1,109	1,927	69.8	57.1	64.1	25.7	19.9	23.6
6. MEMPHIS, TN	312,074	173	313	402	723	99.8	99.6	99.7	43.3	29.2	43.3
7. ATLANTA, GA	292,757	94	354	398	767	82.8	60.2	70.6	54.0	27.0	46.1
8. BALTIMORE, MD	262,211	59	476	810	1,309	55.1	44.7	48.6	41.2	31.7	36.3
9. ST. LOUIS, MO	247,698	160	306	788	1,113	81.0	83.4	82.7	26.9	30.1	27.5
10. CLEVELAND, OH	214,122	106	339	1,055	1,430	63.1	59.7	60.9	24.6	22.4	23.7
11. DALLAS, TX	191,430	60	266	577	971	71.9	53.5	60.1	32.8	19.2	27.4
12. NEW ORLEANS, LA	163,802	13	312	263	601	52.5	47.9	50.7	53.7	50.1	51.9
13. LOS ANGELES, CA[a]	156,975	60	542	595	2,000	28.9	35.3	43.0	18.2	33.8	27.1
14. BIRMINGHAM, AL	133,934	41	169	303	476	79.1	54.1	62.9	44.7	20.1	35.5
15. MIAMI, FL	123,628	19	207	638	1,278	59.8	22.2	27.0	35.9	8.9	16.2
16. INDIANAPOLIS, IN	116,177	40	155	604	772	74.7	68.8	70.0	21.5	17.0	20.1
17. MILWAUKEE, WS	113,056	32	149	678	866	75.9	59.6	63.3	20.6	11.3	17.2
18. OAKLAND, CA	111,149	30	160	129	351	69.3	23.7	50.7	62.3	28.4	45.6
19. CINCINNATI, OH	108,090	62	166	688	865	65.3	67.6	67.1	18.6	20.2	19.2
20. NEWARK, NJ	104,687	51	217	167	455	48.3	83.8	66.6	34.6	73.7	47.6
21. LOUISVILLE, KY	101,362	56	109	566	684	92.7	56.6	62.4	23.8	3.1	16.0
22. CHARLOTTE, NC	98,713	56	103	250	360	95.5	72.9	79.4	34.5	6.3	28.7
23. GARY, IN	92,583	25	108	81	203	86.0	73.8	80.3	56.8	37.7	53.0
24. NASHVILLE, TN	91,823	35	102	277	385	89.8	64.3	71.1	33.5	9.3	26.6
25. JACKSON, MS	89,265	21	99	137	238	89.8	52.4	68.1	55.0	13.3	41.7
26. BATON ROUGE, LA	89,149	18	106	207	322	84.0	53.5	63.6	43.5	14.5	32.9
27. SHREVEPORT, LA	84,163	20	96	181	282	87.3	61.9	70.6	42.2	14.8	34.1
28. RICHMOND, VA	81,481	26	140	301	449	58.1	67.4	64.5	28.2	36.9	31.3
29. COLUMBIA, SC	81,058	12	92	163	262	88.1	75.2	79.2	39.1	20.2	35.1
30. BUFFALO, NY	76,491	71	101	565	684	75.8	81.5	80.8	13.9	18.5	14.8
31. KANSAS CITY, MO	76,106	57	123	388	533	61.8	55.2	57.1	25.0	20.6	23.1

continued

METROPOLITAN AREA	BLACKS LIVING IN WASTE SITE AREAS	# SITES IN AREA	TOTAL POPULATION IN METROPOLITAN AREA WH (TH)			PERCENTAGE OF GROUP WHICH LIVES IN WASTE SITE AREAS WH			BLACK PERCENTAGE OF POPULATION		
			BLK	WH	ALL	BLK	WH	ALL	IN AREAS WITH SITES	W/O SITES	ALL AREAS
32. MOBILE, AL	70,954	27	104	176	285	68.0	59.6	62.7	39.8	31.4	36.7
33. FLINT, MI	69,052	6	72	183	264	95.3	44.0	58.5	44.7	3.1	27.4
34. BOSTON, MA	67,234	65	147	1,378	1,611	45.8	47.6	47.2	8.9	9.4	9.1
35. JACKSONVILLE, FL	66,978	40	140	417	574	47.8	60.0	56.8	20.6	29.5	24.4
36. FT. LAUDERDALE, FL	65,066	15	67	410	497	97.0	45.7	53.0	24.7	0.9	13.5
37. SAVANNAH, GA	59,037	33	77	113	194	76.5	36.0	52.0	58.4	19.5	39.8
38. EAST ST. LOUIS, IL	56,848	14	70	46	116	81.7	21.2	57.6	85.1	25.9	60.0
39. TAMPA, FL	55,763	24	75	325	459	74.1	50.5	53.3	22.8	9.1	16.4
40. MONTGOMERY, AL	55,218	18	73	111	187	75.6	53.6	62.2	47.6	25.3	39.2
41. CHATTANOOGA, TN	54,021	57	54	147	203	99.5	79.2	84.7	31.4	0.8	26.7
42. OKLAHOMA CITY, OK	53,761	71	63	431	527	85.3	67.3	70.2	14.5	5.9	12.0
43. WINSTON-SALEM, NC	53,583	23	58	130	190	92.9	65.1	73.5	38.4	8.1	30.4
44. ROCHESTER, NY	52,272	26	68	415	501	77.4	64.2	66.5	16.7	9.1	13.5
45. GREENSBORO, NC	51,643	36	56	146	205	92.9	84.8	87.1	28.9	14.9	27.1
46. TOLEDO, OH	50,560	33	63	334	412	80.9	84.3	84.0	14.6	18.1	15.2
47. SAN ANTONIO, TX	50,129	36	67	422	950	74.6	46.2	52.5	10.1	3.8	7.1
48. COLUMBUS, OH	48,187	25	128	567	704	37.6	41.6	40.7	16.8	19.2	18.2
49. SEATTLE, WA	46,819	83	49	575	694	95.2	74.4	76.8	8.8	1.5	7.1
50. RALEIGH, NC	45,449	18	48	152	204	94.9	74.6	79.4	28.1	5.8	23.5

Note:

a Covers only geographic area within 900 3-digit ZIP code (more).

BRIDGE OVER THE MONONGAHELA RIVER, PITTSBURG, PENN.

Figure 6.1 "Bridge Over the Monongahela River, Pittsburgh, Penn." (1857). Source: *Ballou's Pictorial*, February 21, 1857. Courtesy of the Center for Historic American Visual Culture at the American Antiquarian Society.

As Joel Tarr notes in his essay, "The Metabolism of the Industrial City," Pittsburgh earned a reputation as the "smoky city" early in the nineteenth century. This view of the city's busy waterfront in 1857 illustrates how smoke from steamboats, factories, and other sources obscures the impressive 1,500 foot bridge connecting Pittsburgh to Birmingham across the Monongahela River.

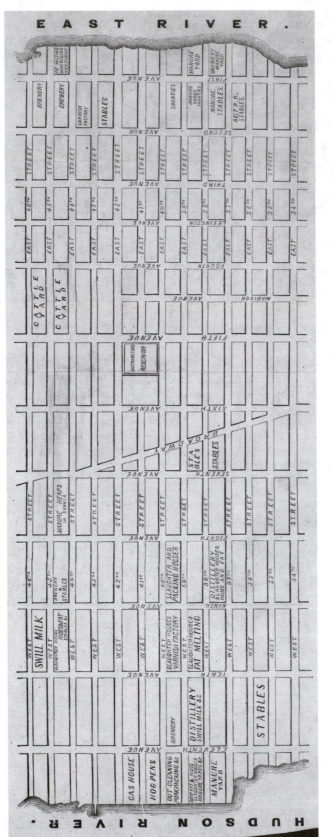

Figure 6.2 "Encroachment of Nuisances Upon Populous Up-Town Districts" (1864) Citizens' Association of New York. Source: Citizens' Association of New York, Report of the Council of Hygiene and Public Health of the Citizens' Association of New York Upon the Sanitary Condition of the City (New York: D. Appleton and Company, 1865). Courtesy of the Lionel Pincus and Princess Firyal Map Division, The New York Public Library, Astor, Lenox, and Tilden Foundations.

The mixed use of space characterized American cities before the rise of zoning and urban planning in the early twentieth century. This map identifies the location of "special nuisances," such as breweries, animal rendering plants, manure yards, and animal pens, in one of the most desirable residential areas of New York City during the middle of the nineteenth century. Contemporary public health reformers considered these nonresidential endeavors to be sources of disease and campaigned to have them relocated to less populated areas.

Figure 6.3 "Demolished and Tilted by the Earthquake, Homes on Howard Street at 17th, 1906. (544–7961) Stereopticon view. Kelly and Chadwick." San Francisco Earthquake of 1906. Courtesy of the Center for Historic American Visual Culture at the American Antiquarian Society.

Figure 6.4 "Smog, Salt Lake City, Utah, November 11, 1950." Courtesy of the United States Department of Health and Human Services, Center for Disease Control and Prevention/Barbara Jenkins, National Institute for Occupational Safety and Health.

PART VII

*T*RANSPORTATION AND PHYSICAL MOBILITY

EDITORS' INTRODUCTION TO PART VII

Most courses in urban history and urban studies are not complete without the inclusion of materials related to transportation and physical mobility across and through the metropolis. Cities in the eighteenth century and earlier found physical growth circumscribed by the distance a person could easily traverse—a radius from the central city of about two miles. Our early, compact cities, normally crossed on foot, are referred to as "walking cities" by urbanists for this reason. Population pressures, the need for more extensive business sectors, and the economic ability of some (originally only the middle and upper classes) to live in the countryside and commute into the city for work fostered to the evolution of a modern transportation network, serving both residents of the city and commuters from the metropolitan region as a whole.

Urban history and urban studies, as taught and researched today, are as much about metropolitan and suburban growth as they are about central cities. Thus many urban academic programs are renaming themselves "metropolitan and community studies" programs or adopting similar monikers. By the 1990s, about half of the American population lived in areas that might be termed "suburbs." Suburban life did not change the fact that most Americans connected with "urban" culture on a daily basis, whether it be through commuting into the city for jobs and recreation, or through the multiple doorways of mass popular culture, streaming at us from the Internet, cable television, satellite radio, and the like. The subject of the modern suburb is somewhat outside of the scope of this reader, and already is ably handled in *The Suburb Reader* (New York: Routledge, 2006) by historians Andrew Weise and Becky Nicolaides. Yet some aspects of suburban growth must be touched on here. In the mid-nineteenth century, central cities grew increasingly differentiated from outlying hinterlands, while at the same time better transportation linked the widening city together. The wealthy and then the middle class took advantage of increased transportation options to relocate away from cities plagued with overcrowding, seemingly relentless noise, and growing levels of airborne and waterborne pollution.

The first city dwellers to realize the dream of residing beyond the central city were the wealthy, as depicted in Ernest W. Burgess' concentric zone model of 1920. Wealthy people could afford to keep their own horses and carriages, providing private means for them to move out from the city centers during the 1800s. Popular forms of mass transit allowed for the upper middle class, the middle class, and ultimately portions of the working class to afford daily commutes in some American cities. The earliest form of rudimentary travel within a metropolitan region (drawing on the model of the stagecoach, which offered privately owned service between cities with a set route and set stops) was the horse-drawn omnibus, a privately owned vehicle open to all that could pay the fare, that traveled a set route. Omnibuses were first used in New York City in 1827. Chicago featured omnibuses as a means to transport travelers between hotels and railroad stations in 1852. Modifications followed, including the introduction of rails, and the rail-reliant cars came to be known as horsecars or horse-drawn streetcars. Chicago opened its first horsecar line in 1859. Urban commuters also relied on trains headed for distant locations for local service, although this form of transportation was not designed for the local commuter. In 1873, San Francisco implemented the cable car, which became popular in many American cities. Even Chicago, which did not have San Francisco's daunting hills, relied on the cable car technology it acquired from San Francisco beginning in 1882, but the entire system had been converted to electric trolleys by 1906.

It was the electric trolley, whereby overhead wires transferred electricity to the vehicle, that transformed most American cities. This technological form caught on quickly in cities throughout the United States. Experiments with the trolley had been ongoing since the 1830s, but the power supply initially had proved inadequate and too unreliable for a city-wide system. Montgomery, Alabama put a rudimentary system in place in 1886, and one was built for the city of Richmond, Virginia by Frank J. Sprague in 1888. By the 1890s, almost all cities of substantial size had a trolley system. The business of transportation systems was rife with corruption, for transportation made more money if lines were consolidated and politicians had to approve of licensing. Philadelphian Charles T. Yerkes, Chicago's own "robber baron," consolidated streetcar systems there by 1900, and had his business exploits fictionalized in the Theodore Dreiser works, *The Financier* (1912), *The Titan* (1914), and *The Stoic* (published posthumously in 1947). Trolleys ultimately became unprofitable, and were dismantled in most cities due to the pressures of the automobile, intense regulation, and population relocation to the suburbs. [See Transportation Revolution Photo Essay in this part.]

For some cities, urban congestion was so overwhelming that innovators sought a means to get mass transit off the city streets entirely. Trolleys added greatly to urban congestion, and having to cross the tracks proved to be a highly dangerous, yet disturbingly frequent, urban activity. So many were killed or maimed by trolleys that some wondered if trolley drivers were *trying* to injure pedestrians. By 1870, New York City had elevated its steam-powered railway system, eliminating the need for grade-crossings of at least one form of transportation. Unfortunately, elevating train systems blocked light to the street below, brought trains perilously close to second and third floor apartments, and occasionally contributed to stunning accidents (as was the case when an car derailed from the elevated tracks in New York City in 1919.) Other cities realized the potential of placing mass transit underground. Boston implemented the first, albeit limited, system in 1897, when the local streetcar franchise established a limited subway route under Tremont Street. New York City followed this lead in 1904, building an extensive system that transformed the city. No major subway projects followed until Chicago's work of the 1930s, for subways proved prohibitively expensive. Buses became popular in many cities in the 1950s, replacing streetcar systems. Chicago's red cars, operated by Chicago Surface Lines (CSL), carried almost 900 million riders per year, but were decimated by the implementation of a bus system in that city in the 1950s.[1]

The automobile radically transformed cities, in their reshaping of the central cities (now filled by parking lots, parking spaces, parking meters, gas stations and other car-related businesses), crowded the roads, and expanded the spaces made available to the individual driver. Commuting became a way of life for millions of Americans, and the house with the backyard became a reality for more former urbanites. By the 1920s, cars had become an essential component of the American lifestyle. Cars were so entrenched in the United States that many held on to their cars in the midst of the Great Depression. Americans considered cars a necessity, even as they re-evaluated the need for three square meals a day. By the time urban planners realized the full extent of the spatial changes the private car would bring to our cities and regions, the American reliance on the car was seemingly irreversible. By 1940, thirteen million American homes were not served by public transportation.

Once we had made cars the standard form of transportation in the United States, Americans found their roads inadequate; the nation's roads were not efficient for travel within a city, travel between cities, or travel in the rural regions. Under the Eisenhower Administration, Congress authorized the Federal Highway Act of 1956 [see **Document 7.1**], which allowed for $27 billion dollars to be spent over what was initially to be a ten-year effort to build 40,000 miles of interstate highway. Monies in part came from a "trust fund" of taxes pulled from the purchase of fuel, cars, trucks, and tires. But this unprecedented public works initiative cost far more in terms of time and money than first understood. Upkeep on these roads would be a struggle passed down for generations. And the highways did not lessen traffic problems, but rather encouraged movement. Once built, it was possible for city dwellers to move away from dwellings near their jobs and to acquire the trappings of suburban life. The interstate highway system was designed for projections on highway needs for 1972, but was not completed until the early 1990s. The highways also created physical and psychological scars within cities, tearing apart neighborhoods and disrupting surface traffic. One remedy came in the form of the Central Artery/Tunnel Project in Boston that placed portions of Interstate 93 underneath the city and its harbor. The so-called "Big Dig" cost in upwards of $14.6 billion [see **Document 7.2**].

In Part VII, three authors offer analyses of the changing city. Sam Bass Warner's "From Walking City to the Implementation of Street Railways," a portion of his work, *Streetcar Suburbs: The Process of Growth in Boston, 1870–1900* (Cambridge, MA: Harvard University Press, 1962) provides a classic reading of the way in which streetcars transformed Boston, leading to the creation of suburbs later formally annexed by the city. Warner's work opens a way into the discussions of physical and economic mobility that so preoccupied the emerging "new social historians" of the 1960s and 1970s and still shapes the field of social and urban history today. Clifton Hood's "The Subway and the City," taken from his book, *722 Miles: The Building of the Subways and How They Transformed New York* (New York: Simon & Schuster, 1993) documents the opening of the New York City subway system—the most important local transportation system in the United States—and demonstrates how this system restructured this massive city. The excitement at the grand opening of the subway is palpable through the stories Hood relates. Finally, Robert Fogelson's "Wishful Thinking: Downtown and the Automotive Revolution," from his book, *Downtown: Its Rise and Fall, 1880–1930* (New Haven: Yale University Press, 2001) examines how urban leaders worked to provide better access to the downtown business district, and watched as its relevance seemed to slip away, despite their best efforts.

NOTE

1.   David M. Young, "Street Railways," in James R. Grossman, Ann Durkin Keating, and Janice L. Reiff, eds., *Encyclopedia of Chicago* (Chicago: University of Chicago Press, 2004), 791–792.

From Walking City to the Implementation of the Street Railways

Sam Bass Warner, Jr.

Source: *Streetcar Suburbs: The Process of Growth in Boston, 1870–1900*
(Cambridge, MA: Harvard University Press, 1962).

EDITORS' INTRODUCTION

Despite its reputation for traditionalism and a conservative outlook, Boston, as portrayed by Sam Bass Warner, Jr., in his classic work *Streetcar Suburbs*, is a city of "ceaseless change." Warner notes that in the second half of the nineteenth century, the city experienced a dramatic evolution, in which city leaders, home builders, transportation entrepreneurs, and enthusiastic new suburbanites transformed the city's physical form. Warner states, "In fifty years it changed from a merchant city of two hundred thousand inhabitants to an industrial metropolis of over a million. In 1850 Boston was a tightly packed seaport; by 1900 it sprawled over a ten-mile radius and contained thirty-one cities and towns."[i] Boston had a rapid metamorphosis from a "walking city" (a city of approximately two miles in radius easily accessible by foot) to a city reliant on transportation. The central city, which once housed people from all socioeconomic backgrounds, lost its middle-class and upper-class population to the lures of suburban life. The central business district—the city area devoted to financial and business matters—grew up upon the increasingly expensive real estate of the central city. Thus the city and its related areas, or hinterlands, grew into a metropolis more and more divided by class. In an examination of the suburbs of Roxbury, West Roxbury, and Dorchester, all of which would come to be annexed by Boston in the late 1800s, Warner provides information on the origins of the suburb and the now well-known figure of the commuting worker.

Warner's work, originally published in 1962, is still assigned in college classrooms and underpins much of the work done on suburban growth and the impact of transportation on American cities. Warner demonstrates how sprawl preceded the advent of the automobile. His work relates with that of the Chicago School's Ernest W. Burgess, whose concentric zone model set the stage for much of the thinking about the evolution of urban physical space and differentiation by class within a city. **[See Mike Davis, "Beyond *Blade Runner*," in Part I.]** The upper class find themselves with the access to the largest quantity of physical space, space they need only divide among a limited number of people. Suburbanites in effect create their own individual parks, and have many of the advantages of country life, including fresh air, physical beauty of landscape, and quiet. As the middle class grew and took advantage of their financial wherewithal to purchase suburban homes, the metropolitan lifestyle grew untenable, with very long, stress-inducing commutes, choked highways, and a loss of open land. As geographer John Corbett writes about the continued relevancy of Warner's argument, "Decades later, we are still dealing with the forces of development that Warner first unlocked, and [are] as far as ever from finding a solution."[ii]

---

i Sam Bass Warner, Jr., *Streetcar Suburbs: The Process of Growth in Boston, 1870–1900* (Cambridge, MA: Harvard University Press, 1978), 1.

ii John Corbett, "Sam Bass Warner: Modeling the Streetcar Suburbs, 1962," Center for the Spatially Integrated Social Science (CSISS) Classics, accessed at www.csiss.org/classics/content/49.

Sam Bass Warner, Jr., is Professor of History Emeritus at Brandeis University and Visiting Professor at the Massachusetts Institute of Technology (MIT). In addition to *Streetcar Suburbs*, Warner has written and contributed to a number of books, including *Planning for a Nation of Cities* (Cambridge, MA: MIT Press, 1969), *The Private City: Philadelphia in Three Periods of Growth* (Philadelphia: University of Pennsylvania Press, 1987), *To Dwell is to Garden: A History of Boston's Community Gardens* (Boston: Northeastern University Press, 1987), and *The Urban Wilderness: A History of the American City* (Berkeley: University of California Press, 1995).

THE LARGE INSTITUTIONS

At any given time the arrangement of streets and buildings in a large city represents a temporary compromise among such diverse and often conflicting elements as aspirations for business and home life, the conditions of trade, the supply of labor, and the ability to remake what came before.

The physical plan of metropolitan Boston in 1850 rested upon a primitive technology of urban transport: Boston was a city of pedestrians. Its form reflected a compromise among convenience and privacy, the aspirations of homeownership, and the high price of land. The arrival of the street railway freed the elements of the compromise from their former discipline of pedestrian movement and bound them together again by its own new discipline. By 1900 the transformation of Boston had been completed. The patterns made by this new compromise are what today is recognized as the suburban form of the metropolitan city.

The Walking City

In 1850 the area of dense settlement hardly exceeded a two-mile radius from City Hall. It included only portions of the towns and cities of Boston, Brookline, Cambridge, Charlestown, Chelsea, Dorchester, Roxbury, and Somerville. Before the invention of the telephone in 1876 and the introduction of street railways in the 1850's, face-to-face communication and movement on foot were essential ingredients of city life.

One can only guess just how large metropolitan Boston would have grown had there been no invention of new communication devices. If the spread of the city had begun to exceed the distance a man might walk in about an hour, say a three-mile radius, the shops and offices of the metropolis would have fallen out of easy daily communication with each other. The result would have been the destruction of a single unified communication network and the development of semi-autonomous subcities which would have had to duplicate many of the services and facilities offered in other parts of the city. One of the principal contributions of nineteenth century transportation and communication technology was to preserve the centralized communication of the walking city on a vastly enlarged scale.

In 1850 carriages were a prominent sight on Boston's downtown streets. They moved only a small proportion of the city's population, however, because few people could afford to maintain a private horse and carriage. The omnibus and the steam railroad were likewise supplements to walking. The omnibus, an urban version of the stage coach, was first introduced in 1826. It moved slowly, held relatively few passengers, and cost a lot. The stream railroad, in operation since 1835, was also expensive and accomplished, during its first fifteen years, little to change the old pattern of the city. At best it was a limited method of mass transportation. The railroad was fast but its infrequent stops and its single terminal, often located at some distance from passengers' ultimate destinations, prevented it from offering the great variety of choices of entrance and exit that streetcar systems ultimately provided. Prior to the Civil War the principal contribution of the railroad lay in its joining of the port of Boston, with its wharves and warehouses, to the manufacturing and farming towns of New England. The result was to accelerate the industrialization of both the trading center and its hinterland. For residents of the Boston region the railroad simplified business transactions with outlying industrial cities like Lynn and Waltham. The railroad also enabled some men of wealth and leisure to settle permanently at their summer estates which lay in scattered clusters about the hills beyond Boston.[1]

Before 1850 Boston's geography had inhibited easy expansion. Marshes, rivers, and the ocean restricted the paths of pedestrian communication. Boston itself was a rough, hilly peninsula set on the end of a narrow strip of land that connected it to the mainland at Roxbury. In the general area where the wharves now stand, against the eastern and northern part of the peninsula, lay the deep-water harbor. The rest of the peninsula was surrounded by tidal basins and enormous marshes. So confined by the harbor, Boston land had always been expensive, and almost from the beginning of its settlement men cramped for space began damming and filling the marshes and flats, first for commercial, and later for residential, purposes. As the city prospered and housing standards rose, more extensive works became profitable. Hills were leveled and sea walls built. By the 1850's developers had reclaimed the area around Charles street, parts of the North End, and much of the South End, and had cut down a good deal of Beacon and other hills.

In the succeeding twenty years Boston's two most ambitious land filling schemes were executed: the South End and the Back Bay. The South End was almost completely taken up with houses by 1880; the Back Bay, by 1900. Only the rich and the prosperous segment of the middle class could afford most of the new houses in these sections even though the common design of narrow row houses, three and one-half to four and one-half stories high, required but small parcels of land.[2]

Under such circumstances speculators turned their attention to land just beyond the main peninsula. What they wanted was property that could be more easily developed and therefore sold at lower prices. The search for cheap land began long before central Boston was filled. In 1804 South

Boston was opened as a housing speculation. Its progress remained slow, however, until the 1830's when the growth of Boston created a shortage of land sufficient to persuade people to move beyond the old peninsula and walk the added distance.[3] Similarly, Charlestown, parts of Cambridge, East Boston, and the nearby sections of Roxbury filled up rapidly in the period from 1830 to 1850 when Boston's industrial prosperity and expansion began to make headway.

These peripheral communities were not simple bedroom towns for commuters, not exact early models of the modern middle class residential suburb; rather they were mixed settlements of Boston commuters and local workers. All these communities lay at the edge of the harbor and possessed considerable industrial and mercantile potential. Charlestown and East and South Boston developed large shipbuilding and wharf facilities, while Cambridge and Roxbury became manufacturing centers.[4] Promoters of these areas, used to the tight scale of the walking city, saw no incompatibility between residences and factories; they wished to re-create the conditions of Boston.

Throughout the tiny metropolitan region of 1850, streets of the well-to-do lay hard by workers' barracks and tenements of the poor; many artisans kept shop and home in the same building or suite; and factories, wharves, and offices were but a few blocks from middle class homes. The wide physical separation between those who could afford new houses and those who could not awaited the expansion of the city that accompanied the introduction of the street railway.

Despite the peripheral towns' imitation of the central city some architectural differences marked the two areas. On the filled land of the main peninsula close copies of the brick London town row house predominated. In the peripheral areas, detached houses, continuations of eighteenth century American wooden construction, were the rule. These latter structures were often smaller and generally cheaper than their intown opposites. Today, after detached wooden styles have dominated residential fashions for over eighty years, the little wooden houses of South and East Boston appear to be significant alternatives to the brick row house. In the early nineteenth century, however, these houses were but a continuation of old habits. They were the products of a class of people who had yet to earn the wealth, had yet to learn the modes, of city life.

Compared to the enlarged lots, the picturesque houses, and the planted streets of the streetcar suburbs of the last third of the nineteenth century, the architecture of Boston in 1850 was strongly urban. The houses of the central city and the peripheral towns, set as they were on small narrow lots and generally placed against the street, created a town environment of dense settlement. Building in both areas was eminently suited to a city short of land, a city which depended on people's walking for its means of transportation, a city which depended upon face-to-face relationships as its means of communication.[5]

The Street Railways

The history of Boston's street railways in the nineteenth century is the story of fifty years of aggressive expansion. During both the early years of the horsecar and the later years of the electric, lines were rapidly lengthened and service frequently increased. This continuous expansion of surface transportation had a cumulative effect upon the city. The pace of suburbanization, at first slow, went forward with increasing acceleration, until by the 1890's it attained the proportions of a mass movement.

From 1852 until 1873 the horse railroads of Boston merely stretched out the existing city along already established paths. The outer boundary of dense settlement moved perhaps half a mile, so that at the time of the great Depression of 1873 it stood two and a half miles from Boston's City Hall. During the next fourteen years, from 1873 to 1887, horsecar service reached out about a mile and a half farther, bringing the outer edge of good transportation to four miles from City Hall. Lines of suburban settlement began to appear in what were formerly distant places. In the late 1880's and 1890's the electrification of street railways brought convenient transportation to at least the range of six miles from City Hall. The rate of building and settlement in this period became so rapid that the whole scale and plan of Greater Boston was entirely made over.

Boston's first street railway had but one car which began service between Harvard Square, Cambridge, and Union Square, Somerville, around 1852. The success of this experiment and the example of profitable lines in other American cities brought on a wave of entrepreneurial enthusiasm. To the local investment public, used to the relatively long periods necessary to realize profits on large-scale land speculations, the rapid construction of horse railroads seemed to promise a generous and immediate harvest. To real estate men the simple procedure of placing a coach on iron rails seemed a miraculous device for the promotion of out-of-town property.

The experience of the three towns of Roxbury, West Roxbury, and Dorchester was typical. The first line in this section of the metropolis commenced running in 1856. It followed the seventeenth century path which ran from downtown Boston along Washington street in the South End to Roxbury Crossing. In effect, the new service merely replaced the existing omnibus and supplemented the main traffic of pedestrians and carriages. In the short period from the first incorporation of 1852 to the Depression of 1873, seven companies were formed to serve the outlying towns of Roxbury, West Roxbury, and Dorchester. Only four ever operated. By 1873 only two companies, the Metropolitan Street Railway, and the Highland Street Railway, survived.

Some of Boston's street railways had been projected for routes with too light settlement and traffic, others were badly financed, and some were bogus companies put together to lure investors or to harass operating companies. The scramble for franchises, which were granted by the Boston Board of Aldermen, and for charters of incorporation, which were granted by the state legislature, further confused the ever shifting rivalries of the city's street railway companies.

These early difficulties of franchise and capitalization were soon superseded by the problems of the downtown. Boston's streets were just too narrow to carry all the needed cars. The downtown squeeze made necessary complicated lease arrangements for competitors' use of each other's tracks. The tempers of street railway employees were not always equal to this requirement of cooperation in a field of intense competition. All too often rival drivers raced for switches, stalled, and in general interfered with each other's progress. Nevertheless, despite early confusion, chicane, and false starts, by 1873 the main streets of the old city had become the new horsecar thoroughfares. During the years from 1852 to 1873 the periphery of dense settlement moved from 2 to 2.5 miles from City Hall.[6]

For the next fourteen years service in Greater Boston expanded steadily outward. Then, in 1887, Henry M. Whitney, a steamship operator and speculator in Brookline real estate, formed a syndicate out of his small West End Street Railway and began to purchase stock in the other five operating companies of Boston. After he had bought up large amounts of stock, especially in the biggest line, the Metropolitan, he offered by an exchange of stock and bonds to combine all the companies into one. Minority stockholders, probably helpless, and at any rate anticipating great profits from the rationalization of Boston service under one giant company, agreed to the merger. At the same time, the promise of rapid expansion of service and relief to downtown traffic jams persuaded the public and the legislature to allow the creation of the traction monopoly. Consolidation did in fact accelerate the rate of improvements in transportation.

Whitney continued two historic policies of street railway management. First, he was more interested in increasing the total number of fares on his system than in watching the relationship of distance, cost, and fare per ride. He, like his fellow streetcar managers the state over, was so convinced that the key to profit lay in the endless expansion of the numbers of passengers that, with little regard to costs, he constantly expanded the service area of the West End. As a result, by 1900 the outer limits of Boston's electric railways lay at least six miles from the downtown.

Second, Whitney, like all horsecar managers before him, was an ardent believer in the five-cent fare. Thus expansion of service took place without additional charge to the commuter. As crosstown lines were built, free-transfer points were added, so that the nickel fare was almost universal in 1900. During the 1870's and 1880's eight cents had been required for many transfer rides; two full fares had been required where riders moved to the cars of different companies.[7]

In his speeches before city clubs and regulatory agencies Whitney often pointed to these twin policies of rapid service expansion and the uniform five-cent fare as the proper basis for a public transportation system. He was an ardent champion of the suburban city. He frequently appealed to the popular belief that the rapid suburbanization of modern industrial cities was perhaps the most important single contribution of the street railway. Like his listeners, also, Whitney did not wish to control the form and direction of this suburban expansion, but rather to leave the development of suburbs to individual builders and homeowners. Though statistics of 1890 and 1900 showed that only one quarter of Boston's suburbanites owned their houses,[8] he, like his contemporaries, felt that the continued suburbanization of the city would bring a substantial increase in homeownership. He liked to use as a typical example of the coming benefits the rather untypical case of the workingman buying a lot of land in the suburbs upon which would be built his own home. Whitney's speeches were also full of comparisons to conditions in Europe and references to the old pre-streetcar sections of Boston where multi-family tenements and crowded old wooden houses were the rule.

Whitney made these appeals to what was then termed the "moral influence" of street railways both from personal conviction, and from the need to answer the numerous critics of his monopoly. He was continually before state and city agencies defending the profits and schedules of the West End Street Railway. Most important for the growth of the suburban city, criticism always took for its point of departure the same view of public transportation that Whitney's management undertook to carry out. For critics, the trouble with the West End Company was that its very vigorous performance was not vigorous enough: new service was not added fast enough, profits were too high, and fares not cheap enough.[9]

The demise of Whitney's West End Street Railway as an operating company was due not to the shortcomings of its suburban service, but to continued strife over downtown traffic conditions. The details of the decade of controversy over the control and pricing of tunnels and elevateds are not relevant to this history. In the end, in 1897, a group of rival capitalists formed the Boston Elevated Street Railway Company, and, under the supervision of the state-created Boston Transit Authority, leased the West End system in its entirety. With this new operating company the great subway and elevated projects were undertaken in a belated effort to solve downtown traffic problems. The Boston Elevated's suburban policy remained that of its predecessors: expand for more total passengers.

During the entire second half of the nineteenth century two things made possible this continuous expansion of service under all kinds of managements. The first was the declining costs of materials; the second was electrification. In 1888 the West End began experimenting with electric cars and in 1889 introduced its first trolley service. The electric car moved at least twice as fast as the horse drawn one and soon was perfected to carry three times the number of passengers. Of course offsetting these advantages, the new machines required a great deal more investment in heavy equipment than the horse and his carbarn.

In the center of the system, where traffic was heavy, the electric car was cheaper to operate per passenger mile than the horsecar. It seemed reasonable to run the electric car from the intown segment of a line out to the suburban terminal, especially since in the outer areas of less frequent stops the

electric could really show its speed. In this way the electric-powered streetcar beguiled traction men who were careless about costs into spinning out the web of their service even beyond profitable limits.[10]

NOTES

1. At the time of writing Professor Charles J. Kennedy of the University of Nebraska was about to publish his history of the Boston and Maine Railroad. This book will contain a complete discussion of the early steam railroad and its associated commuting patterns. I am indebted to Professor Kennedy for a citation of *Hunt's Merchant Magazine* (December 25, 1851, p. 759), which published a one-day traffic count of Boston. This count showed three equally popular means of entering and leaving the city: walking, riding the railroad, and traveling by carriage or omnibus.

2. The common mid-century South End land plan located single-family row houses on the side streets and mixed these row houses with tenement and store combinations on the main traffic streets. Tremont and Washington streets and Columbus, Shawmut, and Harrison avenues offered some moderately priced small rental units before the wholesale conversion of the single-family houses. Walter Muir Whitehill, *Boston: A Topographical History* (Cambridge, 1959), pp. 119–140; Suffolk Deeds, Liber 626, plan at end.

3. The original South Boston grid was broken in 1822 when narrow alleys were built behind the main streets. The alley lots were sold off for workers' housing. The resulting cramped land plan has provided a source of discomfort for 140 years. These alleys turn up in Harold K. Estabrook, *Some Slums in Boston* (Boston, 1898), pp. 21–23. Some alleys of houses have been replaced by federal housing projects; others still can be seen—for example, West 4th and 5th streets between E and F, and Silver and Gold streets. For the development of South Boston: Thomas C. Simonds, *History of South Boston* (Boston, 1857), pp. 72–104, 194–204, 300–313.

4. William H. Sumner, *A History of East Boston* (Boston, 1858), pp. 421–471; Suffolk Deeds, L. 401, end; Francis S. Drake, *The Town of Roxbury* (Roxbury, 1878), pp. 397–441; Woods and Kennedy, "The Zone of Emergence," chapters on Charles-town, South Boston, East Boston, Cambridgeport, East Cambridge and Roxbury.

5. Good examples of the popular varieties of pre-streetcar city housing may be seen in Boston proper at Porter street; and in the lower South End, the blocks from Castle street to Worcester Square between Harrison avenue and Tremont street. Examples of the cheaper styles of the peripheral towns: in East Boston at Saratoga,

Princeton, Lexington, and Trenton streets, between Marion and Brooks; in South Boston on West 4th and 5th streets; in Roxbury from Madison to Vernon streets between Tremont and Washington street; in Charlestown from Chelsea street to the Bunker Hill Monument; in East Cambridge, 3rd to 5th streets between Cambridge and Charles street.

6. Prentiss Cummings, "Street Railways of Boston," *Professional and Industrial History of Suffolk County, Mass.* (Boston, 1894), III, 289–290; Richard Herndon, *Boston of Today* (Boston, 1892), pp. 310–311; *Boston Evening Transcript*, November 24, 1882, editorial, p. 4; Robert H. Whitten, *Public Administration in Massachusetts* (New York, 1898), pp. 112–126.

7. Roswell F. Phelps, *South End Factory Operatives, Employment and Residence* (Boston, 1903), pp. 18–19.

8. For further discussion of tenure, see Warner, "Residential Development," Appendix D.

9. The street railwayman's credo: Henry M. Whitney and Prentiss Cummings, *Additional Burdens upon the Street Railway Companies, etc.* (Boston, 1891); the critics: *Citizen's Association of Boston Explaining Its Position. Statement of the Executive Committee Regarding ... the Franchise Bill* (Boston, 1891).

10. The foregoing economic analysis of street railways is taken from Edward S. Mason, *The Street Railway in Massachusetts* (Cambridge, 1932), pp. 1–7, 71–113, 118–121.

The Subway and the City

Clifton Hood

Source: *722 Miles: The Building of the Subways and How They Transformed New York* (New York: Simon & Schuster, 1993).

EDITORS' INTRODUCTION

New York City is a metropolis inextricably linked with the subway. Once the subway opened in 1904, the city was forever transformed. The subway inevitably affected the city's physical spaces. Subway stops defined real estate values, making some locations prime sites for retail, and some neighborhoods more enticing residential options for commuters. The subways became part of an elaborate transportation system whereby millions of people moved within and through the city's five boroughs (legally merged as a whole in 1898) and the Greater New York metropolitan area. The subway became the setting where New Yorkers spent a considerable amount of time. Friendships were formed, love interests encountered, business deals secured, newspapers and books read, and people entertained by other riders on the subway. As Hood notes here, residents and tourists alike enjoyed the decorative tiles and other fine touches of the carefully designed subway stations, at least until the residents became blasé about the scenery after months of routine commuting. Subway riders balked at the initial installation of extensive advertisements within the stations, although that too became commonplace. In today's subways, advertisements have moved inside the trains themselves, and creative marketers think of seemingly endless ways to draw the attention of the commuter. As Clifton Hood notes, the subway, by knitting together once far-flung neighborhoods in unforeseen ways, "changed New York City almost beyond recognition."[i]

New York was not the first city in the United States to construct a subway, although New York rightly claims a special relationship with subway history for devising the fastest urban mass transit system in the world at the time. As Hood straightforwardly describes, "Although rapid transit engineering was quite sophisticated, there were just six other subways in the world by 1904, and the only other one in the Western Hemisphere was a short Boston line that had been in service for a mere seven years."[ii] Boston's subway, opened in 1897 and initially running just one and two-thirds miles under Tremont Street, was an off-shoot of the city's electric trolley franchise. As we have seen in Sam Bass Warner, Jr.'s essay, Boston was a city defined by its above-ground commuter trains. **[See Sam Bass Warner, Jr., "From Walking City to the Implementation of the Street Railways," in this part.]**

The excitement New Yorkers experienced at the dedication and grand opening of the subway on October 27, 1904, from Mayor George B. McClellan's refusal to give up the controls on the train filled with dignitaries, to the crowds of spectators waiting to see a glimpse of the subway cars on the viaduct between 122nd to 135th streets, testifies to the city's strong connection to its subway system. The Interborough Rapid Transit Company, or IRT, was one of three separate subway lines ultimately established in New York City. The IRT later merged with the BRT (Brooklyn Rapid Transit Company) to form

---

i Clifton Hood, *722 Miles: The Building of the Subways and How They Transformed New York* (New York: Simon & Schuster, 1993), 111.

ii Hood, *722 Miles*, 92, 98.

the BMT (Brooklyn-Manhattan Transit Company) in 1923, and then Mayor Fiorello H. La Guardia combined the BMT with the IND (Independent Subway System) in 1940 to form one city-wide transit system.

Clifton Hood joined the faculty of Hobart and William Smith Colleges in 1992, and now serves as a professor of history. He is at work on a book on New York City's economic elites, and is serving as co-editor with Kenneth T. Jackson on an historical atlas of New York City. Hood was interviewed for the 1997 PBS/American Experience series, *New York Underground*, as well as a number of other documentaries.

THE SUBWAY AND THE CITY

October 27, 1904

Mayor George B. McClellan switched on the motor, turned the controller, and headed north from the city hall station for a tour of the new Interborough Rapid Transit subway. The underground railway had been dedicated earlier that day in October 1904 during a ceremony at city hall, and it would be opened to the general public four or five hours later; people were already waiting outside the stations for their first ride on the new subterranean wonder. For now, however, Mayor McClellan and a select group of the city's most distinguished leaders had it to themselves.[1]

Although Mayor McClellan was supposed to surrender the controls to a regular motorman once the excursion got under way, he was enjoying himself so much that he adamantly refused to step aside and insisted on running the train himself, despite the fact that, as he admitted with a boyish grin, he had never driven a railway car before.

McClellan's decision startled the two top Interborough executives on board the train, Vice-President E. M. Bryan and General Manager Frank M. Hedley. Although they naturally wanted to indulge a politician as powerful as the chief executive of New York City, Bryan and Hedley feared that McClellan might cause a serious accident which would turn the public against the IRT. Bryan and Hedley were concerned because the Interborough was so novel that city residents might not accept it. Although rapid transit engineering was quite sophisticated, there were just six other subways in the world by 1904, and the only other one in

the Western Hemisphere was a short Boston line that had been in service for a mere seven years. Indeed, one wag had predicted years earlier that a New York subway was bound to flop because people would go below ground only once in their lifetimes—and that was after death.

Bryan and Hedley were particularly worried about the possibility of an accident because many prominent individuals were riding this special excursion train: President Nicholas Murray Butler of Columbia University and Chancellor Henry Mitchell McCracken of New York University; Archbishop John M. Farley of the Catholic Church and Bishop Coadjutor David H. Greer of the Episcopal Church; and bankers Jacob Schiff, Morris K. Jesup, and Henry Clews. These men represented elite groups that ruled New York City, and their participation in these opening day ceremonies underscored the importance of the subway. To these leaders the IRT belonged in the tradition of grand civic projects that made New York the greatest metropolis in North America, such as the Erie Canal, the Croton Aqueduct water system, and the Brooklyn Bridge.[2]

But George B. McClellan was having the time of his life driving the train, and he did not share the IRT executives' anxieties. Mischievously ignoring the pained expressions on the faces of Bryan and Hedley, McClellan pressed the controller and sent the special train shooting through the tunnel. General Manager Hedley nervously glued himself to the emergency brake and kept blowing the whistle to alert track workers to the danger, while Vice-President Bryan stationed himself directly behind the mayor, ready to take charge in a crisis. At a point near Spring Street, Hedley tried to coax

McClellan into ending his joyride by asking, "Aren't you tired of it? Don't you want the motorman to take it?" "No, sir!" McClellan replied firmly. "I'm running this train!"[3]

So he was. One mishap did occur when McClellan accidentally hit the emergency brake, bringing the four-car train to a violent stop that sent the silk-hatted, frock-coated dignitaries flying through the air. But McClellan confidently settled back at the controls after a few tense moments and, despite Hedley's panicked cries—"Slower here, slower! Easy!"—raised the train's speed even higher.[4] Up Elm Street (now Lafayette Street) and Fourth Avenue (now Park Avenue) to Grand Central Terminal, across Forty-second Street to Times Square on the West Side, and then up Broadway through the Upper West Side, the train roared on the straightaways and careened around the curves at over forty miles per hour. Afterward the "motorman mayor," as he was now called, attributed his success to his mastery of "automobiling."

Mayor George B. McClellan's escapade was hardly the only reason this trip was memorable, for the IRT subway ranked as the world's best rapid transit railway. A British transit expert who inspected the Interborough in 1904 concluded that it "must be considered one of the great engineering achievements of the age" and acknowledged that it was more advanced technologically than London's underground.[5] The IRT was not yet the largest subway in the world—London still held that distinction—but it was the longest ever completed at a single time, covering twenty-two route miles. Because the northern sections were still under construction, the special reached only as far uptown as 145th Street and Broadway on its run. [...]

The subway had been created not merely as a pedestrian municipal service but as a civic monument. The architects were Heins and La-Farge, who had designed America's largest church, the Cathedral of St. John the Divine, on New York's Morningside Heights, and made some of the subway stations works of art in themselves. For example, the flagship station at city hall was an underground chapel in the round that had beautiful Guastivino arches, leaded glass skylights, and chandeliers. Although the other stations were utilitarian boxes that could not compare to city hall's, they nonetheless had colorful tile mosaics, natural vault lighting, and oak ticket booths with bronze fittings that created an elegant impression. Their most popular feature was ceramic bas-relief name panels that depicted neighborhood themes: The Astor Place plaque had a beaver in honor of fur trader John Jacob Astor; Fulton Street showed Robert Fulton's pioneering steamboat, the *Clermont*; Columbus Circle had Christopher Columbus' flagship, the *Santa Maria*; and 116th Street (Broadway branch) displayed the Columbia University seal.

The Interborough was equally attractive above the surface. For instance, McKim, Mead & White had turned the facade of the IRT powerhouse—a colossal brick and terra-cotta structure on the Hudson River at Fifty-ninth Street where coal-burning furnaces generated electricity for the subway—into a classical temple that paid homage to modern industry. Still more impressive were the cast-iron and glass kiosks that covered the station entrances and exits. These ornate kiosks, which were patterned after similar structures on the Budapest metro, soon became an Interborough trademark, and for good reason. Cleverly designed to enhance rider comfort, the kiosks marked the entrances to the stations so that patrons could find the subways without getting lost on the street; they also shielded the passageways so that people were not drenched in rainstorms and segregated incoming from outgoing pedestrians so that traffic would flow more smoothly and riders going downstairs did not have to fight those going up.[6]

After the initial V.I.P. activities, the celebration took on a democratic air. In the words of a newspaperman who observed the festivities, New York City went "subway mad" over the IRT's inauguration. For the preceding few weeks, hundreds of New Yorkers had held "subway parties" to celebrate the big event. On October 27 courthouses, office buildings, shops, and private homes were decked out with flags and bunting just as on the Fourth of July; church bells, guns, sirens, and horns resounded all day long. Thousands of people began to gather around city hall early in the morning, waiting to see the dedication ceremony that would be held upstairs in the aldermanic chamber. Thousands more queued up at the kiosks, waiting for their first subway ride.[7]

The only place where the official train ran in full public view was on the viaduct over Manhattan Valley, from 122nd to 135th streets. A huge crowd of spectators went there for a look, blanketing rooftops, vacant lots, street corners, and fire escapes for blocks around. When the special emerged from the tunnel and started across the trestle, these onlookers began to cheer. The train slowed down and blew its whistle in response; sirens from local factories and from ships on the Hudson River let loose, too. The noise continued until the train reentered the tunnel and disappeared from sight.

The rest of the trip was uneventful, largely because Hedley and Bryan had finally persuaded Mayor McClellan to relinquish the controls. Very proud of himself, McClellan puffed away at a cigar and bantered with the other guests all the way back to city hall.

Finally, at 7:00 P.M., the IRT opened its doors to the public. Men and women who had been waiting all afternoon for this moment streamed down the stairways and onto the cars. A new era had begun in the history of New York City.[8]

More than 110,000 people swarmed through subway gates that evening and saw the stations and platforms for themselves. New Yorkers were so excited by their discovery of the IRT that they coined a phrase to describe the experience: "doing the subway."

The night took on a carnival atmosphere, like New Year's Eve. Many couples celebrated in style by putting on their best clothes, going out to dinner, and then taking their first subway ride together. Some people spent the entire evening on the trains, going back and forth from 145th Street to city hall for hours. Reveling in the sheer novelty of the underground, these riders wanted to soak up its unfamiliar sights and sensations for as long as possible. In a few instances

high-spirited boys and girls took over part of a car and began singing songs, flirting, and fooling around. The sheer exuberance of opening night proved to be too much for others; although they bought their green IRT tickets and entered the stations like everyone else, these timid passengers were so overwhelmed by their new surroundings that they did not even attempt to board a train. All they could do was stand on the platform and gawk.

This popular hoopla climaxed three days later, on Sunday, October 30. Most New Yorkers still worked six days a week and had only Sundays to themselves. On this particular Sunday, almost one million people chose to go subway riding. The IRT was like a magnet, attracting groups from the outskirts of Brooklyn and Queens, two or three hours away. Unfortunately, the IRT could accommodate only 350,000 a day, and many people had to be turned away. The lines to enter the 145th Street station stretched for two blocks, and people grew so frustrated that police reserves had to be summoned to break up fights and restore order.[9]

That same week a public controversy erupted when the Interborough Rapid Transit Company suddenly began to install advertising placards in the stations. Although the Rapid Transit Commission had evidently always intended to permit advertising, it withheld this information from the public. Even the subway's architects, Heins and LaFarge, did not know about it. So when workers for the Interborough's advertising firm, Ward & Gow, began driving nails into the ornamental tilework and covering the walls with large, tin-framed signs, New Yorkers reacted with surprise and anger. Many thought these unsightly billboards—for products such as Baker's Cocoa, Evans Ale ("Live the Simple Life"), Coke Dandruff Cure, and Hunyadi János ("A Positive Cure for Constipation")—detracted from the subway's stature as a noble civic monument. The *Real Estate Record and Builders Guide* blasted the placards as "an outrage" that "mar the appearance of an appropriate and admirable piece of interior decoration," while Rapid Transit

Commissioner Charles Stewart Smith called them "cheap and nasty."[10] Both the Architectural League and the Municipal Art Society condemned the ads and demanded their removal. Aroused by this strong negative reaction, the municipal government filed a lawsuit against the Interborough to eliminate the ads. The Interborough expected to earn about $500,000 from this concession and vigorously defended its contractual rights; the company won the case several years later. The signs remained, an early indication that the subway was assuming a more pedestrian place in the life of the city.[11]

The initial thrill eventually wore off for the passengers, too, and a subway ride became nothing more than a daily habit. Elmer Rice, a twelve-year-old who had been badgering his parents to take him on the IRT, finally got his chance one Sunday afternoon late in November. Young Rice, his parents, his grandfather, and his uncle embarked on a family expedition through the subway. Years later Rice, by then an accomplished playwright, treasured this trip as a highlight of his boyhood. "So this was the subway!" he exclaimed, remembering how awed he had been by the beautiful tile mosaics and how he had pressed his face against the window glass and watched the station pillars flash by. But the excitement faded away when Rice began taking the subway to school every day. "At the end of six months," he admitted, "I had even stopped looking at the tiling."[12]

Long after most New Yorkers became bored with it, the IRT continued to fascinate out-of-towners. For years popular guidebooks put the subway high on their list of sights that travelers should see in New York. "The tourist," Rand McNally advised in 1905, "will be well repaid by a trip through the bore of this greatest of all underground railways," while the *Banner Guide & Excursion Book* strongly encouraged visitors to experience the subway's "surprising roominess and apparent rush and hustle and, especially, the fine finish and cheeriness of its stations."[13] As these guidebooks recognized, the IRT was an essential part of the metropolis. Along with the Brooklyn Bridge,

the Statue of Liberty, the Flatiron Building, and Wall Street, the IRT embodied the wealth, power, and modernity that distinguished New York from all other cities.

For residents and tourists alike, the IRT represented a completely new kind of urban environment. Unlike the els and streetcars where the rest of the city was always in view, the underground railway enabled passengers to travel across New York without ever catching sight of the surface. For instance, riders could pass through the city hall subway station and never know what city hall, the Tweed courthouse, or the surrogate courthouse looked like. According to the *Utica Saturday Globe*, the subway had transformed New York into "the city of human prairie dogs." The paper noted that "just as the little burrowers of the West dart into their holes in the ground," so New Yorkers had developed a habit of disappearing beneath the surface and then reappearing somewhere else.[14]

A ride in the subway thus meant entering a separate and sometimes disorienting sphere, particularly in the long stretches between stations where the trains were shrouded in darkness. Isolated from their familiar surroundings and dependent on steel rails, track switches, electrical conduits, signals, and other mechanical devices, passengers thought of the subway as a realm of impersonal, complicated technology.[15]

Observers agreed that the IRT's most important technical attribute was its high speed. In fact, the Interborough was renowned for being the fastest urban mass transit railway in the world. The reason for this impressive performance was that it was the first rapid transit railway to have separate express and local service. Many other railways employed some kind of express service before 1904, but none could compare to the Interborough. For example, the Manhattan Railway Company's Ninth Avenue elevated route extended all the way from Cortlandt Street at the foot of the island to the Harlem River, but its expresses were confined to one part of this route, from Fourteenth Street to 116th Street, and to a single track. Consequently, Ninth Avenue expresses headed south during the morning rush hour and back uptown at night. In comparison, the Interborough's four tracks permitted permanent two-way express service, significantly improving the speed and range of its trains.[16] The Interborough expresses exceeded forty miles per hour, three times faster than the city's steam-powered els and six times faster than its streetcars.

NOTES

1. *New York Times*, October 28, 1904. *New York Evening Post*, October 27, 1904.
2. August Belmont to William Barclay Parsons, July 17, 1904, PL 79, BFP.
3. *New York Times*, October 28, 1904.
4. Ibid.
5. London County Council, *The Rapid Transit Subways of New York: A Report by Mr. J. Allen Baker, Chair man of the Highways Committee, of the Inspection made by him of the Rapid Transit Subways of New York* (London: Southwood, Smith & Company, 1904): 5.
6. Interborough Rapid Transit Company, *The New York Subway, Its Construction and Equipment* (New York: n. p., 1904): 15, 23–26.
7. *New York Times*, October 28, 1904. *New York Mail & Express*, October 28, 1904. *Brooklyn Eagle*, October 27, 1904. Elmer Rice, "Joy-Riding in the Subway," *New Yorker* 4 (December 29, 1928): 21–23.
8. *New York Times*, October 28, 1904. *New York Evening Post*, October 27, 1904. Although the capacity of the original subway was six hundred thousand, only part of the route was opened on October 27.
9. *New York Times*, October 30 and 31, 1904. *New York Commercial*, October 31, 1904. *New York Tribune*, October 29, 1904. Abraham Lincoln Merritt, "Ten Years of the Subway," in Electric Railroaders Association, *Interborough Bulletin* 77 (November 1987): 12. The capacity of 350,000 was for the portion of the subway that was opened on October 27, 1904, not the entire IRT.
10. *Real Estate Record and Builders Guide*, November 5, 1904: 949. *New York Times*, November 19, 1904.
11. *New York Times*, October 29 and November 2, 5, 11, 18, 19, and 29, 1904; June 17, 1990.
12. Rice, "Joy-Riding in the Subway," 22, 23.
13. *Rand McNally & Co.'s Handy Guide to New York City*, 18th ed. (Chicago: Rand McNally & Company, 1905): 23. *Banner Guide & Excursion Book* (New York: John D. Hall, 1904): 4.
14. *Utica Saturday Globe*, November 5, 1904.
15. *New York Commercial*, October 31, 1904. *New York Times*, October 29 and 31, and November 2, 1904.
16. The IRT express service was so innovative that the subway's planners did not foresee its significance and originally assumed that the locals would carry the greater part of the passenger load, hence their decision to restrict express operations to built-up areas south of Ninety-sixth Street. Original specifications had called for building only two local tracks above Ninety-sixth Street, but a third track for one-way express service was added after construction began, partly in response to the traffic increases caused by electrification of the elevateds. "Diary of William Barclay Parsons, Chief Engineer, Rapid Transit Commission, from the beginning of work, March 26, 1900, to his resignation as Chief Engineer, December 31, 1904," entry for January 28, 1901, Rare Book and Manuscript Library, Butler Library, Columbia University, New York, NY.

Wishful Thinking: Downtown and the Automotive Revolution

Robert Fogelson

Source: *Downtown: Its Rise and Fall, 1880–1950* (New Haven: Yale University Press, 2001).

EDITORS' INTRODUCTION

In the preceding articles by historians Sam Bass Warner, Jr., and Clifton Hood, downtown access is discussed as a matter of mass transportation. In Warner's classic text, transportation changes led to a movement away from the city center. Warner's wealthy and upper middle class Bostonians accessed the countryside by means of a newly constructed streetcar system; they had previously been living downtown. These new neighborhoods would later be considered suburbs. Hood demonstrates how the New York City subway system—so intriguing on an imaginative level—also made original contributions to the city's physicality, by transforming the far-flung city into a coherent whole and irrevocably changing neighborhoods. But the transformative power of the streetcar and the subway was dwarfed by the influence of the car. By the 1920s, the automobile had radically altered urban concerns. At this time, Fogelson reveals, many Americans ceased using mass transportation. Some of these people, comfortably ensconced in the suburbs, were relying on the growth of new secondary business districts close to their homes. Others chose to access the central business district, yet got there by means other than mass transit. Since the dawn of the omnibus in the early nineteenth century, shared transit had often meant uncomfortable transportation; the omnibus was too cold in the winter, too warm in the summer, and continually overcrowded. And as if to add insult to injury, mass transportation oftentimes was unreliable and slow. In every city other than New York, the "riding habit," or the reliance on public transportation, tended to dwindle, while the "driving habit" swiftly increased.

Urban business leaders and boosters promoting the use of downtown areas conceived of the problem as one of access, misunderstanding the variety of reasons people had stopped heading downtown. This contingent believed people wanted to get downtown, but were stymied. These urban leaders turned their focus to improving downtown accessibility. They considered the means by which to increase the flow of traffic in downtowns, the employment of traffic regulations, street widening, throughways for non-local traffic, and the implementation of the modern highway system. Proposals were made for garages at the edge of cities, served by train lines. Others suggested banning "pleasure" vehicles, but how could one ultimately gauge the intent of each driver? Some wondered if setting limits on building height could affect downtown overcrowding. Certainly designs for higher buildings led to much more populated central business districts. Others argued the opposite, noting that high urban concentrations led to a reduced need to crisscross the city on daily business; everything that one needed, especially if businesses were clustered by type, could be accessed on foot in a highly dense business district. Planning ideas grew increasingly creative, including dreams of multi-level roads. Versions of a multi-level road were constructed in many cities (this includes Wacker Drive in Chicago, proposed in Daniel Burnham's 1909 Plan of Chicago and in use by 1926 as the nation's first modern double-level boulevard, separating regular and commercial vehicles) but many of these ideas were too fanciful to warrant real consideration.[i] Ultimately, the road builders would find it impossible to adequately anticipate the need for roads and build enough of them. Once a city constructed a road, people used it, and then moved out to the often less expensive suburbs and commuted in to their downtown jobs. Far sooner than expected, gridlock returned.

In 1956, the United States Congress, with the support of President Dwight Eisenhower, passed the Federal Highway Act. With this legislation, Washington, D.C. unequivocally backed the automobile as the preferred type of transportation, and undercut the health of the nation's downtowns. The more than 41,000 miles of interstate highway created by the act, ostensibly as a means by which to get people more quickly and easily to the central cities, actually made many downtowns largely irrelevant to regional growth. **[See Document 7.1, "National Interstate and Defense Highways Act."]**

Robert Fogelson is a professor of history and urban studies and planning at the Massachusetts Institute of Technology (MIT). *Downtown: Its Rise and Fall, 1880–1950*, was awarded the prize for the best book in urban history by the Urban History Association in 2002. Additionally, *Downtown* won the 2001 Lewis Mumford Prize for Best Book in American City and Regional History given by the Society for American City and Regional Planning. Fogelson is also the author of *Bourgeois Nightmares: Suburbia, 1870–1930* (New Haven: Yale University Press, 2005). This book won Honorable Mention for the 2006 Peter C. Rollins Book Award sponsored by the Northeast Popular Culture/American Culture Association.

WISHFUL THINKING: DOWNTOWN AND THE AUTOMOTIVE REVOLUTION

In May 1941 the newly formed Downtown Committee, an organization of about thirty of downtown Baltimore's largest property owners, sent G. Harvey Porter, director of the committee's Downtown Study, on a trip to find out what other cities were doing about decentralization. Porter visited Oakland, Los Angeles, Kansas City, and St. Louis, "each of which," said the *Baltimore Sun*, "has taken more or less elaborate steps to combat the process." On his return he made several recommendations, most of which were later adopted by the committee. Porter's trip was enlightening. But it was also superfluous. On the basis of studies in other cities and reports by the Urban Land Institute, Porter and his associates had already made up their minds about how to curb (and, if possible, to reverse) decentralization. "The principal objective," Porter said shortly before leaving, "is to get

persons in and out of the downtown area as quickly and easily as possible, by whatever means." Once downtown was made more accessible, business would pick up, values would rise, capital would flow in, and decentralization would slow down (or even stop).[1] Underlying this belief was the assumption that people were not going downtown because they were unable to—that, as a leading Los Angeles reformer (and sometime real estate speculator) pointed out when decentralization first appeared there two decades earlier, "They wanted to[,] but they couldn't."

The belief that accessibility was the key to the well-being of downtown had emerged in the second half of the nineteenth century and became part of the conventional wisdom in the first half of the twentieth. But between 1915 and 1925 the meaning of accessibility changed. Before then it had been synonymous with mass transit. For down through the 1910s most people used it to go downtown, the large majority traveling on streetcars (and, in a few cities, els and subways)

---

i James R. Grossman, Ann Durking Keating, and Janice L. Reiff, *The Encyclopedia of Chicago* (Chicago: University of Chicago Press, 2004), 31–32. Additional portions were added to Wacker Drive in subsequent years. In one section, there is a third level of street.

and a small minority on ferries and commuter trains. The rest came by automobiles, trucks, taxis, bicycles, and horse-drawn vehicles (or on foot). None of these vehicles, not even the automobile, carried nearly as many people as the streetcar. According to early cordon counts, straphangers outnumbered motorists by close to five to one in San Francisco (1912), more than six to one in Denver (1914), and roughly four to one in Chicago (1921)—and almost twice again as much if the els and commuter trains are counted. That an effective system of mass transit was vital to the well-being of a highly compact and extremely concentrated business district was taken for granted before 1920, especially by the downtown businessmen and property owners. Witness their support for the attempts to build subways. Witness too their backing of the street railways in their efforts to drive the jitney out of business. A commercial motor vehicle that was faster than a streetcar and cheaper than a taxi, the jitney "stole" so many riders from the street railways that the railway companies saw them as a threat to their long-term solvency.[2]

Starting around 1920, however, many Americans stopped using mass transit to go downtown—some because they stopped going downtown, opting to patronize outlying business districts instead, and others because they stopped using mass transit. The growth of these business districts took Americans by surprise. So did the decline of the riding habit. According to the conventional wisdom about the relation between transit patronage and population growth, the riding habit should have gone way up in the 1920s, a decade during which big cities grew even bigger. But in every city except New York, where it went up about 15 percent, or around two-thirds as much as the population, the riding habit went down. Between 1920 and 1930 it fell 10 to 20 percent in Boston, Philadelphia, Chicago (the only cities other than New York with a rapid transit system), and San Francisco, whose riding habit was the highest in the country until 1927, when it dropped below New York's. Elsewhere the riding habit fell more sharply—20 to 30 percent in Pitts-

burgh and Milwaukee, 30 to 40 percent in Baltimore, Cincinnati, and St. Louis, and 40 to 50 percent in Buffalo, Cleveland, and Los Angeles. In general it fell even more sharply in small and medium-sized cities. During the 1930s, a terrible time for the transit industry, the riding habit dropped still further. By the end of the decade it was lower than it had been at any time since the turn of the century. As a result of gas rationing and other fallout from World War II, the transit industry regained some of its riders in the early and mid 1940s. But shortly after the war ended, it resumed its long and irreversible decline.[3]

Of the many Americans who stopped using mass transit but kept going downtown, most traveled by private automobiles (as opposed to taxis or other commercial vehicles). What might be called the driving habit soared in the late 1910s and 1920s, more than doubling in some cities, more than tripling in others. By 1930, 50,000 to 100,000 autos poured into downtown Boston, downtown Philadelphia, and downtown Detroit on a typical weekday. More than 100,000 poured into downtown Chicago, more than 250,000 into downtown Los Angeles. (Autos carried over three-fifths of the daytime population of downtown L.A. in 1931, up from under two-fifths in 1924, a period during which the number of people who went downtown by mass transit declined by nearly one-third.) The driving habit rose more slowly in the 1930s, partly because of the Great Depression and partly because of decentralization. Even so, by early 1941, a few months before Baltimore's Downtown Committee was organized, 30 to 40 percent of those who went downtown traveled by auto in Boston, Philadelphia, and Chicago, 40 to 50 percent in Pittsburgh, Detroit, and San Francisco, and more than 50 percent in St. Louis and Los Angeles. Only in New York did less than 20 percent travel downtown by automobile. A larger proportion, from two-thirds to as high as nine-tenths, drove downtown in small and medium-sized cities. In only four cities other than New York did as many as one-half of downtown's daytime population still ride the streetcars, els, subways, and motorbuses, which had replaced many of the streetcars in the 1920s and 1930s.[4]

To understand why a large and growing number of Americans opted to drive downtown after 1920, it is important to bear in mind that many of them had long been dissatisfied with mass transit. The streetcars were extremely crowded, especially during rush hour, when it was very hard to find a place, much less a seat. They were uncomfortable and unreliable, especially in inclement weather. And once they reached the central business district, they moved "at a snail's pace," wrote the *Los Angeles Times*. The els and subways were faster and more reliable, but more crowded and less comfortable. The service, bad before World War I, deteriorated afterward. In an effort to deal with the fiscal crisis triggered by the phenomenal wartime inflation, the railway companies kept antiquated equipment in service, deferred much-needed repairs and maintenance, and abandoned miles of unprofitable lines. They raised fares too. Exacerbating the industry's problems, driving its revenues down and its expenses up, was the proliferation of private automobiles, the number of which soared from 8,000 in 1900 to 500,000 in 1910, 8 million in 1920, and 23 million in 1930. By then, there was one automobile for every five people—and as many as one for every four in Detroit, the home of the auto industry, more than one for every three in Baltimore, and nearly one for every two in Los Angeles.[5] The bane of the transit industry, the automobile was a boon for many Americans, especially once the automakers began to build better and less expensive cars and the authorities began to construct more and better roads. Despite the traffic jams and parking problems, it was not long before many decided that as a way of getting downtown the automobile was preferable to the streetcar and other forms of mass transit.

This decision had a number of momentous consequences, not least of which was that it changed the meaning of accessibility. By the late 1920s, about the time that many downtown business interests first became concerned about decentralization, access-

ibility was no longer synonymous with mass transit. Instead, it was synonymous with private as well as public transit, with automobiles as well as streetcars, with highways as well as railbeds. Thus when G. Harvey Porter said in 1941 that it was imperative to get people "in and out of the downtown area as quickly and easily as possible, by whatever means," he meant that the central business district had to be made more accessible to both electric railways and motor vehicles, and above all to private automobiles.[6] The change was reflected not only in what the downtown business interests said, but also in what they did. Starting in the mid and late 1920s, they intensified their efforts to persuade the authorities to take whatever steps were necessary to enable motorists to drive "quickly and easily" to the central business district and to find a place to park when they arrived. During the 1930s and 1940s they also continued their efforts to persuade the authorities to build rapid transit systems, insisting that in view of the heavy traffic in and around the central business district rapid transit was the only viable form of mass transit. By virtue of these efforts, the downtown businessmen and property owners were drawn into several major controversies, the resolutions of which would have a great impact, not only on downtown, but on other parts of the metropolis as well. And the most momentous was over traffic congestion.

Traffic congestion had long been a serious problem in American cities. As early as the 1870s New York's *Real Estate Record and Builders' Guide* wrote that the narrow downtown streets could no longer handle the growing traffic. "The universal cry down town is for 'more elbow room,'" it said. A product of the tremendous growth of commercial activity, the extreme concentration of the business district, and the growing separation of the business and residential sections, traffic congestion grew much worse in the 1880s and 1890s. And not just in New York. In downtown Boston, *American Architect and Building News* observed, the sidewalks were "jammed to suffocation" with pedestrians, while the streets, as narrow and crooked as any in the United States, were packed with streetcars, wagons, carts, and other horse-drawn vehicles. To make things worse, some of the streets were lined on one side by "a long string of [stationary] carriages" and on the other by "a similar string of miscellaneous vehicles, the horses attached to which munch their oats peacefully" while the traffic inches past them. Despite the electrification of the street railways and, in New York, Brooklyn, and Chicago, the construction of the elevated lines, the traffic problem was as serious as ever at the turn of the century. In 1903 *Scientific American* warned that "unless some heroic measures are taken, we are bound to witness within a few years in the busiest hours of the day a positive deadlock [in lower Manhattan]." In 1909, when only one of every two hundred Americans owned an automobile, the *Los Angeles Times* pointed out that traffic congestion downtown "has become so great that the police and the officials of the street railway companies are at their wits' end to find a solution."[7]

Some Americans believed that the automobile (and truck) would help solve the traffic problem by displacing slower and more cumbersome horse-drawn vehicles. One of them was Thomas Edison. If all of New York's horse-drawn vehicles "could be transformed into motor cars overnight," he remarked in 1908, it would "so relieve traffic [congestion] as to make Manhattan Island resemble 'The Deserted Village'." Other Americans were less sanguine. By the late 1910s it was clear they were right. Motorcars did displace most horse-drawn vehicles, but as more people drove, they flooded the downtown streets, especially during rush hour. Visiting Los Angeles in 1919, a Cleveland doctor commented that at six in the evening it seems that "every automobile owner in the city suddenly decides to motor through the business section." With thousands of cars, trucks, streetcars, and the remaining horse-drawn vehicles fighting for space downtown, traffic often slowed down to a crawl—sometimes to a standstill. Traffic congestion in New York "is growing worse every day," the *Real Estate Record and Builders' Guide* said in 1917. It "[has] become well-nigh unbearable" in Atlanta, a special committee of the chamber of commerce reported three years later. In Chicago traffic congestion "is so great that matters have almost reached a deadlock," observed British city planner Raymond Unwin in 1923. In the business district of many American cities, he pointed out, it was no faster to drive than to walk.[8] The result was that by the early 1920s there was a widespread consensus that the traffic problem was in large part the product of the phenomenal proliferation of private automobiles.

Some engineers, city planners, public officials, and street railway executives held that the only way to solve the problem was to ban private automobiles (or at least "pleasure" vehicles) from the central business district. If a ban was imposed, its sponsors pointed out, motorists could drive downtown, park at the fringe, where garages and lots would be located, and take mass transit to the center. At the heart of this position was the belief that automobiles were a very inefficient means of urban transportation— that they took up more space than streetcars and carried fewer passengers. It was impossible to provide enough space downtown to accommodate the growing number of motor vehicles, a New York street railway executive declared in 1926. To open new streets and widen existing ones would only bring more motor vehicles into the business district, which would increase congestion and thereby encourage decentralization. Even if the city did not impose a ban on motorcars, said Boston mayor Malcolm E. Nichols in the mid 1920s, traffic congestion would force many motorists to use mass transit to get downtown. It was highly unlikely that private automobiles would continue to enjoy "unlimited access" to the central business district much longer, he predicted.[9]

But most Americans—most motorists, automakers, traffic experts, and above all most downtown businessmen and property owners—were opposed to a ban on private automobiles downtown. (A ban on "pleasure" vehicles only was impractical, argued one expert, for the simple reason that "no one but the motorist himself could tell whether the trip was for business or pleasure.") These Americans were well aware that the traffic problem was very serious and that the growing number of motorcars was largely responsible for it. By the mid and late 1920s they were also aware that traffic congestion was widely regarded as the main reason for the decentralization of business. But they were convinced, as the Building Owners and Managers Association of St. Louis put it in 1925, that "the so-called pleasure car is a business necessity." It made downtown more accessible, especially for well-to-do motorists, who were highly prized customers and tenants. The private automobile was "here to stay," most Americans assumed. And as the editors of *Engineering Magazine* put it, any attempt to limit its usefulness would be "altogether undesirable, ill-advised, and futile." "Some means simply will have to be found to make room for necessary auto traffic," said W. W. Emmart, a member of the Baltimore City Planning Commission, in 1925. Surely, most Americans believed, the authorities could do something less draconian to unclog "the arteries of the city" than impose a ban on private automobiles in the central business district.[10]

But what could they do? To find the answer, engineers, planners, and other experts made hundreds of studies of traffic congestion in the early twentieth century. Out of these studies, most of which were commissioned by down-town businessmen or, at their behest, by local officials, emerged a diagnosis, according to which traffic jams downtown were largely a product of four things other than the centralization of business and the proliferation of private automobiles. One was that the streets were too few and too narrow—and, in many instances, poorly paved and badly designed. How, asked a New York City architect, could a street system that was developed when two- and three-story buildings were the rule possibly handle the traffic generated by sixteen- and twenty-story buildings? Another was that there were few traffic regulations—and few police officers to enforce them. And "without proper regulation[s]," a

street railway executive warned, the motorcars will "congest new arteries as fast as they can be opened." Yet another was what experts viewed as nonessential traffic. Many motorists drive downtown not because they have "a desire to go there," a New Jersey engineer observed, but because they do not know "how to get through the city any other way." "They go through the Triangle," wrote a director of the Pittsburgh Chamber of Commerce, "because there is no other convenient way to [get from one part of the city to another]." The fourth was what planners termed "the promiscuous mixing of different types of traffic." By this they meant that all the surface traffic—rail and motor, commercial and pleasure, local and through—ran on the same streets, one type of vehicle blocking the other and the slowest holding down the speed of the fastest.[11]

From this diagnosis, it followed that the authorities could do several things to relieve traffic congestion short of imposing a ban on private automobiles. Perhaps most important, they could open new streets and widen existing ones. The streets should be widened, declared the Cleveland Building Owners and Managers Association, "wherever possible and as rapidly as finances will permit." Almost as important, the authorities could adopt and enforce tough traffic regulations to maintain a steady flow of vehicles. The authorities could also build crosstown highways (and inner and outer belts) to divert nonessential traffic from the business district. "What a rejuvenation down-town business organizations could experience through the removal of [the estimated] 40 to 50 percent of non-business-producing traffic and its replacement by an equal volume of business producing traffic!" proclaimed Pittsburgh's Better Traffic Committee. Last of all, the authorities could segregate the different types of traffic, forcing them to run along separate streets (or possibly on separate grades)—and perhaps even segregate vehicular and pedestrian traffic. Such a move, it was widely held, would not only relieve traffic congestion but also improve traffic safety—a subject of growing concern during the 1920s.[12]

Many Americans opposed these measures, some because they were skeptical of the diagnosis of the traffic problem and others because they were afraid that the solutions might be worse than the problem. Street opening and widening, they argued, was very disruptive, especially to abutting businesses. It was also very expensive. It was prohibitively so in the central business district—where the streets that had the heaviest traffic also had the most valuable real estate, a point that even some advocates of street improvements conceded. It was self-defeating too, opponents contended. No sooner was a street opened or widened than traffic increased and congestion worsened. In the face of such opposition, some proposals were shelved—among them a plan by New York mayor William J. Gaynor to relieve traffic congestion on Fifth Avenue by opening a new avenue that would run between Fifth and Sixth avenues from Washington Square to Fifty-ninth Street. But with the support of downtown businessmen, outlying real estate interests, motorists' associations, and auto manufacturers and distributors, many other schemes were carried out. At a cost of tens and even hundreds of millions of dollars, most of which came from bond issues, special assessments, and motor vehicle taxes, the authorities opened new streets in one city after another. Often laid out according to comprehensive plans prepared by Miller McClintock, Harland Bartholomew, and other experts, most of them were wide, direct, well designed, and well-paved roads that radiated from the central business district to the outlying residential sections. At the same time the authorities widened existing streets in city after city, sometimes by condemning the abutting property and sometimes by narrowing the adjacent sidewalks. By virtue of these measures, the street systems were able to handle far more motor vehicles in the late 1920s than in the early 1900s.[13]

The early attempts to regulate traffic ran into opposition too. It came from merchants who feared that one-way streets would render their stores less accessible and engineers who believed that traffic signals would slow down traffic. It also came from team-sters, taxi drivers, and ordinary motorists—many of whom, historian Clay McShane has written, regarded traffic regulations as "unwarranted intrusions on personal freedom." As a Baltimore reporter later observed, "It was not always easy to persuade citizens to break the habits of a lifetime and to prevent them from cutting corners, parking at random and driving both ways on a one-way street." But as traffic congestion and traffic safety grew worse, traffic experts, auto industry leaders, and downtown business interests forged a consensus that the authorities had to do something to regulate motor vehicles and their drivers. Beginning in the early twentieth century, they adopted a host of regulations, many of which were designed by William Phelps Eno, a well-to-do New Yorker who spent his life working for effective traffic control. All vehicles had to be registered, all drivers licensed. Drivers also had to stay to the right, signal before turning, abide by posted speed limits, and use lights after dark. To facilitate the flow of traffic, the authorities also created one-way streets, first in Philadelphia (1908) and then in Boston (1909), and installed stop signs, which first appeared in Detroit (1915), and traffic signals, at first manual semaphores with "go" and "stop" signs and later on electric lights with their familiar green, yellow, and red glow. To enforce these regulations, most cities formed a special traffic squad, a branch of the police department, and a special traffic court, which removed routine traffic violations from the criminal justice system.[14] Taken together, these measures revolutionized traffic control in America's cities in a short period and at little cost.

The authorities also took steps to divert nonessential traffic from the central business district. To enable motorists to go from one part of the city to another without going downtown first, they built a few crosstown highways, most of which were laid out according to the traditional gridiron plan. By the late 1920s some cities also began to build an outer-belt (or circumferential) highway system. To encourage motorists to drive around the central business district rather than through it, the authorities built a few inner belts, the best known of which was the quadrangle of streets—Roosevelt Road on the south, Michigan Avenue on the east, Canal Street on the west, and South Water Street on the north—that encircled the Chicago Loop. An integral feature of Daniel H. Burnham's famous plan for Chicago, this inner belt was strongly supported by the Chicago Plan Commission, on which the Loop's interests were well represented. Started in the early 1910s, it was completed in the late 1920s. But these crosstown highways and inner and outer belts made up only a small fraction of the major thoroughfares, most of which still converged on the central business district, funneling in tens of thousands of automobiles en route elsewhere.[15] Why were so few of them constructed before 1930? The answer is that the authorities could not build all the proposed bypasses and radial highways without raising property taxes to unacceptable levels. Given the choice, most downtown businessmen favored radial highways over bypasses. So did the many motorists who worked and shopped downtown. And though many planners and engineers thought bypasses were the most economical way to relieve traffic congestion, they also believed radial highways were necessary to make the central business district "directly accessible" to all the other parts.

The authorities took steps to segregate different types of traffic, too. They eliminated grade crossings, the points at which the railroads and highways intersected and the sites of many of the worst traffic jams and traffic accidents. In Atlanta, for example, they persuaded the voters to approve two bond issues, one in 1921 and the other in 1926, to help pay for three north–south viaducts that carried motor vehicles over the railroad tracks that bisected the central business district. Other cities also built viaducts to separate motor traffic at busy intersections. Following the completion of the Bronx River Parkway in 1923, the authorities also created parkways in a handful of cities and suburbs. Most of them not only excluded cross traffic but also banned commercial vehicles. (After a highly

promising start in the late nineteenth century, due in large part to the pioneering efforts of Frederick Law Olmsted, the parkway movement had fallen into disfavor in the early twentieth. And its revival in the late 1920s would be short-lived.) But these measures did little to segregate different types of vehicular traffic, much less to separate vehicular and pedestrian traffic. Most vehicles still ran on the same streets and on the same grade. These efforts were stymied by both financial and political constraints. Building separate street systems would have been prohibitively expensive, especially in or near the central business district. And banning private automobiles from commercial thoroughfares would have been very unpopular—and probably unenforceable. In a country that had already segregated land uses through zoning, and racial and economic groups through deed restrictions, the segregation of traffic may have seemed "inevitable," as the Cleveland Building Owners and Managers Association wrote in 1924.[16] If so, its time had not yet come.

By the late 1920s more automobiles were pouring into the central business district than ever, far more than would have been possible if the authorities had not opened new streets and widened existing ones. And as a result of the new regulations, traffic was more orderly than ever. American motorists are so well disciplined, observed a German visitor, that traffic "regulates itself to a large extent." In New York the policeman does not have "to wave his arms about like a windmill" to direct traffic; "A gesture of the hand and a tweet [of the whistle] are enough." But even though some motorists no longer went downtown to get from one part of the city to another and others no longer went downtown at all, traffic congestion was as bad as ever. "Despite every scheme of traffic control so far devised," midtown Manhattan still "ties itself up in a knot twice a day," wrote the *New Republic* in 1928. Broadway had traffic jams seventy-five years ago. "It has them still." Although Baltimore spent millions of dollars on street widening after the great fire of 1904, traffic conditions downtown were just as bad twenty years later, a special committee informed the mayor. Despite the efforts of Harland Bartholomew, chief planner for St. Louis, traffic downtown "moves slowly and irregularly," wrote the president of the St. Louis street railway system in 1926. "Conditions are bad in the middle of the day, and in the morning rush, but are well nigh intolerable in the evening rush." Conditions were very bad in downtown Los Angeles too, the city's traffic commission acknowledged in 1930, a decade after it had been formed by downtown business interests and civic and commercial groups to solve the city's traffic problem.[17]

Despite a good deal of evidence to the contrary, some Americans remained convinced that the cities could solve the traffic problem by building more and wider streets and imposing more and tougher regulations. But others were beginning to have second thoughts. As they saw it, the cities were caught in "a vicious circle." To relieve traffic congestion, the authorities opened and widened streets; but the new streets attracted more traffic, the additional traffic generated more congestion, and eventually every street system reached what a Minneapolis engineer called "a saturation point," a state of "almost but not quite intolerable congestion," to quote Frederick Law Olmsted, Jr., and two of his associates. Another planner, George A. Damon of Los Angeles, went even further. "Every possible cure [for the traffic problem] seems to be worse than the original disease," he wrote. From this pessimistic prognosis, Americans drew one of two very different conclusions. The first was that the traffic problem could be solved only if the cities reduced the number of motor vehicles that entered the central business district. Banning autos downtown would help. So would imposing height limits, improving mass transit, and encouraging decentralization. The second conclusion, the one favored by most downtown businessmen and property owners, was that the problem could be solved only if the cities took what William J. Wilgus, a New York engineer, called "radical measures" to facilitate the flow of traffic—more expensive, more disruptive, and more far-reaching measures than any taken thus far.[18]

NOTES

1. *Baltimore Sun*, April 21, May 20/21, June 12/25, 1941. See also California Railroad Commission, *Application 1602: Reporter's Transcript* (1921), page 134, California Public Utilities Commission files, Sacramento.

2. San Francisco Department of City Planning, "Daily Trips in San Francisco" (1955), table 6; Roger W. Toll, "Traffic Investigation in Denver," *Electric Railway Journal*, August 21, 1915, page 311; R. F. Kelker, Jr., *Report and Recommendations on a Physical Plan for a Unified Transportation System for the City of Chicago* (1923), pages 39–40; Ross D. Eckert and George W. Hilton, "The Jitneys," *Journal of Law and Economics* (October 1972), pages 293–325.

3. John A. Beeler, "What Price Fares?" *Transit Journal*, June 1932, pages 263–266; American Transit Association, *Transit Fact Book: 1945*, pages 15–19; American Transit Association, *Transit Fact Book: 1951*, pages 7–8. By at any time since the turn of the century, I mean at any time other than the mid 1930s, the worst years of the Great Depression, when the riding habit was even lower.

4. Kelker, *Unified Transportation System*, page 40; Chicago Department of Streets and Electricity, Bureau of Street Traffic, "Cordon Count Data on the Central Business District" (1949), page 2; U.S. Works Progress Administration, *Traffic Survey Data on the City of St. Louis* (1937); Donald M. Baker, *A Rapid Transit System for Los Angeles California* (1933), page 37-e; Coverdale & Colpitts, *Report to the Los Angeles Metropolitan Transit Authority on a Monorail Rapid Transit Line for Los Angeles* (1954), page 62; *Automobile Facts*, January 1941, page 2.

5. Paul Barrett, *The Automobile and Urban Transit: The Formation of Public Policy in Chicago, 1900–1930* (Philadelphia, 1983), pages 104–120; *Los Angeles Times*, July 25, 1909; Robert M. Fogelson, *The Fragmented Metropolis: Los Angeles, 1850–1930* (Cambridge, 1967), chapter 7; Stanley Mallach, "The Origins of the Decline of Urban Mass Transportation in the United States," *Urbanism Past and Present*, Summer 1979, pages 1–15; U.S. Department of Commerce, *Historical Statistics of the United States: Colonial Times to 1970* (Washington, D.C., 1975), part 2, page 716; Baker, *Rapid Transit System for Los Angeles*, page 37-e; Clay McShane, *Down the Asphalt Path: The Automobile and the American City* (New York, 1994), pages 126–127.

6. *Baltimore Sun*, May 21, 1941. See also David Whitcomb, "Maintaining Values in Central Business Districts," *Proceedings of the Twenty-Second Annual Convention of the National Association of Building Owners and Managers: 1929*, page 95.

7. *[New York] Real Estate Record and Builders' Guide*, March 8, 1873, page 107, October 8, 1881, page 940; *American Architect and Building*

News, July 27, 1878, pages 27–28, August 20, 1892, page 109; *Scientific American*, April 25, 1903, page 310; Clay McShane, "Urban Pathways: The Street and the Highway, 1900–1940," in Joel A. Tarr and Gabriel Dupuy, eds., *Techology and the Rise of the Networked City in Europe and America* (Philadelphia, 1988), page 68; *Los Angeles Times*, July 25, 1909.

8. McShane, *Down the Asphalt Path*, pages 122, 193–194; Mark S. Foster, *From Street-car to Superhighway: American City Planners and Urban Transportation, 1900–1940* (Philadelphia, 1981), pages 43–44; Amos Stote, "The Ideal American City," *McBride's Magazine*, April 1916, page 89; Scott Bottles, *Los Angeles and the Automobile: The Making of the Modern City* (Berkeley, 1987), pages 59–60; *[New York] Real Estate Record and Builders' Guide*. February 17, 1917, page 220; Howard L. Preston, *Automobile Age Atlanta: The Making of a Southern Metropolis, 1900–1935* (Athens, Georgia, 1979), pages 116–117; Raymond Unwin, "America Revisited—A City Planner's Impressions," *American City*, April 1923, page 334.

9. John A. Miller, Jr., "The Chariots That Rage in the Streets," *American City*, July 1928, pages 113–114; Stephen Child, "Restricted Traffic District Proposed," ibid., April 1927, pages 507–510; V. R. Stirling and Rensselaer H. Toll, "How to Eliminate Traffic from Downtown Sections," *National Municipal Review*, June 1929, pages 369–371; Robert H. Whitten, "Unchoking Our Congested Streets," *American City*, October 1920, pages 351–354; *Proceedings of the American Society of Civil Engineers*, September 1926, pages 1453–1454; *Boston City Record*, January 23, 1926, pages 100–101.

10. Miller, "The Chariots That Rage in the Streets," page 113; St. Louis Building Owners and Managers Association, *The St. Louis Traffic Problem* (St. Louis, 1925), pages 4, 16; Blaine A. Brownell, "A Symbol of Modernity: Attitudes Toward the Automobile in Southern Cities in the 1920s," *American Quarterly*, March 1972, pages 24–25; E. R. Kinsey and C. E. Smith, *Report on Rapid Transit for St. Louis* (St. Louis, 1926), page 147; *Engineering Magazine*, August 1906, page 738; *Baltimore Sun*, June 14, 1925; Stote, "The Ideal American City," page 89.

11. Julius F. Harder, "The City's Plan," *Municipal Affairs*, March 1898, page 34; *Proceedings of the American Society of Civil Engineers*, September 1926, pages 1459–1460; Louis G. Simmons, "The Solution of Big Cities Traffic Problems," *Illustrated World*, October 1917, page 267; *[Pittsburgh] Progress*, April 1922, page 2; Frederick Law Olmsted, Harland Bartholomew, and Charles Henry Cheney, *A Major Traffic Street Plan for Los Angeles* (Los Angeles, 1924), pages 12–14.

12. Cleveland Building Owners and Managers Association, *Cleveland's Traffic Problem* (Cleveland, 1924), pages 6–7; Harland Bartholomew, "Basic Factors in the Solution of Metropolitan Traffic Problems," *American City*, July 1925, pages 38–39; *Cassier's Magazine*, August 1907, pages 374–375; Morris Knowles, "City Planning as a Permanent Solution of the Traffic Problem," *Planning Problems of Town, City, and Region: Papers and Discussions at the International City and Regional Planning Conference: 1925*, page 60; "The Triangle's 'Thru' Traffic," *Better Traffic*, October 1931, page 6; Ernest P. Goodrich, "The Urban Auto Problem," *Proceedings of the Twelfth National Conference on City Planning: 1920*, page 84; Miller McClintock, *Street Traffic Control* (New York, 1926), pages 70–85.

13. Miller McClintock, *Report and Recommendations of the Metropolitan Street Traffic Survey* (Chicago, 1926), page 48; *[New York] Real Estate Record and Builders' Guide*, September 26, 1908, page 591, May 28, 1910, page 1137; *American Architect*, June 1, 1910, page 15; *Proceedings of the Engineers' Society of Western Pennsylvania*, November 1919, page 488; Sidney Clarke, "Special Report on Traffic Relief," in *Report of the Transportation Survey Commission of the City of St. Louis* (1930), page 117; McShane, "Urban Pathways," page 77; McShane, *Down the Asphalt Path*, pages 213–216; Theodora Kimball Hubbard and Henry Vincent Hubbard, *Our Cities To-Day and Tomorrow* (Cambridge, 1929), chapter 12.

14. Raymond S. Tompkins, "Are We Solving the Traffic Problem?" *American Mercury*, February 1929, page 155; Cleveland Building Owners and Managers Association, *Cleveland's Traffic Problem*, page 6; Barrett, *The Automobile and Urban Transit*, pages 155–161; McShane, *Down the Asphalt Path*, chapter 9; McShane, "Urban Pathways," page 77; *Baltimore Sun*, May 15, 1932; J. Rowland Bibbins, "The Growing Transport Problem of the Masses," *National Municipal Review*, August 1920, pages 517–522. See also McClintock, *Street Traffic Control*, chapters 7–8, 11–12, 14.

15. John Ihlder, "The Automobile and Community Planning," *Annals of the American Academy of Political and Social Science*, November 1924, page 204; E. S. Taylor, "The Plan of Chicago in 1924," ibid., pages 225–229; Arthur A. Shurtleff, "The Circumferential Thoroughfares of the Metropolitan District of Boston," *City Planning*, April 1926, pages 76–84; Hubbard and Hubbard, *Our Cities*, pages 196, 204–205; "By-Pass Highways for Traffic Relief," *American City*, April 1928, page 89; Olmsted, Bartholomew, and Cheney, *A Major Traffic Street Plan for Los Angeles*, page 28.

16. Preston, *Automobile Age Atlanta*, pages 118–125; *American Architect*, May 28, 1919, pages 756–758; McShane, *Down the Asphalt Path*, pages 31–40, 220–223; McShane, "Urban Pathways," pages 71–74, 79–82.

17. Paul Barrett, "Public Policy and Private Choice: Mass Transit and the Automobile in Chicago Between the Wars," *Business History Review*,

Winter 1975, pages 482–483; *Current Affairs in New England*, July 12, 1926, pages 3–4; "The Triangle's 'Thru' Traffic," page 1; Oscar Handlin, ed., *This Was America* (Cambridge, 1949), page 491; "Congested Traffic," *New Republic*, November 28, 1928, pages 29–31; *Report of the Committee on Traffic to His Honor Howard W. Jackson, Mayor of Baltimore, Maryland* (1923), page 5; Clarke, "Special Report on Traffic Relief," page 117; Bottles, *Los Angeles and the Automobile*, pages 101–102, 118–119.

18. "Traffic Problems and Suggested Remedies," *Public Works*, June 1924, pages 177–180; Carol Aronovici, "Down-Town Parking," *Community Builder*, December 1927, pages 28–34; Olmsted, Bartholomew, and Cheney, *A Major Traffic Street Plan for Los Angeles*, page 18; George A. Damon, "Relation of the Motor Bus to Other Methods of Transportation," *Planning Problems of Town, City, and Region: Papers and Discussions at the International City and Regional Planning Conference: 1925*, page 270.

7-1. NATIONAL INTERSTATE AND DEFENSE HIGHWAYS ACT (1956)

Source: National Interstate and Defense Highways Act (PL 627, 29 June 1956), 70 *United States Statutes At Large.*

EDITORS' INTRODUCTION

By the late 1930s, federal government officials were taking increased interest in building a national system of interstate highways. Mobility remained a particular concern of cities, where commerce slowed with snarled traffic. Worries abounded about city evacuation in the event of war, and the outbreak of World War II and the dawn of the nuclear age exacerbated this anxiety. Rural areas also supported an improved transportation infrastructure, in part because the roads gave them better access to urban markets and amenities. In 1956, Congress passed the National Interstate and Defense Highways Act, commonly known as the Federal Highway Act of 1956. President Dwight D. Eisenhower, who had spent a lifetime in the military, championed the cause of the interstate system, which was renamed the Dwight D. Eisenhower System of Interstate and Defense Highways in 1990. The system's construction, first estimated to cost $27 billion dollars and to be completed in about a decade, cost far more than first planned and extended for decades. Although nominally completed during the 1990s, some aspects of the proposed system have yet to be built. The Interstate Highway System is considered the largest public works program in the world. The highways changed cities in vital ways, but did not put an end to traffic problems. The system as initially designed (there were later adjustments) was meant to serve the estimated population of the 1970s.

An Act

To amend and supplement the Federal-Aid Road Act approved July 11, 1916, to authorize appropriations for continuing the construction of highways; to amend the Internal Revenue Code of 1954 to provide additional revenue from the taxes on motor fuel, tires, and trucks and buses; and for other purposes.

Be it enacted by the Senate and House of Representatives of the United States of America in Congress assembled,

TITLE I—FEDERAL-AID HIGHWAY ACT OF 1956
SEC. 101. SHORT TITLE FOR TITLE I.
This title may be cited as the "Federal-Aid Highway Act of 1956".
SEC. 102. FEDERAL-AID HIGHWAYS.
(a) (1) AUTHORIZATION OF APPROPRIA-TIONS.—For the purpose of carrying out the provisions of the Federal-Aid Road Act approved July 11, 1916 (39 Stat. 355), and all Acts amendatory thereof and supplementary thereto, there is hereby authorized to be appropriated for the fiscal year ending June 30, 1957, $125,000,000 in addition to any sums heretofore authorized for such fiscal year; the sum of $850,000,000 for the fiscal year ending June 30, 1958; and the sum of $875,000,000 for the fiscal year ending June 30, 1959. The sums herein authorized for each fiscal year shall be available for expenditure as follows:

(A) 45 per centum for projects on the Federal-aid primary high-way system.

(B) 30 per centum for projects on the Federal-aid secondary high-way system.

(C) 25 per centum for projects on extensions of these systems within urban areas.

(2) APPORTIONMENTS.—The sums authorized by this section shall be apportioned among the several States in the manner now provided by law and in accord-

ance with the formulas set forth in section 4 of the Federal-Aid Highway Act of 1944; approved December 20, 1944 (58 Stat. 838): Provided, That the additional amount herein authorized for the fiscal year ending June 30, 1957, shall be apportioned immediately upon enactment of this Act.

(b) AVAILABILITY FOR EXPENDITURE.—Any sums apportioned to any State under this section shall be available for expenditure in that State for two years after the close of the fiscal year for which such sums are authorized, and any amounts so apportioned remaining unexpended at the end of such period shall lapse: Provided, That such funds shall be deemed to have been expended if a sum equal to the total of the sums herein and heretofore apportioned to the State is covered by formal agreements with the Secretary of Commerce for construction, reconstruction, or improvement of specific projects as provided in this title and prior Acts: Provided further, That in the case of those sums heretofore, herein, or hereafter apportioned to any State for projects on the Federal-aid secondary highway system, the Secretary of Commerce may, upon the request of any State, discharge his responsibility relative to the plans, specifications, estimates, surveys, contract awards, design, inspection, and construction of such secondary road projects by his receiving and approving a certified statement by the State highway department setting forth that the plans, design, and construction for such projects are in accord with the standards and procedures of such State applicable.

[...]

SEC. 108. NATIONAL SYSTEM OF INTERSTATE AND DEFENSE HIGHWAYS.

(a) INTERSTATE SYSTEM.—It is hereby declared to be essential to the national interest to provide for the early completion of the "National System of Interstate Highways", as authorized and designated in accordance with section 7 of the Federal-Aid Highway Act of 1944 (58 Stat. 838). It is the intent of the Congress that the Interstate System be completed as nearly as practicable over a thirteen-year period and that the entire System in all the States be brought to simultaneous completion. Because of its primary importance to the national defense, the name of such system is hereby changed to the "National System of Interstate and Defense Highways". Such National System of Interstate and Defense Highways is hereinafter in this Act referred to as the "Interstate System".

(b) AUTHORIZATION OF APPROPRIATIONS.—For the purpose of expediting the construction, reconstruction, or improvement, inclusive of necessary bridges and tunnels, of the interstate System, including extensions thereof through urban areas, designated in accordance with the provisions of section 7 of the Federal-Aid Highway Act of 1944 (58 Stat. 838), there is hereby authorized to be appropriated the additional sum of $1,000,000,000 for, the fiscal year ending June 30, 1957, which sum shall be in addition to the authorization heretofore made for that year, the additional sum of $1,700,000,000 for the fiscal year ending June 30, 1958, the additional sum of $2,000,000,000 for the fiscal year ending June 30, 1959, the additional sum of $2,200,000,000 for the fiscal year ending June 30, 1960, the additional sum of $2,200,000,000 for the fiscal year ending June 30, 1961, the additional sum of $2,200,000,000 for the fiscal year ending June 30, 1962, the additional sum of $2,200,000,000 for the fiscal year ending June 30, 1963, the additional sum of $2,200,000,000 for the fiscal year ending June 30, 1964, the additional sum of $2,200,000,000 for the fiscal year ending June 30, 1965, the additional sum of $2,200,000,000 for the fiscal year ending June 30, 1966, the additional sum of $2,200,000,000 for the fiscal year ending June 30, 1967, the additional sum of $1,500,000,000 for the fiscal year ending June 30, 1968, and the additional sum of $1,025,000,000 for the fiscal year ending June 30, 1969...

7-2. "$14.6 BILLION LATER, BOSTON'S BIG DIG WRAPS UP" (2003)

Seth Stern

Source: Seth Stern, "$14.6 Billion Later, Boston's Big Dig Wraps Up," *Christian Science Monitor* (December 19, 2003).

EDITORS' INTRODUCTION

The Central Artery/Tunnel Project, also known as the Big Dig, rerouted a portion of Interstate 93, built in the early 1950s. Interstate 93 snaked through downtown Boston, destroying the beauty of an important section of the city and leading to traffic backups. In the early 1980s, planning began for the Big Dig and in 1987, federal funding was approved. The project cost far more than anticipated, and traffic difficulties remained after completion. Subsequent to the publication of this article, the tunnel sprung leaks, a portion of the ceiling collapsed on automobile passenger Milena Del Valle, killing her, and heated debates about how to use the open space created by the removal of the highway abounded.

Beneath Boston—

With a tellingly simple ribbon-cutting ceremony, the last underground segment of Boston's Big Dig project opens Friday—completing major construction on one of the most complex and controversial engineering projects in human history.

It may not look as dramatic as the Hoover Dam, but the revamp of traffic flows in one of America's oldest cities rivals any past US public-works project in complexity—and outpaced them all in cost.

Its effects will be felt for decades and far beyond in Boston: It is changing commuting habits here, may influence the prospects for any similarly large-scale efforts in the future, and has hit the pocketbook of almost every taxpayer in America.

But the Big Dig's scale—at its peak it employed 5,000 construction workers—was rivaled by high costs that have been a source of controversy since the project's inception in 1987—after President Reagan tried unsuccessfully to wield a penny-pinching veto pen.

That's one reason the city will celebrate this weekend with a whimper rather than a bang—or even a pop. The Boston Pops concert scheduled for underground Thursday was canceled. After spending $14.6 billion (up from an initial forecast of about $4 billion

in today's dollars), leaders and taxpayers weren't in the mood to shell out several hundred thousand dollars for the show.

"It will be a mixed legacy," says David Luberoff, associate director of Harvard's Taubman Center for State and Local Government. "For a lot of people in the region it will be seen as a major positive addition. The farther you move from Boston, the less positively people will view the project."

The two-mile-long underground road will ease commutes—at least for a while—reconnect the city with the harbor, and replace the eyesore of a highway with a necklace of green spaces. Already, the spindly Zakim Bridge over the Charles River has become a landmark on the city's skyline.

The city won't reap the full benefits for at least another year, when the hulking overhead highway is finally torn down and traffic patterns are completed. But this weekend's opening is surely the end of an era here. And as traffic flows underground, the city can finally assess whether it was worth the wait—or the price.

Engineering Marvels

No one disputes that the project is an engineering marvel—particularly given the added challenge of building among subway tunnels and steam pipes while the city bustled above.

The statistics are staggering. Making room for 7.5 miles of underground roads required excavating 16 million cubic yards of dirt—enough to fill New England's football stadium 16 times, or just 20 percent less than the Chunnel Tunnel built to connect Britain and France.

"It rivals anything in the history of the world built by men," says Matthew Amorello, chairman of the Massachusetts Turnpike Authority, which oversaw the project. "This is the opening of the Panama Canal. This is an incredible achievement."

Above ground, about half of the rusted carcass of elevated highway nicknamed the 'green monster" has already been demolished and workers are racing to tear down as much as possible before the Democratic Convention arrives in July.

In its place, a 1.5 mile greenspace named in honor of John F. Kennedy's mother, Rose, will sprout. Exact plans aren't finalized but will likely include eight acres of parks as well as housing, shops, and cultural venues.

Among taxpayers, though, it was the price tag that inspired the most awe. The project cost was more than double the Panama Canal's in today's dollars. Citizens here and nationwide—60 percent of the tab was federal—wound up paying far more than expected. Revelations about hidden cost overruns angered many, as statewide highway tolls climbed. The Massachusetts Turnpike Authority is planning a $150 million lawsuit against firms that managed the project.

The controversy is less important to many who helped build the tunnels, such as Patrick Mogauro, who has worked underground on the project for six years. Underneath his hard hat and layers of dirt-encrusted sweatshirts, the electrician is feeling wistful as he puts some finishing touches on the Big Dig.

Disappearing Jobs

He won't miss pulling heavy lines of wire through four-foot ducts. But Mogauro notes, "it kept a lot of families fed." At the project's height, 730 members of Mogauro's union alone found steady work installing lighting, ventilation, and alarms. These days, with the project winding down, the job sheet at the local union hall is empty and 1 in 10 members are out of work.

As the opening neared, the median lines were dry, highway signs installed, and all that was missing were commuters. "Another job like this wouldn't be bad," says electrician's union representative Michael Calder. "But I don't see it happening again in my lifetime."

Figure 7.1 "Clic-Clac Des Omnibus," Street Scene on Sheet Music, 1835. Courtesy of the Center for Historic American Visual Culture at the American Antiquarian Society.

Figure 7.2 "Whitehall, South and Staten Island Ferries and Revenue Barge Office, New York." Circa 1850s–1860s. Courtesy of the Center for Historic American Visual Culture at the American Antiquarian Society.

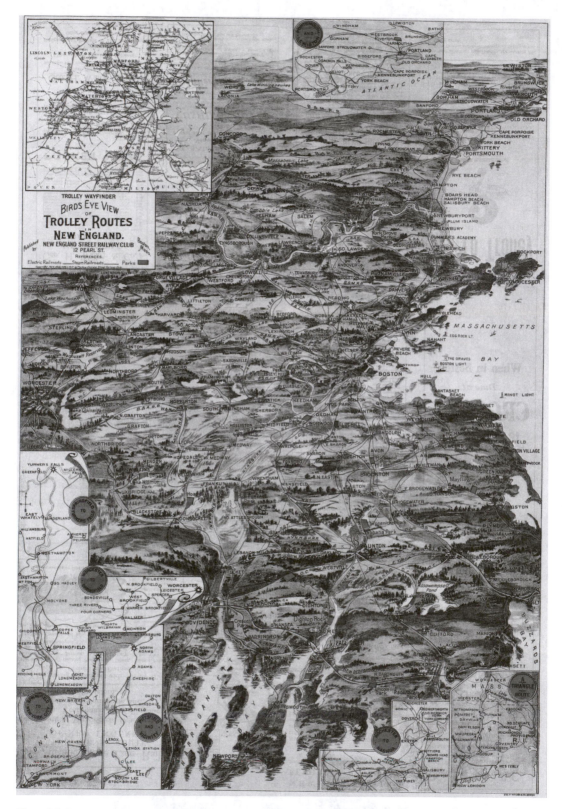

Figure 7.3 Trolley Wayfinder, "Bird's Eye View of Trolley Routes in New England," New England Street Railway Club, 1907. Courtesy of the Center for Historic American Visual Culture at the American Antiquarian Society.

Figure 7.4 Horsecar, New York City, 1908. Library of Congress, Prints and Photographs Division.

Figure 7.5 Norfolk, Virginia, Granby Street, c. 1915. Library of Congress, Prints and Photographs Division.

Figure 7.6 Trolley Car, Hyde Street Hill, San Francisco, c. 1970s. Library of Congress, Prints and Photographs Division.

Figure 7.7 Creeping Sickness. *American City.* April 1929.

PART VIII

Urban Migrations and Social Mobility

EDITORS' INTRODUCTION TO PART VIII

There are four general ways in which a city can increase in population: (1) natural increase through higher numbers of births than deaths, (2) migration of people from the country-side, towns, and other cities into the city in question, (3) immigration from foreign nations, and (4) annexation of surrounding territories. Biological increase is well understood, and the annexation of population through political restructuring and the redrawing of maps, while an interesting aspect of urban history, does not of course bring any new people into the region. Immigration, a process vital to the understanding of cities and an integral part of the American mythology, was the subject of Part III. Migration, the study of the flow of people from within the national borders into a city, has extensively transformed cities, yet is under-acknowledged.

Migration proves to be a confusing term, because scholars apply it in a variety of ways. Defining migration as a movement of people within national borders keeps the term straightforward enough to be meaningful. Yet others have used the term migration to refer to the act of emigration (leaving one's country of origin) or immigration (entering into a new country), complicating the word's usage. In urban studies and urban history, migration most often refers to intra-national movements, unless another context is clear. Referring to migration as regional migration might help clarify its meaning. Scholars recognize the major migration or migrations of African Americans out of the South and to the West and North during the twentieth century. The movement of blacks began right after Emancipation, but gathered momentum around the time World War I broke out in Europe. Historians differ on where to put the emphasis—some highlight the importance of migration within the South,[1] others focus on the movement westward, and still others look at the people moving north. Those relocating from rural locations in the South often lived temporarily in a southern city before heading on to other regions. Some scholars note that some of those moving north settled in rural areas or small cities. But the millions moving into major cities played a highly influential role in redefining American culture and transforming the political landscape of the century. The migration north is often, but not always, divided into two major movements divided by the Great Depression, a period in which migration slowed. As with any social movement, the dates of the migration are approximate. Scholars date the First Great Migration, the movement of close to 1.5 million from the South to the North, as approximately 1914–1930, with some using 1916 as a starting date. The Second Great Migration, a movement of approximately five million people, is normally defined as occurring between 1940–1960 or 1940–1970.

This part opens with Arnold R. Hirsch's blockbuster work, *Making the Second Ghetto: Race and Housing in Chicago* (Chicago: University of Chicago Press, 1998; first published in 1983 by Columbia University Press). Hirsch offers a multi-faceted study of the Second Great Migration, when hundreds of thousands of African Americans came to Chicago.

Once in Chicago, blacks were forced by convention and law into tightly restricted neighborhoods on the South Side and, ultimately, on the West Side of the city. Even with expanded boundaries, the black belt could not adequately accommodate all the migrants, who made their homes in inadequate spaces. Many lived in one-room kitchenette apartments with extended family members; the very desperate carved out spaces in tenement basements and subdivided the rooms with highly flammable cardboard. Because of the city's decision to keep housing segregated, even in the face of increased numbers of African Americans, Chicago created a new ghetto on top of its old one, a place that became associated with rampant poverty, political corruption, and crime. The influence of Hirsch's arguments cannot be overstated; all those studying race in modern urban America have been influenced by this important work.

When scholars study watershed historical movements, they often do not pause to consider the movement as a gendered experience. With the growing strength of the subfield of women's history, the time has come to examine migration from the perspective of women. As migration within the United States and immigration to the United States have so often been fueled by employment opportunities, men's concerns have figured centrally in studies of the movements. This is beginning to change. Following in the steps of immigrant historians Hasia Diner, Elizabeth Ewing, and Donna Gabbacia, Suellen Hoy makes a persuasive argument in her work, *Good Hearts: Catholic Sisters in Chicago's Past* (Urbana: University of Illinois Press, 2006) of the significance of Irish nuns to the story of Irish immigration to the United States. In a similar fashion, urban historian Lisa Krissoff Boehm reconceptualizes African American migration by placing women front and center in the story. Krissoff Boehm's book, *Making a Way out of No Way: African American Women and the Second Great Migration* (Jackson: University Press of Mississippi, 2009) demonstrates the power of oral histories in broadening historical understanding. Archival resources on the Second Great Migration, 1940–1970, are slim, especially in terms of women migrants. Luckily, Krissoff Boehm had the opportunity to conduct oral histories with the migrants themselves, and add their voices to the historical record. The oral histories collected for this study are archived at the Bentley Historical Library at the University of Michigan and the Schlesinger Library for the History of Women in America at Harvard University.

Concurrent with the movement of millions of African Americans to the North, but less often documented in historical literature, was the migration of southern whites. This migration often surpassed—in terms of numbers—the migration of southern blacks. Yet the southern whites are more difficult to track, and proved more willing to relocate back to the South. Southern migrants faced ridicule in their new homes based on cultural stereotypes, yet they had an easier time than blacks at assimilating after a few generations. Southern whites bequeathed their own cultural legacy to their new region, for instance in the flowering of a new, commercially-appealing popular music with rural roots. In Chad Berry's influential *Northern Migrants and Southern Exiles* (Urbana: University of Illinois Press, 2000), we again see oral history put to good use in shedding light on a modern historical phenomenon. We also see how urban history and labor history are difficult to disentangle. Berry's work provides us with a new framework of understanding social history of midwestern cities in the mid and late twentieth century.

All major cities, not just those of the North and West, proved popular destinations for migrants. Southern cities were increasingly popular places to relocate in the second half of the twentieth century. The inflow of migrants was joined by new immigrants to urban areas, particularly after the legal changes of 1965, which eased immigration restrictions. Asian and Asian Indian immigrants came in increased numbers to American cities, along with additional settlers from such places as the Middle East, Eastern Europe, and Central and South America. Debates about bilingual education and assimilation raged as they had in the early twentieth century. In crystal clear prose, Melanie Shell-Weiss deepens our understanding of modern urban life with her book *Coming to Miami: A Social History*

(Gainesville: University of Florida Press, 2009). Providing a model for a new form of synthetic urban scholarship, Shell-Weiss combines urban, immigration, migration, and labor history for a new look at modern society. We see that we cannot understand the history of one ethnic group without surveying the larger social landscape of metropolitan life.

The documents in this part reflect the tensions stemming from the growing social diversity of cities in the twentieth century. In Tulsa, Oklahoma violence erupted in 1921 when whites destroyed the city's black business district, killing scores of people. White Protestant fears of Catholics, Jews, and blacks reached their apex with the open membership in the Ku Klux Klan in the 1920s. Klan meetings, such as the one in Worcester, Massachusetts in October 1924, were widely attended by entire families. During World War II, white servicemen in California targeted and attacked Hispanic youth who wore eye-catching zoot suits.

Migrants and immigrants bravely moved to unknown locations seeking better economic and social opportunities. In Harriette Arnow's bestselling novel, *The Dollmaker* (1954), Gertie Nevels leaves Kentucky for the industrial city of Detroit, but finds the new setting impersonal and unappealing. Author Richard Rodriguez, plagued by language and cultural differences, found the transition to his Sacramento, California elementary school complex difficult despite the fact that he was a second generation American. Migration and immigration are processes that lack finite beginnings and ends. Second and third generation family members are also affected by relocation. William H. Frey demonstrates that northern-born blacks left northern cities for southern cities, reversing the previous generation's migration.

NOTE

1. See Bernadette Pruitt, "For the Advancement of the Race: African-American Migration to Houston, 1914–1941," *Journal of Urban History*, 31(4) (May 2005): 435–478.

The Second Ghetto and the Dynamics of Neighborhood Change

Arnold R. Hirsch

Source: *Making the Second Ghetto: Race and Housing in Chicago,
1940–1960* (Chicago: University of Chicago Press, 1998; first published in
1983 by Columbia University Press).

EDITORS' INTRODUCTION

Chicago was a major destination for the First and Second Great Migrations, the historic flow of African Americans from the South to the urban North launched by the pull of industrial work during the world wars. The First Great Migration (approximately 1914–1930) is generally thought to have numbered about 1.5 million, and the Second (approximately 1940–1970), approximately five million people. Yet these numbers are difficult to gauge, as some migrants came in and out of the city repeatedly, and many migrants left little historical evidence in their wake. African Americans also migrated before and after these major waves. While it is important to understand this movement as transformative in a variety of ways (including economically, politically, socially, and culturally) to major cities, some migrants also settled in small towns and rural areas. By 1920, at least 110,000 blacks had settled in Chicago. The U.S. Census concluded there were 812,637 African Americans in Chicago in 1960, making up over 22 percent of the population.[i] As we will see later in this part, the black migration occurred contemporaneously with a sizable white migration, a movement that most likely exceeded the black migration. **[See Chad Berry, "The Great White Migration, 1945–1960" in this part.]** Historian James N. Gregory writes that "More than 28 million southerners left their home region during the course of the twentieth century."[ii] Although black women were largely restricted from war work—even during these times of national crisis—the world wars provided black men with an unprecedented opportunity to find industrial employment, albeit often in the most dangerous and distasteful aspects of industry. This expanded opportunity ultimately helped to bring many African American migrants into the middle class. But others found themselves stuck in newly reinforced ghettoes in northern cities. As Hirsch emphasizes, black settlers of longer duration had already lived in Chicago ghettoes; Hirsch chronicles the establishment of Chicago's startlingly narrow (three miles long by only a quarter mile wide) ghetto between 1890 and 1930. The ghetto, rather than being dismantled, was *reinforced* during the dawn of the Second Great Migration. Although the black population of Chicago grew, and the boundaries of the black belt expanded due to the pressures of this growing

---

i Arnold Hirsch, *Making the Second Ghetto: Race and Housing in Chicago, 1940–1960* (Chicago: University of Chicago Press, 1998), 3, 17.

ii James N. Gregory, *The Southern Diaspora: How the Great Migrations of Black and White Southerners Transformed America* (Chapel Hill: University of North Carolina Press), 19.

population, black isolation intensified, with the majority of African Americans living in almost completely black neighborhoods.

Chicago's highly segregated neighborhoods were not created by accident. Public policy dictated that blacks could not buy or rent homes in most Chicago neighborhoods, and where any doubt remained, the organizational practices of realtors' professional associations and pressures by institutions assured that neighborhoods would not be integrated. Public housing projects adhered to the "neighborhood composition rule" promulgated by Chicagoan Harold Ickes, head of the housing division of the New Deal creation, the Public Works Administration. Only with the Supreme Court decision *Shelley* v. *Kraemer* of 1948, which upended the use of restrictive covenants, and the Fair Housing Act of 1968, would the well-fortified palisades of segregation begin to crack. Hirsch explains, "The ghetto was to be reinforced with taxpayers' dollars and shored up with the power of the state."[iii]

As Hirsch explores, the renewed efforts at segregation in response to the increased flow of African Americans to the North during World War II ultimately created an untenable situation in Chicago, leading to the establishment of a city within a city, with redundant businesses and services and an increasingly powerful black political leadership. The area became associated with intense poverty, and the highly controversial term, "underclass," assigned to families who seemed mired in poverty generation after generation. Contemporaneous observers began to assign some of the causation for this deep poverty to the culture of the southern migrants, although recent studies like the quantitative work of sociologist Stewart Tolnay, now offers evidence to refute these accusations.[iv] We can clearly see, however, how the pressures of a large flow of migrants into a highly restricted space encouraged devastating housing conditions within the black belt and great tension with the bordering white neighborhoods, which often ignited violence.

Hirsch's work follows on from an earlier generation of historiographical works on the ghettoization of American blacks in northern cities, such as the influential work of Allen H. Spear.[v] Hirsch's work intrigued urban scholars for its analysis of public policy's role in creating what Hirsch terms a "Frankenstein's monster," a highly regrettable artifact of incorrect assumptions and a host of prejudices. Post-war urban development, in an attempt at "urban renewal," created deep segregation, generations of poverty, and nearly impenetrable physical divides within the city.[vi]

Arnold R. Hirsch is the Ethel and Herman L. Midlo Professor for New Orleans Studies and University Research Professor in the department of history at the University of New Orleans. Hirsch has written articles on a variety of urban topics and served as the co-editor and contributor to *Creole New Orleans: Race and Americanization* (Baton Rouge: Louisiana State University Press, 1992) and *Urban Policy in Twentieth-Century America* (New Brunswick: Rutgers University Press, 1993).

---

iii Hirsch, *Making of the Second Ghetto*, 9–10. **[See Thomas J. Sugrue, "Class, Status, and Residence: the Changing Geography of Black Detroit," in Part IX of this volume.]**

iv Stewart E. Tolnay, "The Great Migration and Changes in the Northern Black Family, 1940–1990," *Social Forces* 75 (June 1997): 1213–1238.

v See Allen H. Spear, *Black Chicago: The Making of a Negro Ghetto, 1890–1920* (Chicago: University of Chicago Press, 1967) and St. Clair Drake, Horace Roscoe Cayton, and Richard Wright, *Black Metropolis: A Study of Negro Life in a Northern City* (New York: Harcourt, Brace, and Company, 1945).

vi For an extended analysis of the impact of Hirsch's work, see a group of essays in the *Journal of Urban History* (March 2003).

THE SECOND GHETTO AND THE DYNAMICS OF NEIGHBORHOOD CHANGE

I have walked the South Side Streets (Thirty-first to Sixty-ninth) from State to Cottage Grove in the last 35 days searching for a flat.

Anonymous to the *Chicago Defender*, November 28, 1942

Something is happening to lives and spirits that will never show up in the great housing shortage of the late '40s. Something is happening to the children which might not show up in our social records until 1970.

Chicago Sun-Times, undated clipping, Chicago Urban League Papers, Manuscript Collection, The Library, University of Illinois at Chicago

The race riot that devastated Chicago following the drowning of Eugene Williams on Sunday, July 27, 1919, was notable for its numerous brutal confrontations between white and black civilians. White hoodlums sped through the narrow sliver of land that was the Black Belt, firing their weapons as they rode, wreaking havoc and killing at least one person.[1] Nor was that all. Aside from the many assaults and casualties taken in the Stock Yards district immediately west of the Black Belt, serious clashes occurred in the Loop and around the Angelus building, a rooming house that remained the abode of white workers in the predominantly black area around Wabash Avenue and 35th Street. Blacks retaliated by attacking whites unfortunate enough to be caught on their "turf."[2] By the time the riot ended, 38 persons – 23 blacks and 15 whites – lay dead and 537 were injured.[3]

In early April 1968, following the assassination of Dr. Martin Luther King, Jr., Chicago was again the scene of serious violence. Although labeled a "race riot," the events of 1968 differed sharply from those of 1919. Instead of an interracial war carried on by black and white citizens, the "King riot," largely an expression of outrage by the city's black community, was characterized by the destruction of property. The deaths that did occur during the riots (there were nine) resulted primarily from confrontations between black civilians and the police or National Guard.[4]

There were other significant differences as well. The worst rioting in 1968 occurred on the West Side. Merely a minor black enclave in 1919, by the time of Dr. King's assassination Chicago's West Side housed more than twice the number of blacks resident in the entire city during the earlier riot. A vast ghetto of relatively recent origin, the West Side thus established itself as a scene of racial tension to rival the older, and larger, South Side Black Belt. Moreover, the Loop, where blacks were viciously hunted in 1919, was now subjected to roving groups of black youths who had walked out of nearby inner-city high schools. This time, however, harassment of pedestrians and petty vandalism replaced the deadly violence of the earlier era. Confrontations such as the one around the Angelus building were impossible in the more rigidly segregated city of the 1960s, and white injuries, reportedly few in number, generally occurred as motorists were unluckily trapped in riot areas. There were no armed forays into "enemy" territory. In sum, clashes between black and white Chicagoans (other than the police) were infrequent, fortuitous, and not lethal. The prevailing image of the 1968 disorder was evoked not by mass murder but by the flames that enveloped stores along a 2-mile stretch of Madison Street and those that engulfed similar structures along Western, Kedzie, and Pulaski avenues.[5]

The close relationship between the growth of the modern black metropolis and the changing pattern of racial disorder is clear. After an era of tremendous ghetto expansion and increasing racial isolation, "communal" riots on the scale of those that shook the nation in 1919 became impossible. The thought of white mobs attacking the black ghettos of the 1960s boggles the imagination. Additionally, the large concentration of blacks in the inner city rendered exceedingly unlikely the stalking and killing of individual blacks on downtown streets. The burning and looting of primarily white-owned property in massive black ghettos was the most visible manifestation of racial tension permitted in the modern city. Able to quarantine black neighborhoods, police were much less able to control actions taken within them. The eruption of the "commodity" riots of the 1960s heralded the existence, in Chicago at least, of that city's "second ghetto."[6]

The reasons for making a distinction between the "first ghetto" of the World War I era and the "second ghetto" of the post-World War II period are quantitative, temporal, and qualitative. As Morris Janowitz noted in his analysis of racial disorders in the twentieth century, the "commodity" riots of the 1960s took place in black communities that had grown enormously in both size and population.[7] Ten times as many blacks lived in Chicago in 1966 as in 1920. Representing but 4% of the city's population in the latter year, blacks accounted for nearly 30% of all Chicagoans by the mid-1960s. The evolution of the West Side black colony, from enclave to ghetto, was a post-World War II development. And the South Side Black Belt's expansion between 1945 and 1960 was so pronounced that its major business artery shifted a full 2 miles to the south, from 47th Street to 63rd.[8]

There is a chronological justification for referring to Chicago's "second ghetto" as well. The period of rapid growth following World War II was the second such period in the city's history. The first, coinciding with the Great Migration of southern blacks, encompassed the years between 1890 and 1930. Before 1900, the earliest identifiable black colony existed west of State Street and south of Harrison; an 1874 fire destroyed much of this section and resulted in the settlement's reestablishment between 22nd and 31st streets. By the turn of the century, this nucleus had merged with other colonies to form the South Side Black Belt. Where, according to Thomas Philpott's meticulously researched *The Slum and the Ghetto*, "no large, solidly Negro concentration existed" in Chicago until the 1890s, by 1900 the black population suffered an "extraordinary" degree of segregation and their residential confinement was "nearly complete." Almost 3 miles long, but barely a quarter mile wide, Chicago's South Side ghetto – neatly circumscribed on all sides by railroad tracks – had come into being.[9]

By 1920 the Black Belt extended roughly to 55th Street, between Wentworth and Cottage Grove avenues. Approximately 85% of the city's nearly 110,000 blacks lived in this area. A second colony existed on the West Side between Austin, Washington Boulevard, California Avenue, and Morgan Street. More than 8,000 blacks, including some "scattered residents as far south as Twelfth Street," lived here. Other minor black enclaves included the area around Ogden Park in Englewood, Morgan Park on the far South Side, separate settlements in Woodlawn and Hyde Park, and a growing community on the near North Side. Between 1910 and 1920 three additional colonies appeared in Lilydale (around 91st and State streets), near the South Chicago steel mills, and immediately east of Oakwood Cemetery between 67th and 71st streets.[10]

Ten years later it was possible to speak of an almost "solidly" black area from 22nd to 63rd streets, between Wentworth and Cottage Grove. Whole neighborhoods were now black where, according to Philpott, "only some buildings and some streets and blocks had been black earlier." By 1930 even such gross measuring devices as census tracts documented a rigidly segregated ghetto. In 1920 there were no tracts that were even 90% black; the next census revealed that two-thirds of all black Chicagoans lived in such areas and 19% lived in "exclusively" (97.5% or more) black tracts. The West Side colony grew as well. Although it expanded only two blocks southward to Madison Street, it went from only 45% black to nearly all black in the same period; and a new colony appeared in an area previously occupied by Jews near Maxwell Street. By the time of the Depression, Black Chicago encompassed five times the territory it had occupied in 1900. Its borders were sharp and clear, it had reached maturity, and all future growth would spring from this base.[11]

The Depression, however, marked a relaxation in the pace of racial transition, in the growth of Chicago's Black Belt. Black migration to the Windy City decreased dramatically, thus relieving the pressure placed on increasingly crowded Black Belt borders. The period of the 1930s, consequently, was an era of territorial consolidation for Chicago's blacks. Over three-quarters of them lived in areas that were more than 90% black by 1940, and almost half lived in areas that were more than 98% black. On the eve of World War II, Chicago's black population was, according to sociologist David Wallace, "very close to being as concentrated as it could get."[12]

This meant that the 1930s and early 1940s produced only slight territorial additions to the Black Belt (such as the opening of the Washington Park Subdivision). Such stability provoked few black–white clashes, and a similar calm prevailed in the border areas surrounding the other enclaves. The colony in Englewood saw whites replace the few scattered blacks on its periphery, whereas its core around Ogden Park became increasingly black. The Morgan Park community grew in both numbers and area, but its population became virtually all black, and its expansion was accomplished through new construction on vacant land rather than the "invasion" of white territory. The Lilydale enclave followed the same pattern. The South Chicago and Oakwood settlements likewise grew in numbers but actually decreased in size as they became more solidly black.[13] By 1940, St. Clair Drake and Horace R. Cayton were able to assert that the Black Belt "had virtually ceased to expand."[14]

The two decades between 1940 and 1960, and especially the fifteen years following the conclusion of World War II witnessed the renewal of massive black migration to Chicago and the overflowing of black population from established areas of residence grown too small, too old, and too decayed to hold old settlers and newcomers alike. It was during the 1940s and 1950s that the Black Belt's boundaries, drawn during the Great Migration, were shattered. To the east, the Cottage Grove Avenue barrier – which had been buttressed by the activity of local improvement associations after the 1919 riot – fell as blacks entered the communities of Oakland, Kenwood, Hyde Park, and Woodlawn in large numbers. To the south and southwest, Park Manor and Englewood also witnessed the crumbling of what were, by 1945, traditional borders. On the West Side, the exodus of Jews from North Lawndale created a vacuum that was quickly filled by a housing-starved black population. The first new black settlement since the 1920s, the North Lawndale colony was the largest of several new black communities created in the post-World War II period.[15]

Every statistical measure confirmed that racial barriers that had been "successfully defended for a generation," in Allan Spear's words, were being overrun after World War II. The number of technically "mixed" census tracts increased from 135 to 204 between 1940 and 1950. The proportion of "non-Negroes" living in exclusively "non-Negro" tracts declined from 91.2% in 1940 to 84.1% in 1950, reversing a twenty-year trend. Moreover, of the city's 935 census tracts, only 160 were without a single non-white resident in 1950; there were 350 such tracts just ten years earlier. Such startling figures prompted the Chicago Commission on Human Relations to hail them as signifying a reversal of the city's march toward complete segregation. Their conclusion, however, was hastily drawn.[16]

The census figures for 1950 revealed not a city undergoing desegregation but one in the process of redefining racial borders after a period of relative stability. Black isolation was, in fact, increasing even as the Black Belt grew. Nearly 53% of the city's blacks lived in exclusively black census tracts in 1950 compared with only 49.7% in 1940; more people moved into the Black Belt than were permitted to leave it. As overcrowded areas became more overcrowded, the pressure of sheer numbers forced some blacks into previously all-white areas. Thus, whereas blacks were becoming more isolated from the white population generally, a large number of whites found themselves living in technically "mixed" areas. Segregation was not ending. It had merely become time to work out a new geographical accommodation between the races.[17]

If, however, the territorial arrangement forged by the end of the 1920s needed revision, the postwar era provided, theoretically at least, an opportunity for dismantling, instead of expanding, the ghetto. That such a possibility existed has been obscured by the dreadful air of inevitability that permeated the ghetto studies produced in the 1960s and that sped analysis from the Stock Yards to Watts.[18] Such telescopic vision blurred what occurred in between, placed an unfair measure of responsibility on those living in the World War I period for what later transpired, and provided absolution through neglect for those who came later. Indeed, the real tragedy surrounding the emergence of the modern ghetto is not that it has been inherited but that it has been periodically renewed and strengthened. Fresh decisions, not the mere acquiescence to old ones, reinforced and shaped the contemporary black metropolis.

Certainly close observers of the housing situation in the years following World War II saw nothing inevitable about the continued expansion of preexisting ghetto areas. Robert C. Weaver, a member of the Mayor's Committee on Race Relations and later the

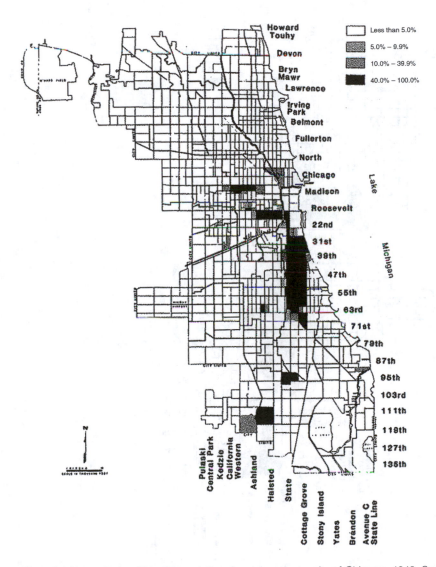

Figure 8.1 Percentage of black population, in census tracts, city of Chicago, 1940. Source: U.S. Bureau of the Census, *Population and Housing Characteristics*, 1960.

first secretary of the Department of Housing and Urban Development, emphasized the malleability of the future in *The Negro Ghetto*, the most significant contemporary survey of the problem. Viewing the increased involvement of government on all levels in urban affairs, he expressed with some trepidation the notion that postwar redevelopment could be either a "threat or an opportunity." "Provision of more space for minorities is the most immediate need," Weaver wrote, "and it will be accelerated by a sound national housing program which insists upon widespread participation by all elements in the population." "But it is extremely important," he warned, "that we avoid the creation of additional ghettos."[19] Weaver's sense of uncertainty and opportunity were genuine. The 1960s fires, which illuminated the past as well as the present (and thus facilitated the use of hindsight), should not be permitted to obscure the fact that paths other than the one eventually taken were available. Moreover, by stressing the role to be played by government intervention in urban affairs, Weaver pinpointed the qualitative distinction that separated the second ghetto from the first.

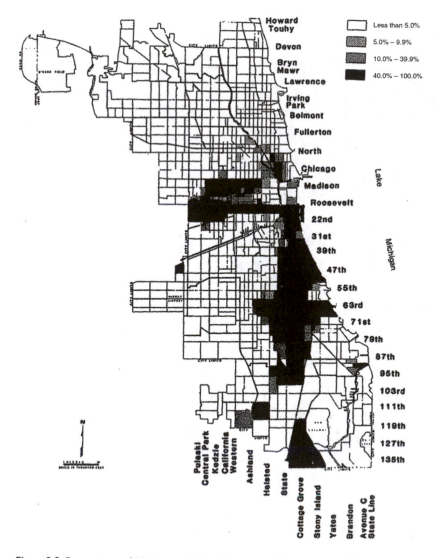

Figure 8.2 Percentage of black population, in census tracts, city of Chicago, 1960. Source: U.S. Bureau of the Census, *Population and Housing Characteristics*, 1960.

The most distinguishing feature of post-World War II ghetto expansion is that it was carried out with government sanction and support. As black migration northward increased in the first quarter of the twentieth century and racial lines began to harden, it was apparent that white hostility was of paramount importance in shaping the pattern of black settlement. Sometimes violent, sometimes through the peaceful cooperation of local real estate boards, white animosity succeeded, informally and privately, in restricting black areas of residence.[20] Direct government support for segregation, before the New Deal, consisted primarily of the judicial enforcement of privately drawn restrictive covenants.

After World War II, however, government urban redevelopment and renewal policies, as well as a massive public housing program, had a direct and enormous impact on the evolution of the ghetto. In Chicago such programs reshaped, enlarged, and transformed the South Side Black Belt. Decaying neighborhoods were torn down, their inhabitants were shunted off to other quarters, and the land upon which they stood was used for middle-class housing and institutional expansion. High-rise public housing projects, created, in large part, to rehouse fugitives from "renewed" areas, literally lined State Street for miles as a new, vertical ghetto supplemented the old. To the east, Hyde Park became first a new area of black settlement and later, after implementation of an urban renewal program designed specifically to meet the challenge of racial succession, an obstacle around which most blacks had to move en route to accommodations farther south. The peculiar characteristics of Chicago's racial geography – the Black Belt's concrete northern end, the white thorn in its flank, and its newly occupied southern and western provinces – were all, in some measure, acquired through government action after World War II.

Increased government concern with housing was apparent, of course, before the postwar period. Beginning in the 1930s, and continuing thereafter, the operation of national agencies such as the Home Owners Loan Corporation (HOLC) and the Federal Housing Administration (FHA) reflected prevailing segregationist attitudes. Indirectly at least, they furthered the racial segmentation of metropolitan America and inner-city decay by supporting the flight of the white, middle-class population to the suburbs (which, despite government support, remained closed to blacks). A contemporary survey revealed, for example, that of 374 FHA-guaranteed mortgages in metropolitan Chicago, only 3 were in the central city.[21] More direct and immediate, however, were the federal government's attempts to clear slums and provide public housing to the urban poor. Although these programs were limited in scope and halting in practice, they pointed the way to the future. The ghetto was to be reinforced with taxpayers' dollars and shored up with the power of the state.

The first signs that this was happening in Chicago came with the construction of the Ida B. Wells housing project in the late 1930s. Covering 47 acres and costing nearly $9 million, the Ida B. Wells Homes provided shelter for 1,662 black families. Like similar projects in Cleveland, this black development was located in the ghetto, between 37th and 39th streets, South Parkway (now Martin Luther King Drive), and Cottage Grove. Opposition to the project came only from realtors and others outside the black community. Never once raising the issue of segregation, the Chicago *Defender* claimed that nearly "all of our political leaders, our ministers, social workers and civic organizations have united their resources to combat the opposition." The completion of the project, the black press asserted, was a "brilliant climax to Mayor Kelly's fight to see to it that the people of Chicago are properly housed." The reasons for such enthusiasm were apparent. Conditions within the Black Belt were so appalling that decent housing, wherever it was located, was desperately desired by the community, leaders and masses alike. The huge Wells development was a gift horse (albeit a Trojan one) not to be scrupulously examined. And, in some ways, the project did represent a gain for "the race." Black contractors, technicians, engineers, draftsmen, architects, and skilled and unskilled laborers were all employed in the construction process. Nonwhite plumbers, lathers, steam fitters, and structural-steel workers were granted temporary union cards so that they, too, could labor at the Wells Homes. Such "firsts," the promise of decent, safe, and sanitary dwellings, and the prospect that slum areas would be redeemed were more than enough to assure the undivided support of Black Chicago.[22]

This pattern of federal action, which became firmly established with the wartime emergency, soon generated bitter denunciations, however. As early as 1943 black Chicagoans were calling for the dismissal of the National Housing Agency's John Blandford for his "deference to the principle of residential segregation." There was truth to the charge. Federal respect for restrictive covenants and the delegation of site selection responsibilities to local interests vitiated all efforts to house black war workers. By 1944, despite the documented presence of 500 "emergency" cases and 10,000 other eligible in-migrants, the NHA had contributed but 93 units to the black housing supply. Blandford, the *Defender* charged, lacked even the "backbone of a jellyfish."[23]

Proposed solutions to the problem emphasized this growing black concern and awareness of the potential impact of government action. One possibility was temporary housing; yet the mere mention of such quarters sparked stinging rebuttals from blacks who suspected the units would be placed in their areas and who, like Chicago Housing Authority (CHA) chairman Robert R. Taylor and onetime alderman Earl Dickerson, rejected "any palliative that preserved [the] ghetto." Well-meaning whites hesitated before suggesting these emergency measures in 1944, knowing that their counsel "place[d] us under suspicion by Negroes, because they place segregation above all other problems." Similarly, proposals to rebuild the ghetto with high-rise apartment buildings "so that the same area can take care of a greater number of people" led Robert Weaver to denounce them as "inconsistent" with the American creed. Moreover, Weaver felt, once the "existing Negro population became accommodated" to such an

arrangement, "bars to its future expansion would become more inflexible than they are now."[24]

However, the Depression-era and wartime government building programs were not particularly large, and their significance lay elsewhere. By the end of the war the Chicago Housing Authority operated 7,644 permanent low-income housing units, including the nearly 4,000 that segregated blacks in the Ida B. Wells, Robert H. Brooks, and Altgeld Gardens projects. But this was merely a fraction of the nearly 40,000 such units in existence by 1976 (contained in 1,273 separate buildings and housing roughly 5% of the city's population).[25] The significance of these early government efforts lay in their demonstration of the difficulty in breaking established racial patterns. The building of ghettos was a cumulative process. The existence of the first ghetto made the rise of the second much easier, if it did not, in fact, produce overwhelming forces assuring its appearance. Ultimately, the dismantling of the ghetto in postwar Chicago under the hammerblows of a massive, nondiscriminatory government building program proved an insurmountable challenge. Local and federal authorities sustained, rather than attacked, the status quo.

At times the ties between the first and second ghettos were close and direct. Charles S. Duke, an architect and consulting engineer on the Wells Homes, as well as one of the select black group that had originally sponsored the project, was also the author of *The Housing Situation and the Colored People of Chicago, with Suggested Remedies and Brief References to Housing Projects Generally*. Published in April 1919, shortly before the riot of that year, Duke's treatise condemned "all attempts at racial segregation" but called for new construction and "decent living conditions" within existing black communities as a means of relieving both their distress and the pressure they placed on adjacent white neighborhoods. Duke was concerned not only with housing but also with the economic benefits such activity would bring to black realtors and businessmen; it was an attempt – in the context of the racial hatreds of that era – to deal constructively with the fact of segregation and real black needs. His approach was emulated by the governor's riot commission, which investigated the ensuing holocaust. The commission's report, *The Negro in Chicago*, denounced *forcible* segregation while proposing, in Thomas Philpott's words, a "dual solution" to the city's racial and housing difficulties; it recommended "not open housing but better *Negro* housing" as the solution to racial tension. For a decade after the riot, reformers, philanthropists, and entrepreneurs tried to provide more and decent housing for blacks and working-class whites while observing both the color line and the bottom line. The construction of the Garden Homes, the Marshall Field Garden Apartments, and the Michigan Boulevard Garden Apartments (Rosenwald Gardens), however, was testimony only to their good intentions, the strength of the "business creed," and their futility – except for their success in leaving the prevailing pattern of segregation intact. If the private sector's "dual solutions" proved abortive in the twenties, though, they were substantially resurrected and brought to fruition in the modern era through the exercise of public power. One need only look, in 1980, at the unbroken wall of high-rise public housing along State Street, stretching all the way from Cermak Road (22nd Street) to 55th, to realize that the riot commission's recommendations were followed in spirit, if not in detail, more than a generation after they were made.[26]

Similarly, forces at work on the national level stretched back to the age of Progressive reform. Former settlement house resident, NAACP leader, and Chicagoan Harold Ickes headed the housing division of the Public Works Administration (PWA). Perhaps wishing to make the novel federal presence in urban America as unobtrusive as possible, it was Ickes who promulgated the "neighborhood composition rule," which prevented government projects from altering the racial composition of their host neighborhoods. Progressive willingness to work within the constraints of the color line, so evident at the beginning of the century, thus left its mark on the early federal programs

as well. Not only were the "black" projects located in ghetto areas, but Chicago's Lathrop and Trumbull Park Homes, located in white areas, excluded blacks; and the Jane Addams Homes, which adhered to a racial quota in keeping with previous black presence on the site, was alone in its mixed clientele in the prewar era.[27] Federal policy later changed, of course, but these precedents were difficult to overcome and they became sources of controversy in the postwar period.

Other links between the first and second ghettos were less visible but equally important. The emergence of Chicago's "black metropolis" gave rise to institutional, economic, and political forces that had their roots, and therefore a stake, in the ghetto. The white hostility that isolated blacks spatially necessitated the creation of an "institutional ghetto," a city within a city, to serve them. It also produced a leadership class eager, or at least willing (as suggested by Duke's approach to housing), to pursue separate development rather than total assimilation – which is to say it created interests that could only view the ghetto's destruction with grave misgivings.[28]

In the late 1940s and 1950s, given the growing significance of government action, the conservative nature of black politics and politicians was of particular importance. Throughout the period, Chicago's black leadership was fragmented by the issues of redevelopment and renewal, and those who joined the opposition received little help in the political arena from William L. Dawson's black "sub-machine." Constrained by their accommodation to Chicago's brand of ethnic and machine-style politics, and their subordination to the dominant, white-controlled Cook County Democratic Organization, the professional black politicians lacked the desire or ability to fight those forces shaping the postwar ghetto. They would, according to political scientist Milton Rakove, "rather gild the ghetto than break it up." Such action, Rakove asserted, "insure[d] their tenures of office, indebt[ed] their constituencies to them, and enable[d] them to advance themselves within the Democratic machine in the city." The ghetto was a self-sustaining organism, which, politically at least, could not effectively challenge the forces that preserved and enlarged it.[29]

It was the sheer presence of the first ghetto and the white reaction to it, though, that did the most to produce the second. In creating it, white Chicago conceived a "Frankenstein's monster," which threatened to "run amok" after World War II. The establishment of racial borders, their traditional acceptance, and the conditions spawned by unyielding segregation created an entity that whites feared and loathed. Those who made it were soon threatened by it, and, desperately, they both employed old techniques and devised new ones in the attempt to control it. Others elected to flee to the suburbs, thus compounding the difficulties of those left behind. In any event, the very process of racial succession, dormant for nearly a generation, inspired both the dread and the action that called forth the second ghetto.

NOTES

1. Chicago Commission on Race Relations (hereafter cited as CCRR), *The Negro in Chicago* (Chicago: University of Chicago Press, 1922), pp. 6, 18–19; William M. Tuttle, Jr., *Race Riot: Chicago in the Red Summer of 1919* (New York: Atheneum, 1970), pp. 33–4, 40.
2. CCRR, *The Negro in Chicago*, pp. 6–7, 19–20, 31–2, 655–67; Tuttle, *Race Riot*, pp. 41, 46.
3. Of the injured, 342 were black and 195 were white. See Tuttle, *Race Riot*, p. 64.
4. *Report of the Riot Study Committee to the Honorable Richard J. Daley* (Chicago: City of Chicago, 1968), passim.
5. Ibid., pp. 5–20, 27, 36–8, 66.
6. Morris Janowitz, "Patterns of Collective Racial Violence," in Hugh Davis Graham and Ted Robert Gurr, eds., *Violence in America: Historical and Comparative Perspectives* (New York: New American Library, 1969), pp. 412–44; August Meier and Elliott Rudwick, "Black Violence in the 20th Century: A Study in Rhetoric and Retaliation," in ibid., pp. 399–412.
7. Janowitz, "Patterns of Collective Racial Violence," pp. 424–5.
8. Allan H. Spear, *Black Chicago: The Making of a Negro Ghetto, 1890–1920* (Chicago: University of Chicago Press, 1967), pp. 223–4; St. Clair Drake and Horace R. Cayton, *Black Metropolis: A Study of Negro Life in a Northern City*, 2 vols. (New York: Harcourt, Brace, 1945; reprint ed., New York: Harper & Row, Harper Torchbooks, 1962), 2:xvi.
9. David A. Wallace, "Residential Concentration of Negroes in Chicago" (Ph.D. dissertation, Harvard University, 1953), p. 64; Thomas L. Philpott, *The Slum and the Ghetto: Neighborhood Deterioration and Middle-Class Reform, Chicago, 1880–1930* (New York: Oxford University Press, 1978), pp. 119, 121, 130, 146.
10. Spear, *Black Chicago*, pp. 142, 146; CCRR, *The Negro in Chicago*, pp. 106–8; Otis Duncan and Beverly Duncan, *The Negro Population of Chicago* (Chicago: University of Chicago Press, 1957), p. 92; Wallace, "Residential Concentration of Negroes," p. 69, claims no new communities came into being between 1910 and 1920.
11. Duncan and Duncan, *The Negro Population*, pp. 95–6; Wallace, "Residential Concentration of Negroes," p. 111; Philpott, *The Slum and the Ghetto*, p. 121.
12. Duncan and Duncan, *The Negro Population*, pp. 95–7.
13. Drake and Cayton, *Black Metropolis*, 1:184–7; Frederick Burgess Lindstrom, "The Negro Invasion of the Washington Park Subdivision" (M.A. thesis, University of Chicago, 1941); Wallace, "Residential Concentration of Negroes," pp. 79–80.
14. Drake and Cayton, *Black Metropolis*, 1:174.
15. Wallace, "Residential Concentration of Negroes," pp. 85, 88, 148, 149n.
16. Spear, *Black Chicago*, pp. 223–4; Wallace, "Residential Concentration of Negroes," p. 113; Duncan and Duncan, *The Negro Population*, pp. 96–7; Chicago Commission on Human Relations (herefter cited as CHR), *Fourth Chicago Conference on Civic Unity: Abridged Report of Proceedings* (Chicago: CHR, 1952), p. 7.
17. Duncan and Duncan, *The Negro Population*, pp. 95–6.
18. The previously mentioned works of Spear and Philpott, which were both written in the aftermath of the 1960s riots, have clear implications for contemporary race relations but halt their analysis at 1930 – or earlier. The same is true for Gilbert Osofsky, "The Enduring Ghetto," *Journal of American History* 55 (September 1968): 243–55, and idem, *Harlem: The Making of a Ghetto; Negro New York, 1890–1930* (New York: Harper & Row, 1966); David M. Katzman, *Before the Ghetto: Black Detroit in the Nineteenth Century* (Urbana: University of Illinois Press, 1973); and Kenneth L. Kusmer, *A Ghetto Takes Shape: Black Cleveland, 1870–1930* (Urbana: University of Illinois Press, 1976).
19. Robert C. Weaver, *The Negro Ghetto* (New York: Harper & Row, 1948), pp. 275, 324, 369.
20. For the impact of white hostility on black residential patterns in Chicago, see Spear, *Black Chicago*, pp. 6–8, 20–3, 26, 201, 208–13, 219–21; Tuttle, *Race Riot*, pp. 157–83; CCRR, *The Negro in Chicago*, pp. 113–35; Drake and Cayton, *Black Metropolis*, 1:213–74; Philpott, *The Slum and the Ghetto*, pp. 146–200; Kusmer similarly emphas-

izes white hostility in restricting the choices of black Clevelanders; see his *A Ghetto Takes Shape*, pp. 46–7, 165, 167–70; see also Katzman, *Before the Ghetto*, pp. 69–80, and Osofsky, *Harlem*, pp. 46–52, 81. It also should be noted that Spear and Wallace feel that the blacks' weak economic position was relatively unimportant as a cause for their segregation. See Spear, *Black Chicago*, p. 26, and Wallace, "Residential Concentration of Negroes," p. 195.

21. Kenneth T. Jackson, "Race, Ethnicity, and Real Estate Appraisal: The Home Owners Loan Corporation and the Federal Housing Administration," *Journal of Urban History* 6 (August 1980): 419–52; Mark I. Gelfand, *A Nation of Cities: The Federal Government and Urban America, 1933–1965* (New York: Oxford University Press, 1975), p. 123.

22. *Chicago Defender*, October 26, 1940, has a special section devoted to the Ida B. Wells Homes. For the Cleveland experience, see Christopher G. Wye, "The New Deal and the Negro Community: Toward a Broader Conceptualization," *Journal of American History* 59 (December 1972): 621–39.

23. *Chicago Defender*, June 12, 1943; Horace R. Cayton and Harry J. Walker, Memorandum to Mr. Blandford and Mr. Divers, National Housing Agency, January 14, 1944; Metropolitan Housing [and Planning] Council (MHPC), Minutes of the Executive Committee Meeting, November 21, 1944, both in the Metropolitan Housing and Planning Council Papers (hereafter cited as MHPC Papers), Manuscript Collection, The Library, University of Illinois at Chicago (UIC). The Metropolitan Housing Council changed its name to the Metropolitan Housing and Planning Council in 1949. To avoid confusion, the amended name will be used throughout this study.

24. *Chicago Bee*, May 14, 1944; Eugene O. Shands to John Blandford, n.d.; Metropolitan Housing [and Planning] Council, Minutes of the Executive Committee Meeting, November 21, 1944; Metropolitan Housing [and Planning] Council, Minutes of the Regular Meeting of the Board of Governors, April 4, November 1, 1944; Ferd Kramer to Robert Taylor, May 19, June 2, 1944; Ferd Kramer to Louis Wirth, May 31, 1944; Robert R. Taylor to Ferd Kramer, May 24, 1944, all in the MHPC Papers.

25. Devereux Bowly, Jr., *The Poorhouse: Subsidized Housing in Chicago, 1895–1976* (Carbondale: Southern Illinois University Press, 1978), pp. 17–54, 221.

26. Philpott, *The Slum and the Ghetto*, pp. 209–27; 244–69; *Chicago Defender*, October 26, 1940.

27. For the willingness of Chicago Progressives to observe the color line, see Philpott, *The Slum and the Ghetto*, pp. 271–347.

28. Spear, *Black Chicago*, pp. 71–89; 91–126; 181–200.

29. Ibid., pp. 111–26; Milton Rakove, *Don't Make No Waves – Don't Back No Losers: An Insider's Analysis of the Daley Machine* (Bloomington: Indiana University Press, 1975), pp. 256–81; James Q. Wilson, *Negro Politics: The Search for Leadership* (New York: Free Press, 1960); Harold F. Gosnell, *Negro Politicians: The Rise of Negro Politics in Chicago* (Chicago: University of Chicago Press, 1935; reprint ed., 1967); Ira Katznelson, *Black Men, White Cities* (New York: Oxford University Press, 1973); Charles Branham, "Black Chicago: Accommodationist Politics Before the Great Migration," in Melvin G. Holli and Peter d'A. Jones, eds., *The Ethnic Frontier: Essays in the History of Group Survival in Chicago and the Midwest* (Grand Rapids, Mich.: Eerdmans, 1977), pp. 211–62.

Making a Way out of No Way: African American Women and the Second Great Migration

Lisa Krissoff Boehm

Source: Lisa Krissoff Boehm, *Making a Way out of No Way: African American Women and the Second Great Migration* (Jackson: University Press of Mississippi, 2009).

EDITORS' INTRODUCTION

This essay asks us to reconsider the history of the Second Great Migration by rethinking periodization and questions of gender. The First (1914–1930) and Second (1940–1970) Great Migrations brought approximately 6.5 million African Americans from the South to northern cities.[i] The migrations are often explained as the time in which African Americans gained access to industrial work, and thus at long last secured the types of salaries necessary to gain a foothold in the middle class. Yet the story is rarely told from the *female* migrant's perspective. While men migrated for a chance at finding industrial work, African American women were largely excluded from jobs at the major war factories, especially in the early years of World War II. The much lauded "Rosie the Riveter" figure was usually white. Thus the advent of war industry had less effect on the work lives of African American women than other workers of the time period. The women did not simply follow men northward; a regional migration was a monumental life change, and required considerable planning and decision making. Women numerically predominated among the migrants, and, while many moved due to the wishes of their husbands or male relatives, in other cases it was women themselves who led the migration to northern cities.[ii]

We see here the extensive use of oral histories that reveal a once obscured historical story. The voices of African American women migrants show up only intermittently in the historical record, and most often then in the context of strife, such as in court records. Oral history projects of African Americans, like oral history projects in general, began recording the voices of prominent citizens, overlooking lesser-known, more representative, individuals. Boehm demonstrates how powerful oral histories can be when used as historical evidence.[iii] She presents the voices of migrants in extended edited transcripts throughout her book, allowing the migrants to tell their own stories. In this essay, we encounter the edited transcript of migrant Ella Sims, a migrant from Mississippi who came to Michigan in 1946 and joined the cleaning staff of the C & O Railroad.

Although pockets of misunderstanding remain in academic circles, oral historians have proven that oral histories are no less reliable than other historical sources and

---

i The periodization of these two migrations are approximate, and a variety of dates are employed by scholars. This reflects the complexity of social movements in general. African Americans have experienced a great deal of mobility since the end of the Civil War. Some moved within the South, while others sought residence in the North, or even relocated to Africa.

ii Leslie Brown, "Sisters and Mothers Called to the City: African American Women and an Even Greater Migration," in Catherine Higgs, Barbara A. Moss, and Earline Rae Ferguson, eds., *Stepping Forward: Black Women in African and the Americas* (Athens, OH: Ohio University Press, 2002).

iii See "Oral History Evaluation Guidelines," at www.oralhistory.org/network/mw/index.php/Evaluation_Guide. Also available as a pamphlet from the Oral History Association.

indeed offer unique windows onto the past. Oral histories greatly expand our understanding of urban history. Indeed, the vagaries of personal memory, instead of presenting roadblocks to research, can provide compelling openings for analysis. Analyzing what is said, how it is said, and what goes unsaid, provides invaluable insight into the past. Such techniques are becoming known as the "history of memory."[iv]

Lisa Krissoff Boehm, co-editor of this volume, is a professor of urban studies and the director of the honors program at Worcester State College. In addition to *Making a Way out of No Way*, she is the author of *Popular Culture and the Enduring Myth of Chicago, 1871–1968* (New York: Routledge, 2004). She has been awarded oral history fellowships from the Baylor University Institute for Oral History and the Schlesinger Library, Radcliffe Institute of Advanced Study, at Harvard University. Krissoff Boehm served as the guest editor of the January 2010 volume of the *Journal of Urban History* dedicated to the teaching of urban history.

AFRICAN AMERICAN WOMEN AND THE SECOND GREAT MIGRATION

This essay showcases and analyzes recently collected oral histories with forty African American women, most of whom were born in the southern United States in the first part of the twentieth century and then migrated to northern cities in the movement known as the Second Great Migration, 1940–1970. The Second Great Migration brought approximately five million black migrants to northern cities, leaving these cities, and the migrants themselves, forever transformed. The essay presents an analysis of the life stories of women migrants, with a focus on their reasons for moving and their thoughts on how work shaped their lives. Although the First and Second Great Migrations have been the subject of a number of wonderful books, the woman migrant herself has rarely been placed in the foreground within these works. Analysis of the oral histories demonstrates how black women forged purposeful lives for themselves despite multifaceted pressures. As migrant Inez Smith said in characterizing her own mother, a talented businesswoman who supported her daughters by the efforts of her hard work, the women featured here "made a way out of no way."

Social historians seek to understand trends in American culture and lived experience. Yet it is difficult for scholars to truly comprehend a trend if the supporting documents have not yet made their way to the archives. Documentation regarding the Second Great Migration has not yet been assiduously collected. Oral histories with black women who were not famous are found in only a limited number of library collections. Thus, to better understand the way in which African American women viewed the migration, I went and asked them, tape recorder in hand. Many black migrants were born in rural parts of the South, while others began their lives in cities. Some transitioned from rural settings to southern cities before making the trek to the North. The North figured centrally in their dreams and hopes, yet the region rarely lived up to expectations.

To understand this migration, a movement in which women predominated, we are well served to consider individual stories. Examination of personal narratives proves particularly weighty when the narrators represent a people and a gender whose documents are underrepresented in the archives. Although millions made the choice to migrate, each individual migrant made the decision to uproot on her own, weighing

---

iv For more on the history of memory, see Jacques LeGoff, *History and Memory*, translated by Steven Randall and Elizabeth Claman (New York: Columbia University Press, 1992), John Bodnar, *Remaking America: Public Memory, Commemoration, and Patriotism in the Twentieth Century* (Princeton: Princeton University Press, 1993), Barbara Misztal, "Memory and Democracy, *American Behavioral Scientist*, 28 (June 2005): 1320–1338 and *Theories of Social Remembering* (Philadelphia: Open University Press, 2003), James Fentress and Chris Wickham, *Social Memory: New Perspectives on the Past* (Cambridge: Blackwell, 1992).

carefully what she knew of American social structures, pay scales, living conditions, and family concerns. Due to the limits society placed on African American women, the majority of the respondents in this study worked as domestic laborers during at least a portion of their work lives. A great many African American women undertook domestic work, and many used the work as a bridge to other fields or as an expedient measure between more desirable careers.

The Migration

Ella Sims

Grand Rapids, Michigan
Ella Sims and I met in her lovely, second-floor apartment in Grand Rapids, Michigan, on a warm summer day. It was Sims's leadership roles at the local Office of Economic Opportunity in the 1960s and in later years as an employee and trustee of Aquinas College, a local Catholic institution, that had garnered her great respect in the city.

Sims explored her motivations for moving to Michigan. Like many migrants, she came north on a vacation and stayed. She came to Grand Rapids for a short-term visit to her female cousin and was offered a job. Blue-collar jobs were relatively easy to locate and obtain.

Well, I was born in the South. My parents were sharecroppers—we grew cotton and corn. One of three girls, and I'm the middle girl. My daddy was a Baptist preacher. We moved a heck of a lot. Because they always say the preacher's always moving, and I think that was the truth. But I guess we had a normal childhood. We used to go and sing while my daddy preached.

When I went over to Arkansas and went to high school,[1] I married right out of high school in my senior year, when I was seventeen. I met him right there in high school; he was just a grade ahead of me, and I guess that's how come it was so easy to talk me into getting married.

I was married for three years before I got pregnant. I had a baby boy. And my baby lived to be ten months old and died very suddenly one night. Soon after that I got

pregnant again. So then my second son was born. And he was born the twenty-eighth day of September, and on Thanksgiving morning my husband woke up sick. So the baby was about two months old. And my husband was just sick five days, and he died.

When we went to bed that night, I woke up the next morning with him calling me, and he said, "Oh, I'm as sick as I could be." Now this is what's strange—from the moment when he said that until he died, he never had another pain. He was just very sick. Something had burst in his ear. We had a very hard time getting a doctor on Thanksgiving, and so I finally got a doctor out to the house, and he didn't tell me much, just to give him some pills. And so then our doctor, who was gone Thanksgiving, was back in town. My husband's uncle went to his house. You know, a little small town, everybody knows everybody.

I knew there was something very serious by the way the doctor put his tube in my husband's ear, and he wasn't saying anything. The doctor said these words to me, he said, "We're going to see if we can save his life. We're going to take him to the hospital right now, and we are going to start giving him this new drug [penicillin]." Now, after he died, the doctor put on the death certificate "abscess in the brain." And with my children, if somebody says they have an earache, I am scared to death.

I remember saying over and over, "I'm twenty-two years old and my life is over." By March, I was in such terrible shape. My doctor asked me if I had any relatives anywhere so I could just take a vacation. And that's how I came to Michigan. Incidentally, my cousins that had moved to Grand Rapids, Michigan, was the same cousins that I went to live with to go to high school in Arkansas.

I came for vacation. My cousin said, "Oh, why don't you stay for the summer?" I said, "Well, I think I will." She said, "I bet you could get hired at the Pantlind Hotel." And so, I got hired at the Pantlind Hotel. Back then, even if you went to General Motors, you could get hired the same day. I came here in March of 1946. My husband died December 1945. My baby was born September 1945.

And so, when I started working, I had to have a babysitter. A neighbor, she sat keeping the baby for me. And so one day she said to me, she was asking me if everything was okay, and I said, "Well, I don't know." I wasn't getting the check from Social Security then. She said, "They are hiring at the railroad." And she told me how to get out there on the bus. And I went out there and got hired! They hired me on the second-shift job, and they wanted me to come to work that night. And she still kept the baby, because she just stayed two doors from my cousin's. So I could pick the baby up—I didn't get off until eleven at night. I must've maybe worked out there for a year before I got on days. But she was a good friend and she kept the baby. After that I got an apartment away from my cousin, and I also met my future husband. I'd been there a year when I met him.[2]

Existing archival collections feature few stories of the Second Great Migration, and only rarely has the movement been considered from the female viewpoint in oral histories. Of the resources that exist, few could rival the specificity and wrenching emotion of Sims's memories. An examination of the broad array of reasons for African American women's migration expands our understanding of this key American movement. Sims's tale of her difficult southern life, including the frightening details of her first husband's illness, makes her need for a Michigan vacation clear. Her recollection of an almost accidental decision to remain in Grand Rapids bears noticing; so often major life moments "fall into place" as this regional shift does for Sims. Darlene Clark Hine, in her article "Black Migration to the Urban Midwest: The Gender Dimension, 1915–1945," argues that historians must focus much more effort on analyzing the story of the female migrant. She writes:

we need micro-studies into individual life, of neighborhoods, families, churches, and fraternal lodges in various cities. Examination of these themes makes imperative an even deeper penetration into the internal world of Afro-Americans. Perhaps, even more dauntingly, to answer fully these questions requires that the black woman's voice and experience be researched and interpreted with the same intensity and seriousness accorded that of the black man.

Information derived from statistical and demographic data on black midwestern migration and urbanization must be combined with the knowledge drawn from the small, but growing, numbers of oral histories, autobiographies, and biographies of twentieth century migrating women … Actually these sources, properly "squeezed and teased," promise to light up that inner world so long shrouded behind a veil of neglect, silence, and stereotype, and will quite likely force a rethinking and rewriting of all of black urban history.[3]

This study adds a somewhat overlooked element to the history of African American migration: analysis of women's personal reasons for the migration. Certain societal structures, including the economics of southern society, political disfranchisement, the raging, daily insults of a discrimination defended by law, and the threat and reality of violence—a violence for which few whites were ever punished—pushed families from their homes. Simultaneously, the pace of the northern industrial world and the culture of the northern cities pulled individuals to the bus depots, train stations, and highways. However influential such factors were for southern African Americans, every migration began with a very private and personal discussion. Although everyone follows trends, we do not choose to comprehend the great changes in our lives as defined by the grand structures or systems in place in society, but as our very own, very private history. Only the individual truly understands the interplay of factors contributing to the watershed moments in his or her life; oral history proves to be an excellent way of documenting what individuals know about these factors.

Historian Peter Gottlieb argues that frequent movement within the South became a critical means by which African American families negotiated the almost nonnegotiable economic structures there. Blacks had long considered changes in physical location as a reasonable, feasible means by which to better their lives. Migration out of the region followed a long-lived practice of moving within the region. Since the dawn of Reconstruction, African Americans had relocated. Gottlieb focuses on the First Great Migration, which began about the time World War I broke out in Europe. He writes, "Long experience in moving to jobs within their native regions gave southern blacks added traction as they began moving toward new job openings during the war."[4] For Gottlieb, the move north came as a result of a combination of the inequities of the South and the migrants' culture, which at times encouraged migration as a response to difficulties. Just generations ago, any movement whatsoever had been solely at the discretion of the slave owner. For black sharecroppers, moving to another farm brought the hope of a fairer share of the crop yield, a better accounting in the books kept at the plantation commissary, or more humane treatment by area whites. Migration to southern cities brought access to a broader array of jobs and the delights of urban life. And migration northward brought even wider job opportunities, access to the glittering entertainment venues of the cities, and the whispered promise, often unrealized, of a more just society. Unfortunately, the North had its own system of legalized and de facto discrimination and segregation. Recent scholarship has taken to calling this formalized system "northern Jim Crow."[5]

Family ties figured strongly in the moves. Some migrants moved primarily because of the decisions of male family members. In traditionally oriented families, male heads of households often had the most weight in decision making. Yet some husbands did follow their wives to the North. Although almost all the women of this study were part of tight-knit family units, the women consciously structured their economic choices and weighed their options regarding physical location—these women did not "end up" living in the North, but deftly negotiated the narrow labor market open to them as well as their migratory path. Few of the study's respondents claimed to be the very first family member to make the move,

however. Almost all followed siblings, cousins, husbands, or other relatives to their intermediate and final destinations. This "chain migration" brought the approximate six and a half million migrants north during the First and Second Great Migrations.

As shown in Ella Sims' history, some of the women came north without male guidance, following a female family member to the northern city. With historical hindsight, this appears to be quite revolutionary behavior. Fitting the definition of "women adrift," the term put forth by historian Joanne Meyerowitz to describe unchaperoned women in the city, the women made history by traveling unfettered by male bonds, but they did not envision their moves as atypical. Meyerowitz's term uses historical language to describe the women's lack of male supervision; she does not imply that these women were literally lost or adrift, and the oral testimony demonstrates that the migrants felt fairly secure traveling and relocating without men. Acting on their own seemed a reasonable solution and, in most instances, perfectly within the bounds of propriety for the era. Sims, for example, surely would have preferred to remain within a household with a male head, but her husband had died. The female-oriented chain migration resembles a female pattern for women immigrants, particularly the women of Ireland.[6]

Florence Allison, born in Livingston, Alabama, in 1926, represents those migrants who moved primarily due to the wishes of their husbands. Her husband, a marine who later worked at the Chrysler assembly plant in Detroit, led the way in this particular choice. Allison explained, "After being in the army he didn't want to be back in the country anymore so he decided to move."[7] Annie Benning, born in Georgia in 1911, came to River Rouge, Michigan, so her husband could work in the auto industry. Her husband's brother had already arrived. Benning remembered, "Well, he had a brother that lived here and his brother wanted him to come here and to work with him in the steel mill but he didn't like working in no mill. He come here and got him a job as a mechanic and that's where he stayed until he passed." Mr. Benning made a comfortable living in a garage of a car dealership. Benning continued, "He couldn't get no job working down there [in the South] and he wanted to come where he could make it. It didn't make no difference to me and he come to find him a job. I stayed home about three months and then I come to Michigan." Benning's husband also disliked the way black men were treated in the South. She said, "He did [face discrimination] when he was in the southern states, so that's when he come here, but he didn't have no trouble here." The Bennings proved typical in that the husband got settled in his position and established a living space for the couple before the wife made the move. Such systems also were typical of many immigrant groups coming to America in the early twentieth century. Like many African American men, Annie Benning's husband located a job quickly. Benning characterized her view of Detroit by saying, "It was real nice and you could get jobs. No job was too hard to find here."[8]

The majority of the respondents reported that their husbands had initiated the migration. The women did not express displeasure at the move, but in their patriarchal homes, the husband's plans dominated. Such male leadership is not unusual, even today. Because men still tend to earn higher salaries than their spouses, it proves reasonable for families to favor finding the most lucrative position possible for male workers. It remains highly unusual for families to relocate regionally for a female's job.

In the world of blues music, the oft-repeated tale told by migrant and blues vocalist Koko Taylor represents the sharp distinction between southern and northern pay rates, and the number of hopes and dreams bound up in the decision to migrate. Taylor, interviewed in 1993, recounted her future husband's announcement that he was heading to Chicago in 1953. Taylor refused to be left behind. Robert "Pops" Taylor landed a position at the Wilson Packing Company, a real achievement. Koko found work as a housekeeper for a Wilmette family, where she would earn $5.00 for an eight-hour day. In Tennessee, Taylor had had to care for white families for $1.50 a day, and sometimes just $3.00 a week. The couple was thrilled with their new city, yet they had arrived with very little in their pockets. Taylor said, "We rode from Memphis to Chicago with 35 cents in our pockets and a box of Ritz crackers."[9]

Faith Richmond boarded a train in North Carolina to go and live with her husband's family. Yet her family of origin warned her about the difficulty of living with in-laws. Richmond related, "He brought me up to Boston and [I] had to live with his family. I remember my aunt saying, if you must live with your in-laws, try very hard to get along."[10] Lillian Clark followed her husband to Detroit soon after he secured a job at Uniroyal. Her husband had followed his brother-in-law to Michigan. Clark's husband's joy at arriving in the Midwest has become a favorite family anecdote. Clark related, "When he got off the train, he was so excited he left the bags on the train."[11] Minnie Chatman depicted her migration story as a rather passive part of her life; in keeping with her husband's leadership position in the household, he made most of the decisions for the couple. His position at U.S. Rubber, far better than he could hope for in Mississippi, launched the family's migration. Chatman recalled, "He came first and he was working and then I stayed and later he sent for me." Chatman's husband had no desire to live in the South again. Chatman said, "He was looking around to see if we could find a place because he say we never going back there and he didn't go back there." Chatman remained in Michigan although her husband passed away about a decade after she arrived.[12]

Mattie Bell Fritz moved to the North immediately after she married, motivated by her husband's wishes. Fritz, born in Montgomery, Alabama, in 1927, married Andrew Fritz shortly before he headed off to the army. Fritz admits, "I got married on a Sunday and left [the South] on a Monday. He [Andrew Fritz] is originally from Pittsburgh, but his family was in Alabama so they moved back and then he moved here [Detroit] and he went into the army from here." Her father balked at the sudden wedding and move. At just eighteen and a recent high school graduate, Mattie Bell married in the recreation center near her home. She recalled, "I told my dad, he say, 'But baby, why do you want to get married so early?' I said, 'He swept me off my feet.'" Mattie Bell settled in near her husband's cousins in Ecorse, Michigan, outside of Detroit, and visited the cousins often. She entered into her husband's tight-knit family.[13]

Liddie Williams came to Chicago from Mississippi in 1954; she was just seventeen years old. Newly married, Williams accompanied her mother-in-law to the big city; Williams's husband had already relocated. Perhaps because of her young age at the time, she found the migration difficult. She said, "It was pretty hard. My mother was in the South. A couple of years later, she came here." Williams also revealed that her stepfather's behavior contributed to her desire to move north. She intimated, "I had kind of [a] mean stepfather, that's why I wanted to leave, but I hated to leave my mother." Many years earlier, Williams's parents' divorce had come as a direct result of her father's move to Chicago. She explained, "Her and my father, the reason they separated, it wasn't that they didn't get along, he wanted to come to Chicago and she wouldn't come with him. So they separated." Williams's story demonstrates that a wife's relocation was not a foregone conclusion; all married women did not dutifully follow their spouses. The married women also weighed the consequences, and determined if the migration fit their own needs as well as their husband's.

Of the migrants who admitted to misgivings, homesickness for family members played a significant role.[14] Rosa Young, who followed her father to Michigan from Mississippi in 1944 (she was about seventeen), recalled sadness over leaving her small town. Young's father came to Grand Rapids to attend his son's wedding, and found work in a railroad yard during his vacation. Young mused, "I was glad, I guess I was glad to come, but I hated to leave my home, you know, my homeland, Holly Springs, because that was really tough for me, you know."[15]

Esther Woods presented the decision to migrate as her own, but also cited her brother's need for help with his nieces and nephews, who lived with him in Grand Rapids. Woods's sister had entered the state hospital, leaving the children without a parent to care for them. One of the nieces ended up living with Woods for much of her childhood. Woods admitted, "And I came here—frankly that's why I came here—to help him with those kids." Yet this pressing need only provided the catalyst for the move. Woods believed the migration to be her only reasonable option for a solid economic future. Note that her language points to a return to the South constituting more than a visit; her relocation did not occur all at once. "I wouldn't have stayed there," she said bluntly, "because there was nothing there to do. I worked in York, Alabama, which was about eight miles from my home, before I ever left there *the first time*. But it is a small town—wasn't very much work there for me any longer, so I figured it was time for me to move on for something better." Members of Woods's family migrated to many cities, including Los Angeles, Toledo, Detroit, and New York City. Her personal inclination to move was in keeping with the decisions made by the rest of her family, yet she came to her decision over a matter of years and with considerable personal reflection.[16]

It is important to highlight the significant minority of the respondents who followed other women to northern cities. Annie Evelyn Collins of Detroit migrated due to female ties. Like Sims and other migrants, Collins meant to come to Michigan for a visit, yet she stayed permanently. She joked a little about the casual beginning of this major life change. Economics greatly influenced her decision. Collins sought to keep a female relative company. Collins's mother proffered important advice. In the passage below, Collins worked through a degree of incredulity at the way in which small choices end up affecting people's lives in major ways. Her words attest to a degree of ambivalence about the migration. She clearly had not worked through her ideas on the migration fully, and perhaps had not been asked about it for some time. Collins explained at length:

My sister was here and my mother [felt] that she shouldn't be by herself. She had two sisters in Kentucky and one sister in Cincinnati and she [her mother] told me to come to Detroit so this sister wouldn't be here by herself. I come to stay two weeks and then have fifty years. Ain't that terrible. Now, ain't that terrible. Come to spend two weeks and then get fifty-three years. Fifty-three years, now that's terrible, ain't it. No, that's good, I like living here.

Well, coming here you had better ways of living and making money. The houses was different and the money was different and it was different than the South, even though it wasn't all bad living in the South. There is more money in Michigan, you know. I didn't work that much, but I had more chance to work.[17]

Mary Smith also relied on a network of female relatives to help her decide where to live. Smith, born in 1938 in Sylvester (Worth County), Georgia, moved to find better-paying work. Her quest led her on a circuitous journey—to New York City, back to Georgia, back to New York, on to Miami, Florida, back to Georgia, and finally to Boston. Childbearing also played a part in helping Smith choose her location, because she returned to Georgia to give birth to her babies in a familiar location. The children all stayed with her mother in Georgia for most of their lives. An aunt and a sister had found work in Miami before she arrived. Smith said of her job hunt, "The jobs were very easy to find. All you do is get the paper and you call, and you go for an interview, and most of the time, you know, they hire you." Smith lived in a female-centered world. Although she mentioned off-handedly that she had married, she raised all of her three children with only her mother's assistance, and seemed to provide the sole economic support for her family. Smith made her way to Boston, where she ran a day care center out of her three-decker home. The three decker, a common housing type in New England, consists of three separate apartments, arranged one per floor. Smith owned the building, and she resided on the top floor, where she also located the day care. Smith came to Boston at her sister's urging. Smith said straightforwardly, "She sent for me and I came here."[18]

Work also led Rebecca Strom from Alabama to Boston. Strom, born in 1944, stood out as the only respondent not to mention another relative blazing the trail north ahead of her. She did not remember how she heard of the option of working in Boston, guessing only that someone she knew had probably made the trip. Strom also remained one of the few respondents, joining Mary Smith, Anniese Moten, and a handful of others, who labored as a live-in domestic. Most domestics had abandoned live-in work for day work by this time. The fight for the right to live out had been undertaken by an earlier generation of domestic workers, such as the Washington, D.C., workers chronicled by historian Elizabeth Clark-Lewis.[19] As with any social practice, however, change came incrementally. Not all employers allowed workers this advantage, and some women did not desire this option. For a very young woman like Strom, rent for an apartment would have proved prohibitive at this stage of her career. Strom stated, "Well, see there was not a lot of work there [in Alabama], and we heard about working for families that would pay for you to come here. So, you would work for them to pay them back, and then you would have your regular money." The systematized approach to migration mentioned here allowed Strom to move without even having to come up with travel fare. Working to pay off travel costs echoes the technique employed by many immigrants from abroad, who had employers advance the cost of their ship fare. Strom's reference to "we" in the above excerpt indicates her understanding of the great flow of migrants she joined by heading to the North. Strom remembered, "They met you at the bus station and you went to their home. That was our home till I met some other people who told me about Freedom House on Crawford Street, and how you got a regular job outside of living in with a family." (Freedom House, a social service agency run by social workers Otto and Muriel Snowden, drew together the white and black residents of its Dorchester neighborhood in Boston.)[20] All of Strom's siblings left Alabama, leaving her parents behind. Strom felt that she would have eventually located work or entered college if she had remained in her home state. Boston brought her alternative work and an alternative future, but relocation to the city was not the only option open to her. By the time she left, in the last decade of the Second Great Migration, the South was, according to her, a region with some economic opportunities. Like Mary Smith, Strom made a living at the time of the interview by operating a home day care.[21]

Migrants could move back and forth between regions, taking jobs in the North for a time, yet returning to family and friends in the South for several years or more. African American migrants undertook this form of "shuttle migration" to a lesser extent than the white, southern migrants detailed in Chad Berry's excellent study, *Southern Migrants, Northern Exiles*. Most African American migrants did not carry quite the case of "divided heart" that the white migrants did. White migrants considered the South home, but needed the heavier pay packets to be found in northern industry. African American migrants' searing memories of southern Jim Crow restrictions somewhat tempered any warm feelings for their home states. Despite some of the pleasant childhood memories held by the migrants, many believed strongly that the North offered them the possibility of a more just society along with the higher pay.[22]

Yet, the study respondents did report some cases of shuttle migration that mirrored that of the white southern migrants. Not only did Dean move between a number of cities and towns around the United States, but her relocation was motivated by her desire to further her education and career. Dean, a domestic worker turned hair stylist born in Mississippi in 1928, moved frequently between South and North. She characterized the moves as fitting her own needs, rather than complying with the wishes of a male family member. Dean related her convoluted path: "I worked in Alabama and had a [beauty] shop. I lived in Alabama and moved to Inkster [Michigan]. I moved back to Alabama and stayed seven years. My big girl was born in Alabama. I went to Nashville and got another diploma. I wanted to bob hair and I didn't know how. Then I moved back to Michigan and married my sweetheart in 1955. I have been here ever since."[23]

Beatrice Jackson moved to Michigan to join her family, and, unusually, her fiancé followed her to their new home. Jackson traveled to Michigan to live near her brother and his family. Years before, she had joined her sister in Tulsa. The sister needed her help because her husband had entered a sanitarium; during Jackson's years in Tulsa, she worked as a domestic and earned a college degree in elementary teaching, which she never utilized directly in her employment. Jackson did not think highly of the Motor City. "The summer of 1941," Jackson said in her low, tired voice, "I went to Detroit and my husband-to-be followed me. My brother was in Detroit. He didn't have a job at that time. His wife didn't have a job. They had two kids—I was disgusted with Detroit."[24]

Jerliene "Creamy" McKinney followed a female family member northward, and also drew her boyfriend along with her. McKinney, born in Alabama in 1940, followed her sister to New York City. Anticipating her move, McKinney's boyfriend (and later husband), Theodosis, moved to the Bronx. McKinney detailed, "My sister moved from Florida to New York because she used to do jobs of living in with peoples, doing housekeeping and stuff like that. So she moved from Florida to New York, and when I got old enough, I kept asking my mom, 'Can I come to stay with her for a while?' So, when I got older, my mom let me come up to New York to stay with her." After about four years, Creamy and Theodosis married, and had four children in New York. "Then the peoples that she was living there with moved here [to Massachusetts]," McKinney explained, "and they wanted my husband and her husband to come to live with them here." Both husbands found jobs at Boston's airport, while Creamy and her sister worked for the family. Eventually McKinney moved her family to Worcester, Massachusetts, and her sister followed.[25]

The interviewees who shared their memories for this study add considerably to our understanding of the Second Great Migration. Although many did move north at the behest of their husbands or other male relatives, their stories reveal important facts about the men's roles as family leaders and the women's views of themselves. In the twenty-first century, it remains highly unusual for women to initiate cross-country migrations for their families. In the mid-twentieth century, it would have been atypical for families to travel hundreds of miles solely to pursue better-paying work for the females of the family. Black women made more money in the North than the South, but they largely remained in domestic positions until the last decades of the twentieth century.

Stories like that of Creamy McKinney and Beatrice Jackson, however, document that some men did follow their girlfriends and wives northward. McKinney and Jackson, both exceedingly motivated, knew the region would improve their economic security. Their male counterparts refused to be left behind. Other women, including Mary Smith and Rebecca Strom, came north without any male companion at all. Smith would remain the sole breadwinner for her family, and Strom would meet her husband only after settling permanently in Boston. Some women, like Liddie Williams's mother, divorced their husbands rather than follow them to the North.

Viewing the Great Migration through a feminine lens upsets our previous understanding of what was arguably the most historically important movement of people in the United States before the present era. Although millions relocated, the decision to do so stemmed from highly personal life choices. Each family struggled, sometimes for decades, over where to best make a life. And for many families, the decision to head north was never truly conceived of as permanent. In the late twentieth and early twenty-first centuries, hundreds of thousands of African Americans have been migrating to the South. Many are the children and grandchildren of migrants. Migrants themselves have returned to their region of origin. In this period, African American college graduates are more likely to settle in the South than the North after graduation. The vast majority of the new migrants settle in the southern suburbs.[26] The South draws new residents of all races with its job opportunities and sunny weather. Interestingly, many of the African Americans flowing south to follow their dreams envision the move as a "return" rather than a simple migration. The South still figures as an actual or metaphorical homeland for a significant number of African American families.

NOTES

1. Ella Sims's father sent his children to board with relatives in Helena, Arkansas, to attend school, there being no high school for black children in their Mississippi town.
2. Ella Sims, interview with Lisa Krissoff Boehm, Grand Rapids, Michigan, July 2, 2002.
3. Darlene Clark Hine, "Black Migration to the Urban Midwest: The Gender Dimension, 1915–1945," in Joe William Trotter, Jr., ed., *The Great Migration in Historical Perspective: New Dimensions of Race, Class, and Gender* (Bloomington: Indiana University Press, 1991), 129.
4. Peter Gottlieb, "Rethinking the Great Migration: A Perspective from Pittsburgh," in Trotter, Jr., ed., *The Great Migration in Historical Perspective*, 71.
5. See Davison M. Douglas, *Jim Crow Moves North: The Battle over Northern School Segregation, 1865–1954* (New York: Cambridge University Press, 2005).
6. Suellen Hoy, *Good Hearts: Catholic Sisters in Chicago's Past* (Urbana: University of Illinois Press, 2006), 12, 20, 30–31.
7. Florence Allison, interview with Elizabeth Cote, Detroit, Michigan, July 31, 2002.
8. Annie Benning, interview with Lisa Krissoff Boehm and Elizabeth Cote, Detroit, Michigan, June 26, 2002.
9. Katherine Aldin, "Koko Taylor: Down in the Bottom of that Chitlin' Bucket," *Living Blues* (July/August 1993), 13.
10. Faith Richmond (pseudonym), interview with Lisa Krissoff Boehm and Patricia Burke, Boston, Massachusetts, October 3, 2002.
11. Lillian Clark, interview with Lisa Krissoff Boehm and Elizabeth Cote, Southfield, Michigan, January 2, 2003.
12. Minnie Chatman, interview with Lisa Krissoff Boehm and Elizabeth Cote, Detroit, Michigan, October 19, 2001.
13. Mattie Bell Fritz, interview with Lisa Krissoff Boehm and Elizabeth Cote, Detroit, Michigan, August 4, 2001.

14. Liddie Williams, interview with Lisa Krissoff Boehm, Chicago, Illinois, November 16, 2001.

15. Rosetta "Rosa" Lewis Young, interview with Lisa Krissoff Boehm, Grand Rapids, Michigan, January 4, 2003.

16. Esther Woods, interview with Lisa Krissoff Boehm, Grand Rapids, Michigan, June 10, 2000. Statistics for York, Alabama, in 2005 found median household income in this town of less than three thousand people to be close to nineteen thousand dollars. The town was 78.3 percent African American. See www.citydata.com.

17. Annie Evelyn Collins, interview with Elizabeth Cote, Detroit, Michigan, January 11, 2003.

18. Mary Smith, interview with Lisa Krissoff Boehm, Audrey Kemp, and Patricia Burke, Boston, Massachusetts, October 12, 2002.

19. Elizabeth Clark-Lewis, *Living In, Living Out: African American Domestics and the Great Migration* (New York: Kodansha American, 1994), 124–146.

20. For more on Freedom House, see www.freedomhouse.com.

21. Rebecca Strom, interview with Lisa Krissoff Boehm, Audrey Kemp, and Patricia Burke, November 12, 2002.

22. Chad Berry, *Southern Migrants, Northern Exiles* (Urbana: University of Illinois Press, 2000), 21.

23. Avezinner Dean, interview with Lisa Krissoff Boehm and Elizabeth Cote, Detroit, Michigan, June 25, 2002.

24. Beatrice Jackson, interview with Lisa Krissoff Boehm and Elizabeth Cote, June 23, 2002.

25. Jerliene "Creamy" McKinney, interview with Lisa Krissoff Boehm, Worcester, Massachusetts, January 9, 2003.

26. Roderick J. Harrison, "The Great Migration South," *New Crisis* (July/August 2001): 20; William H. Frey, *The New Great Migration: Black Americans' Return to the South, 1965–2000*, Center on Urban and Metropolitan Policy, Brookings Institution, May 2004.

The Great White Migration, 1945–1960

Chad Berry

Source: *Southern Migrants, Northern Exiles*
(Urbana: University of Illinois Press, 2000).

EDITORS' INTRODUCTION

In his book, historian Chad Berry offers an extended study of the white migration from the southern United States to the North. Heretofore, this migration of white southerners, which reached its peak in the 1950s, had been largely overlooked. Declining opportunities for small farmers and the precarious position of coal mining sent many upland southerners towards northern cities. As historian James N. Gregory demonstrates in his important book, *The Southern Diaspora: How the Great Migrations of Black and White Southerners Transformed America* (Chapel Hill: University of North Carolina Press, 2005), we cannot truly understand the history of the twentieth century without a careful accounting for these massive movements of people. More than twenty-eight million people from the South left their homes during the twentieth century. The numbers of whites flowing out of the South each decade dwarfed the numbers of black migrants, although the black migrants were more evident to the long-term residents of the receiving cities. Still, searing anti-southern attitudes were directed towards the white newcomers, who were branded with the term "hillbillies" (although, as Berry warns us, not all were from Appalachia).[i] **[See Document 8.4 Harriette Arnow, *The Dollmaker* (1954).]** The newcomers faced hiring discrimination and found themselves relegated to certain neighborhoods. So many southerners transplanted themselves in the West and North that these regions were transformed culturally. Berry's edited collection, *The Hay Loft Gang: The Story of the National Barn Dance* (Urbana: University of Illinois Press, 2008) tells the story of how the largest city in the Midwest, Chicago, served as an early home of country music, with its nationally broadcast National Barn Dance. The National Barn Dance even preceded Nashville's Grand Ole Opry, for which the midwestern program served as a model.[ii]

Certainly white southerners had a different connection with their homeland than black southerners. Berry argues that the migrants had "divided hearts," for they missed the land of their childhood and came almost entirely for economic reasons. They relocated out of dire need, however, thus Berry terms them exiles. Yet he also finds evidence of "shuttle migration," frequent movements between the South and North, with some families migrating back home each year between April and October for the planting season. African Americans had a host of reasons for leaving the South, including the restrictions of Jim Crow, rampant violence, mechanization of farming, and disenfranchisement. As Lisa Krissoff Boehm has shown in *Making a Way out of No Way: African American Women and the Second Great Migration* (Jackson: University Press of Mississippi, 2009) **[see Krissoff Boehm essay in this part]**, black women revealed a closer connection with their southern homes than is usually acknowledged and were at times also shuttle migrants. The fact that white and black southern migration occurred simultaneously had

---

i   Chad Berry, *Southern Migrants, Northern Exiles* (Urbana: University of Illinois Press, 2000), 104, 110.
ii James N. Gregory, *The Southern Diaspora: How the Great Migrations of Black and White Southerners Transformed America* (Chapel Hill: University of North Carolina Press), 15, 19.

some negative repercussions for black migrants, who found southern racial prejudice (as well as the northern variety), in cities like Detroit.

White southern migration also has connections with the movements of Hispanic and Caribbean peoples, for, like Mexican immigrant farm workers, southern whites segued from harvesting crops in locations like southeastern Michigan to becoming permanent residents. Some of these migrants went on to work for corporations in the area—such as, Berry documents, the Whirlpool plant in Benton Harbor, Michigan—and settled permanently. Likewise, seasonal Mexican workers, formerly just passing through, came to make their homes in small cities like Holland, Michigan, taking on industrial jobs in the Heinz pickle factory and the Haworth office furniture plant, and forever changing the demographics of this once predominantly Dutch settlement. Berry concludes that the new group of southern, white industrial workers was much more open to union activism than has previously been assumed.[iii]

Relying on sixty oral histories and extensive archival research, Berry provides a compelling new way to view the southern migration. His book puts the start of significant migration at the beginning of the twentieth century, quite a bit earlier than other scholars. The work also confronts stereotypes regarding southerners. Berry considers anew the success rate of southern white transplants, who were considered ill-fit for northern urban life. He demonstrates that the southerners adapted to their new homes far more successfully than anti-southern, contemporaneous observers reported.

Chad Berry is the Goode Professor of Appalachian Studies and Coordinator of Appalachian Studies at Berea College, as well as an associate professor of history. Berry is the author of *Southern Migrants, Northern Exiles* (Urbana: University of Illinois Press, 2000), and the editor of and contributor to *The Hay Loft Gang: The Story of the National Barn Dance* (Urbana: University of Illinois Press, 2008). Before coming to Berea, Berry taught for eleven years at Maryville College. Berry is at work on a project examining the development of Appalachian Studies after World War II.

THE GREAT WHITE MIGRATION, 1945–60

IN THE LATE 1940s, Knott County, Kentucky, had a peculiar problem. The county, with plenty of youngsters around, was having a hard time finding teachers to staff its schools. Simeon Fields was only seventeen years old when he "took one of these schools on the emergency basis." As Fields explained, "There were about six schools in the county that were not able to get on their way because they had no teachers. These were the days when young seventeen- and eighteen-year-old boys were finishing high school and buying a coal truck, and some were going to Detroit and Cleveland and Cincinnati—the great out migration was in full swing, 1947, '8, and '9."[1]

By the mid-1950s, nearly three thousand people born in Cocke County, Tennessee, deep in the Smoky Mountains, had settled in Cleveland, Ohio. Jack Shepherd, who edited the county's *Plain Talk-Tribune*, published in Newport, Tennessee, said that he had more than four hundred subscribers who were living in Cleveland who "pass the paper around for other Cocke families up there." One Lorain Avenue furniture store in Cleveland ran advertisements in the Tennessee paper simply to reach migrants in Ohio. "Cleveland," said Cocke County Judge Benton Giles, "gets more people from Cocke County than any other city, but Detroit runs a close second." Alluding to the divided heart of the exiles, he declared, "They'd all rather stay here if they had jobs. I have a nephew who is happier here making half the money he made in Cleveland. They don't like living in a big city." Between 1940 and 1960, the 201 counties of the Tennessee Valley region lost more than 1.3 million people to migration. Out-migration had become such a problem in the state by the

iii Berry, *Southern Migrants, Northern Exiles*, 108.

mid-1950s that Tennessee proclaimed the annual loss of ten thousand young people its number-one social problem.[2]

These are but two examples of the great white migration that resumed with unprecedented force after World War II. As the northern economy was booming, pockets of the southern economy, particularly mining, were as depressed as ever, and out-migration began again, reaching a peak during the 1950s. In the urban Midwest, industry was beckoning southerners northward, and southerners were arriving by the bus load. The Brooks Bus Line, for example—only one of a number of small bus lines that serviced people moving between the North and South—made daily round-trips between Detroit and Paducah, Mayfield, and Fulton, in western Kentucky. Since for many years throughout the South, particularly in depressed regions, what occurred outside determined whether, in the sociologist James S. Brown's words, "there will be a great or a greater movement out," southern whites responded to the calls in droves. In the late 1940s, Brown had studied the Beech Creek community in Clay County, Kentucky, for his doctoral dissertation. In 1961, Brown returned to Beech Creek, which had become something of the Middle-town of southern Appalachia, to reinterview residents and was stunned by the extent of migration: more than half had relocated outside Appalachia, and of these, almost two-thirds had moved to southern Ohio and the rest elsewhere in Ohio and Indiana. "You are just thunderstruck," he said, "by how many people have left that part of the country. There are many more people … that I knew 15 years ago on Beech Creek in Clay County now in South Lebanon, Ohio, than there are on Beech Creek itself today." When he asked Beech Creek members whether they would want their children to stay in the community or move away, the answer was "*outside* for more *opportunity*."[3]

The period of upland southern out-migration between 1945 and 1960—one of the largest internal migrations in the history of the United States—has four important characteristics. First, although the migration has been portrayed as a hegira from the hills, in reality people from throughout the Upland South left the region for the Midwest between 1945 and 1960. It is incorrect, in short, to speak of this migration as exclusively "Appalachian." Second, census data show the extraordinary numbers involved in what previous scholars have called the "invisible minority" of migrants in the Midwest. Considering such stunning numbers, one wonders how such a horde of people could remain invisible. Third, kinship determinism often characterized this migration. People from the Appalachian Mountains, for example, have long been (mis)understood as being too cemented to kindred relationships to search out a better place to live. Those who migrated disproved this view often by making sure that kin came along with them. Finally, even during this period, upland southerners were beginning to find economic success, again debunking the idea that those who did leave the South remained mired in poverty in the Midwest.

Cheap Labor to Sustain the Boom

Economically, of course, one of the most important results of massive southern white out-migration was that the biggest economic boom in U.S. history was sustained, in part, by the sweat, muscles, and backs of southern migrants, many of them young, thus ensuring years of labor for their employers. The boom in the economy and the subsequent need for cheap labor were the primary reasons the "migrant problem" ceased after World War II. Indeed, a personnel manager for the Randall Company in Cincinnati, which employed about eight hundred people, more than half of whom were migrants, said that "they're proving they can be adaptable and can be a worthwhile addition to the community and to labor." "Industry," he summed, is "better off with them." Journalists in several cities began writing series on southern migration that actually attempted to revise commonly held stereotypes about southerners. By the 1960s, for example, a survey of hourly workers in Columbus, Ohio, discovered that a third were from "Appalachia" and that almost half of these workers had been at their current jobs for more than six years; two-thirds of those from the South had lived in Columbus longer than ten years. Others estimated that for Ohio as a whole, one in three workers had been born in southern Appalachian counties.[4]

The demand for workers in the Midwest strengthened the migration between the North and the South. When times were good, the flow of people went northward, and when times were bad, the flow often reversed, as it had in the Great Depression; the needle that indicated northerly or southerly flows of people was very sensitive. Take, for example, Harlan County, Kentucky, and Detroit. In the 1950s, the county was losing as many as one thousand people annually; the majority, it seemed, were headed to Detroit, since a bus line ran daily departures for Detroit. In the recession of 1957–58, however, the northward flow of people reversed, as laid-off autoworking southerners assumed they could make a better living in the South. Requests for surplus food, for example, in Black Mountain, near Harlan, soared by 30 percent the month after auto industry layoffs in 1957. A report in Chicago, too, noted:

> Former coal miners and farmers from the South are the most visible evidence of shuttle migration: when jobs are available in Chicago, the streets of the Uptown area are lined with cars bearing licenses from Kentucky, Tennessee, West Virginia, Alabama, etc. Conversely, when jobs are very limited, the roads in these home states are filled with cars carrying Illinois, Indiana, and Michigan licenses. Nothing has yet improved the job situation at home, so the southern whites continue to move restlessly from town to town and home again.[5]

In 1950, a West Virginian traveled to Chicago to find work, thinking he would return once he saved up some money or if conditions back home improved. When things in West Virginia began to look promising, he quickly returned. His sojourning continued for ten years, until September 1960, when he moved his family permanently to Chicago, realizing that things would never again look promising in West Virginia. While many southerners made return trips to avoid harsh winters, especially during winter slowdowns, others from rural areas returned in April to plant a crop and then came north in October once the harvest was in. In Chicago's Uptown in the 1950s, for example, school attendance among migrant children was highest in November and lowest in April.[6]

Hundreds of white migrants flocked to both agricultural and industrial areas to fuel the economy. Southwestern Michigan, south-central and east-central Indiana, and western Ohio continued to see large numbers of white farm migrants, though by the 1950s farm owners began looking farther south to Texas and Mexico for their labor needs, particularly in Ohio, where Kentuckians who struck the Scioto Marsh's onion fields in the 1930s had left a pungent memory among landowners. Many migrants who began as agricultural workers, of course, moved into factory work.[7]

Take, for example, the case of Adolph Lacy, who grew up in Cleburne County, in north-central Arkansas, the child of farmers. In 1942, Adolph, his three siblings, his parents, Clarence Lackey, Gyle Lacy, and Luther Vance and his wife piled in a pickup truck "like a bunch of cattle" and traveled to Milburg, Michigan, in Berrien County, to harvest fruit. The families returned to Arkansas after the harvest and used the money earned to send their children to school. "Michigan farmers loved to hire southern people," Adolph explained, "because they would work." Each of his family members was paid fifteen cents an hour. Just after World War II, he said, large numbers of Arkansans migrated northward because all there was to do in Arkansas was farm or work in timber, and by the end of the war most of the timber had been cut. In Berrien County, they worked for Wesley Miller picking cherries, apples, strawberries, and peaches and planting tomatoes. They were housed in little "huts", chicken coops and cow pens were common homes for the migrants. Initially, migrants were happy to harvest fruit, but the Whirlpool Corporation's giant plant in nearby Benton Harbor became the employment dream of many migrant pickers. Whirlpool, Adolph said, would "rather hire a southerner than their own. The only problem they had is most of the time they'd get a little money in their pocket and they'd want to go back south."[8]

On August 21, 1949, Adolph, now married with two children, left Cleburne County for Benton Harbor with a friend. "This is the God's truth: When I left Arkansas," he said, "I had thirty-seven dollars and a half in my pocket. I had two pairs of blue overalls, two blue denim shirts, and my underwear—the wife had made them out of V.C. fertilizer sacks. It had the V.C. still on the hip back there." It took them two days to get to Michigan. Once they arrived, Adolph and his friend stayed in a chicken house near his parents, who had been there since the early summer picking fruit. By the end of the first week, he had a job working the night shift at Kaywood Corporation in Benton Harbor making venetian blinds for $1.04 an hour. It was Adolph's first factory job. During the day, he picked fruit for 75 cents an hour. Even with his parents nearby, he said, "I got so homesick I thought I couldn't stay there. But I didn't have no other choice." In October, his wife, Jemae, arrived with their children. She had come with her brother, who was moving to Mishawaka, Indiana, about forty miles south, to do carpentry work. She also longed for home, but not nearly as badly as Adolph. They were living in a furnished three-room apartment in adjacent St. Joseph for seven dollars a week and were able to laugh about their northern "home" when interviewed. In January, Adolph was laid off, but he found a job in St. Joseph at Leeco Platers. After four consecutive days of nosebleeds, he quit and found a job at Auto Specialists, pouring crankshafts for $1.25 an hour. "Of course, they had piece work there," he said:

> They were pouring crankshafts then. They'd make four at a time. And them guys there on them core machines, it was piece work. And I asked somebody about them coremakers if they made any money. They said, Yeah. They was making a hundred bucks a week. And I said, "Boy, that's for me!" And the foreman happened to hear me, and that's all he wanted to hear, you know. The next day I went in and he said, "How would you like to have one of

them machines over there?" And I said, "Man, you're looking at the guy that would like to have one of them." And I went to work on that thing and I'll tell you what: I'm no coremaker. I'd work myself to death. I'd get up in the morning and my hand—I had a pound-and-a-half hammer; you had to beat that machine to pack that thing. She'd have to soak my hand in hot salt water to get it back where I could use it the next day. And I think the most I ever made was fifty-eight dollars a week.

Frustrated, Adolph went to Whirlpool in Benton Harbor to complete an application, and on April 8, 1950, he went to work, much more comfortable around the many southern transplants working there. "It was full of them," he said, most of whom had gone first to pick fruit and ended up in a factory job.[9]

Elements of associational life often eased the adjustments of the exiles. One of the strongest examples was union activity. As more southerners migrated, they filled the ranks of union rolls, duping industrialists, many of whom looked favorably upon southern whites because they were thought to be "independent" enough to resist unionization. Few migrants became labor radicals; most seem to have been typical postwar bread-and-butter unionists, eager primarily to gain higher wages and more benefits. Southern migrants were not only active rank and filers but also leaders, again not so much because they were radicals but because they were willing to answer the call of fellow workers. Earl Cox was active at TRW, Daymon Morgan in the UAW at Chrysler, Joe Clardy was a union steward at Studebaker, as was Adolph Lacy at Whirlpool, while Grady Roberson, who began work at Dodge Brothers in Mishawaka in 1959 as a lathe operator, soon became the shopwide set-up man. Eventually, he was elected president of the Steelworkers' local there, though he emphasized modestly that it was others in the plant who forced him into becoming a steward and then ultimately voted him president. John Weatherford also worked at Dodge during the Korean War but says he was never greatly involved with the union because of the "family" atmosphere at

Dodge—a feeling of separation between management and labor did not exist, according to him. In 1952, he went to Bendix, and six years later was asked to run for steward. Although also nominated without wanting the job, he won and remained in the position for eleven years, at which time he was "talked into" running for the bargaining committee. Since that time, he has served the UAW as committee member, vice-president, and most recently as president. Clardy, Roberson, and Weatherford pointed out that it was others in the plant (including natives and ethnics) who pushed them into union leadership, mostly because of their social qualities, not their militancy. Roberson and Weatherford, for example, said they socialized with everyone after arriving in the North. Weatherford maintained that his base was much larger than southern whites; native whites, Poles, Hungarians, and African Americans often voted for him more often than southerners did.[10]

My research reveals little of the coolness toward unions that previous scholars have ascribed to migrants. Roscoe Giffin and William W. Philliber, for example, maintain that southern newcomers were not active in unions because of their independence. The sociologist Harry Schwarzweller writes that "Appalachian people just aren't good joiners," feeling "uncomfortable in formal gatherings, and their participation in union activities is in most cases minimal. A general behavioral apathy prevails." He continues:

> Participation in union meetings and activities outside of the immediate job situation are seen as interfering with home life and most migrants are unwilling to allow this to happen. They accept union membership in much the same way as they accept other, more discomfiting aspects of factory work life, and they obey union dictums in much the same way that they obey shop regulations or the orders of a foreman. Further involvement demands a social commitment over and above that for which the familistically-oriented mountaineer is prepared.

Not every migrant became an avid unionist (some may have seen themselves as only temporary sojourners, not permanent employees),

but many did, even among the agricultural workers. Although many mountaineers and western Kentuckians came to northern urban areas believing John L. Lewis stood on the right side of God, some southerners, particularly from undeveloped areas outside the Appalachian South, undoubtedly came north with little if any understanding of labor unions. Many, however, were soon converted, as Grady Roberson pointed out: "Well, after you get into a place and you get to working and you understand the jobs and know that the company's really making a lot of money and you're not getting much, you're going to go fighting for more money; that's just all there is to it." Frank Plemons agreed: "Of course, down South, even today there's a lot of places down there that's nonunion. These companies today, they don't want no unions. But I can see what the union's done for the people, you know, over the years. I mean, the things that the company give me, there's no way they'd give it to me if they didn't have to. The company is just common sense." "The company," he concluded, "don't give you nothing if they don't have to, I don't think."[11]

The Upland Southern Hegira

The coalfields continued to transform southerners into exiles following World War II. Although coal mining enjoyed prosperity during World War II, by the 1950s coal mining operations, using their profits from the war, were scrambling to buy automated equipment, and thousands of miners, whose existence had always been precarious, were expelled from the mines. Company stores closed, movie theaters shut their doors, and train and bus services stopped. Ironically, many ex-miners were going to such places as Columbus, Ohio, and getting jobs with the Joy Company, which manufactured much of the equipment that was replacing miners. "It was kind of like watching the place die around me," the novelist Denise Giardina recalled of her youth in West Virginia's coalfields. "The older I got the more things left," including people. "Mostly I remember people leaving and not coming back, or they might have come back to another place where they had relatives. It seemed like everybody left at the same time," she said. "People did try to stay around—sometimes they moved to another coal camp like we did for a while. Sometimes they moved to the next county or something, but probably just as many left for good." When the mine that employed her father closed, the family moved to a nearby coal camp when she was twelve; a year later they moved to Charleston, West Virginia.[12]

The statistics speak for themselves. Between 1950 and 1955, for example, the number of miners in Kentucky fell by almost one-half, hemorrhaging 22,000 people. In McDowell County, West Virginia, 30,000 miners were employed in 1945; ten years later less than half that number were still mining coal. Farther south, Campbell County, Tennessee, was suffering a similar fate. In 1946, 6,000 people were employed in the mines; by 1955, the figure had dropped to 4,000 and by 1958, said C.J. Daniels, editor of the *LaFollette Press*, "I doubt if there are a thousand miners working today." Some of the mines, he explained, were played out, "but the chief reason for the great decline in the industry is automation in the mines." Many of the people were leaving Tennessee for Cleveland and Dayton. Frank Bradburn, pastor of the local Baptist church, said 47 of his 200-member congregation left for northern jobs in 1957 alone. A Bluefield, West Virginia, bus line was selling a hundred tickets each week for Cleveland. Between 1950 and 1960, over half a million people left West Virginia; more than 67,000 people left the state for Cleveland alone between 1955 and 1960. Estimates on the number of ex-miners and other southern whites in Cleveland ranged between 35,000 and 50,000—as many as one in every eighteen people—clustered mainly on the west side.[13]

The zenith years of upland southern white migration to the Midwest were dawning. In the southern Appalachian region alone, 704,000 people left between 1940 and 1950 compared with a paltry 81,000 between 1935 and 1940. Between 1950 and 1957, another 784,000 fled; between 1940 and 1970, a total of 3.2 million mountaineers bolted. Although the southern Appalachian

birthrate had actually begun to fall, out-migration was significant enough to produce losses through interstate migration for each southern state.[14]

Kentucky, always one of the big suppliers of migrants northward, lost almost 400,000 people through migration during the 1940s; during the 1950s, thirteen out of every one hundred people—from western areas and eastern areas—were leaving the state. The high birthrate and limited opportunity left many Kentuckians with little choice but to leave. Harlan County alone lost more than 23,000 people between 1940 and 1950, almost a third of its population, and Leslie County, long having the dubious distinction of the nation's highest birthrate, lost almost a third of its population the following decade. Seven other eastern Kentucky counties (Breathitt, Elliott, Jackson, Magoffin, Owsley, Rockcastle, and Wolfe) between 1940 and 1950 lost 40 or more percent of their populations to migration. While demographers seemed to focus on eastern counties, western and central counties were also losing people to migration: nine western and south-central counties lost more than 30 percent of their 1940 population figures, proving that migration was a *southern*, not exclusively an *Appalachian*, phenomenon—not a hegira from the hills but rather from the Upland South. Data indicate that more western than eastern Kentuckians were leaving the state.[15]

But it was the southern Appalachian person who was getting all of the attention in the media, beginning in the late 1950s. Census data, however, reveal that almost twice the number of people left western Tennessee than eastern Tennessee between 1955 and 1960, most of whom were bound for Chicago. More western Kentuckians migrated to Indiana than eastern Kentuckians during the same period, although twice as many Tennesseans bound for Indiana left middle and eastern areas than western areas. Of white migrants from Kentucky to Illinois, a little more than half of whom were bound for Chicago, more than twice the number came from western counties than from eastern ones, although slightly more eastern Kentuckians and Tennesseans went to

Detroit than did their western counterparts. In spite of these data, Lewis Killian writes that "the stereotype of the hillbilly definitely includes the notion that he is a mountaineer, a white southerner whose caricature is to be seen in Snuffy Smith of the comic strip."[16]

NOTES

1. Fields interview, 2.
2. Shepherd and Giles quoted in "Cocke County Boasts Scenery and Moonshine," mimeographed clipping (from *Harlan Daily Enterprise*), Urban Migrant Project, folder 3, box 278, Records of the Council of the Southern Mountains (hereafter CSM Collection), Southern Appalachian Archives, Hutchins Library, Berea College, Berea, Ky.; Tennessee Valley Authority, *Tennessee Valley Region*, n.p.; Norma Lee Browning, "Poverty Spurs Hill Folk on Road to North," *Chicago Daily Tribune*, May 11, 1957. For more on Cleveland's migrants, see Julian Krawcheck, "Smile When You Say 'Hillbilly!'" *Cleveland Press*, Jan. 29-Feb. 4, 1958.
3. James S. Brown, "Migration within, to, and from the Southern Appalachians, 1935–1939," 18, 20, Urban Migrant Project, folder 3, box 278, CSM Collection. For the original study, see Brown, "Social Organization of an Isolated Kentucky Mountain Neighborhood."
4. William Collins, "Your Neighbor!" clipping (from *Cincinnati Enquirer*), Migrants II folder, CSM Collection (quote); Roscoe Giffin, "Newcomers from the Southern Mountains," 3, Southern Appalachia—General, folder 8, box 3, Roscoe Giffin Collection, Southern Appalachian Archives; "Appalachian Workers in Columbus Surveyed," 37. For journalistic revisionism, see the series by Kraw-check, "Smile When You Say 'Hillbilly.'" There were exceptions, of course, particularly in Chicago, such as Norma Lee Browning's series on "Otter Hollow, Appalachia, U.S.A.," the first of which was printed in the *Chicago Daily Tribune* on May 5, 1957. The complete collection of articles is in Newspaper Clippings, folder 15, box 293, CSM Collection. See also one of the most notorious articles: Votaw, "Hillbillies Invade Chicago," 64–67. Not surprisingly, when the economic boom slowed in the 1960s, voices once again began to clamor about the migrant problem, a focus of chapter 7.
5. Drake, "Recession Is Far from Over in the Southern Mountains," 36–37; Chicago Commission on Human Relations, *1960 Annual Report of the Migration Services Department*, 3, 6 (quotation), Urban Migrant Project, folder 2, box 283, CSM Collection.
6. Lake View Newcomer Committee, *Summary of Visits to Southern White Families*, 4; Killian, *White Southerners*, 106.
7. Mary Ellen Wolfe, "Migrants Loyal, Easily Adjust to Jobs," *Dayton Journal Herald*, Feb. 26, 1960; Hundley, "Mountain Man in Northern Industry," 34–38.
8. Lacy interview.
9. Ibid.
10. Roberson interview; Weatherford interview.
11. Giffin, "Appalachian Newcomers to Cincinnati," 79–84; Philliber, *Appalachian Migrants in Urban America*, 89; Schwarzweller, "Occupational Patterns of Appalachian Migrants," 136; Roberson interview; Plemons and Collins interview, 22. James Gregory found "little reluctance" and "considerable enthusiasm for workplace organization" among "Okies" in California. See Gregory, *American Exodus*, 163.
12. Stroud interview; Giardina interview.
13. Daniels quoted in Browning, "Poverty Spurs Hill Folk on Road to North"; "Industry Comes, but Workers Quit Tennessee," clipping, Urban Migrant Project, folder 3, box 278, CSM Collection, "'Bloody Harlan' Hit Hard by Strike," clipping, Urban Migrant Project, folder 3, box 278, CSM Collection; Krawcheck, "Smile When You Say 'Hillbilly'"; Julian Krawcheck, "Coal Industry Decline Sends Southerners Here," *Cleveland Press*, July 20, 1959; Schweiker, "Some Facts and a Theory of Migration." Many ex-miners, of course, also traveled to Chicago. See Chicago Fact Book Consortium, *Local Community Fact Book*, 6.
14. Brown, "Migration within, to, and from the Southern Appalachians," 10. Southern-born people constituted ever increasing percentages in midwestern states, including 12 percent of Ohio's total population, 11 percent of Indiana's, 10 percent of Michigan's, and 9 percent of Illinois's. See U.S. Bureau of the Census, *U.S. Census of Population: 1950*, vol. 4, *Special Reports*, part 4, chap. A, State of Birth, tables 4, 8, 9, and 14. See also U.S. Bureau of the Census, "Estimates of the Population of States and Selected Outlying Areas of the United States, July 1, 1957 and 1956."
15. James S. Brown and Paul D. Richardson, "Changes in Kentucky's Population by Counties: Natural Increase and Net Migration," 1–4, manuscript, Southern Appalachian Studies—Roscoe Giffin, folder 7, box 3, Faculty and Staff Collection, Berea College Archives; "Exodus from the Hills," *Hazard (Ky.) Herald*, Feb. 28, 1963; Jim Hampton, "Exodus," *Louisville Courier-Journal*, June 16, 1962; "Area Still Gets Steady Stream from South," *Dayton Journal Herald*, July 22, 1961; Mary Ellen Wolfe, "Daytonians Accept South's Migrants," *Dayton Journal Herald*, Feb. 22, 1960. For exact out-migration numbers, contact author.
16. U.S. Bureau of the Census, *U.S. Census of Population: 1960, Subject Reports, Mobility for State Economic Areas*, Final Report PC (2)-2B, tables 33–36; Donald Janson, "30,000 Hill People Now Cluster in Chicago," *New York Times*, Aug. 31, 1963; Killian, *White Southerners*, 103.

Citizenship and Civil Rights, 1964–1974

Melanie Shell-Weiss

Source: *Coming to Miami: A Social History*
(Gainesville: University Press of Florida, 2009).

EDITORS' INTRODUCTION

In the articles written by Hirsch, Krissoff Boehm, and Berry, the white and black divisions in American urban society are highlighted. We know however, that the racial and ethnic palette of our cities was highly complex. As the twentieth century unfolded, increasing numbers of Spanish-speaking and Portuguese-speaking (not to mention French-speaking) migrants and immigrants came from Mexico, South America, and the Caribbean. As Shell-Weiss reminds us, Latin Americans complicated understandings of race and efforts at segregation because Latin Americans themselves comprise language and cultural groups, rather than a racial category. Latin Americans who settled in the United States at times found themselves divided by skin color—darker skinned Latin Americans encountered a greater degree of prejudice. However, Latin Americans could at times traverse the color line, where African Americans could not. Members of Miami's long-standing African American community, made up of migrants, Caribbean immigrants, and their descendents, balked at being placed at the bottom of the city's three-tiered hierarchy. Miami's multifaceted population mix offered challenges in terms of how to best orchestrate a fight for increased civil and economic rights.

In one of the few book-length studies of Miami, Shell-Weiss offers a brand-new, and much needed synthesis of that city's migration, immigration, and labor history. She demonstrates how from its earliest days, Miami had a mixed race population. The book showcases the city's evolution "from a new, primarily 'southern' city to a broadly international, even global, one."[i] Like Krissoff Boehm's and Berry's essays, Shell-Weiss' scholarship alters historical periodization, beginning the Latinization of Miami—once tied solidly to the post-1960s—approximately two decades earlier. Shell-Weiss writes that "by the mid-1950s, local officials estimated that 46,000 Cubans, 30,000 Puerto Ricans, 3,500 Colombians, 2,000 Venezuelans, 1,200 Ecuadorians, 800 Mexicans, and an additional 2,000 people from elsewhere in Central American made their homes in Miami-Dade County. Most had arrived in the last five years."[ii] These new Miami residents were a combination of migrants (having been born in Puerto Rico or having already settled in the mainland United States) and immigrants. Miami was at once both representative and unique; like many American cities, Miami was becoming an increasingly multi-lingual city, but, unlike other cities, its immigrant population was almost entirely made up of peoples of Caribbean origins.

Melanie Shell-Weiss is Visiting Assistant Professor of History at Johns Hopkins University. She is an editor of H-Migration, a listserv dedicated to discussion of migration and issues of race and ethnicity (www.h-net.org/~migrate/). In addition to *Coming to Miami*, her work includes, *Florida's Working Class Past: Current Perspectives on Labor from Spanish Florida to the New Immigration*, edited with Robert Cassanello (Gainesville: University Press of Florida, November 2008), *Translators Wanted in Dixie: Immigration and Race Relations in the Twentieth Century South* (forthcoming), and *Reconstructing America: Evaluating the Legacy of the Dillingham Commission on Immigration Reform* (forthcoming).

---

i Melanie Shell-Weiss, *Coming to Miami: A Social History* (Gainesville: University Press of Florida, 2009), 1.
ii Shell-Weiss, *Coming to Miami*, 152.

CITIZENSHIP AND CIVIL RIGHTS, 1964–1974

María Espinoza came to Miami in December 1965. She was part of the second major wave of Cubans to leave the island in less than a decade.[1] María was twenty-three years old at the time. Like a small but growing number of immigrants from this period, she was Afro-Cuban and had dark skin and tight, curly hair. She made the trip with her two young sons, Carlos and Manolo. They traveled to join her husband, who was already living in Miami, having left Cuba two years earlier. This was María's third attempt to leave the island in as many years.

Compared to the Cubans who came to Miami in the immediate wake of the Cuban Revolution, those who left after 1964 were less likely to be highly educated or to work in white-collar professions.[2] María was no exception. Her husband was a plasterer. She worked as a maid in several Havana hotels and a few wealthy homes. In the first years after the Revolution, María supported Fidel Castro and hoped that his presidency would provide a real democratic alternative to the violence and corruption of Fulgencio Batista's regime.

Her family had always enjoyed having ample food and their material needs met. Still, as the Cuban economy transitioned, they often were unable to buy even basic food staples like beans, rice, flour, or oil. Household supplies like toilet paper, aspirin, and toothpaste were increasingly hard to come by. International embargos further limited the goods that were available on the island. Worried about what the future held for her sons, and skeptical that Castro's rule would ultimately prove more democratic than Batista's, María left for Miami.

Once in Miami, she went to work in a garment factory. "It was a matter of eating or not eating," María recalled. "Besides, when you leave Cuba you are so desperate that any work, anything that will let you get a few dollars is OK." But María also found that she liked garment work and certainly preferred it to working as a maid. The hours were more regular. The pay was higher and

more predictable. She could also take work home to earn a little extra, and spend more time with her sons. Perhaps, María thought, she might even be able to attend school to become a secretary or a clerk if she remained in Miami.

In Miami, María joined a growing community of Cuban immigrants. But the contours, occupations, and demographics of this community were very different from the one she left on the island. Here, Afro-Cubans like herself were found in far fewer numbers than in her homeland. And while the proportion of immigrants who were coming from Cuba and who held jobs in service occupations or the skilled trades was increasing, this development was still relatively new and reflected which jobs were available more than the prior work experience and education levels of the men and women who filled them. This shaped how María interacted with other Cubans in Miami. It also affected how María saw herself. In Miami, she gladly signed a union card and joined ILGWU Local 415–475. Although there were some African Americans in the union, the vast majority of the members were Cuban, and she was pleased to join with her fellow countrywomen to ensure the best possible working conditions for themselves.[3]

What surprised María was the hostility she encountered once in Miami. At the point she arrived, divides of race, class, and nativity had never been more pronounced. For the first time, Miami was an immigrant city. Most of these new immigrants were from the Caribbean and Latin America. Like María, most were Spanish-speakers. But María's race made her especially anxious about the move. When she applied for an exit permit, officials in Havana showed María pictures of lynchings and police with dogs brutalizing African Americans who looked like her. "This is what you will find in America," they said.[4] What María experienced, however, was even more unexpected. Cubans like María were the focus of a growing split between immigration advocates and civil rights activists. While María's initial fear was that she would not be able to reap the benefits of the civil rights progress being made in the city, she was surprised to find herself the object of so much hostility from native-born black and white residents alike. What did this mean for her future in Miami? she wondered. What kind of life would her children enjoy there? Where did they fit in the social order of this rapidly internationalizing city? Here, debates over civil rights and immigration played no small role.

National Policies, Local Outcomes, 1964–1965

Civil rights and immigration advocates had not always been at odds with each other. In the immediate postwar period, these causes were intertwined. Although there were some public figures like A. Philip Randolph who continued to oppose an open door policy on immigration, the NAACP was among the most vocal proponents of more open borders and an end to the national quota system, due in no small part to the large number of West Indians among their members. They, along with the National Urban League and the Harlem congressman Adam Clayton Powell, lobbied hard to prevent the passage of the McCarran-Walter Act, which ended the Western Hemisphere exemptions. As Executive Director Roy Wilkins told the U.S. Congress in 1952, "Citizens of Trinidad, Jamaica, and other West Indian colonies, most of whom are Negroes, at present have relatively free access to the United States." If passed, he argued, the bill would "reduce Negro immigration from the West Indies by 90 percent" and also "prove harmful ... in Latin America and in the Caribbean."[5] The NAACP intervened on behalf of Asian wives of American servicemen who were denied entry to the United States in the immediate postwar period.[6] They also joined with the American Jewish Congress to press U.S. President Eisenhower to open the door to all global refugees from brutal political regimes, and to limit the provisions allowing deportation of foreign-born people living within the United States.[7] Noting that federal immigration restrictions had "significant racial implications," in the view of organizations like the NAACP, civil rights and immigration rights were interwoven.

By the mid-1960s, however, these ties began to fray. Florida's NAACP took no public stance on the Cuban refugee issue. But internally, leaders expressed worries that Cubans were fast replacing African Americans in many entry-level service and manufacturing trades, growing the gap between working- and middle-class blacks.[8] In Florida and an assortment of western states, NAACP chapters joined with Mexican American and Filipino civil rights activists, and the AFL-CIO, in calling for an end to the Bracero and British West Indies labor programs. The NAACP national headquarters soon followed suit, adding this demand to the list of their annual convention resolutions in 1961. When the U.S. Congress finally abolished the programs, Florida's NAACP touted it as being among their most important victories.[9] The union of civil rights and immigration advocates was showing deep signs of strain.

As the U.S. Senate worked to hone the Civil Rights Act, which was signed into law in July 1964, the House discussed repealing the national origins system. Editorials published in the *New York Times* and *Washington Post* condemned the system, comparing it to Jim Crow legislation across the South. Jewish leaders similarly opposed the quotas, noting the anti-Semitic ideologies that undergirded them.[10] Arguing that the quota system was "a gratuitous insult" to many nations and an impediment to world leadership, New York Congressman Emmanuel Celler, himself the child of both German Catholic and Jewish parents, became one of its most vocal critics, with strong support from the NAACP headquarters. "The NAACP is on record, and will continue to be on record, for the elimination of the presently existing national origins quotas as enforced by our immigration laws," the NAACP assistant executive director John Morsell wrote in December 1964. "Anything which sets up such restrictions on the basis of race or national origin is in conflict with our philosophy." But the NAACP's support was no longer unequivocal. "Whether the overall number of immigrants permitted to come in should be restricted and what effects such immigrants have on our domestic employment situation are totally different matters and should be discussed on that basis," Morsell continued.[11]

As pressure from local chapters in areas of the nation most affected by new waves of immigrants grew, the shift toward economic as well as legal equality brought organizations like the NAACP into further conflict with immigration advocates. Quoting Frederick Douglass, one NAACP member put it most bluntly: "Every hour sees the black man elbowed out of employment by some newly arrived immigrant … whose hunger and whose color are thought to give him better title to the place." She continued:

It was because of the millions of immigrants with a Latin tradition who came to the United States during the early years of this century that there arose a concern over the possible consequences such a tradition would have on the country's democratic institutions and individual rights. And it is neither intolerant nor bigoted to point out that where Americans of this background have gained political control, the tendency has been to give little or no consideration to the rights of others on a number of basic issues—birth control, censorship, divorce, etc. Moreover, their increasing demands for the use of public funds to promote their own particular ideas and activities, as well as their current attempts to change some of our state constitutions to make it easier to obtain these funds, grows yearly more disturbing.[12]

With hostility toward immigrants on the rise, the NAACP found itself in an awkward position and began to back away from immigrant advocacy altogether.[13]

A Pivotal Year

In Florida, these debates were impassioned. Noting that economic opportunities for the state's African Americans lagged far behind nearly every place in the nation, in January 1965, the Florida NAACP director Robert Saunders declared job opportunities to be the focus of their annual campaign. "[D]espite the laws, appointments, winning of elections by Negroes, and spread of the poverty program, Negroes in Florida are still the last to be hired and the first to be fired," Saunders wrote.

They are still receiving less training than the white person and are still the victims of the propaganda piece that "industry and business have jobs and opportunities but just can't find qualified people to fill them…." There is still discrimination and it is becoming "Northern style." There is still police brutality and there is still a need for the NAACP.[14]

Florida, Saunders argued, was poised to become a national model for black economic opportunity. The state's tourism and entertainment industries, in particular, provided a widely publicized meeting ground for civil rights, and now Black Power, advocates. Less than one year earlier, for example, Muslim minister and Black Power advocate Malcom X, British pop giants The Beatles, and African American singer-songwriter Sam Cooke all converged in Miami over a single weekend, talking and socializing, brought together by the heavyweight boxing match between Cassius Clay, who had recently joined the Nation of Islam, and world heavyweight champion Sonny Liston. Their meeting made headlines across the nation, assuming almost mythic proportions. Many within the civil rights movement believed that this showed what was possible in the city. But Florida's reliance on tourism also meant that it could not afford too much of the wrong kind of publicity.[15] For these reasons, Saunders believed Florida activists could force economic integration on a scale not seen anywhere else in the nation.

No other state experienced immigration on the scale of Florida over this short period. Never in U.S. history had immigration taken the particular form it did in Florida. Nor had the federal government ever before mobilized on such a large scale to support a single group of newly arrived immigrants. Yet as immigrants from Vietnam and Indochina also began pouring in, and as discussion of civil rights was linked to economics and national origins, many wondered if Florida might no longer be exceptional after all, but a harbinger of challenges that would soon face cities all over America. In these respects, Miami made history. But whether or not this history would produce the kind of liberation for African Americans that Robert Saunders hoped was unclear.

Then in August 1965, the City of Miami broke ground for a new extension to the North-South expressway, Interstate 95. Plans for the highway extension had been in the works since the World War II era. Initially, the proposed route was to follow the Florida East Coast Railway corridor and would largely have kept Miami's existing neighborhoods intact. Advocates of slum clearance, however, argued that this was unacceptable. So the city instead approved a plan proposed by the Florida State Road Department rerouting the new highway directly through the heart of Overtown. Proponents of the revised plans, including some members of the Greater Miami Urban League, argued this change was necessary to allow adequate room for future growth.[16] Their advocacy caused a major rift within the organization. But plans for the highway went ahead on schedule. In a move reminiscent of the forced relocations of the 1930s and 1940s, residents who lived in the path of the new highway were given little warning that their homes were to be razed and few option for where to go. Some tenants had notice of fewer than twenty-four hours before their homes were boarded up and torn down.[17]

The federal government opened an Office of Economic Opportunity in Miami to aid those displaced by the highway development. But that help was often too little, too late. "These people are pretty much lost when the man comes and says, 'You have to get out,'" Bob Wyrick, the spokesman for the agency recalled.[18] Several Overtown residents filed lawsuits and stays to stop city contractors from tearing down their homes. It was not enough. Construction on the highway continued unabated.

Many African Americans were furious at the power a core of wealthy white business leaders continued to hold over urban development and the seeming ease with which the City of Miami forcibly displaced scores of black residents. Calls for change became more militant. In early September 1965, roughly two and a half years before similar strikes in Memphis made headlines across the United States, African American garbage handlers in Miami and Miami Beach walked

off the job. Theirs was the first in a series of work stoppages that reverberated across the city's service industries that fall, from the Biscayne dog-racing tracks to janitors, maids, and restaurant staff on Miami Beach.[19] Like these other workers, garbage handlers lacked the support of a national union. But they understood that their labor was essential to maintaining Miami's pristine image for tourists even if the importance of their work was not reflected in their pay or working conditions. The sanitation workers' demands were also modest.[20] They asked for a pay increase from $1.48 an hour, which was barely above the federal minimum of $1.25, to $2.10, working toilets, and no more overtime hours without overtime pay.

The Public Works Departments of Miami and Miami Beach found replacement workers from wherever they could, rounding up unemployed men from across the city and offering them jobs. Policemen armed with rifles rode in the cabs of the trucks to protect these replacement workers from retaliation by the strikers.[21] None came. But the fear proved a powerful disincentive to prospective strikebreakers. Then, on September 7, Hurricane Betsy struck Miami. A Category 3 storm, with winds of up to 130 miles per hour, it remains one of the single most powerful hurricanes to ever hit the city. With no sanitation workers to help clean up the storm damage, the Miami and Miami Beach mayors declared a "state of emergency."[22] The next day Fidel Castro opened the door to any Cubans who wished to leave the island and had relatives living in the United States. Once again, one of the city's major civil rights demonstrations coincided with a massive influx of new immigrants.

Thousands of Cubans already living in Miami flooded into the offices of Cuba's Interior Ministry, requesting exit visas for their relatives. In a series of press releases and radio spots, the U.S. State Department tried to discourage Cubans from sailing on their own from Florida to Cuba. Still, many Cuban exiles chartered tugboats, pleasure craft, shrimp boats—"anything that would float," as one local observer put it—with the goal of bringing family members out of Cuba to the United States.[23] Faced with mounting public pressure, and fearing that they would indeed lose their jobs once a new influx of Cuban immigrants reached Miami's shores, the city's sanitation employees returned to work. Cuban Americans, meanwhile, increased their pressure on the executive arm of the federal government to intervene on behalf of their family members and fellow countrymen and women.[24]

On October 2, one day after the Immigration and Nationality Act was signed into law, President Lyndon Johnson addressed the people of Florida in a nationally televised speech from the foot of the State of Liberty on New York's Ellis Island. He said:

> I want all of the people of this great land of ours to know of the really enormous contributions that the compassionate citizens of Florida have made to humanity and to decency. And all States in this Union can join with Florida now in extending the hand of helpfulness and humanity to our Cuban brothers. And today we can all believe that the lamp of this grand old lady is brighter today—and the golden door that she guards gleams more brilliantly in the light of an increased liberty for the people from all the countries of the globe.[25]

If Ellis Island had symbolized early-twentieth-century immigration, it seemed Miami was poised to replace it.

In place of the national origins quotas, the new immigration law established a seven-tiered preference system for determining admission. Occupation and skill constituted one primary criterion. Professionals, scientists, and artists "of exceptional ability" were also given preference, as were workers in occupations where there were labor shortages. The act also gave priority to parents, children, and spouses of immigrants already living in the United States. Political refugees were the last in the list of preferred groups. Western Hemisphere countries were not subject to any separate quotas, although total migration from the region was capped at 120,000 (slightly less than total migration from the region in 1964). Eastern Hemisphere countries were given a quota of 20,000. Family members were exempted from this limit.

The bill represented a significant number of compromises. Preferences for more highly educated, middle-class immigrants reflected the interests of organized labor. The Johnson administration steadfastly refused to ratify the refugee convention proposed by the United Nations (UN) on the grounds that it defined "refugee" too broadly, making the United States and Canada the only two Western democracies that had failed to ratify the convention.[26] While many groups were pleased to see refugees permanently included in U.S. federal immigration policies, they called the definition of political migrants "unnecessarily limiting" and "restrictive" because it applied only to those leaving Communist nations or countries in the Middle East. Here the bill was very much a product of the Cold War period in which it was birthed. Above all, the Johnson administration emphasized that this bill was strictly designed to remove racial, ethnic, and religious biases from the nation's immigration laws; it would *not* expand the volume of legal admissions to the United States.

The NAACP's national headquarters praised the bill as marking another important victory over legalized racism. But Florida activists responded much differently. Some found less than compelling the argument that immigrants from Communist nations should be exempted from any entry limits. The specter of communism had been used to convict Miami civil rights leaders like Reverend Theodore Gibson and to harass countless others. It had caused the collapse of groups like the Civil Rights Congress and undermined the work of countless others.[27] Instead, Miami civil rights leaders argued, these exemptions essentially undercut the economic protections the seven-tier preference system were supposed to provide. They also argued that it gave unfair advantage to immigrants from predominantly Spanish-speaking nations that were not extended to West Indians.

Within days of Johnson's public address, Donald Wheeler Jones, head of Miami's NAACP, sent a strongly worded letter to President Johnson and Florida officials expressing his indignation. "The United

States must exercise its responsibilities toward the economically oppressed of this community as well as toward the politically oppressed of Cuba," he wrote, adding that earlier Cuban refugees were already displacing Miami's African Americans as waiters, doormen, bellhops, maids, and kindred service workers.[28] "[D]espite efforts at resettlement," he continued, "a great majority of these newly arrived refugees will remain in the Miami area." Jones also pledged the support of the NAACP's services with the resettlement, however, noting that he was certain that "the Cuban people and the Negroes of this area can live and work together as brothers." The same day Jones's comments were published in papers across the country, authorities announced that another fifty thousand Cubans were poised to leave the island.

The shift in emphasis among civil rights activists toward economics also brought the views of groups like the NAACP more in line with that of the AFL-CIO, which had long favored immigration restrictions like literacy tests, preferential treatment for highly educated immigrants, and the national quota system, all issues traditionally opposed by civil rights groups. Although the ILGWU and the NAACP had long shared a publicly adversarial relationship, on the subject of Cuban immigrants, Miami labor and civil rights leaders agreed.[29] Two days after the Immigration Act was signed into law, Robert Gladnick wrote an impassioned plea to ILGWU President David Dubinsky:

> We have come through five of the most painful years of the Miami Market. [T]he refugees of the past few years were beginning to learn to protect themselves from local employers' abuses and we were looking forward to finally start an organization campaign.... But President Johnson's offer of permitting some 5,000 refugees per month to enter, will ruin everything we have planned in Miami.... Of the 50,000 refugees expected, half will be women and obviously, they will flood the garment market. President Dubinsky, you have always said that I pay too much attention to the Cuban problem, but with this deluge, what can I do?[30]

This opposition to immigration was not rooted in a strictly economic logic. Few black women were employed in Miami's garment shops by this period. Nor was there statistical evidence to support accusations of displacement in other industries.[31] But each group still perceived immigration as undercutting their individual aims. For this reason, these groups became united by their increasingly nativist stance.

Cuban immigrants, however, were elated. Within months, thousands of people worked to bring friends and relatives from overseas. But even with these benefits, the process of claiming a relative in Cuba could be difficult.[32] Cubans already residing in the United States first had to contact the Cuban Refugee Center in Miami and file a request. Located in the skyscraper that previously housed the headquarters of the *Miami Daily News*, the refugee center sat on Biscayne Boulevard at Sixth Street. Staff at the center compared requests made by family members to the list of Cubans who had requested exit visas and been approved to leave by the Cuban government.[33] If the names matched, the Miami office informed Cuban immigrants that their family members were approved for immigration. But the center did not know when they would arrive. Some Cubans in Florida received letters from loved ones informing them of their travel dates. Miami's Spanish-language radio stations also read out the names of the immigrants airlifted to Miami each day. Lists and names of new arrivals were also published in the daily newspapers. Often this amounted to more than four thousand individuals a month.[34]

Since the First World War, federal immigration policy emphasized resettling immigrants in diverse areas, believing that this approach would lessen the burden of incorporation on local economies and encourage newcomers to assimilate more rapidly. Between 1959 and 1965, the Cuban Refugee Center relocated well over 200,000 Cubans in areas outside of Miami. Most were sent to New York and New Jersey. Other leading destinations included Puerto Rico, California, Illinois, Massachusetts, Texas, the District of Columbia, Pennsylvania, Louisiana,

Ohio, and Maryland. But after 1965, thousands of Cubans began moving back to Miami. Surveys conducted by refugee and resettlement agencies indicated that there were roughly 181,000 Cubans living in Dade County. Of these, 56,050 had entered the United States before the Cuban Revolution.[35] Others were new arrivals who either preferred to stay in Miami or who had returned to the city after being placed by refugee agencies elsewhere in the United States. Increasingly, it seemed, Cubans preferred Miami to any other place in the United States.

While Cubans made the most headlines, they were not the only foreign-born to seek refuge in Miami. In the Dominican Republic, an April 1965 coup engineered by groups wanting to return the former president Juan Bosch to power clashed with rivals. The U.S. government quickly intervened. Vowing that they did not want "another Castro-type takeover," the United States sent in troops. Dominicans soon began leaving the island, seeking refuge on the U.S. mainland. "Traffic to the U.S. from the Dominican Republic has increased considerably since the revolution," one report in the *Miami Herald* read. "Long lines of Dominicans seeking to leave the country form daily outside the U.S. consulate."[36] The report hinted that of the 18,000 people who left the island each month, Miami would soon become a choice destination for Dominicans as well.

Haitians also fled their nation after François "Papa Doc" Duvalier declared himself "President for Life" in 1964. As in Cuba five years earlier, many of the first to leave were relatives of politicians who opposed Duvalier's rule and political philosophy. But dire economic circumstances across the island, which showed no sign of improving, also began to push urban and rural residents from their homes in search of better opportunities abroad. The average life expectancy for Haitians was thirty-two years, the lowest of any nation in the Western Hemisphere. Over 80 percent of Haitians were illiterate. Population density was 415 people per square mile, the highest of any nation in Latin America.[37] On December 12, 1965, one of the first groups of Haitian refugees landed at Pompano Beach, just north of Miami.[38]

For all these reasons, 1965 proved a pivotal year. By December, it seemed that Miami's ethnic communities were divided into two separate camps: On the one side were those advocating for equal economic rights for all U.S. citizens; on the other were those arguing for the right of foreign-born peoples to enjoy the opportunity of citizenship extended to earlier generations of immigrants.

Civil Rights, Immigrant Rights, Economic Rights, 1966–1967

This divide troubled national leaders like Reverend Martin Luther King Jr. In April 1966, Reverend King came to Miami at the invitation of the Ministerial Alliance. In public talks and private meetings, he urged Miami's African Americans to look beyond nativity and cautioned against pitting African Americans against Cuban refugees in the local job market.[39] The response was decidedly lukewarm. Some Miami residents called King "blind" to decades of civil rights work across the city. "Few metropolitan areas in the nation have a more diligent program going for race relations than Miami," one *Miami Herald* columnist wrote. The Dade Council on Community Relations seconded that view.[40] Rather than coming closer together, the immigration debate grew the gulf separating the national headquarters from local chapters of the NAACP and the SCLC.

Activists, meanwhile, continued to make important gains. The Florida state NAACP launched a major campaign for better job opportunities, emphasizing the need to increase black employment in areas where African Americans had previously been excluded. Richard H. Powell of Miami's NAACP was appointed to chair the state NAACP's Labor and Industry Committee. The city hosted a major conference on migrant labor, organized jointly by the NAACP and the AFL-CIO, where they discussed strategies to improve working conditions and pay for agricultural workers.[41]

CORE's voter registration campaign registered more black voters than at any previous point in Dade County history.[42] For the first time, an African American was appointed to serve as the Metropolitan Dade County welfare coordinator. This was the highest-ranking position ever held by a black person within Miami-Dade's metropolitan government.

But even the most committed activists could do little to counteract the cumulative effects of the city's decades-old relocation policies. Unlike in northern cities where the postwar period created a large, concentrated black ghetto like New York's Harlem or Chicago's South Side, Miami's urban renewal policies dispersed the city's black community to far-flung places across the metropolitan area. Slum clearance continued to erode the city's African American voting base, breaking up neighborhoods and moving black residents farther and farther apart from each other. The number of businesses in Overtown dropped 29 percent from just a decade earlier. Fewer than ten thousand residents now lived in Overtown. At least twelve thousand residents had been forced out. Others had simply gotten out as soon as they could. Although black residents made up 18 percent of the Miami community, not a single African American had ever been elected to the Board of County Commissioners or any other elected office in Dade County.[43] Even though civil rights were now a federal promise, structural measures enacted by Miami officials and developers undercut these gains.

They soon created an institutional vacuum, too. Even as the NAACP's national headquarters looked to Florida as the center of its "Closing the Economic Gap of the Masses" campaign, and the state office launched a major membership drive and model city and job opportunity pilot programs in cities from Jacksonville, Tallahassee, and Gainesville, to St. Augustine, Clearwater, Tampa, and Pensacola, membership in Miami's NAACP and Urban League chapters fell off steadily.[44] Conflict over urban renewal further undermined the ability of the Urban League to mobilize new members. When Executive Director James Whitehead stepped down, saying he felt that the appointment of an African American to the position was essential, the Greater Miami Urban League stopped meeting altogether.[45]

As members were forced from the central city, Miami's NAACP chapter also stopped meeting. "The downtown is not a suitable place for meeting due to the hazardous conditions that exist," Thelma Vernell Albury, treasurer of Miami's chapter, wrote to the national office.[46] National organizers who came to the city were aghast at the conditions faced by Miami activists, noting that even when meetings were set up, they were held in neighborhoods "far removed from most people and in an area of severe blight where many people fear going at night."[47] Other chapters of the NAACP were established in Liberty City, Carol City, and Opalocka. But they never achieved the size of Miami's chapter or its broad membership base.

The Florida NAACP field director, Marvin Davies, noted that he found it "deeply shocking" that Miami's membership could fall off so steeply even as so many gains were being made.[48] As other groups like the CORE and the Student Non-Violent Coordinating Committee (SNCC) adopted new platforms calling for Black Power and a closing of ethnic ranks, the possibility of cross-ethnic alliance seemed ever more remote. Davies, in turn, became more and more vocal about his own hostility toward federal immigration policies. "[I]f the same amount of government financing was given to aid the Negro community here as has been spent on Cuban refugees," Davies told the *Miami Herald*, "there would be no black problem in Miami."[49]

Labor unions like the ILGWU, which had supported a Latina majority among its rank-and-file for nearly two decades, also suffered major losses. By 1967, it was clear that Cubans were flooding into Miami's garment shops not just as workers, but as owners. Because work in the industry was so often "under-the-table," exact numbers or lists of subcontractors do not exist, making it impossible to pin down just how many Cubans immigrants had moved from being plant employees to subcontractors. But anecdotal evidence is extensive and suggests that patterns of Cuban ownership in Miami mimicked those seen in Puerto Rico a decade earlier. As the sociologist José A. Cobas described, it was not uncommon to hear Cubans referred to as the "Jews of Puerto Rico," for their disproportionate presence in the retail, real estate, construction, and garment trades.[50] Aided by a shared language, low start-up costs, and a ready supply of available labor, Cubans entered the garment industry first as laborers and then as subcontractors.[51] For Puerto Ricans who, not unlike African Americans, believed that as U.S. citizens they should be entitled to basic protections and economic rights, this angered them as well.

After nearly fifty years of work in the ILGWU, Robert Gladnick resigned, writing simply: "I am in a blind alley."[52] The alliances among Miami's Latino workers he had worked so hard to build were crumbling before him. Gladnick also expressed dismay with the politics of these new arrivals, predicated on a kind of transnational identity, focused as much on Cuban politics as those in the United States. Instead, Gladnick accepted a position with the American Institute for Free Labor Development's Latin American Division, a joint initiative of the American Federation of Labor and the Central Intelligence Agency. It would be more than a decade before the ILGWU would even hire on another Spanish-speaking manager. From an all-time peak of nearly eight thousand members in more than twenty factories, membership in the union in Miami fell off steadily after Gladnick's departure.[53]

New Alliances

It was at this critical time that the Service Employees International Union (SEIU) launched an organizing campaign in Miami. The SEIU began in Chicago as the Flat Janitors Union.[54] In 1921, they incorporated window washers, maids, and a whole host of kindred service workers, both men and women, into the organization, renaming themselves the Building Service Employees International Union. Unlike other labor organizations that relied primarily on trade- or industry-based alliances, the SEIU used a different approach. Janitors, they argued, were not only important to their employers but served a critical public health and safety role. Thus the union sought partnerships between janitors and public service employees, as well as social service agencies.

After World War II, the SEIU extended their efforts both geographically and occupationally. As Sunbelt migration expanded the range of service occupations, the West Coast and the South became major foci of activism, including a drive to organize hospital workers, groundskeepers, and other occupations practiced by a large number of women, African Americans, Asian Americans, and Latinos. At a time when many labor unions were segregated, the SEIU was fully integrated.[55] In 1961, the SEIU became one of first unions to organize their own Commission on Civil Rights and to mandate that all local chapters follow suit by appointing a representative to specifically focus on civil rights and equal representation. They also were far more decentralized than other unions, allowing individual locals a degree of autonomy not typically found in other unions.

Although the national SEIU was a part of the AFL-CIO, individual locals were given the choice of whether or not to formally affiliate with the AFL-CIO. Many did. But Florida locals did not for a variety of reasons. Some members objected to the AFL's bureaucracy and top-down structure. Others noted the AFL's mixed history on support for African Americans or its anti-immigration stance. Others simply preferred local autonomy and the right to respond to local circumstances as those directly involved saw fit. All these features put the SEIU in an ideal position to move into Florida and play an active role among Miami's service workers.

By 1966, the SEIU had six separate locals in the Miami area.[56] The largest were Locals 337 and 362. Local 337 was made up primarily of pari-mutuel clerks, who handled the bets placed at Miami's racetracks and jai alai facilities. Local 362 included service workers like janitors, skycaps, and baggage handlers at Miami International Airport, window washers, maids, and kindred workers at hotels, groceries, and a range of other locations across the city. Under the direction of the organizer James O'Halloran, the SEIU set its sights on organizing school janitors and hospital employees, and enlarging the service workers' local to include kindred workers at retail establishments and hotels. Two members of the rank-and-file became especially instrumental in forging this movement: Vernon H. Clark and Rafael M. Estévez.

Clark was an African American pari-mutuel clerk who worked at the Biscayne Dog Track and was a member of Local 337. He had also earned a reputation for his commitment to civil rights, and was respected across the communities of Coconut Grove and Liberty City.[57] Clark proposed that the SEIU focus a major campaign on the city's health-care workers, beginning with the Coral Gables Veteran's Hospital. As a federally owned and run institution, the Veteran's Hospital clearly fell under the purview of Executive Order No. 10988, which gave all federal employees the right to form, join, and assist unions without fear of penalty or reprisals.[58] It also proved an excellent way to bring friends and family members of already unionized workers into the fold. In many families, husbands and sons worked for the city's various gambling establishments or the airport, while wives and daughters worked as maids, laundresses, and aides at the hospital. Together with help from Reverend Theodore Gibson and Cecil Rolle, they launched a major organizing campaign starting in January 1967.[59] Open meetings were held in several area churches, as well hotels. They drew in national figures like A. Philip Randolph to discuss the particular challenges facing Miami's African American workers. They also partnered with the SEIU International organizer John Gore, himself a black Bahamian and Miami resident, who in May 1968 was appointed to help organize workers in the Bahamian tourist industry and West Indians who worked in Miami hotels, as taxi drivers, and in local hospitals.[60]

With that effort underway, the SEIU moved forward on another front: forging stronger collaborations among Cuban, African American, and West Indian workers. One way they hoped to do this was by establishing a mandatory minimum wage. The other was to unionize the Cuban immigrants who accepted jobs in the city's service occupations, rather than allowing employers to pit workers of different ethnic backgrounds against each other.[61] Here Rafael M. Estévez emerged as a second important leader.

Like Clark, Estévez worked as a pari-mutuel clerk and was a member of Local 337. Estévez had moved to Miami in 1964. Where Clark's connections were strongest in Coconut Grove and Liberty City, Estévez's ties ran deep in Hialeah, spanning Cuban Americans, Puerto Ricans, and newcomers alike. In late 1966, Estévez wrote to Jim O'Halloran asking if he might help the union to mount an organizing campaign at some of the other racetracks and jai alai establishments that were hiring more and more newly arrived Cubans.[62] Estévez then started working to make this happen. But it was far from easy, as the "Miami Hi-Li" case demonstrates. By 1967, nearly 40 percent of the pari-mutual clerks employed at Miami Hi-Li were Cuban. In much the same way that employers threatened African American and Puerto Rican workers that their jobs would be given to noncitizens if they unionized or asked for more pay, owners at Miami Hi-Li used similar techniques to intimidate their Cuban workers. Cubans were told that if they unionized, "their jobs would go to Americans."[63] Estévez worked hard to win the workers' trust. Employers responded by mounting a smear campaign and hiring a notorious anti-labor lawyer to charge organizers with violating the state's right-to-work laws. They were unsuccessful, and Estévez's work to organize the Miami Hi-Li clerks continued undeterred.

Next Estévez and Clark extended the campaign to janitors, maids, and gardeners at the University of Miami.[64] Like the Veteran's Hospital, the University of Miami was hiring a growing number of newly arrived

Cubans to work in low-level service jobs. Many African Americans were also working in these same trades. As at the other companies, Estévez and Clark worked to gain the workers' trust, educate them on their rights, and to convince Cubans, African Americans, and West Indians to work together toward the common goal of achieving pay that was commensurate with experience, shorter hours, and better working conditions.

Their efforts coincided with a burgeoning of labor activism among black workers across the city. In late March 1967, janitors for Greyhound Lines, the interstate bus company, went on strike.[65] Garbage handlers walked off their jobs on April 3 for the first time in nearly two years. In October, Miami city bus drivers also walked off the job, drawing on the support of the SCLC, who had begun working with sanitation workers in Memphis, Tennessee, in their efforts.[66] But as Estévez and Clark experienced, even at a moment when so many workers were demonstrating their willingness to demonstrate and calling for change, forging alliances among Latinos and Blacks proved challenging.

Estévez and Clark were able to amass a core group of Cuban and African American employees who were willing to join the union and who pledged to work together. But even those Cubans who joined the union expressed skepticism that other newly arrived immigrants would be willing to do the same. When SEIU organizers fell back on appeals to nativity, this isolated Latino workers and frayed existing alliances. Equally important, it appeared to undermine the confidence of all workers in the union. For example, in early 1968, after months of struggle, owners of Miami Hi-Li fired several union employees and hired Cubans newly arrived from the Freedom Flights in their place. Frustrated, Jim O'Halloran set up a meeting with George Johnson of the Florida Racing Commission, hoping that the commission would enforce a new statewide rule that 85 percent of employees at all racing establishments had to be native-born.[67] Not only was the approach ineffective, but it was unpopular with the rank and file. Member-

ship dropped off steadily. By 1970, nearly all of the shop's clerks were newly arrived Cubans.[68]

In August 1968, the Republican National Convention was held on Miami Beach, a place the novelist Norman Mailer dubbed the "materialism capital of the world." In the weeks leading up to the convention, Miami became a staging ground for a range of political figures from George Wallace—an independent candidate for the U.S. presidency, former governor of Alabama, and ardent segregationist—to Malcolm X. Representatives of Miami's chapters of CORE, the SCLC, the United Black Students (UBS), the Black Association for Total Equality (BATE), the Black Panther Party, and the Afro-Republicans determined they needed to bring these events to the awareness of those in the convention. They set up a meeting for the night of August 4 and gathered at the SCLC headquarters in the heart of Liberty City, intending to begin with a Vote Power rally on August 7. Instead, when the day for the rally came, what began as a peaceful demonstration quickly deteriorated into a full-blown riot. Miami's rioters did not try to provoke more direct action from police. Investigators concluded that the Miami riots stemmed directly local frustrations. Loss of jobs, forced displacements, and the "accumulation of grievances" against the police were cited repeatedly.[69]

While it was the riots that grabbed most national headlines, meetings among Cuban and African American hospital aides, nurses, janitors, and maids continued. SEIU members handed out bumper stickers promoting Democrat Hubert Humphrey's bid for the U.S. presidency. They also campaigned on behalf of Congressmen Claude Pepper and Dante Fascell, both of whom were known for their support of labor issues in Dade County.[70] Partnering with the Dade Council on Community Relations, in early 1969, Vernon Clark extended the organizing campaign among hospital and health-care workers to Dade County nursing homes as well. Four years later, Clark also led a drive to unite Locals 337 and 362. With Local 337 housing a majority of Cuban workers by the early 1970s, the merger provided a basis for collaboration, rather than competition, among Miami's Latino, West Indian, and African American service workers.[71]

In this way, the SEIU broke important ground. But it was unclear how long these tentative collaborations would last because the union's members disagreed about most other issues not narrowly related to work. The same month that Clark pushed to extend the nursing home organizing campaign and renewed efforts to organize University of Miami workers, the *Liberty News* published a series of calls to end the Cuban Refugee Program and the Freedom Flights altogether.[72] Nixon's well-publicized support for Cuban immigrants, along with his long-standing reputation as an ardent Cold Warrior, made him far more popular with Miami's Cubans than Humphrey. On issues of workplace fairness, the SEIU managed to forge a common ground among these very diverse groups of service workers. But without more fully integrating the issues that mattered most to workers, from the pressure of feeding and housing newly arrived relatives from abroad to federal and state policies, it was unclear just how much momentum these efforts could sustain.

Much to the frustration of the national SEIU office, as late as 1970, the city's locals remained unaffiliated with the AFL-CIO or the Florida State Council of Labor Unions. They also neglected to establish a formal civil rights committee, one of the few mandates from the national body.[73] Instead, the strength of Miami's SEIU locals seemed to rest in their more disperse, deeply local, less formalized structure. Coming at a time when immigration and civil rights were increasingly at odds, the SEIU thus provided one example of how class-based alliances could unite rather than divide these causes. But their sustainability was uncertain.

A City of Immigrants

By 1970, more than 50 percent of new immigrants arriving in Miami were working-class, compared to less than 5 percent one decade before.[74] Because men of working or military age were more often held back in Cuba, the proportion of women and the elderly among new Cuban immigrants increased. Even after the Freedom Flights ended in 1973, Cubans who had been relocated elsewhere in the United States moved back to Miami. Forty percent of Miami's residents were now born outside of the United States, compared to only 12 percent in 1960.[75]

This massive rise in immigration set Miami apart from nearly every other major metropolis in the United States. Even long-standing immigrant meccas like New York, Los Angeles, and San Francisco, or border communities like El Paso and San Diego, did not come close.[76] It was not just the scale, but the way these new waves of immigrants transformed, and were transformed by, Miami that made it unique. Unlike earlier periods where a polyglot assortment of immigrants made their homes in the city, Miami had become more than ever a Caribbean American city. Mexican Americans, who were now the second-largest ethnic minority in the United States, made up only a small fraction of Miami's Latinos. Cubans, Dominicans, Haitians, and West Indians comprised more than three-quarters of the city's foreign-born.[77] Where Mexican Americans had been living in the United States for generations, the bulk of Miami's Latinos had arrived within the past ten years. Jewish immigrants made up another 15 percent of Miami's residents, less than in earlier decades. And, for the first time in several decades, the proportion of African American residents grew rather than declined.[78]

Not only was Miami an immigrant city, it was now a minority-majority city, where Latinos and African Americans outnumbered Anglos.[79] With legalized segregation dismantled, many Anglos felt they had lost the last remaining protections of their advantage in the social hierarchy and so moved north to other cities in Florida and neighboring states. Individuals with less than a college education left in especially high numbers.[80]

Where a generation earlier it had been Jewish Americans and Jewish immigrants who moved from the margins of Miami's socioeconomic structures to the core, by the 1970s, Cubans and Cuban Americans surpassed any earlier models. The combination of federal support, Miami's strong ties to the Caribbean, and the educational resources many Cubans were able to amass before moving to the United States made this transformation possible for many. Without it, as the sociologist Alejandro Portes has noted, the "economic activities of these exiles would not have amounted to much more than a series of rags-to-riches stories."[81]

But not all Cubans and Cuban Americans shared in this upward mobility. Cubans continued to face significant downward occupational mobility once in the United States.[82] Where nearly half of all Cuban immigrants held professional jobs in Cuba, only about 13 percent were able to enter kindred professions once in the United States. Tradesmen and -women fared slightly better. Less than 12 percent of immigrants held "skilled" jobs in Cuba compared to 17.3 percent in the United States. The percentage of those in "unskilled," more low-paying positions also increased, more than doubling. This remained the case a decade after immigration.[83] Cubans were also vastly underrepresented among staffers in both the Dade County government and Dade County public schools. Many key public agencies, including the Miami and Dade County police and fire departments, local hospitals, and nursing homes had few employees who could speak Spanish. The result was often tragic, with the most vulnerable members of the community, like the elderly, disabled, and adolescents, hurt the most. As one study conducted by the University of Miami in 1974 noted, among adolescents who had been experiencing trouble or conflict in school, "discrimination was the most frequently mentioned source of unhappiness."

For some, this inspired a closing of ranks and an emphasis on self-sufficiency, as it had for black Americans. By the 1970s, Latinos, and Cubans especially, had one of the highest rates of self-employment of any ethnic group in the city. Many Cubans worked to establish independent labor organizations and lobbied successfully to have Miami-Dade County become officially bilingual and bicultural.[84] Rates of political representation also climbed quickly. Cuban Americans were elected to chair the state Democratic Party and to two city council seats in Hialeah. In 1973, Miami elected its first Latino mayor, a Puerto Rican named Maurice Ferré, a descendent of one of South Florida's oldest Puerto Rican families. Thus, while the overall picture for Cuban immigrants in Miami was not entirely rosy, it did represent some important gains made all the more remarkable by the relative newness of this latest immigration stream to Miami.

African Americans, however, continued to struggle. Unemployment for black residents in Miami remained around 10.2 percent, compared to 5.8 per cent for native-born whites and 6.2 percent for Latinos.[85] Latinos' median income, rates of home ownership, and overall education level also exceeded that of African Americans. Only among Puerto Ricans in Miami did rates of unemployment, education, and home ownership compare to that of African Americans.[86]

Civil rights advocates thus found themselves in a quandary. If new immigrants were not displacing working-class African Americans, then why did Cuban immigrants seem to fare so much better than the non-white, native-born in Miami? Structural factors, like skills obtained prior to migration and federal aid, provided one explanation. But as Miami transformed into an international city, many marveled at the persistence of racism toward African Americans even in a city where Anglo residents were fast becoming a minority. Afro-Cubans experienced this discrimination as well. Given the history of exceptional treatment granted to Spanish-speaking over English-speaking blacks, it was perhaps no surprise that the rapid influx of new immigrants embittered many. Thus fewer Afro-Cubans ultimately chose to settle in Miami than elsewhere in the United States. Only 5.5 percent of Miami's Cubans identified themselves as being either Afro-Cuban or of mixed race. In New York City, the population of Afro-Latinos was 8 percent. In New Jersey, it was even higher, at close to 12 percent.[87]

The persistence of racial discrimination was one striking feature of the post-1965 period. The fact that Miami's working class was more readily identified by its pink collars than blue was another. Women like María Espinoza remained the backbone of industries like garment manufacturing. Among service workers, too, women comprised over 60 percent of the city's workforce, the vast majority of them black or Latina.[88] They were especially vulnerable to the same patterns of exploitation used to divide ethnic workers one from another. When the Freedom Flights ended in 1973, many of Miami's industrialists complained once again that they faced a labor shortage. Newly arrived immigrants provided an answer. "Thank God for the Nicaraguans and Central Americans!" one manufacturer proclaimed in 1976, in comments eerily reminiscent of what was said about Cuban immigrants just a decade or so before. "Without them we'd really be in trouble."[89]

Just like the New York manufacturers who first came to Florida hoping to take advantage of its "right-to-work" legislation, by the mid-1970s many Florida manufacturers began using subcontractors beyond the U.S. borders. "When you consider that labor costs in Haiti or Central America can be as low as 20 cents an hour you are talking about a substantial number of manufacturers operating abroad that should be staying here," one ILGWU official explained.[90] Where in Miami workers were guaranteed the federal minimum of $2.60 an hour, hourly wages in other Latin American and Caribbean nations were as low as 20 cents. As one disgruntled contractor put it: "Here for 17 cents the manufacturer gets a zipper. In Haiti or Colombia, he pays 17 cents for a whole dress."[91] Where immigrants taking jobs from the native-born was one of the issues most often described as a threat in the 1950s and 1960s, by the 1970s, that issue had been replaced by the perceived threat of jobs moving overseas.

But unlike manufacturing, service industries stayed put. It was here that labor organizers realized they would need to train their energies if cross-ethnic alliances were going to be built. It was also here that most newcomers to the city, whether they arrived from abroad or elsewhere in the United States, first worked in Miami. For all of these reasons, service employment and the organization of service workers became a new focus of community-based activism in the decades ahead.

NOTES

1. María Espinoza, interview by the author.
2. Pedraza, "Cuba's Exiles"; Pérez, "Cubans in the U.S."
3. This recollection is supported by union organizers. See Anita Cofina, interview by Bruce Nissen and Guillermo Grenier, 1988, quoted in Nissen and Grenier, "Union Responses to Mass Immigration," 93.
4. Many Afro-Cubans had similar experiences. See *New York Times*, June 8, 1969.
5. Alex Brooks, "McCarran's Iron Curtain," clippings, 1952, NUL, Box C17, file: Immigration, 1951–1954; Roy Wilkins, NAACP, Testimony, President's Commission on Immigration and Naturalization, September 30, 1952, NAACP Papers, Supplement to pt. 1: 1951–1955, reel 2.
6. "Report of the Exec. Secretary to the Board of Directors for the Month of January 1951": 2, NAACP Papers, Supplement to pt. 1: 1951–1955, reel 2.
7. Memo, Joseph Robison, American Jewish Congress to Roy Wilkins, NAACP, January 2, 1956, NAACP Papers, pt. 24, ser. B, reel 1; Roy Wilkins to Joseph Robison, January 10, 1956, NAACP Papers, pt. 24, ser. B, reel 1; Roy Wilkins to Julius Edelstein, U.S. Senate, May 4, 1956, NAACP Papers, pt. 24, ser. B, reel 20.
8. Robert Saunders to Roy Wilkins, Gloster Current, and Ruby Hurley, November 3, 1961, NAACP Papers, Supplement to pt. 13, reel 6, box A186, folder: Florida.
9. Herbert Hill, NAACP, testimony before the U.S. Department of Labor Public Hearing, Miami, November 5, 1963, NAACP Papers, Supplement to pt. 13, reel 16; "52nd Annual Convention Resolutions," July 15, 1961, Philadelphia, NAACP Papers, Supplement to pt. 1, 1961–1965, reel 3. See also Diamond, "African-American Attitudes towards U.S. Immigration Policy." On Florida NAACP response, see Clippings, NAACP Papers, pt. 4, box A39, folder: Florida, 1966–1967, LOC.
10. *New York Times*, January 18, 1965; *Washington Post*, October 1, 1965. On the response of Jewish leaders, see *Congressional Record* (April 23, 1952): 4247; *Congressional Bi-Weekly Record* (February 1, 1965): 3; *Joint Hearings before the Subcommittees of the Committees on the Judiciary*, 563.
11. Statements, Congressman Emmanuel Celler, January 13, 1964, quoted in E. Kennedy, "The Immigration Act of 1965," 141; John A. Morsell to Doreen Taylor, New York, December 4, 1964,

NAACP Papers, pt. 24, ser. B, roll 20. Celler's comments were not published by the subcommittee.

12. Doreen Taylor, New York, to Whitney M. Young, Jr., National Urban League, New York, November 30, 1964, NAACP Papers, pt. 24, ser. B, roll 20. Douglass originally penned these words in an editorial published in the *Northern Star* in May 1853. See the *African Repository* 34 (May 1853): 136–38.

13. Letter to the editor, I. Theodore Peters, Committee on Race Relations, *Pittsburgh Courier*, February 1, 1965.

14. Robert Saunders, Annual Report (Dec. 1965), NAACP Papers, pt. 6, box C29, folder: Saunders, Reports 1965–1966, LOC.

15. *Florida Times Union*, July 25, 1966.

16. Miami Planning and Zoning Board, *The Miami Long-Range Plan*. For a detailed discussion, see Mohl, "Shadows in the Sunshine," 72–77. On the initial proposal, see Wilbur Smith and Associates, comp., *A Major Highway Plan*, 33–44. See also Greater Miami Urban League Report, n.d., NUL, I.A.107, folder: 1959 Miami, LOC.

17. *Miami Daily News*, August 19, 1965, November 19, 1965.

18. *Miami Herald*, November 25, 1965. See also *Miami Daily News*, February 13, 1967.

19. David Sullivan to James O'Halloran, April 20, 1966, Sullivan Papers, box 33, folder 21, SEIU Archives, RL-WSU.

20. *Miami Herald*, September 3, 1965.

21. Ibid., September 11, 1965.

22. Ibid., September 8–10, 1965.

23. *Time Magazine*, December 31, 1965.

24. García, *Havana, U.S.A.*, 40–45; C. Wong, *Lobbying for Inclusion*, 44–63.

25. *Public Papers of the Presidents of the U.S.: Lyndon B. Johnson*, 1965, vol. 2, no. 546, 1037–40.

26. "National Quotas for Immigration to End," 475–82.

27. On the national response, see press release, September 30, 1965, NAACP Papers, pt. 24, ser., B, reel 20; telegram, Philip Hart, U.S. Senate, to Roy Wilkins, September 22, 1965, NAACP Papers, pt. 24, ser., B, reel 20. On the Florida NAACP, see Robert Saunders to Roy Wilkins, February 26, 1965, NAACP Papers, Supplement to pt. 13, reel 6; *Report on Discrimination in Florida Agriculture*, May 10, 1965, NAACP Papers, Supplement to pt. 13, reel 6; *Miami Herald*, February 29, 1965; Mohl, *South of the South*, 43–47.

28. *Miami Herald*, October 16, 1965. Jones's comments were published in newspapers across the United States. See *Florence (S.C.) Morning News*, October 17, 1965; *Hagerstown (Md.) Daily Mail*, October 4, 1965; *Sunday Lincoln (Neb.) Journal and Star*, October 17, 1965.

29. The NAACP was sharply critical of the ILGWU's leadership, calling it "a trade union controlled by a rigid bureaucracy that long ago lost contact with its rank and file members." See testimony of Herbert Hill, House Committee for Education and Labor, August 17, 1962, NAACP Papers, Supplement to pt. 13, reel 3.

30. Robert Gladnick to David Dubinsky, October 4, 1965, ILGWU SERO Records, 3062/10, SLA-GSU.

31. Fetzer, *Public Attitudes toward Immigration*.

32. The historian María Cristina García provides the most detailed description of this process (García, *Havana, U.S.A.*, 39–41). See also *Miami Herald*, October 13, 1965.

33. Cuba barred several specific groups from exit altogether. These included young men of military service age, and professional, technical, and skilled workers whose exit was deemed to cause a major disruption in production or a shortage in key social services, such as teaching or medicine. See J. Clark, "The Exodus."

34. *Miami Daily News*, December 2, 1965, December 19, 1967.

35. *Miami Herald*, August 21, 1967. See also Amaro and Portes, "Una sociología del exilio."

36. *Miami Herald*, December 11, 1965.

37. Mats Lundahl, *Peasants and Poverty*, 623–47.

38. *Miami Herald*, December 13, 1965.

39. Martin Luther King Jr., "Statement on Resolutions Passed at the Annual SCLC Board Meeting," Miami (April 14, 1966), Martin Luther King, Jr. Papers, 1950–1968, box 118, 66–414–001, Martin Luther King, Jr. Center for Nonviolent Social Change, Inc.

40. *Miami Herald*, n.d., 1966, Clippings, SCLC Papers, pt. 1, reel 15.

41. Marvin Davies, field director, State of Florida, *Annual Report: May–Dec. 1966*, NAACP Papers, pt. 6, box C26, folder: Davies Annual Reports, 1966–1967, LOC.

42. Greater Miami CORE, "Voter Education Project, Monthly Report, Part I," October 8, 1962, CORE Papers: Addendum: 1944–1968, reel 22; Weldon J. Rougeau to Marvin Rich, May 27, 1964, CORE Papers, reel 19.

43. Dluhy, Revell and Wong, "Creating a Positive Future." Some popular accounts have estimated that as many as forty thousand people were displaced by the building of highway. Statistical evidence places that number around twelve thousand over the 1960s. See Dluhy et al., *The Historical Impacts of Transportation Projects*. See also Zimmerman, "Metropolitan Reform," 538.

44. Marvin Davies, Annual Reports: 1966 and 1967, NAACP Papers, pt. 6, box C26, folder: Davies Annual Reports, 1966–1967, LOC. One of the largest was a pilot project called "The Economic Security Project (ESP)," launched in Pinellas County in 1967.

45. T. W. Fair to Betti Whaley, March 5, 1965, NUL Papers, II.C.2, LOC; interview record, Ella Campbell, August 3, 1965, NUL Papers, box II.C.2, LOC.

46. Thelma Vernell Albury to Lucille Black, November 13, 1968, NAACP Papers, pt. 6, box C29, folder: M. Davies Correspondence, 1968, LOC.

47. Memo, Ruby Hurley, June 11, 1974, NAACP Papers, pt. 6, box C83, folder: Florida Miami Branch, 1967–1977, LOC.

48. Ruby Hurley to Marvin Davies, January 30, 1969, NAACP Papers, pt. 6, box C29, folder: M. Davies Correspondence, 1968, LOC; M. Davies to R. Hurley, February 3, 1969, NAACP Papers, pt. 6, box C29, folder: M. Davies Correspondence, 1968, LOC.

49. *Miami Herald*, June 24, 1966. See also testimony of Marvin Davies, U.S. Department of Labor Public Hearing, Miami, December 7, 1966, NAACP Papers, pt. 6, box A39, folder: Labor, Florida, LOC; *St. Petersburg Times*, August 4, 1966, July 27, 1966; *Fort Lauderdale News*, July 28, 1966. Davies's black nationalist views, including a public speech arguing that "[o]ur women need to produce more babies … until we comprise 30 to 35 percent of the population," drew sharp criticism from black women leaders as well. See Marlene Fried, Silliman, and Ross, *Undivided Rights*, 55.

50. Carr, *Puerto Rico*, 263; Cobas, "A New Test," 438.

51. Cobas, "A New Test," 438–41. Reports by the Greater Miami Urban League allude to this development as early as 1962. See H. Daniel Lang, "Testimony given at the Senate Sub-committee Hearing on Refugees and Escapees," December 26, 1961, NUL, II.A.71, LOC.

52. Robert Gladnick to Louis Stulberg, September 23, 1966, ILGWU Archives, Coll. #5780/008, box 53, folder 5, KCCU.

53. The AIFLD became very active in Latin America over this period, and launched a number of initiatives through the University of Miami's Center for Advanced International Studies. See J. Lovestone Collection, box 350, folder: AIFLD, Hoover Institution. On local membership, see Anna Cofino, interview by Bruce Nissen and Guillermo Grenier, in Nissen and Grenier, "Union Responses to Mass Immigration."

54. The most comprehensive history of the SEIU to date is Beadling, Cooper, and Palladino, *A Need for Valor*.

55. In Miami, employees at Pan American Airlines were the first to desegregate in the 1940s. See Lichtenstein, "Putting Labor's House in Order."

56. These included Local 291, Local 306 (Miami greyhound trainers), Local 337 (parimutuel employees), Local 362 (service employees), Local 468 (Dade County Metro employees), and Local 507 (guards and watchmen). See SEIU Archives, RL-WSU.

57. J. O'Halloran, Activities Report, October 11, 1966, Sullivan Office Files, box 65, folder 32, SEIU Archives, RL-WSU.

58. *Liberty News*, February 2, 1967.

59. Meeting Report, December 1966–February 1967, Sullivan Papers, box 65, folder 33, SEIU Archives, RL-WSU.

60. J. O'Halloran, Activities Report, March 8, 1967, Sullivan Papers, box 65, folder 33, SEIU Archives, RL-WSU. Records of Gore's work in the Bahamas are especially detailed and include numerous collaborations in Dade County.

61. See J. O'Halloran, Activities Report, April 24–25, 1964, May 12, 1965, October 5, 1967, Sullivan Papers, box 65, folders 30 and 34, SEIU Archives, RL-WSU.

62. Rafael M. Estévez, Hialeah, to J. O'Halloran, Miami, September 14, 1966, Sullivan Papers, box 33, folder 21, SEIU Archives, RL-WSU.

63. J. O'Halloran, Activities Report, March 25–27, April 3, 17, September 27, 1967, Sullivan Papers, box 65, folders 33 and 34, SEIU Archives, RL-WSU.

64. J. O'Halloran, Activities Report, May 18, 20–21, 1967, June 8, 16, 23, 1967, July 27, 1967, Sullivan Papers, box 65, folders 33 and 34, SEIU Archives, RL-WSU.

65. *Miami Herald*, March 31, 1967.

66. Ibid., October 15, 1967.

67. J. O'Halloran, Activities Report, December 26 and 27, 1967, Sullivan Papers, box 65, folder 35, SEIU Archives, RL-WSU.

68. J. O'Halloran, Activities Reports, December 20 and 22, 1968, Sullivan Papers, box 65, folder 36, SEIU Archives, RL-WSU.

69. National Commission on the Causes and Prevention of Violence, Miami Study Team, "Miami Report," 26–27.

70. J. O'Halloran, Activities Report, September 20, 28–29, October 23, November 5, December 17, 1968, Sullivan Papers, box 65, folder 36, SEIU Archives, RL-WSU.

71. George Hardy to J. O'Halloran, October 13, 1974, Hardy Papers, box 35, folder 49, SEIU Archives, RL-WSU.

72. *Liberty News*, March 22, 1969.

73. Fairchild to O'Halloran, December 16, 1970, Hardy Papers, box 35, folder 47, SEIU Archives, RL-WSU.

74. Pedraza, "Cuba's Exiles," 18; J. Clark, "The Exodus," 235–37.

75. In 1970, 41.2 percent of Miami residents were foreign-born. See C. Gibson and Lennon, "Historical Census," table 19.

76. The next-highest proportion of foreign-born in other metropolitan areas remained around or below 20 percent. These included New York City (18.2), Chicago (11.1) Los Angeles (14.6), Philadelphia (6.5), San Diego (7.6), San Francisco (21.6), Boston (13.1), and El Paso (13.8). See C. Gibson and Lennon, "Historical Census," table 19.

77. *U.S. Census of Population: 1970*, Subject Reports: National Origin and Language, table 15, 224–29.

78. The *American Jewish Yearbook* lists 187,500 Jewish residents in Miami in 1971. See *American Jewish Yearbook*, vol. 73, table 3, 388; *U.S. Census of Population: 1970*, Characteristics of the Population, Florida, section 1, chapter B, table 16, Florida 11–57; *U.S. Census of Population: 1980*, General Population Characteristics, Florida, chapter B, table 15: Florida 11–21.

79. Calculations based on the Miami SMSA show that in 1970 non-Hispanic whites made up 64 percent of Miami's population. By 1980, they made up just 47 percent. There was also a numerical decline of approximately fifty thousand non-Hispanic whites. In Miami, the percentage of non-Hispanic whites was even lower: 19.4 percent in 1980, and between 33 and 35 percent in 1970 (for 15 and 5 percent samples, respectively). See C. Gibson and Jung, "Historical Census Statistics," table 10.

80. *U.S. Census of Population: 1970*, Supplementary Report: Interstate Migration by State, no. 47, table 44, 318–20; *U.S. Census of Population: 1970*, Subject Report: Migration between State Economic Areas, table 1, 5.

81. Portes, "The Social Origins," 341.

82. "Occupations in Dade County and in Cuba," in *The Cuban Immigration, 1959–1966.*

83. Prohías and Casal, "The Cuban Minority in the U.S," 10, 12–14, 42. Their study notes 44.6 percent of Cuban immigrants working in unskilled trades.

84. *U.S. Census of Population: 1970*, Subject Reports: Persons of Spanish Origin, tables 15–18, 170–190; Grenier, "Ethnic Solidarity"; Lavender, "A History of Jewish and Hispanic Interaction," 72–73.

85. U.S. Department of Labor, *Area Trends in Employment and Unemployment*, October 1965; ibid., October 1966; U.S. Department of Labor, *Employment and Earnings* (1960–66).

86. U.S. Bureau of the Census, *Persons of Spanish Origin*, tables 15–18, 170–90.

87. Only 3 percent of Cubans living in the United States in 1970 were of African descent (U.S. Bureau of the Census, *Persons of Spanish Origin*, ix, 7–10).

88. The garment industry employed more Latinas than any other job sector in the state of Florida. The second was clerical/technical work (U.S. Bureau of the Census, *Persons of Spanish Origin*, table 9, 111; *U.S. Census of Population: 1970*, chapter C, Florida, table 46, 213–14).

89. *Miami News*, September 15, 1976.

90. *Miami Herald*, January 22, 1978.

91. U.S. Department of Labor, Wage and Hour Division, *History of Federal Minimum Wage*; *Miami News*, September 13, 1976.

DOCUMENTS FOR PART VIII

8-1. TULSA RACE RIOTS, 1921

Source: John Hope Franklin and Scott Ellsworth, "History Knows No Fences: An Overview," in *Tulsa Race Riot: A Report by the Oklahoma Commission to Study the Tulsa Race Riot of 1921*, February 28, 2001. Courtesy Research Division, Oklahoma Historical Society, Oklahoma City, Oklahoma.

EDITORS' INTRODUCTION

On May 31 and June 1, 1921, riots broke out in the city of Tulsa, Oklahoma resulting in the destruction of more than 1,000 homes, the annihilation of the black business area of the city, and an unspecified number of deaths, likely in the range of seventy-five to one hundred people, or more. This horrible event, which historians John Hope Franklin and Scott Ellsworth declare might be better termed a pogrom or an attempt at racial cleansing than a riot, was, unbelievably, largely forgotten by many Tulsans for decades. In 2001, the state issued a formal report which called for restitution to the riot victims and their families.

The late John Hope Franklin (1915–2009), was a native of Rentiesville, Oklahoma and professor of history at numerous colleges including Howard University, Brooklyn College, the University of Chicago, and Duke University. He was the author of numerous books, including *From Slavery to Freedom: A History of African Americans* (New York: Knopf, 1947). He was the past president of the American Historical Association, the Organization of American Historians, the Southern Historical Association, and the American Studies Association. In 1995 he was awarded the Presidential Medal of Freedom by President William J. Clinton. Scott Ellsworth is a visiting lecturer in Afroamerican and African Studies at the University of Michigan. He wrote *Death in a Promised Land: The Tulsa Race Riot of 1921* (Baton Rouge: Louisiana State University Press, 1992) and worked for the Duke University Oral History Program, the Smithsonian Institution, and various national news organizations.

History Knows No Fences: An Overview

As the centennial of Oklahoma statehood draws near, it is not difficult to look upon the history of our state with anything short of awe and wonder. In ninety-three short years, whole towns and cities have sprouted upon the prairies, great cultural and educational institutions have risen among the blackjacks, and the state's agricultural and industrial output has far surpassed even the wildest dreams of the Boomers. In less than a century, Oklahoma has transformed itself from a rawboned territory more at home in the nineteenth century, into now, as a new millennium dawns about us, a shining example of both the promise and the reality of the American dream. In looking back upon our past, we have much to take pride in.

But we have also known heartaches as well. As any honest history textbook will tell you, the first century of Oklahoma statehood has also featured dust storms and a Great Depression, political scandals and Jim Crow legislation, tumbling oil prices and truckloads of Okies streaming west. But through it all, there are two twentieth century tragedies which, sadly enough, stand head and shoulders above the others.

For many Oklahomans, there has never been a darker day than April 19, 1995. At two minutes past nine o'clock that morning, when the northern face of the Alfred P. Murrah Federal Building in downtown Oklahoma City was blown inward by the deadliest act of terrorism ever to take place on American soil, lives were shattered, lives were lost, and the history of the state would never again be the same.

One-hundred-sixty-eight Oklahomans died that day. They were black and white, Native American and Hispanic, young and old. And during the weeks that followed, we began to learn a little about who they were. We learned about Colton and Chase Smith, brothers aged two and three, and how they loved their playmates at the daycare center. We learned about Captain Randy Guzman, U.S.M.C., and how he had commanded troops during Operation Desert Storm, and we learned about Wanda Lee Howell, who always kept a Bible in her purse. And we learned about Cartney Jean McRaven, a nineteen-year-old Air Force enlistee who had been married only four days earlier.

The Murrah Building bombing is, without any question, one of the great tragedies of Oklahoma history. And well before the last memorial service was held for the last victim, thousands of Oklahomans made it clear that they wanted what happened on that dark day to be remembered. For upon the chain-link fence surrounding the bomb site there soon appeared a makeshift memorial of the heart—of teddy bears and hand-written children's prayers, key rings and dreamcatchers, flowers and flags. Now, with the construction and dedication of the Oklahoma City National Memorial, there is no doubt but that both the victims and the lessons of April 19, 1995 will not be forgotten.

But what would have come as a surprise to most of the state's citizens during the sad spring of 1995 was that there were, among them, other Oklahomans who carried within their hearts the painful memories of an equally dark, though long ignored, day in our past. For seventy-three years before the Murrah Building was bombed, the city of Tulsa erupted into a firestorm of hatred and violence that is perhaps unequaled in the peacetime history of the United States.

For those hearing about the 1921 Tulsa race riot for the first time, the event seems almost impossible to believe. During the course of eighteen terrible hours, more than

one thousand homes were burned to the ground. Practically overnight, entire neighborhoods where families had raised their children, visited with their neighbors, and hung their wash out on the line to dry, had been suddenly reduced to ashes. And as the homes burned, so did their contents, including furniture and family Bibles, rag dolls and hand-me-down quilts, cribs and photograph albums. In less than twenty-four hours, nearly all of Tulsa's African American residential district — some forty-square-blocks in all — had been laid to waste, leaving nearly nine-thousand people homeless.

Gone, too, was the city's African American commercial district, a thriving area located along Greenwood Avenue which boasted some of the finest black-owned businesses in the entire Southwest. The Stradford Hotel, a modern fifty-four room brick establishment which housed a drug store, barber shop, restaurant and banquet hall, had been burned to the ground. So had the Gurley Hotel, the Red Wing Hotel, and the Midway Hotel. Literally dozens of family-run businesses—from cafes and mom-and-pop grocery stores, to the Dreamland Theater, the Y.M.C.A. Cleaners, the East End Feed Store, and Osborne Monroe's roller skating rink — had also gone up in flames, taking with them the livelihoods, and in many cases the life savings, of literally hundreds of people.

The offices of two newspapers — the *Tulsa Star* and the *Oklahoma Sun* — had also been destroyed, as were the offices of more than a dozen doctors, dentists, lawyers, realtors, and other professionals. A United States Post Office substation was burned, as was the all-black Frissell Memorial Hospital. The brand new Booker T. Washington High School building escaped the torches of the rioters, but Dunbar Elementary School did not. Neither did more than a half-dozen African American churches, including the newly constructed Mount Zion Baptist Church, an impressive brick tabernacle which had been dedicated only seven weeks earlier.

Harsher still was the human loss. While we will probably never know the exact number of people who lost their lives during the Tulsa race riot, even the most conservative estimates are appalling. While we know that the so-called "official" estimate of nine whites and twenty-six blacks is too low, it is also true that some of the higher estimates are equally dubious. All told, considerable evidence exists to suggest that at least seventy-five to one-hundred people, both black and white, were killed during the riot. It should be added, however, that at least one credible source from the period — Maurice Willows, who directed the relief operations of the American Red Cross in Tulsa following the riot — indicated in his official report that the total number of riot fatalities may have ran as high as three-hundred.[1]

We also know a little, at least, about who some of the victims were. Reuben Everett, who was black, was a laborer who lived with his wife Jane in a home along Archer Street. Killed by a gunshot wound on the morning of June 1, 1921, he is buried in Oaklawn Cemetery. George Walter Daggs, who was white, may have died as much as twelve hours earlier. The manager of the Tulsa office of the Pierce Oil Company, he was shot in the back of the head as he fled from the initial gunplay of the riot that broke out in front of the Tulsa County Courthouse on the evening of May 31. Moreover, Dr. A. C. Jackson, a renowned African American physician, was fatally wounded in his front yard after he had surrendered to a group of whites. Shot in the stomach, he later died at the National Guard Armory. But for every riot victim's story that we know, there are others — like the "unidentified Negroes" whose burials are recorded in the now yellowed pages of old funeral home ledgers — whose names and life stories are, at least for now, still lost.

By any standard, the Tulsa race riot of 1921 is one of the great tragedies of Oklahoma history. Walter White, one of the nation's foremost experts on racial violence, who visited Tulsa during the week after the riot, was shocked by what had taken place. "I am able to state," he said, "that the Tulsa riot, in sheer brutality and willful destruc-tion of life and property, stands without parallel in America."[2]

Indeed, for a number of observers through the years, the term "riot" itself seems somehow inadequate to describe the violence and conflagration that took place. For some, what occurred in Tulsa on May 31 and June 1, 1921 was a massacre, a pogrom, or, to use a more modern term, an ethnic cleansing. For others, it was nothing short of a race war. But whatever term is used, one thing is certain: when it was all over, Tulsa's African American district had been turned into a scorched wasteland of vacant lots, crumbling storefronts, burned churches, and blackened, leafless trees.

Like the Murrah Building bombing, the Tulsa riot would forever alter life in Oklahoma. Nowhere, perhaps, was this more starkly apparent than in the matter of lynching. Like several other states and territories during the early years of the twentieth century, the sad spectacle of lynching was not uncommon in Oklahoma. In her 1942 master's thesis at the University of Oklahoma, Mary Elizabeth Estes determined that between the declaration of statehood on November 16, 1907, and the Tulsa race riot some thirteen years later, thirty-two individuals — twenty-six of whom were black — were lynched in Oklahoma. But during the twenty years following the riot, the number of lynchings statewide fell to two. Although they paid a terrible price for their efforts, there is little doubt except by their actions on May 31, 1921, that black Tulsans helped to bring the barbaric practice of lynching in Oklahoma to an end.

But unlike the Oklahoma City bombing, which has, to this day, remained a high profile event, for many years the Tulsa race riot practically disappeared from view. For decades afterwards, Oklahoma newspapers rarely mentioned the riot, the state's historical establishment essentially ignored it, and entire generations of Oklahoma school children were taught little or nothing about what had happened. To be sure, the riot was still a topic of conversation, particularly in Tulsa. But these discussions — whether among family or friends, in barber shops or on the front porch — were private affairs. And once the riot slipped from the headlines, its public memory also began to fade.

Of course, any one who lived through the riot could never forget what had taken place. And in Tulsa's African American neighborhoods, the physical, psychological, and spiritual damage caused by the riot remained highly apparent for years. Indeed, even today there are places in the city where the scars of the riot can still be observed. In North Tulsa, the riot was never forgotten — because it could not be.

But in other sections of the city, and elsewhere through out the state, the riot slipped further and further from view. And as the years passed and, particularly after World War II, as more and more families moved to Oklahoma from out-of-state, more and more of the state's citizens had simply never heard of the riot. Indeed, the riot was discussed so little, and for so long, even in Tulsa, that in 1996, Tulsa County District Attorney Bill LaFortune could tell a reporter, "I was born and raised here, and I had never heard of the riot."[4]

How could this have happened? How could a disaster the size and scope of the Tulsa race riot become, somehow, forgotten? How could such a major event in Oklahoma history become so little known?

Some observers have claimed that the lack of attention given to the riot over the years was the direct result of nothing less than a "conspiracy of silence." And while it is certainly true that a number of important documents relating to the riot have turned up missing, and that some individuals are, to this day, still reluctant to talk about what happened, the shroud of silence that descended over the Tulsa race riot can also be accounted for without resorting to conspiracy theories. But one must start at the beginning.

The riot, when it happened, was front-page news across America. "85 WHITES AND NEGROES DIE IN TULSA RIOTS" ran the headline in the June 2, 1921 edition of the New York Times, while dozens of other newspapers across the country published lead stories about the riot. Indeed, the riot was even news overseas, "FIERCE OUTBREAK IN OKLAHOMA" declared The Times of London.[5]

But something else happened as well. For in the days and weeks that followed the riot, editorial writers from coast-to-coast unleashed a torrent of stinging condemnations of what had taken place. "The bloody scenes at Tulsa, Oklahoma," declared the Philadelphia Bulletin, "are hardly conceivable as happening in American civilization of the present day." For the Kentucky State Journal, the riot was nothing short of "An Oklahoma Disgrace," while the Kansas City Journal was revolted at what it called the "Tulsa Horror." From both big-city dailies and small town newspapers — from the Houston Post and Nashville Tennessean to the tiny Times of Gloucester, Massachusetts — came a chorus of criticism. The Christian Recorder even went so far as to declare that "Tulsa has become a name of shame upon America."[6]

For many Oklahomans, and particularly for whites in positions of civic responsibility, such sentiments were most unwelcome. For regardless of what they felt personally about the riot, in a young state where attracting new businesses and new settlers was a top priority, it soon became evident that the riot was a public relations nightmare. Nowhere was this felt more acutely than in Tulsa. "I suppose Tulsa will get a lot of unpleasant publicity from this affair," wrote one Tulsa-based petroleum geologist to family members back East. Reverend Charles W. Kerr, of the city's all-white First Presbyterian Church, added his own assessment. "For 22 years I have been boosting Tulsa," he said, "and we have all been boosters and boasters about our buildings, bank accounts and other as sets, but the events of the past week will put a stop to the bragging for a while."[7] For some, and particularly for Tulsa's white business and political leaders, the riot soon became something best to be forgotten, something to be swept well beneath history's carpet.

What is remarkable, in retrospect, is the degree to which this nearly happened. For within a decade after it had happened, the Tulsa race riot went from being a front-page, national calamity, to being an incident portrayed as an unfortunate, but not really very significant, event in the state's past. Oklahoma history textbooks published during the 1920s did not mention the riot at all — nor did ones published in the 1930s. Finally, in 1941, the riot was mentioned in the Oklahoma volume in the influential *American Guide Series* — but only in one brief paragraph.[8]

Nowhere was this historical amnesia more startling than in Tulsa itself, especially in the city's white neighborhoods. "For a while," noted former Tulsa oilman Osborn Campbell, "picture postcards of the victims in awful poses were sold on the streets," while more than one white ex-rioter "boasted about how many notches he had on his gun." But the riot, which some whites saw as a source of local pride, in time more generally came to be regarded as a local embarrassment. Eventually, Osborn added, "the talk stopped."[9]

So too, apparently did the news stories. For while it is highly questionable whether — as it has been alleged — any Tulsa newspaper actually discouraged its reporters from writing about the riot, for years and years on end the riot does not appear to have been mentioned in the local press. And at least one local paper seems to have gone well out of its way, at times, to avoid the subject altogether.

During the mid-1930s, the *Tulsa Tribune* — the city's afternoon daily newspaper — ran a regular feature on its editorial page called "Fifteen Years Ago." Drawn from back issues of the newspaper, the column highlighted events which had happened in Tulsa on the same date fifteen years earlier, including local news stories, political tidbits, and society gossip. But when the fifteenth anniversary of the race riot arrived in early June, 1936, the *Tribune* ignored it completely — and instead ran the following:

Fifteen Years Ago

Miss Carolyn Skelly was a charming young hostess of the past week, having entertained at a luncheon and theater party for Miss Kathleen Sinclair and her guest, Miss Julia Morley of Saginaw, Mich. Corsage bouquets of Cecil roses and sweet peas were presented to the guests, who were Misses Claudine Miller, Martha Sharpe, Elizabeth Cook, Jane Robinson, Pauline Wood, Marie Constantin, Irene Buel, Thelma Kennedy, Ann Kennedy, Naomi Brown, Jane Wallace and Edith Smith.

Mrs. O.H.P. Thomas will entertain for her daughter, Elizabeth, who has been attending Randolph Macon school in Lynchburg, Va.

Central high school's crowning social event of the term just closed was the senior prom in the gymnasium with about 200 guests in attendance. The grand march was led by Miss Sara Little and Seth Hughes.

Miss Vera Gwynne will leave next week for Chicago to enter the University of Chicago where she will take a course in kindergarten study.

Mr. And Mrs. E.W. Hance have as their guests Mr. L.G. Kellenneyer of St. Mary's, Ohio.

Mrs. C.B. Hough and her son, Ralph, left last night for a three-months trip through the west and northwest. They will return home via Dallas, Texas, where they will visit Mrs. Hough's homefolk.[11]

Ten years later, in 1946, by which time the *Tribune* had added a "Twenty-Five Years Ago" feature, the newspaper once again avoided mentioning the riot. It was as if the greatest catastrophe in the city's history simply had not happened at all.[12]

That there would be some reluctance toward discussing the riot is hardly surprising. Cities and states — just like individuals — do not, as a general rule, like to dwell upon their past shortcomings. For years and years, for example, Oklahoma school children were taught only the most sanitized versions of the story of the Trail of Tears, while the history of slavery in Oklahoma was more or less ignored altogether. Moreover, during the World War II years, when the nation was engaged in a life or death struggle against the Axis, history text-books quite understandably stressed themes of national unity and consensus. The Tulsa race riot, needless to say, did not qualify.

But in Tulsa itself, the riot had affected far too many families, on both sides of the tracks, ever to sink entirely from view. But as the years passed and the riot grew ever more distant, a mindset developed which held that the riot was one part of the city's past that might best be forgotten altogether. Remarkably enough, that is exactly what began to happen.

When Nancy Feldman moved to Tulsa during the spring of 1946, she had never heard of the Tulsa race riot. A Chicagoan, and a new bride, she accepted a position teaching sociology at the University of Tulsa. But trained in social work, she also began working with the City Health Department, where she came into contact with Robert Fairchild, a recreation specialist who was also one of Tulsa's handful of African American municipal employees. A riot survivor, Fairchild told Feldman of his experiences during the disaster, which made a deep impression on the young sociologist, who decided to share her discovery with her students.[13]

But as it turned out, Feldman also soon learned something else, namely, that learning about the riot, and teaching about it, were two entirely different propositions. "During my first months at TU," she later recalled:

I mentioned the race riot in class one day and was surprised at the universal surprise among my students. No one in this all-white class room of both veterans, who were older, and standard 18-year-old freshmen, had ever heard of it, and some stoutly denied it and questioned my facts.

I invited Mr. Fairchild to come to class and tell of his experience, walking along the railroad tracks to Turley with his brothers and sister. Again, there was stout denial and, even more surprising, many students asked their parents and were told, no, there was no race riot at all. I was called to the Dean's office and advised to drop the whole subject.

The next semester, I invited Mr. Fairchild to come to class. Several times the Dean warned me about this. I do not believe I ever suffered from this exercise of my freedom of speech ... but as a very young and new instructor, I certainly felt threatened. For Feldman, such

behavior amounted to nothing less than "Purposeful blindness and memory blocking." Moreover, she discovered, it was not limited to the classroom. "When I would mention the riot to my white friends, few would talk about it. And they certainly didn't want to."[14]

While perhaps surprising in retrospect, Feldman's experiences were by no means unique. When Nancy Dodson, a Kansas native who later taught at Tulsa Junior College, moved to Tulsa in 1950, she too discovered that, at least in some parts of the white community, the riot was a taboo subject. "I was admonished not to mention the riot almost upon our arrival," she later recalled, "Because of shame, I thought. But the explanation was 'you don't want to start another.'"[15]

The riot did not fare much better in local history efforts. While Angie Debo did make mention of the riot in her 1943 history, *Tulsa: From Creek Town to Oil Capital*, her account was both brief and superficial. And fourteen years later, during the summer of 1957, when the city celebrated its "Tulsarama" — a week-long festival commemorating the semi-centennial of Oklahoma statehood — the riot was, once again, ignored. Some thirty-five years after it had taken the lives of dozens of innocent people, destroyed a neighborhood nearly one-square-mile in size in a firestorm which sent columns of black smoke billowing hundreds of feet into the air, and brought the normal life of the city to a complete standstill, the Tulsa race riot was fast becoming little more than a historical inconvenience, something, perhaps, that ought not be discussed at all.

Despite such official negligence, however, there were always Tulsans through the years who helped make it certain that the riot was not forgotten. Both black and white, sometimes working alone but more often working together, they collected evidence, preserved photographs, interviewed eyewitnesses, wrote about their findings, and tried, as best as they could, to ensure that the riot was not erased from history.

None, perhaps, succeeded as spectacularly as Mary E. Jones Parrish, a young African American teacher and journalist. Parrish had moved to Tulsa from Rochester, New York in 1919 or 1920, and had found work teaching typing and shorthand at the all-black Hunton Branch of the Y.M.C.A. With her young daughter, Florence Mary, she lived at the Woods Building in the heart of the African American business district. But when the riot broke out, both mother and daughter were forced to abandon their apartment and flee for their lives, running north along Greenwood Avenue amid a hail of bullets.[17]

Immediately following the riot, Parrish was hired by the Inter-Racial Commission to "do some reporting" on what had happened. Throwing herself into her work with her characteristic verve — and, one imagines, a borrowed typewriter — Parrish interviewed several eyewitnesses and transcribed the testimonials of survivors. She also wrote an account of her own harrowing experiences during the riot and, together with photographs of the devastation and a partial roster of property losses in the African American community, Parrish published all of the above in a book called *Events of the Tulsa Disaster*. And while only a handful of copies appear to have been printed, Parrish's volume was not only the first book published about the riot, and a pioneering work of journalism by an African American woman, but remains, to this day, an invaluable contemporary account.[18]

It took another twenty-five years, however, until the first general history of the riot was written. In 1946, a white World War II veteran named Loren L. Gill was attending the University of Tulsa. Intrigued by lingering stories of the race riot, and armed with both considerable energy and estimable research skills, Gill decided to make the riot the subject of his master's thesis.[19]

The end result, "The Tulsa Race Riot," was, all told, an exceptional piece of work, Gill worked diligently to uncover the causes of the riot, and to trace its path of violence and destruction, by scouring old newspaper and magazine articles, Red Cross records, and government documents. Moreover, Gill interviewed more than a dozen local citizens, including police and city officials, about the

riot. And remarkably for the mid-1940's, Gill also interviewed a number of African American riot survivors, including Reverend Charles Lanier Netherland, Mrs. Dimple L. Bush, and the noted attorney, Amos T. Hall. And while a number of Gill's conclusions about the riot have not withstood subsequent historical scrutiny, few have matched his determination to uncover the truth.[20]

Yet despite Gill's accomplishment, the riot remained well-buried in the city's historical closet. Riot survivors, participants, and observers, to be certain, still told stories of their experiences to family and friends. And at Tulsa's Booker T. Washington High School, a handful of teachers made certain that their students — many of whose families had moved to Tulsa after 1921 — learned at least a little about what had happened. But the fact remains that for nearly a quarter of a century after Loren Gill completed his master's thesis, the Tulsa race riot remained well out of the public spotlight.[21]

But beneath the surface, change was afoot. For as the national debate over race relations intensified with the emergence of the modern civil rights movement of the 1950s and 1960s, Tulsa's own racial customs were far from static. As the city began to address issues arising out of school desegregation, sit-ins, job bias, housing discrimination, urban renewal, and white flight, there were those who believed that Tulsa's racial past — and particularly the race riot — needed to be openly confronted.

Few felt this as strongly as those who had survived the tragedy itself, and on the evening of June 1, 1971, dozens of African American riot survivors gathered at Mount Zion Baptist Church for a program commemorating the fiftieth anniversary of the riot. Led by W.D. Williams, a longtime Booker T. Washington High School history teacher, whose family had suffered immense property loss during the violence, the other speakers that evening included fellow riot survivors Mable B. Little, who had lost both her home and her beauty shop during the conflagration, and E.L. Goodwin, Sr., the publisher of the *Oklahoma Eagle*, the city's black newspaper. Although the audience at the ceremony — which included a handful of whites — was not large, the event represented the first public acknowledgement of the riot in decades.[22]

But another episode that same spring also revealed just how far that Tulsa, when it came to owning up to the race riot, still had to go. The previous autumn, Larry Silvey, the publications manager at the Tulsa Chamber of Commerce, decided that on the fiftieth anniversary of the riot, the chamber's magazine should run a story on what had happened. Silvey then contacted Ed Wheeler, the host of 'The Gilcrease Story,'' a popular history program which aired on local radio. Wheeler — who, like Silvey, was white — agreed to research and write the article. Thus, during the winter of 1970–71, Wheeler went to work, interviewing dozens of elderly black and white riot eyewitnesses, and searching through archives in both Tulsa and Oklahoma City for documents pertaining to the riot.[23]

But something else happened as well. For on two separate occasions that winter, Wheeler was approached by white men, unknown to him, who warned him, "Don't write that story." Not long thereafter, Wheeler's home telephone began ringing at all hours of the day and night, and one morning he awoke to find that someone had taken a bar of soap and scrawled across the front windshield of his car, "Best check under your hood from now on."

But Ed Wheeler was a poor candidate for such scare tactics. A former United States Army infantry officer, the incidents only angered him. Moreover, he was now deep into trying to piece together the history of the riot, and was not about to be deterred. But to be on the safe side, he sent his wife and young son to live with his mother-in-law.[24]

Despite the harassment, Wheeler completed his article and Larry Silvey was pleased with the results. However, when Silvey began to lay out the story — complete with never-before-published photographs of both the riot and its aftermath chamber of commerce management killed the article. Silvey appealed to the chamber's board of directors, but they, too, refused to allow the story to be published.

Determined that his efforts should not have been in vain, Wheeler then tried to take his story to Tulsa's two daily newspapers, but was rebuffed. In the end, his article — called "Profile of a Race Riot" — was published in *Impact Magazine*, a new, black-oriented publication edited by a young African American journalist named Don Ross.

"Profile of a Race Riot" was a hand-biting, path-breaking story, easily the best piece of writing published about the riot in decades. But is was also a story whose impact was both limited and far from city-wide. For while it has been reported that the issue containing Wheeler's story sold out "virtually overnight," the magazine's readership, which was not large to begin with, was almost exclusively African American. Ultimately, "Profile of a Race Riot" marked a turning point in how the riot would be written about in the years to come, but at the time that it was published, few Tulsans — and hardly any whites — even knew of its existence.[25]

One of the few who did was Ruth Sigler Avery, a white Tulsa woman with a passion for history. A young girl at the time of the riot, Avery had been haunted by her memories of the smoke and flames rising up over the African American district, and by the two trucks carrying the bodies of riot victims that had passed in front of her home on East 8th Street.

Determined that the history of the riot needed to be preserved, Avery begin interviewing riot survivors, collecting riot photographs, and serving as a one-woman research bureau for anyone interested in studying what had happened. Convinced that the riot had been deliberately covered-up, Avery embarked upon what turned out to be a decades-long personal crusade to see that the true story of the riot was finally told.[26]

Along the way, Avery met some kindred spirits — and none more important that Mozella Franklin Jones. The daughter of riot survivor and prominent African American attorney Buck Colbert Franklin, Jones had long endeavored to raise awareness of the riot particularly outside of Tulsa's black community. While she was often deeply frustrated by white resistance to confronting the riot, her accomplishments were far from inconsequential. Along with Henry C. Whitlow, Jr., a history teacher at Booker T. Washington High School, Jones had not only helped to desegregate the Tulsa Historical Society, but had mounted the first-ever major exhibition on the history of African Americans in Tulsa. Moreover, she had also created, at the Tulsa Historical Society, the first collection of riot photographs available to the public.[27]

None of these activities, however, was by itself any match for the culture of silence which had long hovered over the riot, and for years to come, discussions of the riot were often curtailed. Taken together, the fiftieth anniversary ceremony, "Profile of a Race Riot," and the work of Ruth Avery and Mozella Jones had nudged the riot if not into the spotlight, then at least out of the back reaches of the city's historical closet.[28]

Moreover, these local efforts mirrored some larger trends in American society. Nationwide, the decade of the 1970s witnessed a virtual explosion of interest in the African American experience. Millions of television viewers watched *Roots*, the mini-series adaptation of Alex Haley's chronicle of one family's tortuous journey through slavery, while books by black authors climbed to the top of the bestseller lists. Black studies programs and departments were created at colleges from coast-to-coast, while at both the high school and university level, teaching materials began to more fully address issues of race. As scholars started to re-examine the long and turbulent history of race relations in America — including racial violence — the Tulsa riot began to receive some limited national exposure.[29]

Similar activities took place in Oklahoma. Kay M. Teall's *Black History in Oklahoma*, an impressive collection of historical documents published in 1971, helped to make the history of black Oklahomans far more accessible to teachers across the state. Teall's book paid significant attention to the story of the riot, as did Arthur Tolson's *The Black Oklahomans: A History 1541–1972*, which came out one year later.[30]

In 1975, Northeastern State University historian Rudia M. Halliburton, Jr. published *The Tulsa Race War of 1921*. Adapted from an article he had published three years earlier in the *Journal of Black Studies*, Halliburton's book featured a remarkable collection of riot photographs, many of which he had collected from his students. Issued by a small academic press in California, Halliburton's book received little attention outside of scholarly circles. Nonetheless, as the first book about the riot published in more than a half-century, it was another important step toward unlocking the riot's history.[31]

In the end, it would still take several years — and other books, and other individuals — to lift the veil of silence fully which had long hovered over the riot. However, by the end of the 1970s, efforts were underway that, once and for all, would finally bring out into the open the history of the tragic events of the spring of 1921.[32]

Today, the Tulsa Race Riot is Anything but Unknown

During the past two years, both the riot itself, and the efforts of Oklahomans to come to terms with the tragedy, have been the subject of dozens of magazine and newspaper articles, radio talk shows, and television documentaries. In an unprecedented and continuing explosion of press attention, journalists and film crews from as far away as Paris, France and London, England have journeyed to Oklahoma to interview riot survivors and eye-witnesses, search through archives for documents and photographs, and walk the ground where the killings and burning of May 31 and June 1, 1921 took place.

After years of neglect, stories and articles about the riot have appeared not only in Oklahoma magazines and newspapers, but also in the pages of the *Dallas Morning News*, *The Economist*, the *Kansas City Star*, the *London Daily Telegraph*, the *Los Angeles Times*, the *National Post of Canada*, the *New York Times*, *Newsday*, the *Philadelphia Inquirer, US. News and World Report, USA Today*, and the *Washington Post*. The riot has also been the subject of wire stories issued by the Associated Press and Reuter's. In addition, news stories and television documentaries about the riot have been produced by ABC News *Nightline*, Australian Broadcasting, the BBC, CBS News' *60 Minutes II*, CNN, Cinemax, The History Channel, NBC News, National Public Radio, Norwegian Broadcasting, South African Broadcasting, and Swedish Broadcasting, as well as by a number of in-state television and radio stations. Various web sites and Internet chat rooms have also featured the riot, while in numerous high school and college classrooms across America, the riot has become a subject of study. All told, for the first time in nearly eighty years, the Tulsa race riot of 1921 has once again become front-page news.[33]

What has not made the headlines, however, is that for the past two-and-one-half years, an intensive effort has been quietly underway to investigate, document, analyze, and better understand the history of the riot. Archives have been searched through, old newspapers and government records have been studied, and sophisticated, state-of-the-art scientific equipment has been utilized to help reveal the potential location of the unmarked burial sites of riot victims. While literally dozens of what appeared to be promising leads for reliable new information about the riot turned out to be little more than dead ends, a significant amount of previously unavailable evidence — including long-forgotten documents and photographs — has been discovered.

None of this, it must be added, could have been possible without the generous assistance of Oklahomans from all walks of life. Scores of senior citizens — including riot survivors and observers, as well as the sons and daughters of policemen, National Guards men, and riot participants have helped us to gain a much clearer picture of what happened in Tulsa during the spring of 1921. All told, literally hundreds of Oklahomans, of all races, have given of their time, their memories, and

their expertise to help us all gain a better understanding of this great tragedy.

This report is a product of these combined efforts. The scholars who have written it are all Oklahomans — either by birth, upbringing, residency, or family heritage. Young and not-so-young, black and white, men and women, we include within our ranks both the grandniece and the son of African American riot survivors, as well as the son of a white eyewitness. We are historians and archaeologists, forensic scientists and legal scholars, university professors and retirees.

For the editors of this report, the riot also bears considerable personal meaning. Tulsa is our hometown, and we are both graduates of the Tulsa Public Schools. And although we grew up in different eras, and in different parts of town — and heard about the riot, as it were, from different sides of the fence — both of our lives have been indelibly shaped by what happened in 1921.

History knows no fences. While the stories that black Oklahomans tell about the riot often differ from those of their white counterparts, it is the job of the historian to locate the truth wherever it may lie. There are, of course, many legitimate areas of dispute about the riot — and will be, without a doubt, for years to come. But far more significant is the tremendous amount of information that we now know about the tragedy — about how it started and how it ended, about its terrible fury and its murderous violence, about the community it devastated and the lives it shattered. Neither myth nor "confusion," the riot was an actual, definable, and describable event. In Oklahoma history, the central truths of which can, and must, be told.

That won't always be easy. For despite the many acts of courage, heroism, and selflessness that occurred on May 31 and June 1, 1921 the story of the Tulsa race riot is a chronicle of hatred and fear, of burning houses and shots fired in anger, of justice denied and dreams deferred. Like the bombing of the Murrah Federal Building some seventy-three years later, there is simply no denying the fact that the riot was a true Oklahoma tragedy, perhaps our greatest.

But, like the bombing, the riot can also be a bearer of lessons — about not only who we are, but also about who we would like to be. For only by looking to the past can we see not only where we have been, but also where we are going. And as the first one-hundred years of Oklahoma statehood draws to a close, and a new century begins, we can best honor that past not by burying it, but by facing it squarely, honestly, and, above all, openly.

NOTES

1. For the so-called "official" estimate, see: Memorandum from Major Paul R. Brown, Surgeon, 3rd Infantry, Oklahoma National Guard, to the Adjutant General of Oklahoma, June 4, 1921, located in the Attorney Generals Civil Case Files, Record Group 1–2, Case 1062, State Archives Division, Oklahoma Department of Libraries.

    For the Maurice Willows estimates, see: "Disaster Relief Report, Race Riot, June 1921," p. 6, reprinted in Robert N. Hower, *"Angels of Mercy": The American Red Cross and the 1921 Tulsa Race Riot* (Tulsa: Home stead Press, 1993).

2. *New York Call*, June 10, 1921.

3. Mary Elizabeth Estes, "An Historical Survey of Lynchings in Oklahoma and Texas" (M.A. thesis, University of Oklahoma, 1942), pp. 132–134

4. Jonathan Z. Larsen, "Tulsa Burning," *Civilization*, IV, I (February/March 1997), p. 46.

5. *New York Times*, June 2, 1921, p. 1. [London, England] The *Times*, June 2, 1921, p. 10.

6. *Philadelphia Bulletin*, June 3, 1921. [Frank fort] *Kentucky State Journal*, June 5, 1921. "Mob Fury and Race Hatred as a National Disgrace," *Literary Digest*, June 18, 1921, pp. 7–9. R.R. Wright, Jr., "Tulsa," *Christian Recorder*, June 9, 1921.

7. The geologist, Robert F. Truex, was quoted in the *Rochester* [New York] *Herald*, June 4, 1921. The Kerrquote is from "Causes of Riots Discussed in Pulpits of Tulsa Sunday," an unattributed June 6, 1921 article located in the Tuskegee Institute News Clipping File, microfilm edition, Series 1, "1921 — Riots, Tulsa, Oklahoma," Reel 14, p. 754.

8. Joseph P. Thoburn and Muriel H. Wright, *Oklahoma: A History of the State and Its People* (New York: Lewis Historical Publishing, 1929). Muriel H. Wright, *The Story of Oklahoma* (Oklahoma City Webb Publishing Company, 1929–30). Edward Everett Dale and Jesse Lee Rader, *Readings in Oklahoma History* (Evanston, Illinois: Row, Peterson and Company, 1930). Victor E. Harlow, *Oklahoma: Its Origins and Development* (Oklahoma City: Harlow Publishing Company, 1935). Muriel H. Wright, *Our Oklahoma* (Guthrie: Co-operative Publishing Company, 1939). [Oklahoma Writers' Project] *Oklahoma: A Guide to the Sooner State* (Norman: University of Oklahoma Press, 1941), pp. 208–209.

9. Osborn Campbell, *Let Freedom Ring* (Tokyo: Inter-Nation Company, 1954), p. 175.

10. In 1971, a *Tulsa Tribune* reporter wrote that, "For 50 years The *Tribune* did not rehash the story [of the riot]." See: "Murderous Race Riot Wrote Red Page in Tulsa History 50 Years Ago," *Tulsa Tribune*, June 2, 1971, p. 7A. A very brief account of the riot that not only gave the wrong dates for the conflict, but also claimed that "No one knew then or remembers how the shooting began — appeared in the *Tulsa World* on November 7, 1949.

    On the reluctance of the local press to write about the riot, see: Brent Stapes, "Un earthing a Riot" *New York Times Magazine*, December 19, 1999, p. 69; and, oral history interview with Ed Wheeler, Tulsa, February 27, 1998, by Scott Ellsworth.

11. *Tulsa Tribune*, June 2, 1936, p. 16.

12. *Ibid.*, May 31, 1946, p. 8; and June 2, 1946, p. 8.

    The *Tulsa World*, to its credit, did mention the riot in its "Just 30 Years Ago" columns in 1951. *Tulsa World*. June 1, 1951, p. 20; June 2, 1951, p. 4; and June 4, 1951, p. 6.

13. Telephone interview with Nancy Feldman, Tulsa, July 17, 2000. Letter from Nancy G. Feldman, Tulsa, July 19, 2000, to Dr. Bob Blackburn, Oklahoma City.

    On Robert Fairchild see: Oral History Interview with Robert Fairchild, Tulsa, June 8, 1978, by Scott Ellsworth, a copy of which can be found in the Special Collections Department, McFarlin Library, University of Tulsa; and, Eddie Faye Gates, *They Came Searching: How Blacks Sought the Promised Land in Tulsa* (Austin: Eakin Press, 1997), pp. 69–72.

14. Feldman letter, op. cit.

15. Letter from Nancy Dodson, Tulsa, June 4, 2000, to John Hope Franklin, Durham, North Carolina.

16. Angie Debo, *Tulsa: From Creek Town to Oil Capital* (Norman: University of Oklahoma Press, 1943).

    On the "Tulsarama," see: Bill Butler, ed., "Tulsarama! Historical Souvenir Program," and Quentin Peters, "Tulsa, I.T.," two circa-1957 pamphlets located in the Tulsa history vertical subject files at the Oklahoma Historical Society library, Oklahoma City.

17. Mary E. Jones Parrish, *Events of the Tulsa Disaster* (N.p., n.p., n.d.). in 1998. A reprint edition of Parrish's book was published by Out on a Limb Publishing in Tulsa.

    Tulsa City Directory, 1921 (Tulsa: Polk-Hoffhine Directory Company, 1921).

18. Parrish, *Events of the Tulsa Disaster* (rpt. ed.; Tulsa: Out on a Limb Publishing, 1998), pp. 27, 31–77, 115–126.

    Prior to the publication of Parrish's book, however, a "book let about the riot was issued by the Black Dispatch Press of Oklahoma City in July, 1921. Written by Martin Brown, the booklet was titled, "Is Tulsa Sane?" At present, no copies are known to exist.

19. Loren L. Gill, "The Tulsa Race Riot" (M.A. thesis, University of Tulsa, 1946).

20. *Ibid.* According to his thesis adviser, William A. Settle, Jr., Gill was later highly critical of some of his original interpretations. During a visit to Tulsa during the late 1960s, after he had served as a Peace Corps volunteer, Gill told Settle that he had been "too hard" on black Tulsans.

21. Scott Ellsworth, *Death in a Promised Land: The Tulsa Race Riot of 1921* (Baton Rouge: Louisiana State University Press, 1982), pp. 104–107. Gina Henderson and Marlene L. Johnson, "Black Wall Street," *Emerge,*) 4 (February, 2000), p. 71.

    The lack of public recognition given to the riot during this period was not limited to Tulsa's white community. A survey of back issues of the *Oklahoma Eagle* — long the city's flagship African American newspaper — revealed neither any articles about the riot, nor any mention of any commemorative ceremonies, at the time of the twenty-fifth anniversary of the riot in 1946. The same also applied to the thirtieth and fortieth anniversaries in 1951 and 1961.

22. *Oklahoma Eagle*, June 2, 1971, pp. 1, 10. *Tulsa Tribune*, June 2, 1971, p. 7A. Sam Howe Verhovek, "75 Years Later, Tulsa Confronts Its Race Riot," *New York Times*, May 31, 1996, p. 12A. Interview with E.L. Goodwin, Sr., Tulsa, November 21, 1976, in Ruth Sigler Avery, *Fear: The Fifth Horse man — A Documentary of the 1921 Tulsa Race Riot*, unpublished manuscript.

    . See also: Mable B. Little, *Fire on Mount Zion: My Life and History as a Black Woman in American* (Langston, OK: The Black Think Tank, 1990); Beth Macklin, "'Home' Important in Tulsan's Life," *Tulsa World*, November 30, 1975, p. 3H; and Mable B. Little, "A History of the Blacks of North Tulsa and My Life (A True Story)," type script dated May 24, 1971.

23. Telephone interview with Larry Silvey, Tulsa, August 5, 1999. Oral history interview with Ed Wheeler, Tulsa, February 27, 1998, by Scott Ellsworth. See also: Brent Stapes, "Unearthing a Riot," *New York Times Magazine*, December 19, 1999, p. 69.

24. Ed Wheeler interview.

25. *Ibid.* Larry Silvey interview. Ed Wheeler, "Profile of a Race Riot," *Impact Magazine*, IV (June–July 1971). Staples, "Unearthing a Riot," p. 69.

26. Avery, *Fear: The Fifth Horseman*. William A. Settle, Jr. and Ruth S. Avery, "Report of December 1978 on the Tulsa County Historical Society's Oral History Program," type script located at the Tulsa Historical Society. Telephone interview with Ruth Sigler Avery, Tulsa, September 14, 2000.

27. Mozella Jones Collection, Tulsa Historical Society. John Hope Franklin and John Whittington Franklin, eds., *My Life and An Era: The Autobiography of Buck Colbert Franklin* (Baton Rouge: Louisiana State University Press, 1997). John Hope Franklin, "Tulsa: Prospects for a New Millennium," remarks given at Mount Zion Baptist Church, Tulsa, June 4, 2000.

    Whitlow also was an authority on the history of Tulsa's African American community. See: Henry C. Whitlow, Jr., "A History of the Greenwood Era in Tulsa," a paper presented to the Tulsa Historical Society, March 29, 1973.

28. During this same period, a number of other Tulsans also endeavored to bring the story of the riot out into the open. James Ault, who taught sociology at the University of Tulsa during the late 1960s, interviewed a number of riot survivors and eyewitnesses. So did Bruce Hartnitt, who directed the evening programs at Tulsa Junior College during the early 1970s. Harnitt's father, who had managed the truck fleet at a West Tulsa refinery at the time of the riot, later told his son that he had been ordered to help transport the bodies of riot victims.

    Telephone interview with James T. Ault, Omaha, Nebraska, February 22, 1999. Oral history interview with Bruce Hartnitt, Tulsa, May 30, 1998, by Scott Ellsworth.

29. John Hope Franklin and Alfred A. Moss, Jr., *From Slavery to Freedom: A History of African Americans*, 7th edition (New York: Alfred A. Knopf, 1994), p. 476. Richard Maxwell Brown, *Strain of Violence: Historical Studies of American Violence and Vigilantism* (New York: Oxford University Press, 1975). Lee E. Williams and Lee. E. Williams 11, *Anatomy of Four Race Riots: Racial Conflict in Knoxville, Elaine (Arkansas), Tulsa and Chicago, 1919–1921* (Hattiesburg: University and College Press of Mississippi, 1972).

30. Kay M. Teall, ed., *Black History in Oklahoma: A Resource Book* (Oklahoma City: Oklahoma City Public Schools, 1971). Arthur Tolson, *The Black Oklahomans: A History, 1541–1972* (New Orleans: Edwards Printing Company, 1972).

31. Rudia M. Halliburton, Jr., *The Tulsa Race War of 1921* (San Francisco: R and E Research Associates, 1975).

32. Following the publication of Scott Ellsworth's *Death in a Promised Land* in 1982, a number of books have been published which deal either directly or indirectly with the riot. Among them are: Mabel B. Little, *Fire on Mount Zion* (1990); Robert N. Hower, *"Angels of Mercy": The American Red Cross and the 1921 Tulsa Race Riot* (Tulsa: Homestead Press, 1993); Eddie Faye Gates, *They Came Searching* (1997); Dorothy Moses DeWitty, *Tulsa: A Tale of Two Cities* (Langston, OK: Melvin B. Tolson Black Heritage Center, 1997); Danney Goble, *Tulsa!: Biography of the American City* (Tulsa: Council Oak Books, 1997); and, Hannibal B. Johnson, *Black Wall Street: From Riot to Renaissance in Tulsa's Historic Greenwood District* (Austin: Eakin Press, 1998).

    The riot has inspired some fictionalized treatments as well, including: Ron Wallace and J.J. Johnson, *Black Wall Street. A Lost Dream* (Tulsa: Black Wall Street Publishing, 1992); Jewell Parker Rhodes, *Magic City* (New York: Harper Collings, 1997); a children's book, Hannibal B. Johnson and Clay Portis, *Up From the Ashes: A Story About Building Community* (Austin: Eakin Press, 2000); and a musical, "A Song of Greenwood," book and music by Tim Long and Jerome

Johnson, which premiered at the Greenwood Cultural Center in Tulsa on May 29, 1998.

And more books, it should be added, are on the way. For as of the summer of 2000, at least two journalists were under contract with national publishers to research and write books about the riot and its legacy. Furthermore, a number of Tulsans are also said to be involved with book projects about the riot.

33. Oklahoma newspapers have, not surprisingly, provided the most expansive coverage of recent riot-related news. In particular, see: the reporting of Melissa Nelson and Christy Watson in the *Daily Oklahoman*; the numerous non-bylined stories in the *Oklahoma Eagle*; and the extensive coverage by Julie Bryant, Rik Espinosa, Brian Ford, Randy Krehbiel, Ashley Parrish, Jimmy Pride, Rita Sherrow, Robert S. Walters, and Heath Weaver in the *Tulsa World*.

For examples of national and international coverage, see: Kelly Kurt's wire stories for the Associated Press (e.g., "Survivors of 1921 Race Riot Hear Their Horror Retold," *San Diego Union-Tribune*, August 10, 1999, p A6); V. Dion Haynes, "Panel Digs Into Long-Buried Facts About Tulsa Race Riot," *Chicago Tribune*, May 16, 1999, Sec. 1, p. 6-, Frederick Burger "The 1921 Tulsa Race Riot: A Holocaust America Wanted to Forget," *The Crisis*, CVII, 6 (November-December 1999), pp. 14–18; Arnold Hamilton, "Panel Urges Reparations in Tulsa Riot," *Dallas Morning News*, February 5, 2000, pp. IA, 22A; "The Riot That Never Was," *The Economist*, April 24, 1999,

p. 29; Tim Madigan, "Tulsa's Terrible Secret," *Ft. Worth Star-Telegram*, January 30, 2000, pp. 1G, 6–7G; Rick Montgomery, "Tulsa Looking for the Sparks That Ignited Deadly Race Riot", *Kansas City Star*, September 8, 1999, pp. A1, A10; James Langton, "Mass Graves Hold the Secrets of American Race Massacre," *London Daily Telegraph*, March 29, 1999; Claudia Kolker, "A City's Buried Shame," *Los Angeles Times*, October 23, 1999, pp. A1, A16; Jim Yardley, "Panel Recommends Reparations in Long-Ignored Tulsa Race Riot," *New York Times*, February 5, 2000, pp. A1, A10; Martin Evans, "A Costly Legacy," *Newsday*, November 1, 1999; Gwen Florio, "Oklahoma Recalls Deadliest Race Riot," *Philadelphia Inquirer*, May 31, 1999, pp. A1, A9; Ben Fenwick, "Search for Race Riot Answers Leads to Graves," Reuter's wire story #13830, September 1999; Warren Cohen, "Digging Up an Ugly Past," *U.S. News and World Report*, January 31, 2000, p. 26; Tom Kenworthy, "Oklahoma Starts to Face Up to '21 Massacre," *USA Today*, February 18, 2000, p. 4A; and Lois Romano, "Tulsa Airs a Race Riot's Legacy," *Washington Post*, January 19, 2000, p. A3.

The riot has also been the subject of a number of television and radio news stories, documentaries, and talk shows during the past two years. The more comprehensive documentaries include: "The Night Tulsa Burned," The History Channel, February 19, 1999; "Tulsa Burning," *60 Minutes II*, November 9, 1999; and, 'The Tulsa Lynching of 1921: A Hidden Story", Cinemax, May 31, 2000.

8-2. KU KLUX KLAN INITIATION, WORCESTER, MASSACHUSETTS (1924)

Source: *Worcester Sunday Telegram*, October 19, 1924. Reprinted with permission of the Worcester Telegram & Gazette Corporation.

EDITORS' INTRODUCTION

Millions of Americans eagerly supported the 1920s hate-mongering organization known as the Invisible Empire, Knights of the Ku Klux Klan (KKK). Unlike the previous incarnation of the group, which was southern and rural in orientation, support for the new Klan was national and heavily urban. While numerous factors account for the Klan's resurgence, its simplistic message of "one hundred percent Americanism" hit a chord with many white Protestants who felt threatened by blacks, Catholics, Jews, and immigrants who flocked to cities in large numbers. On Saturday, October 18, 1924, approximately 15,000 Klan supporters attended a "klonvocation" at the New England Fairgrounds in the Greendale section of Worcester, Massachusetts. This KKK gathering, the largest in New England during the 1920s, took place in an industrial city with a population that was heavily immigrant (over 70 percent were foreign-born or the children of immigrants). Incredibly, despite the KKK's hostility to immigrants, roughly one-third of Worcester's Klan membership was itself foreign-born. The bulk of these immigrant Klansmen were Protestant Swedes. The description below is of an initiation ceremony, one of several that took place during the klonvocation, which brought 2,600 new members into the Klan.

PARADE OF KNIGHTS COLORFUL SCENE

The evening's parade and initiation was colorful in character, with 5,000 Knights in full regalia carrying red torches and marching about the track singing "Onward Christian Soldiers."

The initiation exercises at which 1,000 new members were added to the Klan organization were conducted with elaborate ceremony. The initiates were divided into two classes at separate ends of the field and repeated the Klan oath after officers, who conducted the ceremonies from temporary stagings erected on the inner rim of the tracks.

During the exercises an airplane bearing the red cross of the Klan sailed over the grounds several times. The big cross glowing like a ruby in the sky thrilled the great crowd more than the speeches or even the constant display of fireworks had done.

Klavern yesterday was distinctly a family affair, and it seems to be largely rural in character. Many small children wearing full Klan regalia paraded about the track.

Scores of babies cried constantly during the ceremonies and the crowd was not unlike that seen at the New England fair on one of the closing days.

No reporters were observed in the press box, however. In that respect the general character of the observance was distinctly different. Newspaper men were escorted to the exits many times during the course of the afternoon.

The exhibition building was used for registration headquarters, and as an application bureau for new members. Names of all the counties in Massachusetts appeared on large placards along the wall and each county had its own clerks to assist in the new membership drive.

8-3. ZOOT SUIT RIOTS (1943)

Source: Memo from Commander Clarence Fogg to District Patrol Officer, Downtown Los Angeles, June 8, 1943. United States Navy, Eleventh Naval District, San Diego, California.

EDITORS' INTRODUCTION

During the early 1940s, a new style of clothing called the zoot suit took hold in cities across the country. Baggy pegged pants, a knee-length jacket with wide lapels and padded shoulders, and a wide-brimmed, low-crowned hat typified the zoot suit look. Despite wartime restrictions imposed in April 1942 on excessive material in clothing—such as cuffs, pleats, and long coats—zoot suits remained in style with urban youth, especially African Americans in Harlem (New York City) and Chicanos in Los Angeles.

During the spring of 1943, a series of altercations broke out between Chicanos wearing zoot suits and white servicemen stationed at military bases in southern California. Racial tensions ran high in the area following a murder trial a year earlier, referred to as the Sleepy Lagoon case, in which seventeen Chicano youths were convicted of murdering a man. Newspaper accounts sensationalized the trial, playing on anti-Mexican stereotypes and fanning racial fears.

Riots broke out when white servicemen and civilians attacked Chicanos to remove their zoot suits and cut off their long hair. Chicanos fought back and full-scale rioting erupted, as roving bands of sailors and soldiers (which often numbered into the hundreds) hunted down their victims. The rioting eventually stopped in June 1943, when the U.S. military authorities suspended all leave and ordered personnel to return to base. The following document is a copy of one such order from Naval Commander Clarence Fogg to the Senior Patrol Officer in Downtown Los Angeles.

The following message for information to the District Patrol Officer.

Dictated by Senior Patrol Officer downtown Los Angeles.

0045, June 8, 1943

Quote:

Continued disorder.

Hundreds of service men prowling downtown Los Angeles mostly on foot—disorderly—apparently on prowl for Mexicans.

Have by joint agreement with Army Provost Marshall declared following Los Angeles city territory out of bounds to all Navy-Marines, Coast Guard, and Army personnel. — Main Street east to Los Angeles city limits.

All shore patrol are concentrated in the downtown area.

Disorderly personnel are being arrested by shore patrol.

Expect adverse publicity in morning newspaper.

Los Angeles Police have called in all off-duty men and auxiliary police to handle situation.

Naval Reserve Armory did not grant liberty. Men involved are from Marine activities, San Diego and El Toro, Navy activity composed of Roosevelt Base, Port Hueneme, and Destroyer Base, San Diego.

Situation under control at present except for widely separated incidents.

Groups vary in size from 10 to 150 men and scatter immediately when shore patrol approach. Men found carrying hammock clues, belts, knives, and tire irons when searched by patrol after arrest.

Army personnel are predominate tonight at ration [sic] of 4 or 5 to 1.

Senior Patrol Office will call District Patrol Officer at about 1000 today, June 8, 1943, if there is anything additional to report.

Given by R. O. Smith, C.M.M. Commander Fogg

8-4. *THE DOLLMAKER* (1954)

Harriette Arnow

Source: Harriette Arnow, *The Dollmaker* (New York: Avon Books, 1954).

EDITORS' INTRODUCTION

Harriette Arnow's bestselling and critically acclaimed novel, *The Dollmaker*, offers insight into the emotional effects of migration and immortalizes the important, but often overlooked, massive migration of white southerners to northern farms and cities. Arnow focuses on the white southern migration accompanying American entrance into World War II. Chad Berry brought out the importance of white southern migration in his essay, "The Great White Migration, 1945–1960," included in this section. Arnow, born in Kentucky in 1908, attended Berea College and graduated from the University of Louisville. Arnow's writing blossomed while she lived in Cincinnati, and she and her husband, newspaperman Harold B. Arnow, eventually settled on a farm in Ann Arbor, Michigan. In this section, the novel's main character Gertie Nevels and her children Reuben, Amos, Clytie, Cassie, and Enoch travel from Kentucky to Detroit, to reunite with Gertie's husband Clovis who labors in a war factory. They leave the train, only to hear comments of "hillbilly" around them, and take a cab through the surprising urban sights to their new lodgings.

The children fell silent as the driver, after much slow turning and slow driving through the narrow, crowded streets, came at last to a straight wide street, half buried in the ground, bounded by gray cement walls and crowded with cars and monstrous truck-like contraptions such as none of them had ever seen. Here there were no lights to stop them, and they went so fast that Gertie could only sit, shivering, staring straight ahead, or blinking and crouching over Cassie when they shot under bridges carrying more cars, buses, and even trains. The wind pried at the doors and the windows, finding every crack; and as there seemed to be no heat in the cab all of them were as cold, almost, as when they had waited on the sidewalk.

The unbroken rush past the gray walls and under the bridges ended at last. There followed more turnings down narrow streets, strange streets that, though crowded, seemed set at times in empty fields until one saw a slowly moving switch engine or a mountainous pile of coal blown free of snow. The smoke thickened, and through it came sounds such as they had never heard; sometimes a broken clanking, sometimes a roar, sometimes no more than a murmuring, and once a mighty thudding that seemed more like a trembling of the earth than sound. "Boy, I'd hate to live by one of them big press plants," the driver said, then asked of them all, "Don'tchas know where youses at? Right in u middle a some a Detroit's pride and glory—war plants."

Enoch kept twisting around to see, but there was little to be seen save blurred shapes through the snow and smoke. The railroad tracks multiplied, and twice jangling bells and red lights swinging in the wind held them still while long freight trains went by with more smoke rolling down and blotting out the world. It seemed suddenly to Gertie as if all the things she had seen—the blurred buildings, the smokestacks, the monstrous pipes wandering high above her, even the trucks, and the trains—as if all these were alive and breathing smoke and steam as in other places under a sky with sun or stars the breath of warm and living people made white clouds in the cold. Here there seemed to be no people, even the cars with their rolled-up windows, frosted over like those of the cab, seemed empty of people, driving themselves through a world not meant for people.

They drove for a long while through the sounds, the smoke and steam, past great buildings which, though filled with noise, seemed empty of life. They were stopped again on the edge of what looked to be an endless field of railroad tracks, to wait while a long train of flat cars went by. Each car carried one monstrous low-slung, heavy-bodied tank, the tank gray green, wearing a star, and holding, like the black feelers of some giant insect reaching for the sky, two guns. Gertie, hoping for something better to see, scratched another hole in the window frost. She was just turning away in disappointment when the whirling snow, the piles of coal, the waiting cars, the dark tanks moving, all seemed to glow with a faint reddish light. The redness trembled like light from a flame, as if somewhere far away a piece of hell had come up from underground.

8-5. *HUNGER OF MEMORY* (1982)

Richard Rodriguez

Source: Richard Rodriguez, *Hunger of Memory: The Education of Richard Rodriguez* (New York: Bantam Books, 1982).

EDITORS' INTRODUCTION

Author Richard Rodriguez' work, *Hunger of Memory*, relates the tale of his educational journey from elementary school to graduate school, and pauses to consider the teaching of religion in his early schooling and the state of his religious conviction as an adult. Rodriguez' life is shaped by his status as the child of immigrants. In this piece, he remembers the trials of the first days of school as a non-English speaker. Perhaps surprisingly, he speaks out against bilingual education. All children, he argues, learn a different language at school than they do at home. In the passage below, we see how the children's acquisition of English language skills ultimately tears at the fiber of Rodriguez' family. In every American household, parents and children come to feel they are metaphorically "speaking different languages" due to generational differences; in immigrant families, the generations are literally thinking and speaking in different tongues, and this may complicate inter-family relations. Examining the generational differences between immigrants and the children of immigrants is a classic topic within social science and social history.

Latinos comprise the largest minority group within the United States, and experts predict the group will triple between 2005–2050.[i] Rodriguez' personal struggles to define his place within his family and in society represent those of millions of others. *Hunger of Memory* found a number of critics who faulted Rodriguez for his arguments against bilingual education. Others expressed dismay at his actions; Rodriguez explains in his memoir that he left his Ph.D. program and turned down the offer of a university professor position out of concerns he had landed the job due to affirmative action. Rodriguez has published widely, including essays in *American Scholar* and *Harper's Magazine*. He provides regular commentary for the *PBS NewsHour*. His books include the Pulitzer-nominated *Days of Obligation: An Argument With My Mexican Father* (New York: Viking, 1992) and *Brown: The Last Discovery of America* (New York: Viking, 2002).

I remember to start with that day in Sacramento—a California now nearly thirty years past—when I first entered a classroom, able to understand some fifty stray English words.

The third of four children, I had been preceded to a neighborhood Roman Catholic school by an older brother and sister. But neither of them had revealed very much about their classroom experiences. Each afternoon they returned, as they left in the morning, always together, speaking in Spanish as they climbed the five steps of the porch. And their mysterious books, wrapped in shopping-bag paper, remained on the table next to the door, closed firmly behind them.

An accident of geography sent me to a school where all my classmates were white, many the children of doctors and lawyers and business executives. All my classmates certainly must have been uneasy on that first day of school—as most children are uneasy—to find themselves apart from their families in the first institution of their lives. But I was astonished.

The nun said, in a friendly but oddly impersonal voice, 'Boys and girls, this is Richard Rodriguez.' (I heard her sound out: *Rich-heard Road-ree-guess.*) It was the first time I had heard anyone name me in English. 'Richard,' the nun repeated more slowly, writing my name down in her black leather book. Quickly I turned to see my mother's face dissolve in a watery blur behind the pebbled glass door.

Many years later there is something called bilingual education—a scheme proposed in the late 1960s by Hispanic-American social activists, later endorsed by a congressional vote. It is a program that seeks to permit non-English speaking children, many from lower-class homes, to use their family language as the language of school. (Such is the goal its supporters announce.) I hear them and am forced to say no: It is not possible for a child—any child—ever to use his family's language in school. Not to understand this is to misunderstand the public uses of schooling and to trivialize the nature of intimate life—a family's 'language.'

Memory teaches me what I know of these matters; the boy reminds the adult. I was a bilingual child, a certain kind—socially disadvantaged—the son of working-class parents, both Mexican immigrants.

---

i "U.S. Population Projections," Pew Hispanic Center, www.pewhispanic.org.

In the early years of my boyhood, my parents coped very well in America. My father had steady work. My mother managed at home. They were nobody's victims. Optimism and ambition led them to a house (our home) many blocks from the Mexican south side of town. We lived among *gringos* and only a block from the biggest, whitest houses. It never occurred to my parents that they couldn't live wherever they chose. Nor was the Sacramento of the fifties bent on teaching them a contrary lesson. My mother and father were more annoyed than intimidated by those two or three neighbors who tried initially to make us unwelcome. ('Keep your brats away from my sidewalk!') But despite all they achieved, perhaps because they had so much to achieve, any deep feeling of ease, the confidence of 'belonging' in public was withheld from them both. They regarded people at work, the faces in crowds, as very distant from us. They were the others, *los gringos*. That term was interchangeable in their speech with another, even more telling, *los americanos*.

[...]

Following the dramatic Americanization of their children, even my parents grew more publicly confident. Especially my mother.

She learned the names of all the people on our block. And she decided we needed to have a telephone installed in the house. My father continued to use the word *gringo*. But it was no longer charged with the old bitterness or distrust. (Stripped of any emotional content, the word simply became a name for those Americans not of Hispanic descent.) Hearing him, sometimes, I wasn't sure if he was pronouncing the Spanish word *gringo* or saying gringo in English.

Matching the silence I started hearing in public was a new quiet at home. The family's quiet was partly due to the fact that, as we children learned more and more English, we shared fewer and fewer words with our parents. Sentences needed to be spoken slowly when a child addressed his mother or father. (Often the parent wouldn't understand.) The child would need to repeat himself. (Still the parent misunderstood.) The young voice, frustrated, would end up saying, 'Never mind'—the subject was closed. Dinners would be noisy with the clinking of knives and forks against dishes. My mother would smile softly between her remarks; my father at the other end of the table would chew and chew at his food, while he stared over the heads of his children.

Figure 8.3 The New Great Migration: Black Americans' Return to the South, 1965–2000 (2004). Source: William H. Frey, "The New Great Migration: Black Americans' Return to the South, 1965–2000" (Washington, DC: Center on Urban and Metropolitan Policy, The Brookings Institution, May 2004).

William H. Frey's important work offers perspective on the First and Second Great Migrations discussed in this part's articles. Frey, a demographer and sociologist at the prestigious Brookings Institution, examines late twentieth-century migration using the last four decennial censuses in the century. He concludes that the South saw net gains in black migrants coming from other U.S. regions in the late 1990s, ending a thirty-five year trend of South–North migration. College educated African Americans in particular chose to relocate to the South. The movement south demonstrates the importance of cities like Atlanta and Washington D.C. in the twenty-first century economy, and the considerable ties black migrant families had retained with extended family remaining in the South.

Black Net Migration, Metropolitan Areas with Largest Gains and Losses, 1965–2000

Rank	1965–70 Period		1975–80 Period		1985–90 Period		1995–2000 Period	
Largest Gains								
1	Los Angeles	55,943	Los Angeles	32,764	Atlanta	74,705	Atlanta	114,478
2	Detroit	54,766	Atlanta	27,111	Washington-Baltimore	29,904	Dallas	39,360
3	Washington-Baltimore	34,365	Houston	24,267	Norfolk-Virginia Beach	27,645	Charlotte	23,313
4	San Francisco	24,699	San Francisco	16,034	Raleigh-Durham	17,611	Orlando	20,222
5	Philadelphia	24,601	San Diego	15,621	Dallas	16,097	Las Vegas	18,912
6	New York	18,792	Dallas	12,460	Orlando	13,368	Norfolk-Virginia Beach	16,660
7	Dallas	16,384	Norfolk-Virginia Beach	10,141	Richmond	12,508	Raleigh-Durham	16,144
8	Houston	16,301	Washington-Baltimore	9,998	San Diego	12,482	Washington-Baltimore	16,139
9	Chicago	14,061	Kileen-Temple	9,959	Minneapolis-St. Paul	11,765	Memphis	12,507
10	Cleveland	10,914	Columbia	9,082	Sacramento	10,848	Columbia	10,899
Largest Losses								
1	Birmingham	–12,177	New York	–139,789	New York	–190,108	New York	–193,061
2	Memphis	–8,498	Chicago	–44,884	Chicago	–69,068	Chicago	–59,282
3	Mobile	–8,017	Philadelphia	–16,678	Detroit	–22,432	Los Angeles	–38,833
4	Pittsburgh	–5,003	Cleveland	–13,483	New Orleans	–17,395	San Francisco	–30,613
5	New Orleans	–4,886	St. Louis	–12,030	Los Angeles	–11,731	Detroit	–15,095
6	Montgomery	–4,635	Buffalo	–5,371	Cleveland	–11,553	New Orleans	–13,860
7	Charleston	–4,595	New Orleans	–4,889	St. Louis	–10,374	San Diego	–9,970
8	Jackson	–4,096	Boston	–4,576	San Francisco	–7,078	Miami	–7,772
9	Lafayette	–4,061	Pittsburgh	–3,022	Shreveport	–5,503	Pittsburgh	–7,425
10	Shreveport	–4,047	Kansas City	–2,795	Pittsburgh	–4,987	Boston	–7,018

Source: Author's analysis of 1970, 1980, 1990, and 2000 decennial censuses

Notes

* Metro areas are CMSAs, MSAs, and (in New England) NECMAs, as defined in Census 2000. Names are abbreviated.

PART IX

RACE AND THE POST-WAR METROPOLIS

EDITORS' INTRODUCTION TO PART IX

In the epilogue to his important American history survey, *America Becomes Urban: The Development of U.S. Cities & Towns, 1780–1980*, the late Eric H. Monkkonen cautions against the reduction of urban history to a set of problems. This warning is well-taken. Urban history contains the story of sexual scandal, political imbroglios, mobsters and gangsters, weather-related disasters, devastating fires, clashes between rich and poor, inter-racial violence, inadequate housing, dire poverty, families in crisis, and the like. Monkkonen concludes however, that "American cities are far more successful than we sometimes realize." American cities are the sites of considerable progress—technological, social, economic, political, and otherwise. Cities are simply large settlements of people, centers for human experiment, failure, and sometimes, success. Monkkonen posits that by studying the cities:

> We learn that our cities are highly flexible, that they have never experienced stasis, that diffuse sprawl and blurred boundaries are their heritages, that a hustling support of private enterprise is a long tradition, and that numerous multiple and small governments have been with us from the start. We also learn that American taxpayers have always been stingy as we tried to pass on the costs of services to the future through growth, but that we have historically been willing to create the service providing city and to indebt ourselves for infrastructural expansion, which in turn has promoted technological change. It is a complex legacy, one without easily identified heroes and villains. But the promise is there of an adaptive and potentially humane future.[1]

It is easy to only see the troubling aspects of the post-war metropolis. The promise of the post World War II economic recovery never translated into concrete, long-term improvements for urban civic life. Scholars have highlighted the weighty issues facing the post-war city as a corrective to the rampant myth-making about the period, much heralded as the heyday of the "greatest generation," who, after coming home from fighting in World War II, settled into pretty, multi-colored homes in the suburbs, raised their baby-boomer children, and held weekend barbeques. In the main, national and civic leaders of the period perpetuated racism in the housing market despite strong legal challenges and unsuccessfully turned to consumerism as a way to solve American problems.

The part opens with essays by Thomas J. Sugrue and Robert O. Self, who in their case studies of Detroit and Oakland leave us astounded by the exclusionary practices of the housing market. Sugrue and Self build on Arnold R. Hirsch's "second ghetto thesis" to explain how segregation continued on into the late twentieth century. The third essay is an excerpt from *American Project, the Rise and Fall of an American Ghetto* by sociologist Sudhir Alladi Venkatesh. While a graduate student, Venkatesh conducted a participant-observer study of the Robert Taylor Homes in Chicago in the style of Herbert Gans' *The Urban Villagers: Group and Class in the Life of Italian-Americans* (1962).

Optimism abounded in post-war America, but what largely resulted was a retreat from civic involvement and a failure to create the racially integrated neighborhoods necessary for a stronger nation. Urban renewal, launched in 1949 with the Housing Act of that year, promised a revitalized effort to improve our cities but led to the warehousing of the poor in high-rise public housing that later came to be torn down in most cities. The lessons learned in the Great Depression regarding care for the poor and the elderly largely fell from the public consciousness as good times returned for the white majority. Suburbanites started refusing to pay the bill for increased social services in the 1950s, a trend that only grew as the century went on. Californians voted for President Lyndon Baines Johnson in 1964, but voted against fair housing, one of Johnson's major issues. The contradictions of the post-war years are definitely difficult to grasp. Jon C. Teaford surmises that the period is best understood not as a time of triumph or of strife, but of a difficult road to an unrealized renaissance. Some of the best American minds tried to alleviate the problems of the city, but the battle was surely not won outright. Teaford writes, "Along that road there were enough pitfalls to warrant serious consideration whether the journey was worth the effort and whether the billions of dollars spent on physical and social renewal were wasted. To the perceptive observer the road was lined with ample monuments both to the possibilities and limitations of recent public policy."[2] For more by Jon Teaford see the essay "Messiah Mayors and the Gospel of Urban Hype" in Part V.

The documents in this part expand on the theme of social and economic tensions of post-war America, specifically conflicts that arose from the quest for fair and decent housing, good public schools, and civil and economic rights. **Document 9.3** on the Watts Riots of 1965 demonstrates how quickly a Los Angeles neighborhood ignited when black motorist Marquette Frye was arrested by white police officers. American Indians displaced from reservations by the unfulfilled promise of urban jobs sought justice throughout the 1960s [see **Document 9.4**]. The actions of the Oakland Black Panther Party for Self-Defense riveted the nation in the late 1960s; they set out their platform for equity, the Ten Point Plan, in 1966 [see **Document 9.5**].

In a movement that began in the late nineteenth century and gained momentum in the 1950s, white families fled the cities and moved to the suburbs to escape perceived urban disorder. Sloan Wilson's bestselling book, *The Man in the Gray Flannel Suit* [**Document 9.2**] portrays the story of a New York City businessman who commutes daily to and from his home in Connecticut. After decades, this suburban lifestyle became so firmly entrenched that suburbanites grew estranged from the urban center. Some balked at paying taxes, especially those that might fund social services and other programs to benefit city residents. Many urban dwellers who were white and/or middle- to upper-class, abandoned urban public education, once a linchpin of upward mobility, and sent their children to private and parochial schools. [See **Documents 9.6** *All Souls* and **9.8** "**Hispanic Communities and Urban Public Schools.**"]

NOTES

1. Eric H. Monkkonen, *America Becomes Urban: The Development of U.S. Cities & Towns, 1780–1980* (Berkeley: University of California Press, 1988), 238, 243–244.
2. John C. Teaford, *The Rough Road to Renaissance: Urban Revitalization in America, 1940–1985* (Baltimore: Johns Hopkins University Press, 1990), 9.

Class, Status, and Residence:
The Changing Geography of Black Detroit

Thomas J. Sugrue

Source: *The Origins of the Urban Crisis: Race and Inequality in Postwar Detroit* (Princeton: Princeton University Press, 1996).

EDITORS' INTRODUCTION

With its riot of 1943, Detroit rocketed into the forefront of national public consciousness. Known as the "Arsenal of Democracy" for its substantial role in providing industrial goods for the war effort, racial tensions ran extremely high in this midwestern metropolis. Detroit's symbolic power heightened even further with the city's riots in 1967. Detroit's resonance as a symbol gained strength in the early twenty-first century. As the American auto industry, centered in Detroit, faltered, the city remained in the national news. Just uttering the city's name "Detroit," quickly summoned a variety of themes, including white flight, deindustrialization, and the financial ramifications of global competition. Pundits and scholars continue to debate the extent to which this largely one-industry city is a bellwether of the rise and fall of American industrial cities.

Detroit, in the early post-war years, was primarily a black and white city, with few Hispanic or Asian residents. In Detroit, racial politics and the harsh effects of high levels of "white flight" play out in dramatic ways. The city certainly provides a window onto the great inequities of American life, inequities whose ramifications are only just being grasped by middle-class Americans many decades later. The post-war years were much heralded as a time of prosperity for millions of white Americans, but as Michael Harrington's 1962 book, *The Other America*, points out, the seeds of disquiet were planted in the 1950s. The industrial belt of the United States, stretching from the Middle Atlantic states on through the Middle West, began to atrophy during the 1950s. Industry moved southward, as Melanie Shell-Weiss notes in *Coming to Miami*, or moved overseas. **[See Melanie Shell-Weiss, "Citizenship and Civil Rights, 1964–1974," in Part VIII.]** It was once said of Detroit, "When Detroit sneezes, other cities catch pneumonia." Detroit, linked to one of the most important national industries, seemed a stable place to be. By the early twenty-first century, the saying no longer applied. Michigan led the nation's unemployment ratings and felt the impact of the economic downturn deep to its core.

Sugrue brings much-needed historical perspective to the history of the generationally poor, oftentimes referred to as the underclass (but not without substantial debate). Those, like Daniel Patrick Moynihan and E. Franklin Frazier, who have connected the existence of the underclass with what they perceive to be problems within the black family, have been successfully refuted. Those scholars, such as William Julius Wilson and Douglas Massey, who attribute the existence of generational poverty to structural issues within American society, have received more positive attention.[i] Sugrue steps into

---

i See E. Franklin Frazier, *The Negro Family in the United States* (Chicago: University of Chicago Press, 1939), Lee Rainwater and William L. Yancey, eds., *The Moynihan Report and the Politics of Controversy* (Cambridge, MA: MIT Press, 1967), William Julius Wilson, *The Truly Disadvantaged: The Inner City, the Underclass, and Public Policy* (Chicago: University of Chicago Press, 1987), and Douglas Massey and Nancy Denton, *American Apartheid: Segregation and the Making of the Underclass* (Cambridge, MA: Harvard University Press, 1994).

this treacherous intellectual ground confidently. As he points out, we can benefit by adding political analysis to this discussion. Sugrue writes, "This book is a guide to the contested terrain of the postwar city, an examination of the unresolved dilemmas of housing, segregation, industrial relations, racial discrimination, and deindustrialization. I argue that the coincidence and mutual reinforcement of race, economics, and politics in a particular historical moment, the period from the 1940s to the 1960s, set the stage for the fiscal, social, and economic crises that confront urban America today."[ii]

Sugrue's work draws on the findings of Arnold R. Hirsch's "second ghetto" thesis and brings our understanding of the segregated city further forward in time. **[See Arnold R. Hirsch, "The Second Ghetto and the Dynamics of Neighborhood," in Part VIII.]** Like Hirsch, Sugrue concluded that the segregated city was not inevitable, but carefully created through public policy. Analyzing Sugrue's maps of the expanding black neighborhoods of Detroit echoes the expansion of Chicago's black belt as seen in the maps in the Hirsch essay. In this article, Sugrue opens with the landmark *Sipes* v. *McGhee* case, challenging the legality of the restrictive covenants that allowed for segregated neighborhoods. The case joined with three other similar court battles to constitute the U.S. Supreme Court case, *Shelley* v. *Kraemer* (1948), which at long last invalidated restrictive covenants with racial restrictions.

Thomas J. Sugrue serves as the Edmund J. and Louise W. Kahn Professor of History and Sociology at the University of Pennsylvania. He is also the author or editor of the books *W.E.B. DuBois, Race, and the City: The Philadelphia Negro and its Legacy* (Philadelphia: University of Pennsylvania Press, 1998), *The New Suburban History* (Chicago: University of Chicago Press, 2006), and *Sweet Land of Liberty: The Forgotten Struggle for Civil Rights in the North* (New York: Random House, 2008). *The Origins of the Urban Crisis* garnered a number of awards, including the Bancroft Prize in American History (1998), the Philip Taft Prize in Labor History (1997), the Social Science History Association's President's Book Award (1996), the Best Book in North American Urban History Award, Urban History Association, of 1997, and one of *Choice*'s Outstanding Academic Books for 1997. He is currently at work on three new books, including a history of twentieth century America to be published by W. W. Norton.

CLASS, STATUS, AND RESIDENCE: THE CHANGING GEOGRAPHY OF BLACK DETROIT

The family who moves in next door to you or down the block, whether white or colored, is not the advance guard of an invasion. They are just folks following the old American custom of bettering their living conditions by seeking a finer place to live.

—Maceo Crutcher, president of the Detroit Realtist Association, and Walker E. Smith, Chairman of the Committee on Race Relations, the Detroit Realtist Association (1948)

THE SCENE was tense with drama. The place was the Wayne County Circuit Court in May 1945. The case was a civil suit against a middle-class black couple who had bought a house in an all-white West Side neighborhood. The defendants, Minnie and Orsel McGhee, were upwardly mobile, better off than most Detroit blacks at the end of World War II. She was one of Detroit's two hundred black school teachers, he was a relatively well-paid automobile worker. The plaintiffs were Benjamin and Anna Sipes and other members of the Northwest Civic Association. With the assistance of the NAACP and two leading black lawyers, Willis Graves and Francis Dent, Minnie and Orsel McGhee used the defense to challenge racially restrictive covenants, agreements that covered virtually all

---

ii Thomas J. Sugrue, *The Origins of the Urban Crisis: Race and Inequality in Postwar Detroit* (Princeton: Princeton University Press, 1996), 4–5.

Detroit neighborhoods outside the center city. Their immodest goal was "to wipe out Detroit's ghetto walls."[1]

When the McGhees bought a house on Seebaldt Street, in a white neighborhood just beyond the black enclave near Grand Boulevard and Tireman Avenue, Benjamin Sipes, their next-door neighbor, along with a delegation from the all-white Northwest Civic Association, sent the McGhees a letter asking them "to kindly vacate the property." When the McGhees refused, Sipes and the Northwest Civic Association filed suit to prevent them from moving in, on the grounds that the entire neighborhood was covered by a covenant that specified that houses could not be "sold nor leased to, nor occupied by any person other than one of the Caucasian race." Sipes testified that Orsel McGhee "appears to have colored features," and that Minnie McGhee "appears to be the mulatto type." Attorneys Dent and Graves tried to challenge Sipes's testimony, to no avail, on the grounds that "there is no simple way to determine whether a man is a member of the Mongoloid, Caucasoid, or Negroid race." The Wayne County Circuit Court held that the McGhees were indeed "colored" and that the covenant was valid.

That was only the beginning of the McGhees' legal assault on Detroit's ghetto walls. With the assistance of the NAACP Legal Department, they appealed to the Michigan State Supreme Court, this time deploying a more powerful legal weapon. They argued that the convenants violated state antidiscrimination laws and were unconstitutional under the Fourteenth Amendment. Again, their arguments fell on deaf ears. Michigan's conservative senior jurists denied their appeal and wrote an opinion reaffirming the validity of restrictive covenants. Still confident of the merits of their case, the McGhees' lawyers appealed to the United States Supreme Court.

Sipes was one of dozens of restrictive convenant cases that the NAACP and other civil rights groups argued before the courts in the 1940s (including several others in Detroit), with the hopes of undermining residential Jim Crow throughout the United States. Judges around the country had regularly upheld such convenants as necessary and proper to protect the rights of property owners. In addition, the Home Owners' Loan Corporation and Federal Housing Administration used racial restrictions to determine the actuarial soundness of a neighborhood. FHA underwriting manuals, in fact, encouraged developers to put racial restrictions on their properties to protect the "character" of a neighborhood and to maintain high housing values.[2]

In 1948, the U.S. Supreme Court heard arguments on *Sipes* along with three other covenant cases, including *Shelley* v. *Kraemer*, a similar case from Saint Louis after which the court's decision would be named. A team of lawyers, led by the NAACP's talented Thurgood Marshall, argued against racially restrictive convenants using both sociological evidence about the impact of convenants on black housing opportunities, and constitutional arguments about the illegality of state action that sanctioned racial discrimination. Persuaded by the NAACP's effective combination of constitutional and sociological arguments, the Vinson court unanimously ruled that restrictive covenants, including that at issue in *Sipes*, could not be enforced by the state. Detroit blacks were elated at the decision. "We Can Live Anywhere!" ran a banner headline in the *Courier*. "This far reaching decision means that a mortal blow has been struck at racial restrictions in homes, artificially created ghettoes,... and countless other jim-crow manifestations made possible because of heretofore enforced segregation in home ownership." The attack on restrictive covenants raised blacks' hopes that their housing woes would soon be over. And it inspired blacks in Detroit to move forth more boldly, looking for housing in the predominantly white neighborhoods beyond the city's racial frontier.[3]

In the era of *Sipes* v. *McGhee*, civil rights activists were optimistic that Detroit would soon be a racially integrated city. The wartime rhetoric of pluralism, tolerance, and antiracism, forged in response to Nazi atrocities, promised a future free of racial conflict. Even though the failure of public housing was a portent of resistance to racial change, the creation of a "second ghetto" in Detroit hardly seemed inevitable to observers of the postwar city. Liberals pointed to statistics showing mixed racial composition in certain neighborhoods as the herald of an era of equality. And civil rights groups clung to the hope that a combination of litigation, legislation, and moral suasion would break down the barriers of race that had kept blacks confined to the inner city. Just five years after the *Shelley* decision, Charles Wartman, editor of the *Michigan Chronicle*, Detroit's most important black weekly, believed that "private housing has become the means of bringing the Negro housing problem nearer solution, with every indication that ultimately it will solve the whole problem of the ghetto."[4]

Motivated by a hopeful vision of an interracial metropolis, civil rights organizations and city officials took an active role in challenging Detroit's racial boundaries. At the same time that African Americans battled to gain access to equal opportunities in the workplace, civil rights organizations directed their energies toward the private housing market. Their beneficiaries were growing numbers of black "pioneers" like the McGhees. Many were members of the city's African American elite.

Beginning in the late 1940s, black Detroit began to expand outward from the prewar concentrations on Detroit's East Side and the outlying enclaves (Map 7.1). Detroit blacks moved beyond the inner city to the east, and especially to the northwest. Between 1940 and 1950, the number of census tracts in Detroit with more than five hundred blacks increased from 56 to 73; between 1950 and 1960, the number increased to 166. The impact of the movement out of the traditional ghetto was mixed. Between 1948 and 1960, black housing conditions in Detroit improved significantly. The number of blacks in substandard buildings (dilapidated buildings or those that lacked running water or indoor toilets) plummeted between 1950 and 1960 from 29.3 percent to only 10.3 percent, and the number of overcrowded residences fell from 25.3 percent to 17.5 percent. The reason for the decline was simple: blacks

moved out of the oldest, most run-down sections of the city into newer neighborhoods, including some that contained some of Detroit's finest housing stock, that had been all-white through World War II.[5]

Even though black housing conditions improved, patterns of residential segregation remained intact. Virtually all of Detroit's blacks—regardless of class and education, occupation, age, or place of birth—shared the experience of discrimination in the city's housing market. Only a handful of blacks ever lived for any significant period of time within predominantly white sections of the city, unless they were living-in servants. But to describe the experience of blacks after World War II as a single process of "ghettoization" is to simplify a complex reality. Within the constraints of the limited housing market, Detroit's blacks created distinct subcommunities. The universality of the experience of segregation should not obscure other aspects of the residential life of black Detroiters. An unintended consequence of the opening of Detroit's housing market was a hardening of class divisions within black Detroit. As white movement increased the housing options available to black city dwellers, blacks began the process of sifting and subdividing, replicating within Detroit's center city the divisions of class that characterized the twentieth-century metropolis as a whole.[6]

In the rapidly changing economic climate of postwar Detroit, blacks had two increasingly divergent residential patterns. Those who were able to obtain relatively secure, high-paying jobs were able to purchase their own homes. Increasingly, they put pressure on the racial boundaries that confined them to the center city. But those who were trapped in poor-paying jobs and thrown out of work by deindustrialization remained confined in the decaying inner city neighborhoods that had long housed the bulk of Detroit's black population.

Pushing at the Boundaries: Black Pioneers

As one observer noted in 1946, "it is physically impossible to keep the Negro population imprisoned in its present warren."[7]

Families with resources found the housing shortage especially frustrating, because their expectations far exceeded the reality of housing in the city. As sociologists Alfred McClung Lee and Norman D. Humphrey observed: "Take an already crowded situation, add half again as many people, give them a great purchasing power, and still attempt to confine them within ... the old area, and the pressures developed within the increasingly inadequate 'container' will burst the walls."[8] Adequate housing for African Americans remained one of the great unfulfilled promises of postwar Detroit.

First to push at the city's racial boundaries was the rapidly growing black bourgeoisie. Since the early twentieth century, black entrepreneurs in Detroit had carved out an important niche in the city's economy by providing services to a clientele that white businessmen largely ignored. Because of systematic discrimination in public facilities, blacks created a separate system of "race" businesses—black-owned private hospitals, hotels, restaurants, and funeral homes. Hotelier A. G. Wright made his fortune through his ownership of Detroit's Hotel Gotham, known for providing luxurious accommodations to black travelers who were closed out of Detroit's white-owned hotels. Democratic political leader and U.S. Representative Charles Diggs had followed the typical trajectory of Detroit's black bourgeoisie, starting his career in his family's enormous "House of Diggs" Funeral Home. In addition, many African Americans in the city moved into the black elite through the traditional route of the ministry or education, and a growing number of women joined the ranks of the professions, primarily teaching and social work, after World War II.[9]

As the city's black population grew in the 1940s and 1950s, Detroit's black bourgeoisie kept pace. In 1953, Detroit boasted the largest number of independently owned black businesses of any city in the United States. Most black business leaders continued to find opportunities in traditional "race" businesses, which grew to meet the needs of the city's expanding African American population. As blacks joined the

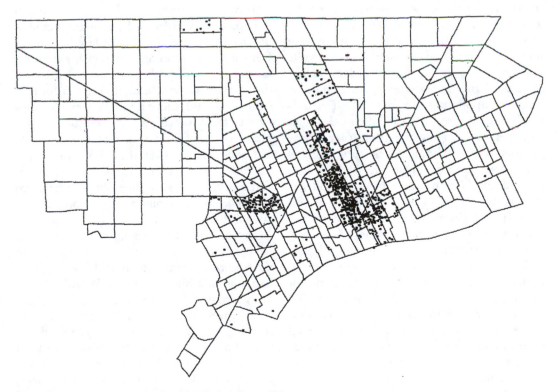

Figure 9.1 Black Population in Detroit, 1940. 1 Dot = 200.

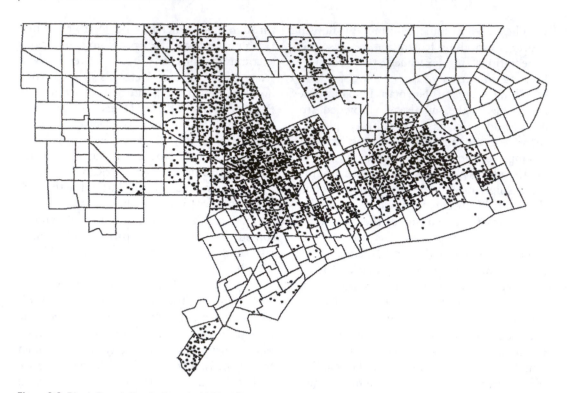

Figure 9.2 Black Population in Detroit, 1970. 1 Dot = 200.

postwar consumer culture with the same fervor, if not the same resources, as whites, a number of black entrepreneurs began to cross over into sectors of the economy that had been white-dominated. Like white Americans, if they could afford it, blacks purchased radios, televisions, cars, and new electric appliances. Some of Detroit's wealthiest African Americans made their fortunes by bringing the fruits of postwar prosperity to well-paid black auto workers and their families. One, Edward Davis, opened the nation's first black-owned car dealership in Detroit on the brink of World War II and profited handsomely from the postwar boom. Another, Sidney Barthwell, followed the trend of franchising and consolidation that reshaped the postwar retail industry. He owned a ten-store chain of pharmacies in black neighborhoods, catering to a rapidly growing base of customers that white-owned firms ignored. Black-owned savings and loan associations and insurance companies filled the niche left by bankers and actuaries who relentlessly redlined African American neighborhoods. Real

estate brokers and developers like Pete W. Cassey, Jr., James Del Rio, and Samuel Gibbons profited from the growing demand of Detroit blacks for single-family homes. Detroit was also home to two of the nation's largest black-owned financial institutions: the Great Lakes Mutual Life Insurance Company and the Home Federal Savings and Loan Association. And cultural entrepreneurs also fueled a creative expansion of the consumer market in radio and music, starting the city's first black radio station, and marketing (to an increasingly interracial audience) the Detroit sounds of blues, jazz, and Motown.[10]

Detroit's black elite sought the status and security of residence in districts outside of the traditional inner-city neighborhoods that had confined blacks through World War II. They looked for houses of the size and grandeur appropriate to their economic and social status. Paradise Valley, reported the elite, boosterish *Color* magazine, "can no longer hold the ambitious Negro. He wants to get out of this mecca for card sharks, numbers players, cult leaders, 'prophets,' and shady entertainment." By the late 1940s, Detroit's well-to-do blacks had the desire and the means to flee the overcrowded and decrepit inner city.[11]

Detroit's high-status blacks were not alone in their aspirations to escape the inner city. Also seeking to escape Detroit's "rat belt" were black city employees and automobile and defense workers, especially those who were able to obtain seniority in relatively high-paying factory jobs. Chrysler worker James Boggs recalled that "everybody saved some money during the war. That's how they bought all those houses when the war was over, because people had four years there when they just worked and there wasn't nothing to buy." For the first time, as a city race relations official reported in 1946, black workers had "sufficient funds ... to free themselves from the tragic overcrowding" in inner-city Detroit.[12] Working-class blacks looked in white neighborhoods on the periphery of black enclaves, whose streets, lined with modest frame and brick houses, had fulfilled the aspirations of a generation of blue-collar homeowners. In addition, by the early 1950s, they hoped to benefit from the new housing opportunities in outlying Detroit neighborhoods and suburbs. Thousands of new houses were constructed on vacant land in northeast and northwest Detroit, and in the booming suburbs to the north and west of the city. Once the Detroit housing market became fluid, the pent-up black demand for housing spilled over racial boundaries. As the housing market opened, black "pioneers" with more modest incomes began moving into neighborhoods on the periphery of black Detroit. By the late 1940s, several neighborhoods, most on the city's near Northwest Side, attracted upwardly mobile blacks fleeing the inner city. Many who moved into the older neighborhoods being abandoned by whites did not view their new homes as permanent residences, but instead treated their purchases or rentals as "a temporary route to the 'best' neighborhoods." Movement to older, formerly white areas gave black strivers a boost in status, while allowing them to build up equity or savings to fund the purchase of a better home in the future.[13] They hoped that eventually they would have the opportunity to live anywhere in the city, and that, like whites, they would enjoy unrestricted residential mobility.

The Open Housing Movement

The aspirations of Detroit's black elite and steadily employed working-class blacks coincided with the rapidly growing integrationist movement. Civil rights activists believed that blacks should have equal access to the housing market, but more than that, they should live side by side with whites to create a racially harmonious city. Only daily contact between the races would solve the nation's pressing dilemma of racial prejudice and inequality. Beginning modestly in the late 1940s, and expanding dramatically in the 1950s, a coalition of civil rights groups, religious organizations, and African American leaders directed their energies toward desegregating the city's housing market. They found a powerful ally in the Detroit Mayor's Interracial Committee (MIC), which had been founded after the race riot of 1943 to monitor racial tension in the city and advocate civil rights reform. Dominated by liberal whites and blacks who had close ties with civil rights organizations, the MIC consistently opposed segregation in public housing and other facilities, worked to abolish restrictive covenants, and investigated incidents of racial conflict in the city. The MIC, despite its name, was a largely independent city agency whose members were protected by civil service laws. Under Jeffries and Cobo, it became a refuge for a small, dedicated band of integrationists, who maintained close ties with civil rights groups throughout the country. In the late 1940s, the MIC spearheaded a joint campaign with civil rights and religious groups around the city to open the housing market to blacks.[14]

Inspired by the victory in *Shelley* v. *Kraemer*, open housing advocates hoped that with concerted action, they could abolish residential segregation once and for all. At first their attempts were primarily educational. The Coordinating Council on Human Relations (CCHR), founded in 1948, brought together the MIC and dozens of religious and civil rights organizations to persuade whites that they should support racial integration for moral and economically rational reasons. Throughout the 1950s, the CCHR held meetings with white church groups, parent-teacher associations, and community organizations. The primary goal was to convince whites to "act with intelligence and courage" when blacks moved in. Open housing activists attempted to persuade skeptical white homeowners that "racial change was inevitable," and that it was in their self-interest to "work for a sound, stable, liveable community." The CCHR's primary task was to challenge the conventional wisdom that "the movement of Negroes into your community will inevitably cause depreciation of value." If whites acted rationally rather than panicking and fleeing, their property values would remain stable or rise.[15]

To further their goal, civil rights organizations published pamphlets, brochures, and booklets extolling the virtues of integrated housing. They wrote articles and letters for local newspapers on the dangers of racial division and the benefits of racial integration, and published materials attempting to assuage homeowners' fears of property depreciation and crime following black movement into their neighborhoods. They looked to other cities for models of successful racial change. Open housing groups in Philadelphia, Cleveland, and Chicago shared materials with their Detroit counterparts. Detroit open housing advocates also assiduously cultivated contacts with national newspapers and magazines and worked with authors to develop stories on successful racial integration. A typical story, authored by NAACP head Walter White in *Saturday Evening Post* in the summer of 1953 and reprinted by civil rights groups around the country, added an interracial twist to typical 1950s depictions of family life. Included as an example of how "Detroit is now setting an example" of integration were photographs of black and white children playing together, and black and white housewives amiably chatting on their lawns.[16]

Religious leaders also joined together in an ecumenical call for racial harmony, even if many of their rank-and-file clergy members and coreligionists did not support them. In 1957, Edward Cardinal Mooney, the Roman Catholic Archbishop of Detroit, Reverend G. Merrill Lenox of the Detroit Council of Churches, and Rabbi Morris Adler of the Jewish Community Council issued a joint call for integration. To "deny the right of homeownership" to blacks, they argued, "is contrary to our American Constitution and an affront to the righteousness of God." In a typical exchange with a correspondent who denounced racial integration as "the hysterical championing of the primitive black minority," the Reverend Lenox challenged her to avoid the "course that is comfortable and in line with our accustomed thinking," and to act "in agreement with the will of God." But because most Protestant churches were congregationally controlled, many of their members paid little heed to the exhortations of the Detroit Council of Churches, particularly those that challenged conventional racial wisdom. As a result, Presbyterian, Congregationalist, Baptist, and Reformed churches tended to move quickly from racially changing neighborhoods.[17]

The Catholic response was somewhat different. Unlike Protestants, the vast majority of Catholics lived in territorial parishes, whose boundaries were strictly defined and whose churches were permanent fixtures on the cityscape. Local priests and their parishioners had long resisted black encroachment onto parish turf. Yet in the 1950s, a growing number of Catholic bishops and clergy, and a vocal minority of laypeople, began to speak out on civil rights issues. In 1957, Cardinal Mooney met with the pastors of St. Brigid and St. Cecilia parishes to work out a strategy to dampen white parishioners' resistance to blacks moving into their area. Liberal Catholic clerics like University of Detroit Professor John Coogan, S.J. joined in calls for racial equality. Taking a stand alongside Coogan were members of the small but vocal Catholic Interracial Council, and in the late 1950s, the Archdiocesan Council for Catholic Women. And in 1960, then-conservative Archbishop John Dearden (Mooney's successor) heeded the voices of racial liberalism in the Church and established a Commission on Human Relations. The hierarchy's growing racial tolerance brought it into conflict with parishioners who lived in racially changing neighborhoods and with pastors who often shared racial prejudices and looked with chagrin on white flight from their parishes. Angry Catholics barraged Father Coogan, a longstanding member of the Commission on Community Relations, with hate mail. And parishioners often greeted Catholic interracial activists with suspicion and hostility.[18]

Motivated by the burgeoning national civil rights movement, open housing groups moved beyond moral suasion to political action. In the mid-1950s, DUL officials lobbied the Federal Housing Administration and Home Owners' Loan Corporation to allow blacks to purchase foreclosed houses in white neighborhoods. United Automobile Workers officials also supported behind-the-scenes efforts to open the housing market to blacks (although they worked quietly, so as to avoid rankling the white rank and file who had so vocally repudiated the union on public housing issues in the 1940s). And by the late 1950s, civil rights groups began targeting the racially exclusionary practices of real estate brokers. Civil rights groups allied with liberal Democrats in the state legislature to extend the principles of the FEPC to the real estate market. In 1958 and 1959, Michigan's Senate and House of Representatives debated bills that would have fined real estate brokers who failed to sell or rent to anyone because of race. The bills did not pass, but increasing pressure from civil rights groups kept the issue on the table for the next decade.[19]

The challenge to real estate discrimination in Detroit burst onto the national scene in 1960, in the wake of revelations that realtors in suburban Grosse Pointe used a "point system" that ranked perspective home buyers by race, nationality, occupation, and "degree of swarthiness." Blacks and Asians were excluded from Grosse Pointe altogether, and Poles, Southern Europeans, and Jews needed higher rankings than families of northwestern European descent to be approved to move into the community. Private detectives, paid with

money from assessments on property owners and real estate brokers, investigated the backgrounds of potential residents, excluding them for such offensive practices as using outdoor clotheslines or painting their houses in gaudy colors. Even though the "point system" affected a relatively small segment of the metropolitan area's housing market, it brought the issue of discriminatory real estate practices to the center of political debate. In the wake of public hearings on Grosse Pointe, the state corporation and securities commissioner issued a regulation that would prevent the issuance of licenses to real estate brokers who discriminated on the basis of race, religion, or national origin.[20]

More importantly, the Grosse Pointe revelations led to a dramatic expansion of open housing activity in Detroit. In 1962, Catholic, Protestant, and Jewish leaders formed the Open Occupancy Conference (later renamed the Religion and Race Conference) to promote housing integration, particularly in suburban communities. The Conference had as its primary goal "to assist middle-class blacks to move into the larger community." As Leonard Gordon, one of the Conference's organizers, noted, "the inner city areas per se were not a programmatic focus." Like earlier open occupancy efforts, the Conference targeted the "small part of the Negro community that could afford outer-city and suburban housing." To that end, conference organizers embarked on a "challenge to conscience" campaign "to teach whites their moral duty" to support integration. A related open housing group, the Greater Detroit Committee for Fair Housing Practices, also appealed to religious sentiments. Greater Detroit Committee organizers handed out fair housing "Covenant Cards" in white churches, that churchgoers could sign and carry as proof of their commitment to housing integration. Committee members also assisted blacks trying to move to white areas and escorted blacks to real estate offices in Detroit's suburbs. Beginning in 1964 and 1965, open housing advocates began using testers—paired black and white home buyers who met separately with real estate brokers—to document discriminatory sales practices. Their efforts ensured that open housing remained a central issue in discussions of race, politics, and civil rights in Detroit throughout the 1960s.[21]

NOTES

1. Materials on *Sipes v. McGhee* can be found in NAACP, Group II, Boxes B135–137. Quotes from *Benjamin J. Sipes and Anna C. Sipes, James A. Coon, and Addie A. Coon, et al. v. Orsel McGhee and Minnie S. McGhee*, January 7, 1947. On other restrictive covenant cases, see Gloster Current to Shirley Adelson, July 12, 1946, ibid., Box B135, Folder: Sipes v. McGhee, 1946; Memorandum to Mr [Thurgood] Marshall from Marian Wynn Perry, May 1, 1946, ibid., Box B74, Folder: Legal, Detroit, Mich., General 1946, 1947; *Michigan Chronicle*, October 26, 1946; John C. Dancy, *Sand Against the Wind: The Memoirs of John C. Dancy* (Detroit: Wayne State University Press, 1966), 215–16; Marshall Field Stevenson, "Points of Departure, Acts of Resolve: Black-Jewish Relations in Detroit, 1937–1962," (Ph.D. diss., University of Michigan, 1988), 346–49; Clement Vose, *Caucasians Only: The Supreme Court, the NAACP, and Restrictive Covenant Cases* (Berkeley: University of California Press, 1959), 125–27.

2. See especially ibid.; also Charles Abrams, *Forbidden Neighbors: A Study of Prejudice in Housing* (New York: Harper, 1955).

3. *Shelley v. Kraemer*, 334 U.S. 1 (1948); *Pittsburgh Courier* (Detroit edition), May 8, 1948; for similar articles, see *Michigan Chronicle*, May 8, 1948; for an overview of the NAACP's strategy, see Mark V. Tushnet, *Making Civil Rights Law: Thurgood Marshall and the Supreme Court, 1936–1961* (New York: Oxford University Press, 1994), 81–98.

4. On wartime racial liberalism, see Philip Gleason, "Americans All: World War II and the Shaping of American Identity," *Review of Politics* 43 (1981): 483–518; and Gary Gerstle, "The Working Class Goes to War," *Mid-America: An Historical Review* 75 (October 1993): 303–22. Civil rights organizations and observers of race relations in the city retained a remarkable confidence in the possibility of integration. See George Schermer, "The Transitional Housing Area" (A Statement Prepared for the Housing Workshop Session of the 1952 NAIRO Conference, Washington, D.C.), November 10, 1952, DUL, Box 38, Folder A2–8; *Michigan Chronicle*, February 28, 1953; this and other interesting articles on black Detroit in the 1950s are reprinted in Charles J. Wartman, *Detroit—Ten Years After* (Detroit: Michigan Chronicle, 1953). As late as 1964, the *Detroit News* ran an article, "Housing Bias Crumbling in Detroit, Expert Finds," which cited city race rela-

tions official Richard Marks criticizing the cynicism of those who argued that "integration is the period between the arrival of the first Negro and the departure of the last white" (*Detroit News*, March 22, 1964).

5. Bernard J. Frieden, *The Future of Old Neighborhoods: Rebuilding for a Changing Population* (Cambridge: MIT Press, 1964), 24, 26, Tables 2.4 and 2.5.

6. For a general discussion of the social geography of cities, see Thomas J. Sugrue, "The Structures of Urban Poverty: The Reorganization of Space and Work in Three Periods of American History," in *The "Underclass" Debate: Views from History*, ed. Michael B. Katz (Princeton, N.J.: Princeton University Press, 1993), 85–117.

7. Henry Lee Moon, "Danger in Detroit," *Crisis* 53 (January 1946) 28.

8. Alfred McClung Lee and Norman D. Humphrey, *Race Riot* (New York: Dryden Press, 1943), 93.

9. For a thorough discussion of Detroit's black-owned businesses, see Richard W. Thomas, *Life for Us Is What We Make It: Building Black Community in Detroit* (Bloomington: Indiana University Press, 1992), 201–23. On the growing number of black women professionals (most of whom were schoolteachers), see Appendix B, Table B. 2.

10. *Detroit Free Press*, March 3, 1953, June 20, 1957; "Detroit's Top 100 Negro Leaders: Aces Who Help Build World's Motor City," *Color*, August 1948, 24–25; "Detroit's Top 100 Negro Leaders, Second Installment," ibid., October 1948, 38–39. Ed Davis, *One Man's Way* (Detroit: Edward Davis Associates, 1979); "Why Detroit is the Money City for Negroes," *Color*, December 1955, 16–21 (thanks to Eric Arnesen for this reference). On the rise of Motown, see Suzanne Smith, "Dancing in the Street: Motown and the Cultural Politics of Detroit" (Ph.D. diss., Yale University, 1996). The proportion of black men who were professionals, managers, proprietors, and officials did not rise until the 1960s, but it grew in absolute numbers as Detroit's black population rose. The number of black women managers, proprietors, and officials remained very small. See Appendix B, Tables B.1 and B.2.

11. "Why Detroit is the Money City," 16.

12. City of Detroit Interracial Committee, "Demonstrations Protesting Negro Occupancy of Houses (Area Bounded by Buchanan Street, Grand River Avenue, Brooklyn Avenue, Michigan Avenue, and Maybury Grand), September 1, 1945 to September 1, 1946," 2, 4, in CCR, Part I, Series 1, Box 3.

13. Mayor's Committee—Community Action for Detroit Youth Report, "A General Introduction to the Target Area," n.d.[c. 1963], DNAACP, Part I, Box 23.

14. For an overview of the MIC's history, see Tyrone Tillery, *The Conscience of a City: A Commemorative History of the Detroit Human Rights Commission and Department, 1943–1983* (Detroit: Detroit Human Rights Department, 1983).

Cincinnati (and a number of other cities) had similar organizations. See Robert A. Burnham, "The Mayor's Friendly Relations Committee: Cultural Pluralism and the Struggle for Black Advancement," in *Race and the City: Work, Community, and Protest in Cincinnati, 1820–1970*, ed. Henry Louis Taylor, Jr. (Urbana: University of Illinois Press, 1993), 258–79. The notion that integration was a solution to America's racial "dilemma" was most forcefully articulated by Gunnar Myrdal, *American Dilemma* (New York: Harper, 1944).

15. Schermer, "The Transitional Housing Area," 5–6.

16. Walter White, "How Detroit Fights Race Hatred," *Saturday Evening Post*, July 18, 1953, 26–27; "Buyer Beware," *Time*, April 16, 1956, 24; "Prejudice is Not Sectional," *Christian Century*, April 18, 1956, 477; "A Northern City Sitting on the Lid of Racial Trouble," *U.S. News and World Report*, May 11, 1956, 34–40; "New Carpetbaggers," *The New Republic*, July 30, 1956, 6; "Detroit Collision," *Ebony*, August 1961, 77–80; *New York Times*, April 22, 1962 (reprinted in "The Bagley Community: A Good Place to Live in Near-Northwest Detroit," copy in DUL, Box 53, Folder A17–2). On the open housing movement in Chicago, see James R. Ralph, Jr., *Northern Protest: Martin Luther King, Jr., Chicago, and the Civil Rights Movement* (Cambridge, Mass.: Harvard University Press, 1993).

17. In southwest Detroit, for example, a Methodist Church fled from a racially changing neighborhood, while members of the Catholic parish held fast. See Mayor's Interracial Committee, Minutes, April 17, 1950, CCR, Part III, Box 25, Folder 25–114; "Joint Statement," March 8, 1957, MDCC, Part I, Box 8, Folder: Press Releases—Civil Rights, 1952–64; G. Merill Lenox to Dorothy L. Tyler, April 19, 1956, ibid., Box 9, Folder: Civil Rights Activity Feedback; *Michigan Chronicle*, March 14, 1953; *Detroit Free Press*, June 24, 1957. On Jewish civil rights efforts, see Sidney Bolkosky, *Harmony and Dissonance: Voices of Jewish Identity in Detroit, 1914–1967* (Detroit: Wayne State University Press, 1991), 368–71.

18. "Activities Report, February 1–March 1, 1957, Cherrylawn Case," DUL, Box 38, Folder: A2–23; Detroit Urban League Board of Directors, Annual Meeting Minutes, February 28, 1957, CCR, Part III, Box 11, Folder 11–19; Interview with Mel Ravitz, in *Untold Tales, Unsung Heroes: An Oral History of Detroit's African American Community, 1918–1967*, ed. Elaine Latzmann Moon, (Detroit: Wayne State University Press, 1994), 334–35; Gerhard Lenski, *The Religious Factor: A Sociological Study of Religion's Impact on Pol-*

itics, Economics, and Family Life (Garden City, N.Y.: Doubleday, 1961), 65, 148, 190. Lenski's study was primarily based on Detroit research. See also John T. McGreevy, "American Catholics and the African-American Migration" (Ph.D. diss., Stanford University, 1992), 61, 159–62; Leslie Woodcock Tentler, *Seasons of Grace: A History of the Catholic Archdiocese of Detroit* (Detroit: Wayne State University Press, 1990), 308–9. For more on Catholics and racial change, see Chapters 8 and 9 below.

19. William H. Boone, "Major Unmet Goals that Suggest Continuing Attention," March 9, 1956, DUL, Box 38, Folder A2–16; Draft of Letter from UAW Legal Department to Thomas Kavanagh, Michigan Attorney General, July 18, 1956, ibid., Folder A2–17, "Election Warning" [1958], CCR, Part III, Box 13, Folder 13–28; *DREB News*, April 24, 1959, copy ibid., Box 14, Folder 14–5; "Your Co-operation Asked" [1959], flyer attached to letter from Robert Hutton to Merrill Lenox, March 31, 1959; Merrill Lenox to Robert Hutton, April 8, 1959, MDCC, Part I, Box 10, Folder: Housing-Detroit Real Estate Board; Detroit Branch NAACP, Board of Directors Meeting, September 14, 1959, NAACP, Group III, Box C65, Folder: Detroit, Michigan, Sept.–Dec. 1959.

20. *Detroit Free Press*, April 21, 1960, June 22, 1960; *New York Times*, June 5, 1960; *Detroit News*, August 5, 1960, October 19, 1960, November 28, 1960; "Memorandum in Opposition to Proposal 1007," December 6, 1961, in DNAACP, Part I, Box 14; Kathy Cosseboom, *Grosse Pointe, Michigan: Race Against Race* (East Lansing: Michigan State University Press, 1972).

21. Detroit Urban League, Department of Housing, Second Quarterly Report, April–June 1964, in DUL, Box 53, Folder A27–2; Eloise Whitten, "Open Occupancy: A Challenge," ibid., Folder A17–7; *Detroit News*, January 3, 1963, July 28, 1963, September 19, 1963; Citizens for a United Detroit, "Why We Oppose the Proposed Home Onwer's Ordinance," MDCC, Part I, Box 10, Folder: Housing—Home Owners' Ordinance, Citizens for a United Detroit; Leonard Gordon, "Attempts to Bridge the Racial Gap: The Religious Establishment," in *City in Racial Crisis: The Case of Detroit Pre- and Post- the 1967 Riot* (n.p.: William C. Brown Publishers, 1971), 18–24, quotes 23–24; see also Mayor Jerome Cavanagh, Richard Marks, and Charles Butler, "Messages to the Open Occupancy Conference," ibid., 29–33; materials on "Operation Open Door," March 1965, RK, Box 5, Folder 5–24. For resistance to open housing efforts in the wealthy suburb of Birmingham, see *Brightmoor Journal*, March 17, 1966.

White Noose

Robert O. Self

Source: *American Babylon: Race and the Struggle for Postwar Oakland*
(Princeton: Princeton University Press, 2003).

EDITORS' INTRODUCTION

Robert O. Self's book on post-war Oakland demonstrates that Detroit was not alone in its racial strife. Unlike Detroit, however, Oakland and the surrounding area had a more diverse demographic, containing a high number of Hispanics and Asians in addition to white and black residents. Still, in Self's narrative, major issues do come down largely to a black and white divide.

Self deftly employs the framework of property to provide us with a nuanced understanding of the Bay Area, a pivotal battleground in the long civil rights movement of the twentieth century and a growing white activism, which, according to the author, cannot be solely seen as a backlash movement. The whites, to some (perhaps high) degree disingenuously, described their own efforts with the rhetoric of individual rights. As a state, California faced the challenges of great growth, struggling with open access to public housing and the costs of other social programs for its poorer residents. Groups like the California Real Estate Association (CREA) argued that the free ownership of private property allowed for the greatest social good, and that housing should be unregulated. Self writes that the homeowner populism of the time "precipitated a series of suburban counterrevolutions in these two decades that lay the groundwork for the so-called tax revolt of 1978. The price of California's extraordinary growth had to be met, but not, if suburban homeowners had their way, by them."* The largely white suburbs came to form a physical and metaphorical noose around Oakland, strangling the city in terms of housing needs and economic viability. Those taking part in the white flight to the suburbs refused to pay higher taxes for the social and economic support of the city and the less affluent residents there. They refused to acknowledge their own tax benefits, coming from such governmental agencies as the Veteran's Administration and the Federal Housing Administration, which offered loan guarantees to white home buyers to a much higher degree than home buyers of color. Once families had purchased housing, of course, the interest on the mortgage payments became tax deductable. Additionally, continued racist controls of housing access helped suburban properties gain market value at a rate unmatched in Oakland itself.

The region's initial promise of serving as a post-war industrial garden—a region replete with jobs, fine housing options, and a pleasing metropolitan setting—would not unfold as many had hoped. At the two extremes, the dream ended in the radical politics of the separatist Black Panther Party, born in the area, and the individualistic, anti-tax conservative politics of the white homeowners. **[See Document 9.5.]** The latter view quickly became common throughout the nation, and ushered in the Reagan Revolution of the 1980s. Although American cities had long featured suburbs, the city–suburb dualism came of age in these decades, defining the period's politics and lived reality.

---

* Robert O. Self, *American Babylon: Race and the Struggle for Postwar Oakland* (Princeton: Princeton University Press, 2003), 259.

Robert O. Self is an associate professor of history at Brown University. *American Babylon* was awarded four major prizes: the James A. Rawley Prize, Best Book on U.S. Race Relations (2005) from the Organization of American Historians; the Best Book in Urban Affairs from the Urban Affairs Association (2005); the Ralph J. Bunche Award, Best Book on Ethnic Pluralism (2004) from the American Political Science Association; and the Best Book in North American Urban History (2004) from the Urban History Association. Self is at work on a new book, provisionally titled, *A New Political Order: Gender and Sexuality in America From Watts to Reagan.*

A WHITE NOOSE

THE SUBURBAN "white noose" surrounding the urban black community stood metaphorically for metropolitan inequality and segregation. Unwelcome in the South County (Southern Alameda County) suburbs, African Americans in Oakland were denied access to the region's fastest growing employment and housing markets. Suburban Alameda County, from San Leandro through Fremont (and across the Santa Clara County line into Milpitas) *was* closed to black homebuyers in most important respects through the middle 1970s. But the denial of access was only one story. It must be joined to others. Suburban homeowners shaped regional distributions of opportunity and resources in more ways than just policing racial boundaries. Indeed, by the 1970s white East Bay homeowners were more interested in reducing taxes than in managing race. But unequal metropolitan development meant that fighting taxes represented the reproduction of racial disadvantage by other means — and therefore the reproduction of race by other means. In the 1960s and 1970s the suburban politics of property were an extension, under changing economic conditions, of the processes that underlay city building in the 1940s and 1950s. Even as they remained major beneficiaries of public subsidy, South County suburban homeowners nonetheless claimed that they were under siege and victimized. In their view, the industrial garden had begun to show signs of wilting, the suburban dream signs of malaise. Keeping it alive and flourishing remained their overriding objective.[1]

The pace and reach of postwar suburbanization had transformed California in a single generation. Between 1950 and 1970 the state's population doubled, from just over ten million to just under twenty. Men and women from every state, Mexico, and, after 1965, Southeast Asia poured into California in these two decades, dwarfing even the enormous World War II migration. To accommodate them, three and a half million new housing units were built — double the number that existed in 1950 — in a twenty-year construction bonanza of enormous scope. The new population was overwhelmingly young. As the median age in the state dropped from thirty-two to twenty-seven, the percentage of people over sixty-five years of age fell from 8 to 3, and the percentage of school-age children shot up from 17 to 25. In all, the number of California school-age children quadrupled in two decades. Population growth and development fed a real estate boom in which the median home price jumped by 50 percent — and it would increase even more dramatically during the 1970s. In the space of twenty years, California had become the nation's economic engine and population magnet.[2]

In the late 1960s the East Bay suburban corridor, from Oakland to San Jose, looked like much of postwar California. Two decades of industrial-garden city building had made the "Metropolitan Oakland Area" one of Northern California's leading poles of growth. A forty-mile river of concrete, the Nimitz Interstate Highway, spanned its length and stitched together the landscape in linear regularity (map 3.2). South of Oakland, Nimitz exits led first to San Leandro and its booming industrial districts. Fifteen thousand blue-collar workers labored here, at Caterpillar Tractor, International Harvester, National Can, Frieden Calculators, Simmons Mattresses, the Latchford Glass Company, and dozens upon dozens of small, ten- and fifteen-employee machine shops and light assembly plants. They drove to work on the Nimitz and parked on vast asphalt acreages. Others arrived on surface streets through San Leandro neighborhoods, patchworks of ranch homes and stucco bungalows that looked much like Oakland's. Outside the city limits lay San Lorenzo, one of the largest subdivisions in Northern California, five thousand wartime ranch homes on unincorporated county land with a population of seventeen thousand. Filled with World War II veterans turned machinists, welders, teachers, civil servants, clerks, and salespeople, San Lorenzo's government was its homeowners association, its downtown the Bayfair Mall in San Leandro. Here, and in neighboring Castro Valley, racial segregation was a given, and homes appreciated ahead of inflation every year.

Further south, exit ramps led east into Hayward, by the late 1960s a city more than double its prewar physical size. Ethnic Mexican *colonias*, once on marginal land, had been incorporated through annexation, as had acres of Anglo tract homes. Near Hayward's prewar downtown, the giant Hunt Foods canneries hummed with seasonal activity and four thousand workers. Hunt's large ethnic Mexican workforce lived in *barrios* in Hayward, Union City, Milpitas, Alviso, and even on San Jose's Eastside. Surrounding downtown and the canneries were new subdivisions with names like Fairway Greens and Holiday Estates, and new shopping malls indistinguishable at a distance from factories and warehouses with their low-slung, horizontal design and gargantuan parking lots. In Hayward, Okie and Arkie migrants and their descendants lived in close proximity to Mexican migrants and their families, with multiple subdivisions of white-collar WASPs in between, in a city that symbolized the sudden and often jarring confluence of an agricultural past and a suburban future. Hayward was the most eclectic South County suburb, a mish-mash of working-class and ethnic cultures stirred together with an ascendant managerial and commercial Anglo middle class.

Leaving Hayward, the Nimitz passed quickly through Union City and then into the largest municipality in Northern California, Fremont. In the 1960s Fremont's population more than doubled, from forty-three thousand to just over a hundred thousand — within corporate limits larger than either San Francisco or Oakland. Horizontal, diffuse, uncentered, Fremont lived up to America's suburban clichés. On the far south side of town, Nimitz traffic buzzed along within a hundred yards of the sprawling General Motors plant, set in near-perfect industrial garden coincidence against the vacant, verdant hillside. Back in the city proper, wide boulevards criss-crossed one another in a broad latticework that linked each new subdivision to the next. Nearly devoid of any pre-World War II structure, Fremont boasted the newest housing stock in the country, cul-de-sac after cul-de-sac of ranch-style homes set back behind front lawns and rows of freshly planted maple trees. By far the greenest South County suburb, Fremont's parks, lake, nearby hills, huge blocks of undeveloped land, and plentiful crabgrass on both public and private property, along with the ubiquitous sunshine common in the southern part of the Bay Area, gave the city literally the feel of a garden. Past Fremont lay the autoworker suburb of Milpitas and San Jose's sprawling Eastside, the center of Mexican and Chicano life in Northern California.

The Nimitz provided one possible viewing frame of this emerging landscape. By the 1970s, BART offered another. With its multiple stops along the length of the East Bay, BART took managers to work in Oakland from Fremont, but also auto-workers to Fremont assembly lines from Oakland. Nurses at Kaiser Hospital in Oakland or San Francisco traveled from their homes in Hayward. Seasonal cannery workers in Hayward commuted from their homes near the Fruitvale stop in Oakland. Workers passed back and forth across one another's paths in a complex set of daily migrations that did not always correspond to the organization man model — commuting to central city jobs from bedroom suburbs. Two long bridges across San Francisco Bay in South County, intersecting with the Nimitz at Hayward and Fremont, respectively, multiplied the commuting combinations. They made it possible for aerospace engineers at Lockheed in Sunnyvale or electrical engineers at the Stanford Industrial Park to live in Fremont, which many did. The bridges also carried ethnic Mexicans from the barrio in Redwood City south of San Francisco to work in Hayward or Union City or, by the 1970s, at General Motors in Fremont and Ford in Milpitas. Black autoworkers Jim Crowed out of Fremont and Milpitas in the 1960s lived in East Palo Alto, at the foot of the Dumbarton Bridge. Shopping malls and factories on the fringe, multicity commutes, and vast subdivisions spread life, labor, and leisure horizontally across the spaces of the flatlands.

The most powerful frame in which to understand South County, however, remains property. Underneath the commuting, subdivisions, and development lay a history of property markets and the politics that shaped them. The expectations of racial segregation and low taxes produced in suburban South County after World War II could not be contained by the boosters and public officials who helped to construct them. They would take on a life of their own. Homeowners in the 1960s and 1970s remained focused on how property would be developed and taxed, how space would be mobilized for social and political ends. That concern, animated by the homeowner populism that was a foundation of suburban city building in the 1950s, precipitated a series of suburban counterrevolutions in these two decades that lay the groundwork for the so-called tax revolt of 1978. The price of California's extraordinary growth had to be met, but not, if suburban homeowners had their way, by them. On three key issues — racial segregation, affordable housing, and taxes — suburbanites in the East Bay joined with their counterparts statewide in a political retrenchment with far-reaching consequences. Suburban homeowners in Alameda County presented themselves as protecting their economic future and preserving the promises of the industrial garden, but their actions, embedded in already skewed metropolitan structures of opportunity, continued to shift a disproportionate share of the costs of postwar capital-

ism to Oakland. Furthermore, they participated in the creation of a narrative of victimization, which appealed to increasing numbers of homeowners over these decades, that may have reflected genuine feeling but belied the enormous privileges they enjoyed. The suburban break with liberalism, so evident in the East Bay by the late 1960s, changed California politics within a decade and national politics within another.[3]

The Suburbs in Black and White

In November 1964 tens of thousands of southern Alameda County suburbanites drove to the polls. They voted in overwhelming numbers for the figurehead of mid-1960s liberalism, President Lyndon B. Johnson, while casting ballots in equal proportion against one of California liberalism's signature achievements, fair housing. Two million Californians statewide joined in this performance, making a contradictory case to the nation about where the state stood on race and equality. But the results likely did not appear contradictory to residents of South County, because they had come to understand the limits of liberalism and the American welfare state through the lens of property. Property and homeownership organized a set of primary concerns and issues for suburban voters. It also structured the mechanics of political participation — who was heard and which groups defined the debate. Homeownership dominated the framing of social and political questions. But homeowners were not alone in setting forth these parameters. Leaders of the real estate industry — at every level, from local to national — kept watch on the California housing market, one of the most dynamic and profitable in the nation, carefully and deliberately. That industry's investment in residential racial segregation had ebbed little by the early 1960s. In 1964 no threat to property markets seemed greater to either homeowners or the real estate industry than the Rumford Fair Housing Act, passed in 1963 after a decade of work by Byron Rumford, the East Bay Democratic Club, and the statewide liberal coalition.[4]

The California Real Estate Association (CREA) brought Proposition 14, repeal of the Rumford Act, before voters in 1964. Part of the CREA's broad antiliberal agenda, Proposition 14 made California "a battleground for a national showdown on housing legislation," in Byron Rumford's phrase. One of the most important social movement organizations in the postwar United States, the CREA organized people on the presumption that property, as space that produces capital, is the highest social good and should remain the least regulated, most "free," arena of human activity. The CREA campaign in 1964 emphasized the sanctity of private property and its centrality to Americanism. "I want to talk about the preservation of this *real* American," a CREA representative explained in 1964, "an individual who, at least up until now, has been endowed with personal freedom as to choice." Co-opting the rights language of the national black liberation movement, the CREA and its political supporters aggressively shaped public discussion of fair housing. "If we believe in the American democratic system," a Republican state senator explained, "we must acknowledge that it is the right of the people to tell the government what to do." He concluded his defense of Proposition 14 by warning that "[w]hen the government tells the people what to do and think, we have a dictatorship." In place of the "traditional right" of property ownership, the president of the National Association of Real Estate Boards asserted, the Rumford Act supposedly established "a new so-called right for individuals of a minority group."[5]

This individual rights language represented a profound dissembling on the part of real estate interests. Industry leaders had long shaped segregation with institutional bulwarks and market manipulation. Through its buying and selling policies, the CREA controlled local real estate boards and set standards for segregation in hundreds of local communities statewide. The Southern Alameda County Board of Realtors, a CREA member, determined, for example, which homes in the East Bay would be advertised as "white only." Prior to 1948 the CREA used racial covenants to prevent the sale of homes to "non-Caucasians," and after 1948 it endorsed "corporation contract agreements" like those used in the East Bay by M. C. Friel to keep communities white. The CREA also maintained a powerful presence in the state legislature in Sacramento, where it influenced property tax legislation, state building codes, and a host of other property-related matters. Indeed, the CREA remained a more consistent reservoir of conservative politics in 1960s' California than the Republican Party and stood as the principal force in the state opposing liberal or social democratic claims on private property. On the eve of the 1964 election, the CREA had 2,600 member realtors in Alameda County and a statewide grassroots network of realtors, realty boards, and business connections that rivaled any political party. A late-1960s report by the California Committee for Fair Practices estimated that "the California Real Estate Association is, among profit-making trade groups, without parallel in power and prestige."[6]

Proposition 14 passed in southern Alameda County by an overwhelming margin. In an election in which Lyndon Johnson won the county by a margin of two to one, and voters returned Democrats to seats in the state legislature and U.S. Congress, Proposition 14 received a stunning endorsement. San Leandro, for instance, voted to repeal the Rumford Act 80 percent to 20 percent while endorsing Johnson over Goldwater nearly two to one. In Hayward, three-fourths of the voters favored repeal, with two to one margins for Johnson as well. Only in Union City, where the Mexican American community remained a near majority, and in Milpitas (in Santa Clara County), where Ben Gross and the UAW campaigned relentlessly against Proposition 14, was the vote against fair housing reasonably close; however the proposition still won in both cities. The San Leandro–Oakland municipal border offered the most striking instance of Proposition 14's intersection with local racial segregation. In San Leandro precincts along the Oakland city line, Proposition 14 passed with slightly more than 80 percent of the vote — in three precincts it was as high as 85 percent. In parallel precincts direclty across the city line, African American neighborhoods in East Oakland voted *against* Proposition 14 by more than 92 percent — in one precinct the vote to defeat the referendum was 204 to 3. Such patterns, and the remarkable totals for Alameda County as a whole, belied the CREA's insistence that Proposition 14 was a race-neutral issue of "freedom." South County voters endorsed the CREA discourse of property rights as a rhetorical standing for resistance to desegregation. Byron Rumford lamented that "the whole proposition was built on fear and discrimination and racism," such that even "those who expressed themselves as liberals" believed they needed Proposition 14 "in order to protect their homes." Nationally, Proposition 14's victory was widely regarded as a severe blow to the civil rights movement, what "No on 14" advocate Edward McHugh called "the severest setback to the forces of fair housing since the current phase of the civil rights struggle began."[7]

Homeowners, however, were not Proposition 14's only constituents, nor was the measure a transparent expression of homeowner political objectives. In Alameda County, as in all developing localities in California and nationwide, dense home finance and construction networks linked a variety of individuals and institutions to the process of community building. Land speculators and developers, as well as the banks that lent them money, were in this group. Real estate brokers and home mortgage brokers, as well as the banks that lent them money, were in it too. The process of home building, from the subdivision planning stage to the handshake over the final sale, involved attorneys, title companies, professional planners, and a host of other subsidiary planning and finance institutions. These multiple constituencies symbolized the range of both personal and structural investments in segregation. At the same time, the uproar over the Rumford Act was ignited and fueled by the CREA and the National Association of Real Estate Boards, not by a spontaneous homeowner revolt. Both the CREA and the NAREB had been

fighting fair housing in the California Assembly and promoting segregated communities for decades. When the Rumford Act passed in a close vote in 1963, CREA representatives, not homeowners' organizations, were on hand in Sacramento to declare their intention to repeal it. Proposition 14 *engendered* a grassroots response, with hundreds of thousands of homeowners enthusiastically championing the campaign. But the campaign itself was organized and directed by the CREA and its affiliates.[8]

Indeed, if there was a grassroots dimension to the 1964 campaign, it came from Proposition 14's opponents. The measure passed in South County despite enormous public efforts to defeat it. "The 'No on 14' campaign," according to one postelection assessment "was strongly endorsed, relatively well financed, and backed by a hard-working army of volunteers." Outside of San Leandro, which remained the most segregationist city in the county, virtually every major public official — from state legislators to mayors and city council members — opposed the measure. "In the interests of justice and common decency, it should be defeated," declared the Tri-Cities Committee Against Proposition 14, a group that included the mayor and city council of Fremont, South County's congressional and assembly representatives, and Union City's major public figures. Another prominent member added that the referendum "would create a new kind of right — alien to our state and not found in any other state, including Mississippi ... the absolute right to discriminate." Governor Brown called it "the segregation initiative" and referred to it as "legalized bigotry." Californians Against Proposition 14, the umbrella organization for the anti-14 forces, drew on the same grassroots networks of churches, labor unions, and civil rights organizations that had come together to defeat the right-to-work measure in 1958. Proposition 14 "would erect a Jim Crow Wall around the ghettoes of California," opponents of the measure emphasized. In press releases, public debates, radio announcements, and innumerable public meetings and information sessions, Alameda County's political, religious, and business leaders vigorously opposed Proposition 14. Only realtors and homeowners associations were absent from the No on 14 coalition. But they, operating through institutional networks cultivated over two decades of city building, proved far more able to convince and mobilize voters than the county's political leadership.[9]

The CREA framed Proposition 14 as a decision between "freedom of choice" and "forced housing" and asked California homeowners to choose segregation under a different name. Naming was especially important in the election. Opponents of the Rumford Act rehearsed in California a well-worn rhetorical strategy that would become increasingly popular in national conservative circles in the late 1960s and early 1970s: employing a putatively race-neutral civil rights language. The Rumford Act's detractors discussed race only to place liberal supporters of fair housing on the defensive and accuse them of "naiveté." Encouraged by the CREA, those aligned against Rumford used a discourse of property rights to argue that the law "forced" property owners to rent or sell to a specific group, namely, African Americans. Further, the CREA claimed in public that they had no influence over housing markets and could not control the racial preferences of property owners or renters. "When one of the so-called minority groups moves in, the majority group moves out," Oscar Brinkman, a lobbyist for the National Apartment Owners Association and its California affiliates, told the House Judiciary Committee in 1963, "and the end result will be financially calamitous to an owner who had no racial prejudice of his own." While such claims may have contained an element of truth, given the segregationist prejudice of most whites, their larger duplicity was evident. After decades of lobbying both state and federal governments against fair housing, and decades of promoting segregation in local communities, representatives of the real estate industry then claimed that they were merely looking out for the "rights" of their constituents and were innocent of any complicity in discrimination. This purposeful deception underscored the lengths to which industry representatives would go to preserve their control over one of the most lucrative real estate markets in the nation.[10]

That control had three principal dimensions. First, since well before the New Deal, NAREB and the CREA had segregated property markets using racial covenants. This allowed the industry both to manipulate the racial prejudice of home buyers and to create predictable markets. The real estate industry wanted reliable control over any market fluctuations created by white prejudice. This emerged as an even more pressing issue within New Deal housing policy. Under Home Owners Loan Corporation (HOLC), FHA, and VA guidelines, the most profitable real estate strategy was to treat black and white housing markets as entirely distinct entities. There was a second, related dimension. Open housing threatened real estate industry control because it raised the possibility of chaotic market fluctuations. Rapid white turnover and property devaluation, wholesale white abandonment of rental properties, or the refusal of developers to build or banks to finance mixed-race developments, to name a few select fears, introduced market factors that undermined steady, predictable, upwardly trending property valuations — the real estate industry's chief concern. Finally, there was a third dimension to industry control. African American residential mobility was always understood in negative terms, because it forced ever wider readjustments of property values in white neighborhoods. Among other factors, white home values were affected by their proximity to African American neighborhoods. Containment is not too strong a word for the industry's desire to minimize these readjustments. In all, the real estate industry came to see the promotion, preservation, and manipulation of racial segregation as central — rather than incidental or residual — components of their profit-generating strategies.[11]

To dramatize the industry's promotion of segregation in suburban Alameda County, in the summer of 1963, a year before Proposition 14, African American leaders from Oakland had appealed to suburban Alameda County in an effort to dramatize suburban segregation and lay the groundwork for application of the Rumford Act. They delivered prescient warnings of impending social distress in Oakland and pleas for justice in the language of liberalism and progressive Americanism. In a major speech before the Southern Alameda County Bar Association, Don McCullum explained that the condition of impoverished black Oaklanders was made worse by the "rigid housing discrimination in Southern Alameda County — beginning at the San Leandro city limits." "This is not good — not good for America, not good for yourselves individually or for your children," he continued. He related his own frustration at being turned down by South County housing developments in a three-year search for a new home. "The minority people cannot break out of the city because of the irresponsibility of the suburban areas," he told the audience of journalists. Clinton White, an Oakland attorney and NAACP official, also toured South County communities urging residents to accept integration. "Fairness in jobs, housing, and education can give Fremont a 'welcome wagon' appearance," White told the Fremont Council of Social Planning in the summer of 1963. That same summer, Berkeley and Oakland CORE chapters staged "Operation Windowshop" in East Bay suburbs, demonstrations in which black home buyers strolled through all-white neighborhoods where homes were listed for sale. In these and other instances, beginning in 1963 and continuing well into the 1970s, South County communities were under constant pressure from Oakland's black leaders to open housing to African American buyers and, in a more general sense, to improve their relationship with African American Oakland.[12]

Black leaders from Oakland could reprimand and cajole suburban residents and appeal to what McCullum called the "responsible white community," but moral rhetoric was virtually their only leverage. McCullum could insist that the notion of property rights articulated by the CREA preserved segregation and trampled on the rights of African Americans, but he and the community he represented were positioned at great remove from the levers of municipal power in places like San Leandro and Fremont. Here was the national civil rights dilemma writ small. The geographic concentration of the African American political community and the structure of American political authority — around municipal, state, and federal, but not regional, poles — made addressing regional problems extraordinarily difficult. State laws like the Rumford Act and federal civil rights legislation represented the best hope that these political boundaries could be superceded. In places like Oakland, there was a constituency for civil rights legislation, especially for the federal Civil Rights Act of 1964, every bit as large, vocal, and determined as in Birmingham and Selma, a constituency that hoped to turn moral suasion into political leverage. But their adversary was not "massive resistance," the South's campaign against desegregation. It was sunbelt metropolitanization and its structure of property markets, homeowner politics, and segregated municipal enclaves.[13]

Resistance to open housing in southern Alameda County rested simultaneously on both willful action and a rhetoric of innocence. Willful acts included Proposition 14, homeowners association agreements, and, prior to the 1960s, all of the architecture of suburban apartheid. These cleared the way for inaction, including homeowners' protestations in 1963 and afterward that no "civil rights problems" existed in South County suburbs. In San Leandro, for instance, when Democratic Mayor Jack Maltester proposed a Committee on Human Rights and Responsibilities in the civil rights heat of 1963, he was stonewalled by the city council. The council, controlled by the city's homeowners associations, three separate times refused to create such a committee, the last two after direct appeals from Don McCullum. "I feel that the great majority of the residents of San Leandro feel that we have no problem that requires the establishment of any committee on human rights," a typical letter to the editor read. Indeed, when David Creque, a San Leandro resident, spoke in support of establishing the civil rights commission, the homeowners association of which he was president quickly dismissed him, claiming that his statements "do not necessarily reflect the views of the board of directors." Homeowners contended that the absence of African Americans meant the absence of a "civil rights problem," much as an earlier generation of whites had denied complicity in a "Negro problem." Such willful inaction and its rhetoric of innocence underscored the physical and social remove that were the privileges of San Leandro's whiteness as well as the power of segregation to perpetuate racism and false consciousness among whites. Combinations of action and inaction sustained suburban segregation in the East Bay for two postwar generations.[14]

Homeowners were not innocent. In conjunction with their real estate industry patrons, they participated in the construction of a new white racial ideology with sweeping implications. Across the middle of the twentieth century, classic forms of white supremacy in the United States slowly gave way in public forums to a right-based language of individualism and freedom. The discourse was not itself new. It had been used for at least two centuries to buttress private property claims, including those of former slaveholders in the postbellum South and those of homeowners who placed racial covenants on their property in cities like Chicago, Detroit, and San Francisco in the first half of the twentieth century. But the aggressive assertion of this rights language as the dominant discourse through which white racial privilege was articulated was new. The Proposition 14 campaign in California played an important role in this larger, mid-twentieth-century development. On the eve of the 1964 election, California Assemblyman Robert Stevens gave voice to this language in a television debate. Claiming that prejudice and discrimination were "not the issue before us," Stevens likened the Rumford Act to the "witch hunts" of early colonial times, insisted that it denied "freedom of choice," and asserted the primacy of "the right to acquire and protect property." Labeling white resistance to open housing in the 1960s a "backlash," as many historians and other commentators have done, distracts attention from the central fact of that resistance: it took the form of rights-based counterclaims. These claims were intended to inoculate segregation and white privilege against charges of racism through appeals to hallowed American rights traditions. Homeowners in California in 1964 helped to advance this project, one that would increasingly come to shape how racial equality was debated and contested in the national political culture.[15]

The California Supreme Court declared Proposition 14 unconstitutional in 1966, but desegregation advocates had lost three years fighting the CREA. Finally enforceable, the Rumford Act eventually became a critical tool for equal rights in California. But lost time, coupled with the long legacy of housing discrimination, meant that change came slowly. In 1971 a national report brought South County's history of racial exclusion to the surface. That year, the National Committee against Discrimination in Housing (NCDH) published the results of a study warning that "developing Bay Area suburbs will be racist enclaves in the image of San Leandro if the segregated housing development and marketing policies are not reversed." Focusing on San Leandro, the NCDH report blamed federal housing policy, homeowners associations, the city government, and the county real estate board for racial restriction, the familiar cast of characters in what NCDH Chief Executive Ed Rutledge called "typical of the situation across the nation." "The Veterans Administration guaranteed more than $1.6 million in home loans" in San Leandro, the report observed, "while the Federal Housing Administration insured more than $1.7 million in home mortgages." All went to white buyers. Those loan guarantees became, in the hands of real estate brokers and homeowners associations, bulwarks against desegregation, subsidized apartheid. In the 1970 census more than three quarters of Oakland census tracts along the San Leandro city line had a black majority. San Leandro itself was less than one-tenth of 1 percent African American. Here was a racial gradient as steep as any in the nation, preserved deep into the 1970s by both custom and structure.[16]

Segregation in suburban housing markets raised concrete economic questions about how resources were distributed in the divided metropolis. "Ironically," sociologist Wilson Record wrote in a 1963 study, "San Leandro may get [industrial] plants which, if located in Oakland, would provide the tax base upon which Oakland needs to draw in order to service the Negroes excluded by San Leandro." A major study of California housing in the early 1960s predicted that segregation would ultimately force older cities like Oakland "to look largely for their revenues to poorer groups of taxpayers who will require higher outlays for social services." Advocates of racial justice made their case against suburban segregation in these concrete economic terms. Trapped in declining cities, they argued, poor African Americans required a greater share of public resources but received a lesser. "Our cities are already virtually bankrupt," Whitney Young, executive director of the Urban League, wrote in his 1969 *Beyond Racism*, citing "the mushrooming demand for costly social services required by the impoverished slums" as the principal reason. Of all the consequences of unequal metropolitan development, the redistribution of the tax base was ultimately one of the most severe and consequential. Even as housing and employment barriers lifted in degrees after the 1960s and metropolitan boundaries became more porous for African Americans, property markets changed slowly. Property value differentials hardened across space, and gaps between the urban and suburban per capita revenue from municipal property taxes widened, creating vast inequalities that functioned to reproduce racial disadvantage — especially in key property tax-supported urban services like education and health and welfare.[17]

Exclusion and containment kept African Americans from making substantial inroads in South County housing markets through the 1960s. Black workers enjoyed slightly more success in obtaining employment in the suburban East Bay, but these gains were limited to the General Motors and Ford plants in Fremont and Milpitas and the U.S. Naval Air Station in Alameda. In the late 1960s the GM plant was thought to employ between 1,500 and 2,000 black workers out of a fluctuating total employment of between 5,000 and 6,000. The Ford plant employed a similar figure. Both hired large numbers of Mexican Americans as well, increasingly so during the 1970s. The Naval Air Station employed between 1,600 and 1,800 black workers out of a total work force of about 8,000. Outside of the automobile factories and the Naval Air Station, however, black workers could be found in only a few corners of the suburban East Bay labor market. A Federal Civil Rights Commission study of San Leandro in 1967 revealed that only 5 percent of employees in the city's industries were black. A similar study for Fremont, Union City, and Newark found 6 percent. Both studies, however, were limited by their reliance on companies required to file reports with the Equal Employment Opportunity Commission. Companies outside of the EEOC's purview may well have employed even fewer African American workers.[18]

Employment discrimination against black workers in the East Bay was capricious and demoralizing. In blue collar fields, East Bay suburban communities were dominated by a few medium-sized employers — like GM and Ford, but also Trailmobile, Caterpillar Tractor, Pacific States Steel, Peterbuilt, and International Harvester — and an enormous number of smaller companies, plants, and establishments that employed less than one hundred workers. For black job seekers, the mixed-industrial landscape envisioned by both the MOAP and suburban city-builders could be almost impossible to navigate. Local offices of the California State Employment Service, for instance, filled jobs in Fremont, Union City, and other South County cities with local residents first. Only then were unfilled jobs forwarded to offices in Oakland. For those who could not afford an automobile, suburban work was especially difficult to secure, because the tasks of finding an opening and appearing for an interview required transportation. After finding a job announcement and driving (or taking BART or a bus) into a suburban city, an African American applicant still might be told that the position had been filled. Race entered the decisions of managers, employment agencies, owners, and others in control of hiring in unpredictable ways. Furthermore, Bay Area employment in the manufacturing, transportation, and wholesale trade sectors was highly unionized, over 90 percent in many industries. In general, African Americans fared best in those sectors of the suburban labor market where they had gained a foothold in plants previously located in black population centers — Ford in Richmond and GM in Oakland, for instance — and in federal military installations.[19]

Between 1963 and 1970, after a decade of attempts to reclaim and revitalize Oakland's neighborhoods, African Americans there looked outward. They turned toward the East Bay suburbs, the lengthy residential and industrial landscape stretching from San Leandro to Milpitas, McCullum's white noose. "The flight to the suburbs is the highest form of social irresponsibility," McCullum charged in 1969, in his most stinging indictment of suburbanization. The metaphor of white strangulation of the black city was powerful precisely because it reduced the complexity of metropolitan patterns of residence and industry to an essential trope of American race and cast the metropolis in black and white. In instances like Proposition 14, the noose seemed very much in evidence. But the trope itself raised questions about how best to address regional racial inequality. Was it a product of overt racism, market economics, or both? Would appeals to suburban whites make a difference? How could African Americans develop a regional program to change the distribution of resources while remaining politically isolated in Oakland? Searching for the answers would occupy Oaklanders for a generation.

With remarkable speed in the mid-1960s, the city-suburb dualism replaced the bigoted southern sheriff, the lynch mob, and the lunch counter as the archetypal national symbol of American racial inequality. Oakland experienced this shift in metaphor and language with the nation. Beginning as early as the 1950s, northern civil rights,

nationalist, and grassroots radical leaders alike had adopted variations on the city-suburb contrast in their speeches, writings, and interviews. The center of these efforts was initially battles over open housing in the industrial Northeast and upper Midwest, where indices of segregation were higher than anywhere in the nation. Confined largely to local political arenas in the 1950s, by the mid-1960s these voices found a national stage with two dramatic episodes in California. The first was Proposition 14. The second came the following summer, with rebellions in Watts in Southern California. Though African Americans across the nation had been pointing to the destructive effects of white suburbanization and the hardening of segregation in "second ghettoes" since World War II, the national press was slow to take the issue seriously. Indeed, as late as 1960 the *Saturday Evening Post* was writing of the "great human tides, made up of middle-income Americans ... flowing out of the cities. Into the cities, to take their place, dark tides were running." Such rhetoric not only buttressed segregationist thinking ("dark tides running"), it also reinforced the widespread white interpretation of black migration as a cause of urban decline. Not until Proposition 14 and the eruption of violence between 1964 and 1968 did either the national press or the federal government begin to discuss with some seriousness the postwar trend toward metropolitan segregation.[20]

Between 1961 and 1968 official white circles slowly took notice of this segregation in ways that black leaders had been urging for decades. In 1961, reports of the U.S. Commission on Civil Rights used the term "white noose" to describe suburbanization, introducing that term into white policy arenas for the first time. Four years later, when the McCone Commission report on Watts in 1965 blamed African Americans for instigating the violence and made no mention of the Proposition 14 election from the previous fall, African Americans in California and elsewhere scathingly criticized the commission. A near total "whitewash," in the words of one local black critic, the report was also criticized by white federal officials. The U.S. Commission on Civil Rights called it "elementary, superficial, unoriginal and unimaginable." Though weak-kneed and retrograde, the McCone report had the effect of generating a national discussion among both whites and blacks over the segregated metropolis. In 1968 the report of the Kerner Commission (National Advisory Commission on Civil Disorders), the federal government's official interpretation of the urban violence of 1967, appeared. The commission's indictment of white America — "[w]hite institutions created it [ghetto], white institutions maintain it, and white institutions condone it" — represented what African American leaders in major cities had been saying for decades, but it took Proposition 14, four summers of violence, the glare of national publicity, and multiple government reports to reorient white discussion of civil rights to a metropolitan (and northern/western) context.[21]

For white East Bay suburban homeowners, Proposition 14 represented the early phases of a long engagement with the changing nature of California. That engagement only occasionally took explicit racial form, though race was nonetheless embedded in every stage. The rhetoric of Americanism and "free" property encouraged by the CREA thinly veiled a resistance to desegregation. More typically, homeowners joined causes that kept racial assumptions and prejudices at a greater remove even as their politics reverberated with profound racialized consequences. Ensuring ever rising property values while keeping other housing costs, especially taxes, as low as possible in the midst of the state's convulsive growth remained homeowners' dominant political objective. In the name of that objective, they collectively resisted the broad structural changes necessary to desegregate the housing market, and they fought other claims on the financial resources of their segregated communities.

NOTES

1. As a description of suburbanization, "white noose" gained popular attention in 1961, when it appeared in *Volume 4: Housing, 1961 United States Commission on Civil Rights Reports* (Washington, DC, 1961). By the late 1960s it was in common usage across the country.

2. U.S. Department of Commerce, *Census of Population: 1950, Characteristics of the Population, California* (Washington, DC, 1951); *1970 Census of the Population, Characteristics of the Population, California* (Washington, DC, 1973).

3. For distinct, but similar, political stories in Southern California, see Nicolaides, *My Blue Heaven*; McGirr, *Suburban Warriors*.

4. See newspaper clippings and other material in "Fair Housing — 1963" and "Fair Housing Bill" folders, Box 1, Rumford Papers. See also Casstevens, *Politics, Housing, and Race Relations*; Denton, *Apartheid American Style*.

5. *California Real Estate Magazine*, May, June, July, August, and December 1964; *NYT*, 10 May 1964; *CV*, 17 May and 9 August 1963; state senator quoted in *California Real Estate Magazine*, February 1964, 5; Rumford quoted in Regional Oral History Office, *William Byron Rumford: Legislator for Fair Employment, Fair Housing, and Public Health* (Berkeley, 1973), 120, 124.

6. *California Real Estate Magazine*, May, June, July, August, and December 1964; *NYT*, 10 May 1964; *CV*, 17 May and 9 August 1963; California Committee for Fair Practices, "Public Education and the CREA — Control by the Subsidized," manuscript, Box 2 Rumford Papers; Clare Short, "What Are the Obligations of the Housing Industry to Resolve Such Conflicts as Exist in This Area?" speech manuscript, University of California, Berkeley Library; Raymond Wolfinger and Fred Greenstein, "The Repeal of Fair Housing in California: An Analysis of Referendum Voting," *American Political Science Review* 62 (September 1968): 753–69.

7. *William Byron Rumford* [??274] of All Votes Cast, General Election, November 3, 1964" (Sacramento, 1964); Wolfinger and Greenstein, "The Repeal of Fair Housing in California."

8. *Ramparts*, April 1966, 7; Denton, *Apartheid American Style*; "Remarks on the Rumford Act and the Housing initiative," by State Senator Albert S. Rodda, and "California's New Fair Housing Law," by Carmen H. Warschaw, Box 7, Rumford Papers.

9. *Ramparts*, April 1966, 7; *FNR*, 23 July, 10 September, 26 October 1964; Alameda County Committee Against Proposition 14, *News*, Central Labor Council of Alameda County Collection, Box 88, Folder 7, CLCAC/LARC; *California Real Estate Magazine*, April 1964, 5; "Proposition 14 — Campaign Flyers," Box 7, Rumford Papers.

10. Denton, *Apartheid American Style*, 30, 32–37.

11. For evidence of these practices and the real estate industry's investment in control of racial segregation in California, see ibid. For the nation as a whole, see Massey and Denton, *American Apartheid*; Bruce D. Haynes, *Red Lines, Black Spaces: The Politics of Race and Space in a Black Middle Class Suburb* (New Haven, 2001). See also any

volume of the *Hearings Before the National Commission on Urban Problems* (Washington, DC, 1968), where these issues received an open hearing in cities across the country.

12. *SLMN*, 27 March, 26 July, 8 August 1963; *FNR*, 25 June, 26 August, 5 and 6 September 1963.

13. I owe these last observations to Martha Biondi and Matthew Lassiter.

14. *SLMN*, 9, 23, 24, 26, and 27 July, 1,17,29, and 31 August, 17 September, 21 November 1963; 10 January, 1 May 1964.

15. Transcript of a debate on Proposition 14 and the Rumford Act, 19 September 1964, KNXT TV, Box 2, Rumford Papers.

16. *SLMN*, 14 and 15 May 1971; *FNR*, 1 September 1971.

17. *OT*, 5 January 1969; Wilson Record, "Minority Groups and Intergroup Relations in the San Francisco Bay Area," 1963, 22–23, IGS; "Draft Report to the Governor's Advisory Committee on Housing Problems," ms., 1962, Box 7, Catherine Bauer Wurster Collection, Bancroft Library, 4; Young, *Beyond Racism*, 6.

18. *Hearings Before the U.S. Commission on Civil Rights*, 587, 687, 1036; *FNR*, 25 June, 5 and 6 September 1963.

19. Oakland Chamber of Commerce, Research Department, "Fifty Largest Private Employers in Alameda County," April 1970; Bay Area Council, "A Guide to Industrial Locations in the San Francisco Bay Area," 1964. For a discussion of the relative weight historians should place on union versus employer discrimination in labor markets, see the set of essays in *International Review of Social History* 41 (1996): 351–406.

20. Harold H. Martin, "Our Urban Revolution, Part I: Are We Building a City 600 Miles Long?" *Saturday Evening Post* 232 (January 2, 1960): 15.

21. Gerald Horne, *Fire This Time: The Watts Uprising and the 1960s* (New York, 1995).

The Beginning of the End of a Modern Ghetto

Sudhir Alladi Venkatesh

Source: *American Project: The Rise and Fall of a Modern Ghetto*
(Cambridge, MA: Harvard University Press, 2000).

EDITORS' INTRODUCTION

For many Americans, large-scale public housing projects are synonymous with poverty and decaying inner-city neighborhoods, or "ghettos." Although the word ghetto originally referred to those sections of European cities where Jews were required to live, it now broadly connotes any physical area, or even social network, where people of similar social and economic backgrounds reside or congregate. More often than not, though, in the United States a ghetto specifically describes a slum or rundown section of city that has a large concentration of minority residents. It was in these physically dilapidated areas that many cities built public housing projects, which began in earnest with the New Deal of the 1930s, to provide decent and affordable homes for low income, working families. However, through a combination of tepid political support for public housing, poor building design, spotty government funding, misguided management policies, and fluctuating tenant regulations, by the late 1960s and 1970s several notable—although by no means all—housing complexes evolved into veritable prisons that isolated tenants from the rest of society. As fewer and fewer residents of these projects were able to leave for better accommodations, public housing itself became associated with government failure.

The story of the Robert Taylor Homes in Chicago, Illinois, illustrates the promising rise and ignominious fall of large public housing projects in the United States. In the 1950s, the Chicago Housing Authority (CHA) conceived of the Robert Taylor Homes as a means to provide affordable, modern housing to residents of Bronzeville, an African American neighborhood located in the city's South Side, also known as the Black Belt, or more pejoratively as the "ghetto." The CHA originally designed the Robert Taylor Homes to contain 2,500 units in a series of low-rise structures, located near the shores of Lake Michigan. However, the federal government, which was paying for two-thirds of construction, favored larger high-rises as more cost effective. In addition to saving money, modernist architecture also influenced the decision of federal housing officials, especially the work of Swiss-born architect and urbanist Le Corbusier who envisioned an urban future full of large buildings surrounded by open spaces. When completed in 1962, the Robert Taylor Homes was the largest housing project in the United States with 4,400 apartments packed into twenty-eight identical buildings, each sixteen-stories high.

Another reason for the immense size of the Robert Taylor Homes was the fact that white aldermen in the city blocked attempts to build public housing units open to black residents within white neighborhoods. As such, the CHA had no choice but to concentrate housing for low-income African Americans within the very same "ghetto" they sought to eradicate. The city, quite ironically, decided to name the Robert Taylor Homes after the CHA's first African American director, who fought for the integration of public housing units throughout the city. Despite the optimism that surrounded the beginning of the Robert Taylor Homes, physical and social conditions quickly deteriorated as poverty, overcrowding, and crime consumed the projects. In the early 1960s, most tenants were members of two-parent families who held steady employment. By the mid-1970s, changes in tenant screening processes and a declining economy meant that single, unemployed parents headed the majority of households. CHA mismanagement, combined with changing tenant attitudes and declining rent revenues, led to the deterioration of buildings and grounds. As historian D. Bradford Hunt contends, the Robert Taylor Homes were arguably the worst place to live in Chicago by 1990.[i] Given the staggering cost to renovate each building, in the mid-1990s, the CHA decided to raze the entire complex and give residents housing vouchers for use elsewhere in the city. The CHA destroyed the very last Robert Taylor structure in 2007, and in its place began building a new mixed-income, combination rental and owner-occupied venture named "Legends South."

The following essay, an excerpt from the conclusion of sociologist Sudhir Alladi Venkatesh's book, *American Project*, chronicles the beginning phases of the Robert Taylor Home demolition. While a graduate student at the University of Chicago, Venkatesh began his study of the Robert Taylor Homes, interviewing and befriending people in the projects. In addition to *American Project*, Venkatesh has produced a documentary film on the Robert Taylor Homes called *Dislocation* (2005) with follows three families through their eviction and relocation process.[ii]

Sudhir Alladi Venkatesh is the William B. Ransford Professor of Sociology at Columbia University where he also serves as Director of the Institute for Social and Economic Research and Policy, and Director of the Charles H. Revson Fellowship Program. His research interests include ethnographic investigations of urban neighborhoods in New York, Chicago, and Paris, France. In addition to *American Project*, Venkatesh's other works include *Off the Books: The Underground Economy of the Urban Poor* (Cambridge, MA: Harvard University Press, 2006), which received a Best Book Award from Slate.com in 2006 and the C. Wright Mills Award in 2007, as well as *Gang Leader for a Day: A Rogue Sociologist Takes to the Streets* (New York: Penguin Press, 2008).

THE BEGINNING OF THE END OF A MODERN GHETTO

A Dream Deferred

In the autumn of 1996, Edith Huddle rested her sore leg on a large cardboard box in the center of her living room and stared out the window of the fourteenth-floor apartment that had been her home for thirty years. Filled with photographs, letters, newspaper clippings, and personal mementos, the box was a record of her days in the Robert Taylor Homes. She had been visiting with neighbors and exchanging her photos for those of her friends. The box was the only remaining item in the apartment that had to be carried away before this chapter in her life could be closed. The walls and cupboards were bare, the closets had been cleaned, and her possessions were now in her daughter's house. Edith Huddle looked down at the box and at the empty space around her, glancing occasionally at her daughter. As she picked up her mementos and walked out the door, a line of well-wishers stood in the hallway, waving goodbye to "Ms. Huddle." "Woman was a fighter," said Kenny Davenport, as Huddle walked by. "The woman *is* a fighter, shit!" said his friend Christie Woodson. In the coming months, the same event would be repeated throughout the buildings in the Robert Taylor Homes as tenants packed their belongings, some departing voluntarily, others evicted by the Housing Authority. The clearance of tenants was the first phase of the eventual "demolition and redevelopment" of the largest public housing development in the world.

---

i D. Bradford Hunt, "Robert Taylor Homes," *Encyclopedia of American Urban History*, Volume 2 (Thousand Oaks, CA: Sage, 2007): 687–688.

ii Sundhir Venkatesh, *Dislocation* (New York: Genco Film Company, 2005),video, www.dislocationfilm.com.

The departure of these families would appear to be the penultimate nail in the coffin of the original 1930s notion of public housing, that is, as a viable "waystation" for poor families from which they could climb the American social and economic ladder. This New Deal–era ray of hope for the American working and poor classes now seemed a broken promise, a naive experiment that was doomed to fail. After 1995, as Americans rendered their verdict on public housing with phrases celebrating the end of a "nightmare," a "mistake," and the worst example of government social engineering, residents looked as though they had lost something more than a roof and four walls—perhaps the dream of better days ahead. Public housing, no matter its problems, still signified to tenants that they were not forgotten in the national promise of freedom and mobility for all citizens, black and white, rich and poor. Many were not leaving public housing completely; most were probably moving to a government rent-subsidized apartment in the private market–reports indicated that they could find housing primarily in the poorest, racially segregated areas, farthest from job growth and adequate city services. Of those who left for the more expensive private market, many envisioned their move as temporary, for they hoped to return to a subsidized apartment soon in order to start their journey again. For the moment, anyway, the dream of public housing as guaranteed shelter and waystation to better days ahead had been deferred.

Plans to demolish the Robert Taylor Homes had circulated with greater frequency beginning in 1995. In June of that year, the Department of Housing and Urban Development had declared that the CHA Board of Commissioners was unfit to govern the city's public housing developments. HUD officials placed the municipal agency in receivership and formed a new interim management team, citing mismanagement and the failure to ensure decent living conditions as their ostensible motives. To tenants, the takeover was a sure sign that their community may not be around much longer. "The national system of public housing is on trial in Chicago," declared HUD Secretary Henry Cisneros, making Chicago the guinea pig for the future of American public housing.[1] Tenants' fears were justified, for in the ensuing months Congress passed legislation mandating that local housing authorities across the nation conduct "viability" studies to determine the more prudent long-term course of action for their larger developments: rehabilitation or demolition and the "scattered" relocation of tenants throughout the city. There had always been calls to destroy Robert Taylor because it was crime-ridden, a less-than-optimal use of city land, or simply an eyesore (even before its construction was completed, CHA officials publicly regretted their decision to build the development), but the federal takeover and the congressional mandates lent an air of certainty to tenant speculation regarding demolition. The CHA determined that 17,859 of its public housing units across the city failed viability standards. Thirty-four thousand residents would have to be moved out so that all the high-rises in Robert Taylor "could be toppled, some within five years," the rest within ten.[2]

The reaction in the tenant body was mixed. One segment of the population wanted to move out and participate in the CHA's "Section 8" program, whereby eligible individuals receive federal certificates and vouchers to subsidize private-market rents. Another, equally vocal constituency wanted to remain, preferring modernization and up-keep to resettlement. A third camp notified the CHA of its willingness to leave, contingent on relocation to a new public housing dwelling in the neighboring Greater Grand Boulevard community. Because the city and the Housing Authority had no plans to rebuild much new housing locally, tenants either placed themselves on the Section 8 waiting lists (which had exceeded twenty thousand families) or waited to hear whether their own high-rise would escape the wrecking balls.[3]

The redevelopment decision affected daily life by dissolving social networks and peer associations, and thereby disrupting whatever support systems households depended upon to make ends meet. Some tenants spent their time and energy looking for new housing elsewhere in the city, and others were relocated to a different building within Robert Taylor, where they met new neighbors and some unfamiliar challenges. In this atmosphere of perpetual change, it was difficult to sustain the informal ties of reciprocity through which material resources, emotional support, and protective services had traditionally been exchanged. In addition to the tenant body, groups and organizations suffered the impact of reshuffling and the loss of members. Bible-reading groups, senior citizens' clubs that ran errands together, tenant patrols, and block clubs were either reconstituted or disbanded altogether. Churches and other service providers lost clients, shifted their resources to conduct outreach and recruit new tenants, and made new needs assessments to ensure adequate service delivery within the complex.

The Black Kings street gang also changed its daily activities as redevelopment began. Prince Williams took advantage of a federal indictment that had dismantled the organizational structure of the Sharks gang to expand the Black Kings' presence into Sharks territory. He negotiated with BK leaders to the southeast, who agreed to absorb Black Kings members displaced by the CHA's resettlement. While the exodus of gang members had a dampening effect on the visibility of the local gangs, fights between remaining Sharks members and colonizing BK factions continued. The drug trade, now dominated by both crack cocaine and heroin sales, continued to flourish, with one estimate citing "$45,000 worth of drug business done in the Robert Taylor Homes each day."[4]

The Grace Center was still in operation, but its Board of Directors decided to limit programming to children and adolescents under sixteen years of age. The Board prohibited center staff from servicing Robert Taylor's youth and young-adult population—for whom there was no other such center within one mile of the housing development—and it expressly forbade its staff to have dealings with street gangs. The well-known individuals who could successfully mediate gang-related conflict had also left.

Will Jackson had resigned, both Christie Woodson and Kenny Davenport moved their families out of Robert Taylor, and Ottie Davis and his wife left the city altogether. Owing to the gang wars, Prince's relationship with the new LAC officers became stilted, and he did not initiate any formal attempts to mollify them or seek collaboration.

As plans for demolition and redevelopment were under way in 1995, the Housing Authority cleared buildings of tenants and placed large cardboard placards on windows to mark the exodus; the city labored to determine the significance of its high-rise public housing communities, including whether the experiment in modernist urban planning should ever be replicated. In their debates over the relative merits of outright destruction of high-rise complexes versus rehabilitation, some asked whether demolition signaled the end of the nation's commitment to housing the poor. Many wondered what would happen to the households evicted from Robert Taylor and other large Chicago public housing complexes. The talk in the streets and in the press, similar to the discourse after the Second World War, when the high-rises were first conceived and built, was emotional and at times contentious. Those favoring the demolition of Robert Taylor cheered the plans while others proclaimed the initiative to be a "conspiracy to remove blacks from their voting power in the inner city and move them to the suburbs."[5] There were public calls to raze the entire complex so that "the nightmare [could be] ended once and for all."[6]

In the ongoing debate, considerations of the habitability of places like the Robert Taylor Homes have been overshadowed by the concerns of parties interested only in the reconfiguration of public housing land. The motives of governments and real estate firms have invaded public discourse and challenged the tenants' rights to remain in their respective areas. Discussions in the most visible media arenas, such as press conferences, talk shows, and the editorial pages of city newspapers, have become shrouded in political posturing and public accusation. Contention is to be expected. Developers thirst for an opportunity to profit from Robert Taylor's valuable real estate tracts, and the mayoral administration is similarly attracted by new prospects for commercial and residential revenue (and the cost savings on social-service delivery). Moreover, given that its own energies are refocused on low-rise and "scattered site" housing, the CHA has expressed relief at the opportunity to leave high-rises behind.

The need to weigh practical concerns of economic productivity and governance are important; however, their introduction has had the effect of replacing concerted examination of the viability of public housing complexes with a more technocratic dialogue regarding the most effective means to meet the interests of developers, tenants, the surging middle and upper class, and the city government. Public rhetoric now regards each party as having an equal stake in the future use of the ninety-six-acre space on which Robert Taylor sits. To claim that public housing developments are a functional or even plausible mode of urban settlement now seems wrongheaded, and perhaps even ignorant, given that public discourse has moved to considerations of how to redevelop, not whether to redevelop.

Despite its prevalence, this framework is not necessarily the best approach to determining the viability of public housing. By almost any criteria that one could use to measure a functional community, it is possible to identify historical periods when Robert Taylor and much of Chicago's public housing were viable, such as the 1940s through the early 1960s. Crime was largely under control—it was not much greater, if at all, than in other areas of the city; public housing provided decent shelter for families, with many leaving eventually for a private-market unit; and management and screening techniques, as well as support from many community organizations and providers, kept its house-holds integrated into the social life of the wider area. Moreover, even in the contemporary period, there are public housing complexes in the largest cities that continue to embody these traits. There is great variation in the functionality of public housing, and whereas Chicago and Los

Angeles have been criticized in recent decades, New York's public housing has been celebrated as viable and well planned.

Beneath the histrionics of public debate and the "theatrical manipulation" over land use in Chicago, the impending demise of Robert Taylor, Cabrini Green, Henry Horner, and other famous high-rise communities has provided an opportunity for self-reflection and evaluation.[7] Chicagoans take great pride in being a "city of neighborhoods," and the elimination of Robert Taylor and its West- and North-Side counterparts has put this self-representation to the test. That high-rise developments will no longer be part of the city's neighborhoods is a moot point. However, the significance of this erasure is still a matter of debate—will it signal the abdication of a local and national commitment to the welfare of the poor, or will it mean that high-rise public housing is ultimately unworkable as a solution to America's low-income housing needs, thus making demolition a painful but necessary circumstance to improve tenants' lives?

The consensus view is that Robert Taylor is an unmistakable failure. This view focuses on two practices, the racism and negligence of mid-twentieth-century participants in the creation and administration of the housing development, and the behavioral pathology of the tenant body itself. That is, Robert Taylor was initially the "victim of racist white politicians and white real estate agents who forced construction in black areas, misguided architects who were captivated by modernist high-rise designs, and an American society unwilling to address the roots of impoverishment."[8] Subsequently, gangs and crime, vandalism, single-parent families, and general disrepair reached intractable levels, well beyond the capacity of tenants and administrative agencies to cope and resteer the housing development toward the mainstream. According to this perspective, then, the first mistake was to build Robert Taylor, the second to allow it to remain when its residents became overwhelmingly destitute and its problems uncontrollable. The lesson in this view is that high-rise public housing is a mistaken means by which to provide for the housing needs of America's urban poor.

To be sure, racism in Chicago and unrest among the tenant body did not enhance the quality of life in Robert Taylor, but these factors do not fully explain the genesis and development of social life in this American project over three decades. It is important to note that the housing development was designed, constructed, and then managed not simply by racist or misguided individuals but by people who had good intentions and who seemed sincere in their efforts to house Chicago's poor and needy. Designers thought that high-rises would free the poor from urban ills, not compound their hardships, and their faith was grounded in the science of urban planning. Black politicians made the difficult choice of ghetto public housing versus no low-income housing at all. Well before racist city officials rejected their proposals to locate low-income housing in white communities, CHA officials had wanted to build public housing in ghettos to address local housing shortages. Later, CHA managers fought for the needs of their constituents while their budgets decreased, and politicians tried to infuse the housing development with law enforcement resources in an effort to increase household security.

The consensus view must be modified to reflect the fact that the fate of Robert Taylor—and the potential of "project living" generally—is inseparable from the housing development's involvement in the ongoing transformations of the larger society. Politicians, designers, CHA officials, and service providers operated in social structures that limited their ability to improve conditions at the complex. Some forces that stymied their efforts were local, such as the law enforcement agencies that refused to police, enforce, and secure the housing development. Others were national in scope, perhaps the most important being the dramatic cuts to the nation's public housing program after the mid-1960s. Moreover, not all developments impacting Robert Taylor were ostensibly related to public housing; these would include the economic disenfranchisement of members of the black working class; who lost jobs and avenues for reemployment, and the government's "redlining" practices that failed to subsidize the homeownership

aspirations of working- and middle-class blacks, some of whom were trying to move out of Robert Taylor. This would suggest that decisions by those whose actions shaped life for Robert Taylor's tenant body were motivated not only by their own prejudices, but also by the institutionalized racism embedded in surrounding political and economic structures.

The consensus view of public housing habitability also ignores the fact that many urban communities face continuous challenges owing to declining economic health, lowered public and private institutional resources, and household hardships, but that the outcome is not the same in each. In the postwar era, a massive city conservation and renewal program sought to stem the deterioration of neighborhoods throughout Chicago. At the time, Chicago was a decaying, drab, and graying place, a testament to the writer Nelson Algren's description, "an October sort of city, even in the spring." Not only the black ghetto, but also white-ethnic poor and working-class areas of the city, and even middle-class communities, suffered a decaying physical infrastructure as well as hardships that threatened family economic stability. In these locales, there was a tremendous infusion of city, state, and federal dollars to ensure that "tipping" neighborhoods on the verge of "blight" did not become slums. By using state-funded "community-conservation" initiatives, the city built schools and parks, increased street lighting, and ensured adequate sanitation service, all in an effort to create clean, livable neighborhoods. Mayor Richard J. Daley exclaimed proudly as he guided Chicago's reconstruction. "When I walk down the street where I live, I see every street in the city of Chicago."

Apparently, the mayor had not seen the streets of the city's black ghetto, which at that time was a segregated place, filled with middle and upper classes, all of whom lived in a cramped and deteriorating physical space that the historian Arnold Hirsch has described uncompromisingly as a composite of "rabbit warrens" and "death traps." The black ghetto was almost wholly ignored in the conservation movement and instead given the vertical high-rise as a solution to its misery and the cries of its residents for decent, affordable housing.

In the late 1960s, as industrial outmigration and job loss took their toll, Robert Taylor was one of many neighborhoods, black and white, that were threatened. Whereas the housing development and the surrounding black community became a space of overwhelmingly unemployed residents, this did not occur throughout Chicago because unions, city politicians, and private capitalists all redirected resources in ways that favored the city's white residents (and select, politically resourceful middle-class black constituents).[9] Again, between 1970 and 1983, the entire city faced a sluggish national economy, but corporate investment and the municipal support of neighborhoods were being targeted to regions containing predominantly white communities, ensuring that the predominantly black areas on the city's South and West Sides would receive no support.[10]

The example of Chicago suggests that government, civic, and private-sector support plays a key role in the viability of *any* community, not just that of public housing—the inability to perceive this connection being perhaps the most glaring error of the consensus view. Yet in the popular deliberations on public housing in the mid-1990s, few thought seriously about the many resources available to mainstream communities—wherever they might be—that enabled these spaces to function and that allowed them to address problems with young people as well as with household hardship. These purportedly normative, private-market neighborhoods will not have rates of vandalism and crime to match those of public housing. Even so, it is doubtful that residents there are tackling problems that may include gangs, truancy, and criminality largely on their own; instead, they are relying on police, whom they trust and who are responsive and responsible in their enforcement. It is doubtful that many of these mainstream communities suffer compromised public spaces, overwhelmingly littered and hazardous parks and play areas, and a negligent city government. Instead, residents can call their elected representatives to remedy such issues, and they probably feel that they can rely on local organizations to provide sufficient social, recreational, educational, and other human services. It is doubtful that these areas will ever reach unemployment rates of nearly 90 percent or have to resort to hidden income and creative hustling schemes; working and middle-class households across America are no doubt fragile and have a "fear of falling," but they are usually embedded in social networks and possess the requisite political capital to locate new employment sources and ensure that their basic needs are being met.

This is to imply not that some American communities are free of problems, but that we ask more of the poor, and particularly those in public housing, than we expect from other citizens. Would residents of a suburb, to offer only one example, be expected to work largely on their own to curb gang activity, and, if they failed to do so, would most Americans then ask whether suburbs were no longer viable planned spaces of residence? Certainly, suburban residents may call for families to assume more responsibility in their children's lives, but it goes without saying that they would demand that their government provide the protective services to which they are entitled, that their schools educate and ensure that their children are sheltered from gang activity, and that social-service providers bolster their resource allocation and provide counseling, drug treatment, and diversionary programming.

By contrast, in discussions of public housing communities, the onus is placed on families, and even the most well-intentioned observers project onto the tenants the need for heroic, independent action that they would never expect of themselves and their own communities. In too many instances, the very same struggles by public housing tenants to procure basic services that are available in the mainstream are not cast as a sign that tenants lack basic entitlements and that the institutions servicing the community need restructuring. Compassionate sentiments turn in the worst case to anger, as in the calls that public housing be ended, that police be allowed to suspend constitutional protections and civil rights, and that tenants stop harboring the gangs. At best, these sentiments express pity for those caught in the middle of the debate over public housing.

This leaves open the question whether Robert Taylor would have been a community capable of responding to its challenges— as it did during the first decade of its existence—if the city's political leaders had devoted adequate resources and attention to the development. It is not difficult to document that leaders at the federal and local level made explicit decisions to rescind resources for public housing, thereby forcing tenants and their management to make do with less. At the least, judgments of its habitability cannot be divorced from this climate of neglect and should not occur without full recognition that, from the middle of the 1960s, Robert Taylor was playing catch-up, never able to garner the resources or commitment necessary for household stability. One of the most important foundations for a sustainable community, namely, the presence of a minimum level of support from the state, was lost, and with few signs that it would be restored, each passing year lent credence to arguments that Robert Taylor was facing problems beyond the capacity of its tenants to manage. Notwithstanding the tenants' destructive behavior, the difficulties faced by residents of Robert Taylor in every period of its existence can be seen as a result not of behavioral pathology but of institutional neglect. How the behavior of administrative agencies and tenants is given weight in any explanation, then, is a matter of debate and is influenced by ideology and politics.

Perhaps the determination of the habitability of public housing—or of any community for that matter—is best sought in the capacity of residents to resolve problems and meet their personal and collective needs. Using this measure, the tenants of the Robert Taylor Homes must be acknowledged for their impressive efforts to cope and make life meaningful amid a dearth of resources. From day-care provision to street-gang inter-vention, the tenant body devised innovative techniques and fought when necessary to ensure their own safety and welfare. The result was the creation of fairly strong, cohesive networks, wherein individuals worked with one another to respond as best they could to their ever-present challenges. Ultimately, however, the resilience they displayed could never provide a permanent basis to foster habitability. Working outside the law and continually sharing resources were short-term solutions that, for Robert Taylor's poor families, proved to be inadequate as hardships continued and assistance from the broader society withered. If these innovative survival strategies had been buttressed with government resources and adequate economic development in public housing neighborhoods, perhaps tenants' networks and associations could have been strengthened and the capacity of the overall community to meet its needs could have been restored.

The larger lesson is that it may be impossible for a community to create its own law and order. Wherever communities develop a quasi-juridical foundation to cope with extremely dangerous practices such as gang wars and drug trafficking, a rapid, responsible initiative that recreates the presence of mainstream legal institutions may be the best course to chart. Recent community policing efforts have suggested that an approach that embeds the police and the judicial system within the community— often, quite literally, by placing courts and jails there—may be a means by which to staunch outlaw justice and create more effective relationships between the poor and the wider world.

Even as they developed internal procedures to address their needs, the tenants of Robert Taylor did not necessarily live in complete isolation, that is, in a "city within a city," effectively disconnected from the wider world. Throughout their attempts to supplant their lack of mainstream resources with informal support systems, tenants lobbied and demanded their fair share of goods and services from the organizations that were neglecting them. Tenants were "unemployed," but they still participated in the local economy as part-time and hidden workers, consumers, and taxpayers. Police ignored Robert Taylor relative to other neighborhoods, but law enforcement officers were nevertheless part of an informal system of localized policing and redress. Similarly, while service providers and government agencies did not respond to all the needs of households, tenants still asked them to be of assistance and welcomed staff members who could help individual families.

To remember the struggles of Robert Taylor's tenants is important, but not at the price of pitying those who have passed through the 4,500 apartments or, in the final instance, rendering them as victims of an uncaring world. There is no community in which ongoing collective labor is not required to ensure livability, though the resources available to communities will differ. In its first three years, Robert Taylor was a success by any definition, in large part because the CHA and tenants had the freedom and resources to meet household needs. The two parties screened applicants rigorously, mixed working and poor families in the high-rises, and drew on the resources of the wider community to support tenants and decrease their sense of isolation. By the mid-1960s, the deluge of impoverished households that came to the Housing Authority seeking shelter made this conscious planning and social engineering unworkable. Buildings soon became filled with households in poverty, the CHA and organizations in the complex were stretched beyond their capacities, and those in the surrounding communities themselves were coping with a growing population of poor families. The conditions worsened as the years passed, and by the end of the 1980s, few could predict how the community would survive. The rising hardship did not, however, eclipse the spirit of the tenants; nor for that matter did it fully erase the habitability of the housing development. Residents' hopefulness is apparent in their acute awareness of their past, the ways in which they celebrate their collective history, and the meaningful and sometimes deliberate ways they keep this history alive in their current actions.

One of the most difficult challenges of representing tenants' personal and collective histories has been to ensure that their experiences and outlooks make their way onto these pages. This has taken on a greater urgency given that, at the time of this writing, only one-half of the twenty-eight buildings in the Robert Taylor Homes are occupied, and even in those high-rises, families are being evicted, relocated, and displaced so that the development may soon be razed. As the individual buildings come down, one by one, the community should be remembered for the ways in which tenants took sustenance from both the joy and the struggle of "project living."

NOTES

1. In the Chicago newspaper coverage of the proposed redevelopment of Robert Taylor, few editorials and articles defended high-rise public housing. The most vituperative attacks came in the *Chicago Tribune* (see "Rethinking Public Housing," July 7, 1996, and "Editorial," October 11, 1995), which has always had the reputation of being pro-development and anti-public housing. Although metro reporters at the *Chicago Sun-Times* offered more balanced coverage, its editorial staff also fully supported high-rise demolition ("Editorial," September 12, 1996). The most informative coverage on the politics of redevelopment was David Peterson, "A Great Chicago Land Grab," *Z Magazine*, April 1997, pp. 34–37.

2. "CHA May Demolish Most of Its Units," *Chicago Tribune*, October 23, 1997.

3. A lawsuit was filed in 1966 in the U.S. District Court by the American Civil Liberties Union against the CHA, on behalf of seven black tenants, including Dorothy Gautreaux. The "Gautreaux" ruling found that the CHA "deliberately and with intent" discriminated against public housing tenants by not placing them in available apartments in white neighborhoods. As a result of the ruling and subsequent negotiations between the federal government and the CHA, the Housing Authority has had to seek housing for black applicants in non "racially impacted" areas, that is, predominantly African American, poor communities. The consequence has been an inability to build housing in existing African-American communities.

4. "The Education of Miss Kelly," *Chicago Tribune Magazine*, September 18, 1999.

5. "U.S. Lends Hand on Plan to Raze, Rebuild Taylor," *Chicago Tribune*, October 9, 1996.

6. This was the opinion of the *Chicago Tribune* editorial staff ("Plan for a City sans CHA Rises," *Chicago Tribune*, September 12, 1996).

7. Gerald D. Suttles, *The Man-Made City: The Land-Use Confidence Game in Chicago* (Chicago: University of Chicago Press, 1990), p. 83.

8. D. Bradford Hunt, "What Went Wrong with Public Housing?" paper delivered at the Newberry Urban History Group, Chicago, May 16, 1998, p. 1.

9. This could occur in different ways, including direct preference for whites, such as hiring by municipal departments or acceptance to union-controlled training and vocational apprenticeship programs, the creative redirection of government financing for areas of "severe economic distress" into projects benefiting largely white middle-class constituents, and subsidization of redevelopment outside of inner-city areas. (For an extended discussion, see Joel Rast, *Remaking Chicago: The Political Origins of Urban Industrial Change* [DeKalb, Ill.: Northern Illinois University Press, 1999]). A white constituency not faring well during these moments of economic decline is based on the city's North Side, in areas where rural Appalachian migrants once settled.

10. "Industrial investor choices in the period 1970–1983 are progressively oriented away from the region's black community which is concentrated on Chicago's West and South Sides and in the northern portion of Lake County, Indiana" (Suttles, *Man-Made City*, p. 42).

9-1. HOUSING ACT OF 1949

Source: Housing Act of 1949 (PL 171, 15 July 1949), 68 *United States Statutes At Large*.

EDITORS' INTRODUCTION

In 1949, Congress passed the Housing Act of 1949, one of the most important laws in the federal government's toolbox for promoting change in urban areas. This act, part of President Harry Truman's Fair Deal, established the idea of urban renewal—that areas considered under-utilized could be razed and set to another purpose. In addition to urban renewal, the Housing Act of 1949 called for the Federal Housing Authority to back mortgages, build more public housing, and extended FHA loan guarantees to rural dwellers.

The Housing Act of 1949 uses the terms "blight" and "slums" in reference to places where poor people resided in substandard housing. Much of the housing for the impoverished in urban areas was highly inadequate. As these terms had loose definitions, however, there were instances in which government officials employed them in reference to physically appealing neighborhoods out of political expediency. The question of slums is further confused because of the highly-segregated nature of American cities. High segregation meant that minority group members of all classes tended to reside in a single neighborhood; if such a neighborhood was completely torn down, the homes of doctors, politicians, and other leaders of the community were razed along with the homes of the financially insecure. As this portion of the law states, the federal government encouraged partnerships with private entities, like business, whenever possible. The Housing Act of 1949 and other related housing acts came to be equated with "Negro removal," as so many of the actions targeted African American neighborhoods. In 2005, the U.S. Supreme Court dealt with the Takings Clause of the Fifth Amendment in the case of *Kelo* v. *City of New London* (Connecticut) and upheld the controversial practice of eminent domain (citing public good) and the use of this property for a private purpose (like building a shopping center). By a vote of 5–4, the court maintained eminent domain yet signaled a growing discomfort with the practice.

An Act

To establish a national housing objective and the policy to be followed in the attainment thereof, to provide Federal aid to assist slum-clearance projects and low-rent, public housing projects initiated by local agencies, to provide for financial assistance by the Secretary of Agriculture for farm housing, and for other purposes.

Be it enacted by the Senate and House of Representatives of the United States of America in Congress assembled, That this Act may be cited as the "Housing Act of 1949".

DECLARATION OF NATIONAL HOUSING POLICY

SEC. 2. The Congress hereby declares that the general welfare and security of the Nation and the health and living standards of its people require housing production and related community development sufficient to remedy the serious housing shortage, the elimination of substandard and other inadequate housing through the clearance of slums and blighted areas, and the realization as soon as feasible of the goal of a decent home and a suitable living environment for every American family, thus contributing to the development and redevelopment of communities and to the advancement of the growth, wealth, and security of the Nation. The Congress further declares that such production is necessary to enable the housing industry to make its full contribution toward an economy of maximum employment, production, and purchasing power. The policy to be followed in attaining the national housing objective hereby established shall be: (1) private enterprise shall be encouraged to serve as large a part of the total need as it can; (2) governmental assistance shall be utilized where feasible to enable private enterprise to serve more of the total need; (3) appropriate local public bodies shall be encouraged and assisted to undertake positive programs of encouraging and assisting the development of well-planned, integrated residential neighborhoods, the development and redevelopment of communities, and the production, at lower costs, of housing of sound standards of design, construction, livability, and size for adequate family life; (4) governmental assistance to eliminate substandard and other inadequate housing through the clearance of slums and blighted areas, to facilitate community development and redevelopment, and to provide adequate housing for urban and rural nonfarm families with incomes so low that they are not being decently housed in new or existing housing shall be extended to those localities which estimate their own needs and demonstrate that these needs are not being met through reliance solely upon private enterprise, and without such aid; and (5) govern- mental assistance for decent, safe, and sanitary farm dwellings and related facilities shall be extended where the farm owner demonstrates that he lacks sufficient resources to provide such housing on his own account and is unable to secure necessary credit for such housing from other sources on terms and conditions which he could reasonably be expected to fulfill. The Housing and Home Finance Agency and its constituent agencies, and any other departments or agencies of the Federal Government having powers, functions, or duties with respect to housing, shall exercise their powers, functions, and duties under this or any other law, consistently with the national housing policy declared by this Act and in such manner as will facilitate sustained progress in attaining the national housing objective hereby established, and in such manner as will encourage and assist (1) the production of housing of sound standards of design, construction, livability, and size for adequate family life; (2) the reduction of the costs of housing without sacrifice of such sound standards; (3) the use of new designs, materials, techniques, and methods in residential construction, the use of standardized dimensions and methods of assembly of home-building materials and equipment, and the increase of efficiency in residential construction and maintenance; (4) the development of well-planned, integrated, residential neighborhoods and the development and redevelopment of communities; and (5) the stabilization of the housing industry at a high annual volume of residential construction.

9-2. THE MAN IN THE GRAY FLANNEL SUIT (1955)

Sloan Wilson

Source: Sloan Wilson, *The Man in the Gray Flannel Suit* (New York: Simon & Schuster, 1955).

EDITORS' INTRODUCTION

Sloan Wilson published this best-selling novel, largely believed to be autobiographical, in 1955. The novel provided its readers with a recognizable portrait of the 1950s suburban lifestyle. The phrase, "the man in the gray flannel suit," became a common expression in American popular culture and vernacular language. The phrase denoted a middle class or upper middle class man who was forever tied to his job and financial obligations. In the novel, the main character, Tom Rath, was a graduate of Harvard University and a World War II veteran (Sloan Wilson shared these characteristics with Rath). Rath's life, including his grinding workday, his daily train commute, his tense relationship with his unfulfilled wife, and his growing financial responsibilities for his three children, was one shared by many Americans. Novelist Sloan Wilson, who published fifteen books, as well as articles and essays, had worked as a reporter for *Time* and as a professor of English at the University of Buffalo. *The Man in the Gray Flannel Suit* was made into a 1956 film starring Gregory Peck and Jennifer Jones. *The Man in the Gray Flannel* suit provided fodder for the popular television program *Mad Men* (2007–), and the title phrase was even employed within the script to describe the program's main character, Don Draper, as played by Jon Hamm.

By the time they had lived seven years in the little house on Greentree Avenue in Westport, Connecticut, they both detested it. There were many reasons, none of them logical, but all of them compelling. For one thing, the house had a kind of evil genius for displaying proof of their weaknesses and wiping out all traces of their strengths. The ragged lawn and weed-filled garden proclaimed to passers-by and the neighbors that Thomas R. Rath and his family disliked "working around the place" and couldn't afford to pay someone else to do it. The interior of the house was even more vengeful. In the living room there was a big dent in the plaster near the floor, with a huge crack curving up from it in the shape of a question mark. That wall was damaged in the fall of 1952, when, after struggling for months to pay up the back bills, Tom came home one night to find that Betsey had brought a cut-glass vase for forty dollars. Such an extravagant gesture was utterly unlike her, at least since the war. Betsey was a conscientious household manager, and usually when she did something Tom didn't like, they talked the matter over with careful reasonableness. But on that particular night, Tom was tired and worried because he himself had just spent seventy dollars on a new suit he felt he needed to dress properly for his business, and at the climax of a heated argument, he picked up the vase and heave it against the wall. The heavy glass shattered, the plaster cracked, and two of the laths behind it broke. The next morning, Tom and Betsey worked together on their knees to patch the plaster, and they repainted the whole wall, but when the paint dried, the big dent near the floor with the crack curving up from it almost to the ceiling in the shape of a question mark was still clearly visible. The fact that the crack was in the shape of a question mark did not seem symbolic to Tom and Betsey, nor even amusing—it was just annoying. Its peculiar shape caused people to stare at it abstractedly, and once at a cocktail party one of the guests who had had a little too much to drink said, "Say, that's funny. Did you ever notice that big question mark on your wall?"

"It's only a crack," Tom replied.

"But why should it be in the form of a question mark?"

"It's just coincidence."

"That's funny," the guest said.

Tom and Betsey assured each other that someday they would have the whole wall replastered, but they never did. The crack remained as a perpetual reminder of Betsey's moment of extravagance, Tom's moment of violence, and their inability either to fix walls properly or to pay to have them fixed. It seemed ironic to Tom that the house should preserve a souvenir of such things, while allowing evenings of pleasure and kindness to slip by without a trace.

The crack in the living room was not the only reminder of the worst. An ink stain with hand marks on the wallpaper in Janey's room commemorated one of the few times Janey had ever willfully destroyed property, and the only time Betsy ever lost her temper with her and struck her. Janey was five, and the middle one of the three Rath children. She did everything hard: she screamed when she cried, and when she was happy her small face seemed to hold for an instant all the joy in the world. Upon deciding that she wanted to play with ink, she carefully poured ink over both her hands and made neat imprints on the wallpaper, from the floor to as high as she could reach. Betsey was so angry that she slapped both her hands, and Janey, feeling she had simply been interrupted in the midst of an artistic endeavor, lay on the bed for an hour sobbing and rubbing her hands in her eyes until her whole face as covered with ink. Feeling like a murderess, Betsey tried to comfort her, but seven holding and rocking her didn't seem to help, and Betsy was shocked to find that the child was shuddering. When Tom came home that night he found mother and daughter asleep on the bed together, tightly locked in each other's arms. Both their faces were covered with ink. All this the wall remembered and recorded.

A thousand petty shabbinesses bore witness to the negligence of the Raths. The front door had been scratched by a dog which had been run over the year before. The hot-water faucet in the bathroom dripped. Almost all the furniture needed to be refinished, reupholstered, or cleaned. And besides that, the house was too small, ugly, and almost precisely like the houses on all sides of it.

The Raths had bought the house in 1946, shortly after Tom had got out of the army and, at the suggestion of his grandmother, become an assistant to the director of the Schanenehauser Foundation, an organization which an elderly millionaire had established to help finance scientific research and the arts. They had told each other that they probably would be in the house only one or two hears before they could afford something better. It took them five years to realize that the expense of raising three children was likely to increase at least as fast as Tom's salary at a charitable foundation. If Tom and Betsy had been entirely reasonable, this might have cause them to start painting the place like crazy, but it had the reverse effect. Without talking about it much, they both began to thing of the house as a trap, and they no more enjoyed refurbishing it than a prisoner would delight in shining up the bars of his cell. Both of them were aware that their feelings about the house were not admirable.

"I don't know what's the matter with us," Betsey said one night. "Your job is plenty good enough. We've got three nice kids, and lots of people would be glad to have a house like this. We shouldn't be so *discontented* all the time."

"Of course we shouldn't!" Tom said.

Their words sounded hollow. It was curious to believe that that house with the crack in the form of a question mark on the wall and the ink stains on the wallpaper was probably the end of their personal road. It was impossible to believe. Somehow something would have to happen.

Tom thought about his house on that day early in June 1953, when a friend of his named Bill Hawthorne mentioned the possibility of a job at the United Broadcasting Corporation. Tom was having lunch with a group of acquaintances in The Golden Horseshoe, a small restaurant and bar near Rockefeller Center.

"I hear we've got a new spot opening up in our public-relations department," Bill, who wrote promotion for United Broadcasting, said. "I think any of you would be crazy to take it, mind you, but if you're interested, there it is…"

Tom unfolded his long legs under the table and shifted his big body on his chair restlessly. "How much would it pay?" he asked casually.

"I don't know," Bill said. "Anywhere from eight to twelve thousand, I'd guess, according to how good a hold-up man you are. If you try for it, ask fifteen. I'd like to see somebody stick the bastards good."

It was fashionable that summer to be cynical about one's employers, and the promotion men were the most cynical of all.

"You can have it," Cliff Otis, a young copy writer for a large advertising agency, said. "I wouldn't want to get into a rat race like that."

Tom glanced into his glass and said nothing. Maybe I could get ten thousand a year, he thought. If I could do that, Betsey and I might be able to buy a better house.

9-3. WATTS RIOT, AUGUST 11–15, 1965

Source: *Report of the National Advisory Commission on Civil Disorders* (Washington D.C.: U.S. Government Printing Office, 1968).

EDITORS' INTRODUCTION

The National Advisory Commission on Civil Disorders was informally referred to as the Kerner Commission, named after its chairman, former Illinois governor Otto Kerner. The Kerner Commission concluded in this report that the United States was "moving toward two societies, one black, one white—separate and unequal."[i] The eleven-member committee had been formed in July 1967 to study the series of riots that had swept the United States in the twentieth century. The tension seemed to be building in the 1960s, and President Lyndon B. Johnson expressed great concern. In April 1968, just a month after the issuance of the Kerner Commission report, Martin Luther King was assassinated, and cities across the nation again erupted in violence. In this section of the report, the committee tells the story of the Watts Riot of 1965. Watts, by this point a low-income, largely African American section of Los Angeles, broke out in riots following the arrest of a young African American man, Marquette Frye, and his brother Ronald Frye. The story of Watts was first officially documented in the McCone Report, published in December 1965 and named after the riot investigation committee chairman, John McCone. Thirty-three years later, the National Advisory Commission on Civil Disorders issued a follow-up to the Kerner Commission report. The 1998 addendum demonstrated that many American cities still faced racial strife, but African Americans and other minority groups had also resettled in the suburbs in significant numbers.

As late as the second week of August, there had been few disturbances outside the South. But, on the evening of August 11, as Los Angeles sweltered in a heat wave, a highway patrolman halted a young Negro driver for speeding. The young man appeared intoxicated, and the patrolman arrested him. As a crowd gathered, law enforcement officers were called to the scene. A highway patrolman mistakenly struck a bystander with his billy club. A young Negro woman, who was erroneously accused of spitting on the police, was dragged into the middle of the street.

When the police departed, members of the crowd began hurling rocks at passing cars, beating white motorists, and overturning cars and setting them on fire. The police reacted hesitantly. Actions they did take further inflamed the people on the streets.

The following day the area was calm. Community leaders attempting to mediate between Negro residents and the police received little cooperation from municipal authorities. That evening the previous nights' pattern of violence was repeated.

Not until almost 30 hours after the initial flareup did window smashing, looting, and arson begin. Yet the police utilized only a small part of their forces.

Few police were on hand the next morning when huge crowds gathered in the business district of Watts, two miles from the location of the original disturbance, and began looting. In the absence of police response, the looting became bolder and spread into other areas. Hundreds of women and children from five housing projects clustered in or near Watts took part. Around noon, extensive fire-bombing began. Few white persons were attacked; the principal intent of the rioters now seemed to be to destroy property owned by whites, in order to drive white "exploiters" out of the ghetto.

---

i *Report of the National Advisory Commission on Civil Disorders* (Washington, D.C.: U.S. Government Printing Office, 1968), 1.

The chief of police asked for National Guard help, but the arrival of military units was delayed for several hours. When the Guardsmen arrive, they, together with police, made heavy use of firearms. Reports of "sniper fire" increased. Several persons were killed by mistake. Many more were injured.

Thirty-six hours after the first Guard units arrived, the main force of the riot had been blunted. Almost 4,000 persons were arrested. Thirty-four were killed and hundreds injured. Approximately $35 million in damage had been inflicted.

The Los Angeles riot, the worst in the United States since the Detroit riot of 1943, shocked all who had been confident that race relations were improving in the North, and evoked a new mood in the ghettos around the country.

9-4. URBAN INDIANS (1964–1969)

Adam Fortunate Eagle

Source: Adam Fortunate Eagle, *Alcatraz! Alcatraz!* (California: Heyday Books, 1992). Reprinted with permission of Adam Fortunate Eagle.

EDITORS' INTRODUCTION

Adam Fortunate Eagle was born Adam Nordwall. A member of the Red Lake Minnesota Chippewa, Eagle played an instrumental role in the occupation of Alcatraz Island, located in San Francisco Bay, between 1969–1971, bringing considerable publicity to the cause of Native American rights. He contributed to the writing of the group's manifesto, "The Alcatraz Proclamation to the Great White Father and his People." The 1969 Alcatraz takeover actually began in 1964, when a group of Sioux sailed to Alcatraz and claimed its land under the auspices of the Sioux Treaty of 1868. So much land had been taken from native peoples, and the Alcatraz occupation was an attempt to take some back again or at least garner media attention. The Alcatraz proclamation offered $24 in glass beads and red cloth for the land, at that time not in use by the federal government, and urged the creation of the Bureau of Caucasian Affairs, for the care of any white people on the island. In addition to *Alcatraz! Alcatraz!*, Eagle is the author of *Heart of the Rock: The Indian Invasion of Alcatraz* (Norman: University of Oklahoma Press, 2002) and an upcoming memoir, *Pipestone: A Boy's Life in an Indian Boarding School* (Norman: University of Oklahoma Press). He narrated the film *Sitting Bull: A Stone in My Heart*, directed by John Ferry, in 2007, and is the subject of a new film by Ferry and Lillimar Films, *Contrary Warrior: The Life and Times of Adam Fortunate Eagle*, released in 2009.

Urban Indians

I remember that as we were heading back to the mainland that March day in 1964, one of the non-Indians asked another non-Indian, "What are a bunch of Sioux Indians doing here in the Bay Area? Why aren't they back in the Midwest, or wherever they're from?"

I am sure he wasn't the only one wondering why we Indians would be so concerned about a little rock in the middle of San Francisco Bay when we supposedly had vast reservations to live on and the government was reportedly paying us to do nothing. Why would we leave such a paradise and move to the big city where we might even have to work?

If you visit a reservation today you will probably see poverty, alcoholism, and desperation. These problems persist despite improvement due to recent Indian activism, such as the Alcatraz occupation. In 1964, the reservations were much worse. Corruption in the Bureau of Indian Affairs (BIA) and the tribal governments often allowed greedy speculators to purchase tribal resources such as land and mineral deposits; Indians remained poor and their reservations remained undeveloped.

In 1968, a Senate subcommittee stated that "50,000 Indian families live in unsanitary, dilapidated dwellings, many in huts, shanties, even abandoned automobiles." The report went on to state that the average annual Indian income was $1500, 25% of the national average; the unemployment rate among Indians was 40%, more than ten times the national average; the average age of death for American Indians was 44 years and for all other Americans 65 years; infant mortality was twice the national average; and thousands of Indians had migrated or been relocated into cities only to find themselves untrained for jobs and unprepared for urban life. Many returned to their reservations more disillusioned and defeated than when they left. And this report appeared after several years of "Great Society" programs, none of which seemed to be directed towards helping the Indians. For many, reservation life was one of hopeless poverty and ongoing misery.

Many people think that these conditions were due to laziness, a sort of welfare mentality. They don't realize the conditions were a deliberate creation of the U.S. Government, the result of decades of manipulation, contempt, and control.

The government and the speculators knew that the tribes held vast amounts of natural resources. In 1952 the government prepared an 1800-page report on Indian conditions. Indians called it the "Doomsday Book." The report discussed the complicated task of eliminating the reservation system and concluded that the expense and difficulty were justified by the prospect of gaining control of the natural resources held by the tribes. In addition to timber and water, it was estimated that the 23 Western tribes controlled 33 percent of the country's low-sulfur coal, 80 percent of the nation's uranium reserves, and between 3 and 10 percent of the gas and petroleum reserves. I have never seen the monetary value of these tribal holdings quoted in any report, but the amount would have to be very large.

Considering all these natural resources, one would think that the BIA would have trained Indians to develop these resources to create jobs and wealth for all the Indians on the reservation. Self-sufficiency would have been the humane solution, but it might have interfered with the profit that stood to be made. The report stated that by withdrawing federal services to the tribes and eliminating the reservation system the government would save millions of dollars every year. Without any Indian lands to administer, the BIA, the oldest bureau in the federal government could be shut down. This rearrangement would allow the large corporate structure which operated in convert with the federal government to quickly grab up the natural resources. The last vestige of Indian country would disappear into the history books, which could then proudly proclaim that "the American Indian has finally become fully assimilated into the mainstream of American society." It all sounded like a twist on the "final solution" idea proposed by another government just a few years earlier.

The next year the government put these plans into action and passed what is referred to as the Termination Act, which allowed them to begin removing the tribes' status as political entities. The process of dismantling 200 years of a relationship between the U.S. Government and the American Indians lurched into motion like a giant steam roller. But when the government began to look at closing down the reservations, they ran into an interesting problem: the Indian reservations were full of Indians!

The political leaders in Washington then put their collective heads together and dreamed up another scheme—they would reduce the reservation populations by relocating Indians to urban areas. Of course, this would all be done under the guise of helping the Indians. So by 1958 the decision had been made to establish eight relocation centers in major U.S. cities. Four of those centers were set up in California cities: Los Angeles, San Francisco, San Jose, and Oakland.

The BIA had the responsibility of running an employment assistance program for relocated Indians. Unfortunately the program was really a carrot on a stick to entice the Indians on the reservations, where many lived in great poverty. The BIA sent agents to the reservations to talk to the unemployed young men and women and even the older unemployed family men. The agents offered to help the Indians find work in a "meaningful job." The hitch was that the jobs weren't on or near the reservations as the Indians hoped, but often more than a thousand miles away from their homes and families.

The Indians that signed up for the program were given bus tickets to whichever center they had chosen. For instance, say a young Indian man chose the Oakland center. When he and his family arrived they immediately reported to the relocation office, which found them an apartment, usually in a ghetto. Every morning the young man checked into the relocation office where he was instructed to sit down and wait until called. He sat in a waiting room with a small television set and a bunch of old magazines while an "employment assistance officer" tried to line up a job interview. He was told that if he didn't report to the office each day his subsistence allowance would be cut off. In the meantime, his wife and kids locked themselves in their apartment, because they were afraid to go out by themselves into the crime-ridden streets. When the BIA found a job for their Indian "client," he was cut off from BIA services after his first paycheck. Many of the jobs were temporary. It didn't take long for the Indian to realize he had been trapped.

After the BIA "cut the cord" with the relocated Indians, those who had been given only temporary jobs had to turn to city, county, and state agencies. But the agencies seldom wanted anything to do with the Indians. They were considered the responsibility of the federal government, not local agencies. It was a terrible dilemma to be told, "You're an Indian, you go to the federal government for help." Or, as one Indian declared, "It's damn tough to go around to these different agencies looking for help and they pretend you don't exist."

In a hearing for the Committee on Urban Indians, sponsored by the National Council of Indian Opportunity in the late spring of 1969, an attorney testified to this problem by stating, "Discrimination is implicit in most of the programs for urban areas." Needy urban Indians found themselves in a new type of entrapment—too poor to go back to the reservation and too "Indian" to receive the benefits of society.

For some, the transition was simply too much to take. The government provided the bus ticket from the reservation to the city, but many Indians hitch-hiked back, more bitter than ever about what they felt was another government trick.

For others who stayed, the adjustment from reservation life to an urban existence proved to be chaotic at best. The pressures of adapting and the frustration of dealing with the agencies were too much for many young Indians trapped in the cities. In one eighteen-month period, there were four suicides reported among Indians in the Bay Area. One year in San Francisco, my own sister was counted among the despairing numbers who could not cope with the urban trap. She slipped a plastic bag over her head and filled it full of a greaseless cooking spray.

9-5. OAKLAND BLACK PANTHER PARTY FOR SELF-DEFENSE, TEN POINT PLAN (1966)

Source: Ten Point Plan, Black Panther Party, October 1966.

EDITORS' INTRODUCTION

The Black Panther Party, originally the Black Panther Party for Self-Defense, was formed in 1966 and disbanded in 1976. In May 1967, the group famously staged a march on the California State Capitol in Sacramento, demonstrating in support of their claimed right to bear arms. The symbol of the party, the crouching black panther, originated with the Lowndes County (Mississippi) Freedom Organization, which had fought for the right of

African Americans to vote. Drawing from the ideological teachings of Malcolm X, and a symbol of the black power movement of the late 1960s and 1970s, the party coalesced under the leadership of such figures as Huey P. Newton, Bobby Seale, and Eldridge Cleaver, and had a strong association with Angela Davis. Alongside the North Oakland Neighborhood Anti-Poverty Center, the group worked on behalf of African American causes, such as sickle-cell anemia and poverty. The Black Panther Party caught on in cities throughout the country, and even inspired the founding of modern groups with similar ideals. By the time of the party's disbanding in the 1970s, police forces around the country had grown significantly more integrated.

What We Want

What We Believe

1. *We want freedom. We want power to determine the destiny of our Black Community.*
   We believe that black people will not be free until we are able to determine our destiny.

2. *We want full employment for our people.*
   We believe that the federal government is responsible and obligated to give every man employment or a guaranteed income. We believe that if the white American businessmen will not give full employment, then the means of production should be taken from the businessmen and placed in the community so that the people of the community can organize and employ all of its people and give a high standard of living.

3. *We want an end to the robbery by the CAPITALISTS of our Black Community.*
   We believe that this racist government has robbed us and now we are demanding the overdue debt of forty acres and two mules. Forty acres and two mules was promised 100 years ago as restitution for slave labor and mass murder of black people. We will accept the payment as currency which will be distributed to our many communities. The Germans are now aiding the Jews in Israel for the genocide of the Jewish people. The Germans murdered six million Jews. The American racist has taken part in the slaughter of over twenty[1] million black people; therefore, we feel that this is a modest demand that we make.

4. *We want decent housing, fit for shelter of human beings.*
   We believe that if the white landlords will not give decent housing to our black community, then the housing and the land should be made into cooperatives so that our community, with government aid, can build and make decent housing for its people.

5. *We want education for our people that exposes the true nature of this decadent American society. We want education that teaches us our true history and our role in the present-day society.*
   We believe in an educational system that will give to our people a knowledge of self. If a man does not have knowledge of himself and his position in society and the world, then he has little chance to relate to anything else.

6. *We want all black men to be exempt from military service.*
   We believe that Black people should not be forced to fight in the military service to defend a racist government that does not protect us. We will not fight and kill other people of color in the world who, like black people, are being victimized by the white racist government of America. We will protect ourselves from the force and violence of the racist police and the racist military, by whatever means necessary.

7. *We want an immediate end to POLICE BRUTALITY and MURDER of black people.*
   We believe we can end police brutality in our black community by organizing black self-defense groups that are dedicated to defending our black

community from racist police oppression and brutality. The Second Amendment to the Constitution of the United States gives a right to bear arms. We therefore believe that all black people should arm themselves for self-defense.

8. *We want freedom for all black men held in federal, state, county and city prisons and jails.*
We believe that all black people should be released from the many jails and prisons because they have not received a fair and impartial trial.

9. *We want all black people when brought to trial to be tried in court by a jury of their peer group or people from their black communities, as defined by the Constitution of the United States.*
We believe that the courts should follow the United States Constitution so that black people will receive fair trials. The 14th Amendment of the U.S. Constitution gives a man a right to be tried by his peer group. A peer is a person from a similar economic, social, religious, geographical, environmental, historical and racial background. To do this the court will be forced to select a jury from the black community from which the black defendant came. We have been, and are being tried by all-white juries that have no understanding of the "average reasoning man" of the black community.

10. *We want land, bread, housing, education, clothing, justice and peace. And as our major political objective, a United Nations-supervised plebiscite to be held throughout the black colony in which only black colonial subjects will be allowed to participate for the purpose of determining the will of black people as to their national destiny.*

When in the course of human events, it becomes necessary for one people to dissolve the political bands which have connected them with another, and to assume, among the powers of the earth, the separate and equal station to which the laws of nature and nature's God entitle them, a decent respect to the opinions of mankind requires that they should declare the causes which impel them to the separation.

We hold these truths to be self evident, that all men are created equal; that they are endowed by their Creator with certain unalienable rights; that among these are life, liberty, and the pursuit of happiness. *That, to secure these rights, governments are instituted among men, deriving their just powers from the consent of the governed; that, whenever any form of government becomes destructive of these ends, it is the right of the people to alter or to abolish it, and to institute a new government, laying its foundation on such principles, and organizing its powers in such form, as to them shall seem most likely to effect their safety and happiness.* Prudence, indeed, will dictate that governments long established should not be changed for light and transient causes; and, accordingly, all experience hath shown, that mankind are more disposed to suffer, while evils are sufferable, than to right themselves by abolishing the forms to which they are accustomed. *But, when a long train of abuses and usurpations, pursuing invariable the same object, evinces a design to reduce them under absolute despotism, it is their right, it is their duty, to throw off such government, and to provide new guards for their future security.*

NOTE

1. In March 1972, the platform was revised to include the number of fifty million.

9-6. *ALL SOULS* (1999)

Michael Patrick MacDonald

Source: *All Souls: A Family Story from Southie* (Boston: Beacon Press, 1999).

EDITORS' INTRODUCTION

The decision in the landmark civil rights case, *Brown* v. *Board of Education* (1954) began to erode the long practice of segregated schools within the United States. Yet this Supreme Court ruling proved to be just the beginning of the movement to desegregate American public schools. Many of our school systems were segregated because the neighborhoods they served were themselves segregated. A lesser known Supreme Court case, *Swann* v. *Charlotte-Mecklenburg Board of Education* (1971) instituted the concept of busing between school districts to disrupt entrenched segregation, while the case *Milliken* v. *Bradley* (1974) lessened the effects of *Swann* somewhat by requiring proof of *de jure* segregation across multiple school districts.

Boston became the site of great unrest in the mid-1970s, following federal judge W. Arthur Garrity, Jr.'s decision to desegregate city schools by busing students out of their neighborhoods. Garrity's plan did not combine wealthy white schools with struggling minority schools, but rather by-and-large mixed students from white inner city schools with minority inner city schools. Memoirist and activist Michael Patrick MacDonald remembered how upset his largely white neighborhood in Southie felt about the decision to bus children to different schools. Violence erupted in the streets. The author himself threw a rock at a school bus. Many white families, like the MacDonalds, pulled children out of public school in preference for parochial education. Louise Day Hicks organized South Boston into a protest movement, Restore Our Alienate Rights (ROAR), and held a National Boycott Day, marching on Judge Garrity's home. The movement to desegregate schools in Boston was never fully successful; whites abandoned the cities in significant numbers or pulled their children out of the public school system, leaving the city with a largely minority student base. In Boston, as was the case throughout the nation, people grew less enamored with the idea of desegregation and the term was infrequently employed in public discourse.

Michael Patrick MacDonald is also the author of *Easter Rising: An Irish American Coming Up From Under* (New York: Houghton Mifflin, 2006). He is at work on a screen-play for a film based on *All Souls*.

That September, Ma let us skip the first week of school. The whole neighborhood was boycotting school. City Councilor Louise Day Hicks and her bodyguard with the bullhorn, Jimmy Kelly, were telling people to keep their kids home. It was supposed to be just the high school kids boycotting, but we all wanted to show our loyalty to the neighborhood. I was meant to be starting the third grade at St. Augustine's School. Ma had enrolled Kevin and Kathy in the sixth and seventh grades there as well. Frankie was going to Southie High, and Mary and Joe were being sent to mostly black Roxbury, so they really had something to boycott. But on the first day, Kevin and Kathy begged Ma not to send them. "C'mon Ma, please?" I piped in. It was still warm outside and we wanted to join the crowds that were just then lining the streets to watch the busloads of black kids come into Southie. The excitement built as police helicopters hovered just above our third-floor windows, police in riot gear stood guard on the rooftops of Old Colony, and the national news camped out on every corner. Ma said okay, and we ran up to Darius Court, along the busing route, where in simpler times we'd watched the neighborhood St. Paddy's Day parade.

The whole neighborhood was out. Even the mothers from the stoop made it to Darius Court, nightgowns and all. Mrs. Coyne, up on the rooftop in her housedress, got arrested before the buses even started rolling through the neighborhood. Everyone knew she was a little soft, and I thought the excitement that day must have been a bit too much for her. She ran up to the roof and called the police "nigger lovers" and "traders," and started dancing and singing James Brown songs. "Say it loud, I'm black and I'm proud!" She nearly fell off the roof before one cop grabbed her from behind and restrained her. Everyone was laughing at that one: big fat Mrs. Coyne rolling around on the rooftop kicking and screaming, with a cop in full riot gear on top of her. Little disturbances like that broke out here and there, but most people were too intent on seeing the buses roll to do anything that might get them carted away.

I looked up the road and saw a squadron of police motorcycles speeding down Dorchester Street, right along the curb, as if they would run over anyone who wasn't on the sidewalk. The buses were coming. Police sirens wailed as hundreds of cops on motorcycles aimed at the crowds of mothers and kids, to clear the way for the law of the land. "Bacon . . . I smell bacon!" a few people yelled, sniffing at the cops. I knew that meant the cops were pigs. As the motorcycles came closer I fought to get back onto the sidewalk, but it was too crowded. I ran further into the road to avoid one motorcycle, when two more came at me from the middle of the street. I had to run across to the other side of the road, where the crowd quickly cleared a space for me on the sidewalk. All the adults welcomed me, patting me on the shoulder. "Are you all right?" "Those pricks would even kill a kid." "Pigs!" someone else shouted. I thought I'd lost Kevin and Kathy, but just then I saw them sitting on top of a mailbox up the street for a good view of the buses. They waved to me, laughing because they'd seen me almost get run over.

The road was cleared, and the buses rolled slowly. We saw a line of yellow buses like there was no end to them. I couldn't see any black faces though, and I was looking for them. Some people around me started to cry when they finally got a glimpse of the buses through the crowd. One woman made the sign of the cross and a few others copied her. "I never thought I'd see the day come," said an old woman next to me. She lived downstairs from us, but I had never seen her leave her apartment before. I'd always thought she was crippled or something, sitting there in her window every day, waiting for Bobby, the delivery man who came daily with a package from J.J.'s Liquors. She was trembling now, and so was everyone else. I could feel it myself. It was a feeling of loss, of being beaten down, of humiliation. In minutes, though, it had turned to anger, rage, and hate, just like in those Irish rebel songs I'd heard all my life. Like "The Ballad of James Connolly": "God's curse on you England/You cruel hearted monster/Your deeds they would shame all the devils in Hell." Except we'd changed it to "God's curse on you Garrity."

Smash! A burst of flying glass and all that rage exploded. We'd all been waiting for it, and so had the police in riot gear. It felt like a gunshot, but it was a brick. It went right through a bus window. Then all hell broke loose. I saw a milk crate fly from the other side of the street right for my face. More bricks, sticks, and bottles smashed against the buses, as police pulled out their billy clubs and charged with their riot shields in a line formation through the crowds. Teenagers were chased into the project and beaten to the cement wherever they were caught.

I raced away about a block from the fray, to a spot where everyone was chanting "Here We Go Southie, Here We Go," like a battle cry. That's when I realized we were at war. I started chanting too, at first just moving my lips because I didn't know if a kid's voice would ruin the strong chant. But then I belted it out, just as a few other kids I didn't know joined the chorus. The kids in the crowd all looked at each other as if we were family. *This is great*, I thought. I'd never had such an easy time as this, making friends in Southie. The buses kept passing by, speeding now, and all I could see in the windows were black hands with their middle fingers up at us, still no faces though.

The buses got through the crowd surrounded by the police motorcycles. I saw Frankie running up toward Southie High along with everyone else. "What are you doing out here!" he yelled. "Get your ass home!" He said there was another riot with the cops up at the high school, and off he ran with the others. Not far behind were Kevin and his friends. He shouted the same thing at me: "Get your ass home!" I just wanted to find Ma now and make sure she wasn't beaten or arrested or anything, so I ran home. The project was empty—everyone had followed the buses up the St. Paddy's parade route. Ma wasn't home, but the TV was on, with live coverage of the riots at Southie High. Every channel I turned to showed the same thing. I kept flipping the dial, looking for my family, and catching glimpses of what seemed to be all the people I knew hurling stones or being beaten by the police, or both. *This is big*, I thought. It was scary and thrilling at the same time, and I remembered the day we'd moved into this neighborhood, when Ma said it looked just like Belfast, and that we were in the best place in the world. I kept changing the channels, looking for my family, and I didn't know anymore whether I was scared or thrilled, or if there was any difference between the two anyhow.

The buses kept rolling, and the hate kept building. It was a losing battle, but we returned to Darius Court every day after school to see if the rage would explode again. Sometimes it did and sometimes it didn't. But the bus route became a meeting place for the neighborhood. Some of my neighbors carried big signs with RESIST or NEVER or my favorite, HELL NO WE WON'T GO. There was always someone in the crowd keeping everyone laughing with wise-cracks aimed at the stiff-looking state troopers who lined the bus route, facing the crowds to form a barrier. They never moved or showed any expression. We all wanted to get them to react to some-thing. But we wanted a reaction somewhere between the stiff in-human stance and the beatings. When my friends and I tried to get through to them by asking questions about their horses and could we pet them, they told us to screw. And it wasn't long before some kids started trying to break the horses' legs with hockey sticks when riots broke out. One day the staties got distracted by a burning effigy of Judge Garrity that came flying off a rooftop in the project. That's when I saw Kevin make his way out of Darius Court to throw a rock at the buses. A trooper chased him, but Kevin was too fast. His photo did end up in the *Boston Globe* the next day, though, his scrawny shirtless body whipping a rock with all his might. It looked like the pictures we'd always seen of kids in war-torn countries throwing petrol bombs at some powerful enemy. But Kevin's rock hit a yellow bus with black kids in it.

I threw a rock once. I had to. You were a pussy if you didn't. I didn't have a good aim, though, and it landed on the street before it even made it to the bus. I stared at my rock and was partly relieved. I didn't really want it to smash a bus window. I only wanted the others to see me throwing it. On that day there were so many rocks flying that you didn't know whose rock landed where, but everyone claimed the ones that did the most damage. Even though I missed, a cop came out of nowhere and treated me just like they treated the kids with good aim. He took me by the neck and threw me to the dirt. I sat there for a few minutes to make sure that everyone had seen that one. I was only eight, but I was part of it all, part of something bigger than I'd ever imagined, part of something that was on the national news every night.

Every day I felt the pride of rebellion. The helicopters above my bedroom window woke me each morning for school, and my friends and I would plan to pass by the TPF on the corners so we could walk around them and give them hateful looks. Ma and the nuns at St. Augustine's told me it was wrong to hate the blacks for any of this. But I had to hate someone, and the police were always fracturing some poor neighbor's skull or taking teenagers over to the beach at night to beat them senseless, so I hated them with all my might. SWAT teams had been called into the neighborhood. I'd always liked the television show "S.W.A.T.," but they were the enemy now. We gave the SWAT sharp-shooters standing guard over us on the rooftops the finger; then we'd run. Evenings we had to be off the streets early or else the cops would try to run us down with their motorbikes. No more hanging out on corners in Old Colony. A line of motorbikes straight across the street and sidewalks would appear out of nowhere and force everyone to disappear into hallways and tunnels. One time I had to jump into a bush because they were coming from both ends of the street. I was all cut up, and I really hated them then.

It felt good, the hate I had for the authorities. My whole family hated them, especially Frankie, Kathy, and Kevin, who got the most involved in the riots. I would've loved to throw Molotov cocktails myself, along with some of the adults, but I was only a kid and the cops would probably catch me and beat me at the beach. So I just fantasized about killing them all. They were the enemy, the giant oppressor, like Goliath. And the people of South Boston were like David. Except that David won in the end, and we knew we were going to lose this one. But that made us even more like the Irish, who were always fighting in the songs even if they had to lose and die a glorious death.

9-7. ADDRESS TO THE NATION ON THE CIVIL DISTURBANCES IN LOS ANGELES, CALIFORNIA (1992)

George H. W. Bush

Source: *Public Papers of the Presidents of the United States, George Bush, 1992–93*, Book I—January to July 31, 1992 (Washington D.C.: United States Government Printing Office, 1993).

EDITORS' INTRODUCTION

On April 29, 1992, a jury in Simi Valley, California acquitted four Los Angeles police officers in the brutal beating of African American Rodney King. Millions of Americans who saw the widely broadcast videotape of the incident, which took place in March 1991, were surprised at the verdict; thousands of Los Angelinos even took to the streets in anger. Violence eventually erupted and engulfed the city for the better part of a week, resulting in fifty-three deaths and approximately $1 billion in property damage, making it one of the most costly civil disturbances in American history. Other small riots and protests took place in cities across the United States, with notable acts of violence in San Francisco, Seattle, and Atlanta.

On the third day of rioting, May 1, 1992, President George H. W. Bush addressed the nation from the Oval Office at the White House. In his comments, excerpted below, President Bush noted the urgent need to restore order and for further investigation by the United States Department of Justice into the violation of Rodney King's civil rights. He also recounted the inspiring story of how four African Americans came to the aid of a beaten white truck driver (Reginald Denny) and helped get him safely to a hospital. In his concluding remarks, President Bush harkened back to John Winthrop's "A Model of Christian Charity" sermon **[see Document 2.1]** in reminding Americans of their special place in the world.

Address to the Nation on the Civil Disturbances in Los Angeles, California

May 1, 1992

Tonight I want to talk to you about violence in our cities and justice for our citizens, two big issues that have collided on the streets of Los Angeles. First, an update on where matters stand in Los Angeles.

Fifteen minutes ago I talked to California's Governor Pete Wilson and Los Angeles Mayor Tom Bradley. They told me that last night was better than the night before; today, calmer than yesterday. But there were still incidents of random terror and lawlessness this afternoon.

In the wake of the first night's violence, I spoke directly to both Governor Wilson and Mayor Bradley to assess the situation and to offer assistance. There are two very different issues at hand. One is the urgent need to restore order. What followed Wednesday's jury verdict in the Rodney King case was a tragic series of events for the city of Los Angeles: Nearly 4,000 fires, staggering property damage, hundreds of injuries, and the senseless deaths of over 30 people.

To restore order right now, there are 3,000 National Guardsmen on duty in the city of Los Angeles. Another 2,200 stand ready to provide immediate support. To supplement this effort I've taken several additional actions. First, this morning I've ordered the Justice Department to dispatch 1,000 Federal riot-trained law enforcement officials to help restore order in Los Angeles beginning tonight. These officials include FBI SWAT teams, special riot control units of the U.S. Marshals Service, the Border Patrol, and other Federal law enforcement agencies. Second, another 1,000 Federal law enforcement officials are on standby alert, should they be needed. Third, early today I directed 3,000 members of the 7th Infantry and 1,500 marines to stand by at El Toro Air Station, California. Tonight, at the request of the Governor and the Mayor, I have committed these troops to help restore order. I'm also federalizing the National Guard, and I'm instructing General Colin Powell to place all those troops under a central command.

What we saw last night and the night before in Los Angeles is not about civil rights. It's not about the great cause of equality that all Americans must uphold. It's not a message of protest. It's been the brutality of a mob, pure and simple. And let me assure you: I will use whatever force is necessary to restore order. What is going on in L.A. must and will stop. As your President I guarantee you this violence will end.

Now let's talk about the beating of Rodney King, because beyond the urgent need to restore order is the second issue, the question of justice: Whether Rodney King's Federal civil rights were violated. What you saw and what I saw on the TV video was revolting. I felt anger. I felt pain. I thought: How can I explain this to my grandchildren?

Civil rights leaders and just plain citizens fearful of and sometimes victimized by police brutality were deeply hurt. And I know good and decent policemen who were equally appalled.

I spoke this morning to many leaders of the civil rights community. And they saw the video, as we all did. For 14 months they waited patiently, hopefully. They waited for the system to work. And when the verdict came in, they felt betrayed. Viewed from outside the trial, it was hard to understand how the verdict could possibly square with the video. Those civil rights leaders with whom I met were stunned. And so was I, and so was Barbara, and so were my kids.

But the verdict Wednesday was not the end of the process. The Department of Justice had started its own investigation immediately after the Rodney King incident and was monitoring the State investigation and trial. And so let me tell you what actions we are taking on the Federal level to ensure that justice is served.

Within one hour of the verdict, I directed the Justice Department to move into high gear on its own independent criminal investigation into the case. And next, on Thursday, five Federal prosecutors were on their way to Los Angeles. Our Justice Department has consistently demonstrated its ability to investigate fully a matter like this. [...]

We owe it to all Americans who put their faith in the law to see that justice is served. But as we move forward on this or any other case, we must remember the fundamental tenet of our legal system. Every American, whether accused or accuser, is entitled to protection of his or her rights.

In this highly controversial court case, a verdict was handed down by a California jury. To Americans of all races who were shocked by the verdict, let me say this: You must understand that our system of justice provides for the peaceful, orderly means of addressing this frustration. We must respect the process of law whether or not we agree with the outcome: There's a difference between frustration with the law and direct assaults upon our legal system.

In a civilized society, there can be no excuse, no excuse for the murder, arson, theft, and vandalism that have terrorized the law-abiding citizens of Los Angeles. Mayor Bradley, just a few minutes ago, mentioned to me his particular concern, among others, regarding the safety of the Korean community. My heart goes out to them and all others who have suffered losses.

The wanton destruction of life and property is not a legitimate expression of outrage with injustice. It is itself injustice. And no rationalization, no matter how heartfelt, no matter how eloquent, can make it otherwise.

Television has become a medium that often brings us together. But its vivid display of Rodney King's beating shocked us. The America it has shown us on our screens these last 48 hours has appalled us. None of this is what we wish to think of as American. It's as if we were looking in a mirror that distorted our better selves and turned us ugly. We cannot let that happen. We cannot do that to ourselves. [...]

Among the many stories I've seen and heard about these past few days, one sticks in my mind, the story of one savagely beaten white truck driver, alive tonight because four strangers, four black strangers, came to his aid. Two were men who had been watching television and saw the beating as it was happening, and came out into the street to help; another was a woman on her way home from work; and the fourth, a young man whose name we may never know. The injured driver was able to get behind the wheel of his truck and tried to drive away. But his eyes were swollen shut. The woman asked him if he could see. He answered, "No." She said, "Well, then I will be your eyes." Together, those four people braved the mob and drove that truck driver to the hospital. He's alive today only because they stepped in to help.

It is for every one of them that we must rebuild the community of Los Angeles, for these four people and the others like them who in the midst of this nightmare acted with simple human decency.

We must understand that no one in Los Angeles or any other city has rendered a verdict on America. If we are to remain the most vibrant and hopeful Nation on Earth we must allow our diversity to bring us together, not drive us apart. This must be the rallying cry of good and decent people.

For their sake, for all our sakes, we must build a future where, in every city across this country, empty rage gives way to hope, where poverty and despair give way to opportunity. After peace is restored to Los Angeles, we must then turn again to the underlying causes of such tragic events. We must keep on working to create a climate of understanding and tolerance, a climate that refuses to accept racism, bigotry, anti-Semitism, and hate of any kind, anytime, anywhere.

9-8. HISPANIC COMMUNITIES AND URBAN PUBLIC SCHOOLS

Arne Duncan

Source: Secretary Arne Duncan's Remarks to the National Council of La Raza, Department of Education, Released July 28, 2009.

EDITORS' INTRODUCTION

Public schools in major cities have suffered significantly in the late twentieth and early twenty-first century, often perceived as falling behind the quality of education offered at private educational facilities. Public schools are funded by a combination of federal, state, and local taxpayer dollars and this can create disparities, with wealthier communities spending more on public education than poorer ones. Neighborhoods with a high level of minority and/or immigrant groups often struggle to keep children in school and meet the standardized testing benchmarks set during the George W. Bush presidency with the *No Child Left Behind Act* (2002). This legislation reduces federal funding for underperforming schools. This speech, made by United State Secretary of Education Arne Duncan in 2009, reflects the challenges American Hispanic communities face with their public schools.

Hispanic Communities and Urban Public Schools

It is a great pleasure to be here to speak to the National Council of La Raza, which is one of our national leaders in promoting the importance of education in the Hispanic community. La Raza was one of the first progressive organizations to nurture and support a large network of charter schools. You have also actively promoted early childhood education and preschool education for Hispanic children, who historically have been underrepresented in these vital programs.

Your CEO, Janet Murguia, has been a leader in working with other civil rights organizations to close the achievement gap as well. President Obama and I believe that reducing dropout rates and boosting student achievement among Hispanic students is absolutely essential to the future of our economy and the future of our nation. And it's especially critical that many more Hispanic students enroll and graduate from college.

I want to call on you today to help work with us to strengthen the college-going culture in Hispanic communities across the U.S. The statistics, the big picture is well known. For the last decade, Hispanic students have been the biggest minority group in our public schools. As the superintendent of Chicago's public schools for seven years, I saw firsthand that the success of many of our reforms depended on our Hispanic students. Last year, just over 40 percent of students in the city's public schools were Hispanic. Yet we all know that nationwide, almost half of Latino students drop out of high school—and those students will have to compete for jobs in a global economy.

It is no secret that education is more important today than ever to getting a good job. By 2016—in just eight short years—four out of every 10 new jobs will require some advanced education or training. Thirty of the fastest growing fields in the economy today require a minimum of a bachelor's degree.

Now, the Hispanic work ethic is legendary. But I want Latinos to not only be known as the backbone of the economy but its brains as well. And that is going to require many more Hispanics students to enroll in and complete college. I don't know if there has ever been an administration in Washington that is as personally committed to boosting educational attainment in the Hispanic community as the current administration.

A little more than a year ago, Barack Obama spoke to the National Council of La Raza convention in San Diego. And he said that the election was "about the Latino students who are dropping out of school faster than nearly anyone else, and the children who attend overflowing classes in underfunded schools." When the President gave his speech laying out his education reform agenda this year he didn't do it at the U.S. Chamber of Commerce. He spoke before the U.S. Hispanic Chamber of Commerce. The President has already appointed Juan Sepulveda as the director of the White House Initiative on Educational Excellence for Hispanic Americans. Juan is well-known to many of you. He has already started a series of town hall discussions around the country about increasing educational attainment among Latino students.

My Assistant Secretary for Legislation and Congressional Affairs, Gabby Gomez, is well-versed in the problems that confront Hispanic students and districts that are majority Latino. And I'm pleased to tell you that just last Friday, Thelma Melendez, was confirmed as the Assistant Secretary for Elementary and Secondary Education.

Thelma will be the first Hispanic to serve in that position in the department's history. It is hard for me to think of someone more familiar with the needs of Hispanic students than Thelma. She was an ELL student herself growing up in California, where she had her high school counselor tell her that she would never get in to UCLA. Well, she did get into UCLA—and got a Ph.D. in language and literacy. She went on to teach ELL and became the superintendent of the Pomona Unified School District—a district that is predominantly Hispanic and low-income.

Thelma knows that bilingualism can be a great asset for students and workers in a globally competitive market. But I'll tell you something you might not know. In the Chicago public schools, we had the largest Chinese language program in the country—and many of the students taking Chinese were Latino.

So I want you to know that this administration doesn't just hear the voice of Latino leaders. In fact, we are convinced that improving educational attainment among Hispanic students is critical to our nation's future.

That is one reason why I am convinced that we have a unique opportunity to reform our schools that we cannot afford to miss. I've called this the perfect storm for reform. For the first time, we have governors stepping up around the country to agree to common, rigorous standards in math and English. They have said no more to lying to students—they have rejected the dumbed-down standards that led students to believe they were college-ready when they weren't. For the first time, we have union leaders who are stepping outside their comfort zones to challenge the status quo, and we have congressional leaders committed to reform. And for the first time the U.S. Department of Education has the resources to incentivize far-reaching reforms in our nation's schools. Last week, the President announced the draft guidelines to the $4.35 billion Race to the Top fund. That's a bigger pot of discretionary money for reform than all of my predecessors at the department had combined. The Race to the Top is a com-

petition, and only the states with the most effective and comprehensive reform plans will be funded.

We have four core reforms or assurances that we are seeking from states. We want states to work toward setting common, internationally benchmarked standards and assessments that really tell us whether students are college-ready. We want states to develop data systems that allow them to do a better job of tracking growth in student learning and tailoring instruction to the needs of students. It is no secret that talent matters tremendously. And to boost the quality of teachers and principals—especially in high-poverty schools and hard-to-staff subjects—states and districts should be able to identify their most effective and least effective teachers, and put the best teachers where they are needed most.

And finally, to turn around the lowest-performing schools, states and districts must be ready to institute far-reaching reforms, replace school staff, and change the school culture. We cannot continue to tinker in high schools that are little more than "dropout factories" where students fall further behind, year after year. All of these four reforms are essential if we are going to start to close the achievement gap and make the dream of equal educational opportunity a reality.

But we have one other unique force in our favor. I call it the "Barack Effect." The president—and the First Lady—have made education cool and hip again. I hear kids say all the time they not only want to be the president, they want to be smart like the president. I hope that in Latino communities, parents and kids are going to start talking soon about the "Sotomayor effect." Judge Sotomayor's story is impressive in so many ways. But I love what she has said about the power of education. Judge Sotomayor's father was a factory worker with a third grade education. He died when Sonia was just nine years old—and Sonia's mother had to work six days a week to raise Sonia and her brother in a Bronx housing project on her nurse's salary. But Sonia Sotomayor's mother told her two children that education was the key to success in America. Her children were the only kids in their housing project that had a set of the *Encyclopedia Britannica*.

At night, Sonia's mother sat at the kitchen table with her kids, studying side-by-side so she could become a registered nurse. And I think you know the rest of the story. Sonia Sotomayor was the valedictorian of her high school, top of her class at Princeton, and an editor at the Yale Law Journal. And I expect that she will soon become the first Hispanic member of the United States Supreme Court! I think Judge Sotomayor put it best when she said that "my brother and I grew up in the projects. But through my mother's emphasis on education, we are living wonderful, full lives, liberated from the shackles of poverty." I want every child to have the opportunity to fulfill their potential like Sonia Sotomayor and not be held back by the color of their skin or the burden of poverty.

The administration wants to turn those dreams into reality for many more students. And we're going to make an unprecedented effort to increase not only college enrollment but college completion. President Obama's goal is for the U.S. to again have the highest proportion of college graduates in the world. And he wants every American to have at least one year of college or technical training. The department's budget, and the American Recovery and Reinvestment Act enacted earlier this year, provide the largest commitment to higher education funding since the GI Bill sent World War II veterans to college and built the American middle class.

The cash value of Pell Grant awards for low-income students will increase by about 10 percent. And we are boosting the number of students receiving Pell Grants from 6 million to 7 million students. All told, we are going to be increasing Pell Grant funding by almost $42 billion over the next five years.

I'm pleased to report that we have also simplified the form for federal financial aid and will soon make this new version available in Spanish. I am a big supporter of the Dream Act because every child, regardless of their status, deserves an equal opportunity to a high-quality college education. President Obama worked to pass the Illinois state version of the Dream Act, and he worked hard with Senator Durbin to move the federal version of the bill through the Senate. Still, all of these new resources will not be enough if parents and communities don't do a better job of encouraging and supporting kids to college graduation.

While our public schools have more Hispanic students than black students, just the opposite is true in college. Hispanic students are less likely than black students to enroll in college or get a degree. In 2005, only 11 percent of undergraduate students were Hispanic. I know that the low rate of college attendance and completion among Hispanic students has complicated roots. The Hispanic community has so many strengths to draw upon—a strong work ethic, and strong religious and family values. But there are times when some of these very strengths do not help students climb the mountain to college. When young Latino males drop out of high school to take jobs to support their family, they are ultimately limiting their potential. When working parents keep their kids at home to do babysitting because they don't believe in organized day care, those students are losing out. I believe we need to create a stronger culture of college-going in low-income Hispanic communities. We need more parents like Sonia Sotomayor's mother, who said you will study hard and you will succeed at college and you will graduate—even if I have to work six days a week to make it happen. We need more parents who will tell their kids to not only turn off the X-box but to get out the *Encyclopedia Britannica* and hit the books.

So I want to challenge parents and communities to become more involved in cultivating that culture of college-going and celebrating the importance of academic achievement. And as part of that mission I want to encourage you to develop a new generation of Hispanic teachers. Twenty percent of all public school students in the U.S. are Latino. But only 5 percent of their teachers are Latino. In Chicago, the numbers are just as lopsided—41% of students are Latino but only 15% of teachers are

Hispanic. I know that change of the sort I'm asking for does not come easily. But it can be done. From 2004 to 2008, the college enrollment rate for Latino graduates of the Chicago Public Schools rose nine percentage points, much faster than the small uptick in college enrollment among Hispanics nationally.

So as you go back to your communities at the end of this conference, I thank you for your service and celebrate the extraordinary contributions of La Raza and the Hispanic community. But I also want to challenge you to help us, to help take the next step of making college an expectation for our young Latino students, and not an exception available to the lucky minority.

We are moving toward realizing the dream of equal educational opportunity. It has taken us a long time to get there. But together, for the good of our children, let's seize this unique moment in the history of education reform.

Thank you for all you have done—and continue to do—to improve our nation's schools.

PART X

EXURBIA AND POSTINDUSTRIAL CITIES

EDITORS' INTRODUCTION TO PART X

Following World War II, the suburbs emerged as a new home to millions of people who once lived in densely populated city neighborhoods. Given their location on the periphery of major cities, most suburbs are located in municipalities large enough for classification as urban by census definitions. A small but conspicuous number of people moved directly from cities to exclusive residential enclaves known as "exurbs." Auguste Spectorsky used the term exurb, and its derivatives, in his 1955 book *The Exurbanites*, as a label for displaced New Yorkers who moved to the country to escape the "rat race" of their highly competitive professions.[1] Although housed in a country setting, exurbanites still identify themselves vis-à-vis the city.

The economic base of the nation also underwent dramatic transformation after World War II. Accompanying the decentralization of the population to the suburbs was the establishment of numerous factories, warehouse and distribution centers, along with regional malls and freestanding retail outlets outside of the city. Owners of these businesses were able to take advantage of the nation's new highway system and less expensive land. They also benefited from their proximity to the growing suburbs. By the 1970s, transformation in the global economy resulted in mass deindustrialization in the United States. The loss of well-paying manufacturing jobs led to high levels of unemployment and underemployment in former industrial centers. Particularly hard hit were the Midwest, Middle Atlantic states, and parts of the Northeast known as nation's "rust belt." In place of once bustling industry, service, retail, and knowledge-based economics emerged. Many cities in the Southeast and West that had bypassed the nineteenth- and twentieth-century model of industrial economic development fared better and even witnessed overall growth in the 1980s and 1990s.

The essays in this part explore the nature of postindustrial urbanization. In "Commerce: Reconfiguring Community Marketplaces," Lizabeth Cohen demonstrates the unwanted side effects of that alluring temple to consumerism, the seemingly endless regional mall. Cohen shows us how the mall reconstructed American conceptual and spatial realities, and it proves interesting to connect her work with that of Robert Fogelson's on the sustainability of downtowns in Part VII. In the essay, "Inventing Modern Las Vegas," the late Hal Rothman examines how a small desert oasis became the prototype twenty-first century city by building upon the gaming and tourist industry. Finally, in "Polo Ponies and Penalty Kicks," sociologist Corey Dolgon uses sports to explore the social and cultural dimensions of class differences and demographic changes in the Hamptons, arguably the most talked about exurban enclave in America popular culture.

The documents and figures in this part provide a comparison of efforts to reform the use of urban space from the late nineteenth and early twentieth centuries with the present. Edward Bellamy, a socialist philosopher, and Ebenezer Howard, a pioneer of regional planning, influenced generations of thinkers. They both sought to take advantage of industrialization and technological innovation to improve the lives of all people, not just the privileged few. A century later, this kind of imaginative take on urban planning was recreated with the Congress for the New Urbanism, which attempted to enhance the urban setting with innovative design. Hana Rosin's controversial article "American Murder Mystery," however, reminds us that there can be unintended consequences from social and political reforms. Issues of design, equity, and political sensitivity even pervade attempts to remember and commemorate the tragic events of September 11, 2001 at the former World Trade Center site in Manhattan.

NOTE

1.   A. C. Spectorsky, *The Exurbanites* (Philadelphia: J. B. Lippincott Company, 1955), 4, 6, 12.

Commerce: Reconfiguring Community Marketplaces

Lizabeth Cohen

Source: *A Consumer's Republic: The Politics of Mass Consumption in Postwar America* (New York: Random House, 2003).

EDITORS' INTRODUCTION

In Robert O. Self's essay in Part IX, we learned about the way in which California's Bay Area can be seen through the lens of the highway, BART (Bay Area Rapid Transit) mass transit, and property ownership. Lizabeth Cohen's New Jersey serves as a case study that allows for insight into America's twentieth-century mass culture. America left behind its preoccupation with frugality and, following World War II, leapt into a lifestyle defined by easier credit terms, ubiquitous shopping options, government-backed mortgages, and government-built highways. In Cohen's elegant and complex analysis of this consumers' republic, we see how commerce came to define public space for suburban-ites. Devoid of the traditional downtown, the suburbs, once simply bedroom communit-ies, increasingly found their retail needs met by the regional mall. Anchored by two to three major retailers, these palaces of commerce offered ample parking and a faux-communal experience to the thousands of suburbanites located within a half an hour's drive of the mall's open air or air-conditioned environs.

Cohen urges her readers to think carefully about a way of life many have taken for granted for decades. Material consumption comprised the American paradigm, where citizens could not truly perceive the searing effects of consumerism on their culture and landscape. What was the impact of this "malling of America?"[i] Certainly the pre-existing, albeit limited, shopping in small and medium sized towns withered in the face of this beguiling new competition. More and more Americans spent their time away from home at the mall, which likely was not a good replacement for the civic engagement they would have experienced in a downtown shopping district. Gone were the leafleters and speech-makers of the public square, not to mention the poor. Malls catered to whites, and lacked many representatives from minority groups. Unattended youngsters were heavily monitored and often shooed away altogether. Malls, with their enormous physical footprints, took an environmental toll as well. The high degree of stability needed for the mall's tenants led to the favoring of national chain stores, which could more reliably pay the rent, and offered financial guarantees new start-ups and personal businesses could not extend. The tastes of the middle class and the upper middle class were catered to, as shoppers of this caliber promised higher revenue per square foot. Cohen does not blame the regional shopping centers for sprawl, rightly noting that the construction of malls followed residents out to the suburbs, rather than leading the way. Real estate investments of such magnitude could not afford to be pioneers; they had to locate in areas that were safe bets. Once built, successful malls often improved the property values of those within a short driving distance, and lessened the home values of those located at too far a distance.

The malls helped encourage the establishment of "edge cities," neo-cities containing very high concentrations of retail space and office space.[ii] Unlike traditional suburbs,

---

i   William Severin Kowinski, *The Malling of America* (Bloomington, IN: Xlibris, 2002).
ii Joel Garreau, *Edge City: Life on the New Frontier* (New York: Random House, 1992).

edge cities are less defined by suburban tract homes than they are by office parks. Oftentimes they transcend actual urban or suburban boundaries, straddling two or more places on the map. They often take their physical cues from highways, the availability of off-ramps (sometimes built specifically to service new malls), and the ease of access from a variety of bedroom communities. Unexpectedly, they came to be plagued by the kind of traffic problems that once only beset downtowns.

In the early twenty-first century, the tide began to turn away from the regional mall. Americans increasingly met their shopping needs through the Internet. First hit were the less stable malls in lower-income suburbs. But the retail decline spilled over into the middle class and upper class establishments, and even affected the newest competitor on the retail network, the "big box chain store." Today suburbs scramble to find ways to reuse the abandoned, hulking structures that line their highways and major intersections.[iii] Americans began to critically reevaluate the consumer culture that so engulfed the nation, and looked so promising, in the years after World War II.

Lizabeth Cohen is the Howard Mumford Jones Professor of American Studies and currently serves as the chair of the history department of Harvard University. Cohen is also the co-author of the textbook, *The American Pageant* (Wadsworth) and of the influential *Making a New Deal: Industrial Workers in Chicago, 1919–1939* (Cambridge: Cambridge University Press, 1990), winner of the Bancroft Prize in American History (1991). She is at work on a new book on Edward J. Logue, an influential figure in urban renewal.

COMMERCE: RECONFIGURING COMMUNITY MARKETPLACES

By the 1950s the shopping center … had become as much a part of suburbia as the rows of ranch houses, split-levels, and Cape Cods," political scientist Robert Wood stated matter-of-factly in his *Suburbia: Its People and Their Politics* of 1959. And indeed, attention within the Consumers' Republic to promoting consumer spending reshaped much more than the character of residential communities in the postwar metropolitan landscape. The physical arrangement of American commercial life became reconfigured as well. As existing suburban town centers proved inadequate to support all the consumption desired by the influx of new residents, as suburbanites more and more attached to their cars increasingly viewed returning to urban downtowns to shop as inconvenient, and as retailers came to realize that suburban residents, with their young families, new homes, and vast consumer appetites, offered a lucrative frontier ripe for conquer, the regional shopping center emerged as a new form of community marketplace. Wood underscored the tremendous increase in suburban share of total

metropolitan retail trade from 4 percent in 1939 to 31 percent by 1948; by 1961 it would total almost 60 percent in the ten largest population centers. But as significant as the volume of commerce transacted in suburbia was the setting where that consumption took place.[1]

The development of a new, distinctive kind of metropolitan marketplace suited to mass suburbia lagged behind the construction of residences. New suburbanites who had themselves grown up in urban neighborhoods walking to corner stores and taking public transportation to shop downtown had to contend with inadequate retail options until at least the mid-1950s. Only in the most ambitious suburban tracts built after the war had developers incorporated stores into their plans. In those cases, developers tended to place the shopping district at the core of the residential community, much as it had been in the prewar planned community of Radburn in Fair Lawn, New Jersey, and in the earliest shopping centers such as Kansas City's Country Club Plaza of the 1920s. These precedents, and their descendants in early postwar developments in Park Forest, Illinois, Levittown, New York, and Bergenfield, New Jersey, repli-

---

iii Julia Christiansen, *Big Box Reuse* (Cambridge, MA: MIT Press, 2008).

cated the structure of the old-style urban community, where shopping was part of the public space at the settlement's core and residences spread outward from there.[2] But most postwar suburban home developers made no effort to provide for residents' commercial needs. Rather, suburbanites were expected to fend for themselves by driving to the existing "market towns," which often offered the only commerce for miles, or by returning to the city to shop. Faced with slim retail offerings nearby, many new suburbanites of the 1940s and 1950s continued to depend on the big city for major purchases, making do with the small, locally owned commercial outlets in neighboring towns for minor needs.

It was not until the late 1950s that a new market structure appropriate to this suburbanized, mass consumption society prevailed. Important precedents existed in the branch department stores and prototypical shopping centers constructed between the 1920s and 1940s in outlying city neighborhoods and in older suburban communities, which began the process of decentralizing retail dollars away from downtown. But the scale required now was much larger. By 1957, 940 shopping centers had already been built. That number more than doubled by 1960, and doubled again by 1963; by 1976 the 17,520 shopping centers in the nation would represent an almost nineteenfold increase over twenty years.[3] With postwar suburbanites finally living the motorized existence that had been predicted for American society since the 1920s, traffic congestion and parking problems discouraged commercial developers from expanding in central business districts of major cities and smaller market towns, already hindered by a short supply of developable space.[4] Rather, retailers preferred catering to suburbanites on the open land where they now lived and drove, deeming it a unique opportunity to reinvent community life with their private projects at its heart.[5]

Merchandisers at first built stores along the new highways, in retail "strips" that dispersed consumers could easily reach by car. By the 1950s, however, commercial developers—many of whom owned department stores—devoted themselves to constructing a new kind of marketplace, the regional shopping center, aimed at satisfying suburbanites' consumption *and* community needs, which had similarly been paired in the old town centers. Strategically located at highway intersections or along the busiest thoroughfares, the regional shopping center aimed at attracting patrons living within half an hour's drive who would come by car, park in the abundant lots provided, and then proceed on foot (although there was usually some bus service as well). Here was the "new city" of the postwar era, a community center suited to an economy and society built around mass consumption. Well-designed regional shopping centers, it was thought, would provide the ideal core for settlements that grew by adding residential nodes off major roadways rather than concentric rings from downtown, as in cities and earlier suburban communities. After spending several months in the late 1950s visiting what he called "modern-day downtowns," *Women's Wear Daily* columnist Samuel Feinberg was moved to invoke Lincoln Steffens's proclamation on his return from the Soviet Union in the 1920s: "I have seen the future and it works."[6]

Although the shift in community marketplace from town center to shopping center was a national phenomenon, Paramus, New Jersey, a postwar suburb seven miles from the George Washington Bridge that became the home of the largest shopping complex in the country by the end of 1957, provides an illuminating case.[7] Within six months, R. H. Macy's Garden State Plaza and Allied Stores Corporation's Bergen Mall opened three-quarters of a mile from each other at the intersection of Routes 4, 17, and the soon-to-be-completed Garden State Parkway. Both department store managements had independently recognized the enormous commercial potential of Bergen and Passaic Counties. Although the George Washington Bridge had connected the area to Manhattan in 1931, the Great Depression and the war had postponed major housing construction until the late 1940s. By 1960 each shopping center had two to three department stores as anchors (distinguishing it from many prewar projects built around a single anchor), surrounded by fifty to seventy smaller stores. Attracting half a million patrons a week, these shopping centers dominated retail trade in the region.[8]

The Paramus malls have special significance because of their location adjacent to the wealthiest and busiest central business district in the nation. If these malls could prosper in the shadow of Manhattan, the success of their counterparts elsewhere should come as no surprise. Furthermore, the Paramus case illuminates three major effects of shifting marketplaces on postwar American community life: in commercializing public space, they brought to community life the market segmentation that increasingly shaped commerce and residence; in privatizing public space, they privileged the rights of private property owners over citizens' traditional rights of free speech in community forums; and in feminizing public space, they enhanced women's claim on the suburban landscape while circumscribing the power they wielded there.

Commercializing Public Space

Developers, department stores, and big investors such as insurance companies (who leapt at the promise of a huge return on the vast amounts of capital they controlled) built shopping centers to profit from what seemed to be ever rising levels of consumption. As Macy's board chairman, Jack Isidor Straus, who oversaw the development of the Garden State Plaza, confidently explained in 1965, "Our economy keeps growing because our ability to consume is endless. The consumer goes on spending regardless of how many possessions he has. The luxuries of today are the necessities of tommorrow."[9] Why not, then, situate new stores as accessible as possible to the most dynamic sources of demand fueling the thriving economy of postwar America—the new, high-consuming suburbanites? Already a decade earlier, an article in the *New York Times Magazine* marking the growing interest in building shopping centers had concluded, "There is a widely held belief that American households are ready to do more buying than they pres-

ently do.... They would do it more readily but for the difficulty of getting to the 'downtowns' where the full range of goods is available." The solution proposed: "Bringing the market to the people instead of people to the market."[10]

Focusing on the obvious economic motives developers and investors shared in constructing shopping centers, however, can mask the visionary dimension of their undertaking, which led them to innovate a new retail form. When planners and shopping center developers envisioned this new kind of consumption-oriented community center in the 1950s, they set out to perfect the concept of downtown, not to obliterate it, even though their projects directly challenged the viability of existing commercial centers like Hackensack, the political and commercial seat of Bergen County adjacent to Paramus.[11] They felt that they were participating in a rationalization of consumption and community no less revolutionary than the way highways were transforming transportation or tract developments were delivering mass single-family housing. "Shopping Centers properly planned by developers and local communities are the rational alternative to haphazard retail development," the International Council of Shopping Centers explained.[12]

The ideal was still the creation of centrally located public space that integrated commerce with civic activity. Victor Gruen, one of the most prominent and articulate shopping center developers, spoke for many others when he argued that shopping centers offered dispersed suburban populations "crystallization points for suburbia's community life." "By affording opportunities for social life and recreation in a protected pedestrian environment, by incorporating civic and educational facilities, shopping centers can fill an existing void."[13] Not only did Gruen and others promote the private construction of community centers in the atomized landscape of suburbia, but their earliest shopping centers idealized—almost romanticized—the physical plan of the traditional downtown shopping street, with stores lining both sides of an open-air pedestrian walkway that was landscaped and equipped with benches. Regional shopping centers would create old-style community with new-style unity and efficiency; statements like "the shopping center is ... today's village green" and "the fountain in the mall has replaced the downtown department clock as the gathering place for young and old alike," dominated planning for new centers.[14]

Designed to bring many of the best qualities of urban life to the suburbs, these new "shopping towns," as Gruen called them, sought to overcome the "anarchy and ugliness" characteristic of many American cities. A centrally owned and managed Garden State Plaza or Bergen Mall, it was argued, offered an alternative model to the inefficiencies, visual chaos, and provinciality of traditional downtown districts. A centralized administration made possible the perfect mix and "scientific" placement of stores, meeting customers' diverse needs and maximizing store owners' profits. Management kept control visually by standardizing all architectural and graphic design and politically by requiring all tenants to participate in the tenants' association. Common complaints of downtown shoppers were directly addressed: parking was plentiful, safety was ensured by hired security guards, delivery tunnels and loading courts kept truck traffic away from shoppers, canopied walks and air-conditioned stores made shopping comfortable year-round, piped-in background music replaced the cacophony of the street. The preponderance of chains and franchises over local, independent stores, required by big investors such as insurance companies, brought shoppers the latest national trends in products and merchandising techniques.

Garden State Plaza and Bergen Mall provide good models for how shopping centers of the fifties followed Gruen's prescription and became more than miscellaneous collections of stores. B. Earl Puckett, Allied Stores' board chair, went so far as to boast that Paramus's model shopping centers were making it "one of the first preplanned major cities in America," an urban innovation that also maximized profits.[15] As central sites of consumption, they offered the full range of shops and services that would previously have existed downtown. They not only sold the usual clothing and shoes in their specialty and department stores—Stern Brothers and J. J. Newberry at Bergen Mall, Bamberger's (Macy's New Jersey division), JCPenney's, and Gimbel's at Garden State Plaza—but also featured stores specifically devoted to furniture, hardware, appliances, groceries, gifts, drugs, books, toys, records, bakery goods, candy, jewelry, garden supplies, hearing aids, tires, and even religious objects. Services grew to include restaurants, a post office, Laundromat, cleaners, key store, shoe repair, bank, loan company, stock brokerage houses, barbershop, travel agency, real estate office, "slenderizing salon," and Catholic chapel. Recreational facilities ranged from a 550-seat movie theater, bowling alley, and ice-skating rink to a children's gymnasium and playground.

Both shopping centers made meeting rooms and auditoriums available to community organizations and scheduled a full range of cultural and educational activities to legitimize these sites as civic centers, while also attracting customers. Well-attended programs and exhibitions taught shoppers about such "hot" topics of the fifties and sixties as space exploration, color television, modern art, and civics. Evening concerts and plays, ethnic entertainment, dances and classes for teenagers, campaign appearances by political candidates, and community outreach for local charities were some of the ways that Bergen Mall and Garden State Plaza made themselves indispensable to life in Bergen County.

In sum, it was hard to think of consumer items or community events that could not be found at one or the other of these two shopping centers in Bergen County. (In the 1970s a cynical reporter cracked that "the only institution that had not yet invaded" the modern shopping mall was the funeral home.) To a regional planner like New Jersey's Ernest Erber, these postwar shopping centers represented a new kind of urbanism appropriate to the automobile age: the "City of Bergen," he dubbed the area in 1960. Seven years later the New Jersey Federation of Planning Officials was still encouraging its members and their communities to use "appropriate zoning and site development controls to encourage this desirable trend" of making centers "real downtowns for the surrounding area." In time, the *New York Times* would proclaim Paramus's commercial complex the real thing: "It lives a night as well as a day existence, glittering like a city when the sun goes down." In fact, shopping centers prided themselves on their greater "night existence" than most downtowns, as their stores and services were open to patrons from 10 a.m. to 9:30 p.m., at first four nights a week, and by the 1960s six nights.[16]

Making the shopping center a perfection of downtown entailed more than building idealized pedestrian streets, showcasing a full range of goods and services, and staying open long hours. Developers and store owners also set out to exclude from this new public space unwanted urban elements, such as vagrants, prostitutes, disruptive rebels, racial minorities, and poor people. Market segmentation became the guiding principle of this mix of commercial and civic activity, as the shopping center sought, perhaps contradictorily, to legitimize itself as a true community center and to define that community in exclusionary socieconomic and racial terms.

The simple demographics of postwar America helped, as metropolitan areas were becoming polarized between poorer, blacker cities and more prosperous, whiter suburbs.[17] But shopping centers did not inadvertently exclude simply by virtue of their suburban location. Rather, developers deliberately defined their communities through a combination of careful site selection, marketing, and policing. Locating a center in a prosperous area was the first priority. As the chairman of the board of Bamberger's New Jersey put it bluntly in 1964, "There are many kinds of people, and we must, therefore, consider the qualitative as well as the quantitative composition of the population." Once established in an affluent community, moreover, centers needed to be respectful of their neighbors. "A shopping center which fails to consider its relationship to residential areas," the shopping center developer Victor Gruen warned, "will soon be surrounded by blighted and slum neighborhoods and will find itself with a greatly reduced business potential."[18]

Once well situated, most branch department stores and new shopping centers worked to secure a white middle-class clientele. Macy's reminded its stockholders in 1955 as it was building its first shopping center, Garden State Plaza, "We are a type of organization that caters primarily to middle-income groups, and our stores reflect this in the merchandise they carry and in their physical surroundings."[19] By the late 1950s retailers were getting expert advice from publications such as the *Journal of Marketing* to ensure that the "tone and physical character of the[ir] advertising permit the shopper to make social-class identification." As suburbs were "quickly becom[ing] stratified along social-class and mobility dimensions," this article elaborated, it was imperative that stores "acquire a status definition." Almost all suburban shopping centers built in this early period sought to appeal to what Macy's called the "middle-income groups," who, it was widely assumed, would also be white.[20] Baltimore's Planning Council exposed the racial overtones to commercial reconfiguration under way in this era more explicitly than merchants ever would: "Greater numbers of low-income, Negro shoppers in Central Business District stores, coming at the same time as middle and upper income white shoppers are given alternatives in … segregated suburban centers, has had unfortunate implications for Central Business District merchants."[21]

When shopping centers located in prosperous communities, moreover, their presence only augmented that prosperity, exacerbating the inequalities that already characterized suburbia. As one bank assured its investors, property values in residential communities are "enhanced by the presence of a regional shopping center," while location at a distance from stores lessened a town's desirability. Nor did the benefit end there. The bank's monthly newsletter continued, "Regional shopping districts are surplus areas yielding far more in taxes than they cost in municipal services." Imposing "no costs for schools, parks or recreation areas and a minimum of cost per dollars of assessed value for street maintenance, police or fire protection ... at least three-fourths of the taxes received are a net surplus to the city or taxing district." And, indeed, Paramus boasted in 1960, three years after Bergen Mall and Garden State Plaza had opened, that "business pays taxes accounting for 43 percent of the town's total revenue."[22] In other words, a town well enough off to attract a shopping center was rewarded with higher property values and a big boost to its property tax and sales tax revenues, resulting in improved local services and potentially lower tax rates for residents.

Carefully controlled access to suburban shopping centers further supported the class and color line. The operating assumption in planning centers was always that patrons would travel by car. The debate among developers, played out in retailer trade journals and planning conferences, revolved instead around how long that drive could feasibly be; articles like "The Influence of Driving Time Upon Shopping Center Preference" were legion.[23] But not everyone living in metropolitan areas had cars. A survey of consumer expenditures in northern New Jersey in 1960–61 revealed that while 79 percent of all families owned cars, fewer than one-third of those with incomes below $3000 did, and that low-income population included a higher percentage of non-white families than the average for the whole sample.[24] Although bus service was available for non-drivers, only a tiny proportion arrived that way (in 1966 a daily average of only 600 people came to Garden State Plaza by bus compared to 18,000 to 31,000 cars, many carrying more than one passenger). The small number traveling by bus was not surprising, as bus routes were carefully planned to serve non-driving customers, particularly women, from neighboring suburbs, not low-income consumers from cities like Passaic, Paterson, and Newark. Meanwhile, studies of African-American mobility as late as the 1970s documented their great dependence on public transportation to get to work or to stores.[25]

Whereas individual downtown department stores had long targeted particular markets defined by class and race, some selling, for example, to "the carriage trade" at the upper end and others to the bargain hunters at the lower, shopping centers took market segmentation to the scale of a downtown, much the way suburbs converted distinctive urban neighborhoods into homogeneous municipalities. In promoting an idealized downtown, shopping centers like Garden State Plaza and Bergen Mall tried to filter out not only the inefficiencies and inconveniences of the city but also the undesirable people who lived there.

If developers and retailers envisioned the regional shopping center as the new American city of postwar suburbia, what actually happened? How successful were shopping centers in attracting the patrons they sought and displacing existing urban centers? The behavior of consumers, on the one hand, and retail businessmen, on the other, reveals the impact of Bergen Mall and Garden State Plaza on the commercial and community life of Bergen County.

Consumer surveys of the late 1950s and early 1960s, carried out by sociologists and market researchers interested in evaluating the changes wrought by the new regional shopping centers, provide a remarkably good picture of consumer behavior in the era. Before Bergen Mall and Garden State Plaza opened in 1957, Bergen County shoppers satisfied their immediate needs on the Main Streets of Hackensack and of smaller surrounding towns like Ridgewood, Fair Lawn, Bergenfield, and Englewood. For more extensive shopping, people went to branches of Sears and Arnold Constable in Hackensack; Meyer Brothers and Quackenbush's department stores in Paterson; Bamberger's, Hahne's, and Kresge's in Newark, and quite often to the big stores in Manhattan. Even before the regional shopping centers opened, the huge influx of new suburban dwellers had raised retail sales in Bergen County from $400 million in 1948 to $700 million in 1954, an increase of 75 percent. By 1958 sales had increased another

23 percent to $866 million. Nonetheless, Bergen County residents in 1954 were still spending $650 million outside the county, almost as much as inside.[26]

Samuel and Lois Pratt, professors at Fairleigh Dickinson University, surveyed Bergen County consumers living within a ten-minute drive of the two new shopping centers in 1957, 1958, and 1959 to follow changes in their shopping habits over time. Prior to the opening of the shopping centers, seven in ten of the suburban families surveyed shopped in New York City to some extent. One year after the centers opened, the numbers shopping in New York dropped to six in ten, and two years after, fewer than five in ten families shopping there at all. In other words, one-fourth of the entire sample formerly had shopped in New York City but had now entirely stopped. The loss was even more substantial than that; the 15 percent of suburban families who formerly did most of their shopping in New York City—people the Pratts labeled "major shoppers"—showed the sharpest decline, 50 percent by 1958, 80 percent by 1959. Moreover, those who continued to shop in New York City were spending much less money there; the average annual expenditure in New York by suburban families dropped from $93 to $68 after the regional shopping centers opened. Furthermore, consumers were much less likely to shop in the New York stores that had opened suburban branches. By the end of the first year, the number of Bergen County families who had traded in the New York Macy's or Stern's dropped by half.

A similar study of 1100 shoppers by the New York University School of Retailing confirmed the Pratts' findings: shoppers for women's wear were half as likely to go to New York and a third as likely to go to Hackensack just one year after the shopping centers had opened. By the early 1960s a survey of New York area shoppers by a Harvard Business School professor concluded that more than 80 percent of residents of the New Jersey suburbs were most likely to shop close to home for clothing and household items, while only 20 percent went most often to Manhattan and 38 percent to New Jersey cities. (Some multiple answers

brought the total over 100 percent.) Nationwide the trend was the same. Retail sales in central business districts declined dramatically between 1958 and 1963, even while overall metropolitan sales mushroomed from 10 to 20 percent.[27]

The reasons consumers routinely gave for shifting from downtown stores to shopping centers varied, but the overwhelming motivation they articulated was convenience—the ability to drive and park easily, more night hours, improved store layouts, increased self-service, and simplified credit with the charge plate, more available at suburban stores. The Pratts concluded that shoppers were not so much dissatisfied with New York and Hackensack stores as attracted to the ease and "progressiveness" of shopping center shopping. They seemed to share the developers' sense that shopping centers were the modern way to consume.[28]

While overall patronage of stores in surrounding downtowns declined as shopping center patronage increased, researchers discovered that the story was not so simple. Some local stores were benefiting as Bergen County residents became less dependent on New York. Small purchases that shoppers would have made alongside larger ones in New York were now handled closer to home, often in locally owned shops in small downtowns. A Hackensack, however, did not benefit as much as a Ridgewood or Englewood, since it was being displaced as a major shopping site by the shopping centers, and its stores were less likely to foster the same kind of loyalty to merchants as shops in small towns. In fact, within a year of the shopping centers' opening, major shoppers used Hackensack a third less; as a consequence, 50 percent of the retail establishments on Main Street reported they had done less business than in the previous year. By 1960 the competition had caused 10 percent of the stores on Hackensack's Main Street to close. Bergen County residents were restructuring their consumption patterns by substituting the new shopping centers for New York and for closer, large shopping towns like Hackensack, while continuing to shop—mostly for convenience goods and services—in the small town centers near their homes.[29]

While it is hard to evaluate the extent to which people viewed the shopping centers as more than places to shop—as the community centers that developers aimed to build—anecdotal evidence suggests that many did.

NOTES

1. Robert C. Wood, *Suburbia: Its People and Their Politics* (Boston: Houghton Mifflin, 1959), p. 63; 1961 statistic from Bert Randolph Sugar, "Suburbia: A Nice Place to Live, but I Wouldn't Want to Define It There," *Media/Scope* 11 (February 1967): 50; for further analysis, see James D. Tarver, "Suburbanization of Retail Trade in the Standard Metropolitan Areas of the United States, 1948–54," in William M. Dobriner, ed., *The Suburban Community* (New York: Putnam's, 1958), pp. 195–205. Estimates of the number of shopping centers before the International Council of Shopping Centers was founded in 1957 vary; Janet L. Wolff, author of *What Makes Women Buy: A Guide to Understanding and Influencing the New Woman of Today* (New York: McGraw-Hill, 1958), p. 223, claims that in 1952 "there were only about 100 organized shopping centers." Historians of suburbanization have paid far less attention to the restructuring of commercial life in the postwar period than to the transformation of residential experience.

2. Ann Durkin Keating and Ruth Eckdish Knack, "Shopping in the Planned Community: Evolution of the Park Forest Town Center," unpublished paper in possession of author; Howard Gillette, Jr., "The Evolution of the Planned Shopping Center in Suburb and City," *American Planning Association Journal* 51 (Autumn 1985): 449–60; Daniel Prosser, "The New Downtowns: Commercial Architecture in Suburban New Jersey, 1920–1970," in Joel Schwartz and Prosser, eds., *Cities of the Garden State: Essays in the Urban and Suburban History of New Jersey* (Dubuque, IA: Kendall/Hunt, 1977), pp. 113–15; "Park Forest Moves into '52," *House and Home: The Magazine of Building* 1 (March 1952): 115–16; William S. Worley, *J. C. Nichols and the Shaping of Kansas City: Innovation in Planned Residential Communities* (Columbia: University of Missouri Press, 1990); Richard Longstreth, "J. C. Nichols, the Country Club Plaza, and Notions of Modernity," *Harvard Architecture Review*, vol. 5, *Precedent and Invention* (New York: Rizzoli, 1986), pp. 121–32; William H. Whyte, Jr., "The Outgoing Life," *Fortune*, July 1953, p. 85; Michael Birkner, *A Country Place No More: The Transformation of Bergenfield, New Jersey, 1894–1994* (Rutherford, NJ: Fairleigh Dickinson University Press, 1994), pp. 174–77; Special Foster Village Edition, *BR*, Aug. 10, 1949.

3. Statistics compiled by the International Council of Shopping Centers, in advertising supplement to the *NYT*, "Shopping Centers Come of Age: International Council of Shopping Centers Observes 20th Anniversary," 1977, GSD, p. 7.

4. Richard Longstreth, "The Mixed Blessings of Success: The Hecht Company and Department Store Branch Development After World War II," Occasional Paper No. 14, January 1995, Center for Washington Area Studies, George Washington University.

5. Kenneth T. Jackson, *Crabgrass Frontier: The Suburbanization of the United States* (New York: Oxford University Press, 1985), pp. 255–61. On precedents in the pre-World War II period, see Richard Longstreth, "Silver Spring: Georgia Avenue, Colesville Road, and the Creation of an Alternative 'Downtown' for Metropolitan Washington," in Zeynep Celik, Diane Favro, and Richard Ingersoll, eds., *Streets: Critical Perspectives on Public* (Berkeley: University of California Press, 1994), pp. 247–57; Longstreth, "The Shopping Center in Washington, D.C., 1930–1941," *Journal of the Society architectural Historians* 51 (March 1992): 5–33; Longstreth, "The Perils of a Parkless," In Martin Wachs and Margaret Crawford, eds., *The Car and the City: The Automobile, the Built Environment, and Daily Urban Life* (Ann Arbor: University of Michigan, 1992), pp. 141–53.

6. Samuel Feinberg, "Story of Shopping Centers," *What Makes Shopping Centers Tick*, printed from *Women's Wear Daily* (New York: Fairchild, 1960), p. 1. For background on the development of regional shopping centers, see William Severini Kowinski, *The of America: An Inside Look at the Great Consumer Paradise* (New York: Morrow, 1985); Neil Harris, *Cultural Excursions: Marketing Appetites and Cultural Tastes in Modern America* (Chicago: University of Chicago Press, 1990), pp. 7, 76–77, 278–88; Margaret, "The World in a Shopping Mall," in Michael Sorkin, ed., *Variations on a Theme: The New American City and the End of Public Space* (New York: Noonday Press/Hill Wang, 1992), pp. 3–30; Gillette, "Evolution of the Planned Shopping Center." For a useful case study of the development of suburban shopping centers in the Philadelphia region, see Stephanie Dyer, "Markets in the Meadows: Department Stores and Shopping Centers in the Decentralization of Philadelphia, 1920–1980" (Ph.D. diss., University of Pennsylvania, 2000).

7. On the postwar growth of Paramus and Bergen County, New Jersey, see Raymond M. Ralph, *Bergen County, New Jersey History and Heritage*, vol. 6, *Farmland to Suburbia, 1920–1960* (Hackensack, NJ: Bergen County Board of Chosen Freeholders, 1983), pp. 62–71, 76–90; Catherine M. Fogarty, John E. O'Connor, and Charles F. Cummings, *Bergen County: A Pictorial History* (Norfolk, VA: Donning, 1985), pp. 182–93; *Beautiful Bergen: The Story of Bergen County,*

New Jersey (Ridgewood, NJ: s.n., 1962); Patricia M. Ryle, *An Economic Profile of Bergen County, New Jersey* (Trenton, NJ: Office of Economic Research, Division of Planning and Research, New Jersey Department of Labor and Industry, March 1980); League of Women Voters of Bergen County, *Where Can I Live in Bergen County?: Factors Affecting Housing Supply* (Closter, NJ: League of Women Voters, 1972).

8. Feinberg, *What Makes Shopping Centers Tick*, pp. 2, 94–102; Ralph, *Farmland to Suburbia*, pp. 70–71, 84–85; Mark A. Stuart, *Bergen County, New Jersey History and Heritage*, vol. 7; *Our Era, 1960-Present* (Hackensack, NJ: Bergen County Board of Chosen Freeholders, 1983), pp. 19–22; Prosser, "New Downtowns," pp. 119–20; Edward T. Thompson, "The Suburb That Macy's Built," *Fortune*, February 1960, pp. 195–200; "Garden State Plaza Merchant's Manual," May 1, 1957, and certain pages revised in 1959, 1960, 1962, 1963, 1965, 1969, GSP.

9. "The Economy: The Great Shopping Spree," *Time*, Jan. 8, 1965, pp. 58–62 and cover.

10. C. B. Plamer, "The Shopping Center Goes to the Shopper," *NYT Magazine*, Nov. 29, 1953, p. 40.

11. On the financing of shopping centers, and the great profits involved, see Jerry Jacobs, *The Mall: An Attempted Escape from Everyday Life* (Prospect Heights, IL: Waveland, 1984), p. 52.

12. ICSC, "Shopping Centers Come of Age," p. 2.

13. Victor Gruen, "Introverted Architecture," *Progressive Architecture* 38 (1957): 204–208; Gruen and Larry Smith, *Shopping Towns USA: The Planning of Shopping Centers* (New York: Reinhold, 1960), pp. 22–24; both quoted in Gillette, "Evolution of the Planned Shopping Center." For more on Gruen, see Kowinski, *Malling of America*, pp. 118–20, 210–14; "Exhibit of Shopping Centers," *NYT*, Oct. 19, 1954. For profile of Martin Bucksbaum, another shopping-center builder, see Paul Goldberger, "Selling the Suburban Frontier," *NYT Magazine*, Dec. 31, 1995, pp. 34–35.

14. ICSC, "Shopping Centers Come of Age," pp. 1, 39. One Florida architect whose firm built several shopping centers referred to making the department store the focal point of a center as the "Main Street Plan": Clinton Gamble, "Shopping Centers! A Modern Miracle," *Miami Herald*, Oct. 23, 1955. In a talk to the Urban History Seminar of the Chicago Historical Society, February 17, 1994, Robert Bruegmann made the same point about the way the earliest design of suburban shopping centers resembled downtown shopping streets.

15. Quoted in Feinberg, *What Makes Shopping Centers Tick*, p. 101. In addition to sources already cited on the control possible in a shopping center versus a downtown, see "Shopping Centers Get Personality," *NYT*, June 29, 1958. For a notion of shopping centers as an "integrated organism," see Howard T. Fisher, "The Impact of New Shopping Centers Upon Established Business Districts," talk at National Citizens' Conference on Planning for City, State and Nation, May 15, 1950, GSD, pp. 3–4. Chains were also favored over independents in shopping centers because they more easily reaped the big bonuses for depreciation of new store upfitting, while small independents had little surplus income to shelter and less specialized tax accounting expertise: e-mail correspondence with Thomas W. Hanchett, Nov. 20, 1996.

Insurance companies made no secret of why they were attracted to investing in shopping centers. John D. W. Wadhams, senior vice president of Aetna, explained that insurance companies saw buying a center "as a way of saying to policy holders that their company is aggressively seeking those equities which will have ever-increasing rates of return and can some day be sold at a good profit, increasing overall yield": ICSC, "Shopping Centers Come of Age," p. 54. Teachers Insurance and Annuity Association–College Retirement Equities Fund (TIAA-CREF) explained why it favored chain stores in centers: "TIAA normally requires a certain proportion of national tenants in the shopping centers it finances. This means that if a particular center does not turn out well, the leases held by its major tenants will be supported by other stores in that system around the country": William C. Greenough, *It's My Retirement Money, Take Good Care of It: The TIAA-CREF Story* (Homewood, IL: Irwin, 1990), p. 175. In a 1971 publication, TIAA boasted that with shopping center loans accounting for 43 percent of its total conventional mortgage loans, "today [it] is recognized as being one of the leaders among the institutions that finance shopping centers": *TIAA Investment Report for 1971*, pp. 8–9. A year later TIAA would claim investments in 133 shopping centers in 30 states: *The Participant* (Policyholder Newsletter), November 1972, p. 4.

16. Ernest Erber, "Notes on the 'City of Urban,'" Erber, Box B; Dean K. Boorman, "Shopping Centers: Their Planning and Control, Federation Planning Information Report," vol. 2, no. 4 (New Jersey Federation of Planning Officials, September 1967), p. 6, GSD; "Paramus Booms as a Store Center," *NYT*, Feb. 5, 1962; "The Mall the Merrier, or Is It?" *NYT*, Nov. 21, 1976. For details on particular stores and activities at Bergen Mall and Garden State Plaza, see Feinberg. *What Makes Shopping Centers Tick*. pp. 97–100; Fogarty et al., *Bergen County*, p. 189; Prosser, "New Downtowns," p. 119. Almost every issue of the *BR* beginning in 1957 yields valuable material (in articles and advertisements) on mall stores, services, and activities. The discussion here is based particularly on issues from Nov. 8, 13, 19, 1957, Jan. 8, 1958, June 10, 1959, and Mar. 2, 1960. Also see "Shoppers! Mass Today on Level 1," *NYT*, June 14, 1994; press release on Garden

State Plaza's opening in GSP, folder "GSP History"; "It Won't Be Long Now ... Bamberger's, New Jersey's Greatest Store, Comes to Paramus Soon," promotional leaflet, stamped Aug. 22, 1956, file "Bergen County Shopping Centers," Hackensack; "The Shopping Center," *NYT*, Feb. 1, 1976.

For data on the allocation of shopping center space in ten regional shopping centers in 1957, see William Applebaum and S. O. Kaylin, *Case Studies in Shopping Center and Operation* (New York: ICSC, 1974), p. 101. For evidence of the company orientation of shopping centers nationwide, see Arthur Herzog, "Shops, Cultural Centers—and More," *NYT Magazine*, Nov. 18, 1962, pp. 34–35, 109–10, 112–14; in *NYT*: "A Shopping Mall in Suffolk Offering More Than Goods," June 22, 1970; supermarkets Hub of Suburbs," Feb. 7, 1971; "Busy Day in a Busy Mall," Apr. 12, 1972. the community relations efforts of branch stores, see Clinton L. Oaks, *Managing Urban Branches of Department Stores*, Business Research Series No. 10 (Stanford, CA: Graduate School of Business, Stanford University, 1957), pp. 81–83.

17. George Sternlieb, *The Future of the Downtown Department Store* (Cambridge: Center for Urban Studies of the Massachusetts Institute of Technology and Harvard University, 1962), p. 10.

18. Arthur L. Manchee, "Retailing," excepts from statement during a panel discussion "Industrial Growth in New Jersey in the Next Decade," *New Jersey Economic Review* 6 May-June 1964): 5; Victor Gruen Associates, *Shopping Centers of Tomorrow: An Architectural Exhibition*, circulated by the American Federation of Arts, n.d. but c. 1954, p. 16.

19. R. H. Macy & Co., *Annual Report for 1955; The Times-Advocate*, Mar. 14, 1976, argues that Bamberger's, Macy's store at the Garden State Plaza, was at the forefront of the chain's appeal to the middle- to upper-income shopper. On market segmentation of shopping centers, also see William H. Whyte, Jr., *The Organization Man* (New York: Simon & Schuster, 1956), pp. 316–17; Jacobs, *The Mall*, pp. 5, 12; and Albert Bills and Lois Pratt, "Personality Differences Among Shopping Centers," *Fairleigh Dickinson University Business Review* 1 (Winter 1961), which had already begun making finer socioeconomic distinctions among the middle-class customers of the Bergen Mall and Garden State Plaza. Crawford's "The World in a Shopping Mall" discusses the sophisticated strategies that market researchers used to analyze trade areas and pitch stores to different kinds of customers; pp. 8–9.

20. Pierre Martineau, "Social Classes and Spending Behavior," *JM* 23 (October 1958): 126–27; also see Manchee, "Retailing," p. 5, on "middle income" customers.

21. George Sternlieb, "The Future of Retailing in the Downtown Core," *AIP Journal* 24 (May 1963),

as reprinted in Howard A. Schretter, *Downtown Revitalization* (Athens: Institute of Community and Area Development, University of Georgia, 1967), p. 95. Before the shopping centers were built and the Baltimore area's white shoppers had few options besides downtown stores, African Americans accused these stores of discriminating; see, for example, a letter to Clarence Mitchell, director of the Washington, D.C., Bureau of the NAACP, reporting a complaint that "the Baltimore Lane Bryant store would not serve Negroes": NAACP, II, B 64, "Discrimination, General, 1950–55."

22. First Federal Savings and Loan Association of Chicago newsletter, "Savings and Homeownership," August 1951, pp. 2–3, GSD; Samuel Feinberg, "Metropolis in the Making," *Women's Wear Daily*, Mar. 1, 1960; also see Wood, *Suburbia*, p. 211; and in *NYT*: "The Incredible Expanding Mall," Aug. 11, 1996, and "Suburban Comforts Thwart Atlanta's Plans to Limit Sprawl," Nov. 21, 1999.

23. For example, James A. Brunner and John L. Mason, "The Influence of Driving Time Upon Shopping Center Preference," *JM* 32 (April 1968): 57–61; William E. Cox, Jr., and Ernest F. Cooke, "Other Dimensions Involved in Shopping Center Preference," *JM* 34 (October 1970): 12–17; Pierre D. Martineau, "Customers' Shopping Center Habits Change Retailing: Secondary Areas and Scatter Zones Important with Mobility," *Editor and Publisher*, Oct. 26, 1963, p. 16.

24. U.S. Department of Labor, Bureau of Labor Statistics, "Consumer Expenditures and Income, Northern New Jersey, 1960–61," BLS Report No. 237–63, December 1963, Schomburg, clipping file "Consumer Expenses & Income—NJ."

25. "The Wonder on Routes 4 and 17: Garden State Plaza," brochure, file "Bergen County Shopping Centers," Hackensack; "Notes on Discussion Dealing with Regional (Intermunicipal) Planning Program for Passaic Valley Area (Lower Portion of Passaic Co. and South Bergen," n.d., Erber, Box A, Folder 3; "Memorandum to DAJ and WBS from EE," Nov. 22, 1966, Erber, Box B; National Center for Telephone Research (a division of Louis Harris and Associates), "A Study of Shoppers' Attitudes Toward the Proposed Shopping Mall in the Hudson County Meadowlands Area," conducted for Hartz Mountain Industries, February 1979, Rutgers.

On African-American dependence on public transportation, see Greater Newark Chamber of Commerce, "Survey of Jobs and Unemployment," May 1973, "Q" Files, NPL, "Greater Newark Chamber of Commerce," p. III-2; Donald E. Sexton, "Black Buyer Behavior," *JM* 36 (October 1972): 37. In another New York suburban area, Long Island, highway builder Robert Moses made sure that buses carrying poor and black city residents were unable to reach beaches, parks, and other sites of consumption and recreation by constructing overpasses too low to allow buses underneath: Robert A. Caro, *The Power Broker: Robert Moses and the Fall of New York* (New York: Vintage, 1975), pp. 318–19, 546, 951–52. As recently as 1995, a black teenager was killed crossing a seven-lane highway which had no light or crosswalk because the suburban mall where she worked would not allow her bus from inner-city Buffalo to enter mall property and drop off passengers: "Mall Accused of Racism in a Wrongful Death Trial in Buffalo," *NYT*, Nov. 15, 1999; "Galleria Oks City Bus Access," *Buffalo News*, Jan. 30, 1996; "Mall Bus Policy Called Anti-City," *Buffalo News*, Jan. 28, 1996; I am grateful to Katie Barry for alerting me to this case.

26. Stuart, *Our Era*, p. 20; Lois Pratt, "The Impact of Regional Shopping Centers in Bergen County," unpublished conference paper delivered April 23, 1960, in possession of the author. A survey of shopping habits in suburban Montclair, New Jersey, in 1945—before any shopping centers were built—revealed that Newark drew the biggest share of non-Montclair shoppers, with New York second: "Montclair Studies the Shopping Experiences of Its Residents," *JM* 10 (October 1945): 165–70.

27. Samuel Pratt and Lois Pratt, "The Impact of Some Regional Shopping Centers," *JM* 25 (October 1960): 44–50; S. Pratt, "The Challenge to Retailing," address to the 1957 annual meeting of the Passaic Valley Citizens Planning Association, Apr. 24, 1957, in possession of the author; L. Pratt, "Impact of Regional Shopping Centers in Bergen County"; S. Pratt and James Moran, "How the Regional Shopping Centers May Affect Shopping Habits in Rochelle Park (Preliminary)," *Business Research Bulletin* 1, Bureau of Business Research, Fairleigh Dickinson University, 1956; New York University study cited in Thompson, "Suburb

That Macy's Built," pp. 196, 200; Regional Plan Association, Committee on the Second Regional Plan, "Work Book for Workshops," Princeton, NJ, May 25–26, 1966, Erber, Box D, pp. V, 7, 9; Stuart U. Rich, *Shopping Behavior of Department Store Customers: A Study of Store Policies and Customer Demand, with Particular Reference to Delivery Service and Telephone Ordering* (Boston: Division of Research, Graduate School of Business Administration, Harvard University, 1963), particularly pp. 133–56, 228; Plan One Research Corporation, New York City, for the Bergen Evening Record Corporation, *The Mighty Market* (Hackensack, NJ: The Record, 1971). For national statistics on the decline of retail sales in central business districts while they mushroomed in metropolitan areas between 1958 and 1963, see Jon C. Teaford, *The Rough Road to Renaissance: Urban Revitalization in America, 1940–1985* (Baltimore: Johns Hopkins University Press, 1990), pp. 129–31.

28. S. Pratt and Moran, "How the Regional Shopping Centers May Affect Shopping Habits in Rochelle Park"; S. Pratt, "Challenge to Retailing," pp. 13–15. For surveys of consumers outside of the New York area, see C. T. Jonassen, *Downtown Versus Suburban Shopping*, Ohio Marketing Studies, Ohio State University Special Bulletin Number X-58 (Columbus: Bureau of Business Research, Ohio State University, 1953); Sternlieb, *Future of the Downtown Department Store*, pp. 33, 131–33; Rich, *Shopping Behavior of Department Store Customers*; and several important studies described in S. Pratt, "Challenge to Retailing," pp. 15–19.

29. See all the Pratts' studies listed in note 27, as well as "Hackensack Faces Year of Decision," *BR*, Jan. 10, 1958.

Inventing Modern Las Vegas

Hal Rothman

Source: *Neon Metropolis: How Las Vegas Started the Twenty-First Century*
(New York: Routledge, 2003).

EDITORS' INTRODUCTION

Las Vegas is like no other place in the United States. A desert city, initially made infamous by the investments and influence of a wide cast of characters including Benjamin "Bugsy" Siegel, Meyer Lansky, and Howard Hughes, it came to be associated with popular entertainers such as Frank Sinatra and the Rat Pack, Elvis Presley, Wayne Newton, Celine Dion, and the quirky acrobats of Cirque du Soleil. Las Vegas is the heart of a sprawling gaming, entertainment, and recreation metropolis surrounded by an inhospitable desert. During the 1990s, the region was one of the fasting growing in the United States. In that decade, the city's population doubled to almost 500,000 residents. Las Vegas enjoys an international reputation as a tourist destination, fueled by the highly successful "Only Vegas" advertising campaign from the Las Vegas Convention and Visitors Authority that helped draw nearly forty million people to the region in 2007. With its glitzy casinos, extravagant theme resort hotels, amusement rides, and simulations of other world travel destinations—notably New York City, Venice, and Egypt—Las Vegas defies easy categorization.

This postindustrial, postmodern city is a new type of place that scholars are struggling to define. Like Los Angeles, the city of Las Vegas has a short history compared to municipalities in the East, South, and Midwest. Los Angeles has been the quintessential symbol of cities coming of age in the twentieth century. In *The City: Los Angeles and Urban Theory at the End of the Twentieth Century* (1996), Edward W. Soja and Allen J. Scott write that, "the historical geography of Los Angeles invites continuing debate between those who see in it the achievement of some sort of urban utopia and the American Dream, and those who see little more than the dystopia nightmares of 'Hell Town' grown to gargantuan proportions."[i] Las Vegas shares this oversized personality and beguiling reputation. Its economy centers on activities that are, or at least at one time were, frowned upon or outright illegal.

In the following essay, the late historian Hal Rothman (1959–2007), explores how Las Vegas went from being a seasonal outpost and railroad depot in the middle of nowhere to "a paradigm of the postindustrial city." Rothman writes, "Las Vegas anticipated the transformation of American culture not out of innate savvy, but as a result of a lack of other options in the city."[ii] Cities as diverse as Detroit and New Orleans now face a similar dearth of options and have no other choice but to adopt Las Vegas' once suspect gaming industry model.

Hal Rothman was a professor and chair of the department of history at the University of Nevada, Las Vegas. He was the author or editor of over a dozen books on the American West and a frequent commentator, writer, and guest for newspapers and television.

---

i Edward W. Soja and Allen J. Scott, *The City: Los Angeles and Urban Theory at the End of the Twentieth Century* (Berkeley: University of California Press, 1996), 1–2.

ii Hal Rothman, *Neon Metropolis: How Las Vegas Started the Twenty-First Century* (New York: Routledge, 2003), 31, 323.

As one of the guiding members of the American Society for Environmental History (ASEH), he served as editor of *Environmental History* and its predecessor *Environmental History Review*. In addition to *Neon Metropolis*, his works include *On Rims and Ridges: The Los Alamos Area Since 1880* (Lincoln: University of Nebraska Press, 1992), *Devil's Bargains: Tourism in the Twentieth Century American West* (Lawrence: University of Kansas Press, 1998), *Saving the Planet: The American Response to the Environment in the Twentieth Century* (Chicago: Ivan R. Dee, 2000), and *LBJ's Texas White House: "Our Heart's Home"* (College Station, TX: Texas A&M Press, 2001), and *Blazing Heritage: A History of Wildfire in the National Parks* (New York: Oxford University Press, 2007).

INVENTING MODERN LAS VEGAS

THE NUMBERS ARE THERE, BUT THEY DON'T MEAN MUCH. HOW DO YOU explain a town that began as a railroad land auction in 1905, reached eight thousand in 1940, and topped one million people in 1995? There's no precedent for Las Vegas, no way to put its experience into the framework of other American cities. Distinct from the American whole, away from the arrows of progress and prosperity, Las Vegas was an insignificant part of the great government-industry matrix that defined the twentieth century. No set of circumstances led to Las Vegas. It didn't have fertile land or rich mineral veins; railroads didn't meet, highways didn't cross there. Banks didn't seek out Las Vegas, developers didn't fashion it into the next paradise, corporations didn't come to the desert to establish new headquarters, and people certainly didn't come looking for the little oasis to put down roots. Las Vegas's attractiveness was lost on Americans until after World War II and to the mainstream until well after 1975.

The reasons are obvious. Las Vegas was nowhere, a "miserable dinky little oasis town," the mobster Meyer Lansky supposedly called it, and without transportation that made it easy to reach or air-conditioning to make the stay bearable, Las Vegas's appeal was as seasonal as any ski resort. Before 1945, it had little to recommend it. Las Vegas had no markets, no hinterland to colonize. Even today, nearby St. George and southern Utah, heavily Mormon, look north to Salt Lake City; Kingman, Arizona, is a highway crossroads of its own; Flagstaff is fast becoming a suburb of Phoenix; and Barstow occupies its own dystopic universe. Las Vegas did not even have enough water to make it prey for Los Angeles. At its twentieth-century birth, Las Vegas was podunk, weak, and dependent, an inconsequential speck on the map.

The new town was typical of the small-town West. Modern Las Vegas began atop the remains of a nineteenth-century Mormon settlement that left only a few cantankerous ranchers. It started as a railroad town, a repair shop for the San Pedro, Los Angeles, and Salt Lake Railroad. Like so many other places in the West, its sustenance came from the rails, and when they prospered, as they did with the opening of the silver mines in Bullfrog and Rhyolite before 1910, so did the town. By 1910, Fremont Street, the heart of the old downtown, was paved, guttered, and flagged with sidewalks, and ten miles of local dirt road had been oiled to reduce the dust. The company built sixty-four workers' cottages and offered easy terms to workers who wanted to build their own. When the railroad's fortunes dipped, so did the town's. A track washout in 1910 sent the population spiking downward from twelve hundred to eight hundred. Only an upsurge in regional fortunes redirected the number upward. A pattern that typified the rural West in this period and ever after defined Las Vegas was set: the town was dependent on decisions made in other places.

Las Vegas's circumstances mirrored the history of the state. Nevada has always been a colony, dependent on the whims and needs of other larger, more powerful states some adjacent like California, others farther away. Shoehorned into the Union to guarantee Abraham Lincoln's reelection in 1864, Nevada enjoyed the privilege of statehood at the cost of its dignity and, some said, its independence. [...]

For two decades, Las Vegas was a simple small western town. Its main industry was the Union Pacific, which bought out the San Pedro, Los Angeles, and Salt Lake in 1921, kept the maintenance shop, and became master of the railroad town, responsible for its infrastructure as well as for its open social climate. Las Vegas had all the virtues and vices of such places. It was tough, raw, and sometimes mean. The rules of high-tone America not only did not apply, they simply didn't exist. Like many similar towns, Las Vegas did not explicitly forbid prostitution. As long as it was confined to one square block, block 16 of the original town plat, "quasi-legal" best defined its status. Railroad fiat restricted gambling, legal in Nevada until Progressive reformers barred it in 1910 in a prohibition that lasted until 1931 and alcohol to the same area. Illegal but only in a technical sense, such activities were part of the compact the railroad made when it created towns that functioned like the port cities of yore. The railroad brought life and it tacitly condoned behavior at odds with Victorian norms. Railroad companies well understood the advantages and drawbacks of the rails, and towns that grew up along them made accommodation, even in the most moralistic of times.

Las Vegas's circumstances were typical of the rural West and even more characteristic of railroad towns. The railroad provided a capital regime; it was the only consistent source of funding for the town, and its goals determined those of the city. Much like the cattle trade of the nineteenth century, the rails brought a rowdy element with plenty of cash and a feeling of mobility. Workers lived in Las Vegas, but travelers passed through, and the sense of movement along the rails freed people from place and time. Vice flourished and became an integral part of local commerce. Although still considered not quite proper, it was recognized as necessary. Catering to other people's desires proved so lucrative that even the most upright small-town burghers held their noses and looked away, as they had in the cattle towns. The accommodation made life palatable. Without vice there wasn't enough business to eke out a living.

This condition reflected a larger theme in the state's history. While Nevada liked to bill itself as the Old West, where the rules of modern civilization didn't apply, it was equally true that the state had few choices. Neither of its two nineteenth-century industries, mining and railroads, encouraged stability. Mining exploded on the landscape, peaked in great rushes, then left huge visible scars as testimony to its transience. The railroad epitomized nineteenth-century mobility, defying the rooted ideals of the time. Its reputation in American folklore for encouraging transience and license and freedom inspired generations of songwriters and other artists. The state embraced these industries because it had no other choice. If Nevadans seemed more willing to mind their own business than most, this incipient libertarianism was a product of the limits of its land and infrastructure in a harsh climate.

One-owner towns had their drawbacks for the people who lived in them. Even though they allowed locals considerable autonomy and leeway, outside power maintained tremendous control. Early Las Vegas was wise to heed and placate its masters. When it didn't, disaster resulted. After the Union Pacific purchase in 1921, the new owners laid off sixty workers, earning the ire of the town. The next year, an opportunity arose for railroad workers to pay back their new overlords; workers shut Las Vegas down during the national railroad strike in 1922. The new masters were not amused. In retribution, the Union Pacific signed the town's death warrant: it moved the maintenance shop and three hundred jobs to Caliente, about 125 miles track toward Utah. The railroad regime ended as arbitrarily as it had started, and Las Vegas was consigned to the fate of other small western towns. It had to adapt—or diminish, wither, and finally go under. The period just following the railroad's departure was the bleakest in modern Las Vegas's short history. The whistle-stop easily could have become a ghost town.

Only California and its imperial need for water saved the city. Since the remarkable fiction that created modern Los Angeles, the City of Angels became a vacuum for every drop of water it could collect. Southern California's growth demanded ever more water and threatened its neighbors near and far, paralyzing even distant states like Colorado. Largely to prevent California from taking all the water in the Colorado River, the other river states sued for peace. The result was ratification in 1927 of the Colorado Compact, which adjudicated the waters of the Colorado River on a state-by-state basis, and the decision to construct the Boulder Dam, now Hoover Dam, the largest public works project of its time, in Black Canyon about thirty miles from Las Vegas.

The dam was the signal event in the history of southern Nevada with ramifications far beyond the region. Beginning in 1931, construction lasted nearly four years, which meant four years of paychecks to almost five thousand workers at the height of the Depression. When Franklin D. Roosevelt dedicated the dam on September 30, 1935, the 760–foot concrete face presided over a technological miracle: a holding tank for all the water in the river, distributed by legal agreement between haves and havenots. The dam created life, an economy, infrastructure, business, and even tourism. Secretary of the Interior Dr. Ray Lyman Wilbur decided he wanted no part of the sinful railroad town of Las Vegas for the project. A stern moralist, Wilbur preferred the dry style of the Coolidge administration that preceded his tenure. Although Wilbur built a government town called Boulder City, dry and free of gambling, the road to the dam led through Las Vegas. Wilbur's puritanism had inadvertently given Las Vegas a new future.

The synergy the dam created was tremendous. Its success paved the way for the Bureau of Reclamation to become the preeminent federal agency of the 1930s and a powerful engine of federal spending until the 1970s. After Boulder Dam, the Bureau of Reclamation engaged in forty-year orgy of dam building until it controlled the distribution of most of the water west of the Mississippi River and created legions of dependent local oligarchies in the small-town and mini-city West. As the dam revived Las Vegas, it also provided a new master, one that carried other federal beneficiaries in tow.

Las Vegas was entirely typical of other western towns in the 1930s. The region's economy survived or thrived based on the size of the federal contribution.... There was one way that Las Vegas could stand apart from the multitude of similar towns. It possessed a sense of itself as a place out of time, left over from an older western past. A certain amount of the Old West was considered ribald by 1930s standards, but Las Vegas wasn't really sinful, its symbolism seemed to say. It just hadn't changed while everyone else had, and so held a convenient place in memory that allowed it—and you, when you visited—to get away with things that you couldn't at home. In a society quick to condemn aberrant behavior yet nostalgic for its lost roots, ribald could be packaged as individual freedom.

This tradition became the crux of the vaunted Nevada individualism, the most appealing and vexing characteristic of the state then and now. Nevada was and is wide open, a dream for anyone who was ever a sophomore in college and entranced by Ayn Rand, even for a moment. In their rugged self-image, Nevadans pride themselves on having real freedom, not the namby-pamby eighteenth-century Paul Revere—style freedom within the constraints of the community, but the right to do what you want, whenever you want, wherever you want, and with whomever you want. Fusing its rugged history with economic necessity, Nevada put as few constraints on the individual as possible. Your property is *your* property more in Nevada than in any other state in the union; you can carry a concealed weapon with less red tape than in most places, and the concept of self-defense—your right to protect yourself—is carried further in Nevada law than elsewhere in the nation. The desert alone was not the sole attraction for James "Bo" Gritz, the survivalist who negotiated the surrender at Ruby Ridge in Idaho. Nor is it accident that within a mile of the state capitol in Carson City, legal houses of prostitution flourish. Nevada is the home of the Sagebrush Rebellion, an attempt to privatize most federal lands in the West under the pretext of furthering private property rights. Nevada still sells this same nostalgia. All of this individualism pulls on the nation's emotions in an age when we're oppressed by institutions and information and told that the self is all there is. But this romanticism embodies a difficult paradox: with ideals like these, it's hard to run a modern society.

The next capital regime, federal dollars, illustrated the perils of colonial existence. Lacking industry or infrastructure, Las Vegas depended first and foremost on outside money. Almost as an afterthought, the state permitted activities that were regarded as scandalous. Southern Nevadans especially recognized the perils of dependence. An arbitrary change in federal policy could threaten not only individual livelihood, but the economic viability of the entire region. Before air-conditioning, attracting newcomers to a town where summer temperatures routinely topped 110 degrees was a difficult task without the lure of easy prosperity.

As a result, Las Vegas shaped itself to the needs of the outside. In the West of the 1930s and 1940s, this was not unusual. Oklahoma City, Richmond, California, and countless communities did the same. Only Las Vegans recognized that their opportunity to capitalize was time-bound, and that long-term sustenance required other strategies. Southern Nevada especially welcomed the federal money and encouraged those dollars to stay. At the same time, its people looked for new ways to diversify their income base. [...]

As World War II ended, a little red sports car came up Highway 91 from Los Angeles, and from it emerged a strong-jawed if ragged-looking man with hard eyes. Benjamin "Bugsy" Siegel, a mobster and close associate of underworld leader Meyer Lansky, inaugurated the next capital regime in Las Vegas. A vicious and probably psychotic thug and hit man, Siegel had been flirting with Hollywood before he came to Las Vegas. He didn't understand why he hadn't been cast in movies; he was handsome, he thought, rugged-looking, and a good actor to boot. He should be in film.

But his real business called, and Siegel headed down the road.

His arrival was part of a larger plan. Lansky and his associates eyed Las Vegas as early as 1941, but in most accounts Siegel receives credit for envisioning the complicated relationship between gambling and status that turned the Flamingo Hotel into Las Vegas's first national destination. Siegel transformed Las Vegas from a western, institution-free center of vice into a world-renowned spectacle of gambling, entertainment, and fun by blending the themes of Monte Carlo, Miami Beach, and Havana with the resortlike character of the hotels that preceded the Flamingo on Highway 91. Siegel had a bizarre idea of class, but in the process of painting it onto the dinky little oasis, he inaugurated an era in which the capital to fund gaming resorts, the newest dominant industry in Las Vegas, came first from the pockets of organized crime and later from legitimate money the underworld could control. [...]

Locals did not object to this seemingly nefarious involvement in what was becoming the primary local industry. There was only one other significant source of capital in postwar Las Vegas, the Nevada Test Site. Cold War spending in support of aboveground testing between 1951 and 1963 and underground testing afterwards provided as many as nine-thousand jobs. Although certainly significant, such spending only went so far: it provided jobs for the most specialized workforce in the area, offered a considerable number of well-paying but dangerous jobs, and became the baseline for the regional economy. But federal spending after 1945 was only the starting point. In southern Nevada, the need for capital was so great that almost everyone looked the other way when it came to mob dollars. Even the strait-laced Mormon culture welcomed the newcomers. The mobster's arrival opened a new pipeline to the capital for which Las Vegans thirsted. Siegel's well-known association with Murder Incorporated, the sensationalized mob killers from 1930s New York, did not scare away locals. Anyone with money to invest was welcome, even Benny Siegel.

Lansky was perhaps the shrewdest of the mobsters, carefully covering his tracks. When Siegel purchased the El Cortez in 1945, his investors included locals as well as gangsters Lansky, Gus Greenbaum, an Arizona bookmaker, Davie Berman, the mob boss of Minneapolis, and his ne'er-do-well brother Chickie, and Israel "Icepick Willie" Alderman, who ran typical 1930s gaming roadhouses called "carpet joints" in Minneapolis, and Moe Sedway, a Siegel associate from Los Angeles. The purchase of the El Cortez initiated a pattern that marked two decades of Las Vegas development. In every subsequent purchase or development of a resort on the Strip, "connected" illegal gamblers, who became legal in Nevada, participated. In nearly every new casino in the 1940s and 1950s, a visible relationship between locals and newcomers effectively linked outside capital with respectability. Locals who could easily be licensed or individuals with ties to organized crime but no significant criminal record held visible and often sizable percentages of new casinos. Most of these "owners" appeared to have recently come into money. Who truly owned their percentage was not a good question to ask. [...]

The mob and its strange habits with money created the Las Vegas of myth, the town where, as Debbie Reynolds observed, "nobody got killed who didn't deserve it." Las Vegas became a world of shadowy individual investment, usually hidden and always untaxed, with deliveries of the skim, paper bags, and briefcases full of money to distant cities. These individuals held "points" in Las Vegas, percentage investments that were not on the record but that returned monthly profits skimmed off the top of the casino's profits and never recorded in their ledgers, taxed, or made known to aboveground stockholders. Insidious and nefarious to be sure, most of these investments were also small-time, amounting to as little as a few thousand dollars a month in profit. On paper, Jack Entratter, the head of the Sands in the early 1960s, ostensibly owned 12 percent of the operation. A former headwaiter at the Copacabana in Miami Beach who had become a player and philanthropist in Las Vegas—the social hall in the oldest synagogue in town, Temple Beth Sholom, was constructed with his donation and named for him—Entratter owned 2 percent himself. The other 10 points he held for various people, including the real power at the Sands, an old associate of Lansky's named Vincent "Jimmy Blue Eyes" Alo. The mythic Las Vegas was a personal world where everyone knew everyone else and all knew who buttered their figurative bread. [...]

In the open political and cultural climate of southern Nevada, Las Vegas became the center of gaming in the Western Hemisphere. With the rise of Fidel Castro in Cuba and the closure of the Havana casinos, only one location in North America provided legal big-time gambling. Combined with improvements such as the expansion of McCarran Airport in 1963, Las Vegas took advantage of the growing affluence and changing cultural mores of American society. In Nevada, gaming masked its social cost. Despite the reality that many casino employees gambled their pay-checks, most of casinos' winnings came from visitors. The industry consistently produced positive numbers for the state economy.

This new importance led to a much greater demand for capital than had existed during the 1950s. Until 1963, when the Fremont Casino skimming scandal was derailed by illegal Federal Bureau of Investigation wire-taps, Las Vegas was a small-time operator's paradise. Accustomed to seeing their occupation as risky, the individuals who ran casinos operated as fly-by-nights. Skimming was endemic. A piece of the profit went in the celebrated "three for the hotel, one for the government, and one for the boys" formula, and the real powers, mob bosses in other cities, received it in paper bags. They looked at the short-term profit that could be put in their pockets as the best profit, almost instinctively feeling that the idyllic moment could not last. They believed that their run of luck would soon end. The laws would change, the moralists would come out of the woodwork, the police would crack down, and they'd be on the run again, without their increasingly expensive tangible assets, the larger and larger casino hotels along the Strip.

When the hammer fell, as it did repeatedly, its impact was usually negligible. Americans were increasingly willing to experiment with self-indulgence. In a world where leisure and recreation were becoming more important, gambling ceased to be a moral violation and began its road toward acceptance as a legitimate recreational pastime, a journey completed sometime in the 1990s. The new emphasis on gambling as a form of entertainment rather than a tawdry pastime put pressure on operators to cater to a broader audience. To get Mom and Pop America to Sin City demanded that operators see the openness of Las Vegas as more than a moment that would soon end. It also required a lot more money. [...]

The financial markets still eschewed gaming resorts. The only legitimate source of such capital in southern Nevada was a local bank, the Bank of Las Vegas, founded in 1954 and reorganized as the Valley Bank in 1964. An arm of the empire of Walter Cosgriff of the Continental Bank of Utah, the only non-Mormon financial institution of significance in the Beehive State, the Bank of Las Vegas mirrored Cosgriff's willingness to loan money outside of the conventional channels of midcentury America. In the 1950s, the Bank of Las Vegas became a primary local source of capital, but despite its significance and that of banker E. Parry Thomas, growth still outstripped available funding. Casinos lined up for money from Thomas's bank, but the capital needed to transform Las Vegas into a first-class resort would have to come from somewhere else.

Again, the mob was at the center of the story. The Teamsters' Central States, Southeast, and Southwest Areas Pension Fund, run by Allen Dorfman, the stepson of mobster Paul "Red" Dorfman and an associate of the Chicago mob, provided the source. In the early 1950s, the Teamsters boss Jimmy Hoffa hand-picked the younger Dorfman, then a college physical education instructor, to handle the Teamsters' insurance to repay a favor to his stepfather. In 1967, as Hoffa prepared to go to jail, he gave Dorfman complete control of pension fund loans. [...]

Early Teamsters pension fund forays into Las Vegas had little to do with gaming. In 1958 *Las Vegas Sun* publisher Herman "Hank" Greenspun, one of the few American newspaper publishers to challenge Senator Joseph McCarthy's reign of terror and loudly critical of the influence of organized crime on his adopted state, received $250,000 from the pension fund for a golf course. Teamsters money funded other developments. On April 14, 1959, the one-hundred-bed Sunrise Hospital opened, built by the Paradise Development Company, whose officers included Moe Dalitz, casino executive Allard Roen, who had been indicted in the United Dye and Chemical stock fraud case, and two young Las Vegas businessmen, Irwin Molasky and Mervin Adelson. Hoffa ensured its profitability by delivering the Teamsters union health care contracts to the new hospital.

Subsequent construction by the Paradise Development Company, especially the 1967 Boulevard Mall, drew accolades from the community. With access to capital for developing noncasino projects, the company effectively planned the future of nonresort Las Vegas by turning Maryland Parkway, a two-lane road that paralleled the Strip about two miles to the east, into the main commercial thoroughfare for the growing city. Nearly everyone in the city with any kind of aspiration, workers and executives alike, came to live in the area east of the new commercial center. The enclosed Boulevard Mall, the first modern shopping center in Las Vegas, capped this process. With its completion, Las Vegans needed only a little self-deception to believe that their city had amenities for its residents to match those of the resorts that catered to visitors.

This was the most complicated dimension of mob rule in southern Nevada. In a colony lacking internal capital, in the middle of substantial growth, and dominated by an industry that the mainstream would not fund, Las Vegas hungered for fresh capital, no matter what its origins. Largely invisible to the public, unconventional financing helped shape the direction of the city. Teamsters pension fund money invested in social projects, albeit profitable ones like the hospital and the mall, made that capital even more palatable. To most of greater Las Vegas, which had grown from roughly 8,000 in 1940 to 269,000 in 1967 and was comprised of casino workers who regarded legalized gaming as the solution to legal woes they experienced elsewhere, the hospital and mall were community assets. Similar developments continued to normalize Las Vegas, offering people a sense of typicality that had been hard to sustain in the 1950s. For that, Las Vegans were grateful, and they were usually willing to overlook the unusual origins of the money that financed their normalcy. [...]

By 1966, the pension fund had become the dominant source of development capital in southern Nevada. The rising cost of resort development, particularly after Caesars Palace, demanded more than $100 million in development capital. The traditional means of capital formation, stock offerings and bonds, were still blocked. Wall Street was not ready, leaving gambling's lucrative rewards to the pension fund and the organized crime bosses who ran it. That made Las Vegas beholden not to conventional financial powers in America, but to the parasitic forces that preyed upon it. People in gaming were not bothered by the prospect of silent and powerful control. In the 1960s, Las Vegas's veneer of typicalty was thin. Although Las Vegans insisted that behind the glitz, they lived in a "normal" town, their definition of normal was quite at odds with the one held by the rest of the nation. [...]

The transformation of Las Vegas from a mob-dominated gambling town to corporate-owned modern resort began with two related events. The first was the arrival of reclusive billionaire Howard R. Hughes at a suite atop the Desert Inn in Las Vegas in his typically bizarre fashion on the eve of Thanksgiving, 1966. Hughes had been a frequent visitor to Las Vegas in the 1950s, living there for a year, often talking of bringing his entire business empire to Nevada. In 1966, the billionaire was ferried from his private railroad car and hustled upstairs to the floor of penthouse suites reserved for the high rollers on whom the casino depended. After a few weeks, the

management of the Desert Inn sought to persuade Hughes to leave; they'd expected an increase in gambling as a result of the presence of the world's richest man and were sorely disappointed. Hughes had so far cost them money. They couldn't put the high rollers they needed in the hotel because Hughes insisted on having the entire floor. Gamble or leave, they told Hughes's representatives.

Instead of doing either, Hughes bought the place for about $13 million and remained cloistered in the penthouse for four years. The purchase was the first in a buying spree that included the Frontier, for which Hughes paid $14 million, the Sands, $14.6 million, Castaways, $3 million, the $17 million Landmark and its nearly $9 million Teamsters pension fund loan, and the Silver Slipper. All of Hughes's purchases had been Lansky-dominated casinos. Hughes added a television station, airlines, small airport facilities, one hundred residential lots at the Desert Inn Country Club, and thousands of acres of undeveloped land, including more than twenty thousands acres called "Husite," where Hughes promised the federal government a guided missile base in return for the nearly free land. Hughes made overtures to purchase Caesars Palace, the Riviera, and the Dunes in Las Vegas as well as Harrah's in Reno and Lake Tahoe, but an antitrust suit halted negotiations. Before the Nixon administration received a bribe and overruled Justice Department objections to Hughes's purchase of Harold's Club in Reno and the Landmark Hotel, the tycoon controlled about one-seventh of the state's gaming revenue, one-quarter of that in Las Vegas, and more than one-third of the revenue generated on the Strip. [...]

Hughes served as a harbinger of a new era, the first set of truly deep pockets to seek to make Las Vegas his own. He arrived at the ideal moment for a newcomer, exactly as the fortunes of his predecessors began to give way. The first generation of mob impresarios, men such as Meyer Lansky and Jimmy Alo, were aging, and some grew tired of the constant federal surveillance and other hassles that accompanied a move to the legitimate American economy. Selling out to Hughes, whom they regarded as the quintessential sucker, seemed a good idea. They took their profit and departed.

In some ways, Hughes was more like the gangsters he replaced than the corporate America that revered him. Gaming was a natural for Hughes. He was a confirmed risk-taker who flaunted rules all his life, he was beholden to no one, and even more important, owed no one. Hughes was the sole stockholder of Hughes Tool Company, meaning that only he had to pass gaming commission investigations. A man of his stature and wealth had little problem manipulating regulatory bodies in a state with weak government. As was the case with the development of the Flamingo and its peers, Hughes's capital was private and personal. The reclusive and idiosyncratic billionaire's vast empire had no public association with organized crime. A forerunner of the new Las Vegas whose patterns resembled the old, Hughes's interest helped legitimize investment in the gaming industry.

The second change made the mobsters who sold out wince. In 1967, at the behest of William F. Harrah and Baron and Conrad Hilton, with the support of Nevada governor Paul Laxalt, the state passed the Corporate Gaming Act, which eliminated the requirement that each stockholder had to pass a Gaming Control Board background check. Governor Grant Sawyer had fought this law while in office, believing it would only institutionalize organized crime, but Laxalt had no such qualms. Passage of the law opened the door for an infusion of corporate capital and raised the stakes in gaming. Corporations could now invest, inaugurating a new capital regime that brought Las Vegas closer to the primary avenues of capital formation. [...]

In this climate, organized crime suddenly became financially obsolete. Hotel chains pioneered the way, and financial markets slowly changed their view of gaming. In a few seconds, Wall Street could muster a great deal more money than organized crime ever could. The $269 million of Teamsters pension fund money in late-1960s Las Vegas might have remained the largest investment in southern Nevada, but it ceased to represent the growth sector of gaming capital. In an instant, the passage of the revised Corporate Gaming Act redistributed power in Las Vegas away from mob-controlled dollars and toward Wall Street. [...]

Clearing the mob out was easier said than done. In 1979, after a nearly three-year battle to rid the Aladdin of James Tamer, an affiliate of the Lebanese underworld, and Sorkis Webbe, its legal counsel, the Gaming Commission suspended the Aladdin's state gaming license. Later the Gaming Commission gave the Aladdin a sell-or-close order. On August 6, 1979, gaming control agents entered the Aladdin casino and sealed the slot machines and the tables. It was a sad fate for the hotel where Elvis and Priscilla married. Even though Judge Harry Claiborne, who was later impeached by the Senate, issued an injunction a few hours later and the casino reopened, never before had a mob casino been shut down simply for being a mob casino. The closure was revolutionary. A little more than a decade after the Corporate Gaming Act, Nevada state government was making unprecedented efforts to rid its primary industry of organized crime.

The 1980s completed the process of excising the mob. The arrival of FBI agent Joe Yablonsky as special agent in charge in Las Vegas led to a half-decade of vigorous prosecution. The city became tense, and city leaders screamed that Yablonsky pursued a vendetta against them. Senator Paul Laxalt, a close confidant of President Ronald Reagan, squawked so loudly about Yablonsky that it attracted attention to corruption in Las Vegas. A scandal at the Tropicana led to further prosecutions, and the mob's hold, always tenuous, convulsed and released. [...]

Throughout the 1970s, national banks generally shied away from Las Vegas, but large profits in Atlantic City persuaded a few East Coast and California banks that Las Vegas might be a legitimate investment. Through the Del Webb Company, the Sahara received $135 million in 1979 from New York banks for improvements to the resort, $25 million more than the hotel requested. At about the same time, Aetna Insurance Company loaned Caesars World, the parent corporation of Caesars Palace, $60 million. Soon after, First Interstate Bank developed a sizeable casino and gaming loan portfolio. By 1980 the state's five dominant gaming entities, Harrah's, the MGM, Del Webb, the Hilton, and Caesars World, were all publicly traded corporations.

Las Vegas was yet again transformed by the nearly unlimited capital that public financing could generate. Impresario Steve Wynn, a protégé of Parry Thomas, raised the ante of casino financing, laying the foundation of a new and presumably competition-proof Las Vegas. Large-scale funding meant that Las Vegas could become more than the mecca of glitz and excess. Once its capital came from the mainstream, its attractions could be shaped to the tastes of the mainstream audience. Las Vegas promised a luxury experience at a middle-class price; now it could offer that price to the entire middle class. The gradual easing of the stigma of gaming and the willingness to merge gaming with conventional postwar attractions on the scale of Disneyland increased Las Vegas's reach. Not only did gamblers come to the transformed desert town, so did people who wanted to see the spectacle and have a vacation in a classic but updated sense of the word. Sin City became more palatable and maybe even marginally less sinful. [...]

The combination of widespread credit, the new availability of cash, and the great stock run-up of the 1990s extended the market for gaming and leisure. In the late 1970s, consumer interest rates were deregulated and companies located in states that permitted high interest rates could export them to customers in states with lower ceilings. The credit card revolution began. Within a few years, anyone with halfway decent credit and the prospect of paying back at least part of what they borrowed received offers of credit cards with limits that sometimes exceeded their annual income. With credit, people could truly attain the be-all and end-all of post-1960s culture: they could have whatever they wanted now and pay for it later, if at all. Cash flow was no longer a barrier to a weekend in Las Vegas. [...]

In a 1994 cover story, *Time* magazine declared that Las Vegas had become an All-American city, the new American hometown. The rest of the nation had become more like its former capital of sin, Kurt Andersen of the magazine averred, granting Las Vegas a leading role in the service economy that has become, for better and worse, the future of the nation. What this glitzy and superficial analysis failed to note was that at the same time, Las Vegas had become a lot more like the rest of the nation.

Las Vegas had solved one of the major problems of the transition from industrial to postindustrial economy. In this mecca of gaming, unskilled individuals with barely a high school education could still earn a middle-class income. The Culinary Union helped keep wages high, and some hotels provided wages and benefits that exceeded union contract in order to discourage unionization. Las Vegas had become the "Last Detroit" in the way it provided solid pay for unspecialized work; for anyone with a modicum of skill and grace, it was an easy place to do well in service positions.

The transformation was completed by the way in which the Las Vegas experience became a part of the business of professional leisure. By the 1990s ITT-Sheraton, Hilton, and other major hotel chains owned major casino-hotels. Graduates of Wharton Business School made decisions, and the gaming industry developed a hierarchy that resembled the army's. Special training was required before anyone received the opportunity to lead. There was even a glass ceiling in gaming, but its defining trait wasn't gender: dealers could no longer work their way off the floor to management positions. In the large resorts, the upward mobility that being "connected" once ensured disappeared. Pit boss was now as high as a dealer or floor worker could expect to go. The management positions were filled by MBAs, professional businesspeople who did not truly understand the gaming industry. The personal side of gaming, where a floor manager recognized and took care of regular patrons, disappeared as gaming became an industry like any other. [...]

As the twenty-first century gathers momentum, Las Vegas is finally sharing greater commonality with the rest of the nation. It depends on the same sources of capital that other communities do and has accepted many of the same rules and regulations. It's not only that the rest of the nation normalized the behaviors that used to make Las Vegas exceptional; in its hierarchy, distribution of wealth and status, demography, and stratification of its labor force, Las Vegas has become more like the rest of the nation as well. Once a pariah, Las Vegas has become a paradigm of the postindustrial economy. As gaming spreads throughout the nation—usually run by Las Vegas companies—the colony is being transformed. Las Vegas has become a colonizer, exporting its version of the new economy to New Orleans, Missouri, Detroit, and elsewhere. Las Vegas has always reflected America onto itself. It has always been the mirror people held up to their faces to see what they hoped for and, equally, what they feared. As it became normative, the entire historical equation of the city was thrown on its head. Las Vegas is the first city of the new century, the one that owes its allegiance to the shape of the new universe, to the signs and symbols of a culture of entertainment.

Polo Ponies and Penalty Kicks: Sports on the East End

Corey Dolgon

Source: *End of the Hamptons: Scenes from the Class Struggle in America's Paradise* (New York: New York University Press, 2005).

EDITORS' INTRODUCTION

Few communities in America enjoy a reputation for extraordinary wealth, fame, and glitzy social events as do "the Hamptons," a sobriquet for the hamlets and villages located in the towns of East Hampton and Southampton, New York, on the eastern end of Long Island. The Hamptons may seem like a strange place to end an anthology on the American city, but as the following essay by Corey Dolgon illustrates, they recently have transformed from world-famous summer resorts to the year-round home of Manhattan's new "ultra rich," or "hyper-bourgeoisie." Like all urban areas, though, the Hamptons are much more. They are also socially and culturally diverse, much to the dismay of those who cultivate an image of exclusivity.

In the *End of the Hamptons*, Dolgon explores the historic pattern of invasion and succession—beginning with the Puritans who grabbed land from the Shinnecock and Montaukett tribes—which has defined land use and cultural hegemony on the eastern end of Long Island. However, as Dolgon notes, each dominant group eventually comes to feel inundated by new migrants who are inspired by the very success of those who came before them. As a result, social commentators have routinely read challenges to the status quo and any harbingers of change as the "end of the Hamptons" as they know it.

In order to differentiate those who belong from those who do not, wealthy Hampton residents attempt to set themselves apart from everyone else with an odd and somewhat perverse mixture of what is old (bourgeoisie) and new (hyper-bourgeoisie). At the same time, newcomers to the area, such as Latino workers whose cheap labor helps the elite maintain their social façade, adapt themselves to their new lives in a new country by mixing their cultural histories and ethnic heritages. One area where both groups express their hybrid adaptations is with sports; polo tournaments for the rich and soccer matches for newly arrived Latinos. Dolgon examines each one of these arenas of leisure and popular culture within the context of global transformations of the economy and the changing nature of exurbia in the Hamptons.

Corey Dolgon is the Director of Community-Based Learning and a professor of sociology at Stonehill College in Easton, Massachusetts. He is past president of the Association for Humanist Sociology (AHS) and served as editor for its journal, *Humanity and Society*. He was a professor and chair of sociology at Worcester State College in Worcester, Massachusetts. *The End of the Hamptons* won book-of-the-year honors from both the American Sociological Association's Marxist Section and from the AHS. He has just finished two other books, *Living Sociology: Social Problems, Service Learning and Civic Engagement* (Thousand Oaks, CA: Pine Forge Press, 2010) and *Pioneers in Public Sociology: The First Thirty Years of Humanity and Society, The Journal of the Association for Humanist Sociology* (forthcoming, 2010).

POLO PONIES AND PENALTY KICKS

Sports on the East End

The Walentas family estate and horse farm in Bridgehampton is home to the Bridgehampton Polo Club and the new Mercedes-Benz Polo Challenge, a professional polo tournament that now stands, according to one former professional, as "the best polo played in America." As exciting as polo may be, however, most press and spectator attention is paid to the special celebrity guests who congregate under a large tent off to one side of the field. Here, famous entertainers, models, designers, CEOs, and politicos sip champagne and nosh on gourmet snacks before they mix with the hoi polloi during half-time, when the whole audience is asked to stomp down divots on the field.

Well off to another side of the farm is a soccer field that the Manhattan real estate magnate David Walentas had built for his landscapers and stable workers, many of whom come from Mexico or Central or South America. While this field hosts informal "pick-up" games for employees and friends, some of the players also participate in a variety of competitive soccer leagues that have sprung up on the East End. Teams with names such as Team Mexico, Team Colombia, Team Costa Rica, and Team Ecuador wear brightly colored uniforms sponsored by a variety of the area's landscaping firms and building contractors. League games are often played on small, poorly manicured fields surrounded by families with children kicking soccer balls and radios blasting banda music.

The Hamptons have experienced rapid economic, political, and demographic changes over the past three decades. Once regarded as one of the world's best-known summer resort areas for the rich and famous, the area has become an increasingly primary residence for some of Manhattan's newly "ultra-rich." Much of this ascendant class (whom I will call the "hyper-bourgeoisie") has made its fortunes in the 1990s stock market boom and dot.com explosion, as well as in Madison Avenue's advertising firms, the media, the film industry and from the cult of celebrity that surrounds them.

They bring to the East End an insatiable and now year-round demand, not for inconspicuous peace and quiet but for publicity and conspicuous consumption. Heliports, expanded jet service, luxury bus lines, cell phones, and "telecommuting" have facilitated this transformation to what one *Newsweek* reporter dubbed the "Hollywood-Wall Street Hamptons.

The burgeoning economy of wealthy homeowners in the Hamptons has created a huge labor demand in construction and landscaping, as well as in retail and other services. While some businesses have gone so far as to recruit workers directly from Colombia and Ecuador, others have run morning bus services to poorer communities in western Suffolk County to facilitate the commuting of lower-wage, predominately Hispanic labor that works in the Hamptons but cannot afford to live there. Informal "labor halls" have sprung up on busy street corners, vacant lots, outside delicatessens, 7-Elevens, and building supply stores throughout the eastern region of Suffolk County. Also notable are the ways in which more permanent populations of Latino workers have established their own informal networks of job placement, transportation, van services, carpooling, and child care.

In this essay, I examine the social and cultural impact of these major economic and demographic changes through the lens of sports. Although I'm concerned with specific population shifts, real estate patterns, land use, and labor markets, I focus on how these phenomena are both reflected and rearticulated through cultural activities and events. In particular, I argue that the cultural politics of sports in the Hamptons represents the struggles of both groups—an ascendant hyper-bourgeoisie and a burgeoning Latino working class—as they adapt, jostle, and thrive amid the area's rapid changes. For polo enthusiasts, the sport represents a new elite's attempt to legitimize and propagate its wealth and power by resurrecting historical images of "old" money within a contemporary setting of new wealth and celebrity. For soccer players and fans, sport and leisure activities reflect efforts to preserve and promote traditional social practices and identities within the political borders and cultural contexts of their new homes. [...]

Polo and the Cultural Politics of a New Bourgeoisie

Polo is a sport for rich people. The game itself requires huge plots of land—a regulation field is at least 160 by 300 yards. To prepare for the game requires even larger tracts; most Hamptons horse farms that train the "ponies" cover between twenty and fifty square acres of the most expensive real estate in the region. The Walentas's farm spreads out over one hundred acres and costs almost $1.5 million a year just to operate. To compete in "high goal" polo (the top level of international play) costs each player anywhere between $300,000 and $1 million for horses and maintenance, equipment, travel, and other expenses. Often referred to as the "game of kings," polo has always been closely associated with colonial power and great wealth ever since the British appropriated it from southern Asia in the mid-1800s. Therefore, the sport also possesses a kind of cultural capital whose regal history of empire bestows legitimacy to newly arrived social achievers. To play polo is both a sign of one's actual wealth and an indication of one's class position.

But sports are not only reflective of class relations; they are also constitutive. Playing exclusive sports such as polo once helped reproduce an aristocratic class by serving as what the sociologists H. E. Chehabi and A. Guttmann described as the means of socialization by which rulers can "develop those traits of character and leadership necessary for dominion at home and abroad."[1] Some of these characteristics are obvious. For example, riding on a stately horse in front of a high-society viewing stand reinforces one's command over troops while simultaneously reaffirming in the popular imagination one's fitness to rule. Yet, the performance of class, both reflected and reproduced by sports, is also temporal. At the dawn of the twenty-first century, on the East End of Long Island, the old aristocracies of nineteenth-century Britain and early-twentieth-century America are being supplanted by a new bourgeoisie. While playing polo carries with it a historical element of prestige and power, the dominant characteristics that must be acquired by this new class of polo players and, perhaps even more important, packaged for a new public's consumption, require a new narrative of changing symbols and values. [...]

Despite polo's expression of bourgeois distinction, the events themselves do integrate the players with their spectators. In particular, Bridgehampton polo unites players with three groups: their hyperbourgeois peers under the "Members and Special Guest Tent"; the upper-middle-class summer tourists and local professionals who pay $10 per ticket to sit in the spectator stands across the field from the celebrity tent; and the general regional and metropolitan audience that reads stories about the events in glossy magazines like *Dan's Papers, Hamptons* magazine, *The Hamptons Sheet*, and *Montauk Life*. While this relationship is, in part, generated by pre- and postgame mingling, players also demonstrate their good will toward the general population through their sponsorship of the sport itself. As southeast Indian polo-playing royalty sought to achieve popular legitimacy through sport, players not only participate to show their physical prowess but also express their social grace by "giving back" to their communities (according to the sociologist Peter Parkes, "Sponsorship of new polo grounds, together with the hosting of communal feasts at sporting festivals, were essential policies of populist legitimation for tyrannous princes" in India).[2] Bridgehampton players make up more than a third of the largest individual contributors to the Club, and their own companies often sponsor the tournaments, the teams, and even the publications.[3]

In Bridgehampton, each tournament game is accompanied by a charity auction or drawing that usually benefits a local organization such as Southampton Hospital or Long Island Cares, a group that helps feed homeless people. The charity events, however, were late additions to the polo club's schedule. In early 1996, residents of homes adjacent to the Walentas farm complained to Town Board members that the previous year's polo tournaments had created a "carnival-like" atmosphere, "ruining their entire summer." When the board refused to halt the permit for the 1996 tournament, the residents took the matter to court, filing first with the State Supreme Court (where the suit was dismissed) and then with the Supreme Court's Appellate Division, where they lost as well. Despite their success in the courts, polo enthusiasts recognized that "special events permits" granted by the town were much more flexible if the planned activities were charitable fund-raisers rather than simple amusements or commercial events. [...]

Nowhere is the democratic sentiment more evident at polo matches than when spectators from both sides of the field are asked to enter the field of play between the third and fourth chukkers and stamp down the divots of turf pulled up by horses during the game. Despite the effort of many club professionals and their publications, however, few spectators come primarily to watch the riders swat a ball across an open field. As the journalist Peter Fearon writes, most attendees are engaged "in a less arcane spectator sport: watching each other.... Most of the 'Tent People' are so involved in their own spectacle that the chukker in progress, between [the magazine publisher] Peter Brant's White Birch, ranked fourth in the world, and Revlon, owned by [Wall Street broker-age firm] Bear Stearns partner Mickey Tarnopol, ranked sixth, seems almost an afterthought."[4] Many of the polo enthusiasts speak begrudgingly about the "tent mentality" of the audience.[5] Even the Club's own guide admits that the spectators are as impressive as the polo matches themselves. And, as the stadium announcer periodically reminds the crowd about the day's sponsor, *Town and Country* magazine, the event, too, is "for and about the affluent." [...]

Yet, Bridgehampton spectators have little, if any, interest in team loyalties; polo's popularity is based predominately on the cultural capital of the spectacle itself. Therefore, the appearance of upscale merchandisers suggests a parallel strategy that has more to do with the players' and organizers' own social sophistication than with corporate marketing plans. To be connected with cars such as Mercedes-Benz and BMW, jewelers such as Cartier and Tiffany, or designers such as Calvin Klein, Ralph Lauren, or Giorgio Armani is an important sign of social superiority. In other words, it is the major corporations whose long history of serving a bourgeois clientele offers the tournament players and their entourage "prestige by association." The appearance of these corporate names is a major part of the total spectacle of the event itself, and polo players and guests reap the distinction associated with such icons of upscale lifestyles as much as (if not more than) the corporations themselves benefit from their act of sponsorship. [...]

While the Hamptons are still far from urban, their inherent link to New York City's upscale metropolitan culture is fundamental to this wealthy migrant group's worldview. The spectacle of polo, and its emphasis on publicity and marketing, makes it an important public site for displaying commercial power and prestige. Cultural capital itself is being shopped, and its production and distribution are vital to the creation of the Hamptons as an upscale exurban landscape. [...]

Many of the Latinos who work on the East End live "up-island" (west of the Hamptons), in the towns of Riverhead and Brookhaven. Many Hamptons large-chain retailers such as Caldor (now T.J. Maxx) department stores and King Kullen food markets cannot find enough local low-wage workers and run morning buses to up-island neighborhoods.[6] Similarly, an entire informal economy has risen around transportation as many Latino entrepreneurs have saved money and invested in large passenger vans. These vehicles provide transportation for workers who cannot afford automobiles and who find that the few public buses and trains that do service the area don't stop anywhere near regular job sites. While workers pay between $20 and $30 a week for rides, one driver explained, "I pick them up at home and I pick them up at work, and if I have to take their children to the babysitter I do it, too. All for the same price.... We have to help each other because it's tough to survive earning less than minimum wage."[7] But, even with help from one another, Latino workers can find the East End of Long Island an inhospitable place.

On July 24, 1998, health officials and sheriff's deputies in Brookhaven forced forty-four Latino men out of the two houses they were sharing. The Town Council had received numerous complaints from neighbors who had formed the Farmingville Civic Association (eventually known as Sachem Quality of Life) in an attempt to pressure legislators to rid "their neighborhood" of an increasing number of multifamily rental units occupied by Latinos. While some homeowners claimed they were just as concerned about the workers, who "may have been exploited" by landlords, white neighbors began circulating flyers asking, "Tired of seeing hundreds of people hanging around? Afraid to walk down the streets?" The Association president betrayed this convergence of racism and compassion as she told one *Newsday* reporter, "If you had twenty-two dogs in one small area, people would be concerned on a humane level." But, as one Latino worker explained, "If you close the houses where ten, fifteen, twenty people live, where are you going to find other houses to redistribute them? ... We wait here in the morning because this is a zone the *patrones* know we'll be. If they don't want us on the street they have to help us find a place where we don't bother them."[8] [...]

Even more noticeable to the area's majority population has been the new Latinos' impact on various aspects of social and cultural life. Many clubs throughout the Hamptons have instituted meringue and salsa nights, attracting an almost exclusively Latino population: Large grocery market chains such as King Kullen and IGA have set aside large sections for Spanish and Mexican foods. Small markets and take-out eateries specializing in Mexican and South and Central American cuisine have appeared around the Hamptons. Almost ten years ago, Tom Desmond opened the Embassy Market, a Latino deli in the center of Montauk's business district. As he told a reporter

from *Dan's Papers*, "If you asked me twenty years ago if I'd have a Latino deli in Montauk, I'd say, 'What, are you kidding me? There aren't enough Latinos around.' " But, when Desmond wanted to start a business, he explained, "I was looking for a sign. It was Sunday, and I drove past the baseball field where I used to play little league, and there it was—the field packed with Latinos playing soccer. So I looked up and said, 'Gracias a Dios!' and decided to go ahead and open a deli."[9] Now, Latinos themselves own restaurant-markets such as Chiquita Latina, in Amagansett, and El Mundo Latino, in Southampton, as well as the Azuca nightclub in Bridgehampton. Throughout the East End, Latino workers, entrepreneurs, and their families are changing the permanent character and cultural landscape of the area. And nowhere has this impact been felt as much as on the region's soccer fields and the resulting conflicts over their use.

Since the mid-1980s, many of the Latino workers who settled on the East End have created soccer teams to compete in the official East Hampton summer soccer leagues. In recent years, these leagues have expanded to service the growing interest among predominantly Latino players, resulting in the creation of a Latino League. This popular league has its games on a small field just outside the Montauk central business district. From just about noon until well after 8:00 p.m. on Sundays, the field is filled with two opposing teams and at least three or four dozen spectators cheering them on. Each team is composed primarily of players who share a particular national origin; there is Team Mexico, and Team Costa Rica, and Team Ecuador. The referees speak Spanish, the crowd speaks Spanish, and the sound of Latin music and sometimes the smells of Spanish foods fill the air.

Many of the soccer players say they play the game because it is fun. While soccer has been played in the United States for many years, some players claim it is a "Spanish" sport, imbuing its performance with an ethnic quality or a sense of national or regional pride. Other players openly admit that playing the game reminds them of home and, like other special celebrations or festive occasions, gives them a sense of "who they are." For the spectators, the soccer games are an integral part of the community's activities and represent an intergenerational family event where older men can be seen kicking soccer balls with young boys and girls while women sit in the stands or on picnic blankets and talk. Some watch the players intently, but, not unlike polo, the games share a kind of status as community events, not just as sporting competitions.

While polo's fundamental purpose emanates from its public spectacle, soccer games offer the Latino communities of Colombian, Mexican, Guatemalan, and Ecuadorian people a chance to see and converse with one another, reaffirming both their common heritage and their evolving immigrant identities and communities. Although the players often say that they "play to win," both participants and nonparticipants use the games as a place to create a solidarity based on their shared experiences in a new land and a shared sense of cultural history and origin. There are no major corporate sponsors, no player profiles, no paparazzi, only seventy-five to a hundred primarily Latino immigrants celebrating their struggle to negotiate new lives in a new place. [...]

According to one Colombian player, the merchants in Montauk are happy to have Latinos work for them washing dishes in their kitchens and cleaning rooms in their hotels. Yet, the same employers don't like to see these same workers have fun in town. He asked, "Why do they want us here when we are workers but not when we are soccer players?" A player from Mexico stated that some of the business people are "O.K., and others don't want to look at you." And even in their small communities, white neighbors are always complaining to the police about noise. But he continued, "we always eat and talk and relax outside whenever we can. That is how we do it at home [in Mexico]. Here, people don't like to see so many people hanging around, especially Latinos."[10]

Local media coverage of the games is scanty at best, and when pictures of the game do appear, they rarely have names below the photos of the players. One local sportswriter, Jack Graves, covers the Latino League with regularity and does a meticulous job of keeping track of goal scorers and other stars of the game. In his columns, he has argued that the level of play is excellent and that the League itself should be able to stay in Montauk, despite the local protests. He wrote, "[The League] should remain right where it is, and the powers that be should see to it that the grass is cut regularly."[11] In gratitude for Graves's support, the League organizers put together a special game after the season a few years ago to honor him. The group presented Graves with a trophy that called him a "friend to soccer." More important, though, Graves's reportage treats the Latino players with respect and gives their presence a kind of legitimacy; he has been a friend to them as well as their game.

As soccer leagues on the East End continue to grow as the Latino population grows, government officials will be faced with increasing conflicts over land use. Some contests will be fought over which sports are permitted in which locations. Other battles will occur because many white residents are unfamiliar with or intolerant of the kinds of cultural practices that Latino immigrants bring with them. And struggles will take place because some image-conscious merchants and racist home-owners would prefer that Latinos be as invisible in their leisure time as they are at work. As the recent economic slowdown wreaks havoc on the kind of second-circuit economic investment represented by some of the Hamptons exurban development, tensions over jobs and wages may fuel struggles that will play themselves out in social and cultural conflicts over sports and leisure activities.

Polo and soccer represent a complex set of cultural practices and politics for the fastest-growing populations on Long Island's East End. The permanent migration of the hyper-bourgeoisie and of Latinos to the region has already resulted in a variety of changes in both the physical and the cultural landscape as large-scale economic and social transformations and regional and local dynamics converge. The ways in which the people of the Hamptons face these changes will determine future government policies, as well as the use and design of public space. Part of the process will reflect the struggles of new populations to establish their own sense of identity and place. For polo players, armed with public relations experts and the economic resources to conquer huge tracts of land, the image of the Hamptons will continue to reflect and reinforce their elite identity of celebrity and privilege as they claim their historical ascendancy and a post-modern sense of natural right. The soccer players whose hands work the land, clean the mansions, and serve the wealthy, however, will continue to struggle to shape the region's everyday physical environment in a way that reflects their own experience, culture, pride, and dignity.

NOTES

1. H. E. Chehabi and A. Guttmann, "From Iran to All of Asia: The Origin and Diffusion of Polo," in *Sport in Asian Society: Past and Present*, edited by Fan Hong (London: Frank Cass, 2003), p. 390.
2. David Rubin, Interview with Author, New York, NY, 15 August 1999.
3. Peter Parkes, "Indigenous Polo and the Politics of Regional Identity in Northern Pakistan," in *Sport, Identity and Ethnicity*, edited by J. MacClancy (New York: Berg, 1996).
4. David Rubin, Interview with Author, New York, NY, 15 August 1999.
5. Anthony Rosalia, Interview with Author, Southampton, NY, 3 August 1998; Quentin Dante, Interview with the Author, Bridgehampton, NY, 6 July 1998.
6. Caldor went out of business in the Bridgehampton Commons in 2000 and has been replaced by K Mart.
7. *Newsday*, 2 August 1998.
8. *Newsday*, 24 August 1998.
9. *Dan's Papers*, 10 June 1999.
10. Interviews with soccer players.
11. *East Hampton Star*, 7 October 1993.

10-1. *GARDEN CITIES OF TO-MORROW* (1902)

Ebenezer Howard

Source: Ebenezer Howard, *Garden Cities of To-Morrow* (London: Swan Sonnenschein & Company, 1902).

EDITORS' INTRODUCTION

English-born Ebenezer Howard (1850–1928), created a powerful legacy with his idea of mixing open pastoral spaces with urban living in his plan for "garden cities." Howard, deeply influenced by the ideas of Edward Bellamy's 1888 novel *Looking Backward* **[see Document 10.2]**, penned his visionary ideas for a new city with *Garden Cities of To-Morrow*, originally published as *To-morrow: A Peaceful Path to Real Reform* (1898), and founded the Garden Cities Association in 1899. His publication brought his ideas to the general public and two garden cities, Letchworth Garden City and Welwyn Garden City were built in the United Kingdom during his lifetime. America's 1930s greenbelt towns, England's New Town's Act of 1946, and the open land movement in modern American cities also drew upon Howard's planning ideas. The garden cities, greenbelt towns, and England's new towns were built outside of major urban areas like London and Washington, D.C. Critics of these newly planned communities point out that they draw people

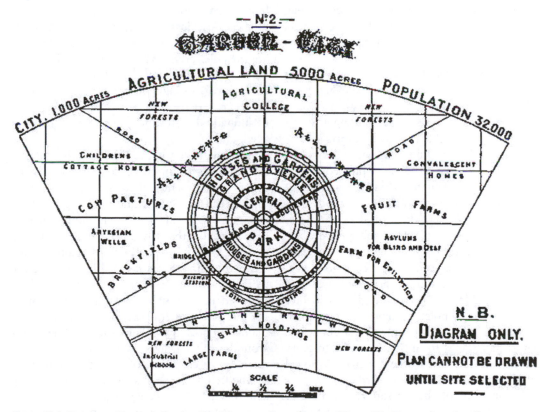

Figure 10.1 Ebenezer Howard, Garden-City Diagram, From *Garden Cities of To-Morrow* (London: Swan Sonnenschein & Company, 1902).

and resources away from nearby traditional urban centers. Although designed to be self-contained urban villages, they often become bedroom communities of major metropolitan areas and serve to intensify urban sprawl. New Urbanists who tout projects within existing cities (often referred to as "infill projects") are in fact similarly criticized for the high number of New Urbanist developments built on remote greenfields.

Garden City, which is to be built near the centre of the 6,000 acres, covers an area of 1,000 acres, or a sixth part of the 6,000 acres, and might be of circular form, 1,240 yards (or nearly three-quarters of a mile) from centre to circumference.

[...]

Six magnificent boulevards—each 120 feet wide—traverse the city from centre to circumference, dividing it into six equal parts or wards. In the centre is a circular space containing about five and a half acres, laid out as a beautiful and well-watered garden; and, surrounding this garden, each standing in its own ample grounds, are the larger public buildings—town hall, principal concert and lecture hall, theatre, library, museum, picture-gallery, and hospital.

The rest of the large space encircled by the 'Crystal Palace' is a public park, containing 145 acres, which includes ample recreation grounds within very easy access of all the people.

Running all round the Central Park (except where it is intersected by the boulevards) is a wide glass arcade called the 'Crystal Palace', opening on to the park. This building is in wet weather one of the favourite resorts of the people, whilst the knowledge that its bright shelter is ever close at hand tempts people into Central Park, even in the most doubtful of weathers. Here manufactured goods are exposed for sale, and here most of that class of shopping which requires the joy of deliberation and selection is done. The space enclosed by the Crystal Palace is, however, a good deal larger than is required for these purposes, and a considerable part of it is used as a Winter Garden—the whole forming a permanent exhibition of a most attractive character, whilst its circular form brings it near to every dweller in the town—the furthest removed inhabitant being within 600 yards.

Passing out of the Crystal Palace on our way to the outer ring of the town, we cross Fifth Avenue—lined, as are all the roads of the town, with trees—fronting which, and looking on to the Crystal Palace, we find a ring of very excellently built houses, each standing in its own ample grounds; and, as we continue our walk, we observe that the houses are for the most part built either in concentric rings, facing the various avenues (as the circular roads are termed), or fronting the boulevards and roads which all converge to the centre of the town. Asking the friend who accompanies us on our journey what the population of this little city may be, we are told about 30,000 in the city itself, and about 2,000 in the agricultural estate, and that there are in the town 5,500 building lots of an average size of 20 feet x 130 feet-the minimum space allotted for the purpose being 20 x 100. Noticing the very varied architecture and design which the houses and groups of houses display—some having common gardens and co-operative kitchens—we learn that general observance of street line or harmonious departure from it are the chief points as to house building, over which the municipal authorities exercise control, for, though proper sanitary arrangements are strictly enforced, the fullest measure of individual taste and preference is encouraged.

Walking still toward the outskirts of the town, we come upon 'Grand Avenue'. This avenue is fully entitled to the name it bears, for it is 420 feet wide, and, forming a belt of green upwards of three miles long, divides that part of the town which lies outside Central Park into two belts. It really constitutes an additional park of 115 acres—a park which is within 240 yards of the furthest removed inhabitant. In this splendid avenue six sites, each of four acres, are occupied by public schools and their surrounding playgrounds and gardens, while other sites are reserved for churches, of such denominations as the religious beliefs of the people may determine, to be erected and maintained out of the funds of the worshippers and their friends. We observe that the houses fronting on Grand Avenue have departed... from the general plan of concentric rings, and, in order to ensure a longer line of frontage on Grand Avenue, are arranged in crescents—thus also to the eye yet further enlarging the already splendid width of Grand Avenue.

On the outer ring of the town are factories, warehouses, dairies, markets, coal yards, timber yards, etc., all fronting on the circle railway, which encompasses the whole town, and which has sidings connecting it with a main line of railway which passes through the estate. This arrangement enables goods to be loaded direct into trucks from the warehouses and workshops, and so sent by railway to distant markets, or to be taken direct from the trucks into the warehouses or factories; thus not only effecting a very great saving in regard to packing and cartage, and reducing to a minimum loss from breakage, but also, by reducing the traffic on the roads of the town, lessening to a very marked extent the cost of their maintenance. The smoke fiend is kept well within bounds in Garden City; for all machinery is driven by electric energy, with the result that the cost of electricity for lighting and other purposes is greatly reduced.

10-2. *LOOKING BACKWARD* (1887)

Edward Bellamy

Source: Edward Bellamy, *Looking Backward, 2000–1887* (Boston: Ticknor and Company, 1887).

EDITORS' INTRODUCTION

Edward Bellamy's bestselling *Looking Backward, 2000–1887* launched the Nationalism movement that called for a reformation of U.S. social systems, including the physical reorganization of the city. Born in Chicopee Falls, Massachusetts in 1850, Bellamy attended Union College in Schenectady, New York. Bellamy's work, which is now a staple in college classes, offers ideas for a socialist overhaul of society. The main character of the novel, the insomniac Julian West, seeks the services of a "quack" doctor who hypnotizes him to sleep. The year is 1887, and West is a thirty-year-old living in Boston. Unfortunately, during the night his house burns down, leaving West in a trance state in his secretive basement chamber. He is not awakened until the year 2000. At first West believes he is the subject of an elaborate hoax. He is startled to find the city much transformed. Rather than the economic hardships and labor struggles of 1887, there are no labor issues of any kind. Men (Bellamy does not consider the possible employment of women) toil at labor they are best suited for, and the system of national ownership of industry works so cleanly that no labor shortages exist. In the first scene, West's host, Dr. Leete, shows the city to his incredulous time-travelling guest. In the second excerpt, West dines with his host and his daughter Edith Leete, while learning more about the absence of class distinction in the modern society. Bellamy's imagined society of 2000 is a far cry from the reality of class division as depicted by sociologist Corey Dolgon, in his work on the Hamptons. **[See Corey Dolgon's "Polo Ponies and Penalty Kicks" essay in Part X.]**

He [Dr. Leete] led the way up two flights of stairs and then up a shorter one, which landed us upon a belvedere on the house-top. "Be pleased to look around you," he said, as we reached the platform, "and tell me if this is the Boston of the nineteenth century."

At my feet lay a great city. Miles of broad streets, shaded by trees and lined with fine buildings, for the most part not in continuous blocks but set in larger or smaller inclosures [*sic*], stretched in every direction. Every quarter contained large open squares filled with trees, among which statues glistened and fountains flashed in the late afternoon sun. Public buildings of a colossal size and an architectural grandeur unparalleled in my day raised their stately piles on every side. Surely I had never seen this city nor one comparable to it before. Raising my eyes at last towards the horizon, I looked westward. That blue ribbon winding away to the sunset, was it not the sinuous Charles? I looked east; Boston harbor stretched before me within its headlands, not one of its green islets missing.

I knew then that I had been told the truth concerning the prodigious thing which had befallen me.

[…]

The waiter, a fine-looking young fellow, wearing a slightly distinctive uniform, now made his appearance. I observed him closely, as it was the first time I had been able to study particularly the bearing of one of the enlisted members of the industrial army. This young man, I knew from what I had been told, must be highly educated, and the equal, socially and in all respects, of those he served. But it was perfectly evident that to neither side was the situation in the slightest degree embarrassing. Dr. Leete addressed the young man in a tone devoid, of course, as any gentlemen's would be, of superciliousness, but at the same time not in any way deprecatory, while the manner of the young man was simply that of a person intent on discharging correctly the task he was engaged in, equally without familiarity or obsequiousness. It was, in fact, the manner of a soldier on duty, but without the military stiffness. As the youth left the room, I said, "I cannot get over my wonder at seeing a young man like that serving so contentedly in a menial position."

"What is the word 'menial'? I never heard it," said Edith.

[…]

"To understand why Edith is surprised," he [Dr. Leete] said, "you must know that nowadays it is an axiom of ethics that to accept a service from another which we would be unwilling to return in kind, if need were, is like borrowing with the intention of not repaying, while to enforce such a service by taking advantage of the poverty or necessity of a person would be an outrage like forcible robbery. It is the worst thing about any system which divides men, or allows them to be divided, into classes and castes, that it weakens the sense of a common humanity. Unequal distribution of wealth, and still more effectually, unequal opportunities of educa-

tion and culture, divided society in your day into classes which in many respects regarded each other as distinct races. There is not, after all, such a difference as might appear between our ways of looking at this question of service. Ladies and gentlemen of the cultured class in your day would no more have permitted persons of their own class to render them services they would scorn to return than we would permit anybody to do so. The poor and the uncultured, however, they looked upon as of another kind from themselves. The equal wealth and equal opportunities of culture which all persons now enjoy have simply made us all members of one class, which corresponds to the most fortunate class with you. Until this equality of condition had come to pass, the idea of the solidarity of humanity, the brother hood [sic] of all men, could never have become the real conviction and practical principle of action it is nowadays. In your day the same phrases were indeed used, but they were phrases merely."

"Do the waiters, also, volunteer?"

"No," replied Dr. Leete. "The waiters are young men in the unclassified grade of the industrial army who are assignable to all sorts of miscellaneous occupations not requiring special skill. Waiting on table is one of these, and every young recruit is given a taste of it. I myself served as a waiter for several months in this very dining-house some forty years ago. Once more you must remember that there is recognized no sort of difference between the dignity of the different sorts of work required by the nation. The individual is never regarded, nor regards himself, as the servant of those he serves, nor is he in any way dependent upon them. It is always the nation which he is serving. No difference is recognized between a waiter's function and those of any other worker. The fact that his is a personal service is indifferent from our point of view. So is a doctor's. I should as soon expect our waiter to-day to look down on me because I served him as a doctor, as think of looking down on him because he serves me as a waiter."

After dinner my entertainers conducted me about the building, of which the extent, the magnificent architecture and richness of embellishment, astonished me. It seemed that it was not merely a dining-hall, but likewise a great pleasure-house and social rendezvous of the quarter, and no appliance of entertainment or recreation seemed lacking.

"You find illustrated here," said Dr. Leete, when I had expressed my admiration, "what I said to you in our first conversation, when you were looking out over the city, as to the splendor of our public and common life as compared with the simplicity of our private and home life, and the contrast which, in this respect, the twentieth century bears to the nineteenth century. To save ourselves useless burdens, we have as little gear about us at home as is consistent with comfort, but the social side of our life is ornate and luxurious beyond anything the world ever knew before. All the industrial and professional guilds have clubhouses as extensive as this, as well as county, mountain, and seaside houses for sport and rest in recreation."

10-3. CHARTER OF THE NEW URBANISM (1996)

Congress for the New Urbanism

Source: Congress for the New Urbanism, www.cnu.org/charter. Copyright 1996, Congress for the New Urbanism.

EDITORS' INTRODUCTION

New Urbanism arose in the early 1990s through the efforts of a small group of architects who drafted a set of principles emphasizing diversity, pluralism, and environmentally friendly design in local and regional planning. These architects formally incorporated as the nonprofit group Congress for the New Urbanism (CNU) and held their first meeting in 1993. At their fourth annual gathering in 1996, the organization ratified the Charter of the New Urbanism with twenty-seven principles to guide public policy makers, planners, architects, and others committed to reducing automobile sprawl and the inefficient use of space by building more viable and sustainable communities. For a visual representation of CNU principles, see **Figure 10.2 The Rural-Urban Transect**.

Charter for the New Urbanism

The Congress for the New Urbanism views disinvestment in central cities, the spread of placeless sprawl, increasing separation by race and income, environmental deterioration, loss of agricultural lands and wilderness, and the erosion of society's built heritage as one interrelated community-building challenge.

We stand for the restoration of existing urban centers and towns within coherent metropolitan regions, the reconfiguration of sprawling suburbs into communities of real neighborhoods and diverse districts, the conservation of natural environments, and the preservation of our built legacy.

We recognize that physical solutions by themselves will not solve social and economic problems, but neither can economic vitality, community stability, and environmental health be sustained without a coherent and supportive physical framework.

We advocate the restructuring of public policy and development practices to support the following principles: neighborhoods should be diverse in use and population; communities should be designed for the pedestrian and transit as well as the car; cities and towns should be shaped by physically defined and universally accessible public spaces and community institutions; urban places should be framed by architecture and landscape design that celebrate local history, climate, ecology, and building practice.

We represent a broad-based citizenry, composed of public and private sector leaders, community activists, and multidisciplinary professionals. We are committed to reestablishing the relationship between the art of building and the making of community, through citizen-based participatory planning and design.

We dedicate ourselves to reclaiming our homes, blocks, streets, parks, neighborhoods, districts, towns, cities, regions, and environment.

We assert the following principles to guide public policy, development practice, urban planning, and design:

The Region: Metropolis, City, and Town

1. Metropolitan regions are finite places with geographic boundaries derived from topography, watersheds, coastlines, farmlands, regional parks, and river basins. The metropolis is made of multiple centers that are cities, towns, and villages, each with its own identifiable center and edges.

2. The metropolitan region is a fundamental economic unit of the contemporary world. Governmental cooperation, public policy, physical planning, and economic strategies must reflect this new reality.

3. The metropolis has a necessary and fragile relationship to its agrarian hinterland and natural landscapes. The relationship is environmental, economic, and cultural. Farmland and nature are as important to the metropolis as the garden is to the house.

4. Development patterns should not blur or eradicate the edges of the metropolis. Infill development within existing urban areas conserves environmental resources, economic investment, and social fabric, while reclaiming marginal and abandoned areas. Metropolitan regions should develop strategies to encourage such infill development over peripheral expansion.

5. Where appropriate, new development contiguous to urban boundaries should be organized as neighborhoods and districts, and be integrated with the existing urban pattern. Noncontiguous development should be organized as towns and villages with their own urban edges, and planned for a jobs/housing balance, not as bedroom suburbs.

6. The development and redevelopment of towns and cities should respect historical patterns, precedents, and boundaries.

7. Cities and towns should bring into proximity a broad spectrum of public and private uses to support a regional economy that benefits people of all incomes. Affordable housing should be distributed throughout the region to match job opportunities and to avoid concentrations of poverty.

8. The physical organization of the region should be supported by a framework of transportation alternatives. Transit, pedestrian, and bicycle systems should maximize access and mobility throughout the region while reducing dependence upon the automobile.

9. Revenues and resources can be shared more cooperatively among the municipalities and centers within regions to avoid destructive competition for tax base and to promote rational coordination of transportation, recreation, public services, housing, and community institutions.

The Neighborhood, the District, and the Corridor

1. The neighborhood, the district, and the corridor are the essential elements of development and redevelopment in the metropolis. They form identifiable areas that encourage citizens to take responsibility for their maintenance and evolution.

2. Neighborhoods should be compact, pedestrian-friendly, and mixed-use. Districts generally emphasize a special single use, and should follow the principles of neighborhood design when possible. Corridors are regional connectors of neighborhoods and districts; they range from boulevards and rail lines to rivers and parkways.

3. Many activities of daily living should occur within walking distance, allowing independence to those who do not drive, especially the elderly and the young. Interconnected networks of streets should be designed to encourage walking, reduce the number and length of automobile trips, and conserve energy.

4. Within neighborhoods, a broad range of housing types and price levels can bring people of diverse ages, races, and incomes into daily interaction, strengthening the personal and civic bonds essential to an authentic community.

5. Transit corridors, when properly planned and coordinated, can help organize metropolitan structure and revitalize urban centers. In contrast, highway corridors should not displace investment from existing centers.

6. Appropriate building densities and land uses should be within walking distance of transit stops, permitting public transit to become a viable alternative to the automobile.

7. Concentrations of civic, institutional, and commercial activity should be embedded in neighborhoods and districts, not isolated in remote, single-use complexes. Schools should be sized and located to enable children to walk or bicycle to them.

8. The economic health and harmonious evolution of neighborhoods, districts, and corridors can be improved through graphic urban design codes that serve as predictable guides for change.

9. A range of parks, from tot-lots and village greens to ballfields and community gardens, should be distributed within neighborhoods. Conservation areas and open lands should be used to define and connect different neighborhoods and districts.

The Block, the Street, and the Building

1. A primary task of all urban architecture and landscape design is the physical definition of streets and public spaces as places of shared use.

2. Individual architectural projects should be seamlessly linked to their surroundings. This issue transcends style.

3. The revitalization of urban places depends on safety and security. The design of streets and buildings should reinforce safe environments, but not at the expense of accessibility and openness.

4. In the contemporary metropolis, development must adequately accommodate automobiles. It should do so in ways that respect the pedestrian and the form of public space.

5. Streets and squares should be safe, comfortable, and interesting to the pedestrian. Properly configured, they encourage walking and enable neighbors to know each other and protect their communities.

6. Architecture and landscape design should grow from local climate, topography, history, and building practice.

7. Civic buildings and public gathering places require important sites to reinforce community identity and the culture of democracy. They deserve distinctive form, because their role is different from that of other buildings and places that constitute the fabric of the city.

8. All buildings should provide their inhabitants with a clear sense of location, weather and time. Natural methods of heating and cooling can be more resource-efficient than mechanical systems.

9. Preservation and renewal of historic buildings, districts, and landscapes affirm the continuity and evolution of urban society.

10-4. "AMERICAN MURDER MYSTERY" (2008)

Hanna Rosin

Source: Hanna Rosin, "American Murder Mystery," *The Atlantic* (July/August, 2008): 48–50.

EDITORS' INTRODUCTION

The nation's overall crime rate has declined since the early 1990s, with the violent crime rate for New York City at its lowest level since the early 1960s. The economic downturn that began in the latter part of the George W. Bush administration, also known as the "Great Recession," may have been responsible for some changes in the pattern of crime statistics. According to experts cited by Hanna Rosin in her highly controversial article "American Murder Mystery," violent crime has increased in several communities. Hanna Rosin asks if the Section 8 housing voucher program, supported by the federal government, bears any responsibility for the rise in crime. The release of her article created a stir in housing policy circles and evoked numerous critiques of the attempt to pin the cause of crime on a generally successful program. Most contentious is her assertion that we reconsider the premise that mixing neighborhoods by income levels always results in positive outcomes.

In the most literal sense, the national effort to diffuse poverty has succeeded. Since 1990, the number of Americans living in neighborhoods of concentrated poverty—meaning that at least 40 percent of households are below the federal poverty level—has declined by 24 percent. But this doesn't tell the whole story. Recently, the housing expert George Galster, of Wayne State University, analyzed the shifts in urban poverty and published his results in a paper called "A Cautionary Tale." While fewer Americans live in high-poverty neighborhoods, increasing numbers now live in places with "moderate" poverty rates, meaning rates of 20 to 40 percent. This pattern is not necessarily better, either for poor people trying to break away from bad neighborhoods or for cities, Galster explains. His paper compares two scenarios: a city split into high-poverty and low-poverty areas, and a city dominated by median-poverty ones. The latter arrangement is likely to produce more bad neighborhoods and more total crime, he concludes, based on a computer model of how social dysfunction spreads.

Studies show that recipients of Section8 vouchers have tended to choose moderately poor neighborhoods that were already on the decline, not low-poverty neighborhoods. One recent study publicized by HUD warned that policy makers should lower their expectations, because voucher recipients seemed not to be spreading out, as they had hoped, but clustering together. Galster theorizes that every neighborhood has its tipping point—a threshold well below a 40 percent poverty rate—beyond which crime explodes and other severe social problems set in. Pushing a greater number of neighborhoods past that tipping point is likely to produce more total crime. In 2003, the Brookings Institution published a list of the 15 cities where the number of high-poverty neighborhoods had declined the most. In recent years, most of those cities have also shown up as among the most violent in the U.S., according to FBI data.

The "Gathering Storm" report that worried over an upcoming epidemic of violence was inspired by a call from the police chief of Louisville, Kentucky, who'd seen crime rising regionally and wondered what was going on. Simultaneously, the University of Louisville criminologist Geetha Suresh was tracking local patterns of violent crime. She had begun her work years before, going blind into the research: she had just arrived from India, had never heard of a housing project, had no idea which were the bad parts of town, and was clueless about the finer points of American racial sensitivities. In her research, Suresh noticed a recurring pattern, one that emerged first in the late 1990s, then again around 2002. A particularly violent neighborhood would suddenly go cold, and crime would heat up in several new neighborhoods. In each case, Suresh has now confirmed, the first hot spots were the neighborhoods around huge housing projects, and the later ones were places where people had moved when the projects were torn down. From that, she drew the obvious conclusion: "Crime is going along with them." Except for being hand-drawn, Suresh's map matching housing patterns with crime looks exactly like criminologist Richard Janikowski and sociologist Phyllis Betts's.

Nobody would claim vouchers, or any single factor, as the sole cause of rising crime. Crime did not rise in every city where housing projects came down. In cities where it did, many factors contributed: unemployment, gangs, rapid gentrification that dislocated tens of thousands of poor people not living in the projects. Still, researchers around the country are seeing the same basic pattern: projects coming down in inner cities and crime pushing outward, in many cases destabilizing cities or their surrounding areas. Dennis Rosenbaum, a criminologist at the University of Illinois at Chicago, told me that after the high-rises came down in Chicago, suburbs to the south and west—including formerly quiet ones—began to see spikes in crime; nearby Maywood's murder rate has nearly doubled in the past two years. In Atlanta, which almost always makes the top-10 crime list, crime is now scattered widely, just as it is in Memphis and Louisville.

In some places, the phenomenon is hard to detect, but there may be a simple reason: in cities with tight housing markets, Section8 recipients generally can't afford to live within the city limits, and sometimes they even move to different states. New York, where the rate of violent crime has plummeted, appears to have pushed many of its poor out to New Jersey, where violent crime has increased in nearby cities and suburbs. Washington, D.C., has exported some of its crime to surrounding counties in Maryland and Virginia. Much research has been done on the spread of gangs into the suburbs. Jeff Rojek, a criminologist at the University of South Carolina, issued a report in 2006 showing that serious gang activity had spread to eight suburban counties around the state, including Florence County, home to the city of Florence, which was ranked the most violent place in America the year after Memphis was. In his fieldwork, he said, the police complained of "migrant gangs" from the housing projects, and many departments seemed wholly unprepared to respond.

After the first wave of housing-project demolition in Memphis, in 1997, crime spread out, but did not immediately increase. (It takes time for criminals to make new connections and to develop "comfort zones," Janikowski told me.) But in 2005, another wave of project demolitions pushed the number of people displaced from public housing to well over 20,000, and crime skyrocketed. Janikowski felt there were deep structural issues behind the increase, ones that the city was not prepared to handle. Old gangs—the Gangster Disciples and the LeMoyne Gardens gang—had long since reformed and gotten comfortable. Ex-convicts recently released from prison had taken up residence with girlfriends or wives or families who'd moved to the new neighborhoods. Working-class people had begun moving out to the suburbs farther east, and more recipients of Section8 vouchers were taking their place. Now many neighborhoods were reaching their tipping points.

Chaotic new crime patterns in suburbia caught the police off guard. Gang members who'd moved to North Memphis might now have cousins southeast of the city, allowing them to target the whole vast area in between and hide out with relatives far from the scene of the crime. Memphis covers an area as large as New York City, but with one-seventeenth as many police officers, and a much lower cop-to-citizen ratio. And routine policing is more difficult in the semi-suburbs. Dealers sell out of fenced-in backyards, not on exposed street corners. They have cars to escape in, and a landscape to blend into. Shrubbery is a constant headache for the police; they've taken to asking that bushes be cut down so suspects can't duck behind them.

10-5. REFLECTING ABSENCE (2003)

Michael Arad and Peter Walker

Source: Lower Manhattan Development Corporation, World Trade Center Site Memorial Competition, www.wtcsitememorial.org. Courtesy of the Lower Manhattan Development Corporation and the Department of Housing and Urban Development.

EDITORS' INTRODUCTION

In April 2003, the Lower Manhattan Development Corporation (LMDC) announced a public competition for the design of the World Trade Center Memorial. The competition called for plans for the site of the former World Trade Center, which was destroyed in the tragic events of the terrorist attack of September 11, 2001. The LMDC received 5,201 entries from sixty-three nations across six continents, making this the largest design competition in history. In January 2004, the World Trade Center Memorial jury awarded first prize to Michael Arad and Peter Walker for their design "Reflecting Absence."

This memorial proposes a space that resonates with the feelings of loss and absence that were generated by the destruction of the World Trade Center and the taking of thousands of lives on September 11, 2001 and February 26, 1993. It is located in a field of trees that is interrupted by two large voids containing recessed pools. The pools and the ramps that surround them encompass the footprints of the twin towers. A cascade of water that describes the perimeter of each square feeds the pools with a continuous stream. They are large voids, open and visible reminders of the absence.

The surface of the memorial plaza is punctuated by the linear rhythms of rows of deciduous trees, forming informal clusters, clearings and groves. This surface consists of a composition of stone pavers, plantings and low ground cover. Through its annual cycle of rebirth, the living park extends and deepens the experience of the memorial.

Bordering each pool is a pair of ramps that lead down to the memorial spaces. Descending into the memorial, visitors are removed from the sights and sounds of the city and immersed in a cool darkness. As they proceed, the sound of water falling grows louder, and more daylight filters in from below. At the bottom of their descent, they find themselves behind a thin curtain of water, staring out at an enormous pool. Surrounding this pool is a continuous ribbon of names. The enormity of this space and the multitude of names that form this endless ribbon underscore the vast scope of the destruction. Standing there at the water's edge, looking at a pool of water that is flowing away into an abyss, a visitor to the site can sense that what is beyond this curtain of water and ribbon of names is inaccessible.

The names of the deceased will be arranged in no particular order around the pools. After carefully considering different arrangements, I have found that any arrangement that tries to impose meaning through physical adjacency will cause grief and anguish to people who might be excluded from that process, furthering the sense of loss that they are already suffering.

The haphazard brutality of the attacks is reflected in the arrangement of names, and no attempt is made to impose order upon this suffering. The selfless sacrifices of rescue workers could be acknowledged with their agency's insignia next to their names. Visitors to the site, including family members and friends of the deceased, would be guided by on-site staff or a printed directory to the specific location of each name. For those whose deceased were never physically identified, the location of the name marks a spot that is their own.

In between the two pools is a short passageway that links them at this lower level. A single alcove is located along this passageway, containing a small dais where visitors can light a candle or leave an artifact in memory of loved ones. Across from it, in a small chamber, visitors might pause and contemplate. This space provides for gatherings, quiet reflection, and memorial services.

Along the western edge of the site, a deep fissure exposes the slurry wall from plaza level to bedrock and provides access via a stairway. Descending alongside its battered surfaces, visitors will witness the massive expanse of the original foundations. The entrance to the underground interpretive center is located at bedrock. Here visitors could view many preserved artifacts from the twin towers: twisted steel beams, a crushed fire truck, and personal effects. The underground interpretive center would contain exhibition areas as well as lecture halls and a research library.

In contrast with the public mandate of the underground interpretive center is the very private nature of the room for unidentified remains. It is situated at bedrock at the north tower footprint. Here a large stone vessel forms a centerpiece for the unidentified remains. A large opening in the ceiling connects this space to the sky above, and the sound of water shelters the space from the city. Family members can gather here for moments of private contemplation. It is a personal space for remembrance.

The memorial plaza is designed to be a mediating space; it belongs both to the city and to the memorial. Located at street level to allow for its integration into the fabric of the city, the plaza encourages the use of this space by New Yorkers on a daily basis. The memorial grounds will not be isolated from the rest of the city; they will be a living part of it.

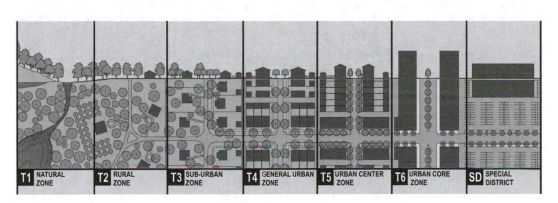

Figure 10.2 The Rural-Urban Transect. Source: Courtesy of Duany Plater-Zyberk & Company.

A transect is a cut or cross section of the environment that illustrates diverse features and habitats. In 2003, the planning firm of Duany Plater-Zyberk & Company, new urbanist visionaries, developed the "Rural-Urban Transect" with six T-zones (transect zones) and one special district. The transect is for use on zoning maps in conjunction with their "SmartCode." New urbanists hope to redesign urban space in a manner that minimizes sprawl and promotes close-knit communities. They envision the SmartCode as an alternative to traditional zoning regulations. Tzones are defined by the ratio and intensity of their natural, built, and social components. The top layer of the "Rural-Urban Transect" is a ground-level view of each zone, while the middle and bottom portions illustrate how each zone appears from an aerial perspective.

Figure 10.3 Celebration, Florida, 2008. Photograph by Lisa Krissoff Boehm.

REFERENCE AND SUGGESTED BIBLIOGRAPHY

*Books may overlap categorization and are generally listed under one heading.

I. Overview Works

Anthologies

Binder, Frederick and David M. Reimers. *The Way We Lived: Essays and Documents in American Social History, Volume I: 1607–1877*. Second Edition. Lexington: D.C. Heath, 1993.

Callow, Alexander B. Jr., ed. *American Urban History: An Interpretive Reader With Comments*. Third Edition. New York: Oxford University Press, 1982.

Chudacoff, Howard P. and Judith E. Smith. *The Evolution of American Urban Society*. Sixth Edition. Upper Saddle River, NJ: Pearson Prentice Hall, 2005.

Jackson, Kenneth and Stanley K. Schultz, eds. *Cities in American History*. New York: Knopf, 1972.

Kantor, Paul and Dennis R. Judd. *American Urban Politics in a Global Age: The Reader*. Fifth Edition. White Plains, NY: Pearson Longman, 2008.

Mohl, Raymond. *The Making of Urban America*. Wilmington: SR Books, 1997.

Sennett, Richard, ed. *Classic Essays on the Culture of Cities*. Upper Saddle River, NJ: Pearson Prentice Hall, 1969.

Sennett, Richard and Stephan Thernstrom. *Nineteenth-Century Cities: Essays in the New Urban History*. New Haven: Yale University Press, 1969.

Theory

Abrahamson, Mark. *Urban Enclaves: Identity and Place in America*. New York: St. Martin's Press, 1996.

Anderson, Benedict. *Imagined Communities: Reflection on the Origins and Spread of Nationalism*. New York: Verso, 1983.

Boyer, M. Christine. *The City of Collective Memory: Its Historical Imagery and Architectural Entertainments*. Cambridge, MA: MIT Press, 1996.

——. *CyberCities*. Princeton: Princeton Architectural Press, 1996.

Channing, Edward. *A History of the United States*. New York: Macmillan Company, 1922.

Durkheim, Emile. *The Division of Labor in Society*. New York: The Free Press, 1984.

Ghent Urban Studies Team. *Post Ex Sub Dis: Urban Fragmentations and Constructions*. Rotterdam: 010 Publishers, 2002.

Hall, Peter (Sir). *Cities in Civilization*. New York: Pantheon Books, 1998.

Harvey, David. *The Condition of Postmodernity: An Enquiry into the Origins of Cultural Change*. Cambridge, MA: Blackwell, 1990.

Hozic, Aida. *Hollyworld: Space, Power, and Fantasy in the American Economy*. Ithaca: Cornell University Press, 2001.

Lears, T.J. Jackson. *No Place of Grace: Antimodernism and the Transformation of American Culture, 1880–1920*. New York: Pantheon Books, 1981.

Levine, Lawrence W. *Highbrow/Lowbrow: The Emergence of Cultural Hierarchy in America*. Cambridge, MA: Harvard University Press, 1988.

Marsh, Margaret, "Old Forms, New Visions: New Directions in United States Urban History," *Pennsylvania History* 59, no. 1 (1992): 21–40.

Marx, Leo. *The Machine in the Garden: Technology and the Pastoral Ideal in America*. New York: Oxford University Press, 1964.

Mumford, Lewis. *The Culture of Cities*. New York: Harcourt, Brace & Company, 1938.

Sassen, Saskia. *Cities in a World Economy*. New York: Pine Forge Press, 2006.

——. *The Global City: New York, London, Tokyo*. Princeton: Princeton University Press, 2001.

Scott, Allen and Edward Soja. *The City: Los Angeles and Urban Theory at the End of the Twentieth Century*. Berkeley: University of California Press, 1998.

Sennett, Richard. *The Fall of Public Man*. New York: W.W. Norton, 1976.

Smith, Henry Nash. *Virgin Land: The American West as Symbol and Myth*. Cambridge, MA: Harvard University Press, 1978.

Soja, Edward. *Postmetropolis: Critical Studies of Cities and Regions*. Wiley-Blackwell, 2000.

——. *Thirdspace: Journeys to Los Angeles and Other Real-and-Imagined Places*. Hoboken: Wiley-Blackwell, 1996.

Sorkin, Michael, ed. *Variations on a Theme Park: The New American City and the End of Public Space*. New York: Hill and Wang, 1992.

Strong, Josiah. *Our Country: Its Possible Future and Its Present Crisis*. New York: Baker & Taylor, 1885.

Trachtenberg, Alan. *The Incorporation of America: Culture and Society in the Gilded Age*. New York: Hill and Wang, 1982.

Turner, Frederick Jackson. *The Frontier in American History*. Tucson: The University of Arizona Press, 1986.

White, Morton and Lucia White. *The Intellectual Versus the City: From Thomas Jefferson to Frank Lloyd Wright*. Cambridge, MA: Harvard University Press and MIT Press, 1962.

Wiebe, Robert H. *The Search for Order, 1877–1920*. New York: Hill and Wang, 1967.

Zukin, Sharon. *The Culture of Cities*. Cambridge, MA: Blackstone Publishers, 1995.

——. *Landscapes of Power: From Detroit to Disney World*. Berkeley: University of California Press, 1991.

Urban Overviews & General U.S. History

Bender, Thomas. *Community and Social Change in America*. Piscataway: Rutgers, 1978.

Fishman, Robert. *Urban Utopias in the Twentieth Century*. Boston: MIT Press, 1982.

Gillette, Howard, Jr. and Zane L. Miller, eds. *American Urbanism: Historiographical Review*. New York: Greenwood Press, 1987.

Goldfield, David. *Cotton Fields and Skyscrapers: Southern City and Region, 1607–1980*. Baton Rouge: Louisiana State University Press, 1982.

Goldfield, David R. and Blaine A. Brownell. *Urban America: A History*. Second Edition. Boston: Houghton Mifflin, 1990.

Green, Constance McLaughlin. *American Cities in the Growth of the Nation*. New York: John De Graff, 1957.

——. *The Rise of Urban America*. New York: Harper & Row, 1965.

Hall, Peter (Sir). *Cities in Civilization*. New York: Pantheon Books, 1998.

Hofstadter, Richard and Michael Wallace. *American Violence: A Documentary History*. New York: Vintage Books, 1970.

Howells, Frederic C. *The City: The Hope of Democracy*. New York: Charles Scribner's Sons, 1906.

Jacobs, Jane. *The Death and Life of Great American Cities*. New York: Vintage Books, 1961.

Kleniewski, Nancy. *Cities, Change & Conflict: A Political Economy of Urban Life*. Belmont, CA: Thompson/Wadsworth, 2006.

Kotkin, Joel. *A City: A Global History*. New York: Modern Library, 2005.

Macionis, John J. and Vincent N. Parrillo. *Cities and Urban Life*. Upper Saddle River, NJ: Pearson/Prentice Hall, 2007.

Monkonnen, Eric. *America Becomes Urban: The Development of U.S. Cities and Towns, 1780–1980*. Berkeley: University of California Press, 1990.

Mumford, Lewis. *The City in History: Its Origins, Its Transformations, and Its Prospects*. New York: Harcourt Brace, 1961.

Palen, John J. *The Urban World*. New York: McGraw Hill, 1997.

Schlesinger, Arthur. *Paths to the Present*. New York: MacMillan, 1949.

——. *The Rise of the City*. New York: Macmillan, 1933.

Warner, Sam Bass, Jr. *The Urban Wilderness: A History of the American City*. New York: Harper & Row, 1972.

II. Urban History by Time Period

Colonial

Bonomi, Patricia U. *Under the Cope of Heaven: Religion, Society, and Politics in Colonial America*. New York: Oxford University Press, 1986.

Bridenbaugh, Carl. *Cities in Revolt: Urban Life in America, 1743–1776*. New York: Knopf, 1955.

——. *Cities in the Wilderness: The First Century of Urban Life in America, 1625–1742*. New York: Oxford University Press, 1938, rev. 1966.

Bushman, Richard. "Family Security in the Transition from Farm to City, 1750–1850," *Journal of Family History*, 6 (1981): 238–252.

Cronon, William. *Changes in the Land: Indians, Colonists, and the Ecology of New England*. New York: Hill and Wang, 1983.

Deetz, James. *In Small Things Forgotten: The Archeology of Early American Life*. New York: Anchor, 1977.

Demos, John. *A Little Commonwealth: Family Life in Plymouth Colony*. New York: Oxford University Press, 1970.

Fries, Sylvia Doughty. *The Urban Ideal in Colonial America*. Philadelphia: Temple University Press, 1977.

Lemisch, Jessie. "Jack Tar in the Street: Merchant Seamen and the Politics of Revolutionary America," *William and Mary Quarterly* 3rd Series, vol. 25 (1968): 371–407.

Lemon, James. *The Best Poor Man's Country: Early Southeastern Pennsylvania*. Baltimore: Johns Hopkins University Press, 2002.

Lockridge, Kenneth A. *A New England Town: The First Hundred Years*. New York: W. W. Norton, 1970.

Maier, Pauline. "Boston and New York in the Eighteenth Century," *Proceedings of the American Antiquarian Society* 91, Part 2 (Oct. 21, 1981): 177–195.

Nash, Gary. *The Urban Crucible; Social Change, Political Consciousness, and the Origins of the American Revolution*. Cambridge, MA: Harvard University Press, 1979.

Reps, John W. *Town Planning in Frontier America*. Princeton: Princeton University Press, 1969.

Teaford, Jon C. *The Municipal Revolution in America: Origins of Modern Urban Government, 1650–1825*. Chicago: University of Chicago Press, 1975.

Ulrich, Laurel Thatcher. *A Midwife's Tale: The Life of Martha Ballard*. New York: Alfred A. Knopf, 1990.

Nineteenth Century

Allen, Robert C. *Horrible Prettiness: Burlesque and American Culture*. Chapel Hill: The University of North Carolina Press, 1991.

Badger, R. Reid. *The Great American Fair: The World's Columbian Exposition and American Culture*. Chicago: Nelson Hall, 1979.

Bender, Thomas. *Towards an Urban Vision: Ideas and Institutions in Nineteenth Century America*. Baltimore: Johns Hopkins University Press, 1991.

Blumin, Stuart M. *The Emergence of the Middle Class: Social Experience in the American City, 1760–1900*. Cambridge: Cambridge University Press, 1989.

——. *An Urban Threshold: Growth and Change in a Nineteenth-Century American Community*. Chicago: University of Chicago Press, 1984.

Boyer, Paul. *Urban Masses and Moral Order in America, 1820–1920*. Cambridge, MA: Harvard University Press, 1978.

Bridges, Amy. *A City in the Republic: Antebellum New York and the Origins of Machine Politics*. Cambridge: Cambridge University Press, 2008.

Brown, Julie K. *Contesting Images: Photography and the World's Columbian Exposition*. Tucson: The University of Arizona Press, 1.

Burg, David F. *Chicago's White City of 1893*. Lexington: The University Press of Kentucky, 1976.

Cohen, Patricia Cline, Timothy J. Gilfoyle, and Helen Lefkowitz Horowitz. *The Flash Press: Sporting Male Weeklies in 1840s New York*. Chicago: University of Chicago Press, 2008.

Cronon, William. *Nature's Metropolis: Chicago and the Great West*. New York: W. W. Norton & Company, 1991.

Ebner, Michael and Eugene Tobin, eds., *The Age of Urban Reform: New Perspectives on the Progressive Era*. Kennikat Press, 1977.

Ethington, Phillip. *The Public City: The Political Construction of Urban Life in San Francisco, 1850–1900*. New York: Cambridge University Press, 1994.

Feldberg, Michael. *The Turbulent Era: Riot and Disorder in Jacksonian America*. New York: Oxford University Press, 1980.

Flanagan, Maureen. *Seeing with Their Hearts: Chicago and the Vision of the Good City, 1871–1933*. Princeton: Princeton University Press, 2002.

Gamber, Wendy. *The Boardinghouse in Nineteenth-Century America*. Baltimore: Johns Hopkins University Press, 2007.

Gilfoyle, Timothy. *City of Eros: New York City, Prostitution and the Commercialization of Sex, 1790–1920*. New York: W. W. Norton, 1994.

——. *A Pickpocket's Tale: The Underworld of Nineteenth-Century New York*. New York: W. W. Norton, 2006.

Ginzberg, Lori D. *Women and the Work of Benevolence: Morality, Politics, and Class in the 19th-Century United States*. New Haven: Yale University Press, 1990.

Goldfield, David R. *Urban Growth in the Age of Sectionalism: Virginia, 1847–1861*. Baton Rouge: Louisiana State University Press, 1977.

Harris, Neil, Wim de Wit, James Gilbert, and Robert W. Rydell. *Grand Illusions: Chicago's World's Fair of 1893*. Chicago: Chicago Historical Society, 1993.

Johnson, Paul. *A Shopkeeper's Millennium: Society and Revivals in Rochester, New York, 1815–1837*. New York: Hill and Wang, 1978.

Lebsock, Suzanne. *The Free Women of Petersburgh: Status and Culture in a Southern Town, 1784–1860*, New York: W. W. Norton, 1984.

Miller, Zane. *Boss Cox's Cincinnati: Urban Politics in the Progressive Era*. Columbus: Ohio State University Press, 2000.

Monkonnen, Eric. *Police in Urban America, 1860–1920*. Cambridge: Cambridge University Press, 2004.

Rosenberg, Charles E. *The Cholera Years: The United States in 1832, 1849, and 1866*. Chicago: University of Chicago Press, 1962, 1987.

Ryan, Mary P. *Cradle of the Middle Class: The Family in Oneida County, New York, 1790–1865*. New York: Cambridge University Press, 1981.

Smith, Carl. *Urban Disorder and the Shape of Belief: The Great Chicago Fire, the Haymarket Bomb, and the Model Town of Pullman*. Chicago: University of Chicago Press, 1995.

Stansell, Christine. *City of Women: Sex and Class in New York, 1780–1860*. New York: Knopf, 1982, 1986.

Trachtenberg, Alan. *The Incorporation of America: Culture and Society in the Gilded Age*. New York: Hill and Wang, 1982, 2007.

Wade, Richard. *The Urban Frontier: The Rise of Western Cities, 1790–1830*. Cambridge, MA: Harvard, 1959.

——. "Urban Life in Western America, 1790–1830," *American Historical Review* LXIV (1957): 14–30.

Warner, Sam Bass. *The Private City: Philadelphia in Three Periods of Growth*. Philadelphia:" University of Pennsylvania Press, 1968.

Wilentz, Sean. *Chants Democratic: New York City and the Rise of the American Working Class, 1788–1850*. New York: Oxford University Press, 1984.

Late Nineteenth to Twentieth Century

Benson, Susan Porter. *Counter Cultures: Saleswomen, Managers, and Customers in American Department Stores, 1890–1940*. Urbana: University of Illinois Press, 1986.

Bergreen, Laurence. *Capone: The Man and the Era*. New York: Touchstone, 1994.

Biles, Roger. *Big City Boss in Depression and War: Mayor Edward J. Kelly of Chicago*. DeKalb, IL: Northern Illinois University Press, 1984.

——. *Richard J. Daley: Politics, Race, and the Governing of Chicago*. DeKalb, IL: Northern Illinois University Press, 1995.

Bloom, Nicholas Dagen. *Suburban Alchemy: 1960s New Towns and the Transformation of the American Dream*. Columbus: Ohio State University Press, 2001.

Cohen, Lizabeth. *A Consumer's Republic: The Politics of Mass Consumption in Postwar America*. New York: Vintage Books, 2003.

Davis, Allen F. *Spearheads for Reform: The Social Settlements the Progressive Movement, 1890–1914*. New York: Oxford University Press, 1967.

Davis, Mike. *City of Quartz: Excavating the Future in Los Angeles*. New York: Vintage Books, 1992.

——. *The Ecology of Fear: Los Angeles and the Imagination of Disaster*. New York: Metropolitan Books, 1998.

Dolgon, Corey. *End of the Hamptons: Scenes from the Class Struggle in America's Paradise*. New York: New York University Press, 2005.

Findlay, John M. *Magic Lands: Western Cityscapes and American Culture after 1940*. Berkeley: University of California Press, 1992.

Gans, Herbert. *The Levittowners: Ways of Life and Politics in a New Suburban Community*. New York: Pantheon, 1967.

——. *The Urban Villagers; Group and Class Life of Italian Americans*. Free Press, 1962.

Gelfand, Mark I. *A Nation of Cities: The Federal Government and Urban America, 1933–1965*. New York: Oxford University Press, 1975.

Jackson, Kenneth. *The Ku Klux Klan in the City*. New York: Oxford University Press, 1967.

Kessner, Thomas. *Fiorello H. LaGuardia and the Making of Modern New York*. New York: Penguin Books, 1989.

Miller, James. *Democracy is in the Streets: From Port Huron to the Siege of Chicago*. New York: Simon and Schuster, 1987.

Mowry, George E. *The Urban Nation, 1920–1960*. New York: Hill and Wang, 1965.

Palen, John J. *The Suburbs*. New York: McGraw Hill, 1995.

Pritchett, Wendell, *Brownsville, Brooklyn: Blacks, Jews, and the Changing Face of the Ghetto*. Chicago: University of Chicago Press, 2002.

Riordan, William. *Plunkitt of Tammany Hall: A Series of Very Plain Talks on Very Practical Politics*. New York: Dutton, 1983.

Rosen, Ruth. *The Lost Sisterhood: Prostitution in America, 1900–1918*. Baltimore: Johns Hopkins University Press, 1982.

Rothman, Hal. *Neon Metropolis: How Las Vegas Started the Twentieth Century*. New York: Routledge, 2003.

Self, Robert O. *American Babylon: Race and the Struggle for Postwar Oakland*. Princeton: Princeton University Press, 2005.

Sugrue, Thomas J. *The Origins of the Urban Crisis: Race and Inequality in Postwar Detroit*. Princeton: Princeton University Press, 1996.

Teaford, Jon C. *Cities of the Heartland: The Rise and Fall of the Industrial Midwest*. Bloomington: Indiana University Press, 1993.

——. *The Rough Road to Renaissance: Urban Revitalization in America, 1940–1985*. Baltimore: Johns Hopkins University Press, 1990.

Wilder, Craig Steven. *A Covenant with Color: Race and Social Power in Brooklyn*. New York: Columbia University Press, 2000.

Wilson, William Julius. *The Declining Significance of Race: Blacks and Changing American Institutions*. Chicago: University of Chicago Press, 1978.

——. *When Work Disappears: The World of the New Urban Poor*. New York: Vintage Books, 1996.

III. Urban History By Topic and Place

Architecture and Space

Hayden, Dolores. *The Power of Place: Urban Landscapes as Public History*. Cambridge, MA: MIT Press, 1995.

Rybczynski, Witold. *Home: A Short History of an Idea*. New York: Penguin, 1987.

Stilgoe, John R. *Outside Lies Magic: Regaining History and Awareness in Everyday Places*. New York: Walker and Company, 1998.

Downtowns

Isenberg, Alison. *Downtown America: A History of the Place and the People that Made It*. Chicago: University of Chicago Press, 2004.

Fogelson, Robert. *Downtown: Its Rise and Fall, 1880–1950*. New Haven: Yale University Press, 2001.

Environment, see Urban Environmental

Gay and Lesbian Urban History and Related Works

Chauncey, George. *Gay New York: Gender, Urban Culture, and the Making of the Gay Male World, 1890–1940*. New York: Basic Books, 1994.

Duberman, Martin. *Stonewall*. New York: St. Martins Press, 1993.

Krahulik, Karen Chistel. *Provincetown: From Pilgrim Landing to Gay Resort*. New York: New York University Press, 2005.

Yoshino, Kenji. *Covering: The Hidden Assault on our Civil Rights*. New York: Random House, 2006.

Planning History, Planning Practice, Highways, see Urban Infrastructure

Housing

Bauman, John F. *Public Housing, Race, and Renewal: Urban Planning in Philadelphia, 1920–1974*. Philadelphia: Temple University Press, 1987.

Bauman, John, Roger Biles, and Kristin Szylvian. *From Tenements to the Taylor Homes: In Search of an Urban Housing Policy in Twentieth Century America*. College Station: Pennsylvania State University Press, 2000.

Cowie, Jefferson and Joseph Heathcott. *Beyond the Ruins: The Meanings of Deindustrialization*. Ithaca: Cornell University Press, 2003.

Hunt, D. Bradford. *Blueprint for Disaster: The Unraveling of Chicago Public Housing*. Chicago: University of Chicago Press, 2009.

Venkatesh, Sudhir Alladi. *American Project: The Rise and Fall of a Modern Ghetto*. Cambridge, MA: Harvard University Press, 2000.

Wright, Gwendolyn. *Moralism & the Model Home: Domestic Architecture and Cultural Conflict in Chicago, 1873–1913*. Chicago: University of Chicago Press, 1985.

Immigration

Antin, Mary. *The Promised Land*. New York: Penguin Books, 1997.

Antler, Joyce. *The Journey Home: How Jewish Women Shaped Modern America*. New York: Schocken Books, 1997.

Barton, Josef. *Peasants and Strangers: Italians, Rumanians, and Slovaks in an American City, 1890–1950*. Cambridge, MA: Harvard University Press, 1975.

Bayor, Ronald H. *Neighbors in Conflict: The Irish, Germans, Jews, and Italians of New York City, 1929–1941*. Baltimore: Johns Hopkins University Press, 1978.

Binder, Frederick M. and David Reimers. *All the Nations Under Heaven: An Ethnic and Racial History of New York City*. New York: Columbia University Press, 1995.

Bodnar, John. *The Transplanted: A History of Immigrants in Urban America*. Bloomington: Indiana University Press, 1985.

Bodnar, John, Roger D. Simon, and Michael P. Weber. *Lives of Their Own: Blacks, Italians, and Poles in Pittsburgh, 1900–1960*. Urbana: University of Illinois Press, 1982.

Conzen, Kathleen Neils. *Immigrant Milwaukee, 1836–1860: Accommodation and Community in a Frontier City*. Cambridge, MA: Harvard University Press, 1976.

Daniels, Roger and Otis L. Graham. *Debating American Immigration, 1882-Present*. New York: Rowman and Littlefield, 2001.

Diner, Hasia. *Erin's Daughters in America: Irish Immigrant Women in the Nineteenth Century*. Baltimore: Johns Hopkins University Press, 1983.

——. *Hungering for America: Italian, Irish, & Jewish Foodways in the Age of Migration*. Cambridge, MA: Harvard University Press, 2001.

Dinnerstein, Leonard and David M. Reimers. *Ethnic Americans: A History of Immigration*. New York: Columbia University Press, 1999.

Ewen, Elizabeth. *Immigrant Women in the Land of Dollars: Life and Culture on the Lower East Side, 1890–1925*. New York: Monthly Review Press, 1985.

Gabaccia, Donna R. *From the Other Side: Women, Gender and Immigrant Life in the U.S., 1820–1990*. Bloomington: Indiana University Press, 1994.

——. *From Sicily to Elizabeth Street: Housing and Social Change Among Italian Immigrants, 1880–1930*. Albany: State University of New York Press, 1984.

Jacobson, Matthew Frye. *Whiteness of a Different Color: European Immigrants and the Alchemy of Race*. Cambridge, MA: Harvard University Press, 1998.

Kessner, Thomas. *The Golden Door; Italian and Jewish Immigrant Mobility in New York City, 1880–1915*. New York: Oxford University Press, 1977.

Meagher, Timothy J. *Inventing Irish America: Generation, Class, and Ethnic Identity in a New England City, 1880–1928*. Notre Dame: University of Notre Dame Press, 2001.

Miller, Thomas. *Immigrants and the American City*. New York: New York University Press, 1993.

Powers, Vincent E. *Invisible Immigrants: The Pre-Famine Irish Immigrant Community in Worcester, Massachusets from 1826–1860*. New York: Garland, 1989.

Reimers, David M. *Still the Golden Door: The Third World Comes to America*. New York: Columbia University Press, 1985.

——. *Unwelcome Strangers: American Identity and the Turn Against Immigration*. New York: Columbia University Press, 1998.

Riis, Jacob. *How the Other Half Lives: Studies Among the Tenements of New York*. New York: Scribner & Sons, 1890.

Takaki, Ronald. *A Different Mirror: A History of Multicultural America*. Boston: Little, Brown and Company, 1993.

——. *Strangers from a Different Shore: A History of Asian Americans*. New York: Penguin, 1998.

Labor in Urban Settings

Barrett, James R. *Work and Community in the Jungle: Chicago's Packinghouse Workers, 1894–1922*. Urbana: University of Illinois Press, 1987.

Blewett, Mary H. *The Last Generation: Work and Life in the Textile Mills of Lowell, Massachusetts, 1910–1960*. Amherst: University of Massachusetts Press, 1990.

Brecher, Jeremy. *Strike*. Boston: South End Press, 1972.

Cohen, Lizabeth. *Making a New Deal: Industrial Workers in Chicago, 1919–1939*. New York: Cambridge University Press, 1990.

Dawley, Alan. *Class and Community: The Industrial Revolution in Lynn*. Cambridge, MA: Harvard University Press, 1976.

Dublin, Thomas. *Women at Work: The Transformation of Work and Community in Lowell, Massachusetts, 1826–1860*. New York: Columbia University Press, 1979.

Faue, Elizabeth. *Community of Suffering and Struggle: Women, Men, and the Labor Movement in Minneapolis, 1915–1945*. Chapel Hill: University of North Carolina Press, 1991.

Gerstle, Gary. *Working-Class Americanism: The Politics of Labor in a Textile City, 1914–1960*. New York: Cambridge University Press, 1989.

Green, Hardy. *On Strike at Hormel: The Struggle for a Democratic Labor Movement*. Philadelphia: Temple University Press, 1990.

Green, James. *Death in the Haymarket: A Story of Chicago, the First Labor Movement, and the Bombing that Divided Gilded Age America*. New York: Pantheon Books, 2006.

Hareven, Tamara, and Randolph Langenbach. *Amoskeag: Life and Work in an American Factory City*. New York: Pantheon, 1978.

Jones, Jacqueline. *American Work: Four Centuries of Black and White Labor*. New York: W. W. Norton, 1998.

——. *The Dispossessed: America's Underclasses from the Civil War to the Present*. New York: Basic Books, 1992.

——. *Labor of Love, Labor of Sorrow: Black Women, Work, and Family from Slavery to the Present*. New York: Vintage Books, 1985.

Kessler-Harris, Alice. *Out to Work: A History of Wage Earning Women in the United States*. New York: Oxford University Press, 1982.

Lichtenstein, Nelson. *The Most Dangerous Man in Detroit: Walter Reuther and the Fate of American Labor*. New York: Basic Books, 1995.

Meyerowitz, Joanne. *Women Adrift: Independent Wage Earners in Chicago, 1880–1930*. Chicago: University of Chicago Press, 1988.

Orleck, Annelise. *Storming Caesar's Palace: How Black Mothers Fought Their Own War on Poverty*. Boston: Beacon Press, 2005.

Peiss, Kathy. *Cheap Amusements: Working Women and Leisure in Turn of the Century New York*. Philadelphia: Temple University Press, 1986.

Rosenzweig, Roy. *Eight Hours For What We Will: Workers and Leisure in an Industrial City, 1870–1920*. Cambridge: Cambridge University Press, 1983.

Ross, Robert. *Slaves to Fashion: Poverty and Abuse in the New Sweatshops*. Ann Arbor: University of Michigan Press, 2004.

Smith, Carl. *Urban Disorder and the Shape of Belief: The Great Chicago Fire, the Haymarket Bomb, and the Model Town of Pullman*. Chicago: University of Chicago Press, 1995.

Tentler, Leslie Woodcock. *Wage-Earning Women: Industrial Work and Family Life in the United States, 1900–1930*. New York: Oxford University Press, 1979.

Trotter, Joe William, Jr. *Black Milwaukee: The Making of an Industrial Proletariat, 1915–1945*. Urbana: University of Illinois Press, 1985.

Native Americans

Eagle, Adam Fortunate. *Alcatraz! Alcatraz!* California: Heyday Books, 1992.

Jaffee, David. *People of the Wachusett: Greater New England in History and Memory, 1630–1860*. Ithaca: Cornell University Press, 1999.

LeGrande, James. *Indian Metropolis: Native Americans in Chicago, 1945–1975*. Urbana: University of Illinois Press, 2005.

Thrush, Coll. *Native Seattle: Histories from the Crossing-Over Place*. Seattle: University of Washington Press, 2007.

Novels

Algren, Nelson. *The Man with the Golden Arm*. New York: Doubleday & Company, Inc., 1949.

——. *Never Come Morning*. New York: Four Walls Eight Windows, 1987.

Angelou, Maya. *I Know Why the Caged Bird Sings*. New York: Bantam Books, 1993.

Arnow, Harriette. *The Dollmaker*. New York: Macmillan Publishing, 1954.

Bell, Thomas. *Out of This Furnace*. Pittsburgh: University of Pittsburgh Press, 1941.

Bellow, Saul. *Adventures of Augie March*. New York: Penguin Books, 1984.

Brown, Claude. *Manchild in the Promised Land*. New York: Touchstone, 1995.

Cahan, Abraham. *The Rise of David Levinsky*. New York: Harper & Row, 1960.

Dreiser, Theodore. *Jennie Gerhardt*. New York: Penguin Books, 1994.

——. *Sister Carrie*. New York: Bantam Books, 1992.

——. *The Titan*. New York: Meridian Classic, 1984.

Gelernter, David. *1939: The Lost World of the Fair*. New York: Avon, 1995.

Lehan, Richard. *The City in Literature: An Intellectual and Cultural History*. Berkeley: University of California Press, 1998.

Lewis, Sinclair. *Babbitt*. New York: Harcourt, Brace, & Co., 1922.

Masters, Edgar Lee. *Spoon River Anthology*. New York: Dover, 1992.

Niles, Blair. *Strange Brother*. London: Liveright Press, 1931.

Norris, Frank. *The Pit: The Epic of Wheat*. New York: Penguin Books, 1994.

Petry, Ann. *The Street*. Boston: Houghton Mifflin, 1974.

Simon, Kate. *Bronx Primitive: Portraits in a Childhood*. New York: Penguin, 1982.

Sinclair, Upton. *The Jungle*. New York: Penguin, 1985.

West, Dorothy. *The Living is Easy*. New York: The Feminist Press, 1948.

Wilson, Sloan. *Man in Gray Flannel Suit*. New York: Simon and Schuster, 1955.

Wright, Richard. *Black Boy (American Hunger)*. New York: HarperPerennial, 1993.

——. *Native Son*. New York: Harper & Row Publishers, 1966.

Yates, Richard. *Revolutionary Road*. New York: Vintage Books, 2008.

Yezierska, Aniza. *The Bread Givers*. New York: Persea Books, 2003.

Planning History, Planning Practice, Urban Infrastructure

Abrams, Charles. *The City is the Frontier*. New York: Harper & Row, 1965.

Bluestone, Barry. *Constructing Chicago*. New Haven: Yale University Press, 1993.

Boyer, M. Christine. *Dreaming the Rational City: The Myth of American City Planning*. Cambridge, MA: MIT Press, 1986.

Bruegmann, Robert. *Sprawl: A Compact History*. Chicago: University of Chicago Press, 2005.

Fairfield, John D. *The Mysteries of the Great City: The Politics of Urban Design, 1877–1937*. Columbus: Ohio State University Press, 1993.

Gilfoyle, Timothy. *Millennium Park: Creating a Chicago Landmark*. Chicago: University of Chicago Press, 2006.

Gillette, Howard Jr. *Between Justice and Beauty: Race, Planning, and the Failure of Urban Policy in Washington, D.C.* Philadelphia: University of Pennsylvania Press, 2006.

Hirsch, Arnold R. and A. Lee Levert, "The Katrina Conspiracies: The Problem of Trust in Rebuilding an American City," *Journal of Urban History*, 35, no. 2 (January 2009): 207–219.

Hood, Clifton. *722 Miles: The Building of the Subways and How They Transformed New York*. New York: Simon & Schuster, 1993.

Jacobs, Jane. *The Death and Life of Great American Cities*. New York: Vintage Books, 1961.

Kunstler, James Howard. *The Geography of Nowhere: The Rise and Decline of America's Man-Made Landscape*. New York: Touchstone, 1993.

——. *Home From Nowhere: Remaking our Everyday World for the 21st Century*. New York: Simon & Schuster, 1996.

Leazes, Francis J. and Mark T. Motte. *Providence, the Renaissance City*. Boston: Northeastern University Press, 2004.

Levy, John D. *Contemporary Urban Planning*. Eighth Edition. Englewood Cliffs, NJ: Pearson, Prentice Hall, 2009.

Mayer, Harold and Richard C. Wade. *Chicago: Growth of a Metropolis*. Chicago: University of Chicago Press, 1969.

McShane, Clay. *Asphalt Nation: How the Automobile Took Over American and How We Can Take It Back*. Berkeley: University of California Press, 1998.

Molotch, Harvey and John J. Logan. *Urban Fortunes: The Political Economy of Place*. Berkeley: University of California Press, 1987.

Platt, Harold L. *The Electric City: Energy and the Growth of the Chicago Area, 1880–1930*. Chicago: University of Chicago Press, 1991.

Rosenzweig, Roy and Elizabeth Blackmar. *The Park and the People: A History of Central Park*. New York: Henry Holt, 1992.

Rybczynski, Witold. *A Clearing in the Distance: Frederick Law Olmsted and America in the 19th Century*. New York: Simon & Schuster, 1999.

Smith, Carl. *The Plan of Chicago: Daniel Burnham and the Remaking of the American City*. Chicago: University of Chicago Press, 2006.

Poverty

Adams, Jane. *Twenty Years at Hull-House*. New York: Signet Classic, 1981.

Katz, Michael. *In The Shadow of the Poorhouse: A Social History of Welfare in America*. New York: Basic Books, 1986.

Levenstein, Lisa. *A Movement Without Marches: African American Women and the Politics of Poverty in Postwar Philadelphia*. Chapel Hill: University of North Carolina Press, 2009.

Pleck, Elizabeth. *Black Migration and Poverty in Boston, 1865–1900*. New York: Academic Press, 1979.

Thernstrom, Stephan. *The Other Bostonians: Poverty and Progress in the American Metropolis, 1880–1970*. Cambridge, MA: Harvard University Press, 1973.

——. *Poverty and Progress: Social Mobility in a Nineteenth-Century City*. Cambridge, MA: Harvard University Press, 1964.

Traverso, Susan. *Welfare Politics in Boston, 1910–1940*. Amherst: University of Massachusetts, 2003.

Venkatesh, Sudhir Alladi. *Off the Books: The Underground Economy of the Urban Poor*. Cambridge, MA: Harvard University Press, 2006.

Wilson, William Julius. *When Work Disappears: The World of the New Urban Poor*. New York: Vintage Books, 1996.

Primary Documents

Boller, Paul F., Jr. and Ronald Story. *A More Perfect Union: Documents in U.S. History Volume II; Since 1865*. Third Edition. Boston: Houghton Mifflin, 1992.

Marcus, Robert D. and David Burner. *America Firsthand. Volume II: From Reconstruction to the Present*. New York: St. Martins, 1992.

Rock, Howard B. *The New York City Artisan, 1789–1825: A Documentary History*. Albany: State University of New York Press, 1989.

Smith, Wilson, ed. *Cities of Our Past and Present: A Descriptive Reader*. New York: John Wiley & Sons, 1964.

Still, Bayard. *Urban America: A History with Documents*. Boston: Little Brown, 1974.

Wade, Richard C. *Cities in American Life*. Boston: Houghton Mifflin, 1971.

Race and Identity in Urban Areas

Anderson, Elijah. *Against the Wall: Poor, Young, Black, and Male*. Philadelphia: University of Pennsylvania Press, 2008.

——. *Streetwise: Race, Class, and Change in an Urban Community*. Chicago: University of Chicago Press, 1990.

Ardizzone, Heidi and Earl Lewis. *Love on Trial: An American Scandal in Black and White*. New York: W. W. Norton, 2002.

Baldwin, Davarian L. *Chicago's New Negroes: Modernity, the Great Migration, and Black Urban Life*. Chapel Hill: The University of North Carolina Press, 2007.

Boehm, Lisa Krissoff. *Making a Way out of No Way: African American Women and the Second Great Migration*. Jackson: University Press of Mississippi, 2009.

Boyle, Kevin. *Arc of Justice: A Saga of Race, Civil Rights, and Murder in the Jazz Age*. New York: Henry Holt, 2004.

Clark-Lewis, Elizabeth. *Living In, Living Out: African American Domestics and the Great Migration*. New York: Kodnasha America, 1994.

Douglas, Davison M. *Jim Crow Moves North: The Battle Over Northern School Desegregation, 1865–1954*. New York: Cambridge University Press, 2005.

Frey, William H. "The New Great Migration: Black American's Return to the South, 1865–2000." Center on Urban and Metropolitan Policy, Brookings Institution, May 2004.

Gillette, Howard Jr. *Between Justice and Beauty: Race, Planning, and the Failure of Urban Policy in Washington, D.C.* Philadelphia: University of Pennsylvania Press, 2006.

Gottlieb, Peter. *Making Their Own Way: Southern Blacks' Migration to Pittsburgh, 1916–1930*. Urbana: University of Illinois Press, 1987.

Green, Adam. *Selling the Race: Culture, Community, and Black Chicago, 1940–1955*. Chicago: University of Chicago Press, 2009.

Gregory, James N. *The Southern Diaspora: How the Great Migrations of Black and White Southerners Transformed America*. Chapel Hill: University of North Carolina Press, 2005.

Grossman, James R. *Land of Hope: Chicago, Black Southerners, and the Great Migration*. Chicago: University of Chicago Press, 1991.

Harrison, Alferdteen, ed. *Black Exodus: The Great Migration from the American South*. Jackson: University Press of Mississippi, 1991.

Hirsch, Arnold R. *Making the Second Ghetto: Race & Housing in Chicago, 1940–1960*. New York: Cambridge University Press, 1990.

Jacoby, Tamar. *Someone Else's House: American's Unfinished Struggle for Integration*. New York: The Free Press, 1998.

Jaffe, Harry S. and Tom Sherwood. *Dream City: Race, Power, and the Decline of Washington, D.C.* New York: Simon & Schuster, 1994.

Jelks, Randal Maurice. *African Americans in the Furniture City: The Struggle for Civil Rights in Grand Rapids*. Urbana: University of Illinois Press, 2006.

Kotlowitz, Alex. *There Are No Children Here: The Story of Two Boys Growing Up in the Other America*. New York: Anchor Books, 1991.

LeBlanc, Adrian Nicole. *Random Family: Love, Drugs, Trouble and Coming of Age in the Bronx*. New York: Scribner, 2003.

Lemann, Nicholas. *The Promised Land: The Great Black Migration and How it Changed America*. New York: Vintage Books, 1992.

Lewis, Earl. *In Their Own Interests: Race, Class and Power in Twentieth-Century Norfolk, Virginia*. Berkeley: University of California Press, 1993.

Marks, Carole. *Farewell—We're Good and Gone: The Great Black Migration*. Bloomington, IN: Indiana University Press, 1989.

Patillo, Mary. *Black on the Block: The Politics of Race and Class in the City*. Chicago: University of Chicago Press, 2007.

Phillips, Kimberley L. *AlabamaNorth: African-American Migrants, Community, and Working-Class Activism in Cleveland, 1915–1945*. Urbana: University of Illinois Press, 1999.

Pruitt, Bernadette. "The African American Experience in Slavery and Freedom: Black Urban History Revisited." *Journal of Urban History* 33, no. 6 (September 2007): 1033–1047.

Rodriguez, Richard. *Brown: The Last Discovery of America*. New York: Viking, 2002.

——. *Hunger of Memory: An Autobiography*. New York: Bantam Books, 1992.

Santiago, Esmeralda. *When I Was Puerto Rican*. New York: Vintage Books, 1993.

Sitkoff, Harvard. *The Struggle for Black Equality, 1954–1992*. New York: Hill and Wang, 1993.

Takaki, Ronald. *A Different Mirror: A History of Multicultural America*. Boston: Little, Brown and Company, 1993.

——. *Strangers from a Different Shore: A History of Asian Americans*. New York: Penguin, 1998.

Tolnay, Stewart E. "The Great Migration and Changes in the Northern Black Family, 1940–1990." *Social Forces* 75 (June 1997): 1213–1238.

Trent, Alexander J. "The Great Migration in Comparative Perspective: Interpreting the Urban Origins of Southern Black Migrants to Depression-Era Pittsburgh." *Social Science History* 22 (Fall 1998): 349–376.

Trotter, Joe William, Jr., ed. *The Great Migration in Historical Perspective: New Dimensions of Race, Class, and Gender*. Bloomington, IN: Indiana University Press, 1991.

Trotter, Joe W., Jr., Earl Lewis, and Tera W. Hunter. *The African American Urban Experience*. New York: Palgrave Macmillan, 2004.

Tuttle, William M. *Race Riot: Chicago in the Red Summer of 1919*. New York: Athenaeum, 1970.

Religion

Bonomi, Patricia U. *Under the Cope of Heaven: Religion, Society, and Politics in Colonial America*. New York: Oxford University Press, 1986.

Orsi, Robert A., ed. *Gods of the City: Religion and the American Urban Landscape*. Bloomington, IN: Indiana University Press, 1999.

——. *The Madonna of 115th Street: Faith and Community in Italian Harlem, 1880–1950*. New Haven: Yale University Press, 1985.

Working Class/Radical America/Mass Culture

Avrich, Paul. *The Haymarket Tragedy*. Princeton: Princeton University Press, 1984.

Kasson, John F. *Amusing the Million: Coney Island at the Turn of the Century*. New York: Hill and Wang, 1978.

Kessler-Harris, Alice. *Out to Work: A History of Wage-Earning Women in the United States*. New York: Oxford University Press, 1982.

Lamphere, Louise. *From Working Daughters to Working Mothers: Immigrant Women in a New England Industrial Community*. Ithaca: Cornell University Press, 1987.

Nasaw, David. *Children of the City: At Work and At Play*. New York: Oxford University Press, 1985.

——. *Going Out: The Rise and Fall of Public Amusement*. New York: Basic Books, 1993.

Painter, Nell Irvin. *Standing at Armageddon: The United States, 1877–1919*. New York: W. W. Norton, 1987.

Reiss, Steven A. *City Games: The Evolution of American Urban Society and the Rise of Sports*. Urbana: University of Illinois Press, 1991.

Specific Cities and Regional Urban Histories

Boston

Binford, Henry. *The First Suburbs: Residential Communities on the Boston Periphery, 1815–1860*. Chicago: University of Chicago Press, 1985.

Conzen, Michael and George K. Lewis. *Boston: A Geographical Portrait*. Cambridge, MA: Ballinger, 1976.

Gans, Herbert. *The Urban Villagers; Group and Class Life of Italian Americans*. New York: Free Press, 1962.

Handlin, Oscar, *Boston's Immigrants, 1790–1880*. Cambridge, MA: Harvard University Press, 1941.

Knights, Peter R. *Yankee Destinies: The Lives of Ordinary Nineteenth-Century Bostonians*. Chapel Hill: North Carolina University Press, 1991.

Kreiger, Alex and David Cobb, with Amy Turner, eds. *Mapping Boston*. Cambridge, MA: MIT Press, 1999.

MacDonald, Michael Patrick. *All Souls: A Family Story from Southie*. Boston: Beacon Press, 2007.

O'Connor, Thomas. *The Hub: Boston Past and Present*. Boston: Northeastern University Press, 2001.

Thernstrom, Stephan. *The Other Bostonians: Poverty and Progress in the American Metropolis, 1880–1970*. Cambridge, MA: Harvard University Press, 1973.

Traverso, Susan. *Welfare Politics in Boston, 1910–1940*. Amherst: University of Massachusetts, 2003.

Warner, Sam Bass, Jr. *Streetcar Suburbs: The Process of Growth in Boston, 1870–1900*. Cambridge, MA: Harvard University Press, 1962.

Buffalo

Yans-McLaughlin, Virginia. *Family and Community: Italian Immigrants in Buffalo, 1880–1930*. Urbana: University of Illinois Press, 1982.

Chicago

Bluestone, Daniel. *Constructing Chicago*. New Haven: Yale University Press, 1991.

Boehm, Lisa Krissoff. *Popular Culture and the Enduring Myth of Chicago*. New York: Routledge, 2004.

Cohen, Lizabeth. *Making a New Deal: Industrial Workers in Chicago, 1919–1939*. New York: Cambridge University Press, 1990.

Conzen, Michael and Diane Dillon. *Mapping Manifest Destiny: Chicago and the American West*. Chicago: Newberry Library, 2008.

Cronon, William. *Nature's Metropolis: Chicago and the Great West*. New York: W. W. Norton, 1991.

Einhorn, Robin. *Property Rules: Political Economy in Chicago, 1833–1872*. Chicago: University of Chicago Press, 1991.

Findling, John E. *Chicago's Great World Fairs*. Manchester: Manchester University Press, 1994.

Gilbert, James. *Perfect Cities: Chicago's Utopias of 1893*. Chicago: University of Chicago Press, 1991.

Ginger, Ray. *Altgeld's America: The Lincoln Ideal Versus Changing Realities*. New York: Markus Wiener Publishing, 1958.

Hoy, Suellen. *Good Hearts: Catholic Sisters in Chicago's Past*. Urbana: University of Illinois Press, 2006.

Kirkland, Joseph. *The Story of Chicago*. Chicago: Dibble Publishing Company, 1892.

Larson, Erik. *The Devil in the White City: Murder, Magic, and Madness at the Fair That Changed America*. New York: Vintage Books, 2003.

Mayer, Harold M. and Richard C. Wade. *Chicago: Growth of a Metropolis*. Chicago: University of Chicago Press, 1969.

Meyerowitz, Joanne J. *Women Adrift: Independent Wage Earners in Chicago, 1880–1930*. Chicago: University of Chicago Press, 1988.

Miller, Donald L. *City of the Century: The Epic of Chicago and the Making of America*. New York: Simon & Schuster, 1996.

Miller, Ross. *America Apocalypse: The Great Fire and the Myth of Chicago*. Chicago: University of Chicago Press, 1990.

Royko, Mike. *Boss: Richard J. Daley of Chicago*. New York: E. P. Dutton and Company, Inc., 1971.

Ruth, David E. *Inventing the Public Enemy: The Gangster in American Culture, 1918–1934*. Chicago: University of Chicago Press, 1996.

Rydell, Robert W. *All the World's a Fair: Visions of Empire at American International Expositions, 1876–1916*. Chicago: University of Chicago Press, 1984.

——. *World of Fairs: The Century-of-Progress Expositions*. Chicago: University of Chicago Press, 1993.

Sawislak, Karen. *Smoldering City: Chicagoans and the Great Fire, 1871–1874*. Chicago: University of Chicago Press, 1995.

Smith, Carl J. *Chicago and the American Literary Imagination, 1880–1920*. Chicago: University of Chicago Press, 1894.

——. *Urban Disorder and the Shape of Belief: The Great Chicago Fire, the Haymarket Bomb, and the Model Town of Pullman*. Chicago: University of Chicago Press, 1995.

Terkel, Studs. *Chicago*. New York: Pantheon Books, 1986.

Dallas

Hill, Patricia Evridge. *Dallas: The Making of a Modern City*. Austin: University of Texas Press, 1996.

Detroit

Babson, Steve, with Ron Alpern, Dave Elsila, and John Reville. *Working Detroit*. Detroit: Wayne State University Press, 1986.

Chafets, Ze'ev. *Devil's Night and Other True Tales of Detroit*. New York: Vintage Books, 1991.

Meier, August, and Elliott Rudwick. *Black Detroit and the Rise of the UAW*. New York: Oxford University Press, 1979.

Sugrue, Thomas J. *The Origins of the Urban Crisis: Race and Inequality in Postwar Detroit*. Princeton: Princeton University Press, 1996.

Thomas, June Manning. *Redevelopment and Race: Planning a Finer City in Postwar Detroit*. Baltimore: Johns Hopkins University Press, 1997.

Thomas, Richard W. *Life is For Us What We Make It: Building Black Community in Detroit, 1915–1945*. Bloomington, IN: Indiana University Press, 1992.

Thompson, Heather Ann. *Whose Detroit? Politics, Labor, and Race in a Modern American City*. Ithaca: Cornell University Press, 2001.

Widick, B.J. *Detroit: City of Race and Class Violence*. Detroit: Wayne State University Press, 1989.

Wolcott, Virginia. *Remaking Respectability: African American Women in Interwar Detroit*. Chapel Hill: University of North Carolina Press, 2001.

Durham

Brown, Leslie. *Upbuilding Black Durham: Gender, Class, and Black Community Development in the Jim Crow South*. Chapel Hill: University Press of North Carolina, 2008.

Houston

Melosi, Martin and Joseph Pratt. *Energy Metropolis: An Environmental History of Houston and the Gulf Coast*. Pittsburgh: University of Pittsburgh Press, 2007.

Platt, Harold L. *City Building in the New South: The Growth of Public Services in Houston, Texas, 1830–1920*. Philadelphia: Temple University Press, 1983.

Los Angeles

Avila, Eric. *Popular Culture in the Age of White Flight: Fear and Fantasy in Suburban Los Angeles*. Los Angeles: University of California Press, 2004.

Gottlieb, Robert. *Reinventing Los Angeles: Nature and Community in the Global City*. Cambridge, MA: MIT Press, 2007.

Hise, Greg. *Magnetic Los Angeles: Planning the Twentieth Century Metropolis*. Baltimore: Johns Hopkins University Press, 1999.

Scott, Allen J. and Edward Soja. *The City: Los Angeles and Urban Theory at the End of the Twentieth Century*. Berkeley: University of California Press, 1998.

Straus, Emily. *The Making of the American School Crisis: Compton, California and the Death of the Suburban Dream*. Brandeis University Dissertation, 2006.

Miami

Shell-Weiss, Melanie. *Coming to Miami: A Social History*. Gainesville: University Press of Florida, 2009.

The Midwest/Middle America

Atherton, Lewis. *Main Street on the Middle Border*. Bloomington, IN: Indiana University Press, 1954.

Bloom, Stephen G. *Postville: A Clash of Cultures in Heartland America*. New York: Harcourt, Inc, 2000.

Jelks, Randal Maurice. *African Americans in the Furniture City: The Struggle for Civil Rights in Grand Rapids*. Urbana: University of Illinois Press, 2006.

Kotlowitz, Alex. *The Other Side of the River: A Story of Two Towns, a Death, and America's Dilemma*. New York: Doubleday, 1998.

Lynd, Robert and Helen. *Middletown: A Study in Contemporary American Culture*. New York: Harcourt Brace, 1929.

——. *Middletown in Transition*. New York: Harcourt Brace, 1937.

Minneapolis

Faue, Elizabeth. *Community of Suffering and Struggle: Women, Men, and the Labor Movement in Minneapolis, 1915–1945*. Chapel Hill: University of North Carolina Press, 1991.

New York City

Abu-Lughod, Janet L. *From Urban Village to East Village: The Battle for New York's Lower East Side*. Oxford: Blackwell, 1994.

Bender, Thomas. *New York Intellect: A History of Intellectual Life in New York City, From 1750 to the Beginning of Our Time*. Baltimore: Johns Hopkins University Press, 1987.

——. *The Unfinished City: New York and Metropolitan Idea*. New York: New York University Press, 2002.

Binder, Frederick M. and David Reimers. *All the Nations Under Heaven: An Ethnic and Racial History of New York City*. New York: Columbia University Press, 1995.

Blackmar, Elizabeth. *Manhattan for Rent, 1750–1850*. Ithaca: Cornell University Press, 1989.

Burrow, Edwin G. and Mike Wallace. *Gotham: A History of New York City to 1898*. New York: Oxford University Press, 1999.

Day, Jared N. *Urban Castles: Tenement Housing and Landlord Activism in New York City, 1890–1943*. New York: Columbia University Press, 1999.

Douglas, Ann. *Terrible Honesty: Mongrel Manhattan in the 1920s*. New York: The Noonday Press, Farrar, Straus, and Giroux, 1995.

Gilfoyle, Timothy J. *City of Eros: New York City, Prostitution, and the Commercialization of Sex, 1790–1920*. New York: W. W. Norton & Company, 1992.

Gronowicz, Anthony. *Race and Class Politics in New York Before the Civil War*. Boston: Northeastern University Press, 1998.

Hammack, David C. *Power and Society: Greater New York at the Turn of the Century*. New York: Russell Sage, 1982.

Henkin, David M. *City Reading: Written Words and Public Spaces in Antebellum New York*. New York: Columbia University Press, 1998.

Kessner, Thomas. *Fiorello H. LaGuardia and the Making of Modern New York*. New York: Penguin Books, 1989.

Mandelbaum, Seymour J. *Boss Tweed's New York*. New York: J. Wiley, 1965.

Mele, Christopher. *Selling the Lower East Side: Culture, Real Estate, and Resistance in New York City*. Minneapolis: University of Minnesota Press, 2000.

Mollenkopf, John Hull. *A Phoenix in the Ashes: The Rise and Fall of the Koch Coalition in New York City Politics*. Princeton: Princeton University Press, 1992.

Mollenkopf, John Hull. and Manuel Castells, eds. *Dual City: Restructuring New York*. New York: Russell Sage, 1991.

Osofsky, Gilbert. *Harlem: The Making of a Ghetto*. New York: Harper & Row, 1963.

Page, Max. *The Creative Destruction of Manhattan, 1900–1940*. Chicago: University of Chicago Press, 1999.

Rieder, Jonathan. *Canarsie: The Jews and Italians of Brooklyn Against Liberalism*. Cambridge, MA: Harvard University Press, 1985.

Rosenzweig, Roy and Elizabeth Blackmar. *The Park and the People: A History of Central Park*. Ithaca: Cornell University Press, 1992.

Sanjek, Roger. *The Future of All of Us: Race and Neighborhood Politics in New York City*. Ithaca: Cornell University Press, 1998.

Sayre, Wallace and Herbert Kaufman. *Governing New York City: Politics in the Metropolis*. New York: Russell Sage, 1960.

Scherzer, Kenneth. *The Unbounded Community: Neighborhood Life and Social Structure in New York City, 1830–1875*. Durham, NC: Duke University Press, 1992.

Schneider, Robert. *Voice of the City: Vaudeville and Popular Culture in New York*. New York: Oxford University Press, 1989.

Stansell, Christine. *City of Women: Sex and Class in New York, 1780–1860*. New York: Knopf, 1986.

Still, Bayrd. *Mirror for Gotham: New York as Seen by Contemporaries from Dutch Days to the Present*. New York: New York University Press, 1956.

Taylor, William R., ed. *Inventing Times Square: Commerce and Culture at the Crossroads of the World*. Baltimore: Johns Hopkins University Press, 1991.

Wallace, Mike. *A New Deal for New York*. New York: Bell and Weiland, 2002.

Wilentz, Sean. *Chants Democratic: New York City and the Rise of the American Working Class, 1788–1850*. New York: Oxford University Press, 1984.

Philadelphia

Bauman, John F. *Public Housing, Race, and Renewal: Urban Planning in Philadelphia, 1920–1974.* Philadelphia: Temple University Press, 1987.

Hershberg, Theodore. *Philadelphia: Work, Space, Family, and Group Experience in the 19th Century.* New York: Oxford University Press, 1981.

Levenstein, Lisa. *A Movement Without Marches: African American Women and the Politics of Poverty in Postwar Philadelphia.* Chapel Hill: The University of North Carolina Press, 2009.

Warner, Sam Bass, Jr. *The Private City: Philadelphia in Three Periods of Its Growth.* Philadelphia: University of Pennsylvania Press, 1968.

Pittsburgh

Bodnar, John, Roger Simon and Michael P. Weber. *Lives of Their Own: Blacks, Italians, and Poles in Pittsburgh, 1900–1960.* Urbana: University of Illinois Press, 1982.

Serrin, William. *Homestead: The Glory and Tragedy of an American Steel Town.* New York: Random House, 1992.

San Francisco/Silcon Valley/Oakland

Lemke-Santangelo, Gertrude. *Abiding Courage: African American Migrant Women and the East Bay Community.* Chapel Hill: University of North Carolina Press, 1996.

Matthews, Glenna. *Silicon Valley, Women, and the California Dream: Gender, Class and Opportunity in the Twentieth Century.* Palo Alto: Stanford University Press, 2003.

Pellow, David Naguib and Lisa Sun-Hee Park. *The Silicon Valley of Dreams: Environmental Justice, Immigrant Workers, and the High-Tech Global Economy.* New York: New York University Press, 2002.

Self, Robert. *American Babylon: Race and the Struggle for Postwar Oakland.* Princeton: Princeton University Press, 2005.

St. Louis

Sandweiss, Eric. *St. Louis: The Evolution of an American Urban Landscape.* Philadephia: Temple University Press, 2001.

Suburbia and Consumerism

Avila, Eric. *Popular Culture in the Age of White Flight: Fear and Fantasy in Suburban Los Angele* Los Angeles: University of California Press, 2004.

Binford, Henry. *The First Suburbs: Residential Communities on the Boston Periphery, 1815–1860.* Chicago: University of Chicago Press, 1985.

Cohen, Lizabeth. *A Consumer's Republic: The Politics of Mass Consumption in Postwar America.* New York: Vintage Books, 2004.

Duany, Andres and Elizabeth Plater-Zyberk, and Jeff Speck, *Suburban Nation: The Rise of Sprawl and the Decline of the American Dream.* New York: North Point Press, 2000.

Fishman, Robert. *Beyond Suburbia: The Rise of the Technoburb.* New York: Basic Books,1987.

——. *Bourgeois Utopias: The Rise and Fall of Suburbia.* New York: Basic Books, 1987.

Fogelson, Robert M. *Bourgeois Nightmares: Suburbia, 1870–1930.* New Haven: Yale University Press, 1995.

Frantz, Douglas and Catherine Collins. *Celebration U.S.A.: Living in Disney's Brave New Town.* New York: Henry Holt, 1999.

Garreau, Joel. *Edge City: Life on the New Frontier.* New York: Anchor Books, 1991.

Halberstam, David. *The Fifties.* New York: Fawcett Columbine, 1993.

Hayden, Dolores. *Building Suburbia, Green Fields and Urban Growth, 1820–2000.* New York: Vintage Books, 2004.

Hudnut, William H. *Halfway to Everywhere: A Portrait of America's First-Tier Suburbs.* Washington, D.C.: Urban Land Institute, 2003.

Jackson, Kenneth. *Crabgrass Frontier: The Suburbanization of the United States.* New York: Oxford University Press, 1987.

Kelly, Barbara, ed. *Suburbia Re-Examined*. Westport, CT: Greenwood, 1989.

Lewis, Tom, *Divided Highways: Building the Interstate Highways, Transforming American Life*. New York: Penguin, 1999.

Low, Setha. *Behind the Gates: Life, Security, and the Pursuit of Happiness in Fortress America*. New York: Routledge, 2003.

Marsh, Margaret. *Suburban Lives*. Piscataway: Rutgers University Press, 1990.

Marshall, Alex. *How Cities Work: Suburbs, Sprawl and the Roads Not Taken*. Austin: University of Texas Press, 2000.

May, Elaine Tyler. *Homeward Bound: American Families in the Cold War Era*. New York: Harper Collins, 1988.

Meyerowitz, Joanne. *Not June Cleaver: Women and Gender in Postwar America*. Philadelphia: Temple University Press, 1994.

Nicolaides, Becky. *My Blue Heaven: Life and Politics in the Suburbs of Los Angeles*. Chicago: University of Chicago Press, 2002.

Rome, Adam. *The Bulldozer in the Countryside: Suburban Sprawl and the Rise of American Environmentalism*. Cambridge: Cambridge University Press, 2001.

Ross, Andrew. *The Celebration Chronicles: Life, Liberty and the Pursuit of Property Value in Disney's New Town*. New York: Ballantine Books, 1999.

Warner, Sam Bass. *Streetcar Suburbs: The Process of Growth in Boston, 1870–1920*. Cambridge, MA: Harvard University Press, 2004.

Wiese, Andrew. *Places of Their Own: African American Suburbanization in the Twentieth Century*. Chicago: University of Chicago Press, 2005.

Tulsa

Ellsworth, Scott. *Death in a Promised Land: The Tulsa Race Riot of 1921*. Baton Rouge: Louisiana State University Press, 1982.

Urban Environmental

Burnstein, Daniel Eli, *Next to Godliness: Confronting Dirt and Despair in Progressive Era New York City*. Urbana: University of Illinois Press, 2006.

Cronon, William. *Changes in the Land: Indians, Colonists, and the Ecology of New England*. New York: Hill and Wang, 1983.

——. *Nature's Metropolis: Chicago and the Great West*. New York: W. W. Norton, 1991.

Cumbler, John. *Reasonable Use: The People, the Environment, and the State, New England, 1790–1930*. New York: Oxford University Press, 2001.

Elkind, Sarah S. *Bay Cities and Water Politics: The Battle for Resources in Boston and Oakland*. Kansas City: University of Kansas Press, 1998.

Melosi, Martin V. *The Sanitary City: Urban Infrastructure in America from the Colonial Times to the Present*. Baltimore: Johns Hopkins University Press, 2000.

Pellow, David Naguib and Lisa Sun-Hee Park. *The Silicon Valley of Dreams: Environmental Justice, Immigrant Workers, and the High-Tech Global Economy*. New York: New York University Press, 2002.

Steinberg, Theodore. *Acts of God: The Unnatural History of Natural Disaster in America*. New York: Oxford University Press, 2000.

——. *Nature Incorporated: Industrialization and the Waters of New England*. Amherst: University of Massachusetts Press, 1991.

Stradling, David. *Smokestacks and Progressives: Environmentalists, Engineers, and Air Quality in America, 1881–1951*. Baltimore: Johns Hopkins University Press, 2002.

Sze, Julie, *Noxious New York: The Racial Politics of Urban Health and Environmental Justice*. Cambridge, MA: MIT Press, 2007.

Tarr, Joel. *The Search for the Ultimate Waste Sink: Urban Pollution in Historical Perspective*. Akron: Ohio University Press, 1996.

Young, Paula Lee, ed. *Meat, Modernity, and the Rise of the Slaughterhouse*. Dover, NH: University of New Hampshire Press/University of New England, 2008.

Washington, D.C.

Gillette, Howard Jr. *Between Justice and Beauty:Race, Planning, and the Failure of Urban Policy in Washington, D.C.* Philadelphia: University of Pennsylvania Press, 2006.

Jaffe, Harry S. and Tom Sherwood. *Dream City: Race, Power, and the Decline of Washington, D.C.* New York: Simon & Schuster, 1994.

White Southern Migration

Arnow, Harriette. *The Dollmaker.* New York: Macmillan Publishing, 1954.

Berry, Chad, ed. *The Hayloft Gang: The Story of the National Barn Dance.* Urbana: University of Illinois Press, 2008.

Berry, Chad. *Southern Migrants, Northern Exiles.* Urbana: University of Illinois Press, 2000.

Gregory, James N. *The Southern Diaspora: How the Great Migrations of Black and White Southerners Transformed America.* Chapel Hill: University of North Carolina Press, 2005.

Women and the City

Boehm, Lisa Krissoff. *Making a Way out of No Way: African American Women and the Second Great Migration.* Jackson: University Press of Mississippi, 2009.

Deutsch, Sarah. *Women and the City: Gender, Space, and Power in Boston, 1870–1940.* New York: Oxford University Press, 2000.

Jones, Jacqueline. *American Work: Four Centuries of Black and White Labor.* New York: W. W. Norton, 1998.

——. *The Dispossessed: America's Underclasses from the Civil War to the Present.* New York: Basic Books, 1992.

——. *Labor of Love, Labor of Sorrow: Black Women, Work, and Family from Slavery to the Present.* New York: Vintage Books, 1985.

Kessler-Harris, Alice. *Out to Work: A History of Wage Earning Women in the United States.* New York: Oxford University Press, 1982.

Kunzel, Regina. *Fallen Women, Problem Girls: Unmarried Mothers and the Professionalization of Social Work, 1890–1945.* New Haven: Yale University Press, 1995.

Lebsock, Suzanne. *The Free Women of Petersburgh: Status and Culture in a Southern Town, 1784–1860.* New York: W. W. Norton, 1984.

Lemke-Santangelo, Gertrude. *Abiding Courage: African American Migrant Women and the East Bay Community.* Chapel Hill: University of North Carolina Press, 1996.

Levenstein, Lisa. *A Movement Without Marches: African American Women and the Politics of Poverty in Postwar Philadelphia.* Chapel Hill: The University of North Carolina Press, 2009.

Matthews, Glenna. *Silicon Valley, Women, and the California Dream: Gender, Class and Opportunity in the Twentieth Century.* Stanford: Stanford University Press, 2003.

Meyerowitz, Joanne. *Women Adrift: Independent Wage Earners in Chicago, 1880–1930.* Chicago: University of Chicago Press, 1988.

Muncy, Robyn. *Creating a Female Dominion in American Reform, 1890–1935.* New York: Oxford University Press, 1991.

Orleck, Annelise. *Storming Caesar's Palace: How Black Mothers Fought Their Own War on Poverty.* Boston: Beacon Press, 2005.

Peiss, Kathy. *Cheap Amusements: Working Women and Leisure in Turn of the Century New York.* Philadelphia: Temple University Press, 1986.

Rosen, Ruth. *The Lost Sisterhood: Prostitution in America, 1900–1918.* Baltimore: Johns Hopkins University Press, 1983.

Stansell, Christine. *City of Women: Sex and Class in New York, 1780–1860.* New York: Knopf, 1986.

Wolcott, Virginia. *Remaking Respectability: African American Women in Interwar Detroit.* Chapel Hill: University of North Carolina Press, 2001.

"Vesey Slave Revolt, Charleston, South Carolina" in *An Account of the Late Intended Insurrection among a Portion of the Blacks of this City*. Second Edition (Charleston: Corporation of Charleston, Printed by A. E. Miller, 1822). Courtesy of the American Antiquarian Society.

"Debates on Chinese Immigration" from *Immigration of Chinese, Speech of Hon. Aaron A. Sargent of California, In the Senate of the United States*, May 2, 1876 and *Facts Upon the Other Side of the Chinese Question, With a Memorial to the President of the U.S., From Representative Chinamen in America, 1876*. Courtesy of the American Antiquarian Society.

"Triangle Shirtwaist Fire, New York City," from *The Ladies' Garment Worker*, April 1911. Permission of the Kheel Center at Cornell University.

Part IV: City Life From the Bottom Up, 1860s–1940s

Gilfoyle, Timothy J., "The 'Guns' of Gotham" from *The Pickpocket's Tale: The Underworld of Nineteenth-Century New York*. Copyright © 2006 by Timothy J. Gilfoyle. Used by permission of W. W. Norton and Company, Inc.

Gamber, Wendy, *The Boardinghouse in Nineteenth-Century America*. pp. 1–5, 7–9, 12–17. Copyright © 2007 by The Johns Hopkins University. Reprinted with permission of The Johns Hopkins University Press.

Chauncey, George, "Urban Culture and the Policing of the 'City of Bachelors'" in *Gay New York: Gender, Urban Culture, and the Making of the Gay Male World*. Copyright © 1994 by George Chauncey. Reprinted by permission of Basic Books, a member of Perseus Books Group.

Part V: Managing the Metropolis

Rosenzweig, Roy and Elizabeth Blackmar, "The 'Spoils of the Park' in *The Park and the People*. Copyright © 1998 by Roy Rosenzweig and Elizabeth Blackmar, published by Cornell University Press. Reprinted with permission with the Carol Mann Agency.

Kessner, Thomas, "New Deal City" in *Fiorello H. La Guardia and the Making of Modern New York*. Copyright © 1989 by Thomas Kessner. Reprinted with permission of Thomas Kessner.

Teaford, Jon C., "Messiah Mayors and the Gospel of Urban Hype," in *The Rough Road to Renaissance: Urban Revitalization in America, 1940–1985*. pp. 253–259, 267–269, 272, 274, 280–282, 297, 306–307. Copyright © 1990 by The Johns Hopkins University Press. Reprinted with permission of The Johns Hopkins University Press.

Hirsch, Arnold and A. Lee Levert, "The Katrina Conspiracies: The Problem of Trust in Rebuilding an American City," *Journal of Urban History*, 35, no. 2 (January 2009): 207–219. Copyright 2009 by SAGE Publications. Reprinted with permission of SAGE Publications.

"On the Way Up: Charlotte and Kansas City" from "On the Way Up: Four Cities Show How it Can Be Done," *U.S. News and World Report* (5 April 1976): 62–64. Copyright © 1976 U.S. News and World Report, L.P. Reprinted with permission.

Part VI: The Urban Environment

Tarr, Joel A., "The Metabolism of the Industrial City: The Case of Pittsburgh," *Journal of Urban History* 28, no. 5 (July 2002): 511–545. Copyright © 2002 by SAGE Publications. Reprinted with permission of SAGE Publications.

Melosi, Martin V. and Joseph A. Pratt, "Houston: The Energy Metropolis," originally published as the "Introduction" from *Energy Metropolis: An Environmental History of Houston and the Gulf Coast*, edited by Martin V. Melosi and Joseph A. Pratt. Copyright © 2007. Reprinted with permission from the University of Pittsburgh Press.

Pellow, David Naguib and Lisa Sun-Hee Park, "The Emergence of Silicon Valley: High-Tech Development and Ecocide, 1950–2001," in *The Silicon Valley of Dreams*. Copyright © 2002 by New York University. Reprinted with permission of New York University Press.

Toxic Wastes and Race in the United States: A National Report on the Racial and Socio-Economic Characteristics of Communities with Hazardous Waste Sites. Copyright © 1987. Reprinted with permission of the Pilgrim Press, the United Church of Christ.

Part VII: Transportation and Physical Mobility

Warner, Sam Bass, Jr., "From Walking City to the Implementation of the Street Railways." Reprinted by permission of the publisher from *Streetcar Suburbs: The Process of Growth in Boston, 1870–1900*, Second Edition, by Sam Bass Warner, Jr., pp. 15–29, Cambridge, MA: Harvard University Press, Copyright © 1962, 1978 by the President and Fellows of Harvard College.

Hood, Clifton, "The Subway and the City," from *722 MILES: The Building of the Subways and How They Transformed New York*. Copyright © 1993 by Clifton Hood. Abridged by permission of Simon & Schuster, Inc.

Fogelson, Robert, "Wishful Thinking: Downtown and the Automotive Revolution,' in *Downtown: Its Rise and Fall, 1880–1950*. Copyright © 2001 by Robert M. Fogelson. Reprinted with permission of Yale University Press.

Stern, Seth, "$14.6 Billion Later, Boston's Big Dig Wraps Up." Reproduced with permission from the December 19, 2003 edition of *The Christian Science Monitor* (www.CSMonitor.com). Copyright © 2003 The Christian Science Monitor.

Part VIII: Urban Migrations and Social Mobility

Hirsch, Arnold, "The Second Ghetto and the Dynamics of Neighborhood Change," in *Making the Second Ghetto: Race and Housing in Chicago, 1940–1960*. Copyright © 1983, 1998 by Arnold R. Hirsch. Reprinted with permission of the University of Chicago Press.

Boehm, Lisa Krissoff, *Making a Way out of No Way: African American Women and the Second Great Migration*. Copyright 2009 by the University Press of Mississippi. Reprinted by permission of the author.

Berry, Chad, "The Great White Migration, 1945–1960," from *Southern Migrants, Northern Exiles*. Copyright © 2000 by the Board of Trustees of the University of Illinois. Used with permission of the University of Illinois Press.

Shell-Weiss, Melanie, "Citizenship and Civil Rights, 1964–1974," from *Coming to Miami: A Social History*. Copyright © 2009 by Melanie Shell-Weiss. Reprinted with permission of the University Press of Florida.

"Ku Klux Klan Initiation," from "Klansmen Beaten in Street, Cars Stoned, Women Injured," *Worcester Sunday Telegram*, October 19, 1924. Reprinted with permission of the Worcester Telegram & Gazette Corp.

Arnow, Harriette, *The Dollmaker*. Copyright © 1954, 1982 by Harriette Simpson Arnow. Reprinted with permission from the Estate of Harriette Arnow.

Rodriguez, Richard, *Hunger of Memory*. Copyright © 1982 by Richard Rodriguez. Reprinted with permission of David R. Godine, Publisher, Inc.

Frey, William, "The New Great Migration: Black Americans' Return to the South, 1965–2000." Copyright © 2004 Brookings Institution. Courtesy of the Brookings Institution and William H. Frey.

Part IX: Race and the Post-War Metropolis

Sugrue, Thomas J., "Class, Status and Residence: The Changing Geography of Black Detroit," from *The Origins of the Urban Crisis*. Copyright © 1996 by Princeton University Press. Reprinted by permission of Princeton University Press.

Self, Robert Owen, "White Noose," from *American Babylon*. Copyright © 2003 by Princeton University Press. Reprinted by permission of Princeton University Press.

Venkatesh, Sudhir Alladi, "The Beginning of the End of the Modern Ghetto." Reprinted by permission from *American Project: The Rise and Fall of a Modern Ghetto* by Sudhir Alladi Venkatesh, pp. 263–277, Cambridge, MA: Harvard University Press, Copyright © 2000 by the President and Fellows of Harvard College.

Wilson, Sloan, *The Man in the Gray Flannel Suit*. Copyright © 1955, 1983 by Sloan Wilson. Reprinted with permission.

"Urban Indians (1964–1969)," from Adam Fortunate Eagle, *Alcatraz! Alcatraz!* Copyright © 1992 by Adam Fortunate Eagle. Reprinted with permission of Adam Fortunate Eagle.

MacDonald, Michael Patrick, *All Souls*. Copyright © 1999 by Michael Patrick MacDonald. Reprinted by permission of Beacon Press.

Part X: Exurbia and Postindustrial Cities

INDEX